For Kenny

Tuck in!

love

Introduction by
HUGH FEARNLEY-WHITTINGSTALL

Essays and recipes by
PAM CORBIN
MARK DIACONO
NIKKI DUFFY
HUGH FEARNLEY-WHITTINGSTALL
NICK FISHER
STEVEN LAMB
TIM MADDAMS
GILL MELLER
JOHN WRIGHT

Photography by
SIMON WHEELER

Illustrations by
MICHAEL FRITH

RIVER COTTAGE

Our Favourite Ingredients,
& How to Cook Them

BLOOMSBURY
LONDON · OXFORD · NEW YORK · NEW DELHI · SYDNEY

A
B
C
D
E
F
G
H
J
K
L

M
N
O
P
Q
R
S
T
V
W
Y
Z

Introduction

The River Cottage story began almost exactly twenty years ago when I rented a tiny lock-keeper's cottage near Netherbury in Dorset. Surrounded by woodland, the murmuring of the River Brit audible from the very basic kitchen, my plan was to use it as a weekend bolt-hole from London. But River Cottage soon got under my skin, and weekends started stretching into weeks as I found it ever harder to return to the city. I started putting down roots – principally those of my favourite edible plants.

In such an idyllic and unspoiled spot, my long-standing interest in wild foods couldn't help but burgeon. And of course I began to raise my own home-grown ingredients – both animal and vegetable. When you can catch your own fish at the bottom of the garden, pausing on the way back to the house to pick some herbs and vegetables to cook it with, you begin to look at the world with a new clarity.

River Cottage inspired me to seek out a more sustainable way of eating – a way that was better for me, my young family, the local economy and the global environment. The River Cottage television series, which began in 1997, chronicled my trials and many errors as I foraged, fished, farmed and fumbled my way towards greater self-sufficiency. Meanwhile, I spent much of my time thinking about those ingredients that I had, like most of us, once bought shrink-wrapped and scrubbed to within an inch of their lives from the supermarket. I determined, from thereon in, that the ingredients I cooked with, and fed my family with, would be the best they could possibly be.

My experiences at River Cottage seemed to hit a nerve with a legion of viewers who shared my worries about the uglier realities of industrial food production and craved a more direct, honest and fulfilling relationship with their ingredients. During those early years I was lucky to encounter many kindred spirits, and I even managed to persuade a handful of them to join forces with me, becoming part of the team that would eventually create this book – though none of us realised that at the time.

I met the naturalist John Wright, who has since taught me more about wild food than I'd have ever thought possible. I also started my collaboration with Nick Fisher – whose knowledge of and passion for fishing is incomparable. That partnership led to *The River Cottage Fish Book* – still one of the books of which I'm most proud.

I set up the first River Cottage HQ in a set of recently vacated dairy barns near Bridport. Very recently in fact – I watched the cows walk out for the last time, then set to work scraping decades of their friendly deposits from the base of the walls and the corners of the yard. This rich matter became the first fertiliser for the veg beds that sprang up around the buildings.

As the fledgling business found its feet, I met a brilliant young local chef named Gill Meller. We bonded over the battered second-hand Falcon stove which occupied the dairy-turned-kitchen. Gill instantly became my culinary right-hand man, indispensible to the entire River Cottage operation.

In 2006, River Cottage HQ leapt across the county boundary to its current, long-term home in East Devon. Park Farm, comprising sixty acres of rolling farmland in a valley near Axminster, became the site of our cookery school, kitchen garden and smallholding. We began hosting regular dinners and teaching courses: 'A Pig in a Day', 'Catch and Cook' and 'Build and Bake' set the tone. Steven Lamb, another early addition to the team, soon became an absolute lynchpin in pulling together these events. Today, as our principal host, and resident expert on smoking and curing, his knowledge of all things River Cottage is truly encyclopaedic.

Meanwhile, the indefatigable Mark Diacono came on board to lead our garden team while simultaneously running his own ground-breaking climate change garden project down the road at Otter Farm. Local entrepreneur Pam 'the Jam' Corbin was recruited to share her considerable wisdom, and her pickling and preserving days became some of our most popular courses. I also invited the hugely talented food writer Nikki Duffy to work with me on a broad portfolio of projects and, along with Gill, she has been my collaborator in devising recipes ever since. And after Tim Maddams joined us as head chef at the very first River Cottage Canteen in Axminster, he also became a valued culinary sounding board – and fishing companion.

During the fifteen years since *The River Cottage Cookbook* came out, my co-authors and I have published a veritable library of books – twenty-eight, at last count. These have included *The River Cottage Meat Book*, *River Cottage Veg Every Day* and a whole panoply of handbooks which encompass everything from foraging to fishing, herbs to home-curing. We are nothing if not prolific. So you might be forgiven for wondering why we have chosen to bring another hefty tome into the world?

The truth is, a River Cottage 'bible' focusing on ingredients is something that's been in my mind for a very long time. After all, if you remove ingredients from the equation there would be no River Cottage at all. It's the same for all cooks, domestic or professional: every culinary endeavour starts with ingredients – and the best start with the best. This volume, I hope, will help you gain familiarity with, and confidence in, the finest raw materials. I believe there is no better recipe for successful cooking.

As with all the best reference books, I knew that such a volume needed to be the work of more than one person – certainly more than just me. Topics this broad demand a range of knowledge and experience – a stellar team of experts. Happily, I knew exactly where to find them.

Not only are my co-writers among the most knowledgeable people you could ever meet in their fields of expertise, they are qualified in the most important sense of all… they are avid cooks and enthusiastic eaters. We are all on the same page – or, you might say, the same plate. At the end of the day, there is nothing we enjoy more than sitting down and tucking into something simply delicious – but we want to do so with peace of mind and a clear conscience. Finding, sourcing or growing the best food possible is a shared ambition – even an obsession, you might say. We get excited about producers who are doing things really well, just as we become angry about the (all too many) things that are wrong with the world of food.

And we all recognise how essential good ingredients are in our lives. They are more than the tools of the cook's trade, more even than the basis of the daily meals we all consume. Ingredients are, quite literally, us. They physically become part of our bodies, and the bodies of those for whom we cook. The food we choose is the very matter that underpins our life, our health and our well-being. What could possibly be more fundamental than that?

It is the cook's role, and pleasure, to take these life-giving materials and make them life-affirming too. Ingredients are our sensory palette – the box of tricks from which we select the flavours and textures we most desire, in order to produce meals that will not just sate hunger, but will delight, comfort, refresh and excite. Once you know your way around ingredients, you have a wondrous power at your disposal: the power to express care, passion or love through a plate of food. That's pretty amazing.

Ingredients have meaning on a quite different level too: they don't just exist in a culinary, nutritional space, but are part of a political, economic and environmental web. The choices we make when we select one ingredient over another – Fairtrade bananas, organic eggs, sustainably caught fish – are immensely significant. They send ripples. The message carries through to producers and retailers: 'I care about animal welfare' or 'I prefer to buy locally' or even just 'I'm very happy to buy carrots that aren't perfectly straight'. More importantly still, they are votes – and votes that count – in the arena of food production. If we keep buying organic cabbages, farmers will keep growing them. And if we don't, they won't.

In my introduction to *The River Cottage Cookbook* I wrote, only slightly tongue-in-cheek, about a 'food acquisition continuum' – a spectrum of ways of getting food into our kitchens, or into ourselves. As I envisaged it, this spectrum ranged from those consumers who entirely subsisted on industrially produced food to, at the opposite end, those single-minded individuals who had achieved a state of total self-sufficiency. Of course, as I acknowledged, the vast majority of us lie somewhere between the two polar extremes; my avowed ambition was to nudge my readers along the continuum in the direction of self-sufficiency, to encourage them to get as close as possible to the source of their own food. This remains at the heart of my professional mission in the world of food.

At River Cottage we take pride in resisting the influence of the multinational producers and mammoth retailers who control vast swathes of the foods we buy to eat. We have learned, and now we teach, what's truly involved in the production of food – what happens to the raw materials before they get to you, particularly if those 'raw materials' are living creatures. We love being, and encouraging others to be, part of the process of producing good ingredients, whether that means catching, gutting, filleting and cooking a fish, growing a windowbox full of veg, or just grazing a few blackberries from a late summer hedgerow. I believe this reclamation of responsibility for our own food is crucial. It leads to lower environmental impacts and better welfare for animals; it also makes us better cooks, healthier eaters and more empowered individuals. It nurtures our self-reliance, and our ability to take care of others.

If you've been following what we do at River Cottage for any length of time, you'll already have an instinctive understanding of our culinary style. But for those who are less familiar with our work, allow me to sum it up: it's a kind of cooking that's rooted firmly in British soil, and celebrates the liberation and sheer satisfaction that comes from finding, growing and preparing ingredients yourself. And it enthusiastically embraces seasonality, and the constantly changing inspiration that the British calendar brings.

You won't be surprised to see that our preference for local foods is reflected throughout the following pages. But we have never been fundamentalist about it. So you'll also find a good smattering of foreign ingredients here. These are the ones we would find it especially hard to deprive ourselves of – citrus fruits, spices, coconut, coffee, soy sauce and olive oil, for instance. You might notice that we often suggest using imported foodstuffs as seasonings to make our own native produce particularly delicious. We cannot close our hearts to a truly useful ingredient just because it hails from south of Dover. But if we can eat it with potatoes, apples or herring, that is very much the better. And if we can source the best examples of those exotics, according to the same principles of sustainability and fairness that we apply at home, better still.

Although this compendious book encompasses 333 of our best-loved and most-used ingredients, from A to Z, it is not entirely comprehensive. We've deliberately left out ingredients that we think are best avoided. So you'll find no entry on tuna – we don't use it, because many tuna species are currently in big trouble, and those that aren't do not swim in British waters. We believe that there is always going to be a better, more sustainable, more local choice of fish – and we've got plenty to say about coley and gurnard and sardines. There are also native ingredients so broad in their variety that we simply couldn't include every one – among them the more unusual herbs, wild mushrooms and seaweeds. While many entries are rapturous hymns to favourite foods, there are others that do not represent an unquestioning endorsement. There are complexities.

Some ingredients – such as bread, or soya, or any animal product you care to think of – are controversial, to a greater or lesser degree. With these we have done our best to give you the latest information, so that you can make an informed choice about which versions to choose – or whether or not to consume them at all.

Food may be freighted with political significance, but it should never be fraught with personal anxiety. We see this book, more than anything, as a celebration of the amazing spectrum of fruit, veg, herbs, spices, meat and fish that surrounds us. It's all too easy to get stuck in a rut with food – to buy the same things, week in, week out, and to cook the same recipes. When so many great ingredients are available to us, that seems a shame. And so, when it comes to the original recipes we have devised for this volume, our design is to inspire you to try new foods, or new ways to cook your old favourites. Where some culinary reference books can feel a little dry and dusty, this one aims to be your hard-working kitchen companion, nudging you to expand your repertoire.

We would like to think that some people will want to settle down in a comfy chair and read this book whole chunks at a time. But for most cooks, we hope it will be an everyday resource, always ready to be consulted for a burst of inspiration or guidance, whether you're planning what to grow, thinking about what to buy, or dreaming about what to cook. We trust that you will soon be able to count the *River Cottage A to Z* among your most faithful friends in the kitchen (which is always the nicest place for your friends to be).

HUGH FEARNLEY-WHITTINGSTALL, EAST DEVON, JUNE 2016

Sourcing your ingredients

We think your first port of call for any ingredient you have not grown yourself should be a local, independent retailer – be that a farm shop, market, fishmonger, butcher, veg box delivery scheme, health food shop or greengrocer. To help you source ingredients that may be hard to find locally, we've listed some suppliers, many of whom offer mail order. These represent just a selection of producers; a little internet research will invariably turn up more.

MCS ratings

The Marine Conservation Society's ecological rating system for fish and shellfish is used throughout the book. A rating of 1 or 2 indicates sustainably produced seafood from healthy and well-managed fisheries or farms. A rating of 3 or 4 suggests some concern regarding the stock or management and/or environmental impact of the fishing or farming method in use. Fish rated 5 should be avoided.

Following the recipes

» All spoon measures are level unless otherwise stated: 1 tsp = 5ml spoon; 1 tbsp = 15ml spoon.

» All herbs are fresh unless otherwise suggested.

» Use freshly ground black pepper unless otherwise listed.

» The recipes use medium eggs. Anyone who is pregnant or in a vulnerable health group should avoid dishes using raw or lightly cooked eggs.

» If using the zest of citrus fruit, choose unwaxed fruit.

» Oven timings are provided for both conventional and fan-assisted ovens. These are intended as guidelines, with a description of the desired final colour or texture of the dish as a further guide. Individual ovens can deviate by 10°C or more either way from the actual setting. Get to know your oven and use an oven thermometer to check the temperature.

Alexanders

LATIN NAME
Smyrnium olusatrum

SEASONALITY
November–April/May

HABITAT
Coastal, often at roadsides. Largely southern distribution, particularly common in the Southwest

At precisely the time that every other plant is settling down for the winter, alexanders bursts into vigorous green life as though it were the first day of spring. The plant was introduced by the Romans as winter fodder for horses but, unlike the Romans, has refused to leave. Now it fills coastal roadsides with its celery-like stems and leaves, content with the temperate climate that the coast provides. Alexanders enjoys a southern distribution, becoming increasingly common south of Blackpool in the West and The Wash in the East. However, it seems most at home in the Southwest; the coastal verges of Devon being bright with its yellow flowers in spring.

While the whole alexanders plant down to its root is edible, it is generally only the young stems that are used. Pick the long side stems while they are soft and pliable – certainly before they toughen to the consistency of bamboo. Like the celery of old, these need to be (rather laboriously) peeled of their string-like skin to reveal the succulent flesh beneath.

What does alexanders taste like? Highly aromatic and bittersweet, it's a little like angelica (see page 22). Like many wild foods, the flavour is a powerful shock to the modern palate and truly an acquired taste. Fortunately (or not, if you have robust tastebuds) the strong taste is moderated dramatically with 5 or 6 minutes' steaming. The softened stems are then excellent served with butter and black pepper.

Having a sweet tooth, I like to follow the path trodden by angelica and candy the stuff. It takes 5 minutes of your time each day for 10 days, but the resultant sweetmeats are worth your dedication.

For gin and tonic enthusiasts, I recommend (real!) gin alexanders. Crush the stems and squeeze out a thimble-full of juice through muslin into gin laced with a little caster sugar. Add soda and crushed ice.

ALEXANDERS GRATIN WITH BACON AND OATS

150–200g young alexanders side stems

2 tbsp white wine

25g butter

6 rashers of smoked streaky bacon, chopped

4 shallots, thinly sliced

25g plain flour

200ml double cream

FOR THE TOPPING

50g skinned hazelnuts, bashed

2 tbsp porridge oats

About 2 tbsp grated Parmesan or similar hard, matured cheese

Olive or rapeseed oil, to trickle

Sea salt and black pepper

This takes very simply cooked alexanders stems and elevates them to a rather luxurious level. Serves 4 as a starter

Preheat the oven to 190°C/Fan 170°C/Gas 5.

Wash the alexanders stems well. Peel away the fibrous strands that run down their length, then cut the stems into roughly 2–3cm pieces. Set a medium pan (that has a lid) over a high heat. Add the wine with 2 tbsp water and bring to a simmer. Add the alexanders stems, with a twist of black pepper and a pinch of salt, and put the lid on. Cook for 5–10 minutes, until tender. Strain, reserving the cooking liquor.

Meanwhile, set a separate medium pan over a medium heat. Add the butter and, when foaming, add the bacon and shallots. Cook for 6–8 minutes until the bacon is golden and the shallots are softened. Stir in the flour and cook for another minute.

Stir in the reserved alexanders' cooking liquor and the cream. Bring to a simmer and cook over a low heat, stirring from time to time, for 4–5 minutes or until the sauce has thickened slightly. Add the alexanders to the sauce, stir to combine and season to taste with salt and pepper. Divide between 4 shallow ovenproof dishes.

For the topping, toss the hazelnuts, oats and cheese together in a bowl with a good trickle of oil. Scatter a quarter of this mixture over each dish and bake for 10–12 minutes or until golden and bubbling. Serve straight away.

Allspice

LATIN NAME
Pimenta dioica

ALSO KNOWN AS
Jamaica pepper,
Jamaican pimento

MORE RECIPES
Buckwheat and apple fritters
(page 103); Eccles cakes
(page 340)

Allspice is one of those spices that every cook seems to have in their cupboard but seldom uses. And yet, most of us eat it all the time without even knowing, because it lends its peppery, aromatic quality to many off-the-shelf ketchups and sauces.

As the name suggests, the flavour is a complex one – a mingling of cloves, cinnamon, pepper and bay. It starts life as a fresh berry on an evergreen shrub, which is picked and then dried in the sun until hard and brown. In the hot climates where it flourishes, including the Caribbean and Central America, fresh allspice leaves are used in much the same way as bay. The wood is also used for smoking and barbecuing, lending a soft, sweet aroma to the foods being cooked.

Allspice can be overpoweringly hot and astringent if you're heavy-handed with it. It's a good idea to taste it (or any unfamiliar spice) on a little piece of buttered bread to get to know the flavour, then add a tiny amount of salt and see what changes. Try it with a little sugar instead and you'll soon have a good grasp of the spice's characteristics.

Allspice is the cornerstone of dishes such as jerk chicken and goat curry and very good in home-made ketchups and chutneys. But I also like to use it in more unexpected places, such as ice creams and broths, or sprinkle it on to fresh flatbreads with chilli flakes and good olive oil.

Allspice is not the same thing as mixed spice, which is a proprietary blend – usually including cinnamon, cloves, nutmeg and ginger. Pure allspice has a much hotter, more peppery character, but it does have its uses in baking. A touch of allspice can be fabulous in cakes with orange and ginger, and it often makes an appearance in German *pfeffernüsse* biscuits.

As with most spices, I urge you to buy whole berries and grind them yourself. The result will be far more vibrant and lively than the ready-ground spice.

ROAST JERK CHICKEN

1 free-range chicken
(about 1.75kg)

A glass of water or white wine

FOR THE JERK SEASONING
1 tbsp allspice berries

1 tbsp black peppercorns

Leaves from a small bunch
of thyme

4 spring onions, roughly
chopped

4 garlic cloves, roughly chopped

1–2 medium-hot red chillies,
to taste, deseeded and chopped

1 tbsp dark brown sugar or
honey

2 tbsp tamari or soy sauce

Finely grated zest and juice
of 1 lime

A good pinch of sea salt

Allspice is one of the defining flavours in Caribbean jerk chicken, which is usually made with a jointed bird. But it does a great job of spicing up a simple roast too. Serve with 'rice and peas' (rice cooked in coconut milk, mixed with kidney beans). Serves 4

For the jerk seasoning, crush the allspice and peppercorns well using a pestle and mortar, then tip into a food processor. Add the thyme, spring onions, garlic, chilli, sugar or honey, tamari or soy, lime zest and juice, and salt. Blitz to a fairly smooth paste.

To prepare the chicken, pull the legs away from the body slightly and lift the wings out from under the bird to help hot air circulate during cooking. Rub the spice paste all over the bird. Leave to stand in a cool place but out of the fridge for about an hour to come up to room temperature and allow the flavours to penetrate. Preheat the oven to 180°C/ Fan 160°C/Gas 4.

Put the chicken into a roasting tin and roast for 30 minutes, then pour the water or wine into the base of the tin. Return to the oven and roast for a further 50–60 minutes. To check that the bird is cooked, pull at one leg. It should come away from the body with relative ease and the juices between the leg and breast should run clear. If the leg is reluctant and the juices still pink, give it another 10 minutes and test again. When you're happy your bird is done, leave it to rest in a warm place for 10–15 minutes.

Tip up the bird so any juices from inside run out into the roasting tin. Work these into the spicy sauce that's formed in the tin. Serve the chicken with its juices and 'rice and peas'.

Almonds

LATIN NAME
Prunus amygdalus

SEASONALITY
British-grown nuts harvested
in October

MORE RECIPES
Roasted chilli mole (page 173);
Spicy brown rice and broccoli
(page 535); Pear and celeriac
stuffing (page 454); Creamy
spelt and almond pudding
(page 596); Prune, almond
and caraway tart (page 505);
Roasted plum fumble (page 479);
Lemon, honey and courgette
cake (page 347); Raspberry
almond streusel cake (page 526);
Cherry, thyme and marzipan
muffins (page 154)

These nuts are largely the fruit of far-flung, sun-drenched lands, although almond trees will bear fruit in the warmer parts of the British Isles, providing they have a sunny, sheltered location. California is the biggest producer these days, but they grow in Mediterranean Europe, the Middle East and North Africa as well.

Almonds conjure up thoughts of frangipane and syrupy cakes, fluffy pilaus and rich tagines, salty tapas and unctuous sauces, but for all this exotic allure they are without doubt the most hard-working and versatile nut. At any one time, my storecupboard is likely to contain them in at least three different forms: perhaps a tub of the whole nuts with their dusty brown skins still on, a packet of golden flaked almonds and, always, a bag or two of the ground nuts, ready for baking.

As for the pungent marzipan tang that puts so many people off the idea of almonds, this comes not from the nuts we eat but from benzaldehyde, a chemical extracted from bitter almonds (which are otherwise toxic). It is used in ready-made marzipan, amaretti biscuits and almond liqueurs, and as a cheap flavouring. The sweet almonds we cook with have little or none of this flavour. Make your own marzipan or macaroons and you can get a mild and delicate result. Conversely, those of us who do love that unique, bitter-sweet perfume can add a few drops of bottled almond extract whenever sweet almonds are used.

Almonds are laden with monounsaturated fats and antioxidant vitamin E. They stay fresher for longer than many other nuts, too. Unblanched almonds, with their brown skins intact, are the most nutritious form because the skin contains flavonoids. It is thought that soaking the nuts in water for several hours before eating activates enzymes in the skin and makes the nutrients in the nuts much easier to absorb. I've not found actual scientific evidence for this but, on an intuitive level, it makes sense – presumably, the nut thinks it's about to start growing. Soaked almonds swell, their skin changes from dry bark to a lustrous mahogany veneer and they are juicy and tender in the mouth.

A brief soaking is also essential if you want to skin or 'blanch' almonds yourself. Cover them with just-boiled water for 5 minutes then test a couple – the soaking will have loosened the skins and you should be able to peel them off easily. Return them to the hot water for a minute or two longer if they are stubborn.

As with most nuts, a light roasting unlocks the flavour of almonds and makes them crisper. Roast blanched almonds at 180°C/Fan 160°C/Gas 4 for 5–8 minutes, shaking them once or twice and watching them like a hawk, just until golden. Tossed in a lick of olive oil and sprinkled with salt, they make an excellent nibble (especially if served with a cold beer or a bone-dry sherry). Add a touch of spice – a pinch of cayenne pepper or smoked paprika – and they are even better. Spanish 'Marcona' almonds, a round, flat variety with a fine flavour and buttery texture, are exceptionally good served in this way.

Fragrant, golden toasted almonds can also be chopped roughly, then added to veg dishes. Try them on a plateful of blanched green beans, with a little garlic-infused olive oil, or throw them into a salad with roasted red peppers, rocket and a trickle of plain yoghurt.

Slivered or flaked almonds add alluring crunch to cakes, muffins and breads. You can buy slivered almonds ready-toasted and these are fine for baking (as long as they won't be in the oven too long), but they're most useful for throwing straight into grainy dishes such as couscous or pilaus.

To sliver your own whole almonds, use a large sharp knife and a lot of care. You may well get shards and splinters rather than neat slices, but these are arguably even more appealing.

And then there are ground almonds, a storecupboard ingredient of unrivalled versatility. Used alone, they produce close-textured, almost fudgey results. Marzipan, the familiar paste of almonds, sugar and eggs, is the densest example of all. It's very easy to make your own: just combine 250g ground almonds with 250g icing sugar and 1 large, lightly beaten egg, adding a little almond extract if you want that penetrating, bitter almond flavour. Use it as a cake covering (leave it plain or lightly brown the surface under the grill), or as a filling for Christmas stollen, or to make little *petits fours*. Add 50g sifted cocoa powder to the almonds for chocolate marzipan.

When combined with wheat flour (or gluten-free polenta), ground almonds contribute a unique, moist texture to cakes and soda breads. Meanwhile, a measure added to shortcrust pastry (say 50g ground almonds for every 250g wheat flour) yields particularly rich and tender results – perfect for mince pies.

Ground almonds are also essential to many savoury dishes: they thicken curries, enrich piquant romesco sauce (with chillies and tomatoes) and form the basis of the wonderful garlicky Spanish *ajo blanco* soup.

To grind your own almonds, blitz them in a food processor (roasted or not, and even skin on, if you like) until you have a fairly fine consistency. You won't achieve the even texture of commercially ground almonds, but in most things, the coarser, more interesting texture of home-ground nuts works beautifully. Don't over-process though – after a few minutes the nuts will start to release their oil and develop a 'damp' texture. If this does happen, take advantage. Add a little more oil (I like coconut or rapeseed), a pinch of salt and a spoonful of honey and process into a nutritious nut butter to slather on your breakfast toast.

ROASTED ALMOND AÏOLI

50g whole blanched almonds

2 medium egg yolks

2–3 garlic cloves, grated or crushed

½ tsp English mustard

2 tsp balsamic or sherry vinegar

275ml light olive oil OR 200ml sunflower oil and 75ml extra virgin olive or rapeseed oil

Sea salt and black pepper

Almonds lend body, texture and their nutty sweetness to this classic garlic mayonnaise. Serve with crudités or chunky home-made chips, or alongside fish. Serves 4–8

Preheat the oven to 180°C/Fan 160°C/Gas 4. Scatter the almonds on a small baking tray and sprinkle with a pinch of salt. Roast for about 5 minutes, until golden, keeping an eye on them to ensure they don't burn. Remove and allow to cool completely.

Put the almonds in a food processor and blitz until finely ground (a few chunky bits are fine). Add the egg yolks, garlic, mustard, vinegar and a generous pinch each of salt and pepper. Blitz until thoroughly combined.

Put the oil(s) into a jug. With the processor motor running on the lowest speed, slowly pour in the oil through the funnel in a very thin trickle, so that it forms an emulsion with the egg yolks. Go slowly and stop frequently to scrape down the sides – this also helps to stop the processor generating too much heat, which can cause the aïoli to curdle.

When you've added about half the oil, the mix should be looking very thick and oily. Stop and add 2 tbsp warm water to 'let it down' to a looser, creamier consistency, then continue to add the remaining oil. Add a little more water at the end if it still seems excessively thick. Taste and adjust the seasoning if necessary.

Store the aïoli in the fridge and eat within 48 hours.

LATIN NAME

European anchovy: *Engraulis encrasicolus*. Peruvian anchovy: *Engraulis ringens*

SEASONALITY

Usually sold preserved; fresh anchovies best eaten outside spawning seasons (see goodfishguide.org for details)

HABITAT

European anchovies usually from Mediterranean and Atlantic coast of mainland Europe, but range can extend from South Africa to Norway; Peruvian anchovies are from the southeast Pacific

MCS RATING

Some stocks not assessed, otherwise 2–3. Argentine anchovies and Cantabrian Sea (Bay of Biscay) anchovies have MSC certification

MORE RECIPES

Crispy lentil and roasted squash salad with salsa verde (page 352); Pissaladière (page 419); John Dory with creamed radicchio (page 318); Plaice with rosemary, caper and anchovy butter (page 476); Rabbit with anchovies, rosemary and cream (page 516)

SOURCING

goodfishguide.org; msc.org; fish4ever.co.uk

Anchovies – filleted, salted and usually preserved in oil – are to European cooking what pungent *nam pla* (fish sauce) is to Thai cuisine, or intense shrimp paste to Malaysian. Little powerhouses of piquancy, they're bursting with fishy umami flavours and extremely useful in the kitchen. Both substance and seasoning, their gift is to deepen, enhance and enrich a vast array of dishes.

These silver fish do sometimes shoal in significant quantities off the British coast, usually in the Southwest in November and December, but the catch is sporadic and most are sold to Italy and Spain. It's definitely worth telling your fishmonger you'll buy fresh anchovies if they can get them – they're delicious dusted in a little flour and fried until crisp. But such a treat is a matter of luck.

In their preserved form, however, anchovies can easily be an everyday ingredient. They're certainly one I reach for with dependable regularity.

If the thought of eating anchovies straight from the jar (as I sometimes do) makes you wrinkle up your nose, try using them in tiny amounts. A fillet or two 'melted' in hot oil contributes a wonderful, savoury depth to a tomato soup or sauce – even to a spaghetti bolognese – and won't make it taste fishy at all. A few slivers of anchovy pressed into slits in the skin of a lamb joint for roasting, along with slivers of garlic and needles of rosemary, works wonders in seasoning both the meat and the gravy. If that's too much for you, remember that as well as being essential to those powerful Southeast Asian fish sauces, anchovy is among the ingredients that give Worcestershire sauce its seasoning power.

To enjoy this little fish in more generous quantities, try a bowl of plain spaghetti anointed with hot, anchovy-and-garlic laced oil. Food doesn't get much more comforting. A simple pizza is another perfect anchovy vehicle, and these wee fish are fantastic in dressings and dips.

Vinegared anchovies – the *boquerones* beloved of the Spanish – are not my cup of tea. Some people love them as tapas, but they're too sharp and not flavourful enough to find their way into my repertoire.

Tinned anchovies can be a sustainable choice if you shop discriminately. There is a big sustainability question mark over mainstream brands but those with the MSC's blue 'eco-label' are a good option. And I like Fish4Ever's anchovies, caught in the Mediterranean by small boats.

Look out also for tinned Peruvian anchovies in oil – they're cooked rather than salted, and come up like miniature tinned sardines. These are from the same Pacific stock that is heavily plundered for fishmeal, for the aquaculture industry. These stocks are currently assessed as sustainable, though clearly they are under heavy pressure. It's far better, in my view, that they should be eaten by people, rather than farmed fish.

TOMATO AND ANCHOVY SAUCE

6–8 large, ripe tomatoes (about 400g), or 400g tin tomatoes

2 tbsp olive or rapeseed oil, or the oil from the anchovies

6 anchovy fillets in oil

A pinch or two of dried chilli flakes (optional)

A small sprig of rosemary

3 garlic cloves, thinly sliced

½ tsp sugar

Sea salt and black pepper

This very easy, richly flavoured sauce is delicious with fresh pasta or gnocchi. Serves 2

If you're using fresh tomatoes, skin them: nick the skins in a couple of places then put the tomatoes into a large bowl and pour over boiling water to cover them. Leave to stand for 2–3 minutes, then lift out the tomatoes and peel away the skin – it should come away easily. Chop the tomatoes into 1–2cm pieces.

Heat a smallish, heavy-based frying pan over a medium heat. Add the oil, followed by the anchovy fillets, chilli, if using, and rosemary sprig. Fry gently for 1–2 minutes until the anchovies start to break down. Drop in the garlic and sizzle for 30 seconds.

Now add the tomatoes, sugar, a generous twist of black pepper and a little salt. Bring to a simmer and cook gently for 20–25 minutes, stirring from time to time, until reduced and rich-tasting. Add more salt or pepper if required. Serve straight away.

Angelica

LATIN NAME
Angelica archangelica

SEASONALITY
May–September

If you think of angelica as that lurid green, candied stuff that you can buy in packets, cut into diamonds and chuck on a trifle, think again. You can still buy that product (a specialist cake-decorating supplier is your best bet) but with its sickly-sweet taste and odd colour, I'm not sure why anyone would want to.

Instead, go back to the source. Candied angelica begins life as the stem of one of the most magnificent and statuesque herbs you can grow in your garden. This big, lustrous plant gives you pom-pom flowers, luxuriant leaves, that thick, ridged stem and a significant root, all imbued with a unique, slightly musky, aromatic flavour. Angelica is one of the botanicals used to perfume gin – and if that's your tipple, you'll be familiar with its edgy perfume.

Growing angelica requires a little bit of commitment: it needs space (it can reach 2 metres), depth (for its long tap root) and patience. It is one of the few common culinary herbs that likes a shady spot in the garden. As a biennial, it doesn't flower until its second year, though you can use the stems and leaves sooner. Those leaves, which can be harvested from May onwards, can be eaten raw or cooked. However, even when young, I find them bitter.

The stems are the prized part. Candying your own angelica will give you something much more subtle and flavourful than the commercial version. Choose stems fairly early in the season: at least 2cm in diameter but still flexible, not woody. Candying is a long-winded but straightforward process that involves soaking the stems over several days in sugar syrup and then drying them in the oven. The resulting sweetmeat makes a lovely nibble to serve with coffee, and a great addition to cakes and cookies (put it in them, not on them). You'll create a fragrant angelica syrup too.

However, far more instant gratification can be had by chopping the fresh stems and adding them to fruit compotes, puddings and preserves. This herb has a magical affinity with blackcurrants, gooseberries, rhubarb or, indeed, any tart fruit. It lightens, brightens and reduces acidity, while adding a subtle tang of its own. Use around 2 tbsp finely chopped angelica stem per 1kg fruit and, with the exception of jams, reduce the sugar by 25–30 per cent. Your first apple and angelica pie will open your eyes to the true worth of this lovely herb.

RHUBARB COMPOTE WITH ANGELICA AND HONEY

2 tsp chopped tender angelica stem and leaf

50g clear honey

350g rhubarb, trimmed and cut into 3–4cm pieces

The angelica here is subtle and lovely, and its inclusion allows for a little less sweetening and therefore a more vibrant rhubarb flavour. Serves 4

Put the angelica into a wide-based pan (that will hold the rhubarb in a shallow layer) with the honey and 2 tbsp water. Bring to a gentle simmer, stirring, and cook for 5 minutes.

Add the rhubarb, cover the pan and continue to cook very gently, turning the pieces over once or twice, as carefully as you can, so they keep their shape. It should take about 10 minutes for the rhubarb to become tender.

Leave to cool completely then serve the compote with a spoonful of cream.

Apples

LATIN NAME
Malus domestica

SEASONALITY
July–October off the tree; later
season apples can be stored
for many months

MORE RECIPES
Buckwheat and apple fritters
(page 103); Griddled fennel and
apple with ricotta (page 255);
Cheddar, apple and celeriac
salad (page 140); Lancashire,
apple and leek pizza (page 151);
Coconut, spinach and apple
sambal (page 192); Mussels
in vinegar with apple and carrot
(page 399); Coley with bacon,
apples and hazelnuts (page 197);
Roast grouse with barley, apples
and squash (page 290); Venison
salad with apple, celeriac and
hazelnuts (page 660); Tongue,
kale and apple hash with horseradish (page 643); Cranberry
and pear sauce (page 213);
Creamed apple and horseradish
sauce (page 316); Roasted
apples with rosemary (page 543);
Spotted dick with apple-brandy
raisins (page 522); Green
tomato, cumin and green chilli
chutney (page 642)

SOURCING
brogdalecollections.org (home
to the national fruit collection);
englandinparticular.info;
charltonorchards.com;
crapes.wordpress.com;
orangepippintrees.co.uk

The apple is my best fruity friend in the kitchen – raw or cooked. And its glorious potential for variety and individuality is realised here, on Britain's apple-friendly soils, more than anywhere else in the world. Not that you would necessarily know it when you're out shopping. Go to the supermarket – or even to most greengrocers – and you'll find your apple choice limited to a short list of varieties that suits the retailer's concerns for uniformity and shelf-life. They're not all bad, but the supermarket fruit shelves are at once a reductive and a weirdly overblown representation of what apples are – so little choice, but so ubiquitously available.

Yet our finest English apples are a highly characterful bunch. The sheer range of colours – every shade of red, green and yellow, and endless blushing combinations thereof – is a pretty good indicator that there is a vast spectrum of qualities to enjoy. That's not to mention the subtle and not-so-subtle russeting, which somehow always speaks of flavour.

In fact, we have around two thousand native varieties, differing widely in their sweetness, sharpness, crispness, tenderness, juiciness and aromatic tartness – yet all quintessentially appley. For me, there is no greater pleasure than biting into a favourite variety of dessert apple, just as it comes. But almost equally exciting is the knowledge of what can be done in the kitchen to transform this most obliging of fruits into crumbles, compotes, caramels or crisps.

The harvest of early varieties may begin as early as July: you can enjoy them in thin slices with a bowl of summer raspberries or even strawberries – and indeed, the fragrant flavour of many early apples has a hint of berry about it. Some varieties even stain pink just beneath the skin. These early varieties don't keep well and should be eaten as soon as possible after picking.

Mid-season apples are picked in September and early October, and the late-season varieties should all be in by Halloween. On the whole, the later the variety, the better it will store – 6 months is achievable for a good late apple in refrigeration.

A fruit bowl in a warm kitchen is not the ideal holding facility for apples, however, not for more than a week or so. And, though most varieties sweeten a little as they age, the texture also softens, which is certainly not to my taste. A wrinkled specimen is on its way out.

If you have a glut of mid to late apples, store (unbruised specimens only) in a cool, dry, frost-free place such as a garage, shed, dry cellar or unheated spare room. Arrange them in a single layer, not touching. They do well sat on newspaper, though proper, slatted storage trays are even better. The latest apple varieties actually benefit from a few weeks' storage in order to come to perfection. A mild autumn and winter will of course speed their demise, so keep an eye on them.

Commercially, it's steady refrigeration at 4–6°C that keeps the best of the home-grown crop going to Easter and beyond. This is not really a domestic option on any kind of scale. But I have taken to storing prize specimens of my most beloved eating varieties (particularly 'Ashmead's Kernel' and 'James Grieve') in the bottom of our family fridge. I can get several dozen in there and, once their garage-stored brethren have begun to lose their charms, I release them at the rate of a couple a day, through January and into February.

Thankfully, British apples in all their wonderful variety and abundance are enjoying a resurgence. Orchards are being revived and old varieties rehabilitated; you'll find some of them, come autumn, at farmers' markets and fruit farms. You can order mixed

FAVOURITE APPLE VARIETIES

In very rough seasonal order, these are my favourite apple varieties:

Discovery One of the earliest apples, and quite widely available, Discovery is rosy red – the pink hue often penetrating deep into the crisp flesh. The flavour has a delicious hint of strawberry. (Pictured left.)

Tydeman's Early Worcester This is a beautifully shiny, red, aromatic early apple. 'Worcester Pearmain', one of its parents, is another good early.

James Grieve Picked from early–mid September, this is a good dual-purpose apple: the tarter, early fruits cook well and those left longer on the tree to sweeten are very good raw.

Bramley's Seedling This is *the* most popular cooking apple and one of the finest. It is sour and needs sweetening, but the bright white flesh cooks down to a uniquely appealing, silky golden purée, which is perfect for sauces, compotes, pies etc. Picked in September or October, it stores well, and British Bramleys are available now for most of the year.

Lord Lambourne This mid-season apple (late September–early October) is crisp, juicy and aromatic, with hints of lemon and rose.

Charles Ross A lovely all-rounder, this large mid-season apple has slightly streaked red-over-gold colouring and very sweet, firm flesh that is as good baked in a tart as eaten raw. Ready from early October.

Blenheim Orange A large, handsome fruit and a great dual-purpose apple. Picking usually begins in October.

Cox's Orange Pippin One of the few British apples to achieve broad distribution in the shops, this is a fine October fruit. The best examples have a wonderful, slightly spicy tang. An ideal partner to cheese, Cox's also cook well, the slices keeping their shape – perfect for an apple tart.

Ashmead's Kernel My all-time favourite. Crisp and nutty to the bite, the juice is fragrant, perfumed and almost sherbet-fizzy. This is a late cropper, available from mid-October, and will store well into the new year.

Orleans Reinette A richly flavoured, late-season apple with lovely citrus notes, dense in texture and nutty, rather than classically crisp.

Egremont Russet Very sweet and nutty with a subtly granular crunch, this golden apple is perfect munched with walnuts and a hunk of Cheddar. It's also ideal for cooking where you want the apple pieces to hold their shape.

boxes of apples from specialist suppliers too (see page 23). I'd urge you to try as many as you can. You're in for a tasty treat, at the very least. At best, your engagement with the delightful world of apples will be transformed forever. Likewise, if you see a British variety you haven't seen before on a supermarket shelf, grab it. You'll be casting a vital vote for apple diversity.

I reckon I munch an English apple 'in hand' almost every day from August to April. But I'm free with them in the kitchen too: roasting, baking or frying, juicing or drying, or stewing them down to a bubbling golden geyser of a compote. And raw apple slices find their way into a lot of my salads: for breakfast with bananas, clementines or kiwis; as a lovely savoury side dish with parsley leaves and matchsticks of celeriac; or as a raw lunch or supper with bittersweet chicory, crunchy hazels or walnuts and a crumbling of blue cheese or Cheddar.

When actually cooking with apples, you need to have an idea whether a given variety will hold its shape, or collapse into a purée. At entry level, it's worth knowing you can always rely on a Bramley to break down, whereas most crisp eating apples hold their shape pretty well – in a tart, say.

But not all apples described as 'cookers' behave like a Bramley, and not all 'eaters' hold fast under fire. Apple suppliers and nurseries can give you more detailed information on specific varieties and their culinary properties, and the websites of some apple tree specialists also touch on this vital matter (see page 23). In the end, though, if you have an unnamed apple, and you want to know how it's going to react to heat, fry a few sample slices gently in butter and you'll soon get an idea. Either way, finish with a sprinkle of brown sugar and a squeeze of lemon or orange juice, and tuck in. Soft or firm, apples pan-cooked like this are as delectable on breakfast pancakes as they are with a pork chop, or snuggling beside melting ice cream.

Roasting is another favourite apple-cooking technique of mine – particularly skin-on wedges of tart eating apple combined with roast roots (try carrots and/or parsnips) for the last 20–30 minutes of their cooking time. These are wonderful alongside roast pork, venison or goose.

But for classic pies and crumbles, I like to partly pre-cook peeled, sliced cookers (ideally good old Bramleys) with a splash of water (or the juice of an orange or two) to stop them catching, and just enough sugar to sweeten without masking their natural acidity. For an occasional change of scene, I'll add peeled slices of a firm eater, such as a Cox, too.

And don't forget the joys of apple juice. Never mind the cartons of pee-coloured clear juice that comes from concentrate. Fresh-pressed, unfiltered apple juice should be cloudy and sweet-sharp. Farm shops and orchards are ideal places to buy; or if you have a juicer, make your own. The intensity of the juice (if I'm drinking it, I often dilute it with a little water) can be amazingly useful in recipes – forming the basis of a sweet-and-sour liquor for braising meat or even fish, for instance. A splash is often useful in balancing all kinds of sauces and dressings, sweet and savoury, too. In fact it's a vanishingly rare moment in my kitchen when I taste something and say 'hmmm… too much apple.'

APPLE AND CHESTNUT CRUMBLE

1kg ripe cooking apples, a variety that collapses on cooking, such as Bramley or early James Grieve

400g crisp eating apples, such as Cox, Ashmead's Kernel or Lord Lambourne

Finely grated zest and juice of ½ lemon

100g caster sugar

FOR THE CRUMBLE TOPPING

100g chestnut flour

75g caster sugar

75g chilled butter, cut into small cubes

25g pumpkin seeds

A pinch of salt

Chestnut flour and pumpkin seeds give this gluten-free crumble a lovely sweet, crunchy topping. The filling makes the most of both eating apples and cookers: the cooking apples break down to a tender purée, while the eating apples retain their form, giving a delicious contrast in texture. Serves 6

Preheat the oven to 180°C/Fan 160°C/Gas 4. Have ready a shallow baking dish, about 25cm in diameter and 5cm deep.

Peel, quarter and core all the apples, then cut the fruit into slices, 5–10mm thick. Put into a large saucepan with the lemon zest and juice, sugar and 2 tbsp water. Bring to a simmer and cook gently, stirring often, for about 10 minutes, until tender but not mushy. Tip into the dish and level out. Set aside.

To prepare the crumble topping, mix the chestnut flour and sugar together in a large bowl. Add the butter cubes and rub into the flour mix with your fingertips until everything is well combined and the mixture is beginning to clump together. Stir in the pumpkin seeds and a pinch of salt.

Scatter the crumble topping over the apple mixture in the dish. Bake for 30–35 minutes until golden and bubbling. Serve hot, with custard or ice cream.

Apricots

Mark Diacono

LATIN NAME
Prunus armeniaca

SEASONALITY
British crop July–September;
European fruit imported
May–August

MORE RECIPES
North African shepherd's pie
(page 335); Apricot and honey
filo pie (page 314)

Legend has it that the nectar of the gods drunk on Mount Olympus was the juice of the apricot. I can believe it. Cousins of cherries, almonds, plums and peaches, apricots represent a heavenly hybrid of the last two in terms of flavour and use. Where peaches taste like the essence of high summer, all juice and freshness, and plums are altogether more autumnal, apricots taste like the balmy but shortening days between the two – rich, warm and almost spicy.

As with peaches, you should not hesitate to lift apricots to your nose before buying them – and taste them if you can. They ripen little once off the tree, so don't expect more fragrance or sweetness to come. A good apricot should have a delicate fruity scent and yield slightly to the touch, but with no hint of bagginess to the skin. Although the fruit's colour can intensify a little as it matures, depth of colour has more to do with variety than ripeness. You may find that greengrocers or good market stalls, who deal in relatively small quantities and can buy fruit that has ripened longer on the tree (and has a shorter shelf-life), will have better fruit than supermarkets.

Apricots from Israel and the US begin to appear on our shelves in mid-May, followed by the Spanish crop and, through July and August, by French apricots. The later season fruit have far less distance to travel to reach our shelves, and as a result are typically allowed to ripen more before picking, developing additional sweetness and flavour; not surprisingly, these are the best. It's worth waiting for them because apricots in their prime are the loveliest of fruits – as wonderful eaten raw as they are made into ice creams or sorbets, or infused in brandy.

If, following the mildest of springs and hottest of early summers, you see English apricots for sale, snap them up. Once rare, Kentish growers have recently succeeded in producing a small but commercially viable crop. They are likely to be the finest you'll taste unless you grow them yourself.

An under-ripe apricot can be coaxed at least a little way along the flavour line with some artificial sunshine in the form of heat and sugar. Poaching works wonders. Halve each fruit, removing the stones, and poach in half wine/half water with a little sugar added, depending on the sweetness of the wine. You can add star anise and/or a vanilla pod but don't overdo it: apricots pair beautifully with both but can easily be overpowered by either. For a subtle variation, crack a few of the apricot stones using a nutcracker and add them to the poaching syrup for a hint of almond. Eat the poached apricots as they are, warm or cold, perhaps with yoghurt for breakfast or dessert, or blitz the fruit to a purée in a little of the poaching liquor and enjoy in fools or cranachans.

Pies, tarts, crumbles, clafoutis and cobblers are among the many desserts suited to apricots. Given their affinity with almonds, I often like to add ground almonds to the pastry or crumble topping for an apricot pud, or to pair the fruit with almondy frangipane in a tart.

If you're looking for a quick breakfast, apricots on toast is hard to better. Set your grill to high and toast 2 slices of bread on one side only. Melt 60g each of butter and honey together in a small pan, add ½ split vanilla pod and 3 cardamom pods and boil for 30 seconds, then remove from the heat. Halve and stone 8 apricots, place them cut side down on a baking sheet and grill for a minute or two until they start to colour. Lay the toast, untoasted side up, on another baking sheet, and place the apricots, cut side up, on the toast. Spoon the honey butter over the fruit and grill for 3–5 minutes until soft and cooked through. Serve immediately, with a little cream or crème fraîche if you fancy.

Apricots originated in China and moved gradually westwards through the Middle East and Africa before they arrived in Europe. The herbs and spices of those early countries (cinnamon, ginger, anise and thyme, in particular) remain classic and fitting partners for apricots. They work together even in savoury recipes: most famously in the sweet spiciness of a lamb tagine, though the sweet/tart taste of apricots suits pork and duck beautifully too.

For a quick stuffing that works brilliantly for a rolled breast of lamb (or a rolled shoulder if you double the quantities), gently fry 4 finely chopped shallots and 4 finely chopped garlic cloves in a little butter until soft then mix with 130g breadcrumbs, 80g chopped apricots (fresh or dried), the grated zest of 2 lemons, a good pinch of salt and plenty of pepper, a small handful of thyme leaves and a lightly beaten egg.

Dried apricots can be fabulous, especially those without the addition of sulphur dioxide, which is used with non-organic fruit to maintain a light colour, and as an antibacterial. A simple rule of thumb: the lighter coloured the fruit, the more sulphur dioxide is likely to have been used.

Unsulphured apricots have a richer, more complex flavour. Fantastic in flapjacks, chopped into fruit cakes or just on their own as a snack, they are perhaps at their best when bathed in a tangy syrup. Soak them in hot tea or orange juice, which draws some of the sugary loveliness out of the fruit, then boil down the soaking liquid to concentrate its flavour and sweetness, before pouring it back over the apricots and leaving to cool. Wonderful with sweetened crème fraîche or mascarpone.

If you live in the south of England, and have the sunniest of sheltered spots and/ or you have the benefit of the extra warmth of a town or city garden, you have the chance of perfect, sun-ripened apricots, fresh from the tree. Although new varieties flower later and may in theory have a greater chance of dodging the last frosts, I prefer two old favourites, 'Moorpark' and 'Albert', which will have more colour, aroma, sweetness and richness than anything in the shops.

ROASTED APRICOT ETON MESS

4 ripe apricots, halved and stoned

1 tbsp brandy

2 tsp caster sugar

150ml double cream

About 25g meringue, home-made or shop-bought, broken into pieces

1 tbsp toasted flaked almonds

This apricot spin on the classic strawberry Eton mess is a great way to make the most of apricots that need the heat of the oven to enhance their flavour and sweetness. Serves 2

Preheat the oven to 190°C/Fan 170°C/Gas 5.

Place the stoned apricot halves, cut side up, in a small roasting tin and sprinkle over the brandy and sugar. Roast for 15–20 minutes, or until the fruit is tender and juicy (the time will depend on how ripe the fruit is). Leave to cool completely then cut each half into 2–4 pieces.

Whip the cream until it holds soft peaks. Fold in the broken meringue pieces followed by the apricots and any of their roasting juices.

Spoon into small glasses or bowls, top with toasted flaked almonds and serve.

Artichoke, globe

Mark Diacono

LATIN NAME
Cynara scolymus

SEASONALITY
May–September

Inside the immature flowerhead of this most majestic of veg patch plants lies a heart of the most incredible, succulent, sweet, earthy loveliness. Unfortunately, however, globe artichokes seem to have been created with the sole aim of denying us their delicious centre.

They come with armour plating, their petals ranging from deeply scarring to outright digit-removing in their sharpness and, once you get past those obstructions, you'll find a furry, irritating layer – not for nothing called the 'choke'. All of this can be tackled, however, with a little robust knifework and a bowl of water with the juice of a lemon added (to prevent the prepared artichokes discolouring).

For artichokes the size of a cricket ball or larger, cut the stem to 2cm in length, lay the artichoke on its side and slice through the petals about 4cm up from the base of the flower. I find a serrated bread knife is the best tool to use for this tough task, but do watch your fingers. Strip off all the remaining petals and remove any tough remnants of them with a knife. Use a sharp teaspoon to wheedle out the furry choke from the centre of the flower. What remains should resemble a wide, squat, pale green wine glass: this is the heart.

Most often, I poach artichoke hearts in a little wine and water until they just take the point of a sharp knife. They are wonderful in salads, in pasta sauces, and eaten with good bread, cheese, pickles and so on. The same can be said for the oil-preserved artichoke hearts you can buy in the shops – and perfectly good they are too, albeit lacking a little of the subtlety of the freshly prepared variety. I tend to go for roasted or char-grilled jarred artichokes, which have a richer flavour, and I look for those preserved in olive oil – more expensive but much more delicious than those in bland sunflower oil.

Vignarola – a light, bright stew – is perhaps my favourite recipe for freshly prepared artichoke hearts and is one of those delicious and satisfying dishes that bend to whatever the season and your larder offer. Soften a few sliced spring onions in a generous splash of olive oil, along with a couple of finely sliced garlic cloves. Add a handful of chopped pancetta or bacon and cook, stirring often, until it is lightly browned. Cut your raw artichoke hearts into quarters and add to the pan then pour in enough wine, cider, water or stock to cover them. Cook, covered, for 15 minutes or so. Season and add a couple of handfuls of whatever vegetables you fancy – broad beans, peas, mangetout, runner beans, etc. – and cook until the veg are just tender. Serve warm, scattered with gremolata, or chopped mint and parsley, and trickle with olive oil and lemon juice.

You can eat the petals of the artichoke too – or, at least, the fleshy base of the petals. I have to confess, I love the celebratory kerfuffle that comes with serving whole, cooked globe artichokes for those around the table to demolish themselves. Preparation is straightforward: slice through the base of the artichoke just above the stem, only enough to ensure a small flat base, not to release all the petals. Cook in plenty of boiling water until the base takes the point of a sharp knife – this can be 20–50 minutes depending on the artichoke's size and freshness.

The artichokes are then ready to be served with a simple dressing – try a vinaigrette, anchovy butter, or melted butter with lemon thyme – and plenty of salt and pepper. Each head can be stripped of its armour, one petal at a time, and dipped into the dressing. You then scrape the succulent flesh from the base of each petal with your teeth. It makes for a slow, satisfying, convivial and messy feast, made all the finer by

a glass of crisp white wine. (When eating artichokes like this, better to concentrate more on the wine and less on the shirt you're wearing.)

Artichokes can also be barbecued. Boil them whole until just shy of readiness, halve lengthways and scrape out any choke. Brush with olive oil, sprinkle with salt and pepper (and a little smoked paprika if you fancy) and barbecue, cut side down, for 3–5 minutes. Serve with a good, punchy vinaigrette.

For small artichokes, roughly the size and shape of a large egg, strip off the petals and any leaves, until only a smooth, bullet-like, pale green-yellow centre remains. Cut away any pieces of hard petal from around the base, then cut the artichoke in half lengthways, removing any just-developing choke.

At their smallest, youngest and freshest like this, globe artichokes can be left uncooked, and dipped in whichever dressing takes your fancy. They are a fabulous early-season treat, largely reserved for those who grow them. This is, thankfully, a very easy project if you start with small plants (much easier than raising them from seed). Any artichokes that you leave unharvested produce the most gorgeous purple flowers that will draw bees and any number of other pollinators into your garden.

ARTICHOKE HEART AND POTATO SALAD

8 globe artichokes (roughly cricket-ball size)

About 400g young new potatoes, scrubbed

A small bunch of mint, leaves finely chopped, stems reserved

Juice of 1 lemon, plus extra for preparing the artichokes

2 tbsp hempseed oil

½ tsp caster sugar

2 tsp shelled hempseeds, toasted

Sea salt and black pepper

Make this in early summer when the first of the new potatoes and globe artichokes arrive. Mint and lemon work well with both, while the use of pungent hemp oil takes the dish in a deliciously nutty direction. Serve on its own with bread, or as a side dish with air-dried ham or salami, or grilled flatfish. Serves 4 as a starter

For this recipe, you want to start with the raw hearts of the artichokes, so prepare them as described on page 30 (third paragraph). Cut each prepared raw heart in half (or quarters, if they are particularly large) and drop into water acidulated with the juice of a lemon.

Meanwhile, bring a large pan of salted water to the boil, add the potatoes and mint stalks and cook for 12–15 minutes or until just tender. Remove the potatoes with a slotted spoon and set aside.

Add the artichoke hearts to the same simmering pan of water and cook for 8–10 minutes, or until just tender.

When the potatoes are cool enough to handle, slice them thickly into a bowl. Once cooked, drain the artichokes and add them to the potatoes.

Combine the lemon juice, hempseed oil, chopped mint leaves and sugar with some salt and pepper. Trickle this dressing over the warm potatoes and artichokes, tumble everything together and finish with a scattering of toasted hempseeds. Allow to cool to room temperature, which will help all the flavours to develop, before serving.

Artichoke, Jerusalem

Mark Diacono

LATIN NAME
Helianthus tuberosus

SEASONALITY
October–March

MORE RECIPES
Carrot soup with ginger and coriander (page 123); Black bream with Jerusalem artichoke purée (page 91)

In season during our bleakest months, Jerusalem artichokes have a distinctive earthy sweetness which helps to offset the worst winter weather. When these knobbly tubers are to be found in the shops, they are relatively expensive, but they are easy and rewarding to grow. They'll give you glorious sunflowers (the Italian for which is *girasole*) to attract beneficial insects, including bees and other pollinators, and to cut for the house. By virtue of their summer foliage, they will also provide a 2-metre-high seasonal windbreak. What's more, if you save a few tubers or leave some in the ground, they will regrow the following year so you only need buy them once.

As with most of the winter tubers and roots, Jerusalem artichokes were made for roasting: scrub them free of soil, cut into chunks, toss in olive or rapeseed oil, salt and pepper, and roast for 30–40 minutes at 190°C/Fan 170°C/Gas 5. Alternatively, roast them whole: they will steadfastly refuse to crisp like a potato, instead quietly losing their solidity while soaking up the flavours around them. Lamb, beef and other roast vegetables are the pairings that spring to mind.

Jerusalem artichokes are surprisingly versatile. Thinly sliced and gently cooked in butter, they soften, ready to purée into one of my favourite bases for risotto; they make a superb creamy soup; and when raw their water-chestnut-like texture takes to pickling perfectly – making a particularly good preserve to serve with Boxing Day ham.

Jerusalem artichokes discolour quickly when their flesh is exposed; if slicing or chopping them, submerge them immediately in water acidulated with a little lemon juice to preserve their colour.

JERUSALEM ARTICHOKE AND SEAWEED TART

The earthy flavour of the artichokes pairs amazingly well with the savoury depth of seaweed in this delicious tart. Serves 6

FOR THE SHORTCRUST PASTRY
250g plain flour
A pinch of salt
125g cold butter, diced

FOR THE FILLING
400g Jerusalem artichokes
A knob of butter
1 tbsp olive or rapeseed oil
1 medium onion, sliced
10–15g dried seaweed, such as dulse or wakame
2 garlic cloves, thinly sliced
50g hard, matured cheese, such as Lord of the Hundreds, Quickes hard goat's cheese or Parmesan, grated
2 medium eggs
2 medium egg yolks
150ml whole milk
150ml double cream
Sea salt and black pepper

For the pastry, put the flour and salt in a food processor and blitz briefly to combine (or sift into a bowl). Add the butter and blitz (or rub in with your fingers) until the mix resembles breadcrumbs. Add just enough cold water (50–60ml) to bring the mix together into large clumps. Knead lightly into a ball, wrap and chill for 30 minutes. Preheat the oven to 180°C/Fan 160°C/Gas 4.

Roll out the pastry to a 3–4mm thickness and use to line a 20cm tart tin; leave the excess pastry overhanging the rim. Prick the base of the pastry with a fork. Bake for 20 minutes or until the base looks dry and lightly coloured. Trim away the excess pastry.

Peel the artichokes and cut into roughly 2cm chunks. Place a frying pan over a low to medium heat. Add the butter and oil followed by the artichokes and onion. Season well and sauté, tossing occasionally, for about 15 minutes until the artichokes are tender but still a little nutty.

Meanwhile, rehydrate the seaweed according to the packet instructions (different types and brands vary). Drain the seaweed and squeeze out excess water with your hands. Discard any tough stalks and then, if it is not already in small pieces, chop it roughly.

Add the garlic to the pan of artichokes and cook for another couple of minutes, then add the seaweed and stir well. Check the seasoning. Scatter the artichoke and seaweed mix into the cooked pastry case and scatter over the grated cheese.

Whisk together the eggs, egg yolks, milk and cream. Add salt and pepper, then carefully pour into the tart case. Bake for 30 minutes or until set and golden. Leave to stand for 20 minutes before slicing and serving.

Asparagus

LATIN NAME
Asparagus officinalis

SEASONALITY
April–June

MORE RECIPES
St George's mushroom and
asparagus pizza (page 609);
Green garlic, asparagus
and oven-scrambled eggs
(page 270)

SOURCING
britishasparagus.co.uk

It's possible to buy asparagus at any time of year. You could, if you wanted, char-grill it on the barbie in August, slather it with hollandaise for your Christmas dinner, or take full advantage of its suggestive form and dunk it seductively into a soft-boiled egg on Valentine's Day. But, while I strongly believe you should explore all these methods of serving asparagus, you'll be selling yourself, and this glorious vegetable, very short if you eat it in any month that isn't April, May or June. So draw a metaphorical black line through the rest of the year and instead cram all the joy of asparagus-eating into the brief but blissful period when the British crop is being cut.

When it comes to what you might call seasonal sensitivity – the degree to which the quality of a vegetable is dependent on the time it's harvested – asparagus has to be at the top of the tree. A member of the lily family, an asparagus plant is formed of a matted, rooty 'crown' beneath the surface of the soil, from which the spears are sent forth in the late spring. The crown depletes its supplies of natural sugars as the weeks progress, so the spears become less sweet: early season asparagus is always the best.

Once cut, asparagus spears deteriorate quickly too because they continue to consume whatever sugars they have at an astonishing rate, particularly in the first 24 hours. Flavour and tenderness diminish at a pace: asparagus eaten more than 3 days after cutting (I'd include pretty much all imported asparagus in that bracket) is likely to be bland and coarse.

If you're starting off with freshly cut asparagus, keeping the spears wrapped in a wet tea towel in the fridge will buy you a little time – perhaps 12 hours of extended sweetness. Some people store it upright in a jug of water, which also helps. Should you manage to bag some very fresh asparagus that you can't eat straight away, you can also preserve its flavour by blanching it in boiling water for 2 minutes then plunging it into cold water before storing it in the fridge for up to 2 days. Blanch the asparagus again before eating, or roast or griddle it.

Timing, then, is everything with asparagus. But our climate and countryside are particularly well suited to producing this unique vegetable and, if you catch it early and fresh, it is extraordinarily good. Its flavour is exquisite and unlike anything else. As well as all that natural sugar, the taste is delicately informed by sulphur-containing compounds, making it not just sweet, but earthy and ever-so-slightly farmyardy (in a good way).

If cut from your own garden and cooked immediately, asparagus is sublime. If you don't grow your own, at least start looking for it very close to home – and if you can buy it from the producer themselves, so much the better. There are lots of growers who sell at the roadside, at farmers' markets or directly into farm shops; some even offer a pick-your-own option.

You may find such fresh, local asparagus a little pricey, but there's good reason for that. It takes 3 years of nurturing before a crown produces its first usable crop. That crop is just a handful of slender spears – maybe a dozen per plant. The season spans barely 70 days and the stuff has to be cut by hand: it's incredibly labour-intensive. View it as the delicacy it is: a seasonal treat, not a year-round staple.

While I'm always looking for tempting new ways to enjoy asparagus, I do think that when you have a bunch of the very sweetest, super-fresh, early season spears in your hands, you should do as little to them as possible. That initial, glorious bundle should be enjoyed, reverentially, in the simplest ways. I eat the very first baby stems from my own patch raw, with just a simple dressing.

For anything thicker than a toddler's thumb, bring a large pan of lightly salted water to the boil. Snap off the woody ends, which will break naturally at the point where the stem becomes tender, and give the spears a thorough rinse (the feathery tips often harbour grains of grit). Drop into the boiling water and cook just until the tip of a knife pierces a stem without effort – with really fresh stuff, you're looking at 2–3 minutes. Spears that are 1 or 2 days old need more like 5–6 minutes. Drain, trickle over a little melted butter, season and you're away.

Dunking just-cooked asparagus into the hot, golden yolk of a soft-boiled egg, into which I've first added a nut of butter, a few drops of cider vinegar and a pinch of salt and pepper (for a kind of instant, improvised hollandaise sauce), is another favourite way to eat the season's first, finest stems. And after that, I'll move on to roasting, griddling and barbecuing (in all cases, lightly blanching the spears first).

When buying, look for asparagus with a bright green colour and very firm, undamaged stems. Many varieties have a beautiful, purplish blush to their tips that makes them look like just-dipped paintbrushes. You may also come across completely purple varieties. All are good (though some of this colour will be lost on cooking).

White asparagus, now being grown in the UK, is produced by 'blanching' – banking the soil up against the spears as they develop. I find its popularity a little mysterious: it tastes milder or, in other words, less of asparagus, than its green cousin – and why would anyone want that?

RAW ASPARAGUS AND RADISH SALAD

250g asparagus

75g radishes

2–3 spring onions

2 tbsp shredded mint

A few shavings of Parmesan or other hard, salty cheese, or a few nuggets of ricotta (optional)

FOR THE DRESSING

3 tbsp extra virgin olive or rapeseed oil

2 tsp cider vinegar

¼ tsp English mustard

Sea salt and black pepper

This super-simple, colourful dish is a real celebration of early summer and an ideal way to use very fresh, reasonably slender spears of asparagus. Serves 2 as a starter or side dish

To make the dressing, put all the ingredients into a jam jar, screw on the lid and shake vigorously to emulsify.

Snap off the woody ends of the asparagus. Slice the spears as thinly as you can, either using a vegetable peeler and working along the spears to produce 'ribbons', or cutting across the spears with a sharp knife at a sharp angle to create elongated, oval slivers. Any odd bits of asparagus left over can be used in a soup or risotto. Put the slivered asparagus in a bowl. Add the dressing and toss well.

Trim and thinly slice the radishes and add them to the asparagus. Trim and finely slice the spring onions and add these too, along with the mint. Toss gently to combine, then taste and add more seasoning if necessary. You can leave the salad now for anything up to a few hours – the veg will soften and 'relax' in the dressing – or serve it straight away.

Spoon on to serving plates and finish, if you like, with some wafers of salty cheese, or a few little nuggets of ricotta. Give it a final little grinding of black pepper, and serve.

Aubergine

Mark Diacono

LATIN NAME
Solanum melongena

ALSO KNOWN AS
Eggplant

SEASONALITY
British crop August–October;
imported all year round

MORE RECIPES
Roasted sweet potatoes and
aubergine (page 628)

Aubergines love sunshine. It seems likely they originated in India but, centuries ago, they made the hop to Europe and are now to be found flourishing in the heat around the Med too, soaking up the rays through their glossy black skins. Their love of heat means that the best ones are those in the shops at the tail end of summer and in early autumn, when they've basked as much as they can. It also means that there is a rich heritage of aubergine recipes that use other sun-loving ingredients as well. Tomatoes, capers, olives, peppers, garlic, olive oil and the sunny herbs of the Mediterranean – rosemary, thyme and basil – are especially good with aubergines. They also pair deliciously with many earthy spices of the East; their affinity with cumin, for instance, can lead to some particularly heavenly combinations.

It's perhaps tomatoes that most commonly, and beautifully, join the dots with aubergines. A simple tomato sauce brings aubergine together with mozzarella in an Italian *parmigiana* (see below), with fried green peppers in the Turkish dish *patlican biber kizartmasi*, with lamb in the classic moussaka, with peppers and courgettes in a ratatouille, and with celery and capers in sweet and sour Sicilian caponata, to name but a few.

For a while, the culinary delights of these beautiful vegetables (technically fruits) passed us by. A member of the nightshade (Solanaceae) family, aubergines were grown largely as ornamentals because, like their close relatives tomatoes and potatoes, they have flowers and stems that are poisonous in substantial doses. Even putting that aside, you can understand how an aubergine's pleasures might be overlooked. That firm black skin doesn't appear overly appetising. A raw aubergine is unremarkable of flavour and rubbery of texture, so it's not immediately apparent how it might become something delectable to eat. However, roasted, stewed or fried, its firmness is transformed into a delightful silkiness.

Frying needs a little care: a single slice of aubergine will soak up a glug of olive oil in a second, though this is considerably reduced if you get the oil nicely hot before you add the aubergines. Salting is another method that seems to work. Aubergines were traditionally sliced and salted to draw out moisture and any bitterness with it. Modern varieties are much less bitter and don't require salting for that reason, but the process does break down their sponge-like texture, saving you a small fortune in olive oil. Cut aubergines into 5–10mm slices, sprinkle the cut sides with salt and leave for 30–60 minutes. Rinse and pat dry before using.

There are two simple but delicious aubergine recipes that everyone should have in their arsenal. *Parmigiana di melanzane* is a fabulous, meat-free halfway house between lasagne and moussaka that mingles aubergines, tomatoes and mozzarella in a hugely satisfying combination. Slice, salt, rinse and dry 3 large aubergines then fry the slices in hot oil for 2–3 minutes each side until golden. In a 25 x 20cm baking dish, arrange the fried aubergines in layers with tomato sauce, torn mozzarella and freshly grated Parmesan (probably 3 layers of each), topping with more grated Parmesan. Bake for 30–40 minutes at 180°C/Fan 160°C/Gas 4 and serve with plenty of salad leaves and a good, sharp dressing.

And then there's baba ganoush, a wonderfully smoky dip that is ridiculously moreish with flatbreads. Roast 3 aubergines over a barbecue or the flames of a gas ring, or grill them, turning frequently to blacken the skin, until the core is soft and collapsing on itself. Allow to cool a little, then peel away the charred skin, or scoop the flesh out if that's easier. Mash the smoky flesh in a bowl with 3 finely chopped garlic cloves, then

stir in 3–4 tbsp tahini, 1 tsp dried chilli flakes, 50g plain wholemilk yoghurt and lemon juice to taste (I like a lot – up to 2 lemons' worth). Season and spoon into a bowl to serve, dusted with ground cumin and finely chopped parsley and finished with a trickle of olive oil. Try not to eat it all at once.

The classic, elongated purple-black aubergine is by far the most common, but you can also buy a plump, spherical variety which tastes, arguably, even better and forms lovely slices for frying. The extra silkiness and flavour may be due to the shape: more flesh to skin. I find the increasingly common striped aubergines, often sold as 'Graffiti' aubergines, generally less bitter than black ones. This may be due to the specific variety but I have a hunch it could be down to the pigments in the skin: this is backed up by one of my favourite varieties for home-growing, 'Rosa Bianca', which is white, blushed with pale purple, and particularly sweet. Baby aubergines look wonderful and make for quick cooking without the need for anything more than halving, but I've found their much higher proportion of skin to flesh can sometimes make them bitter.

You may find tiny 'pea aubergines' in the shops these days too; these mini-fruits are popular in Thai cooking in particular, and have a wonderful, almost crunchy texture. They are small enough to be thrown into a curry sauce to cook without salting, slicing or pre-cooking.

In all cases, when buying aubergines, scent will not help you, but texture will. A good one should be as taut as a birthday balloon.

Aubergines are well worth growing yourself. Don't expect home-grown examples to reach the same dimensions as commercial ones, but you'll be rewarded in flavour if not in enormity. Fresh off the vine they have a particular richness matched only by the very best bought in the shops. Grafted aubergines – where a variety is joined on to a separately grown root system – are increasingly available as young plants, and seem to produce well in our climate. 'Moneymaker', 'Black Beauty' and 'Rosa Bianca' are my favourite varieties – each with its own distinct flavour, rich and complex when cooked. They won't give you much trouble, as long as they get plenty of sun and warmth, and are watered and fed regularly.

GRIDDLED AUBERGINES WITH SPICED YOGHURT

A very simple and delicious side dish – fantastic with lamb or as part of a mezze spread. Pre-salt the aubergine slices if you have time (see page 37). Serves 4 as a side dish

4 medium aubergines (about 1kg), cut into 8mm thick slices

Olive or rapeseed oil, for brushing

Sea salt and black pepper

FOR THE DRESSING

1½ tsp cumin seeds (or 1 tsp ready-ground cumin)

1½ tsp coriander seeds (or 1 tsp ready-ground coriander)

150g plain wholemilk yoghurt

¼–½ garlic clove, crushed

Juice of ½ lemon

A pinch or two of dried chilli flakes, to taste

TO FINISH

2 tbsp finely shredded mint leaves

2 tbsp pumpkin seeds

If you are toasting your own cumin and coriander seeds for the dressing, put them in a dry frying pan and toast over a medium heat for a few minutes until fragrant. Tip out on to a plate and leave to cool, then crush or grind fairly finely, using a pestle and mortar or spice grinder. Set aside.

Heat a griddle pan, or a heavy-based, non-stick frying pan over a medium-high heat. Brush a few of the aubergine slices on both sides with oil and sprinkle with salt and pepper, then place them in the pan. Cook for about 3 minutes each side until tender and golden, then transfer to a large serving platter. Repeat until all the aubergine slices are cooked.

For the dressing, mix the yoghurt with the ground spices, garlic, lemon juice, chilli flakes and some salt and pepper.

Spoon the dressing over the aubergine slices and sprinkle with the pumpkin seeds and shredded mint to serve.

Note You can use the same ingredients to make a silky aubergine dip: grill the whole aubergines until blackened and soft (as for baba ganoush, see page 37), remove the skins and purée the flesh with the spices, garlic, lemon juice and chilli, then top with the yoghurt, mint and pumpkin seeds.

Avocado

Nikki Duffy

LATIN NAME
Persea americana

ALSO KNOWN AS
Avocado pear

SEASONALITY
Imported all year round

MORE RECIPES
Kiwi, spinach and avocado smoothie (page 325); Lime and coconut mousse (page 358)

The creamy, crushable flesh of the avocado, rich in vitamin E and monounsaturated fat, is healthy and versatile. It gives you an almost instant dressing or dip, vegan 'butter' or smoothie. It is the very thing to put in a raw salad to make it feel substantial – and it can even be whipped into thick, rich, dairy-free mousses, icings and cake batters. For a quick lunch, roughly mash avocado and spread thickly on garlicky sourdough toast with a sprinkling of Parmesan, a trickle of olive oil and some salt and pepper.

Undeniably, there are food miles attached to this fruit. None of us in the UK are likely to buy locally grown avocados. They're imported, year round, from countries including Africa, Central and South America, Spain and Israel. On the plus side, however, very few these days are air-freighted – most come by ship or by road.

There are several varieties of avocado in the shops. Greenskin types, such as 'Fuerte', are smooth skinned and elongated, while 'Hass', the most common variety, is plump and round, with distinctive, dark green, rough-textured skin. Its flesh, having a higher oil content than some other varieties, is particularly rich.

Another point in the Hass's favour is that its skin darkens as it ripens – and anything that helps pinpoint an avocado's fleeting moment of perfect ripeness is to be welcomed. The disappointment of slicing this fruit open to find it either unpalatably hard or turning softly black is sadly not uncommon. Give your avocado a gentle squeeze at the stem end: if it's ripe, it should give a little. If it's completely unyielding, it will need ripening – just leave it in the fruit bowl for a few days, ideally near some ethylene-producing bananas. Any real softness or black patches on the skin signal that it's well past its best. A perfectly ripe avocado can be preserved in the fridge for a few days.

To prepare an avocado, slice it lengthways through the middle, all the way round, and twist apart. Now take a large heavy knife, and drop it smartly downwards with a flick of the wrist, into the heart of the stone. It should bite and, with a slight lift and twist, you'll be able to pull the stone out.

For mashed avocado, just scoop it out of the skin. For slices, quarter the fruit and peel off the skin first. That rich flesh quickly discolours so use it up fast. Blending or sprinkling it with lemon or lime juice is the best way to slow down the browning.

CHILLED AVOCADO SOUP WITH TOMATOES

2 large, ripe avocados

1 cucumber (about 400g)

½ small red onion, chopped

½ garlic clove, finely chopped (optional)

1 medium-hot red chilli, deseeded and finely chopped, or a pinch of dried chilli flakes

Grated zest and juice of 1 lime

3–4 tbsp roughly chopped coriander, plus extra to serve

1 tbsp tamari (or soy sauce)

150–200g cherry tomatoes

Extra virgin olive or rapeseed oil

Sea salt

Rich, cool and refreshing, this smooth soup has all the flavours of guacamole. Serves 3–4

Halve, stone and peel the avocados. Roughly chop the flesh and put it into a blender. Peel and roughly chop the cucumber. Add to the blender with all the other ingredients except the tomatoes, oil and salt. Pour in 150ml water and blend to a thick, smooth soup. Taste and add salt and more lime juice as needed.

Transfer to a bowl, cover and refrigerate for at least an hour, to chill and allow the flavours to develop. Meanwhile, cut the tomatoes into quarters or eighths.

Serve within 48 hours, topped with the tomatoes, a little coriander and a trickle of oil.

Bacon & pancetta

Hugh Fearnley-Whittingstall

SOURCING

dorsetcharcuterie.co.uk; peelham.co.uk; trealyfarm.com

In my book, a great British bacon bap rivals the street food of any other nation – from Italy to Indonesia – for sheer, indulgent deliciousness. Tender bread, a splash of tangy ketchup and a few hot, crisp rashers releasing their delectably salty, savoury fat as you dig in. Few, surely, are above such pleasure.

It's a pitiful shame, then, that this totemic treat is so often ruined by rubbish bacon. Introduce limp, insipid, weirdly pink rashers to heat and they release a mix of briney liquid and sinister white goo that prevents them ever achieving the desired crispness.

If, like me, you expect more of your bacon, you've got to start with the pig. Intensive pig farming is a profoundly miserable business (see page 488). And it produces miserable pork: fast-grown, flaccid and flavourless. Such meat is bullied into becoming 'bacon' with a dose of preservatives and flavouring chemicals. So if your pack doesn't have the words 'free-range' or 'organic' on it, or the RSPCA's Assured label at the very least, I'd put it back on the shelf. Vote for a better class of bacon, from a happier pig.

If you can, buy your bacon from a farm shop, butcher's or market where you can chat to the person who actually made it. Find out about the breed of pig, the way it was reared, and the curing process. Bacon is special enough – and pigs are smart enough – to warrant such consideration.

Sample some of the old British varieties such as the sweet-cured Suffolk or the traditional wet-cured Wiltshire and you will be reminded what bacon is: a punch-packing, meaty game-changer. Richly flavoured, salty, sweet and tangy, robust in texture and deliciously crisp when fried, it's an ingredient so full of character that just a little of it transforms a recipe. Hot shards of sautéed, smoked bacon can season a big dish of veg or pulses, for instance. A whole rasher or two, with nothing more than a slice of bread and a creamy egg, make for breakfast heaven.

Bacon is a very simple thing: pork belly and/or loin, salted and left to cure so that moisture is drawn out of the meat as salt travels in. The salt enhances the flavour and vastly increases its keeping qualities. Salting may be done via a 'dry-cure' rubbed on to the meat, or it may be 'wet-cured' by immersion in brine.

Dry-curing produces particularly good bacon precisely because it takes longer: flavour develops as the meat matures. It also gives a good, firm texture. There's nothing wrong with wet-curing, though, as long as you use a good brine and allow it to penetrate slowly. It produces slightly more tender bacon with a shorter shelf life. Commercial bacon production, at its worst, involves injecting additive-laden brine directly into the meat. This speeds up the process but makes for flabby bacon – and liquid forced into the meat in this way is bound to make an unwelcome reappearance in the frying pan.

Streaky bacon is all belly meat. It forms long, narrow rashers that may have as much fat as lean, which makes it a superb ingredient in countless dishes. Chopped and fried, it releases that flavoursome fat to permeate, lubricate and season soups, stews, pasta and risottos. Back bacon includes the loin and a section of belly, giving the characteristic breakfast slice with a large, lean 'eye' of meat and a fattier 'tail'. Either kind may be smoked. Whether you use smoked or unsmoked is entirely up to you. I prefer the simplicity and sweetness of an unsmoked cure in my bacon butties, but I use smoked to impart flavour to soups and sauces, and I particularly like smoked bacon in beany-pulsey stews.

Pancetta is Italian-style streaky bacon. It also uses the belly, but the traditional curing process is slightly different. Pancetta may be cured flat (*tesa*), just like streaky, and can be used in all the same ways. Or it may be rolled (*arrotolata*).

If this is re-whetting your appetite for really great bacon, I'd urge you to take the porky plunge and rustle up some rashers yourself. It's incredibly easy, delicious and one of the most satisfying steps you can take away from industrially produced food.

You need good, fatty pork belly – cuts from rare-breed pigs such as 'Gloucester Old Spot' or 'Middle White' are best. A whole belly divides neatly into three pieces of a good size for salting. But a much smaller single piece, weighing 1.5–2kg, is perfect for your first foray.

Mix a cure of 50:50 fine salt and brown sugar and add some aromatic flavourings: shredded bay leaves, cracked black pepper and crushed juniper berries are my standards. Scatter a generous handful of cure in a deep-sided plastic tray, add the pork belly and rub another handful of cure over it. Cover and leave in the fridge or a very cool place for 24 hours. Pour off the liquid that has leached from the meat, apply a fresh layer of cure and repeat daily for 3 or 5 days. For a sweeter, lighter cure – perfect for breakfast rashers – opt for 3 days. The 5-day cure gives you an old-school farmhouse bacon, which is on the salty side but perfect for slow-cooked soups and stews.

In either case, rinse the bacon well, wipe the surface with a cloth soaked in vinegar, then pat dry. Now hang to dry in a well-ventilated, cool, dry place (or return to the fridge, wrapped loosely in a tea towel) for 5–10 days. Then it's ready to go. Three-day cured bacon should be refrigerated, loosely wrapped, and used within a fortnight. Five-day cured will keep out of the fridge, hung on a hook at cool room temperature, for up to 3 months (getting firmer and drier). If spots of mould appear, just wipe them off with a vinegar-dipped cloth.

Freeze any bacon you don't use within these time frames. But I think you'll be hard-pushed to leave it alone.

BACON AND CELERIAC TART

400g celeriac, peeled and roughly chopped

Olive or rapeseed oil, for cooking

225g smoked streaky bacon, chopped

1 large or 2 medium onions, finely sliced

Leaves from a large sprig of thyme (optional)

320g ready-made all-butter puff pastry (ready-rolled is convenient)

A little milk, to glaze

A handful of parsley leaves, finely chopped

Sea salt and black pepper

This works equally well with parsnip or swede. Serves 4–6

Preheat the oven to 190°C/Fan 170°C/Gas 5 and grease a large baking sheet.

Simmer the celeriac chunks in salted water for 10–12 minutes until tender. Drain and allow to steam-dry in the colander.

Heat a large frying pan over a medium heat. Add a splash of oil and the bacon and fry briskly for a few minutes until starting to brown. Add the onion with the thyme, if using. Stir, reduce the heat and cook for about 10 minutes until the onion is soft and golden.

If it's not already rolled, roll out the pastry to a rectangle, about 32 x 25cm and 3mm thick. Lift the pastry on to the baking sheet and score a margin around it, 2cm in from the edge.

Roughly mash the celeriac and spread it over the pastry, leaving the margin clear. Season lightly with salt and pepper. Spoon the bacon and onion mixture evenly on top, trickling over a little of the bacon fat from the pan too; press lightly down into the celeriac.

Brush the pastry rim with milk. Bake for 20–25 minutes or until the pastry is golden and the topping browned. If the topping looks as though it is browning too much, place a piece of foil loosely over it, leaving the pastry rim uncovered.

Leave the tart to stand for around 10 minutes before slicing and serving, scattered with chopped parsley.

Baking powder & bicarbonate of soda

Nikki Duffy

ALSO KNOWN AS
Baking soda (bicarbonate of soda)

MORE RECIPES
Wild garlic fritters (page 273); Spotted dick with apple-brandy raisins (page 522); Drip scones (page 237); Summer savory scones (page 569); Cherry, thyme and marzipan muffins (page 154); Rye and caraway scones (page 114)

Bicarbonate of soda, aka baking soda, is an alkaline powder that, when combined with liquid and an acid such as lemon juice, vinegar, honey or the lactic acid in yoghurt, releases carbon dioxide. It's quite a powerful reaction, as you can see if you pour a little vinegar on to some bicarbonate in a cup. It's fast too, which is why batters made with bicarb need to be got into the oven without delay. Those bubbles of gas, caught within a dough or batter, cause it to swell and rise. As the heat of the oven sets the crumb, the bubbles are trapped and a light, airy texture is created.

Baking powder, which made its first appearance around 1850, is a ready-blended combination of bicarbonate of soda with an acid. This always used to be cream of tartar but is now more likely to be another chemical such as a phosphate, which will only react once heated. So getting your cake into the oven quickly isn't as important as it used to be.

Baking powder also includes a 'buffer' such as maize or rice flour (occasionally wheat flour) to prevent any reaction happening in the tub. Some reaction will inevitably take place, however, which is why it's not wise to use baking powder that's out of date.

One of the disadvantages of bicarbonate of soda is that if acidic ingredients aren't present in the right quantities alongside it, they won't completely neutralise the bicarb and vestiges of its slightly bitter, soapy taste may remain in the finished item. If you find this, try reducing the quantity of bicarbonate slightly, or increasing the acidic ingredient in the mix just a touch.

Some recipes use a combination of the two agents. Baking powder will do a reliable job of leavening the batter but, as long as there's something acidic in the mix, the bicarbonate will contribute a little extra oomph. In addition, because of its alkalinity, it also contributes to a complex process called the Maillard reaction, which enhances colouring and the development of 'toasty' flavours in food. For instance, a buttermilk muffin made with bicarbonate as well as baking powder will be browner and more richly flavoured than one made with baking powder alone.

HONEYCOMB

1 tsp bicarbonate of soda

100g caster sugar

60g clear honey

This classic sweet treat capitalises on the voluminous reaction of bicarbonate of soda when added to a slightly acidic medium (in this case, a solution of sugar and honey). The Maillard reaction is at work here too, contributing to the honeycomb's rich golden colour. Sprinkle the broken comb on creamy and/or fruity puds, or just munch straight from the jar. Makes enough to sprinkle on a pudding for at least 8

Line a baking tray with a sheet of baking parchment or a silicone liner. Have your bicarbonate of soda measured out ready.

Put the sugar, honey and 2 tbsp water in a medium, heavy-based saucepan. Place over a medium heat, stirring a few times until the sugar has dissolved and you have a dull, pale brown liquid, then increase the heat. Once the solution is boiling, boil it for about 3 minutes until golden brown and just starting to give off a burnt sugar smell.

Immediately remove from the heat, add the bicarbonate of soda and stir vigorously as the mixture foams and froths up. Once all the bicarbonate is worked in, tip the foaming mixture on to the prepared baking sheet.

Leave for half an hour or so until completely set and cold, then break up and store in an airtight container, such as a Kilner jar or plastic box.

Banana & plantain

Hugh Fearnley-Whittingstall

LATIN NAME
Musa species

SEASONALITY
Imported all year round

MORE RECIPES
Mango and banana salad
(page 374); Upside-down
chocolate plum pudding
(page 189); Linseed, banana and
chocolate muffins (page 359)

I don't think I could ever by-pass bananas, they're a pretty much permanent fixture on my shopping list. I press them into service for breakfast, baking, drinks and even savoury dishes. Their less-sweet brethren, the plantains, are a more occasional but worthwhile purchase – with their many savoury possibilities, they make an interesting tropical alternative to potatoes.

Although botanically almost identical, bananas and plantains are quite different when it comes to eating. Bananas, with their irresistibly sweet and silky flesh, are so good that we eat them raw without thinking (although they can be excellent cooked too). Some of us may reach for a banana two or three times a day. Their flavour is delicately floral and grassy, developing into something rich, honeyed and slightly yeasty as they ripen. Those flavours can be brought out by pairing them with everything from chocolate to chicken.

Plantains are considerably more starchy – you certainly wouldn't want to eat one raw. When cooked, however, their mild sugars and tender texture come to the fore in a very appealing way. If you enjoy sweet potatoes, squashes and parsnips, I'll take a punt that plantains will please you too. You can find them in some supermarkets, but shops that cater to African, Asian, West Indian and South American cooks are the best hunting grounds. There are several different varieties, of varying shape, colour and sweetness, but the general rule is that the greener they are, the starchier they are, and the yellower (or in some cases redder) the sweeter.

Ripeness is of course the key with bananas too. They become sweeter and more deeply aromatic as they develop from green to yellow to speckled to black. When choosing a banana to eat *au naturel*, we all like to intercept that transformation at different points: I'm a just-starting-to-speckle man myself. You can hold that point of perfection for a couple of days, by putting them in the fridge once they've reached (or got very close to) the magic moment. That will slow the ripening right down, though the skin will discolour so they won't look so good. But the joy of bananas is that wherever they're at on the ripeness spectrum, there's always some delicious use to which they can be put.

Starchy plantains ripen more sedately. Green or just-yellow ones are good baked whole in their skins, at 200°C/Fan 180°C/Gas 6 for an hour or so, until black and tender. Slice open the skins and serve rather like a jacket spud: the hot, crumbly flesh trickled with melted butter or good oil and sprinkled with salt and pepper. Fried plantain is another good dish, that works particularly well when the skin of the fruit is yellowish and well-blotched with black – or even heading for over-ripeness.

Whatever stage a plantain is at, slice off the tip and tail. If it is ripe, you'll be able to remove the peel fairly easily. With under-ripe plantains, a small knife may be needed to pare the skin away.

Green bananas can be cooked rather like plantains. They take well to the frying pan and love a bit of spice. I've added them, peeled and sliced, to kedgeree, and to fish in a foil parcel with coconut milk, tamarind and chilli. An over-ripe specimen, on the other hand, is just what you need for cakes, muffins, ice creams and smoothies. The riper the banana, the more flavour and sweetness it will give.

I buy organic bananas when I can find them, and Fairtrade bananas (see overleaf) when I can't. It's gratifying to see how widely available they have become – a great example of the positive changes that happen when conscientious consumers vote with their shopping trolleys.

Fairtrade

The Fairtrade mark, which you'll find on many bananas as well as other goods, indicates that the producers have received fair terms of trade and a fair price, whatever the conventional market price. Fairtrade producer organisations also receive a premium to be used for business or social development projects.

Having been largely welcomed since its inception in 1992, Fairtrade has come in for criticism in recent years. It aims to offer better working conditions and a sustainable future for producers in developing countries. 'Normal' trading arrangements keep many such communities in poverty. Growers produce their crops in challenging circumstances and, with scant commitment from their trading partners to their long-term economic well-being, they're at the mercy of volatile international markets and exploitative multinationals who are in a position to push prices very low. For these growers Fairtrade certification can make the difference between destitution and survival.

Some critics argue that the Fairtrade endorsement is misleading, that only a small percentage of the extra money paid for Fairtrade goods reaches farmers and workers in the developing world and Fairtrade focuses on relatively well-off producers so that the poorest miss out. I welcome this scrutiny into the administration and application of Fairtrade resources and I've no doubt there are things that can be improved. But the basic principle of Fairtrade seems to me unshakeably sound.

More subtle economic arguments describe Fairtrade as a short-term solution that could actually harm developing world economies by encouraging producers to maintain their reliance on low-value commodities, such as bananas, rather than diversifying into higher value products, like avocados, or beginning to process their own raw goods (roasting coffee, for example). The answer to this is that there is little hope of diversification or investment (both risky and expensive) if farmers struggle on with non-Fairtrade prices. The resources, long-term trading relationships and stability needed for diversification are exactly what Fairtrade seeks to create.

I'd concede that buying Fairtrade is not a cure-all. The issues of supply, demand, workers' rights, market economics and global politics are far too complex to be 'solved' by our choice of one banana over another. For the conscientious consumer, an ideal complement to buying Fairtrade is to research products and companies individually in order to choose those which are most traceable, sustainable and ethically sound.

But, while Fairtrade is not by any means a universal panacea, buying certified products has been shown to have concrete positive effects in individual communities. I don't doubt that if we all stopped buying Fairtrade, things would go backwards. Fairtrade bananas are still going into my basket – along with FT coffee, chocolate, tea, dried fruits and many other products from far-flung agricultural communities.

BANANA AND PEANUT BUTTER ICE CREAM

2 large, sliced frozen bananas

80g crunchy, no-sugar-added peanut butter

2–3 tsp clear honey, to taste

If you have an excess of ripe or slightly over-ripe bananas, peel, slice and freeze them spread out on a plate. The frozen banana purées to a velvety ice 'cream', which is dairy-free. Peanut butter and honey add texture and flavour, but it works with bananas alone. Serves 3–4

Place all the ingredients in a blender or food processor and blitz until smooth and creamy, stopping several times to scrape down the sides. It might look unpromising at first, but it will soon come together. Scoop into bowls straight away before the ice cream 'melts', or put it back in the freezer.

Barley

Gill Meller

LATIN NAME
Hordeum vulgare

ALSO KNOWN AS
Pot barley, pearl barley

MORE RECIPES
Roasted beetroot orzotto with lavender (page 68); Walnut, barley, rocket and blue cheese salad (page 666); Minted spelt and tomato salad (page 386); Roast grouse with barley, apples and squash (page 290); Saffron speltotto with black pudding and parsley (page 548)

Barley is one of the world's most ancient cultivated grains and, in Britain, its use can be traced back to the dense loaves of the Iron Age. In recent decades, it has fallen out of favour – suffering from a rather dull image. Most of our barley crop currently goes for animal feed or for making beer and whisky. However, this robust grain is being rediscovered as a thrifty and hearty ingredient. It's certainly a favourite at River Cottage.

Barley grains have a tough, inedible outer casing. To produce pot barley, just this outer layer is removed, while the bran layer is left on. This makes for a nutty, chewy, nourishing wholegrain, albeit one that takes up to an hour to cook.

The barley we use most is pearl barley, which has the bran partially or entirely removed, making it a bit quicker to cook. It needs to be rinsed then simmered in lots of water for 30–40 minutes, until tender. Pre-soaking it in cold water for several hours can knock 10–20 minutes off the cooking time.

Barley is traditionally used for thickening soups and stews. Throw pearl or pot barley into a pan of slow-braising shin of beef and bacon, or into a Scotch broth or mutton soup with greens. You only need a small handful: the grains can absorb up to four times their weight in liquid, taking on all the hearty flavours you cook them with.

Pearl barley is delicious as a substitute for rice in a pilaf or a barley version of a risotto, known in Italy as *orzotto* (see page 68). The beauty of barley is that it's almost impossible to overcook: it seems to just swell and swell, without turning to mush.

Cooked pearl barley is especially good in autumnal salads with mushrooms (see below), and with roasted squash. Cooked barley grains add texture and character to home-made bread, particularly alongside seeds such as sunflower; they're great in stuffings too. Try loosely stuffing chicken or game birds with cooked barley flavoured with cinnamon, honey, thyme, raisins and lemon zest. A grainy barley version of a vegetarian nut loaf works well too, using onion, apple and sage.

Today's lovely malted grain bread flours include nutty, malted barley to lend flavour and sweetness. Steamed and rolled barley flakes can be used in similar ways to porridge oats (but be aware that barley does contain gluten). And barley flour is used to make traditional Scottish flatbreads called bannocks.

BARLEY AND RAW MUSHROOM SALAD

100g pearl barley, rinsed

A small bunch of flat-leaf parsley, leaves picked, stalks reserved

A small bunch of mint, leaves picked, stalks reserved

4–5 large chestnut mushrooms

3 tbsp extra virgin olive or rapeseed oil, plus extra to finish

Finely grated zest and juice of 1 lemon

A small bunch of chives

100g ricotta or fresh, mild ewe's or goat's cheese

A handful of dill fronds, chopped

Sea salt and black pepper

This celebrates the contrast of nutty barley, earthy raw chestnut mushrooms and freshly cut herbs. The aniseedy flavour of dill is especially good here but you could use fennel or chervil instead. Serves 2

Put the barley into a pan with a pinch of salt and the parsley and mint stalks. Cover with plenty of water and bring to a gentle simmer. Cook, uncovered, for 30–40 minutes or until tender. Drain and leave to cool.

Cut the mushrooms into 5mm thick slices and arrange in a single layer on large serving plates. Trickle with 2 tbsp oil and the juice of ½ lemon. Season lightly with salt and pepper.

Chop the parsley and mint leaves, and the chives, and add to the barley along with the lemon zest, a dash of lemon juice, the remaining 1 tbsp oil and plenty of salt and pepper. Stir gently.

Scatter the dressed barley over the mushrooms and crumble the cheese on top. Finish with a scattering of chopped dill, a final trickle of oil and another squeeze of lemon. Serve with bread or crostini.

Basil

Mark Diacono

LATIN NAME
Ocimum basilicum

SEASONALITY
June–September

MORE RECIPES
Razor clams with cherry tomatoes and basil (page 528); Strawberry salad with raspberry basil sauce (page 616)

If any herb encapsulates a season, then surely basil is summer. Its sweet aniseed fragrance and flavour please the nose as much as the tastebuds, and pair with so much of what is good in the hottest months of the year.

Its many natural partners include cucumber, tomatoes and courgettes (raw or griddled) in salads. Basil also has an affinity with a wide variety of cheeses, from the deliciously bland (such as mozzarella or ricotta) to the saltily pungent, such as goat's cheese and halloumi.

The most common basil variety found in the shops is 'Sweet Genovese' (pictured right), named after its coastal Italian home, but there are many others to consider. Most are stronger and more pungent than Genovese and, to varying degrees, can be used as much to add a spicy note as a herby flavour. Rub a leaf up close and you'll find the scent can be really quite cinnamon-like, carry quite a hit of cloves, or be dominated by aniseed. These spicy basils accentuate tomatoes quite differently to Genovese – drawing out their fruitiness in a more dessert-like way. Try a leaf of each of these with a strawberry to see how the varieties take fruit in different directions, and you might well find basil appearing in your fruit salads too. Basil also makes a lovely ice cream or sorbet that goes particularly well with peaches or nectarines, and raspberries.

Whichever variety of basil you buy, trim the end of the stems, stand the bunch in a jug of water, keep it in a cool spot out of the fridge and use it soon after purchasing.

There are a couple of things you really need to know in order to get the best out of basil. The first is that, for all that it loves soaking up the summer sun when growing, it really doesn't take well to heat in the kitchen. A gentle warming-through for a pasta sauce is about the most it can stand, so add it late to cooked food, on serving, to retain the fullness of its scent and piquancy.

The second thing to understand about basil is that Mediterranean heat is needed to bring its spicy aniseed and clove notes to the fore, allowing them to dominate the more subtle, floral tones. This is why it is difficult to replicate the truly amazing pesto to be had in Italy with our home-grown basil.

That's not to say a British basil pesto can't be good but I prefer it cut with other herbs: parsley and basil pesto, for instance, has more character and a better balance. It's also worth using a stronger variety of basil, such as Greek, in conjunction with 'Sweet Genovese' in pesto. The flavour of the oil makes a big difference too: go for a grassy, not-too-heavy extra virgin olive oil, so as not to mask the basil. And if you have time, make pesto using a pestle and mortar rather than a processor, for a more complex, multi-layered result.

POPULAR BASIL VARIETIES

Sweet Genovese With its full but not overpowering flavour this is excellent paired simply with mozzarella and good tomatoes, marrying the two in a way no other herb does. It's also lovely in sweet dishes.

Greek basil Tiny-leafed and intensely flavoured, this variety is increasingly available in the shops. It goes even better with tomatoes than Genovese.

Thai basil This is so aniseedy, it is almost in a different category of herb. Perfect in curries and laksas.

Lemon basil The variety for infusing as tea, it's even better paired with fish (gurnard, especially), or cucumbers.

Purple basils These often carry more of a hint of clove than green varieties. Infusing them in white wine vinegar makes an excellent basil vinegar to use for summer salad dressings.

However, a quick pesto can be made in a food processor in seconds: blend together 3 good handfuls of basil and flat-leaf parsley leaves (or just basil if you prefer), a garlic clove and a good pinch of salt. Add a handful of lightly toasted pine nuts and process until fairly smooth, while slowly pouring in a little olive oil until the sauce is thickish and glossy. Once blitzed, stir in a handful of grated Parmesan (or other hard salty cheese, such as Godminster Cheddar or Lord of the Hundreds). Tasting is crucial. Add more salt and pepper, and the juice of ½ lemon, if needed. Taste again and adjust as you like: the key is finding the balance you prefer.

Pistou is a classic Provençal sauce, similar to Italian pesto, although traditionally it doesn't contain pine nuts or cheese (modern versions sometimes include cheese). It is lovely with pasta and in soups. Just prepare the pesto recipe above, omitting the cheese and nuts, and add a little grated lemon zest for an optional edge. Add some grated cheese on serving if you fancy.

Basil grown slowly at home in a pot in the sun will develop greater depth of flavour and aroma than a supermarket herb. This plant needs heat and light. Start it off in modules, from seed, no earlier than May, under cover – on a warm windowsill is fine. Once germinated, give the seedlings as much sunshine as possible, keeping the growing plants well watered too – water the compost (rather than the plant) in the morning, to see them through the warmth of the day. When the roots begin to poke through the base of the modules, transplant them into 9cm pots (or their final place of growing) and re-pot as the basil grows.

BASIL PANNACOTTA WITH MINTED RASPBERRIES

150ml whole milk

300ml double cream

50g caster sugar

3 large sprigs of basil

Enough sheets of leaf gelatine to set 285ml liquid (different brands vary)

150ml plain wholemilk yoghurt

FOR THE MINTED RASPBERRIES

200g raspberries

1 tsp caster sugar

1 tbsp shredded mint leaves

Basil's intoxicating aniseed character makes it a wonderful ingredient in sweet dishes. You can replace the raspberries with loganberries or wineberries. Serves 6

Combine the milk, cream and sugar in a saucepan. Heat to dissolve the sugar and bring to just below a simmer; don't let it bubble. Add the basil sprigs, take off the heat and leave to infuse for an hour. Remove and discard the basil stalks.

Calculate how many gelatine leaves you need to set 285ml liquid (see note). Soak the gelatine in cold water for 5 minutes, until soft and floppy.

Meanwhile, reheat the cream mixture until almost boiling, then remove from the heat. Drain the gelatine leaves and squeeze out excess water, then add to the hot cream mixture, stirring to dissolve.

Leave to cool to room temperature, stirring from time to time. Once cooled, stir in the yoghurt until thoroughly combined. Pour the mixture into six 100ml moulds and chill in the fridge for at least 4 hours, or until set.

Meanwhile, put the raspberries and sugar into a bowl and roughly crush with a fork. Add the mint and set aside to macerate.

To turn out the pannacottas, dip each mould very briefly into hot water to slightly soften the outside of the pannacotta, then invert on to a serving plate and give it a shake; if necessary, run a knife around the edge of the pannacotta to help release it. Serve with the macerated raspberries.

Note In order to achieve the perfect, just-set consistency in this creamy, yoghurty mixture, you'll need less gelatine than you would to set the same volume of a simple jelly.

Bay

Hugh Fearnley-Whittingstall

Laurus nobilis

SEASONALITY
All year round

MORE RECIPES
Braised white beans with greens (page 55); Potted carp (page 118); Lemon-cured herring (page 310); Roast guinea fowl with onions and sage breadcrumbs (page 291); Braised rabbit with turnips (page 652); Salt beef with carrots and potatoes (page 559); Quince in star anise and honey syrup (page 512); Bay syllabub (page 217)

The idea of running out of bay leaves sends a shiver down my spine. I am well insured against such a prospect, since I have bay trees flourishing both at home and in the River Cottage garden, but still the thought slinks up on me every now and again, to give me the culinary creeps. The antidote is to grab a leaf whenever I pass, and have a quick scrunch-and-sniff hit of aromatherapy. It perks me up every time.

In my book, bay is the undisputed king of herbs. I use it almost every day: tucking a few leaves into the cavity of a bird or fish before roasting; stirring them into a slow-simmered stew; infusing them in milk for a white sauce or even a sweet custard. All these dishes, made without bay, would still be perfectly serviceable, but this perfumed leaf makes them sing.

With its intense, woody, citrus aromatics, caught pleasingly between the herb world and the spice world, bay has the power to deepen flavour, to round out a dish, seasoning it subtly yet significantly. It's the kind of ingredient that turns a plate of food from something workmanlike into something memorable, a way to almost effortlessly ratchet up the deliciousness factor a couple of notches.

Bay's heady perfume has long been seen as mysterious and magical. It was once used as a strewing herb to purify the air in medieval and Tudor homes. And Nicholas Culpeper wrote in his herbal of 1653 that bay, 'resisteth witchcraft very potently… neither witch nor devil, thunder nor lightning, will hurt a man in the place where a bay-tree is.' It's not hard to see how the bay's lovely scent could have been invested with such powers. I am so fond of this leaf that my younger daughter Louisa's middle name is Bay – as she gets older, she may be grateful that my favourite herb wasn't basil or borage.

Were you to pop a bay leaf into your mouth and chew it, the experience would not be pleasant. Sharing flavour compounds with both eucalyptus and cloves, bay in its neat form is bitter and harsh. But if you put the leaves next to, inside or underneath the thing you want to eat, soak them in hot liquid, infuse them in salt, oil or fat, even set fire to them, then you're talking.

My personal passion for it aside, bay is probably the single most versatile – and therefore most useful – culinary herb of all. It is an essential ingredient in a classic bouquet garni, along with thyme and parsley. It goes into every stock I make, whether meat-, fish- or veg-based, and most of my soups and stews too. You can even add it to the water for boiling potatoes. Tomato sauces always benefit from a leaf or two, as do tagines and curries – Indian cooks often crackle a few bay leaves in hot oil with spices such as mustard or cardamom at the very outset of cooking.

Bay is a great pickling spice too, and also lifts and perfumes beans and lentils as they cook. I always add bay to the milk when making a béchamel sauce. I stuff bay leaves into and under joints of meat before roasting and I love to cook them with fish. Mackerel fillets fried with bay and garlic are a favourite of mine: where the bay has contact with the fish skin and gets slightly charred, it creates an amazing, smoky-sweet flavour. This comes out, too, when you thread bay on to skewers between cubes of lamb and vegetables for cooking on a barbecue – or just strew some dampened leaves over the hot coals to imbue your food with its delicious smoke.

Bay also works beautifully in sweet recipes, where it can be infused in a hot liquid such as cream, milk or wine to add an intoxicating, fragrant thread of flavour. Try it in rice puddings, ice creams and syrups – particularly if they are to be served with fruit. Bay is especially delicious with apples and pears.

Dried bay used to be the norm in this country – the fragile leaves dropped into a simmering bolognese or bourguignon – but this leaf is even better used fresh. You can now buy packs of leaves in the fresh herb sections of some supermarkets (they may be British but are more likely to be from Spain, Israel or another hot country) but quality is patchy. It's not until you get the packet home, tear a leaf in half and inhale its scent that you'll get a good idea of how perfumed that particular batch is. Still, a couple of mild leaves is better than no bay at all.

The ideal, however, is to grow your own. There is something wonderful about being able to pick the leaves whenever you need them. Native to the eastern Mediterranean, bay trees have spread throughout southern Europe and grow quite well in less balmy northern climates such as ours. They need shelter, warmth and free-draining soil. A young bay tree can be finished off by a few serious frosts or too much rain, which is why it's a good idea to start them off in a pot. Once established, however, bay can grow into a majestic tree up to about 9 metres tall – though you can keep it pruned back as a smaller, attractive evergreen bush in a herb or flowerbed.

Having a tree to hand, whether potted or planted, will encourage you to use the herb often – and in quantity. And that is a boon. Because whenever a recipe calls for a bay leaf, I would use two… or three, or more. No cook should ever be without them.

BAY-SPIKED PEARS WITH SHALLOTS AND LEMON

6 large, medium-ripe pears

24 bay leaves

4 small (or 3 large) shallots, thinly sliced

Finely pared zest of 1 small lemon

1 tbsp olive or rapeseed oil

A large knob of butter

A pinch of dried chilli flakes (optional)

Sea salt and black pepper

The sweetness and silky texture of these aromatic pears makes them a superb foil to rich meats. Try them with roast partridge, venison or pork. Alternatively, make them part of a warm salad with some bitter leaves such as chicory, crumbled blue cheese and any juices from the pan trickled over. Serves 6 as a side dish

Preheat the oven to 180°C/Fan 160°C/Gas 4.

Peel the pears, then quarter them and remove the cores. Make a slit down the centre of the curved 'back' of each piece of pear and insert a bay leaf.

Place all the bay-spiked pears in a roasting tray. Scatter over the shallots and lemon zest, and trickle over the oil. Dot the butter around the pears and, if using, add a pinch of chilli flakes. Season well with salt and pepper.

Roast in the oven for 20–30 minutes or until the pears are tender, turning them once or twice with a spatula. Serve warm.

Beans, dried & tinned

Nikki Duffy

MORE RECIPES
Hempy hummus (page 308);
Roasted broccoli, red onion
and cannellini salad (page 99);
Pollack with courgettes and
cannellini beans (page 484);
Cuttlefish with fennel and white
beans (page 228); Squirrel
and beans on toast (page 608);
White beans with chorizo and
tomato (page 180)

SOURCING
hodmedods.co.uk (for British-
grown dried beans)

Glossy, compact and beautifully coloured, beans are so full of potential. From the rich, crusted cassoulets of France to the bubbling bean and pasta soups of Italy and the spicy *frijoles refritos* of Mexico, these little pellets of protein are nutritious, filling and cheap – a framework around which the very best kind of everyday eating can be built.

Dried beans are the food of the frontiersman. They can rattle around in your saddle bag (or kitchen cupboard) for months, but can be swollen by an hour or two's cooking into creamy, tender sustenance. While essentially bland, they soak up other flavours and form a lovely, starchy counterpoint to spices, salty meats or earthy greens.

The vast majority of the beans we eat are imported from Africa, Europe, America and China, in particular. Some beans, however, are grown in the British Isles.

Age does matter with dried beans – the longer they've sat on the shelf, the more desiccated they'll be. Older beans will still be usable – they'll just take longer to cook – though if they're really ancient, they may never reach a state of perfect tenderness.

Whereas dried beans need a bit of forethought because of the soaking and simmering they require, tinned ones are ready in an instant because they're already cooked. Use them straight from the tin in salads or hummus, or warm them through in garlicky oil, a brothy soup or a tomato sauce. I prefer organic tinned beans, packed in water alone. It's ok to include the starchy liquid from the tin in a dish but, if you don't like its gloopy consistency, drain and rinse the beans first.

Don't get too hung up about which beans to use for a particular dish. The differences between them, culinarily speaking, are pretty subtle and many are closely related. In most recipes you can happily replace one kind of bean with another. And you can, of course, use freshly cooked dried beans in any recipe that specifies tinned beans.

COMMON BEAN VARIETIES

Aduki beans Oxblood red, these little pulses are much-used in Japan – particularly in sweet dishes. They also work well in salads and other dishes with grains such as rice, or with small pasta.

Badger peas A British-grown pulse, also called carlin peas, pigeon peas or maple peas, traditionally eaten in the North on bonfire night, liberally seasoned with salt and vinegar. For a modern take, dress while still warm with a rich vinaigrette.

Black beans Also called black turtle beans, these are much used in the US and South America. Make the most of their dramatic good looks in beany chillies or salsas.

Black eye beans or black eyed peas These are white, with a black 'eye'. In Hoppin' John, a dish from the southern US, they pair very tastily with rice.

Borlotti beans Also known as cranberry beans, these are very similar to pinto beans. Prized when fresh (see page 81), they are a favourite dried, too. Creamy and rich, they are just what you want in a big soup or stew.

Butter beans These big, fat pulses are great for crushing and bashing to form a rough sort of mash, best served doused in plenty of olive or rapeseed oil.

Cannellini beans A great all-rounder – perfect for simply dressing with oil and serving on bruschetta but also for a lovely, creamy, hummus-style dip.

Fava beans The dried form of the broad bean, used to make Egyptian *ful medames*.

Flageolet beans A young, slightly under-ripe form of haricot bean (hence their delicate green colour), these are superb stewed with fatty meats.

Haricot beans Also called navy beans, these are what you find in a tin of baked beans. Use them in a home-made version for something far richer and more delicious.

Kidney beans Dark red, these are traditional in Jamaican rice and peas, and generally used in chilli con carne.

Mung beans These tiny green beans are a top choice for sprouting – they're what you tend to get when you buy a pack of fresh beansprouts. But their dinky size and nutty texture makes them delicious in curries too.

Pinto beans Popular in the US and Mexico, pinto (or 'painted') beans are so named because of their pretty, mottled skins.

This often gives good results because still-warm, cooked beans soak up dressings and sauces particularly well. To replace one 400g tin of beans, start with 150g dried beans before soaking and cooking. In both cases, the yield of cooked beans is about 250g.

Cooking beans

Dried beans should be soaked before cooking to partially rehydrate them. Cover them with lots of cold water (they will swell considerably) and leave for at least 8 hours, ideally overnight. Red kidney beans need at least 12 hours' soaking.

A little bicarbonate of soda added to the soaking water will shorten the beans' cooking time by about 25 per cent. Adding salt to the soaking water will also reduce the cooking a little, because it affects pectins in the cell walls. However, it will give you beans with a slightly more fluffy, floury inner texture. In a hard-water area, beans take longer to cook, so bicarb and/or salt in the soaking water is a useful addition. There's no reason not to use both; allow 1 tsp bicarbonate and 2 tsp salt to 1 litre of water. After soaking, drain the beans and rinse (very thoroughly if you've used bicarb or salt).

If time is short, you can also 'speed-soak' your beans: boil the dried beans (without bicarb or salt) for a couple of minutes then turn off the heat and leave them in the hot water for an hour or so before draining, rinsing and cooking.

Put your soaked, rinsed beans into a saucepan, cover with plenty of cold water and bring to a fast boil. Many beans contain a substance called phytohemagglutinin, which is toxic at high levels. Red kidney beans have large amounts and should be boiled hard for 10–15 minutes, to destroy the toxin, before being cooked at a more gentle simmer. Cannellini beans contain about a third as much of the toxin as red kidney beans, and fava beans have 5–10 per cent. I like to give these the hard-boil treatment too.

Simmer your beans until tender, which could be anywhere between 45 minutes and 2 hours, depending on their age and your water.

BRAISED WHITE BEANS WITH GREENS

This is simple, hearty winter food – absolutely delicious finished with a simple chilli- and garlic-infused oil. Serve with bacon or sausages, or with fish. Serves 4

250g cannellini, haricot or butter beans, soaked overnight

10cm length of leek, halved lengthways

1 celery stalk, cut into 3–4 pieces

1 carrot, cut into 3–4 pieces

½ head of garlic (sliced across)

2–3 bay leaves

A large sprig of thyme

200g spring greens or cabbage

Sea salt and black pepper

FOR THE GARLIC-CHILLI OIL

4 tbsp extra virgin olive or rapeseed oil

2 garlic cloves, finely chopped

1 medium-hot red chilli, deseeded and finely chopped

1 tsp hot smoked paprika

Preheat the oven to 170°C/Fan 150°C/Gas 3. Drain the beans, rinse well and tip them into a large flameproof casserole. Add the leek, celery, carrot, garlic, herbs and 1.2 litres fresh water. Bring to the boil, skim off any foam from the surface, then boil hard for 10 minutes.

Put the lid on the casserole, transfer to the oven and cook until the beans are tender; this might take as little as 25 minutes, or up to 2 hours. Allow plenty of time and, if the beans are done before you are planning to eat, you can reheat them gently later on. Check the beans now and then and if they look as though they are getting dry, add a little more boiling water. By the end of cooking, there should be 5–10mm cooking liquor in the pan.

Meanwhile, put the oil in a small saucepan over a medium-low heat and add the chopped garlic, chilli and paprika. Fry gently for 2 minutes, then turn off the heat and leave to cool.

Remove the thick stalk bases from the greens, then slice the leaves into 1–2cm ribbons. When the beans are cooked, add the greens, poking them down among the beans. Return to the oven and cook for about 5 minutes, until the greens are tender.

Just before serving, season the beans and greens with salt and pepper. Spoon them, with their savoury cooking liquor, into warmed dishes (pick out the herbs and veg as you go, or eat them!). Trickle generously with the garlicky chilli oil and serve.

Beef

MORE RECIPES

Fragrant beef curry (page 350); Salt beef with carrots and potatoes (page 559); Szechuan-spiced venison steak (page 461)

SOURCING

pastureforlife.org; browncoworganics.co.uk; cotswoldbeef.com; eversfieldorganic.co.uk

If you have ever visited a county show and watched the bulls in the exhibition ring, you will know what powerful and magnificent beasts they are. A prime female example of the species is barely less imposing. Beef cattle are hefty conglomerations of hard-working brawn and sinew, with tongues the size of hobnail boots, and huge hearts that pump litres of blood round their great bodies. Many of our native breeds are resilient and hardy, able to survive outdoors in the harshest of winter weather and to convert grass into kilo upon kilo of muscle and fat. I've always been impressed by fine cattle, and I find the best beef deeply impressive too. With the right care and cooking, it is for me the most show-stopping meat in our culinary canon.

I'm convinced that the best-tasting beef – and the beef that is best for us – is from the highest welfare herds. Generally that means traditionally bred and traditionally fed animals of established native beef breeds. These animals are well adapted to their environment and live outside for at least 8 months of the year (though not necessarily all year round, due to cattle's propensity to churn up wet, muddy ground). Some may get a top-up treat of barley, oats or a compound feed in cold weather or in the last few months before slaughter. But they thrive, for the most part, on pasture: good green grass in the summer, hay and silage in the winter.

In fact, a small proportion of the very best British beef is raised on pasture alone – a great boon since grass-fed animals, in comparison to their grain-fed counterparts, have been shown to produce meat with higher levels of many beneficial nutrients including omega-3 fatty acids and conjugated linoleic acid. If you are after beef from 100 per cent grass-fed cattle, the 'Pasture for Life' label, a fairly new certification issued by the Pasture-Fed Livestock Association, will tell you that your beef was 100 per cent pasture-fed right up until slaughter.

Excellent British beef breeds include 'Aberdeen Angus', 'Hereford', 'Longhorn', 'Shorthorn', 'Red Poll', 'Devon Ruby' (my favourite), 'Sussex' and 'Belted Galloway', though there are many more. When grass-fed, these single-breed 'pedigree' cattle grow relatively slowly but produce beautifully flavoursome and well-marbled meat. Such beef is certainly not the norm. You may see some of those breed names on packs of supermarket meat, but the chances are it isn't from single-breed animals since beef can be described as 'Aberdeen Angus' or 'Hereford' if only the sire (bull) is of that breed.

In fact, the bulk of our beef in this country comes from animals 'finished' indoors on concentrate feeds derived from wheat, maize, peas, beans or soya. This is a way of maximising returns. Feeding these high-energy fodders to cattle means more meat, more fat, and a marketable weight, more quickly.

Some of this meat is from beef-cross cattle, often involving huge Continental breeds such as 'Limousin'. But a lot of British beef – around 50 per cent – is from dairy animals, largely the mainstay breed in the domestic milking industry, the 'Holstein-Friesian'. This meat comes from male calves not needed on dairy farms, or from offspring of dairy cows cross-bred with beef bulls to produce 'dairy-cross' meat.

Much as I value the excellence of traditional, pasture-fed beef, I think we *should* also be eating meat from dairy breeds. At least we should if we're consuming milk, butter and cheese, because the market for dairy beef is helping to reduce the appalling waste of male calves from the dairy industry. Since 2006, the number of male dairy calves retained for rearing in Britain (rather than being sent abroad for fattening) has increased by 58 per cent, and the number of calves being killed shortly after birth has declined by 36 per cent.

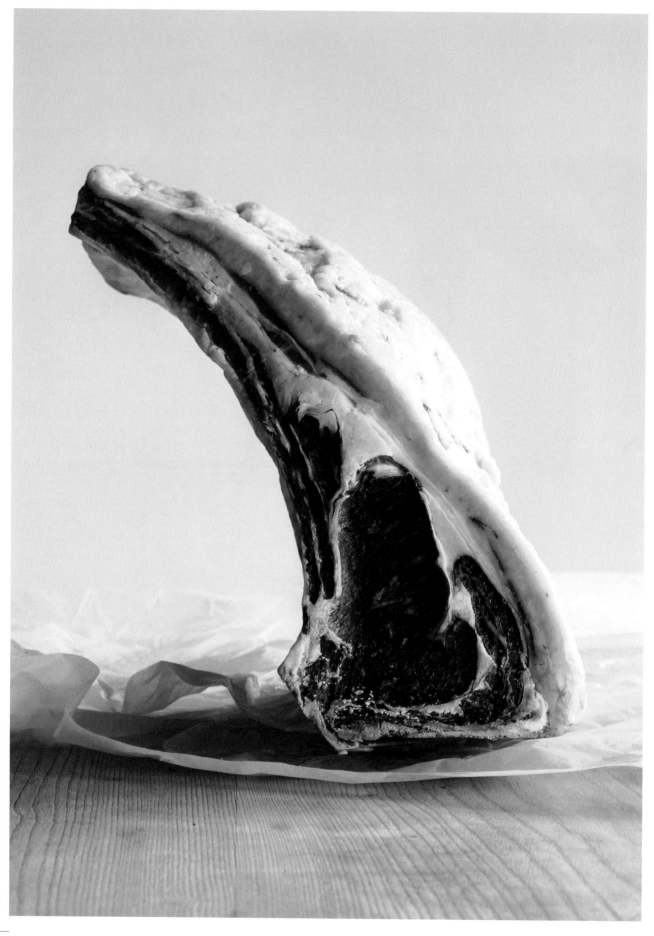

Dairy beef can be of reasonable – and, if grass-fed, sometimes excellent – quality. It seems like a sensible use of the male cattle (and indeed surplus females) that inevitably arise from the dairy industry. The problem is that for many dairy beef cattle, welfare is compromised. Some are raised completely indoors, without access to open pasture. In the very best of these modern systems, I would accept that much is being done to keep the animals clean and comfortable, but this is not a natural way to raise cattle. And in a worrying new development, some British cattle are being raised on grass-less, American-style 'feedlots', where they are outside but confined in large numbers without proper shelter until they have munched enough grain-based 'concentrates' to reach the required weight – a sorry consequence of the demand for cheap meat.

Hanging and ageing

The best beef is richly flavoured, the muscle – even from the leaner quarters – visibly marbled with fat. With correct cooking, any cut, from tail to T-bone, can be made tender and tempting. But before you even get your beef in the kitchen, you can put yourself at an advantage by choosing properly aged meat.

Dry-ageing – hanging the quartered carcass in a cold store – is the optimum way to mature the best, grass-fed beef for the finest flavour. When kept in a cold, slightly humid atmosphere for anything up to a month (I think you can safely hang it longer, and some butchers do), beef undergoes subtle but crucial changes. Enzymes in the meat act on the flesh, breaking down protein, fat and other substances into their constituent parts which, as luck would have it, have an array of rich flavours. As part of the same process, protein and collagen structures are weakened, making the meat more tender.

Because dry-aged beef is left uncovered, it also loses moisture, which concentrates its flavour. That is why a vac-packed joint, even if you 'hang' it in the fridge for 4 weeks, will never achieve the same deliciousness as a dry-aged equivalent.

Favourite beef cuts

Braising/stewing cuts Many of the less tender cuts of lean beef respond well to stewing: consider leg of beef, top rump and silverside. Chuck steak is often what's sold as 'braising steak' and can be delicious in a pie or stew, but buy it in the piece if you can. Pre-cut braising steak is often cut too small, meaning that the meat dries out during cooking. In all cases, these relatively lean cuts benefit from lubrication – cubes of fried streaky bacon added to the pot are ideal.

Brisket Fatty and flavoursome, this has a beautiful, open-grained texture and makes a fabulous slow roast. Ask your butcher for the thick end of the brisket, boned and rolled, and make sure they don't trim off all the fat. Brisket is the cut to use for home-made salt beef – a delicacy that I highly recommend – and also for what my grandmother would have called boiled beef. Served with carrots, this simple dish is supremely pleasing. Don't, however, *actually* boil it – at least not hard or for any length of time. Beef, like any meat, will dry out irretrievably if cooked at a rolling boil. The liquor should remain at a tremulous simmer, no more. You will almost certainly find a foamy 'scum' comes to the surface when simmering this, or any meat. This is albumin, a protein – it's perfectly ok to eat it, or you can skim it off if you prefer.

Forerib The ultimate, flag-waving, John Bull roasting joint, this is a spectacular and expensive cut. It's one for Christmas dinner or a very special gathering. I love to roast it on the bone: it guarantees more flavour and succulence and looks very impressive too. But a rolled rib joint is still hard to beat and, of course, easier to carve.

Mince The best minced beef gives tender burgers, glorious ragus and golden-crusted cottage pies. Basic supermarket mince is too fine and sometimes too fatty for my taste. Minced steak, about 10 per cent fat, is the best option if you're buying it pre-packed, but this can become rather dry and granular in a slow-cooked dish such as chilli con carne. Much better is to buy one of the cheaper cuts, trim it well and mince it coarsely yourself (or chop it finely). Your butcher can do this for you too. For quick cooking – burgers, for instance – I like minced silverside, topside or even rump steak. For longer cooking, such as in a bolognese or chilli, I prefer chuck, leg of beef or top rump.

Ox cheek A wonderful, plump piece of meat, the cheek is tough and fibrous in character (you can imagine the work it's had to do, helping that great jaw grind grass into mush). But slow-cooking takes care of that, rendering it spoonably tender and gloriously, beefily rich in flavour. Braise cheeks whole for at least 3 hours (see recipe on page 64), or cube them and use in slow-cooked curries or casseroles.

Oxtail Along with tongue, kidney and cheek, this is one of the few beef cuts to retain the epithet 'ox', an Old English word in currency long before the Norman *boeuf* infiltrated the language. The two words reflect the social divide in English society post 1066. Less luxurious cuts kept their old Saxon names while the Norman nobility dined on beef. Like shin, tail is an unprepossessing cut that nevertheless yields superb flavour and texture. A couple of tails will make a fine stew for up to 8 people. Expect to cook it for 3–4 hours. You'll get particularly good flavour if you soak oxtail in well-salted water for 1–2 hours before using. When cooking, it will initially release lots of scum, which you should skim off as it rises to the surface.

Shin This is an inexpensive piece of meat that I regularly turn to for stews and braises. The shin is usually sold in thick cross-sections, sometimes with the bone still running through the centre. It's low in fat but high in tough, connective tissue, which you should leave on the meat, rather than trim off. Long, slow cooking allows that tissue to break down, releasing body into the broth, and the bone gives bags of flavour and body too. You can buy it boned if you prefer, or remove the bone yourself, and leave the meat in thick slices or cut into smaller chunks – say for a beef and kidney pie. Keep those chunks reasonably large though (around 4cm in any direction) so they don't lose too much of their juice as they braise. Shin needs lots of cooking – more than some other stewing cuts. Give it at least 2½ hours.

Steak Should you decide to push the boat out and treat yourself to a steak dinner, I'd recommend sirloin as the most fail-safe option, offering the best balance of flavour and texture. Rump can be great too, though if it is not well hung it may be on the tough side. Fillet, for me, is wasted as steak – tender, yes, but flavoursome, no. Far better to roll a whole fillet in something piquant and punchy – like a mix of crushed spices and salt – roast it hot and quick and serve it practically raw in the middle. A skirt steak can be another great choice (see recipe on page 64). Also known as bavette, skirt is lean, open-textured and less tender than other steaks but as long as it is properly trimmed of the membrane that covers it, and rested after cooking, it can be very good.

Topside Taken from the top of the rear leg of the animal, this is a lean cut but tender enough to eat as a roast, provided you bard it well with fat and roast it slowly (as low as 150°C/Fan 130°C/Gas 2 after an initial hot 'sizzle'). I vastly prefer it cold to hot, however – it's perfect for beef sandwiches and salads.

Beef stock

Beef bones, with all but a few crucial scraps of meat removed, make the most magnificent stock. Full-bodied, dark and beefily savoury, it's too powerful for risottos or soups but will anchor any beef stew, pie or braise firmly in heavenly territory. Good home-made beef stock also makes mind-bendingly good gravy (see right), or a classic beef 'reduction' (see below).

You need fresh beef bones – and lots of them. You can produce a litre or so of stock with as little as 1kg bones, but it makes sense to use as many bones as you can get into your largest pan. Buy a new stockpot if necessary: 5 litres of beef stock is so much more useful than 1 litre, not least because this is such a valuable commodity to keep in your freezer. Raw beef bones can be obtained from your butcher. Some online meat suppliers sell them too – though they can be rather expensive. Rib bones and marrow bones (from the leg) are the best to use.

It is essential to roast at least some of the raw bones, as this will create the rich, caramelised meat flavour that will be the backbone of the liquor. Put the beef bones into a large roasting tray and roast at 200°C/Fan 180°C/Gas 6 for 20–30 minutes until well browned. Transfer the bones to a stockpot and add 2–4 carrots, 2–4 onions and 2–4 celery stalks, all roughly chopped. Add a few bay leaves, a sprig of thyme and some peppercorns. Cover the whole lot with water, bring to a simmer and skim off the scum from the surface. Cook very gently, at never more than a tremulous simmer, for 4–5 hours minimum, ideally 6 or 7.

Strain the stock through a fine sieve, discarding the vegetables and bones. Leave to cool then place in the fridge or leave in a cool place, ideally overnight, so the stock turns to jelly and the fat separates out and sets hard on the surface. Carefully remove all the fat (this beef dripping can be used too, of course).

The stock will keep in the fridge for up to a week or it can be frozen. If you've made several litres of beef stock, it makes sense to reduce it by at least half or two-thirds, for freezing. Defrost and bring back to the boil before using.

Beef reduction

Reducing a beef stock (or any stock), to intensify the flavour, is simply a matter of boiling it hard to evaporate some of the liquid. But you should only do this with a stock that is completely 'clean', as any impurities will compromise the flavour. That means removing the fat as above, warming the stock back to a free-flowing liquid, and passing it through a muslin-lined sieve (a fine chinois is not good enough).

Once 'clean' you can boil and reduce your stock as hard or as fast as you like, until you get the intensity of flavour you require. Never add salt (or other strong seasonings) until the end or it will be much too salty.

A classic chef's reduction or 'meat glaze' is the kind of lip-sticking, intense, almost syrupy, dark sauce that is served with meat in high-end restaurants. It is usually made by adding red wine (about 1 bottle to 3 litres stock) and reducing by anything up to 90 per cent. The final tweaks – of salt and pepper, a hint of sweetness (typically from redcurrant jelly), acidity (from wine vinegar), aroma (by dropping in a few thyme leaves, then straining them out again) – add character. A little unsalted butter is sometimes whisked in at the end to add gloss.

Although invested with a certain arcane mystery, gravy-making is actually pretty straightforward. It does require the cook to use a little judgement, but confidence in this area is easily built (and no one is going to mind sampling a few roast dinners while you perfect your technique). The key is to start with a dish of very flavoursome meat juices – something you can't really help but create whenever you season and roast any decent piece of meat. So really, the bulk of the work is done for you there. The basic principles, which apply to making gravy from any joint of meat or roast bird, are then to remove excess fat, add volume with more liquid, and season to taste.

After roasting, remove the meat to a warm dish, cover and leave to rest while you make the gravy.

With beef (and lamb, pork, duck and goose), the amount of fat floating on top of the meat juices may be significant – less so with poultry and game. You want a couple of tablespoonfuls of fat, max, to be left in the roasting tin. To remove excess, pour it off, or skim off with a tablespoon. You can also use a gravy separating jug – pouring all the liquor from the tin into the jug, then pouring off most of the fat. Return the juices to the roasting tin.

Put the roasting tin over a medium-low heat and use a spatula to scrape up any meaty residues from the base of the tin, stirring them into the juices. If there's very little juice, add a splash of water or wine to help with this 'deglazing' process.

At this point you may wish to add a little plain white flour to absorb the fat and thereby thicken and emulsify the gravy; I usually do with chicken and lamb, but usually don't with beef and game. Sprinkle in 1–2 tsp flour and work it into the liquid in the tin using a spatula. It is important to 'cook out' the flour at this stage: allow it to bubble, stirring for a minute or two, to form a smooth brown 'roux' (the thickness will vary according to how much liquid you started with).

Now increase the volume of your gravy as necessary by adding good, hot stock. Stock made from a stock cube will do, but it can be too salty and never has the depth of flavour that a home-made meat stock achieves. Shop-bought fresh stock is an option, if you can find a good one. Decent chicken or veg stock does good service for any gravy, but a stock made from the same species you are roasting is of course the perfect choice. Add enough stock to loosen and make generous your gravy, but not so much as to dilute those intense meaty flavours. Taste as you go.

I like to strain my nearly-finished gravy through a chinois (fine sieve) into a small pan. Here I can control the final seasoning, while tasting with a teaspoon. Salt and pepper may or may not be needed, depending on how well seasoned the joint was. As with the chef's reduction (see left), a dash of wine, a blob of redcurrant jelly, a few drops of vinegar (even a few drops of strong coffee, to develop the rich dark flavours) can all be deployed to tweak your gravy to perfection.

SKIRT STEAK AND CHIPS

About 600g large floury potatoes, such as Maris Piper

Vegetable oil (refined rapeseed oil), or clarified beef dripping, for frying

A piece of skirt steak (about 300g), 2–3cm thick, trimmed

Sea salt and black pepper

An underused cut, open-textured skirt makes fabulous steak. The chips are great with a rose veal steak too. Serves 2

Peel the potatoes and cut them into long chips, about 1cm square in cross-section. Put them in a colander and rinse under cold running water to remove some of their starch. Tip into a large pan and cover with water. Add 1 tsp salt and bring to a simmer, then cook for 4–5 minutes. Drain and allow to steam-dry in the colander for 5–10 minutes.

Heat a 4–5cm depth of oil or dripping in a wide, deep, heavy-based saucepan to 130°C (or use a deep-fat fryer); use a cook's thermometer to check the temperature. Carefully add the part-cooked potato chips (they will be fragile). Do this in batches if your pan is not large. Cook the chips for 5–6 minutes, then scoop them out and leave to drain on kitchen paper for a few minutes while you prepare the steak.

Using a sharp knife, split the steak in half horizontally to give 2 thin steaks, 1–1.5cm thick.

Put the chip pan back on the heat and bring the oil up to 180°C. Return the part-cooked chips to the pan and cook for a further 6–8 minutes or until crisp and golden. Scoop out the cooked chips and put them in a bowl lined with kitchen paper. Toss in a good pinch of salt and keep warm.

Place a heavy-based frying pan over a high heat and add a little oil or dripping. Season the steaks with salt and pepper. When the pan is really hot, add the steaks and cook for about 1–1½ minutes on each side for rare, 2–2½ minutes on each side for medium rare, depending on thickness. Rest the steaks on a warm plate for 4–5 minutes before serving, with the chips.

ALE-BRAISED OX CHEEKS WITH PARSNIPS

Olive or rapeseed oil, or beef dripping, for cooking

2 ox cheeks (about 1kg in total), trimmed of any sinew and fat

1 medium onion, chopped

2 garlic cloves, crushed

4 medium parsnips, peeled, trimmed and quartered lengthways

500ml amber-coloured, not-too-bitter ale

Leaves from 4 sprigs of thyme

2 bay leaves

Finely grated zest of 1 orange

Sea salt and black pepper

Cheeks are a fabulous braising cut. Simmered in ale, they become forkably tender and form a gloriously rich and beefy sauce. Serves 4

Preheat the oven to 140°C/Fan 120°C/Gas 1.

Heat a large flameproof casserole over a medium-high heat and add 1 tbsp oil or dripping. Once hot, add the ox cheeks and brown well all over (do them separately if necessary). Place the browned cheeks in a large bowl.

Reduce the heat to medium-low and add a dash more oil to the casserole if needed. Add the onion with a pinch of salt and sweat gently for 10 minutes or so, until softened. Now add the garlic and cook for a further 2–3 minutes. Spoon into the bowl with the meat.

Put the parsnips into the casserole dish and turn up the heat a little. Cook, stirring them around in the oil and juices for 4–5 minutes, until browned lightly. Transfer to the bowl.

Pour the ale into the casserole and turn up the heat a little. Simmer for 3–4 minutes, scraping up any bits stuck to the bottom of the dish. Then add 500ml water, the thyme, bay leaves, orange zest and everything from the bowl. Season with salt and pepper. Bring up to a simmer, then put the lid on, leaving a slight gap.

Place the casserole in the oven. Cook, turning the cheeks occasionally, until the meat is tender enough to separate with a spoon – start testing after 3 hours, but be prepared for it to take up to 4 hours. Be careful not to break up the parsnips when you turn the cheeks.

Remove from the oven, taste and adjust the seasoning with more salt and pepper as necessary. Cut the braised ox cheeks in half. Serve one half per person, with a few pieces of parsnip on the side and the juices spooned over. Accompany with mash and greens.

Beer

MORE RECIPES
Pot-roasted mallard with celeriac and watercress (page 241); Ale-braised ox cheeks with parsnips (opposite); Seedy stoneground loaf (page 263)

SOURCING
camra.org.uk; bestofbritish.co.uk

To most of us, beer is for drinking, but the hoppy, malty, slightly bitter character of a good beer adds a unique quality to food too: pleasantly bitter, a little sweet and, most important of all, richly aromatic. However, as with other alcoholic drinks such as wine and cider, the alcoholic effects are sadly negated during the cooking process.

There are two main sources of the flavour in beer: malted grain, which gives sweet, toasty, chocolatey, caramel notes; and hops, which are bitter, fragrant and sometimes citrusy. Both can contribute to the flavour of a dish. Which particular beer you use is a matter of judgement and culinary instinct: there are thousands to choose from.

Bear in mind that medium to strong, amber-coloured beers (for example bitter, IPA and porters) will always be sweet and aromatic; stouts will be very bitter with burnt qualities; and light beers such as pale ale and lager are likely to be fizzy and, in the case of pale ale, hoppy as well. I suggest light beers for batters, stout only for the darkest of beef dishes and amber-coloured beers for everything else.

Beer is classically used in stewy, braised things: beef and ale pie, for instance, because the sweet and bitter notes in the beer complement all that rich meatiness so well. It is also very good in a bread dough (where it helps the rise), and superb with cheese in sauces, fondues or rarebit toppings.

Beer is usually reduced during the cooking process, which intensifies its aromatic qualities but also its bitterness. For this reason, it should be combined with other liquids such as stock or water, or even milk or cream, to soften and round out its flavour.

In a sweet dish, one can emphasise those aromatics by using hops late on in the cooking process. For beer toffee, for example, I make a standard butter toffee but use concentrated ale instead of water, adding a muslin bag containing a tablespoonful of hops (available from home-brew shops) a couple of minutes before the toffee reaches setting temperature. Even better is the following beer ice cream. Hand on heart, it is the best ice cream in the world.

BEER ICE CREAM

330ml full-flavoured beer

300ml whole milk

225ml double cream

1 tbsp dried hops (optional)

6 medium egg yolks

135g light muscovado or soft light brown sugar

This caramel-coloured ice cream is fragrant and aromatic with a bittersweet quality. It works best if you use a beer that is not too bitter to start with, so taste it beforehand. The hops are optional but they do make the finished ice cream particularly stellar. Serves 6

Pour the beer into a saucepan and boil until reduced to about 75ml of intensely flavoured beery liquor. Add the milk and cream to the beer, along with the hops, if using. Bring back to a gentle simmer.

Meanwhile whisk the egg yolks and sugar together in a large bowl. Pour the hot, beery cream through a fine sieve on to the egg mixture, whisking as you go.

Pour this custard back into a clean saucepan and cook over a moderate heat, stirring continuously, until thickened. Don't let it boil or it will 'split'. Pour the custard into a bowl and cover the surface directly with baking parchment or cling film to stop a skin forming. Leave to cool and then chill.

Churn the mixture in an ice-cream machine until soft-set, before transferring to a freezer container and freezing until solid. (Alternatively, freeze the mixture in a plastic container for about an hour until the sides start to solidify, then mash with a fork, mixing the frozen sides into the liquid centre; put back in the freezer for another hour. Repeat this at hourly intervals until soft-set then let the ice cream set solid.)

Either way, transfer to the fridge about 30 minutes before serving to make scooping easier.

Beetroot

LATIN NAME
Beta vulgaris

SEASONALITY
May–October; stored roots
are available until February

MORE RECIPES
Beetroot, strawberry and
rocket salad (page 537);
Spiced horse mushroom and
beetroot 'burger' (page 315);
Quinoa with cumin-roasted
roots and parsley (page 514);
Foil-baked trout with baby
beetroot and spring onions
(page 647); Hot mackerel,
beetroot and horseradish
sandwich (page 373)

Beetroot sits uneasily in our culinary canon. It's never quite gained the everyday status of its rooty brethren, the potato and the carrot (not that it's related to either, being a member of the spinach family). We seem to approach its shocking purple hues with instinctive caution. Many wrinkle their nose at it; it's almost an assumption that children will not like it. I have encouraged mine to get over their infant antipathy by declaring a 'purple tongue competition' every time beetroot comes to the table. It's worked in 3 out of 4 cases (4-year-old Louisa has yet to be convinced).

The national suspicion of beetroot has been a wasted opportunity of epic proportions. So I'm pleased to note that we seem to be getting over it. We must. For beetroot – sweet, juicy, richly flavoured, superbly versatile and of course stunningly coloured – is one of the finest vegetables we have.

It's true that this venerable root does have a distinct pungency and responds far better to some treatments than others. One of the main reasons it's fallen out of favour in some circles is that cursed, vinegared stuff in jars that used to blight salads in the 1970s. No vegetable could be expected to come out of such an experience well.

But it's not hard to hit the right note with beetroot. Firstly, consider size. Young roots – golf ball to snooker ball size – are the sweetest and mildest. Though traditionally an autumn/winter root, modern plant-breeding and seed-sourcing have expanded the growing season, and beetroot is now a summer ingredient too. Small, succulent roots are easy to find as early as late May in good grocers and farmers' markets. Beetroot continues to be harvested up until October, by which time it develops a certain, not unwelcome, earthy bitterness. The roots on sale through the winter come from store.

Those first sweet little roots are delicate enough to eat raw. And raw beetroot is a revelation: sweet, nutty and aromatic. The crucial thing is to cut it fine. Big chunks of it are hard to negotiate, but grated or slivered into round purple wafers, its texture becomes deliciously crisp and crunchable. I love it simply dressed with good oil, lemon juice, salt and pepper. Combine it with a little garlic-laced yoghurt, perhaps some dill, a scattering of crunchy walnuts, a posy of watercress and you've got a sumptuous salady starter. Raw beetroot is great for juicing too.

Cooked beetroot, of any size, has a much deeper, more rounded flavour and is again wonderful in salads or blitzed into a soup with stock and soured cream. It's also excellent as a side dish in its own right, especially with pigeon or other game.

You can boil it, but roasting it in a foil parcel is my preferred method. It concentrates the flavour and sweetness. Add a little roughly bashed garlic, perhaps a couple of bay leaves or a sprig of thyme to the parcel, along with a splash of oil or butter and some salt and pepper. Put it in a fairly hot oven – around 190°C/Fan 170°C/Gas 5 – and give it at least an hour, maybe 1½ hours, to become yielding and tender. Leave to cool a little, then peel the skins from the cooked roots (a gloriously messy job), dress them with the purple, buttery juices and use warm or cold.

If you see bunched young beetroot with the leaves still attached – and those leaves look lush and healthy – grab them. These beet tops are a fantastic vegetable in their own right, a lot like Swiss chard (which is a different form of the same *Beta vulgaris* species). Separate the stems from the leaves because they cook at different rates. Sauté the chopped stalks with garlic for about 10 minutes, then add the shredded leaves and wilt them down for a further 5 minutes or so. This delicious combination can be dished up just as it is, lubricated with a little cream as a pasta sauce, topped with breadcrumbs and cheese and gratinated, or used in a tart filling.

Beetroot has a high sugar content for a vegetable, and the practice of using it in sweet dishes – an avenue we've explored with great success at River Cottage – is a fruitful one. Cooked then grated or puréed, it adds an uncloying sweetness, a delicate moistness and a whisper of distinctive aromatic flavour to puds and cakes. It pairs particularly well with chocolate: beetroot brownies and beetroot chocolate ice cream are two of my favourite sweet beet treats.

These days, it is the dark purple-crimson, globe-shaped beetroot that is most familiar to us (though this type was only introduced in the seventeenth century). Its extraordinary colour makes it my personal favourite and its visual appeal should not be underestimated: that deep, dramatic red will turn a risotto into a talking point and a soup into a spectacle before you've even tasted it.

But other forms of beetroot are available. Rather hard to resist is the spectacular 'Chioggia' variety, which reveals pink-and-white layers like psychedelic tree rings when sliced open. There are white and egg-yolk yellow beets to be had too. All taste similar to the classic deep red beet and look very beautiful, particularly when combined, raw, in a glorious multi-coloured salad. They regularly crop up (so to speak) at farmers' markets and are also widely available as seeds if you fancy growing your own.

ROASTED BEETROOT ORZOTTO WITH LAVENDER

About 500g small or medium beetroot, scrubbed

3 tbsp olive or rapeseed oil

50g butter

1 onion, finely chopped

2 garlic cloves, finely chopped

A few strips of finely pared lemon zest

300g pearl barley, or pearled spelt, rinsed and drained

A glass of dry white wine

1 litre hot chicken or vegetable stock

1 tsp finely chopped lavender leaves (or rosemary)

200g soft goat's or ewe's cheese, crumbled

A little extra virgin olive or rapeseed oil, to finish

Sea salt and black pepper

Orzotto is like risotto, only made with pearl barley rather than rice (pearled spelt works well too). Fragrant lavender has a great affinity with earthy, sweet beetroot but rosemary or one of the savories will be equally complementary. Serves 4

Preheat the oven to 190°C/Fan 170°C/Gas 5.

Place the beetroot in a small roasting tin, season well with salt and pepper and trickle with 1 tbsp oil. Cover with foil and roast for 1–1½ hours, longer if necessary, until tender. When cool enough to handle, remove the skin from the beetroot. Cut the flesh into cubes or slim wedges.

Heat the remaining 2 tbsp oil and half the butter in a large saucepan over a medium heat. Add the onion, garlic and lemon zest and cook gently for 10 minutes until the onion is soft but not coloured. Add the beetroot and stir well. Now add the barley or spelt and cook, stirring occasionally, for a further 2 minutes.

Pour in the wine and let it reduce, stirring until it has bubbled away to almost nothing. Now start adding the hot stock, a couple of ladlefuls at a time, stirring as you go, adding each new addition after the previous one has been absorbed.

It should take about 40 minutes for all the stock to be incorporated and the barley to become tender (spelt will cook more quickly). If your barley is stubborn, just add a little more stock or hot water and keep cooking until it is done. Take the orzotto off the heat. Sprinkle the lavender and half the cheese over it and dot with the remaining butter.

Cover and leave the orzotto to stand for a few minutes before stirring in the lavender, cheese and butter. Season with salt and pepper to taste. Serve with the rest of the cheese crumbled over the top and a final trickle of extra virgin oil.

Bilberries

LATIN NAME
Vaccinium myrtillus

ALSO KNOWN AS
Blaeberries, huckleberries, whinberries, whortleberries

SEASONALITY
August–September

HABITAT
Heathland, moors and open woodland in the north and west of the British Isles, with a few populations in the south

MORE RECIPES
Chicken and blueberry salad with coriander dressing (page 77)

Why just sit around on a piece of heathland in August and September enjoying the fine weather when you could be usefully employed picking bilberries? Gathering this fruit, characteristic of acid uplands across the British Isles, is a foraging task that takes some time as each bilberry bush will generally bear but a few fruit, and they are considerably smaller than the brazen cultivated blueberry (see page 76). However, there are likely to be several thousand of the shrubs in any one location, so a substantial collection can be made with a little dedication.

If your intention is to take them back for tea you'll need the self-control of a saint not to eat every last one on the spot, and it is true that not a single bilberry among the thousands I have picked has ever made it home. But I have a dream that one day I will bring back sufficient to cover a cheesecake or previously cooked flan. It would certainly be worth it – these berries are quite superb.

With thicker skins and less juice than their cultivated cousins, bilberries are more intense, sharper and richer in the mouth. They are bracingly delicious raw but also cook well – with a splash of water and a sprinkling of sugar to make a versatile compote. For more elaborate recipes, turn to *Jane Grigson's Fruit Book*, which contains one of the most erudite paeans to the fruit you're likely to find, celebrating the traditional bilberry pies of the English North as well as French dishes for mountain *myrtilles* – including ices, sauces and pastries. Bilberry jam is exceptional too, I am told, but the idea of ever gathering enough for the preserving pan must remain, for me, a fantasy.

PEAR AND BILBERRY CRUMBLE TART

This makes the most of even the smallest haul of bilberries (or blackberries, or cultivated blueberries), which go exceptionally well with pears. The addition of thyme gives a delightful, sweet fragrance, but it is optional. Serves 6–8

FOR THE PASTRY
200g plain flour

35g icing sugar

A pinch of salt

100g cold unsalted butter, diced or coarsely grated

1 medium egg yolk

2–3 tbsp cold milk (or water)

FOR THE FILLING
4 ripe pears

100–200g bilberries

1 tbsp soft brown sugar

Leaves from 1 sprig of thyme

2 tbsp clear honey

FOR THE CRUMBLE TOPPING
100g plain flour

80g cold butter, cubed or coarsely grated

75g porridge oats

50g caster sugar

25g walnuts, crushed or chopped

For the pastry, put the flour, icing sugar and salt into a food processor and blitz briefly to combine (or sift into a bowl). Add the butter and blitz (or rub in with your fingers) until the mixture resembles breadcrumbs. Add the egg yolk and just enough milk or water to bring the mix together into large clumps. Knead lightly into a ball, wrap in cling film and rest in the fridge for 30 minutes. Preheat the oven to 180°C/Fan 160°C/Gas 4.

Roll out the pastry to a circle, 3–4mm thick, and use it to line a 20cm tart tin, about 4cm deep; leave the excess overhanging the rim. Prick the pastry base with a fork. Stand the tart tin on a baking tray and line the pastry case with baking parchment and baking beans. Bake for 15 minutes, then remove the beans and parchment and return the pastry case to the oven for about 10 minutes until it looks dry and lightly coloured. Trim away the excess pastry. Turn the oven up to 190°C/Fan 170°C/Gas 5.

For the filling, peel, quarter and core the pears, then cut each quarter into 2 or 3 wedges. Lay the pear wedges in the pastry case. Scatter over the bilberries, sugar and thyme leaves, and trickle over the honey.

For the crumble topping, put all the ingredients into a bowl and work together with your hands until you have a well-combined, lumpy mix. Spoon this over the pears and bilberries (if you have a little left over, freeze it for another pud).

Bake the tart in the oven for 25–30 minutes or until the crumble is golden brown. Allow to cool slightly, or completely, before serving with plain yoghurt or cream.

Black pudding

ALSO KNOWN AS
Blood pudding

MORE RECIPES
Saffron speltotto with black pudding and parsley (page 548); Roasted sprouts with black pudding and chestnuts (page 102)

SOURCING
pipersfarm.com;
trealyfarm.com

Black pudding is, for me, one of the most delicious products a pig can provide. It is made with their blood (although some varieties of this traditional sausage are made with the blood of sheep or cows). Today, black pudding tends to be made with dried, powdered blood, which is practical and economical on a commercial scale, but it's never quite as good as puddings made using fresh blood. At River Cottage we make fresh blood pudding every time we send a pig to slaughter. The blood is collected in a clean container and stirred to stop it coagulating. Once cool, it can be used.

In a traditional English recipe, the blood is thickened with cereals such as oatmeal and barley, as well as rusk or breadcrumbs, flavoured with plenty of spices and combined with a generous amount of chopped pork fat, which lends moisture and richness. The River Cottage recipe includes mace, coriander seed and cayenne pepper, as well as finely chopped onions, brandy and double cream. We fill the mixture into casings, usually beef intestines, known as 'runners'. Once tied at the ends, the sausages are steamed or poached to cook the blood, then cooled.

Boudin noir, the French version of black pudding, does not include cereals, so it's particularly rich. *Morcilla* is a Spanish blood sausage which may be thickened with rice.

Good black pudding has a light, just-firm texture and a deeply savoury, slightly spicy flavour. It is usually cooked further before serving. You'll typically have it sliced and fried as part of a full English breakfast – it pairs well with eggs and tomatoes. However, this rich sausage has a multitude of other uses. Like other forms of highly seasoned pork, it goes beautifully with seafood, particularly seared scallops or squid.

In the colder months fried black pudding is delicious in salads with roast squash or sweet root veg, crunchy nuts and bitter leaves such as radicchio. And it has a wonderful affinity with fruit, including apples, rhubarb, gooseberries and peaches. It also makes a fantastic alternative to sausagemeat in Scotch eggs.

All the welfare issues attendant on pork are of course relevant to black pudding (see page 488). There's not a huge range of organic or free-range black pudding to be had, but it is out there. The alternative, of course, is to make your own. If you keep your own pigs, or know someone who does, then getting hold of fresh blood after slaughter is straightforward. Otherwise, ask your butcher if they can source some for you. Dried blood is available online, but there's generally little information on its provenance, and it may well come from abroad.

BLACK PUDDING AND GOOSEBERRIES ON TOAST

200g gooseberries, topped, tailed and halved

3–4 tsp sugar

About 1 tbsp cider vinegar

1 tbsp chopped flat-leaf parsley

A little olive or rapeseed oil

350g black pudding, thickly sliced

4 slices of bread

Butter, for spreading

Sea salt and black pepper

The fresh acidity of raw, ripe gooseberries both cuts the richness of blood and pork fat, and complements their sweetness. Serves 4

Combine the gooseberries with 3 tsp sugar, 1 tbsp vinegar and the parsley. Season with a little salt and pepper, then taste. If your gooseberries are particularly ripe, you might need a dash more vinegar; if they are very sharp, a sprinkle more sugar might be in order. You are looking for a pleasantly sweet-sour balance that will contrast with the richness of the pudding. Set the gooseberries aside to macerate for 20 minutes.

Heat a medium frying pan over a medium heat and add a dash of oil. When hot, add the black pudding slices and cook for 3–4 minutes on each side. Meanwhile, toast and butter the bread.

Pile the black pudding on to the hot buttered toast, top with the gooseberries and serve.

Blackberries

John Wright

LATIN NAME
Rubus fruticosus

SEASONALITY
July–October

HABITAT
Widespread throughout the British Isles except the Scottish Highlands, in woods, hedgerows, gardens and on waste ground

MORE RECIPES
Wineberries with peaches and custard (page 317); Damson ripple parfait (page 231); Pear and bilberry crumble tart (page 69); Raspberry almond streusel cake (page 526); Peach slump (page 448)

The humble bramble on which the blackberry grows is amongst the most giving of wild foods, providing free fruit by the kilo and endless opportunities for the cook to experiment. Picking such large quantities takes time and a certain amount of dogged fearlessness. Heavy-duty apparel is advisable, and an assortment of buckets, baskets and crooked walking sticks for reaching those really fat, juicy berries that are just a little too far away. Since brambles sport backward-pointing thorns of vicious intent, I don a leather gardening glove on my left hand to hold the fruit-bearing stem and pick with my right.

The blackberry has a long season, from as early as mid-July to as late as mid-October. Weather and location play a part, but there is also the innate variability of our native plants. The bramble is an apomictic species encompassing over 300 micro-species in this country alone. Each reproduces without resort to messy sexual mechanisms and its offspring are clones. The upshot of this is that there are over 300 different types of bramble, each with its own characteristics of fruitiness, berry-size, sweetness and season. If you find a good bush, remember where it is and go back next year.

The cultivated blackberries you find in shops are usually monsters compared to their wild counterparts but pretty juicy and tasty enough. There's nothing wrong with them apart from their high price but, in season, I would much rather eat wild fruit. And out of season, I'd rather eat something else altogether. Garden-grown blackberries can be a nice option though: many modern varieties are thornless, sweet and fecund.

One thing I never worry about is the nonsense about not picking blackberries after Michaelmas, which falls on 29 September, though the superstition probably refers to Michaelmas by the old calendar, which was 10 October. The devil is said to spit on the berries and turn them bad – infected with the grey mould *Botrytis cinerea*. Since mouldiness is perfectly obvious, I will not be swayed by timetables and sometimes keep picking until early November.

Wild blackberries do not keep. Even a day in the fridge is too much for them, so it is worth planning their culinary destination even before you set off to pick them.

Squashed, they will barely make it through the day, so collect in several containers, not all piled into one. It is possible, of course, to freeze them, but there are much better ways of preserving blackberries – bottling the whole berries in sweetened blackberry juice, or with sugar and cheap whisky, for instance. The juice can be served with the blackberries, the blackberry whisky partaken of at leisure and the whisky-soaked berries used in a trifle.

The enormous quantity of blackberries that results from an entire family spending an afternoon in their pursuit can overwhelm even the most inventive cook. Of course, the very best blackberries (usually the fat one at the end of the stem) are best eaten raw on the day they are picked, in a fruit salad, but what to do with the rest? Well, lots.

Blackberry jelly made with *real* fruit tastes divine. Crush the raw blackberries and push them through a fine sieve. Warm the juice in a pan with sugar to taste and add leaf gelatine (about 1 water-softened leaf for every 120ml juice, but do check because brands of gelatine vary). Pour into wine glasses, leave to set and serve with cream.

Blackberry mousse is another favourite, made by adding a little gelatine to cooked, sieved blackberry juice then whisking it into an egg-and-sugar mousse with a generous amount of double cream. But there is no end to the blackberry's potential: fool, sorbet, soufflé, summer pudding, blackberry and apple crumble, muffins and pancake filling.

Finally, a country wine: blackberry is one of the few really exceptional home-made wines. Make it when the fruit is abundant: you will need 1.5kg for a 4.5-litre demi-john. It is among the easiest of country wines to make and I have never known it go wrong.

BLACKBERRY YOGHURT SOUFFLÉ CAKE

4 medium eggs, separated

100g caster sugar

400g plain wholemilk yoghurt

Finely grated zest of 1 lemon

50g plain flour

150g blackberries

FOR THE BLACKBERRY SAUCE

500g blackberries

75g caster sugar

Juice of ½ lemon

This melt-in-the-mouth cake is an elegant treatment for blackberries (or their hybrids, such as loganberries and tayberries). The tangy-sweet accompanying sauce is also lovely trickled over ice cream or pancakes. Serves 6–8

Preheat the oven to 150°C/Fan 130°C/Gas 2. Grease a 23cm springform cake tin and line the base and sides with baking parchment.

Using a stand mixer or electric hand whisk, whisk the egg yolks with 65g of the sugar for 4–5 minutes until the mixture is very thick, pale and creamy; it should be thick enough to 'hold a trail' when you lift the beaters.

Carefully fold in the yoghurt and lemon zest. Now sift the flour over the mixture and fold this in too. (Don't worry if you can't get rid of every little lump of flour at this point.)

In a clean bowl, whisk the egg whites with the remaining 35g sugar until they hold soft peaks. Carefully fold the whites into the batter then fold in about two-thirds of the berries.

Tip the mixture into the prepared cake tin, give it a shake to level it out and dot the remaining blackberries over the top. Bake for about 50 minutes until risen and golden with a slight wobble.

Leave to cool completely in the tin (it will sink, but don't worry), then refrigerate.

Meanwhile, make the sauce. Put the blackberries, sugar and lemon juice into a pan and heat gently, stirring, until the juices start to run, then simmer gently for about 10 minutes; the fruit will release lots of juice. Leave to cool in the pan, then rub through a sieve into a bowl; you will have a thick, smooth blackberry sauce. Taste: it should be nicely tangy, but if it seems too sharp, whisk in a little icing sugar. Chill the sauce.

Serve the cake in thick wedges, with the sauce poured generously over the top.

Blewits

LATIN NAME
Wood blewit: *Lepista nuda*.
Field blewit: *Lepista saeva*

ALSO KNOWN AS
Field blewit: blue legs

SEASONALITY
Late autumn–early winter
(wood and field blewits)

HABITAT
Wood blewit: common
in woodland, hedges,
mature grassland.
Field blewit: uncommon
but locally abundant in
areas of mature grassland

MORE RECIPES
Hedgehog mushroom and
bacon omelette (page 306);
Woodcock with wild
mushrooms (page 678)

In late October, just when the ceps and chanterelles are fading from the woods, my favourite of all the mushrooms, wood and field blewits, begin to appear.

The fragrant wood blewit (pictured right) is bluish all over, flushing brown on the cap, and has an unusual, slightly damp feel and soft rubbery texture. There is little to confuse it with but, if you are unsure, check that it produces a pinkish spore print, not one that is rust coloured. Cut off a cap and lay it, gills down, on a sheet of white paper then leave for a few hours to allow the spores to accumulate to visibility.

Unsurprisingly, this mushroom grows in the leaf litter of woods, but I very often find them in enormous, productive rings in old pasture. Sometimes I pick several kilos at a time and, since they neither dry nor keep well, it's time for a mushroom feast.

The field blewit is cream coloured all over except for the substantial, short stem which is a remarkable, brilliant lilac. It grows in permanent pasture, though parks and lawns sometimes sport them. It is less common than its cousin, at least in the Southwest. In the Midlands they were, and sometimes still are, sold in markets as blue legs, making them one of the few wild fungi that have made a mark in British cuisine.

Both types of blewit must be cooked, not eaten raw. They are particularly delicious served with garlic and cream. Slice them straight across the cap and gently sauté for a few minutes until the abundant juices have started to flow. Take the mushrooms out of the pan and keep them to hand. Strain any maggots out of the juice, swearing never to tell your guests what you have done, and return the juice to the pan with a little salt. Simmer until the water has mostly evaporated, then add some crushed garlic and the partially cooked mushrooms. Sauté until lightly browned, then stir in some cream and simmer for another minute. Serve on toast, of course.

BLEWIT, PIGEON AND ENDIVE SALAD

Olive or rapeseed oil, for frying

8 pigeon breasts

6 rashers of streaky bacon
(smoked or unsmoked),
roughly chopped

About 400g blewits, brushed,
trimmed and thickly sliced

A sprig of thyme

25g butter

1 garlic clove, crushed

1 curly endive (or other crisp
lettuce), leaves separated

Sea salt and black pepper

FOR THE DRESSING

1 tsp Dijon mustard

3 tbsp extra virgin olive
or rapeseed oil

1 tbsp red wine vinegar

A pinch of sugar

Blewits, with their lovely firm texture, are perfect with pigeon in this earthy sauté. You could use other mushrooms here, especially field mushrooms or, in spring, St George's mushrooms. Serves 4 as a light meal

Set a large frying pan over a medium-high heat and add a dash of oil. Season the pigeon breasts with salt and pepper and add to the hot pan. Cook them for 1 minute each side, if you like them quite rare, or 2 minutes each side for a medium finish. Remove all the breasts and leave to rest on a warm plate.

Using the same pan, fry the chopped bacon until starting to colour and crisp a little. Add the mushrooms, thyme and butter and sauté for 6–7 minutes, or until the liquid released by the mushrooms has evaporated and they are starting to caramelise. Throw in the garlic about a minute before the end of cooking and season well with salt and pepper.

For the dressing, put the ingredients into a small jar (or bowl). Add a twist each of salt and pepper and any juices released by the pigeon breasts while resting. Shake (or whisk) to emulsify, then pour over the endive and toss carefully.

Divide the dressed leaves between 4 plates. Slice the pigeon breasts thinly. Scatter the pigeon, mushrooms and bacon over the leaves and serve right away.

Blueberries

Mark Diacono

LATIN NAME
Vaccinium species

SEASONALITY
British crop July–September;
imported all year round

MORE RECIPES
Strawberry salad with raspberry
basil sauce (page 616); Pear and
bilberry crumble tart (page 69)

SOURCING
dorsetblueberry.co.uk;
blueberrypicking.co.uk

Next time you have a punnet of blueberries in your hand, check out the base of one of the fruit. You'll see a rather beautiful, round-lobed, five-pointed star. This was taken by Native Americans as a sign that the Great Spirit had bestowed 'starberries' on his subjects to ease famine and disease. They were on to something: high in vitamins A and C, as well as anti-inflammatories and antioxidants, blueberries are one of those foods where the nutritional value is just as great as the pleasure of their eating.

A blueberry is intensely fruity, as if a few blackcurrants, a blackberry and a strawberry were rolled into one and condensed. It's a flavour I never tire of, and the sweet/acidic balance is as good as in any fruit. It seems that I'm not the only who thinks so: a couple of years ago, blueberries overtook raspberries as the nation's second favourite fruit, behind strawberries.

Nevertheless, there's no denying that blueberries remain expensive (see below for the reasons why). So it's handy that their flavour is intense and even a few can make a real impact: a small handful added to a bowl of banana and yoghurt, or steaming porridge, lifts an otherwise plain breakfast, and takes even a perfectly fine fruit salad into the extraordinary. Muffins and pancakes are much more appealing with blueberries punctuating that gorgeous creamy batter – just a few in each one is all you need.

As lovely as blueberries are eaten raw – popped one-by-one like biblical grapes – they are excellent in cooked dishes. For a clafoutis, they run cherries a very close race: sift 75g plain flour and a pinch of sea salt into a large bowl and whisk in ½ tsp vanilla extract and 180ml milk. Beat in 2 medium eggs (one by one), 40g caster sugar and an additional 170ml milk until smooth. Scatter 300g blueberries over the base of a greased and floured 25cm baking dish, pour in the batter and dot the surface with cubes of butter. Bake at 230°C/Fan 210°C/Gas 8 (yes, really that hot!) for around 25 minutes until plump and lightly golden. Allow to cool and dust with icing sugar. You have the option to court a little controversy here: man-made blueberry flavouring shares a compound with coriander seed, and a twist or two of ground coriander either in the clafoutis batter or dusted on with the icing sugar at the end gives a little extra blueberry taste. It works beautifully in blueberry muffins too, and the recipe opposite.

Similarly, a blueberry and sliced strawberry salad – equal amounts of each fruit, with 2 tsp each of caster sugar and lemon juice – is marvellous scattered with fresh coriander flowers (you'll not find these in the shops, but you'll be familiar with them if you've tried growing coriander, which bolts so easily (see page 198). Other herbal flavours that enhance blueberries, whether in sweet or savoury dishes, include basil, mint and tiny amounts of thyme.

We've got used to blueberries being ever-present on the shelves, with Chile, France, Poland and Spain supplying most. (The fruits are fragile and need careful handling during transport, which goes some way to explaining their cost.) But there is an increasing home-produced crop, available through the height of summer and into early autumn – you'll find British blueberries on some supermarket shelves, as well as in veg/fruit boxes and specialist suppliers. The Dorset Blueberry Company first brought blueberries across the pond just after the war and the increasing demand in the last 10 years has seen production swell to over 1,200 tonnes annually.

There's a limit as to how much we can produce, however. Blueberries thrive in very acidic soil – the sort that tends to be covered by protected heathland in the British Isles. It means that home-grown fruit is likely to remain a very seasonal, relatively small crop and all the more precious because of it.

When buying blueberries, look for fruit that is firm: softening is no indication of ripeness, just that the berries are reaching the end of their lifespan. Good ones will keep for a week or more in the fridge – much longer than many berries. And frozen ones can be dropped straight into muffin batters, smoothies or compotes. Size is also an important consideration. The skin carries a great deal of a blueberry's flavour, so smaller fruit (where the ratio of skin to flesh is higher) can be considerably more flavoursome, though this varies with variety to a degree. 'Bluecrop', 'Duke' and 'Draper' are about the best varieties in the supermarkets, so keep an eye out for them.

This is a fruit definitely worth growing yourself. The plants are easy to raise as long as you provide their favoured acidic conditions, so grow in containers filled with ericaceous compost – widely available at garden centres and garden suppliers. Give them a place in the sun and out of the worst of the winds and frosts, water them with rainwater if you can, as it's mildly acidic, and you should be in blueberries mid-summer. They fruit more heavily if cross-pollinated, so two or more plants, of different varieties, will give you the heftiest harvest.

Blueberries have wild relatives, including native bilberries (see page 69) which thrive on heathlands such as Exmoor, and the *myrtilles sauvages* of the Ardèche and Vosges mountains in France. These fruits are pippy and don't keep well, but they are intensely flavoured and perfumed.

CHICKEN AND BLUEBERRY SALAD WITH CORIANDER DRESSING

About 200g cold, cooked chicken, shredded

75g blueberries

2 handfuls of lamb's lettuce (or another mild green leaf)

FOR THE DRESSING

1 tsp coriander seeds

Juice of ½ lemon

½ medium red chilli, deseeded for less heat if preferred, finely chopped

3 tbsp extra virgin olive or rapeseed oil

Sea salt and black pepper

This is a lovely illustration of the happy marriage that can be made between blueberries and spice – and this recipe is also great made with wild bilberries. Cold, leftover pork or duck work well here as alternatives to chicken. Serves 2

For the dressing, in a small, dry pan over a medium heat, toast the coriander seeds gently until they begin to release their aroma. Tip on to a plate to cool, then grind using a pestle and mortar or spice grinder, as finely as you can.

Tip the ground coriander into a large bowl, mix in the lemon juice and chilli, then whisk in the oil. The dressing should taste a touch sour at this point; the sweetness of the berries in the salad will balance it out. Season with salt and pepper.

Add the shredded chicken and blueberries to the bowl and toss to coat in the dressing. Toss in the lamb's lettuce, then transfer to plates and serve immediately.

Borage

Mark Diacono

LATIN NAME
Borago officinalis

SEASONALITY
April–October

There comes a point early each spring when the weather can't seem to make up its mind if it should be winter or something more civilised. At such times, you need a little encouragement to be outside and borage gives you – and the early pollinators – just that. Springing lively and bright, in blue or white, before much else has even thought of growing, and producing right through the summer, borage flowers are spectacular. Miniature, but spectacular nevertheless. Strewn on to leafy salads, sprinkled over strawberries or Eton mess, floated on cocktails or frozen in ice cubes and popped into summer drinks, their light, cool, cucumber flavour lends a fresh contrast.

The lightly furry leaves also carry that fabulous cucumber flavour, but they have to be harvested when young and tender, before they become tough rabbit's ears. At their tiniest, they bring cool punctuation to a salad (leafy or fruity), make a fine accompaniment to smoked fish when sliced and stirred into crème fraîche, and bring freshness and visual loveliness to warm runner beans dressed with olive oil. Not to mention Pimms, where borage leaves and flowers are pretty special.

I've never seen borage flowers or leaves for sale – the flowers are very delicate – but they are easy to grow and you'll only need to buy the seeds once. Sow the seed in spring or summer, cover with the thinnest smattering of compost and they will appear in a few short weeks. In an ideal world, it would be a well-drained sunny spot, but I've seen borage grow in such unwelcoming places that I suspect it would germinate in your shoe. Unless you are meticulous in removing all the flowers before they go to seed, borage will reappear next year. Just pull up any plants you don't want.

COURGETTE SALAD WITH HAM, BORAGE AND EWE'S CHEESE

1 courgette (200–250g)

1 tbsp extra virgin olive or rapeseed oil, plus extra to finish

1 lemon

50g soft, mild ewe's cheese, crumbled or cubed

4 slices of air-dried or cooked ham, roughly torn into shreds

A handful of very young, tender borage leaves, shredded (optional)

A handful of borage flowers

Sea salt and black pepper

This delicate dish is simple and quick to throw together. If your borage plant has any very young, tender leaves, use some of these – otherwise, just use the flowers. If you can't find soft ewe's cheese, any mild, slightly salty, fresh white cheese will work for this salad. Serves 2

Using a vegetable peeler, cut the courgette into ribbons, working from top to bottom. Go as far in as the seeds on one side, then turn the courgette and pare ribbons from the other side.

Put the courgette ribbons into a bowl and add the oil, the juice of ½ lemon and a sprinkle of salt and pepper. Turn to coat the ribbons with the dressing, then allow to stand for 5–10 minutes.

To serve, divide the marinated courgette between serving plates, spooning over all the lovely juices too. Scatter over the cheese, ham and any shredded borage leaves you may have, and finish with the flowers. Add a touch more black pepper, a squeeze more lemon and a trickle more oil, and serve.

Borlotti beans

Mark Diacono

LATIN NAME
Phaseolus vulgaris

ALSO KNOWN AS
Cranberry beans

SEASONALITY
August–September
(fresh beans)

MORE RECIPES
Hempy hummus (page 308);
Roasted broccoli, red onion
and cannellini salad (page 99)

If you are lucky enough to live near a shop or market where fresh borlottis are sold, don't move – you are in a very special minority. The cream-coloured beans are splashed with crimson – usually, mysteriously, in inverse proportion to the pods – making them superficially similar to pinto beans. But you'll not mistake the flavour of borlottis; their creamy nuttiness is the most satisfying of all the late-season beans.

Borlottis' ability to take on full flavours such as garlic, chilli, bay and rosemary, while retaining something of themselves, makes them perfect partners to meat (notably pork, bacon and chorizo), fish (salt cod, in particular) and shellfish (especially mussels), not to mention many vegetables.

Fortunately, borlottis are simple to grow. In mid-April, start the seeds off in pots or root trainers, planting them out 5–6 weeks later. Planted in pairs, they will climb steadily, two-to-a-cane, to a couple of metres tall. Give them a spot out of the wind and water them through extended dry spells.

Picked soft in August, they don't take long to cook and make a superb hummus, give delicious substance to a warm summer salad, and add bite and texture to soups. As summer dips into autumn, the beans are demi-sec (half dry); the chill seems to draw out their flavour and firm up their texture, so this is a good time to pick them. Cook your podded borlottis in boiling water – anything from 15–40 minutes, depending on their size and maturity. (Sadly, they do lose their lovely speckles.)

The beans, at any age, also take wonderfully to drying – string up pods somewhere sheltered and, once they are completely dry, pluck out the beans and store. The dried borlotti beans are wonderful added (after overnight soaking) to winter soups, stews and casseroles.

BORLOTTIS WITH FENNEL SEEDS AND ONION

You can make this with fresh or dried borlottis and it's also a delicious way to serve freshly cooked chickpeas. Serves 4–6 as a side dish

300g dried borlotti beans, soaked overnight in water OR 500g fresh borlotti beans (about 1kg in the pod)

A bouquet garni (1 bay leaf, 1 sprig of thyme and 3 parsley stalks, tied together with string), optional

4 garlic cloves, peeled

1½ tsp fennel seeds

3 tbsp olive or rapeseed oil

1 medium onion, thinly sliced

Sea salt and black pepper

A little extra virgin olive or rapeseed oil, to finish

Drain the dried beans, if using. Put the fresh or soaked dried beans into a large saucepan and add enough water to cover them by about 5cm. Add the bouquet garni, if using, and 2 garlic cloves. Bring to the boil, then reduce the heat a little and simmer until the beans are tender. Fresh beans will cook in 15–40 minutes; dried beans can take anywhere from 45 minutes–1¼ hours, depending on their age. Top up the water if necessary.

Drain the beans and return them to the pan to keep warm. Remove the bouquet garni and garlic.

Finely slice the other 2 garlic cloves. Toast the fennel seeds in a small frying pan over a medium heat for 2–3 minutes until they give off their aroma. Lower the heat a little and add the oil. Throw in the onion and let it sweat for 10 minutes, then add the sliced garlic and cook for a further 3–4 minutes.

Tip the onion and fennel mixture over the warm beans, making sure you get every last drop of oil from the pan, and give them a gentle toss. Season with salt and pepper and add a drizzle of extra virgin oil before serving, if you like. Best served warm, but still good at room temperature.

Brains

Brains used to be eaten quite often in this country, but fell out of favour, along with most other offal, after the Second World War. Their popularity suffered further when, in 1989, in response to BSE, the sale of sheep's and cow's brains was banned. The ban was lifted in 1998, but it is still illegal to sell the brains from either animal once over a year old (the restriction does not apply to pig's brains). All brains for sale must be inspected at the abattoir before they are allowed to enter the food chain.

Brains are very tasty and less pungent than a lot of other offal, and it is well worth seeking them out. Butchers can get them for you but you may need to order in advance. Do make sure that any calf's brains you buy are from British-raised animals, as Continental calves may be raised in low-welfare conditions.

From a culinary aspect, the differences between the brains of different species are minimal. They all have a soft, rich, creamy texture. There's a hint of beef, pork or lamb flavour but the most noticeable difference is size. A lamb's brain is about the size of a small apple, a pig's brain roughly the size of an avocado and a calf's brain a little larger.

To prepare, wash brains carefully and thoroughly to remove bone shards, soak them to draw out any blood, then poach lightly in a liquor flavoured with bay, pepper, perhaps ½ onion and a splash of white wine. Mild and tender, brains can then be used in various ways. Some cultures eat them curried. Many traditional preparations have them dusted in flour or breadcrumbs and fried (as in the recipe below).

Lamb's brains are particularly good poached, chilled, sliced, dusted in mustard-and-cayenne-spiked flour and fried in butter with a few coriander seeds. I finish them by tossing a little chopped garlic and parsley into the pan and serve them on bread fried in lamb fat, with a little lemon juice squeezed over.

Pig's brains have a subtle sweetness that can even take them into dessert territory. After soaking, de-vein with tweezers, then cook briefly in reduced, sweetened milk and serve on toasted brioche with a little nutmeg grated over and a drizzle of caramel.

SAUTÉED BRAINS WITH PARSLEY AND CAPER SAUCE

The classic approach of pairing lightly fried brains with a piquant green sauce produces reliably good results. You can cook and serve sweetbreads in exactly the same way, after soaking and poaching them as described on page 629. Serves 2

2 lamb's or pig's brains

2 bay leaves

1 tsp black peppercorns

2–3 tbsp plain flour

1 tbsp olive or rapeseed oil

A knob of butter

Sea salt and black pepper

FOR THE SAUCE

Leaves from a small bunch (about 25g) of flat-leaf parsley

2 tsp small capers, rinsed and drained

Finely grated zest and juice of ½ lemon

1 small shallot, very finely diced

3–4 tbsp extra virgin olive or rapeseed oil

Wash the brains gently in a bowl of cold water. Then put them to soak in a bowl of fresh water for 15–20 minutes.

Meanwhile, to make the sauce, chop the parsley leaves, capers and lemon zest together on a board to a fine texture. Place the mixture in a bowl and stir in the lemon juice, shallot and enough extra virgin oil to form a loose sauce. Season with salt and pepper to taste.

Drain the brains and carefully peel away the dark, frail membrane that covers them; it may tear, but do your best to remove it all.

Bring a small saucepan of water to a simmer, add the bay and peppercorns, then lower in the brains. Poach for 5–6 minutes over a very low heat. Remove the brains to a plate to cool. When cool, cut each one in half or, if they are quite big, into quarters.

Season the flour generously with salt and pepper and use to dust the brain pieces, coating them well. Heat a medium non-stick frying pan over a medium-high heat and add the oil and butter. When hot, add the floured brains to the pan and fry for 2–3 minutes on each side or until golden. Serve straight away, with warm toast and the piquant sauce.

Brandy

MORE RECIPES
Devilled parsnips (page 128);
DIY prawn cocktail (page 502);
Spiced liver pâté (page 362);
Snipe with swede and bacon
(page 587); Roasted apricot
Eton mess (page 28); Chocolate,
brandy and star anise ice cream
(page 178); Spotted dick with
apple-brandy raisins (page 522);
Prune, almond and caraway tart
(page 505); Crêpes Suzette
(page 422)

SOURCING
ciderbrandy.co.uk;
thecornishcyderfarm.co.uk

There is no substitute for brandy when it comes to adding layers of depth and richness to a dish, not to mention a warming alcoholic twang. It has a fantastic affinity with all kinds of sweet things – lending flavour to puddings, fresh and dried fruit, cakes and chocolate truffles. Flambéeing the spirit, as for crêpes Suzette or Christmas pudding, not only looks impressive, it also imparts a subtle, toasted caramel note.

Brandy is great for deglazing savoury pans, too. A small quantity will dissolve meaty or fishy residues, reducing and intensifying in the heat as it does so, before stock and/or cream is added and cooked down to a rich sauce. Grape brandies (see below) work particularly well for deglazing pans used for beef, and I love cider brandy with shellfish. Watch out when adding brandy to a hot pan: the brandy vapours are quite likely to spontaneously ignite.

Brandy is produced by distilling an already fermented liquor and can have an alcohol content anywhere between 35 and 60 per cent. Grape (wine) brandies are the most common and popular type, aged in oak casks to develop flavour and colour. Some are named after the region from which they come, the famous French examples being Cognac and Armagnac.

Fruit brandies are derived from other fruits, including apples, pears and plums. Apple or cider brandies are made in apple-growing regions, including our own West Country and all over Normandy, where they go under the name of Calvados. A lovely tipple is apple brandy mixed with equal quantities of good apple juice, served over crushed ice. And an apple brandy and blackberry posset is a thing of wonder, made simply by heating cream with lemon juice until it thickens, and then adding a sweetened purée of raw blackberries and brandy before chilling.

Pomace brandy is made from the remains of grapes after their juice has been extracted for wine. The French version is *marc* and the Spanish *orujo*, with the most famous being Italian *grappa*.

For cooking, there's no need to splash out on expensive brandy, but nor should you cook with anything you wouldn't happily drink. The finest, well-aged brandies should be enjoyed at room temperature – in a warmed glass to release their aroma. More 'rugged' brandies should be drunk with ice – or very, very quickly.

BRANDY AND RAISIN TRUFFLES

75g raisins

50ml brandy

200g dark chocolate
(at least 70% cocoa solids)

150ml double cream

20g unsalted butter

Cocoa powder, to dust

Ideally, put the raisins to soak in the brandy the day before, to give them plenty of time to plump up. Serve the truffles with coffee. Makes about 24

Put the raisins into a bowl, add the brandy, stir and then leave to soak for 4–5 hours, or overnight. Line a shallow 24 x 15cm baking tray (or similar) with cling film.

Chop the chocolate into small pieces and place in a bowl. Put the cream and butter in a small pan over a medium heat and bring to a low simmer, then immediately pour over the chopped chocolate. Leave to stand for several minutes until the chocolate is melted.

Once melted, stir gently until glossy and smooth, then add the raisins, along with any brandy remaining in the bowl, and stir to combine. Pour the mixture into the prepared tray and refrigerate for 2–3 hours until set.

To serve, turn the truffle mixture out of the tray and cut it into small cubes. Place a few cubes in a sieve set over a bowl. Scatter over a few teaspoonfuls of cocoa and shake gently to coat. The cocoa that falls through into the bowl can be used for the next batch.

Brazil nuts

Nikki Duffy

LATIN NAME
Bertholletia excelsa

These are the luxurious, gob-stopping treats of the nut world: fat bullets so packed with oil that they break between the teeth like a piece of crystalline fudge. Their texture is a little like fresh coconut flesh, with a crisp, snapping, sweet-rich quality. In fact, they go exceptionally well *with* coconut and, like it, sit firmly at the indulgent end of the health-food spectrum.

Brazil nuts are the swollen seeds of a jungle fruit and do indeed come from Brazil, as well as other South American countries. Growing high on vertiginous trees, they're managed and gathered rather than cultivated – the huge, dense, nut-filled fruits falling murderously to the ground when ripe.

The wise nibbler should limit Brazil consumption to moderate levels. At around 25 calories per single nut, they are, shall we say, energy-dense – though what great energy it is, with lots of magnesium, as well as vitamin E, zinc, copper and phosphorus. They are also a rich source of selenium, a mineral required for many things including healthy thyroid and immune function, but we need only a trace amount; a mere 2 or 3 Brazil nuts will give you your daily recommended dose.

The granola below is one way to sprinkle the nuts judiciously into your day. Salads are another option but I have never found Brazils to behave particularly well as a team-player in savoury recipes; somehow, they're just too sweet and creamy. They're a destination nut. A few, eaten just as they come, will always be my favourite Brazil treat – perhaps with a couple of squares of salted dark chocolate as a chaser…

Because of their high oil content, Brazils can become rancid rather quickly so buy them in small quantities, and with a long sell-by date. However, one stale Brazil (and you'll know when you get one because it will have a curious, chemical 'off' taste) does not necessarily mean the whole packet is doomed.

BRAZIL NUT, CACAO AND ORANGE GRANOLA

350g porridge oats

150g whole Brazil nuts, each chopped into 2 or 3 pieces

150g pumpkin seeds or sunflower seeds, or a mix

A pinch of salt

50ml extra virgin rapeseed oil

Finely grated zest and juice of 1½ oranges

4 tbsp clear honey

50g cacao nibs

The bitter chocolate taste of cacao (see page 177) is a nice counterpoint to sweet, buttery Brazils (pecans work well here, too). You can also stir some dried fruit into the granola before eating, if you like, such as raisins, chopped dried pears or apricots, or dried cherries. Makes about 8 servings

Preheat the oven to 150°C/Fan 130°C/Gas 2 and line a couple of shallow baking trays with baking parchment.

Put the oats, nuts, seeds and salt in a large bowl and mix thoroughly. Pour on the oil and mix it in, getting it evenly distributed.

Mix together the orange zest, orange juice and honey until combined, then pour over the oats. Mix thoroughly – you might find it easiest to do this with your hands.

Spread the mixture out in the baking trays. Bake for 45–50 minutes or until golden brown, giving the mix a good stir halfway through.

Leave the granola to cool completely and crisp up, then stir in the cacao nibs. Store in an airtight container. Serve for breakfast with a couple of good spoonfuls of plain wholemilk yoghurt, or milk if you prefer.

Bread

Hugh Fearnley-Whittingstall

SOURCING
realbreadcampaign.org
(includes listing of good
bakeries); breadmatters.com

Bread is a staple of such universal importance, such ubiquity, that the name itself has come to stand as a synecdochal representation for all food. If you could somehow, retrospectively, uninvent bread, culinary cultures all over the world would collapse in on themselves, suddenly devoid of that daily, starchy building block. There would be no tender, puffy naans, hot from the wall of the tandoor oven; no dark, dense ryes to chew with smoked fish and aquavit; no coarse-textured *pane pugliese* to soak in some olive-oil-swirled stew. Bread can have a place at every meal, in every season: it's cheap, easy to use and filling, so often the alpha and omega of our daily diets.

Why then, is it so damn hard to buy good bread these days? Why do supermarkets, high-street bakers and sandwich shops stock bread that fails to satisfy? Flavourless and pappy, with an insignificant crust and crushable cotton-woolly interior that cleaves annoyingly to your palate, it's bread that leaves you hungry 30 minutes after eating it.

The answer is that bread has been a victim of its own success. We want plenty of it and we want it to be cheap; in order to answer that demand, manufacturers have given us quantity at the expense of quality. Before the Second World War, British bread was largely made with imported North American wheat flour, which possesses the high level of protein required to give body and bounce to a traditional loaf. And our bread was made – much as home-bakers still make it now – with a long period of rising before baking.

However, in 1961, the Chorleywood Process was born. This method of bread-making, now responsible for the vast majority of bread in the UK, is also dubbed the 'no-time method'. Which tells you a lot. It means that lower protein British wheat can be used to produce a packaged, sliced loaf from raw ingredients in less than 4 hours – and a lot of that is cooling down time. The mixing and proving only take about an hour. In order for that to be possible, the dough is mixed at high speeds using powerful machinery. It requires extra yeast, and solid vegetable fats to help maintain structure. The bread often contains preservatives and may also include enzymes that help ensure a consistent result (these don't have to be listed on the packaging because they are categorised as 'processing aids', not ingredients). This is industrial baking: accelerated and soul-less.

Chorleywood lies behind the wrapped, sliced bread that dominates supermarket shelves – the antithesis of hand-made, slow-risen bread. In between these two extremes are the high-street bakers and supermarket in-store bakeries who may not use the Chorleywood process but who will still be mixing their bread in bulk, and using some of the same additives and preservatives. Supermarket bakeries often buy in their bread part-baked and frozen, then 'bake it off' in store.

Our bread has changed vastly and I don't believe it's an accident that more and more people are having difficulties digesting it. It's not just the process of bread-making that has altered in the last half-century, but the ingredients too. The standard wheat flour we use nowadays is ground from modern, high-yielding strains, rather different from the wheat we were using even 50 years ago. There's evidence that it's both lower in minerals and higher in substances known to cause a reaction in people with coeliac disease (a severe auto-immune response to gluten). Some mass-produced bread also includes soya flour. Most modern flours are roller-milled, which creates heat and may affect the nutrients in the flour. (Stoneground flours are subjected to less heat.) And refined white flour, of course, lacks the greater part of the nutrients found in the whole grain (see page 262 for more information).

And then there's the yeast. The earliest leavened breads, thousands of years ago, were sourdoughs, relying on the action of the natural yeasts that live in the air around us. Sourdough baking has survived to this day. It remains one of the great miracles of the kitchen that you can leave a simple paste of flour and water sitting on the counter for a few days and watch it start to gently bubble and breathe, coming alive with active yeasts which, when nurtured and fed with fresh flour, can not only rise a loaf of bread but imbue it with fantastic flavour.

Now, however, the vast majority of bread uses commercially bred yeast, cultured in carefully controlled conditions, then dried and granulated, to puff up dough in next to no time. But speed is the enemy of good bread. The more sedate the action of the yeast, the more time for fermentation – and fermentation equals flavour, even in a loaf made with commercial yeast.

In a naturally leavened sourdough, the much longer, slower rising time allows the development of lactobacilli bacteria (also present in live yoghurt). These bacteria release acids which produce a rich array of flavours, but they are also beneficial in other ways. They may help the body absorb nutrients from bread. There is evidence that long-fermented sourdough causes less of a spike in blood sugar than standard bread, and also that the cultures in sourdough help to break down the gluten proteins in dough.

A few years ago, I made the decision to eat less bread, but better bread. So I often go for a few days without bread, and I feel much better for it. When I do eat bread, it's a choice, not a default, so it brings me more pleasure – and I don't have to go further than my own kitchen for it. I'm lucky enough to be married to someone who regularly turns out delicious, crisp-crusted sourdough loaves, mainly of spelt and rye.

But you don't have to get your hands floury to enjoy great bread. The UK is peppered with artisan bakers who are making loaves the old-fashioned way, and a great variety of them. Seek out rye loaves: these are characteristically dense and, especially if made with a sourdough culture, amazingly flavourful. Look for proper, shiny-crusted baguettes, traditional barm breads and sweet, enriched fruit loaves. If it's a soft bap or a tender bloomer you're after (and I'd agree that bacon sandwiches and barbecued burgers are much more pleasurable to eat in soft bread), these can still be made using traditional, slow methods and good ingredients.

Some well-made bread is available in supermarkets but it's very much the exception. Be particularly wary of 'sourdough' breads on supermarket shelves: these may contain added commercial yeasts, so they're not sourdoughs in the true sense at all. In the absence of reliable information, one bite of the crumb is likely to give you a good idea: true sourdough is chewy, with an open, slightly waxy crumb, a robust crust and that rich, characteristically tangy flavour.

Making your own bread, even occasionally, is the best way to put yourself back in the driving seat. And home-baking affords a great opportunity to explore the effects of using organic, stoneground flours, seeds and nuts, and healthy fats such as rapeseed oil. Whether you use dried yeast or experiment with sourdough, you'll be getting back to the basics of this amazing food, and you will learn a lot.

If you're new to bread-making, start with simple flatbreads that you can cook in minutes in a frying pan on the hob. Graduate to basic rolls and tin loaves, then start to explore the brown-skinned, big-bubbled, beautifully flavoured wonders of sourdough. Like so many of the very simplest foodstuffs, sourdough bread takes a modicum of skill in the making. But even a slightly heavy, lopsided first attempt will remind you what bread really ought to taste like. For bruschette, toast or soup-dunking, I promise you, there is nothing finer.

Leftover bread

One of the things I appreciate about good bread is that it goes stale. Indeed, the simple dishes that have evolved over the centuries as ways to use yesterday's loaf are among the best-loved in the comfort food repertoire. A particular favourite is *pain perdu*, otherwise known as eggy bread or French toast. Simply slightly stale bread sliced thickly and soaked in beaten egg with a dash of milk and fried until it has a golden crust, it is as delicious with a simple sprinkling of sugar as it is with something a little more elaborate, such as caramelised apples or flambéed bananas. You can give it a savoury spin too, and serve it with bacon and tomatoes.

Then there's the glory of a juice-soaked, berry-filled summer pudding – simply not achievable with soft, structure-less bread – and the classic bread and butter pudding. On the savoury front there are Glamorgan sausages, golden-crusted cassoulet and *panzanella* – the lovely Italian salad. Sausages and meatballs are always better for a measure of fat-and-flavour-holding breadcrumbs, and there are all the stuffings, toppings, croûtons and crumb coatings that require a dryish loaf.

Chorleywood bread has a preternaturally long shelf-life and a woolly texture that just doesn't crumb well. But if you buy a decent loaf you can look forward not just to its fresh incarnation, but to days of potential culinary reward as it matures into a dignified middle age.

Bread stores best for a few days loosely wrapped in paper in a bread bin – or, for longer keeping, in the freezer. In the fridge, it will quickly go hard. Don't eat bread that's gone mouldy – some bread moulds can be harmful.

MIGAS

250g good, coarse-textured bread, 1–2 days old

About 75g cooking chorizo

2 rashers of bacon

2 tbsp olive oil or lard

4 garlic cloves, peeled

A squeeze of lemon juice

A handful of flat-leaf parsley leaves (optional)

Sea salt and black pepper

This delectable Spanish use for slightly stale bread is often served as part of a spread of tapas. You can also serve it with poached or fried eggs, or with green leaves as a warm salad. Serves 4 as a tapas dish

Slice the crusts off the bread, then cut it into 2cm cubes. If the bread is very hard, sprinkle with a little water, cover and leave for an hour. Slice the chorizo into half-moons, about 3mm thick. Roughly snip the bacon into pieces.

Heat the oil or lard in a large frying pan over a medium heat. Add the whole garlic cloves and fry, turning often, for a few minutes until they start to turn golden. Add the chorizo and bacon and fry for a few minutes until crisp. Scoop the chorizo, bacon and garlic out of the pan with a slotted spoon, leaving most of the fat behind.

Add the cubed bread to the pan and stir well to coat it in the fat. Fry for 5 minutes or so, tossing often, until golden brown. Return the chorizo, bacon and garlic to the pan and stir. Season with a squeeze of lemon, and salt and pepper if it needs it (the chorizo and bacon may have contributed enough). Serve straight away, scattered with parsley if you like.

Bream, black

Nick Fisher

LATIN NAME
Spondyliosoma cantharus

ALSO KNOWN AS
Bream, sea bream, porgy

SEASONALITY
Avoid during April–May
when spawning

HABITAT
Eastern Atlantic. Usually found
around the south coast of Britain,
but sometimes further north.
Also the Mediterranean

MCS RATING
3–4

REC MINIMUM SIZE
23cm

MORE RECIPES
Cod with fennel, capers and
tomatoes (page 194); Red mullet
with roasted red pepper mayo
(page 393); Roast gurnard with
pepper, lemon, thyme and chilli
(page 292); Steamed sea bass
with kale and ginger (page 573);
Garfish with olives, oregano
and garlic (page 267); Dill salsa
verde (page 235)

SOURCING
goodfishguide.org

If God were to create the perfect fish flesh, it would be some heavenly mixture of mackerel, cod and bass. It would be a little oily, with firm muscular flakes, as delicious served raw as sashimi as it would be soused in citrus juices for ceviche, or simply fried and served with samphire and butter-lashed, waxy new potatoes. In short, it would be exactly like the flesh of the black bream.

The only downside to this fish is that it's elusive. It's rare to find any for sale on fish counters, because few commercial fisheries target it. If it does turn up, it's as by-catch in bass, plaice or sole fisheries. But it's worth asking or even *begging* for. Black bream does get landed at Brixham, Newquay and other southern harbours and occasionally trickles into fishmongers.

In addition, boat anglers can catch this fish around the rocks, reefs and wrecks of the south coast. Some black bream come to the eastern end of the English Channel to breed in spring, but most only visit in the summer when our inshore waters offer plenty of squid, crustaceans and bait-fish to gorge upon. Line-caught is the most sustainable capture method for black bream (bottom trawling can destroy their eggs and sea-floor nests). Bream from Cornwall, Sussex, North Wales and the Northwest are currently the most sustainable.

Black bream has a stiletto-sharp, spiny dorsal fin, which makes it tricky to handle when alive, and armour-tough scales that need to be removed before cooking. If you're baking one whole, snip off all the fins with a sturdy pair of scissors first. Fillets can be skinned to avoid descaling, although, personally, if I've gone to the trouble of catching a beautiful black bream, I want to eat that skin too.

Any bream or sea bream you find on a fish counter will almost certainly be gilthead – usually a farmed fish. Fed on pellets and grown to a uniform half-kilo size, it is distinguished by a gold stripe across its nose. A *wild* gilthead bream would be a thing to cherish, but farmed gilthead are just a pale, flabby imitation of the real thing.

If you find true black bream on sale, *buy* them. Lots of them. They freeze very well and, even when defrosted weeks later, will still taste better than most fresh fish flesh.

BLACK BREAM WITH JERUSALEM ARTICHOKE PURÉE

Fillets of John Dory, bass, gurnard, pouting or red mullet would also work well here. Serves 4

4 black bream fillets, descaled and pin-boned

Olive or rapeseed oil, for cooking

2 bay leaves

1–2 garlic cloves (unpeeled), bashed

Sea salt and black pepper

FOR THE PURÉE

750g Jerusalem artichokes

1 bay leaf (optional)

75g butter

A squeeze of lemon juice (optional)

For the Jerusalem artichoke purée, peel the artichokes, cut into chunks and drop straight into a large pan of water. Add salt and the bay leaf, if using, bring to the boil, then lower the heat. Simmer for 15–20 minutes, until the artichokes are completely tender. Drain and remove the bay leaf.

Tip the artichokes into a food processor (or into a clean pan if you have a stick blender). Add the butter, some seasoning and the lemon juice, if using. Blitz until smooth. Keep warm in a pan over a very low heat, stirring occasionally.

Season the fish with salt and pepper. Heat a frying pan large enough to take all 4 fillets over a medium-high heat (or use two smaller pans) and add a trickle of oil. Add the bay and garlic, and cook briefly to flavour the oil. Push them to one side and add the fish, skin side down. Cook for 4–5 minutes or until the skin is crisp and the fish is almost cooked through. Flip the fillets over and take the pan off the heat. Leave for 1–2 minutes – the fish will finish cooking in the residual heat.

Place the fish on warmed plates and spoon over some of the pan juices. Add a spoonful of artichoke purée and serve with kale 'crisps' (see page 322) or simply cooked greens.

Brill

LATIN NAME
Scophthalmus rhombus

SEASONALITY
Avoid during spring and
summer when spawning

HABITAT
Eastern Atlantic. Found around
the south and west coasts of
Britain and in the North Sea.
Also the Mediterranean

MCS RATING
3–4

REC MINIMUM SIZE
30cm

MORE RECIPES
Plaice with rosemary, caper and
anchovy butter (page 476);
Turbot with white wine, lemon
zest and thyme (page 648)

SOURCING
goodfishguide.org

Everyone's heard of turbot, it's the chef's favourite. And yet brill, the turbot's almost-twin, is left skulking anonymously in the shadows. But brill is not only every bit as good as turbot, I would say it's better. A little firmer of flesh, its whole overlooked-underdog persona also makes it feel more of an original choice.

Brill is in fact *so* similar to its more expensive, more famous flatfish cousin that the two even interbreed occasionally. Both are Premier League flatfish: big, ripped, aggressive predators that can grow up to 9kg. And because they're so partial to eating prawns and crabs, their flesh tastes of the firm, white place where lobster meets scallops to talk about veal. In terms of price and cache, they soar above plaice, dab, flounder and even sole, with only the mighty halibut to keep them company in the higher echelons of bottom feeders.

Brill is sold whole, or in tranches (slices across the body), or as fillets. A whole fish will be pricey and definitely something for a special occasion but it takes some beating, flaking off the bone in an easy-to-serve, forktastic fashion. For two people, try a single, large fillet instead. The tight, muscular, robust flesh can stand any manner of sensible cooking: baking, grilling, frying or even poaching in a fresh herby liquor. A double-skin-sided tranche will even survive the rigours of barbecuing. Sorrel, sage, basil, parsley butter, black butter, capers and salsa verde are all great friends of brill.

Like turbot and skate, brill is, surprisingly, not at its best on the day it is caught. When very fresh, the flesh is slightly jellified and bland. So, if you're lucky enough to catch your own brill or buy one direct from a day-boat, don't cook it immediately. Leave the flesh to rest and knit and settle in the fridge for 24–48 hours. Don't be afraid to freeze it either. Tightly wrapped fillets freeze well, tranches even better, and this helps 'mature' the flesh in the same way as a little quality fridge-time.

It's no surprise that such a Class-A fish is under threat of overfishing. Hard evidence about stock health is lacking but tread with care and avoid buying trawled brill. Local day-boat catches are best, with line-caught being the most conscientious option. The bigger (i.e. more mature) the brill, the better; avoid anything under 30cm.

ROAST BRILL WITH AIR-DRIED HAM AND PARSLEY SAUCE

A little olive or rapeseed oil

Leaves from a large bunch of
flat-leaf parsley (about 100g),
finely chopped, stalks reserved

1 whole brill (1.5–2kg), gutted
and trimmed

2–3 garlic cloves, sliced

8 slices of air-dried ham

50g butter

30g plain flour

400ml hot ham, veg, chicken
or fish stock

1 tsp Dijon mustard

250ml double cream

Sea salt and black pepper

A spectacular but comforting way to eat this superb fish – or any other large flatfish, such as plaice or turbot. Serves 4

Preheat the oven to 220°C/Fan 200°C/Gas 7.

Oil a large roasting tray, big enough to take your fish, sprinkle with salt and pepper, and scatter over the parsley stalks. Place the fish on top, dark side up, and scatter over the garlic. Trickle the fish with more oil and massage it into the skin, then season all over with salt and pepper.

Lay the ham slices over and around the fish. Bake for 25 minutes or until the fish is just cooked through and the white flesh lifts away from the bone.

Meanwhile, melt the butter in a medium saucepan over a medium-low heat. When it's bubbling, stir in the flour and cook for 1–2 minutes. Now add the hot stock, a third at a time, whisking it in to avoid any lumps. Stir in the mustard and simmer over a low heat for 8–10 minutes, stirring occasionally. Add the cream and bring back to a simmer, then take off the heat. Add the chopped parsley, and season with salt and pepper to taste.

Bring the whole brill to the table and serve with the warm sauce and some good mash.

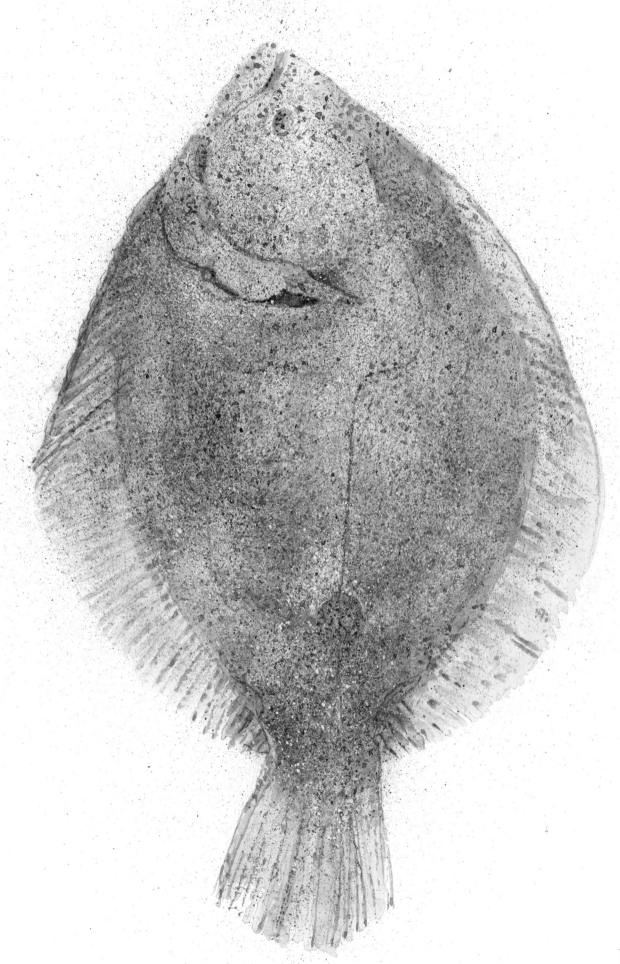

Broad beans

Hugh Fearnley-Whittingstall

LATIN NAME
Vicia faba

ALSO KNOWN AS
Ful or fava beans (when dried)

SEASONALITY
June–July is peak season

MORE RECIPES
Hempy hummus (page 308);
Little Gem with crushed broad
beans and Parmesan (page 433);
Garlicky pea ravioli with brown
butter (page 444); Risi e bisi
with pea shoot pesto (page 457);
Scallops with cauliflower
purée and green peppercorns
(page 572)

I'm not one to put all my produce in one basket but, if I had to name my favourite vegetable of all, broad beans just might be it. When picked young and cooked lightly, these emerald green niblets are exquisite: a little bit bitter, a little bit sweet. Lubricated with a lick of butter and piqued with pepper, they're a veg treat like no other.

Unfortunately, these beans don't hold up well to the storing and travelling involved in selling them on any scale. It's not impossible to get good broad beans in the shops, but it's all too easy to find yourself with a bagful of rather limp and weary examples, or with pods containing giant beans well past their sweet and silky youth. Farmers' markets and veg box schemes can be a decent source – though it's not always possible to ascertain how much time has elapsed since they were picked, which is a crucial factor in their deliciousness. At any time outside the mid-summer peak bean season, frozen broad beans, usually processed straight after picking, can actually be a better, sweeter bet.

Although broad beans may be harvested as early as late April (for a polytunnel or greenhouse crop) and as late as September, the main season is generally June and July. Wherever you're buying, look for bright green, firm, slightly glossy pods. It's normal for a few black fronds from the withered flower to remain at the stalk end, but any brown on the stalk or pod itself suggests the beans were harvested when over-mature.

A few pioneering pick-your-own farms offer broad beans, enabling you to access the beans at their fresh, young best. But if no such place exists near you, your best bet is growing your own. Climbing upwards rather than spreading outwards, they can be raised in a fairly tight space. They will grow on most soils and do as well in a large container as in an open bed.

Some varieties (particularly any called 'Aquadulce') can be autumn-sown directly into the soil for a May crop. But don't worry if you miss this window. If you start sowing (under cover) in February, then plant out your seedlings in late March or early April, you should have sweet little beans by early June. Later sowings will take you through to September – and you certainly won't find good, fresh broad beans in the shops that late in the year.

One of the wonderful things about home-grown beans is the generosity of the harvest. Before a single bean can be seen, the plant will give you a treat. It is horticultural good practice, once the flowers have just wilted to black, sooty curls, to pinch out the little cluster of leaves at the top of the plant. This directs the energy of the plant into the developing pods. But it's also your first harvest: those leafy bean tops, wilted in butter, are a delicious side dish. They also make a fine filling for a tart or omelette.

Sometime around late May, the swelling green pods start to tip from an upward to a downward trajectory. As soon as they are 5cm or so long, you can pick them and cook them whole, pod and all. And then, when the dangling pods start to reach hand-span length, you can finally begin the beanfeast itself. Inside the pods, you'll find ranks of tiny beans, smaller than a thumbnail. When this young and fresh, you can eat them raw, but cooking (just 2 minutes in lightly salted simmering water) will bring out maximum sweetness. Sometimes I just pour boiling water from the kettle over podded beans, leave them for a minute, and drain. The first pick of the year, prepared like this, and tossed with an indulgent knob of butter, is a high point of early summer.

Such is the pod's ability to camouflage itself among the leaves and stalks of the plant that you're always confronted, at the last few picks of the summer, by bulging pods containing hard, swollen beans. This is the point at which a home-grown bean

is most like the majority of shop-bought ones. Large and starchy rather than sweet, they are past the stage at which a simple buttering renders them exquisite. But worry not: remove them from their pods and drop them into boiling water. The amount of time they'll take to reach tenderness depends on size and age, but start at 3 minutes' simmering and work up to 10. Drain them and, when cool enough to handle, slip them out of their leathery grey skins. A bit of a faff this may be (or a soothing, meditative kitchen task, depending on your view), but it makes all the difference. It's only the very youngest, smallest beans that don't need skinning.

Rather than trying to turn mature beans into a delicate salad or side dish, purée them into a creamy broad bean hummus. Just whiz the cooked, skinned beans with a scrap of crushed garlic, a squeeze of lemon and a glug of your best olive oil. Here, their starchy nature is an asset. Soup is another delicious option for the same reason.

Broad beans are also known as fava beans. And, when mature beans are allowed to dry fully (something else you can do with your own crop), they become the *ful* of Middle Eastern cuisine – used for classic dishes including garlicky *ful medames*.

When buying broad beans in the pod, remember there's a huge volume discrepancy between bean and pod. You'll need a good 1kg of full pods to yield 300–400g naked beans. The great pile of green-skinned, velvet-lined debris that you'll amass when podding can be alarming. It does of course make great compost fodder but you can also cook up a light stock with at least some of it: add onions, celery, bay leaves and peppercorns to boost the flavour.

BROAD BEAN AND FETA FALAFEL

400g podded broad beans

6 spring onions (about 75g), white and pale green parts only, trimmed and finely sliced

1–2 garlic cloves, chopped

1 tsp ground cumin

Finely grated zest of 1 lemon

1 tbsp finely chopped flat-leaf parsley or mint

1 tbsp plain flour

60g feta or feta-style cheese, such as Homewood, chopped or crumbled

Olive or rapeseed oil, for frying

Sea salt and black pepper

It might be a bit of a crime to blitz the very youngest, sweetest broad beans into falafel, but for slightly older beans, this works an absolute treat. The slight bitterness of the beans is offset by the sweet saltiness of the feta cheese – though you can leave that out if you prefer a vegan falafel. Makes about 12

Bring a pan of water to the boil. Drop in the broad beans, return to a rolling boil, then drain. You don't want to cook the beans much (they should still be quite firm), but you do need to be able to get the skins off. Let the beans cool, then slip them out of their skins.

Put the beans into a food processor with the spring onions, garlic, cumin, lemon zest, parsley or mint and a pinch each of salt and pepper. Blitz to a coarse purée, stopping a few times to scrape down the sides of the bowl. Sprinkle in the flour and blitz briefly, to work it in.

Tip the bean purée into a bowl, add the feta and work it into the mixture roughly with a fork; you still want bits of feta to be visible.

Take a dessertspoonful of the mix, roll into a ball between your palms, then squash gently to form a patty, about 5cm in diameter and 1.5cm thick. Repeat with the rest of the mix.

Pour enough oil into a non-stick frying pan to just cover the base, then place over a medium heat. When hot, add the falafel and fry for about 8 minutes, turning a few times, until golden brown on both sides and steaming hot in the middle. (Alternatively, you can brush the falafel with oil and bake them at 200°C/Fan 180°C/Gas 6 for 20 minutes, flipping them over halfway through.)

Leave to cool at least a little before serving. Like any falafel, these are delicious with hummus and/or yoghurt, a tomato salad and some warm pitta bread.

Broccoli & purple sprouting broccoli

Gill Meller

LATIN NAME
Brassica oleracea var. *italica*
(both types)

SEASONALITY
PSB: December–April.
Calabrese: June–February

MORE RECIPES
Sweet and sour barbecued
courgettes (page 201); French
beans with shallots and black
olives (page 265); Spicy brown
rice and broccoli (page 535)

Common-or-garden broccoli – also known as calabrese, after the Calabria region of Italy – is a perfectly decent vegetable. Highly nutritious (like all brassicas), widely available and easy to cook, it's a great green ingredient. And I'll come back to it. But first, let me celebrate its close cousin, purple sprouting broccoli or 'PSB', which is in a different league altogether.

One of the great attractions of PSB is that it is abundant during the 'hungry gap', early in the year, when not much fresh produce is around. It comes good in late winter and early spring and brings much-needed freshness to the table. But even if it came at a more plentiful time, PSB would still be magnificent. Its slender form is so appealing and the flavour is fantastic – more delicate than standard broccoli (see overleaf) but beautiful, with a hint of the mildly bitter earthiness that all brassicas share.

Once a fairly obscure seasonal treat, the development of new varieties means PSB can now be harvested from December through to April at least, and is widely available. But the stems are still best picked often and eaten very fresh: requirements that don't really fit in with the standardised supermarket supply chain. This is why PSB in the shops can be disappointingly thick-stemmed and fibrous.

The sooner you can cook the stalks after picking, the better – like so many tender vegetables, the stems lose their juicy sweetness as their sugars turn to starch. So look for PSB in farm shops where it is sold fresh from the field. Check for bright leaves, firm stems and dense, compact florets. In some shops, they put the stem ends in water to help keep them fresh. If your only option is the supermarket, you may have more joy with 'Tenderstem' – a hybrid of broccoli and Chinese kale – which, as the name suggests, is reliably tender, if a tad less interesting than PSB.

Sprouting broccoli isn't difficult to grow – it even thrives in containers – but it takes almost a year to mature, requiring a period of cold weather before it starts to crop. Once flourishing, however, it's a cut-and-come-again veg that benefits from regular harvesting. While the beautiful purple varieties are most common, you can get white spouting broccoli too. Sow the seeds under cover in March or April and plant them out in June and July, or sow directly outside in April to May and thin out the seedlings.

In restaurants, sprouting broccoli is sometimes heavily trimmed before serving but I always cook all the dark, khaki-emerald leaves along with the stem and floret. They have got loads of flavour and give a fabulous contrast of textures, which is one of PSB's great selling points. PSB is always best cooked simply: boiled or steamed for a few minutes, until the stem is just turning tender. The freshest stems cook in just 3 minutes or so. If it's a few days old, you'll need 5–6 minutes of cooking to help bring out its sweetness.

The lovely, complex flavour of sprouting broccoil means that it works well with both delicate accompaniments and punchier tastes. Like asparagus, you can serve PSB draped with hollandaise or with soft-boiled eggs, or eat it with olive oil, lemon juice and shavings of salty cheese. Alternatively, melt a tub of buttery potted shrimps over it, and season it up with an extra shake of cayenne. Cooked sprouting broccoli is great as a canapé with the Italian garlicky anchovy dip known as *bagna cauda*.

Lightly cooked purple sprouting is also delicious combined with softened shallots, reduced white wine, cream, grated Parmesan and a little finely chopped chilli and rosemary, topped with a scattering of breadcrumbs and baked as a gratin. Alternatively, try tossing the florets into a pan of fried chorizo slices and turn to coat in the tasty oil, or coat them, still raw, in a light batter and deep-fry for tempura.

The stems are also lovely tossed with olive oil, garlic and anchovies and roasted in a hot oven for 10–15 minutes, until the leaf and florets crisp and blister; served with poached eggs, this is a great supper.

Standard broccoli has something of a tarnished reputation as a bland vegetable, all too often overcooked in school canteens and served up waterlogged. Served with everything from fish fingers to roast chicken, it has become *the* veg to persuade children to eat their greens. But, while far from glamorous, this type of broccoli is still useful and tasty. Cooked lightly, it is firm and sweet and children often really *do* like it. It's a great first vegetable for babies to pick up and chew. And as they grow up, there are many ways to add interest to those perky florets.

For a good broccoli experience, cook it until the tip of a sharp knife can just pierce the stems – a few minutes of steaming or boiling is enough. Leave the cooked broccoli in a colander for a few minutes to let the water evaporate, thereby avoiding sogginess. Alternatively, if you cut the broccoli into small florets and use a bit less stem, it can go into a dry frying pan to char-cook in 5–6 minutes.

However you cook it, broccoli partners strong flavours well: it loves mature cheeses, chilli, spices, garlic. It's good incorporated into macaroni cheese, or tossed with toasted cashews and a lime and tamari dressing, or served raw with tangy dips (like the one on page 464).

Unlike sprouting broccoli, standard broccoli can be planted in the spring and picked later in the same year, making it less 'greedy' on space in the veg plot. And if you can't grow your own, the commercial calabrese season now extends from June to February, meaning you can eat British broccoli, in one form or another, pretty much all year round.

ROASTED BROCCOLI, RED ONION AND CANNELLINI SALAD

This is a great, one-tray roasted salad – fresh, healthy and tasty. Serves 4

2 slices of stale bread (about 60g), cubed

4 tbsp olive or rapeseed oil

Leaves from 1 sprig of rosemary

2 red onions, peeled and cut into small wedges

1 tbsp balsamic vinegar

1 head of broccoli (400–500g with stalk), or about 400g PSB

400g tin cannellini (or borlotti) beans, drained and rinsed

Leaves from 2 sprigs of thyme, chopped

A pinch of brown sugar

Finely grated zest and juice of ½ lemon

50g soft ewe's or goat's cheese

Sea salt and black pepper

Preheat the oven to 180°C/Fan 160°C/Gas 4.

Put the bread cubes in a roasting tray with 1 tbsp oil, the rosemary leaves and a pinch of salt and toss together. Bake for 10 minutes, tossing once or twice, until golden brown. Tip the bread cubes into a bowl and set aside.

Add the red onion wedges to the roasting tray with another 1 tbsp oil and the balsamic vinegar. Season with salt and pepper, toss to mix and roast for 15 minutes.

Meanwhile, cut broccoli florets from the central stalk and quarter each floret; or snap off any woody ends from PSB and cut each spear into 2 or 3 lengths. Put the broccoli in a bowl, trickle with 1 tbsp oil and season lightly with salt and pepper. Add to the onions, mix well and roast for 15 minutes, stirring twice, until the broccoli is tender but still with a little bite.

In a bowl, combine the cannellini beans with the thyme, sugar, remaining 1 tbsp oil and the lemon zest and juice. Season and mix well. Add to the tray of tender onions and broccoli and put back in the oven for a further 5 minutes to roast the beans a little.

Meanwhile, roughly break up the rosemary croûtons – either in a food processor, or bash them in a bag with a rolling pin, keeping them coarse.

Remove the tray of veg from the oven and check the seasoning – you may want a little more lemon juice, salt or pepper. Transfer to a serving dish, crumble over the cheese and scatter over the broken croûtons to serve.

Brussels sprouts

Gill Meller

LATIN NAME
Brassica oleracea var. *gemmifera*

SEASONALITY
October–March

MORE RECIPES
Cheddar, apple and celeriac salad (page 140); Fried cabbage wedges with caraway (page 112); Tongue, kale and apple hash with horseradish (page 643)

'Abacus', 'Cronus', 'Revenge', 'Maximus', 'Diablo': these could be the names of powerful horses that once pulled Caesar's chariot through the streets of ancient Rome; or gladiators. In truth, they are varieties of Brussels sprout, which I find an equally thrilling thought. This vegetable is incredibly versatile and deserves to be championed in all its possible guises, to persuade sprout-doubters to give them a second chance.

Sprouts are often victims of overcooking, and regularly brought to the table grey, mushy and smelly. Traditionally, a cross is cut in their base before cooking (supposedly to speed up heat penetration), but this is unnecessary. If you do want to boil them, give them no more than 4 or 5 minutes, until tender but not soft. But this under-rated little emerald of a brassica deserves so much more, or perhaps I should say less – less time in a pan of boiling water, and more time being cooked in other, more interesting, ways.

Roasting sprouts brings out their complex, bittersweet charm. Give them around 30 minutes at 190°C/Fan 170°C/Gas 5, until tender and slightly caramelised, then augment them with good chorizo, hazelnuts, garlic and fresh thyme.

Or try barbecuing them: turn whole sprouts through olive oil with crushed garlic, toasted cumin seeds, chilli, lemon zest and sumac, then thread on to skewers, season with crunchy salt and grill over glowing embers. Blistered and tenderised, smoky, nutty and sweet, they are fantastic eaten off the stick with mint and yoghurt, as a side dish to barbecued lamb.

Creamed sprouts is a great classic: simmer sprouts with sweated shallots, thyme and chicken stock, then purée with a dash of cream. It's a velvety embrace of a dish, which is particularly good served alongside roast goose or earthy fried fish. It can be spiked with lovage or green peppercorns, or topped with smoky pancetta or salty chestnuts, for fragrance and texture.

And another fantastic way to eat fresh spouts is raw, when they are at their sweetest and their most nutritious – like all brassicas, sprouts are packed with vitamins and minerals. To enjoy your Brussels without cooking them, choose the youngest, freshest specimens and make sure you slice them thinly: I like them tossed with sliced raw apple, lemon juice, olive oil and tarragon – or in the Asian-inspired dish overleaf.

Early sprout varieties were cultivated in Rome a few thousand years ago (which may explain why they have such dramatic names today). They are now grown throughout much of Europe – with the UK being one of the larger producers – and harvested in the winter months. They are quite strange plants to look at: with a thick, heavy stem, up to a metre in height, from which the little buds grow in a helical fashion from bottom to top. The plant culminates in an open, leafy crown, known as the Brussels top, which is a beautiful vegetable in its own right. Try blanching the leaves, then draining them and tossing into a hot pan of sizzling, garlicky butter.

Sprouts are relatively easy to grow in a veg patch but planning is required. You should have Brussels on your mind by mid-May. Propagate the seeds indoors then, when the plants are 10–15cm tall, plant them out into free-draining, firm, fertile soil; they like a sheltered, sunny spot. Keep them well watered. When the plants reach maturity, the little buds can be picked in small batches as and when required. Alternatively, the whole stem can be cut at its base and taken into the kitchen in its entirety. The sprouts keep beautifully fresh this way.

Sprouts are sweetest after a frost as they produce more natural sugars at lower temperatures. Seek out sprouts that are on the small side, and nice and firm, as these will cook and taste better than older ones.

B

ROASTED SPROUTS WITH BLACK PUDDING AND CHESTNUTS

500g Brussels sprouts, trimmed

2 sprigs of rosemary, roughly torn

2 sprigs of thyme, roughly torn

6 garlic cloves, peeled and bashed

2 tbsp olive or rapeseed oil

200g black pudding, chopped or broken into 1–2cm pieces

100g cooked chestnuts, halved

2 tsp clear honey

A squeeze of lemon juice

A handful of parsley leaves, chopped (optional)

Sea salt and black pepper

Roasted with hearty black pudding and chestnuts, Brussels sprouts are a meal in themselves. This also makes a fantastic winter side dish. Serves 3–4 as a light lunch, 4–6 as a side dish

Preheat the oven to 190°C/Fan 170°C/Gas 5.

Halve the Brussels sprouts and put them into a large roasting tin. Add the rosemary, thyme, garlic, oil and some salt and pepper, and toss everything together well. Roast for 15 minutes, stirring once.

Add the black pudding and chestnuts to the roasting tin, trickle over the honey and toss together again. Roast for a further 15–20 minutes, until the sprouts are tender but still have a little bite.

Taste for seasoning, adding more salt and pepper if needed and a squeeze of lemon juice. Scatter over some chopped parsley if you like, then serve.

RAW SPROUT SALAD WITH SESAME, GINGER AND LIME

200g firm young Brussels sprouts

2 tsp sesame seeds

½ small red chilli, deseeded and finely diced, or 1 tsp dried chilli flakes

½ garlic clove, crushed or grated

1 tsp finely grated root ginger

Juice of ½ lime

4 tsp tamari (or soy sauce)

2 tsp clear honey

This is the antithesis of the over-boiled, soggy Brussels sprout. Cooked not at all, these sprouts are finely shredded then tossed in the zingiest of dressings – vibrant with chilli, lime, ginger, garlic and tamari. It makes a fabulous starter before a big winter meal, or a great side salad with leftover Christmas meats. You can use the same dressing on finely shredded raw cabbage. Serves 2 as a starter or side dish

Trim the very base off each Brussels sprout, then peel away any tired outer leaves. Use a sharp knife to shred each sprout thinly. Place the shredded sprouts in a bowl.

Toast the sesame seeds in a small dry, hot pan over a medium heat for 1–2 minutes until they start to pop in the pan. Tip the seeds into a small bowl.

Add the chilli to the sesame seeds, along with the garlic, ginger, lime juice, tamari and honey. Whisk well to combine.

Pour three-quarters of the dressing over the shredded sprouts and toss together. Divide the dressed sprouts between plates, trickle over the remaining dressing and serve.

Buckwheat

Tim Maddams

LATIN NAME
Fagopyrum esculentum

ALSO KNOWN AS
Kasha, soba

MORE RECIPES
Chive buckwheat blinis with hard-boiled eggs (page 175); Tortillas with cumin and garlic oil (page 221); Noodles with seaweed, smoked mackerel and soy (page 407)

Not a form of wheat at all, buckwheat is actually the seed of a flowering plant. The black hull is removed to reveal a pale seed with a characteristic triangular shape. This is used whole (as 'groats'), rolled into flakes, or milled into flour. The popularity of buckwheat is on the rise as more of us seek out wheat- and gluten-free foods. This renaissance is well deserved: buckwheat has a delicious nutty, earthy flavour and to cook with it is to be transported to a time before wheat ruled the roost. Note that although buckwheat is naturally gluten-free, it may be 'contaminated' by being processed alongside wheat: check the packet if you are avoiding gluten.

Buckwheat is a fast-maturing crop that grows even in poor conditions and, until wheat became more popular, it was used wherever it could be grown, particularly in cold and mountainous regions. It was a mainstay in Russia and Eastern Europe and remains the basis for traditional staples such as northern Italian pizzoccheri pasta and Japanese soba noodles.

Used alone, buckwheat flour won't produce cakes with a tender sponge, owing to the absence of gluten, but it can be combined with some wheat flour, or mixed with other non-wheat flours or ground nuts, along with eggs and/or raising agents, to make good cakes and scones. Buckwheat also makes great batters with a characteristic, slightly 'gloopy' consistency, which produce excellent fritters (see recipe below) and pancakes. Both Breton galettes and Russian blinis owe their distinctive, earthy flavour to buckwheat flour.

Buckwheat can be used in place of bulgar wheat in tabbouleh: cook the groats in lightly salted boiling water for 8–12 minutes until tender, then drain, cool under cold running water and drain again. Dress the cooked grains with spices such as smoked paprika, coriander and cumin, then add diced onion, garlic, tomato and lots of vibrant herbs such as mint, parsley and coriander. Season well with chilli and lemon juice and finish with hemp or olive oil. This makes a fantastic accompaniment to any barbecue.

Buckwheat seed may also be roasted for a stronger, earthier flavour – when it is sometimes called 'kasha'; it is used in the same way as the raw groats.

BUCKWHEAT AND APPLE FRITTERS

1 medium eating apple (125–150g)

1 medium egg

50g caster sugar

100g buckwheat flour

A pinch of salt

1 tsp baking powder

Vegetable oil (refined rapeseed oil), for frying

TO FINISH

4 tbsp caster sugar

A good pinch of ground allspice or ground cinnamon

These little fritters – light and moreish and very quick to make – are delicious with coffee.
Serves 4–6 as a snack

Peel the apple and grate it coarsely into a bowl. Add the egg and beat to combine. Add the sugar, buckwheat flour, salt and baking powder and beat to form a batter.

Heat a 1.5cm depth of oil in a fairly deep, heavy pan to about 170°C, or until ½ tsp of the batter dropped in turns a rich golden brown in just under 1½ minutes.

Cook the fritters in batches, 4–6 at a time. Spoon teaspoonfuls of the batter into the hot oil and cook for about 1½ minutes, turning the fritters over in the oil once or twice, until puffed up and dark golden brown. Drain on kitchen paper.

Mix the sugar and ground spice together in a small bowl. Sprinkle over the hot fritters and turn to coat. Pile the fritters into a bowl and serve straight away.

Bulgar wheat

Tim Maddams

LATIN NAME
Triticum spp.

ALSO KNOWN AS
Burghul, bulgur

MORE RECIPES
Spiced couscous with lemon and sultanas (page 202); Minted spelt and tomato salad (page 386)

Bulgar, also known as burghul, is wheat that has been par-boiled, dried and 'cracked' to form pale golden-brown nuggets. It can be milled to various degrees to form fine, medium or coarse granules. Medium works well for most purposes.

One of the great things about this grain is that it is quick and easy to cook. The basic preparation is simple: for 4 people, bring 300ml water to the boil in a medium saucepan. Add 1 tbsp olive oil, 200g medium bulgar wheat and some salt and pepper. Stir, then simmer for 3 minutes. Take off the heat, cover and leave for 10 minutes to plump up. (Fine and coarse bulgar will require a little less or more simmering, respectively.) Fluff up the grains with a fork – they should be *al dente* rather than soft. You can serve the bulgar plain, alongside something spicy, or dress it: just olive oil or butter and some salt and pepper will do, but a zesty, blended herb and garlic number is a winner every time.

Bulgar has a lovely, virtuous texture but, as with many grains, it is essentially bland. The more flavour, spice and seasoning you can give it – or accompany it with – the better. Traditionally, it's a North African and Eastern European ingredient, popular particularly as an addition to spiced stews, soups and rissoles such as kibbeh.

I mostly use bulgar in a similar way to couscous, as an accompaniment to tagines or stews. It also makes an excellent last-minute stand-in for pearl barley in soups. Tossing a handful or two of cooked bulgar (see above) into bread doughs and batters, meanwhile, is a great way of adding extra fibre and texture.

Try using bulgar instead of breadcrumbs in stuffings for rich meats like pork belly. Cooked as above, seasoned and mixed with lots of chopped herbs and minced meat offcuts, it works well and lends a more interesting texture.

Look out for organic and/or fairly traded bulgar. The biggest supply is from Canada but it's often processed in other countries.

MUJADARA

3 tbsp olive oil

4 large onions, thinly sliced

100g Puy lentils

150g medium bulgar wheat

1 tbsp cumin seeds, toasted and crushed (or 2 tsp ground cumin)

2 tbsp chopped flat-leaf parsley

Juice of ½ lemon

50g toasted sunflower seeds or shelled hemp kernels

Sea salt and black pepper

This comforting combination of grain, nutty lentils and golden, fried onions is a traditional Lebanese dish. Classically, it's made with rice, but bulgar works beautifully too. Serves 4

Heat a large frying pan over a medium heat and add 2 tbsp olive oil. Toss in the onions, sprinkle with a generous pinch of salt and give them a good stir. Cover and cook gently for about 30 minutes or until the onions are very soft and tender.

Meanwhile, rinse the lentils in a sieve under cold running water. Tip them into a pan and add enough water just to cover. Bring to the boil, then immediately drain and return to the pan. Add the bulgar wheat to the pan too. Cover with water and bring up to a gentle simmer. Cook for 8–10 minutes, or until the lentils and bulgar are tender but still with a little bit of bite. Drain and place in a bowl.

Stir the cumin through the softened onions, turn up the heat and cook, uncovered, for a few minutes until golden and caramelised. Remove from the heat.

Stir half the onions through the cooked lentils and bulgar, along with the parsley, lemon juice, remaining olive oil and some salt and pepper.

Serve garnished with the remaining onions and toasted seeds, as a side dish, or on its own, with a spoonful of thick yoghurt.

Bullace, wild plum & cherry plum

John Wright

LATIN NAME
Bullace: *Prunus domestica*
subsp. *insititia*.
Wild plum: *Prunus domestica*.
Cherry plum: *Prunus cerasifera*

SEASONALITY
Bullace and wild plum:
August–September.
Cherry plum: July–August

HABITAT
Bullace and wild plums: Found
on lowlands throughout Britain.
Cherry plums: Mainly southern
and eastern distribution

MORE RECIPES
Damson ripple parfait (page
231); Damson and rosemary
vodka (page 663)

Few things cause as much confusion as the various types of wild plum that can be found in the hedgerow. All are purple. But where the bullace is small and round, rather like a big sloe, the wild plum is large and oval. (The wild damson, on the other hand, is small and oval.) These are all, basically, plums, *Prunus domestica*, although bullace and damson are usually considered to be the subspecies *insititia*.

Bullace and wild plums are found from mid-August to mid-September. Both have the potential to be quite delicious, though you never quite know until you take a bite. They may be just as sweet and tasty as a good orchard plum, or they may not. They can be eaten raw or cooked, just like cultivated plums, and the tiny bullace is wonderful used in place of sloes in a sloe gin recipe, with the bonus that the fruit is even tastier after its long sojourn steeped in alcohol. Leave the fruit in the gin or vodka for at least 3 months for the best effect.

The cherry plum, a different species, is hugely abundant where it has been planted as a roadside tree. It fruits earlier than the other plums – from the first week or two of July until the end of August. The fruit are about 3cm in diameter and cluster like grapes around the branches. You can pick a hundred kilos in an afternoon with a bit of help. They come in yellow and red and I hesitate to say which is better, as the flavour varies so much from year to year and tree to tree (though, if pressed, I would go for the yellow ones).

What also varies is whether or not you will find cherry plums at all. Their early flowering leaves them vulnerable to bad weather and they often fail, sometimes for several years. When there is a glut, it is well worth making jam, and some cherry plum wine. It can be a tricky wine to pull off, going sour very easily during fermentation, but scrupulous cleanliness should pull you through.

GRILLED CHEESE SALAD WITH BULLACE COMPOTE

250g ripe bullace (or other wild plums)

4 slices from a baguette (or other loaf of your choice)

1 tbsp olive or rapeseed oil, plus extra for brushing

2 tsp clear honey, plus a little extra if needed

4 tsp cider vinegar, plus a little extra if needed

½ tsp thyme leaves

1 small or ½ large head of radicchio, leaves separated

1 tbsp extra virgin olive or rapeseed oil

4 thick slices of soft, rinded ewe's or goat's cheese

Sea salt and black pepper

Tangy, plummy bullace marry beautifully with salty ewe's or goat's cheese. You can use any wild plum or damson here, or try the compote with tart cherries – just vary the sweet/acid seasonings according to the flavour of the fruit. Serves 4 as a light meal

Stone the bullace using a cherry stoner, or by halving the fruit with a small, sharp knife and prising out the stone.

Preheat the grill to medium. Brush both sides of the bread slices with a little oil and toast lightly on both sides.

Heat a small pan over a medium heat and add 1 tbsp oil. Add the bullace, 2 tsp honey, 3 tsp cider vinegar, the thyme leaves and 2 tbsp water. Cook over a medium heat, stirring occasionally, for 8–10 minutes or until the bullace start to break down. You want the compote to be quite loose, so don't overcook it. Add a splash more water if necessary.

Taste the compote and adjust the sweetness and acidity with a little more honey or vinegar if required. Keep warm.

Put the radicchio leaves into a large bowl and add the remaining 1 tsp cider vinegar, 1 tbsp extra virgin oil and some salt and pepper. Toss to coat the leaves with the dressing, then divide between salad bowls or plates.

Lay a slice of cheese on each slice of toast. Grill until the cheese is golden, then place a cheese toast on each pile of radicchio. Spoon over the warm bullace compote and serve.

Butter

Gill Meller

SOURCING
abernethybuttercompany.com; hookandson.co.uk; quickes.co.uk

There is nothing quite like hot toast, spread with fridge-cold butter and good marmalade. As a source of saturated fats, butter has received a bad press over the years, but recent analysis has questioned the link between saturated fats and heart disease. Also, butter is a source of fat-soluble vitamins, including vitamin A, and of conjugated linoleic acid (CLA). Eaten in moderation, butter can play a role in a healthy diet.

I find it amazing to think that cows produce rich, creamy milk from a simple natural diet of grass. Butter is made by skimming off the cream from that milk and agitating it. The agitating (or churning) process damages the fat globules in the cream, which begin to break down. The fat leaks out of the globules and masses together, into 'grains' of butter, and the liquid that remains is called buttermilk.

You can make butter easily in your own kitchen. All you have to do is fill a large jam jar two-thirds full with double cream – ideally a few days old, but still fresh – and shake it up. Eventually it will 'split' and you will be left with home-made butter and a quantity of thin buttermilk too (see page 109). It takes a little more elbow grease than buying it, but it's much more fun.

The process is basically the same on a commercial scale, albeit most butter these days is produced in huge 'continuous churning' machines. These accelerate the process and allow manufacturers to precisely control moisture content by injecting water into the butter if necessary; they can also remove air from it to increase shelf-life. Factory-made butter may also include milk or milk powder, besides pure cream.

As an alternative, there are some wonderful butters still made in small batches in the traditional way. Their texture is delightfully dense and where standard supermarket butter is 80–82 per cent butterfat, a good artisanal butter may be up to 86 per cent. Such rich butter is particularly good for baking and pastry-making.

The flavour of the cream – and therefore of the resulting butter – varies subtly depending on the breed of the cow, the food it eats and the time of year that it is milked (although these fluctuations are what industrial butter-making aims to iron out).

The flavour of butter is also influenced if bacterial cultures are allowed to grow in it. In pre-industrial times, raw, unpasteurised cream would be collected over several days of milking before it was churned. Left to stand for this time, the bacteria in the milk produced lactic acid and other flavour compounds, giving the cream a slightly sour, fermented edge. This culturing of the cream gave the butter a deeper, fuller taste, which is still preferred in much of Europe.

Today nearly all butter is made with pasteurised cream but cultures may be added once the butter is churned. Many French butters – both artisan butters and mainstream brands – are cultured, and have a characteristic, full, lactic flavour. British butters are not usually cultured and have a slightly sweeter taste.

You can buy goat's milk butters from most supermarkets and farm shops. The cream is churned in a similar way but the butter has a sweet, grassy flavour with the merest hint of 'goat'. It is nearly always lighter in colour than a cow's milk butter – often almost white – so many producers add a colouring to give it a more familiar yellow hue. It can be used in exactly the same way as cow's butter, though as with all goat dairy products, it's hard to find free-range (see page 280).

When butter melts in a hot pan it 'splits'. Most of it is pure fat, which turns clear and golden, but a layer of milk solids will separate from the fat and sink to the bottom of the pan, while residual water contained in the butter will evaporate as it sizzles away. The butter will re-solidify if cooled, but it won't re-combine into a smooth mass.

This heating and separating is referred to as 'clarifying' the butter. The advantages are that the milk solids can be discarded, leaving pure butterfat which has a higher smoke point, making it great for frying.

Ghee, a form of clarified butter, is widely used in Indian cuisine, probably because pure butterfat keeps much better in a hot climate than creamy butter itself. The melted butter is cooked, rather than just melted, giving ghee a deeper, richer flavour than simple clarified butter. The flavour also varies depending on where the butter is from and how the ghee has been made (some ghee is made from buffalo milk). It can be spiced or otherwise flavoured and is particularly popular in Northern India.

Sometimes it's desirable to retain the milk solids in melted butter and allow them to burn slightly. *Beurre noisette*, or brown butter, is made by gently heating melted butter so that the milk solids develop a nutty, aromatic flavour and rich brown colour. Much-loved by the French, *beurre noisette* is used in baking (see below) as well as for making a simple and delicious sauce or dressing for fish, roast meats and vegetables.

At River Cottage we use organic unsalted butter on a daily basis. We find it is more versatile than salted butter, especially when it comes to delicate puddings and sweets that may call for little or no salt. It's also better for sautéeing as it has a slightly higher smoke point than salted butter. But when it comes to hot crumpets or breakfast toast, a good salty butter is hard to beat.

Buying organic offers an assurance that the cows who have produced the milk have spent much of their time grazing outdoors on untreated pasture. Butter from grass-fed animals is higher in CLA and other beneficial nutrients than that from grain-fed cows. And I believe that natural, grassy diet is reflected in the quality of the butter, and in the flavour of the delicious pastries, biscuits and cakes we make with it.

BROWN BUTTER SHORTBREAD

225g plain flour
75g caster sugar
¼ tsp fine sea salt
150g unsalted butter

Devilishly moreish, these biscuits have a wonderfully rich flavour thanks to the nutty brown butter used to make them. Makes 8 wedges

Preheat the oven to 170°C/Fan 150°C/Gas 3. Lightly butter a 20cm loose-bottomed cake tin and line the base with a disc of baking parchment.

Put the flour, sugar and salt into a large bowl and whisk together thoroughly.

Put the butter into a medium saucepan over a low heat. Let it melt completely, then increase the heat a fraction so that it starts to simmer. Cook for about 7 minutes, swirling it around often. It will release steam to start with, then simmer for a bit. Watch it carefully until it gets to the point where it starts to foam and the butter solids on the base of the pan turn brown. Quickly, before the solids blacken, take off the heat.

Immediately pour the melted butter into the flour, scraping in the browned butter solids too, and mix well until it comes together into a crumbly dough. Tip this into the prepared tin and smooth out with the back of a spoon into an even disc. Prick all over with a fork, right through to the base. Bake for 35–40 minutes, or until just starting to turn pale golden brown at the edges.

Leave in the tin, marking it into 8 wedges after it has cooled for a few minutes. Leave to cool completely in the tin. The shortbread will keep for a week in an airtight tin.

Buttermilk

MORE RECIPES
Peach slump (page 448); Cherry, thyme and marzipan muffins (page 154)

SOURCING
ivyhousefarmdairy.co.uk; longleyfarm.com

Most buttermilk these days is not really buttermilk; it is an approximation of what it once was. In days gone by, the cream used for butter-making would be 'ripe', i.e. several days old and slightly fermented (see page 106). When it was churned for butter, the liquid that drained off the creamy, fatty buttery solids – the original buttermilk – was alive with bacteria and a little sour. This acidity made it very useful, not least because it meant it kept better than fresh milk. It was enjoyed as a refreshing, tangy, nourishing drink and was good for cooking too, particularly as a baking ingredient, where it reacted with agents such as bicarbonate of soda to produce a good rise.

However, the vast majority of buttermilk available now on supermarket shelves has never seen the inside of any kind of churn. It's not derived from cream and has nothing to do with butter-making. Instead, it is skimmed milk to which a bacterial culture has been added in order to create a thicker texture and slightly sour flavour – a mimicking of the original ingredient it's named after. (The actual buttermilk produced in modern butter-making goes into prepared products such as spreads and milkshakes.)

There are a few dairies producing buttermilk in a more authentic way, by draining the liquid from churned butter. But rather than starting with a fermented cream, they also add controlled amounts of specifically chosen cultures *after* the buttermilk is drawn off. These more traditional buttermilks have a slightly smoother, richer mouth-feel because they contain a tiny amount of fat (about 1 per cent), whereas skimmed milk-based 'buttermilk' has almost no fat at all.

While modern buttermilks may be rather different from their ancestor, their uses are nevertheless similar. They are still low-fat, acidic dairy products and you can employ them in all the old-fashioned ways. In muffins, pancakes and Irish soda bread, buttermilk gives a great rise. You can use it in marinades as a meat tenderiser, or whip it into a smoothie in place of yoghurt. Buttermilk has a special place in the cooking of the American Deep South, where it was once as common as 'normal' milk because its fermented, acidic nature meant it kept well in the heat. It's still used in Dixie cooking to coat classic fried chicken and to lift batters and doughs, including those for cornbread, 'biscuits' (scones) and hush puppies (cornmeal dumplings).

BUTTERMILK AND SAGE ONION RINGS

2 large onions

1 tbsp finely chopped sage leaves

200g plain flour

150ml buttermilk

Vegetable oil (refined rapeseed oil), for frying

Sea salt and black pepper

Flaky sea salt, to finish

The buttermilk and flour form an instant light, crisp batter on these onion rings. Sprinkle with salt and serve them up hot with a burger, or just devour a bowlful with a cool beer. Serves 4–6

Peel the onions and slice each one into 7–8 thick rounds, then separate the rings.

Combine the chopped sage with the flour, a generous pinch of salt and some black pepper. Pour the buttermilk into a bowl.

Heat a 3–4cm depth of oil in a medium, heavy-based pan to about 175°C, or until a cube of bread dropped in turns golden brown in about a minute.

Cook the onion rings in batches. Dust a handful individually in the sagey flour, coat in buttermilk, then dip them straight back into the sagey flour again to coat thoroughly. Immediately lower into the hot oil and fry for 45–60 seconds, or until golden brown.

Drain on kitchen paper, then sprinkle with a little flaky salt. Keep warm while you cook the rest in batches. Serve while still warm and crunchy.

Cabbages

Tim Maddams

LATIN NAME
Brassica oleracea var. *capitata*

SEASONALITY
Different varieties all year round

MORE RECIPES
Stir-fried cabbage with turmeric and garlic (page 651); Braised Savoy cabbage with mustard (page 400); Braised white beans with greens (page 55); Raw sprout salad with sesame, ginger and lime (page 102); Cheddar, apple and celeriac salad (page 140); Tongue, kale and apple hash with horseradish (page 643)

This brassica is often taken for granted, viewed as a dull side dish, or disregarded altogether, but it is an ingredient we should be making more of. High in fibre and rich in vitamins C and K, cabbage is also a good source of minerals and disease-fighting antioxidants (red cabbage in particular). It is inexpensive and in season most of the year in one form or another. Depending on how you cook it (or don't cook it), cabbage can be earthy or sweet, crisp or silky, and is a fantastic counterpoint to rich, creamy, salty or starchy foods. There are hundreds of different varieties, which can be split into two broad categories, summer and winter.

Winter cabbages are usually harvested from late autumn onwards. Because they are frost-hardy and won't continue to grow under about 7°C, they can be left in the ground, in a sort of stasis, and harvested to meet demand. These cabbages keep well in cold storage, particularly the harder headed varieties, but they are always sweeter eaten soon after harvesting.

Summer cabbages are altogether different from their wintry brethren, with notably smaller, more open heads, softer leaves and a sweeter flavour.

Cabbages are a satisfying crop to grow, although, I would say, not a project for the novice. They have a tendency to bolt for a variety of reasons, including exposure to frost. They are also rather prone to cabbage diseases like club root – and don't even mention caterpillars. But if you have plenty of space, rich, slightly alkaline soil, and the time and inclination to be attentive, you should be able to produce a crop of deliciously flavourful specimens.

As for cooking, boiling is not the best way to go, as most of the sweetness and a lot of the flavour leaches out of the cabbage into the water, which is then discarded. It's far better to steam, sweat, stir-fry or braise cabbage.

Hard red or white varieties are ideal for braising: cut the cabbage evenly into slices the thickness of a £1 coin, stalks and all. Sweat in a little oil in a large saucepan for about 10 minutes, then add some crushed garlic, a few spices, a spoonful of honey and some cider. Cover and cook gently, stirring occasionally, for an hour or so, until tender. Then remove the lid, simmer until the liquid is reduced to a coating consistency and add a knob of butter before serving.

POPULAR CABBAGE VARIETIES

January King With beautiful red-tinged leaves, this variety of Savoy is a superb winter ingredient. I use it for all sorts of cabbage dishes, particularly with pasta: sweat down the finely sliced leaves with onion, carrot, bacon and garlic for a good 15–20 minutes before adding a sprinkling of dried chilli flakes and plenty of extra virgin olive oil, and tossing with a robust pasta such as orecchiette.

Hispi Also called 'Sweetheart', this is a pointed green cabbage that starts to appear early in the spring and is good right through the summer. It has a delicious, sweet flavour and is great simply steamed but also very good sautéed.

Green cabbage This smooth-leaved, compact-headed, glossy green cabbage is a great all-rounder. Be careful not to overcook it – it can lose its appeal very quickly.

Red cabbage This beautifully coloured cabbage is harvested from July to December and stores pretty well for some time thereafter. It's suitable for everything from a raw, punchily dressed coleslaw to a long, slow braise with cider, apples and spices.

Savoy This is a popular variety, with characteristically ridged and wrinkled leaves. It has a robust texture and an excellent flavour – more complex than that of some of the hard-headed, smooth-leaved varieties. An excellent cold-weather staple.

White cabbage A hard-headed tightly packed cabbage with a mild flavour, this is typically used raw – finely shredded for coleslaw and other salads. But it is just as good as red cabbage for slow-cooking and also brilliant in stir-fries.

Slightly looser, green cabbages, including Savoy, are best steamed: shred finely into 2mm thick slices and cook in a steamer for about 5 minutes. Season well with white pepper and sea salt and toss with plenty of butter.

Raw cabbage dishes – slaws – can be really exciting and vibrant. Hard red and white cabbages are ideal, but you can use any variety. Keep it a cabbage-only affair, or add in raw root veg, such as celeriac, carrot or beetroot, or celery. Finely shred your cabbage, ideally using a mandoline slicer, then toss in a dressing that will cling, such as mayonnaise, yoghurt or oil balanced with some acidity in the form of vinegar, citrus juice or finely sliced spring onion, red onion or shallot. A handful of crunchy toasted seeds will lift the texture.

I tend to dress slaws at the last minute to keep them fresh and crisp. However, you may prefer to dress them ahead and put them in the fridge to soften a little. Just remember that salt and acid break down the cells in the leaves, releasing moisture and making the dressing much looser.

My all-time favourite slaw is red cabbage and shredded raw beetroot, dressed with 4 parts rapeseed oil to 1 part soy sauce and 1 part lime juice, with a healthy scattering of toasted sesame seeds over the top.

Another option for cabbage is fermentation. Sauerkraut, the classic fermented cabbage, is enjoying new popularity, not least because, if unpasteurised, it is rich in beneficial bacteria. Raw sauerkraut can be bought and is also simple to prepare at home by combining shredded raw cabbage with salt, which draws out its juices to form a simple brine. Try eating sauerkraut with smoked sausage and a rich cream and mustard sauce; or with a little smoked herring, plain yoghurt and some good rye bread for a healthier option. And if you like it, try pungent Korean kimchi, another form of fermented cabbage with a much spicier character.

Unless you are lucky enough to have a very cold, dry shed or larder, cabbages should be stored in the fridge: they will quickly degrade at room temperatures. Aside from not overcooking them, the key to getting sweetness from cabbages is freshness: the longer they are left after picking, the more of the plant's sugars will turn to starch and the more dull and unrewarding it will be.

FRIED CABBAGE WEDGES WITH CARAWAY

1 firm, medium cabbage, such as Hispi or Savoy (about 400g)

20g butter

1 tbsp olive or rapeseed oil

2 tsp caraway seeds, lightly bashed

2 small garlic cloves, peeled and bashed

Sea salt and black pepper

Cabbage cooked in this way is sweet and tender, yet rich and caramelised at the same time. The cabbage quarters are great on their own or with good sausages or lamb chops. Halved Brussels sprouts can be cooked in the same way. Serves 2–4

Trim the very base from the cabbage, but keep the leaves attached at the base. Peel off any rough or damaged outer leaves. Quarter the cabbage from stem to tip. Cook in a steamer for 3–4 minutes, then remove.

Heat a medium-large frying pan over a medium-high heat and add the butter, oil, caraway and bashed garlic. When the butter is foaming, add the wedges of steamed cabbage and season all over with salt and pepper. Cook for 2 minutes on each side or until caramelised. Serve straight away.

Capers

Steven Lamb

LATIN NAME
Capparis spinosa

MORE RECIPES
Dill salsa verde (page 235); Celery and walnut tapenade (page 133); Crispy lentil and roasted squash salad with salsa verde (page 352); New potato and egg salad with gherkins and capers (page 276); Spider crab salad (page 208); Plaice with rosemary, caper and anchovy butter (page 476); Cod with fennel, capers and tomatoes (page 194); Sautéed brains with parsley and caper sauce (page 82)

Capers have a unique flavour: tangy, pungent and herbaceous. They come in various shapes and sizes but all are the preserved flowerbuds of the same Mediterranean plant *Capparis spinosa*, which resembles a shrubby rose.

In general, the quality of a caper is related to its size. Capers can be picked as tiny buds, almost before their journey has begun. These *nonpareille* (meaning 'without peer') capers are certainly among the best. Larger capers are left on the plants until just before they flower. And sometimes, the caper makes it all the way through flowering and is picked as a fruit. These caperberries are usually brined or vinegared. They resemble olives in size and shape and can be used as an alternative to them, but their flavour is less piquant and punchy than that of the smaller capers.

No caper is much good straight off the bush. Prior to preserving, the fresh buds have a strong flavour of cabbage and radish. Pickling in vinegar or packing in salt brings out sour and salty notes. I would argue that dry-salted capers are the best. The bud retains a better texture and the salt brings out a fruity floral aroma that isn't present after pickling in vinegar.

However they come, it is good practice to rinse capers then drain or pat them dry before adding them to a dish, so that the brine, pickle or salt in which they were suspended does not overpower other ingredients. Even so, capers still contribute a salty kick, so you will probably need to add less salt to the dish. Capers are an essential ingredient in a classic tartare sauce. They are also delicious with lamb and roasted vegetables, and in pasta sauces. They make a crisp and irresistible garnish too – simply fry for a minute or so in about 1cm of very hot oil.

While there's no such thing as a British caper, you can produce something very similar with the seed pods of the nasturtium. From late July to early September, the knobbly pods form as the flowers fade. Brine the nasturtium pods, then jar them in vinegar to produce a good caper alternative with a particularly hot, peppery character.

ROASTED CAULIFLOWER WITH CAPERS

1 small cauliflower (about 500g), trimmed

1 medium onion, finely sliced

2–3 garlic cloves, peeled and bashed

1 tsp roughly chopped rosemary

A pinch of dried chilli flakes (optional)

2 tbsp olive or rapeseed oil

2 tbsp capers, rinsed and drained

A knob of butter

Sea salt and black pepper

Extra virgin olive oil, to finish

Salty little capers go deliciously with earthy cauliflower, which is served here two ways: as both a creamy purée and as whole, roasted florets. You can skip the puréeing step if you prefer and keep all the roasted cauliflower florets whole. Serves 2 as a starter

Preheat the oven to 180°C/Fan 160°C/Gas 4.

Cut the cauliflower into golf-ball-sized florets and place in a roasting tin with the onion, garlic, rosemary, chilli, if using, oil and capers. Season with salt and pepper and stir well. Roast for 35–40 minutes until the cauliflower is tender and starting to colour, giving it a stir halfway through.

Put half the roasted cauliflower and caper mixture into a food processor with a knob of butter and 2 tbsp water and blitz to a thick purée. Add a little more water if necessary. Taste and add more salt and pepper if needed.

Spread the warm cauliflower purée over individual plates, scatter over the whole roasted cauliflower florets, onion and capers and finish with a trickle of olive oil.

Caraway

Pam Corbin

LATIN NAME
Carum carvi

SEASONALITY
Home-grown caraway produces leaves May–June and seeds in the autumn of its second year

MORE RECIPES
Fried cabbage wedges with caraway (page 112); Sunflower seed and caraway corn crackers (page 623); Prune, almond and caraway tart (page 505)

Caraway, with its complex, lively tones, is a friend to both sweet and savoury ingredients and its use is ancient and widespread. With a hint of aniseed, it has a deep aroma, with a subtly citrusy note, and an intoxicating, nutty sweetness. (The related anise seed has a more powerfully liquorice-like flavour, but can be substituted for caraway in sweet recipes.)

A member of the aromatic, feathery-leaved carrot family, Apiaceae (or Umbelliferae), caraway is easy to grow. A biennial, flowering and producing seedheads in its second season, it enjoys sunshine and a well-drained soil. Both leaf and root can be eaten – the leaves snipped into salads, and the roots, dug in their second autumn, treated like parsnips – but it is the elegant brown seeds we are most familiar with. Harvest these towards the end of the summer, cutting off the seedheads when they are dry and beginning to turn brown. Pop the seedheads, upside down, in a paper bag, hang in an airy place to dry for a week or so until they start to release the seeds, then collect and store these in a sealed jam jar in a cool, dark place.

Whether home-grown or shop-bought, kitchen use for these curvaceous seeds is diverse. To get the very best from them, toast them gently in a dry pan. They can then be used whole, roughly crushed or finely ground – releasing more flavour the more you break them down.

Caraway pairs well with rich, salty flavours. Sprinkle it on to cheesy biscuits before baking, add to Welsh rarebit mixes or blend with Seville orange marmalade to glaze a baked ham. Caraway is also a principal player in North Africa's merguez spice mix and fiery harissa paste. It brings an earthy fragrance to lightly cooked brassicas and is often used to spice up sauerkraut and other fermented veg.

It has plenty of sweet applications too. Mix caraway seeds into melt-in-the-mouth shortbread, toss into the topping mix for an apple or pear crumble, or add a teaspoonful to a favourite carrot cake recipe. And of course, caraway is the traditional choice for a classic seed cake. This spice also gives its distinctive flavour to the Prussian liqueur, kummel, a soothing digestif.

RYE AND CARAWAY SCONES

1 tbsp caraway seeds, plus extra to finish

125g dark rye flour

125g plain white flour, plus extra to dust

2 tsp baking powder

¼ tsp salt

4 tbsp plain wholemilk yoghurt

2 tbsp extra virgin rapeseed oil

1 tbsp clear honey

A little milk, to finish

These little scones have a lovely flavour and a nice, crisp crust. Split them, spread with salty butter and serve with soup or a dish of beans. Makes 8

Preheat the oven to 210°C/Fan 190°C/Gas 7. Line a baking tray with baking parchment.

Lightly toast the caraway seeds in a hot, dry pan for a minute or so, until fragrant. Tip into a mortar and leave to cool for a few minutes, then bash roughly with the pestle. You're not trying to grind them to a powder, just break them up a bit to help release their flavour.

Combine the flours, baking powder, salt and bashed caraway seeds in a large bowl.

In a jug, whisk together the yoghurt, 3 tbsp water, the rapeseed oil and honey. Tip the mixture into the dry ingredients and mix to a firm dough – start mixing with a spoon and then finish off with your hands.

Tip the dough on to a lightly floured surface and pat into a disc, about 15cm in diameter and 2cm deep. Cut into 8 wedges and transfer to the baking tray.

Brush each scone wedge with a little milk and sprinkle with a few more caraway seeds. Bake for about 20 minutes until risen and golden brown. Leave to cool (at least a little) before serving. Eat within 24 hours, or freeze.

Cardamom

Elettaria cardamomum

MORE RECIPES
Fragrant beef curry (page 350);
Indian spiced grilled quail
(page 510); Masala chai doodh
(page 384)

Split open a green cardamom pod and you'll find a knot of brown seeds, which may not look promising, but it's their seductive aroma you're after. The extraordinarily exotic scent, almost minty in its fresh sweetness with a deep background warmth, carries through into the taste. It's hardly surprising cardamom has held cooks in thrall for millennia, firstly in its Indian homeland and then in Europe and the Middle East.

Cardamom is exceptional with fruit, especially mangoes and oranges – in a frozen kulfi or chilled lassi, for example, while its flavour is essential in a cup of hot chai or Arabic coffee. A rice pilaf is enhanced by the addition of a few pods and they are called for in countless Indian recipes. The Vikings took a shine to cardamom in Constantinople and shipped it homewards. Used lavishly in baking as well as drinks such as glogg and aquavit, it remains a classic spice in Scandinavian cooking.

In savoury dishes, cardamom pods are often used whole. Biting into one halfway through a curry is not to everyone's taste, but it's all part of the experience. Ready-ground cardamom is not easy to find but this is no great loss – it lacks the fresh perfume of the whole seeds. It's easy (though a little fiddly) to grind the seeds yourself: give each pod a light whack with a pestle or rolling pin to split it, then use your thumbnail or the tip of a sharp knife to open the pod and excavate the seeds. Bash the seeds with a pestle until powdered. You'll need about 20 pods to get 1 tsp ground cardamom.

Black cardamom is the big, brash cousin of green cardamom. The pods are about four times the size, earthy brown and with a distinct smoky scent that comes from the traditional practice of drying them over a fire. The seeds have a strong flavour of camphor so the pods are often thrown whole into curries to give a smoky depth. But the whole seeds can be used in chutneys or ground in small amounts into spice mixes; both black and green cardamom seeds are traditional in garam masala (see page 225).

PULLA

40 cardamom pods

175ml whole milk

50g butter, cubed, plus a little
extra, melted, to grease

80g caster sugar

½ tsp salt

Finely grated zest of 1 orange

300g strong white bread flour

125g plain white flour

7g fast-acting dried yeast

1 medium egg

TO FINISH

1 egg white, beaten with
a splash of water

10g flaked almonds

1½ tsp demerara sugar

This cardamom-scented brioche-style bread is made in Finland at Christmas. It's best the day it is made, but slightly stale slices are great toasted. Makes 14–18 slices

Put the cardamom pods into a mortar and give them a good bashing with the pestle: you want to break open the pods, release the seeds and roughly crush them.

Heat the milk in a pan to just below boiling, then take off the heat. Add the butter, sugar, salt, orange zest and bashed cardamom, pods and all. Stir until the butter has melted, then set aside to cool until lukewarm. In a bowl, whisk the flours together with the yeast.

Beat the egg into the infused milk mixture, then strain into a separate large bowl, pressing the cardamom in the sieve to extract the flavour. Using a wooden spoon, beat in half the flour mixture to form a batter. Mix in the rest of the flour. Turn the dough out on to a lightly floured surface and knead for 10 minutes, until smooth and glossy. (Or use a mixer with a dough hook.) Form the dough into a ball, coat lightly in melted butter and place in a large bowl. Cover and leave in a warm place until almost doubled in size, at least 4 hours.

Line a baking sheet with baking parchment and lightly butter it. Turn out the dough on to a lightly floured surface, deflate it with your fingers, then divide into 3 equal pieces. Roll each piece into a sausage, 40cm in length, and braid into a plait, securing the ends. Place on the baking sheet, cover and leave in a warm place until doubled in size – another 2 hours or so. Preheat the oven to 190°C/Fan 170°C/Gas 5.

Brush the loaf with the egg white, sprinkle on the flaked almonds and sugar, and bake for 25–30 minutes until golden brown. Transfer to a wire rack and leave to cool before slicing.

Cardoons

Mark Diacono

LATIN NAME
Cynara cardunculus

SEASONALITY
Usually October–November
for blanched stalks; a spring
crop is sometimes available

Cardoons are magnificently huge, with an edible part that's relatively small, and are only at their best for a short period in autumn, so if you're feeding an expanding family and have limited space, they may not be high on your list of things to grow.

However, if you are looking for something which adds architectural splendour to your garden every week of the year, and where the edible part is delicious, or you have need of a sturdy mace (the spiky flowerheads) for smiting unwanted visitors, cardoons are just the ticket.

Even to the experienced gardener, cardoons are hard to tell apart from globe artichokes. Their jagged, silver-green leaves and spiky flowers, carried aloft on long stalks, are visually identical, but where you eat the core of the immature flowerheads of globe artichokes, it is the celery-like ribs from the leaves that are cardoons' edible treasure. Cardoons may be 'blanched', as celery often is, the leaves tied up to form a 'trunk', excluding light from the centre. Blanching is not essential, but the resulting new growth is paler, sweeter and more tender than unblanched stalks.

To prepare cardoons, strip off the leafy, spiky parts, leaving the crisp, ribbed central stalks. At their very young and tender best, these can be eaten raw, finely sliced, but usually it's good to pare away the tough, outer fibres with a veg peeler, then cook them. Lightly blanched, cardoons retain quite a crunch, rather like celery. Roasted or stewed, they become tender and yielding (the time they take to do this can vary considerably).

Cardoons' flavour is subtle yet distinctive: earthy, sweet, yet faintly bitter, with a hint of celery, globe artichoke heart and salsify. Fabulous lightly blanched and dressed in vinaigrette, as a crudité, or deep-fried as tempura, I find I use them most in gratins, either as the sole vegetable or with leafy greens such as chard or spinach.

I've never seen cardoons in the shops, but some online food specialists sell them. They are, however, easy to grow – either from seed or bought plants. Allow them space: a 2-metre spread is usual, and the flowerheads can easily reach 2–3 metres high. They are gorgeous, perennial, require no maintenance and you can dig up, separate and replant the young plants that spring up at the base of the 'mother' to give you more.

CARDOON BRUSCHETTA WITH HONEY AND THYME

3–4 cardoon stalks

Juice of 1 lemon

4 slices of sourdough or other robust bread

1 garlic clove, halved

Extra virgin olive oil, to trickle

1–2 tsp clear honey

Leaves from a couple of sprigs of thyme

Sea salt and black pepper

This bruschetta is very good made with plain sourdough bread, but if you happen to have something a little fruity to hand, such as a good raisin and walnut bread, it will make the dish particularly delicious. Another tasty addition is cheese: try a little ricotta, soft ewe's cheese or blue cheese crumbled on top. Serves 2–4

To prepare the cardoons, strip off the leaves and spiky edges, leaving the ribbed stalks (wearing gloves will protect you from the spiky leaves). Add the lemon juice to a large pan of cold water. Working one stalk at a time, use a veg peeler to peel off the tough strings that run the length of the stalk, effectively reducing the ridged stalk to a smooth one. Slice into 2 or 3 pieces and drop into your pan (the lemon juice will prevent discoloration).

Bring the pan of cardoons to the boil, lower the heat and simmer gently until tender – as little as 10 or as much as 40 minutes. Drain and let them steam-dry in the colander for a minute or two.

Slice the stalks thinly, on the diagonal. Toast the bread. While still hot, rub the toast lightly with the cut surface of the garlic. Trickle over a little extra virgin oil, then pile the sliced cardoons on to the toast and season well with salt and pepper. Finish with a trickle of honey and the thyme leaves and serve straight away.

Carp

LATIN NAME
Cyprinus carpio

SEASONALITY
England and Wales: closed
season on rivers generally
15 March–15 June

HABITAT
Rivers and still waters across
the British Isles

MCS RATING
Not rated

REC MINIMUM SIZE
25cm

SOURCING
fishsociety.co.uk

There are plenty of people in this country who are nuts about catching carp – and then putting them back in the water. Freshwater fish doesn't seem to have the appeal of its marine cousins nowadays, but we used to love eating this fish. Native to Eastern Europe, where it is still heartily enjoyed, it was welcomed in Britain when the Romans introduced it precisely because it was such good eating. With its rich flesh (it's classed as an oily fish, and is a good source of omega-3s) and curdy flakes of meat, it can be quite delicious.

I'm particularly interested in carp because it could potentially reduce the pressure on some of our other, more high-profile fish. Carp is unusual in that it can easily be farmed in an organic, sustainable way. It is a fast-growing omnivore, happy to graze in inland ponds and, crucially, does not require vast quantities of other fish in order to thrive. It does very well on grains, seeds, worms and insects. This is in marked contrast to the high water and protein requirements of some other farmed species, including trout and salmon.

Carp is already being farmed in Britain but most of it goes to stock angling lakes. However, farmed carp can be bought online, in Asian-run fishmongers, and in some supermarkets around Christmas, when it's considered a traditional treat by many Eastern Europeans. I think every curious fish cook should give it a try.

Carp has scales that need to be removed and, while the basic skeleton is uncomplicated, it sports a row of y-shaped pin bones down the centre of each fillet. In carp-eating countries, these are either dealt with via special machines, or accepted as part and parcel of the carp experience, as with herring and sardines. The feared 'muddy' flavour in carp can be dealt with by 'cleaning' the fish in a tank of fresh water for a couple of days before dispatch – something that good carp farms will do.

Whole or filleted, carp is very good baked in a foil parcel with aromatic seasonings such as garlic, ginger and soy. Or, Italian style, baked with pancetta and tomatoes.

POTTED CARP

1 gutted carp (700g–1kg),
no need to descale

1 large garlic clove, peeled
and roughly bashed

2 large sprigs of thyme

4 bay leaves

6–8 juniper berries, bashed

200g unsalted butter

Juice of ½ lemon

Sea salt and black pepper

Delicately scented with thyme and juniper, this is lovely served on hot brown toast. Try it with other fish too, such as trout or perch. Serves 4–6 as a starter

Preheat the oven to 180°C/Fan 160°C/Gas 4.

Place the carp on a baking tray and put the bashed garlic clove, thyme and bay into the cavity. Roast the fish for 20 minutes or until the flesh is just cooked; check by gently lifting the flesh from the bone – it should come away easily.

When the carp is cool enough to handle, remove and reserve the garlic, thyme and bay from inside. Now carefully peel away the skin and scales from the fish: they should come away easily. Flake the cooked carp flesh into a large bowl, removing and discarding the bones as you go – including the y-shaped pin bones.

Put the reserved bay, thyme and garlic in a small pan with the juniper and butter. Melt over a gentle heat. When bubbling, take off the heat and leave to infuse for 5–10 minutes.

Pour the butter through a sieve over the carp meat. Gently combine the fish with the butter, trying not to break up the flakes of fish too much, and giving it one last check for bones. Season well with salt, pepper and lemon juice as you go.

Put the mixture into a sealable jar or 4–6 ramekins or small pots. Leave to cool, then refrigerate to set before serving. It will keep in a sealed jar in the fridge for up to 7 days.

Carrot

Hugh Fearnley-Whittingstall

C

LATIN NAME
Daucus carota subsp. *sativus*

SEASONALITY
Traditionally May–November but now available nearly all year round

MORE RECIPES
Roots and fruits salad with rapeseed dressing (page 524); Quinoa with cumin-roasted roots and parsley (page 514); Curried new potatoes, red onion and lettuce (page 226); Spiced horse mushroom and beetroot 'burger' (page 315); Halloumi and roasted carrot salad with pomegranate (page 486); Mussels in vinegar with apple and carrot (page 399); Pot-roasted mallard with celeriac and watercress (page 241); Salt beef with carrots and potatoes (page 559)

Despite the fact that the epithet 'humble' is often attached to it, the carrot is actually a mighty and magnificent root. It may not be glamorous but I struggle to think of anything bad to say about it. So let's say something good: the carrot is arguably the most useful vegetable we have.

Cheap as chips (well almost) and widely grown across Britain, carrots are overall very low-impact in terms of the energy needed to produce them. They're also packed with nutritious stuff, including fibre, vitamins and, of course, carotenoids (powerful antioxidants). They're good for you raw (when they retain more of their vitamin C) and they're good for you cooked (when they release more of their beta-carotene). Their healthy and ethical credentials are unimpeachable.

But there's so much more to carrots than that. Sweet, nutty, earthy and aromatic, they offer one of the most complex flavour profiles of any root. They open the door to a hugely varied range of dishes, from boiled-and-buttered-beside-your-Sunday-roast carrots to the irresistible Indian *gajar burfi* – a kind of aromatic carrot fudge.

Carrots are so versatile that, if you don't like them one way, I bet you will another. After all, raw, grated carrot is a world away from a smooth, blended carrot soup, while caramelised, roasted carrots are quite unlike lightly steamed ones. Even the way you cut them makes a difference – chunky batons are the preferred form in our home, but you may find the coin-shaped cross-section more acceptable.

Carrots are bold in flavour, which means they marry nicely with assertive partners. Orange and ginger speak to their aromatic qualities; thyme, tarragon and parsley match their earthy, vegetal notes; while lemon and garlic balance their sweetness. For me, the popular carrot and coriander leaf soup is not the finest way to use this vegetable, having a slightly cloying flavour. But throw some coriander seed or other warming, savoury-edged spices into a carrot soup and you've got my attention. Cumin, paprika and turmeric all balance carroty sweetness gorgeously. Cook the spice gently with sweated onion and garlic before adding chopped carrot and stock. Simmer until tender, then purée. A swirl of crème fraîche or yoghurt is a wonderful finishing touch – especially if you sprinkle over a final pinch of your chosen spices too.

It's the sweet and aromatic qualities of carrots that make them such an important ingredient in home-made stocks. They provide the ideal top-note to balance the earthy savouriness of celery and the sweet piquancy of onion. But one roughly chopped large carrot to, say, each chicken carcass is enough; any more can make the stock a little too penetratingly sweet.

Raw carrot salads are ubiquitous across Europe and the Middle East, sometimes sweetened with raisins or apple, sometimes perfumed with orange flower water, perhaps pepped up with mustard or vinegar. Usually the carrot is grated but a favourite technique of mine is to sliver the roots with a vegetable peeler, as in the recipe overleaf. Those raw, wafer-thin orange ribbons seem to meet the tongue in a particularly pleasing way. Dress them with olive or rapeseed oil, a whisper of lemon juice and some salt and pepper. Great as they are, they can also be combined with fresh mint or parsley, or with slivered almonds and toasted cumin.

Occasionally, more through neglect than planning, I manage to grow a few monster carrots. I like to celebrate this achievement by braising them, peeled and halved lengthways, in a shallow flameproof oven dish in a 2–3cm depth of veg stock with a few sprigs of thyme (and lovage if it's to hand), a good knob of butter, and some salt and pepper. Bring to the boil on the hob, then cover tightly with a lid or foil and roast

120

C

in the oven at 120°C/Fan 110°C/Gas ½ for a couple of hours, basting every half hour, until very tender but still holding their shape. Serve the carrots with the liquor from the dish, boiled to reduce and intensify the flavours for a minute or two.

For centuries, English cooks have been mixing carrot into cakes and puddings, though perhaps not in the same way we do now. Both Eliza Acton and Mrs Beeton provided recipes for sweet, steamed puddings packed with cooked, puréed carrot. In fact, the use of carrot as a pudding ingredient probably dates back as far as the Middle Ages.

Modern carrot cakes are more likely to employ the root raw and grated straight into the batter, which is certainly more convenient. It contributes body, and also some sweetness, so that adding carrot to a cake provides an opportunity to reduce the amount of sugar. I've experimented lately and found that you can safely cut the sugar in most carrot cake recipes by up to half – and when you do, you really start to taste the vegetable.

Even a fully sugared classic carrot cake at least provides a little more fibre and beta-carotene than your average sweet treat – and the tender-but-textured nature of a carroty crumb is very hard to beat. Carrot works beautifully in muffins and fat-free cakes too.

Thanks to our differing climate from north to south, and to techniques such as bedding the crop with straw through the winter, British carrots are available pretty much all year round (late spring being the only time of dearth). But they do of course have a traditional season – something you will be aware of if you grow them yourself.

I start sowing carrots in March and harvest the first babies in late May. I try not to overdo it with these tinies, though, because carrots get tastier as they get older. By late June, they'll be finger-thick adolescents – perfect for eating raw and whole, or sliced into slender halves, lengthways. They're great lightly cooked, too – boiled for 3 minutes max with a sprig of mint and a dash of salt in the water.

Later in the summer, and well into the autumn, I'll move on to the mature, more generously girthed chaps, and when my garden supply runs out I'll get a kilo or two delivered every week from our local box scheme. They'll be hardly less sweet than the youngsters, and deeply full of carroty flavour.

Supermarket carrots are washed and 'polished', which can damage and weaken their outer layer, making them more susceptible to rotting. Keep them, in their opened plastic bag, in the fridge.

I prefer to buy slightly grubby farm shop or veg box carrots, not least because their unscrubbed skin, and the vestiges of earth that cling to it, help to protect them and minimise moisture loss. They're still best kept in the fridge, wrapped in a paper bag, unless they are really muddy, in which case, a cool, dark larder or shed is ideal. They should keep well there for a good couple of weeks. Gardeners can store their carrots for longer packed in sand.

Bunches of carrots with luxuriant leafy tops look wonderful – but shear those leaves off as soon as you get them home because they will draw moisture out of the carrot as long as they are attached, leading quickly to the dreaded bendy root syndrome.

CARROT SOUP WITH GINGER AND CORIANDER

500g carrots

2 tbsp olive or rapeseed oil

1 large leek (white and pale green part only), trimmed and finely sliced

2 celery stalks, finely sliced

50g piece of root ginger, finely sliced

2 fat garlic cloves, sliced

2 tsp coriander seeds

1 litre light chicken or veg stock

Juice of 1 small lime

Sea salt and black pepper

TO FINISH

3–4 tbsp crème fraîche

A small handful of parsley leaves, chopped

Full-flavoured, yet mellow, this soup has a lovely warmth from the ginger – perfect for a cold day. The recipe also works well with sweet potato or Jerusalem artichokes. Serves 4

Peel and halve the carrots lengthways, then cut into 1cm slices.

Heat the oil in a large saucepan over a low heat. Add the leek and celery and sweat gently for 5 minutes without browning. Add the carrots and ginger, season lightly with salt and pepper, then cover and sweat for a further 10 minutes. Stir in the garlic and coriander seeds and cook for another couple of minutes.

Pour in the stock, bring to a simmer and put the lid on. Cook for about 25 minutes until the carrots are completely tender. Remove from the heat.

Add the lime juice, then tip the contents of the pan into a blender or food processor and blitz until velvety smooth. Taste and add salt and pepper as needed.

Serve the soup in warmed bowls, topped with a generous grind of pepper, a swirl of crème fraîche and a scattering of parsley. Rye bread is a good accompaniment.

RAW CARROT SALAD WITH PEANUT AND CUMIN DRESSING

3 medium carrots

FOR THE DRESSING

2 tsp cumin seeds

½ garlic clove, crushed or grated

2 heaped tsp no-sugar-added crunchy peanut butter

Juice of 1 lemon

1 tbsp tamari (or soy sauce)

1 tsp clear honey

Sea salt and black pepper

TO FINISH (OPTIONAL)

A little chopped mint or coriander

This delicate carrot salad is simple and very speedy to prepare. It's wonderful on its own as a starter, or as a side dish with some grilled lamb or a few fried scallops. Serves 4

Using a veg peeler, first peel the carrots then shave the roots along their lengths into tender ribbons. Divide these between individual plates.

For the dressing, lightly toast the cumin seeds in a dry frying pan for a couple of minutes, until fragrant. Let them cool slightly, then crush fairly finely, using a pestle and mortar or a spice grinder. Transfer the crushed cumin to a bowl, add all the other ingredients and whisk to emulsify, seasoning with salt and pepper to taste.

Spoon the dressing over the carrots. Scatter over a little chopped mint or coriander if you like before serving.

Cashew nuts

Gill Meller

LATIN NAME
Anacardium occidentale

MORE RECIPES
Roots and fruits salad with rapeseed dressing (page 524); Roasted chilli mole (page 173)

Cashews are one of the most valuable and widely traded nuts in the world, which is remarkable, considering their complex production. A single cashew grows at the end of a fruit called a cashew apple. This ripe fruit spoils quickly, yet it is more prized than the nut in some places, and is made into preserves and drinks. Elsewhere, the nuts are the main prize, and one that is hard-won. You never see a cashew sold in its shell because that casing contains an oil so caustic that it is used to burn off warts (among other medicinal uses). Extraction must be done carefully.

Somehow, humans worked out how to use this tricky Amazonian plant and it was taken to India and Africa in the fifteenth and sixteenth centuries. Vietnam, Africa and India are now the main exporters.

From Brazil to Goa, finely ground cashews are used to thicken curries, soups and stews, and across India cashew curries are made using the whole nut. Cashews have also long been eaten as simple snacks, either raw or toasted. However, the current trend towards replacing dairy and meat with plant foods has led to new-found uses for this most tender and creamy of nuts.

Soak raw cashews – either whole ones or broken pieces – for several hours in water, then blitz in a blender with fresh water to get a creamy liquid. For cashew milk, simply strain the pale, cashew-thickened liquid off the nut pulp. Use as an all-round alternative to cow's milk, whether in a white sauce, on cereal, in milkshakes or for soup bases.

For cashew cream, use less water for soaking, then pulverise the nuts with the liquor to a purée. The cream goes a treat with puddings – virtuous or otherwise. Both cashew milk and cashew cream keep for around 4 days in the fridge.

If you're eating the nuts whole – in a salad, say – toasting helps develop their flavour and give a slight crunchiness. Toast the nuts in a hot, dry pan, or on a baking sheet in the oven at 180°C/Fan 160°C/Gas 4 for 6–8 minutes, shaking or stirring once or twice to ensure they don't burn.

CASHEW PANNACOTTA

200g raw cashew nuts

75g clear honey

½ vanilla pod, split lengthways and seeds scraped out

2 heaped tsp agar agar flakes

A classic pannacotta is made with double cream and set with gelatine. This healthy version is dairy-free, set with the seaweed extract agar agar and uses no refined sugar. Serves 4

Put the cashew nuts into a bowl, cover with cold water and leave to soak for 2–3 hours. Drain, rinse and place in a blender.

Put the honey into a small pan with 150ml water, the vanilla seeds and empty pod. Bring to a gentle simmer, then add the agar agar flakes and whisk to combine. Cook, stirring, for 1–2 minutes, then remove the vanilla pod.

Pour the hot liquid over the cashews in the blender and purée until very smooth, scraping down the sides of the jug once or twice.

Place 4 ring moulds, roughly 6cm in diameter and 3cm deep, on small serving plates. Divide the cashew cream between the moulds, levelling off the tops. Place in the fridge for 3–4 hours to set.

To serve, run a thin sharp knife around the inside of each mould to free the pannacotta, then carefully turn out on to plates. Serve with fresh seasonal fruit – strawberries or raspberries tossed in a little lemon juice are particularly good.

Cauliflower

Tim Maddams

LATIN NAME
Brassica oleracea var. *botrytis*

SEASONALITY
Home-grown generally available all year round; also imported

MORE RECIPES
Cauliflower and nigella soup (page 405); Roasted cauliflower with capers (page 113); Scallops with cauliflower purée and green peppercorns (page 572)

In the extended family of veg, I think of cauliflower as the exotic cousin of the cabbage, hiding its beauty inside its leaves in a coy, almost flirty way. Cauliflower is, after all, a thwarted flower – its curds are under-formed blooms and within the plant's flesh is a high concentration of nutrients, intended for flowers and fruits that will never be. One of the few white foods we should eat more of, cauliflowers, along with other cruciferous veg (another umbrella term for the Brassica family), are an excellent source of vitamins and minerals, as well as valuable antioxidants and phytonutrients that may help protect against cancer.

Like cabbages, cauliflowers come in two main types, summer and winter. Within these categories, there are different varieties, flourishing at different times of the year, which means you never need be without a cauli. In theory at least, there should be a pretty much year-round crop, though gaps in supply are filled with cauliflowers from other countries sometimes.

In addition to the classic white cauliflowers, there are some more unusual types to seek out. 'Romanesco' (sometimes described as broccoli rather than cauliflower) is a great autumn cauli, outlandish-looking but very tasty. Its distinctive, pale green spirals have a sweet, delicate vibrancy that makes it a stand-out variety for using raw.

Purple-hued cauliflower varieties, such as 'Violetta Italia' and 'Purple Cape' look, frankly, a little odd but again deliver well on sweetness, harbouring little of the bitter after-taste of some varieties. Purple cauli is good raw but also makes a tasty purée and a great addition to a summer-garden *minestra* (soup).

In all cases, look for cauliflowers with firm, tight heads and plenty of lush-looking leaf – which is just as tasty as the florets, and an indication of freshness. A bright white stalk also suggests recent cutting. Summer varieties tend to be a little sweeter and more suited to eating raw.

There is nothing wrong with good old cauliflower cheese but this vegetable really comes to life when used in other ways. Cauliflower makes a wonderful, silky purée or soup, for instance: it contains lots of pectin in its cell walls, which contributes to a smooth texture. Cook the cauliflower without water, sweating it in butter until softened and browned, before blending with a little milk or veg stock if needed.

Indeed, you should never be afraid to get some colour on your cauliflower. This is a vegetable that responds deliciously to being fried, grilled or roasted so that it caramelises. Fresh, sweet cauliflower is fantastic barbecued, for instance. Remove the leaves and halve the heads, then cut each half into 3 wedges, making sure they are firmly held together by a useful amount of stalk. Dress with a little olive oil, some salt, pepper, a sprinkle of smoked paprika and a few thyme leaves, then grill on the barbecue (or roast in a hot oven) until just tender and turning golden. Finish with more oil, chopped raw garlic, lemon juice and plenty of chopped parsley and mint.

Cauliflower loves spices, and a cauliflower pakora is a thing of joy. Cut wedges, stem and all, into slices the thickness of a £1 coin, toss in spiced gram (chickpea) flour, then moisten the mixture with a little beer to create a sticky but not runny mess that will hold together on deep-frying (adding the liquid *after* the flour results in a thinner, crisper batter). Deep-fry spoonfuls of the mix until golden and serve straight away with a little garlicky yoghurt, chopped spring onions and flaky salt as a starter.

The caramelisation and sweetening that you get by cooking cauliflower suits it perfectly but, for all that, a superbly fresh, sweet summer specimen is excellent raw – marinated with a little citrus and chilli and made into a salad. Cut the florets off the

C

stalk (save the stalk and trimmings for a soup or curry) and cut the florets very small, no bigger than a marble. You can also simply grate the cauliflower against the coarse side of a box grater or blitz it in a food processor. Dress with the juice of a lemon and a good glug of rapeseed oil, season with a sprinkling of dried chilli flakes and salt and leave to marinate for an hour or so before serving. The raw crunch is seriously good – a lovely dish for a late-summer mezze.

However you're cutting your cauliflower, don't discard the leaves. The really tough-ribbed outer ones can go to your pig, rabbit or compost heap, but those beautifully curved, inner, tender leaves are great in slaws or even steamed as a side veg.

If you don't know how fresh your cauliflower is, taste a little of it, raw. You can't make a silk purse of a sow's ear and long-stored cauli which is bitter or turning soft won't be any good raw. It will, however, pass muster in a roasted cauliflower purée.

CAULIFLOWER CLAFOUTIS WITH HAM AND PARSLEY

75g plain flour

3 medium eggs

300ml whole milk

2 tbsp chopped parsley, plus a little extra to serve

50g Parmesan, or a similar hard, mature cheese, grated

2 tbsp olive or rapeseed oil

1 cauliflower (about 800g), trimmed and cut into medium florets

50g air-dried ham, torn into large shreds (or use cooked ham or scraps of fried bacon)

Sea salt and black pepper

For this quick supper dish, little florets of roasted cauliflower nestle in a light, Parmesan-seasoned batter, along with shreds of salty ham. Serves 4

Put the flour into a large bowl with a generous pinch of salt. Beat the eggs and milk thoroughly together, then gradually whisk into the flour to form a smooth batter. Stir in the chopped parsley and half the grated Parmesan. Leave to rest for 30 minutes.

Preheat the oven to 210°C/Fan 190°C/Gas 7. Spoon the oil into a roasting dish and place in the oven for a few minutes to heat up.

Add the cauliflower florets to the roasting dish and shake them to coat in the oil, then season lightly with salt and pepper – go sparingly with the salt as the ham will add more.

Add the shredded ham, then quickly pour in the batter. Give the dish a shake to distribute the batter evenly, then sprinkle over the remaining cheese and place it straight in the hot oven. Cook for about 30 minutes until puffed and golden.

Serve immediately, with some more chopped parsley sprinkled over, and a green leafy salad on the side if you like.

Cayenne pepper

Steven Lamb

LATIN NAME
Capsicum annuum

MORE RECIPES
Crumbed whiting goujons with curried egg tartare (page 673); Endive with chicken livers and bacon (page 250); Roasted chilli mole (page 173); Hazelnut and cheese biscuits (page 304)

Cayenne pepper is the Porsche of the spice world, fast-tracking any recipe across the hot-line. Registering in the region of 30,000–50,000 on the Scoville scale, it is not destructively hot, but it will certainly raise your pulse rate. That is no glib metaphor: cayenne pepper is dried, powdered chilli and, as with all chilli, the active ingredient is capsaicin. Once ingested, capsaicin dilates blood vessels and makes the heart beat faster. It is also said to be an aphrodisiac.

What is the difference between cayenne pepper and standard chilli powder? Well, the answer is not much. Cayenne chillies get their name from a city in French Guiana, and were traditionally a variety of *Capsicum frutescens*, the same genus that gives us fiery piri-piris, bird's eye and Tabasco chillies. However, these days it may be fruits of the *Capsicum annuum* genus that are called cayenne, and cayenne pepper may be a blend of different ground dried chillies, mixed to ensure a consistent heat. So the name is more a generic catch-all than a specific indicator of provenance. It's all about heat, really: the term 'cayenne pepper' signifies 'fiery'. You can certainly substitute hot chilli powder in its stead – or vice versa. But a mild chilli powder won't match it.

In short, cayenne pepper is the easiest way to add chilli heat to a dish and a little goes a long way. It is almost always used as a seasoning in chorizo and other spicy sausages, perks up a host of spicy dishes including devilled kidneys, and is lovely added to a warming hot chocolate drink in winter.

You can produce your own cayenne pepper – cayenne seeds are easy to buy and to cultivate. The chillies are fabulous when fresh, or you can dry and grind them yourself (see page 172). However, there will be an element of pot luck regarding what you get because flavour and heat vary with different growing conditions, even from chilli to chilli. If it's a reliable blast of deliciously mouth-tingling heat that you want, a little pot of cayenne pepper fits the bill.

DEVILLED PARSNIPS

500g parsnips

2 tbsp olive or rapeseed oil

2 small shallots, finely sliced

40ml Somerset cider brandy (or any brandy or sherry)

2 tbsp cider vinegar

2 tbsp Worcestershire sauce

2 tsp redcurrant jelly

1 tsp Dijon mustard

A pinch of cayenne pepper

75ml double cream

Sea salt and black pepper

Chopped parsley, to finish

This is an indulgent way to enjoy parsnips: roasted, then bathed in a rich creamy sauce with a bit of a kick. Enjoy them just as they are, with a leafy salad, or as a great accompaniment to almost any meat. Serves 2–4

Preheat the oven to 190°C/Fan 170°C/Gas 5. Peel, trim and halve the parsnips, then cut into 4–5cm long wedges.

Put the parsnips into a roasting tin, scatter with some salt and pepper and toss with 1 tbsp oil. Roast for 40 minutes, or until they are tender and starting to caramelise, turning halfway through.

When the parsnips are nearly done, make the sauce. Heat the remaining 1 tbsp oil in a large frying pan over a medium heat. Add the shallots and sweat for 2 minutes, until soft. Add the brandy and let it bubble until reduced by half; be careful – it may ignite as the vapours rise.

Add the vinegar, Worcestershire sauce, redcurrant jelly, Dijon mustard and a good pinch of cayenne pepper. Simmer for 1–2 minutes, stirring so that the jelly dissolves then add 50ml water and the cream. Simmer for a further 2–3 minutes until thick and creamy, then add salt and pepper to taste.

Add the hot parsnips to the sauce and toss to combine. Serve straight away, scattered with chopped parsley.

Celeriac

Nikki Duffy

LATIN NAME
Apium graveolens var. *rapaceum*

ALSO KNOWN AS
Celery root

SEASONALITY
October–March

MORE RECIPES
Cheddar, apple and celeriac salad (page 140); Roots and fruits salad with rapeseed dressing (page 524); Field mushroom and celeriac pie (page 258); Pear and celeriac stuffing (page 454); Pan-roasted oysters with celeriac and thyme (page 425); Pot-roasted mallard with celeriac and watercress (page 241); Snipe with swede and bacon (page 587); Venison salad with apple, celeriac and hazelnuts (page 660); Bacon and celeriac tart (page 42)

The subtle, savoury and completely unique smell of celeriac is right up there with leeks and bay leaves when it comes to comforting kitchen aromas, evocative of cold weather cooking and steamy kitchens on crisp, frosty mornings. Celeriac is at its best from November through to January and if you don't soup it, roast it, curry it, mash it or slice it raw into a salad at least a few times during those months, you're missing a trick.

Celeriac is closely related to crisp, crunchy celery, which explains why it is sometimes known as celery root. Indeed, they share a common ancestor – smallage. While delightfully named, this wild plant is harshly flavoured, having, as one fifteenth-century writer put it, a bitter and 'ungrateful' flavour. Ungrateful is certainly not an appropriate word to describe celeriac, however: mild, nutty and amenable is more like it. What celeriac shares with its relatives are phthalides: compounds that have been shown to have a unique flavour-enhancing ability. In short, it tastes great, and it makes everything else taste great too.

So, while it may look like the vegetable equivalent of the back end of a bus, and it may fox the cook with its fiendishly knobbly, corrugated, dirt-trapping exterior, celeriac is a superb ingredient to pop on your chopping board in winter. Set to with your sharpest knife, whittling away that rough and root-riddled rind. Eventually you will expose a glimmering white globe of creamy beauty that offers more culinary options than, dare I say, even the potato can muster.

You can't, for instance, eat a potato raw. At least, not happily. But there are a hundred delicious uses for raw celeriac, before you even get it as far as a saucepan or a roasting dish. The most famous is celeriac rémoulade, for which you need only julienne your raw celeriac (speedily if you have a mandoline slicer), then mix it with well-seasoned, mustard-spiked mayonnaise. The key is not to swamp it with too much dressing, so use judiciously – you can always add more – and cut the richness with a spoonful of yoghurt or crème fraîche, or a splash of vinegar.

You can take the same basic idea in many different directions. Swap the mayo for a good, mustardy vinaigrette (3 tbsp olive or rapeseed oil, 2 tsp cider vinegar, ½ tsp English mustard, salt and pepper), add a heap of herbs – chopped parsley is particularly good – and you have a little salad that will accompany anything from cold ham to oysters, crumbled Cheddar or flaked mackerel, with aplomb.

To either of these dressed raw celeriac salads, you can add other ingredients. Fruit is always a winning partner: try raisins or slivers of dried apricot, crisp slices of apple or pear, or juicy segments of orange. Celeriac loves leaves – peppery rocket or watercress, bitter chicory or crisp Cos are the best – and it laps up salty flavours, whether little black olives or capers, scraps of crisp bacon or nuggets of blue cheese. Raw fennel, celery and carrot work a treat in the mix too.

A particular favourite of mine is roughly equal quantities of celeriac and raw apple, both coarsely grated and dressed with olive or rapeseed oil, lemon juice, salt and pepper, then finished with a scattering of capers and some crumbled Cheddar. I put a bowl of it in the fridge, where the root and the fruit slowly wilt and relax – it lasts a few days if it's lucky.

When cooked, celeriac has a superb flavour, smooth texture and an incredibly accommodating nature: it can be mild and understated, or big and bold, as you prefer. It works well as a mash, combined roughly 50:50 with potato, which always seems to highlight celeriac's gentle earthiness. As celeriac cooks a little more quickly, either add it in chunks to a pan of potatoes once they're already boiling, or cook the two

vegetables separately. Drain and leave to steam-dry, then mash them together, with a good measure of butter, salt and pepper. You will create a mash that is no bland backdrop, but a sumptuous side dish for any – and I mean literally *any* – meat or fish. You can ditch the potato and stick to a pure, buttery celeriac purée if you prefer. It's all good.

Celeriac and potato are excellent sliced and combined in a creamy gratin too – just follow a good dauphinoise recipe, replacing up to 50 per cent of the potato with celeriac.

When cut into chunky cubes, celeriac roasts beautifully. Try roasting it in goose fat with thyme and lots of salt and pepper, or in rapeseed oil with a generous sprinkling of curry spices; in either case, the celeriac is good with potatoes, as well as other roots such as parsnip, or on its own.

If you have a sunny bit of garden with rich, moisture-retaining soil, you should be able to grow celeriac with no problems. Start the seedlings off in modules, then plant out in May for harvest in the autumn. You can leave mature roots in the ground over the winter and lift them as you need them.

Alternatively, shop for heavy but not-too-big celeriacs (1kg max), as larger ones can have a slightly spongy centre. Keep them in the fridge and they'll last at least a fortnight. If the green stems are still attached, trim them off and use in stocks, to which they impart a celery-like note. The trimmings from the outside of the root, if cleaned of all dirt, can go into stocks too.

CELERIAC SOUFFLÉS

500g celeriac

A large knob of butter, plus extra for greasing

1 medium onion, thinly sliced

2 garlic cloves, thinly sliced

1 tsp thyme leaves

200ml veg stock

50g well-flavoured hard cheese, or blue cheese, grated or finely chopped

4 medium eggs, separated

Sea salt and black pepper

These delicious little soufflés are light, yet full of flavour. Free from flour, they are great if you're avoiding wheat. You can use any good, strongly flavoured cheese that you have to hand. Serve as a starter or as a side to chargrilled steak. Makes 8

Peel the celeriac and cut into 1–2cm pieces. Set a large saucepan over a medium heat and add the butter. When it is bubbling, add the celeriac, onion, garlic, thyme and some salt and pepper. Cook, stirring regularly, for 10 minutes or until the vegetables are starting to soften and smell fragrant.

Add the stock, bring to a simmer and put a lid on the pan. Cook for about 15 minutes, by which time the celeriac should be really tender and giving.

Use a slotted spoon to scoop about half the celeriac and onion out of the pan into a bowl and set aside. Tip the remaining contents of the pan (including all the liquid) into a jug blender and purée (or do this in the pan with a stick blender). Fold the whole chunks of celeriac back into the purée.

Let the mixture cool a little, while you preheat the oven to 200°C/Fan 180°C/Gas 6 and butter 8 ramekins (about 175ml capacity). Put a baking tray into the oven too, to make it easy to get the ramekins in and out.

Stir the cheese and egg yolks into the warm celeriac purée. Whisk the egg whites in a clean bowl until they hold firm peaks. Stir 1 tbsp whisked egg white into the cheesy celeriac mixture to loosen it, then carefully fold in the rest. Try and keep the batter as light and airy as possible, to help ensure the soufflés rise well in the oven.

Spoon the mixture into the buttered ramekins, but don't overfill them: the mixture should come 1–2cm from the top. Transfer them to the hot baking tray and bake for 12–15 minutes until puffed up and golden brown. Serve straight away (they will soon start to sink).

Celery

Mark Diacono

LATIN NAME
Apium graveolens var. *dulce*

SEASONALITY
June–December

MORE RECIPES
Chicken broth with parsley and celery seed spaetzle (page 163); Carrot soup with ginger and coriander (page 123); Hare ragu (page 301); Salt beef with carrots and potatoes (page 559); Barbecued tripe (page 644)

Love it or hate it, celery has much to offer, and it comes with the bonus of being high in numerous vitamins (B1, B2, A and K in particular), potassium, phosphorus and other blood pressure lowering beneficials, as well as being virtually calorie-free.

A lifelong celery sceptic, it took a perfectly balanced, truly delicious salad of raw celery, orange segments and flaked, smoked mackerel to make me appreciate the qualities of this vegetable. One of the keys is to cut it carefully: thin, even translucent, slices of raw celery are so much nicer than clumsy chunks.

With its peppery crunch, fresh, raw celery has many happy partners: blue cheese and apples, a handful of toasted hazelnuts, Cheddar, borlotti beans, broad beans, even olives. My favourite celery-mate though, has to be Asian pears (which I have recently started growing). Somehow juicy and crisp in equal measure, these have a honeyed, spicy pear flavour, which contrasts and complements celery's crunch and taste.

When cooked, celery softens in taste as well as texture: the flavour is not diminished so much as altered. It is still bold, but its edges are rounded a little. As well as lending that characteristic flavour of its own to a dish, celery boosts the flavour of others. Cooks have been aware of this for generations but recently scientists have backed them up, identifying flavour-enhancing compounds – phthalides – in celery and its relatives (see page 129).

This explains why celery is pretty much indispensable in a stock – of whatever persuasion. And it is one of the holy quartet that makes up a classic *soffritto* (if you're in Italy) or *mirepoix* (if you're in France) – a mix of finely chopped celery, carrots, onions and garlic, gently softened in olive oil with bay, rosemary and seasoning. This is the base for endless sauces, soups and stews and is adaptable, depending on what you have in your kitchen. The onion can be a leek or shallot, if that's what is to hand, and you can skip the carrot if necessary – but don't be tempted to leave out the celery. It adds the balancing bitterness, the crucial savouriness to the whole.

Celery makes one of the great soups, and either pre-blanched or roasted, it can be turned into a fabulous gratin. It is also an essential ingredient in caponata, the lovely Sicilian antipasto dish. And celery hearts can be braised in stock or cider with herbs until meltingly tender to serve as a side dish.

English celery is quite magnificent. The rich, peaty soils of the Fens are perfect for growing it. And it is still produced there using traditional methods, whereby the plants are grown in long trenches, making it easy to push the soil up against them (known as 'earthing up'). This excludes light, resulting in paler, sweeter celery, with a splendid nutty flavour. Fenland celery was the first UK crop to be awarded PGI status and is really worth seeking out during its short October to December season. It is not the easiest vegetable to grow well at home, though modern self-blanching varieties give fairly reliable results.

When you are buying celery, buy organic, if you can. It is not uncommon for the conventional crop to be heavily sprayed as celery needs to be in the ground a long time: it hates competition from weeds, and is prone to various diseases and pests. Organic or not, don't be tempted by the trimmed celery that's increasingly available on the shelves: it is much more expensive by weight and those 'trimmings' are actually a vital part of what you're after. Celery leaves, which are a little more peppery and bitter than the stems but rammed with flavour, work beautifully when simmered down with other veg in a stock, but also make a good, bracing finish for creamy, earthy soups and risottos or winter salads.

The long fibres that run along celery stems can be rather tough in the large outer stalks – the outer 3 or 4 stems of a head of celery are usually best reserved for stock. Alternatively, you can shave off the ridges with a potato peeler (you'll have to go quite deep), or slice the stems very finely before cooking. In a puréed soup, any fibrous bits can be sieved out. For salads and raw dishes, prioritise the more tender, inner stems.

If you find yourself falling in love with the nutty, savoury flavour of celery, explore some kindred ingredients too: celeriac (see page 129) has leaves which carry much of the same characteristic celery taste; celery leaf is a soft herb that's increasingly cropping up at farmers' markets and in veg boxes, and easy to grow if you fancy it; and lovage leaves and seed (page 368) carry more than a passing resemblance in flavour. Celery salt is a fine way to season and add celery flavour; and if you have space for a pot or two, give par-cel – a herb that tastes like a blend of parsley and celery – a go.

CELERY AND WALNUT TAPENADE

50g walnuts

200g celery (see note, below)

½ garlic clove, crushed or finely grated

100g stoned good black olives, such as Kalamata

2 tbsp capers, rinsed, drained and patted dry

2 tbsp extra virgin olive oil

1 tsp thyme leaves

Black pepper

Serve this deeply savoury mix on oatcakes or on strips of toasted sourdough or ciabatta (or untoasted if it's super-fresh) as mini bruschette. It's very good topped with a little crumbled salty cheese, too. A spoonful will also lift a piece of fish. Serves 6–8

Preheat the oven to 180°C/Fan 160°C/Gas 4. Scatter the walnuts on a baking tray and toast in the oven for 5–8 minutes, until fragrant, then tip on to a plate and set aside to cool. Blitz the walnuts in a food processor until finely ground.

Slice the celery finely, across the stems. Add to the nuts in the food processor with all the other ingredients except the pepper. Blitz to a coarse paste, stopping a few times to scrape down the sides. Keep the tapenade a little coarse and chunky – if you make it very fine it can become quite wet.

Season with pepper to taste (the olives and capers should provide enough salt), then it's ready to serve.

Note Avoid using the fibrous, outer celery stems for this recipe. Break off the outermost 4 or 5 stems from the bunch and set aside for stock or soup, then start weighing the celery from there – include the leaves too.

Ceps

John Wright

LATIN NAME
Boletus edulis

ALSO KNOWN AS
Porcini, penny bun

SEASONALITY
Summer and autumn

HABITAT
Open ground near oak, beech and, particularly in Scotland, coniferous trees

MORE RECIPES
Woodcock with wild mushrooms (page 678)

Few foraging experiences are as exciting as walking into an autumnal woodland glade to find a dozen or more enormous ceps in perfect condition. They always occur under or near trees – usually oak, sometimes beech or pine. People quite rightly worry about picking the wrong mushroom, but with the cep you're safe. The nut-brown cap, cream-turning-to-greenish-yellow tubes underneath the cap, and the cream, often-swollen stem with fine, whitish, net-like markings at the top, make it very distinct. The main problem with picking them is to get there before anyone else does, and to stop yourself picking every last one. I leave the small specimens and the really big ones which are producing their spores in vast numbers and likely to harbour ecologically important invertebrates (i.e. maggots).

The cep is considered the king of mushrooms, and I can understand why. The flesh is meaty and contains a great deal of protein, while the flavour is beyond compare – it is so very, well, mushroomy. Ceps take considerably more cooking than you might suppose: about 10 minutes, thickly sliced, in the sauté pan to bring out their flavour.

If you manage to collect a large number you should slice some of them thinly and lay them out on racks to dry in a low oven (see page 315). This intensifies the flavour and they can be used throughout the year – just steep them in hot water first for a few minutes, remembering to use the highly flavoured water in your dish too. Dried ceps can be ground to a powder which you can add to very nearly any dish you turn your hand to. The umami flavour they provide works miracles.

If you don't have your own dried ceps for a recipe, they're easy to buy. You are quite likely to find them labelled 'porcini', the Italian name for this mushroom.

POTATO AND CEP DAUPHINOISE

30g dried ceps/porcini

30g butter

1kg floury potatoes, such as Maris Piper

400ml double cream

100g well-flavoured hard cheese, such as Quickes hard goat's cheese, Berkswell or Parmesan, finely grated

2 large garlic cloves, crushed

¼ tsp freshly grated nutmeg

Sea salt and black pepper

Dried ceps give an intense flavour to this indulgent dish – although it also works with fresh ceps (use about 250g, slice them thinly and toss in with the potatoes and cream).
Serves 4–6

Preheat the oven to 160°C/Fan 140°C/Gas 3.

Put the dried ceps/porcini into a small bowl, pour on just enough boiling water to cover them and leave to soak for 10 minutes.

Use the butter to liberally grease a gratin dish, about 25 x 20cm. Peel the potatoes and slice them thinly with a sharp knife or mandoline.

In a large bowl, whisk together the cream, cheese, garlic, nutmeg and some salt and pepper. Toss the sliced potatoes in the cream mixture until well coated.

Drain the mushrooms, squeezing out any excess water (save the liquor for a soup or stew) and add to the bowl with the potatoes. Stir gently to distribute evenly.

Layer the potatoes and mushrooms in the buttered dish, spreading the potato slices as flatly and evenly as you can. Season with a little more salt between each layer. Pour over any remaining cream from the bowl.

Bake in the oven for 1¼–1½ hours, pressing the mixture down firmly with a spatula every 15 minutes or so to compress the potatoes and prevent them from drying out on top. The gratin is ready when the top is golden and bubbling and the potatoes are tender (a small, sharp knife inserted into the centre should pass through easily). You may need to turn the oven up to 190°C/Fan 170°C/Gas 5 for the last 5 minutes to colour the top.

Leave to stand for 5 minutes before serving, with some bitter or peppery salad leaves.

Chanterelles

Hugh Fearnley-Whittingstall

LATIN NAME
Cantharellus cibarius

ALSO KNOWN AS
Girolles

SEASONALITY
Late summer–late autumn

HABITAT
Common in woodland, throughout the British Isles

MORE RECIPES
Woodcock with wild mushrooms (page 678)

Small, delicately frilled, and a glorious, egg-yolk gold in colour, chanterelles are the bonny wee things of the mushroom world. They even smell pretty, with their unique scent, which is slightly reminiscent of apricot. However, despite their dainty appearance, they boast a deliciously firm flesh and a wonderful, earthy flavour.

You will find them in woodland, on mossy banks or nudging through the grass in shady, damp glades, potentially in pretty much any part of the British Isles. Your most fertile hunting grounds are likely to be oak and beech woods (particularly in the south) and birch and pine (more in the north). My biggest hauls have come from Scotland. Their prime season is late summer to late autumn. But if the summer has been wet they can be found as early as July, and as our winters grow inexorably milder, they're sometimes to be spotted in December.

A sister mushroom, the winter or trumpet chanterelle (*Cantharellus tubaeformis*) can be found in woodland, usually around November. While it's not as fabulous as the chanterelle, it is still worth eating. Don't be fooled, however, by the aptly named false chanterelle (*Hygrophoropsis aurantiaca*) which is similar-looking albeit with a much more pronounced orange colour and a more symmetrical form. Opinions vary as to whether it's poisonous but it's not nice to eat and is definitely best avoided.

I've found very good chanterelles in markets – particularly in France, where they are often known as *girolles*. High-end greengrocers are another potential source. And increasingly you may also find them being sold online.

Given a quick check-over and a light brush, chanterelles need only to be tumbled into a pan of foaming butter (plus a dash of olive oil if you like) with a scattering of chopped garlic and cooked for a few minutes. If they do release some water (which is likely if the weather has been wet) then just keep tossing until it's cooked away. Season well with salt and pepper towards the end.

Finished with a second knob of butter, a mist of lemon juice and a little chopped parsley, chervil or chives, sautéed chanterelles are perfection on toast. They are also great with eggs (poached or scrambled) or alongside some simply cooked meat (venison or wild duck especially). At a push, I might toss them through pasta – a nicely eggy home-made tagliatelle, for preference.

CHANTERELLE AND CHARD BRUSCHETTA

This earthy and delicious autumnal lunch is just as good with spinach in place of the chard.
Serves 2

About 75g chard

1 tbsp olive or rapeseed oil

150g chanterelles, brushed clean, any large ones halved or quartered

2 garlic cloves, 1 sliced and 1 halved

1 tsp chopped thyme leaves

15g butter

2 generous slices of sourdough or other robust bread

Extra virgin olive or rapeseed oil, to trickle

Sea salt and black pepper

Separate the chard stalks from the leaves. Slice the stalks into 1cm pieces and the leaves into wide ribbons.

Place a heavy-based frying pan, large enough to take all the mushrooms in one layer, over a medium-high heat and add the 1 tbsp oil. When it is hot, add the chanterelles and chard stalks and fry for 1 minute, tossing a few times.

Add the sliced garlic, thyme, butter and a pinch each of salt and pepper. Fry for a few more minutes, stirring now and then, until the mushrooms are just soft. Add the chard leaves, and cook for a minute or two more until the leaves have wilted. Taste for seasoning.

Meanwhile, toast the bread and, while still warm, rub with the cut surfaces of the halved garlic clove. Trickle the toast with a little extra virgin oil and place a slice on each plate. Pile the mushroom and chard mixture on top and serve straight away.

Chard

Mark Diacono

LATIN NAME
Beta vulgaris var. *flavescens*

ALSO KNOWN AS
Swiss chard, rainbow chard, ruby chard

SEASONALITY
All year round

MORE RECIPES
Spear-leaved orache bhajis (page 593); Chanterelle and chard bruschetta (page 137); Mozzarella with nettles and lentils (page 390); Swede with orecchiette (page 624); Cockle and chard rarebit (page 188); Paella (page 163); Velvet crab curry (page 211); Sea beet and smoked pollack pasties (page 574)

However unlikely it may seem, chard is the sister of beetroot. But where beetroot has been selected for the plumpness of its base, chard is all about the top above ground. While beetroot's leaves are delicious, they are relatively small. Chard leaves are much more generous and substantial.

Both Swiss chard, with its broad white ribs, and ruby or rainbow chards (with more slender, coloured stems) can be picked early and small and the leaves (ribs and all) will be tender and sweet enough to pair with lettuce in a leafy salad. Mature leaves can handle cooking and full flavours.

The larger leaves can be shredded finely, crosswise, then stir-fried, sweated or steamed as a simple side dish, but their differing densities mean the central rib and the fleshy leaf are often cooked separately. Strip the leaves from the stalks, slicing both, then sweat the stalks in butter for 5–10 minutes before adding the leaves, which will wilt down quickly. You then have the basis for a fabulous tart – try it with a lively hard cheese or a mild ricotta in the creamy egg filling. Or turn it into a great gratin – just add cream, cooked root veg if you fancy, garlic and chopped thyme, top with breadcrumbs and a little cheese and grill under a high heat until golden. Or make a chardy variation on the traditional cauliflower cheese.

Chard's affinity with potatoes, chickpeas and spices makes it a fabulous ingredient in a veg curry too. Just cook the stalks with the spuds and add the leaves at the end.

There's also a lot of fun to be had in treating the rib and leaf as stand-alone veg in different dishes. The stalks, for example, can be cut into thin batons and simmered in a 4:1 mix of white wine vinegar and caster sugar, with a few pinches of salt, coriander seed, fennel seed, peppercorns and a bay leaf or two, for 10 minutes, to make a delicious quick pickle. It's ready to serve the next day with anything roasted – meat, fish or veg – and will keep in the fridge for a fortnight.

Although fairly widely available in the shops these days, chard is a rewarding thing to grow yourself. Easy, reliable and productive, successive sowing means you can grow it all year round: plant a mix of Swiss and rainbow chard for colour, and once established either pick small leaves or (when larger) cut them 5cm or so above the ground and they'll repeatedly grow back to be harvested again.

CHARD AND NEW POTATOES WITH PAPRIKA AND FENNEL

250g chard

500g cooked new potatoes

2 tbsp olive or rapeseed oil

1 tsp fennel seeds

Finely grated zest of 1 lemon, plus a little of the juice

A sprig of thyme

2 garlic cloves, thinly sliced

1 tsp hot smoked paprika

2 tsp sweet paprika (ideally unsmoked)

Sea salt and black pepper

Extra virgin olive oil, to finish

This is equally good as part of a tapas-style spread or as an accompaniment to chicken, fish or roast pork. You can use shredded sea beet leaves here too (but not the stalks). Serves 4

Separate the chard leaves from the stalks. Slice the stalks fairly finely and roughly shred the leaves, keeping them apart. Cut the cooked potatoes into large cubes.

Place a large frying pan over a medium heat and add the oil. When hot, add the sliced chard stalks, fennel seeds, lemon zest and thyme sprig. Sweat, stirring often, for about 5 minutes.

Add the garlic and both paprikas. Cook, stirring, for 30 seconds, then add the cooked potatoes and toss well. Add the chard leaves with 2–3 tbsp water and season well with salt and pepper. Cover and cook for 5 minutes, tossing occasionally, or until the chard is nice and tender.

Squeeze over a little lemon juice, add a generous trickle of extra virgin olive oil and serve straight away.

Cheddar

Hugh Fearnley-Whittingstall

MORE RECIPES

Celeriac soufflés (page 131);
Walnut and blue cheese soufflés
(page 246); Leek and potato
gratin (page 344); Polenta
croquettes (page 481); Fairy ring
champignon risotto (page 252);
Cockle and chard rarebit
(page 188); Smoked haddock
jacket potatoes (page 294);
Cheddar and onion oatcakes
(page 411); Hazelnut and
cheese biscuits (page 304)

SOURCING

britishcheese.com;
farmhousecheesemakers.com

The finest Cheddar is, I think, the unassailable apex of British cheese-making. But since the name 'Cheddar' can be used by pretty much anyone, whether their cheese hails from Somerset, Staffordshire or, indeed, South Africa, it has also come to represent the worst examples of mass-produced mousetrap.

However, cheese labelled West Country Farmhouse Cheddar, and bearing the PDO (Protected Designation of Origin) label, is the real thing. This true and traditional cheese, produced by a small group of farms, is made to a specified recipe, using West Country milk, often unpasteurised and usually from the farm on which the cheese is made. The crucial 'cheddaring' process – a way of cutting, turning, pressing and maturing the fresh curd in order to produce the right acidity and texture – will have been done by hand, and the cheese will be at least 9 months old.

Age, and the way the ageing happens, is crucial. A young cheese, smothered in plastic almost from the day it was born, will be very different from one more than a year old, that has sat, muslin-swaddled, upon a maturing rack in a cool chamber, respiring gently. As cheese ages, its very chemistry changes and a huge range of interesting flavours develop. If it can 'breathe', its texture alters too.

So, to enjoy this most magnificent of cheeses in its full glory, buy a wedge hewn from a big, cloth-bound, lard-coated, unpasteurised cylinder. It will be firm but fissured and enticingly crumbly, breaking into nibblesome nuggets under your knife.

Traditional Cheddar is nutty, complex, tangy and sometimes mouth-tinglingly sharp. Sample a few to find a variety and an age that you like. A sweet and herbal 9-month cheese may be just right for you, or you may prefer the deep, earthy body of a regal 24-month-old. Some names to conjure up in the world of genuine West Country Cheddars include Gould's, Keen's, Montgomery, Quickes and Westcombe. When you do find one that totally tickles your taste buds, I recommend that you eat a piece unaccompanied, except for a sip of good red wine or cider, or a bite of a crisp apple, between mouthfuls.

I would balk at using my finest extra-mature Farmhouse in a cooked dish and there are certainly some decent cheaper Cheddars that can do good service for sauces, but I don't think it's worth buying anything not labelled 'mature' at the very least.

CHEDDAR, APPLE AND CELERIAC SALAD

8–10 Brussels sprouts or
⅛ medium white or red cabbage

¼ head of celeriac (175–200g)

2 eating apples, such as Russets

200g mature Cheddar

A handful of lightly bashed
walnuts or pumpkin seeds

FOR THE DRESSING

1 tbsp cider vinegar

2 tbsp rapeseed oil

2 tsp clear honey

Sea salt and black pepper

This crunchy winter salad is the perfect way to show off a good, strong mature Cheddar.
Serves 4

Peel away any damaged or rough outer leaves from the sprouts or cabbage, then cut into 2mm slices. Place in a large bowl.

Peel the celeriac and cut it into thin matchsticks, using a sharp knife or mandoline. Add to the sprouts or cabbage.

Quarter and core the apples and cut into slim wedges. Add these to the bowl too. Crumble the Cheddar, or cut it into rough cubes, and add to the salad along with the walnuts or pumpkin seeds.

For the dressing, whisk the ingredients or shake together in a screw-topped jar and add to the salad. Toss to combine, check the seasoning, and it's ready to serve.

Cheese

Nikki Duffy

SOURCING

nealsyarddairy.co.uk; paxtonandwhitfield.co.uk

Cheese has a semi-miraculous quality that inspires respect, if not awe, for the product itself and for the people who make it. As with all the simplest foods, cheese is easy to get wrong: it requires artisanship, passion and patience to get it right. The joyful thing is just how many British producers are doing exactly that.

Made from one essential ingredient – milk – and little else, cheese nevertheless varies hugely depending on when, where and how it is made. It expresses provenance, locality and *terroir* in a unique way. Each of the many decisions taken by a cheese-maker, from the pasture on which a herd grazes right up to the environment in which a finished cheese matures, has a profound effect. That is why the louche butteriness of a ripe Brie differs so greatly from the translucent firmness of a nutty Berkswell. It's why salty, moist Beenleigh Blue is a million miles away from a crumbly, subtle Lancashire. And it's why cheeses such as Cheddar and mozzarella are so securely settled in their own culinary niche that we've given them separate entries in this book.

It seems likely we've been eating cheese, in some form, for many thousands of years. As soon as homo-sapiens worked out how to milk an animal, the potential for cheese was created, and as soon as any surplus milk was produced, the need to preserve it arose. Archaeological evidence suggests that the use of simple tools to strain curds from whey dates as far back as the sixth century BC.

The basics have not changed all that much. All cheeses begin life in the same way, when fresh milk is soured with a bacterial culture. These days, that means a carefully selected, named culture added by the maker – though originally, it would have been the bacteria naturally present in the raw milk. The bacteria begins turning lactose, the sugar in milk, into lactic acid. This helps the milk to curdle, aids the development of flavour and also suppresses the growth of unwanted organisms.

A curdling agent is then added to separate the milk into its solid and liquid parts. Rennet, which comes from the inside of a calf's or kid's stomach, is traditionally used, though non-animal 'rennets', produced from a type of fungus, are now common. A cheese labelled as suitable for vegetarians will use one of these. Milk can also be curdled with an acid such as vinegar or lemon juice (or through the action of lactic acid alone). But acid forms a fragile mass of tiny curds which need to be carefully drained over several hours. Rennet, on the other hand, quickly forms a firm, rubbery curd which is easy to handle and to cut.

Once the solid curds have formed, the watery whey is drained off. Sometimes the whey is turned into a cheese in its own right, as in the case of ricotta, or used to store the finished cheese, as with mozzarella, but usually it is seen as a by-product. The curd is what becomes the cheese. It can be eaten straight after separation from the whey but more commonly, the curd, which contains most of the fat and protein from the milk as well as the fat-soluble vitamins, is salted and moulded into a more or less firm cheese.

The way the curd is treated has a great influence on the final texture of the cheese. The more the curd is cut and pressed, the harder the cheese is likely to be, because it loses more whey during this process. Softer cheeses are cheeses with a higher moisture content, where the curd is less disturbed.

Sometimes specific moulds are introduced to form blue veining or interesting crusts and rinds that extend a ripening action deep within the cheese. And time is probably the most important ingredient of all: as cheese ages, enzymes break down the fats and proteins within it into a range of flavoursome amino and fatty acids.

C

The longer it ages, the more characterful it becomes (though of course any cheese can be taken too far). Via all these small but hugely significant manipulations, the vast panoply of cheese varieties opens up.

There's been a thrilling renaissance in British cheese-making in the last few decades. Along with fine examples of traditional greats, such as Farmhouse Cheddar, Lancashire and Double Gloucester, there are hundreds of modern cheeses, made to new or newly revived recipes by small, independent creameries. These represent a huge diversity of locality, technique and taste and there are very few styles of cheese anywhere in the world that cannot also be found here on our lushly pastured islands. In the pages that follow, I describe many fantastic cheeses (though still barely the tip of the cheese-berg), with an emphasis on British examples, slicing up the huge subject according to the source of the milk from which the cheese is made (cow, sheep or goat), with an additional section on blue cheese, which has its own unique character. But it is also sometimes helpful to categorise cheese according to style, as I have done briefly here.

Hard cheeses These firm, sliceable, grateable cheeses are made by cutting the curd small and pressing it hard so as to drive off lots of whey. Most of the remaining lactose from the milk is contained in the whey, so the more that is removed, the more digestible the cheese is likely to be, particularly once it has been through a maturing process, which further breaks down lactose. Hard cheeses aged for only a few weeks may still be a little crumbly and quite fresh flavoured, as in a young Lancashire, but those matured for many months, like Farmhouse Cheddar, become almost crystalline and deeply savoury.

Holey cheeses Emmenthal and Gruyère, of which there are several varieties (some not very holey), are the best known within this category. They are hard cheeses made by heating the curd enough to cook it, then pressing it very firmly to create a dense, rubbery cheese within which bubbles of carbon dioxide, produced by fermentation, form 'eyes' or holes.

Fresh cheeses These may be just a few days old and have a brief shelf-life. They are usually rindless, fluffy and mild, but often with a lemony, lactic-acid tang. Traditional curd cheese is the youngest of all: the best examples are simply unsalted fresh curd, the first product of cheese-making. Curd cheese is very mild but with a slight acidity that makes it wonderful in sweet or savoury recipes.

Mould-ripened soft cheeses With their characteristic bloomy white rind, these include Brie, Camembert and countless others. They are made with curd that is cut into large pieces then ladled into moulds, from which the whey is allowed to drain naturally. They lose far less whey than a hard cheese, which accounts for their moist, creamy texture. The cheeses are inoculated with a mould, *Penicillium candidum* (and sometimes *Geotrichum candidum* too), which ripens the cheese from the outside in.

Washed rind cheeses These are the most pungently perfumed of all. They include the redolent Stinking Bishop, Irish Ardrahan, Reblochon and Taleggio. Many varieties are soft, but others are relatively firm. Washed rind cheeses are laved with brine, wine, mead, ale or some other flavoursome liquor as they mature, which encourages the growth of certain flavour-producing moulds on the surface of the cheese. The rind becomes creamy orange in colour and the interior of the cheese – technically referred to as the 'pate' or 'paste' – grows silky, sticky and rich. The whole cheese develops a pungent, wild, 'farmyard' aroma. However, the bark is often stronger than the bite – their characters may be complex, floral and earthy, but still subtle and creamy.

Storing cheese

The storing and maturing of cheeses is practised by experienced *affineurs* who manipulate humidity and temperature to bring cheeses on to absolute perfection. At home, most of us just swaddle our cheese in cling film and chuck it in the fridge. In the absence of a stone-floored pantry that stays at a constant 10–14°C, the fridge probably is the best place. However, plastic wrap is not the friend of great cheese – it makes it 'sweat' by trapping moisture. To stop cheese drying out in the fridge, encase it in waxed paper, which allows air and moisture to circulate. Cheese that is to be enjoyed on its own, rather than as part of a recipe, should always be brought up to moderate room temperature before serving, or its flavours will be masked.

Unpasteurised cheese

Pasteurisation, which kills most of the micro-organisms and enzymes in raw milk, is now standard in the UK. As well as killing harmful bacteria, it is useful to cheese-makers who want to achieve a consistent product because it irons out the fluctuations in flavour and aroma that come with different batches of milk. It also increases the life of the milk, allowing manufacturers to store and transport it. However, a growing number of cheese-makers are returning to raw, unpasteurised milk, to produce cheeses with fuller, more complex flavours.

Hard, matured cheeses, pasteurised or not, are not hospitable environments for pathogenic bacteria because of their relative acidity and dryness – and the longer they are aged, the more this becomes so. Softer cheeses carry a higher risk of unwanted bacterial growth because of their damp and alkaline nature; pasteurising doesn't negate that risk because although the process kills many pathogens, milk or cheese can be contaminated after pasteurisation.

The health risk most associated with cheese is listeriosis, caused by a microbe that likes to grow in low-acid, moist conditions. Any soft, mould-ripened cheeses such as Camembert and Brie, mould-ripened soft goat's cheeses, soft washed rind and soft blue cheeses carry a greater risk of listeria, and for this reason they are often avoided by pregnant women and those who are frail or have a compromised immune system. In addition, current advice is for pregnant women to only eat fresh soft cheeses such as ricotta and mozzarella if they are pasteurised (see nhs.uk for a complete list). Listeria infection in healthy adults and children is rare, and listeria is destroyed by cooking.

The cheese you choose

Like any dairy product, cheese begins with an animal and all the ethical and welfare issues that attach to milk (see page 382) are also relevant here. The simplest way to ensure that you are buying cheese produced under the highest welfare standards is to choose organic. But there are non-organic producers who adhere to high-welfare standards too. Smaller producers may keep their own herds and make their cheese on the same site that the animals are milked. Such makers are in control of every aspect of animal husbandry and hygiene.

Producers using milk from their own home herds also avoid having to transport it. This means the milk does not have to be repeatedly pumped, piped and agitated, and many artisan cheese-makers cite this as a crucial factor in cheese quality – the more the milk is 'bashed about', the more its individual fat molecules are broken down, affecting the flavour and texture of the finished cheese.

C

Cow's cheese

Many of the world's great cheeses were first developed as a way to store and preserve surplus cow's milk. Excitingly, the techniques and recipes behind many of these classics are being re-explored and revived, and there are literally hundreds of fantastic British cow's milk cheeses to try now. I could not begin to do them all justice here, so I have instead described some of the classics as well as some notable new cheeses. These represent merely a taster: seek out the finest examples local to you by visiting delis, cheesemongers or online specialists, tracking the award-winners from events such as the British Cheese Awards, and browsing the ever-increasing canon of cheese reviews to be found online and in print.

Brie This is a bit like Cheddar in that it's a cheese which can be made anywhere and whose noble name can be slapped on to the most insipid and disappointing of examples. Poorly made, under-matured Brie is chalky, bland and pretty unpleasant. A good one is cheese heaven – buttery, sweet and silky with a delightful, mild pungency that increases with age. Brie de Meaux is one example that does have a protected identity – an AOC (*Appellation d'Origine Contrôlée*) showing that it is made with raw milk in the town of Meaux, near Paris. British Brie-like cheeses include the acclaimed unpasteurised Brie-de-Meaux-style Baron Bigod, made in Suffolk, the lovely organic Bath Soft Cheese and Godminster organic Brie. Brie is at its best when soft, with little or no dry centre, but not yet runny and liquid. You don't have to eat the rind but do try it: in the best examples, it gives a wonderful earthy, minerally contrast to the sweet, silky inner paste.

Caerphilly A beautiful cheese, this is Welsh in origin but there's a strong tradition of making it in the Southwest too. It's quicker to produce than Cheddar, and became a source of income for Cheddar-makers while their other cheese matured. Mass-produced Caerphilly is dry and chalky but a traditionally made one has a lovely creamy layer under its rind and a tender, lactic centre. Westcombe Dairy's Ducketts Caerphilly and the organic Welsh Caerffili from Caws Cenarth in Carmarthenshire are great examples. The award-winning Welsh Celtic Promise is based on a Caerphilly recipe, but, with a washed rind, is stronger and creamier.

Camembert This white mould-ripened cheese from Normandy is sometimes grouped with Brie but it is much more earthy. Camembert is sold in small rounds, in little wooden boxes which, conveniently, can be used to bake the cheese whole, studded with garlic and thyme, to savour with good bread and cornichons. Mature Camembert is famously pungent on the nose, but the flavour should be approachably buttery, sweet and fruity – and as with Brie, it should be soft but not uncontrollably runny. 'Camembert' is not a protected name, but *Camembert de Normandie* is. That label, and the DOP logo, signifies the most authentic, raw milk examples. However, there are some British Camembert-like cheeses worthy of attention, including Hampshire-made Tunworth, Isle of Wight Soft and the organic Little Ryding (made from unpasteurised ewe's milk).

Gloucester Double Gloucester (illustrated above left) is the more familiar form of this cheese. Single Gloucester, which is made more quickly with less maturing time, was traditionally the worker's cheese. This lesser-known cheese is still made by a few producers, the best examples being pale, milky and mild with a light, lemony freshness. Double Gloucester was regarded as the finer cheese – the one that went to market. Originally, it was made with creamier milk. Nowadays both single and double are made with the same milk but Double Gloucester is heated a little more, giving a firmer, drier result, and the cheese is matured for longer for a richer flavour. It should be pleasingly waxy with a hint of crumbliness and a nutty, savoury, mellow taste. Double Gloucester has for many years been coloured orange with annatto (a dye made from the seeds of a tropical tree), which was originally a way to reproduce the golden tone of the very best cheeses, made with the richest milk. Try cloth-wrapped, unpasteurised Gloucesters, such as those made by Jonathan Crump in Gloucestershire from the milk of the now very rare Gloucester breed of cattle.

Gouda This is not to be confused with Edam, which is a far less interesting Dutch cheese. A buttery, nutty Dutch Gouda, ideally at least 2 years old, is a marvellous thing, with a depth of flavour to rival a mature Cheddar, only smoother, less spicy and sharp. Mature Gouda is ideal for a cheeseboard – perfect for nibbling, slice by thin slice, with a glass of red wine. British Gouda-style cheeses include the unpasteurised Welsh Teifi and the wonderful, deeply fruity Northumbrian Berwick Edge. Irish Coolea, meanwhile, from County Cork, tastes like a delicious cross between a mature Cheddar, an aged Gouda and a Parmesan.

Lancashire Made in the traditional way, this is a semi-hard cheese with a crumbly texture and an excellent flavour. Factory-produced Lancashire is a poor imitation. Thankfully, producers are making this cheese in the traditional, painstaking way again: adding low levels of starter culture so that the milk ripens slowly, then gently pressing and breaking the curd over and over to drive off the whey, and finally mingling the curd from 2 or 3 separate days' milking to achieve just the right level of acidity. A good Lancashire such as Kirkhams, at 3–4 months old, is pale and mildly saltily tangy, with a wonderful, moist, buttery crumbliness. A superb cheese for eating alone or cooking.

Reblochon This soft, washed-rind, unpasteurised cow's milk cheese hails from the Haute-Savoie region of France. It is very rich and has a unique, softly rubbery texture. *Reblocher* means to 'remilk', and the cheese was traditionally made from a second milking, which drew off the richer, fattier hind milk. It's fantastic as a stand-alone cheese to end a meal, but also very good melted – as in the simple, hearty classic *tartiflette*, a gorgeously rich potato, cheese and bacon gratin. Baronet is a British Reblochon-style cheese, made from rich, organic Jersey milk in Wiltshire.

Red Leicester Like Gloucester (see opposite), this is traditionally dyed with annatto. A good, matured Leicester is smoother than a Cheddar in both flavour and texture but rich, nutty and full flavoured. Sparkenhoe Red Leicester, made on the farm from unpasteurised milk, cloth-bound and matured for a minimum of 6 months, is a great traditional example.

Stinking Bishop First made in Gloucestershire in 1994, this washed-rind cheese is based on a very old recipe once used by Cistercian monks. The rind is washed with perry to encourage the development of the 'smear mould'. As the name suggests, this cheese announces its presence without restraint. However, the flavour is exceptionally fruity, buttery, sweet and tangy, rather than pungent.

C

Sheep's cheese

This group contains some of the most interesting and tempting of all cheeses. Sheep's milk is naturally homogenised and relatively rich, being much higher in fat and protein than cow's and goat's milk. It contains approximately 20 per cent solids, as opposed to 10–12 per cent in cow's and goat's milk. This means sheep's milk is ideal for cheese-making, and it produces pale, beautiful examples, often with a translucent quality if they are firm. As with goat's milk, the paleness of ewe's milk is down to beta carotene from grass being fully digested by the animal, rather than passing into the milk.

Sheep's milk does not have the rich concentration of caproic acid found in goat's milk, so sheep's cheeses lack the 'farmyard' smell associated with mature goat's cheeses. Sheep's cheeses can be very subtle, with delicious sweet, floral and nutty characteristics.

One could argue that the potential for ewe's cheese has not fully been realised in the UK – we are, after all, very good at farming sheep. But ewe's milk is much more seasonal than cow's or even goat's. Lambs are removed from their mothers anything between 3 days and 6 weeks after birth, then moved on to cow's milk, so that the ewes can be milked. A ewe will give milk for up to 7 months after lambing, before she 'dries up'. These days, cheese-makers use the milk from both spring- and autumn-lambing flocks to extend the cheese-making period, and sometimes freeze the milk to facilitate this too, so you can buy many sheep's cheeses all year round.

We have relatively few ewe's cheeses to choose from – but they can be superb. There are some European classics too, of course, including Manchego (see below) and Roquefort (see page 150).

Berkswell A hard, unpasteurised Midlands ewe's milk cheese of exceptional, buttery, savoury deliciousness, this is best at around 4 months old. Use it slivered in salads, grated on pasta, or nibbled with fruit.

Duddleswell This firm ewe's milk cheese from High Weald Dairy in Sussex is nutty and rich. It's a great alternative to a medium Cheddar and melts like a dream.

Feta Salty and crumbly, this is made from sheep's milk, but sometimes with some goat's milk added. It's formed into hard blocks and preserved in brine. True feta can only come from Greece, but there are other feta-style cheeses such as the lovely, not-too-salty Homewood pickled ewe's cheese from Somerset.

Halloumi This unique cheese from Cyprus is quite rubbery in texture and salty, with a fairly mild taste. It comes into its own when fried or grilled, forming a delicious golden crust and softening without melting. It is traditionally a sheep's milk cheese, but these days may also be made from goat's or cow's milk. There are some good British halloumis now – try those from Homewood or High Weald.

Lord of the Hundreds This matured, hard ewe's cheese is made in Sussex from ewe's milk brought in from Essex. Nutty and sweet with a lovely tang like a mature Cheddar, it melts nicely, releasing amazingly fruity flavours.

Manchego A hard ewe's cheese from Spain, this is salty, waxy, rigorous and quite delicious with something sweet and fruity. Membrillo (quince paste) is the classic partner but any tart fruit jam or preserve is good. The Scottish Corra Linn is firm, nutty and salty – made in the spirit of Manchego, but with a distinctive character of its own.

Sussex Slipcote A lovely, soft, fluffy organic ewe's cheese, so mild and fresh-tasting that you can eat it for pudding with fruit and honey, or use it in a cheesecake. However, it's also a gentle alternative to soft goat's cheese in salads.

Goat's cheese

Goat's milk can produce wonderful cheeses of hugely varied character. The freshest – just a few days old – are fluffy and mild, and can be used as you would a cow's-milk curd cheese. Slightly older, white-rinded examples retain a zesty, lemony, fresh character, while mature goat's cheeses may have a much deeper, sweeter, more complex flavour.

It is the breakdown of the particular fatty acids in goat's milk – notably capric, caprylic and caproic acids – which gives it its unique aroma and flavour. However, goat's cheese needn't be overpoweringly 'goaty'. How pronounced that farmyard tang becomes is hugely dependent on the way the milk is handled. If it is dealt with gently, without pumping, for instance, or cooled quickly after collection, the goaty flavours do not develop in the same way. And even goat's cheeses with a really pungent aroma tend to taste milder than they smell.

Despite its bucolic image, most British goat's milk – including the milk used by many artisan goat's cheese makers – is produced from 'zero-grazing' herds kept in barns all year round and fed with a controlled ration. This is the easiest way to ensure consistently high production and some producers would argue that in this country, goats are most comfortable in that system as they are not ideally suited to the British climate or terrain. They dislike wet weather, for instance, and their coats lack lanolin so do not offer the same natural waterproofing as, say, a sheep's fleece. And they are browsers, rather than grazers, preferring leaves, hedges, young shoots, bushes and scrub to chomping on grass like cows or sheep. Others counter that the sight of goats happily basking in the sunshine or nibbling at a hedgerow confirms that, in the right conditions, goats love fresh air and free-ranging as much as any creature.

As with dairy calves and lambs, the kids of dairy goats are nearly always removed from their mother a couple of days after birth and fed on formula. Often male kids are put down immediately, but there are a growing number of goat's milk producers now sending their young billies to be raised for meat (see page 280).

At the time of writing, the Soil Association only certify one goat's cheese producer as organic. This is Greenlands in Herefordshire, where they give their goats 24-hour access to the outdoors and allow the kids to stay with their mothers for the first couple of months of life. There are, however, other non-organic producers with small herds who let their goats go outdoors to enjoy a range of natural forage – which of course is reflected in the rich and complex flavours of their milk.

Brinkburn This Northumbrian goat's cheese is pale, firm and salty with a beautifully complex flavour: all new-mown hay and sea breezes. Delicious nibbled piece by slender piece, it's also wonderful when melted and bubbling.

Stawley Mild, dense and creamy, with a wrinkled rind, this is made from the raw milk of free-ranging goats at Hill Farm Dairy in Somerset. Often, it is inoculated with a whey starter (from the previous day's cheese-making), which allows a more complex flavour than a conventional proprietary starter. It's fantastic eaten alone or in salads.

Quickes hard This firm, salty cheese is essentially a goat's Cheddar and tastes only mildly goaty. It has a unique nutty character. Try it in place of Parmesan – it doesn't taste the same, but it works well in similar dishes.

Ticklemore This tender but firm, floral Devon cheese is made from the milk of goats that browse outdoors. Beautiful cut into slivers and served in simple salads with crisp, raw veg or peppery leaves and really good extra virgin oil, it's also excellent with barbecued vegetables.

C

Blue cheese

The fact that curdled milk and mould can together create a foodstuff about which many of us feel quite dizzily passionate is one of the wonders of the world.

In the past, cheese moulds would be allowed to grow naturally, encouraged by siting the cheese in certain places, such as the damp limestone caves of Combalou, where Roquefort is aged; or via creative interventions such as swirling horse tack through the milk. These days, blue cheeses are made in a more controlled way by inoculating the milk, or the freshly formed curds, with a mould – *Penicillium roqueforti* or *Penicillium glaucum*. Unusually, these microbes are able to grow in very low oxygen conditions, such as the interior of a cheese. They do need some oxygen, however, which is why the inoculated cheeses, once shaped, are often pierced with needles, creating an ingress for air, which stimulates the mould into growth. The mould acts on the fats and proteins in the cheese, breaking them down in a way that would happen anyway over time – but faster. These chemical changes result in the characteristic pungent flavours and aromas of blue cheeses.

The best blues, I find, are those where the veining meanders through a paste that is creamy, salty and sweet. Such cheese is a great ingredient, a superb counterpoint to fruity and nutty flavours in salads. But the finest should be enjoyed with just a few simple partners: pears or apples, hazelnuts or walnuts, honey, slivers of celery, maybe bread – though even that is not essential.

Beauvale This is a new blue cheese, made at the Cropwell Bishop Stilton creamery. It is in the realms of Gorgonzola, but gentler, with a wonderful, hazelnutty, buttery flavour all its own.

Beenleigh Blue Made in Devon, this has a strong, spicy flavour and is a great British alternative to Roquefort.

Cornish Blue This moist, sweet cheese is made with milk from the home herd at Knowle Farm near Bodmin Moor. It's a little milder, softer and gentler than your average blue.

Dorset Blue Vinney A River Cottage favourite, this cow's milk blue is crumbly, tender and medium strength. Very good on a cheeseboard, it is also wonderful for cooking.

Harbourne Blue This lovely, pungent cheese (illustrated above left) is made in Devon from goat's milk, which is rare for a blue. It has the creaminess that, for me, is the most wonderful counterpoint to that salty blue kick.

Perl Las A creamy, sweet, organic blue, this is a Welsh beauty.

Roquefort A cheese so great that it gives its name to the mould used to inoculate countless other blues, this French ewe's cheese has a characteristic damp texture and is one of the saltiest and most piquant of all the genre.

Stilton Although never actually made in the village of Stilton, this iconic blue must be produced in Derbyshire, Nottinghamshire or Leicestershire from local milk. It is a little drier and firmer than many blues, becoming creamier as it matures, and at its best has a wonderful nutty flavour alongside its punchy blue tang.

LANCASHIRE, APPLE AND LEEK PIZZA

FOR THE PIZZA DOUGH

250g plain white flour

250g strong white bread flour

1½ tsp fine sea salt

1 tsp fast-acting dried yeast

1 tbsp olive or rapeseed oil, plus a little extra for oiling

FOR THE TOPPING

4 medium leeks

80g butter

1 tsp thyme leaves

4 tsp plain flour

250ml whole milk

3 crisp eating apples, such as Cox or Lord Lambourne

300g Lancashire cheese, crumbled or coarsely grated

3 tbsp extra virgin olive or rapeseed oil

Sea salt and black pepper

This delicious pizza topping celebrates the classic pairing of crumbly, lactic Lancashire with apples. Serves 6

To make the dough, in a large bowl, mix the two flours with the salt and yeast. Add the oil and 325ml warm water and mix to a rough dough. Tip out on to a lightly floured surface and knead for 5–10 minutes, until smooth; it should be a loose, sticky dough, so try not to add more flour. Trickle a little oil into a clean bowl, add the kneaded dough and turn it in the oil so it is covered with a light film. Cover with a tea towel and leave to rise in a warm place until doubled in size – at least an hour, probably closer to two.

Meanwhile, for the filling, slice the leeks into 1cm rounds; wash well and drain. Place in a saucepan with 20g butter, 2 tbsp water, the thyme and some salt and pepper. Cover and bring to a simmer over a medium heat. Cook for 4–5 minutes until the leeks are starting to soften. Add the remaining 60g butter. Once it is melted, stir in the flour and cook for 1 minute, then stir in the milk. Cook, stirring, for 2 minutes until thick and creamy.

Preheat the oven to 250°C/Fan 230°C/Gas 9 (if it goes that high) or at least 220°C/Fan 200°C/Gas 7. Put a baking sheet in to heat up.

When the dough is well risen and puffy, tip it out and 'knock it back' by poking it with your outstretched fingers until it collapses to its former size. Leave to rest for a few minutes on a lightly floured surface then cut it into 3 equal pieces.

Roll out one piece as thinly as you can. Take the hot baking sheet from the oven, scatter it with a little flour and place the dough base on it. Spread a third of the leek mix over the pizza base, leaving the very edges uncovered. Peel, core and thinly slice 1 apple and scatter over the leeks. Then sprinkle over one-third of the cheese. Trickle with oil and season with salt and pepper. Bake for 10–15 minutes, or until the base is crisp and golden.

Repeat with the remaining dough ingredients to make 3 pizzas.

EWE'S CHEESE WITH CHICKPEAS, ROASTED CHILLIES AND OLIVES

200g dried chickpeas, soaked overnight in cold water (or 2 x 400g tins chickpeas, drained)

2–3 bay leaves

1 head of garlic, cut in half horizontally (or just 1 clove, chopped, if using tinned beans)

75ml extra virgin olive or rapeseed oil, plus extra to trickle

Lemon juice, to taste

4–6 fleshy, mild chillies (or 2 red peppers)

Leaves from a bunch of flat-leaf parsley

150g stoned black olives

200g feta-style cheese, broken into chunks

Sea salt and black pepper

Any feta or feta-style cheese works well here. Use fairly mild, fleshy chillies, such as Hungarian hot wax, taste-testing them to ascertain their heat. Serves 4

If using dried chickpeas, drain and put into a pan with the bay and garlic. Cover with plenty of fresh water, bring to a simmer, skim, then lower the heat. Simmer until tender, 1–2 hours, depending on the chickpeas, topping up the water if necessary.

Drain the cooked chickpeas and return to the pan. Squeeze out the flesh from the garlic skins into the pot, add the oil, a good couple of squeezes of lemon juice and lots of salt and pepper; give them a light bash with a potato masher and set aside.

(If using tinned chickpeas, gently heat the oil in a large pan with a chopped garlic clove for a couple of minutes, add the drained chickpeas and heat through, then add the lemon juice and seasoning, and bash as above.)

Preheat the oven to 200°C/Fan 180°C/Gas 6. Halve the chillies and remove the seeds. Put them into a small roasting tin. Season, trickle over a little oil, cover with foil and roast for about 25 minutes, or until tender. Leave until cool enough to handle, then slice thickly.

Meanwhile, chop half the parsley with the olives to a fairly fine texture, add a little oil and mash to a loose paste. Gently reheat the chickpeas.

Divide the chickpeas between warmed plates and scatter over the chillies and cheese. Spoon on the olive mixture, sprinkle with the remaining parsley leaves and serve.

Cherries

Hugh Fearnley-Whittingstall

LATIN NAME
Sweet cherries: *Prunus avium*.
Acidic cherries: *Prunus cerasus*

SEASONALITY
July–September

MORE RECIPES
Grilled cheese salad with bullace compote (page 105); Strawberries with lavender and honey (page 341); Roasted plum fumble (page 479)

SOURCING
kentorchards.org.uk;
cherryfestivalkent.co.uk;
Englishcherry.co.uk;
rentacherrytree.co.uk

It's hard to think of a finer fruity package than the cherry – every headily scented, shiny bauble dangling irresistibly on its little stalk, waiting to explode into juice at a bite. The colours are glorious – from creamy white to midnight black through sunset yellow, lipstick scarlet and deep purple – and the flavour can be quite exceptional. The best cherries are tart-sweet with that unique, aromatic, almost almondy, *griotte* note.

The classic recipes are always a joy: the comforting, juice-stained lusciousness of a clafoutis; the fragrant, golden-crusted pleasure of a downhome cherry pie; a lightly set cherry jam. But cherries boast such a range of fruity flavour that they constantly invite invention.

A raw and naked cherry, for instance – ideally a tart variety – dipped first into clear honey, and then into grated dark chocolate, explodes in the mouth with some intense, surprisingly winey flavours. And cherries make unexpectedly good companions to sheep's and goat's cheese too.

I love cherries warmed in butter with sugar and spices until the juices run, then spooned on to brioche or rice pudding. And I enjoy popping out the stones and dropping the bleeding fruit straight into breakfast yoghurt, to be topped with a lavish trickle of honey. I like dried cherries too – especially the organic, sugar-free variety that bring scintillating, tangy-sharp flavour to granola and flapjacks as well as to savoury salads and slaws.

Cherries are versatile in a savoury context: try them raw in chilli-spiked salsas, or cooked and served up as a sauce for game, pork, duck or even oily fish like mackerel.

There are essentially two types of cherry: the sweet and the sour. The latter are too tart to eat raw and unsweetened but they are brilliant for cooking. The 'Morello' is the most common sour variety. However, it is very hard to buy fresh Morello cherries (and I would pass swiftly over the tinned or jarred option). You'll need to seek out specialist producers or grow your own. Morello trees have the advantages of doing well on a north-facing wall and of being marginally less appealing than sweet varieties to voracious avian cherry connoisseurs. You may occasionally find them frozen in farm shops, frozen food stores and a few supermarkets. If you do, pounce – they should be very serviceable.

As long as they have plenty of flavour, sweet cherries work in recipes designed for sour fruit – just use less sugar and perhaps add more acidity with a squeeze of lemon. The exception to this is preserving, where the character of a sour cherry makes all the difference. A loosely set Morello jam is one of my all-time favourite toast-toppers.

To make the simplest of cherry pickles, pack 300g whole sour cherries into a sterilised jar. Heat 200ml water, 300ml cider vinegar and 250g sugar with a few bay leaves, peppercorns, juniper berries and cloves to a simmer, let simmer for 10 minutes, then pour over the fruit and seal. After a month, you'll have a delicious sweet-sour accompaniment to cheese, smoked mackerel or roast duck.

Cherry kernels lend a subtle almond flavour to any dish they're cooked in and, since stoning is a long-winded job (even with a decent cherry-stoner), I often leave the stones in. Do warn your guests, though.

The British cherry revival

We have a venerable tradition of growing cherries in this country. However, it has been hard to maintain a consistent commercial crop due to our unpredictable weather and the fact that traditional orchards feature very tall trees which are labour-intensive to pick and hard to protect from birds. Even newer varieties, grown on smaller rootstock, introduced at the end of the last century, couldn't provide enough cherries to meet demand. Consequently, our shop shelves have long been dominated by imports.

This is changing, with British cherries making a significant dent in the foreign competition during recent summers. That's not, sadly, because there's been a great revival of our majestic old cherry orchards. A few traditional orchards are still thriving and more are being rehabilitated, but most of the British cherries on sale now are from modern orchards planted with specially bred, heavy-cropping, large and very juicy cherry varieties. Grown on very small trees, they are much easier to manage: the trees are protected in the run-up to harvest by polytunnels, with netting at the ends to keep the birds out.

The planting of these modern orchards goes on apace, and I have mixed feelings about it. Those juicy new varieties are not necessarily the most delicious. And ranks of dwarf trees will never match the charm of an ancient orchard. But, of course, traditional orchards can't hope to meet the national demand for this lovely fruit. Buying from a local or at least an English producer is a pragmatic way forward. One of the great advantages of a home-grown fruit is that it can be left to mature fully on the tree before being whisked to the shops in a matter of hours.

Cherry-growing is largely a southern affair, and the very best fresh English cherries are grown in traditional Kent orchards. However, there are some very northerly cherry farms, including some on the east coast of Scotland. Survey your local farmers' markets and shops between late June and early August, and enquire at pick-your-own farms.

When you buy cherries, look for tight-skinned, glossy fruit with perky stems. They keep better with the stalks on, so leave them in place and don't wash the fruit until you're ready to eat them.

CHERRY, THYME AND MARZIPAN MUFFINS

450–500g fresh cherries

250g plain flour

2 tsp baking powder

½ tsp bicarbonate of soda

A good pinch of salt

100g marzipan, diced

120g caster sugar

120g unsalted butter, melted and cooled slightly

2 medium eggs, lightly beaten

100ml buttermilk

1 tsp chopped thyme leaves

These muffins are crammed with melting nuggets of marzipan and chunks of fresh cherry, beautifully enhanced with a whisper of thyme. Outside the cherry season, you can make them with 200g dried cherries (and they're also very good with chopped dates). Makes 12

Preheat the oven to 190°C/Fan 170°C/Gas 5. Line a 12-hole muffin tray with paper muffin cases (about 5cm across the base and 4cm deep). Stone the cherries, using a cherry-stoner and cut into quarters; you need 250g stoned weight.

Sift the flour, baking powder, bicarbonate of soda and salt together into a bowl. Add the marzipan cubes and toss them in the flour. Stir in the sugar.

In a separate bowl, beat together the melted butter, eggs, buttermilk and thyme until evenly combined. Gently fold into the flour mixture until evenly combined, then fold in the cherries; don't over-mix.

Spoon the mixture into the muffin cases and bake for 18–20 minutes or until pale golden brown and a cocktail stick inserted into the middle of a muffin comes out clean. Transfer to a wire rack to cool. Best eaten within 24 hours.

Chervil

Gill Meller

LATIN NAME
Anthriscus cerefolium

SEASONALITY
All year round

MORE RECIPES
Barley and raw mushroom salad (page 47); Lamb's lettuce salad with poached egg and croûtons (page 336); Pike with leeks and chervil sauce (page 470)

This is a lovely, delicate herb. Its flavour, somewhere between parsley and tarragon, has a fractional bitterness, like that found in young carrot tops or celery leaf. But overall, it's incredibly mild. It's a herb for eating fresh and raw – the leaves whole or chopped. In late spring, serve it with crisp radishes, lemon and goat's cheese. In summer, scatter it generously over oysters and enjoy with aged smoky chorizo and cold white wine. Late autumn calls for torn handfuls of chervil turned through roast pheasant and apples. And in winter, it is excellent with buttery Brussels sprouts and soft roast garlic.

Chervil is a wonderful herb to use in soups made with fish or a light chicken stock because it complements their often delicate nature. Try it in a creamy chicken soup with young carrots and fresh peas. Alternatively, purée fistfuls of freshly picked leaves in a classic leek and potato soup and finish with some flakes of poached fish and a tangle of whole chervil leaves.

The herb's aniseedy note picks out the earthy qualities of the more subtle wild mushrooms, such as chanterelles or ceps. Fry them with butter and salt before scattering with chervil and shaking over a few drops of good cider vinegar. If you want to gild the lily, a poached egg makes a lovely addition to this autumn salad.

Chervil is a hardy annual plant from the carrot family and it can be grown and harvested throughout the year. It's simple to produce at home, from seed. In spring, when it's cooler, sow the seed liberally indoors, into plug trays, or lengths of guttering filled with seed compost. When the plant looks robust, it can be planted out into a herb garden or window box. Through the summer months, you can sow chervil seed directly into rich moist soil.

Regular picking will prevent the plant bolting too quickly and running to seed. That said, I do like using the fragile, pretty white flowers in cooking. They look great in salads or scattered over puddings, adding a subtle floral flavour.

SQUID WITH CHERVIL AND BLOOD ORANGE

Aniseedy chervil and aromatic orange are superb with squid – and this is a great treatment for small cuttlefish too. Should you miss the early spring blood orange season, ordinary oranges or clementines work just as well. Serves 2 as a light meal

400g cleaned squid, cut into 1cm strips or rings, tentacles halved

1 large or 2 small garlic cloves, thinly sliced

1 tsp dried chilli flakes

2 tbsp olive or rapeseed oil

2 blood oranges

1 bunch of chervil (about 20g), coarser stalks removed

Sea salt and black pepper

Extra virgin olive or rapeseed oil, to finish

Place the squid pieces, including the tentacles, in a bowl with the garlic, chilli flakes and oil. Turn the squid to coat in the mixture and then set aside while you prepare the oranges.

Take a little slice off the top and base of one orange. Stand it on a board and use a sharp knife to cut away all the peel and pith, leaving you with a skinless fruit. Working over a bowl, slice out the orange segments from between their membranes and drop them into the bowl. Squeeze any juice from the orange membranes into the bowl too. Repeat with the other orange.

Heat a medium-large frying pan over a high heat. When hot, add the squid in an even layer. Season well with salt and pepper and cook for 2–3 minutes, until opaque and just coloured in places, tossing regularly.

Transfer the squid to a warm serving platter and scatter over the orange segments (holding back the juice). Add the chervil to the orange juice and turn it over gently, then scatter it over the squid. Trickle generously with extra virgin oil and season with salt and pepper. Serve with warm bread, if you like.

Chestnuts

Hugh Fearnley-Whittingstall

LATIN NAME
Castanea sativa

SEASONALITY
October

HABITAT
Park or woodland. Common in England, especially the South; less common in Scotland, Northern Ireland and central Wales

MORE RECIPES
Baked parasol mushroom with Brie (page 430); Roasted sprouts with black pudding and chestnuts (page 102); Pear and celeriac stuffing (page 454); Apple and chestnut crumble (page 26)

To pass an autumn evening nibbling freshly roasted chestnuts, gathered by your own fair hand in some misty woodland, is a seasonal treat that's hard to surpass.

I would be deceiving you, however, if I said it's a completely straightforward mission. First you must find a decent haul of nuts that have escaped the attentions of squirrels; then you need to brave the ferociously spiny outer shells (surely one of nature's most successful coats of armour) in order to release the tear-drop-shaped kernels within. Even then, it's necessary to slit the skin of each before roasting them and, finally, to peel off the tightly clinging inner skin. By the time you get to your chestnut, you have certainly earned it. But the labour of love along the way is one of those comforting seasonal rituals that, as with all foraged foods, roots you that little bit deeper in the land you live on.

The sweet chestnut (not to be confused with the horse chestnut, which produces conkers) is a glorious tree that has enthusiastically taken root all over Europe. In the south of the continent, particularly, chestnuts grow abundantly and were once a staple crop for the working classes – hence the cache of lovely chestnut recipes you'll find in Mediterranean cuisines, from Spanish pork and chestnut stews to dense, sweet chestnut flour cakes like the Italian *castagnaccio*.

Further north, in our cooler climes, the chestnut still grows well. Its magnificent silhouette is a familiar sight in parks, woods and gardens, but it struggles to produce such a plentiful harvest of good-sized nuts. This is one of the reasons it is not cultivated here, and why the chestnuts you find in our shops are nearly all imported European ones. Wild British chestnuts are smaller than their Continental counterparts and fruiting can be erratic – in some years, there aren't many good, plump nuts to be had. But their wonderful flavour, even in small quantities, makes up for this.

Look for wild chestnuts from mid-October onwards, searching in the leaf litter under the trees. Go well prepared, with a stick for rooting about and stout gloves to help you remove the nuts from their prickly beds. Choose the biggest nuts and those that seem fat, firm and full inside their beautiful, glossy skins.

Chestnuts' starchy-sweet character makes them wonderfully versatile. Once peeled, they can be left whole and braised in a stew, or crumbled and sautéed in butter with thyme and salt until crisp and golden (fantastic on risottos or pasta). They can be roughly crushed and folded into a meaty stuffing or a creamy vegetable gratin (especially one that includes Brussels sprouts).

Puréed chestnuts are a luscious ingredient in sweet dishes. Just simmer them in water, milk or a light syrup until nice and tender then blitz with some of the cooking liquor to create a velvety paste. Add sugar or honey to taste.

A sweet chestnut purée is delicious marbled with cooked apple and a little crème fraîche into an autumnal fool, or slathered over the base of a Victoria sponge. Chocolate and meringue also pair well with chestnut, and highly sweetened chestnut purées can be preserved and eaten as a jam.

Ready-made chestnut purées – sweetened and unsweetened – are widely available, as are pre-cooked, vac-packed or tinned chestnuts. These save an awful lot of time and effort, and can be used in place of home-cooked nuts in most recipes, though they're softer in texture. Sugar-soaked, candied chestnuts – *marrons glacés* – are a treat that I can't resist around Christmas time.

Chestnut flour, milled from dried chestnuts, is another useful ingredient – much under-explored in British kitchens. It has a lovely dun colour and rich flavour and is

C

wonderful in cakes, biscuits and pancakes. Combine it with wheat flour or use it alone (or with other gluten-free flours such as buckwheat, rice flour or ground almonds) if you want to avoid wheat. Despite the lack of gluten, you can still produce a surprisingly light, fluffy chestnut sponge by folding the flour into super-whipped eggs and sugar, with a good measure of baking powder.

If ever you land a particularly plentiful haul of nuts, you could follow John Wright's instructions for making your own chestnut flour: pass cooked (but slightly underdone), peeled chestnuts through a mouli grater to produce flakes; dry these out in a very low oven (at 40°C) for several hours; then blitz in a food processor. It is, as he never tires of reminding me, damn good. Chestnut flour has a high moisture content and can go off rather quickly so it's best kept in the fridge after opening.

How to prepare chestnuts

You cannot skin a raw chestnut; they need to be roasted or boiled first. Boiling is quicker but roasting makes them more fragrantly tempting.

In all cases, cut the skin of the chestnuts first to prevent them exploding on cooking: use a small, sharp knife to make a slit through the skin from the tufted tip down to the base of the nut.

To boil, put slit chestnuts in a pan and cover with boiling water. Bring back to the boil and simmer for 5 minutes, then take off the heat. Taking them one at a time, and working while they are still hot, use a small knife to help you remove both the tough outer rind and the thinner, inner skin. The nuts will be cooked but still crunchy and can be cooked further.

For roasting chestnuts over embers, you need a metal receptacle, ideally one with holes. I have been known to use a coal shovel or an empty tin can, punched full of holes and with the lid still attached, but you can buy purpose-made chestnut roasting pans. Fill your roaster no more than half-full of slit chestnuts and place it on the embers. Shake it or poke the nuts every now and then, to turn them. They should be done in about 15 minutes and you can then peel off the skins using your fingers, or a knife. You can also roast chestnuts in a hot oven (at 200°C/Fan 180°C/Gas 6) for 20–30 minutes.

ROASTED SQUASH WITH CHESTNUTS, SAUSAGE AND SAGE

500g squash, such as butternut or sweet onion

2 tbsp olive or rapeseed oil

1 tbsp roughly chopped sage

2 garlic cloves, sliced

4 pork sausages (about 250g)

250g chestnuts, cooked and peeled (see above) or 200g vac-packed chestnuts

Sea salt and black pepper

A perfect autumnal supper dish, this can be made with fresh or vac-packed chestnuts. Serves 4

Preheat the oven to 190°C/Fan 170°C/Gas 5. Peel and deseed the squash, then cut the flesh into 3–4cm pieces. Place in a roasting tray, trickle with the oil and scatter over the chopped sage, garlic and some salt and pepper. Roast in the oven, stirring once, for 30 minutes, or until tender.

Squeeze the sausagemeat out of its skin and crumble it over the squash. Scatter over the chestnuts. Toss everything together, then return to the oven for about 25 minutes until the sausage is cooked and the squash and chestnuts are starting to brown nicely.

Allow to stand for 3–4 minutes before serving, with a crisp autumnal salad – a celeriac and cabbage slaw is good.

Chicken

Mark Diacono

MORE RECIPES
Chicken and blueberry salad with coriander dressing (page 77);
Roast jerk chicken (page 16);
Tea-brined chicken (page 634);
Chicken and cider stew with rosemary dumplings (page 617);
Roasted chilli mole (page 173);
Pheasant with olives and preserved lemons (page 414);
Coriander pork chops (page 198)

SOURCING
providencefarm.co.uk;
rutlandorganics.co.uk;
woolleyparkfarm.co.uk

Chicken is the nation's favourite meat. According to the British Poultry Council, 870 million birds were bred, raised and slaughtered in the UK in 2013. In addition, we imported getting on for half that number from other countries, in one form or another. That's a whole lot of birds, and a whole lot of lives.

Of those hundreds of millions of birds raised for our tables, around 90 per cent will never see daylight, will be unable to exhibit their natural behaviours – dust-bathing, roosting, etc. – and will never walk on grass or have the opportunity to browse, peck, scratch and graze as wild birds would. In almost every sense, they live a life not meant for a chicken. Intensive stocking rates – up to 18 or so birds per square metre – mean they have little room to move. They expend very little energy and so convert their feed, which is constantly available to them, very quickly and cheaply into flesh.

Extraordinarily, many chickens make the journey from egg to Sunday-roast-ready bird in around 5 weeks – hatched, fed, treated, housed, killed, dressed, packaged, transported and on our shop shelves, selling for less than a pint of beer.

In an effort to blur the reality of what life is like for nine out of ten chickens, clear, sound information is sadly lacking on much chicken packaging. Ignore anything other than the words 'free-range', 'organic' or 'RSPCA Assured'. Without any of these, you should assume that the chicken has been raised in a standard intensive system. Phrases such as 'farm fresh', 'farm assured', and even the Red Tractor logo, do not indicate higher welfare.

Free-range chickens have more space, with the freedom to roam outside with proper vegetation provided. They are also able to express their natural behaviours. Many producers of free-range chicken choose slower-growing birds, which usually means a longer (8 weeks minimum) and happier life. Organic chickens are kept to free-range standards as a minimum but additionally enjoy organic, GM-free feed and have a longer life of over 11 weeks. 'RSPCA Assured' chickens enjoy better conditions and lower stocking rates than intensively raised birds, but may still have been raised indoors.

The choices we make when we buy chicken are hugely significant. The decision to buy one chicken over another sends a powerful message to the producers and the retailers who put those birds on the shelves about what we, the consumers, are prepared to accept. The money you spend is also reflected in the quality of what you are eating. However, I wouldn't want to encourage you to buy a cheap, intensively reared bird so that you can compare and contrast it with an organic one. So please take my word for it: the better the life – the more varied the diet, the more exercise allowed, the less stress suffered – the better the flavour.

Another thing to be aware of is how the chicken is plucked. Conventional poultry processing involves immersing the dead birds in simmering water to loosen the feathers. This can make the skin 'soggy' and, as many birds are immersed in the same water, it may lead to a build-up of bacteria therein, which transfers to the birds' skin. Because of this, wet-plucking shortens shelf-life considerably.

Dry-plucking, which is more costly and labour-intensive, gives better results when the bird is cooked and, because it is more hygienic, allows the potential for hanging birds for anything up to 2 weeks to improve flavour and tenderness. Some would argue that because chickens are killed young (and are therefore naturally tender) hanging them doesn't make a real difference. I would say that dry-plucking and at least a brief hanging of a good organic bird (which will be a little more mature anyway) can only lead you closer to chicken nirvana.

Smear a good chicken in olive oil, sprinkle with plenty of salt and black pepper and roast until golden brown. Nothing beats it. And, as much as I love the breast, and indeed the wings and legs, the part I'll savour the most is that crisp, golden skin.

Start with a good, well-raised chicken and you have the basis for perhaps a dozen individual meals. A family of four will demolish most of a fairly large bird but leave perhaps enough meat for a leftover chicken curry for the following night. If you then make stock from the bones (and why on earth wouldn't you?) you'll have the core ingredient for soups, risottos and stews. Even if your chicken is organic, that makes for pretty good value.

Roasting a chicken well is easy, but needs a little more thought than simply popping it in the oven until it's cooked. Season the cavity and add a couple of spent lemon halves, a few bashed garlic cloves or half an onion and a few sprigs of thyme if you have some to hand. The 'butter-under-the-skin' trick is a bit cheffy for some, but it does nurse that delicate flesh tenderly through the roasting process. If you want to give it a go, loosen the breast skin, easing it away from the flesh with your fingers in order to form a pocket, then fill with butter and massage it across the meat; this almost guarantees a succulent chicken. Plain butter is ample, but a herb butter (tarragon and thyme are particularly good) with a little grated lemon zest and/or garlic, will imbue the flesh with fine flavour.

The roasting time is all-important. There's a delicate balance to strike between crisping the skin magnificently and avoiding any danger of the flesh drying out. Start by letting the bird come up to cool room temperature. I give a moderately large (1.5–2kg) bird 20–25 minutes at 210°C/Fan 190°/Gas 7 to start the skin crisping and get heat travelling into the meat, then pour a small glass of wine into the dish, and give it a further 40–50 minutes at 170°C/Fan 150°C/Gas 3. Laying strips of bacon across the roasting bird helps to keep the meat moist, but do allow the chicken its 20-minute sizzle before you lay the bacon across the breast, or the skin will stay pale.

A knife inserted into the joint between leg and body should release juices that run clear, with no hint of blood: if not, cook for another 5–10 minutes and test the other leg. Once it's done, I let the bird rest in the oven, turned off with the door open, for about 10 minutes. I find that the crisp skin can get a little soft if left much longer than that, and I'd rather the dog had the bird than let that catastrophe occur. Some resting is important though, allowing the meat to relax so it retains its juices once cut. Adjust the cooking times a little for a larger or smaller bird.

When it comes to serving your bird, it's very simple: the winey pan juices are a delicious sea into which the carved meat can fall. No other gravy is needed.

In our house, most chicken leftovers go into chicken curry (usually with spinach and cauliflower), chicken pie, or what has become known as 'chicken push-around'. This is a moveable feast, but usually features plenty of slowly softened onions as a base, to which we add shreds and chunks of cooked chicken and whatever is in the fridge, plus a few good storecupboard flavours to liven things up. Chunks of bacon, pancetta or chorizo, leftover potatoes, cooked chard, broccoli or spinach, cherry tomatoes, lemon zest, thyme, tarragon and a little cream are among the usual suspects that might get pushed around the pan until the whole ensemble is cooked through.

While chicken stock underpins many of the soups I make, it gets to take a more prominent role in the broth I make most often in winter. A good home-made stock (see page 611) turns a handful of bits and bobs into, if not quite the elixir of life, then

C

certainly the antidote to man-flu and the winter cold. Simmer 300g in total of peeled, finely diced carrots, parsnips and/or celeriac in about 1.5 litres chicken stock for a couple of minutes. Add a handful or two of smallish pasta shapes such as macaroni and cook for a further 4 minutes or so, then add some shredded greens or cabbage plus a little leftover cooked chicken if you have it (though this is by no means essential). Cook for another 2–3 minutes, season with plenty of pepper and a few pinches of salt and a nourishing feast results. A few handfuls of pearl barley or spelt are fabulous in place of the pasta, though they need a little longer simmering (refer to the packet) before you add the diced vegetables.

Jointing a chicken

This is one of the simplest but most useful and rewarding kitchen skills you can master, opening the door to casseroles, fried, barbecued or baked chicken pieces and wonderful one-pot suppers such as chicken basquaise, with its chorizo, rice, peppers and olives. Jointing a whole chicken yourself is much cheaper than buying it in pieces – and it leaves you with a basic carcass which, though small, makes particularly tasty stock because you cook it from raw.

A clean, sturdy chopping board and a good, sharp knife are essential. First, pull one leg slightly out from the body and cut through the skin (and only the skin) along the line between the leg and the body. Pull the leg further away from the body and downwards, pushing the ball at the base of the leg out of and slightly away from the socket. Cut through the flesh that joins the body to the top of the thigh. If you want to separate the drumstick from the thigh, bend the leg at the knee, cutting through where the crease forms. Repeat with the other leg.

Take hold of a wing and pull it out from the body in a circular motion to free the wing and make the join between it and the body more apparent. Cut through the skin and the ligaments – avoid cutting through bones, there's no need. Repeat with the other wing.

For the breasts, place the chicken on its back. Run your knife from the head end tight alongside the long, central breastbone, feeling the knife tip clicking along the ribs as you move towards the tail end. Ease your knife under the meat and gently work away to release one breast from the ribcage, then repeat for the other.

Any meat left on the carcass should be picked off and popped into a freezer bag if you haven't an immediate plan for it – you'd be surprised at what a difference even a few morsels of chicken can make to a broth, soup or salad.

Keeping chickens for meat

Keeping chickens is a pleasurable and largely stress-free business, but if you're rearing them for meat rather than keeping hens for eggs there is the very real difference of a planned end to their lives. Learn how to dispatch a bird – it's quick and simple – and despite this inevitable conclusion, you can be assured that your chickens will have a happier, healthier and almost certainly a longer life than if raised in commercial conditions – and you'll get incredible meat.

Your birds will need a house, food (including a proper, protein-rich feed), clean fresh water, space to forage, protection from predators (including domestic animals) and shelter from extremes of weather, but you can give them this even in the confines of a small garden.

Chickens can be raised from eggs (bought in or fertilised eggs from your own flock) or young chicks, though you will need an incubator to raise them from eggs and a heat lamp to keep chicks warm as they grow. There are numerous breeds that have been bred to grow well for meat – Sasso and Hubbards, for example. However, dual-purpose birds such as Sussex and Orpingtons grow well for meat but also lay well, giving you the option of raising the hens for eggs and cocks for meat.

PAELLA

2 free-range chicken breasts, skinned

2 free-range chicken thighs, taken off the bone, skinned

1 tbsp olive oil

100g cooking chorizo, cut into small chunks or slices

1 medium red pepper, halved, deseeded and cut into strips

1 onion, thinly sliced

3 garlic cloves, thinly sliced

300g paella rice

A glass of white wine

1 litre hot chicken stock

A pinch of saffron strands

200g cleaned small squid

200g live clams or mussels, scrubbed (optional)

100g chard leaves, off the stalk, roughly torn (use the stalks for another dish)

1–2 tbsp chopped flat-leaf parsley

1 lemon, halved

Sea salt and black pepper

Extra virgin olive oil, to finish

This is a great way to use the breast and thigh meat from a chicken you've jointed yourself. (The drumsticks and wings can be roasted, and the carcass used for stock.) Or use the meat from a guinea fowl. To accommodate all the ingredients, you do need a really big pan – at least 32cm in diameter. Serves 4–6

Cut the chicken breasts and thighs into 4–5cm pieces. Place a paella pan or large shallow frying pan over a medium heat. Add the oil, followed by the chicken and chorizo. Season with salt and pepper and fry for 4–5 minutes, stirring from time to time or until the chicken is browned.

Scatter in the red pepper, onion and garlic and cook for a further 8–10 minutes. Add the rice, fry for a minute or two, then add the wine and let it simmer for a few minutes.

Add the stock and the saffron, bring to a gentle simmer and cook, stirring regularly, for 20–30 minutes. The rice will take up the stock as it simmers away.

Meanwhile, slice the squid pouches into rings and cut the tentacles into 2 or 3 pieces each.

When most of stock has been taken up and the rice is almost tender, add the squid to the pan with the clams or mussels, if using. Add the chard and chopped parsley and stir well.

Cover and cook for a further 4–5 minutes or until all the clams or mussels have opened (discard any that refuse to open) and the greens are nicely wilted. You can add a splash more water or stock if necessary but the paella should have a relatively 'dry' consistency, rather than being soupy like a risotto.

Now turn off the heat and squeeze over some lemon juice. Taste and adjust the seasoning with more lemon, salt and pepper as needed. Cover the paella with a lid or tea towel and leave to stand for 5–10 minutes. Serve trickled with a little extra virgin olive oil, with more lemon wedges for squeezing.

CHICKEN BROTH WITH PARSLEY AND CELERY SEED SPAETZLE

100g plain flour

1 medium egg

1 tbsp finely chopped parsley

½ tsp celery seeds

½ tsp fine sea salt

750ml good chicken stock

Sea salt and black pepper

Extra virgin olive oil, to serve

Somewhere between dumplings and noodles, spaetzle are made by dropping little squiggles of dough directly into a simmering broth. Serves 4

In a large bowl, combine the flour with the egg, parsley, celery seeds and salt. Add enough water (30–40ml) to form a thick batter.

Bring the chicken stock to a simmer in a medium pan. Taste and add salt and pepper if it is needed. Set a colander with large holes over the simmering stock.

Spoon the spaetzle batter into the colander and use a rubber spatula to push lengths of dough through the holes and into the simmering broth. Cook for 3–4 minutes or until the spaetzle rise to the surface. Ladle into bowls, trickle with a little oil, and serve.

Chickpeas

Hugh Fearnley-Whittingstall

LATIN NAME
Cicer arietinum

ALSO KNOWN AS
Garbanzo beans, gram,
ceci, besan (flour)

MORE RECIPES
Borlottis with fennel seeds and
onion (page 81); Spear-leaved
orache bhajis (page 593); Ewe's
cheese with chickpeas, roasted
chillies and olives (page 151)

It's worth mentioning the reputation chickpeas used to have – heavy and wholesome but definitely not hot to trot – if only to rapidly reject it. This sorry misrepresentation stemmed from a lack of familiarity with their traditional uses. Despite the fact that these pulses have been cultivated for around nine thousand years, they only arrived in the UK in the 1970s and were quickly pigeon-holed in the good-for-you-but-boring bracket. Once we started to get to grips with the cuisines of the Mediterranean, Middle East and the Indian subcontinent, we realised just how good this legume could be.

Now millions of Brits eat hummus, falafel and bhajis. And hearty dishes such as spicy Spanish garbanzos with chorizo, or chickpea-studded Moroccan tagines are in the repertoire of many keen cooks. I rarely have fewer than three tins of chickpeas in my kitchen cupboard – along with a pack or two of dried ones.

Inexpensive and packed with protein, they are very useful ballast alongside strong flavours and spicy sauces, but I also enjoy their unique creamy texture and earthy taste. I toss them into a salad, stir them into a stew, or whiz them into hummus at some point every week. They are one of my go-to ingredients whenever I want to cook a meat-free meal. They are cracking in saucy curries – especially fine with sweated-down onions and lots of spinach, kale or chard. But they are also fantastic in a simple, tomatoey veg soup with small pasta.

Dried chickpeas, soaked and cooked, do have the edge for flavour over tinned. The cooking time varies depending on how old they are. I'll happily soak and cook chickpeas that are a few months past their use-by date. But if they've been hanging around for years, they won't become tender, no matter how long you soak or simmer them.

Soak dried chickpeas in plenty of cold water overnight, or for at least 8 hours, adding 1 tsp bicarbonate of soda per 500g chickpeas if you like (this helps them soften a little quicker when cooking). They will swell up considerably. The next day drain and rinse well if you've used bicarb, then put them in a large pan with lots of fresh water because on cooking they will swell up even more. *Don't add salt* at this stage, as it makes the skins tough, or at least slows the softening process.

Bring to a simmer, skimming off any scum that rises to the surface and cook to your liking, whether that's tender-but-nutty or good-and-soft. This can take 2 hours, sometimes more. Leave the chickpeas to cool for half an hour or so in the cooking water (they'll continue to swell a bit), then drain and they're ready. Add them to a dish or enjoy just as they are, still warm, tossed with some extra virgin olive or rapeseed oil, a squeeze of lemon, some chopped parsley, flaky sea salt and black pepper.

In the UK, we always buy chickpeas in their dried or processed form, but in some parts of the world (including areas of Italy, the US and India) you can find them fresh. A delicate pale green, they snuggle two to a pod and are popped out and eaten still raw, or lightly cooked like fresh peas. Grab them if you see them – they are delicious.

Chickpea flour

Also called gram flour or besan, this has a distinctive, rich, beany flavour and is a staple in Indian cuisine; it's also used in Mediterranean cooking. I probably use chickpea flour most often for pakora-style fritters. But I also make Provençal *socca* pancakes from a simple chickpea flour and water batter – they're delicious eaten hot from the pan, trickled with oil and sprinkled with salt. Combined in equal quantities with rice flour and either rye or buckwheat flour, chickpea flour also makes a great wheat-free flour mix for drop scones, pancakes or soda breads.

Hummus

This simple purée of chickpeas, tahini (see page 581), garlic and lemon is ubiquitous – but variable to say the least. At its best it is sustaining, versatile and wholesome, but most supermarket hummus is too salty and can have a curious sweetness.

If you've never tried making it, you should. For the simplest version, just blitz 500g cooked chickpeas (or two 400g tins, drained and rinsed) with around 100ml water – (you can use the cooking water from chickpeas you've cooked yourself), a crushed garlic clove, the juice of at least 1 lemon (and perhaps a few gratings of zest too), around 50g tahini (a heaped tablespoonful), and enough good olive oil (around 100ml) to loosen the mix (plus salt and pepper of course). Or see the recipe below for a delicious riff on the hummus theme. Finishing touches are crucial – an extra glug of your best olive oil is *de rigueur* but I also like a decent sprinkling of paprika, some chopped parsley, or perhaps a spoonful of chopped olives or diced tomatoes.

We mainly think of hummus as a 'dip'. But warmed through, and loosened with a little extra water, it is a great dressing/sauce for kebabs in the broadest sense. In fact, it's good with all kinds of poultry and lamb dishes, from a spiced roast chicken to a barbecued chop.

SMASHED CHICKPEAS WITH PRESERVED LEMON AND RED ONION

A little olive or rapeseed oil, for frying

1 small-medium red onion, thinly sliced

1 small, or ¼ large preserved lemon, seeds removed

1 small garlic clove, crushed

1 tbsp tahini

1 tsp ground cumin

A pinch of hot smoked paprika, plus extra to finish

50ml extra virgin olive oil

250g freshly cooked chickpeas, or a 400g tin, drained and rinsed

Extra virgin olive oil, or hempseed oil, to finish

Sea salt and black pepper

This warm, chunky mix is essentially a coarse hummus. It's great as a dip, but also excellent as an accompaniment to lamb. If you have time to toast and grind a couple of teaspoonfuls of cumin seeds, the flavour will be especially good, but ready-ground cumin is fine to use. You will need 150g dried chickpeas to give the cooked weight you need (250g). Serves 3–4

Place a medium frying pan over a medium heat and add a trickle of oil, followed by the onion. Season lightly with salt and pepper. Cook gently for about 8 minutes, stirring every few minutes, until the onion is soft and starting to caramelise slightly.

Meanwhile, roughly chop the preserved lemon peel and flesh. Put into a food processor with the garlic, tahini, cumin, paprika, 50ml water and the olive oil. Blitz to a thin purée, then add the chickpeas and blitz briefly so they retain a nice chunky texture.

Scrape the mixture into the pan with the onion and warm it through for a minute or two. Taste and add salt and pepper as needed.

Serve warm, trickled with a little olive or hempseed oil and a dusting of paprika.

Chicory

Mark Diacono

LATIN NAME
Cichorium intybus

ALSO KNOWN AS
Belgian endive, witloof

SEASONALITY
October–January

MORE RECIPES
Roast potatoes with radicchio and cheese (page 518); Curried new potatoes, red onion and lettuce (page 226); John Dory with creamed radicchio (page 318); Endive with chicken livers and bacon (page 250); Venison salad with apple, celeriac and hazelnuts (page 660)

We don't generally go for bitterness in our food in the way the French and Italians do – but slowly, slowly we are learning to appreciate it. Chicory is an ingredient that can help us on this journey. The height of the British season is winter – and that's a wonderful coincidence because what this leaf does particularly well is to offset the rich roasts, stews and gratins we eat more of in the cold months.

Some confusion exists over the distinction between chicory and endive. Botanically speaking, chicory is *Cichorium intybus*, and endive is *Cichorium endivia*. For the purposes of gastronomy, chicory (also, befuddlingly, sometimes called Belgian endive) usually has oval leaves held tight in the shape of a bullet, while endive (see page 250) is frilly and loose-leaved.

Most chicory is grown in darkness to produce pale leaves – usually with yellow-green tips, though red-tinged varieties are available too. Look for fresh, firm, crisp heads and be aware that leaves with green tips are likely to be more bitter.

A few young, small leaves of chicory add an enticing, bitter dash to a bowl of mixed leaves. And pairing raw chicory with strong, contrasting flavours can work marvellously: try it in a savoury salad with fruit (perhaps apples, or tart berries such as raspberries or blackberries) and something rich or earthy, like black pudding or roast root veg. Pungent herbs and spices – thyme, paprika, chilli – bring such flavours together nicely. Make the most of raw chicory's shape too: the scoop-like leaves are fantastic with dips or piled high with some lovely, well-seasoned filling.

Chicory takes well to braising, griddling, blanching or roasting. For a gentle chicory experience, season the halved heads and coat in olive oil then griddle over a high heat until beautifully caramelised. This moderates that fabulous bitterness without killing it. With a couple of lamb chops and some mash, it's as effective as a log fire in pushing out the chill. For something more assertive, I've found sage, ginger, honey, mustard, balsamic vinegar, orange and thyme to be excellent partners to this leaf.

But perhaps the most successful approach is to combine chicory's bitterness with rich, lactic creaminess. A gratin using blanched and lightly fried chicory makes for a fine midweek supper or a side dish with any roast. And this leaf pairs beautifully, cooked or raw, with blue cheese, which contrasts with chicory's bitterness rather than masking it. A salad of a couple of chicory heads torn into leaves, with a handful of toasted walnuts and 100g or so of crumbled blue cheese, all tossed with a good mustardy dressing, makes a superb light lunch for four.

ROASTED CHICORY WITH HONEY, MUSTARD AND THYME

4 tbsp olive or rapeseed oil, plus a little extra for oiling

4 heads of chicory

1 tbsp clear honey

1½ tsp Dijon mustard

1 good tsp thyme leaves

Juice of ½ large orange

Sea salt and black pepper

This lovely side dish is also a great topping for bruschetta. Try it with radicchio too. Serves 4–6

Preheat the oven to 180°C/Fan 160°C/Gas 4 and lightly oil a roasting dish. Halve the chicory heads lengthways and remove any discoloured leaves.

In a large bowl, combine the oil, honey, mustard, thyme leaves and a good pinch each of salt and pepper. Toss the chicory in this mix (you may need to do this in batches), coating them with the dressing and working it down between the outer leaves with your fingers.

Transfer the chicory to the prepared dish, pouring any leftover oil mixture over it. Roast for 30–40 minutes, turning the chicory every now and again, until tender and browning nicely on the edges. Remove from the oven, squeeze over the orange juice, add a little more salt and pepper and serve warm or at room temperature.

Chillies

Mark Diacono

LATIN NAME
Capsicum annuum,
Capsicum frutescens

SEASONALITY
Fresh chillies harvested
June–December

MORE RECIPES
Muhammara (page 464); Wilted mizuna with chilli, garlic and sunflower seeds (page 387); Sweetcorn with spring onion, chilli and coriander (page 632); Braised white beans with greens (page 55); Ewe's cheese with chickpeas, roasted chillies and olives (page 151); Grilled squid with chilli, parsley and garlic (page 607); Roast gurnard with pepper, lemon, thyme and chilli (page 292); Zander with coriander and chilli dressing (page 685); Roast jerk chicken (page 16); Slow-roasted goose with star anise, orange and chilli (page 283); Fragrant beef curry (page 350); Hot haw jelly (page 302); Green tomato, cumin and green chilli chutney (page 642)

SOURCING
coolchile.co.uk;
seaspringseeds.co.uk;
southdevonchillifarm.co.uk

My father, born in Sri Lanka, liked chilli in everything. He stopped short of sprinkling dried chillies on his coffee, but only just. Not surprisingly, a dislike of chillies formed part of my teenage rebellion; I'm happy to confirm I have left that far behind. Like many other British cooks and gardeners, I've grown to love chillies. This is largely thanks to a band of specialist growers who now cater to the needs of the spiceophile online or via farmers' markets, selling fresh and dried chillies as well as chilli plants and seeds to grow yourself. These suppliers have opened our eyes to the huge variety of flavours, aromas, textures and degrees of heat that exist beyond the supermarket.

Most of the chillies you find in the shops are the shiny, bullet-shaped 'Serenade' variety, selected partly for their reasonable flavour and moderate heat – measuring 5,000–12,000 on the Scoville Heat Unit scale (SHUs) – but largely for their shelf-life. They are perfectly fine, but when there are chillies out there that measure a mere 200 SHUs or well over a million you can see that the supermarket selection is rather thin. Thankfully, some now stock fiery 'Bird's Eye' chillies or hot 'Scotch Bonnets' but to enjoy the rest, you'll need to find specialist suppliers or grow them yourself. Before you shop, get to know a little about what you're looking for.

Vegetable chillies

These are relatively large, thick-skinned and fleshy, with only a mild heat.

Padrón A superb tapas chilli, this variety accelerates from mild to distinctly lively (around 12,000 SHUs) when mature. My favourite way of enjoying padróns is to fry them in a very hot wok with a little oil, flipping them regularly, until well blistered, then serve them heavily dusted with salt and pepper, accompanied by a cold beer. Be prepared for the occasional more mature, and much hotter, one.

Poblano Large, heart-shaped and mild (1,000–1,500 SHUs), this excellent chilli colours from green to deep chocolate as it ripens. It's fabulous in stews, just halved and deseeded, or roasted and/or stuffed. When dried, it's known as ancho chilli.

Hungarian Hot Wax A long, thin chilli with mild to moderate heat (around 6,000 SHUs) and a good flavour and aroma. Use it in anything from pasta dishes to salsas.

Spice chillies

These are small, thin-skinned and usually pretty hot. Grow a good early-ripening variety such as 'Super Chile', and not only will you get fantastic chillies at around five times the heat of supermarket chillies, but you can expect 200–300 per plant. Their thin skin and small size makes spice chillies very easy to dry.

Bird's Eye These small chillies (illustrated overleaf, middle) are much used in Southeast Asian cuisine. They can be astronomically hot (up to 200,000 SHUs), although those you find in British shops are often relatively tame.

Jalapeño These chillies (illustrated overleaf, bottom) are useful all-rounders. Moderately hot, they become spicier as they mature from green to red (though usually sold green). Very good deseeded and sliced raw into salsas, or stuffed and fried.

Super Chile Hugely productive and easy to grow, this is pretty assertive at 36,000 SHUs. It takes superbly to drying.

Stumpy A variety for those with limited space, this grows like a diminutive bunch of flowers and is perfectly happy on a sunny windowsill. It is highly productive and its hot fruit (27,000 SHUs) are great all-rounders. The stunning 'Fairy Lights' (pictured right), which is even hotter, is another great choice for container growing.

C

Habaneros

These belong to the spice chilli group but their distinctive fruitiness sets them apart. Most are very hot, but I would recommend trying something milder too, such as 'Apricot' or 'Bellaforma'. Try them raw, or in a warm salad of contrasting flavours, such as feta, mangetout and strawberries. These mild varieties also tune you in to the similar fine, fruity, aromatic characteristics in stronger habaneros such as hot Scotch Bonnet, a Jamaican chilli that rates as high as 55,000 SHUs.

Apricot One of my very favourite chillies, this is mild enough to eat like an apple, releasing bursts of apricot and even kiwi flavours and aromas. At their best when pale apricot in colour, apricot chillies are great in salads, stuffed, or raw.

Scotch Bonnet Named for its shape (illustrated right, top) and famed for its heat, in reality, this chilli is milder than many other habaneros. It's good for almost any chilli application but especially in sauces and salsas. If you fancy growing one, search out 'Trinity' (40,000 SHUs), the best I've tried.

Turtle Claw This is a thin, knobbly chilli that ripens not to red but to lemon yellow, offering plenty of the classic habanero fruitiness with a distinctive lemon zestiness. It is very hot (96,000 SHUs) and very good.

Super-hots

These are the hottest of the habaneros, often hitting 500,000 SHUs. The 'Dorset Naga', one of the hottest chillies in the world, can be over 1 million SHUs. I am not remotely interested in eating ultra-hot varieties – what flavour there might be is drowned in pain and discomfort. But some of the less incendiary super-hots can be superb.

Piri-piri This Portuguese hot chilli, ranging from 100,000–250,000 SHUs, is used to make the eponymous sauce for piri-piri chicken.

Usually chillies get hotter as they ripen, but also sweeter. So a red fruit will probably be a little spicier but also less sharp than a green one of the same variety. But heat can vary a lot, even with similar chillies from the same plant. To test a chilli's heat relatively safely, cut off the stem end and run a moistened fingertip across the cut flesh and then on to your tongue: if it's not excruciatingly hot, test again by dabbing the tip of your tongue on the chilli. If the heat needs diluting, remove the seeds and white membrane, both of which hold disproportionate levels of capsaicin, the chemical that delivers that heat. As the heat doesn't dissipate with cooking, it's wise to use chillies judiciously.

If you are ever in need of something to soothe a chillied mouth, resist the temptation to reach for water: something lactic, fatty or starchy such as yoghurt, cheese or bread, will help alleviate chilli burn on the tongue.

Dried chillies

Their water driven off by sun, heat or smoke, dried chillies have their own intense, sweet appeal. They can be used as they are, dropped whole into stews or curries, or coarsely chopped, processed or crumbled first. However, in Mexican cooking, where they are used often, they are typically deseeded and lightly toasted in a pan for a couple of minutes, then soaked in hot water for 20–30 minutes. The reconstituted chillies can then be turned into a paste and added to stews, soups, sauces and salsas.

Chipotle Usually available as whole dried chillies, chipotles (illustrated overleaf) are smoke-dried jalapeños, which, while varying in size and heat, tend to pack a fair punch.

C

They have an incredible smoky flavour and are perfect for slow cooking – in a bolognese or chilli con carne, for example – though I tend to take the chilli out before eating as the combination of heat and smoke is lovely just left as a ghost.

Ancho This is a dried poblano chilli. Mild in flavour, it is a favourite in Mexican cooking where fruitiness and gentle heat are what is desired.

Guajillo A moderate red chilli, this is perfect for most Mexican recipes, from mole to enchiladas, where a little more heat than ancho is required.

Dried chilli flakes Derived from whole dried chillies, these are useful for adding a quick-and-easy blast of heat to a dish, but bear in mind that they lose their essential oils and some of their subtlety much more quickly than whole dried chillies. Buy in small quantities and don't let them hang around in your storecupboard for too long.

Growing your own chillies

Growing chillies is easy as long as you sow them early, and shower them with heat, light and feed. Sow in modules in a propagator, airing cupboard (just until germinated) or on a warm windowsill in February ideally, March at the very latest. Hold your nerve: germination can take a month. Keep the compost lightly damp the whole time. Once germinated, chillies grow best at around 20°C with a minimal drop in temperature overnight. Pot into 10cm pots when the roots show at the bottom of the modules, then feed fortnightly with a good tomato or seaweed feed. When the roots appear at the base of the pot, transplant to the ground or pot in which they will grow to maturity. The earliest ripening varieties may produce fruit when grown outside in a very good summer, but a greenhouse, polytunnel or sunny windowsill is a safer option. Consider starting with seedlings for a slightly easier life.

If you have a good crop, chillies take surprisingly well to freezing, retaining their flavour, aroma and structure well. Freeze in a single layer on a tray, then bag them up. When defrosted, use them as fresh.

Drying your own chillies

If you have a bulk of fresh chillies, it is worth drying them. Chillies will dry spread out on a warm windowsill, but this can take a couple of weeks. For best results, halve the chillies and dry them in a very low oven (below 100°C); this can take anything from 30 minutes to 5 hours – the slower the better.

Other sources of chilli heat

Chilli powders are useful for delivering easily measurable and controllable heat. I particularly like cayenne pepper (page 128), which is fairly hot (30,000–50,000 SHUs), though some generic chilli powders can be worthwhile. Whatever the form of chilli powder, don't be tempted to toast it in a pan as you might other spices, as the dust can become airborne and irritate the throat and eyes.

Chilli sauces abound, with Tabasco perhaps the best known. Made solely using hot tabasco chillies, vinegar and salt, it makes a fine shortcut to heat – sprinkle a little into sauces, stews and even on to pizzas for an instant chilli hit.

Harissa is a North African sauce made from a blend of chillies, sweet peppers, garlic and spices, with some varieties including other flavours such as tomatoes or rose petals. Its sweet, aromatic chilliness is great as a marinade for fish or meat (lamb especially), as a dip, added to stews or with poached or scrambled eggs.

ROASTED CHILLI MOLE

About 10g medium-hot dried chillies, such as 2 guajillos or chipotles

50g hazelnuts

50g almonds or cashew nuts

1 tbsp sunflower seeds

1 large onion, cut into 8–12 wedges

4 garlic cloves, peeled

1 tsp black peppercorns

1 star anise

6 cloves

¼ cinnamon stick

4 large, ripe tomatoes, halved

3 tbsp olive or rapeseed oil

750ml chicken or veg stock

2 tbsp raisins or sultanas

1 free-range chicken (1.5–2kg), jointed, or 4–6 chicken joints, or 2 medium young rabbits, jointed

25g dark chocolate (at least 70% cocoa solids), grated or finely chopped

Cayenne pepper (optional)

Lime juice, to taste

Sea salt

A mole ('mole-ay') is a traditional Mexican chilli sauce for meat, often thickened with nuts and enriched with dark chocolate, to warm, spicy effect. This recipe is delicious with chicken but, if you are lucky enough to be in possession of a couple of young, tender rabbits, they will work well too (the cooking isn't long enough to tenderise older, tougher meat). Use dried chillies of your choice – guajillos are good for a nice medium heat, while chipotles give the sauce a lovely smoky depth as well as real kick. Serves 4–6

Preheat the oven to 180°C/Fan 160°C/Gas 4.

De-stem and roughly chop the dried chillies. Place them in a large roasting tray with the nuts, seeds, onion, garlic cloves and spices. Add the tomato halves, cut side up, and trickle with 2 tbsp oil. Roast in the oven for 25–30 minutes, stirring once or twice.

Add the stock and raisins to the roasting tray, give the mixture a good stir and return to the oven for 20 minutes. Remove and allow to cool slightly.

Tip the contents of the roasting tray into a jug blender and blitz to a purée. A good blender should reduce the sauce to a pretty smooth consistency but if there are large pieces of dried spices or tomato skin remaining in the mix, pass it through a sieve.

Wipe out the roasting tray with kitchen paper, then add the chicken or rabbit pieces. Season them all over with salt and pepper and trickle with a little more oil. Roast in the oven for 25–30 minutes or until sizzling and golden – turn up the heat a little if the meat is slow to colour.

Pour the mole sauce around the meat, lower the oven setting to 160°C/Fan 140°C/Gas 3 and cook for about 45 minutes, turning the pieces once, or until the meat is tender and the sauce nicely thickened. Remove the meat to a warmed serving dish.

Stir the chocolate into the sauce and season to taste with salt. If it's a little thick, you can 'let it down' with a ladleful more hot stock or water. If you're hankering for more heat, give it a pinch of cayenne.

Spoon the sauce over the meat and give it a spritz of lime juice. Serve with freshly cooked rice, plain yoghurt (perhaps with some chopped coriander stirred in) and tortilla chips.

Chives

Pam Corbin

LATIN NAME
Allium schoenoprasum

SEASONALITY
April–October

MORE RECIPES
Barley and raw mushroom salad (page 47); Megrim with crab and chives (page 380); Pike with leeks and chervil sauce (page 470); Dab in a bag (page 230); Herbed pouting fish fingers (page 501); Winkles in oatmeal (page 677)

A neat, perennial, clump-forming herb, chives belong to the ever-useful allium (onion) family. With their pinkish-purple (sometimes white), almost spherical flowerheads and their slender, silky, tubular, blue-green leaves, they are the prettiest herbs in the garden. Standard chives have a delicate, leek-like flavour, while their cousins, garlic chives (aka Chinese chives) predictably yield a more garlicky tang. These sport flat leaves with star-shaped white flowers.

You can buy packets of cut chives but it's hardly worth it because their flavour fades fast once harvested. However, these relatively robust herbs are easy to grow, especially in a rich, moist soil with plenty of sun. A trusted companion plant, chives help scare off carrot fly and deter blackspot. A great cut-and-come-again herb, the chive season extends from mid-spring throughout the summer. To encourage succulent second and third crops, simply cut the chives right back to the ground after flowering, water well and they will supply plentifully until dormancy strikes in the autumn.

Leaf, flower and flower stalk (scape) can all be eaten; the younger the better for optimum flavour. The flowers should be pinched out into their tiny, constituent blooms.

Chives are endlessly useful in the kitchen – either on their own, or as part of the *fines herbes* quartet (with parsley, tarragon and chervil). They work particularly well with eggs; snipped at the last minute into buttery scrambled eggs, omelettes or freshly made egg sandwiches. Mixed with soured cream or cream cheese, they make a lively mix to swirl into beetroot or parsnip soup, or a seafood bisque, or to pile into crisp-skinned jacket potatoes. Add chopped chives to salad dressings and toss the pinched-out flowers into leafy green salads, on to soups or over just-baked pizza.

Chive butter is easily made by blending 3–4 tbsp of freshly chopped chives with 125g butter, a little lemon juice, salt and black pepper. This is great melted over hot boiled potatoes, worked into mash, or served with grilled or poached fish. Chives can be added to cheesy scones or breads and rolled in pastry. This is as much cooking as I'd give them, though – too much heat robs them of their beautiful allium flavour.

CHIVE BUCKWHEAT BLINIS WITH HARD-BOILED EGGS

Fluffy little buckwheat blinis, infused with the flavour of chives, are delicious topped with warm hard-boiled egg and soured cream. They're also a great vehicle for smoked mackerel or trout. Makes 40–50

200ml whole milk

175ml plain wholemilk yoghurt

2 medium eggs, separated

70g buckwheat flour

100g strong white bread flour

1 tsp fine sea salt

5g fast-acting dried yeast

4 tbsp finely chopped chives

A little melted butter or rapeseed oil

TO SERVE

100g soured cream

6 still-warm hard-boiled eggs, chopped

4 tbsp finely chopped chives

Sea salt and black pepper

Warm the milk and yoghurt together in a small saucepan until tepid. Remove from the heat and whisk in the egg yolks.

In a large bowl, combine the flours, salt and yeast, then stir in the milk mix until smooth. Cover and leave to ferment until bubbly and almost doubled in volume – up to 4 hours.

Heat a large, heavy-based frying pan or flat griddle over a medium-high heat.

In a clean bowl, whisk the egg whites until stiff, then gently fold into the batter with the chopped chives, trying to keep as much air in the mix as possible.

Wipe the pan/griddle with a little butter or oil. Drop heaped teaspoonfuls of batter into the pan and gently spread out a little with the back of the spoon. Cook for 1–2 minutes or until bubbles rise to the surface of the blinis, then flip and cook the other side for a similar time. Transfer to a plate once cooked and repeat with the remaining batter.

Smear a small dollop of soured cream on to each blini, top with the chopped egg and scatter over the chopped chives. Season with a little salt and pepper and serve.

Chocolate

Nikki Duffy

SOURCING

chococo.co.uk; divinechocolate.com; seedandbean.co.uk

Rarely has a food been mythologised, desired and deplored in such mercurial measure as this one. What other ingredient stands for so much? Both luxury and cheapness, the sacred and the profane – even good health and bad, depending on how you buy your bar. Chocolate's raw ingredient, cacao, is richly flavoured, devilishly dark, bracingly bitter and contains a stimulant, theobromine. When combined with sugar, it creates a unique foodstuff that many of us crave, covet and adore.

In its pure form, cacao is rich in fats and contains protein, vitamins, minerals and antioxidants. Theobromine is one of its more interesting components (from *theobroma*, the Latin name of the cacao tree, which means 'food of the gods'). This bitter-tasting alkaloid is a stimulant, similar to but weaker than caffeine. It is also the reason why chocolate is toxic to dogs; if a human ate enough chocolate (several kilos), it would finish them off too. The darker the chocolate, the more theobromine it contains. Chocolate also contains phenylethylamine – a neurotransmitter associated with joyful feelings. Some say it's the reason why chocolate makes you happy, but there doesn't seem to be enough to make this plausible, nor is there scientific evidence to support the theory. It's more likely the mouth-feel or taste of chocolate – possibly, just the *idea* of chocolate itself – that gives the sensation that one's soul has, at least briefly, been satisfied.

Chocolate is a child of the American rainforests. Cacao beans were first made into a sustaining drink millennia ago by the Olmec civilisation in ancient Mexico (1500–500 BC), and dark, bitter cacao brews were hugely important to Mesoamerican people for many centuries afterwards. The Maya associated cacao with human blood, used it in their rituals and buried their noble dead with cups of it. They even daubed liquid cacao on their newborn children in an act of theobromic baptism. In fact evidence suggests that for hundreds of years, the inhabitants of this region were knocking back buckets of the stuff, their harsh cacao drinks spiked with chilli and vanilla, herbs and flowers, and often whipped up to a froth. It was the Aztecs, around 600 years ago, who first added honey to their cacao, creating the sweet chocolate flavour we so love today.

Via the brutality of conquest and the labour of slaves, cacao began to cast its spell across the world. The Spanish and Portuguese realised how lucrative a trade in this dark delicacy could be and as the centuries passed, chocolate insinuated its way into the culture of all of Europe. In seventeenth-century London, chocolate was quaffed as an alternative libation in the flourishing coffee houses. It wasn't until the eighteenth century that the idea of eating solid chocolate gained currency but, thereafter, there was no stopping it. The first modern chocolate bar was manufactured by Fry's in 1847.

West Africa is the main source of cacao today, though it is grown in many other places, including Mexico and South America as well as Indonesia. Most of the cacao beans produced are of the 'Forastero' variety – robust and reliable. Finer but more temperamental 'Criollo' cacao is grown in much smaller quantities and used, blended with other beans or sometimes just on its own, to make the very highest-end chocolate. 'Trinitario' is a hybrid of Forastero and Criollo.

Cacao is a commodity, often sold by farmers to manufacturers in other countries, and the price on the international market fluctuates, leaving small producers vulnerable. This is why chocolate is one of the foods most associated with the Fairtrade movement. However, there are other things to look for if you want to make an ethical chocolate choice. If chocolate is processed 'bean to bar' entirely in the country of origin, there are huge benefits to the local economy. There are some fabulous chocolates made sustainably in small quantities in the place where the cacao beans are grown. More expensive than your average bar they may be – but you are paying for quality, expertise, ethics and traceability. The price reflects what chocolate can be at its best – not a sugary, padded-out, quick-fix snack, but a rich and satisfying ingredient, revered since ancient times and imbued with a little bit of dark magic.

Chocolate production

The process begins when mature cacao pods are split open and the seeds and pulp inside scraped out and allowed to ferment in 'sweat boxes' for a few days. Properly managed fermentation is crucial in reducing tannins and beginning the development of all the gorgeous chocolatey flavours that will later be apparent; a brief period of germination occurs during the fermentation process too, so cacao beans are in a sense malted, another reason for their complex flavour.

The fermented beans are then dried, de-husked and broken into little bits; these are cacao or cocoa 'nibs'. With a distinct bitterness as well as a chocolatey flavour, raw cacao nibs are now appreciated as a darkly delicious health food: unsweetened, dairy-free and full of vitamins, minerals and antioxidants. You can buy them as tiny, crunchy nuggets – fantastic in muesli, granola or flapjacks – or as a powder, which can be used in baking, smoothies, or to make virtuous treats such as raw brownies. Raw cacao is pricey but delivers an intense flavour punch.

Most cacao beans are destined for a more indulgent use: roasted before being de-husked, the nibs are then ground into a paste known as cocoa 'mass'. If the natural fat in the mix – cocoa butter – is removed from this, what remains is cocoa powder (see page 189). If, instead, the cocoa mass has further ingredients added to it, such as extra fat, sugar and vanilla, it becomes chocolate as we know it.

Milk chocolate contains milk solids and usually a lot of sugar. Many brands include soya emulsifiers as well as vegetable fats such as palm oil. Dark chocolate does not usually have dairy products added (though it may contain traces of them), but it is generally still sweetened with sugar. White chocolate is not true chocolate as it contains only cocoa butter, milk and sugar. Ultra-sweet, it benefits from the twang of vanilla or other spices to make it appealing.

Cooking with chocolate

For most culinary uses, dark chocolate is the best choice: it packs rich chocolate flavour, without too much sweetness, and the higher cocoa solid content makes it more stable when heated. However, it's not true to say that very high cocoa solids always equates to very high quality. That is determined by the beans themselves, the skill with which they are fermented and roasted, and the ingredients that go into the finished bar.

Chocolate with solids in the region of 70–80 per cent works well in most recipes – higher than that and the chocolate can be very bitter. 'Cocoa solids' is a blanket term that includes the dark, chocolatey element (essentially cocoa powder) and the cocoa butter. In the right measure, cocoa butter makes for a wonderful eating experience.

Chocolate contains a vast spectrum of flavour compounds – berry, nutty, woody, winey, floral, smoky, leathery, buttery, caramely – and the cocoa butter in the mix helps to release those magical tastes upon the tongue. Artisan chocolate producers often add a little extra cocoa butter to their blends, whereas in cheap chocolate, cocoa butter is taken out and replaced with bland vegetable fats.

The complex mix of sugars, liquids and fats within chocolate can sometimes lead to mishaps when it is heated. Melting chocolate should be done gently, with occasional stirring, so that it does not burn. Once this happens, it's pretty much irretrievable. Another problem can occur if molten chocolate comes into contact with a small amount of water – the sugar particles within it stick together and the chocolate 'seizes' into a thick, grainy mass. (Larger quantities of liquid won't have the same effect because the sugar is dissolved.) Seized chocolate can be rescued by reheating it gently while stirring in a little hot cream or a flavourless oil. Sometimes melting chocolate mixed with lots of cream, as for ganache or truffles, can 'split' into grainy cocoa and a pool of oily fat. Try gradually whisking in a little hot milk to rescue it. In both these cases, the consistency of the chocolate is loosened, however, which may affect your recipe.

CHOCOLATE, BRANDY AND STAR ANISE ICE CREAM

3–5 star anise

200ml whole milk

300ml double cream

Finely grated zest of 1 large orange

1 vanilla pod, split lengthways

4 medium egg yolks

100g caster sugar

200g dark chocolate (70–75% cocoa solids), finely chopped

75ml cider brandy or Calvados

A gorgeously grown-up ice cream, this mingles the fruity, bittersweet flavour of chocolate with warming star anise, a hint of orange and a sup of brandy. Serves 6–8

Using a pestle and mortar, bash the star anise to reduce to chunky bits. Tip into a pan with the milk, cream and orange zest. Scrape the seeds from the vanilla pod into the pan; add the pod too. Bring almost to a simmer, then set aside to infuse for 15 minutes.

Beat the egg yolks and sugar together in a bowl until well combined. Strain the hot cream through a fine sieve on to the eggs and sugar, whisking all the time. Pour into a clean pan and cook gently, stirring, for a few minutes, until thickened. Don't let it boil or it will split.

Remove from the heat, add the chocolate and stir gently until it has melted. Stir in the cider brandy, then strain through a sieve into a clean bowl. Lay a piece of cling film or baking parchment on the surface to stop a skin forming, then set aside to cool.

Churn the custard in an ice-cream maker until soft-set, then transfer to the freezer to freeze solid. (Alternatively, pour the mixture into a plastic container and freeze for about an hour, or until starting to solidify around the sides, then mash with a fork, mixing the frozen sides into the liquid centre. Put it back in the freezer for another hour, and repeat at hourly intervals until soft-set, then let the ice cream freeze solid.)

Transfer the ice cream to the fridge 30 minutes before serving, to soften a little.

Chorizo

Steven Lamb

MORE RECIPES
Portuguese paprika potatoes (page 429); Migas (page 89); Oat-coated puffball with sage and pancetta (page 507); Paella (page 163)

SOURCING
dorsetcharcuterie.co.uk; forestpig.com; good-game.co.uk; threelittlepigschorizo.co.uk

Chorizo can be many things: a fresh sausage for cooking, a cured and dried salami, or even a kind of loose meat 'relish'. But it is essentially highly spiced and seasoned minced pork, given a characteristic flavour and colour with rich, red *pimentón* (paprika).

The best chorizos are usually from Spain and the finest are made with pork from the traditional black Ibérico breed (see page 300). There are, however, some great British chorizos too. Be warned: the term 'chorizo' is not protected – anyone can put it on a product, and there are some pretty poor examples out there. Chorizo can legally include horse or donkey meat and, wherever you stand on that, they certainly taste inferior to pork chorizos. Some are coloured with cochineal which, if not objectionable, is unnecessary. Check the labels for information and always buy from a knowledgeable source such as a Spanish food specialist or direct from the producer.

Cured chorizo salami can be used in recipes, but it's at its best uncooked – simply sliced and served as a delicious nibble. A fresh or 'cooking' chorizo, which contains only enough salt to season it rather than preserve it, is the one to chop and fry, so that it releases its glorious, smoky red fat, to which you can add all manner of fish, veg, breadcrumbs, rice or other grains.

A Mexican-style 'loose' chorizo (i.e. not in a sausage skin) can be crumbled and fried then used to enhance omelettes or other egg dishes, heaped into tacos or mixed with veg such as broad beans. It makes a superb accompaniment to a delicate plate of scallops or crab, and you could even use it to pep up home-made Scotch eggs.

Such 'loose' chorizo is hard to buy in this country but it is easy to make up your own. For a good moist mix, you want minced pork containing about 20 per cent fat, which usually means shoulder meat. If possible, get a butcher to prepare it for you (though organic or free-range pork mince will do). For perfect seasoning, chorizo mince should contain salt (1–1.5 per cent), smoked paprika (either hot or sweet/mild or both), cayenne and garlic but, beyond that, you can please your own palate. If you like your chorizo topping the Scoville scale, some harissa or fiery chilli can be added. Softer aromatics such as thyme and fennel seeds work well in the mix too – and a splosh of good red wine dampens the fire and brings a rounder flavour.

WHITE BEANS WITH CHORIZO AND TOMATO

Olive or rapeseed oil, for cooking

200g cooking chorizo, diced (or home-made 'loose' chorizo, see above)

4 medium-large tomatoes

A pinch of sugar (optional)

2 x 400g tins white beans, such as haricot or cannellini, or chickpeas, drained

Lemon juice, to taste

A handful of flat-leaf parsley leaves, roughly chopped

Sea salt and black pepper

This is delicious on toast, or served as a side dish. In the winter, you can use a 400g tin in place of the fresh tomatoes: cook for slightly longer – up to 20 minutes – until reduced down, and add a couple of pinches of sugar to counteract the acidity if needed. Serves 4–6

Heat a trickle of oil in a large, heavy-based pan over a medium-high heat. Add the chorizo and fry, stirring often, until the edges are beginning to crisp and darken.

Halve the tomatoes and grate the flesh side directly into the pan, using a coarse grater; discard the skins. Reduce the heat to medium. Season with a little pinch of salt and a good grinding of pepper and leave to simmer for 6–8 minutes or until thickened and really flavoursome. Taste the tomatoes – you may need to add a pinch of sugar if they weren't at their peak of ripeness to begin with.

Stir the beans or chickpeas into the sauce and heat through for 4–5 minutes. Remove from the heat, taste and adjust the seasoning if needed and add lemon juice to taste. Stir the chopped parsley through and serve.

Cider

Steven Lamb

MORE RECIPES
English onion soup (page 613);
Chicken and cider stew with
rosemary dumplings (page 617);
Braised rabbit with turnips
(page 652)

SOURCING
camra.org.uk;
bristolcidershop.co.uk

Despite living in Dorset in the West Country – the centre of the cider universe – this is rarely my first choice of drink. But when it comes to using cider as a cooking ingredient, I just can't leave it alone. To me, its complex flavours and strong, yeasty character seem more balanced and accessible when they form part of a dish than when they are being glugged along with it.

It's hardly surprising that a drink brewed from apples makes such a great and versatile ingredient: it can be sweet, sour or somewhere in between, and boasts a whole array of toasty, floral, fruity flavours. And, although artisanal cider is mostly made in autumn and quaffed through the summer, it has year-round applications in cooking. It is excellent as a base for gravy, in a creamy sauce to go with pork, or as the steaming liquor for mussels – and really comes into its own in a brine for the Boxing Day ham. In salad dressings, its sharpness can lift any leaf, and I can't think of anything better to add to a gamey stew or casserole. It will even improve the taste of apples in a pie or crumble – just pre-cook the fruit with a glassful before topping. I prefer to use dry, sparkling ciders for cooked dishes and flat, sweet ciders for dressings.

The best ciders are those made using traditional cider apple varieties such as 'Kingston Black' or 'Northern Spy'. When pressed and fermented, these sour fruits develop a range of complex flavours. Old-school, still, cloudy ciders are generally the preserve of real ale pubs or home-brew enthusiasts. The bottled ciders you buy in the shops are usually filtered, fizzed and pasteurised – but they can still be very good. It's the worst of the bunch you want to avoid, i.e. bulk-buy ciders concocted from juice concentrate and heaps of sugar.

Perry is very different from cider. Fermented from pears, it has a fresh and light character, and is often a little sweet. Traditional perry is made from specific pear varieties, such as 'Late Treacle' and 'Dumbleton Huffcap', which are much higher in tannins and acids than dessert pears. Good perry, a speciality of Herefordshire, Gloucestershire and Worcestershire, is quite tricky to find; the much broader term 'pear cider' can cover a multitude of sins as it can be made from any pears, and may be from concentrate.

CIDER ONION GRAVY

1 tbsp olive or rapeseed oil

20g butter

2 large or 3 medium onions, finely sliced

2 garlic cloves, finely chopped

1 tsp thyme leaves

1 tbsp chopped sage

2 tsp plain flour

250ml dry cider

250ml chicken or veg stock

Sea salt and black pepper

Use a sharp, dry cider for this big, bold gravy, to complement the caramelised sweetness of the slowly cooked onions. It's delicious, of course, with sausages – but also with pheasant or pork chops. Serves 4

Place a large heavy-based pan over a medium heat and add the oil and butter. When bubbling, add the onions and garlic and cook, stirring regularly, for 4–5 minutes.

Scatter over the thyme and sage, season with salt and pepper and stir well. Place a close-fitting lid on the pan and turn the heat down low. Cook for 15–20 minutes, stirring occasionally, until golden and tender.

Work the flour into the soft onions and cook for another minute, then stir in the cider and stock and bring back to a simmer, stirring. Allow the gravy to bubble for 10–12 minutes so that it reduces and thickens slightly. Taste and add more salt and pepper if necessary before serving.

Cinnamon

Tim Maddams

LATIN NAME
Cinnamomum verum

ALSO KNOWN AS
True cinnamon, Ceylon
cinnamon

MORE RECIPES
North African shepherd's pie
(page 335); Fragrant beef curry
(page 350); Indian spiced
grilled quail (page 510); Pears
with ricotta, honey and thyme
(page 536); Masala chai doodh
(page 384)

This wonderfully warm, smoky spice has enjoyed great status for a very long time. The Greeks flavoured their wine with it, the Romans threw it on funeral pyres for the rich, while the Egyptians offered it to their gods. I tend to use it more in cakes and curries, but I am no less impressed by it.

Cinnamon is the soft under-bark of the *Cinnamomum verum* tree, shaved and dried into sticks, or quills. You can buy it whole or ready ground. As with any spice, I'd recommend grinding it yourself – or, where appropriate, using it whole and then removing it before serving. However, cinnamon quills are among the most difficult spices to grind at home, being tough and woody. You need a good electric grinder to get a fine result. If you don't have one, recently bought ready-ground cinnamon is the best option.

Cinnamon's sweet, woody aroma comes from compounds including eugenol (also found in cloves and basil) and linalool, which is floral. Its warm, sweet character makes it a classic baking spice. And cinnamon toast is a treat: mix brown sugar, soft butter and ground cinnamon and spread on toast, then grill again until the sugar just starts to caramelise.

However, cinnamon certainly shouldn't be confined to sweet dishes. Its warmth and character are welcome as a background note in spiced stews and sauces, including ketchups, pickles, curries and tagines. It's very good in the meaty layer of a moussaka – and in other aubergine dishes. And it's wonderful with squashes (see below).

Cassia is a similar spice from the same tree family. Often seen as being inferior to cinnamon, it is less delicate, more hot and bitter. Quite a lot of what is sold as cinnamon is actually cassia. It may be declared on the ingredients panel, or it may be described as 'Chinese cinnamon' – but in some cases, there is no way to tell. The best tactic is to look for cinnamon that comes from Sri Lanka or India – it's likely to be the real deal.

SQUASH AND CINNAMON SOUP WITH ROASTED SEEDS

Cinnamon has a legendary affinity with squashes (as in pumpkin pie) and this vibrant soup is a lovely savoury way to exploit it. Serves 4

1 squash, such as butternut or kabocha (700–800g)

2 knobs of butter

1 cinnamon stick, broken in half

1 medium red onion, quartered

2 garlic cloves, peeled

3 tbsp olive or rapeseed oil

2 tbsp pumpkin seeds

2 tbsp sunflower seeds

½ tsp caster sugar

½–1 tsp dried chilli flakes, to taste

1 tsp ground cinnamon

500ml hot veg stock

2–3 tsp clear honey

Sea salt and black pepper

Extra virgin olive or rapeseed oil, to finish

Preheat the oven to 180°C/Fan 160°C/Gas 4.

Halve the squash, scoop out the seeds and place the two halves, cut side up, on a baking tray. Divide the butter, cinnamon stick, onion and garlic between the squash cavities. Trickle the squash with 2 tbsp oil, and season with salt and pepper. Roast for about an hour until soft and caramelised.

Meanwhile, put the pumpkin and sunflower seeds into a bowl and scatter over the sugar, chilli flakes and a pinch of salt. Add 1 tbsp oil and toss to coat the seeds in the mixture. Tip them into a small roasting tin, spread out and toast in the oven alongside the squash for 5–6 minutes, until the seeds are coloured and sizzling. Remove from the oven, scatter over the ground cinnamon then allow to cool.

When the squash is cooked, discard the cinnamon stick. Put the cooked onion and garlic into a blender. Scoop out the flesh from the squash skins and add this to the blender too. Add the stock, honey and a little more salt and pepper. Purée until smooth, adding a little more stock if needed.

Reheat the soup if necessary and pour into warmed bowls. Finish with a trickle of extra virgin oil (or a spoonful of yoghurt), scatter over the spicy roasted seeds and serve.

Clams

Nick Fisher

LATIN NAME
Palourdes: *Ruditapes decussatus*.
Sand-gapers: *Mya arenaria*.
Warty venus: *Venus verrucosa*.
Surf clams: *Spisula solida*.
Manila clams: *Venerupis philippinarum*. Grey hardshell: *Mercenaria mercenaria*

ALSO KNOWN AS
Vongole; palourdes also called cross-cut carpet shell clams

SEASONALITY
Avoid in spring and summer when spawning and when water quality may not be as good

HABITAT
Muddy, sandy and sometimes gravelly lower shore, in sheltered bays and estuaries all around the British Isles

MCS RATING
Most not assessed; farmed manila clams 1

MORE RECIPES
Cockle and chard rarebit (page 188); Paella (page 163)

SOURCING
goodfishguide.org

Clams are a conundrum. Like squid and pilchards, they are largely ignored – at worst, sneered at – on their home turf. When they play away, however, i.e. when some stylish Euro-classy nation has adopted them and renamed them *vongole*, suddenly they're special and cool. But have no doubt: the gorgeous *vongole* you eat with linguine in Venice most probably came from Bognor Regis or Poole Harbour.

Walk on to any mud flat around the south of England or west of Scotland at low tide and you'll be walking over clams. Hidden under the mud, belied only by small, tell-tale holes, are millions of them (and cockles, which are, after all, just another type of clam). We harbour manila clams (pictured right), palourdes, sand-gapers, warty venus, surf clams and various other species under our mud. But you will probably only encounter grey hardshell or manila clams on a fish counter.

The majority of British clams are 'hoovered' or dredged from the sea bed. Although these methods are more selective and less damaging than scallop dredging, since the clams are taken from small sections of ground, usually in muddy harbours and estuaries, hand-raked or farmed clams are always a more sustainable choice – though harder to find in fishmongers.

Shop-bought clams don't need to be purged of sand and grit; this will already have been done before sale. But any you've gathered yourself (see advice on gathering wild shellfish on page 399) should be purged in the same way as cockles (see page 188). Once purged, a good shake in a colander under a fast-running cold tap is generally all the cleaning they need.

The basic cooking techniques are the same as those for cockles and mussels. But first, I'd advise keeping your fresh, live clams safe in the fridge salad drawer, under a damp tea towel, while you make a decent fish stock (see page 612). I love a *spaghetti alle vongole*, but clams do not give this dish its rich *mamma mia* flavour; stock does. Similarly, clam chowder owes its heft to salt pork and sweetcorn. Not that clams are without flavour, but it's a subtle sea-sweet tang.

CURRIED CLAMS

1kg live clams

2 mild green or red chillies

1 tsp fennel seeds

2 tsp virgin coconut oil

1 tsp black mustard seeds

1 small onion, finely chopped

5cm piece of root ginger, grated

2 garlic cloves, crushed

About 20 fresh or 10 dried curry leaves (optional)

1 tsp garam masala

1 tsp ground black pepper

½ tsp mild chilli powder

½ tsp ground turmeric

½ tsp salt

100ml coconut milk

A panoply of spices and aromatics, coupled with creamy coconut milk, make for a sumptuous but very simple clam dish. You can do the same thing with cockles or mussels. Serves 2

Scrub the clams well under cold running water. Discard any with broken shells and any that are open and do not close if tapped sharply against the side of the sink.

Halve the chillies and deseed for less heat if you prefer, then slice thinly. Roughly bash the fennel seeds, using a pestle and mortar.

Melt the coconut oil in a large pan (that has a lid) over a medium heat. Add the mustard seeds and fry for about 30 seconds until they start to pop. Add the onion, chillies, ginger, garlic and curry leaves, if using, and fry for 4–5 minutes.

Add the garam masala, pepper, chilli powder, turmeric, fennel seeds and salt and cook for another 2 minutes. Stir in the coconut milk and 100ml water and bring to a simmer.

Give it a good stir then add the clams, put the lid on and cook for 3–4 minutes, shaking the pan once or twice, or until all the clams have opened. Discard any that refuse to open.

Serve the clams, and all their fragrant juices, with naan bread.

Cloves

Pam Corbin

LATIN NAME
Syzgium aromaticum

MORE RECIPES
Roasted chilli mole (page 173);
Indian spiced grilled quail
(page 510); Figs poached
in red wine (page 259)

C

Cloves have a unique flavour that works well with a variety of ingredients. Shaped like a small tack, their name comes from the Latin *clavus* or 'nail'. In fact, cloves are the unopened flowerbuds of a tall, evergreen Indonesian tree. They are available whole or as a ready-ground powder.

Less is more with ground cloves, so add by the pinch rather than the spoonful. To keep their assertive flavour in check, cloves are often blended and balanced with other spices. But don't be afraid of using them: spicy-hot and bitter, their warming floral tones are expansive and uplifting. They are used in Indian, African, Middle Eastern and European cooking, and they're a major ingredient in many traditional spice mixes – including garam masala, ras el hanout and Chinese five-spice – as well as old-fashioned pickling mixes and classic mixed spice.

Rich in an aromatic compound called eugenol (also found in cinnamon and nutmeg, as well as herbs such as basil), cloves have a particularly good rapport with fruit. They are delicious with citrus, orchard and dried vine fruits and will imbue fruit jellies or marmalade with fragrance and verve (as in the recipe opposite). Cloves also enhance fruit pies, crumbles and breads.

Create a ready-to-use clove sugar by warming 1 tbsp whole cloves for a minute or two in a frying pan, grinding to a powder then mixing with 1kg granulated or caster sugar. Use in cakes, poached fruits and creamy rice puddings.

Cloves are a familiar sight studded into marmalade-coated baked hams. A spoonful of cloves infused in milk with onions and bay makes bread sauce taste awesome, and one or two dropped into a beef stock or stew gives richness.

Mulled in wine with their spice comrades nutmeg and cinnamon, cloves radiate warmth – and a single clove in a mix of macerating gin and sloes will lend character.

SEVILLE ORANGE AND CLOVE MARMALADE

1kg Seville oranges, washed in warm water

About 24 cloves (or more if you prefer)

1 star anise

Juice of 2 lemons, strained

2kg granulated sugar

Cloves give a subtle, fragrant warmth to this preserve. If you want a more vivid spice hit, increase the quantity of cloves to 36, or more. Makes 5–6 x 450g jars

First sterilise your jars by washing them in hot soapy water, rinsing well, then putting them upside down on a baking tray in a very low oven (at 120°C/Fan 100°C/Gas ½) to dry and warm up.

Cut the Seville oranges in half and squeeze the juice and pips into a bowl. Using a sharp knife, slice the peel and pith into strips (thick or thin, as you like) and put into a separate large bowl.

Pass the juice through a sieve, retaining both juice and pips. Take the pips and tie them up in a square of muslin with the cloves and star anise. Add to the bowl of peel with the orange juice. Pour on 2.2 litres cold water and leave to soak overnight.

Transfer the contents of the bowl to a large, heavy-based pan or preserving pan. Bring to the boil, lower the heat and simmer slowly, partially covered, for about 2 hours until the peel is tender. Discard the muslin bag. If you don't have a sugar thermometer, put a saucer in the freezer to chill.

Add the lemon juice and sugar to the pan. Stir over a low heat until dissolved. Increase the heat and boil rapidly for 15–20 minutes until setting point is reached: 104°C on a sugar thermometer. Or, drop a little of the marmalade on to the cold saucer and return to the fridge for a minute, then push your finger through the marmalade. If it wrinkles, setting point has been reached. If not, boil for a few minutes more and test again.

Remove from the heat, leave to cool for 8–10 minutes (a little longer if the peel is chunky), then stir gently to disperse any scum. Pour into the warm jars and seal immediately.

Cockles

LATIN NAME
Cerastoderma edule

SEASONALITY
Avoid in spring and summer
when breeding and when water
quality may not be as good

HABITAT
Muddy, sandy and gravelly
lower shore, in sheltered bays
and estuaries all around the
British Isles

MCS RATING
2–3

REC MINIMUM SIZE
2cm

MORE RECIPES
Curried clams (page 184)

SOURCING
goodfishguide.org; msc.org

Cockles are found all around the coast of Britain, living just below the surface of sand, muddy-sand and gravel/mud/sand mixes. In sand the gentle application of a rake may be needed to extract them. In mud it is a matter of feeling for them – sometimes a little oval hole in the mud's surface provides a clue. Occasionally, no search is needed as they sit on the surface of sand or gravel in full view (though you'll only rarely find large numbers so exposed). They must be taken home fairly quickly in a bucket which contains either lots of sea water, or no water at all (in a bucket containing only a little water they soon drown because they try to breathe and the oxygen is quickly used up).

Wild cockles can accumulate quite a bit of sand inside so, once home, should be placed in a fairly wide container and covered generously with fresh, cold salted water (35g salt per litre of water), or fresh clean sea water. A larger surface area allows in the oxygen they need. You will see them open and close, and the water become slightly murky as they purge themselves, expelling the sand. Change the water every 8–10 hours. Two changes over 24 hours is ideal, but one change and 12–16 hours will do. After purging, rinse the cockles thoroughly in a colander under a fast-running cold tap. (Shop-bought cockles don't require purging but must be rinsed.) They can then be kept wrapped in a cold wet cloth in the fridge for 48 hours, but no longer.

Before cooking, discard any cockles with broken shells and make sure the others are alive by trying to open them – they should stay firmly shut. Steam the live cockles in a lidded pan with a little water or white wine and some garlic and/or herbs. Once cooked they will open; any that remain closed must be discarded. Cockles can also be cooked directly in stews, though you'll need to allow for the salty water they add.

You should never eat wild shellfish raw as they often harbour Norovirus, E. coli, or both. Check with your local Port Health Authority about any specific problems. In the event of an algal bloom, for instance, even cooking will not make shellfish safe.

My favourite time to collect cockles is September – before it gets too cold. It is hard to buy fresh, live British cockles these days. Although we harvest plenty, the vast majority are exported. However, you can sometimes find them in fishmongers and supermarkets and, if you're ever in the vicinity of traditional cockle-picking areas such as the Burry Inlet in South Wales, you may also be lucky.

COCKLE AND CHARD RAREBIT

250–300g chard leaves
(off their stalks), washed
(use the stalks for another dish)

A little olive or rapeseed oil

1kg live cockles

150ml white wine

50g butter

30g plain flour

100ml double cream

50g medium-strong Cheddar
or other well-flavoured hard
cheese, grated

4 slices of wholemeal bread

Sea salt and black pepper

This lovely pairing of cockles and chard works equally well with clams and spinach. Serves 4

Put the chard leaves in a large pan with the water that clings to them from washing and place over a high heat. Add a trickle of oil and season with some salt and pepper. Cover and cook for 3–4 minutes, shaking once or twice, or until the chard is tender. Tip into a colander. When cool, squeeze out the excess liquid from the chard then roughly chop it.

Place a large, wide pan that has a lid over a high heat. Add the cockles and wine, shake the pan and put the lid on. Steam for 2–4 minutes, shaking often, until the cockles have opened; discard any that don't. Tip into a sieve set over a large bowl to catch the liquor. When cool enough to handle, pick the cockle meat from the shells. Measure 150ml of the liquor – pouring it slowly, so any grit settled in the bottom of the bowl is left behind.

Melt the butter in a pan over a medium heat, stir in the flour and cook for 2–3 minutes. Whisk in the cockle juice, cook for 2 minutes until smooth and thick, then add the cream. Cook for a minute or two, then take off the heat. Fold in the cheese, cockles and chard.

Toast the bread and top with the rarebit mix. Grill until bubbling and golden, then serve.

Cocoa

Nikki Duffy

MORE RECIPES
Brandy and raisin truffles
(page 83)

SOURCING
equalexchange.co.uk;
traidcraftshop.co.uk

Once mature cacao pods have been split, the seeds and pulp inside fermented, dried, roasted and ground, and the cocoa fat or 'butter' removed, you are left with cocoa powder. This is the soul of chocolate – the repository for all that rich, fruity, complex flavour, unclouded at this point by sugar and containing very little fat. Cocoa powder is bitter but, combined with other ingredients, it delivers intense chocolatey flavour.

A tub of cocoa powder is a really useful storecupboard ingredient because it can be used with other staples – sugar, flour, butter, eggs – to make ultra-chocolatey things that can be just as luscious as those made with actual chocolate – old-fashioned brownies, for instance, are often cocoa based. In a plain sponge recipe, simply replace a couple of tablespoonfuls of the flour with cocoa to turn it into a chocolate cake.

For a super-quick, thick, hot chocolate sauce for 2–3 people, put 25g (3 tbsp) cocoa powder, 50g caster sugar and 100ml water in a small pan. Bring to the boil, whisking to combine, then simmer for 2 minutes, whisking occasionally so it doesn't stick. Stir in a pinch of salt if you like. A little cocoa can work magic in savoury dishes too, such as chillies, moles and meat rubs, adding smoky, deep flavour without sweetness.

Most of the cocoa powder in the UK is 'dutched'. This means it has been treated with alkaline potassium carbonate to neutralise its natural acidity. Dutched cocoa is darker, more mellow and more obviously chocolatey than untreated 'natural' cocoa. Natural cocoa, which is more fruity and has higher acidity, is the norm in the US. The two types behave differently in recipes where raising agents are involved. Natural cocoa reacts with alkaline ingredients such as bicarbonate of soda to create a rise; dutched cocoa does not. You can swap the cocoas in recipes such as sauces and ice creams (though the flavour will be different) but it's not a good idea in baking.

For cooking, always use an unsweetened cocoa powder. Once sugar and other ingredients are added, it becomes drinking chocolate. Cocoa is subject to the same ethical trade and supply issues as chocolate (see page 176), so choose a Fairtrade brand.

UPSIDE-DOWN CHOCOLATE PLUM PUDDING

100g wholemeal spelt flour
(or plain white flour)

35g cocoa powder

2 tsp baking powder

150g butter, softened, plus
extra for greasing

125g soft light brown or light
muscovado sugar

2 medium eggs

About 3 tbsp milk

FOR THE PLUM LAYER

About 400g ripe or almost-ripe
plums

25g butter

50g soft light brown or light
muscovado sugar

This luscious chocolate pud is also very good made with peeled, quartered, cored pears in place of the plums – or even sliced bananas. Serve it with cream or ice cream. Serves 6–8

Preheat the oven to 180°C/Fan 160°C/Gas 4. Butter a baking dish, about 2-litre capacity – a 20cm square one is ideal. Line the base with a square of buttered baking parchment.

For the plum layer, halve the plums and remove the stones. Arrange the plums, cut side up, in the base of the dish. Distribute the butter between them, putting a nugget of butter in the hollow of each plum half, then sprinkle over the sugar in a generous layer.

Thoroughly combine the flour, cocoa and baking powder and set aside. Beat the butter and sugar together for several minutes until very pale, light and fluffy. Beat in the eggs, one at a time, adding a spoonful of the flour mix with each. Then fold in the remaining flour mix. Fold in enough milk to give a firm dropping consistency.

Carefully dollop this mixture over the sugary plums to cover them and gently spread it out; it needn't reach the edges of the dish. Bake for about 50 minutes until the sponge is firm on top and the pudding doesn't wobble if you tap the dish. The tip of a small, sharp knife inserted into the middle should come out with just a little moist cake batter attached (the finished pud should still be slightly gooey around the fruit).

Leave to stand for 10 minutes or so, then run a knife around the edge of the dish, carefully invert the pudding on to a plate and peel away the parchment. Serve warm.

Coconut

Nikki Duffy

LATIN NAME
Cocos nucifera

SEASONALITY
Imported all year round

MORE RECIPES
Velvet crab curry (page 211);
Curried clams (page 184);
Fragrant beef curry (page 350);
Spinach, egg and potato curry
(page 599); Mango and banana
salad (page 374); Lime and
coconut mousse (page 358);
Linseed, banana and chocolate
muffins (page 359); Passionfruit
and coconut curd (page 441);
Piña colada (page 472)

SOURCING
biona.co.uk; cocozumi.com;
tiana-coconut.com

Until quite recently, coconut was an exotic item, known to most of us only as the basis for piña coladas and a certain confectionery bar. If you'd told me 10 years ago that I'd be waxing lyrical about this imported food, I might have looked doubtful, but coconut is fast becoming one of the hardest working ingredients in the British cook's larder.

Dry scatterings of desiccated coconut flesh are how most of my generation first encountered this giant palm tree seed, but they are probably its least interesting manifestation, as the distinct aroma of fresh coconut flesh is largely lost by the time it has been grated and dried. The creamy white coconut flesh from a whole nut is far superior, though dried coconut is still useful in cakes, lending an interesting texture.

Both crisp and succulent, owing to its oil-rich nature, the flesh of a freshly cracked nut tastes much more toastily coconutty and delicious than anything in a packet. Thinly sliced, that white flesh is fantastic in salads, sweet or savoury, or in a sambal to serve with curries (see overleaf). And shavings of roasted coconut, scattered with a little salt, are about as good as snacking gets.

Coconut milk is even more useful than the flesh – and certainly a little easier to access, since it comes in a tin. This creamy white liquid (not to be confused with clear coconut 'water') is made by adding water to shredded coconut flesh then pressing it. Coconut milk often separates in the tin, forming a thick, or even solid, layer on top and a watery one beneath. A vigorous shake before you open the tin may be enough to resolve this or, if the top layer is solid, scrape the lot into a pan and heat it gently, stirring until recombined.

Coconut milk has a definite but mild coconut flavour that forms a pleasing background in all kinds of dishes – from curries to cakes to cocktails. It's rich, though, (comprising, in part, emulsified coconut oil) so I nearly always temper it with another, lighter liquid such as water or stock. The perfect foil to fiery spices, it has a long tradition of use in curries and laksas but it's also good in humbler dishes – add some to a blenderful of leftover cooked veg, with stock and a pinch of cumin or coriander, and you have a fantastic, impromptu soup. It's a great medium for cooking fish and shellfish too.

At the sweet end of the spectrum, a chilled coconut rice pudding – made with half coconut milk, half dairy milk (or water) – is delicious. I also like a dash of coconut milk in tropical smoothies with fresh mango, lychees, melon, etc.

Do not be concerned if your coconut milk appears slightly grainy when cooked, or separates, forming a layer of oil on the surface. Both these are normal characteristics of the ingredient. You can stir the oil back in, or skim it off.

Tinned 'coconut cream', is a thicker, more coconut-rich version of coconut milk, while 'creamed coconut' is a little different: a solid block of pure, milled coconut that requires grating or dissolving, it can be mixed with hot water to replace coconut milk.

There is a plethora of other coconut products appearing on the shelves of health food shops and even supermarkets. Perhaps the most salient is creamy white, 'virgin' (unrefined) coconut oil (solid at room temperature), a fat with close to miraculous properties according to its fans. To sum up its merits in a (coco)nut shell: it is rich in lauric acid, a medium-chain fatty acid that is both absorbed and burnt off more quickly than most other culinary fats. There are studies that have shown lauric acid to have anti-microbial properties too and claims are made for it as a treatment for everything from acne to Alzheimer's. It's worth noting that there is also scepticism about these claims and the scientific debate about the merits of this product is ongoing.

C

Virgin coconut oil can be very useful in the kitchen: it is stable when heated up to its smoke point of around 177°C (similar to butter) and resistant to oxidisation. In the right context – spicy curries, for example – it imparts a subtle coconutty background flavour. It can also be used instead of butter in cakes and cookies. Although I prefer to use a completely unprocessed coconut oil, you can get steam-treated neutral-flavoured oils.

A noteworthy new storecupboard standby is coconut sugar (or nectar). Dark and with a caramel flavour, it is useful for baking and as a lower-GI alternative to standard sugar. Another is coconut flour, made from ground, dried coconut flesh. High in fibre and protein, it soaks up liquid like a sponge, but combined with lighter flours and/or binding and leavening ingredients such as eggs, it lends a nutty flavour in baking.

Tackling a fresh coconut

A coconut should feel heavy and emit sloshing sounds when shaken. To get at its flesh, first pierce two of the 'eyes' on top of the nut with a screwdriver and drain out the liquid (this is coconut water, which you can drink). Then hold the coconut in one hand and use the back of a large, heavy knife to tap the shell firmly, working round the 'equator', until it splits open (it will eventually). Bake the coconut halves at 200°C/Fan 180°C/Gas 6 for about 20 minutes then leave to cool, before prising the flesh away from the shell with a knife.

How green is your coconut?

It is possible that the boom in demand for coconut products could be cause for ecological concern. After all, coconuts grow in some of the same tropical regions as oil palms – a crop whose cultivation is wreaking environmental havoc.

On the plus side, in many of the regions where we source coconut products, including Indonesia, the Philippines, Sri Lanka and India, coconut palms are already ubiquitous and, because they can cling to poor, sandy soils, often grow where little else will. Many coconuts are still grown by small producers, but there is also evidence that mono-culture plantations of coconut, which are increasingly the way our demand for coconut is met, may not be sustainable as they deplete nutrients in the soil.

Choosing organic and fairly traded products is one way to tackle these concerns. CocoZumi coconut oil, which is sourced from a diverse agroforestry environment (i.e. the coconut palms grow alongside other plants and trees) is a good option.

COCONUT, SPINACH AND APPLE SAMBAL

100g fresh coconut flesh

50g baby spinach leaves, young kale or spring greens

1 medium-sized, hot, red or green chilli, finely chopped (seeds and all)

Juice of 1 lime

1 medium, crisp eating apple, such as Cox

Sea salt and black pepper

A sambal is a chilli-hot relish found in the cooking of Sri Lanka, Singapore, Indonesia and Malaysia. This simple, refreshing example makes a great accompaniment to veg curry or grilled fish. Serves 4

Grate the coconut on a medium grater. Remove any coarse stalks from the greens, then roll the leaves into tight, cigar-like wads and slice into very fine ribbons. Combine the coconut, greens and chilli.

Squeeze the lime juice into a bowl. Quarter, core and finely chop the apple, tossing it straight into the juice, so it doesn't discolour. Combine the juicy apple with the coconut mix and add some salt and pepper. Leave for about 15 minutes for the flavours to mingle, then toss again and serve.

Cod

LATIN NAME
Gadus morhua

SEASONALITY
Avoid February–April
when spawning

HABITAT
Northern Atlantic

MCS RATING
2–5

REC MINIMUM SIZE
50cm

MORE RECIPES
Pollack with courgettes and
cannellini beans (page 484);
Herbed pouting fish fingers
(page 501); Crumbed whiting
goujons with curried egg
tartare (page 673)

SOURCING
goodfishguide.org; msc.org

It's undeniable that cod is a fine fish. People who like fish love cod, and even people who don't really like fish fall for its charms. The big boneless fillets of sweet, meaty flesh have made it the family-friendly choice, for fish fingers, trips to the chippy and home cooking. But cod is, literally, a victim of its own success. It got so big that it became more a brand than a fish. But it's the fish, not the brand, that's in peril.

The collapse of the Newfoundland cod fishery at the end of the last century was a man-made disaster of appalling proportions and illustrated just how very finite fish populations are when faced with the indiscriminate power of today's fishing technologies. Our own North Sea fishery was taken to the brink of collapse too.

Cod are big, lazy bottom-dwellers. They lurk in the icy Atlantic, hoovering up pretty much whatever comes their way with their gaping mouths. They can live for 25 years and reach 90kg or more, but they grow slowly. They don't reach sexual maturity until 4–7 years of age, at around 50cm length, and this sedate pace of development makes them susceptible to overfishing. Voracious, non-selective methods net too many immature cod, eroding the population from the base upwards.

The global response to the cod crisis was, of necessity, dramatic and hard-hitting, from the 1992 moratorium on cod fishing off Newfoundland (still in place) to the decommissioning of huge numbers of UK fishing boats. Coupled with measures such as temporary closures, more selective methods and quota cuts, those actions have had an effect. Cod numbers are recovering in some areas. And other, fairly isolated, parts of the world have fished for cod sensibly pretty much all along. Icelandic stocks, for example, didn't suffer the same drastic drops as other zones.

But there are extreme variations in the condition of cod stocks worldwide. Our own North Sea cod is in recovery but stocks are not healthy yet. Yet, there is already impatience, fuelled by economic factors, for us to ramp up the pressure on cod again.

One reason for cod's continuing precarious status is the iniquitous practice of 'discarding', which sees thousands of tonnes of perfectly edible fish being wasted every year. Since cod are usually found on grounds abundant in other species, boats that have caught their full quota of cod will keep on fishing, hoping to catch other valuable fish for which they still have quota. Any 'over-quota' cod that turn up will be 'discarded' – dead. Tonnes of juvenile fish are also thrown back.

Thanks to pressure from a swathe of NGOs, including Greenpeace, the MCS, Client Earth, and our own Fish Fight campaign, a series of measures that will eventually amount to a ban on discards is being phased in as part of the EU Common Fisheries Policy. Only time will tell if these measures will be effectively and fairly implemented and lead to lasting stock recovery.

ICES (the International Council for the Exploration of the Sea) is a global body of scientists that assesses European fish stocks. They describe cod stocks in Icelandic waters, the northeast Arctic and the eastern Baltic as being at a sustainable level and well managed. Some cod from those regions is ranked as a good choice in the MCS's goodfishguide.org and some has gained accreditation from the MSC's scheme – you'll see it in shops bearing the MSC's blue 'tick' label. If you are set on cod, MSC-certified fish is the way to go – particularly line-caught.

But please consider some of the far less fraught alternatives. Cod is dominant because it's been in the market so long, but there is very little you can do with cod that you can't also do with pollack, coley, pouting or whiting. Their flesh may not match the curdy whiteness of cod and they are often smaller, but they taste just as good.

C

We need to knock cod from its piscine pedestal because, while it may have narrowly avoided extinction, it is still in difficult straits. It's time to cast our nets a little wider.

Fishing methods for cod

Cod are often caught by 'otter' trawl, using a large net, shaped like the top of a bottle. As the net is dragged over the seabed, the wide opening 'herds' the fish, which fall back into the narrow 'cod end'. Like any trawling, this involves some disturbance to the seabed (though it's not as destructive as beam-trawling). However, if the stock is healthy and the fishery well managed, otter-trawled cod is still rated as sustainable by the MCS.

But cod caught on a line is always going to be a sounder option. Line-fishing can target species much more effectively than a huge net and also results in a better quality catch (fish often die or get damaged in nets).

Longline fishing, where an extremely long line, to which many shorter, baited lines are attached, is laid out, is not without its problems. It can pose a particular threat to sea birds, which grab the baited hooks then get pulled underwater. But measures such as bird-scaring devices are alleviating this problem in some fisheries.

Handline fishing is one of the most sustainable methods. These days, that may mean a 200-metre line with eight hooks attached, 'jigged' up and down by computer and automatically reeled in when a set weight of fish is detected, but it doesn't damage the environment.

Salt cod

Although it has never really caught on in Britain, salt cod is popular in much of Europe. The dried fish is hard and leathery but, rehydrated in plenty of fresh water, it regains tenderness. In traditional brandade (where it's beaten with olive oil and soaked bread and/or mashed potatoes) or a rich, fishy stew, it contributes a unique, highly seasoned marine flavour. Happily, other white fish, including coley and pollack, can be salted very successfully – whether 'hard'-salted, or just given a light salting for an hour or two (see recipes on pages 197 and 484).

COD WITH FENNEL, CAPERS AND TOMATOES

1–2 tbsp olive or rapeseed oil

1 fennel bulb, trimmed and finely sliced

2 garlic cloves, sliced

1 tbsp capers, rinsed, drained and roughly chopped

250g cherry tomatoes, halved

2 meaty cod fillets (about 175g each)

2 tbsp crème fraîche

Juice of ½ lemon

Chopped parsley, to finish (optional)

Sea salt and black pepper

This beautifully simple one-pan dish works well with other white fish, such as bream, coley, gurnard, haddock, hake, pollack, pouting and even freshwater zander. Serves 2

Heat 1 tbsp oil in a large frying pan over a medium heat. Add the fennel, with a pinch of salt, and sauté for 5–6 minutes until beginning to soften and colour a little. Add the garlic, cook for a further 2 minutes, then add the capers and tomatoes. Sweat, stirring now and again, for 10–12 minutes or until everything is softened.

Season the cod fillets well on both sides. Push the vegetables to the edges, add a dash of oil to the middle of the pan and place the cod, skin side down, in the pan. Cook over a medium heat for 4–6 minutes, depending on the thickness of your fillets. Flip the fillets over and cook for a further 2–3 minutes or until the fish is just cooked through.

Transfer the cooked fish to warmed plates. Add the crème fraîche to the pan and mix through the vegetables. Taste and season with salt and pepper as needed, adding a squeeze or two of lemon juice to bring together all the flavours.

Spoon the vegetables on to the plates with the fish and sprinkle with chopped parsley, if using. Serve immediately.

Coffee

LATIN NAME
Coffea arabica, Coffea canephora

SOURCING
fairtrade.org.uk;
cafedirect.co.uk;
equalexchange.co.uk

There is nothing quite like the smell of freshly ground coffee beans. Breathe in those aromas of dark, sharp, smoky, chocolatey, barky, fruity loveliness and you realise that coffee can play a role in cooking. Roasted coffee beans are up there with good chocolate, wine, damson plums and bay leaves as a source of gloriously complex, aromatic flavour.

In sweet, baked things, coffee is exceptional, because combining it with sugar and butter or cream eases its sharp edges, and stretches and blends its lovely bitterness, allowing it to provide that wonderful edge that stops confections being sickly. A good coffee and walnut cake is testament to this.

But coffee has other applications. Its roasted, spicy, nutty notes will complement meat. It can even be used to doctor gravy – or in fact any meaty stew or braise that lacks that little bit of body – adding depth and acidity. And coffee can enhance the flavour of a tomato sauce.

In savoury cooking, the coffee you use should always be strong but, because you don't want an actual clear coffee flavour to come through, it needn't be astronomically pungent: espresso strength is fine.

In sweet cookery, it's different: you need rocket-fuel coffee. If you can comfortably drink it, it's definitely not strong enough. In order to concentrate coffee so that you get flavour without lots of liquid volume, you can brew very strong filter or cafetière coffee, then boil it down. And, while I'm usually no fan of instant coffee, it can be an excellent choice in baking: 1 tbsp instant granules dissolved in 1 tbsp boiling water gives you, simply and quickly, something akin to coffee essence. (Sweetened coffee and chicory essences work well too, but these are not Fairtrade.)

The plight of Mexican coffee farmers sparked the launch of the first Fairtrade label in 1988 and coffee remains one of the most problematic commodities in the world, with inequality rife and prices often fluctuating crazily. Check out coffees from companies such as Equal Exchange and Cafédirect – their organic Machu Picchu is a personal favourite.

ORANGE AND GINGER FOOL WITH COFFEE SYRUP

3 oranges

300ml double cream

300g plain wholemilk yoghurt

2 tbsp syrup from the stem ginger jar (or 2 tbsp caster sugar)

40g stem ginger in syrup, finely diced

FOR THE COFFEE SYRUP

150ml freshly brewed strong coffee

75g caster sugar

Good coffee has warm, citrusy notes and spicy overtones, which are played upon in this recipe. To begin with, all the flavours are distinct but, by the time you get to the bottom of the dish, the fool has become one creamy, fruity, tangy melange. Serves 6

To make the coffee syrup, put the coffee and sugar into a small saucepan and stir over a medium heat until the sugar has dissolved, then simmer for 10–15 minutes or reduced by half and syrupy, lowering the heat as necessary. Leave to cool completely.

Take a little slice off the top and base of one orange. Stand it on a board and use a sharp knife to cut away the peel and pith, leaving you with a skinless fruit. Working over a bowl, slice out the orange segments from between their membranes and drop them into the bowl. Repeat with the other oranges.

For the fool, put the cream, yoghurt and syrup or sugar into a large bowl and beat with a hand-held electric whisk until the mixture just holds soft peaks. Fold in the diced ginger.

Put a heaped tablespoonful of the fool in the base of each of 6 glasses. Top with a few orange segments (leave the juice behind for drinking) and a little trickle of coffee syrup. Repeat these layers, using up the remaining ingredients, and serve.

Coley

Nick Fisher

LATIN NAME
Pollachius virens

ALSO KNOWN AS
Saithe, coal fish, gilpin, greylord, sillack, piltlock

SEASONALITY
Avoid January–March when spawning

HABITAT
North Sea, northeast Atlantic

MCS RATING
2–4

REC MINIMUM SIZE
60cm

MORE RECIPES
Cod with fennel, capers and tomatoes (page 194); Pollack with courgettes and cannellini beans (page 484); Herbed pouting fish fingers (page 501); Crumbed whiting goujons with curried egg tartare (page 673)

SOURCING
goodfishguide.org; msc.org

Time has been cruel to coley. Once it was revered all around the British Isles as a versatile staple. In Orkney, it was smoked; in Northumberland, wind-dried. Every region had its own pet name for it – gilpin, greylord, sillack, piltlock – and the most enduring old coley moniker, still used in Scotland, is saithe.

But this cousin of the codfish became less popular as cod became more readily available, even though the only real difference between the two is that cod meat is lily white and coley fillets are a bit grey. That and the fact that coley is currently a far more sustainable choice than cod. Apart from that, both bake, deep-fry and bulk out a fish pie with similar succulent style. In the wild, both grow to a similar size, inhabiting similar terrain and depths, with the coley favouring the cooler waters of the North Sea while cod will happily migrate south to the English Channel and even beyond.

If you've got adventurous guests, the head of a big coley is a great thing to bake, studded with garlic, bay leaves and anchovies. Simple, shallow-fried fillets with lemon and capers take a lot of beating too – but you can do with coley anything you'd do with cod or haddock.

As with much white fish, light salting firms up coley a little, making it particularly good: just sprinkle over 1½ tsp fine salt per fillet, leave to stand for 20–25 minutes then thoroughly wash off and pat dry before cooking (see recipe below).

A friend of mine who spent time on a Swedish commercial cod-fishing boat told me that the crew regularly caught coley too. These, he said, did not go into the hold but were saved for the crew's dinner: they considered it superior to cod, which they thought of as flabby and boring. The Swedes called it by their own pet name, which translated to 'white salmon': a sign of deep respect that goes a little way to righting the wrongs that time has dealt this fine fish.

COLEY WITH BACON, APPLES AND HAZELNUTS

This is a very lovely way to eat this underrated fish (or any other white fish, such as pollack or pouting). The apples add an unusual fruity edge and the hazelnuts a delightful crunch. Serves 2

15g fine sea salt

½ tsp fennel seeds, roughly crushed

2 coley fillets (150–200g each)

2 knobs of butter

100g smoked bacon, chopped

2 eating apples, such as Cox or Orleans Reinette

1 tsp thyme leaves

25g hazelnuts (skin on or off)

Sea salt and black pepper

Lemon wedges, to serve

Scatter a pinch each of the salt and crushed fennel seeds on a plate. Put the fish on top, skin side down, and scatter the remaining salt and fennel over the flesh. Leave to stand for 20–25 minutes.

While the fish is salting, heat a non-stick medium frying pan over a medium heat. Add a knob of butter followed by the bacon. Fry, tossing regularly, until the bacon is beginning to turn golden at the edges.

Meanwhile, peel, quarter and core the apples. Cut the quarters into slim wedges and add them to the pan with the bacon. Add the thyme and hazelnuts and toss well. Cook for 4–6 minutes or until the apples are soft and golden and the bacon is crisping nicely. Remove to a bowl and keep warm.

Return the pan to the hob and increase the heat a little. Wash the salt and fennel off the fish under a gently running tap then pat dry on kitchen paper. Place the fish in the pan, skin side down, and fry for 3–4 minutes or until almost cooked through. Flip the fish over, add the second knob of butter and take off the heat. The residual heat of the pan will finish cooking the fish in about a minute.

Divide the warm apple and bacon mix between two plates and add a fish fillet to each. Serve at once, with lemon wedges. This is very good with a watercress salad on the side.

Coriander, leaf & seed

Mark Diacono

LATIN NAME
Coriandrum sativum

ALSO KNOWN AS
Cilantro

SEASONALITY
Leaves: May–September.
Seeds: September–October

MORE RECIPES
Chilled avocado soup with tomatoes (page 40); Carrot soup with ginger and coriander (page 123); Noodle salad with spicy peanut butter dressing (page 451); Sweetcorn with spring onion, chilli and coriander (page 632); Spiced couscous with lemon and sultanas (page 202); Velvet crab curry (page 211); Zander with coriander and chilli dressing (page 685); Chicken and blueberry salad with coriander dressing (page 77); Pork belly with noodles, coriander and tomatoes (page 494); Grapefruit, tomato and coriander salsa (page 287)

Coriander leaf is as popular and widespread in non-European cooking as parsley is in our continent. It carries a wonderful, complex blend of seemingly contradictory flavours: sweet and astringent, lemony and sagey, earthy yet bright. Different elements of that wide palette dominate, depending on what you put it with. In laksas, noodle salads and soups, its citrusy, fresh notes sing out against lime, ginger, garlic and chilli. Sprinkled on to curries and dhals, its earthiness comes to the fore, while it acts almost like a lemony seasoning in raw recipes like guacamole and salsas or yoghurt-based raitas and fresh chutneys. Coriander leaf is hugely aromatic too, and its fragrance can add as much to a dish as its flavour – the combination makes it fabulously powerful without (usually) being overbearing.

As with many leafy, annual herbs, coriander is best added at the end of cooking, or when serving, as its flavour and aroma dissipate quickly with heat. Don't be mean with it, either – add by the handful, not the teaspoon. The more tender stalks, finely chopped, can happily go in with the leaves.

Coriander seed carries many of the qualities of the leaf, without actually being very much like it. Where the leaf is cooling and light, the seed's faint lemon character enlivens and marries with other herbs and spices readily, adding warmth and a floral, fruity tone. It is virtually compulsory if you are pickling, and it is an essential part of most curry spice mixes, where its brightness adds the yin to cumin's delightfully musty yang. It works beautifully over a berry-heavy fruit salad (or even in a savoury salad, like the one on page 77). It's also great sprinkled sparingly into the mix for blueberry or blackcurrant muffins.

If you've ever grown coriander, you will be familiar with its tendency to run to seed quickly, to which there are a couple of remedies: grow coriander as intensely flavoured microleaves, sowing the seed densely and harvesting them when only 5cm or so tall; or allow nature to take its course and collect the flowers to use fresh in salads and on pizzas.

CORIANDER PORK CHOPS

1 tbsp olive or rapeseed oil

2 free-range pork chops

Sea salt and black pepper

FOR THE SPICE RUB

1 tbsp coriander seeds

2 garlic cloves, crushed

1 tsp dried chilli flakes, or to taste

Finely grated zest of ½ lemon

1 tbsp olive or rapeseed oil

TO SERVE

½ lemon, for squeezing

A handful of coriander leaves

Plain wholemilk yoghurt

This aromatic dish uses both seed and leaf to wonderful effect. You can do the same thing with veal chops. Chicken pieces work well too (though they'll need longer in the oven). Serves 2

For the spice rub, heat a small pan over a medium heat, add the coriander seeds and toast for a couple of minutes, until aromatic. Using a pestle and mortar (or a spice grinder), crush the toasted seeds fairly finely. Add the garlic, chilli flakes and lemon zest to the mortar, along with a good grinding of pepper, and bash everything together (or do this in a bowl, if you've used a spice grinder). Stir in the oil, then rub the marinade all over the pork chops. Cover and leave to marinate in the fridge for 2–6 hours.

Preheat the oven to 180°C/Fan 160°C/Gas 4.

Heat the oil in a large ovenproof frying pan over a medium-high heat. Season the chops all over with a little salt and add to the hot pan. Brown them for 3–4 minutes, turning once or twice, until well coloured on each side. Transfer the pan to the oven and cook the chops for a further 8–12 minutes, depending on their thickness, until just cooked through. Remove from the oven and leave to rest for a few minutes.

Serve the chops with a little lemon juice squeezed over them, scattered with the fresh coriander, and with a dollop of yoghurt on the side.

Courgette & marrow

Mark Diacono

LATIN NAME
Cucurbita pepo

ALSO KNOWN AS
Zucchini

SEASONALITY
July–October

MORE RECIPES
Courgette salad with ham, borage and ewe's cheese (page 78); Barbecued fennel and courgettes with loganberries (page 367); Roasted courgettes and onions with yoghurt dressing (page 684); Pollack with courgettes and cannellini beans (page 484); Lemon, honey and courgette cake (page 347)

Let me get marrows dealt with early, as politely as I can. If you're looking for a flavourless boat in which to metaphorically sail a few handfuls of heavily spiced lamb, then a marrow may be the thing. Otherwise they're chutney fodder. I remain convinced of this, even though I have lost count of the number of people who've told me how a marrow can be transformed into something edible.

Perhaps the most criminal thing about a marrow is that it was once something special: a courgette. And a courgette is everything its overgrown incarnation isn't – most importantly, dense and flavourful. A useful way of thinking about these two vegetables is as little bottles of cordial: there is a fixed amount of flavour in them and beyond a certain point, adding water (i.e. letting the courgette grow too much) just dilutes the taste.

Picked small – either from the shop shelves or your veg patch – courgettes have a sublime flavour and texture. At their fresh best, they have a fine, nutty, pea flavour that's wonderful raw in salads or as a crudité. Sliced thinly and dressed in just olive oil, lemon, basil (or lemon basil) and salt and pepper, these baby courgettes are fantastic.

The current trend for 'spiralising' raw courgettes into a low-carb substitute for pasta is not to be sneezed at – tossed with salsa verde or an intense tomato sauce, they are surprisingly satisfying – but I generally cook my larger courgettes. The process is all about managing their moisture.

A long, slow cooking of finely sliced courgettes with a little salt and garlic is very successful, driving out much of the water and resulting in a silky pulp that's full of flavour. This is the springboard for many fine suppers and lunches. Exploit courgettes' affinity with dairy and add a little cream and Parmesan for a wonderful pasta sauce, or stir in ricotta and Cheddar to add to a lasagne. Courgettes also love lemon and herbs, particularly mint and basil. Add lots of them to this cooked-down courgette mix to make a sumptuous side dish.

Whatever a courgette's size, roasting, barbecuing or griddling will do it all kinds of favours. Slippery with olive oil, courgettes take on a welcome smokiness from fast, hot cooking – those blackened corners or stripes from the grill are their favourite spice. For the griddle or barbecue, I cut them lengthways into slices the thickness of a £1 coin as the high heat will cook them quickly, driving off moisture and intensifying their flavour; for roasting, I cut them into 5cm towers. Thyme, garlic and chilli each work well as complementary flavours, with a squeeze of lemon juice brightening them up perfectly just before serving.

If you are fortunate enough to find courgettes with a flower attached (direct from the grower is your most likely source, given their short lifespan), rejoice, because to my mind this is *the* edible flower, as fine a prize as the vegetable itself. If it's your first one, it is worth being a little forensic in examining it to familiarise yourself with its constituent parts. The petals are green and/or yellow and taste peppery – not unlike rocket, if gentler. Pluck and discard the stamen from the centre of the flower, then bite into the flower's firm base for one of the freshest, greenest-tasting treats of the garden, with a crisp, succulent texture and that peculiarly satisfying type of sweetness that comes only from vegetables.

I love the flowers torn up roughly in salads, but stuffed with leftover risotto or herby ricotta, tempura-battered and deep-fried they are beyond heaven. If it weren't for their delicacy making them difficult to transport and store, the flowers would be the ingredient we all know about, not the vegetable (lovely as it is).

Growing courgettes is famously easy. Buy a single packet of seeds, grow half with only moderate success and you should still produce enough courgettes to feed everyone in your family and more. Start seeds off under cover in 9cm pots in April or May, planting out the seedlings 6 weeks or so later. Water well, especially through dry periods, and feed them with a tomato or seaweed feed.

Growing your own courgettes gives you access to wonderful varieties such as 'Arbarello di Sarzano', 'Rondo di Nizza' (spherical, perfect for stuffing) and the yellow cigars of 'Soleil', with their superior flavour and texture. It gives you control over picking them when they are that their best – which usually means slicing them from the plant when no larger than 15cm, though I'd urge you to take some when half that size. Bear in mind, the more you pick, the more the plant produces – you're not doing yourself out of a greater harvest by picking them early, you're just giving it to yourself in smaller, more delicious parcels.

SWEET AND SOUR BARBECUED COURGETTES

40g unsalted peanuts

Rapeseed oil, for cooking

1 tsp dried chilli flakes

½ small garlic clove, finely grated

2 tsp sesame seeds

2 tsp fish sauce (or use soy sauce)

1 tbsp honey

2 tsp cider vinegar

2 spring onions, trimmed and finely sliced

2 medium courgettes

2 tsp toasted sesame oil

Sea salt and black pepper

Chopped mint, coriander or Thai basil, to finish (optional)

Char-striped courgettes – barbecued or griddled – can take on strong, aromatic flavours. These make a fantastic side dish for grilled meat or fish but also a complete meal served over noodles. Purple sprouting broccoli – roasted or just blanched – can be cooked and dressed in the same way. Serves 2

Toast the peanuts in a dry frying pan over a medium heat for 3–4 minutes, stirring several times to make sure they don't burn. Remove from the pan and leave to cool a little, then chop roughly and set aside.

Put 2 tsp oil in a small saucepan over a low heat. Add the chilli flakes, garlic and sesame seeds. Heat gently for 15–20 seconds until everything just begins to sizzle, stirring all the time. Remove from the heat and allow to cool a little. Then add the fish sauce, honey, vinegar, spring onions and a pinch of salt. Stir to combine and set aside for 10 minutes or so while you prepare the courgettes.

Trim the courgettes then slice them, from top to bottom, into 2–3mm thick lengths.

Before cooking, make sure your barbecue is hot, or preheat a ridged grill pan over a high heat. Brush the courgette slices with a little oil and season lightly with salt and pepper. Lay the slices on the barbecue or grill pan. Cook for 3–4 minutes on each side or until nicely charred and beginning to soften, but retaining a slight bite. Transfer the cooked courgettes to a bowl.

Stir the sesame oil into the dressing, then spoon three-quarters of it over the courgettes, turning them gently to coat.

Arrange the courgettes on a serving dish (or spoon over cooked noodles). Scatter with the toasted peanuts, finish with the remaining dressing – and herbs, if using – and serve.

Couscous

Spicy brown rice and broccoli (page 535); Quinoa with cumin-roasted roots and parsley (page 514)

A traditional part of most North African and Middle Eastern cuisines, couscous is now available all over the world, but remains a misunderstood ingredient. One common complaint is that it lacks any real flavour. In fact, as with pasta, good couscous does have a delicate, wheaty taste of its own that plays its part in a dish. But couscous is classically used as a bed for spicy stews and tagines, adorned with pungent pastes such as harissa – its unassertive, soothing nature is precisely the point.

Couscous is not a grain. It is traditionally made by mixing semolina and wheat flour with water, then rubbing the dough with the hands into tiny rounds. These are sieved so that any too-small pieces of couscous can be picked up and re-rolled. The granules are then left in the sun to dry. There are several types of couscous, with granules of varying sizes, including big pearls of Palestinian couscous or *maftoul*, and also wholemeal varieties.

The old way of preparing and cooking couscous is time-consuming. After the laborious forming of the granules, the couscous is steamed – suspended in a special *couscoussier* over a pot of simmering meat or vegetables – then fluffed up and returned to the pot for more steaming until the 'grains' are swollen and light.

Conversely, these days couscous is usually a very fast food. The type we buy is pre-steamed and re-dried so it takes only a few minutes of soaking in boiling liquid before it's ready to eat (with the exception of Israeli couscous, which will need a quick simmer). When you need something to accompany some meaty leftovers, or you've forgotten to add the pearl barley to a stew, couscous can get you out of trouble.

Couscous can also take more of a central role as a quick salad or light meal, as in the recipe below. Success is dependent on the dressing – focus on seasoning and moisture, to avoid a bland result: think garlic, lots of lemon juice and good olive oil, plenty of spices and a free hand with the salt. I also often like to add chilli flakes or chopped fresh chilli.

Look out for fairly traded and organic varieties of couscous and don't be afraid of the wholemeal stuff – it has greater flavour and texture than the more processed types.

SPICED COUSCOUS WITH LEMON AND SULTANAS

This zingy, fruity couscous goes fantastically with tagines, curries and grilled meats. You can use any kind of couscous but larger-grained varieties may need a quick simmer before you take them off the heat (follow the pack instructions). It's also fantastic made with bulgar wheat, which you should simmer for 5 minutes before the 10 minutes' standing time.
Serves 4–6 as a side dish

2 tbsp olive or rapeseed oil

2 tsp ground cumin

2 tsp ground coriander

1 tsp sweet smoked paprika

2 garlic cloves, finely chopped

200g couscous

75g sultanas

4 tbsp chopped mint

4 tbsp chopped coriander

Finely grated zest and juice of 1 lemon

Sea salt and black pepper

Extra virgin olive oil or hempseed oil, to finish

Heat the oil in a medium saucepan over a low heat. Add the spices and garlic, and cook gently for 2 minutes. Add 300ml water and ½ tsp salt, bring to the boil and simmer for 1 minute. Now add the couscous, give it a quick stir and take off the heat. Cover tightly and leave to stand for 10 minutes.

Use a fork to fluff up the couscous, which should have trebled in volume by now. While still warm, add the sultanas, chopped herbs, lemon zest and juice, some pepper and a good trickle of extra virgin olive or hempseed oil.

Give the couscous a good mix and check the seasoning; you may need to add a little more salt. Serve warm or at room temperature.

Crab apples

John Wright

LATIN NAME
Malus sylvestris

SEASONALITY
September–October

HABITAT
Woods and hedgerows in lowland Scotland, England and Wales

Wild apples can be spotted growing on many roadsides in late summer but few of these are true crab apples. People throw apple cores from car windows or as they walk along, and these sometimes grow into trees. Apples do not breed true, so roadside fruit will possess near random qualities. The great pity of it all is that most wild apples go to waste – most have a use, either in the kitchen or for making cider.

True crab apples are usually found in old country hedgerows by the roadside, internal farm hedges and in open woodland. In October, forest trees will be surrounded by tens of kilos of the fallen fruit. They are distinguished by being small (often no more than 2cm in diameter), hard, and at least a little scabby looking. They are also bitter with tannin, lacking in sugar and filled mostly with pips surrounded by tough membranes.

So what can be done with this unappealing fruit? A great deal. Left whole and packed into a Kilner jar to two-thirds fill it, with sugar and vodka added and with screwed-up foil on top to hold them under, they make a superb apple liqueur, ready to drink after 6–12 months. Crab apples also form the basis of many a fruit leather (see Hawthorn, page 302).

C

Crab apple jelly (see below) is a classic use for this fruit, as is crab apple wine, but their usefulness in cider-making shouldn't be overlooked. If you can get your hands on cider apples, then stick with those, but if you wish to make cider from dessert apples, the addition of one-third crab apples will improve the structure of your pulp, tannin levels and general flavour considerably.

CRAB APPLE JELLY WITH THYME, JUNIPER AND MINT

2kg crab apples, stalks removed

A generous bunch of thyme (about 30g)

5–10 juniper berries, bashed

A large bunch of mint (about 100g), leaves chopped, stalks reserved

About 1kg granulated sugar

This herby jelly is delicious with lamb or game birds. For a plain jelly to accompany pork, leave out the juniper and herbs. For a crab apple and sage jelly, add 4 tbsp chopped sage at the end; this is fantastic with cheese. Makes about 6 x 450g jars

First sterilise your jars by washing them in hot soapy water, rinsing well, then putting them upside down on a baking tray in a very low oven (at 120°C/Fan 100°C/Gas ½) to dry and warm up.

Roughly chop the crab apples, retaining the skin, cores and pips. Put them into a large, heavy-based pan or preserving pan with the thyme, juniper and mint stalks. Add enough water to barely cover the fruit and bring to a simmer. Cook gently until the apples are soft and pulpy, about 15 minutes.

Set up a jelly bag or line a large sieve with muslin. Pour the apple mixture into the bag or sieve and leave to strain for several hours, until the juice stops dripping through. For a perfectly clear jelly, do not squeeze the pulp in the bag or muslin. However, if you want maximum yield and don't mind a cloudy jelly, give the bag a squeeze.

Put a saucer in the fridge to chill. Measure the apple liquid into a clean pan. For every 500ml liquid, add 375g sugar. Stir over a gentle heat until the sugar has dissolved, then bring to a rolling boil. Boil for 8 minutes, then test for setting point. To do this, turn off the heat, drip a little of the jelly on to the chilled saucer and return to the fridge for a couple of minutes. Push the jelly with your fingertip: if it has formed a significant skin that wrinkles, setting point has been reached. If not, boil for another 2–3 minutes before testing again. If unsure, err on the side of caution: a lightly set jelly is far nicer than a solid one.

Once the jelly is ready, add the chopped mint. Leave to cool for about 5 minutes, stirring once or twice.

When the mint is suspended through the jelly rather than all floating on top, pour into the warm jars and seal straight away. Store for up to a year; refrigerate once opened and use within a couple of months.

Crab, brown

Nick Fisher

LATIN NAME
Cancer pagurus

ALSO KNOWN AS
Common crab, edible crab

SEASONALITY
Avoid egg-carrying females
at any time

HABITAT
All around the British coastline

MCS RATING
2–3

REC MINIMUM SIZE
14cm (body width)

MORE RECIPES
Spider crab salad (page 208);
Samphire, crab and new potato
salad (page 560); Megrim with
crab and chives (page 380)

SOURCING
goodfishguide.org; msc.org
association-ifca.org.uk
(for crab potting regulations)

A whole, undressed, brown crab, freshly caught and boiled, is without doubt the best cash-for-fish investment you can make. British brown crabs are impossibly packed, like Doctor Who's tardis, with hidden pockets of ecstasy. When you pull a boiled one apart, you unleash at least five different and distinctive flavours and textures. These include, from the body alone, brown meat, white meat and the crinkly, crenulated reddish meat that fits inside the shell like a jelly in a mould. Then there's the white claw meat and leg meat, and the bright red wobbly meat that fits into the 'toe' of the claw. With each of these individual meat pockets, you can excavate a range of unique textures: flaky, stringy, runny, creamy, chewy. And in the process of this flavour-mining activity, you can enjoy an hour of mouth-watering anticipation and entertainment.

The act of picking a fresh crab is like shellfish-lovers' theatre. It entails pulling, cracking, picking and poking – to plunder all the hidden nooks and crannies. It can be a communal activity, punctuated with gossip and grog, or a solo act of crab worship: a meditative ritual in which a calcium-encased, barnacle-encrusted, locked prison of a crustacean is transformed into a bowl of soft, sensuous, tongue-tingling joy.

To kill and cook a crab

To kill a crab humanely prior to cooking, proceed as follows. Put it in the freezer for about an hour to sedate it. Then lay the crab on its back and lift the tail flap to reveal a cone-shaped indentation in the middle of the crab's undercarriage. Plunge a sharp spike such as an awl, skewer or small screwdriver in here and twist it around to sever tissues in the vital ventral nerve system. Now turn the crab over and spike it a second time through the mouth, between and below the eyes, aiming upwards into the top of the carapace. Again, twist from side to side. Efficiently performed, this kills the crab quickly.

To cook, lower the crab(s) into a big pot of well-salted fast boiling water (about 10g salt per litre of water). Return to the boil and cook, uncovered, for 10–12 minutes for a 1kg crab, adding 3–4 minutes for every 500g over that. Then lift out and let your crabs cool – in the open air if possible – until tepid and easy to handle before picking.

By all means chill your picked meat in the fridge, if you're not going to eat it for a day or more. But bring it back to room temperature before serving to ensure all its ripe, complex character will be evident. Most of the flavour is lost in chilled crabmeat.

To pick a crab

Use your thumbs to prise the body shell away from the hard top shell. Pull out the rows of 'dead men's fingers' from the body; grey, hairy and not something you want to eat, these aren't actually poisonous. Once they're out of the way, start picking.

There really is no wrong or right way to pick a crab. I scoop the brown meat out of the top shell first. Then I like to pull off all the legs from the body shell, trying to get the joints out right up to the 'hip'. The legs and claws should be lightly cracked with a rolling pin to release the meat from the shell. I slice my crab's legless body in half from head end to tail end. This exposes the cavities of white meat.

My favourite tool for picking out the flesh is a cheap teaspoon with a thin, square-ended handle (both ends are useful). Kebab sticks, lobster picks, blunt fruit knives and forks with tines bent at right angles are all good alternatives. Whatever it takes, pick and scrape until all you have left is shell in hand and flesh in bowl. Don't be scared to mix brown and white meat, both are better with a hint of the other.

And so to eating. Some people do like a crab cake, but a very ripe avocado and some splendidly artisanal bread and butter are all I'd ever want. In fact, eating crab straight out of the body, mouthful by exotic, tingly, room-temperature mouthful, in the warm summer sun, takes an awful lot of beating.

After your crab is devoured, you'll be left with a pile of shell and claws that you can roast with a head of garlic, mash and then boil with some fennel-flavoured water to make a bisque-like stock that will open another whole galaxy of culinary delights.

Sadly, most brown crabs from Britain end up in Spain, Italy and France, where shoppers expect to buy them live from tanks in supermarkets or fishmongers, to take home and boil themselves, or have them boiled-to-order in the shop. The only shops where I have found live crabs for sale recently are Chinese supermarkets. Fishmongers tend to only sell them pre-boiled although you can buy live crabs at wholesale markets like Billingsgate, and from some online sellers. The majority of British brown crabs are caught by potting – a good, sustainable method.

Given the choice I'd *always* boil my own crab. Second choice is one that's just been boiled and is still warm; these can be bought in seaside towns where crab fishing is a way of life. The crabs I cook are caught in my own pots, baited with fish heads and frames, dropped from my boat and left for at least 24 hours to 'soak'.

It's not unheard of to catch cookable-sized brown crabs from simple drop nets or hoop nets fished from a pier, and in some places it's even worth wading out on a low spring tide and just placing your baited pot with a buoy attached on rocky ground, then waiting for the tide to come back in and cover it (though you must return to your pot before the outgoing tide fully exposes it again or your catch will perish from lack of water). All crabs have legal minimum landing sizes – even if you've just caught them from the shore; for brown crab that is 14cm. You should also check local byelaws regarding permits and regulations for crab potting.

Good quality prepared brown and white crab meat is an acceptable alternative to a freshly picked crab, but I think buying white-only meat is unforgivable. Why would you exclude 50 per cent of the crab's splendid and sumptuous repertoire?

CRAB TOASTS

This alternative to the conventional crab toast uses pumpkin seeds rather than sesame seeds. Use a mixture of white and brown crabmeat. Serves 2–4

150g fresh crabmeat

15g root ginger, grated

½ garlic clove, grated

¼ small medium-hot red chilli, deseeded and finely chopped

1 egg white

Juice of ½ lemon

1 tsp soy sauce

2 slices of good white or malted bread, 1cm thick

30–40g pumpkin seeds

Vegetable oil (refined rapeseed oil), for frying

Lemon wedges, to serve

Put the crab, ginger, garlic, chilli, egg white, lemon juice and soy into a food processor and blitz briefly, until thoroughly mixed.

Spread the crab mix over the bread, making sure you get it right to the edges. Scatter the pumpkin seeds over the crab mix and gently tap them flat with your fingers.

Heat about a 1cm depth of oil in a frying pan over a medium-high heat. When hot, lay one piece of toast in the pan, crab side down. Fry for about 2 minutes or until golden brown, then turn the toast carefully and cook the other side until crisp and golden. Drain on kitchen paper while you fry the other piece.

Cut the toasts into triangles or fingers, and serve, with lemon wedges for squeezing.

Crab, spider

LATIN NAME
Maja brachydactyla
(formerly *Maja squinado*)

SEASONALITY
Avoid April–July when spawning;
avoid egg-carrying females at
any time

HABITAT
Wales, western Scotland and
Ireland, south and southwest
England

MCS RATING
3–4

REC MINIMUM SIZE
12cm (body width)

MORE RECIPES
Crab toasts (page 207);
Samphire, crab and new potato
salad (page 560)

SOURCING
goodfishguide.org

There is a gathering that takes place on the shoreline of Dorset's Chesil Beach in May each year. It can be an assembly of alarming magnitude: upwards of a thousand spider crabs with powerful, clawed arms and wiry legs protruding from their spiky, irregular shell of mottled pink, orange and white. We really don't know why the crabs congregate like this, but the event does coincide with their annual moult and breeding season. There is safety in vast numbers. Shedding their shells leaves the crabs soft and vulnerable to predators who, unlike the majority of British cooks, value the spider crab's sweet and succulent meat.

I've witnessed blind tastings in which spider crab meat has been unquestionably rated as more delicious than brown crab. So why do we eat so little of it? Maybe it's the spider's alien-like appearance that puts the consumer off. Maybe it's the work involved in picking this fiddly crustacean (which should be cooked and prepared exactly as for brown crab, see page 205). Perhaps we have just forgotten how wonderful this locally caught seafood is. The bulk of British-caught spider crab is exported to Spain and Portugal, where it is prized.

At River Cottage, we love spider crab, with its beautiful, delicate meat, which is lighter in texture than that of brown crab. We choose cock crabs where possible, so as to leave the hens, which can carry thousands of eggs, to replenish the stocks.

To my mind there are only a few simple ways spider crab should be eaten, all of which are enhanced by chilled dry white wine. My favourite is with good sourdough toast, buttered. The crab should be carefully picked and dressed with the best olive oil, salt, lemon juice and pepper, and accompanied by fresh mayonnaise made with a whisper of garlic and possibly a note of tarragon. That's a lunch to be savoured. Or, for an amazing supper, the crabmeat can be combined with double cream, a dash of brandy, some mustard and cayenne, piled back into the shell and baked until hot and bubbling, then served with brown bread and butter.

Netting for spider crabs can result in by-catch of other species so avoid net-caught spider if you can. But if you see a pot-caught spider at your fishmongers, give them a hug and buy it – in fact, buy three. Eating spider crab slows time; it's food to be savoured with friends and family.

SPIDER CRAB SALAD

1 cock spider crab (about 1kg),
cooked

Juice of 1 small lemon

Juice of 1 lime

4 small gherkins, finely diced

3 tbsp capers, rinsed, drained
and roughly chopped

4 tbsp extra virgin olive oil

2 Little Gem lettuce

4 hard-boiled eggs, peeled

1 small fennel bulb, finely sliced,
feathery fronds reserved

Black pepper

Here, the rich, soft brown crabmeat is blended into a piquant dressing. The salad is equally delicious made with brown crab. Serves 4 as a starter, 2 as a main dish

Pick the meat from the crab, keeping the white and brown meat separate.

To make the dressing, put the brown crabmeat in a bowl with the lemon and lime juice, gherkins and capers and whisk together. Then slowly whisk in the olive oil. If necessary, stir in a little water to give a nice, spoonable consistency. Season with pepper to taste; the capers and gherkins will probably have added enough salt.

Separate the lettuce leaves and arrange on individual plates. Cut the hard-boiled eggs into quarters and arrange on the lettuce with the white crabmeat and sliced fennel.

Spoon over the crabmeat dressing, scatter over any fennel tops and serve.

Crab, velvet

Hugh Fearnley-Whittingstall

LATIN NAME
Necora puber

ALSO KNOWN AS
Blue velvet swimming crab, devil crab, witch crab

SEASONALITY
Avoid late winter and spring when spawning; avoid egg-carrying females at any time

HABITAT
Found around most of the British Isles, except the east coast

MCS RATING
Some unrated; pot-caught Cornish velvet crab 3

REC MINIMUM SIZE
6.5cm

SOURCING
goodfishguide.org; msc.org; association-ifca.org.uk
(for crab potting regulations)

This delightful crab has an impressive clutch of monikers. Devil crab, witch crab, blue velvet swimmer – whatever you choose to call it – this crustacean is hugely under-appreciated here in Britain. I think we have a problem with its size – its shell generally only grows to 8–10cm in diameter. We mistakenly think that what's inside 'won't be worth the trouble'. I can assure you it is. In fact, I'd rank it the most delicious of our native crabs. But you'll struggle to find them in British fishmongers.

It seems we've simply never cottoned on – and for years velvets have been thrown back or used as bait. Our Continental cousins know this is madness. To keep them happy, a healthy velvet crab fishery has developed around Scotland in recent years – the 2009 catch was worth over £6 million – and southern Europe snaps it all up greedily. We still see almost nothing of this bounty.

The velvet crab has a blue-ish shell, covered in a curious soft pelt, which gives it its name. It also sports a pair of preternatural-looking, almost glowing red eyes (hence the 'devil' tag). Once cooked, it turns bright orange, and looks pretty impressive in a Provençal bouillabaisse – which is where a lot of it ends up.

It's definitely worth asking a fishmonger if they can get you some velvets – especially if you know they are landed nearby (by a small Cornish fishery, for instance). You can also fish for them with a baited pot or creel. You don't even need a boat for this: just wade out in a wetsuit or chuck your pot off a rock at the low tide mark. You can even grab velvets while snorkelling around kelpy rocks, but take care – they are aggressive and have sharp claws. Avoid immature specimens, with a shell narrower than 6.5cm, as well as any egg-carrying females. You should also check local byelaws regarding permits and regulations for crab potting.

Velvets can be dispatched, cooked and prepared as for brown crab (see page 205), but only need about 5 minutes' cooking. A little lemon juice, good mayonnaise, bread and a glass of cold white wine are all you need on the table as you prise off the top shell, crack the claws and suck, slurp and winkle out every last morsel of sweet flesh.

The body is the secret treasure trove. You can extract the flakes of sweet meat daintily with a pick but the inner parts of the shell here are also soft enough to crunch up with your molars. And crunching a velvet crab is, for me, among the highest pleasures to be had from our native seafood.

VELVET CRAB CURRY

A fragrant, coconutty curry is a great way to make the most of these delicious little crustaceans. Serves 2

8 cooked velvet crabs
(1–1.2kg in total), see left

2 good handfuls of spinach
or chard

A large bunch of spring onions

50g root ginger, chopped

4 garlic cloves, chopped

4 tsp coriander seeds

2 tsp ground turmeric

1 tsp ground fenugreek

A large bunch of coriander,
leaves picked, stalks roughly
chopped

2 tbsp virgin coconut or
rapeseed oil

2 large onions, sliced

1 tsp nigella (kalonji/black
onion) seeds

½–1 hot red chilli, deseeded
(or not for more heat) and
chopped

½ lemongrass stem, split
lengthways and bashed

400ml tin coconut milk

2 tsp fish sauce

2 tsp sugar

Juice of 1 large lime

Sea salt and black pepper

Use the back of a large, heavy knife to crack the larger claws on each crab. This makes it easier to remove the claw shell later on when people are eating the crabs.

Pop the hard upper shell off each crab. If there is any good meat in the upper shell, scrape it out and set aside. Discard the upper shells or keep for stock. Remove and discard the 'dead men's fingers' from the lower body or undercarriage (these are like tiny, feathery quills). Cut the crab bodies in half and set aside while you make the curry base.

Roughly chop the spinach or, if using chard, separate the leaves from the central stalks and slice both separately. Slice the green tops from the spring onions and roughly chop them. Slice the white parts of the spring onions and set aside for serving.

Place the ginger, garlic, coriander seeds, turmeric, fenugreek, spring onion tops, coriander stalks and 1 tbsp of the oil into a food processor and blitz to a fairly smooth texture. Add a little water if you need to, to help it come together. Alternatively, use a pestle and mortar to make the paste, adding one ingredient at a time.

Heat a large pan over a medium heat. Add the remaining oil followed by the onions, nigella seeds and chilli, and the sliced chard stalks if you're using them. Cook, stirring frequently, for 4–5 minutes. Add the fragrant paste and continue to cook for a further 5–6 minutes, stirring regularly.

Add the lemongrass, coconut milk, fish sauce and sugar, and return to a simmer.

Allow to simmer for 5 minutes, then add the spinach or chard leaves. As soon as they have wilted in the hot sauce, add the crabs. Season the curry well with salt and pepper and stir everything together. Place a lid on the pan and cook for 2–3 minutes – you want to just heat the crabs through, but not to cook them further.

When the crab is hot, add most of the coriander leaves and the lime juice. Stir well to combine, then remove from the heat.

Serve the curry with rice, sprinkled with the remaining sliced spring onion and more coriander. To eat, diners can just pick out the crab meat from the body and claws and drop it into the curry. Or – and this is more fun – pick up the crabs with their hands, suck and chew the meat from the body then prise open the claws to reveal the flesh there, before tucking into the saucey, greensy curry left in the bowl. Either way, napkins are definitely required.

Cranberries

Pam Corbin

LATIN NAME
Wild cranberries: *Vaccinium oxycoccos*. American cranberries: *Vaccinium macrocarpon*

SEASONALITY
Wild cranberries: August–October. American cranberries: imported November–December

HABITAT
Wild cranberries are rare and should only be gathered in small quantities, if at all. They can sometimes be found on acid bog and heathland in Scotland, northwest England, west Wales and central Northern Ireland

MORE RECIPES
Whisky and marmalade bread and butter pudding (page 672)

Like early Christmas wishes, fresh cranberries arrive in November to bluster their way into sauces, stuffings, ice creams, puds and tarts. The kind we buy are bold, bright cultivated berries from North America, which, though too tart to eat raw, are still sweeter than wild cranberries – real sourpusses that grow in boggy, isolated parts, in soil as acidic as they are.

The mouth-puckering sourness that bursts from the waxy skins of cranberries is ideal to offset the richness and sweetness of the festive season. Sauces and jellies are the classic recipes for these fat red fruits. Make sure you soften the cranberries before adding any sugar, or their skins will toughen. Poach them in enough water or orange juice to just cover them, until they pop; 4–5 minutes is all it will take.

You can also add cranberries to meaty mixtures: try studding them through sausage rolls and forcemeat stuffings. First slice the raw berries finely (using the slicing blade of a food processor is the easiest way) so they form pretty red-edged pearly buttons. Then work the sliced berries into your mixture, allowing about 75g cranberries for every 500g sausagemeat.

The curfew for fresh cranberries is Christmas Eve, when they disappear from the shop shelves. However, you can use them well into the new year because their acidity makes them long keepers. They will store for 2–3 months in a sealed container in the fridge – but do throw out any softies so they don't contaminate the good berries. I love a few cranberries sliced into a simmering pan of January marmalade (after the peel has softened, but before the sugar goes in).

It's also worth getting a jar of cranberry and bay vodka on the go, for next year's festivities: in a pan, simmer 500g roughly chopped cranberries with 200ml water for a couple of minutes until the berries are soft. Take off the heat and stir in the grated zest of 1 large orange, 250g granulated sugar, 6 bay leaves (crushed in your hand) and 1 tsp pink peppercorns. Leave to cool completely, then add 500ml vodka. Transfer to a large sealable container and shake to mix. Leave for 3 weeks for the flavours to infuse, then strain through muslin and bottle in sterilised, sealable bottles.

Dried cranberries are readily available throughout the year from health food stores and supermarkets. Most have sugar added but do keep an eye out for those sweetened with apple juice – they have a cleaner flavour and are more succulent. Use these tangy-sharp, ruby red jewels to replace raisins and/or dried cherries in fruit cakes, scones and flapjacks, or bake them into home-made oatcakes to partner-up splendidly with creamy Wensleydale or Caerphilly cheese.

CRANBERRY AND PEAR SAUCE

250g fresh or frozen cranberries

250g cooking apple (1 large), peeled, cored, and chopped

250g firm pears (2 medium)

Up to 100g caster sugar

50ml port (optional)

Tart from the berries yet subtly sweet from the pears, this is a brilliant accompaniment to festive roast meats or vegetarian nut roasts. Makes about 750ml

Put the cranberries into a saucepan with 200ml water. Bring to a simmer and cook for a couple of minutes until the skins are just beginning to split. Add the chopped apple and continue to simmer for about 10 minutes, stirring often, until the apple is completely soft.

Meanwhile, peel, quarter and core the pears and chop into 1cm (or smaller) pieces. Add to the pan once the apples have softened. Cook for 2–3 minutes (the pear won't break down like the apple), then take off the heat. Sprinkle in 50g sugar and stir until dissolved. Stir in the port, if using. Taste and add more sugar if necessary, then leave to cool.

Store in the fridge for up to a week, or freeze. Serve at room temperature.

Crayfish

LATIN NAME
Signal crayfish: *Pacifastacus leniusculus*. Turkish crayfish: *Astacus leptodactylus*. White-clawed crayfish: *Austropotamobius pallipes*

ALSO KNOWN AS
Crawfish

SEASONALITY
Signal and Turkish crayfish: all year, but harder to catch in the winter when they burrow

HABITAT
Lakes, rivers, fisheries, gravel pits etc.

SOURCING
signalcrayfishsales.co.uk

The three types of crayfish you're most likely to get your hands on in this country are the American signal, the Turkish and the white-clawed. The first two are invasive alien species run wild. Signal crayfish in particular are something of an ecological disaster. Introduced in the 1970s to be farmed for the catering trade, many escaped and have decimated our native population of much smaller, less aggressive white-claws. The result is plenty of American signals roaming our waterways, but very few indigenous white-claws left. The latter are now a protected species and should never be taken from the water. It's not hard to tell one from the other: signals are big and dark brown with vivid red colouring under their claws. Turks have bumpy brown shells and long pincers. White-claws have pale undersides to their claws. If in doubt, put the critters back.

Live signal crayfish do turn up at Billingsgate market. Cooked crays can be found in top-end fishmongers, and many supermarket freezer sections harbour bags of frozen, peeled tails. Crayfish tails also regularly inhabit pre-packed sandwiches, though sadly these tend to be imported from Europe rather than harvested from our own lakes and rivers. But the best thing, if you fancy a crayfish feast, is to catch your own. Common in freshwater throughout Britain, signals are easily caught with simple traps or baited lines (you do need a licence from the Environment Agency). Some people purge live crayfish before cooking them, which empties the gut. I don't usually bother – I prefer to eat them almost straight away. But you can purge them by keeping them without food for a day in a cage in the stream where they've been caught – or in a large bucket, half-full of water, in a cool place. Rinse them thoroughly before cooking.

Put live crayfish in the freezer for 30 minutes to sedate them. Then drop into a pan of fast-boiling, well-salted water and cook for about 5 minutes, until they turn pillarbox red. Scoop them out and leave to cool. Serve whole and use hammers, nutcrackers and teeth to tear the aliens limb from limb. Or pull the heads from the tails, snip along the underside of the tail shell with scissors, then open up and take out the meat. Crack each claw with the back of a heavy knife and retrieve their meat too.

Slathered in a Louisiana-style spicy sauce, fresh crayfish do have some merit. But the best use of crayfish is in stock. The shells, roasted hard with oil and garlic and then mushed up with a steak hammer and boiled in salty water, create a deep, rich, tangy, velvety stock that will make any paella or pasta dish sing like a diva.

SPICED CRAYFISH TAILS WITH CUCUMBER AND YOGHURT

400–500g cooked crayfish tails

½ small garlic clove, grated

½ tsp dried chilli flakes

1 tsp toasted fennel seeds, crushed

Grated zest and juice of ½ lemon

2 tbsp olive or rapeseed oil

1 medium cucumber

3 tbsp plain wholemilk yoghurt

1 tbsp chopped mint

1 tbsp chopped coriander

Sea salt and black pepper

Chilli and fennel seeds give this fresh-tasting, quick salad a little extra punch: it makes a delicious light lunch or starter. Serves 4

Place the crayfish tails in a bowl and add the garlic, chilli flakes, toasted fennel seeds and lemon zest, along with 1 tbsp oil. Tumble together and set aside for 10–15 minutes.

Peel the cucumber, halve it lengthways and scoop out the seeds, then slice into 1cm thick half-moons. Place in a bowl with the yoghurt, chopped herbs, remaining oil and a good squeeze of lemon juice. Mix gently.

Heat a large frying pan over a high heat. When hot, add the crayfish, season well and toss around the pan. Cook for 1–2 minutes, then remove from the heat. Squeeze over the remaining lemon juice.

To serve, divide the dressed cucumber between individual plates. Add the crayfish tails, then spoon over any pan juices.

Cream

Nikki Duffy

Cream is milk's rich soul: the sweet, luscious top-of-the-bottle treat. It was once skimmed off pans of milk with tin scoops. Now, we harness the power of the centrifuge: whole milk is rotated at speed in a drum, very quickly causing the fat globules to separate from the thinner, but heavier, milk. Cream collects at the centre of the vessel and is drawn off. This efficient process is made longer or shorter depending on the fat content required in the cream.

Before pasteurisation and mechanisation, cream, just like butter, had a slightly tangy taste, the result of bacteria working in it as it stood, sometimes for days, in the dairy. Modern cream – extracted from very fresh milk and then pasteurised – does not have a huge amount of flavour. But it is still immensely useful because of its incomparable texture and consistency. Its unique structure – lots of fat globules suspended within a small amount of liquid – coats the mouth without feeling greasy, making anything you add it to instantly more luxurious.

One of the joys of cream is that you don't need very much of it to make a big difference. Cream-rammed cakes and big, blowsy sundaes are all well and good as occasional treats but it's cream in small amounts – particularly in contrast to other ingredients – that I really find most heavenly. Pale, rich, bland and cool, cream dances

TYPES OF CREAM

Single cream With a mere 18 per cent minimum fat, this is the sort of cream you might pour into your coffee, and there is nothing better to cool your breakfast porridge. It's not much thicker than milk, not rich enough to whip, and prone to curdling if boiled – but is a great way to enrich soups at the last minute or to use in pannacottas.

Whipping cream Cream needs at least 30 per cent fat to whip up satisfactorily. Whipping cream has a minimum of 35 per cent fat, making it lighter than double cream, but still nicely whipable. As with double cream, it fluffs up better when well chilled.

Double cream While rich, double cream retains a very good pouring consistency, making it perfect for draping over puddings. With a minimum 48 per cent fat, it whips up easily to a billowy mousse and is stable enough to boil with other ingredients without curdling – hence its use in rich, reduced savoury sauces. It is essential for a classic custard, whether crème anglaise or for crème brûlée, ice cream or *tarte aux citron*, as well as savoury quiche fillings. For a slightly lighter pudding-finisher, combine double cream with an equal quantity of wholemilk yoghurt and whip to soft peaks.

Soured cream Soured cream is to cream as yoghurt is to milk. A bacterial culture is introduced to single cream and allowed to go to work, producing lactic acid that thickens and sours it. Soured cream is light and sharp enough to work fantastically well in savoury dishes – superb alongside chillies, or stirred into stroganoffs. It's great forked into mashed potato with chives or used to bind a rough and ready smoked mackerel pâté. Soured cream is used in cheesecakes to give that lovely, subtle tang, and is a fine baking ingredient, adding more richness than milk, and reacting with alkaline raising agents to produce great lift.

Crème fraîche Another form of cultured cream, this is hugely versatile. With 30–40 per cent fat, it is richer than soured cream, and not as sour. It is less rich than double cream but, with its glorious, thick texture (a result of the bacterial culturing), you'd never know it. Crème fraîche has great keeping properties too: a tub stored in the fridge at around 3°C will keep for a fortnight, making it very useful for impromptu additions to recipes. I also particularly love the slightly tangy flavour of crème fraîche, which cuts its richness beautifully. Crème fraîche d'Isigny, from northern France, is a particularly fine example.

Clotted cream A West Country speciality, this unctuous, golden-crusted delight is traditionally made by allowing cream to rise to the top of a shallow pan of milk (or, these days, pouring centrifuged cream on to a layer of milk), then heating to 80–90°C. Once cooled, the cream forms a splendid crust and develops a unique, thick, gloopy texture. Clotted cream boasts anything up to a luxurious 64 per cent fat content – it is by far the richest of all the creams, making it fit to take the place of butter in a cream tea with scones and jam. You can mix it into things – a sauce or a batch of fudge, say – but it is best enjoyed just as it comes.

Mascarpone This is actually a kind of unsalted cheese, made largely from cream, with a fat content of around 44 per cent. Its considerable richness is balanced by a delicate acidity, which makes it an excellent ingredient in cheesecakes. It can even be whipped like cream.

a delicious counterpoint to the dark, the sharp, the earthy and the hot: the crisp crunch of meringue, the tartness of poached rhubarb, the heat of a bubbling apple crumble or the sweet, rooty mass of a roasted vegetable soup. Just a spoonful or two of cream turns meaty pan juices into a velvety sauce with which to 'nap' your chop or steak. And a little cream added to spicy curries or devilled sauces balances the heat without blanketing it.

Fresh cream is also legendarily delicious with fresh, raw fruit, of course – its mild sweetness balancing the acidity of strawberries, raspberries, peaches or blueberries to perfection. This is why ridiculously easy puds such as Eton mess and cranachan, which simply augment fruit and cream with something a little crisp or crunchy, are so much greater than the sum of their parts.

Cream is full of saturated fat, of course, and has long been demonised because of this. However, the perceived danger of saturated fats in the diet in relation to heart disease is now being questioned, and the potentially harmful role of other elements, such as excessive sugar and polyunsaturated fats, scrutinised. We cannot eat cream (and lard and butter) with impunity, not least because they are so rich in calories. But I for one would rather enjoy real organic cream in moderation than some 'lite' alternative, rammed with palm oil, emulsifiers and colouring. Calorific it may be, but cream is a deeply satisfying ingredient.

BAY SYLLABUB

100ml dry white wine

8 fresh bay leaves, torn

Finely grated zest of ½ lemon

300ml double cream

50g caster sugar, plus extra to serve

50g fresh blackcurrants, to serve (or other fresh fruit)

The delicate flavour of bay perfumes this creamy pud beautifully. You can serve it with any soft fruit, but the sharp tang of blackcurrants pairs particularly well. Serves 4

Put the wine, bay leaves and lemon zest into a small pan and bring to a gentle simmer. Allow the wine to bubble gently until reduced by about half. Remove from the heat and set aside to cool and infuse.

Whip the cream and sugar together until the cream is holding soft peaks. Pass the cooled wine through a sieve into the cream and whisk to incorporate.

Spoon the fragrant cream into glasses or bowls. If using blackcurrants, toss them in a little sugar, then scatter a few over each syllabub before bringing to the table.

Cucumber

Pam Corbin

LATIN NAME
Cucumis sativus

SEASONALITY
British cucumbers: July–September. Imported all year round

MORE RECIPES
Chilled avocado soup with tomatoes (page 40); Noodle salad with spicy peanut butter sauce (page 451); Spiced crayfish tails with cucumber and yoghurt (page 214); Fried salmon with cucumber and gooseberry salad (page 553)

Long, short, round, knobbly, straight, curvy, green or yellow, cucumbers have been grown as a salad crop for around three thousand years. The Romans cooked them in oil and honey, Columbus brought them to Haiti, and Hannah Glasse revived them in ragouts, while nineteenth-century cooks like Mrs Beeton positively revelled in cucumbers – stuffing, sautéeing and bottling them, or turning them into refreshing soups, sauces, jellies, pickles and even jam. For some reason they fell from fashion and, until recently, were used for little other than slicing into salads, trimming poached salmon or to make dainty, afternoon-tea sandwiches. But cucumbers are now having a refreshing renaissance, with chefs enthusing about their delicately sweet fragrance and flavour.

There's nothing quite like a home-grown cucumber, sun-warmed and freshly picked from a scrambling vine. Given steamy heat, they are relatively easy to grow and are prolific and quick croppers. A cucumber can grow 2cm or more a day! They are happier grown under cover, although some varieties will grow outside in sheltered spots. These types, often referred to as 'ridge' cucumbers, are smaller and have tougher skins that protect against inclement weather. They sometimes have a tendency to bitterness. Bizarrely, female flowers pollinated by males also produce bitter fruits. To avoid this, select seeds or young plants that are self-pollinating females. 'Telegraph Improved' and 'Femspot' are excellent greenhouse varieties, while 'Burpless Tasty', 'La Diva' or 'Crystal Lemon' double up for inside or out.

Imported cucumbers are available throughout the year from supermarkets and greengrocers, but they are so much better in season. Do check out farmers' markets and roadside stalls in the summer for fresh, local cucumbers.

Many cucumbers are coated with a food-grade wax to help retain moisture and ward off mould or bacteria in transit. Waxed cucumbers have an unnaturally glossy sheen to their skin. Unwaxed ones usually appear dull and dark green. Choose these if you can – but do make sure they are unwrinkled and firm from end to end.

Recent research reveals that cucumbers do best stored at 10–15°C, rather than in the fridge. However, it may be hard to achieve such cool, ambient temperatures at home during the summer. If the only alternative is a warm kitchen, store your cucumbers in the salad drawer of the fridge, where they'll keep for about a week. But, to get the most from your cucumbers, don't serve them fridge-cold. These fruits are naturally cool, even at room temperature: their water content keeps their inner temperature lower than the surrounding air. If super-chilled, they are tasteless and rather unpleasant.

Cucumbers are 96 per cent water, boasting the highest moisture content of any vegetable. Salting to draw out excess water is essential if you want to preserve them, but a light salting is worthwhile even with cucumber that you're going to serve straight away. It draws out water, seasons and concentrates the flavour. I even like to lightly salt the cucumber for teatime sandwiches, for instance. Using a sharp knife, slice a large cucumber as thin as you dare – peeling it only if the skin is tough. Place the cucumber slices in a bowl with a good splash of cider vinegar and ½ tsp fine sea salt and toss together. Leave for 30 minutes. Meanwhile, generously spread thin slices of white or brown bread with softened butter, right to the edge. Tip the cucumber slices into a sieve, wicking away excess moisture with a clean tea towel. Cover half the slices of bread with cucumber and sprinkle with black pepper. Top with the remaining bread then slice off the crusts and cut the sandwiches into neat little fingers.

Such sandwiches may be quintessentially British, but the bread and cucumber combination is popular in the US too. Their 'bread and butter pickle' – so named because it's so good with bread and butter – is a very good way to preserve a crop of crunchy cucumbers. Cut 1kg cucumbers (any variety) into 3–4mm slices. Finely slice 2 medium onions and toss together with the cucumber in a bowl. Sprinkle with 2 tbsp fine sea sea salt and leave for a couple of hours. Rinse, drain and dry well. Place 300ml cider vinegar, 200g granulated sugar, 2 tsp ground turmeric, 1 tsp dill seeds, 1 tsp celery seeds, 1 tbsp yellow mustard seeds and 100ml water in a large saucepan. Heat gently until the sugar dissolves, then bring to the boil. Add the cucumber and onion slices and simmer for 3–4 minutes. Pack into warm sterilised jars – with fronds of fresh dill, if you like – and seal with vinegar-proof lids.

To peel or not to peel cucumber? If the skin is tender, then leave it on. Otherwise – and also if the fruit is waxed – remove it with a veg peeler. Or peel off alternating strips for a decorative effect. Removing the seeds is another option, particularly if they seem bitter or you don't want the extra moisture they bring. Once the cucumber is halved or quartered lengthways, they can be easily zipped out with a teaspoon.

We are used to eating crunchy cucumbers raw but cooked as a vegetable, they become softly fragrant and smooth. For a delightful side dish, peel, dice and sauté cucumbers in butter for 15–20 minutes, adding crushed garlic, or fennel, cumin or dill seeds during cooking, or toss chopped herbs over at the end. For a refreshing chilled soup, cook chopped cucumber with sliced onions or leeks and purée with chicken or veg stock and plenty of seasoning, finishing with a swirl of soured cream and a scattering of mint.

But it's raw and fresh that I like cucumber best. A fundamental ingredient in many Mediterranean salads, no Niçoise, Greek salad or Italian *panzanella* would seem right without it. And a slice or two is a welcome addition to a Pimms or G & T. Meanwhile, diced, combined with soured cream or yoghurt and plenty of fresh mint or coriander, cucumbers make gorgeously cooling raitas and dressings to serve with spicy Eastern dishes and curries.

CUCUMBER, SMOKED MACKEREL AND DILL SALAD

½ large cucumber (150–200g)

A large handful of baby spinach leaves

100–150g hot-smoked mackerel fillet, skinned

FOR THE DRESSING

1 tbsp plain wholemilk yoghurt

2 tsp Dijon mustard

2 tsp cider vinegar

1 tbsp chopped dill

A pinch of sugar

2 tbsp extra virgin olive oil

Grated zest of ¼ lemon

Sea salt and black pepper

For this quick and refreshing salad, you could use organic hot-smoked trout or salmon in place of the mackerel, if you can find them. The final flurry of lemon zest really lifts the dish. Serves 4 as a starter, 2 as a main dish

Cut the cucumber into quarters lengthways, then slice it across into little quarter-circles, about 5mm thick. Place these in a bowl with the spinach leaves. Flake over the smoked mackerel, checking for any bones as you go.

For the dressing, in a bowl, combine the yoghurt, mustard, vinegar and half the dill with the sugar and some salt and pepper, then whisk in the extra virgin olive oil. Taste and adjust the sweetness or acidity with a pinch more sugar or a drop of vinegar, as required.

Spoon half the dressing over the fish and cucumber salad. Grate over the lemon zest and tumble it all carefully together.

Divide the salad between individual plates, trickle over the remaining dressing and scatter with the remaining dill. Serve with brown bread and butter.

Cumin

Tim Maddams

LATIN NAME
Cuminum cyminum

ALSO KNOWN AS
Jeera

MORE RECIPES
Mexican pumpkin seed dip
(page 508); Spear-leaved orache
bhajis (page 593); Raw carrot
salad with peanut and cumin
dressing (page 123); Quinoa
with cumin-roasted roots and
parsley (page 514); Griddled
aubergines with spiced yoghurt
(page 39); Mujadara (page 104);
Spiced couscous with lemon
and sultanas (page 202); Spicy
kohlrabi wedges (page 327);
Spicy brown rice and broccoli
(page 533); Spiced horse
mushroom 'burger' (page 315);
Lamb, labneh and spinach
salad (page 335); North African
shepherd's pie (page 335);
Green tomato, cumin and green
chilli chutney (page 642)

Cumin has a distinctive personality. It is warm, pungent and woody, with nutty, peppery, vaguely fennel-like, burnt sesame seed notes. It brings warmth and spicy complexity without biting heat and I use it as happily with fruit and fish as I do meat and vegetables. Cumin-lovers like me can add it by the tablespoon, but small amounts can be just as effective. I often use cumin as a replacement for salt: a few toasted and roughly crushed seeds sprinkled over sliced tomatoes with a smidgen of raw garlic, for instance, pretty much negate the need for salt and create a wonderfully warm, savoury flavour.

It's with Indian food that we perhaps most associate this spice – and rightly so, as India produces 75 per cent of the world's cumin (or *jeera*). It is also the world's largest consumer of this magical flavouring: frying cumin seeds to flavour the oil at the beginning of a dish, crushing them for curries, kneading them into biscuits, and using them as a finishing touch – either whole or ground into a garam masala mix. (There is a related spice, black cumin, or *kala jeera*, which has a stronger, smokier flavour.)

But cumin has its place in many other cuisines, including Middle Eastern, Mexican, European – and nowadays modern British too. It works in tagines, chillies, dhals and kebabs as well as soups and hummus. At River Cottage, we like to flavour roasted root vegetables and squashes with cumin, and we use it in our merguez spice mix (with coriander, caraway, fennel and paprika), which flavours everything from sausages to chickpeas. Cumin is great in sweet recipes too, including ice cream and shortbread. Try adding 1 tsp cumin seeds to a batch of fudge just before beating.

We tend not to think about freshness when buying dried spices but it's of paramount importance. Cumin bought as whole seeds from a specialist shop that sells their spices loose is often more vibrant and better quality than from the supermarket. Cumin seeds should have a lovely rich, warm fragrance, even before they are toasted and crushed.

TORTILLAS WITH CUMIN AND GARLIC OIL

250g plain white flour
(or rye or buckwheat flour)

½ tsp fine sea salt

1 tbsp olive or rapeseed oil

FOR THE GARLICKY OIL

1 garlic clove, peeled

4 tbsp extra virgin olive
or rapeseed oil

TO FINISH

4 tsp cumin seeds

Flaky sea salt

Simple, unleavened wheat tortillas (call them flatbreads or chapatis if you prefer) are easy to make. You can also turn out rye or buckwheat versions. Serve warm from the pan, as a nibble or side dish. Serves 6–8

Combine the flour and salt in a bowl. Add the 1 tbsp oil and then gradually work in about 125ml water. Add more water, a few drops at a time, until you have a firm but not dry dough. Knead for a minute or so until smooth. Leave the dough to rest, covered, for at least 15 minutes – up to 1 hour.

Meanwhile, for the garlicky oil, squash the garlic clove with the flat of a large knife then combine it with the extra virgin oil and leave to infuse.

Toast the cumin seeds in a frying pan over a medium heat for about a minute until fragrant, then crush roughly, using a pestle and mortar.

Shortly before serving, set a large frying pan over a high heat. Divide the dough into 8 equal pieces and form each into a ball. Using flour to prevent sticking, roll out each ball into a disc, about 2mm thick. Shake off excess flour. Lay one tortilla in the hot pan and cook for about a minute, until the underside has toasty brown patches, then flip the tortilla and cook the second side for about 45 seconds or until similarly browned.

Wrap the tortilla in a clean tea towel and keep warm while you cook the rest. Brush the warm tortillas with a little of the garlicky oil, sprinkle with the crushed cumin and a pinch of flaky salt and serve.

Currants, black, red & white

Pam Corbin

LATIN NAME
Blackcurrants: *Ribes nigrum*.
Red- and white currants:
Ribes rubrum

SEASONALITY
June–August

MORE RECIPES
Bay syllabub (page 217);
Redcurrant and red wine jelly
(page 675)

Whether translucent, pearly white, glowing crimson or deepest sapphire-black, these tiny, glossy berries shine like gems. They are the jewels in the crown of the British fruit garden, perfectly suited to our climate. Gorgeous to look at, they are also – as long as you season them with just the right amount of sugar – superb to eat.

Depending on weather and location, these lustrous fruits appear from mid-late June onwards. First to show are the red and white – both less tart and less complex than their bolder, black sibling who ripens a week or so later. Currants grow on 'strigs' – dangling tassels of beautiful, shimmering berries. Usually grown as open, spreading bushes, young plants can also be trained as cordons or 'standards', making for easy picking (easy for nimble birds too, if you're not quick). In their season, you can find blackcurrants in supermarkets, though pick-your-own farms are my favourite place, outside the garden, to gather them.

Blackcurrants do not enjoy global popularity. They were forbidden fruits in the US for most of the twentieth century because the bushes can carry a fungus lethal to white pine trees. Restrictions still apply in some states, so American blackcurrant recipes are few and far between. And aside from using their piercingly sharp fruitiness in the rich blackcurrant liqueur, crème de cassis, their affair with the French has not been one of great love. But in Britain we have appreciated currants for centuries.

Blackcurrants were originally valued for their medicinal rather than their culinary qualities, particularly for their astonishingly high vitamin C content (three times that of oranges). Understandably, these stealthy black knights were utilised in a cordial during Second World War, to help keep disease and illness at bay. While vitamin C is affected by cooking and other forms of processing, it seems that other antioxidants in the fruit help to 'protect' it and useful amounts of vitamins and antioxidants can be retained in blackcurrant compotes and jams.

But these berries are not just good for you, their flavour is incomparable. Early berries are sharp but sweeten up as they mature. Use a fork to zip them off the 'strigs'. In season, you can eat red- and white currants raw, tempering the sharp edge with a little caster sugar. Blackcurrants are best lightly poached and sprinkled with sugar to taste. Pile them into pies, tarts and fruity crumbles, with or without summer berries. Or, for a different type of currant bun, beat together 125g soft butter, 125g caster sugar, 125g sifted self-raising flour and 2 eggs until well combined. Fold in 100g raw black-, red- or white currants. Spoon the mixture into a greased bun tin or 12 paper cases and bake at 180°C/Fan 160°C/Gas 4 for 15–20 minutes until risen and softly golden.

Lightly poached, sweetened and puréed, black-, red- and white currants transform into delicious, tangy coulis to pour over ice cream and meringues or trickle through good plain yoghurt or rice pud. Use the soft fruity sauce as the base of a tart blackcurrant curd. You can also employ a currant purée in a sauce to accompany duck, pork, lamb or oily fish. And of course, the vibrant juice can be sweetened and bottled for your own home-made cordial. Whole currants and currant purées freeze well (prepare as for raspberries, see page 525).

Blackcurrants steeped in vinegar and sweetened make a wonderful fruity vinegar, which is fabulous in salad dressings. And redcurrant juice blended with rum or brandy makes a bright, fruity cordial or 'shrub' for cocktail hour. Black-, red- and white currants can all be successfully fermented into very quaffable country wines.

Along with their superb, tart flavour, currants are packed with pectin and fruit acid and they make glorious jams and clear, sharp jellies. It's hard to make a bad blackcurrant

C

jam – and a good one is exquisite. A useful rule to remember is that the skins of these fruits must be softened by poaching before adding sugar. If not, they are likely to be a little tough.

Whereas blackcurrants are most often used to make whole-fruit jam, it is the juice of the red and whites (extracted by cooking, then straining through a jelly bag) that is valued for fresh-tasting, translucent jellies. Add fresh herbs to the poaching berries for uplifting aromatics – garden mint is a favourite. These piquant preserves are little sparklers in the larder.

Lovely served with ham, poultry and cheeses, a tablespoonful of redcurrant jelly also brings balancing sharpness to a pan of Sunday gravy and gives fruity notes to a spicy tagine. Redcurrant jelly is at the heart of a classic Cumberland sauce – enlivened with port, zesty orange and lemon, cayenne, mustard and a whiff of ginger – this is gorgeous with baked hams or gamey things. It is also perfect, gently 'melted', to glaze the tops of fruit tarts and cheesecakes.

With such expert gelling ability, red- or white currant juice helps low-pectin cherries and strawberries to set in the jam pot: add 150ml currant juice to each 1kg of fruit. The juice will freeze well: best to do so in usable quantities i.e. 150ml or 300ml, so you don't waste any.

Don't forget that blackcurrant leaves have a wonderful flavour all their own. They make the most amazing tisane: place 3 or 4 fresh leaves in a mug (or pot), pour over boiling water and leave to infuse for several minutes. And a cooled infusion makes the basis for a beautifully refreshing sorbet or granita. The leaves are easy to dry – simply place on a wire rack in a warm place. Store in a sealable jar or container to use when winter dormancy arrives.

BLACKCURRANT AND THYME SORBET

500g blackcurrants

5 large sprigs of thyme

175g caster sugar

Juice of 1 lemon, strained

The pungently aromatic notes in blackcurrant work really well with earthy thyme. In this sorbet, the fruit flavour is intense and very much at the fore; the fragrant thyme note comes through subtly towards the end. Serves 6–8

Place the blackcurrants in a pan (don't worry about the odd stem – the cooked fruit will be passed through a sieve). Add the thyme, sugar and 100ml water and bring to a gentle simmer. Cook for 5–10 minutes, or until the blackcurrants are broken down and tender. Bash them up a little with a masher, and then pass through a sieve into a bowl, using the back of a ladle to press the fruity pulp though. Discard the pips and skin.

Add the lemon juice and chill the blackcurrant purée. When cold, churn the mix in an ice-cream machine until soft-set, then transfer to a freezer container and freeze until solid. (Alternatively, freeze the mixture in a plastic container for about an hour until the sides start to solidify, then mash with a fork, mixing the frozen sides into the liquid centre; put back in the freezer for another hour. Repeat this at hourly intervals until soft-set then let the sorbet set solid.)

Either way, transfer to the fridge about 30 minutes before serving to make scooping easier.

Curry powders & pastes

Tim Maddams

SOURCING
citruscentre.co.uk (for curry leaf plants)

When I was a lad, things were very simple: 'curry' meant a meat stew made exotic with a teaspoonful of ancient curry powder from my granny's larder. And some raisins. These days we have a fuller understanding of what 'curry' can be.

Famously, the word itself is not authentic. Some say it comes from *kari*, a Tamil word that denotes a gravy or sauce, others that it has its roots in the Middle English *cury*, simply implying a dish made with a mixture of ingredients. However you gloss it, in one sense, it means nothing – it's not a word that cooks in India use. Yet outside the subcontinent, it's come to have an incredibly broad application, taking in any spicy dish from South or Southeast Asia. And it's this sense of the word that has given rise to the multitude of spiced, aromatic powders, pastes and blends on the shop shelves, all bidding to help us achieve curry greatness.

Generally, I prefer to grind and mix my own spices. But curry powders can be very useful. To select, balance and blend a range of individual spices for a dish takes some skill and experience. There's no shame in giving yourself a helping hand, particularly when you're in a hurry.

Most dry curry powders are a combination of cumin, coriander, turmeric, chilli and fenugreek. This last pungent spice is the one that contributes that distinctive, penetrating 'curry' aroma. Coriander adds a rich, burnt orange, almost caramel note; cumin brings warmth and a fennel-like tang; while turmeric lends its unique, complex, slightly bitter flavour. Chilli provides heat, of course. Many powder mixes also include clove, cinnamon, garlic, ginger, allspice or fennel. Check to see if your curry powder contains salt – this can make quite a difference to the seasoning of a dish.

A good basic guide is to select simple, fiery blends for strong meat curries, but stick to more aromatic blends, heavy on the coriander and fenugreek, for fish. A simple dhal could be flavoured with quite a strong, hot curry powder if you are serving it as a main dish but if you want it to be a soothing accompaniment, you might tone down the heat and season it with aromatic garam masala (see below).

In the UK, curry powders are commonly given a name, such as madras or vindaloo, supposedly relating to their style. Although they give an indication of heat (korma is usually mild, madras hot and vindaloo volcanic) these terms aren't all that useful, as the flavour will vary from one brand to the next.

The only real way to establish which curry powder you like is to try some. If you can do so without causing a scene, take a good sniff or even taste a pinch before purchasing. You want a powder that smells fresh, fragrant and delicious, and has plenty of time left before its use-by date. Slightly coarse-looking mixes are more vibrant, in my experience. Freshness is everything and the spices in the mix can fade at different rates, meaning that the overall flavour profile changes as the powder ages.

Garam masala contains many of the classic curry spices – though, in India, blends differ from house to house. *Masala* means 'mixture of spices' and *garam* means 'hot', in the sense of warming the body. Garam masala is not spicy-hot and it's unusual to find chilli as an ingredient. Instead, it often features particularly fragrant spices such as cardamom and cinnamon or cassia. Traditionally, this blend is added right at the end of cooking, to 'freshen up' the spicing.

Once you've found blends that you like, I'd still urge you to buy whole spices and grind your mixtures yourself. This allows you to tinker and experiment and, with the advent of the electric spice mill, the daily grind need not be an arduous task. Keep your jar of spice mix in a cool, dark cupboard – the fridge, even – but use it up quickly

C

or it will become dull. Aside from traditional uses in curries, I often roast nuts and season them with curry spices, to serve as nibbles. Home-made curry powder is also a delicious way to pep up a soup or a few leftovers. Stirred into mayo or yoghurt, it makes a quick dip, and roasted root veg are enhanced with a sprinkling of curry powder and salt before serving.

Curry pastes are another way to get your spices ready-blended, with the addition of water, oil, garlic, ginger and/or tomatoes. There are three main categories: Indian, Thai and Malay. Indian curry pastes tend to have garlic and ginger, and maybe tamarind and tomato paste. Thai curry pastes almost always contain lemongrass, coriander root and galangal rather than ginger; shrimp paste is often added to the mix too. Malay curry pastes include galangal, shallots, garlic, kaffir lime leaves, ginger and lemongrass. Once opened, shop-bought curry paste is best kept in an airtight container in the fridge and used up quickly, or frozen in small portions.

Useful as prepared pastes are, making your own will always give you a fresher, keener flavour. You don't need to spend ages with a massive pestle and mortar pounding the ingredients together – a food processor can do the job in minutes. However, I've heard more than one Thai cook say that a processed curry paste is always a little different to a pounded one. The ingredients are broken down in a different way, the crushing, rubbing and blending motion of the pestle and mortar producing a more aromatic, vibrant and 'developed' flavour. I think they're right – but a food processor can still give good results.

If added at the start of cooking, you will get a smooth, rounded effect from a curry paste. Stir in a little raw paste towards the end and the effect will be more peppy (you can do both). To 'refresh' a curry a day or two after making, warm a spoonful of paste with a little boiling water and add to the reheating dish. Pastes are also good for instant marinades. Just add a little oil and citrus juice and rub on to meat or fish before grilling.

Curry leaves are another way to impart curry flavour. These highly aromatic, sharp, slightly citrusy leaves from the *Murraya koenigii* tree make a wonderful addition to a spice paste, or can be crackled in hot oil and tipped over a dish as a final 'tempering'. They are also a fabulous way to scent rice. They're best when fresh, though not always easy to find. Dried curry leaves are acceptable at a push – but far less flavoursome.

CURRIED NEW POTATOES, RED ONION AND LETTUCE

1 large or 2 smaller red onions

2 tbsp rapeseed oil

200g cooked new potatoes

1 Cos or 2 Little Gem lettuce(s)

½ tsp freshly grated root ginger

2 garlic cloves, sliced

2–3 tsp curry powder

Juice of 1 lemon

Sea salt and black pepper

TO FINISH (OPTIONAL)
Coriander leaves

Toasted flaked almonds

Curry spices and sweet onions turn a few staples from the fridge into a lovely aromatic salad. Try other cooked roots, such as parsnips or carrots, or other leaves, like watercress or chicory, in place of the potatoes and lettuce. Serves 2

Preheat the oven to 180°C/Fan 160°C/Gas 4.

Peel the onions and cut each into 6 or 8 wedges. Place in a large roasting tin and trickle over half the oil. Season well, cover with foil and bake for 35–40 minutes until soft and beginning to caramelise.

Meanwhile, cut the potatoes into chunks and roughly slice the lettuce. Add to the roasting tin with the ginger, garlic, curry powder and remaining oil. Season again and stir well. Return, uncovered, to the oven for a further 10–15 minutes or until the lettuce is wilted.

Transfer to a warm serving plate, squeeze over the lemon juice and scatter over the coriander and almonds, if using. Serve warm.

Cuttlefish

Sepia officinalis

SEASONALITY
Cuttles tend to be caught during their spawning period, which peaks April–May. If buying at this time, look for cuttles taken in trap fisheries where measures are taken to conserve the eggs

HABITAT
Northeast Atlantic, mostly southern and western coasts of Britain, the Mediterranean

MCS RATING
Some stocks not assessed; otherwise 3–4

REC MINIMUM SIZE
13cm mantle length

SOURCING
goodfishguide.org.uk

MORE RECIPES
Squid with chervil and blood orange (page 155)

The first time I saw a live cuttlefish, I found it mesmerising – shimmering sapphire, emerald, ruby and moonstone as it moved. The skin of cuttlefish is able to polarise light, enabling them to instantaneously camouflage themselves against the ground they're moving over. The first time I ate one of these cephalopods was just as memorable. Cooked slowly with bay, lemon, garlic and tomato, it was fragrant, tender and delicate.

Cuttlefish responds beautifully to slow cooking, but you can also treat it as you would squid flesh, marinating it with a little chilli and fresh coriander then grilling it fiercely and briefly over a barbecue. Or try serving it flash-fried with smoked bacon and rosemary – or pepped up with fragrant ginger, tamari and lime juice.

The cuttlefish catching season begins as they come inshore to breed, in late spring. The Channel is the main area and most are trapped in pots – a very selective method.

Weighing anything from 1–10kg, cuttlefish can appear formidable and preparing one is likely to leave you inky-fingered. But it's worth it. First make a 2–3cm incision across the top edge of the cuttle bone, just behind the head. Press on the base of the single, broad flat bone and ease it out through this opening. Slit the thin skin down the length of the back (not the flesh) and peel it back. At either side of the back is a seam, covered by a membrane, that holds the body together. Run your fingers firmly under these seams to open up the body and enable you to remove the head and innards. If the silvery pouch of ink is intact, carefully set it aside. This can be used to colour pasta, or to flavour a *risotto nero*, or a fish soup. Pull off the wings. Use a knife and your fingers to remove as much skin as possible from the body and wings, as well as any fine membrane left clinging to the pearly white flesh. Rubbing with a damp cloth helps with this.

Cut the tentacles away from the head, just in front of the eyes. Separate the tentacles then use a small knife to carefully cut away the skin and suckers that cover them. Wash the cuttle pieces under a cold tap then pat dry. Body, wings and tentacles are all good to eat – but the wings are best slow-cooked, or they can be tough.

CUTTLEFISH WITH FENNEL AND WHITE BEANS

1–1.5kg cleaned cuttlefish (see above), with tentacles

750g ripe tomatoes, or a 400g tin plum tomatoes

2 fennel bulbs, trimmed

3–4 tbsp olive or rapeseed oil

1 large onion, finely sliced

2 large garlic cloves, crushed

2 bay leaves

2–3 strips of finely pared lemon zest

A glass of red wine

500ml fish or veg stock

400g tin cannellini beans

Juice of ½ lemon

Extra virgin olive oil, to finish

Sea salt and black pepper

This aromatic dish is great served in small portions as a starter, or served in generous bowlfuls, with bread. If you have the cuttle's ink, stir it into the sauce at the end of cooking. Serves 6–8

Cut the cuttlefish into 1cm thick strips. If using fresh tomatoes, skin them (see page 642), then deseed and roughly chop; set aside. Thickly slice the fennel.

Place a large saucepan over a medium-high heat and add 2 tbsp oil. When hot, add the fennel and onion. Cook, stirring regularly, for 8–10 minutes. Add the garlic, bay and lemon zest, cook for 1–2 minutes then add the tomatoes – if you are using tinned ones, crush them first in your hands. Add the wine and stock and bring to a gentle simmer.

Meanwhile, heat a large non-stick frying pan over a medium-high heat. Add a little more oil, followed by a couple of handfuls of the cuttlefish and some salt and pepper. Cook, tossing regularly, for 2–3 minutes or until beginning to caramelise. Transfer the cuttlefish to the sauce and repeat the browning process with the remaining cuttlefish, making sure you don't crowd the pan.

Cover and simmer gently for 1–1½ hours or until the cuttlefish is tender, topping up with a little hot stock or water if necessary. Drain the cannellini beans and add them to the pan about 20 minutes before the end of cooking.

Before serving, taste and add more salt and pepper, if needed. Finish with a generous squeeze of lemon juice and a good trickle of your finest olive oil.

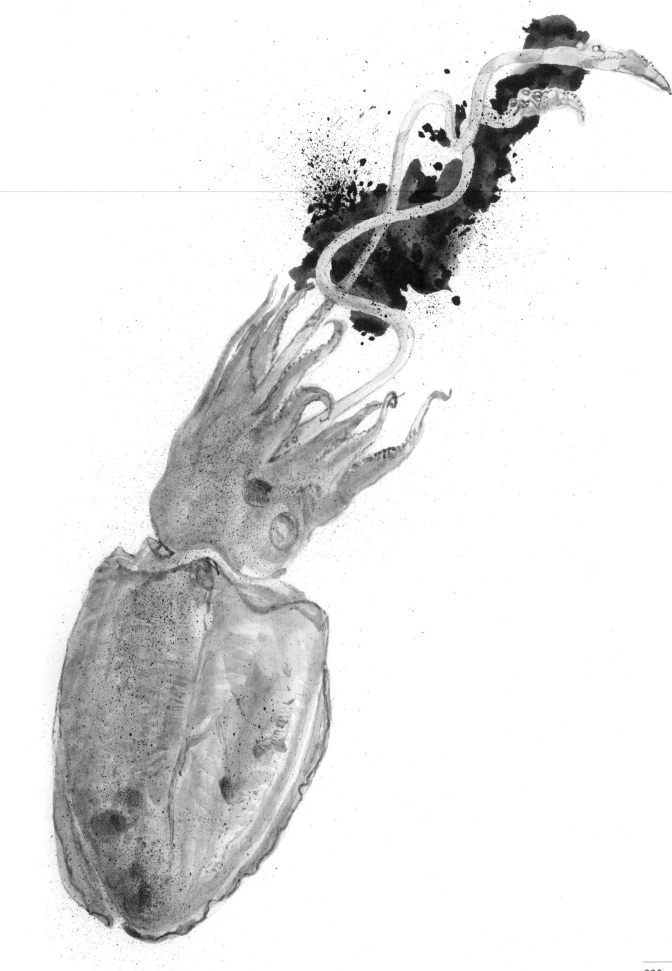

Dab

LATIN NAME
Limanda limanda

SEASONALITY
Avoid April–June when
spawning

HABITAT
Shallow seas all around
the British Isles and
northern Europe

MCS RATING
2–3

REC MINIMUM SIZE
20cm

MORE RECIPES
Grilled flounder and tomatoes
(page 260); Megrim with crab
and chives (page 380); Plaice
with rosemary, caper and
anchovy butter (page 476)

SOURCING
goodfishguide.org

We should all be eating more dab, and here's why. It's cheap, very tasty – on a par with plaice, to which it is related – and, according to the MCS, it's probably the second most abundant fish in the North Sea (the first being sand eels). Yet dab is ridiculously under-utilised – up to 90 per cent of the catch is discarded.

No one could call this fish beautiful. It's a dull, mottled brown creature with rough skin and the mournful bug-eyes that most flatfish share. Dab are often very small too (as little as 150g), but this makes them simple to cook – especially if you get your fishmonger to fillet the fish for you. They can be cooked and dished up, with minimal effort, in about 4 minutes flat.

Dab is also an easy and rewarding fish to cook whole: just scrape off the scales, snip off the fins with scissors then slice off the head and remove the gut that you'll find exposed just below it. It takes only a few minutes, and then your dab is ready to throw into a frying pan. A generous knob of butter in the pan, or rapeseed oil, is all the sauce you need – enhanced perhaps with some chopped garlic, and a few bruised thyme leaves.

Having said that, I do like to sandwich a couple of well-seasoned, butter-fried dab fillets in a bun with lettuce and mayo – and perhaps a few capers. You can also crumb the fillets (dip first in flour, then beaten egg, then breadcrumbs), fry them in oil and serve them with tartare sauce and lemon wedges. And you can even pop your dab into a foil 'bag', as in the recipe below. But that's about as elaborate as I'd get – the simplest approaches bring the best out of this under-appreciated little fish.

Because dab is not a target species (it's mainly by-catch for fishermen looking for plaice and sole) catches may be somewhat erratic. But grab it when you see it – it's well worth having on your radar.

DAB IN A BAG

About 500g waxy salad potatoes, such as Nicola or Pink Fir Apple, scrubbed

2 tbsp olive or rapeseed oil

1 garlic clove, very thinly sliced

2–3 tbsp chopped herbs, such as parsley, chives, dill, fennel and/or basil

2 dab (ideally about 300g each), descaled, trimmed and gutted (see above)

2 large knobs of butter

Finely grated zest and juice of 1 lemon

Sea salt and black pepper

This simple technique is great for both whole fish and fillets – try it also with megrim and witch, trout and sustainable salmon fillets. You could swap the simple herb and lemon flavourings here for chilli, ginger and soy. Serves 2

Put the potatoes in a pan, cover with water, salt well and bring to the boil. Simmer until tender, 8–12 minutes depending on their size. Drain and cool. (You can do this in advance.)

Preheat the oven to 200°C/Fan 180°C/Gas 6. Tear off a couple of sheets of foil, each about 60 x 30cm. Cut the cooked potatoes into thick slices (5–10mm).

Divide the potato slices between the foil sheets, placing them on one half and leaving a good margin of foil around the edge. Trickle the potatoes with oil, tuck in the sliced garlic and scatter over the chopped herbs. Season with salt and pepper.

Season the dabs well all over and lay them on the potatoes. Trickle with a smidge more oil, dot the butter over the fish then scatter over the lemon zest. Finally, give everything a good squeeze of lemon juice. Envelop the fish in the foil as neatly as you can, but not tightly – the parcels should be baggy. Crimp the edges together well.

Place the foil parcels on a large baking tray and cook in the oven for 15–20 minutes, or until the fish is done. Allow the parcels to stand for a few minutes before tearing them open. Serve with a green vegetable such as steamed broccoli.

Damsons

Pam Corbin

LATIN NAME
Prunus insititia

SEASONALITY
August–October

HABITAT
Hedgerows, light woodland

MORE RECIPES
Grilled cheese salad with bullace compote (page 105)

Whether from hedgerow or orchard, damsons are valued for their bold, plummy, wine-rich character. They have a particular allure, subtly different from their fatter, sweeter plum cousins – something to do with their relative scarcity and superb, sharp-sweet depth of flavour. Events such as Cumbria's Damson Day, held each spring as snow-white damson blossom fills the Lyth Valley in Westmorland, attest to the appeal of this fruit. Their dusky darkness is special too: the rich pigment from their skins was employed as a dye in the textile industry, once used to create RAF blue.

At farm shops and pick-your-own farms from late summer, you'll find cultivated damsons – plumper, juicier and sweeter than their wild relatives. They're easier to scoff straight from the tree, or turn into tarts, pies and crumbles with just a little sugar.

The *true* or hedgerow damson, found in hedgerows and woodlands late in August and into autumn, is small, astringent and relatively full of pit. It's distinguishable from other small, dark wild plums by its oval shape (its relative, the bullace, is spherical). These fruits need more sweetening, more cooking and often more added liquid than cultivated damsons, but can be used in many of the same recipes; adjust accordingly.

With good acidity and rich in pectin, damsons are great in jams, jellies, pickles, fruit cheeses and liqueurs. Unlike plums, they are tough to stone when raw, so I rarely bother. On cooking, the stones are released and can be scooped out. An even simpler way to separate the fruit from the stones is to make a damson sauce. Poach 1kg fruit with 300ml water until the fruit collapses, push the mixture through a nylon sieve and sweeten the purée to taste. Freeze in small tubs to make ice creams or sorbets, to pour over poached pears or cheesecakes, or to add port-like richness to game or meat sauces.

DAMSON RIPPLE PARFAIT

The contrast of this snowy, sweet parfait and dark, tangy fruit purée is exceptionally good. Flavourful tart plums or blackberries can be used in place of the damsons. Serves 8

500g damsons

130g caster sugar

3 medium egg yolks

300ml double cream

1 tsp vanilla extract

Line a 1kg loaf tin with cling film, leaving plenty overhanging the edges.

Put the damsons into a saucepan with 2 tbsp water and 50g of the sugar. Bring to a simmer and cook gently, stirring regularly, for about 8 minutes until the fruit has broken down and the stones are coming free. Rub the fruit through a sieve to create a purée. Leave to cool then taste: it should be quite sweet, but with the tartness of the damsons coming through. Add more sugar if necessary. Chill the purée.

Put the egg yolks into the bowl of a stand mixer fitted with the whisk, or into a large bowl with an electric hand whisk at the ready. Put the remaining 80g sugar into a small pan with 125ml water. Stir over a medium heat until the sugar dissolves, then increase the heat and boil, without stirring, until the syrup registers 108°C on a sugar thermometer.

Start whisking the egg yolks, then slowly pour on the hot sugar syrup in a thin stream, whisking continuously. Beat for about 4 minutes, until the mixture is thick, pale and glossy and 'holds a trail' when you lift the whisk. In a separate bowl, whisk the cream with the vanilla to soft peaks, then fold into the egg and sugar mixture.

Transfer to the lined loaf tin and freeze for 1–2 hours, until holding its shape but still pliable. Make several holes in the parfait mix and spoon in the damson purée. Cut and swirl the mixture to spread the purée around, making sure you retain a contrasting ripple effect. Smooth the surface, bring the cling film over the top to cover and freeze until solid.

Allow the frozen parfait to soften in the fridge for 30 minutes or so before turning out on to a board and slicing to serve.

Dandelion

John Wright

LATIN NAME
Taraxacum officinale agg.

SEASONALITY
Leaves: early spring.
Flowers: March–May.
Roots: autumn and winter

HABITAT
Everywhere!

The dandelion is one of the most beautiful flowers to grace the British landscape. In April it can turn a field golden with a million blossoms. Three parts of this abundant plant can be used: leaves, flowers and roots.

As salad leaves go, those of the dandelion take a little getting used to, as they are extremely bitter. To get the sweetest dandelion leaves, pick from close to the centre of a clump – the lower, paler parts of the leaves will be least bitter.

You can also blanch dandelion leaves to lessen their bitterness. If you have dandelions in your garden (and who hasn't?), place an upturned flowerpot (the hole covered with a stone), over any plant in early spring. Over the course of a few days, this will force newly growing leaves to elongated, pink succulence and sweetness.

From late March through April the flowers appear. To make a syrup with these, pack the petals in alternate layers with sugar in a tall jug to extract the barley-sugar-like flavour. After 2 days, pour boiling water into the jug, tip the contents into a pan and heat to dissolve the sugar, then strain and bottle. The golden syrup is great on pancakes or as a flavoured alternative to plain sugar in almost any recipe; adjust the liquid in the recipe to allow for the amount of water in the syrup.

Perhaps the most familiar use of the petals is in dandelion wine – a good country wine. I recommend making it sweet, to enjoy as a dessert wine, as the flavour is strong and heady.

At almost any time of year dandelion roots may be dug up to make 'coffee'. You will be surprised how good this is – and how much it tastes like coffee. Scrub the roots and halve them lengthways if they are thick. Dry in an oven at 60°C for about 3 hours until grey-brown and rubbery, then turn up the oven to 200°C/Fan 180°C/Gas 6 and bake for 25 minutes. They will become smoky – this is a good thing. Allow to cool, grind coarsely and make coffee as usual, preferably a latte.

DANDELION AND RICOTTA SALAD WITH BACON

Salty bacon, creamy ricotta and sweet honey all counteract the bitterness of dandelion. In spring, this salad is lovely garnished with little white hawthorn flowers (see page 302). Serves 2

A little olive or rapeseed oil, for frying

100g streaky bacon or pancetta, cut into lardons

1 tbsp sunflower seeds

2 small handfuls of young, tender dandelion leaves (see above), washed and dried

2 tbsp ricotta

FOR THE DRESSING
Juice of ½ lemon

2 tbsp extra virgin olive or rapeseed oil

1 tbsp clear honey

1 tsp English mustard

¼ garlic clove, grated

Sea salt and black pepper

Place a frying pan over a medium-high heat and add a dash of oil. Add the bacon or pancetta to the pan and fry for a few minutes until golden and starting to crisp. Toss in the sunflower seeds and cook for a further minute. Remove and keep warm.

For the dressing, in a bowl, mix the lemon juice with the extra virgin oil, honey, mustard and garlic, and season with salt and pepper. Mix thoroughly.

Arrange the dandelion leaves on individual plates and scatter over the warm bacon and sunflower seeds. Crumble over the ricotta, then spoon over the dressing and serve.

Dates

LATIN NAME
Phoenix dactylifera

SEASONALITY
Winter (imported fresh dates)

MORE RECIPES
Cherry, thyme and marzipan muffins (page 154); Olive oil and honey flapjacks (page 413)

The date is a fruit that doesn't know it's a fruit. Fudge-tender, toffee-sweet, richly, stickily indulgent, it's louche and luxurious. But, heady with natural sugars as they are, dates also manage to be full of fibre and nutrients such as magnesium and potassium.

Dates grow on palms in arid places, hanging in great, pendulous bunches – maybe 80kg per bunch. In their native lands, they are sometimes eaten when still yellow, firm and crisp; in this under-ripe, fibrous state, the fruit is something of an acquired taste.

Most of the dates we eat have been allowed to ripen fully on the tree, darkening to a rich brown and developing a fleshy, sticky sweetness. Some are harvested at the peak of ripeness, and these 'fresh' dates can be found in shops during our winter, but most are allowed to begin drying out on the tree so they have a longer shelf life when picked.

The most gorgeously soft and fudgy of the dates available in the UK are 'Medjool' dates, which often come from the Jordan Valley area, or from California. It's hard to do anything with these luscious fruits other than eat them straight out of the pack – though they are also superb in salads, savoury or sweet. Mingle them with the bitter and the crisp – chicory and orange, say, with a hint of cumin and toasted seeds. Or with the juicy and sweet: kiwis, bananas, blueberries, honey and a squeeze of lime.

Marginally less sybaritic and a little cheaper is the North African 'Deglet Nour' date. This is the type sold in casket-shaped boxes at Christmas but available in various forms all year round. Deglet Nour are often treated to a gentle steaming before sale to soften and plump them a little. A brief soak in hot water, tea or fruit juice will plump them up further at home. With a slightly firmer flesh than the Medjool, they are ideal for adding to stews and tagines, where they will soak up the cooking liquor. They are also prime baking ingredients.

Dates lend their flavour and sweetness to puddings and baked treats, including sticky toffee pudding, flapjacks and cookies. They can also be blitzed with walnuts into a paste and pressed into a delicious raw crust for virtuous tarts.

STICKY DATE AND PARSNIP CAKE

150g pitted dates, such as Deglet Nour, roughly chopped

150ml hot tea

150g butter, softened

100g light muscovado or soft light brown sugar

3 medium eggs, lightly beaten

1 tsp vanilla extract

150g wholemeal self-raising flour

A pinch of baking powder

1 tsp ground mixed spice

A pinch of salt

150g finely grated parsnip (2–3 medium parsnips)

Dates are very good at absorbing other flavours. Here they carry the subtle aroma of tea into a cake – made moist and tender with grated parsnip. Serves 10

Soak the dates in the hot tea for at least 20 minutes (longer is fine). Preheat the oven to 170°C/Fan 150°C/Gas 3 and line a 20cm springform tin with baking parchment.

Using an electric hand whisk, beat the butter and sugar together for about 5 minutes until light and pale. Gradually add the beaten egg, a little at a time, beating well after each addition. Beat in the vanilla extract.

Sift the flour, baking powder, spice and salt together over the mixture and lightly fold into the butter mixture. Add the grated parsnip and fold in. Drain the dates, saving the soaking liquid, and fold them into the batter.

Spoon the mixture into the prepared tin and spread out evenly. Bake for about 45 minutes or until a skewer inserted into the centre of the cake comes out clean.

Meanwhile, put the date soaking liquid into a small saucepan and boil until reduced to 2–3 tbsp.

As you remove the cake from the oven, prick it all over with a skewer and brush lightly with the reduced tea liquor. Leave to cool completely in the tin.

Dill

Pam Corbin

LATIN NAME
Anethum graveolens

ALSO KNOWN AS
Dillweed

SEASONALITY
Leaves: May–September.
Seeds: September–October

MORE RECIPES
New potato and egg salad with gherkins and capers (page 276); Cucumber, smoked mackerel and dill salad (page 220); Pollack with courgettes and cannellini beans (page 484); Sea beet and smoked pollack pasties (page 574)

Dill is a versatile herb. It can be a soft soother, augmenting rather than dominating other ingredients or, used generously, it can pack quite an aromatic punch. It's lovely when fresh, but perhaps because of its delicate astringency, it is also widely used in pickles and preserves. Leaf, flower and seed all contribute flavour in different ways.

With its feathery, wispy, verdant leaves, fresh dill has a mellow parsley/carrot top/celery flavour, with a faint whisper of anise. A brilliant soulmate to fresh, smoked or preserved fish, dill is the customary cooling partner in piquant, mustardy sauces for oily fish such as salmon or herring, and it's the traditional seasoning for gravlax (cured salmon).

But don't reserve fresh dill for fish alone. It's a great veg-enhancer – particularly delicious snipped over buttery potatoes, carrots, beetroot, tender broad beans or peas. Blended with soured cream or yoghurt, it's very good stirred into a summery veg soup or served as a cooling dip. With cucumbers, fresh or in 'dill pickles', dill truly excels.

Tiny, brown, feather-light dill seeds deliver a more intense, warming punch of sweet aniseed, and are also great with cucumber. They're often used in preserving mixes, and also make a lively addition to home-baked breads – especially if you're going to serve them with smoked fish. The seeds are traditionally used to enhance cabbage dishes, and, like their sister seed caraway (see page 114), are very good in sauerkraut.

Fresh dill and dill seeds are fairly widely available now, but it's worth growing your own – especially if you want to enjoy the lovely flavour of the flowers. The delicate yellow umbel heads proffer something fresh yet sweetly pungent, flavour-wise somewhere between the seeds and the leaves. Snip off just-open flowerheads from the stalk and use them whole in pickles, or separate the tiny umbels and scatter them over leafy salads. They're also very good mixed with mayonnaise and tossed with finely shredded raw cabbage and chopped apple for a vibrant, crunchy coleslaw.

An annual, dill grows easily, thriving in a warm, well-drained site and relatively poor soil. It dislikes being moved, so seeds are best sown directly in the ground or in large pots. For a constant supply, sow in succession during the spring and early summer, keeping it watered when conditions are dry.

DILL SALSA VERDE

Fronds from a 50g bunch of dill, finely chopped

6 tbsp olive or rapeseed oil

A scrap of garlic (¼ clove or less), grated

1 tbsp capers, rinsed, drained and chopped

½ tsp English mustard

Finely grated zest of 1 lemon and a squeeze of its juice

A pinch of sugar

Sea salt and black pepper

This simple sauce is stunning with poached or grilled fish of any kind – especially gurnard or bream. Serves 4

Put all the ingredients into a bowl with a pinch each of salt and pepper. Mix well to combine, then taste and adjust the seasoning with a little more salt, pepper, sugar or lemon juice as needed. Store, covered, in the fridge and use within 4 days.

Dogfish

Nick Fisher

LATIN NAME
Scyliorhinus canicula

ALSO KNOWN AS
Lesser spotted dogfish, small-spotted catshark, roughhound, rock salmon

SEASONALITY
Avoid during spring and early summer when females lay their eggs

HABITAT
Found around the coasts of northern Europe; common around the British Isles

MCS RATING
4

REC MINIMUM SIZE
57cm

SOURCING
goodfishguide.org

Members of the shark family, dogfish are encased in a thick abrasive skin so indestructible it's been used for everything from sandpaper to boot soles. Within this armour lies some surprisingly soft and boneless flesh. The bull huss, a slightly larger shark family member, is sold in chip shops as the poetically named 'rock salmon'.

It's rare to find dogfish on a fish stall. Being such hardy creatures, they often survive being caught in commercial nets, and are released back into the sea because they have no sale value. However, dogfish do get caught a lot on rod and line by anglers. Their omnipresence, and their endless appetite for expensive baits, is rarely welcomed when you're targeting more fancy fish. For this reason, friendly boat anglers may be happy to give you a couple of dogfish.

Removing their tough skins is the trickiest part of their preparation. You'll need a sharp knife, stout pliers and thick gloves. There's a detailed description of dogfish-filleting and skinning in *The River Cottage Fish Book*; but essentially, you need to lay the fish on its back, slice all the way down it with the knife horizontal to the board, from the anal fins to cut away the belly, and then the head. Make a long cut into the skin along the back of the fish, grasp the skin on one side of the cut with pliers and pull it off, then repeat on the other side.

Dogfish have only a spine and no tricky rib or fin bones to deal with, while the flesh has a soft, slightly mushy texture and a more 'fishy' flavour than the other demersal fish, like cod and haddock. Dogfish chunks, cut straight across the spinal cartilage, hold together well during slow-cooking because of a thin membrane that encircles them, so dogfish pieces make a decent curry or stew. They're even good as goujons, deep-fried in a beer batter and dunked in home-made tartare sauce.

Dogfish is something every keen fish cook should try at least once, though in all honesty, I prefer to return any dogfish I catch to the sea.

HOT DOGFISH DOG

1 tbsp olive or rapeseed oil

25–30g butter, plus extra for spreading if required

1 red onion, finely sliced

1 large dogfish, head removed, gutted and skinned (300–400g prepared weight)

2 bay leaves

1 small garlic clove, lightly bashed

Sea salt and black pepper

TO ASSEMBLE

2 large hot dog rolls

Good quality tomato ketchup

Dijon or English mustard

The slender fillets from a dogfish are similar in size and shape to sausages, fitting nicely into a roll with all the trimmings. Makes 2

Heat half the oil and half the butter in a non-stick frying pan over a medium heat. When the butter is foaming, add the onion with a pinch of salt and cook, stirring occasionally, for 10–12 minutes until soft and lightly caramelised. Remove the onion from the pan and give the pan a wipe with kitchen paper.

Meanwhile, remove the cartilaginous spine of the dogfish: cut along the underside of the fish along the central line, going down to the spine, then work the tip of your knife underneath the spine from both sides, releasing the flesh. You should be able to lift out the spine quite easily.

Cut the fish lengthways into a couple of thick goujons. Cut away the membrane that covers them with a sharp knife.

Return the frying pan to a medium-high heat. Add the remaining oil and butter. Season the fish with salt and pepper and add to the pan, with the bay and garlic. Cook for about 2 minutes on each side then turn off the heat and let the fish finish cooking through; discard the bay and garlic.

Slice open the rolls, and butter them if you like. Lay the fish inside and add a generous scattering of onion. Finish with ketchup and mustard. Close the rolls and serve at once, with salad and chips.

Dripping

MORE RECIPES

Skirt steak and chips (page 64); Tongue, kale and apple hash with horseradish (page 643); Ale-braised ox cheeks with parsnips (page 64)

SOURCING

fordhallfarm.com and greenpasturefarms.co.uk (for grass-fed beef dripping)

Dripping is the melted fat that escapes from meat as it cooks. It can, technically, be applied to any meat but generally it refers to beef fat. 'Bread and dripping' is an iconic British snack. Energy-dense and utterly delicious, it's a great way to use the fat rendered from a joint of roasting beef. Spread the solidified dripping on a slice of robust bread (or hot toast if you prefer, so that it melts), sprinkle with salt and tuck in. Like all animal fats, dripping is rich in flavour. The home-rendered variety, lifted from a roasting tin, may well include some meaty residues too, making it even more tasty. In fact, though we generally take 'dripping' to refer to fat alone, the term is sometimes also applied to the rich meaty juices that separate from it. Try mashing some of those together with the fat for a particularly intense topping to your toast.

You can buy dripping ready-rendered in jars, tubs or packets. This is useful if you need a large quantity – for frying chips, say – but collecting your own is easy. After cooking a joint of beef, you can skim off the fat from the juices (leaving those as the base for rich gravy). Alternatively, leave the juices to cool: the fat will harden and form a layer on top of a meaty jelly.

Fattier cuts will of course yield more dripping: try brisket or any visibly well-covered cut from the outside of the animal, including sirloin and rib. In small quantities, dripping can also be gleaned from a stock or stew that has cooled.

You can stockpile dripping in the fridge. If you intend to keep it for any length of time, it should be clarified, removing any solids that may spoil and become rancid. To do this, put warm, liquid dripping in a large bowl and pour over roughly double its volume in boiling water, stirring all the while. Set aside to cool: the clarified fat will float to the top and solidify, and everything else will sink to the bottom.

The flavour and high smoke point of dripping make it ideal for browning meat before roasting or braising. It is also fantastic for roasting potatoes and cooking Yorkshire puddings – and there's nothing better for fried bread.

DRIP SCONES

250g self-raising wholemeal flour

A pinch of baking powder

A couple of pinches of salt

2 medium eggs

About 375ml milk

50g dripping, melted and cooled a little, plus extra for cooking

This savoury version of a simple drop scone is rich and delicious. The scones are fantastic served with leftovers from a joint of roast beef and a little horseradish, or topped with other cold meats or pâtés or even smoked fish. Makes 20–30

Sift the flour, baking powder and salt into a large bowl. Make a well in the centre and add the eggs. Pour in about half the milk. Whisk, gently at first, and then as you start to get a thick, smooth paste, add a little more milk and the 50g melted dripping. Keep beating, adding more milk as necessary, until you have a smooth batter a little thicker than double cream – you might not need all the milk.

Put a large, non-stick frying pan or flat griddle over a medium-high heat and add a small knob of dripping. Once melted, rub a wad of kitchen paper around the pan to oil it lightly. Pour a scant tablespoonful of batter into the pan, to get a disc about 7.5cm in diameter. Repeat until you have 4 or 5 rounds in the pan.

After a minute or two, when little bubbles appear all over the surface of the scones, flip them over. Cook the other side for a minute or so, then transfer the scones to a warm plate and cover with a clean tea towel so they stay warm, or put into a very low oven.

Cook the remaining batter in the same way, adjusting the heat if the scones are browning too quickly and re-greasing with a little more dripping as necessary. To serve, top the warm scones with slices of cold roast beef and a dollop of horseradish, or eat plain.

Duck, farmed

Gill Meller

LATIN NAME
Anas platyrhynchos domestica

MORE RECIPES
Slow-roasted goose with
star anise, orange and chilli
(page 283); Pigeon breasts with
sloe gin gravy (page 584);
Chicken and blueberry salad with
coriander dressing (page 77)

SOURCING
beechridgefarm.co.uk;
providencefarm.co.uk

To me, duck conjures up images of wonderful, rustic food, enjoyed slowly, in quiet places. I remember cooking duck breasts for the first time, for instance, over the embers of a barbecue in an overgrown walled garden down in the South of France. I slashed the fat and cooked the meat slowly with rosemary and salt, the smell of figs and parched earth all around me. There are some meals you never want to let go – that was one. Duck makes me think also of *rillettes* and pâté, and of *confit de canard* – salted duck legs, cooked for hours then preserved in their own fat with shards of garlic and thyme, stored in jars on some rough stone shelf in a cool larder, the meat derived from contented, free-ranging ducks.

Sadly, the reality of much modern duck-rearing casts a heavy cloud over such lovely images. In Britain, in 2012, we raised over 14 million ducks for meat, nearly all of them intensively farmed. We all know that ducks are water birds: their bills are designed to feed in water, their feathers are high in oils so that they shed water, their lungs have evolved to provide buoyancy in water and their webbed feet are, of course, meant specifically for swimming through water.

However, within intensive systems, ducks are denied all access to water, other than what they need to drink – the provision of bathing water would increase the risk of disease, meaning greater costs to the producer. So instead, ducks live by the thousand in artificially lit barns. At this point in time, there is no legislation to enforce the provision of water or address any other significant welfare concerns.

It's the poor Pekin duck, a pretty bird with snow-white plumage and an orange bill, that is seen as the most suitable for indoor intensive farming, superseding most other breeds, including the Aylesbury. It produces not only meat, but eggs and down as well.

I'm glad to say there are alternatives, with many small producers or farmers now raising free-range and organic ducks in Britain. You can buy their wares at the farm gate or at farm shops and traditional butchers, or online. The birds will have led a natural life, splashing freely in the waterways and foraging, as ducks love to do, for insects and worms. Their legs will be strong from swimming and running, and their breasts full and plump.

This is the kind of duck to seek out, a bird worthy of a feast. Ducks carry less meat than chickens, pound for pound: a smaller bird of under 2kg will serve 2–3 people. For a handsome Sunday lunch to feed 4, go for a duck of 2–3kg. The rich meat is particularly delicious when cut with sweet or sharp accompaniments. Something tart and fruity like rhubarb, sweetened with a little honey, works wonderfully, as do roasted apples with a dash of Calvados or even some deep red plums spiked with ginger and chilli. And, of course, there is the timeless classic: duck *à l'orange*.

As with many birds, there is always the risk, when roasting, of the breast meat becoming dry before the legs are cooked to tenderness. Because well-fed ducks carry a good covering of fat, this is less of a problem than with, say, chicken. Nevertheless, when I roast a duck, I like to get the best of both worlds. I first remove the legs and cook them gently for several hours until they are nice and tender, the skin is crisp and much of their fat has been released. I then roast the breasts (or 'crown') quickly in a hot oven. This way, I get slices of moist, still-pink breast meat and yielding, tender leg together on the same plate.

In the likely event that you have eaten all that tender leg meat, pour off the duck fat from the roasting tin and keep it in a jar. Roast potatoes cooked in duck fat are really hard to beat, and the fat can be used for *confit* – not just of duck, but other meats

D

too. Don't jettison the giblets either: these can be used in classic dishes such as confit giblets (or *gésiers*), stuffed duck necks, and of course duck liver parfaits. If you do have any tender leg meat left over from such a feast, it can be used for delicious duck *rillettes*: shred and turn the meat together with salt, pepper, thyme leaves and duck fat, then seal in sterilised jars and store in the fridge.

It is conventional to serve duck breast still slightly pink, rather than well done, to keep it tender and moist. Official advice goes against this, recommending that duck should be cooked as thoroughly as chicken, because it can harbour the same bugs. If you like your duck a little pink, as I do, I think it's particularly important to choose dry-plucked birds from a source you trust.

If you're cooking duck breasts alone, you'll want the skin beautifully golden and crisp. I think it's a mistake, however, to sear it too hot and fast – the outside looks wonderful but a pretty solid layer of fat will remain underneath. I prefer to cook the skin side a little more slowly so the fat renders out (as described below).

The famous delicacy known as foie gras is commonly associated with geese, but in fact most now comes from ducks. It is usually produced by force-feeding the ducks so their livers swell to unnatural proportions and become incredibly fatty and rich; for further information on the welfare issues concerning foie gras and more ethical alternatives see page 360.

BARBECUED DUCK BREASTS WITH ROSEMARY AND FIGS

2 free-range duck breasts (about 350g each)

Leaves from 6 sprigs of rosemary, roughly chopped

1 tbsp olive or rapeseed oil

6 ripe figs

1 tbsp clear honey

Sea salt and black pepper

The secret here is to keep the duck over gently glowing embers rather than a fierce heat, so that the meat cooks without the skin burning. If your figs are a little under-ripe, halve them, oil them lightly, and throw them on to the grill too, towards the end of cooking. Serves 2–3

Heat up your barbecue and let it burn down to gently glowing embers before cooking.

Place the duck breasts on a board, skin side up. Use a sharp knife to make shallow cuts, about 1cm apart, in a criss-cross pattern over the skin, going down into the fat but not as far as the meat. Scatter most of the rosemary over the duck (reserve a little for later), trickle with the oil and sprinkle with salt and pepper. Rub it all into the meat.

Put the barbecue grid at least 10cm above the coals and place the duck breasts on it, skin side down. Cook, skin side down, for 25–30 minutes. Watch carefully in case dripping fat ignites the embers and they flare up – this will burn the meat. It's useful to keep a spray bottle of water on hand in case the coals flare up – or just remove the meat from the grill and allow the flames to die down before you continue cooking.

Turn the duck breasts over and cook for a further 10–15 minutes on the second side. Remove from the heat and allow to rest somewhere warm for 15 minutes.

To serve, slice the duck breasts and divide between warmed plates. Halve the figs and place alongside the duck. Trickle with the honey, season with salt and pepper and scatter with a little more rosemary. Serve with green beans and crushed new potatoes.

Note Rather than barbecue, you can cook the duck breasts in a frying pan, skin side down, over a medium heat for about 12 minutes, until most of the fat has rendered and the skin is golden. Turn the breasts over and cook for a further 2 minutes (for still-pink meat), or until they feel slightly springy when pressed. Leave to rest in a warm spot for 15 minutes.

Duck, wild

Tim Maddams

LATIN NAME
Anas platyrhynchos (mallard)

ALSO KNOWN AS
Mallard (most common species)

SEASONALITY
1 September–late January/
mid-February

MORE RECIPES
Roast grouse with barley, apples and squash (page 290); Partridges roasted with quince and bacon (page 440); Pigeon breasts with sloe gin gravy (page 584); Chicken and blueberry salad with coriander dressing (page 77)

SOURCING
tasteofgame.org.uk

The depth of flavour in ducks that have grazed freely on acorns, grass, wheat, barley, pondweed and insects is superb. Mallard, by far the most plentiful wild duck in the British Isles, is the species you're likely to find at a game dealer or butcher – and the one you are most likely to be able to shoot yourself (for which you need a shotgun certificate, permission from the landowner and a fair bit of luck and skill). The wild population is topped up by thousands of reared mallard, released into the wild for shooting every year. They are also the most easily recognisable of the wild ducks, especially the drakes, which sport that marvellous emerald head and white collar for most of the year.

You may find other duck species for sale, including gadwall, pintail, wigeon, tufted duck, pochard and, the best of all, teal. However, conservation must be considered. Wild duck populations tend to be fluctuating and they are hard to assess so it's best to err on the side of caution. So, with the exception of mallard, view wild duck as a rare treat. Note that wild ducks require more careful handling in the kitchen than their domesticated cousins (see page 239), as they are smaller, tougher and leaner, and they may be shot-damaged.

Versatile mallard is suitable for roasting whole, braising, stewing and barbecuing, and the carcasses make a fantastic stock. I like to slow-roast it with soy, ginger, garlic, spices, honey and a little dry cider, basting until the meat begins to fall off the bone, then serve it to wrap in little pancakes, with shredded spring onions and cucumber.

If you do get your hands on a few teal, a traditional approach is best. You'll need one per person. Season the birds well then start them off in a frying pan on the hob, on their backs. Give them 4–5 minutes, until the backs are golden, then brown on both sides and finally on the breasts. Place back downwards again and pop into a hot oven for around 5 minutes. Allow to rest for at least 10 minutes before serving with the pan juices and a tart fruit jelly.

POT-ROASTED MALLARD WITH CELERIAC AND WATERCRESS

In this fantastic autumn dish, lovely, rich mallard is paired with mellow celeriac and peppery watercress. Grouse also works well cooked this way. Serves 2–4

200g carrots

2 celery stalks

½ small celeriac

1 tbsp olive or rapeseed oil

2 oven-ready mallard

6 small shallots, halved

100g bacon lardons

4 garlic cloves, thinly sliced

3–4 sprigs of thyme

2 bay leaves

250ml dark ale or stout

150ml tomato juice, passata or tinned tomatoes

250ml chicken or game stock, or water

2 large handfuls of watercress, coarse stems removed

Sea salt and black pepper

Preheat the oven to 180°C/Fan 160°C/Gas 4. Cut the carrots and celery into 5cm lengths. Cut the celeriac into 3cm cubes and set aside.

Place a large flameproof casserole, big enough to hold both ducks, over a medium heat and add the oil. Season the mallard with salt and pepper. When the oil is hot, add the mallard and brown well all over. Remove and set aside.

Add the shallots, carrots, celery and bacon to the casserole and fry for 4–5 minutes, until the veg starts to colour, then add the garlic and thyme and fry for another 2 minutes.

Return the mallard to the casserole and add the celeriac, bay leaves, ale, tomato juice and stock. Bring to a simmer, put the lid on and transfer to the oven. Cook for 1 hour.

Remove the mallards from the casserole to a warm platter and leave to rest in a warm place. Place the casserole over a medium-low heat. Add the watercress and let it wilt in the hot juices for 1–2 minutes, stirring once or twice, then taste and add more salt and pepper if necessary.

Carve the birds and divide the meat between warmed plates. Add the bacon, vegetables and watercress and spoon over lots of the rich, meaty sauce to serve.

Eggs

Celeriac soufflés (page 131);
Chive buckwheat blinis with
hard-boiled eggs (page 175);
Lamb's lettuce salad with
poached egg and croûtons
(page 336); Steamed hogweed
with scrambled eggs (page 311);
New potato and egg salad with
gherkins and capers (page 276);
Henakopita with garam masala
and eggs (page 254); Hedgehog
mushroom and bacon omelette
(page 306); Spinach, egg and
potato curry (page 599); Green
garlic, asparagus and oven-
scrambled eggs (page 270);
Sumac eggs (page 622);
Crumbed whiting goujons with
curried egg tartare (page 673);
Wineberries with peaches and
custard (page 317); Rhubarb
crème brûlée (page 532);
Blackberry yoghurt soufflé
cake (page 73); Nutty brown
sugar meringues (page 621);
Meringue with strawberries and
sorrel (page 590); Lemon, honey
and courgette cake (page 347);
Passion fruit and coconut curd
(page 441)

If you have eggs in the house, you have a meal. Boiled, fried, poached… an egg is probably the shortest cut there is to a sustaining plateful. Egg dishes – the simple and the more complex – are some of the best-loved in our repertoire and you'll find many in this book, including poached, scrambled and boiled eggs, omelettes, custards (sweet and savoury), soufflés and meringues.

This familiar, everyday ingredient is a highly nutritious food too. A valuable source of protein, an egg contains every one of the amino acids our bodies require. The white has slightly more protein than the yolk and is rich in selenium and other minerals including zinc and iron. Egg white also gives us B12, an often-deficient vitamin which helps reduce the risk of stroke and heart attack. While an egg is around 10 per cent fat, most of this is unsaturated. The yolk contains most of the calories and fat, and is rich in vitamins A, D, E and K, as well as lecithin, a superb emulsifier, which is the secret behind mayonnaise and hollandaise.

Egg yolks are also rich in cholesterol, but don't be put off by that. It is a substance our bodies require for cell structure and repair, and to manufacture vitamin D. Contrary to the accepted wisdom of previous decades, for most people cholesterol in the diet doesn't significantly raise cholesterol levels in the blood.

Hen's eggs come in a variety of sizes, and as they give moisture and volume to recipes, it's worth being precise about how much you are adding. If you don't know what size your eggs are, weigh them: hen's eggs in the shops are graded as small (under 53g), medium (53–63g), large (63–73g) or very large (over 73g). Unless stated otherwise, most recipes use medium eggs. I prefer these anyway. The hen only produces a certain amount of shell, so a larger egg has a thinner shell, upping the risk of breakages, and in any case I find shop-bought large eggs a touch bland, as if their flavour is diluted. Also, a demand for large or extra-large eggs isn't helpful to hens: it puts farmers under pressure to feed them with more protein (i.e. soya), and it stands to reason that a smaller egg is easier to lay!

Eggs from other birds taste relatively similar to hen's eggs, with some variation in richness and texture. The most obvious difference is in size. Duck eggs, for example, are up to twice the size of a hen's egg and richer in flavour; they are good fried or poached, and excellent for cakes and other baking. Turkey eggs, on average, are about 50 per cent larger than hen's eggs, with more yolk than white, and very rich and creamy; they are superb for baking, but not widely available. Goose eggs are really big, very rich and eggy; try them fried, or use in cake batters.

Guinea fowl eggs are around 30 per cent smaller and stronger in flavour than hen's eggs with tougher shells, though they can be cooked in the same way. Pheasant eggs are about half the size of a hen's egg, flavoursome and rich; they are best served whole – in salads or as Scotch eggs. Quail's eggs are just a quarter of the size of a hen's egg and have delicate shells that break easily. They are good hard- or soft-boiled for use in salads and canapés. Regrettably, the vast majority of quail's eggs are produced by caged birds (see page 510).

Eggs will keep for around a month if stored in the fridge – or for a couple of weeks somewhere cool and out of direct sunlight. They gradually lose flavour and nutritional value during this time, but will still be perfectly edible. They should be stored away from pungent ingredients, such as cheese, as they can absorb other flavours, and they prefer not to be moved – shaking them about can cause the white to thin. Ideally, allow eggs to come up to room temperature before using.

EGGS AND WELFARE

The ink stamp you'll find on most eggs is required by law and the first digit tells you how the egg has been produced.

0 = Organic Birds laying these eggs have access to the outdoors and freedom to express natural behaviours. They are fed an organic, GM-free diet. There is an upper limit of 2,000 birds per flock. No pesticides, herbicides or routine medicines are used in their rearing.

1 = Free-range These chickens have unlimited daylight access to the outdoors (but that is not to say they go outside, as they aren't forced to). Some free-range flocks are very large as there is no upper limit on overall numbers. There is an outdoor stocking rate of 4 birds per square metre, and an overnight indoor stocking rate of 9 birds per square metre.

2 = Barn-reared These birds live their entire lives indoors but not in cages, and can usually express some natural behaviours, such as dust bathing.

3 = Caged These birds are kept indoors in cages. Battery cages were banned in 2012, but the supposedly 'enriched' replacements are, in reality, little better. There are 13 hens or more living in every square metre, which leaves no freedom for them to exhibit their key behaviours. Shockingly, the typical chicken lifespan of around 7 years is likely to be shortened by this highly stressed life to around 18 months. Thankfully, the sales of eggs from caged hens have fallen dramatically to about 50 per cent of the total, and a number of major supermarkets no longer sell eggs from birds kept in these conditions.

The codes explained in the box above are the only meaningful indicators of welfare. Ignore all other distractions. The colour of the shell does not affect the flavour or reflect the hen's living conditions (in fact it's a function of the breed of chicken). Bucolic scenes on the packaging mean nothing; 'farm fresh' means nothing, the presence of tractors (including the Red Tractor) does not indicate that any of the hen's life has been spent outside. The British Lion symbol indicates that the eggs are British, but implies no welfare standards. Trust the first digit of the code on the egg only. Likewise, in processed foods (sandwiches, tarts etc.), assume the eggs were laid by caged hens unless the packaging specifically states the eggs are free-range or organic.

In order to minimise feather-pecking injuries, most British laying hens have part of their beak removed without anaesthetic, using an infra-red burner. Buying Soil Association certified organic eggs or Waitrose free-range British Blacktail eggs is the only way to be sure that the eggs come from hens that have not been beak-trimmed.

Apart from contributing to the chickens' quality of life, buying good eggs gives you a superior ingredient. Crack one open: the colour of the yolk from a happy chicken is likely to be deeper in colour – often almost orange – thanks to their green-heavy diet. Less obviously, the eggs from free-range hens are likely to be higher in omega-3 fatty acids and possess a healthier ratio of unsaturated to saturated fats, so it's not only the hen who gets a better deal when we buy free-range eggs.

If you have even a small space in your garden and the inclination, why not keep a few hens of your own? The eggs will be the finest you ever eat, and the hens will keep you entertained. Depending on the breed, you can expect something like an egg a day per hen for all but the darkest months of the year, when hens naturally stop laying (we have an all-year supply in the shops because some hens are kept in conditions that mimic the longest days of the year).

Cooking with eggs

The fresher the egg the better it is for cooking (except, arguably, for meringues, see right). Eggs have an air pocket inside that expands as they age. To check an egg for freshness, drop it carefully into a bowl of water. A fresh egg, which contains almost no air, will sink to the bottom and lie on its side. If the egg stands on its end at the bottom of the bowl, it's less fresh but ok. If it floats at the top, it's well past its best. Once released from the shell, the yolk of a fresh egg sits proud and tight on a cushion of thick white: a lack of either may indicate an egg approaching its 'best before' date.

It is also important to understand that eggs nearly always like to be cooked gently (a super-crispy, golden-edged fried egg being a notable exception). The proteins in an egg coagulate at surprisingly low temperatures – pure egg white at around 65°C and pure yolk at around 70°C – so you don't need to heat them all that much to set them. For creamy scrambled eggs, for instance, it's almost impossible to have the heat too low. Once you overcook eggs, their proteins start to clump tightly together and force out water – hence the rubbery omelette, the watery scramble and the split custard.

To avoid this, eggs may be stabilised by the addition of flour, as in a cake or batter, or insulated from too much heat with a bain-marie (water bath), as when gently baking a custard or cooking lemon curd. At the simplest though, all you really need when cooking eggs is an eye on the clock, close attention to the pan and practice.

Recipes such as custard, ice cream and hollandaise use just egg yolks. Thankfully egg whites freeze well and once defrosted they work beautifully for meringue. Some say that slightly older whites are best for meringues, and it is true that they whip up quickly as the older proteins are a little looser. Fresh, cold egg whites, with their tight proteins, take longer to whip but create a stable, consistent foam with larger bubbles.

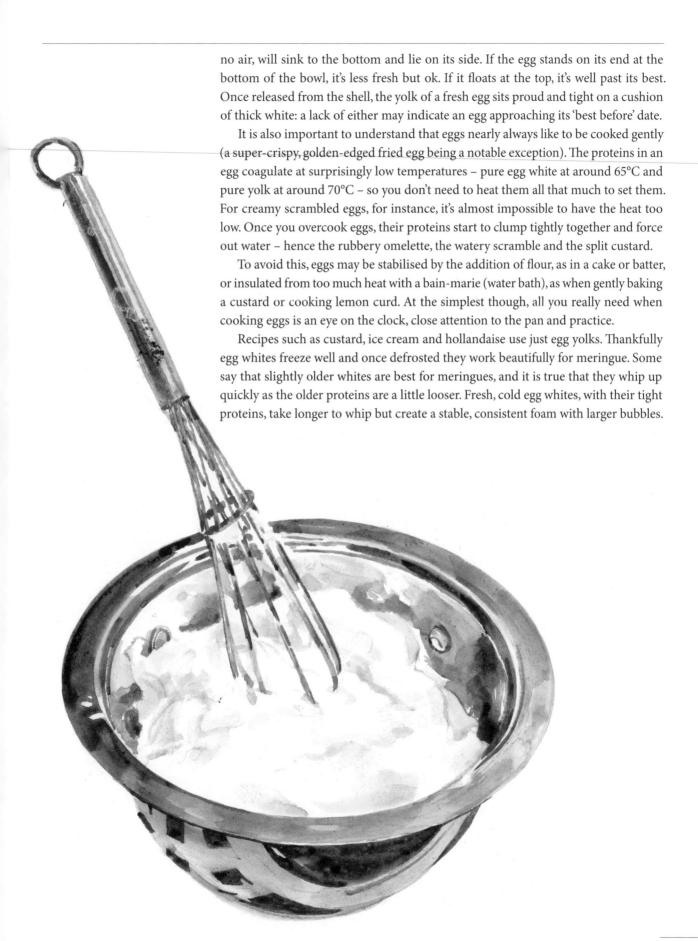

If you find yourself with a surfeit of leftover egg yolks, they keep less well, but can be refrigerated in a sealed container for up to 3 days, their surface covered directly with cling film. Or beat them with a pinch of salt or sugar and then freeze them (making a note of how many yolks you have and whether they're salty or sweet).

Egg safety

Without being paranoid, it's wise to take a little care when using eggs in the kitchen to minimise the slim risk of salmonella. This bacterium may cause illness, which can be particularly serious for pregnant women, the elderly, and the very young. But it is avoidable with a few precautions. Eggs carrying the British Lion mark – almost 90 per cent of British eggs – are from hens that have been vaccinated against salmonella. Vaccination may not be appropriate or cost-effective for small-scale producers, but the risk of salmonella in low-intensity, organic and free-range systems is likely to be lower than in intensive systems.

But in all cases, it makes good sense to wash your hands before and after handling eggs (the bacteria can be carried on the shell as well as inside it). For recipes that call for raw eggs, such as mayonnaise, use eggs that are less than a week old (i.e. have at least 3 weeks left until their 'best-before' date). And avoid serving raw eggs to anyone in a vulnerable group.

WALNUT AND BLUE CHEESE SOUFFLÉS

60g walnuts

60g butter, plus a little melted, for greasing

200ml whole milk

2 sprigs of thyme

1 bay leaf

¼ onion

60g plain flour

250g blue cheese, such as Cornish Blue or Harbourne Blue, crumbled

5 medium eggs, separated

1 tsp Dijon mustard

A pinch of sweet smoked paprika

Sea salt and black pepper

These soufflés are very forgiving – you can make them up to 3 days in advance then reheat them to serve. For a Cheddar soufflé, replace the blue cheese with a mature Cheddar and leave out the walnuts. Makes 6

Preheat the oven to 150°C/Fan 130°C/Gas 2.

Chop the walnuts finely in a food processor, or bash them to fine crumbs using a pestle and mortar. Grease six 10cm diameter ramekins or mini pudding moulds with melted butter, then coat the insides with the chopped walnuts. Stand the ramekins in a roasting tray and place in the fridge.

Put the milk into a pan with the thyme, bay leaf and onion. Bring to a simmer, then turn off the heat and leave to infuse for 5 minutes.

Meanwhile, melt the 60g butter in a saucepan over a low heat. Add the flour and stir to a paste. Cook gently for 2 minutes, stirring all the time. Take off the heat and strain the warm, infused milk into the pan. Beat until smooth. Return to the heat and cook gently for a couple of minutes to create a very thick béchamel sauce.

Let the sauce cool a little, then add the cheese and beat it in until melted. Add the egg yolks, mustard, paprika and a pinch of pepper and beat again until smooth.

Whisk the egg whites in a clean bowl with a pinch of salt until they form firm peaks. Beat about one-third of the egg white into the cheese mix to loosen it, then fold in the remaining egg white very gently, keeping in as much air as possible.

Spoon the mixture into the prepared ramekins. Pour hot water from the kettle into the roasting tray to come halfway up the side of the ramekins. Bake for 45 minutes. Leave to cool slightly then gently tip out the soufflés on to individual plates. Serve straight away, or refrigerate the soufflés for up to 3 days, then put them back in their moulds and reheat at 180°C/Fan 160°C/Gas 4 for 10–12 minutes before serving. They're delicious partnered by a green salad with a herby dressing, or with dressed lentils or green beans.

Elder

Pam Corbin

LATIN NAME
Sambucus nigra

SEASONALITY
Flowers: Late May–early July.
Berries: August–September

HABITAT
Very common, except
in central and northern
Scotland, in hedgerows
and disturbed ground

MORE RECIPES
Gooseberry, cream and honey
pudding (page 286)

They say 'summer only starts when the elderflowers appear'. Festoons of these creamy-white, scented blooms transform hedgerows in early summertime and up until late June. Native to Britain, Europe and Scandinavia, the elder is a small, bushy deciduous tree that grows seemingly everywhere – woods, scrubland, railway embankments, roadside verges.

Aside from its amazing show of flowers and the luminescent black berries that succeed in early autumn, its appearance is rather dull and inconspicuous. But the elder is reputed to be the oldest cultivated herb, used in folk remedies and for culinary purposes since Hippocrates called it his 'medicine chest' well over two thousand years ago. Planted by your door it was said to ward off evil spirits, an infusion of its leaves could repel midges, a swig of its berry wine was a way to cure sneezes and wheezes, while its sap could whip away a knobbly wart.

Today, it is the elder's headily fragrant blossom and juicy berries that are prized. The flowers are best gathered when dry and warmed by the morning sun – damp heads tend to smell unpleasantly of cat's pee! The flowerheads, each a proliferation of tiny clotted-cream blooms, usually look easy enough to reach, from a distance. More often than not, however, they're protected by an intimidating mantle of nettles and brambles. Go prepared.

For the best flavour and fragrance, look for flowerheads with just a few buds still unopened, rather than full-blown ones. When picking, leave some flowerheads for bees and butterflies, and, of course, to develop into berries. Use the flowers as soon as possible after collecting. Don't wash them or you'll lose some of the precious, scented pollen – a gentle shake will remove any insects.

Whole elderflower heads can be turned into glorious, crisp fritters: dip them in a light batter and deep-fry briefly before shaking over a little sugar. However, most commonly, the elder's unique fragrance is captured in a delightful cordial – a zingy combination of floral and citrus notes.

As well as its lovely thirst-quenching properties when simply diluted with iced water, a splash of elderflower cordial will jazz up a glass of sparkling wine, and a few drops will lift a dish of fresh gooseberries, strawberries, raspberries or blueberries. It's also good drizzled over cakes and trifle sponges, mixed into batters for pancakes and griddle cakes, or used in pannacottas and rice puddings. You can also turn this cordial into lollies, refreshing sorbets or delicate jellies (as in the recipe overleaf). Elderflowers can also be lightly fermented to make a sparkling elderflower champagne.

Fortunately, there's always a flush of gooseberries in June when elderflowers are at their peak. A few flowerheads added to the berries while softening for jam or a compote will bring a soft muscat flavour. Either tie the blooms in muslin to infuse, or simply lay the flowerheads on top of the fruit and remove when the berries are cooked. You may get a few of the tiny flowers in your jam or fruit, but that's rather fetching.

Elderflowers are easy to dry, and it's worth taking the time to do so. Lay the flowerheads on a paper-lined baking sheet. Put them somewhere warmish and out of the sun for several days, turning them occasionally, until dry. Then use a fork to zip the flowers off the stalks. Store them in a clean jar. They're great in tisanes, added to cakes and icings, or infused in recipes as if fresh. A handful or two scattered over stored apples will give them a lovely pineapple flavour.

Just as the first flush of creamy elderflowers signals the beginning of summer, so the ripening of the elderberries traditionally marks its end. Thin-skinned and juicy,

the berries are ripe when they droop down in copious purple-black clusters. Flavour-wise, they are a bit of an acquired taste – earthy and astringent but with a little fruity sweetness. They are always best cooked, being mildly poisonous when raw, and are good combined with other autumnal orchard or hedgerow fruits such as apples, pears, plums or blackberries, and used to make fruit pies, jams or jellies. Or use them in lieu of blueberries in muffins and pancakes.

Elderberry juice – rich in vitamin C and health-boosting antioxidants – is underused and undervalued. For home-made wine or cordial, extract the juice by poaching the berries in water. Alternatively, you can cook them with vinegar and spices to make piquant pontack sauce – a worthy storecupboard ingredient that adds body to sauces, gravies and stew.

ELDERFLOWER JELLY

A little rapeseed oil or unsalted butter, for greasing

8 fresh elderflower heads and about 100g caster sugar OR 150ml elderflower cordial

Enough sheets of leaf gelatine to set 500ml liquid (different brands vary)

Juice of ½ lemon (25–30ml)

This is a pudding jelly, rather than a preserve – a lovely, light thing to serve at the end of a meal. You can make it with fresh elderflowers in early summer, or a good elderflower cordial at any other time. Accompany it with a trickle of cream, a few strawberries or perhaps a gooseberry compote. Serves 4

Very lightly oil four 150ml darioles or similar moulds, using a few drops of oil or a smear of butter on a wad of kitchen paper.

If using fresh elderflowers, begin by making an infusion. Snip the elderflowers off the stalks into a small saucepan, pour on 500ml boiling water and leave to infuse for 3–4 hours, making sure they are all submerged.

When you're ready to make the jelly, calculate how many gelatine leaves you need to set 500ml liquid. Soak the leaves in cold water for about 10 minutes until softened.

Meanwhile, remove the elderflowers from the liquid and give them a good squeeze before discarding to get out every last drop of flavour, then bring the infused liquid to a simmer. Take off the heat and stir in 75g caster sugar and the lemon juice. Once the sugar is fully dissolved, taste and add a little more sugar if needed (when cold, the jelly will taste a little less sweet). Pour the liquid through a muslin-lined sieve into a large bowl or wide jug. Squeeze any excess water out of the softened gelatine leaves and add to the hot elderflower liquid. Stir until dissolved.

If using elderflower cordial, calculate how many gelatine leaves you need to set 500ml liquid. Soak the gelatine in a bowl of cold water for about 10 minutes until softened. Meanwhile, combine the elderflower cordial with the lemon juice and 350ml water in a saucepan. Heat gently until steaming but not boiling. Remove from the heat. Drain the gelatine leaves and squeeze out excess water, then add to the hot elderflower liquid and stir until dissolved.

Whether you've used fresh elderflowers or cordial, pour the elderflower liquid into the prepared moulds and leave to cool before refrigerating for at least 4 hours, or until set.

To turn out, first run the tip of a small sharp knife around the edge of each jelly to help release it, then dip the moulds very briefly in warm water to barely soften the outside of the jellies, before inverting on to a plate. If the jellies don't plop out, repeat the warm water dipping.

Endive

Mark Diacono

LATIN NAME
Cichorium endivia

ALSO KNOWN AS
Curly endive, frisée

SEASONALITY
Mid-summer through to spring

MORE RECIPES
Roast potatoes with radicchio and cheese (page 518)

The term 'endive' can mean different things. It may be used interchangeably with 'chicory' – and it is a kind of chicory – but, for the purposes of this book, we shall remain resolutely British in our outlook: endive, aka curly endive, is that shaggy, leafy vegetable that looks rather like a lettuce that has discovered tequila on a long night out. It is also, fittingly, called frisée.

Endive is in season in Britain from the hottest weeks of summer through until spring. Like its relatives chicory and radicchio, endive is naturally bitter. Growers often moderate that quality by 'blanching', i.e. excluding light, by either tying up the heads or covering the whole plant.

You can choose to celebrate the delicate bitterness that remains by leaving endive raw and dressing it lightly. With a lively honey, mustard and orange dressing, it makes a bold salad that's exceptionally good with chicken. Or you can dress it simply with plenty of salt and a good olive oil for an even more bracing partner to something rich.

Alternatively, you can calm down the bitterness by cooking the endive and combining it with creamy, salty and/or bland ingredients. Like chicory, it is delicious braised or sautéed, especially with rich partners such as lamb, duck or winter stews. And it has an affinity with eggs – shredded, wilted endive is lovely with an omelette.

Frying is a particularly good treatment. Briefly blanch a whole head of endive in boiling water, dry it with a good shake and a clean tea towel, then fry in olive oil in a very hot wok, showering it in plenty of salt and pepper, and flipping it as it cooks. It makes a delicious lunch or accompaniment to baked fish. A shredded head of endive, stir-fried with bacon or chorizo, is also excellent in this context. And, unlikely as it sounds, endive leaves are lovely dipped in tempura batter and deep-fried.

ENDIVE WITH CHICKEN LIVERS AND BACON

250g free-range chicken livers

2 tbsp plain flour

A pinch of cayenne pepper

1 tbsp olive or rapeseed oil

150g streaky bacon, diced

1 medium onion, thinly sliced

A knob of butter

½ endive, leaves separated

FOR THE DRESSING

2 tsp Dijon mustard

4 tsp cider vinegar or red wine vinegar

2 tbsp extra virgin olive or rapeseed oil

1 small garlic clove, bashed

Sea salt and black pepper

The richness of liver and saltiness of bacon are superb cut with delicately bitter endive. You could also use chicory or shredded radicchio. Serves 2

Trim away any sinew from the livers and cut larger ones in half. Combine the flour with the cayenne and some salt and pepper; set aside.

For the dressing, put all the ingredients into a jar, screw on the lid and give it a good shake to combine.

Heat a medium frying pan over a medium heat. Add a dash of oil, then scatter the bacon and onion into the pan. Fry, stirring regularly, until the onion is soft and the bacon starts to crisp, 10–12 minutes. Remove both from the pan and keep warm.

Toss the chicken livers in the seasoned flour. Return the frying pan to a high heat. When it is hot, add a dash more oil, then add the livers, in an even layer. Cook for 4 minutes, turning 2 or 3 times.

Now turn the heat down, throw in the butter and return the bacon and onion to the pan. Toss well for about a minute, as the butter melts. By this time, the livers should be nicely done: still a little pink inside, but not bloody or raw-looking. Take the pan off the heat.

Divide the endive between 2 large plates, dress generously with the dressing and spoon on the bacon and livers. Serve straight away.

Fairy ring champignons

John Wright

LATIN NAME
Marasmius oreades

SEASONALITY
Late summer and autumn

HABITAT
Common in lawns, parks and pasture

MORE RECIPES
Hedgehog mushroom and bacon omelette (page 306)

Those who are proud owners of a lawn hate the fairy ring champignon with a passion. It forms rings of mushrooms in the late summer and autumn, and for most of the year disturbs the immaculate green of the grass by forming a ring of lush grass surrounded by a ring of dead grass. This is caused by the fungal mycelium growing outwards, first poisoning the soil to kill the grass, then, as it passes over, releasing nitrogen which stimulates it.

Gardeners may hate them, but fairy ring champignons are among the tastiest of all mushrooms. They are fairly easy to identify from the mess they make but, if you're unsure, they grow to 4cm in diameter, have a honey-coloured top with a broad bump on it when mature, cream-coloured gills and a tough, fibrous stem (which should be removed). In dry weather they do dry out, but the first rain will freshen them quickly. Although the mushrooms are tiny, the rings can be enormous and contain a hundred or more specimens.

Fairy ring champignons should always be cooked. The flavour is mild, sweet and mushroomy and the texture pleasantly firm. Although usable in almost any mushroom dish, they taste and look particularly good in a risotto (see below).

They are also very good pickled: clean the caps, place in a bowl and sprinkle with salt until covered by a thin layer, then stir. Leave for an hour, drain off the liquid and sprinkle on more salt. After a further hour, drain in a sieve, then run water through the mushrooms in the sieve to wash off as much salt as possible – but do it quickly! Pat the mushrooms between clean tea towels to dry. Boil enough cider vinegar or wine vinegar in a saucepan to cover the mushrooms. Add the mushrooms to the vinegar, stir and bring back to the boil. Drain off the vinegar immediately, pack the mushrooms into clean Kilner jars and cover with good olive oil or walnut oil. Keep in the fridge, for up to around 6 months.

FAIRY RING CHAMPIGNON RISOTTO

About 150g open-cap or field mushrooms, cleaned

1 tbsp olive or rapeseed oil

1 medium onion, finely diced

2 garlic cloves, finely chopped

170g arborio rice

2 sprigs of thyme

1 bay leaf

700ml hot veg stock

50ml white wine

150g fairy ring champignons, cleaned, stems removed

50g mature Cheddar, grated

20g butter

½ eating apple, cored and diced

10 hazelnuts, toasted (see page 304) and roughly crushed

Sea salt and black pepper

This is particularly good served topped with a handful of kale 'crisps' (see page 322). If you have cobnuts to hand, use these instead of hazelnuts. Serves 2

Trim and finely chop the open-cap or field mushrooms. Heat the oil in a wide saucepan over a medium-low heat, add the onion and garlic and sweat gently for 8–10 minutes until softened.

Add the chopped open-cap or field mushrooms to the pan. Increase the heat a little and cook for a further 7–8 minutes until nice and soft. Add the rice, thyme and bay, and cook, stirring, for a couple of minutes until the rice is translucent.

Start adding the hot stock, a ladleful at a time, letting the rice simmer gently and adding more stock when the previous ladleful has been absorbed. Stir often. It should take about 20 minutes for the rice to absorb all the liquid and become just tender but not soft.

Add the wine and fairy ring champignons. When the risotto is simmering again, give it a further 3 minutes of bubbling to cook the mushrooms through.

Now add the Cheddar and butter, take the pan off the heat and stir for 1–2 minutes, until the butter and cheese have melted. Pick out the thyme stalks and bay leaf. Add the diced apple and season to taste.

Serve immediately, so the apple retains its crunch, in warmed bowls, and sprinkle with the crushed toasted nuts before serving.

Fat hen

John Wright

LATIN NAME
Chenopodium album

SEASONALITY
May–September

HABITAT
Common in veg patches and other disturbed, cultivated ground, also compost heaps

MORE RECIPES
Spear-leaved orache bhajis (page 593); Spinach, egg and potato curry (page 599)

Every spring, gardeners descend on their vegetable patches to prepare the soil for this year's planting. The first thing they do is dig it over to remove the newly growing annual weeds. Chief among these is fat hen. This is scrupulously removed and spinach, perhaps, is sown. My advice to them is to not bother. Fat hen tastes just as good.

It grows into a substantial plant, but it is the young specimens at around 15cm tall that are the sweetest and most succulent, and at this size, the whole plant is edible. Once you have your first crop, lightly dig the ground and you will get a second crop within a month or two – and a third.

Fat hen is an easily identifiable 'weed', related to spinach. The leaves are pale green and roughly the shape of a cross-sectioned egg, but with shallowly serrated edges. The young leaves, especially those at the top of the plant, are covered in fine granules that glisten.

Vegetable plots are benign locations with few poisonous plants with which fat hen can be confused. However, the leaves of the common black nightshade and the less common datura can appear vaguely similar, to those who are botanically challenged.

The best way to pick fat hen is with scissors, as this avoids bringing roots and dirt into the kitchen.

HENAKOPITA WITH GARAM MASALA AND EGGS

6 eggs

A carrier bagful of young fat hen

2 tbsp olive or rapeseed oil

1 large onion, finely sliced

2 garlic cloves, very thinly sliced

2–3 tsp garam masala

A squeeze of lemon juice

250g ready-made filo pastry (6–8 sheets)

75g unsalted butter, melted

35g hazelnuts or walnuts, roughly bashed

Sea salt and black pepper

Traditionally made with spinach, the Greek dish spanakopita works equally well with fat hen. If you can't find enough of this leaf, make up the difference with young nettle tops and/or spear-leaved orache. It's good with sea beet too. Serves 4–6

Preheat the oven to 180°C/Fan 160°C/Gas 4. Have ready a shallow 1.5 litre baking dish.

Bring a pan of water to the boil, add the eggs and cook for 7 minutes, then remove from the water. Allow to cool, then peel.

Pick over the fat hen, removing any very coarse stalks. Wash thoroughly and chop roughly. Bring a large pan of well-salted water to the boil and throw in the fat hen. Bring back to the boil and blanch for a couple of minutes, then tip into a colander and leave to drain.

Meanwhile, heat the oil in a frying pan over a medium heat, add the onion and sauté for 8–10 minutes to soften. Add the garlic and garam masala, stir and cook for another couple of minutes.

When the fat hen is cool enough to handle, squeeze to extract as much water as possible, then finely chop. Mix with the onion, adding the lemon juice and salt and pepper to taste.

Brush a sheet of filo pastry with a little melted butter and use it, butter side down, to line the baking dish. Let any excess overhang the ends. Place another buttered filo sheet on top and continue until you've used all but one sheet of filo.

Spoon half the fat hen mix into the dish. Halve the boiled eggs and distribute over the greens. Scatter over the nuts, then top with the remaining fat hen. Fold over the pastry ends to enclose the filling, dabbing with a little melted butter to keep the pastry together.

Take the remaining sheet of filo pastry, crumple it lightly in your hands to give the pie a nicely textured top, and place over the filling. Dab a little more butter on top. Bake for 35–40 minutes until golden. Serve immediately.

Fennel, Florence

LATIN NAME
Foeniculum vulgare var. *azoricum*

ALSO KNOWN AS
Bulb fennel

SEASONALITY
July–November

MORE RECIPES
Barbecued fennel and
courgettes with loganberries
(page 367); Cod with fennel,
capers and tomatoes (page 194);
Spider crab salad (page 208);
Cuttlefish with fennel and white
beans (page 228)

Put a couple of fat, creamy white bulbs of Florence fennel in front of me and my culinary synapses start to fire. Crisp, aromatic and fresh-tasting when raw, mellow, melting and rich when cooked, fennel has an incredible range and, in every incarnation, it offers a subtle but delicious aniseed tang.

The Italians, who prize it highly, sauté fennel in oil until tender, then dot it with cheese and butter and grill it. They simmer it in soups and vegetable stews. They fritter it in breadcrumbs and sweat it softly into pasta sauces and risottos. But they also love this ingredient uncooked – simply chopped into wedges and dipped in olive oil or even offered at the end of a meal, alongside fresh fruit.

I love salads with raw fennel – slivered finely and combined with rocket or chicory, radishes or beetroot, apples or oranges, along with a few seeds and something a little salty such as olives or firm ewe's cheese. Thinly sliced and just left to soften for half an hour in a little olive oil, salt and lemon juice, a simple fennel salad goes with everything from smoked mackerel to fresh ricotta to curls of air-dried ham.

Fennel is lovely roasted too – it's superb with pork and poultry, and even better with fish. Thickly slice the bulbs, season with salt and pepper, and trickle with olive or rapeseed oil. Roast, covered with foil, at 190°C/Fan 170°C/Gas 5 for 20 minutes until fairly tender. Then remove the foil and return the fennel to the oven for another 10–15 minutes until beautifully caramelised.

Choose firm, smooth-looking bulbs without wrinkles or brown patches. Slice off the base and the green stalky tops and remove the outer layer (or two), which can be tough (but make a fine addition to home-made stock). For serving raw, slice as thinly as you can. For cooking, keep the fennel reasonably chunky or it will collapse into nothing. The inner core is usually tender and you shouldn't need to cut this out.

GRIDDLED FENNEL AND APPLE WITH RICOTTA

2 large fennel bulbs

Olive or rapeseed oil,
for cooking

1 large or 2 small, crisp
eating apples, such as
Cox or Ashmead's Kernel

75g ricotta

20g pumpkin seeds, lightly
toasted

Sea salt and black pepper

TO FINISH

Extra virgin olive oil or
hempseed oil

A good squeeze of lemon juice

Apple is an excellent partner for fennel and both respond well to grilling. If you do not have a ridged griddle pan, use an ordinary, heavy-based frying pan. Alternatively, you can cook the fennel and apple on a barbecue. Serves 2

Heat a large, ridged griddle pan over a high heat.

Trim the fennel bulbs, reserving any feathery fronds for serving. Cut the bulbs from top to bottom into 5mm thick slices. Put the fennel slices into a bowl, trickle over a little oil and sprinkle with salt and pepper, then toss the fennel to coat well.

Lay the fennel slices in the griddle pan and cook for 3–5 minutes on each side, or until lightly charred.

Meanwhile, core the apple(s) using an apple corer, and slice them into 5mm thick rings. Oil and season the apple rings in the same way as the fennel.

When the fennel is cooked, transfer it to a warm serving platter or divide between warm plates. Add the apple rings to the griddle pan and cook for 3–5 minutes each side or until lightly charred. Arrange the warm apple on and around the fennel.

Dot the ricotta over the apple and fennel. Scatter over the toasted pumpkin seeds and any reserved feathery fennel fronds. Give the salad a final trickle of extra virgin olive oil or hempseed oil, a grinding of salt and pepper and a good squeeze of lemon, and serve.

Fennel, herb & seed

Pam Corbin

LATIN NAME
Foeniculum vulgare

SEASONALITY
Fronds: May–September.
Seeds: September–October

MORE RECIPES

This exuberant herb is not quite the same as the plant that produces fat bulbs of Florence fennel (see page 255) but it shares a similar flavour. Statuesque, with soft, billowing foliage and warm, anise-menthol tones, it is a joyful thing to grow. And necessary too: it's pretty unusual to find the cut herb for sale – though you may happen upon it at a farmers' market.

Perennial and prolific, fennel herb grows well in a sunny, sheltered spot, reaching the heady height of 1.5–2 metres. Dressed in bronze or bright green from late spring, its pretty yellow flowerheads appear in mid-summer, turning into tiny, green berries, which can be chopped or crushed into recipes. These become dry seeds in early autumn, which can be harvested as for caraway seeds (see page 114).

Wild fennel is another option if you live in the South: it can be found in both coastal and urban areas, usually in profuse clumps. Look for its haze of green fronds. The seeds are smaller than those from the cultivated plant but certainly worth collecting.

Fennel fronds are best when young and vibrant, long before the plant has flowered. Renowned for its friendship with fish, fennel is particularly delicious with bream, mullet and mackerel – use the fronds to make a bed on which to roast them. Alternatively, stuff them inside a fish, with slices of lemon, butter and salt to create, once baked, a fennel-scented buttery *jus*. Late in the summer, mature fennel stalks make a fragrant smoke when thrown on the barbecue under mackerel or sardines.

The soothing fronds are lovely snipped into salads too. Like dill (see page 235), to which it is not dissimilar though it has a softer flavour, fennel enhances cucumber, tomato, potato, beetroot and lettuce. At other times, use fronds and seeds to make a pesto – delicious on lentil dishes or swirled into soups.

Fennel seeds (easy to buy if you don't have your own crop) are warm, intense and excellent with meat: dry-fry them to release their fragrance, then smash roughly using a pestle and mortar before rubbing, with flaky sea salt and black pepper, into pork, lamb and duck for roasts and barbecues.

FENNEL AND OLIVE MASH

750g floury potatoes, such as Maris Piper, peeled and cut into large pieces

2 tsp fennel seeds and/or a handful (20–30g) fresh fennel fronds, finely chopped

60g butter

150ml whole milk

150g stoned black olives, chopped

Sea salt and black pepper

This is excellent with fish. Use fennel seeds, or fresh fennel herb – or both. Serves 4

Put the potatoes into a pan with enough cold water to cover them completely. Add a good pinch of salt, cover and bring to the boil. Lower the heat and simmer, partially covered, for about 20 minutes or until completely tender.

Meanwhile, if using the fennel seeds, toast them in a small dry frying pan over a medium heat for a couple of minutes until aromatic. Remove and grind to a powder, using a spice grinder or pestle and mortar.

Put the butter, milk and crushed fennel seeds into a small pan and heat gently so that the butter melts. Turn the heat down very low and leave the milk to infuse while the potatoes finish cooking. Don't let the milk boil. (If you're not using the seeds, just heat the milk and butter shortly before mashing.)

Once the potatoes are cooked, drain and leave to steam in the colander for a couple of minutes, then return to the warm pan. Mash or rice the potatoes until smooth. Add the warm milk and beat until fully incorporated, then add the olives. Taste and season with salt and a good grinding of pepper. If you're using fresh fennel, stir into the mash and serve immediately.

Field mushrooms

Agaricus campestris

SEASONALITY
July–October

HABITAT
Locally common in permanent pasture, usually in rings

MORE RECIPES
Fairy ring champignon risotto (page 252); Sautéed mushrooms with juniper (page 320); Baked mushrooms with rosemary and walnut butter (page 396); Squash, shallot and mushroom tart (page 604); Blewit, pigeon and endive salad (page 74)

I still remember the surge of excitement the first time I found field mushrooms. They looked beautiful and the smell was wonderful. And, of course, their excellent flavour was quite different from that of their cultivated cousins. Although they can be used like a cultivated mushroom, field mushrooms are best treated simply: fried in butter and served on toast.

That single collection heralded a massive glut. I dried as many as I could, but still thousands were left in the field. Sadly, although the field is still there, it fell to the plough – which is often the culprit when a once-productive field becomes barren. Fungi need permanent habitats and field mushrooms require permanent pasture.

When picking wild fungi, some people stick to field mushrooms because they consider that to be a safer option. On the whole, they are quite right. The field mushroom, found between late summer and October, is fairly distinctive as it is almost identical to the cultivated mushroom. Also, fungi that grow in fields are generally safer than those picked in woodland, provided you avoid tree-lined field edges. It is in the woods that the true 'nasties' such as the 'Death Cap' are found.

However, around 95 per cent of poisonings are due to people picking what they think are field mushrooms. It's down to a look-alike called the 'Yellow Stainer'. The key feature of this poisonous mushroom is that the very bottom of the stem, the edge of the cap and the pendulous ring on the stem bruise a brilliant chromium yellow. The effect is less in mature specimens. Also, it smells phenolic (antiseptic), especially when cooking. Despite these startling differences, people sometimes do pick them and have to take a miserable couple of days off to recover.

FIELD MUSHROOM AND CELERIAC PIE

FOR THE RYE PASTRY
100g dark/wholegrain rye flour

100g plain flour

A pinch of salt

100g cold butter, diced

FOR THE FILLING
200g peeled celeriac, roughly chopped

200ml whole milk

3 sprigs of thyme

1 garlic clove, peeled and bashed

1 tbsp olive or rapeseed oil

20g butter

About 400g field mushrooms, trimmed and roughly chopped

1 small onion, chopped

1 small leek, chopped

1 celery stalk, chopped

Sea salt and black pepper

This works well with most other mushrooms too. Eat it warm or cold. Serves 4–6

Preheat the oven to 180°C/Fan 160°C/Gas 4. Grease a baking tray.

For the pastry, put the flours and salt into a food processor and blitz briefly to combine (or sift into a bowl). Add the butter and blitz (or rub in with your fingers) until the mix resembles breadcrumbs. Add just enough cold water to bring the mixture together into large clumps – probably 2–3 tbsp. Knead into a ball, wrap and chill in the fridge.

Put the celeriac in a pan with the milk, thyme and garlic, cover and bring to a simmer. Cook for 15–20 minutes, until the celeriac is tender (don't worry if the milk curdles a little). Remove the thyme stalks and blitz the mixture to a purée. Season and set aside.

Meanwhile, place a large frying pan over a high heat and add the oil and half the butter. Add the mushrooms and season well with salt and pepper. Cook for 6–8 minutes, tossing regularly, until they are starting to caramelise and any moisture has been driven off.

Reduce the heat and add the remaining butter, the onion, leek and celery to the pan. Cook for a further 10–12 minutes until the veg are tender. Stir the mushroom mixture into the celeriac purée, taste to check the seasoning and leave to cool.

Cut the pastry in half. Roll out one piece to a rectangle, about 30 x 15cm and about 5mm thick. Lay it on the baking tray. Spoon the cooled mushroom filling over the pastry, leaving a 3–4cm margin around the edges. Brush this edge with water. Roll out the second piece of pastry in the same way. Lay this over the filling and crimp the edges to seal. Trim the edges. Bake for 45–50 minutes until the pastry is well coloured.

Leave the pie to stand for 15 minutes before serving, with mash and cabbage.

Figs

LATIN NAME
Ficus carica

SEASONALITY
British figs: August–September.
Imported all year round, with
the best Mediterranean fruit
usually available July–October

MORE RECIPES
Barbecued duck breasts with
rosemary and figs (page 240);
Apricot and honey filo pie
(page 314)

The best figs I've ever eaten were purloined from roadside trees in Mallorca during one particularly steamy summer. We ate as many as we could, their bloomy skins warm from the sun, their rosy flesh impossibly aromatic and jammy.

The fig thrives in Mediterranean climates and it doesn't travel well so figs at that peak of perfection are a rare treat in the UK. But I'm still a keen fig-eater. Even when the warmth has to come from my oven rather than the sun, or when a trickle of honey is required to achieve that ambrosial sweetness, they can be exceptionally delicious.

Figs for export are picked when not quite ripe and won't ripen any further so choose the most tender ones you can find and use them straight away. On tasting, you'll have to decide whether they're sweet enough to be enjoyed raw, or require some help.

If it's the former, the simplest, not-even-a-salad assemblies pay dividends. Nip off the little stem-end and slice or quarter the fruits (the skin is edible). Savoury partners that emphasise the figginess of figs include wisps of air-dried ham, salty cheese or slivers of raw fennel, dressed with a little oil and lemon. For pud, try mixing chopped figs with lightly crushed raspberries, trickled with honey.

Those figs that don't quite cut it raw can be redeemed with heat. (If a fig releases milky sap from the stem when trimmed, it's a sign of under-ripeness; rinse the sap away as it can irritate the skin.) Quarter the figs, dot generously with butter and sugar and bake at 190°C/Fan 170°C/Gas 5 for 15–20 minutes, until soft and bubbling. Or make a simple fig compote by simmering the roughly chopped fruit with honey, lemon juice, fresh thyme and a splash of water. Toasted flaked almonds and a blob of crème fraîche turn either of these treatments into a yummy pud.

I love dried figs too. Their rich sweetness and the crunch of their tiny seeds are fabulous in fruit cakes and I often simmer them with wine and spices to make a syrupy compote that's just as good with a slice of baked ham as it is for pudding. These days, dried figs are usually succulent and ready to eat. Any that seem tough can be plumped up with a soak in hot water or fruit juice.

I persist in growing figs at home and every third summer or so I'm rewarded with a modest crop of ripe fruit about half as sweet and figgy as those Mallorcan specimens. It's a mark of how much I love the fruit that these Devon figs still delight me.

FIGS POACHED IN RED WINE

400ml light, fruity red wine,
such as Pinot Noir or Beaujolais

A couple of finely pared strips
of orange zest (no pith)

A couple of finely pared strips
of lemon zest (no pith)

4 tbsp clear honey

1 vanilla pod, split lengthways

2 cloves

1 star anise

8 fresh figs, stalks removed

Thick, plain wholemilk yoghurt,
to serve

This simple recipe turns less-than-perfectly-ripe figs into a delectable pudding. Serves 4

Put the wine, citrus zest strips, honey, vanilla pod, cloves and star anise into a saucepan. Place over a medium heat and bring to a simmer, stirring to dissolve the honey.

Pierce the figs a few times with a cocktail stick or thin skewer, to help the liquid penetrate, then carefully place them in the simmering poaching liquid. Cook, partially covered, for about 20 minutes, gently turning the fruit over once or twice, until the skins are tender.

Remove the figs with a slotted spoon and transfer them to a bowl. Increase the heat under the pan until the liquid is boiling, then boil it for 10–15 minutes until reduced by about two-thirds and syrupy, then pour back over the figs.

Serve the figs warm or at room temperature, with the syrupy juice spooned over the top and a dollop of yoghurt. A sprinkling of granola or 'independent crumble' (page 479) is an excellent finishing touch.

Flounder

Nick Fisher

LATIN NAME
Platichthys flesus

ALSO KNOWN AS
Fluke

SEASONALITY
Avoid February–May when
spawning

HABITAT
European coastal waters

MCS RATING
2–4

REC MINIMUM SIZE
25cm

MORE RECIPES
Plaice with rosemary, caper
and anchovy butter (page 476);
Megrim with crab and chives
(page 380); Lemon sole poached
in butter with thyme (page 589);
Dover sole with seaweed butter
(page 588)

SOURCING
goodfishguide.org

According to the accepted flatfish hierarchy: turbot is king, brill heir to the throne and Dover sole a young prince. Plaice and lemon sole follow, then come megrim and witch, with dab trailing in their wake. And flounder brings up the rear.

It's yet another example of an undervalued fine fish. Like so much of our seafood, flounders receive more accolades in the rest of Europe than here. The Belgians have them smoked and eat them with lemon and soured cream, while the Galician Spanish serve them filleted and fried or steamed in a light creamy saffron sauce.

The best way to get your hands on a fat, fresh flounder… is with your foot. Flounder 'tramping' is a recognised method of harvesting. Every August, Dumfriesshire is home to the Palnackie Flounder Tramping Championships, in which contestants paddle warily out across the muddy estuary, feeling for flounders with their toes. Once located, the fish is held down on the estuary bed with one foot and grabbed by the hand.

Tramping aside, flounder can be a surprisingly easy fish to catch, especially on wide, silty river estuaries. In the whole gamut of flatfish, the flounder has the most robust immunity to fresh water. Even though they can live in deep undersea trenches miles offshore, they'll also happily survive in shallow fresh water. In Holland, flounders are even fattened up in freshwater pools before they're deemed chubby enough to eat.

Flounders look like shrunken, washed-out versions of plaice. They too have fawn skin and orange spots but they're noticeably smaller in stature, and their orange splodges are far fewer and of a much less eye-piercingly Floridian hue.

Because they are by-catch, rather than a targeted species, flounders are rarely seen on Britain's fish counters, which is a great pity: their numbers are healthy, yet many of those caught are discarded. This is an underutilised species you can eat without spoiling your eco-credentials. Should you be so lucky as to spot them for sale, do buy them.

Flounder fillets, coated in egg and breadcrumbs or even just dusted in seasoned flour, then shallow-fried in searing hot oil, are delicious in a freshly baked bap with a slather of tartare sauce, mayonnaise or chive-loaded soured cream.

My favourite way to cook flounder is grilled whole and drizzled with garlic butter and parsley. And, since they cost on average half as much as plaice, I often enjoy double helpings of this foot-stamping steal of a fish.

GRILLED FLOUNDER AND TOMATOES

300–400g ripe, flavoursome
tomatoes (ideally a mix of
varieties, including cherry
tomatoes)

3 tbsp olive or rapeseed oil,
plus a little extra for the fish

2 garlic cloves, sliced

1 tsp ground cumin, plus
a little extra for the fish

2 large flounder (about
500g each), filleted
(i.e. 8 good-sized fillets)

Sea salt and black pepper

This is a super-simple way to make the most of fresh flounder. Try it with fillets of other flatfish too, such as megrim, plaice or sole – or with whole dab. Serves 2

Preheat the grill to high.

Halve cherry tomatoes and cut larger varieties into 1cm slices. Lay the tomatoes out in a single layer on a large, shallow baking tray. Trickle over the oil, then scatter over the garlic and cumin and season generously with salt and pepper.

Place the tomatoes under the grill and cook for 10–12 minutes until tender, juicy and lightly blistered, turning them carefully halfway through.

Meanwhile, rub the flounder fillets with a little oil and season with salt and pepper and a pinch of cumin.

Carefully nestle the fish, skin side up, among the grilled tomatoes. Return to the grill and cook for a further 4–5 minutes or until the fish is just cooked through. Serve the fish with the tomatoes and all their lovely juices, with some salad and good bread on the side.

F

Flour, wheat

Pam Corbin

MORE RECIPES
Pulla (page 115); Pissaladière
(page 419); Tortillas with cumin
and garlic oil (page 221); Rye
and caraway scones (page 114);
Chive buckwheat blinis with
hard-boiled eggs (page 175);
Drip scones (page 237); Chicken
broth with parsley and celery
seed spaetzle (page 163);
Garlicky pea ravioli with brown
butter (page 444); Buttermilk
and sage onion rings (page 109);
Field mushroom and celeriac
pie (page 258); Pruney sausage
rolls (page 447); Summer savory
scones (page 569); Brown butter
shortbread (page 108); Eccles
cakes (page 340)

SOURCING
dovesfarm.co.uk;
shipton-mill.com;
stoatesflour.co.uk

Flour forms the basic structure for many of our staple foods, such as breads, pasta and pastry – as well as cakes, scones, biscuits and sauces. Wheat flour is by far the most commonly used and versatile of all flours.

Britain produces 80–85 per cent of its own wheat, with the balance imported – mainly from Canada, America and Europe. The 'strength' and flavour of wheat is influenced by the soil and climate. More extreme climates than ours tend to produce 'stronger' or 'harder' (i.e. higher protein) wheat.

The protein in wheat is gluten. Gluten proteins, when wet, stick together and start to form stretchy strands, which are developed further by mixing, kneading or otherwise 'working' a dough. A gluten network is uniquely good at binding a dough and allowing it to rise and then hold its shape. The higher the protein, the more stretchy and supple the dough becomes when kneaded. An elastic dough will accommodate the gassy bubbles formed by yeast, which is why bread is made with 'strong' flour. This forms a loaf with a firm crust and a robust, slightly bouncy crumb.

For biscuits, pastry or cakes, a low protein or 'soft' flour is required. These sorts of doughs and batters should only be lightly worked, to avoid developing the gluten too much, and producing a tough, 'bready' crumb.

Wheat grain comprises three parts. The endosperm (the white, floury bit) accounts for about 85 per cent. Traditionally, this was referred to as the 'flower', or finest part, of the wheat grain, which is where our word 'flour' comes from. Then there's the highly nutritious wheat germ, the plant's embryo, forming about 2 per cent of the grain. The remaining 13 per cent is the bran, the protective skin of the seed. This is flavoursome and rich in B vitamins and fibre.

TYPES OF FLOUR

Plain white flour This standard, smooth flour contains only the endosperm of the grain and has a protein content of 9–10 per cent. It is also called 'all-purpose' or 'soft' flour. It's the ideal storecupboard flour for general baking – cakes, biscuits, pastry – as well as pancakes, and savoury batters and sauces.

Self-raising flour Simply plain flour (white or brown) with added raising agents, this is handy for quick-mix cake batters that do not rely on whisking to incorporate air into the mix. You can make your own self-raising flour by mixing baking powder with plain flour (which gives you the freedom to choose white, brown or organic flour). Different brands of baking powder vary and it makes sense to be guided by the manufacturer's suggestion, but 1 generous tsp baking powder to every 100g plain flour is about right.

Plain brown flour This includes some bran and wheatgerm. It is good in fruit cakes and crumbles, and in recipes where part of the flour is replaced with ground almonds or other ground nuts.

Wholemeal flour Comprising the entire grain – endosperm, germ and bran – this has a fuller flavour. With a protein content of around 13 per cent, it is more nutritious than refined white flour; it also contains 5 per cent more fibre.

Malted flour Also called granary flour, this has a distinctive, sweet, nutty flavour owing to the inclusion of malted wheat or barley. Malted flours appear brown but some of them include a large proportion of white flour.

Strong flour This is the best flour to use for baking bread. The strongest, with 15 per cent protein, comes from Canada; some flours from British-grown wheat contain 13–14 per cent. Strong white flour is the most common type, but you can also buy strong brown flour for bread-making.

Durum wheat flour Made from the hardest of all wheats, this has a high gluten content, but the protein does not behave in the same way as the gluten in common high-protein wheats. It is very inelastic, which means it makes great dried pasta, but it is no good for bread-making. The designation '00' on bags of Italian flour signifies that it is very finely milled and has all the bran and wheatgerm removed, but it does not define the type of wheat. '00' pasta flour is often a combination of standard wheat and durum wheat flours.

The process of milling transforms the hard, indigestible nobbles of wheat grain into soft flour. In the past, wind and watermills were used to power millstones, and traditional stoneground flour is still widely available. Stone-grinding crushes the whole grain in one 'pass' and mixes all the parts together. This produces a relatively coarse, 100 per cent wholegrain flour. Even when most of the bran and germ are sifted out to make a white flour, traces of those nutritious parts will remain. Most stoneground flours on the market are intended for bread-making, but you can find lower protein stoneground white flours suitable for cakes and biscuits.

Nowadays, most flour mills are fully automated. The grain travels through a series of steel rollers and sieves that efficiently break it down into its three parts and remove the germ and bran. If a wholemeal or brown flour is desired, the bran and germ are mixed back in. Roller-milling also creates more heat than stone-grinding and this may damage more of the nutrients in the flour. Many bakers view roller-milled flour as a less nutritious and less tasty ingredient. Roller-milling also produces flour with a finer particle size, meaning it is more quickly digested by the body and therefore has a higher GI than stoneground flour.

All of our white wheat flours are fortified with iron, thiamine (vitamin B1), niacin and calcium – nutrients lost when the bran is removed. In some countries white flour is bleached using peroxide and/or chlorine, but this is no longer legal in the UK.

Psocids – tiny bugs that thrive in dark, humid places – love flour. To avoid infestation, store flour in its original packaging or a lidded container in a cool, dry, airy place. White flour (including self-raising) will keep for up to 9 months. Wholemeal and brown are best used within 6 months. Check best-before dates when buying, and avoid mixing old flour with new.

SEEDY STONEGROUND LOAF

Full-flavoured, deliciously nutty and with an irresistible texture, this simple seeded bread is given sweetness and body with ale and honey. The beer also helps to ensure a good rise. Makes 1 large loaf

300g stoneground wholemeal bread flour, plus extra to finish

200g strong white bread flour (ideally stoneground), plus extra to dust

7g fast-acting dried yeast (1 sachet or 1½ tsp)

100g mixed seeds, such as pumpkin, linseed, sesame, poppy and sunflower

10g fine sea salt

350ml ale

4 tsp clear honey

A little rapeseed oil, for oiling

Combine the flours, yeast, seeds and salt in a large bowl. Add the ale and honey and mix to a rough dough. You want a soft, easily kneadable, sticky dough: if it is too wet add a little more flour; if too dry add up to 50ml water. Turn out on to a lightly floured surface.

Knead the dough until smooth, stretchy and no longer sticky, about 10 minutes, then shape into a rough round. Coat it very lightly in oil, place in a large bowl, cover with cling film and leave in a warm place until doubled in size, 1–2 hours.

Tip the dough on to a floured surface and deflate by pressing down on it gently. Form into a thick rectangular shape, about 20 x 25cm, then roll it up from a short edge, nice and tightly. Taper the ends of the loaf with the palms of your hands.

Put the loaf on a floured surface and generously scatter with wholemeal flour. Drape cling film over the top and leave it to rise for a further 40 minutes. Preheat the oven to 220°C/Fan 200°C/Gas 7 and put a heavy baking sheet inside to heat up. Remove the cling film.

Take the hot baking sheet from the oven and carefully lift the loaf on to it. Use a sharp knife to make 4 or 5 slashes across the top of the loaf. Bake in the oven for 20 minutes, then lower the setting to 180°C/Fan 160°C/Gas 4 and bake for a further 20 minutes.

Transfer the bread to a wire rack and leave to cool for at least an hour before slicing.

French beans

LATIN NAME
Phaseolus vulgaris

ALSO KNOWN AS
Green beans, haricots verts

SEASONALITY
May–September

MORE RECIPES
Runner beans with cream and tarragon (page 546); Fragrant beef curry (page 350)

These tasty legumes are usually eaten pod and all, in their infant stage, when the beans within are still undeveloped. Outside our summer season, we fly in tonnes of them from Africa and Egypt, so, if you want to, you can buy them anytime. But they are brought to us by air, then sold plastic-wrapped and often trimmed, which not only wastes huge amounts of bean but also encourages them to turn starchy and bland.

French beans should be eaten so fresh that they break in half with a crisp snap and, if you can find space to grow your own (they are very easy to raise), such freshness is guaranteed. The sweetness they hold in their just-off-the-vine state fades rapidly so even the freshest of beans from a local grower won't be quite as good. They can still be worth buying though. Get them loose and untrimmed if you can and make sure there's no trace of bendiness.

There are many varieties of French bean: some green, some purple, some yellow. Those left on the vine eventually produce a later crop of tasty beans from inside the pods: these are delicious in stews and soups or for home-made baked beans. You can use them fresh or dry them for later use.

Ultra-fresh French beans work brilliantly raw, as crudités. They are also superb simply steamed for a few minutes then buttered. Another delicious approach is to slow-cook the beans, sweating them in a covered pan with lots of olive oil, plus chilli and pancetta, until they're almost falling apart. Stirred through pasta with a handful of grated Cheddar, these are hard to beat.

Green beans are among the many tender vegetables that can be best bought frozen – captured in their just-picked state. For a very quick and easy side dish, sweat a little onion and garlic in butter, then add still-frozen organic beans and cook over a low heat just until the beans are piping hot. If you've got a glut, fresh French beans also make a tasty pickle spiked with coriander, chilli and cardamom, or with turmeric and mustard seeds.

FRENCH BEANS WITH SHALLOTS AND BLACK OLIVES

200g French beans, stalk ends trimmed off

25g butter

2 shallots or 1 echalion (banana shallot), finely chopped

1 large garlic clove, chopped

30g pitted black olives, bashed, smashed or roughly chopped

A small squeeze of lemon juice

Sea salt and black pepper

Quick and easy to prepare, this is a fantastic side dish to a piece of simply cooked fish or almost any meat. It's a great treatment for runner beans, broccoli and purple sprouting broccoli too. Don't skip the lemon juice – it really brings the dish together. Serves 2

Bring a pan of salted water to the boil. Add the French beans, bring back to the boil and simmer for about 4 minutes or until tender but retaining a slight bite. Drain well.

Meanwhile, melt the butter in a saucepan over a low heat and add the shallots and garlic with a pinch of salt and pepper. Sweat them slowly for 6–8 minutes until the shallots are soft and almost transparent, but with no colour.

Add the cooked green beans to the pan, along with the olives and lemon juice. Give it a good stir and taste for seasoning: you may find the olives make it salty enough for you but add salt, pepper or more lemon juice if you like. Serve straight away.

Garfish

Nick Fisher

LATIN NAME
Belone belone

SEASONALITY
Avoid May–June when spawning

HABITAT
Generally in the south and west of the British Isles; found inshore in the summer, often alongside mackerel

MCS RATING
Not rated

REC MINIMUM SIZE
40cm

G

Every fish-lover should give garfish a try, not least because eating a fish with bright green bones is exciting. In contrast, the flesh of the snake-like garfish is a creamy white colour with a firm, flaky, almost tinned-pilchard-like consistency. And, more to the point, garfish grilled and served with salsa verde on toasted sourdough, or poached in butter and lemon juice and heaped over chive-peppered new potatoes, are certain joys we all deserve to experience at some point.

Unlike most fish, garfish like to be seen: they love to travel near the surface and will even leap out of the sea. Nevertheless, most are caught by accident while feathering for mackerel – a species they tend to run with during the spring, summer and early autumn. Those that do get caught are rarely eaten, unless, that is, you're in Jersey or Guernsey, where the true garfish aficionados live. In these islands, the gar is known as 'longnose' or 'greenbones' and is eagerly caught, bought and bartered – to be fried or grilled and served with mushy peas.

The scales and skeleton of the garfish put off plenty of anglers and cooks because they assume the green, which can glow like a radioactive isotope even on a filleted gar, is something poisonous. It's not. The spooky hue is caused by a harmless mineral, vivianite, which occurs naturally in rock formations around the English Channel.

If you don't live in the Channel Islands, the most likely way to cop a gar is to catch one yourself or bend the ear of a friendly mackerel fisherman. If you do avail yourself of a 'greenbones', keep the elongated skeleton after you've filleted off the flesh, dust it in well-spiced flour (I add chilli powder or hot paprika), then shallow-fry the spine in hot oil. It'll crisp up like pork skin and, once drained on kitchen paper, cooled and snapped into sections, provides a fantastic garfish crackling snack.

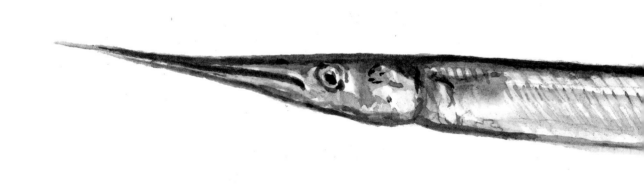

GARFISH WITH OLIVES, OREGANO AND GARLIC

100g stoned black olives, such as Kalamata

1 lemon

1 tbsp oregano leaves

2 garlic cloves, crushed or finely grated

1½ tsp fennel seeds, crushed

1 tsp capers, rinsed and drained (optional)

2 tbsp olive or rapeseed oil

2 garfish (about 300g each), scaled and gutted

Sea salt and black pepper

Earthy, smoky oregano is delicious in the intensely flavoured mix that seasons the garfish here – but slightly more gentle marjoram works just as well, as does rosemary. Red mullet, sardines or bream are also excellent cooked this way. Serves 2

Preheat the oven to 200°C/Fan 180°C/Gas 6.

Place the olives on a large board. Finely grate the zest of half the lemon and add this to the olives with the oregano, garlic, fennel seeds and capers, if using. Using a large knife, chop and scrape everything together until you have a relatively fine mix. Transfer to a bowl (or just leave it on the board), trickle over the oil and fold together.

Make a few deep slashes in the garfish flesh down each side. Put the fish into a small roasting dish and rub all over with the olive and oregano mixture. Season with a little salt and pepper. Quarter the half-zested lemon and throw this into the roasting dish too – the roasting will sweeten and caramelise its juices.

Roast in the oven for 12–15 minutes or until the fish flesh just comes away from the bone when teased with the tip of a knife. Use tongs to squeeze the juices of the hot lemon over the fish and serve with new potatoes and a tomato salad or some peppery rocket.

Garlic, bulb & scapes

Mark Diacono

LATIN NAME
Allium sativum

SEASONALITY
Mature garlic: July–September.
Garlic scapes and green garlic:
May–July

MORE RECIPES
Roasted almond aïoli (page 19);
Hempy hummus (page 308);
Stir-fried cabbage with turmeric
and garlic (page 651); Morels
and potatoes braised with red
wine and garlic (page 388);
Wilted mizuna with chilli, garlic
and sunflower seeds (page 387);
Spring greens with lemon and
garlic (page 601); Garlicky pea
ravioli with brown butter (page
444); Spaghetti with whelks,
garlic and parsley (page 670);
Garfish with olives, oregano
and garlic (page 267); Grilled
squid with chilli, parsley and
garlic (page 607); Garlicky snails
with breadcrumbs (page 586);
Ginger-braised lamb (page 278);
Tortillas with cumin and garlic
oil (page 221)

SOURCING
southwestgarlicfarm.co.uk;
thegarlicfarm.co.uk

It's hard to imagine now, but it wasn't until the middle of the last century that we really embraced garlic, encouraged by food writers such as Elizabeth David and Claudia Roden to use it in pasta, pizza, moussaka, ratatouille, bruschetta, aïoli and so many other great Mediterranean dishes.

It is, like mustard or chilli, something that defies description via other flavours: it is somehow elemental, not only in adding its pungent, aromatic, oniony loveliness to food but in catalysing ingredients it is paired with. It has the curious ability to take something like a tomato off on a tangent (i.e. not taste just like a tomato), while making lamb seem somehow more lamby.

The garlic we are most familiar with is sold as whole dried bulbs, ready to be split into its constituent cloves, stripped of its papery husk and chopped, crushed or used whole to impart its unique loveliness. Garlic loves the cold, growing through at least part of the winter, and maturing in mid-summer. Hence, July and August are when you are most likely to find British garlic in the shops.

That love of the cold means that garlic should never be stored in the fridge – it usually sprouts, and the green shoot that appears often brings an unwelcome bitterness. If a shoot appears, and the clove is still firm and aromatic, slice the clove lengthways, tease the shoot out with the tip of a sharp knife, and use the clove as normal. Ideally you should store garlic at room temperature, in light but not direct sunlight.

Crushing is most effective in releasing maximum, hot, intense garlic flavour because it breaks down the cell membranes, and the fineness of the paste achieved spreads that flavour evenly through butter, mayonnaise, or whatever it is added to.

Chopping releases garlic flavour without the intensity delivered by crushing. Keep that chop coarse and you'll have pockets of garlic to discover, especially if used raw – in gremolata, for example. Or chop it more finely if you want a general impression of garlic through the dish. Increasingly, I favour slivers of garlic: thinly sliced or microplaned garlic has a presence without being overpowering. A clove or two, slivered and scattered on a pizza before it goes in the oven, adds fresh punch and punctuation.

Roasting transforms garlic's hot pungency into mild, aromatic sweetness. Chicken with 40 garlic cloves may sound to the uninitiated like a recipe for estrangement, but on tasting it, you'll be impressed by its subtlety as much as its full flavour. Roasting a whole head of garlic is a great way to enjoy its mellower qualities. Slice off the top centimetre, season with salt and pepper and anoint in olive oil. Wrap loosely in foil and roast at 190°C/Fan 170°C/Gas 5 for 45 minutes. The sweet flesh within makes a wonderful component of a roast dinner but is equally fine smeared on hot toast.

Burning garlic brings out bitterness in both the ingredient and the cook. To avoid this, always fry garlic over a gentle heat, briefly and with a little salt (which draws out liquid, helping to avoid burning). Alternatively, add it to onions or tomatoes that are already cooking.

As with most food, looking beyond what is in the supermarkets can bring great rewards. Elephant garlic, with heads that can be as large as your fist, is, to my mind, the finest garlic for roasting. Although nearer a leek than a true garlic, the bulb carries a mild garlic flavour that sweetens beautifully when roasted, and there's so much of that succulent centre beneath the papery wrapping.

I've been using garlic 'scapes' increasingly in recent years, and before too long I suspect they'll become widely available. As the 'hardneck' type of garlic grows, it throws up a long spike that intends to bear a flower at its top. Chopping this off while

G

this flower-to-be is closed and tear-shaped diverts the plant's energies to the bulb rather than to making a flower. This cut spike – or 'scape' – tastes like gently garlicky asparagus, and is as wonderful as that sounds. Steamed or griddled, it is one of the highlights of spring-into-summer eating, and comes in May/June, just as the British asparagus season goes past its peak.

Black garlic is quite the thing. Whole heads of fresh garlic are baked very slowly – often for over a month – until the cloves turn soft and almost black. The flavour of the flesh is sweet, with a hint of citrus and an umami savouriness that makes it reminiscent of balsamic vinegar. It makes an excellent mayonnaise, is superb in marinades (especially with chicken) and in pasta sauces, or smeared on hot toast.

Elephant garlic, scapes and black garlic are available from specialist suppliers, some farmers' markets and online, but elephant garlic and scapes (as well as standard garlic) can also come from your own garden with little effort.

Hardneck and softneck are the two main types of garlic. If you're going to grow garlic, there are good reasons to choose at least some hardneck varieties. Most are from cold climates and are suited to our often cold, wet conditions. They tend to have a more complex, stronger flavour than softnecks, though they don't store well (hence most of those in the shops are softnecks). And hardnecks are the garlics that produce scapes in May/June.

A couple of weeks later the bulbs will be fully grown, but with the individual cloves not yet formed, and I tend to pick most then. This is 'green' or 'wet' garlic, which is mild, sweet and complex. Roasted whole or used chopped like an onion or leek, it is one of the tastes of early summer. Harvesting most hardnecks as green garlic sidesteps their short storage-life.

Any hardnecks not harvested as green garlic, I leave in the ground with the softnecks, to mature and form cloves. Hardnecks' leaves go yellow and softnecks' leaves flop when they are ready to lift, usually in July. A couple of days in the sun, either outside if the weather suits, or in the greenhouse or on a sunny windowsill if not, dries the bulbs for storing. Use the hardnecks first, as most softnecks will keep well through winter.

GREEN GARLIC, ASPARAGUS AND OVEN-SCRAMBLED EGGS

4 green garlic bulbs, quartered lengthways

1 tbsp olive or rapeseed oil

A knob of butter

About 400g asparagus, woody ends snapped off

8 medium eggs

Sea salt and black pepper

This is a lovely way to celebrate a pair of early summer ingredients – roasting, then bringing them together with lightly scrambled eggs. You can, if you like, replace the asparagus with hogweed shoots (they'll probably need less time in the oven). Serves 4

Preheat the oven to 170°C/Fan 150°C/Gas 3.

Put the garlic into a baking dish. Trickle with the oil, dot with the butter and season with salt and pepper. Roast for 30 minutes or until tender (it might take a little longer).

Take out the dish, add the asparagus and stir well, then return to the oven for about 10 minutes, or until the asparagus is tender. The thin tips of the garlic stalks may brown – don't worry about this, they are chewy and delicious!

Meanwhile, lightly beat the eggs in a bowl and season them with salt and pepper.

Add the beaten eggs to the dish of garlic and asparagus and return to the oven for 4–6 minutes, taking it out and stirring the egg around a couple of times, until the eggs are lightly scrambled and coating the veg nicely. Serve straight away.

Garlic, crow

John Wright

LATIN NAME
Allium vineale

ALSO KNOWN AS
Wild chive, wild onion

SEASONALITY
Leaves: winter and spring.
Bulbs: late spring and early summer

HABITAT
Grassy banks, field edges and cultivated land. Common in southern England; rare in Northern Ireland; largely coastal elsewhere

This common chive-like plant is often ignored as it looks, superficially, just like grass. It is most easy to spot in winter and early spring, when its green/purple, grass-like leaves are visible above the slumbering vegetation, invariably growing in large patches, often on roadsides. Later in the year, its pink/purple flowers and terminal 'bulblets' make its distinct nature clear.

Generally it must be dug up, as pulling usually just breaks off the leaves, the edible bulb being left in the ground. However, there is a legal problem. Although it is perfectly ok to remove leaves, flowers and so on from almost any wild plant, it is not legal to uproot one without permission from the landowner. The landowner of roadsides is likely to be a local highways agency – not known for tolerating the digging up of anything other than pipes and cables. I leave it to your conscience if, or how much, you collect. If you do get permission or you have no conscience, it is possible to gather huge numbers of crow garlic bulbs fairly quickly, which is just as well as they are small – the size of a cocktail onion.

When the leaves are young, they are edible as a rather coarse variety of chives, hence their occasional name of 'wild chives'.

The smell and flavour of the bulb is somewhere between garlic and onion, perhaps a little nearer to the latter, making crow garlic an excellent substitute for either in any wild, or indeed non-wild, dish. You just need to peel and slice the bulb; it can be used raw or cooked. Crow garlic has substantial calorific value, something sadly lacking in most wild foods.

CROW GARLIC AND NIGELLA NAAN

The sweet allium flavours of crow garlic and nigella seeds make for irresistible naan breads. Eat them warm and buttery, alongside any curry. Makes 6–8

5g dried yeast

1 tsp sugar

500g strong white bread flour, plus extra to dust

1 tsp salt

150ml plain wholemilk yoghurt

2 tbsp melted butter, cooled a little, plus extra for brushing

8 crow garlic bulbs and any tender stem, finely chopped

Flour, semolina or polenta, to dust

Nigella (kalonji/black onion) seeds, to finish

Combine the yeast and sugar with 175ml tepid water and stir well to combine. Allow to stand for 10 minutes, until frothy. Meanwhile combine the flour and salt in a large bowl.

Add the yeast mix to the flour, along with the yoghurt and melted butter. Mix to a soft, loose dough, adding a splash more water if necessary.

Turn the dough out on to a lightly floured surface and knead for 5–10 minutes until smooth and pliable, dusting with a little flour if necessary, to prevent sticking.

Add the chopped crow garlic to the dough and work in, for a further 1–2 minutes. Put the dough into a lightly oiled bowl, cover and leave to rise in a warm place for 2–3 hours.

Deflate the dough a little with your fingertips but don't knock it back brutally – you want to keep it puffy. Divide it into 6–8 equal pieces. Roll each out to an oval, about 1cm thick, and leave to rise for a further 15–20 minutes.

Preheat the oven to 220°C/Fan 200°C/Gas 7 and place a large baking tray inside to heat up.

Take out the hot baking tray and scatter it with flour, semolina or polenta. Lay 2 or 3 naans on the tray and bake for 15–20 minutes until puffed and starting to blister. Remove from the oven, brush with a little extra melted butter and sprinkle with nigella seeds; keep warm. Repeat to cook the remaining dough. Serve hot.

Garlic, wild

John Wright

LATIN NAME
Allium ursinum

ALSO KNOWN AS
Ramsons, bear garlic,
wood garlic

SEASONALITY
Leaves: February–May.
Flowers and seedheads:
April–June

HABITAT
Common throughout most
of the British Isles in shady,
damp, wooded places

Few wild foods occur in as great abundance as wild garlic. From late winter until early June, this prolific plant dominates shady roadsides, dark areas of the garden, and woodland. The strong smell of garlic will ensure that you do not confuse the plant with any poisonous look-alike, such as Lily of the Valley. It is easy to pick an entire bin-bag full with no damage to the local population, should you have use for such a large amount. All of the plant is edible, from its narrow root, which of course you should not dig up without the permission of the landowner (see page 271), through the leaves, flowers and immature seedheads. The leaves are the part most used and they are, in effect, garlic in salad form. The flavour is very much that of the garlic bulb with which we are all familiar, though less concentrated and tenacious.

Shredded or chopped, wild garlic leaves can be used instead of ordinary garlic, though they are best cooked only lightly. But their leafy nature opens up many new possibilities. Chief among these is as a shredded addition to a green salad. But a great favourite of mine is wild garlic pesto; you can use any part of the plant for it but the immature seedheads work particularly well. This delicious preparation is great on pasta, with mushrooms, or as a finishing flourish for soups.

The broad leaves are also useful in the making of dolmas or, more properly, sarmas – the leaves wrapped around anything you like and the parcels baked with a light sprinkle of olive oil. One or two wild, shelled mussels (see page 399), cooked with a little wild garlic, make an excellent and thoroughly wild accompaniment to pretty much any fish. As with ordinary garlic, the flavour softens after cooking and will not overwhelm the senses. Late in the season, the pretty, white, star-shaped flowers appear and can be used to garnish this or any other suitable dish.

Not to be confused with wild garlic, but very good in its own right, is hedge garlic (*Alliaria petiolata*), also known as garlic mustard or Jack-in-the-hedge. It is very common (except in northwest Scotland and Northern Ireland) and easy to spot – its tall stalk encompassed by deeply veined, heart-shaped leaves, with little white flowers in the spring. The leaves are good at any point before these flowers are fully out, but the rosettes of basal leaves that form early in the year before the stalk shoots up are particularly tasty. With their garlicky and mustardy overtones, the leaves are good in salads, pesto-style sauces, stuffings or in the recipe below.

WILD GARLIC FRITTERS

About 50g small-to-medium
wild garlic leaves

2 tbsp plain flour

½ tsp baking powder

Iced water, to mix

Vegetable oil (refined
rapeseed oil), for frying

Sea salt

Lemon wedges, to serve

Irresistibly crisp and garlicky, these are a fantastic way to celebrate one of the first wild harvests of the year. Hand them around, hot and salty, as a nibble. Serves 6

Gently wash the garlic leaves and pat dry. Trim the coarser stalks back to the base of the leaf. Cut any larger leaves down to size – you want pieces roughly the size of a bay leaf.

In a large bowl, combine the flour with a pinch of salt and the baking powder. Add just enough iced water to create a batter with a consistency slightly thinner than double cream.

Heat a 3–4cm depth of oil in a heavy-based medium saucepan to 170°C (a little of the batter dropped into the hot oil should fizz and turn golden in about 30 seconds).

Drop a small handful of garlic leaves into the batter, stir around, then lift out little clumps and carefully drop into the hot oil. Fry for 45–60 seconds, until golden and crisp, turning once or twice. Transfer to a plate lined with kitchen paper to drain; keep warm. Repeat to cook the rest. Season the fritters with salt and serve immediately, with lemon wedges.

Gelatine

MORE RECIPES
Basil pannacotta with minted raspberries (page 50); Elderflower jelly (page 249)

SOURCING
therealfoodcompany.org.uk (for organic leaf gelatine)

Completely flavourless, gelatine will reliably set almost any liquid. Mousses, jellies and pannacottas all owe their tempting wobble and firm-but-melt-in-the-mouth texture to this setting agent, as do many jellied meat and fish terrines. The back story of this useful product is, however, less than ethereal: it's made by boiling up vats of bones and skin, the remnants of slaughtered livestock, largely pigs and cows.

Animal-based gelatine comes in two forms. Gelatine granules need to be mixed with water and left to swell, then gently heated. Leaf gelatine, which I favour, is easier to measure and use. The brittle, transparent leaves are first soaked in cold water to soften them, then added to a warm mixture. A little heat is important to melt the gelatine, but it mustn't be boiled or the proteins will be denatured and it won't set.

There is quite a difference in the setting qualities of different brands. A leaf from one brand may set more or less liquid than another. Follow the guidance on the packet, rather than the quantity of gelatine leaves given in a recipe, snipping leaves into halves, thirds or quarters to get the right amount if necessary. You generally want to use as little gelatine as you can get away with, to achieve a gentler set. A pannacotta, for instance, should only just hold its shape, spreading a little as it's released on to a plate.

To make a soft-set fruity jelly, cook slightly over-ripe gooseberries or strawberries in a sugar syrup, flavoured with elderflower, if available, then pass through a sieve and add soaked gelatine leaves while the liquor is still hot. You can use almost any juicy fruits, though you'll need a little more gelatine to set citrus jellies. Pineapple and kiwi fruit are not suitable as they contain enzymes that interfere with the setting process.

Organic gelatine is available but not easy to find. An alternative setting agent is agar agar, which is derived from seaweed. It gives a good set, but it is slightly less reliable. Carragheen, also a seaweed, is another option, but it is rather unpredictable and imparts a slight flavour of its own.

BLACKCURRANT AND RED WINE JELLY

300g blackcurrants

200ml red wine

150g caster sugar

Enough sheets of leaf gelatine to set 500ml liquid (different brands vary)

This simple dessert has a wonderful cassis-like intensity from the red wine. You can use frozen blackcurrants if you haven't any fresh – there is no need to defrost them first. Serves 6

Have ready a 500ml jelly mould or six 80ml individual moulds.

Put the blackcurrants, wine and sugar into a medium pan and bring to a gentle simmer. Cook for 6–8 minutes or until the blackcurrants have broken down and are pulpy.

Pass the contents of the pan through a fine sieve into a large measuring jug, pressing and rubbing the blackcurrants to extract maximum juice. You should have about 500ml liquid. If you have less, top up with water.

Calculate how many gelatine leaves you need to set 500ml liquid. Soak the gelatine sheets in cold water for about 10 minutes to soften. Meanwhile, return the blackcurrant liquid to a clean pan over a low heat.

Squeeze out the excess liquid from the gelatine, then add to the hot (but not boiling) blackcurrant liquid. Stir well to dissolve. Pour the mixture into your mould/s and place in the fridge to set for at least 12 hours, up to 24.

To unmould, run the tip of a small sharp knife around the edge of the jelly to help release it, then dip the mould/s very briefly in warm water to barely soften the outside of the jelly, before inverting on to a plate. If the jelly doesn't plop out, repeat the warm water dipping. Serve alone or with a little cream.

Geranium, scented

Pam Corbin

LATIN NAME
Pelargonium

ALSO KNOWN AS
Scented-leaf pelargonium

SEASONALITY
All year round

SOURCING
fibrex.co.uk; sarahraven.com;
scentedgeraniums.co.uk

Commonly known as scented-leaved geraniums, this group of perennial herbs is quite different from the bright-bloomed, bedding plant geranium. They have rather minimal flowers – mainly in shades of purply-pink – but are surrounded by intricately shaped leaves, which release wonderful bouquets when lightly crushed.

You can find scented geraniums that mimic coconut, eucalyptus, apple, orange, various spices, even chocolate. But it is those awash with the perfume of rose, such as *Pelargonium graveolens* or 'Attar of Roses', or vibrant with lemon, such as 'Mabel Grey', which are most useful.

The easiest way to release the fragrance is to steep a couple of leaves in freshly boiled water to make a soothing floral tisane. But they smooch adoringly with apricots, blackberries, raspberries and peaches. Add them when macerating or poaching these fruits, or use them to expand the flavours of jams and fruit jellies. Just 4 or 5 leaves, added at the start of cooking, are all you need for 1kg fruit. For crème brûlées and custards, 3 or 4 leaves will instil a vivacious new tone in 600ml cream.

Bake ardour into cakes and pastries by lining tins with scented geranium leaves before spooning in cake batter or lining with pastry. For a more pronounced flavour, infuse 3 or 4 leaves in a syrup: dissolve 150g sugar in 150ml water and simmer for 5 minutes, then add a few leaves and let them steep. Drizzle the resultant intensely fragrant syrup over plain cakes or add to fruit salads. In all cases, remove the geranium leaves before serving as it's best not to actually eat them.

Growing your own is the ideal way to access the extravagant aromas of these lovely plants. They'll do well in any sheltered, sunny spot, or on a windowsill. Plants, and sometimes fresh-cut leaves, are available from specialist nurseries.

SCENTED TOMATO JELLY

1kg ripe tomatoes, stalks removed, roughly chopped

Finely grated zest and juice of 1 lemon

10 scented geranium leaves, washed

500g jam sugar with pectin

This fragrant preserve tastes wonderful with cheese or cold meats, the perfume of the geraniums giving it a unique, subtle aroma. Rose-scented leaves work particularly well. Makes about 2 x 350ml jars

First sterilise your jars by washing them in hot soapy water, rinsing well, then putting them upside down on a baking tray in a very low oven (at 120°C/Fan 100°C/Gas ½) to dry and warm up.

Put the tomatoes into a large saucepan along with the lemon zest. Add 100ml water and bring to the boil. Reduce the heat, cover loosely and simmer gently for 20–30 minutes, stirring now and again, until the tomatoes are completely broken down to a pulp.

Rub the tomato pulp through a sieve to remove the skins and seeds. Return the purée to the pan and add the lemon juice and geranium leaves. Bring gently to the boil, then add the sugar and stir until it's fully dissolved. Meanwhile, put a saucer in the freezer to chill.

Cook the mixture at a full boil, stirring regularly to prevent it from sticking, for 7 minutes, then turn off the heat and test for setting point. Drop a small spoonful of the tomato jelly on to the chilled saucer. Leave for a few seconds to cool, and then push your finger through the jelly. If it wrinkles, it is ready. If the jelly floods back into the space where your finger was, it is not, so you will need to return the pan to the heat and cook for a further 2–3 minutes. Place the saucer back in the freezer and test again in the same way.

Once setting point is reached, remove and discard the scented geranium leaves and then pour the jelly into the warm, sterilised jars and seal. Store in a cool, dark cupboard for up to a year. Once opened, store in the fridge and use within 4 weeks.

Gherkins

ALSO KNOWN AS
Cornichon, dill pickle

MORE RECIPES
Spider crab salad (page 208);
Crumbed whiting goujons with
curried egg tartare (page 673)

These crisp, pickled cucumbers are, to my mind, the best condiment ever – and there is no greater sport than trying to fish the tiny, tart torpedoes out of a jar that is always teasingly too narrow in the neck.

The squat, knobbly cucumber varieties from which gherkins are derived differ slightly from the big, smooth, thin-skinned cucumbers we slice into our salads, but they are from the same family. You can buy gherkin seeds but, if you grow your own cucumbers of any type, there is no reason not to pick them young and pickle them. Most recipes call for a simple preserving in brine or vinegar, with dill or other aromatics such as white peppercorns or coriander seeds.

Small gherkins are often referred to as cornichons, though technically this describes a specific French type, grown from certain varieties such as 'Vert Petit de Paris' and harvested young, so that they are particularly tart and firm. In the US, gherkins are referred to as dill pickles, but are essentially the same thing.

Gherkins go with almost anything – pastrami on rye, pâtés, brawn, smoked fish, burgers, etc. Their salty, vinegary sharpness counteracts the richness of cheeses and charcuterie particularly well. For the classic tartare sauce to serve with fish, chopped gherkins are combined with mayonnaise, capers, lemon juice and parsley or tarragon.

The gherkin's gnarly green appearance is a barrier to some – especially the larger varieties you see swimming around in jars of vinegar on chip-shop shelves like sleeping sea slugs. But within that barnacled exterior lies a silky, salty flesh, so wonderful you can eat it solo. The graceful gradient of green in a sliced gherkin visually lifts any dish and belies that direct, snap-punch-kick of flavour. Norman Foster & Partners knew what they were doing aligning their skyscraper design in London's financial district to such a wonder.

NEW POTATO AND EGG SALAD WITH GHERKINS AND CAPERS

This takes its inspiration from the flavours of a classic tartare sauce. Ideal as a barbecue side, it is particularly good with smoky, grilled mackerel. Serves 6 as a side dish

1kg new potatoes, scrubbed, halved if large

4 medium eggs, at room temperature

A bunch of spring onions, trimmed and finely sliced

80g gherkins, chopped

3 tbsp chopped dill (or parsley if you prefer)

50g baby capers, rinsed and drained

Sea salt and black pepper

FOR THE DRESSING

½ garlic clove, finely chopped

1 tsp English mustard

1 tsp clear honey

1½ tbsp cider vinegar

5 tbsp extra virgin olive or rapeseed oil

Put the potatoes in a saucepan, cover with water and add salt. Bring to the boil, then lower the heat and simmer for 8–12 minutes until tender. Drain and allow to cool slightly.

Meanwhile, bring another pan of water to the boil for the eggs. Add the eggs and cook for 7 minutes (this will give you eggs with a still-soft centre). Run the eggs under cold water for a minute or two to stop the cooking, then leave to cool.

For the dressing, whisk all the ingredients together in a bowl and season with salt and pepper to taste.

Once the potatoes have cooled slightly, cut them into bite-sized pieces. Add the dressing to the warm potatoes and mix gently but well. (Adding the dressing while the potatoes are still warm means they soak up more flavour, but it is not essential.) Leave to cool.

Add the spring onions, gherkins, dill and capers to the potatoes. Give it all a good mix and add a little more salt or pepper if needed. Heap into a serving dish. Peel and quarter the boiled eggs, arrange them over the potatoes and serve.

Ginger

Pam Corbin

LATIN NAME
Zingiber officinale

MORE RECIPES
Carrot soup with ginger and coriander (page 123); Raw sprout salad with sesame, ginger and lime (page 102); Spiced spinach with nutmeg (page 408); Spicy brown rice and broccoli (page 535); Crab toasts (page 207); Velvet crab curry (page 211); Noodles with seaweed, smoked mackerel and soy (page 407); Steamed sea bass with kale and ginger (page 573); Fragrant beef curry (page 350); Orange and ginger fool with coffee syrup (page 196); Masala chai doodh (page 384)

There are few baking smells more tempting than warm, sweet ginger. With its sharp, stimulating, citrus and peppery tones, this aromatic spice lends its unique character to traditional gingerbreads, fruit cakes, puddings and snappy biscuits. Used in the British Isles as far back as Anglo-Saxon times, it has been a common spice since the Medieval period. And across Europe, it is essential in many festive baking treats.

All forms of ginger come from the fleshy underground stem, or rhizome, of the plant, which thrives in lush tropical regions. Ginger's warming pungency comes from non-volatile compounds called gingerols; these are comparable to capsaicin and piperine, which give chillies and pepper their heat. In ground ginger, those compounds are concentrated, making it particularly fiery stuff: 1 tsp is equivalent to roughly 6 tsp of the grated fresh root.

Ground ginger is the ideal form for baking purposes and is a component of ground mixed spice, where it combines with cinnamon, coriander, nutmeg, allspice and cloves to give fragrant character to puddings and cakes. However, ground ginger works well in savoury dishes too – it is often found in Indian curry powder blends, for instance.

It's not always possible to ascertain where your ground ginger comes from, but if you know you've got the slightly paler, Jamaican variety, use it for baking first and foremost. Its bite is bright, crisp and fruity. Indian and African ground gingers, with their earthier flavour and richer colour, are perfect for curries and spicy tagines. Sri Lanka is a good source of Fairtrade and/or organic ground ginger.

These days we are fortunate to have easy access to fresh ginger too. The stems are often referred to as 'hands' and they do resemble gnarled fingers. Choose 'hands' that feel firm and taut, with smooth skin – the less wrinkled the better. The 'fingers' should snap off crisply, revealing the juicy, pale yellow flesh inside. Remove the skin by scraping with the rounded edge of a teaspoon – it'll get into all the nooks and crannies, wasting far less of the ginger flesh than if you use a knife or peeler. Peel only what you need for immediate use. Wrap the rest in greaseproof paper or foil and store in the fridge.

Ginger flesh is fibrous. In order to avoid stringy bits in your food, the best way to prepare it is to finely chop or grate it or, for very fine slices, use a mandoline, carefully. Sometimes, it's only the fragrant juice you want – in a fruit salad dressing, say, or a smoothie. You can produce this by simply squeezing a portion of finely grated ginger in your hand until the juice trickles out. Some cooks like to wrap the grated ginger in muslin first and squeeze it dry to get maximum yield.

Fresh ginger is wonderfully versatile in the kitchen. The simplest way to enjoy its warming bite is to steep 2 or 3 wafer-thin slices in piping-hot water for a rousing ginger tea. A knob blitzed with garlic and fresh chilli, meanwhile, will give you the fiery heart of a cracking good curry paste. Finely chopped or grated, ginger adds a spark to stir-fries and noodle recipes, as well as poultry, meat, fish and veg dishes.

It steps brightly into the preserving pan to flavour chutneys, marmalade and other preserves, with a real affinity for rhubarb, apples and pears. Courgette and ginger jam is particularly lovely. In a heavy-based pan, combine 1kg coarsely grated courgette with 100g finely chopped ginger and 100ml lemon juice. Heat gently for 3–4 minutes, then stir in 1kg jam sugar. Continue to stir until the sugar has dissolved. Bring to the boil and boil for about 7 minutes before testing for setting point.

Keep a look-out in March and April for young ginger root, with its pearly white skin and shocking-pink tips. Sweeter and more tender than the mature root, it's a real delicacy. It won't keep long – a couple of weeks in the fridge – but it is perfect to pickle.

G

Pickled ginger is typically packed into little pots in trays of prepared sushi and is a fantastic palate cleanser. It's easy to make: cut 500g young (unpeeled) or peeled mature ginger into wafer-thin slices. Toss in a bowl with 2 tsp fine sea salt and leave for a couple of hours to draw out excess moisture. Rinse the ginger thoroughly, dry and pack into small sterilised jam jars. Heat 300ml rice vinegar and 75g granulated sugar in a saucepan, stirring until the sugar has dissolved, and bring to the boil. Pour the hot syrup over the ginger slices, seal the jars immediately with vinegar-proof lids and leave for a couple of days before using.

Crystallised ginger is made from the young root, by steeping it in sugar syrup, then drying the pieces of ginger and tossing them in sugar. Slices of crystallised ginger dipped in dark chocolate make a lovely sweet treat.

For baking, I prefer to use preserved stem ginger. Preserved in sugar syrup, this has a lively, clean flavour and is excellent added in small pieces to biscuits, cakes, ice creams and puds. And don't waste the gingery syrup – blend it into cake batters or trickle over ice cream.

Ginger is a diva in drinks. Fizzy, fiery old-fashioned ginger beer is punchy and makes a great non-alcoholic pick-me-up. It's also fab mixed half-and-half with proper beer to make a slightly alcoholic shandy. And ginger wine, either neat or with whisky for a whisky mac, is a fine way to warm body and soul on wintry days.

Galangal

This is another member of the ginger family, sometimes known as Thai or Siamese ginger. It is similarly knobbly, but has smoother, paler skin than ginger and the flesh is quite hard and fibrous. More astringent than ginger, with a delightfully citrusy, fragrant character, it is widely used in Thai cooking. You'll find it in specialist Asian stores and some supermarkets but if you can't get it, ginger will do as a substitute in most recipes.

GINGER-BRAISED LAMB

2 tbsp rapeseed oil

1kg scrag end of lamb, on the bone, cut into thick steaks (or use lamb shoulder or neck fillet cut into large cubes)

300ml apple juice

75ml soy sauce

2 tbsp cider vinegar

1 tbsp soft brown sugar

A pinch of dried chilli flakes

4 garlic cloves, thinly sliced

100g root ginger, very thinly sliced

Sea salt and black pepper

This incredibly simple, slow-cooked dish is bursting with flavour. Even after a long spell in the oven, the root ginger retains quite a bit of bite, so it functions almost like a vegetable accompaniment to the rich, savoury lamb. Serves 4

Preheat the oven to 120°C/Fan 110°C/Gas ½.

Heat the oil in a large flameproof casserole over a fairly high heat. Season the lamb pieces with salt and pepper, then colour them well all over in the casserole, giving them a few minutes on each side. You may need to do this in a couple of batches. Set the lamb aside.

Meanwhile, combine the apple juice, soy sauce, vinegar, sugar and chilli flakes in a jug.

Turn down the heat under the lamb browning pan, add the garlic and ginger and cook gently, stirring, for a minute or two until the garlic just starts to colour. Now add the apple juice mixture and bring to a simmer, stirring to dissolve the sugar and release any bits of caramelised lamb from the base of the pan as you go.

Carefully return the lamb to the simmering liquid, with any juices that have seeped from it, cover the dish and transfer to the oven. Cook for 2–2½ hours or until the meat is tender.

Serve the lamb, the ginger and the intensely flavoured juices with rice or noodles, and some wilted greens such as kale.

Goat & kid

MORE RECIPES
Lamb, labneh and spinach salad
(page 335); Roast lamb with
lovage (page 368); North African
shepherd's pie (page 335)

SOURCING
cabritogoatmeat.co.uk;
chestnutmeats.co.uk
(for meat from dairy billies);
goat-meat.co.uk (for non-
dairy goat meat)

Goat meat is eaten all over the world but predominantly in China, Asia and Africa. Some British cooks – particularly those in Asian and West Indian communities – have been buying it for years, but for many of us it is the new kid on the butcher's block.

This meat is, however, catching on. This is partly due to our burgeoning goat dairy industry. As our demand for goat's cheese and milk grows, so does the number of unwanted young male goats born to milking nannies. These young billies have usually been considered a by-product, killed at birth and the carcasses destroyed. But when well looked after, the meat from a billy goat can be a delicacy, on a par with rose veal (the corresponding by-product of the bovine dairy industry), as some enterprising farmers have realised. It's not easy to buy in retailers but it will become so, if shoppers demand it. Most kid meat comes from goats raised indoors (see page 149).

Currently, a lot of goat meat sold in the UK is more mature and comes from the South African Boer breed, or at least from a Boer cross, raised specifically for meat. It's not widely available, but there are some good online suppliers of free-range goat.

Kid goat meat is extremely lean with a milky pinkness and an only mildly 'goaty' tang. Older goat meat is more pungent and dark, like venison. It is to kid what hogget is to lamb – a little less tender but full of flavour, and it responds beautifully to chilli heat and strong spicing.

All goat is low in fat and, without some care, it can toughen under sustained high temperatures. But, handled gently, it is versatile enough to braise, mince, fry or barbecue. The shoulders and legs of older animals are very good slow-roasted, curried or stewed. Kid meat makes delicate chops or cutlets and a whole joint is a lovely Sunday roast. Any goat or kid meat can be minced to create sausages, stuffings, burgers, or a goaty equivalent to shepherd's pie (and will benefit from a certain amount of additional fat, from pork belly, for instance).

I am also fond of a northern Italian recipe for prosciutto-style *violino di capra*. The dry-cured goat 'ham' is traditionally passed around a table of diners who hold it like a violin and slice off the meat using a long knife, like a bow.

GOAT KEBABS WITH ROSEMARY, RED PEPPERS AND ONION

2 red (or orange or yellow)
peppers

2 red onions

750g trimmed goat or kid leg,
cut into large cubes

4 garlic cloves, sliced

2 tbsp olive or rapeseed oil

6–8 sprigs of rosemary,
roughly torn

2 tsp fennel seeds

Sea salt and black pepper

These are a great way to sample goat or kid meat (or you can use rose veal topside). If you grow winter savory, it's a good alternative to rosemary here. You will need a dozen kebab sticks; if using wooden sticks, pre-soak to prevent them burning. Serves 4

Halve the peppers from stem to base and use the tip of a sharp knife to trim out the pale core, stem and seeds. Cut the peppers into bite-sized pieces and place in a large bowl.

Peel the onions, leaving the root end intact. Cut each onion into 12 wedges and add to the peppers along with the goat, garlic, oil, rosemary, fennel seeds and some black pepper. Tumble together gently and refrigerate for at least 6 hours, or overnight.

Add salt just before cooking. Thread the goat, pepper and onions on to your kebab sticks, alternating the different ingredients as you go. You can barbecue the kebabs, or cook them under a hot grill. Either way, heat up the barbecue or grill first. The kebabs will take 12–15 minutes over/under a high heat, with regular turning, to produce nicely browned meat, blistered onion and tender pepper.

Let the kebabs rest in a warm place for 5 minutes before shooting the deliciously charred meat and veg off the sticks. It's delicious stuffed into warm pitta breads and finished with hummus or some thick Greek yoghurt and a sprinkling of chopped green chilli.

Goose

Gill Meller

SEASONALITY
Autumn and winter

SOURCING
goodmansgeese.co.uk;
hostingleyfarmfreerange.co.uk;
organicgeese.com

G

Traditionally, the first geese of the season were eaten at Michaelmas in late September. They were served up on the Feast of St Michael and All Angels, the start of the new farming year, when tenants would pay some of their quarterly rent to their landlord in the form of a fattened bird. You will still find 'Michaelmas goose' on menus – though of course, we eat them in even greater numbers at Christmas. They lost favour at the festive table when turkey began to take precedence in the 1960s, but they are returning.

Proud, elegant and noisy, geese can be aggressive creatures. We keep gaggles of a dozen or so at a time at River Cottage, their white forms highly visible as they waddle around in the darkening days. They do best outdoors and are not intensively farmed in the UK. A fair number of the 250,000 or so free-range birds raised for the Christmas market are in small to medium-sized flocks of 50–5,000.

When alive, geese seem to be mainly neck and wings, but the meat of an average goose is mostly in the breasts, with some on the legs too. All is covered with the softest of fats and magnificent skin that crisps up beautifully in the oven. The weight of an oven-ready goose tends to include the giblets and bagged-up cavity fat. A 4kg bird feeds four comfortably, a 5kg bird feeds six and a 6kg bird feeds eight.

The capacity of a goose to feed a tableful can be greatly enhanced if you cook different parts of it in different ways, and make full use of its fabulous fat. The River Cottage approach is a full-on festive goose feast, most of the preparation for which can be done in the days before Christmas. First the fat is removed from the cavity of the goose, rendered down, then used to confit the legs. The goose's neck skin (specify from the seller that you want your goose 'long-necked') can be removed, the neck itself cooked with the giblets, then chopped into a tasty mix with sausagemeat and herbs, stuffed back into the skin and poached in hot goose fat as a delicious sort of sausage. On Christmas Day, the remaining breast section, or 'crown', can then be roasted and served with all the trimmings. This truly sumptuous spread is a way to get the best of all worlds with your goose – the fabulous legs tender, the succulent crown cooked relatively rare, and all the tasty offal made use of.

I will also, however, happily tuck into a slow-cooked whole goose, the meat dripping with fat and juice as I pull it off the bones (see right).

As with all fat-laden birds, it is key not to use too high a heat. It's very tempting to whack a goose in a high oven to get colour, but a slower approach gives a better result. You want to soften the fat without scorching it. For basic roasting, start your bird off at 200°C/Fan 180°C/Gas 6 for 30 minutes or so, then turn down the heat to 160°C/ Fan 140°C/Gas 3 and cook for a further 1–1½ hours until the goose is done to your liking, depending on its size.

The fatty nature of goose means it also takes well to smoking because it retains a good moisture content, and the flavour of the meat isn't overwhelmed by the smoke. The breasts can be cold-smoked and then roasted. Or they can be cured – perhaps scented with anise, chilli, cloves and cinnamon – and hot-smoked until cooked but still just blushing pink in the middle.

Geese (as well as ducks) are a source of foie gras – one of the most controversial of foods. To produce it, the birds are force-fed so that their liver enlarges, growing to up to ten times its normal size, and becoming creamily rich. More ethical alternatives are available, from geese that are not force-fed, but allowed to follow their instincts to overfeed themselves at certain times of the year. (For further information on foie gras, see page 360.) It's also important not to overlook the fact that goose liver is absolutely delicious in its natural (unfattened) state: excellent included in a pâté or parfait, or just flash-fried in butter with sage and shallots.

Goose fat is another of the great treats of the table, adding luscious richness to earthy ingredients, particularly root veg. It's the ultimate roasting fat for spuds and other roots, including celeriac, parsnips and Jerusalem artichokes. You'll find most of the fat inside the goose's cavity – pull it away and place it in a baking dish, then put into a low oven to gently render down.

You can also collect the fat that renders from a goose as it cooks, and you can buy goose fat in pots too. Goose fat suppliers are not obliged to state on the label if the fat comes from force-fed geese. However, most supermarkets have a policy about this and may well insist on a non-force-fed source. You can contact the retailer to check.

Most of the geese we eat are farmed but small numbers from a few wild geese species are shot by wildfowlers during the winter months. Canada geese can be shot at other times too, as they are considered an agricultural pest. It is illegal to sell wild geese in the UK, though they may be given away. All wild goose meat is darker, leaner and tougher than that of a domesticated bird. Younger or smaller birds can be roasted, but Canada geese are bigger and tougher, so like other older birds they need slower cooking, perhaps in a curry or minced up with some fatty pork for burgers or sausages.

SLOW-ROASTED GOOSE WITH STAR ANISE, ORANGE AND CHILLI

1 free-range, oven-ready goose (about 4kg)

4 star anise

Finely grated zest and juice of 2 oranges (spent orange halves retained)

4 tsp clear honey

2 tsp dried chilli flakes

2 garlic cloves, grated

Sea salt and black pepper

Chopped coriander, to finish

Long cooking in a very low oven renders goose meat gorgeously tender and moist. You could also use a large duck, reducing the low cooking time to 2 hours. Serves 4–6

Preheat the oven to 180°C/Fan 160°C/Gas 4.

Pull the wings and legs away from the goose's body a little so that heat can circulate around. Place the bird in a large roasting tray and prick the skin of the breasts and legs all over with a cocktail stick or thin skewer: don't go through the meat, you just want to create a conduit for the fat to come out. Put the spent orange halves inside the bird, season it all over with salt and pepper and place in the oven for 30 minutes.

Meanwhile, finely crush the star anise using a pestle and mortar. Put the orange zest and juice into a saucepan and add the crushed star anise, honey, chilli flakes and garlic. Bring to a gentle simmer, turn off the heat and set aside to infuse.

After the initial 30 minutes, take the roasting tray out of the oven and brush the goose liberally with the spiced honey and orange mixture, including the legs and wings. Scoop about 3 tbsp fat from the roasting tray and add it to the remaining spiced mixture.

Return the roasting tray to the oven. Lower the oven setting to 120°C/Fan 110°C/Gas ½ and cook the goose, uncovered, for a further 4 hours, brushing it every hour or so with more of the fatty, orangey spice mix (aim to use it all up). To check whether it is cooked, pull at one of the legs: it should feel as though it will come away from the body with ease. If not, put the bird back in the oven for 20–30 minutes and test again. When the bird is completely tender, turn off the oven and allow it to rest there for 30 minutes.

Pull off the leg meat and place on a warmed platter. Cut the breast meat into shards and add to the leg meat, along with the fatty, crispy skin. Season all with a little salt and scatter with coriander.

Serve the goose with pickled cucumber (see page 218) and a green salad, with plain rice on the side if you like.

Gooseberries

Pam Corbin

LATIN NAME
Ribes uva-crispa

SEASONALITY
May–July

HABITAT
Wild gooseberries are not common but may be found in hedgerows, wood margins and river gorges in most parts of the British Isles

MORE RECIPES
Fried salmon with cucumber and gooseberry salad (page 553); Black pudding and gooseberries on toast (page 70); Roasted grapes (page 288); Rhubarb crème brûlée (page 532); Strawberries with lavender and honey (page 341)

It's easy to be smitten by gooseberries and, thankfully, it's love in a cold climate. These bewitching little fruits prefer the cooler, moister climes of the northern hemisphere – the further north the better – where they thrive in the wild as well as in gardens.

The European gooseberry comes early in the year, the first of the summer berries. Fresh, sharp, crisp and exhilarating, this fruit divides into two camps. The tart culinary variety is best for pies, jams and cooked things, while dessert berries are sweet enough to be eaten straight from the bush. However, many varieties double up for both duties and generally, the longer any gooseberry is left on the bush, the sweeter it becomes. If you grow your own, a good ploy is to pick and thin out the small early berries for cooking, then leave the rest to sweeten and mature in the warming sun.

Supermarkets are increasingly selling gooseberries and you can find the fruit on shop shelves in June and July, but I prefer to buy locally grown berries. Lots of pick-your-own farms sell them and they're always worth looking out for at roadside stalls.

These fruits come in all shades from yellow, white and pink to dark, damson red, but are still most commonly gooseberry green. Semi-translucent, slightly hairy and protected by vicious, thorny spines, the berries are usually grown on broad, spreading bushes that can make gooseberry picking a painful affair. It's much easier to harvest them from cordons or lollipop-shaped 'standard' trees. Their main predators are children (and adults) who thrill and shrill at their sourness – as well as blackbird thieves who quite sensibly wait until the berries are riper and sweeter.

Worcesterberries, which are small and red-black, are a form of gooseberry well worth trying, though the bushes are unpleasantly spiny, making picking a little tricky. Jostaberries – the result of a splicing of gooseberries with blackcurrants (sister fruits from the *Ribes* family) – are joyfully spineless, and have a delightful, tangy sharpness. Both these have bags of flavour and plenty of acidity, making them first-class jamming and pudding berries, although, in my eyes, the gooseberry is still the finest of the lot.

Aside from those pop-in-the-mouth, straight-from-the-bush dessert berries, most gooseberries need a bit of softening and sweetening up. But first of all, the flower and stem ends need to be snipped off. This 'topping and tailing' is easily achieved with a pair of scissors – a job best done with cup or glass to hand. (There's no need for this chore when making a purée that's to be sieved, or jelly juice that will be strained).

Once topped and tailed, put the berries in a pan with a splash of water – just enough to stop them catching (gooseberries are very juicy and more than a whisper of water dilutes their lovely liquor). Put the lid on and lightly poach for as few minutes as possible, until the skins and flesh are soft but the berries still whole. To cook evenly, without breaking up the fruit, shake the pan rather than stir it. Add 100g sugar per 1kg fruit to start with (you can always add more). A compote can be made with frozen gooseberries in exactly the same way, but you won't need to add any water as the defrosted berries release lots of juice.

As gooseberries begin to grow and swell in mid- to late May, fragrant hedgerow elderflower is also ready for gathering. There is no greater gooseberry friend. A spray or two placed on the poaching berries will give them a soft-sweet muscat radiance. At other times, a drop of rose or orange blossom water is an alternative way to keep the fruit fragrant and sweet. A simple gooseberry compote, perfumed in any of these ways, is excellent folded through cream or yoghurt with a classic vanilla custard for a tangy fruit fool. Crumbles, pies, tarts and cobblers are all happy destinations for a gooseberry compote too.

G

Gooseberries' clean, sharp qualities work incredibly well with fatty meats and oily fish, the lively tartness lifting the richness vigorously. The French term for gooseberry, *groseille à maquereau* or 'mackerel berry', is no accident. For a quick gooseberry sauce to serve with fresh or smoked mackerel: mix 150–200g lightly poached gooseberries with 1 tbsp caster sugar, 1 tbsp cider vinegar and a pinch of salt. Pep it up a little if you like by adding 1 tbsp horseradish. Similar tart gooseberry sauces can be made to accompany pork, goose or duck – and the whole berries can be added to stuffings for roast meats where their sharp fruitiness will be welcomed.

Alternatively, for a crisp, fresh salsa, roughly slice raw gooseberries and toss with a little sugar and vinegar, and 1 tbsp finely shredded mint or other fresh herb. Allow an hour or two for the flavours to mingle. This works beautifully with feta and young creamy cheeses; it is also brilliant served with a hot curry.

But of all gooseberry's clever tricks, it's in the preserving pan it performs the best. Full flavoured, acidic and packed with pectin, gooseberries have an exceptional jelling ability. They transform easily into heavenly jams and jellies, their sharp-tart qualities holding the sugar in perfect balance. A proportion of gooseberries added to recipes for strawberry jam will enliven the flavour and lend a hand in setting the jam.

And you can use surplus berries to make fruit cheese (a solid, sliceable preserve) to serve as a stylish delicacy with good English Cheddar and soft cheese. Alternatively, sieved gooseberry purée heated gently with fresh eggs, butter and sugar turns into a deliciously soft, smooth fruity curd. The gooseberry can also do sterling service in tangy ketchups, chutneys and pickles to accompany cold meats, smoked fish, cheeses, sausages… almost anything.

Gooseberries freeze well too, so if time is short when they are ready to pick, bag them up and freeze to use later – but do top and tail them first. And, still in the cool zone, gooseberries make gloriously refreshing ice creams and deliciously tart granitas.

GOOSEBERRY, CREAM AND HONEY PUDDING

500g gooseberries, topped and tailed (or frozen gooseberries, defrosted)

2 medium eggs

2 medium egg yolks

200ml double cream

1 generous tbsp clear honey

125g caster sugar, plus extra to finish

75g white breadcrumbs, plus extra to finish

This delicate pudding is a kind of thickened gooseberry custard. If you have some to hand, throw in a few heads of elderflower while the berries cook, for a floral hint. The recipe also works well with frozen gooseberries, with an optional dash of elderflower cordial. Serves 6

Put the gooseberries in a large pan with 2 tbsp water (defrosted frozen berries won't need this extra water). Bring to a gentle simmer, put the lid on and cook for about 10 minutes until the fruit is broken down and soft. Rub the gooseberry pulp through a sieve into a large bowl, to remove the seeds. Leave to cool.

Meanwhile, preheat the oven to 170°C/Fan 150°C/Gas 3 and butter an ovenproof dish, about 25 x 16cm and 5cm deep.

Lightly beat the eggs and egg yolks together, then stir into the cooled gooseberry purée, along with the cream, honey, sugar and breadcrumbs. Pour the mixture into the prepared dish and sprinkle with a little more sugar and a dusting of breadcrumbs.

Stand the dish in a roasting tin and pour in enough hot water to come two-thirds of the way up the sides. Bake for 35–40 minutes, or until just set.

Take the dish out of the tin and leave to cool. Serve the pudding at room temperature or chilled, with cream.

Grapefruit

LATIN NAME
Citrus x paradisi Macfad.

This is a citrus fruit of incomparable fragrance and exceptional juiciness. Although I rather like the cold-baths-and-press-ups appeal of old-school white grapefruit, the pretty ruby and pink varieties offer a much less acerbic experience than white grapefruit, and a more rounded, richer flavour.

The conventional way of dishing up this plump citrus has been to shower it in sugar. But with these rosy modern varieties that's just not necessary: a simple hemisphere of breakfast grapefruit – the dripping segments released from the pith with a little knife and consumed with a spoon – no longer needs sweetening.

One of the few occasions when I would still let sugar rain on grapefruit's parade is when I make it into a sorbet or granita – both exceptionally good. Simply whisk 100g icing sugar into 500ml freshly squeezed grapefruit juice until the sugar is dissolved. Churn in an ice-cream machine to make a sorbet, or freeze solid in a tray, then defrost slightly and scratch up the crystals with a fork for a granita. Finely chopped fresh mint – or a dash of a strong infusion of fresh mint – is a good addition to this lovely ice.

Counterintuitively, the seasoning that grapefruit really loves is salt: it seems to emphasise its bittersweet qualities in the most appealing way. A pinch of salt and a twist of black pepper really bring breakfast grapefruit alive. This savoury affinity can be deployed in all kinds of interesting ways in salads that mingle segments of fresh grapefruit with such partners as olives, bacon or smoked fish. Add peppery salad leaves and/or herbs such as mint, coriander or basil, some crisp raw veg (fennel or celery, for example), and perhaps some slices of buttery avocado, and you've got a very classy dish.

Prepare grapefruit for salads by cutting out the segments, from a knife-peeled grapefruit (as in the recipe below). Work over a bowl to save as much juice as you can and use this in the dressing… or just drink it. Fresh grapefruit juice is great in cocktails (Moscow Mules being the most classic).

There are two relations of the grapefruit to note and explore. The pomelo looks like pear-shaped grapefruit and can grow to a whopping 30cm diameter. It has a pleasing, mild grapefruit flavour, but the pomelo's charm is in the way the segments can be torn up to release the individual 'teardrop' chambers of juiciness, which are great scattered in salads, both savoury and sweet.

The ugli fruit is a cross between a grapefruit and a mandarin. Despite the leathery pitted skin that gives it its harsh name, the fruit is sweet and fragrant on the inside.

GRAPEFRUIT, TOMATO AND CORIANDER SALSA

1 pink or ruby grapefruit

1 small red onion, very finely diced

175g tomatoes, cut into roughly 1cm pieces

1 medium-hot, medium-sized red chilli (deseeded for less heat if preferred), finely chopped

A good handful of coriander leaves, roughly chopped

Sea salt and black pepper

This is fantastic with a fillet of simply fried fish, particularly a robust and flavoursome variety such as bream, gurnard or mackerel. Serves 4–6

Take a little slice off the top and base of the grapefruit. Stand it on a board and use a sharp knife to cut away the peel and pith, leaving you with a skinless fruit. Working over a bowl, slice out the grapefruit segments from between their membranes and drop them into the bowl, letting any juice drip in too. Discard the 'core'.

Take each grapefruit segment out of the bowl, slice it into 3 or 4 pieces and place back in the bowl. Add the onion, tomatoes and chilli, along with a pinch of salt and a good couple of twists of pepper. Mix gently. Taste and add more salt and pepper as needed.

Gently stir in the chopped coriander and the salsa is ready to serve.

Grapes

Mark Diacono

LATIN NAME
Vitis vinifera

SEASONALITY
British grapes: August–October;
imported all year round

Generally, the grapes in our shops represent just a few varieties, including 'Thompson Seedless' (aka 'Sultana'), 'Muscat' and 'Concord'. These are sourced from Continental Europe in autumn, South America and South Africa the rest of the year – places where the growing temperatures suit these sun-lovers. Unfortunately, flavour is less of a priority than disease resistance, uniformity of form and size, and appearance, so the most delicious varieties are rarely available to buy. However, with over 600 vineyards in the UK, table grapes are increasingly being grown as a secondary product for farmers' markets and other local outlets, so do keep an eye out for them. Some supermarkets are also trialling British grapes.

Whether grown for wine, juice or eating fresh, grapes are often subjected to a lot of spraying (they are prone to fungal diseases and a variety of pests). So it's good to prioritise organic grapes if you can. Keep grapes in the fridge to extend their lifespan – they spoil very quickly – but allow them to get to room temperature before eating.

I like to serve grapes in warm salads. The warmth brings out their subtleties of favour and aroma, just as when they are still warm from the vine. And grapes have some wonderful natural partners, notably cheese (Cheddar with sharp grapes, blue cheese with sweet ones), nuts (especially hazels and walnuts), cured meats, roasted cauliflower, rocket and other spicy leaves, parsley and oily fish. A simple vinaigrette will bring together any of these combinations – tweak with honey or mustard to complement the relative sweetness or sharpness of the fruit.

Grapes are also good added late to summer soups or halved and strewn over a pizza with Parma ham and blue cheese. They roast surprisingly well too (see below).

Growing your own grapes opens up a wealth of flavours beyond the usual shop choices. Search for a variety in the area where flavour, outdoor reliability and disease resistance intersect. 'Solaris' and 'Phoenix' are two wonderful white grapes for eating, juicing or wine and can be picked anywhere on the ripeness spectrum from sharpish to fully dessert-wine sweet. 'Rondo' (which, when fully ripe, tastes as close to a mulberry as any fruit) and 'Regent' are superb dual-purpose black grapes. Give them sun and a well-drained spot.

ROASTED GRAPES

500g grapes

2 tbsp olive oil

1 tbsp sherry vinegar or balsamic vinegar

1 tsp clear honey or sugar

8–10 sage leaves, roughly torn, or the leaves from a sprig of thyme

50g hazelnuts or walnuts (optional)

Sea salt and black pepper

Mingled with a few seasonings, these roasted fruits create a lovely, rough, savoury compote. You can serve the grapes plain roasted, or add nuts for even more of a treat. Try this with gooseberries too. Serves 4–6

Preheat the oven to 200°C/Fan 180°C/Gas 6.

Spread out the grapes in a single layer in a shallow baking tray. Sprinkle with a pinch each of salt and pepper and trickle over the olive oil, vinegar, honey or sugar and sage or thyme. Roast for about 15 minutes until the grapes are just starting to burst.

You can eat the roasted grapes like this, perhaps alongside roast chicken or pork chops, or let them cool a little and then transfer them to a bowl (they're very juicy) to serve as an accompaniment to cheese.

Alternatively, scatter the nuts over the grapes and roast for 5 minutes longer before serving, with good bread.

Grouse

Tim Maddams

LATIN NAME
Lagopus lagopus scotica

SEASONALITY
England, Wales and Scotland:
12 August–10 December.
Northern Ireland: 12 August–
30 November

HABITAT
Moorland

MORE RECIPES
Pot-roasted mallard with celeriac
and watercress (page 241)

SOURCING
tasteofgame.org.uk

It's known as the king of game birds and rightly so. In my opinion, grouse – or, more specifically, red grouse – is the tastiest of the tribe. In season from 12 August ('The Glorious Twelfth') until early December, birds shot earlier on are generally of that year's brood (i.e. youngsters), with a greater proportion of older birds taken as the season progresses. It's worth knowing this because age is everything with grouse. This is the most gamey of all game birds, due to its singular diet of heather, and the older the creature, the stronger the flavour.

Grouse are often seen as wild birds and, indeed, they are not reared and released like pheasants and partridges. However, their habitat is carefully managed. In order to ensure the survival of the maximum number, predators and pests are controlled, while heather on every successful grouse moor from Yorkshire to the Highlands is

G

burned on a cyclical basis to rejuvenate the plants, providing ideal cover, nesting and feeding conditions. It's fair to say that the grouse's abundance is somewhat unnatural. However, land managed for grouse is beneficial for many other wild species too.

The very best young birds are wonderfully sweet and aromatic, as well as tender. My favourite way to cook them is simply roasted, served with a frugal garnish of fruit jelly and maybe a root vegetable purée. The roasting should start with a brief browning in a pan and be finished in a hot oven (220°C/Fan 200°C/Gas 7) for a mere 12 minutes or so – and the resting period should be at least as long as that.

Old grouse are far less tender so cooking them becomes a more considered affair. You can roast them, as in the recipe below, as long as you cook them at a lower temperature and for longer than the youngsters. But I often like to cook them slowly to really tenderise them – stewing them gently for pies or pasties, for instance. Pair them with strong flavours. Spices such as cinnamon and star anise work very well and Asian flavours like ginger and soy are up there too. Old grouse are also ideal candidates for smoking.

If you're looking at a plucked bird, assessing the age is difficult. Size is a good indicator – very large grouse will be older birds, and their flesh is a deeper, richer red too. In the feather, it's a little easier: older birds have more ragged plumage, harder, more damaged claws and possibly swelling in the foot joints. These signs are subtle and can be hard to spot at first, but comparison with other birds will quickly teach you the differences.

Hanging for grouse should be kept to a minimum: 2–5 days for older birds, 1–3 for young ones. I often eat young grouse the day after shooting: their sweetness is immense but lessens by the day.

ROAST GROUSE WITH BARLEY, APPLES AND SQUASH

This warming, one-pot dish is game cookery at its simplest and most delicious. Try it with wild duck too. Serves 2

400–500g chunk of squash, such as Crown Prince or butternut

2 tbsp olive or rapeseed oil

2–3 sprigs of rosemary

5–6 sprigs of sage

100g pearl barley, or pearled spelt, soaked for 1 hour

1 oven-ready grouse

A small bunch of thyme

A large knob of butter

2 medium eating apples, such as Russets

½ glass of white wine or water

Sea salt and black pepper

Preheat the oven to 200°C/Fan 180°C/Gas 6.

Peel and deseed the squash, then cut into large-bite-sized pieces and place in a roasting tin. Trickle over 1 tbsp oil, tear over the rosemary and sage leaves and season well with salt and pepper. Roast for 35–40 minutes or until just tender and starting to caramelise around the edges.

Meanwhile, drain the soaked barley or spelt and place it in a pan. Cover with fresh water and bring to a simmer. Cook, uncovered, until just tender but still a bit nutty (it will cook further with the grouse): allow 15–20 minutes for soaked barley, a bit less if you are using spelt. Drain and set aside.

Season the grouse all over and place the thyme in its cavity. Heat a medium pan over a medium-high heat. Add the butter and remaining oil and, when bubbling, add the grouse. Brown it for 6–8 minutes, turning so that all sides are coloured, then remove.

Quarter and core the apples then add them to the squash roasting tin along with the barley or spelt, wine or water and a little more salt and pepper. Place the browned grouse in the middle and return to the hot oven for 20 minutes.

Remove and allow the bird to rest in a warm place for 15 minutes. Serve the grouse legs and slices of the breast with spoonfuls of the barley, squash and apples.

Guinea fowl

Steven Lamb

LATIN NAME
Numidia meleagris (most commonly farmed species)

MORE RECIPES
Paella (page 163); Tea-brined chicken (page 634); Pheasant with olives and preserved lemons (page 414); Poached pheasant with star anise (page 610)

MORE RECIPES
wildmeat.co.uk; woolleyparkfarm.co.uk

The name 'guinea fowl' evokes this bird's original status as game, a wild creature of the jungle. But rather than being hunted down, guinea fowl are mostly now bred for the table. Native to the West African coast, they also do well in our climate, and free-range British birds are increasingly available online and in some supermarkets, butchers and farmers' markets. Guinea fowl are available all year round.

The guinea fowl has a distinctive white face and red wattles and sports a natty, polka-dot plumage, its grey, black and purple feathers peppered with white spots. In silhouette the shape is reminiscent of a partridge (though bigger), a bird with which it shares other similarities, such as being a ground nester.

In terms of flavour and texture, the creamy white meat is not dissimilar to that of lean chicken, and guinea fowl can be used as an alternative to chicken in almost any recipe. However, it is much more than a mere substitute for our most popular poultry, occupying a niche a little closer to that of the game birds. It's lower in fat than chicken and, if hung for a few days after slaughter (as many producers do), it develops a hint of gamey flavour – less assertive than that found in actual game birds, but still present.

Guinea fowl is suitable for braising and casseroles, but it is perhaps best simply roasted – as long as you remember that it is prone to dryness if cooked too hot or too long. I follow the basic times and temperatures for a small roast chicken – giving it an initial hot blast at a high temperature, followed by a more moderate roast – but protect and enhance the super-lean breast meat by barding it with pancetta or bacon.

Guinea fowl tend to make it to the table 10–15 weeks after hatching, at 1.2–1.5kg, which is enough to serve 4 people. As well as size, feeling the breastbone helps to assess age; this is soft in a young bird and much harder in an old one. Also the scales on the feet (if still attached) are coarser and more prominent on an older bird.

ROAST GUINEA FOWL WITH ONIONS AND SAGE BREADCRUMBS

Jointing the guinea fowl (as for chicken, see page 162) and giving the breasts less time in the oven helps to avoid overcooking. Serves 2–4 depending on the size of the bird

4 large onions (red or yellow), peeled and cut into 8 wedges

3 tbsp olive or rapeseed oil

1 free-range guinea fowl, jointed into 6 portions (drumsticks, thighs, breasts)

200ml white wine

150ml chicken (or guinea fowl) stock

8 garlic cloves, peeled but left whole

8 bay leaves

3 tbsp chopped sage

25g butter

100g coarse breadcrumbs

Sea salt and black pepper

Preheat the oven to 160°C/Fan 140°C/Gas 3.

Place the onions in a large roasting tin with 2 tbsp of the oil. Season well with salt and pepper and toss together. Cook in the oven for about 10 minutes.

Meanwhile, heat the remaining oil in a large frying pan over a medium heat. Season the guinea fowl drumsticks and thighs and brown them all over in the hot pan, then set aside on a plate. Deglaze the pan with the wine, scraping to release any meaty residues. Let the wine simmer until reduced by half, then add the stock and bring to the boil.

Take the roasting tin from the oven and add the drumsticks and thighs. Add the garlic, bay, half the sage and the boiling stock. Give the tin a shake to mingle the ingredients, then return to the oven for 45 minutes, turning and stirring everything once or twice.

When the time is nearly up, return the frying pan to a medium heat. Add a trickle more oil and brown the guinea fowl breasts; remove and set aside. Add the butter to the frying pan. Once melted, add the breadcrumbs and remaining sage and stir to coat in the butter.

Take the roasting tin of meat and onions from the oven and add the guinea fowl breasts to it. Scatter the buttery crumbs over the guinea fowl and onions and return to the oven for 20–25 minutes or until the breasts are cooked through and the crumbs are golden.

Let rest for 10 minutes before serving, with mash and cabbage, or rice and wilted chard.

Gurnard

LATIN NAME
Red gurnard: *Aspitrigla cuculus*.
Grey gurnard: *Eutrigla gurnardus*.
Tub gurnard: *Chelidonichthys lucerna* or *Triglia*

SEASONALITY
Avoid in summer when spawning

HABITAT
Usually English Channel, Celtic Sea and west of Scotland

MCS RATING
3

REC MINIMUM SIZE
25cm

MORE RECIPES
Black bream with Jerusalem artichoke purée (page 91); Steamed sea bass with kale and ginger (page 573); Red mullet with roasted red pepper mayo (page 393); Cod with fennel, capers and tomatoes (page 194); Dill salsa verde (page 235)

SOURCING
goodfishguide.org

I've long championed the gurnard, and I use it often. It's delicious, and the curdy, firm flesh of its tapering, almost triangular body, peels obligingly off the bone for serving. Its dragon-like, armour-plated head also adds oomph to fish soups and stews. That's why I like to braise it whole with chunky root veg; or drop meaty cutlets, along with the head, into a coconutty curry or highly seasoned tomato-based stew. But the fillets are very friendly too: fry them with onions and olives; or steam in a foil parcel with Asian flavours. This is one of those accommodating fish, like bream, that can be swapped into almost any enticing fish recipe.

In the UK, most gurnard is caught in the English Channel, the Celtic Sea and off the west coast of Scotland. In the north and east, it's less common. There are several varieties that may crop up on the fishmonger's slab (or on the end of your line, when boat fishing inshore), the most common here in the Southwest being the red gurnard. These are usually a generous, one-per-person size of around 500g. But occasionally a bigger fish of 2kg or more will be found – and that's likely to be either a tub or a grey gurnard. I once baked a 3kg tub gurnard whole for Christmas Eve – it was a spectacular and delicious party piece.

Because a lot of people have heeded advice to try gurnard, fishermen are now landing more of it. In the past it was often discarded but, while it's still not actually a target species, it is now much more likely to be retained when it's reeled in.

In fact, our growing enthusiasm for gurnard has led the MCS to sound a note of warning, pointing out that there's a need for more detailed data on this species as it transmogrifies from disregarded, funny-looking baitfish to desirable dish of the day. But that doesn't mean we have to give up gurnard, just as we are getting a taste for it. It's better that this is recognised as a good table fish, rather than discarded at sea, dead. And of course, eating gurnard also takes the pressure off other species, such as cod. The important thing, as with any seafood, is not to focus on it to the exclusion of all else. As a nation, we have a bad habit of excessive fish fidelity to the same fish species. But when a net comes up, it usually includes more than one type of fish; our eating should show similar variety.

ROAST GURNARD WITH PEPPER, LEMON, THYME AND CHILLI

This full-flavoured fish responds really well to seasoning with big, bold flavours. Here it's marinated with a fragrant, peppery paste. Try this with bream or sardines too. Serves 2

2 tsp black peppercorns

1 large or 2 small garlic clove(s), finely grated

Finely grated zest of 1 lemon

2–3 tsp thyme leaves

2 tsp dried chilli flakes, or to taste

1 tsp flaky sea salt

1 tbsp olive or rapeseed oil

2 gurnard (each about 500g), scaled and gutted

Using a pestle and mortar, grind the peppercorns fairly finely. Add the garlic, lemon zest, thyme, chilli flakes, salt and oil, then pound everything together.

With a sharp knife, make 4–5 slashes, each 1–2cm deep, down each side of the fish. Rub the fragrant peppercorn mixture into the slashes and over the skin. Leave to marinate in the fridge for 2–4 hours, taking the fish out of the fridge half an hour before you want to cook them.

Preheat the oven to 200°C/Fan 180°C/Gas 6.

Place the fish in a roasting tin and roast for 20–25 minutes or until the flesh comes away from the bone easily when teased with the tip of a knife. Serve with sautéed potatoes and a fresh green salad.

Haddock

Nick Fisher

LATIN NAME
Melanogrammus aeglefinus

SEASONALITY
Avoid March–April when spawning

HABITAT
Northern Atlantic

MCS RATING
2–5

REC MINIMUM SIZE
30cm

MORE RECIPES
Cod with fennel, capers and tomatoes (page 194); Herbed pouting fish fingers (page 501); Crumbed whiting goujons with curried egg tartare (page 673)

SOURCING
goodfishguide.org; msc.org

At an early age I was encouraged to think of haddock as a finer fish than cod. It was, my mum told me, a fish for the discerning palate. This early lesson has stayed with me.

For me, a haddock fillet does anything a cod fillet does and just as well – if not slightly better. It's a matter of mouth-feel as much as anything: haddock is a little finer textured and more delicate. To be fair, it's much easier to find a fat, thick fillet of cod. Haddock is normally a smaller fish and so its fillets are thinner. If you're after a doorstep wedge of battered fish, it wouldn't be the fish you'd buy, but I'm certainly happy to plump for a haddie. Go for fish from the right area, and it's a good, sustainable choice too. Haddock from the North Sea, west of Scotland, Iceland and northeast Arctic is generally a safe bet and some Scottish haddock is MSC-certified.

Cold-smoked haddock is a firm favourite of mine. Steamed and served with kale or a few sticks of asparagus, and a poached duck egg, it's a magnificent meal. Cold-smoked haddock should always be the colour of a just-planed oak plank: honey in hue, like the skin on clotted cream before it's stirred. If it's bright orange or as yellow as a bilious banana, it's been dyed before smoking, or dyed instead of smoking.

The colouring generally used to be E104, quinoline yellow, a synthetic coal-tar dye that has been linked to hyperactivity in children. A lot of manufacturers now use curcumin, derived from turmeric, instead. But either way, the dye is a lie – to make the fish look more smoked. I prefer haddock where the flavour speaks for itself.

Arbroath Smokies should be hunted down and coveted with ferocity and passion. These whole, headless, hot-smoked haddock – usually tied together in pairs with string around their tails – can be lightly grilled or steamed, or even just eaten cold with horseradish sauce on toast. Then, you need to save the skins and skeletons to make a light stock, which will give you another experience of haddock joy the next day, when you can use it to cook a handful of pearl barley and lentils into a smoky broth.

SMOKED HADDOCK JACKET POTATOES

2 large baking potatoes

250g smoked haddock fillet

About 250ml whole milk

25g butter

50g well-flavoured hard cheese, such as mature Cheddar or Lancashire, or Quickes hard goat's cheese, grated, plus extra to finish

4–6 spring onions, trimmed and thinly sliced

Sea salt and black pepper

Served with a green salad and perhaps a poached egg, this is great comfort food. Smoked pollack works just as well. Serves 2

Preheat the oven to 200°C/Fan 180°C/Gas 6. Prick the potatoes in a few places with a fork, then sprinkle with a little fine salt. Place on a baking tray and bake for about 1 hour or until completely tender; to test, insert a small, sharp knife into their centres.

Meanwhile, lay the haddock in a medium saucepan and pour on the milk; it should just cover the fish. Put the lid on, bring slowly to the boil, then take off the heat. Flip the fillet over, cover the pan and leave the fish to cook in the residual heat for 3 minutes. Check the fish is opaque and flaking easily from the skin, then remove it from the milk. Flake the cooked flesh into a bowl, checking for any small bones as you go. Reserve the smoky milk.

When the potatoes are cooked, remove from the oven and cut them in half. Scoop out as much hot flesh as you can, without tearing the skin, into a bowl. Add 2–3 tbsp of the fish poaching milk, along with the butter, cheese and some salt and pepper. Mash well, using a potato masher. Carefully fold in the flakes of smoked fish (you don't want to break it up too much) and the spring onions.

Spoon the filling back into the potato skins and top with a sprinkling of cheese. Return to the oven for 12–15 minutes to heat through and crisp slightly on top before serving.

Haggis

SOURCING
blackface.co.uk;
peelham.co.uk

It may not be immediately appealing, but haggis seems to get the creative juices flowing. This savoury pudding, concocted from offal and wrapped in a sheep's stomach, has prompted writers from Homer to Burns to describe and celebrate it. And rightly so.

At the risk of upsetting anyone north of the border, the origins of haggis aren't actually Scottish. The Romans created similar foods, and some believe the haggis as we know it came to us from Scandinavia. However, thanks to the lyricism of Robert Burns the haggis now has tartan DNA running through it.

One of the great things about haggis is that it blends lowly ingredients into a wonderful product, which is certainly more than the sum of its parts. Probably born of necessity – to utilise the whole animal – it is made by cooking the sheep's 'pluck' (lungs, heart and liver) with onions, oatmeal, suet and spices to create a nutty, moist, savoury dish. There is nothing quite like the tender, spicy crumble of haggis spilling from its skin.

Most shop-bought haggis are pre-cooked. To heat them through, simmer in a large saucepan of stock for 45 minutes, or wrap in foil and bake at 180°C/Fan 160°C/Gas 4 for about an hour. At best, haggis is accompanied with potato and swede ('neeps') and celebrated with a nip of single malt whisky as the traditional centrepiece of a Burns Night supper in late January. At worst, it is battered and deep-fried in fast food establishments. In between, there are other worthy uses for haggis: I like it served cold with a fruity chutney, for instance.

If you can get hold of a fresh sheep's pluck, from a butcher or an abbatoir, then making your own haggis is simple and satisfying. The only tricky bit is poaching the pudding gently enough so that it doesn't rupture.

It isn't uncommon for Burns Nights to be celebrated beyond the Scottish border. However, the nature of the haggis itself is often lost in translation, particularly to those visitors to Scotland who believe it to be a wild animal that roams the outer Highlands.

ROASTED HAGGIS, SWEDE AND KALE SALAD

1 small swede (about 500g)

300g haggis

6 rashers of smoked streaky bacon, derinded

Leaves from 3–4 sprigs of rosemary

2 fat garlic cloves, sliced

2 tbsp olive or rapeseed oil

150g curly kale, cavolo nero or Red Russian kale, leaves stripped from the stalk

1–2 tbsp raspberry vinegar or balsamic vinegar

Sea salt and black pepper

Haggis roasts successfully and pairs happily with traditional veg accompaniments in this hearty salad. A generous handful of cooked lentils can be added in place of (or as well as) the kale. Serves 4

Preheat the oven to 190°C/Fan 170°C/Gas 5.

Peel the swede and cut it into roughly 1.5cm cubes. Place in a pan and cover with water. Bring to the boil, then simmer for 10 minutes.

Meanwhile, cut the haggis into roughly 2cm cubes. Cut the bacon into 2cm pieces. Throw both into a large roasting tin.

Drain the swede and toss it into the roasting tin with the haggis and bacon. Scatter over the rosemary leaves and garlic. Trickle with the oil and season lightly with salt and pepper. Roast in the oven for 35–40 minutes, stirring once or twice, until everything is sizzling hot and beginning to caramelise a little.

Meanwhile, bring a large pan of water to the boil. Add the kale leaves and cook for about 3–4 minutes until tender. Drain thoroughly.

Remove the roasting tin from the oven. Add the kale and 1 tbsp vinegar and stir well. Taste to see if it needs more vinegar, salt or pepper then serve warm, with good bread.

Hake

Nick Fisher

LATIN NAME
Merluccius merluccius

ALSO KNOWN AS
European hake

SEASONALITY
Avoid February–July when spawning

HABITAT
In deep water, from Norway and Iceland as far south as Mauritania, and in the Mediterranean

MCS RATING
2–3 (northern stock); Cornish gill-net hake is MSC-certified

REC MINIMUM SIZE
50cm

MORE RECIPES
Cod with fennel, capers and tomatoes (page 194); Steamed sea bass with kale and ginger (page 573); Crumbed whiting goujons with curried egg tartare (page 673)

SOURCING
goodfishguide.org; msc.org

Like sardines, spider crabs, velvet crabs and squid, the hake is a British fish that has lost its national identity. It thinks it's Spanish. Or possibly Portuguese. Because these are the fish-loving nations who make it feel special and wanted. To the Spanish, *merluza* is something of a religion. Cooked with chorizo and fennel, baked with potatoes, cheese and tiny baby leeks, or steamed with asparagus or firm garden peas, it is venerated and adored as much as, if not more than, cod.

In appearance, a hake is not a thing of beauty. It has sharp, wonky, needle-like teeth, a sickly, evil grin, and skin of an unappetising slate grey – a fish of childhood nightmares. But to eat fresh and hot, baked, battered, fried or steamed, it can be superior to its cod, pollack, haddock and ling brethren.

Hake flesh is finer than cod, smaller in muscle flake and bigger in flavour. Its shelf-life is shorter than that of cod or haddock and it can turn slightly mushy if it's not spankingly fresh or been well cared for. It's harder to fillet too, partly due to its snake-like, elongated shape and softer texture, so it's easiest to buy ready filleted or steaked (the bones and head, however, make a fantastic stock so it's worth bagging those too).

Use hake in any of the ways you would use other white fish – fry the fillets, turn them into chunky fish fingers or bake them with a rich tomatoey sauce. Hake is also good added at the last minute to a light, yoghurty fish curry (it will tend to fall apart if stirred about too much), or baked in a foil parcel with herbs, lemon and white wine. And a good, big fresh hake can be magnificent if roasted whole.

Until very recently, European hake was in a mess. Both the southern stock (south of the Bay of Biscay) and the northern stock (from Biscay as far north as Iceland) were overfished and stocks were in tatters. The general advice was pretty simple: don't eat it. However, since the 1990s, a combination of good management and environmental factors have wrought a sea change and the hake population is, thankfully, now booming. Some well-managed fisheries, including the little Cornish gill-net fishery, even have MSC certification. Hake is a great British fish again.

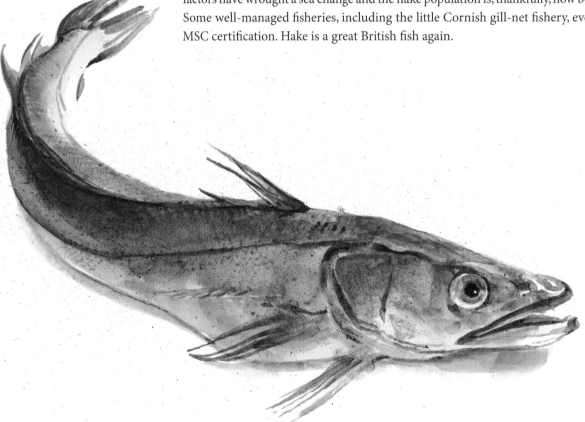

Sadly, nobody in Britain (apart from a few restaurants) seems to really care. At the moment, British fish-eaters consume less than 2 per cent of the national hake catch. The rest, of course, goes to Spain and Portugal. But mature, sustainably caught hake is a great choice for British fish cooks. The southern stock is still being overfished but numbers of hake in the northern stock – including that Cornish catch – are riding high. It's time to wake up and make hake feel loved again.

HAKE WITH ROOT AND SEAWEED BROTH

25g dried seaweed, such as dulse or wakame

1–2 tbsp olive or rapeseed oil

1 medium onion, chopped

2 garlic cloves, finely sliced

1 medium carrot, peeled and cut into 1cm cubes

200g peeled celeriac, cut into 1cm cubes

2 bay leaves

2 sprigs of thyme

750ml fish stock

A knob of butter

4 pieces of hake fillet (about 130g each), pin-boned

Sea salt and black pepper

Extra virgin olive or rapeseed oil, to finish

This broth needs a really good fish stock to give it a depth of flavour. Ask your fishmonger to fillet a hake and give you the skeleton along with the fillets, so you can use the bones to create the stock (see page 612). Serves 4

Soak the seaweed in cold water for 15–30 minutes, depending on the variety and packet instructions (some seaweeds may need cooking too – you need to get the seaweed to the point where it's ready to eat). Drain the seaweed and squeeze out excess water with your hands, then roughly chop it, removing any tough stalks.

Meanwhile, place a large heavy-based saucepan over a medium-low heat and add 1 tbsp oil. When hot, add the onion, garlic, carrot and celeriac. Cook, stirring regularly, for 10–12 minutes, until the vegetables are beginning to soften but not colour.

Add the bay, thyme and fish stock and bring up to a gentle simmer. Cook for a further 10–15 minutes until the veg are just tender. Add the seaweed to the broth and season well with salt and pepper to taste. Turn the heat down low for a few minutes while you cook the fish.

Set a large frying pan over a medium-high heat. Add the butter and a dash more oil. Season the pieces of hake all over with salt and pepper and place in the pan, skin side down. Cook for 4–5 minutes until the skin has a good colour, then flip the fish over and cook for a further minute or so until just cooked through.

Ladle the hot broth, including the veg and seaweed, into warmed, shallow bowls. Place a portion of hake, skin side up, in each bowl and serve straight away, finished with a trickle of extra virgin oil.

Ham

Steven Lamb

MORE RECIPES
Cauliflower clafoutis with
ham and parsley (page 126);
Courgette salad with ham,
borage and ewe's cheese
(page 78); Roast brill with
air-dried ham and parsley
sauce (page 92); Saltimbocca
(page 657)

SOURCING
dorsetcharcuterie.co.uk;
peelham.co.uk; riverford.co.uk

Ham can be a magnificent thing: the whole back leg of a well-reared pig, cured in an aromatic brine, boiled until tender, then baked with a clove-studded glaze of brown sugar and mustard until bubbling and crisp crusted. Such a joint should be the centrepiece of a celebration, then enjoyed, slice by thick juicy slice, for days afterwards. Sadly, however, as with many pork products, ham can be very disappointing.

Ham made from intensively farmed pigs, cured as fast as possible and sliced thin, is the norm on supermarket shelves. Often different pieces of pork are compressed together to make neat circles of ham, which exhibit a curious, iridescent sheen in their packaging. But we should remember what the best ham is: prime meat, a very large set of whole muscles from a slow-grown animal, skilfully butchered and then lovingly cured – a process that takes time and investment.

Ham is, in the broadest sense, a cured (preserved) leg of pork. In the British culinary tradition, the word usually refers to the top part of a pig's hind leg, cured and then cooked. In other cuisines, a ham is the entire back leg, cured then air-dried, as with Serrano or prosciutto ham. However, the term 'ham' can wander: *spalla*, for instance, is a boned, cured and dried Italian ham made from the shoulder. Our own British ham hocks and picnic hams are both taken from the front leg. A hock contains lots of skin and connective tissue, which both release gelatine when cooked – creating a lovely stock that will set into a jelly. Often, the hock meat is picked off and set in this jelly to make a superb terrine.

The word 'ham' has even been extended to encompass other meats. Duck and goose 'ham', for example, are the cured and air-dried breasts of the birds. Gammon is simply a cut of ham traditionally served hot rather than cold.

Brining is the primary procedure for making a traditional ham: pork is immersed in salted liquid with aromatics for several days. The brine slowly penetrates, drawing out the meat's natural moisture and creating an environment that's inhospitable to undesirable bacteria. This stabilises the meat, slowing deterioration and creating a window of opportunity for flavour-producing enzymes to get to work.

There are time-honoured cures specific to different parts of Britain. A traditional Wiltshire cure ham, for instance, is held in a beer and molasses brine, giving it a sweet, intense flavour. Suffolk hams are cured in treacle and stout, then smoked, which further flavours and preserves them. Some British hams, such as Cumberland and York, are cured in dry salt and then air-dried.

The majority of commercial hams these days, however, are injected with salty water rather than left to sit in a brine – a much quicker and therefore cheaper process. These hams do not carry the complex flavours of a slow-cured ham. They also need to be soaked in fresh water for hours before cooking, drawing out some of the salt the brine put there in the first place.

After brining, hams may or may not be smoked, and are then ready to be cooked. This may be done by the producer, and the ham sold ready to eat. But of course you can also buy a whole, cured ham and cook it yourself – by simmering in water. The meat can be eaten straight away, or baked to give it a glorious, caramelised crust.

If you source your ham from a small producer or butcher, you can ask exactly how it's been cured. Otherwise, look for organic or free-range ham and pay particular attention to the additives listed on the label. The lowest quality hams will have 'fillers' or 'meat extenders' such as wheat flour, rusk or cornstarch, as well as binding agents derived from milk proteins.

Brining your own ham is simple and the only equipment you need is a suitably sized plastic tub. A whole leg makes a magnificent ham but this is a huge piece of meat. A half leg – enough for a sumptuous dinner for six, with leftovers – works just as well and will take about 15 days brining. You can flavour the brine as you please: try apple juice or cider; I also like to add cracked black pepper, fennel seeds and star anise. You will need to cook the pork before eating it, but it can stay in your fridge for up to 10 days beforehand. Commercial cures usually include nitrates as an added form of preservative, which maintain a vivid pink colour in the meat. Home-cured hams, without nitrates, tend to revert to a similar colour to roast pork, but are no less delicious.

Dry-cured hams

The classic, air-dried hams of Europe, including Italian *prosciutto di Parma* and Spanish *jamón serrano*, are among the finest cured meats you can eat (at least, the best of them are). Expensive but exquisite, carved into translucent slivers and curls, they are the silky and salty jewels of the cured meat world.

Many of these hams are marked with the EU's PDO (Protected Designation of Origin) label, recognising the particular combination of pig breed, feed, topography, climate and skill that makes hams from that area unique. For example, Spanish Ibérico ham is only from the *pata negra* (blackfoot) pig, and the very best – *jamón ibérico de bellota* – come from pigs that have ranged freely, grazing on acorns (*bellota*) and other wild plants on the plains of Extremadura. Serrano ham, meanwhile, is hung to dry in mountainous regions for 18 months, the air circulating gently and drying the hams in perfect, humid conditions that allow them to develop astonishing flavour. Top-of-the-range hams come with a certificate of authenticity. To source the best of these hams in the UK, you will need to find a good deli.

There is a burgeoning culture of air-drying hams in Britain too, however – and of course, you can produce your own. Dry-curing and air-drying your own ham takes time and requires certain conditions. You need to be able to hang your salted ham in a cool, well-ventilated place, ideally outdoors, for up to a year, protected from insects, birds and squirrels. And you need to have the confidence to let time do its work! But, while you won't replicate the likes of Ibérico or Parma hams, the results can be terrific and you will create a ham that expresses your own *terroir*, technique and climate. The ham will keep for ages, the flavour improving and intensifying as it matures.

POTATO AND HAM RÖSTI

500g floury potatoes, such as Maris Piper

½ large onion, thinly sliced

75–100g cooked ham, roughly chopped

1 tsp thyme leaves

Olive or rapeseed oil, for frying

Sea salt and black pepper

These delicious rösti will make the most of the last scraps from a magnificent cooked ham. Serve with a fried or poached egg for a richly satisfying lunch or supper. Serves 2

Peel the potatoes, rinse, then grate coarsely into a bowl. Pick up a handful of the potato and squeeze out as much of the starchy liquid as possible, then put into a second bowl. Repeat with the remaining potato. Add the onion to the bowl of squeezed-out potato, along with the ham and thyme. Season generously with salt and pepper.

Heat a medium non-stick frying pan over a medium heat. Add a dash of oil, to just coat the base, then spoon in the potato and ham mixture. Spread it out evenly, then use a spatula to press the mixture down flat. Cook gently for 15 minutes until holding together well and crisp and golden on the base, then carefully flip over and cook for a further 15 minutes or so. Serve hot from the pan, with fried eggs or dressed watercress.

Hare

Tim Maddams

LATIN NAME
Brown hare: *Lepus europaeus*.
Mountain hare: *Lepus timidus*.
Irish hare: *Lepus timidus
hibernicus*

ALSO KNOWN AS
Mountain hare: blue hare

SEASONALITY
Brown hare: Scotland and Isle
of Man 1 October–31 January;
Northern Ireland 12 August–
31 January; England and Wales
no closed season with the
exception of moorland and
unenclosed land.
Mountain hare: Scotland
1 August–28 February (or 29);
species rarely found elsewhere

HABITAT
Brown hare: lowland
meadows and downlands.
Mountain hare: mountains
and high moorland

SOURCING
tasteofgame.org.uk

There are three different types of hare living wild in the British Isles: brown hare, mountain hare and the rare Irish hare. Many mountain hare are considered pests in the highlands where they live, and shot as a matter of course. Brown hare were, until recently, in decline but numbers are now on the increase and an abundance in certain areas has led to some small-scale shooting.

The hanging time for hare should be kept to a minimum or it becomes overly gamey: 3 days should be more than enough to tenderise the meat but keep it fresh and sweet.

Hare can be bought skinned, gutted and jointed from online suppliers or butchers. If you are acquiring your hare 'in the fur', from a game dealer or local hunter, it will come with the skin on, head and feet attached, and with the guts still in. Hare, unlike rabbit, is hung entire, in order to preserve the blood, which is traditionally used to thicken the liquid the hare is cooked in (as in 'jugged hare'). It also makes a very tasty blood pudding (you will need the blood from 3–4 hares for this). The blood collects in the chest cavity and can be drained off by carefully opening the belly area before removing the guts.

Be sure to remove the guts before attempting to skin the hare, otherwise a rather foul-smelling explosion can occur. Once skinned, joint the hare into saddle, haunches and shoulders – follow the same technique as for rabbit (see page 516).

The meat of the hare is richer and deeper in flavour and more delicate in texture than rabbit – more like venison, in fact. The saddle roasts very well, as long as you serve it medium rare: you only need to oil and season it, brown it well then put it in the oven at 200°C/Fan 180°C/Gas 6 for 8–10 minutes. The shoulders and haunches require more prolonged cooking – in a stew, braise or confit. I usually cook the shoulders slowly under butter or olive oil, with a little star anise, rosemary and pepper, then shred the meat and recombine it with some of the fat to make hare *rillettes*.

HARE RAGU

A little olive or rapeseed oil

250g pancetta or streaky bacon, cut into large lardons

2 large onions, sliced

3 large carrots, halved lengthways and cut into 2cm pieces

4 celery stalks, cut into 2cm pieces

8–10 sage leaves

6 sprigs of thyme

4 small sprigs of rosemary

3–4 tbsp plain flour

1 hare, jointed into 9–11 pieces

A glass of red wine

2.5 litres game or chicken stock

20g dark chocolate, chopped

Sea salt and black pepper

This is lovely spooned over 'wet' polenta (see page 480). To fit into the casserole, the hare needs to be jointed into fairly small pieces: cut the back legs in half at the knee, the saddle into 3 portions, and the front legs in half if they are large. Serves 6–8

Set a large frying over a medium-high heat, and add a trickle of oil. Add the bacon and cook for about 10 minutes, until well browned, then transfer it to a large flameproof casserole dish, using a slotted spoon.

Add the onions, carrots, celery and herbs to the casserole and sweat over a medium heat for 6–8 minutes, stirring regularly.

Return the frying pan to a medium heat. Season the flour and use to dust the hare pieces, shaking off any excess. Fry them, in batches, in the residual bacon fat, until golden on all sides, adding them to the casserole as they are done.

Over a medium-low heat, deglaze the frying pan with the wine, scraping up any sediment, and let it simmer for a minute or two. Add the liquor to the casserole. Pour in the stock, cover and bring to the boil, then turn the heat down to a very low simmer. Set the lid ajar a little and cook for 2½–3½ hours, until the meat is lovely and tender. Take the hare pieces out of the pan.

Add the chocolate to the sauce and stir until melted, then taste and adjust the seasoning. Take off the heat; keep warm. When the hare is cool enough to handle, pull all the meat off the bones and fold it through the sauce. Serve spooned over 'wet' polenta.

Hawthorn

John Wright

LATIN NAME
Crataegus monogyna

SEASONALITY
Flowers: May–June.
Berries: August–November

HABITAT
Very common in hedgerows,
except in northern Scotland

The lovely hawthorn makes an excellent hedge, and thousands were planted during the nineteenth century as part of the enclosure movement. Hawthorn flowers are quite heady and they can be used to make a wild flower syrup (follow the instructions for dandelion syrup on page 232). They are also good sprinkled judiciously on to salads. Pick the flowers early, in May, when they will be most perfumed.

The hawthorn also produces a vast quantity of fruit, unfortunately referred to as 'haws', causing much infantile sniggering on wild food forays. These tiny round 'pomes' consist of a thin layer of skin and mildly fruity flesh wrapped around a substantial pip; as such, they are a considerable challenge to the chef.

This challenge has been admirably met with crab apple and haw leather, inspired by Pam Corbin. Pam's excellent fruit leathers are a great way to use intractable hedgerow fruit like haws, crab apples, elderberries and sloes. Cook 1kg each of haws and crab or other sharp apples in a lidded saucepan with a little water to stop burning. Once the apples have disintegrated, mash with a potato masher, then press the purée through a sieve into a clean pan. Add sugar to taste and heat, stirring, until it has dissolved. Spread the sweet purée on a tray lined with baking parchment to a 4mm thickness, then dry in a very low oven (50°C). The leather peels off the parchment easily and can be kept rolled in fresh parchment indefinitely.

HOT HAW JELLY

1.5kg ripe haw berries, washed

2 medium cooking apples, roughly chopped (no need to peel or core)

About 500g preserving sugar or granulated sugar

2 hot or medium-hot red chillies, deseeded and finely diced

1 star anise

This wild, spicy preserve is great with lamb or mutton, or with chicken. It's also wonderful with cheese. Choose a couple of hot but not incendiary red chillies such as 'Whippet's Tail' or 'Aji Limon', or a few spicy little 'Stumpies'. Makes 2–3 x 350ml jars

First sterilise your jars by washing them in hot soapy water, rinsing well, then putting them upside down on a baking tray in a very low oven (at 120°C/Fan 100°C/Gas ½) to dry and warm up.

Put the berries and apple into a preserving pan or other large pan with 1 litre water and bring to a gentle simmer. Cook for 45–60 minutes until the fruit is soft and pulpy, breaking it up once or twice with a potato masher during cooking and topping up the water if the mix is very thick – it's got to be wet enough to drip easily through a jelly bag.

Set up a jelly bag or line a large sieve with muslin. Pour the fruity mixture into the bag or sieve and leave to strain for several hours, until the juice stops dripping through. For a perfectly clear jelly, do not squeeze the pulp in the bag or muslin. However, if you want maximum yield and don't mind a cloudy jelly, give the bag a squeeze.

Put a saucer in the freezer to chill. Measure the juice, then pour it into a clean pan. For every 600ml juice, add 500g sugar. Stir over a gentle heat until the sugar has fully dissolved, then bring to the boil and add the chillies and star anise. Boil rapidly for about 10 minutes, then test for setting point. To do this, turn off the heat, drip a little of the jelly on to the cold saucer and return to the fridge for a couple of minutes. Push the jelly with your fingertip: if it has formed a significant skin that wrinkles, setting point has been reached. If not, boil for another 2–3 minutes before testing again. If unsure, err on the side of caution: a lightly set jelly is far nicer than a solid one. Discard the star anise.

Leave the jelly to cool for about 10 minutes, stirring once or twice, which helps to stop the chilli pieces floating to the top. Pour into the warm jars and seal straight away. Store in a cool, dark cupboard for up to a year and refrigerate once opened.

Hazelnuts & cobnuts

Hugh Fearnley-Whittingstall

LATIN NAME
Corylus avellana

SEASONALITY
Fresh nuts: August–September or October

HABITAT
Very common throughout the British Isles

MORE RECIPES
Alexanders gratin with bacon and oats (page 14); Fairy ring champignon risotto (page 252); Henakopita with garam masala and eggs (page 254); Coley with bacon, apples and hazelnuts (page 197); Roasted chilli mole (page 173); Venison salad with apple, celeriac and hazelnuts (page 660); Roasted grapes (page 288); Apricot and honey filo pie (page 314); Nutty brown sugar meringues (page 621)

SOURCING
kentishcobnutassociation.org.uk; cobnuts.co.uk; farnellfarm.co.uk; kentishcobnuts.com

Widespread and common, the hazel is the blackberry of the nut world – or at least it would be if it wasn't for the damn squirrels. Hazel has long been a very important tree in Britain's woodlands, not only as a source of food but also for coppicing. Its springy young branches are useful for building shelters, and it makes fine charcoal.

You have a pretty good chance of finding hazel trees in oak, ash and birch woods, as well as mature hedgerows, almost anywhere in Britain. But you've got to be quick off the mark to get the nuts. August is the likeliest time, when the nuts are still green. As they ripen and darken on the tree (and eventually drop off) they become increasingly irresistible to the squirrels, though in a good year there will be enough for everyone.

Fresh, green hazels are juicy and crisp, almost more like a crunchy vegetable than a rich, oily nut. They are superb in salads – especially with soft cheeses, early apples and roasted roots. When ripe and brown the wild nuts have a richer flavour and denser texture but are still more juicy than a shop-bought hazel, which will have been dried.

In the shops, you can buy hazelnuts whole or shelled, skin-on or blanched. They are drier and sweeter than the fresh nuts and I like to toast them in the oven (as in the recipe below). I love them ground up in cakes, biscuits and crumbles, or coated in caramel and smashed into praline smithereens. You can also chop them roughly, toss them in a pan with a little rapeseed oil, garlic and salt, and scatter them over soups and veg dishes.

Cobnuts are a cultivated form of hazel. Bigger and more consistent, they are sold green-gold and fresh from orchards (mostly in southeast England) in August and September. Farm shops are a good source. You can even find them in some supermarkets, or buy them online. Mature brown cobs should be available all year round from specialist suppliers. They develop a lovely nutty flavour in storage.

Filberts are a similar-looking but slightly different species that you're most likely to come across as a garden tree – although sometimes hazelnuts are called filberts.

HAZELNUT AND CHEESE BISCUITS

50g hazelnuts (skin on or off)

75g cold, unsalted butter, cubed or coarsely grated

75g plain flour

1 tsp Dijon mustard

½ tsp thyme leaves (optional)

25g mature Cheddar or Lancashire, Shipcord or other well-flavoured hard cheese, grated

50g Parmesan or other very hard, salty, crystalline cheese such as Berkswell, Lord of the Hundreds or Pecorino, finely grated

A good pinch of salt

A pinch of cayenne pepper

These delicate, savoury biscuits absolutely melt in the mouth. Makes about 20

Preheat the oven to 180°C/Fan 160°C/Gas 4.

Scatter the hazelnuts on a baking tray and toast in the oven for 5–10 minutes until golden and fragrant. If they are skin-on, bundle them up in a tea towel and rub vigorously to remove the dark brown skins.

When the nuts are cool, tip them into a food processor and pulse to chop coarsely, so there are still some nice chunky bits in the mix. Tip the nuts on to a plate and set aside.

Toss the other ingredients together roughly in a large bowl, then transfer to the food processor and process until the mixture starts to form clumps. It will look dry and crumbly at first, but keep going and it will come together. Add the chopped nuts and process again until the mix forms a dough. Wrap and chill for 15–20 minutes.

Line 2 baking trays with baking parchment. On a well-floured surface, roll out the dough as thinly as the chunks of nut will allow. Stamp out rounds using a 6–7cm cutter. Place the rounds on the baking trays and bake for about 8 minutes or until golden. You can re-roll the trimmings for a second batch, and bake the misshaped offcuts too.

Leave on the baking trays for a minute or two to firm up slightly, then transfer to a wire rack to cool. Store in an airtight tin for 2–3 days.

Heart

Steven Lamb

SOURCING
graigfarm.co.uk;
greenpasturefarms.org.uk

Heart trails behind liver and kidneys in popularity, even among those who are keen on offal. However, organ aficionados would argue that it has untapped potential. It has the dense texture common to other forms of offal, but it is less pungent than liver or kidneys, with a flavour like very lean steak.

Eating your heart out in a restaurant is unlikely to be an option as you'll rarely find it on the menu. Your best bet is a good butcher. The majority of hearts sold for food are taken from sheep and pigs, but hearts from ox, calves, venison and chickens are all available. The size varies, of course, but the general structure and texture are the same.

A heart consists of a set of chambers encased in dense meat with a layering of fat towards the top. Inside are various tubes, valves and connective tissue, which tend to be quite tough in larger hearts. To prepare any heart for cooking, trim away all the connective tissue and collagen and rinse out any coagulated blood left in the chambers. If you are slow-cooking the heart, leave the fat on, as it will help keep the meat moist.

When cooking heart, a slow and gentle braise helps retain moisture while softening the texture. My favourite heart dish is a rustic farmhouse recipe where lamb and calf hearts are marinated in lemon juice then cooked in an apple and cider sauce with crushed coriander. The other option is to sear heart fast and hot, like steak, so it stays pink and juicy, as in the recipe below.

Lamb's heart is the tenderest of the significantly sized hearts, and has a distinctive bright red colour. It can be sliced thinly and flash-fried with just a little garlic and a few herbs such as thyme or bay. Pig's heart is a similar size but tougher and more gristly, so it needs additional trimming and really benefits from slow braising. An ox heart, meanwhile, is big enough to stuff with a rich, flavoursome mix of shallots, breadcrumbs and diced pork belly, seal briefly in a hot pan and then roast in a moderate oven for an hour or so.

Chicken hearts are relatively tender and can be grilled or barbecued. They are also quite delicious devilled or even hot-smoked.

All hearts should look vibrant and not carry too much scent. Avoid any that look grey or pallid: they will probably be too far on from their last registered beat.

SEARED OX HEART

1 ox heart

A little olive or rapeseed oil, for frying

FOR THE CURE

50g fine sea salt

50g soft brown sugar

A good grinding of black pepper

1 bay leaf, shredded (optional)

A couple of juniper berries, crushed (optional)

In this recipe, the heart meat is briefly cured with a mixture of sugar and salt, which seasons it deliciously, then seared hot and fast like a steak. Serves 4

Halve the heart from top to bottom. Trim away any fat from inside and out, the coarse tubes and any connective tissue, leaving just 'clean' dark meat. Rinse it well. Cut the trimmed meat into 1cm thick slabs that can be fried like steaks. Pat dry with kitchen paper.

Mix the cure ingredients together. Put the heart 'steaks' in a shallow dish and sprinkle all over with the cure, patting it on. Leave for 5 minutes, then rinse quickly under a cold running tap and pat dry.

Heat a large, heavy-based frying pan until smoking hot. Trickle a little oil into the pan and then add the heart steaks (cook them in batches, two at a time, if your pan is not large). Sear them for 1 minute on each side (which will leave them rare), then remove to a warm plate and let them rest for at least 2 minutes.

Slice the heart as thinly as you can. Serve with a crisp, crunchy salad, such as thinly sliced raw baby turnips with parsley, lemon juice and olive oil; or watercress, orange segments and a spoonful of yoghurt.

Hedgehog mushrooms

John Wright

LATIN NAME
Hydnum repandum

SEASONALITY
Late summer–early winter

HABITAT
Common in woodland, mostly with oak, beech and spruce

MORE RECIPES
Sautéed mushrooms with juniper (page 320); Woodcock with wild mushrooms (page 678)

People worry about picking wild mushrooms. Sensible people do, anyway. Identifying some wild fungi is notoriously difficult, but it's not necessary to be an expert mycologist to pick all wild mushrooms. To become a mushrooming legend, all one needs to do is learn a dozen or so that are easily identifiable. Top of my list of such fungi is the hedgehog mushroom. It is the mushroom with everything.

Delicious, firm and abundant, with no conservation concerns, it is unmistakeable and invariably maggot-free. It usually grows in large rings in oak, beech, pine and spruce woodlands. Look for it from late summer to mid-autumn. The cap of the hedgehog mushroom is creamy/buff, the texture of chamois leather, irregular in shape and adorned underneath, not by gills or tubes, but by tiny, cream-coloured spines, which break off very easily. Nothing looks remotely like it, except several bracket-like species, which always grow on wood, not the ground, and lack any sort of stem. These are not poisonous, but they are mostly very rare and should be left in peace.

The firm, dry texture of the hedgehog mushroom is unusual, as is the flavour, which is mild but very distinctive. 'Hedgehogs' should always be cooked, as they are slightly bitter raw, but not for very long as they toughen up easily. The cliché mushroom treatment – sautéed with garlic then simmered with cream – is ideal for this find.

The enormous number of hedgehog mushrooms that can be picked in a single foray can be tackled by slicing and drying (as for horse mushrooms, see page 315). They dry very easily, but unfortunately do not reconstitute well. For this reason, after drying hedgehog mushrooms, I blitz them in a blender to create a flavoursome dried mushroom powder, to add to soups, sauces and stews. I particularly like to use this in combination with sweet chestnut flour (see page 156), rather than wheat flour, to thicken the sauce for a game pie.

HEDGEHOG MUSHROOM AND BACON OMELETTE

About 150g hedgehog mushrooms

2 knobs of butter

2 rashers of streaky bacon, derinded and roughly chopped

2 medium eggs, lightly beaten

Sea salt and black pepper

A simple approach is often the best for wild mushrooms, as this lovely dish demonstrates. You could use almost any mushroom here: try blewits or fairy ring champignons. Serves 1

Using a paring knife, trim the mushroom stalks of any roots or earth. Use a pastry brush or mushroom brush to gently brush away any remnants of woodland foliage or fauna, then cut the mushrooms into bite-sized pieces.

Place a small, non-stick frying pan over a medium-high heat. Add a small knob of butter, followed by the bacon. Cook, stirring occasionally, for 2–3 minutes, by which time the bacon should be releasing its fat.

Add the mushrooms, toss them in the bacon fat and cook for 4–6 minutes or until any liquid they release has evaporated and they are turning nice and golden. Tip the contents of the pan on to a plate.

Return the pan to the heat, reduce the heat a little and add the second knob of butter. When foaming, add the beaten eggs. Move the egg around the pan, tilting the pan and lifting and pushing the set egg with a wooden spoon or spatula so the liquid egg can run down to the base of the pan. After 30–40 seconds of this, allow the omelette to settle and cook briefly until it is mostly set but with a little wet egg still on top.

Season the top of the omelette lightly with salt and pepper, then spoon the bacon and mushrooms on to one half of it. After a further 20–30 seconds, use a spatula to flip the other half of the omelette over, enveloping the filling. Slide out of the pan on to a warm plate and serve straight away.

Hempseed

Hugh Fearnley-Whittingstall

LATIN NAME
Cannabis sativa

MORE RECIPES
Artichoke heart and potato salad
(page 32); Smashed chickpeas
with preserved lemon and red
onion (page 165); Mujadara
(page 104)

SOURCING
clearspring.co.uk;
goodhempfood.com

H

I've always enjoyed good olive oil and I always will – but I can't condone the monopoly it seems to hold over our culinary imaginations. Many keen cooks see it as the one and only high-end oil, the answer to every dressing, trickling and dipping requirement. That needs to change. There is a panoply of other delicious and characterful oils – often with nutritional credentials at least as good as olive oil – that I think we should all be exploring. And hempseed oil is among the best of them.

This is strong stuff. It comes from the same family as – you know – the other kind of hemp and, while it certainly won't get you high, its pungent, grassy flavour notes do have something in common with its recreational relative. But in that intense, herbal flavour lies its appeal. It's a complex and rich oil, gloriously grassy green, that is just made to mingle with earthy, fruity, salty flavours.

It makes a barnstorming pesto and turns potato salad into a talking point. Any roasted veg soup – pumpkin, celeriac, parsnip – will be taken to a whole new level with a slosh of this emerald liquid (try adding a crumbling of sheep's cheese or ricotta too). And trickled on to bruschetta with sweet tomatoes, or simply used to dunk bread, it does the job extra virgin olive oil would conventionally do – only with more chutzpah.

It's not great for frying because heating can change the structure of the oil and damage the nutrients. But as a raw cold-pressed oil, hempseed oil is an exciting ingredient. Experiment a little and I predict you'll soon be seduced. You can always try blending it with a gentler oil such as rapeseed, or mixing it into a dressing. Milder tasting 'light' versions are also available.

Consider also hemp oil's environmental and nutritional benefits. British-grown hemp is a very green, low-input crop – it drinks in carbon dioxide, and every part of it can be used. It's also rich in omega-3 as well as omega-6 fatty acids.

The oil is pressed from shiny-shelled little hemp seeds and these are a tasty treat in themselves. You'll find them increasingly in health food shops and delis, and in a few supermarkets too. I use them in salads, granolas and flapjacks. Packed with protein, they have a robust crunchy texture and benefit from being lightly bashed or crushed before use. You can also buy shelled hempseed kernels – expensive, but creamy, nutty and a great sprinkler on everything from salads and soups to porridge and pasta.

HEMPY HUMMUS

400g tin beans, such as
borlotti, butter or cannellini,
drained and rinsed

1 garlic clove, crushed

1 tbsp shelled hempseed
kernels, toasted

½ small-medium red chilli,
deseeded and chopped

3 tbsp hempseed oil, plus extra
to finish

1 tsp finely chopped rosemary,
plus an extra sprig to finish

A little squeeze of lemon juice

Sea salt and black pepper

You can make this in minutes and it keeps in the fridge for days. Nutty hempseed kernels make a great alternative to the traditional tahini (sesame seed paste) and give the dip a rich earthy flavour. Large, mealy broad beans can be used instead of the tinned beans; you'll need 250g skinned, cooked beans. Serves 4–6

Put the beans, garlic, hempseed kernels, chilli, oil, rosemary and a little squeeze of lemon juice in a food processor and blitz to a smooth purée. If it seems a bit thick, add 1–2 tbsp warm water to 'let it down'. Season to taste with salt and pepper.

Spoon the hummus into a bowl, trickle with a little more hempseed oil and finish with a sprig of rosemary. Serve with flatbreads and crudités.

Herring

Nick Fisher

LATIN NAME
Clupea harengus

SEASONALITY
All year round (different populations spawn at different times)

HABITAT
Much of the north Atlantic

MCS RATING
1–5. Generally a very sustainable choice but a few stocks are depleted or under pressure; look for MSC-certified herring

REC MINIMUM SIZE
25cm

MORE RECIPES
Noodles with seaweed, smoked mackerel and soy (page 407); New potato, mackerel and purslane salad (page 509); Grilled sardines with potatoes and rosemary (page 565); Hot mackerel, beetroot and horseradish sandwich (page 373)

SOURCING
goodfishguide.org; msc.org

Today most people's first experience of herring is as a rollmop: an odd, rolled-up grey specimen in a jar of dubious vinegar. Or as a kipper on a B & B menu, although not everyone knows that a kipper is a smoked herring. Or that bloaters, bucklings and Bismarcks are other manifestations of this small, silver British fish. And, sadly, many fail to realise just how much, as a nation, we owe to this oily, pelagic little specimen.

Britain's culture and economy has been enormously influenced by the herring. In 1108, the town of Yarmouth was made a borough by Henry I and its annual crown payment was set at 10 millards, or 1,000 million, herring. The Victorian expansion of the railways network was all about herring: a fish that perished easily needed to be transported quickly.

Herring brought wealth to parts of Britain that were previously mired in poverty. When the Gold Rush was raging in California, Scotland and the east coast of England were basking in a sudden flush of comparable wealth, owing to the massive herring shoals migrating around the coast. But by the 1970s, by dint of modern trawling techniques and the wasteful use of fresh herrings as fertiliser and animal fodder, we managed to totally deplete our once world-famous stocks. Tragically, herring fisheries were forced to close.

But herrings are creeping back. Stocks are growing and there are now some carefully managed individual British fisheries landing great fish, which means herring should be back on our plates. But where to start?

Herring is a uniquely versatile fish and it comes in many guises. I would suggest starting with a kipper. Most supermarkets sell these split, brined and smoked herrings at reasonable prices but my preference is for the Manx or Scottish varieties on the bone, which you are more likely to find at a good fishmonger or online.

I like to cook kippers whole, but if you opt to buy kipper fillets, please make sure they are not dyed. Proper smoking gives the fish a burnished honey colour. Adding paprika or annatto to make them glow-in-the-dark orange is just unnecessary – unless you're trying to compensate for something. Dyeing was a trick used to make kippers look more smoked than they were – the curing process being labour-intensive and costly – and it still makes me suspicious.

Either grill or bake your kipper fast in the hottest part of the oven for no more than 5 minutes. Eat with horseradish sauce, good bread and a poached egg – if you fancy – and tease every last morsel from the spine bones and head. Like crab picking, kipper eating is a tactile, hands-on, sucking, plucking, greasy-chin affair.

Next, try bloater, which is much harder to find than the kipper. They're smoked whole (not split open) with their guts inside to make them a little more 'gamey'. Like kippers, they only need to be lightly cooked and served with hot tea and crusty bread.

If bloater doesn't float your boat, you could try buckling, which is a variation on the theme. It has a stronger, smokier flavour and doesn't always have the guts intact. Buckling comes from a Baltic tradition of curing and more or less does what the bloater does – although in my opinion, not so well.

And beyond smoking, the herring still has other avenues for you to explore: fresh, pickled, marinated or roes. Rollmops are cured herrings rolled around onions (the Bismarck is similar, it's just not rolled-up). Unfortunately, they are curate's eggs: some good, some very bad. Mostly it's the quality of the vinegar that lets them down. A good rollmop, eaten alone sushi-style, will fill your mouth with fishy flavour, underpinned only subtly by vinegar and sour crunchy onion.

Marinated herring is probably the most exciting and progressive new way to eat our ancient species. These are mostly imported from Scandinavia, where they're flavoured with anything from sweet mustard to Marsala.

Roes are, I confess, something of an acquired taste. You either do fish roe – caviar, lumpfish eggs, salmon eggs – or you don't. Herring roes are fairly different in that they're always cooked, whereas other fish roes are eaten salted or raw. There are two types of roe: hard and soft; eggs equals hard; sperm (or milt) equals soft. Some roe lovers adore both. Some are devoted to either soft or hard. I suggest you trial each, cooking them exactly the same way, i.e. fry gently in well-salted butter and serve mushed on toast with black pepper and lemon. You'll soon know if it's your thing.

And finally, fresh herring – one of the finest fish you'll ever eat. Ask your fishmonger to remove the bones. You don't want fillets per se – not the meat cut from the bones but, rather, the meat with the head and bones filleted out. This is done by laying the fish flat, belly down, pressing along the backbone with a firm but fair thumb, flipping over and pulling head and bones out in one.

Yes, there are little bones left over. But, it doesn't matter, because when cooked, they will just crisp and crunch delightfully. There's only one way, other than curing, to cook fresh herrings in my world: dip them in milk or egg, coat with oatmeal, salt and pepper and fry in butter. Delicious…

LEMON-CURED HERRING

8 herring fillets (350–400g in total)

FOR THE BRINE
100g fine sea salt

FOR THE PICKLE
Finely grated zest of 1 lemon and juice of 2 lemons

6 bay leaves

2 sprigs of thyme

6–8 black or white peppercorns

6–8 coriander seeds

4 tsp caster sugar

These piquant fillets keep well in the fridge for up to a week. This technique works well with sardine fillets too. Serves 6–8 as a starter

For the brine, put the salt in a large shallow bowl, add 500ml cold water and mix well to dissolve. Add the herring fillets, skin side up, in a single layer. Leave for 25–30 minutes.

Remove the herring fillets from the brine and rinse under cold running water. Lay them in a clean dish, ideally in one layer and, again, skin side up.

Meanwhile put all the pickle ingredients into a small pan with 200ml water and bring to a gentle simmer.

Pour the hot lemony pickle over the fish. Give the dish a little shake to make sure all the fish is submerged. Leave to stand until cool, then cover with cling film and refrigerate for a minimum of 12 hours – longer if possible.

To serve, lift the fish fillets from their liquid. Eat them just as they are, or chop roughly and toss with cubed apple and a little mayonnaise. Serve with buttered brown bread.

Hogweed

John Wright

LATIN NAME
Heracleum sphondylium

SEASONALITY
Young shoots March–June

HABITAT
Very common, except in
northern Scotland, at roadsides,
field edges, waste ground

MORE RECIPES
Green garlic, asparagus and
oven-scrambled eggs (page 270)

Tough, hairy hogweed does not look particularly appetising, but one part of it at least is extremely good to eat. From early spring to early summer each plant produces its young leaves one or two at a time. These shoots, perhaps 10–15cm long, curl round at the tip where the leaf is forming. A walk along almost any hedgerow will reveal a plant at every other step, and the forager should check each one and pull or cut off any young shoot that has appeared.

The shoots, like the rest of the plant, are hairy and not at all good to eat raw. However, the hairs wilt to nothing with cooking and, for many recipes, they can be treated as honorary asparagus shoots, excepting that the taste is of parsley. They are pleasant steamed and served with butter. I also like to arrange very lightly cooked shoots radially on a quiche just before putting it in the oven. In tempura batter, the stem and curled leaf soften to a perfect succulence, nicely matched by the crunchiness of the batter. A dip to go with it is always welcome and nothing could be more appropriate than wild garlic pesto.

The young flowerbuds are also edible and very good, but they are always covered in a fibrous sheath which needs to be removed unless very young, resulting in the flowerbud falling to pieces.

Hogweed is easy to identify and extremely common, but do not mix it up with the giant hogweed, an invasive species usually found near water, whose sap can cause severe skin damage. Hogweed is also a member of the treacherous carrot family, which includes not only carrots but also the deadly hemlock and hemlock water-dropwort. Fortunately the latter two are not hairy at all.

One further small warning – some people find that, as with giant hogweed and wild parsnip, their skin becomes photo-sensitised by the hairs of hogweed, causing long-lasting scars. Once it is cooked, the hairs are harmless.

STEAMED HOGWEED WITH SCRAMBLED EGGS

This is a quick and simple way to enjoy a small bounty of hogweed. Serves 2

12–14 hogweed shoots,
well washed

4 medium eggs

25g butter

Sea salt and black pepper

Good malted grain or rye bread,
toasted, to serve

Pour a large glassful of water into a medium pan fitted with a steamer basket. Set over a medium heat and bring to a simmer. Add the hogweed to the basket, put the lid on and steam for 4–5 minutes. Test a shoot to make sure it is tender.

Meanwhile, whisk the eggs lightly together in a bowl. Put a medium, non-stick saucepan over a low heat. Add half the butter and allow it to melt and bubble, then add the eggs. Cook very gently for 4–5 minutes, stirring regularly. Good scrambled eggs should be soft, creamy and tender, so take the pan off the heat when they are still a little 'wet' – they will continue to cook off the heat. Season well with salt and pepper.

Toss the hot hogweed shoots with the remaining butter and some salt and pepper. Serve the eggs on toast, topped with your steamed hogweed.

Honey

Nikki Duffy

SOURCING

honeybeehive.co.uk (lists local honey producers)

Honey is a unique ingredient. Produced by bees from nectar, via a process something like digestion, it is stored in perfect hexagonal cells and fanned by the bees' frantic wingbeats until it loses enough water to make it thick and sticky. Even in this raw form, it is intensely sweet – a rare thing in nature. Until a few hundred years ago, when sugar became widely available in the West, honey was all we had to take the bitter edge off the world.

Honey is often seen as a healthier alternative to sugar and you could argue that's true – but only just. Refined sugar is pure sucrose, which is made up of bonded fructose and glucose. In honey, the fructose and glucose are already separate, and there is a little more fructose (precise levels vary in different honeys). On glycaemic index tables (which measure the speed at which foods elevate blood glucose) honey usually ranks below sugar, but not significantly so. However, the fructose means that honey tastes sweeter than sugar, so it can be used in smaller quantities.

In its raw form, honey also contains antioxidants and trace amounts of vitamins and minerals. And it has extraordinary anti-bacterial properties, proving inhospitable to microbes and bacteria because it is low in moisture, very acidic and contains hydrogen peroxide. It has long been applied to wounds as a kind of natural, antiseptic bandage – with modern studies proving its efficacy. And honey has healing effects when ingested too, having been shown to boost immunity and to soothe sore throats. However, honey is still basically sugar – high in calories and destructive to teeth, so it should be consumed in moderation. Note that no honey – not even organic – should be given to babies younger than 12 months because it can cause a disease known as infant botulism.

Cooking with honey is a joy, though. Unlike sugar, it offers not just sweetness but oodles of flavour. It's often the simple, raw applications that are the most satisfying: the spoonful stirred into a garlicky, mustardy vinaigrette, the trickle over a salad of blue cheese and celery, or the dollop spread on to hot toast so it mingles with the melting butter. It is also fantastic in cakes – which it helps to make deliciously moist – with veg as well as fruit, and with meat and even fish, especially smoked fish.

HONEY VARIETIES

Acacia honey Very mild and a pale straw colour, this is ideal if you want sweetness without a strong honey flavour.

Blossom or Wildflower honey These generic terms indicate that the honey is 'polyfloral' and comes from bees that have foraged on a variety of plants. It may well be blended.

Clover honey Clover is one of the most common plants on which bees feed. It produces a gentle, versatile honey.

Cut comb honey Sold still in the comb, this is honey in its most raw and unadulterated form. The comb itself is chewy and doesn't dissolve in the mouth, so you'll need to remove it surreptitiously after getting out all the sweet stuff.

Floral honeys Known as 'mono-floral' in the trade (since all honey is of course floral), these are distinctively scented and flavoured because the bees have largely visited just one type of flower. Orange flower honey is a delicate delight, with a soft perfumed burr. Borage honey is pale and subtle. Scottish heather honey is one of the most characterful of the floral honeys – with a slightly gel-like texture, it is strong, earthy and heavy, and has a lovely pungency.

Manuka honey Honey from New Zealand manuka trees is powerful in flavour and rich in an anti-microbial agent. It is marketed as a potent health food and has been shown to help fight infection in wounds and promote healing.

Organic honeys These are available but certification is difficult to achieve because everything growing within a 4-mile radius of the hives (i.e. the foraging area) must be either organic or wild.

H

However, honey scorches easily, so care must be taken if it is to be exposed to the heat of an oven. Even mixed into a batter, it will brown quickly. Honey also adds considerable liquid to a mixture so you cannot use it as a straight, weight-for-weight replacement for dry sugar. As a rough guide, you'll need around two-thirds less honey than sugar, less additional moisture and less heat in the oven.

Honey is the most locally distinctive of foods. Its flavour, texture and quantity vary markedly depending on the flowers that the bees have fed from, the weather and the season. Honey from the same hive can taste different every week.

This fluctuation is anathema to big brands and major retailers, to whom reliability is key. Consequently, many of the cheaper types are blends of several honeys, often from different countries, mixed to achieve a consistent result. The flavour of blended honeys is often relatively bland. Inexpensive they may be, but they cannot offer the same experience as raw, intense and complex local honey, made by local bees.

Big-brand honey is also more processed than raw honey from local beekeepers and small producers. These extract the honey from the comb in a centrifugal spinner, then warm their honey just enough to liquefy it so it can be passed through a fairly crude filter to remove any debris before it is jarred. In a factory, honey may be heated to a higher temperature and forced through very fine micro-filters to render it clear, free-flowing and resistant to crystallisation. Heating and super-filtering can adversely affect the flavour, and possibly the nutritional value too.

All honey, eventually, will crystallise; raw, unprocessed honeys, or those higher in glucose, do so sooner. This is merely a structural change and does not affect the quality or safety of the honey – gentle warming will get crystallised honey flowing again.

Mead

This wine, made from fermented honey, may be dry or sweet. It can be pretty alcoholic (up to 16 per cent abv), but lighter versions are available. The best meads have a distinct but not overpowering honey character, and are lovely served chilled as an aperitif or dessert wine. Not all British mead is made from British honey, so check before buying.

APRICOT AND HONEY FILO PIE

40g butter, melted and cooled until tepid

10 sheets of ready-made filo pastry

12 large or 16 small apricots, halved and stoned

150g ricotta

2 tbsp roughly chopped hazelnuts

1 tsp chopped thyme leaves

100g clear honey

You can use other fruits in this lovely pud, such as ripe figs or plums, and replace the hazelnuts with pistachios or the thyme with rosemary. Serves 6–8

Preheat the oven to 190°C/Fan 170°C/Gas 5. Butter a shallow baking tray, about 30 x 20cm and 5cm deep (a Swiss roll tin is ideal). Keep the filo sheets covered with a damp tea towel while you work, to stop them drying out.

Lay a sheet of filo lengthways in the tray, leaving the ends overhanging the sides. Brush the filo with more butter and lay another sheet of pastry directly on top. Repeat, brushing each layer, until you have built a pastry base 5 layers deep. Now lay a couple of filo sheets the other way, leaving them overhanging the other sides, and brushing these too.

Arrange the apricots, cut side up, evenly over the pastry base. Spoon the ricotta over the top and into the gaps. Scatter over the hazelnuts and thyme and trickle over the honey. Fold over the crossways layers of pastry, then any edges from the lengthways layers. Top the pie with the remaining layers of filo (you may need to cut them in half crossways), brushing with butter as you go. Bake for about 45 minutes until golden.

Serve warm or at room temperature, cut into squares, with vanilla ice cream or yoghurt.

Horse mushrooms

John Wright

LATIN NAME
Agaricus arvensis

SEASONALITY
Late summer and autumn

HABITAT
Fairly common in fields

MORE RECIPES
Hedgehog mushroom and bacon omelette (page 306); Sautéed mushrooms with juniper (page 320); Field mushroom and celeriac pie (page 258)

The horse mushroom, and the similar but less tasty macro mushroom, are found in similar habitats to that of the field mushroom – fields, and often in rings. They can be enormous, filling an entire frying pan, and this, together with their similarity to very large cultivated mushrooms, makes them easy to identify. Do not be put off by their tendency to bruise yellow. Unlike the poisonous 'Yellow Stainer' (see page 258), the colour change is slow, not instant, and the yellow persists and intensifies, whereas it turns to brown after 15 minutes in the Yellow Stainer.

Since horse mushrooms are so impressive, it seems a shame to chop them up, so I usually fry them whole in well-salted butter, turning them after a few minutes. The texture is a little chewy and the flavour a glorious mixture of mushroom and sweet almond. They also grill beautifully, their surface coated in salt and melted butter. If you grill the top of the cap first, you have the opportunity to fill the gill surface with cheese, breadcrumbs or whatever you fancy when you turn them over.

If you have a glut, horse mushrooms dry very well: slice them thinly (about 2mm) and arrange on a rack. Put them in the oven, on its lowest possible setting, with the door ajar. Leave the mushrooms until completely dry and a little crisp – this should take 5–6 hours. Alternatively, use a dehydrator. Store the dried mushrooms in jam jars, with lids on tight, and use within a year. It is also worth powdering dried horse mushrooms to provide an instant mushroomy burst to sauces and soups.

Unfortunately, these fungi do have a tendency to attract maggots. Everyone has their acceptable maggot to mushroom ratio. Mine is 1:10. When the mushrooms are cooked slowly, the maggots emerge and you have the chance to scoop them out. Horse mushrooms often have mysterious little v-shaped holes in their caps. These are caused by crows, who like maggots more than we do.

SPICED HORSE MUSHROOM AND BEETROOT 'BURGER'

1 medium (tangerine-sized) raw beetroot

½ tbsp cider vinegar

A good pinch of sugar

1 tsp cumin seeds

1 tsp coriander seeds

2 tbsp olive or rapeseed oil, plus an extra dash

2 garlic cloves, thinly sliced

A pinch of dried chilli flakes (optional)

4 large (but not gigantic) horse mushrooms

4 tbsp plain wholemilk yoghurt

2 tbsp chopped mint or coriander, or a mix of both

A bunch of spring onions, trimmed and thinly sliced

Sea salt and black pepper

4 large baps, to serve

This is a positively meaty treat, thanks to the texture and flavour of this beautiful wild mushroom. If you're not a huge beetroot fan, use carrot instead. Serves 4

Peel the beetroot and cut it into very thin matchsticks using a mandoline or sharp knife, or grate it coarsely. Combine with the cider vinegar, sugar and a pinch each of salt and pepper. Set aside (you can do this several hours in advance).

Using a pestle and mortar, roughly bash the cumin and coriander seeds. In a small bowl, combine the 2 tbsp oil with the garlic, bashed seeds, and the chilli, if using. Season with salt and pepper and mix well.

Preheat the grill to high. Place the mushrooms, gill side up, on a baking tray and brush them with the spiced, garlicky oil. Grill for 4–5 minutes, then turn them over, brush on some more oil and grill their tops for another 4–5 minutes.

Meanwhile, combine the yoghurt with the herbs, spring onions and a dash of oil.

Slice open the baps. Lay a whole grilled mushroom on each and trickle over any cooking juices from the baking tray. Top with a spoonful of beetroot and another of herby yoghurt, put the top back on the bap, and serve.

Horseradish

Hugh Fearnley-Whittingstall

LATIN NAME
Armoracia rusticana

SEASONALITY
All year round, once the plant is established (or from September of its first year)

HABITAT
Waste ground, roadsides, field edges (and gardens). Most common in central and southern England; coastal in Wales; rare in Scotland and Northern Ireland

MORE RECIPES
Tongue, kale and apple hash with horseradish (page 643); Hot mackerel, beetroot and horseradish sandwich (page 373)

Preparing fresh horseradish is not so much a labour of love as an act of heroism. It's ferocious stuff: as you grate the gnarled, ribbed root, its powerfully pungent, volatile oils are released, assailing your eyes and nose mercilessly. Is it worth it? Oh, yes!

The flavour of the freshly prepared root is vastly superior to anything you can buy in a jar and the suffering is nothing compared to the pleasure of home-made horseradish sauce. And just try mixing a few gratings into a Bloody Mary…

Peel the root, then attack it with a fine grater, mixing it straight away with a splash of lemon juice or cider vinegar to help 'fix' the flavour. The punchy pulp can then be combined with crème fraîche, a little mustard and some seasoning to make a fiery sauce. Add more of the cooling cream to give a milder dressing for salads, or to stir into soup (particularly beetroot). Don't cook horseradish – the heat kills its heat.

Lengths of fat horseradish root can be found in greengrocers and online, particularly in autumn and winter (usually imported – from Europe or Asia, depending on the season). But horseradish also grows prolifically in the English countryside. Its big, glossy leaves are more robust and pointy than dock leaves, which they resemble. Crushing them in your fingers will release a mild horseradish scent.

The irony is that this food is not easy to gather. Firstly, you are supposed to have the permission of the landowner before uprooting wild plants. Secondly, horseradish roots are big and deep and you need a garden fork to lift them. So, despite the tantalising tracts of horseradish that can often be spotted at field edges or on waste ground in late summer and autumn, if you have neither permission nor the appropriate tools, it might be better to grow your own. This is almost too easy to do.

You can buy young horseradish plants, but just a sliver of root from an existing plant put into the ground will take hold and flourish. Once installed, horseradish is hard to eradicate. Planting it in a large container is one way to control it. The roots can be harvested from autumn onwards and will get more eye-watering as the season progresses. Store scrubbed but unpeeled roots in the fridge and grate as needed.

Prepared, grated horseradish is available in jars or tubes, and may be substituted for the fresh root in recipes. It will contain preservatives, however, and may be less fiery. Don't confuse it with branded horseradish sauces (note that those called 'creamed horseradish' usually have the most horseradish in them). These have their place but they do not deliver the same thrill as the fresh, raw, real deal.

CREAMED APPLE AND HORSERADISH SAUCE

1 very ripe, large cooking apple (275–300g), a variety that collapses on cooking, such as Bramley

1–1½ tbsp caster sugar

Juice of ½ lemon

About 60g fresh horseradish root

½ tsp Dijon mustard

3 tbsp crème fraîche

Sea salt and black pepper

A deliciously fruity version of the classic sauce, this is good with pork or beef, but also with smoked mackerel or fresh fish. Serves 4

Peel, core and slice the apple. Put into a pan with 2 tbsp water and 1 tbsp sugar. Cook over a low heat for about 10 minutes, stirring often, until the apple is partly collapsed but still a bit chunky; add a splash more water if it looks like sticking. Let cool completely.

Put the lemon juice into a bowl. Peel the horseradish then grate it finely into the lemon juice, stopping to stir it into the juice from time to time.

Add the lemony horseradish to the apple purée, along with the mustard and a good pinch each of salt and pepper. Stir in the crème fraîche, then add a pinch or two more sugar, to balance the hot and sour elements. Taste for seasoning, adding more salt or mustard if needed. The sauce will keep, covered, in the fridge, for a few days.

Japanese wineberries

Mark Diacono

LATIN NAME
Rubus phoenicolasius

SEASONALITY
August–September

MORE RECIPES
Barbecued fennel and courgettes with loganberries (page 367); Basil pannacotta with minted raspberries (page 50); Raspberry almond streusel cake (page 526)

Years ago, having just moved house, I was given a Japanese wineberry plant by a new neighbour. I didn't know anything about wineberries and presumed that they were one of the many uninteresting raspberry hybrids: I couldn't have been more mistaken.

When the fruit appeared – perfectly timed in the lull between the peaks of the summer and autumn raspberry harvests – they were a revelation, with the flavour of a slowly ripened autumn raspberry, mixed with a drop or two of cassis and a hint of red wine. They ripen steadily across the plant, so are rarely harvestable in huge numbers, but they do make a delicious treat and they are perfect where a few handfuls of berries add a special touch to a recipe.

I've never seen the fruit for sale, but don't hesitate to plant some yourself: Japanese wineberries almost grow themselves. Simply plant, water in well and come back in late summer to harvest.

Wineberries are their own species, rather than being hybrid, but grow very much like blackberries, throwing up long arching canes that can reach 2–3 metres. In the second year, as well as producing new canes, the existing canes grow side shoots that bear fruit. Cleverly, the papery calyx that surrounds each berry splits open late, just as the fruit is getting ready to turn from green to orange to red-ripe – a process that happens very quickly – meaning that you, rather than the birds, get to eat them. These fruited canes will produce only once and can be pruned off at ground level after picking, though I tend to leave them until spring, as the pink bristles along their length catch the winter light beautifully.

WINEBERRIES WITH PEACHES AND CUSTARD

300g Japanese wineberries

A good squeeze of lemon juice

3–4 medium peaches or nectarines

FOR THE CUSTARD
200ml whole milk

300ml double cream

1 vanilla pod

50g caster sugar

1 tsp cornflour

3 medium egg yolks

This is a simple way to make the most of these glorious fruits. You will need to prepare the custard ahead because it has to be chilled. Other berries such as raspberries, blackberries, mulberries or loganberries all work well here too. Serves 4

For the custard, put the milk and cream into a saucepan. Split open the vanilla pod and scrape out the seeds with the tip of a knife into the pan. Add the scraped-out pod too. Bring to just below simmering, then take off the heat and set aside for 10 minutes.

Meanwhile, whisk the sugar, cornflour and egg yolks together in a bowl until well combined. Pour on the hot milk and cream, whisking as you do so.

Return this mixture to a clean pan and cook gently over a medium heat, stirring constantly, for a few minutes, until the custard thickens. Don't let it boil, or it may 'split'.

Pass the custard through a sieve into a clean bowl or jug and cover the surface directly with cling film or baking parchment, to stop a skin forming. Allow it to cool, then chill in the fridge.

When you are ready to serve, place the wineberries in a bowl and crush them lightly with the back of a spoon. Stir in the lemon juice.

Halve and de-stone the peaches, then slice each half into small chunks. Divide the peach chunks between serving glasses.

Spoon over the crushed wineberries and pour over the chilled custard (you may not need it all). Serve straight away, with shortbread biscuits if you like.

John Dory

Nick Fisher

LATIN NAME
Zeus faber

ALSO KNOWN AS
Dory, St Peter's fish

SEASONALITY
Avoid June–August when
spawning

HABITAT
Widespread in Europe, Africa
and Asia. Around the British
Isles, it is most common in
the English Channel

MCS RATING
3–4

REC MINIMUM SIZE
35cm

MORE RECIPES
Black bream with Jerusalem
artichoke purée (page 91);
Plaice with rosemary, caper
and anchovy butter (page 476);
Steamed sea bass with kale
and ginger (page 573)

SOURCING
goodfishguide.org

A John Dory looks like a flatfish that forgot to lie flat: thin and oval, like a plaice stuck edgeways up. Its flesh is also very similar in texture and taste to flatfish royalty, namely turbot and brill. Meaty, white, succulent and sweet, sometimes it even reminds me of scallop muscle. This makes its fillets perfect for poaching, steaming or gentle frying – while its bizarre skeleton and enormous head are a shoo-in for the stockpot.

There is no specific targeted fishery for John Dory, and so their appearance on British fishmongers' slabs is sporadic. Unlike many British fish, the John Dory cannot be confused with any other species. Apart from its distinctive profile, it has a huge, quill-like dorsal fin that loops majestically upwards and backwards, and which has led to it being called *gallo* (cockerel) in Sicily. This porcupine-quill-like fin spine is its ultimate protection from any predator big enough to tackle it. The spike can lock in the erect position, making JD a painful mouthful for a shark.

Many and varied are the theories as to why this fish ended up with its name – and none of them make much sense. On the Continent, it's most commonly known as 'St Peter's fish', because the black splodges on either side of its body are supposed to be the marks of St Peter's thumb and forefinger, from when he first plucked it out of the Sea of Galilee. Heretics will, of course, tell you that the Sea of Galilee is fresh water and does not contain John Dory, and then point out that the haddock has identical splodges too.

In all fairness though, eating the fillets of a John Dory *is* an uplifting and spiritual experience, although its price tag can be a quick and painful comedown. The fish are caught surprisingly frequently from boat and shore around the English Channel, although they tend to travel alone, not in shoals or schools. The bigger they become, the more lone-wolfish they are. Their huge mouths and violent predatorial tendencies mean they don't usually hang out with other fish. Instead, they tend to eat them.

Personally, when I see a John Dory on a menu I'm quick to indulge, but paradoxically, when I catch one, I can rarely bring myself to dispatch it. Eating them is easy. Killing them, impossible.

JOHN DORY WITH CREAMED RADICCHIO

*The sweet flesh of John Dory works beautifully with the bitter notes of radicchio, or chicory (use a couple of heads). You could serve the creamed radicchio with pan-fried scallops too.
Serves 2*

A knob of butter

1 tbsp olive or rapeseed oil

4 fillets of John Dory (about 300g in total)

½ large head of radicchio (about 175g), coarsely shredded

1 garlic clove, finely chopped

2–3 anchovy fillets in oil

125ml double cream

Sea salt and black pepper

Place a large non-stick frying pan over a medium-high heat. Add the butter and oil and, when foaming, add the fish fillets, skin side down. Fry for about 3 minutes, by which time the fish should be almost cooked through, with just the surface still a touch translucent. Transfer the fillets to a warmed plate.

Add the shredded radicchio, garlic and anchovies to the pan and sauté over a medium heat for 2–3 minutes, stirring to help the anchovies break down. Now add the cream and 75ml water. Turn up the heat a little and bring to a simmer. Cook for 3–4 minutes, until the sauce is quite thick and the radicchio tender. Season with salt and pepper to taste.

Turn the heat off and return the fish fillets, flesh side down, to the pan for a couple of minutes to finish cooking. Serve straight away, with boiled potatoes.

Juniper

Steven Lamb

LATIN NAME
Juniperus communis

SEASONALITY
Berries: August–November

HABITAT
Dry limestone in the south of
Britain, acid ground in the north

MORE RECIPES
Potted carp (page 118);
Seared ox heart (page 305);
Crab apple jelly with thyme,
juniper and mint (page 204)

J

This tiny plump berry has a powdery, frosted blue/black appearance when ripe. The flavour is dominated by piney, resinous notes and there is a hint of citrus about it too. The berries are bitter if you eat them alone; it's what you pair them with that matters. Juniper's unique, fresh and penetrating taste is most commonly employed in the distilling of gin, giving the spirit its characteristic flavour – and its name, which comes from the Dutch word for juniper, *jenever*.

There is also a strong tradition of using juniper's clean, aromatic bite to cut through fatty or gamey meats such as pork, boar, venison or wildfowl. Crushing, then cooking the berries in liquid or combining them with oil or butter is a great way to get that flavour to travel. Juniper is also excellent with pickled or braised cabbage (it's used in sauerkraut), root vegetables, as part of a spice rub or cure for meat or oily fish, and in pâtés or terrines.

Dried juniper berries are easy to buy. Although most pungent in their freshly picked state, they don't lose too much flavour or aroma when dried, and remain slightly soft, so they can be easily crushed.

It's also sometimes possible to gather fresh, wild juniper berries. They are, in fact, cones, rather than berries, more related to a pine cone than a fruit, and grow on straggling bushes or small trees. The slow-ripening berries start off green, gradually turning to bruise-coloured spheres in their second or third year. It is feasible to have berries maturing at different rates on the same branch. Unfortunately, however, they are surrounded by horribly sharp spikes, which limit the ease of picking.

Growing your own juniper is possible (some specialist nurseries sell plants), but somewhat challenging. It requires open, chalky soil and plenty of sun – the more sun juniper gets, the better the flavour. You will need both male and female plants (the latter produce the berries).

Juniper contains a compound that may possibly induce miscarriage, so should not be eaten by pregnant women. It should also be avoided if you have kidney problems.

SAUTÉED MUSHROOMS WITH JUNIPER

500g mushrooms, trimmed

30 juniper berries

1 tbsp olive or rapeseed oil

25g butter

2 shallots, finely sliced

3 fat garlic cloves, slivered

1 tbsp balsamic vinegar

2 tbsp double cream (optional)

Sea salt and black pepper

TO SERVE

4 slices of sourdough or other crusty bread

Extra virgin olive or rapeseed oil

3–4 spring onions, finely chopped

For this full-flavoured, quick dish, buy portobello, chestnut or button mushrooms, or use foraged field, horse, hedgehog or St George's mushrooms. Serves 4

Cut the mushrooms into roughly 1cm slices; set aside. Crush the juniper berries to a rough powder, using a pestle and mortar.

Heat the oil with the butter in a large frying pan over a medium heat until sizzling. Add the shallots and fry for a few minutes until lightly golden. Stir in the garlic and juniper berries and cook for a minute or so.

Add the sliced mushrooms to the frying pan and stir-fry over a fairly high heat for at least 5 minutes until their juices have evaporated and they are well coloured. Remove from the heat and lightly stir in the balsamic vinegar, and the cream if using, then season to taste with salt and pepper.

Meanwhile, toast the bread, then trickle or brush with olive or rapeseed oil. Pile the mushrooms on to the hot toast and scatter over the spring onions to serve.

Kale

Mark Diacono

LATIN NAME
Brassica oleracea var. *acephala*

ALSO KNOWN AS
Borecole

SEASONALITY
June–February

MORE RECIPES
Swede with orecchiette (page 624); Steamed sea bass with kale and ginger (page 573); Roasted haggis, swede and kale salad (page 295); Tongue, kale and apple hash with horseradish (page 643); Sausages with squash and kale (page 568)

Kale comes to us in a variety of guises with leaves that can be almost any combination of wrinkled, ruched and frilled. The ubiquitous green curly kale, with its foppish ruffles, is only one form. Kale leaves may be darkest bottle green and quill-shaped, as with the fantastic, robust cavolo nero, or ragged-edged and purple-stemmed like 'Red Russian'. Any can be simply steamed or boiled and served on the side, but kale can do so much more.

In season in all but March, April and May (and even this gap is filled if you grow perennial varieties), kale lends itself to recipes throughout the year. Use the leaves when they are young and tender: in raw spring salads; blitzed into summer fruit smoothies; shredded and cooked in olive oil with lemon zest and chilli for an autumn pasta sauce; or baked in a gratin with Jerusalem artichokes in the heart of winter.

Of course, there are many other possibilities. For delectable 'kale crisps', toss the torn-up leaves with olive oil and salt, then spread out on a baking tray and roast at 120°C/Fan 100°C/Gas ½ for 25 minutes, turning once or twice. Or shred the leaves and stir-fry with soy, ginger and garlic; or bake in a tart with Jerusalem artichokes.

Unless the plant is very young and tender, remove the tough central stalks from kale leaves before cooking (those supermarket bags of ready-sliced kale are useless because of all the fibrous chopped-up stalk included in the mix). Then all you have to do is not overcook it. A few minutes of simmering, steaming or frying is all it needs.

If you have the space to grow a few kale plants, do so. As good as shop-bought kale can be, you'll have access to far more variety from your garden – and you'll be able to harvest them at any stage of maturity. Red Russian's early green-with-purple-tinged leaves are sweet and delicate enough to enjoy raw, becoming deeply flavoured as the cold toughens their texture. 'Pentland Brig' produces mild, gently curled leaves in the winter and tasty side shoots in the following spring. And 'Redbor', with its dark purple leaves, is as ornamental as it is delicious.

There are even a few perennial kales that grow all year round. 'Sutherland' kale is my favourite; no matter what time of year I tear the leaves off, they are sweet and tender straight from the plant.

RAW KALE WITH YOGHURT AND TAHINI

300g bunch of kale (any variety)

FOR THE DRESSING
Juice of ½ lemon

1 tbsp tahini

2 tbsp plain wholemilk yoghurt

2 tbsp extra virgin olive or rapeseed oil

2 tsp clear honey

A scrap of garlic (about ¼ clove), crushed or finely grated

Sea salt and black pepper

This is a lovely way to eat raw kale: the leaves are 'massaged' with the dressing so they soften and wilt, while still retaining their raw character. Serves 4 as a side dish

Remove the stalks from the kale leaves and tear the leaves into pieces. Wash and spin-dry the kale leaves or pat dry with a clean tea towel, then put them into a large bowl.

To make the dressing, lightly whisk all the ingredients together to combine thoroughly, seasoning with salt and pepper to taste.

Pour the dressing over the raw kale, then massage the dressing into the leaves with your hands, crushing, rubbing and squeezing the leaves so that they darken, soften and wilt. Keep going for 3–4 minutes until the kale is reduced to about half its former volume. Taste and add more salt, pepper or lemon juice if needed.

You can serve the kale straight away or leave it to relax and develop in flavour for a few hours. Either way, it's delicious with some hummus or a beany salad.

Kidneys

SOURCING
coombefarmorganic.co.uk;
graigfarm.co.uk

Glistening like plump, giant beans on the butcher's slab, very fresh kidneys promise, and can deliver, superb flavour – rich and dense, with a sweet-sharp tang. They're not hard to cook and, paired with something a little piquant and/or sweet to match their strong character, they are one of the finest of all offally treats.

As with any offal, kidneys must be chosen carefully. Their function is the elimination of waste from the animal, so it's not hard to see how, if left sitting around, the bacteria they naturally contain can wreak havoc. Freshness is paramount – I wouldn't look at a kidney more than a few days old. They should appear juicy and wet and have a mild, not unpleasant aroma. They keep better if left whole: good butchers display them like this and cut them to order.

To source the finest, freshest kidneys, find out when your local butcher gets their fresh kidneys delivered. Frozen kidneys may seem a pragmatic choice if fresh ones aren't available. But there's always the possibility they were bunged in the freezer after a few days of sitting in the chiller, to avoid wastage.

If you're buying fresh kidneys pre-packed in the supermarket, look for a margin of 3–4 days, at least, before the expiry date and eat them on the day of purchase.

Multi-lobed calf's kidneys are delicious – look for those that come from higher welfare or British rose veal calves (see page 656). The grown-up version, ox kidney, is more robustly flavoured and can be tough. But when cooked long and slow in, say, a steak and kidney pie, it tastes magnificent.

With pig's kidneys, freshness and provenance are particularly important. But bought super-fresh, from organically reared stock, these are my favourite of all.

Lamb's kidneys are the type most often sold. The mildest flavoured of the various types, these are a very good choice, especially if you are a little bit kidney-shy.

To prepare lamb's or pig's kidneys, remove the fine membrane, then slice the kidney in half lengthways and trim out the hard, white, gristly 'core'. This is most easily done by cutting the kidney into bite-sized pieces, trimming out the core as you go. The paler pink part has a slightly more resistant texture than the darker, purply-brown flesh but is quite edible.

Cooking should be either fast and hot, rendering the kidneys nicely browned on the outside but still just pink in the middle, or long and slow, as in a Lancashire hotpot.

LAMB'S KIDNEYS WITH MUSTARD AND CREAM

4 lamb's kidneys

Olive or rapeseed oil, for frying

½ glass of white wine or cider

2 heaped tsp Dijon mustard

About 150ml double cream

Sea salt and black pepper

Chopped parsley, to finish

Toast or rye crispbreads, to serve

Use delicate lamb's kidneys for this dish, or very fresh pig's kidneys if you can get them. Chicken livers also work splendidly. Serves 2

Halve the kidneys lengthways and remove the white core, using the tip of your knife. Lightly season the kidneys with salt and pepper.

Place a medium frying pan over a high heat and add a good trickle of oil. When it is almost starting to smoke, add the kidneys. Don't stir them about initially: let them get some colour. After about 45 seconds, start to turn them over. Cook the kidneys for a further minute, moving them around the pan so they cook evenly.

Now add the wine or cider and the mustard. Let the liquid bubble until reduced by about two-thirds, then add the cream. Let bubble, stirring, until the sauce is reduced to a nice, thick consistency and is coating the kidneys. Take the pan off the heat.

Serve the kidneys scattered with parsley, on toast or rye crispbreads, with a green salad.

K

Kiwi fruit

Gill Meller

LATIN NAME
Actinidia deliciosa

ALSO KNOWN AS
Chinese gooseberry

SEASONALITY
Imported all year round; Italian fruit in season September–April

Although native to East Asia (its other name is Chinese gooseberry), the kiwi was first developed as a commercial crop in New Zealand in the early twentieth century – and Italy is now the largest producer. It's a fantastic fruit, and quite different from anything else. With a wonderful combination of sweet, luscious juiciness and tangy edge, kiwis are delicious eaten on their own or in fruit salads. In particular, they will give sweetness to a salad in place of pears or plums when these home-grown fruits are out of season. A good source of fibre and rich in vitamin C, kiwis offer health benefits too.

Kiwis work well alongside orchard fruits. For a refreshing pudding, combine rounds of kiwi with thinly sliced apple wedges and finely chopped tarragon, then dress with a trickle of honey. They are also great in smoothies, where the surprisingly peppery flavour of their seeds is revealed.

Kiwis are not just at home in sweet dishes, their acid/sweet balance makes them excellent in savoury salads too. Think of them performing a similar role to tomatoes. They make good partners to blue cheese, for instance, and they're brilliant in a new potato salad with bacon and mint. I also like them added to mozzarella with chopped red onion, torn basil and good olive oil.

Kiwi fruit contain actinidin, an enzyme which breaks down protein. This means crushed kiwis are very effective at tenderising squid or cuttlefish before cooking (see page 605). However, the same enzyme attacks gelatine, so a kiwi jelly is an impossibility!

Kiwi fruit can be eaten when they are firm and slightly under-ripe, though they will be quite sharp. But you can happily leave them in the fruit bowl for a week or so, to slowly ripen. Don't leave them too long though, or the flesh will turn dark and develop a fermented quality. Give the fruit a gentle squeeze every so often so you can catch them when they feel gently yielding but not soft – the perfect stage to eat them.

To peel kiwi fruit, first slice off the top and bottom of the fruit, then pare the skin away with a small knife.

KIWI, SPINACH AND AVOCADO SMOOTHIE

2 ripe kiwi fruit, peeled and roughly chopped

½ ripe avocado (about 100g), peeled and diced

75g raw, de-stalked spinach leaves

Juice of 1 large orange

2 tsp honey

8–10 ice cubes

Bright green and bursting with goodness, this velvety smoothie gets creaminess from the avocado and a slight pepperiness from the kiwi seeds (which you can increase by replacing the spinach with watercress). It's great for breakfast or whenever you feel the need for a healthy pick-me-up. Serves 2

Put all the ingredients into a blender and blitz until smooth and silky. If the smoothie seems a little thick, you can 'let it down' with 1–2 tbsp water. Divide between 2 glasses and drink straight away.

Kohlrabi

Mark Diacono

LATIN NAME
Brassica oleracea var. *gongylodes*

ALSO KNOWN AS
Turnip cabbage

SEASONALITY
June–December

MORE RECIPES
Kohlrabi and mushroom salad
with sesame (page 581)

The martian tennis ball, the slug magnet, the devil's testicle – these are just a few of the names I've given kohlrabi over the years. I did try growing it a few times, but the slugs seemed insatiably intent on eating their way through the entire crop. I persisted because, while kohlrabi may not be beautiful to look at, it has so much potential in the kitchen. It gives you two contrasting parts to eat: a turnip-like bulb (usually pale green but occasionally vivid purple) and kale-like leaves.

The bulb has a flavour like the sweetest cabbage heart, and a water-chestnut-like crunch that's perfect for rémoulade and coleslaw, where it combines splendidly with the usual roots and cabbage, but perhaps most happily with apple and Brussels sprouts.

It's hugely adaptable too: roasting peeled and chunked kohlrabi for 30–40 minutes in a little oil with plenty of salt and pepper brings out its nutty brassica flavour brilliantly. Thinly sliced, the bulb makes a very good dauphinoise in place of potatoes – you can even add the shredded leaves. And grated kohlrabi, combined with pork or white fish, makes splendid rösti.

At its freshest, a bulb of kohlrabi contains more vitamin C than an orange and is good enough to munch into like an apple. Or, for a delicious instant pickle, peel, slice into matchsticks and toss with a couple of pinches of sugar and one of salt, along with 2 tbsp cider vinegar.

The leaves can be used in the same way as kale, green cabbage or spring greens, taking particularly well to being finely shredded and sautéed in olive oil with garlic and chilli to go with pasta.

Kohlrabi is in season from mid-summer into early winter. It's just starting to appear on the radar of some supermarkets, but you're more likely to find it in your veg box or local farmers' market. In order to be glad that you took the plunge and tried it, look for leaves that are full of vitality rather than limp, choose bulbs no larger than 6cm across and peel all but the youngest, freshest specimens.

SPICY KOHLRABI WEDGES

750g kohlrabi

2 tsp cumin seeds

1 tsp coriander seeds

1 tsp fennel seeds

½–1 tsp dried chilli flakes

1 tsp hot smoked paprika

20g cornflour

2–3 tbsp olive or rapeseed oil

4 sprigs of rosemary

2 garlic cloves, thinly sliced

Sea salt and black pepper

Soured cream or crème fraîche,
to serve

These wedges are delicious on their own or as an accompaniment to fried fish or home-made burgers. You can give the same treatment to sweet potato, though it may need a little less cooking. Serves 4 as a side dish

Preheat the oven to 200°C/Fan 180°C/Gas 6.

Peel the kohlrabi and cut it into thick wedges. Place in a large bowl.

Set a small frying pan over a medium heat and add the cumin, coriander and fennel seeds, and the chilli flakes. Toast the spices, shaking the pan occasionally, for a couple of minutes until hot and fragrant.

Tip the spices into a mortar and grind with the pestle to a fairly fine texture. Combine the ground spices with the smoked paprika and cornflour, adding some salt and pepper.

Pour the oil over the kohlrabi wedges and toss them to coat, then sprinkle with the spice mixture and tumble everything together. Tip the spice-coated kohlrabi into a roasting tray. Scatter over the rosemary sprigs and place the tray in the oven.

Bake, turning once or twice, for 35–40 minutes, adding the garlic about 10 minutes before the end of the cooking time. The kohlrabi should be golden and crisp on the outside, yet tender on the inside. Serve with a spoonful of soured creamed or crème fraîche – alone, or as a side dish.

Lamb, hogget & mutton

Hugh Fearnley-Whittingstall

MORE RECIPES
Ginger-braised lamb (page 278); Roast lamb with lovage (page 368); Lamb's kidneys with mustard and cream (page 324)

SOURCING
pastureforlife.org; blackface.co.uk; langleychase.co.uk; streamfarm.co.uk

Lamb is some of the best-flavoured meat we can enjoy. Compared with pork and beef, it has a distinctive, strong taste, even when young. Lamb's mild, feral tang makes it not only superb for roasting but also, without doubt, the most rewarding meat to cook over wood or charcoal. One of its flavour-creating constituents is thymol, which is also found in thyme. Combined with something a little piquant, such as mint, cumin or garlic, lamb can reach pretty astronomical levels of savoury deliciousness.

In the British Isles, for the most part, sheep are free-range beasts. They're natural wanderers and grazers, adept at putting on muscle and fat on a diet of even the sparsest vegetation, and no farmer is going to keep them indoors, stoking them up with expensive feeds, if they could be turned out to eat fast-growing grass on marginal pasture that's not much suited to other types of farming.

So most sheep live outdoors, most of the time. While nearly all our breeds are hardy enough to overwinter out-of-doors, lowland sheep are likely to be brought in for 2–3 months during the winter, to avoid them churning up what little grass is still about. Upland animals, such as Welsh and Cumbrian mountain sheep, which graze over much larger areas, are usually outside all the time.

However, although sheep probably live the least unnatural life of all our farm animals, we've still seen fit to alter their inherent cycles when it suits us. Despite the fact that different breeds naturally lamb at different times of year – autumn for some of the southernmost lowland breeds, and spring or early summer for most others – our hunger for lamb on the table at Easter has led to pressure for winter lambing.

I'm extremely wary of anything pitched as 'new season lamb' between March and May. There are a range of methods that can be used to manipulate and control the lambing season. Carefully managed proximity to rams, melatonin implants that mimic the effects of shortening days, or a hormone extracted from pregnant mare's blood can all be employed to bring ewes into season early so that they can start lambing in December and January, producing meat for the Easter market. Going on sale at the time when most breeds would naturally only just be giving birth, these lambs will have been born in the coldest months and raised, quickly, largely on their mother's milk, with some concentrated feed to help them along, because there simply isn't much grass to be had. They will have been slaughtered as young as 12 weeks. Depending on the weather and the breed, the animals may have spent a significant part of their short life – perhaps all of it – indoors.

We've been conditioned by decades of marketing to think of lamb as a quintessential spring food, but as that same marketing spiel points out, new season lamb is 'delicate' and 'mild'. I'd put it a different way: it lacks character. When I eat lamb, I want it to have a rich, full, herby taste. For that it should come from an animal that has felt the sun (and indeed the rain) on its back, and had the good few months of wandering and grass-chomping required to build up fat and flavour. And quite apart from my selfish desires, surely that's the animal's due.

Young spring lamb largely bypasses that process. So if I want to eat sheep at Easter, and be confident it's had some outdoor grazing, I choose hogget (a sheep in its second year) or, at the very least, lamb that is not labelled as 'new season' which may be well on its way to being hogget anyway. Or I might go all-out for mutton, a sheep over 2 years old. Sadly the concept of hogget and mutton barely exists outside old-school butchers' shops and farm-gate or farmers' market sales. But we should continue to champion these meats.

Naturally, the best time to enjoy regular, outdoor-reared lamb is autumn and winter. Spring born, with a good summer of outdoor grazing under its woolly belt, it will be nicely fatted and full of flavour.

All things considered, lamb is the meat I'd be least anxious about buying in a supermarket. Most will be from outdoor-reared flocks, especially from mid-summer onwards. So the average level of welfare is reasonable and the quality of the meat can certainly be good. But for those who like to know as much as possible about the meat they eat, there are questions you won't get answers to in the supermarket: what breed was it? What age was it slaughtered? How long was it hung? Supermarket lamb is usually cut and packed within a few days of slaughter, whereas a good butcher or farm shop may well hang their lamb for a week or so – longer for hogget or mutton. And you will taste the difference.

You should also be able to satisfy your curiosity on most other significant questions of provenance. Of course, the fullest picture of what you are getting when you buy lamb comes when you buy it direct from the producer: that means farm shop, farmers' market or mail order. Many producers sell online, offering big boxes of lamb cuts or whole or half-animals at very reasonable prices.

Much organic lamb is sold wholesale like this. It offers the guarantee of a grass-fed animal that's lived outdoors, and the further reassurance that the grass is grown naturally, without the use of fertilisers or pesticides. If you've been buying your lamb in the supermarket, want to try something different and you have a bit of freezer space, try ordering half a hogget online from an organic supplier.

Breed is another factor influencing flavour. And in the British Isles we are said to have more varied sheep stock than anywhere else in the world – around 100 different breeds are currently farmed within our shores. Our traditional breeds have been developed to do well in specific parts of the country, and it makes sense to look for meat from a breed suited to your locality. This supports better welfare, of course, and our food culture would be far poorer if we were to lose the distinctiveness of different breeds.

The hardy Cumbrian 'Herdwick', for instance, so beloved of Beatrix Potter, ekes sustenance from bilberries, heather and even lichen on the harsh Lakeland hilltops. The sheep are largely left to their own devices and lambs are born relatively late in the year. Allowed to 'grow on' for longer than other breeds, they produce relatively mature lamb, as well as very fine hogget and mutton. Other flavourful traditional breeds include the stocky 'Poll Dorset', which we raise at River Cottage, and the 'Scottish Blackface'. Another wide-ranging mountain sheep with a wonderfully varied diet, the Blackface is the most numerous breed in the British Isles.

Saltmarsh lamb (the term referring not to a specific breed but a method of raising) is usually Welsh but is also reared in other coastal areas all over Britain. It's sometimes romantically portrayed as having a kind of internal seasoning from the salty grasses and shoreline seaweeds it feeds on. In fact, even a minuscule increase in salt levels within an animal's blood and muscle tissues would soon kill it. Nevertheless, the broad range of wild vegetation it grazes on, and the hard work it needs to do to reach it, certainly does lend something rich and unique to the flavour of this meat.

The traditional cuts of lamb are described below. The same terms are applied to hogget and mutton, though you can expect these meats from older animals to have deeper flavours. Besides being more mature, they usually have a greater covering of fat than younger lamb, which is a great advantage because it means they can be hung for a couple of weeks or more, which will develop that flavour further.

It's a mistake to think that hogget and mutton are only fit for stewing and slow cooking. This is not 'old meat', but 'prime meat'. A 3- or 4-year-old mutton wether (the traditional name for a castrated male sheep) is not a clapped-out old timer, but a young adult in its prime. So there's no problem in serving prime cuts of hogget and mutton, such as a leg, rack or loin – and the steaks and chops thereof – a bit pink in the middle, if that is to your taste.

Favourite lamb cuts

Leg This is generally considered the pick of the lamb roasts, because of its tender meat and relative leanness. It can be roasted slowly until the meat falls off the bone, or cooked hot and fast and served still pink in the middle (a technique that tends to work best with more mature meat, such as hogget, that's been hung for several days, rather than very young lamb). Either way, I like to pierce the meat all over and stuff slivers of garlic, sprigs of rosemary and snippets of anchovy into it. This perfect trio of lamb seasonings flavours the meat exquisitely and gives you wonderful juices for gravy (see page 63).

Sometimes the leg is portioned into two pieces to produce half legs. You'll be able to tell from the shape whether you've got the lower shank end or the upper chump end. The latter will be a little more meaty. However, I generally prefer to roast a whole leg, which will easily feed eight or more, not least because leftover roast lamb is a truly joyful thing to have in the fridge.

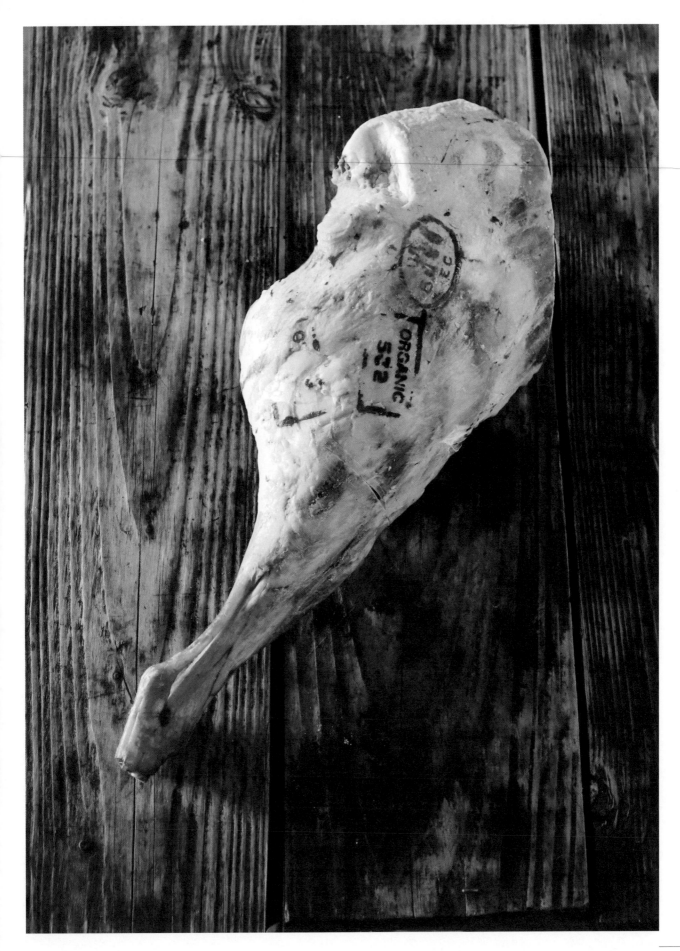

A boned-out and flattened (or 'butterflied') leg of lamb, marinated in yoghurt, garlic and spices, makes a superb centrepiece for a celebratory barbecue. And leg steaks are useful, tender cuts if you want a quick lamb supper. Seared quickly and left to rest for a few minutes, then sliced thickly to reveal their juicy, still-pink interior, they make a superb accompaniment to a really good veg dish. Bone-in leg steaks are sometimes called gigot chops.

Loin This cut comes from the mid-back of the animal. As well as providing good chops (see below), it is used whole as a roasting joint. The loin is often boned out and rolled around a stuffing before being tied, and this makes a pretty posh mini roast. I like it stuffed with a scant but highly flavoured mix of dried fruit, nuts, spices and a little fried onion, held together with a minimal quantity of breadcrumbs. You can roast loin on the bone too.

Chops These can be cut from different parts of the animal's back. Chump chops are cut from the rump end, and are correspondingly chunky and generous, boneless and fairly lean. Loin chops, taken from the middle section of the back, are slightly smaller and fattier, with a small piece of chine bone but no rib. Cutlets are the dainty chop from the neck end of the back, with the convenient handle of rib to hold them by. To get the desirable browning and caramelisation on the outer surface of chops and tender, succulent meat within, sear on both sides in a very hot pan, then reduce the heat and finish them in the pan, or transfer to the oven to cook through. Either way, it's a pretty quick way to get a good bit of meat on the table.

Rack of lamb This is an elegant joint for two, comprising the cutlets still joined together. Also called the best end, it is sometimes 'French-trimmed' so the stripped ribs are exposed. Two racks, trimmed, curved and tied together give you a 'crown roast'.

Fillet This is the little eye of meat taken from the loin, free of fat, bone and sinew. Overcook lamb fillet or under-season it and it's a slightly dull cut, but rolled in tasty seasonings, cooked hot and fast, and served pink, it's a treat. One fillet will serve one or two people.

Shoulder If the leg is the neat and tidy, well-behaved, high-achiever of lamb roasting joints, then the shoulder is its louche, relaxed, decadent cousin. No prizes for guessing which is my favourite. Shoulder is more fatty and therefore tastes richer than the leg. You can cook it for hours to produce magnificently tender, intensely flavoured meat, and smother it with spices or herbs without any fear of it being overwhelmed. The shoulder is pretty ungainly in shape and can be boned and rolled to make a neater package – but I love the intriguing, undulating plane of the whole, bone-in joint. You needn't worry about carving: when slow-roasted, you can just pull the long, sweet shreds of meat from it with your hands (or, of course, with a knife and fork if you prefer). Cubed lamb shoulder is a good stewing meat and makes excellent kebabs too.

Breast of lamb This is the ovine equivalent of belly of pork and has similar characteristics. Incredibly inexpensive, it's great for a cheap and tasty roast. It is a fatty cut, but full of flavour and it responds well to long cooking. However, the breast is not a pretty cut of meat: it's untidy-looking: long, narrow and shallow, with one pointed end, and various layers of flesh and fat running in different directions. To combat this, it is very often rolled around a stuffing for cooking – which conveniently transforms it into a neat cylinder that is easy to carve. A breadcrumb-based stuffing also absorbs some of the flavoursome fat nicely. For rolling, you need a boned-out breast. But you can also roast the breast on the bone, either as a whole piece (once cooked, the bones are

easily removed) or as chunky sections with a few bones each that you can pick up and gnaw. Long, slow cooking is always best; pour off excess fat during cooking and finish with a blast of heat at the end to crisp it up.

Scrag and neck Scrag is the highest cut from the neck of the animal, before you get to the head. Relatively tough, it is packed with flavour and makes a great stewing meat. I like to use it on the bone, in thick steaks, and cook it for at least a couple of hours. Slowly simmered in water with just a few aromatic herbs and vegetables, and finished off with a handful of shredded fresh greens, it produces a thrifty stew, hearty enough to warm anyone's cockles.

Neck of lamb comes from just below the scrag end. Either filleted or on the bone, it also makes a great stew. Don't confuse lamb neck fillet with the more tender fillet from the loin of the animal, which will not respond well to long cooking.

Shank From the rear leg of the animal, the shank is the cut taken from above the knee. The shank forms the lower part of a whole leg of lamb but is also sold separately as a braising cut. And lamb shanks braise beautifully. Rather like shin of beef, they have plenty of body-giving sinew and, when slow-cooked, they become beautifully tender and form a lovely rich liquor. Just brown them in a hot frying pan before placing in a casserole dish. You can then cook them with nothing more than water and some aromatic veg – but add wine, stock, herbs, spices, citrus zest or tomatoes and you can produce an exceptional, warming dish.

Double cuts of lamb Most lamb cuts are taken from 'sides', formed by cleaving the carcass symmetrically down the middle, through the backbone (or 'chine', as it is called). So all the traditional cuts occur twice, once from each side of the animal. However, it is possible to butcher a lamb crossways, and get double cuts. The best known of these are the saddle of lamb – a large celebratory joint comprising the rack and loin from both sides of the animal, still joined at the chine – and the Barnsley chop, which is a double loin or chump chop, also still joined at the chine.

Mince Lamb mince is the bedrock of some of the world's best-beloved comfort food, from shepherd's pie and barbecue burgers to moussaka and merguez sausages. Traditionally, some of these would (and arguably should) be made with leftover cooked lamb, finely chopped, and I still make my shepherd's pie this way. But these days, since we've got out of the habit of cooking big roasts every Sunday, we're more likely to buy our lamb mince fresh and raw than fashion it from our leftover joint.

Pre-packaged lamb mince is usually made from forequarter cuts such as neck, scrag end and breast. It can be very fatty – usually more so than beef or pork mince. This needn't in itself be a problem: fat gives flavour and cogency (important in burgers or koftas, for instance) and any excess is easy enough to drain off. This is one reason why browning mince in a pan before adding it to a dish is a good idea; the terrific amount of flavour you get from browning being another. For a lean mince, you can use leg, though this is relatively expensive. I'd prefer to choose some middle neck and scrag, and trim and mince them myself – or get a butcher to do it.

LAMB, LABNEH AND SPINACH SALAD

300g lean lamb leg steak, about 2cm thick

1 tbsp olive oil

100g baby spinach

150g labneh (yoghurt cheese)

Sea salt and black pepper

FOR THE DRESSING

About 75ml freshly squeezed orange juice

1 tsp cumin seeds, toasted and ground

1 small garlic clove, grated

2 tsp clear honey

2 tbsp extra virgin olive oil

TO FINISH

2–3 tsp sesame seeds, toasted

In this dish, lean lamb leg steak is seared quickly, then marinated in an aromatic orange, cumin and honey dressing. Either buy the labneh from a good deli or make it yourself (see page 684). You could use lamb chops instead of steaks (serving them whole); tender kid chops work well too. Serves 2

For the dressing, put all the ingredients into a jam jar with a little salt and pepper, screw on the lid and shake hard to emulsify.

Heat a medium frying pan over a high heat. Rub the lamb with the olive oil, season it and lay it in the hot pan. Cook for about 7 minutes, turning the meat in the pan a few times, which will give you lamb that is nicely caramelised on the outside and still succulent and pink in the middle.

Take the pan off the heat but leave the lamb to rest in it for a few minutes. Pour the dressing over the lamb and baste it all over. Leave to rest for a further 5 minutes.

Lay the spinach out on a platter or individual plates, then spoon over the labneh. Slice the lamb thinly and scatter over the spinach. Spoon over the warm dressing from the pan and finish with a sprinkling of toasted sesame seeds.

NORTH AFRICAN SHEPHERD'S PIE

2 tbsp olive oil

2 medium onions, chopped

2 medium carrots, chopped

500g lamb mince (or kid goat mince)

3 garlic cloves, grated or crushed

1 medium-hot red chilli, deseeded and finely diced

2 small or ½ large preserved lemon, rind only, finely diced

2 bay leaves

1 tsp chopped rosemary

2 tsp ground cumin

2 tsp ground coriander

1 tsp ground cinnamon

6–8 dried apricots, chopped

400g tin tomatoes

Sea salt and black pepper

FOR THE MASH

500g floury potatoes, such as King Edward

500g chunk of squash

2 tbsp plain wholemilk yoghurt

2 tbsp extra virgin olive oil

Spices, sweet apricots and sour, salty lemon give an aromatic twist to this comforting classic. Serves 4–6

Heat a large saucepan over a medium heat and add 1 tbsp olive oil. When hot, add the onion and carrot, and cook, stirring occasionally, for 6–8 minutes until the veg are softened but not coloured.

Meanwhile, in a large frying pan, heat ½ tbsp oil over a medium-high heat. Add half the lamb mince and cook, stirring frequently, for 5–6 minutes, until nicely browned. Tip into the pan of vegetables, then repeat with the remaining mince.

Add the garlic, chilli, preserved lemon, herbs, spices and chopped apricots, stir well and cook for a further 4–5 minutes.

Tip the tinned tomatoes into a bowl and crush them roughly with your hands, removing any tough stalky ends as you go. Add to the pan of mince with a generous pinch of salt. Fill the tomato tin with water and add this too, then bring to a gentle simmer. Cover and cook, stirring occasionally, for 40 minutes. Taste for seasoning, adding more salt and some pepper if you think it needs it.

Meanwhile, preheat the oven to 200°C/Fan 180°C/Gas 6.

Peel the potatoes and cut into chunks. Peel and deseed the squash, then cut into large chunks. Put the potato and squash into a pan, cover with water, add salt and bring to the boil. Reduce the heat and simmer until tender, about 20 minutes.

Drain the cooked veg and allow to steam-dry in the colander for 5 minutes or so. Return the veg to the pan, add the yoghurt and extra virgin olive oil, season well with salt and pepper and mash until smooth.

Spoon the spiced lamb mince into a baking dish, about 20cm square, and 6–8cm deep. Top with the mash, carefully spreading it over the mince. Bake for 20–25 minutes or until golden and bubbling. Serve with a tomato salad and green leaves.

Lamb's lettuce

Nikki Duffy

LATIN NAME
Valerianella locusta

ALSO KNOWN AS
Mâche, corn salad

SEASONALITY
November–April

MORE RECIPES
Chicken and blueberry salad with coriander dressing (page 77)

Mild, gentle and sweet, the delicacy of this little leaf, paradoxically, makes it stand out a mile among the peppery, bitter, crunchy and crisp leaves that so often populate our salad plates these days. That soft flavour and texture are its finest qualities: so much of the enjoyment of a good meal is to do with pleasing contrasts, and lamb's lettuce can give you the mellow, velvety green counterpoint not just to other leaves, but to anything rich, hot and/or hearty. Since it is a winter leaf, at its best from November to April, this is especially neat.

The paddle-shaped leaves of lamb's lettuce grow in small clumps, and this is the way you buy them. If you pick your own, or get it from a veg box or market, there is often a little wispy root still attached to the base of each leafy sprig, which you can simply pinch off. It's not unusual to find some earth or sand lodged in there at the base too. Thorough but very gentle washing – a soothing swish in a big bowl of cold water – will get rid of any salad-spoiling gritty bits. Then spin or pat it dry.

You can wilt lamb's lettuce in a pan, but I think it loses all its charm. It can simply be used as basic salad bowl padding, tossed with a host of other, more assertive leaves, and there's nothing wrong with that. But my own preference is to pander to the understated nature of this leaf. I like to eat it as a delicate little salad course, barely tampered with. Add a few herbs – the more subtle sorts, such as parsley, chives, or perhaps a tiny bit of soft thyme – a few drops of oil, a little spritz of lemon juice and some salt and pepper, and you have a dish of fresh and cleansing greenness to precede, succeed or accompany heavier, richer things.

Lamb's lettuce is a source of folic acid, iron and omega-3 fatty acids. Like any plant source, these omega-3s are not as easily utilised as those found in fish or meat – but you can always serve your mâche salad alongside a fillet of hot, salty grilled mackerel to boost the content.

LAMB'S LETTUCE SALAD WITH POACHED EGG AND CROÛTONS

2 slices of bread, about 2cm thick, from a medium loaf

1½ tbsp olive or rapeseed oil

2 eggs (at room temperature)

2 handfuls of lamb's lettuce (about 50g)

Leaves from a handful of delicate herbs, such as parsley and chervil

1 tbsp extra virgin olive or rapeseed oil

2 tsp cider vinegar

Sea salt and black pepper

Delicate herbs that grow well through the winter, including parsley and chervil, also happen to make great partners to lamb's lettuce. Very early chives could be added here too, or coriander microleaves (see page 198). Serves 2

Preheat the oven to 180°C/Fan 160°C/Gas 4.

Cut the crusts off the bread, then cut each slice into 2cm cubes. Toss the bread cubes in the 1½ tbsp oil and season with a pinch of salt. Place the bread pieces on a small baking tray and bake in the hot oven, turning once, for 4–6 minutes, until golden. Set aside.

Meanwhile, poach the eggs according to your preferred method. This is the way we do it: pour a 4–5cm depth of water into a wide saucepan or deep frying pan, add a little salt and bring to the boil. Break each egg carefully into a cup or ramekin. When the water is boiling, turn it down very low and slip the eggs into the water. Put the lid on the pan and leave to cook for 2 minutes. Carefully scoop up the eggs using a slotted spoon and check that the whites are set (if not, return them to the water briefly until they are). Lift out the eggs, dab away excess water with kitchen paper, and keep them warm.

Put the lamb's lettuce and herbs into a bowl. Trickle with the extra virgin oil and cider vinegar and toss very lightly together, then arrange in shallow serving bowls. Carefully place a poached egg in each bowl and scatter over the croûtons. Season everything with a little salt and pepper and serve.

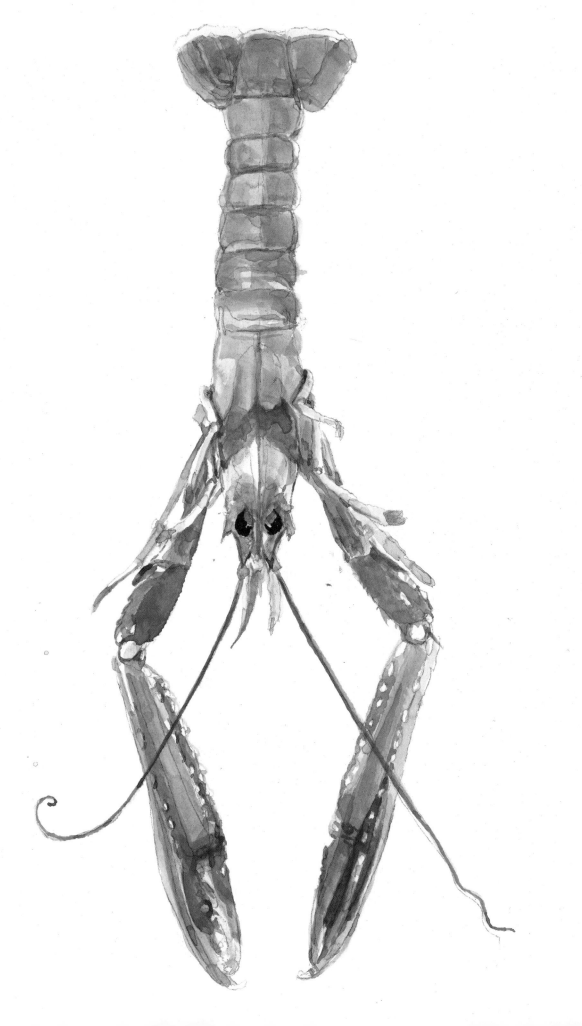

Langoustine

Hugh Fearnley-Whittingstall

LATIN NAME
Nephrops norvegicus

ALSO KNOWN AS
Dublin bay prawns, Norway lobster, scampi

SEASONALITY
Avoid in spring and summer when spawning

HABITAT
Widely found in the northeast Atlantic from Scandinavia to North Africa; also in the Mediterranean

MCS RATING
2–4

REC MINIMUM SIZE
3cm carapace length (from back of eye socket to end of main body shell, not including tail)

MORE RECIPES
Lobster with béarnaise mayonnaise (page 365)

SOURCING
goodfishguide.org

Langoustine, Dublin bay prawns, scampi – whatever you call them, these bug-eyed middleweights of the shellfish world (bigger than a prawn, smaller than a lobster) are a rich seafood treat. They're hugely important to the Scottish fishing industry – currently second only to mackerel. In fact, one-third of all the langoustine landed worldwide come from Scottish waters. A lot of them are packed off to Europe and, until recently, most langoustine that did stay in this country were processed into crumbed scampi.

But we're waking up to the appeal of langoustine served whole in their shells – simply boiled or perhaps smokily barbecued. Confronting a plate of these critters, shell on and unashamedly themselves, is an engaging experience. Crack, peel and dip – into lemony mayonnaise, garlic butter, or a simple dressing of good olive oil, lemon juice, salt and pepper (plus finely chopped chilli and chives if you like).

These shellfish are shy. They live in burrows on silty areas of the seabed and venture out only for feeding or breeding. 'Berried' (egg-bearing) females will stay in their little homes for months while they incubate their eggs – a behaviour that has helped to protect them from the trawlers that seek them out. But trawling for langoustine, which is the primary means of fishing them, inevitably has some negative impacts. The delicate benthic fauna of the seabed is disturbed by the trawl, and untargeted species such as cod, haddock and whiting are still being discarded in some fisheries – though hopefully the new discard ban (see page 193) will reduce this.

Creel-caught langoustine from the west coast of Scotland are the most sustainable choice. If you can source whole, live langoustine, treat them like the mini lobsters they are, first chilling them until insensible in the freezer, then boiling as described in the recipe below.

To get to the sweet, fragile meat, first twist the head off, then pinch the shell of the tail to crack it, before pulling it away from the flesh, as you would with a prawn. Many people discard the heads (or use them in fish stock), but they contain good meat – a delicious, creamy pink paste. A small, thin-ended tool will help you get to it.

If you want to serve pre-cooked langoustine warm, they must be reheated very gently or the delicate flesh will be ruined.

GRILLED LANGOUSTINE WITH LEMON AND PARSLEY BUTTER

The sweet, delicate meat of the langoustine is always at its best when treated simply. If you can only get frozen raw langoustine, defrost them in the fridge, then split and grill them from raw. This recipe also works well with a couple of lobsters. Serves 4

1kg live langoustine

2 lemons

75g butter, softened

1 small garlic clove, grated or crushed

1 tbsp finely chopped flat-leaf parsley

Sea salt and black pepper

To kill the langoustine humanely, first place them in the freezer for about 30 minutes to chill them to the point of torpor. Bring a large pan of well-salted water (about 10g salt per litre) to the boil. Drop in the cold langoustine, bring back to the boil and cook for 3–5 minutes. You'll be able to see the meat inside the tail shells turning white as they cook through. Remove and allow to cool.

Finely grate the zest of 1 lemon and combine it with the soft butter, along with the garlic and parsley. Season with a little salt and pepper, mixing well to combine.

Preheat the grill to high. Place the cooled langoustine on a board and use a sharp, heavy cook's knife to split them in half from head to tail. Lay the halves on a large baking tray, cut side up, and spread a little of the seasoned butter over each half. Grill the langoustine for 5–7 minutes or until bubbling. Serve immediately with the other lemon, cut into wedges, and fresh bread.

Lard

MORE RECIPES

Migas (page 89); Slow-cooked turkey legs with bacon and prunes (page 650); Pheasant pie (page 468); Woodcock with wild mushrooms (page 678); Pork burgers with mace and thyme (page 369); Tagliatelle with lamb's liver, pancetta and sage (page 551)

SOURCING

devonrose.com; greenpasturefarms.co.uk

Lard is rendered pork fat, i.e. fat that has been melted down and re-solidified. The 'raw' fat is usually taken from around the belly of the pig or from the seam of back fat running along the loin.

As a cooking fat, lard can be heated to relatively high temperatures without burning, and gives incomparable flavour to everything from potato cakes to a fry-up. You can also tie pork back fat around lean meats, such as venison, to keep them moist while roasting (a technique called 'barding'). But lard can be an ingredient in its own right – doughy, fruit-studded lardy cake being the most obvious use. It makes good 'shortening' too, creating a unique, melt-in-the-mouth texture in pastry. As it's a source of saturated fat, lard is often avoided, although the link between saturated fats and heart disease is now being questioned. It's worth knowing that lard has less saturated fat than butter.

In Italy, the cured, aged lard from the little village of Colonnata has achieved cult status, but *lardo* is a delicacy you can easily create at home by curing a clean slab of back fat in a fragrant mix of salt, pepper, juniper, garlic and herbs.

Unfortunately, the standard blocks of lard on the supermarket shelf do not come from free-range pigs (see page 488). A few farmers are now producing 'pastured' lard but another option is to render lard yourself. Get some free-range pork back fat from your butcher, cut it into cubes, and put it into a casserole dish. For every 500g fat, add 100ml water; this will evaporate as the lard melts but initially helps moderate the transfer of heat to the fat so that it renders gently and evenly. Put the dish in a very low oven (100°C/Fan 80°C/Gas ¼) and leave to melt over an hour or two. Let it cool a little, then pour into suitable containers. It will keep in the fridge for a couple of months, or in the freezer for a year.

ECCLES CAKES

Lard gives richness and flakiness to the rough puff pastry for these fruity treats. Makes 8

FOR THE PASTRY

400g plain flour

A pinch of salt

100g cold lard, in roughly 1–2cm cubes

100g cold butter, in roughly 1–2cm cubes

FOR THE FILLING

150g currants

40g butter

2 tbsp marmalade

75g caster sugar

½ tsp ground nutmeg

1 tsp ground allspice

TO FINISH

1 egg white, lightly beaten

2 tbsp demerara sugar

To make the pastry, combine the flour and salt in a large bowl. Toss in the lard and butter until coated. Stir in enough ice-cold water (about 250ml) to bring the mixture together and form a very rough, fairly firm, dough (the chunks of fat should still be visible).

Transfer the dough to a well-floured surface and shape into a fat rectangle. Roll out to form a long rectangle, about 1cm thick. Fold the furthest third towards you, then fold the nearest third over that (like folding a business letter). Give the pastry a quarter-turn, so an open edge is facing you.

Repeat the rolling, folding and turning process a further 4 times. If the dough starts to feel soft, chill it between foldings. Wrap the pastry in cling film and rest in the fridge for at least an hour, or up to 24 hours.

For the filling, gently heat all the ingredients together until the marmalade has melted and the butter is bubbling. Leave to cool.

Preheat the oven to 200°C/Fan 180°C/Gas 6 and grease a baking sheet. Take the pastry from the fridge, roll out to a 5mm thickness and cut out 16 circles, 10cm in diameter. Stack up the pastry trimmings and re-roll to cut more circles as necessary.

Top 8 pastry circles with a generous spoonful of the spiced currant mix. Top with the remaining pastry circles and crimp the edges to seal. Flip each cake over and flatten slightly with a rolling pin. Brush the surface with egg white, sprinkle with demerara sugar, then snip a 'V' in the top of each with scissors. Place on the baking sheet and bake for about 20 minutes, or until golden and puffed. Eat warm or cold.

Lavender

Nikki Duffy

LATIN NAME
Lavandula species

SEASONALITY
Fresh leaves and flowerbuds
best for culinary use May–July

MORE RECIPES
Roasted beetroot orzotto with
lavender (page 68)

SOURCING
downderry-nursery.co.uk;
norfolk-lavender.co.uk

Lavender has unfortunate associations with scented drawer sachets and over-perfumed purple soap. But forget that. This is a sexy, heady, exciting herb (all those bees can't be wrong), and a vastly under-used ingredient.

It is similarly aromatic to rosemary and thyme (to which it is related) and works with many of the same foods. But lavender is, of course, more floral and penetrating, and should be used a little more judiciously than those herbs. Lavender features camphor among its flavour compounds. Also found at significant levels in sage and cardamom, camphor gives fantastic resonance and depth, but too much tastes unpleasantly medicinal.

Lavender is lovely with fruit, in syrups, ice creams, shortbread biscuits and sponge cakes. It can also be wonderful with meat – notably lamb – and robustly flavoured vegetables like beetroot. It pairs brilliantly with lemon, which balances its strong perfume. Try beating fresh lavender into butter with grated lemon zest and lots of black pepper, then massaging it under the skin of a chicken before roasting.

Lavender is a great herb mixer too. It combines deliciously with thyme and lemon thyme, with oregano and with garlic. Crushed with any of these (and with lemon zest too), loosened with a little olive oil and used as a rub for meat, it is just what you want for smoke-scented, sun-baked, sensuous summer cooking.

To make the most of lavender, use it fresh. The tender leaves and very young, unopened flowerbuds, picked in spring or early summer, are the best. Chop them finely and add to your dish. They can withstand cooking, or can be eaten raw. Dried lavender flowers are easy to buy (make sure you buy those intended for cooking, rather than for perfuming things) but the flavour is more pungent, less sweet and floral. They will certainly do when fresh lavender is out of season, but you'll need about half as much.

For culinary uses, the *Lavandula angustifolia* varieties are the ones to choose. More delicate and fragrant than other varieties, owing to a lower camphor content, these are the classic, country-garden types with demure, bobbing heads. Buy from a specialist lavender or herb grower and check they have not been sprayed.

Once established, a lavender plant is hard to kill as long as it has light, sandy, well-drained soil (line the hole with fine gravel before planting) and plenty of sun. It should be cut back hard after flowering in late summer but without actually going into the old wood or ridding it of all green growth; reducing the size of the plant by about 50 per cent is ideal.

STRAWBERRIES WITH LAVENDER AND HONEY

500g strawberries

2 tsp lemon juice

1 tbsp clear honey

20 tender young lavender leaves, roughly chopped

4 lavender flowerheads, to finish

Honey is a great partner to lavender, and the two together give a lovely subtle perfume to sweet summer strawberries. You could do the same with dessert gooseberries, halved, stoned cherries, or slices of peach or nectarine. Serves 4

Hull the strawberries then halve them, or, if very big, cut into 5–6mm slices. Place them in a medium bowl with the lemon juice. Add the honey (dip the tablespoon in hot water before measuring it out, so it slips off easily). Now add the chopped lavender leaves and stir very gently. Cover and place in a cool place to macerate for a couple of hours.

When ready to serve, spoon the strawberries into wide-necked wine glasses and serve topped with a lavender flowerhead.

Leek

Mark Diacono

LATIN NAME
Allium porrum

SEASONALITY
September/October–May;
baby leeks from July

This relatively unassuming member of the onion family carries none of the attack of onion, nor the bite of garlic. But what these pale cylinders have in spades is gentle sweetness and savoury depth; they're all sophistication and friendliness, the most warming member of the allium clan.

Leeks have a long and illustrious history. Early forms of the vegetable were enjoyed in ancient Egypt, Greece and Rome, where they were prized for their relative subtlety. No one knows exactly when the leek found its way to our shores but we have certainly been enjoying them for hundreds of years. And, of course, they have a particular association with Wales. The origins of this pairing are now lost in the mists of time, but there are stories that describe sixth- or seventh-century Welsh soldiers engaging in battle with the Saxons in a field full of leeks, and wearing leeks in their hats to identify each other. Sadly, there is no hard evidence to corroborate this – and the Old English word *leac* could signify any member of the allium family – but it's an enticing legend all the same.

The leek is a winter vegetable, one that helps to fill that cold and hungry gap, especially heading into spring, when so little is around. It grows readily in our climate and British leeks are gloriously good from the first frosts in November through to April. If you frequent a local farm shop, or have a veg box delivered, leeks will be a familiar sight in the winter. And you never need wonder what on earth you're going to do with them: like all alliums, they're terrifically versatile.

The sweetest and tastiest leeks are slender; 3–3.5cm diameter is ideal. Preparation is simple but careful washing is important. Leeks usually come with soil between their rings of flesh, deposited there by the rain and wind as they grow. A grain of grit can really spoil the otherwise silky loveliness of this vegetable, so take the time to clean them. Slice off the base of the leek, with its roots, chop off the green leaves, then make a lengthways cut into the heart of the leek, so it's split from top to bottom but not cut in half. Submerge in a bowl of water and agitate gently – a little persuasion with your fingers will release any soil and grit. Shake the leeks dry.

Leeks are usually then best sliced into slim discs, ready to be softened in butter or oil. Some people prefer their leeks chunky, however, where the smaller surface area leads to less caramelisation and a slightly milder, softer flavour. Don't discard the base and green leaves – both are valuable for the grassy onion flavour they release when simmered in a stock or placed in a chicken's cavity with a lemon before roasting.

Leeks are nearly always best when softened gently over a low heat. They don't crisp in quite the same delicious way as onions, and can be tough if they're allowed to brown. Once cooked, and given just a coat of dairy (butter, cream, cheese), leeks are quite self-sufficient as a main course. Complex and satisfying in themselves, they need only some good bread on the side. But leeks are generous in their friendships with other ingredients. Herbs as bold as thyme or as subtle as chervil, salty capers or acidic lemon, comparatively bland potatoes – all marry with leeks beautifully.

This potato-leek friendship is never finer than in a classic leek and potato soup (or *vichyssoise*). The secret of a silky finish is to ease back on the potato and to not cook it for too long. And if the leeks are fresh, the lightest of stocks will suffice – you don't want to overpower those lovely, earthy flavours. For a delightful variation, try celeriac in place of the potatoes: its gentle, rooty bitterness sits perfectly with the sweetness and oniony edge of the leek. A small glass of white wine added during simmering ties the flavours together nicely.

L

And, while we're on the subject of leeks and alcohol: a couple of finely shredded leeks, softened in butter with a clove or two of chopped garlic, and a generous glass of cider or white wine, is about the best base over which to steam mussels that I can think of. A slick of double cream when it's all cooked, and the addition of generous amounts of parsley, and you have one of *the* great lunches.

Cheesy leeks on toast is another fantastic lunch. And this versatile vegetable is a wonderful addition to all manner of soups, risottos and pies (especially with chicken).

If you can find them (or grow your own), baby leeks are extraordinary. Their diminutive size means they take comparatively little time from sowing to harvest – perhaps 4 months – and are in season from July until spring. Looking like plump spring onions, they have that characteristically fabulous, sweet onion flavour. Their size makes them easy to cook quickly on the barbecue or griddle, so they are the exception to the cook-leeks-gently rule. Lightly olive-oiled, infant leeks will turn sweet, smoky and lightly charred in a few minutes, their insides steamed to melting perfection. They are good enough to enjoy on their own in a roll with mayo and a dash of chilli sauce. But next to meat – pork in particular – they are heavenly.

Leeks are relatively expensive to buy, but they are easy to grow. Start them under cover in a length of guttering or a seed tray, sown 3cm apart, and plant out 3 months later, 20cm or so from their neighbour (or just 3cm for baby leeks). Make a hole for each seedling with a pencil, and pop the young plant in but don't back-fill – the seedling should be loose in the hole. Water well. With a combination of early, mid-season and late varieties, you can be in home-grown leeks from September to spring. Any left to flower will look incredible, draw insects to your garden and provide you with seed for the next year.

LEEK AND POTATO GRATIN

30g butter

1 tbsp olive or rapeseed oil

500g potatoes, peeled and cut into 2–3cm cubes

2–3 medium leeks, trimmed, washed and sliced into 1cm rounds

Leaves from a couple of sprigs of thyme

1 tbsp plain flour

250ml veg stock

150ml double cream

1 tsp Dijon or grainy mustard

FOR THE TOPPING

2 handfuls of coarse white breadcrumbs

25g grated Cheddar or other hard flavoursome cheese

Sea salt and black pepper

The familiar combination that works so well in soup is arguably even better in this gratin. Dish up as a comforting autumn or winter supper, or as a side to accompany roast chicken. Serves 2–3 as a supper, 4 as a side dish

Preheat the oven to 180°C/Fan 160°C/Gas 4.

Heat a large, heavy-based pan (with a lid) over a medium heat and add the butter and oil. When bubbling, add the potatoes, leeks and thyme, season well with salt and pepper and give it all a good stir. Put the lid on the pan, reduce the heat to medium-low and sweat the veg for about 10 minutes until the leeks are soft and the potatoes are just beginning to tenderise.

Stir in the flour and cook for another minute. Add the stock, cream and mustard, stirring well so the flour is smoothly combined, and bring back to a simmer. Season if necessary with a little more salt and pepper, then take off the heat.

Tip the mixture into a shallow ovenproof dish, level it off, then sprinkle the breadcrumbs and grated cheese evenly over the top. Bake for 20 minutes or until the top is golden and tempting. Leave to stand for 10 minutes before serving.

Lemon

Gill Meller

LATIN NAME
Citrus limon

SEASONALITY
Available all year round; Italian lemons at their best March–July

MORE RECIPES
Spring greens with lemon and garlic (page 601); Spiced couscous with lemon and sultanas (page 202); Smashed chickpeas with preserved lemon and red onion (page 165); Shrimps on sourdough with paprika and lemon (page 583); Grilled langoustine with lemon and parsley butter (page 339); Turbot with white wine, lemon zest and thyme (page 648); Lemon-cured herring (page 310); Roast gurnard with pepper, lemon, thyme and chilli (page 292); Pheasant with olives and preserved lemons (page 414); North African shepherd's pie (page 335); Bay-spiked pears with shallots and lemon (page 53); Candied orange and lemon peel (page 459)

SOURCING
natoora.co.uk (for unwaxed Italian lemons)

This luscious, sour fruit originated in India (still the largest producer), reaching the West around two thousand years ago. Lemons have come to influence the cooking in almost every part of the world and they are now grown in Asia, the Americas, Africa and the Med. Second only to salt and pepper, they are indispensable in the kitchen.

The 'Eureka' is the standard supermarket lemon that we are all familiar with. It's easy to grow all year round and its robust nature means it stores well once harvested. But the most prized lemons are those that have a touch more sweetness, giving them a much gentler flavour. Lovely generous scented lemons come from Italy – from the sun-scorched groves of Sicily, Sorrento and the Amalfi coast. The peel from these fruits is used to infuse the liqueur known as limoncello.

In California, meanwhile, streets are lined with trees heaving with wonderful little 'Meyer' lemons. This small, thin-skinned variety, the offspring of a standard lemon and a mandarin, is relatively sweet and very aromatic. Sadly, they don't keep or travel well so you are unlikely to come across them, but if you do, grab them – they are wonderful for pickling or making marmalade.

Although lemons keep well, their shelf-life is prolonged further by waxing. Paradoxically, the fruit's natural wax is washed off first, before the artificial one is applied. Waxing stops the lemon drying out, shrinking or wrinkling and gives them an appealing shine. In many cases, the wax is polyethylene-based. Alternatively, it is based on shellac, a resin secreted by the lac bug, processed, liquefied and sprayed directly on to the fruit. If you intend to make the most of your lemons, which means using the lovely zest as well as the juice, then go for unwaxed fruit. Choosing organic is one way to ensure a lemon is wax-free, although you can buy conventionally grown unwaxed fruit. If waxed fruit is the only option, you can remove the wax yourself by dipping the fruit in hot water and giving it a firm rub.

Even wax-free lemons should look good: plump, heavy and firm, with a shine from their own natural wax. Avoid lemons with wrinkled or dull skin, or any with soft or hard patches. Once mould sets into a lemon, it will spread through your fruit bowl like wildfire, so check frequently for spoiling fruits.

Every part of a lemon is useful, but it's the juice we utilise the most. Even in tiny quantities, it has the capacity to bring out the flavour in dishes without making them taste lemony. Very often, it's the final splash of lemon juice that brings a dish together, highlighting the flavours beautifully. The sharpness of lemon also cuts the richness of oils and fats and balances the intense sweetness of sugars, honeys and syrups. The juice is acidic enough to tenderise meat by denaturing the long protein strands in the muscle. When applied to raw fish, it 'cooks' it, firming the texture and making the translucent flesh opaque.

If an intense lemon flavour is required in a dish – a curd, perhaps, or a cake – then the zest, or skin, must be called into play. This is packed with natural oils, intensely fragrant and wonderfully aromatic. It's where the real lemon flavour resides. The oil is held within the skin and is best released with a fine grater or very sharp little knife.

Underneath the skin is the softer, slightly spongy white pith. This is exceptionally bitter, which is why it is generally removed. But combined with lots of sugar, as in candied peel (see page 459), or salt, as in preserved lemons (see overleaf), it can be wonderful. The pith is also rich in pectin.

Despite their sourness, lemons do contain some sugars. You can capitalise on this by caramelising the fruit. Heat a little oil in a non-stick frying pan, then add some

halved lemons, cut side down. Fry them until golden and charred, about 5 minutes. Serve with fish or root veg, squeezing over the gorgeous bittersweet juice.

Preserved whole lemons – pickled and lightly fermented in salt and their own juices – are a unique and fabulous ingredient, showcasing the entire fruit in a feast of bitter, sour, salty and sweet flavour. A key ingredient in North African cooking, the lemons are softened and mellowed both in texture and flavour by the process. Traditionally, it's just the salted rind that's used, chopped in tagines and veg dishes, with the soft, salty scooped-out pulp being discarded. But you can use both – try puréeing the pulp in a soup or dip, or just chopping preserved lemons entire for a rice dish (like the one on page 535).

Making your own preserved lemons is simple. Cut 8 lemons into quarters, top to toe, but without going all the way through the fruit, so the lemon is still joined at the base and the top. Pack fine sea salt into the cuts and squash the salt-packed lemons into a large preserving jar. Seal the jar and leave for a couple of days to allow the salt to draw out the juice. Squeeze more fresh lemon juice over so that the fruit is submerged. Seal it again and store for at least a month before using, turning the jar upside down and back again every now and then. Once opened, keep in the fridge.

And for old-fashioned lemonade, the most refreshing of all summer drinks, pare or grate the zest from 3 lemons and put into a large jug with 100g caster sugar. Pour over 1 litre of boiling water, stir, then leave until cool. Add the squeezed-out juice of 6 lemons, then strain into a clean jug and chill before serving, straight up or slightly diluted, with ice and more lemon slices.

LEMON, HONEY AND COURGETTE CAKE

This lovely, light, fat-free lemony bake is sweetened with honey and made moist with fresh courgette. It's gluten-free too (as long as your baking powder doesn't contain gluten). Makes 8–10 slices

100g fine (not quick-cook) polenta or cornmeal

100g ground almonds

2 tsp baking powder

A pinch of salt

100g clear honey

3 medium eggs

200g peeled and finely grated courgette (1 medium-large)

Finely grated zest of 2 lemons

1 tsp finely chopped thyme (optional)

TO FINISH

50g clear honey

Juice of 2 lemons

Preheat the oven to 180°C/Fan 160°C/Gas 4. Line a 20cm round, deep cake tin with baking parchment.

Put the polenta, ground almonds, baking powder and salt into a bowl and mix well.

Place the honey and eggs in a large bowl or a free-standing mixer bowl. Using a hand-held electric whisk, or the mixer, whisk for about 3 minutes until the mixture is thick, pale and foamy and at least doubled in volume.

Using a spatula or large metal spoon, carefully fold the polenta and almond mix into the egg mix. Add the grated courgette, lemon zest, and thyme if using, and gently fold these in too.

Gently pour the mixture into the prepared tin and bake for 25–30 minutes or until the cake is lightly golden and a skewer inserted into the centre comes out clean.

Meanwhile, whisk together the honey and lemon juice. As you take the cake out of the oven, pierce the surface all over with a fine skewer or toothpick, then carefully trickle the lemony honey mix over it. Leave to cool before removing from the tin.

Lemon verbena

Pam Corbin

LATIN NAME
Aloysia triphylla

ALSO KNOWN AS
Lemon beebrush

SEASONALITY
May–October

The elegant, lanceolate leaves of lemon verbena are heady with an exquisite citrus-floral scent. It's hardly surprising the perfume industry values it almost as highly as we do.

This is one herb you definitely need to grow yourself because you won't find it in the shops – and it will reward you with refreshing notes to perfume a profusion of dishes and thirst-quenching drinks. A deciduous perennial, lemon verbena loves sun and shelter: a south- or west-facing situation is ideal. The glossy, shapely foliage is late to show, appearing in early summer, with the delicate, pale lilac flowers following a little later.

This is a pungent herb. It contains much more of the lemony tasting compound citral than you find in an actual lemon. Sometimes you only need to infuse freshly cut verbena leaves in liquid to enjoy their flavour. To make a soothing herbal tea, brew 2 or 3 leaves – alone, or with a sprig of mint in the cup. Scale up the quantities to form the base of a vibrant verbena cordial. Or steep verbena in warm milk or cream to make fragrant crème brûlées and ice cream (1 leafy sprig will suffice for 500ml).

The scented leaves can be pummelled with a pestle and mortar, then added to vinegar and salad dressings. Or you can chop them finely and mix them into stuffings for chicken and pork, or fold them into couscous or grain dishes. Alternatively, chopped and frozen into ice cubes, they will uplift soft drinks and cocktails.

The leaves are waxy and can be slightly tough, so use a sharp, heavy knife to deal with them efficiently. Their robust quality makes them the ideal mould for chocolate leaves. Carefully coat the underside of each leaf thickly and evenly with melted chocolate, then place on baking parchment to set, before peeling off the leaf to reveal a perfect chocolate specimen.

The leaves are also easy to dry, and retain their gorgeous fragrance well. Pick stems on a sunny day, lay them on a wire rack and dry in an airing cupboard or very low oven. Use to make tisanes or crumble and add to caster sugar for cake-baking.

LEMON VERBENA PILAF

1 tbsp olive or rapeseed oil

1 large garlic clove, grated

1 tsp ground coriander

1 tsp ground turmeric

200g basmati rice, well rinsed and drained

500ml light veg stock

12 lemon verbena leaves

1 red onion

A knob of butter

Sea salt and black pepper

This fragrant, lemony rice is beautiful with a Thai green curry but also good on its own.
Serves 4 as a side dish

Heat the oil in a medium saucepan over a medium heat. Add the garlic, coriander and turmeric with a twist each of salt and pepper, and fry gently, stirring, for about 30 seconds. Add the rice, stir well and cook for another 2 minutes.

Add the stock and verbena leaves and bring to a simmer. Reduce the heat, put the lid on the pan and cook gently for 15–18 minutes until the rice is tender and the stock has been absorbed.

Remove the pan from the heat, fluff the rice up with a fork, then replace the lid and let the pilaf sit for 10 minutes.

Meanwhile, thinly slice the red onion from root to tip. Heat a small knob of butter in a medium frying pan over a medium heat. Add the sliced onion and fry for 8–10 minutes, stirring regularly, until just starting to crisp.

Heap the rice into a warmed serving dish (you can leave the lemon verbena in it but you probably won't want to actually eat the leaves, as they are quite tough). Top with the fried onion and serve.

Lemongrass

Tim Maddams

LATIN NAME
Cymbopogon citratus

ALSO KNOWN AS
Citronella

SEASONALITY
Home-grown lemongrass
best May–October

MORE RECIPES
Velvet crab curry (page 211)

The moment you get a whiff of lemongrass, you know a treat is in store. Simply bashing up one of the fibrous stems is enough to get the mouth watering: it's incredibly lemony. That pungent aroma comes from citral, which is also found in lemon verbena, coriander and ginger. In the mouth, lemongrass has a palate-teasing friskiness but also a delicate earthiness that underlies the citrus zing.

This perennial grass is native to the tropics and Australia, and strongly associated with the cooking of Thailand, Malaysia and Indonesia. But these days it is used all over the world and not just as an ingredient. The oil of the plant is a natural fungicide, a pesticide (hence its most common use – citronella candles) and a perfume. It's even employed to trick bees into swarming in a specific place because it closely approximates a bee pheromone.

As soon as you start cutting lemongrass, you will discover that it is very fibrous. It will stay that way no matter how long you cook it. You can leave the stalks whole and just bruise or bash them so they can be easily removed from the finished dish. Alternatively, and for a stronger hit of flavour, peel off the tough 2 or 3 outer layers of the stem (it might seem like you're losing a lot, but these trimmings can be used in infusions) then slice, chop or pound the tender inner lemongrass very finely.

There are many culinary uses for lemongrass. I think its most pleasing role is the traditional one: in curries and spicy broths. It is often chopped and pounded into complex, multi-layered Thai and Malay curry pastes but you don't have to go to quite so much trouble: finely sliced or minced, it is delicious paired with just a few pungent bedfellows, such as cumin, coriander (seed, leaf and root), chilli and garlic. Fry the mix gently, add coconut milk and/or stock, season with a whisper of salty fish sauce and you have the base for a simple curry, a rich, noodly laksa or an Asian-inspired dish of steamed mussels or clams. You can mix those aromatics into soft butter too, to dot over fish or shellfish before grilling, making the most of lemongrass' wonderful affinity with seafood.

Lemongrass stems can also be infused into tea, into custard for making ice cream, or into a syrup to flavour cakes. And finely chopped lemongrass is a wonderful way to scent barbecue marinades and dipping sauces.

As with all aromatics, success with lemongrass lies in balancing it with other ingredients. To understand its flavour, make a simple infusion by pouring boiling water over a few slices of lemongrass, then try adding sugar or salt, and see how the flavour changes, then add a little chilli and taste again to appreciate its full potential.

Lemongrass can be bought dried and chopped but this rather sawdust-like form is best avoided. Fresh is the way to go. Don't worry too much if the stems look a little woody, they should still be tender within.

You can get most shop-bought stems of lemongrass to sprout roots by simply leaving them in a glass of water. Grow them on in a pot and you will be able to harvest the fresh leaves, which are excellent.

FRAGRANT BEEF CURRY

Loosely based on an Indonesian rendang (but much quicker) this curry is fragrant with lemongrass as well as garlic and ginger, and hot with chilli. You can adjust the heat with more or less chilli, to taste. Check the heat of your chillies first (see page 170), before you start cooking. This curry is also very good made with rose veal. Serves 4

To prepare the spice paste, put all the ingredients into a food processor, add 50ml water and blitz to a fine paste. (If you prefer, you can pound the ingredients thoroughly using a large pestle and mortar.)

To make the curry, heat the oil in a large saucepan over a medium-low heat. Add the spice paste and the cardamom pods and cook gently for 3–4 minutes, until fragrant, stirring so the paste does not catch. Add the coconut milk, tamarind paste, sugar, some salt and pepper and 100ml water. Simmer gently for 5 minutes.

Add the beans and simmer, stirring now and again, for another 10 minutes or so, until they are approaching tenderness.

Meanwhile, heat a frying pan over a medium-high heat and add a little oil. Season the steak strips, add to the pan and fry quickly for 1–2 minutes, until browned: they should be still a little rare in the middle.

Add the beef to the sauce and simmer for a further 5 minutes. Meanwhile, if using tomatoes, halve, deseed and cut into strips. Take the curry off the heat and add the fresh coriander and tomato strips, if using. Serve with rice.

2 tbsp rapeseed or coconut oil, plus a little extra for the beef

6 cardamom pods, bashed

400ml coconut milk

1 tbsp tamarind paste

1 tbsp brown sugar

100g French beans, trimmed and cut in half

800g top rump or frying steak, cut into thin strips

Sea salt and black pepper

FOR THE SPICE PASTE

1–3 bird's eye chillies, roughly chopped

3 shallots, roughly chopped

4 large garlic cloves, roughly chopped

30g root ginger, roughly chopped

3 lemongrass stems, tough outer layers removed, finely chopped

6 kaffir lime leaves, shredded if fresh, crumbled if dry (or the zest and juice of 1 lime)

2 tsp garam masala

2 tsp ground coriander

2 tsp ground turmeric

½ tsp ground cinnamon

2 tbsp rapeseed or virgin coconut oil

TO FINISH

3 medium tomatoes (optional)

Coriander leaves

Lentils

Gill Meller

LATIN NAME
Lens culinaris

MORE RECIPES
Mujadara (page 104); Dhal with crispy seaweed (page 579); Mozzarella with nettles and lentils (page 390); Roasted haggis, swede and kale salad (page 295)

Lentils are a fantastic ingredient. With a whopping 25 per cent protein, these little pulses boast a range of earthy flavours – not strong, but distinct – and partner a huge range of other ingredients beautifully too. They have the advantage over other pulses that they are quick to cook. If prepared properly and dressed the right way, they can form the basis for a multitude of deeply satisfying dishes.

Lentils are legumes and like their relatives, beans and peas, they grow in pods. They are harvested when the pods are already dry and the lentils hard (though some are dried further once picked). This is the form we buy them in – which means they keep well for ages. You can buy ready-cooked lentils in cans or vac-packs too. But as dried lentils take so little time and effort to cook, and since freshly cooked lentils absorb the flavours of dressings and seasonings so well, they don't offer a huge benefit. Lentils, unlike dried beans, do not require pre-soaking. It's always worth giving them a thorough rinse in a sieve, but then they can go straight into the pot.

There are many different types of lentil, but the most prized are the very small, firm and slightly round variety grown in the volcanic soils of Le Puy in Southwest France, and around Castelluccio in Umbria, Italy. However, Puy-style lentils are grown elsewhere and can be excellent: they are often labelled as 'French green lentils' or *lentilles vertes*.

Puy (and similar) lentils have a wonderful creamy, almost peppery earthiness. As well as using them to add protein, nutty texture and subtle substance to vegetable dishes and salads, they make a really good simple accompaniment to fish or meat.

To cook them as a side dish, put the rinsed lentils in a pan, cover with water, bring up to a simmer, then drain to get rid of the slightly scummy water (the 'scum' is just protein from the lentils, so you can skip this step if you're pushed for time). Cover with fresh water and add a few stock veg (roughly chunked carrots, onion and/or celery), a couple of bay leaves, some parsley stalks if you have any and perhaps a couple of bashed garlic cloves. Bring back to a simmer and cook for 10–15 minutes, until tender but with a slight bite, then drain. It's quite easy to overcook Puy-style lentils – and different batches do vary – so start checking early.

Dress the lentils while they are still warm – this will increase their absorption of the flavours. To enhance their nuttiness, use a nice peppery extra virgin olive oil, plus a dash of something acidic such as cider vinegar or lemon juice to bring out their hidden notes and, of course, season with plenty of salt and pepper. Or toss lentils with a mustardy dressing, chopped parsley and shallots – a great combination with fried mackerel, lamb, beef or game. For an exceptional treat, try lentils and meat with a piquant salsa verde.

In the autumn, try a warm salad of roasted parsnips, chorizo, kale and lentils. I even use Puy-style lentils in Asian-inspired dishes such as stir-fries or salads. Try combining them with cashew nuts, then dressing with chilli, garlic and tamari and finishing with lime juice and coriander. Another good trick with cooked Puy-style lentils is to fry them until light and crisp (see recipe overleaf).

Puy or green lentils are great to sprout at home. Put them in a Kilner jar, soak overnight, drain and then let them sit in the jar, covered by a piece of cloth rather than a lid. Rinse with fresh water morning and night for 4–5 days. Quite quickly, these dormant and dry pulses sprout sudden shoots of life. When they have 2cm tails, rinse and store in the fridge for up to 5 days. Use sprouted lentils raw to add character to salads, sandwiches or stir-fries, or to finish soups.

Where Puy lentils are prized for holding their shape, red lentils are appreciated for precisely the opposite quality. These bright orange pulses are hulled and split so they collapse easily into a fluffy, golden purée, which makes them great in soups, where they give a comforting thickness, and essential for Indian dhals.

For a filling lentil soup, fry onions and tomatoes with cumin, coriander seed and chilli, then add red lentils and stock and simmer for 25 minutes or so. You can either purée the soup or leave it coarsely textured. Finish with a few scraps of fried ham or spoonfuls of thick natural yoghurt, or a sprinkle of smoked paprika and olive oil.

Lagging behind Puy-style and red lentils in the popularity stakes, but nevertheless very respectable and economical ingredients, are plain brown or green lentils. These are slightly larger and flatter than Puys, with a thinner skin. They don't collapse like a red lentil, but cook to a greater softness than Puys, and have a less distinctive flavour. They're exactly what you want, however, in a big lentil bake or curry.

Split peas closely resemble lentils. Yellow or green in colour, they are derived from the same type of pea that we eat green and fresh (although eating them as a dried pulse is a much older practice). Once dried, the skins are removed and the two halves of the seed divide. They behave like lentils too: you don't need to soak them, and they soften to the point of collapse when cooked.

CRISPY LENTIL AND ROASTED SQUASH SALAD WITH SALSA VERDE

1 squash, such as butternut or onion (about 1kg)

2 garlic cloves, bashed

4 sprigs of rosemary

3 tbsp olive or rapeseed oil

150g cooked Puy (or similar) lentils

Sea salt and black pepper

FOR THE SALSA VERDE

1 small garlic clove

25g picked parsley leaves

2 anchovy fillets in oil

2 tsp capers, rinsed

1 tsp English or Dijon mustard

2 tsp lemon juice

4 tbsp extra virgin olive oil

Crisp, nutty, fried Puy lentils complement tender roasted squash beautifully. You can use sweet potato here in place of squash, and embellish this lovely autumn salad further with some crisp-fried leftover lamb, chicken or ham. In the spring or summer, the crisp lentils and salsa verde go beautifully with some blanched or roasted broccoli. Serves 4

Preheat the oven to 190°C/Fan 170°C/Gas 5.

Halve the squash and scoop out the seeds. Place the squash halves, cut side up, in a roasting tin. Place a bashed garlic clove and a couple of torn rosemary sprigs in each squash-half hollow. Season the squash with salt and pepper and trickle over 1 tbsp oil. Roast for 45–50 minutes or until the flesh is lovely and tender.

Meanwhile, make the salsa verde. Finely chop the garlic on a large board. Add the parsley, anchovies and capers and chop them all together until well mixed and fairly fine in texture. Transfer to a bowl and mix in the mustard, lemon juice, some black pepper and enough extra virgin olive oil to give a spoonable consistency. As you add these last ingredients, taste and tweak the mixture until you are happy with the balance of flavours.

Place a large non-stick frying pan over a medium-high heat. Add the remaining 2 tbsp olive or rapeseed oil, followed by the lentils. Fry, tossing regularly, for 10–12 minutes or until the lentils are really crisp (they will shrink too). Season well with salt and pepper.

Peel the warm, cooked squash (or just scoop the tender flesh out of the skin). Cut into bite-sized pieces and tip into a large serving bowl or divide between individual bowls. Scatter over the lentils, then spoon over the salsa verde. Serve straight away.

Lettuce

Mark Diacono

LATIN NAME
Lactuca sativa

SEASONALITY
Main season May–October but
lettuce can be grown in the
British Isles all year round

MORE RECIPES
Nasturtium and pink
peppercorn soup (page 401);
Little Gem with crushed broad
beans and Parmesan (page 433);
Curried new potatoes, red onion
and lettuce (page 226); Spider
crab salad (page 208); Chicken
and blueberry salad with
coriander dressing (page 77)

The selection of lettuce in our shops and markets is ever-increasing. And, of course, if you grow your own lettuce, you'll have an even greater range of flavours, colours and textures to call on.

There are two main types of lettuce. Most prevalent are those that form definite heads (firm, at least in the centre). Among the best-known 'heading' types are the Romaine (or Cos) varieties, which can be tall and elegant, or quite compact, as with 'Little Gem'. Romaines hold a dressing exceptionally well, making them great salad all-rounders, whether in a simply dressed leaf-fest, or a more substantial affair such as a classic Caesar or Niçoise.

Crispheads (also heading types) are firm and round, and often pale or even white in the centre. Moist, crisp and crunchy, they give a refreshing bite to a salad. 'Iceberg' is the ubiquitous crisphead but there are more exciting examples. 'Reine de Glace' is the queen – a spike-edged leaf with elegance, lots of flavour and a refined texture. You may find it in a box scheme or market, or you could try growing some yourself.

Butterheads (pictured left) are altogether more relaxed, with thin, almost oily leaves. These are the old-fashioned lettuce we used to eat with tomatoes and salad cream. They have been superseded to a large extent by the crunchy and the crisp, but try a tender butterhead and you'll be reminded how lovely and flavoursome they can be. 'Buttercrunch' (old-school green in colour) and the multicoloured 'Marvel of Four Seasons' are the stand-out butterheads. Soft and, yes, buttery, they are fabulous dressed only in good olive oil and salt.

The second main category of lettuce comprises those with loose leaves. Far too idle to create a centre, these loll about in the sun, their often deeply lobed leaves moving with the wind. Don't let that fool you: the likes of 'Lollo Rosso' and green (or red) 'Oak Leaf' are delicious and come with a certain delicacy of texture.

The main British lettuce season runs from mid-May until October, though different varieties and protected growing – using fleece or polytunnels – can extend the season.

Whichever lettuce you are using, the importance of the dressing is hard to overstate. Few lettuces have a full-on flavour. They are more often subtle, even borderline bland, but with the right dressing – be it a classic vinaigrette, a honey-mustard dressing or a lively blue cheese and orange mix – the leaves are taken in quite different directions.

The very best, sweetest lettuce should be eaten raw as soon after harvest as possible, though kept in the bottom of the fridge, its lifespan can be extended by a few days. But lettuce can be cooked successfully too, which is a good option if it's a little past its best, or you have a glut on your hands.

Romaine (or Cos) varieties are the ones for griddling or barbecuing, Little Gems especially. Their substantial physique stands up to the intense heat. Halve the whole lettuce lengthways, coat in a slick of olive oil and sear on a griddle or over charcoal until they start to blacken. Plenty of salt and pepper is all they need to become a great snack or side dish.

The more flavoursome lettuces – often the loose-leaved ones – make superb soups. For the simplest of quick lunches, soften a handful of chopped spring onions in a little butter, then add 3 shredded lettuces and a couple of handfuls of frozen peas and cover with 400ml light stock (chicken or vegetable). Bring to the boil, simmer for 5 minutes and then purée in a blender. Season and reheat to serve. For a touch more refinement, top with a few slices of lightly fried chorizo, and/or add a little lovage to the spring onions, or sprinkle with a little celery salt.

Lettuce also works wonderfully as a kind of light green, where you might otherwise use, say, chard or spinach. It can be used to finish a curry, for example, and firm heads can be quartered, lightly cooked, then baked with onions and cheese in a savoury tart. Lettuce makes a fabulous braised side dish with peas and shallots (*petits pois à la française*) too, and it's one of my favourite ingredients in a summer risotto. You can even use flavoursome butterheads to make a light pesto.

Lettuce is easy to grow. Sow seed outside from March, or a month earlier under cover, in modules, then plant out when a few centimetres tall. Lettuce likes cool temperatures to germinate, so in summer either sow direct in shade or a cool indoor spot. As well as being uprooted entirely, once they've grown to full size, many lettuces can be cut (or plucked), leaf by leaf, 5cm or so above ground, leaving the base and roots to drive new growth.

This cut-and-come-again method gives you maximum return from your seeds, effort and space and it means you can pretty much create your own salad bag, using whichever varieties you like. Mix your 'Australian Yellow Leaf' (large, gorgeous, bright green/yellow crinkled leaves with a good crunch and sweet flavour) with a little 'Really Red Deer Tongue' (deep red-black and nutty), or your 'Flashy Butter Oak' (splashes of deep red on pale green), with the red/purple, crisp Romaine leaves of 'Devil's Tongue'. They go as well together in the kitchen as they do in the garden.

LETTUCE AND SPRING ONION TARTE TATIN

Dense, sweet Little Gem lettuces work well in this radical departure from the classic tarte tatin. Serves 4

250g ready-made puff pastry or home-made rough puff pastry (see page 447)

3 Little Gem lettuces (about 250g)

20g butter

1 tbsp cider vinegar

30g caster sugar

2 garlic cloves, thinly sliced

Leaves from 1 sprig of thyme

About 100g spring onions, trimmed and cut into 2–3cm pieces

Sea salt and black pepper

TO SERVE (OPTIONAL)

75g soft ewe's or goat's cheese, sliced or crumbled

1 tbsp chopped parsley

1 tbsp chopped mint

Juice of ½ lemon

1 tbsp extra virgin olive oil

Preheat the oven to 200°C/Fan 180°C/Gas 6.

If the pastry is not already rolled, roll it out to a 4–5mm thickness. Invert a 20cm non-stick ovenproof frying pan or tarte tatin dish on the pastry and cut out a circle to fit the top of the pan. Put the pastry in the fridge to rest.

Slice the lettuces in half lengthways and trim back the stalks to the base of the leaves.

Put the frying pan or tarte tatin dish over a medium heat and add the butter and cider vinegar. Once the butter has melted, sprinkle over the sugar and cook for 3–4 minutes, shaking the pan now and then as it bubbles, until the mix starts to turn golden brown. Remove from the heat.

Sprinkle the garlic slices and thyme leaves over the buttery caramel in the pan. Now add the lettuce halves, cut side down, fanning them out in a circle with the hearts towards the middle. Fill in the gaps between the lettuces with the cut spring onions. Season with salt and pepper.

Drape the circle of puff pastry over the top of the veg and tuck in the edges around the lettuce. Prick the pastry surface all over with a fork and bake for about 30 minutes, until it is golden brown.

Leave the tart to cool slightly in the pan for 5–10 minutes, then invert a plate over the top, hold the plate and pan firmly together and turn over, so the tart is unmoulded on to the plate. Pour any juices left in the pan back over the tart, along with any sticky bits that have adhered to the pan.

Serve the tarte just like this or, to make even more of a meal of it, top it with some cheese, chopped parsley and mint, a squeeze of lemon juice and a trickle of extra virgin olive oil.

Lime

Nikki Duffy

LATIN NAME
Tahiti lime: *Citrus latifolia*.
Key lime: *Citrus aurantifolia*.
Kaffir lime: *Citrus hystrix*

ALSO KNOWN AS
Persian lime (Tahiti lime)

SOURCING
citruscentre.co.uk (for British-
grown kaffir lime leaves);
kaffirlimes.co.uk (for fresh
leaves and fruit)

Significantly sharper than lemon, lime is a lesson in the transformative power of acidity. Thriving best in hotter, steamier conditions than their big yellow cousins, limes are used in the cooking of many tropical countries, where the refreshing effect of their aromatic sourness is particularly appreciated.

Fruits with minimal acidity tend to disappoint, and no more so than the lime. The acid-less nature of a breed known as the 'Palestine Sweet' lime makes them easy to consume in quantity. The British navy exploited this in years gone by, feeding them to its 'limey' sailors in order to ward off scurvy, but the flavour is insipid.

The common-or-garden supermarket lime is the 'Tahiti'. Big, juicy and seedless, this is the one to juice into a lusciously cooling minty mojito, to squeeze over perfectly ripe papaya flesh or sprinkle into a banana smoothie. In fact, lime juice has a wonderful seasoning effect on all very sweet fruits: it's lovely with ripe strawberries, and whole lime segments can be mingled with mango in a salad. Lime combines beautifully with coconut in any number of cakes and cookies and is a surprisingly good playmate for dark chocolate too.

This citric powerhouse is also a great balancer in savoury dishes. In the raw fish dish ceviche, it effectively cures the fish. It is also lovely tossed – in slivers – through a salad of shaved fennel to serve alongside smoky barbecued fish. Alternatively, beat the zest, along with garlic and chilli, into butter to be melted on steak or chicken, or hot cobs of corn.

The 'Key' lime (also known as the West Indian lime) is very small – not much bigger than a walnut – and tart, with a spicy quality. Their sharp flavour is famously used to cut through all the sugar, condensed milk and egg yolk in a classic key lime

pie (although you can use ordinary limes for this) and their aromatic character was the original basis for the iconic Rose's lime juice and marmalade. They are also *de rigueur* in a good rum punch. I've never found key limes for sale in the UK but you can buy the plants and raise them yourself.

The kaffir lime, also called the makrut lime, is another hard-to-find speciality. It has an intensely floral, perfumed flavour – less fresh and bright than a standard Tahiti lime. The fruit and leaves are chock-full of fragrant essential oils and you will see them ooze from the skin if you squeeze it. The leaves, with their distinctive, figure-of-eight shape (two lobes on one stalk), prevail in authentic Thai and Laotian cooking. In fact, some would say that if you don't make your Thai curry with fresh kaffir lime leaves, then it's not really a Thai curry at all. Unfortunately, fresh kaffir lime leaves are almost impossible to find in the UK. You can buy them dried but these are a poor substitute – worth using, but only just.

You can order kaffir lime leaves 'fresh' from online specialists but, if they are imported (as most are), they will have been previously frozen in order to meet strict EU regulations (freezing kills off bugs and bacteria that could infest other plants). They can still be good but often lack the verve of the freshly picked leaves. Luckily, there are a few growers producing properly fresh kaffir lime leaves in the UK. Sometimes these find their way into supermarkets, but your best bet is to buy direct from a specialist nursery. One or two growers also sell the fruit itself when in season (from August through the autumn).

Whole dried limes look somewhat unappealing (brown and shrunken), but they are a flavoursome ingredient in Arabian and Iranian cooking. Sometimes pierced and added whole to simmering stews or boiling rice, they are also crushed into a zesty, citrus-spicy powder.

The skin of a lime can range from deep forest green to sunshine yellow, or be a mottled amalgam of both, depending on the maturity of the fruit. The best way to tell if a lime is likely to be good and juicy is if it feels full and heavy in your hand and has just a little give when you squeeze it. Nevertheless, even plump limes rarely give up their juice quite so readily as lemons or other citrus fruits. To really set it loose and maximise yield, roll the lime over a hard surface, pressing down firmly with your hand, to rupture some of the membranes inside. As with all citrus, if you want to use the zest, it's best to buy unwaxed fruit.

LIME AND COCONUT MOUSSE

3 ripe avocados

2 tbsp virgin coconut oil

4 tsp clear honey

½ tsp vanilla extract

A pinch of salt

3 limes

A little grated or slivered fresh coconut, to finish

This dairy-free mousse, thickened with avocado, is light and creamy with a lovely limey tang to it. It's also very quick and easy to make. Serves 4

Peel, halve and de-stone the avocados. Put the flesh into a blender or food processor along with the coconut oil, honey, vanilla and salt.

Finely grate the zest from 1 lime and set it aside.

Juice all 3 limes and add the juice to the blender. Blitz for up to 5 minutes to achieve a really smooth, silky paste.

Spoon the mousse into 4 small dishes and sprinkle with the coconut and reserved lime zest. Serve straight away or refrigerate, covered, for up to 48 hours.

Linseed

Nikki Duffy

LATIN NAME
Linum usitatissimum

ALSO KNOWN AS
Flaxseed

MORE RECIPES
Seedy stoneground loaf
(page 263)

Linseed and flaxseed are the same thing. Confusingly, the terms are used pretty much interchangeably, whether applied to the whole seed, the ground seed or the oil.

Whatever you call it, linseed/flaxseed is prized for its high content of omega-3. It's also a rich source of lignans, one of the many components of plant foods that may help protect against heart disease and cancer. Linseed is a rich source of fibre, which of course helps with healthy digestion. It's important not to have too much linseed, though – more than 45g a day can lead to unwelcome outcomes.

While it's unwise to look at linseed as some kind of tiny, shiny magic health bullet, it is true that diets rich in seeds, nuts, wholegrains etc. are generally associated with better health. Linseeds can certainly be enjoyed as a valuable addition to a rich and varied menu.

The whole seeds are tiny and leaf-shaped. They may be golden or brown – the brown seeds supposedly being more robustly flavoured, though the difference is hardly discernible. Both have very tough, glossy shells. These are quite hard for the body to break down, which is why ground or milled linseed is so popular. The milled seed is also very useful because it acts like a flour and is a good binder in gluten-free recipes.

Both whole seeds and ground can be added to breads, muesli or flapjacks, or sprinkled on to cereals, salads or soups.

Linseed oil is also easier to absorb than the whole seeds. It's rich in those omega-3s, but doesn't contain lignans, as they stay in the solid part of the seed. Make sure you buy a culinary-grade oil, not one intended for seasoning cricket bats, and use it for trickling or for dressings rather than heating it.

LINSEED, BANANA AND CHOCOLATE MUFFINS

150g self-raising gluten-free flour

1 tsp baking powder

A pinch of salt

75g soft brown sugar

2 tbsp milled linseed (flaxseed)

½ tbsp whole linseeds (flaxseeds)

125ml coconut milk

1 medium egg

60g virgin coconut oil, melted and slightly cooled

1 ripe, medium banana (150g), peeled and roughly mashed

25g dark chocolate (at least 70% cocoa solids), chopped

Deliciously moist and simple to make, you can easily knock these muffins up for breakfast. The recipe is gluten- and dairy-free but, if you are avoiding either, do check your ingredients, especially baking powder and dark chocolate, as some brands may contain traces. Try replacing the banana and/or chocolate with other fresh or dried fruit. Makes 10

Preheat the oven to 180°C/Fan 160°C/Gas 4 and line a muffin tray with 10 paper muffin cases (about 5cm diameter across the base and 3cm high).

Sift together the flour, baking powder and salt into a large bowl and then stir in the sugar, milled linseed and whole seeds.

In a separate bowl, whisk together the coconut milk, egg and melted coconut oil, then pour into the dry ingredients and quickly mix together. Stir in the mashed banana and chopped chocolate until just combined.

Divide the mixture between the muffin cases and bake for 15–20 minutes or until a skewer inserted into the centre of a muffin comes out clean. Serve warm or cold.

Liver

SOURCING

eversfieldorganic.co.uk; graigfarm.co.uk

Liver is the most commonly eaten type of offal – the first organ most of us ever taste – and so tends to be the catalyst for dividing us into pro- and anti-offal camps.

Liver carries very little fat and, while it is powerful in flavour, it's incredibly delicate in texture. Long cooking can sometimes work – a good ox liver will be beautiful if gently braised for a few hours or so – but usually it is best cooked fast and hot.

Preparing liver is quick and simple. Some recipes suggest pre-soaking in milk or lemon water but you should only do this if you want to mellow the taste. Any visible connective tissue should be removed. All livers are made up of lobes that have ventricles – bile ducts – running through them, though it's only in larger livers, such as ox, pig and lamb, that these are really noticeable. Removing these ducts is worth it if you want a completely silky liver. Otherwise, larger livers should be sliced across the lobes, rather than along them, so that the ventricles are reduced to very short sections.

It is always preferable to choose liver from an animal that has led a free-range or organic existence, because the general health of any animal will be reflected in its organs. The quality of any meat will suffer if the animal was raised in a polluted environment, but there is evidence that toxins and heavy metals accumulate in the liver and kidneys more than other parts.

Go to a butcher who keeps liver whole. It is easier to judge the freshness of a whole liver as opposed to small pieces swimming in blood, oxidising and going stale. Liver should really be consumed within 3 days of slaughter. It does freeze quite well but if you have very fresh liver it makes sense to cook and eat it straight away.

Calf's liver is the type most commonly served in restaurants. It is much milder than a robust pig or lamb's liver. Rose veal calf's liver offers a particularly sweet and delicate flavour.

At the other end of the scale in terms of popularity and price is ox liver. Typically from intensively farmed beef cattle, it is often poorly cooked, yet ox liver from a grass-fed, organic animal is an exceptional slow-braised ingredient (due to its enormity, it can be tough if flash-fried).

Pig's liver (pictured right) is less common. Firmer than most livers, it should be served pink or it will be dry. A piece of spankingly fresh, free-range pig's liver is great in a classic liver and bacon dish, a pâté, or just thinly sliced and dusted with a little flour and chopped sage then flash-fried.

If you love the strong, almost metallic flavour of liver, lamb's liver is the one for you. The most robust of all, it can easily take on big flavours from spices and chilli.

Venison liver can be fantastic. It's most often wild or free-range and its rich, dark deliciousness reflects a good life, well spent, with an added gamey note to the subtle liver flavour. A good butcher should be able to source venison liver.

Livers from poultry and game birds offer a much gentler flavour experience, but the welfare concerns that apply to whole chickens (see page 159) apply to chicken livers too. Fortunately free-range and organic chicken livers are easy to find these days. These are delicious quickly fried with a little onion and garlic and perhaps bacon, or sautéed then blitzed with shallots, cream and sage to make a simple pâté.

When it comes to foie gras – the fattened liver of over-fed ducks or geese – there are huge welfare issues. The liver of these birds is genetically disposed to store fat for long migration but, in foie gras production, that trait is exploited to an extreme degree: a programme of force-feeding via a tube, and restricted exercise (i.e. the birds cannot fly), is used to swell the liver well beyond its normal size. A finished goose liver can

weigh up to 700g (of which 80 per cent is fat). The resulting liver has a delicate flavour and exotic richness, but many people believe that traditional foie gras production is unacceptably cruel. Force-feeding is prohibited under animal welfare laws in many countries (including the UK).

Most foie gras sold in the UK is produced on an industrial scale in France and elsewhere on the Continent, the birds raised intensively and fed mechanically. It's not for me. So-called 'ethical' foie gras is produced without force-feeding. In this system, free-range geese are allowed to follow their instincts to gorge themselves at will, at certain times of year, resulting in a liver that is still enlarged, but to a lesser degree. Of course, normal unfattened livers from free-range geese or ducks are a delicious option that should not be overlooked.

SPICED LIVER PÂTÉ

This smoky pork pâté, spiked with paprika and fennel seed, is incredibly tasty. Using a mincer to chop the meat will give a nice, even texture. If you use a food processor, take care not to reduce the mix to an homogeneous paste. Makes a 1kg terrine, to serve 10–12

Butter or lard, to grease

400g very fresh free-range pig's liver

400g free-range fatty pork belly, cut into 1–2cm chunks (or strips if using a mincer)

100g streaky bacon, cut into 1–2cm pieces

1 onion, chopped

4 garlic cloves, grated

100g fresh breadcrumbs

1 tbsp chopped rosemary

1 tbsp chopped thyme

50ml port or red wine

30ml cider brandy (optional)

1 tbsp redcurrant, crab apple or other tart fruit jelly

1 medium egg, lightly beaten

3 tsp fennel seeds, toasted and ground

1 tsp coriander seeds, toasted and ground

A good pinch of dried chilli flakes or cayenne pepper

1 tbsp sweet smoked paprika

1 tsp fine sea salt

Black pepper

Preheat the oven to 170°C/Fan 150°C/Gas 3 and grease a 1-litre terrine or loaf tin (about 22 x 11cm base measurement).

Trim out any tough ventricles from the liver, then chop it into 1–2cm pieces. Combine the liver with the pork belly, bacon and onion, then put them through a mincer: use a coarse plate (8mm) for a chunky, country-style pâté, or the fine plate (2–3mm) for a smoother texture. Alternatively, process the meat mixture in a food processor, in a couple of batches, until well mixed and chopped, but not reduced to a paste. Transfer to a large bowl.

Add all the remaining ingredients and mix well (it's easiest to do this with your hands). To check the seasoning, break off a little walnut-sized ball of the mixture and fry it until cooked through. Leave to cool, then taste it and adjust the seasoning of the main mixture accordingly, adding more salt or chilli/cayenne as needed.

Spoon the mixture into the prepared terrine and level the surface. Cover the terrine with greased foil or a well-fitting lid. Place in a large roasting tray and pour hot water into the tray to come about halfway up the sides of the terrine. Cook in the centre of the oven for 1½ hours, or until a cook's thermometer inserted into the centre registers at least 72°C. The pâté should feel firm to the touch and be coming away from the side of the terrine.

You now need to press the pâté as it cools in the terrine, to give it a nice, firm texture. Some terrines come with their own platform that fits snugly on top, which you can then place weights on. Alternatively, you can place another loaf tin on top and fill that with weights such as tins of food. Don't apply too much weight, though, or you'll squeeze out all the lovely meat juices. Leave until completely cool, then remove the weights.

Refrigerate the pâté until thoroughly chilled. It will keep for up to a week in the fridge. Eat with good bread, boiled eggs and gherkins.

Lobster

Gill Meller

LATIN NAME
Homarus gammarus

SEASONALITY
Lobsters can spawn at any time; avoid egg-carrying females at any time

HABITAT
All around the British Isles and across Europe, extending to Norway and North Africa

MCS RATING
2–4 Lobsters from the Southwest or the Channel Islands are the best choice

REC MINIMUM SIZE
9cm carapace length (from back of eye socket to end of main body shell, not including tail)

MORE RECIPES
Grilled langoustine with lemon and parsley butter (page 339); Samphire, crab and new potato salad (page 560)

SOURCING
goodfishguide.org; association-ifca.org.uk (for lobster potting regulations)

Lobster is a sweet, meaty, succulent crustacean – a real treat, though arguably no more delicious than less expensive crab. In the Southwest, the best time to eat it is from early summer into autumn, when it is landed sustainably by inshore potters, who catch it within 6 miles of the coast. Only mature lobsters may be landed; other fish or young lobsters in the pot are released alive. They cannot land 'berried' (egg-carrying) females.

Fishermen who catch lobsters in nets cannot be so selective. Nevertheless, even with potting, lobsters can be overfished. This is currently the case in many parts of the British Isles, and Mediterranean and Scandinavian stocks are depleted. Broadly speaking, pot-caught lobsters from the Southwest or the Channel Islands are the best choice.

Lobsters can grow up to a metre in total length, but a smaller specimen is always preferable on the plate. Lobsters weighing 800g–1.5kg are best: sweet and tender. There's nothing sweet and tender about the lobster's nature, however. They attack like prize fighters with their big claws, which is why lobster ranching is more difficult and less developed than other forms of shellfish farming – and why a lobster's pincers are held closed with rubber bands when the creatures are put in a vivarium.

Avoiding those claws is one of the challenges you will face should you decide to fish for a few lobsters yourself, using a pot (or creel). If you have a boat it's pretty straightforward. Lobster pots should be baited with fish scraps – the stinkier the better. Drop your pots (which must have floating markers, of course) over rocky ground, in water 10 metres deep or more. You could also walk and then wade out as far as you can at low tide to place and collect your pots – but most lobsters will be a bit further out than this. It's essential to collect your catch at the next low tide, too, so they don't die. You must observe the minimum landing size for lobster (see left) and return egg-carrying females, or lobsters with a v-notch cut in their tail (a conservation measure that identifies breeding females). You should also check local byelaws regarding permits and regulations for lobster potting.

Before cooking, you must first kill the lobster. Our recommended method is to first sedate the lobster by putting it in the freezer for about an hour (but no more than 2 hours, or the flesh may start to freeze solid). Then drop the insensate crustacean into a large pan of well-salted boiling water and cook for 10 minutes for a 500g lobster, 15 minutes for one weighing 750g, and allow an extra 5 minutes for each 500g after that. Lift the lobster out of the pan and leave to cool until warm or at room temperature.

To serve, split the lobster down the middle as described in the recipe overleaf. Remove the gills, small stomach sac behind the mouth and the digestive tract that looks like a black vein running the length of the tail. But leave in the liver, known as tomalley, which may not look appetising but is one of the most delicious and rich parts. A halved lobster is great for grilling (see page 339), or you can simply pick the meat out.

Most of a lobster's meat is in the big front claws and tail. These are two quite different textured meats but with a similar flavour. The meat comes easily out of the tail, but to access the claw meat you need to crack open the shells. Put the claw on a board and tap hard with the heel of a sharp chef's knife so the blade goes into the claw. Give it a twist and you can usually crack the claw straight in half with a nice clean break (though with large lobsters, you might need to use a hammer or give the claw a blow with the back of a heavy knife). You can then tease out the meat from the claws with a little fork.

Like other shellfish, lobster shells make great stock. To maximise the flavour, you can toast the crushed shells in butter and oil in a pan for 2–3 minutes before simmering, or, for a lighter stock, just put them straight in a pan with lots of tasty veg and herbs,

including fennel, celery, onions, thyme and parsley. Like a fish stock, lobster stock should be simmered for only 30 minutes or so.

Lobster cooked on a barbecue is particularly special – the charring shell releases a rich, savoury flavour. Put the lobster in the freezer for an hour to sedate it, then split in half and remove the unwanted parts (see recipe below). Brush the lobster meat with oil and cook cut side down for 2–3 minutes, then turn over, dot with butter (flavoured with herbs, citrus zest and chilli, ideally) and cook for another 1–2 minutes, until the butter has melted into the flesh and the meat is cooked; take care to avoid overcooking.

Generally, lobster is best eaten very simply. A grilled one is perfect with a nice home-made mayonnaise, some dressed new potatoes and salad. But you can dress it up more – for example in the classic lobster thermidor, which is sumptuously rich with cream, brandy, egg yolks, mustard and grilled cheese. Lobster is quite a well-flavoured, robust meat and can take such a treatment. It also works well with other sweet or bitter ingredients. Lobster with apple and tarragon, or apple and cucumber, makes a lovely summer salad, with the sliced shellfish turned through a simple dressing of mayo, yoghurt, fresh mint and lemon juice.

For an autumnal dish, try a lobster and cep risotto. Boil the lobster and take the meat from the shell and claws. Use the shell to make a light stock (see above), then follow the classic risotto method, cooking sliced fresh ceps (or soaked, dried ones) with the onion and garlic. Finish with the lobster meat, parsley, butter and Parmesan.

LOBSTER WITH BÉARNAISE MAYONNAISE

The unique, delicately aniseedy flavour of tarragon is essential to a classic béarnaise sauce. Here it's used similarly in mayonnaise to produce a lovely rich dressing for freshly cooked lobster. Langoustine are also delicious served in this way. Serves 4

2 live lobsters (800g–1kg each)

FOR THE MAYONNAISE
25g unsalted butter

1 shallot or small onion, finely diced

2 tbsp medium white wine

1 tbsp white wine vinegar or cider vinegar

2 medium egg yolks

1 heaped tsp English mustard

200ml light olive oil OR 150ml sunflower oil plus 50ml extra virgin olive or rapeseed oil

Juice of ½ lemon

2 tbsp chopped tarragon

Sea salt and black pepper

Put your lobster in the freezer for about an hour before cooking to sedate them.

For the béarnaise, melt the butter in a small pan over a medium heat. Add the shallot or onion and cook gently for 8–10 minutes to soften without colouring. Turn up the heat a little and add the wine and vinegar. Simmer until reduced to a scant 2 tsp liquid. Let cool.

Put the egg yolks, mustard, a pinch of salt, the shallot and its liquor into a blender and blitz for 25–30 seconds. Then, with the motor running on the lowest speed, slowly trickle in the oil, so that it forms an emulsion with the egg yolks, stopping frequently to scrape down the sides. Alternatively, you can whisk the oil into the egg yolks gradually by hand.

When you've added all the oil and have a thick, glossy mayonnaise, add the lemon juice and chopped tarragon. Blitz briefly to combine, then taste and adjust the seasoning as required. If the mayonnaise is a little thick, stir in 1–2 tsp warm water. Refrigerate while you boil the lobster.

Bring a large pan of well-salted water to the boil and cook the lobsters as described on page 363. Remove them from the pan and leave to cool for 15–20 minutes.

Put one lobster on a board with the head towards you. With the tip of a sharp, heavy knife on the cross on the lobster's head, press down firmly, cutting through the head towards you. Turn the lobster round so the tail is now facing you. Carefully cut from the split in the head down though to the tip of the tail in one firm motion. Keep the blade central so you end up with two even halves. Repeat with the second lobster. Remove the gills, sand sac from behind the lobster's mouth and the intestinal tract that runs the length of the tail.

Serve the warm lobster with the mayo, bread and a salad dressed with lemon and olive oil.

Loganberries, tayberries & boysenberries

Mark Diacono

LATIN NAME
Loganberry: *Rubus ×
loganobaccus*. Tayberry:
Rubus fruticosus × idaeaus.
Boysenberry: *Rubus
ursinus × idaeaus*

SEASONALITY
July–September

MORE RECIPES
Wineberries with peaches and
custard (page 317); Blackberry
yoghurt soufflé cake (page 73);
Mulberry and walnut cranachan
(page 391); Basil pannacotta with
minted raspberries (page 96);
Raspberry almond streusel cake
(page 526)

Some people dedicate a lifetime to the pursuit of an invention or ideal. Others, like James Logan, just get lucky. He accidentally created the loganberry by crossing a particular strain of raspberry with a certain variety of blackberry. Looking like a long raspberry but with blackberry dominating the flavour, loganberries have a fine balance of sweet and sharp. They ripen gradually across the plant, which means that they are rarely grown commercially, so you'll need a nearby pick-your-own farm, or a plant in your garden, to enjoy them. Relishing loganberries at their very best demands patience. Don't be tempted to pick the raspberry-red fruits, which will still be a little too acidic. Instead, wait for them to turn wine-coloured, almost purple, when they will reveal their full, sensuous sweetness and aromatic depth.

Tayberries are another blackberry/raspberry cross – larger than loganberries and with a sweeter taste (which doesn't make them better, just differently delicious). But boysenberries are my favourite among these berry hybrids. The product of a three-way cross between loganberries, raspberries and American dewberries, they are both sweet and sharp, with a gorgeous winey depth. They are as close to a mulberry as any other fruit gets, and that is a very desirable adjacency as far as I'm concerned (see page 391). They also share with the mulberry a real delicacy of texture: once ripe, you get a couple of days at best to enjoy them, before they dismantle themselves under the weight of their own luscious juice.

None of these berries are widely available in the shops. They are tricky to harvest mechanically and/or too delicate to stand the journey to the shelves and beyond. But they are simple to grow and reliably productive. As with blackberries, these hybrids grow canes one year that fruit the next, in an ongoing cycle of fruity productivity.

You don't need telling what to do with such lovely berry fruits. Start with some or all of: cream, pastry, meringue, custard, honey, toasted oats and crushed nuts and you'll end up somewhere in the happy land of fools, trifles, cranachans, tarts, Eton messes and knickerbocker glories. Not forgetting ice creams, granitas, jams and so on.

BARBECUED FENNEL AND COURGETTES WITH LOGANBERRIES

2 small-medium courgettes
(about 300g in total)

2 medium fennel bulbs

Finely grated zest and juice
of 1 lemon

2 tbsp olive oil

1 tbsp chopped mint

Extra virgin olive oil, to trickle

150g loganberries

2–3 tbsp ricotta, or mild, fresh
ewe's or goat's cheese

Sea salt and black pepper

You can use raspberries or wineberries here, but the full, complex flavour of loganberries is particularly good with the smoky vegetables. Serves 4

Top and tail the courgettes and cut them into long strips, 2–3mm thick.

Trim the very base from the fennel bulbs and remove the tough outer layer. Stand the bulbs upright on a board. Slicing downwards, cut the bulbs into slices the same thickness as the courgette. Don't worry if they break up a little.

Put the prepared vegetables into a bowl and add the lemon zest, the 2 tbsp olive oil and some salt and pepper, and toss lightly together.

Prepare your barbecue, or preheat the grill.

When ready to cook, lay the courgette and fennel pieces on the barbecue grid or grill pan (keep the bowl with the seasonings in it to hand). Cook the veg for 5–10 minutes on each side, depending on the heat of the coals, until just tender and lightly charred.

Place the veg back in the bowl of seasoned oil and allow to cool a little. Add the chopped mint, a trickle of extra virgin olive oil, some more salt and pepper and half the lemon juice and mix lightly. Lay the veg out over a large serving platter.

Put the loganberries in a bowl with the remaining lemon juice and crush roughly with a fork, then scatter over the veg. Dot with the cheese and serve.

Lovage

Nikki Duffy

LATIN NAME
Levisticum officinale

SEASONALITY
April–September

MORE RECIPES
Radishes with chicken livers
and lovage (page 520)

Lovage is a herb that can offer more powerful, punch-packing, aromatic heft than any of its leafy brethren. The flavour combines notes of celery, fenugreek and pepper. It's intensely savoury, distinctly spicy, a little bitter and very penetrating – ably lending character to everything from cheese on toast to a meaty pie.

This is not a herb to fling, scatter and shower about with abandon but it works wonders in small quantities, or combined with other, more delicate, grassy herbs such as chives and, particularly, parsley.

The best-flavoured leaves are the youngest and most tender, those that unfurl themselves in spring or early summer, or that reappear after the plant has had a vigorous cutting back. Chop this baby foliage finely and add just a pinch or two to anything eggy – an omelette, quiche or frittata, say – to understand its incredible seasoning power. Use a few leaves in a vegetable soup – adding them at the beginning for a mellow background flavour, at the end for a more sharp, assertive effect – or use half a dozen leaves to build flavour in a stock.

Lovage is great with red meats – again, giving a different effect depending on when and in what quantity you add it. It can spicily dominate a burger mix or subtly round out a slow-cooked stew. And this herb is also fabulous with cheese: later in the year, when the plant is getting leggy and leafy, the big leaves can be used to wrap chunks of Cheddar or Lancashire. After a few days, the leaves' intense aroma will have subtly flavoured the cheese.

You occasionally see lovage for sale as a cut herb, but growing it is the best, if not the only, way to guarantee a good supply. A robust perennial, it favours sunshine and rich soil, but it's not too fussy and will make its presence felt in a herb patch – shooting up from tiny plantlet to tall, muscular bush in just a few seasons. You can keep it in check with regular cutbacks, or by growing it in a large pot but, in the garden as in the kitchen, lovage is impossible to ignore.

ROAST LAMB WITH LOVAGE

This is a great use for lovage that's gone a bit leggy in the garden. It's a nice way to cook a leg of kid or goat too. Serves 6–10

Preheat the oven to 220°C/Fan 200°C/Gas 7.

Put the lamb in a roasting tin, rub it with a little oil and season well with salt and pepper. Give it an initial 'sizzle' in the hot oven for 35 minutes.

Remove the lamb from the oven and tuck the sliced onion, garlic and lovage around and under the meat. Pour a glass of water around (not over) the meat. Turn down the oven to 180°C/Fan 160°C/Gas 4, return the joint and roast for a further 1–2 hours depending on how pink you like your lamb. An hour will leave it quite rare, 2 hours will take it close to well done. Remove the lamb from the tin and allow it to rest on a warm plate.

Pick out the lovage stems (don't worry about the odd few leaves) then set the roasting tin over a medium heat on the hob. If there is more than 2–3 tbsp of fat in the tin, skim off the excess. Sprinkle in the flour and work it into the juices with a spatula, crushing the garlic, onion and any lovage leaves at the same time. Cook gently for 1–2 minutes, then add the stock and stir well. The gravy will thicken as it comes back to a simmer. Cook for 2–3 minutes, then taste for seasoning. Pass through a sieve into a warmed jug.

Carve the lamb and serve with the gravy, and some roast potatoes and boiled carrots.

1 leg of lamb, hogget or mutton on the bone (about 2kg), at room temperature

Olive or rapeseed oil, for cooking

1 onion, sliced

1 head of garlic, halved through the equator

A couple of good handfuls of lovage (leaves and stems)

1 tbsp plain flour

400ml hot lamb or chicken stock, or water

Sea salt and black pepper

Mace

Steven Lamb

LATIN NAME
Myristica fragrans

MORE RECIPES
Pear and celeriac stuffing
(page 454); Spotted dick with
apple-brandy raisins (page 522)

Mace is a traditional flavouring for meat products like sausages, pork pies and pâtés, and a classic pickling spice, yet it is something of a forgotten spice these days. It is sometimes confused with nutmeg, which is hardly surprising because it is in fact the dried aril, or outer covering, of the nutmeg seed. The flavour profiles are similar but mace is softer, less intense and a little more floral than nutmeg.

Mace is commonly dried and ground into a powder, but it can also be sold in whole 'blades', which look like tattered, orange flower petals. These blades can be infused in a dish, then removed before serving. You can grind down the hard mace blades in a spice grinder or coffee grinder (it's pretty tricky to do it with a pestle and mortar).

Mace is ideal if you're looking for a delicate, fragrant and smooth spiciness. It works particularly well with meat dishes and especially so in a cure mix for pancetta, cotechino or mortadella sausage. Mace is also very good in slow-cooked casseroles or stews, although it should be added towards the end of cooking because it can become slightly bitter if heated too long.

Like nutmeg, mace adds a lovely defining edge to milky or creamy dishes. Infuse a blade in the milk for a béchamel sauce, or add a pinch of ground mace to savoury custards for tarts. It's good in any sweet dish that involves cream, milk or eggs too.

Mace (and raw nutmeg) contains a substance called myristicin, which can have psychoactive effects and cause convulsions, palpitations and nausea, if consumed in large doses. The amount of mace in a pork terrine or a chutney, however, is highly unlikely to be any cause for concern.

PORK BURGERS WITH MACE AND THYME

500g minced free-range
pork belly

50g fresh breadcrumbs

2 tsp ground mace

2 tsp thyme leaves

1 tsp fine sea salt

Black pepper

Rapeseed oil or lard, for frying

Whether you serve these in buns or just as they come, they're great with just a smidgen of mustard. Or, for something more substantial, top them with sweated leeks and crumbled blue cheese. You could also cook the burgers on a barbecue. Makes 4–5 burgers

Put the mince and breadcrumbs into a large bowl with the mace, thyme, salt and a generous grinding of pepper and work together thoroughly with your hands. To check the seasoning, break off a small nugget of the mixture and fry it in a hot pan until cooked through. Taste it and then adjust the seasoning of the main mixture with more salt and pepper if necessary.

Divide the mixture into 4 or 5 portions and form into burgers about 3cm thick, using your hands to mould them into a good, firm shape. Chill in the fridge for at least half an hour before cooking.

Heat a large pan over a medium heat and add a trickle of oil or 1 tsp lard. When hot, add the burgers and cook gently for 8–10 minutes each side, or until cooked through. Take the pan off the heat but leave the burgers in it to rest in for 5 minutes before serving.

Mackerel

Hugh Fearnley-Whittingstall

LATIN NAME
Scomber scombrus

SEASONALITY
Avoid March–July when
spawning

HABITAT
This wide-ranging pelagic
species roams the northeast
Atlantic from North Africa to
Iceland and Norway, including
the Black Sea, Mediterranean
and western Baltic

MCS RATING
2–4

REC MINIMUM SIZE
30cm

MORE RECIPES
Mackerel with tamari and
sesame glaze (page 592); New
potato, mackerel and purslane
salad (page 509); Cucumber,
smoked mackerel and dill salad
(page 220); Noodles with
seaweed, smoked mackerel
and soy (page 407); Fried
salmon with cucumber and
gooseberry salad (page 553)

SOURCING
goodfishguide.org; msc.org;
fish4ever.co.uk

Mackerel has had a rough ride over the past few years. This sleek, oily fish – one of the most delicious, versatile and health-giving we have at our disposal – has been the subject of a sea storm of doubt and dispute and you could be forgiven for feeling pretty confused about it. Fast-growing, plentiful and long championed as the A1 sustainable choice, it was on the MCS's 'Fish to Eat' list and many chefs and food writers (including me, of course) promoted it with unqualified enthusiasm.

Then politics and greed got in the way and the northeast Atlantic mackerel fishery, of which British fishers are part, became the scene for some rather ugly in-fighting. Iceland, the Faroe Islands and Greenland unilaterally opted to start taking more mackerel from the sea. They failed to agree catch limits with the EU and Norway, with whom they share that area, and the resulting fishing pressure far exceeded what was scientifically advised, jeopardising the entire international fishery. Consequently, in 2012, all the Atlantic fisheries lost their MSC sustainable status. This meant that for a period of 4 years, no mackerel landed in the UK could carry the MSC's blue logo.

Thankfully, Norway and the EU countries who fish from the North Atlantic stock responded to the crisis by banding together. They formed a body called MINSA (Mackerel Industry Northern Sustainability Alliance), and committed themselves to getting mackerel back on track. They've been successful: following a reassessment of the MINSA fisheries (which includes the vast majority of British and Irish fisheries), MSC-certified mackerel is available again. This is fantastic news and means that mackerel – some of it, anyway – has regained its status as the perfect fishy storm of sustainability, good health and great eating.

The correct management of mackerel stocks for the future is vitally important. This is a fast-maturing fish, so stocks can recover relatively quickly from a dip. But because they are such fine eating, fishing pressure is increasing too. All the countries fishing the northeast Atlantic stock need to adhere to the scientific advice put in place to protect this fantastic natural resource.

As with any fish, the method by which mackerel is caught is also crucial. That is why I eat line-caught, local mackerel; if it's not fish I have caught myself, it will be from the South-West Handline fishery. This Cornish fishery was groundbreaking, being among the first to achieve certification from the MSC as being sustainable, back in 2001. Since then, the fishery has taken the decision to stop seeking certification, for financial reasons. But, along with the MINSA fisheries, it remains the source of the most sustainable commercially caught mackerel you can put on your plate.

Mackerel is one of my all-time favourite fish. It's got everything going for it, being rich in crucial omega-3 fats, and simpler to prepare than its oily-fish colleagues, sardines and herring. It's easy to slice the plump fillets off the fish yourself (though, of course, a fishmonger can do this for you) and easy to either excise its single line of pin bones by removing a slim wedge of flesh from the centre of the fillet, or to eat round them once the fillet is cooked.

Mackerel is a full-flavoured, lightly oily fish, with a beautiful, firm flesh that takes very well to strong partners. I've served it with everything from gooseberries to mint and oranges to fennel (in fact it's particularly good with gooseberries *and* mint, or oranges *and* fennel!). I don't think mackerel does well with rich or creamy sauces – they can't compete with its natural richness. But I've soused it, smoked it, pickled it, potted it, oat-coated it, roasted it with all kinds of different fruit, veg and herbs, cooked it in a chilli-spiced brew of soy sauce and apple juice, and even dished it up raw, dabbed

M

with hot English mustard, as a sort of Southwest sashimi. It has never let me down. But for all its astonishing versatility, my favourite treatments for this favourite fish are the most basic and primal. Gutted, seasoned with salt and thrown in a hot pan with some garlic and a few bay leaves, or lain on the barbecue to char over hot coals, it cooks to a delicious, moist-fleshed, crisp-skinned finish. With something a little hot or sharp on the side – horseradish, gooseberries, mustard, rhubarb or just lemon juice – I don't think it can be beaten by any other fish.

Beneath its glorious, tiger-striped coat, mackerel's rich flesh deteriorates quickly and it should ideally be eaten within 48 hours of being caught, assuming it has been hand-line caught and chilled immediately and continuously to the point of purchase.

A properly fresh mackerel should smell sea-sweet, not fishy, and have firm flesh, glossy skin and bright eyes. It should have no hint of sliminess around the gills. You may not get to handle and closely appraise your fish at the fishmongers, but you can ask when and where it was landed. Avoid any mackerel that's more than 48 hours out of the water.

At the supermarket, you may actually be better off with a gutted, beheaded and cling-wrapped tray of mackerel fillets than the whole fish on the ice display. That sounds counterintuitive, I know. But the pack of fillets will have run the gauntlet of a super-efficient, well-chilled packing plant and transport system. If it still has a couple of days' leeway on its use-by date, it's probably good to go. Whereas the whole fish on ice may simply be tired window-dressing.

For me, a smoky, salty barbecued whole fresh mackerel is the apex of fish-eating pleasure, but I'm aware that some people are more comfortable with mackerel fillets that have been hot-smoked and vac-packed, or tinned in oil. I certainly have time for these processed forms of mackerel and, of course, they are convenient: all the work has been done for you.

Hot-smoked mackerel is generally available in fat fillets, though I often smoke the fish whole. Either way, the flavour of smoke and the tang of salt get tremendous purchase in that rich oily flesh, making this an ingredient of wonderful depth and character. Just a few mouthfuls of it transform a salad (try flakes of it tossed with cold roast beetroot, flat-leaf parsley and, if you like, a scattering of cold cooked Puy lentils). And, of course, it makes a superb pâté.

Tinned mackerel is a great storecupboard standby too. Mashed with a spoonful of crème fraîche, and a little mustard and onion, it's a brilliant toast-topping quick lunch or supper. It's also delicious flaked and tossed into hot pasta, along with its oil, a squeeze of lemon juice and a sprinkling of dried chilli flakes. It works on pizza, in potato salads and on jacket potatoes as well.

Both tinned and smoked mackerel can be sustainably sourced; I like the Fish4Ever brand of tinned mackerel fillets. When it comes to smoked, look for the promise of line-caught fish, or the MSC blue logo.

Scad

Scad, or horse mackerel, is a species little seen on fish counters or in restaurants in the UK. It's not mackerel at all (it's actually a 'jack', from the Caringidae family), but it does have a similarly high omega-3 content and is very tasty – the flesh a little milder and meatier than mackerel. It does end up in commercial catches (it sometimes swims among mackerel), but it's usually sent for processing into fertiliser and fishmeal. However, other cultures, notably in Japan and Africa, love this fish and serve it reverently, raw, dried or cooked. There's not enough information on this species to declare it sustainable or otherwise, and what evidence there is tends to point to it being fully fished – i.e. we really shouldn't be increasing our catch of it. But if you find it – either in a fishmongers or flapping at the end of your own line, it is most certainly worth eating. Treat it just as you would mackerel.

HOT MACKEREL, BEETROOT AND HORSERADISH SANDWICH

This is such a good way to serve mackerel, and other fish for that matter, such as herring or red mullet. The basic technique for cooking fillets outlined here will serve you well for countless dishes (you could also use the hot flesh from whole baked or barbecued mackerel). Serves 2

Fillets from 1 large or 2 small mackerel

Olive or rapeseed oil, for cooking

A few garlic cloves, thickly sliced (optional)

A few bay leaves, roughly torn (optional)

4 slices of granary bread or 2 soft, white baps or 1 ciabatta, split

Butter, softened, for spreading

A little freshly grated horseradish, or 1 tbsp creamed horseradish sauce from a jar

A squeeze of lemon juice

About 100g roasted beetroot, hot or cold (see page 68), or vac-packed cooked beetroot

Sea salt and black pepper

Season the mackerel fillets with salt and pepper. Heat a thin film of oil in a frying pan over a medium heat. When it is fairly hot, scatter in the garlic and/or bay leaves, if using, then lay the mackerel fillets in the pan, skin side down. Cook for 2–3 minutes until the fillets are almost completely opaque, then turn them over and finish cooking for just a minute.

Lift the mackerel fillets from the pan and leave them to cool slightly while you butter the bread and spread on the horseradish. (If using fresh horseradish, mix it with a few drops of lemon juice.)

Flake the hot flesh from the mackerel skin, being careful to remove the bones as you go, then pile on to the base of each sandwich. Give the fish a squeeze of lemon juice and a scattering more salt and pepper. Slice the cooked beetroot into thin discs or wedges and lay on top of the fish. Sandwich together with the top slices of bread and serve.

Mango

Nikki Duffy

LATIN NAME
Mangifera indica

SEASONALITY
Different varieties imported all year round; Indian Alphonso mangoes April–June

A ripe 'Alphonso' mango is as tempting as food gets. Small and yellow-skinned, like plump, golden hearts, these Indian fruits contain a flesh so buttery, honeyed and juicy that it's hard to believe it's good for you. But it is. Like all mangoes, Alphonsos are rich in antioxidants, vitamins including A and C, and potassium.

Sadly Alphonsos (pictured right) are not the mango norm in the UK. During their short season, April to June, you will find them in Asian grocers, but for the most part we sink our teeth into the much larger 'Keitt' and 'Kent' varieties. Nothing wrong with that. These are luscious too when ripe – if a little less ambrosial.

To ascertain ripeness in your mango, ignore the skin colour. They can be red-blushed but still hard, or green all over and still almost rotting inside. Instead, press the fruit gently at the stem end, where it should give a little, without feeling mushy.

Completely under-ripe, green-fleshed mango is excellent julienned or grated in a salad with a punchy, Thai-influenced dressing. Although you can get these from specialist suppliers, mangoes are not widely sold this way in the UK. Instead, one can end up with a disappointingly halfway-house mango, which is neither green nor drippingly ripe. Don't despair, such firm mango flesh is still a fantastic salad ingredient – try it where you might otherwise use pear or plum.

To liberate the flesh from a mango, you can go the 'hedgehog' route, first slicing off the 'cheek' on either side of the big central stone. Score the flesh side of the cheeks into squares before pushing the cheek inside out, as it were, causing the cut mango to bristle up in easy-to-slice-off chunks. Cut off the remaining flesh from the stone with a small, sharp knife.

Alternatively, you can simply peel the whole fruit with a veg peeler or paring knife and slice off the flesh in chunks, slivers and wedges. Either way, you're left with a flesh-clothed stone. Hold this over a jug and squeeze it to extract every last bit of juice, but not too hard or the slippery stone will shoot upwards.

Dried mango is marvellous: like a very tender kind of fruity-tangy, sweet leather. Strips of it make great, chewy snacks and are fantastic snipped into little pieces and tossed through couscous, bulgar or rice salads with spices, pomegranate seeds and lots of mint or coriander. Dried mango also makes an amazing chutney.

MANGO AND BANANA SALAD

1 large mango, ripe but not too soft

1 large, medium-ripe banana

2 tsp clear honey

Juice of ½ large lime

50g fresh coconut flesh (see page 192)

This super-quick, healthy salad is a brilliant breakfast. You could make it with papaya in place of the mango if you like. Try serving with thick yoghurt and a few toasted seeds. Serves 2

Remove the flesh from the mango in your favoured way (see above), cutting as close to the stone as possible to get the maximum amount of flesh. Remove any skin from the liberated flesh, then cut the flesh into slivers or chunks and place in a large bowl.

Peel the banana and cut into slices, on a slight angle, about 5mm thick. Add to the mango. Trickle over the honey and squeeze over the lime then turn the fruit over very gently. Leave to macerate for a few minutes.

Turn the fruit again, then divide between individual bowls or plates. Using a medium grater or potato peeler, grate or sliver the coconut over the fruit. Serve straight away.

Maple syrup

Nikki Duffy

When the snow falls from the branches with a particular kind of wet thud, the farmers of the Beauce know it's time to start tapping their trees. In this part of Quebec, and other parts of Canada and the eastern US, the first stirrings of the spring thaw signal the advent of the maple season. The thin, clear sap of the maple trees begins to rise, even while their branches are bare. A simple tap, inserted into the trunk, is all that's required to siphon off this mild nectar.

Maple syrup is rarely produced outside North America. Maple trees will certainly grow in other places, but rather specific seasonal temperature fluctuations are required to get the sap flowing. And some would say the sap just doesn't seem to taste the same without that frontier *terroir*.

At first, the sap looks like water and is barely sweet. To transform it into the richly flavoured, burnt-gold liquor with which we love to douse our pancakes, it is boiled to concentrate (it takes 30–40 litres of sap to produce 1 litre of syrup). This is a more efficient way of producing syrup than the ancient method, but not much more complex. Native Americans used to reduce maple sap by dropping hot stones into it.

That's pretty much all there is to it. Pure maple syrup really is pretty pure. It's hardly a health food, being largely sucrose, but it does contain some antioxidants and nutrients, including vitamin B2, manganese and zinc. And then there's the incomparable flavour – sweet but slightly tangy – it's like butterscotch with tannins.

Maple syrup is graded according to its colour and character, ranging from golden through amber, to dark and very dark. The darker the syrup, the more robust the taste. I prefer amber or dark syrups – they have such intensity. What you definitely don't want is anything labelled maple 'flavoured' syrup. A poor synthetic imitation, it tastes thin and artificial. The real thing is undeniably pricey – but it's worth it.

Maple syrup is delicious poured generously on to hot pancakes, perhaps with a smear of butter or crisp bacon to add that irresistible salty co-flavour, but it has endless other possibilities too. In glazes, marinades, stews and bean dishes, it adds a unique sweetness with woody, earthy undertones. This syrup does, however, burn easily, so you need to take care when cooking with it – combining it with other wet ingredients is the answer.

Like honey, maple syrup can be a good partner to strong cheese – try trickling it over a blue cheese rarebit. It loves salty things, earthy pulses and lots of spice. In baking, it pairs well with nuts and with bananas. It is very liquid – more so than honey – so in conventional baking it is often combined with dry sugar, and in less conventional raw recipes with dried fruit such as dates.

BACON AND MAPLE COOKIES

100g derinded unsmoked streaky bacon (about 4 rashers)

125g unsalted butter

100g granulated sugar

75g maple syrup (amber or dark)

1 medium egg

170g plain flour

½ tsp baking powder

The moreish combination of bacon and maple syrup works brilliantly in these large cookies. Try adding chopped hazels or walnuts for an extra dimension. Makes 12

Preheat the oven to 170°C/Fan 150°C/Gas 3 and line 2 large baking sheets with baking parchment.

Lay the bacon rashers on a small rack set over a roasting tin and cook in the oven for 30–35 minutes – a little longer if necessary – until completely crisp. Remove and allow to cool. Turn the oven up to 190°C/Fan 170°C/Gas 5.

Melt the butter in a small saucepan over a low heat. Meanwhile, chop the bacon finely and set aside.

Put the sugar and maple syrup into a large bowl, pour on the melted butter and beat well. Add the egg and beat until well combined. Sift the flour and baking powder over the mixture and stir in. Finally, stir in the crisp bacon.

Drop heaped dessertspoonfuls of the mixture on to the baking sheets, leaving plenty of space in between them – these cookies really spread out. Bake for 10–12 minutes, until they are just turning golden brown.

Leave on the baking sheets for a couple of minutes to firm up, then carefully lift the cookies on to a wire rack. Leave to cool completely.

Medlar

Mark Diacono

LATIN NAME
Mespilus germanica

SEASONALITY
October–November

Resembling a small apple with a wide, shallow crater at the calyx (non-stem end), the medlar is traditionally harvested after the first frosts begin to transform its firm, pale flesh into dark, rich pulp, in a process known as 'bletting'. Imagine a good cooking apple crossed with a date and you'll be in the ballpark of a bletted medlar's flavour.

These fruits may turn up once in a while at a November farmers' market, but it is unusual to find them for sale, so your best bet is to get to know someone with a tree. However you come by your medlars, it's likely that you'll have at least some still firm or only partially bletted fruits. These are great for cooking with.

Medlars make the prince of jellies. Prepared with equal amounts of bletted and unbletted fruit (or medlars that are halfway though the process), it has richness yet enough pectin from the unbletted fruit to ensure a good set. Venison, duck and cheese were made for it.

You can also produce a lovely, datey purée from medlars at pretty much any stage, or stages, of ripeness by gently simmering the quartered fruit in a little water until they collapse. Sieved free of seeds and skin, and sweetened or not to your taste, this works well in anything from carrot cake to Eton mess, sticky toffee pudding to fool.

Nevertheless, since a perfectly bletted medlar is much to be coveted, and can be eaten raw (as in the recipe below), it's worth knowing how to bring them on at home. Simply arrange any still-firm medlars on a large tray, stalk upwards, and leave at room temperature, giving them a little squeeze every day or so to gauge their progress. They're ready when they are soft and yielding.

Bletting is of course the beginning of decay, so it's important to catch the medlars before they go too far. They are best when they give readily between your finger and thumb, without collapsing. Once broken open, they should have a thin outer layer of still-white flesh, with a soft, fudgey-brown interior. If they are completely brown and collapsing, or black or showing any signs of mould, they are past their best. A handy tip: freezing then thawing medlars will mimic the frost and get them bletting beautifully.

Medlars are easy to grow, even if you have room only for a large pot. Their delightful, irregular demeanour, large flowers (which, while prolific in spring, can also appear in random handfuls throughout the year) and autumnal leaf colour make them worthy of the space on looks alone. They rarely exceed 2–3 metres in height and need no pruning. All varieties taste the same, but some, such as 'Royal', have larger-than-usual fruit which are especially good baked, and served with a little cream and honey.

MEDLAR AND HONEY FOOL

About 500g bletted medlars

Grated zest of ½ lemon

About 1 tbsp caster sugar

About 4 tbsp crème fraîche

Clear honey, to serve

The soft, creamy-brown flesh of nicely bletted medlars, sweetened with a little sugar, swirled with crème fraîche and topped with a trickle of honey, makes an elegant pud. Serves 2

Break open the medlars and scoop their fudgey-brown flesh into a sieve. Rub through the sieve to remove the pips and any scraps of skin, and produce a thick, brown purée. Stir in the lemon zest and then enough sugar to make it pleasantly sweet – start with 2 tsp and add more as needed – but remember there's a trickle of honey to come.

Swirl roughly the same volume of crème fraîche through the purée and serve, trickled with a little honey.

M

Megrim & witch

Nick Fisher

LATIN NAME
Megrim: *Lepidorhombus whiffiagonis*. Witch: *Glyptocephalus cynoglossus*

ALSO KNOWN AS
Megrim: Cornish sole. Witch: Torbay sole; witch flounder

SEASONALITY
Megrim: avoid January–April when spawning. Witch: avoid March–September when spawning

HABITAT
Megrim is common throughout the northeast Atlantic; witch is found all around Europe

MCS RATING
Megrim 3–4; witch 4

REC MINIMUM SIZE
Megrim 25cm; witch 28cm

MORE RECIPES
Dab in a bag (page 230); Grilled flounder and tomatoes (page 260); Lemon sole poached in butter with thyme (page 589)

SOURCING
goodfishguide.org

Megrim – and its slightly less ugly cousin, witch – are possibly fish you've never even heard of, yet thousands are landed by trawlers and gill netters all around the West Country coast every year. They are generally regarded as lesser members of the sole family. While Lemons and Dovers are soles with supermodel-like features and eye-pleasing, exquisitely camouflaged bodies, megrim and witch are squashy-eyed, big-nosed and tatty-finned species.

So why don't we know about them? Because, like so many of our great species, they're exported to Spain and Italy. Over 90 per cent of the megrim and witch caught around our coastline goes abroad without ever making an appearance on the fish slabs of Blighty.

I'm not going to argue they are every bit as good as a Dover to eat, because they aren't. But they are a quarter of the price and, looks aside, they are still fine fish to cook. Personally, I like to crisp mine first in a searing hot pan, and then finish them off in the oven, smeared with wild garlic pesto or paprika and tomato sauce – they pair up well with stronger and more exciting flavours than some of the more refined flatfish.

Generally both of these fish are by-catch so there is a lack of accurate data about their numbers and no management plan for them. Some are brought in by bottom-dragging beam trawlers (otter-trawled fish is always preferable) and discarding is an issue in some of these trawl fisheries. However, these species are still a great alternative to some of the more glamorous, under-pressure species like cod. Sales of megrim and witch are beginning to increase, which is great – let's learn to love our uglier soles. The more economic value they have, the greater the motivation to monitor these fisheries.

Occasionally, in order to make megrim and witch sound more attractive, fish merchants sell them pre-filleted and call them pretty things like Torbay Sole, Rockall Sole or even Cornish Sole. Frankly, I'd urge you to forget the names and the faces, and just concentrate on the flesh.

MEGRIM WITH CRAB AND CHIVES

A dash of olive or rapeseed oil

A knob of butter

1 large or 2 small megrim, filleted (500–600g in total)

1 shallot or ½ small onion, finely diced

75ml double cream

50g fresh crabmeat (brown and white)

A small bunch of chives, finely chopped

Sea salt and black pepper

With its rich, crabby sauce, this dish makes megrim magnificent. You could use witch too, of course, or fillets of sole, flounder or dab. Serves 2

Place a large non-stick frying pan over a medium heat and add the oil and butter. When it's foaming, add the fish fillets, skin side down, and season with salt and pepper. Cook for about 1 minute, then sprinkle the shallot or onion around the fillets. Keep the shallot or onion moving around the pan then, after a further minute, turn the fillets over with a spatula. After another minute, remove the fillets to warmed serving plates.

Turn the heat up under the pan and add ½ small glass of water and the cream, followed by the crabmeat. Bring to a simmer and cook for about 1 minute until the sauce has thickened. Season the sauce to taste then stir in the chives.

Spoon the rich crab sauce over the megrim fillets and serve straight away. This is good with potatoes, or with lemon verbena pilaf (see page 348).

Melon

Mark Diacono

LATIN NAME
Cucumis melo

SEASONALITY
Different varieties imported all year round; European Galias and Cantaloupes imported early summer–early autumn

The quality of melons has improved in recent years. Whether it's the varieties grown or the fact that they now get pretty rapidly from field to shelf (allowing the fruit to be picked at a riper stage), shop-bought melons generally have more flavour, a more intense aroma and a finer texture these days.

Nevertheless, improved as they may be, care is still crucial when choosing these voluptuous fruits. Pick your variety carefully. The Cantaloupe group is the closest you'll get to melon heaven – the orange-fleshed 'Charentais' especially. 'Galia' is another excellent choice. Both have a depth of flavour and perfume that are irresistible invitations to turn them into sorbets, granitas and summer cocktails. Sunshine-yellow honeydew melons look inviting but don't quite deliver on the flavour scale. And big, bright, juicy watermelons are really best viewed as fun, refreshing summer coolers.

Melons may soften once harvested, but any change in flavour is very limited, so choosing one in prime condition is vital to your enjoyment. Lift one to your nose and inhale – at the ends, especially. Cantaloupes and Galias should be fragrant. Press a little – the melon should just surrender to the merest pressure. If not, choose another. Check for a stalk: a melon that's ready to be picked will separate from the vine cleanly, whereas one picked early will have to be cut and leave the melon with a 'tail'.

Melons' loveliest fruity partners are those that share some of the same, intensely sweet, aromatic character – pineapple, mango, or a good ripe pear. I would, however, always season such combinations with orange or lime juice. The citrus contrasts beautifully with melons' musky taste and cuts across the fruity sweetness to prevent it from becoming cloying. A little juice squeezed from freshly grated ginger does the same thing.

Emphasising melons' honeyed fruitiness in sweet dishes is only one way to go. You can also contrast it very successfully with salt – the classic pairing with Parma ham is a fine example. Slivers or crumblings of nutty cheeses – Manchego or a hard goat's cheese, say – also make great melon partners.

Store ripe melons in the bottom of the fridge or a very cool place for up to a week, and scrub the skins under running water before you dive in with your knife.

MELON AND MILK SORBET

300ml whole milk

250g caster sugar

1 ripe Charentais or Galia melon (about 1kg)

Juice of 1 lemon

This is clean-tasting and very refreshing. The addition of milk gives a creamy finish but keeps the sorbet light. Serves 6–8

Put the milk and sugar into a pan, bring to a simmer, stirring to dissolve the sugar, then turn off the heat. Leave to cool completely.

Halve the melon and scoop out the seeds. Cut each half into wedges, then cut the juicy flesh away from the skin and put it into a blender. Pour over the sweetened milk and blitz until smooth. Transfer the purée to a bowl and stir in the lemon juice. Chill well.

Churn the mixture in an ice-cream machine until soft-set, then transfer to a freezer container and freeze until solid. (Alternatively, pour into a plastic container and freeze for about an hour or until the sides start to solidify. Mash up the mixture with a fork, mixing the frozen sides into the liquid centre. Put back in the freezer straight away for another hour. Repeat this at hourly intervals until soft-set then let the sorbet set solid.)

Either way, transfer the sorbet to the fridge about 30 minutes before serving to make scooping easier. Serve with raspberries or strawberries, bananas, apples or cherries.

Milk

We've drunk milk for thousands of years and cooked with it for centuries. It is an everyday staple, a food so thoroughly embedded in our way of life – and indeed, so cheap – that it flies under our radar. Sloshing milk on to our cornflakes, or adding a dash to our tea or coffee, for most of us, are barely conscious actions.

Yet milk comes with its share of issues. While it is nutritious and a good source of calcium – and while dairy marketing boards have done their best to convince us otherwise – we don't need it. It's not meant for human systems (obviously) and the larger part of the world's population do not produce the enzyme, lactase, needed to digest it properly. (People of European and Scandinavian descent are much more likely to be able to digest milk comfortably than Asians or Africans.)

And then there's animal welfare. Dairy farming is one of the most exploitative of all forms of animal agriculture. Dairy cows are bred to produce large quantities of milk. They are in calf roughly once a year, their calves removed from them almost immediately after birth, and they are then milked for about 10 months before a 2-month 'dry' period prior to them giving birth again. A dairy cow can go through up to thirteen of these cycles in her lifetime.

It's incumbent on those of us who want to consume milk to minimise the discomfort of the animals who produce it. For me, that means choosing organic milk from pasture-fed cows kept in small herds. Cows are supposed to graze; they are designed to digest grass. In modern systems, cows' feed is supplemented with other ingredients, known as 'concentrates', that are much higher in energy and protein, in order to boost their milk production. Most dairy cattle are brought indoors during the winter when grass is not growing, where they may be fed on silage or hay – again often supplemented with other feeds.

Organic standards state that cows must spend the majority of their lives outdoors and that their diet must contain a minimum 60 per cent forage, such as grass and clover or roots. Average yields for organic dairy cows are around one-third less than for conventional cows – a statistic which might make some farmers shudder but that I find reassuring. Take into account that organic milk has been shown to contain higher levels of nutrients such as omega-3 and vitamin E, and it seems an obvious choice.

Milk is an ingredient I have cut back on but I still enjoy organic milk, as it offers something unique: the velvety sweetness of dairy without the richness of cream. At around 4 per cent fat, even whole milk is still a relatively low-fat food and I don't see much point in skimmed or semi-skimmed milks, where, for the sake of losing a few calories, you also lose flavour, body and a small dose of fat-soluble vitamins. Whole milk tastes better and cooks better too: béchamel sauces, bubbling, cheesy rarebits, mellow rice puddings and wobbling crème caramels all owe their character to milk.

Milk heated with even mildly acidic ingredients, including fruits and vegetables, is prone to curdling. Milky soups such as chowders can have a slightly grainy appearance because of this. To tackle it, a very small measure of flour can be stirred into the soup base – mixed into well-sweated onions, for instance – to help stabilise the milk.

Sometimes, however, that characteristic curdling is just what you want. You can produce a simple home-made cheese (very similar to the Indian paneer) by warming whole milk with lemon juice until it 'splits', then draining the whey from the curdy solids through muslin. The traditional Italian dish *arrosto di maiale al latte* is another way to celebrate the split, by braising pork in milk until it curdles and cooks down to nutty sweetness.

Non-cow's milk and unpasteurised milk

Other milks – from goats, sheep and buffalo – are becoming increasingly popular because some people find them easier to tolerate than cow's milk. You might assume that these 'alternative' milks are produced in less intensive systems than cow's milk, but this is not necessarily the case. Most of our dairy goats are raised in zero-grazing systems and are far less likely to be allowed outside than dairy cows. Organic goat's milk is available, though rare, and there are some free-range producers. Dairy sheep (as with sheep bred for meat) and buffalo tend to do well outdoors for most of the year – but it's worth researching how the animals are kept before you buy.

There's a small but passionate following for raw milk in this country. In England, Wales and Northern Ireland, you can buy it direct from the producer, for example at farmers' markets and farm shops, though in Scotland it's banned altogether.

Pasteurisation kills off most of the bacteria and enzymes in milk and, some believe, turns it into a lifeless and less nutritious product. I can certainly vouch for the fact that unpasteurised milk has good flavour and character.

There is always a risk attached to drinking unpasteurised milk because it can contain seriously nasty bacteria including campylobacter, E. coli and listeria. Producers have to follow very stringent hygiene rules but raw milk does, occasionally, cause food poisoning. These outbreaks are rare but potentially very serious, especially for people with other health problems, or pregnant women.

A1 and A2 milk

The latest debate about cow's milk centres on the identification of two different types, labelled A1 and A2 according to the form of protein they contain. All cow's milk used to be A2. The A1 protein arose as the result of a genetic mutation, but is now found in milk from many modern breeds – including 'Holstein-Friesian', which dominates our market. Some other breeds (including Channel Island cows) still produce largely A2 milk. The issue now at large concerns a 'peptide' produced in the gut when you drink A1 milk, that some believe can affect digestion, immunity and even the nervous system. More scientific evidence is needed but, if you're persuaded of its merits, you can now buy A2 milk in many UK supermarkets.

MASALA CHAI DOODH

1 heaped tsp loose-leaf
Assam tea

4 cardamom pods, crushed

4cm piece of root ginger, bashed

A large pinch of ground
cinnamon (optional)

400ml cold whole milk

1–2 tsp sugar, or to taste

Doodh means milk in Hindi and masala chai doodh is milky, spiced tea – or spicy tea-ey milk, to be more accurate. Fragrant and sweet, it's equally refreshing drunk piping hot or icy cold. Serves 2

Put the tea in a medium pan with the cardamom, ginger and cinnamon, if using. Add 100ml boiling water, swirl the tea and spices in the water and place over a medium heat. As the water comes to the boil, add a big splosh of the cold milk. Bring back to the boil. Repeat this process, adding milk and heating 3 or 4 times until you have added it all.

Add sugar to taste and give the chai a final fierce boil for about 2 minutes – watch it carefully all the time and whip it off the heat for a moment if it threatens to boil over.

Strain the chai into cups and drink piping hot, adding more sugar if you like. Alternatively, strain, cool and chill the chai, skim off any skin that forms, and serve it over ice (you could call this a spicy cool doodh).

Mint

Hugh Fearnley-Whittingstall

LATIN NAME
Mentha species

SEASONALITY
April–October

MORE RECIPES
Artichoke heart and potato salad (page 32); Griddled aubergines with spiced yoghurt (page 39); Raw asparagus and radish salad (page 36); Broad bean and feta falafel (page 96); Roasted courgettes and onions with yoghurt dressing (page 684); Barley and raw mushroom salad (page 47); Noodle salad with spicy peanut butter dressing (page 451); Fried salmon with cucumber and gooseberry salad (page 553); Spiced papaya salsa (page 428); Crab apple jelly with thyme, juniper and mint (page 204)

Mint is a herb used prolifically in cuisines across the globe so it seems fitting that it also grows promiscuously – rampaging over the poorest ground, pushing its way through cracks and crevices and elbowing other plants out of the way.

I couldn't possibly be without mint – several kinds of mint – in my garden, but I have to keep it trammelled and controlled, planting it in large pots, or in bottomed-out containers sunk into the soil. Otherwise, perhaps in league with nettles and horseradish, mint would simply take over the world.

Indeed, this is a herb that recognises few frontiers. It would be easy to draw a minty map that spans the earth, from our own, cherished mint sauce to the kofte of Turkey and the dolmades of Greece, taking in the tisanes and tagines of Morocco, the minty salads and soups of the Middle East, and the pungent sambals of Southeast Asia on the way. Mint has an ability that not all herbs share – to grace sweet and savoury dishes with equal charm. It is assertive enough to be noticed, mild enough to mingle.

I see mint as a quintessentially summery herb, perfectly at home with fresh berries, cooling cocktails, salads and grilled meat. And if you grow your own, summer will be the best time to use it. However, keep it well watered, trim back regularly and pinch out flowering stems, and you'll be able to extend your mint season from early spring well into the autumn.

The alternative is to buy mint in the supermarket – a touch-and-go affair as it can sometimes be very disappointing – or, much better, to go to a farm shop or market stall. Shops that specialise in Asian or Middle Eastern ingredients may well have properly generous bunches too: it pays to ask, because savvy shopkeepers don't always have it on display, preferring to keep it fresh and cool out back. Mint is not a herb that does well on the shelf; once cut, it soon wilts. At home, trim off the dried stem ends to 'open' them and keep in a jug of cold water to prolong their life. You'll get 10 days from a big cut bunch at the cooler end of the kitchen.

Pretty much the only mint you're likely to be able to buy as a cut herb is spearmint, i.e. the softer and sweeter type. It's also called 'common' or 'garden' mint and is the most versatile and useful variety, perfect for everything from a tabbouleh to a mojito.

As soon as you visit the garden centre rather than the grocers, however, you'll discover how much more there is to mint. For a start, there are many sub-types of spearmint, such as the glorious, sweet Moroccan mint, which is perfect for mint tea (and doubles for most garden mint applications). And then there is the other main type of mint, peppermint, which, as the name suggests, has a much more piquant, menthol bite. It can be overpowering if used in the wrong dish (a delicate cucumber salad, say) but to some, it's even better for tea than spearmint. It's also great for making minty syrups to trickle over fruit or cakes, or in chocolatey puds such as mousses.

Many of the multiplicity of 'flavoured' mints that await you are forms of peppermint too. Chocolate mint, 'berries and cream' mint, basil mint, orange, lemon, lime or grapefruit mint – it's a tempting catalogue. I've found ginger mint (with fruit) and pineapple mint (in Pimms) to be worthwhile, but don't get too carried away – you really cannot beat basic garden spearmint for everyday deliciousness. Also, don't grow different mints together as they can cross-pollinate and lose their distinctive flavours.

Other forms of mint you may come across include watermint, which grows wild near streams and in other damp places. Well worth seeking out if you don't grow your own mint, it has a strong flavour – more like peppermint than spearmint – and makes a stunning sorbet, and a pleasingly quirky mojito.

And, while I'm not a huge fan of dried herbs, a good, strong dried mint – such as you'll be able to get from a decent herb and spice specialist or stores catering to Greek, Turkish and Arab communities – is an intriguing ingredient. With a smoky, earthy character, it's essential for authentic flavour in dishes such as dolmades and tzatziki. It tastes different to fresh mint – the bitter notes are more to the fore – but in these contexts, that is how it should be.

When it comes to using fresh mint, don't be confined by convention. It's fabulous, of course, in the simple jellies and vinegary sauces that we love with roast meat, particularly lamb. But raw, torn mint is like gustatory gilding on the gutsy, smoky, rough-hewn deliciousness of barbecued meat too. This herb is also marvellous with veg, especially spring and summer veg, from asparagus, broad beans and peas in June to courgettes and aubergines in August. Just chop it or roll up the leaves into a tight 'cigar' and slice finely into ribbons then scatter over the veg – or stir into yoghurty sauces or simple dressings. Try mint in place of other herbs in favourite dishes – swap it for parsley in gremolata or use it to usurp basil in your tomato salads. It will totally reinvigorate the old cliché, 'a refreshing change'.

Mint's cool sweetness can be superb with raw fruit – it has a subtle seasoning effect, almost like lemon juice (although it's delicious with a spritz of lemon or lime juice *as well*). Top partners for mint include strawberries, raspberries, peaches, apples, mangoes and pineapple.

And then, after all that feasting, do try that cup of mint tea – the best herbal infusion (and digestif) there is. On a hot day, lightly sweetened, cooled and poured over ice, it manages to be both soothing and refreshing at the same time.

MINTED SPELT AND TOMATO SALAD

200g pearled spelt

A large bunch of spearmint (about 100g)

400g ripe, flavoursome tomatoes (any size, including cherry)

A bunch of spring onions

2 tbsp extra virgin olive oil

1 tbsp cider vinegar

½ tsp caster sugar

Sea salt and black pepper

This is a tabbouleh-style dish and, like any tabbouleh, it should be all about the herbs. In this case, it's mint alone, which is a surprisingly good partner to tomatoes. You could replace the pearled spelt with pearl barley (which will take a little longer to cook), or use the traditional bulgar wheat, or even gluten-free quinoa. Serves 4

Put the spelt in a sieve and rinse well. Tip into a pan and cover with cold water. Pick the mint leaves from the stems and add the stems to the spelt pan; reserve the leaves. Bring to a simmer and cook until tender but nutty, about 20 minutes.

Drain the spelt in a colander. Chop the tomatoes into roughly 1cm pieces and slice the spring onions thinly.

While the spelt is still warm, tip it into a large bowl, add the olive oil, vinegar and sugar and season generously with salt and pepper. Now add the tomatoes and spring onions.

Take several mint leaves at a time, roll them into 'cigars' and cut them into thin ribbons. Scatter the mint into the salad. Use your hands to tumble everything together thoroughly. The warmth of the spelt will bring out all the flavours in the mint and tomatoes. Allow the salad to stand for 15–20 minutes, check the seasoning, then serve.

Mizuna & other oriental leaves

Mark Diacono

LATIN NAME
Mizuna and Mibuna: *Brassica rapa japonica* or *Brassica rapa nipposinica*. Giant Red Mustard: *Brassica juncea*. Green in Snow: *Brassica juncea multiceps*. Mustard Red Frills: *Brassica juncea crispifolia 'Rubra'*. Kai-lan: *Brassica oleracea alboglabra*. Chop Suey Greens: *Glebionis coronaria*

SEASONALITY
Various, but many do well in the winter

It's only the constraints of space that have grouped mizuna and the other oriental leaves together here, for, in fact, they form a diverse and fascinating corner of the leafy world. Most of them do, however, share common characteristics.

Almost all have a certain peppery spiciness that can range from the pleasantly mild ('Mibuna'), through the delightfully, nose-ticklingly lively ('Green in Snow') to the downright horseradish (mature 'Giant Red Mustard').

All are easy to grow too: sow them straight into prepared soil or start in modules in spring, growing them in a sunny spot and spaced according to the packet's instructions. Equally importantly, many are hardy, surviving the worst that winter can throw at them. I remember one freezing January day when the few of us that had made it to River Cottage HQ brushed away the foot of snow that sat on top of the giant red mustard plants, cut a few handfuls and wilted them to serve in rolls with hot rare beef – it was as good a lunch as I have had.

Oriental leaves are increasingly appearing in mixed salad bags: 'Mizuna' is the jagged-edged green leaf; the narrow, spindly purple leaf will be 'Mustard Red Frills'; and the saw-edged balloon leaf is likely to be young 'Giant Red Mustard'. Good as they are, this is a slender selection from the possibilities. Allow me to suggest a few of my other favourites.

'Kai-lan' is not peppery but seems in flavour and looks to be a cross between asparagus and sprouting broccoli and loves all the same treatments and sauces as either of its parents. 'Chop Suey Greens' (aka shungiku) is an edible chrysanthemum, with a most peculiar flavour – slightly medicinal, part aniseed – that certainly shouldn't be over-used, but as a bit-part in a leafy stir-fry adds something quite wonderful. Its flowers are edible too. Green in Snow is perhaps my favourite of the oriental leaves. Mild, yet bright and characterful when young, it gathers peppery punch as it grows, allowing you to harvest it (like all oriental leaves, it takes well to cut-and-come-again) at the size that gives the flavour you require.

Raw oriental leaves make a delicious, sparing punctuation in a salad of milder leaves, and are superb wilted or stir-fried as a side veg. They share a certain robustness with leafy greens such as chard and spinach, and so take easily to pasta sauces and work well as a peppery substitute in dishes such as creamed spinach.

WILTED MIZUNA WITH CHILLI, GARLIC AND SUNFLOWER SEEDS

50g sunflower seeds

3 tbsp tamari or soy sauce

1 tbsp rapeseed oil

3 medium garlic cloves, sliced

1 medium-hot red chilli, deseeded (or not for more heat) and sliced

350g mizuna, leaf and stalk

Juice of 1–2 limes

If you grow your own leaves, this is a great way to deal with excess – or anything that looks like it might bolt. It works beautifully with mizuna but is good with other peppery oriental leaves too. Serves 2 as a main dish with noodles or rice, 4 as a starter

Toast the seeds in a large dry frying pan over a medium-high heat for 30 seconds. Add 2 tbsp of the tamari or soy and cook, tossing regularly, until the liquid has evaporated and the seeds are dark and fragrant. Remove the seeds to a plate.

Return the pan to a high heat and add the oil. When hot, toss in the garlic and chilli and stir-fry for 1–2 minutes. Throw in the mizuna and, using two forks or some tongs, toss well for 3–4 minutes or until the leaf is well wilted. Squeeze over some lime and the remaining tamari or soy.

Serve over rice or noodles, sprinkled with the tamari-toasted sunflower seeds and another squeeze of lime.

Morels

John Wright

LATIN NAME
Morchella esculenta.
Black morel: *Morchella elata*

SEASONALITY
April–May

HABITAT
Uncommon; occasionally found on waste ground, in gardens and woodland (particularly near habitation)

M

Unlike the bulk of wild mushrooms, which are autumnal, morels are denizens of spring, typically April and May. There are two principle species: the morel, and the darker and more conical black morel. Both have an intensely mushroomy flavour and, unfortunately, both are fiendishly hard to find. Despite some heroic searches, I have never found any truly in the wild, only in gardens and parks.

The morel often forms permanent colonies in mature gardens, usually pushing themselves untidily out of lawns. The black morel was once quite rare, but since the introduction of woodchip mulches in the late 1980s has found a new lease of life in rose beds and around car parks. Black morels can sometimes appear in their hundreds, but only in fairly fresh mulch. Unlike their cousin, they seldom make a return visit to the same location. If you find wild morels, of either type, then do be sure to clean them quickly but thoroughly in cold water as they will be full of leaf litter and wildlife.

The honeycomb appearance to the cap is very distinct in both species. If you discover something that looks a bit like a morel with the honeycomb replaced by what seems to be a piece of screwed-up brown leather, then you have found the deadly poisonous false morel (*Gyromitra esculenta*). Surprisingly, these can be eaten but only if prepared in a special way. Morels themselves are poisonous raw and must be well cooked before eating (this goes for dried morels too, and the soaking liquid from dried morels).

Fresh morels are available from specialist suppliers between early March and late May. They are food-miles heavy, though. It is not possible to cultivate them reliably, so they are picked wild in Turkey, China, North America and many other places. And they're not cheap! Also expensive, but more readily available and very useful, are dried morels. These can be reconstituted by soaking in cold water for an hour or two, and used as fresh morels – the flavour is just as intense, if not more so, though they do not regain their firmness. Make sure you keep the soaking water for sauces or stocks.

Morels, being hollow, are just asking to be stuffed (when fresh) and are frequently served this way, the filling being piped in. Two classic dishes are morels *à la crème*, and morels in a herb sauce. They also go famously well with veal.

MORELS AND POTATOES BRAISED WITH RED WINE AND GARLIC

750g small new potatoes or waxy salad potatoes, such as Charlotte or Anya

Olive oil, for frying

150g fresh morels, cleaned and trimmed, or 25g dried morels soaked in cold water for about 2 hours

4 garlic cloves, chopped

150ml red wine

A large knob of butter

1 tbsp chopped parsley

Sea salt and black pepper

The season for fresh morels coincides nicely with the beginning of the new potato harvest, and the two work deliciously together in this dish (though you can use rehydrated dried morels here too). Bashing the potatoes to crack them open before you cook them helps them take on the flavours of the wine and garlic. Serves 3–4

Using a pestle or rolling pin, whack each potato – to crack them open (not to pulverise them). You might find it easier to loosely wrap each potato in a tea towel first.

Cover the base of a large, wide saucepan with a 2mm film of olive oil and place over a high heat. Add the bashed potatoes and fry them hard, stirring from time to time, for at least 10 minutes – they should start to brown. Add the morels and continue to fry for a further 5 minutes. Add the garlic to the pan and stir well for a minute; don't let it colour.

Add the wine (be careful, it will spit) and stir well, then reduce the heat to a simmer. Put a lid on the pan and cook, stirring occasionally, for about 20 minutes or until the potatoes are almost tender. Now remove the lid and cook for up to 10 minutes, until the wine has reduced to a syrupy glaze. Stir in the butter and take the pan off the heat.

Taste and add more salt and pepper if needed, then serve, scattered with chopped parsley.

Mozzarella

Gill Meller

SOURCING
laverstokepark.co.uk

A plate of fresh mozzarella with sourdough bread, good olive oil and salt is one of my all-time favourite dishes. I love the purity of mozzarella's form, its light and milky texture and its delicate, cool flavour.

The majority of mass-produced mozzarella is made with cow's milk. But the far richer milk of the water buffalo makes the very best – *mozzarella di bufala*. Buffalo mozzarella from the Campania region carries a DOC (controlled designation of origin) label, meaning it must be made in the traditional way in that area of southern Italy.

The process of making this stretchy cheese is relatively straightforward. Citric acid is first added to pasteurised milk to raise the acidity. Rennet is used to separate the curds from the whey (in the case of traditional Italian buffalo mozzarella, this is animal rennet, but vegetarian rennet is used in some other mozzarellas). The curds are cut or torn into pieces, a process the Italians call *mozzatura*, meaning 'cutting by hand'.

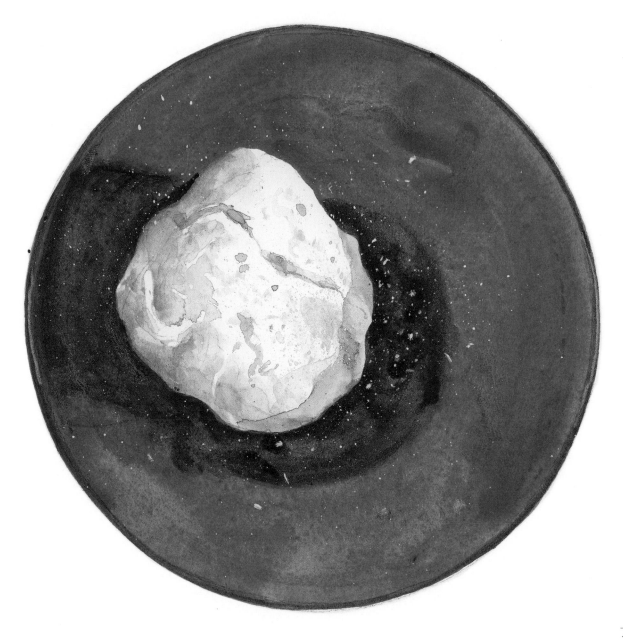

The whey is heated and when it reaches 80°C the curds are re-submerged in it to soften them before being stretched and folded, then shaped into balls. It's this heating and stretching process that gives the cheese its celebrated texture. The cheese is usually packaged in its own whey, and has a short shelf-life.

Burrata is another unbelievably delicious Italian fresh cheese. It's very similar to traditional mozzarella (though usually made with cow's milk) but is filled with rich cream. It's softer and even milkier than mozzarella, and almost flows when you tear into it. Burrata is best eaten fresh, within 24 hours of making, and purists would say it should not be refrigerated.

Good burrata and buffalo mozzarella cost a bit more but are well worth it. Well-made cow's milk mozzarella can be decent, but blocks of cheap, highly processed pizza mozzarella are likely to be rubbery and hard. Concerns have been raised over the welfare of some farmed buffalo in Italy and there are very few organic Italian buffalo mozzarellas, but good quality organic British buffalo mozzarella is now available.

Mozzarella is well known as a pizza topping and it does melt rather deliciously into soft, milky strings: it's hard to resist when torn and stirred into a hot risotto or stuffed inside rice patties and fried to make *arancini*. But I think the best buffalo mozzarellas, with their subtle, lactic tang, beg to be enjoyed uncooked. The combination of mozzarella with ripe tomatoes or thinly sliced prosciutto has delighted families throughout Italy for hundreds of years. These pairings are hard to beat. However, mozzarella is also wonderful with sweet roasted beetroots, chargrilled asparagus or, if you're up for a bit of foraging, with wilted nettles and olive oil (see below).

MOZZARELLA WITH NETTLES AND LENTILS

100g freshly picked nettle tops, well washed

1 small garlic clove, grated

4 tbsp extra virgin olive oil, plus a little extra to finish

1 tbsp red wine vinegar

4 balls of buffalo mozzarella or burrata (125g each), or 2 larger ones

50g cooked Puy lentils

5–6 spring onions, trimmed and cut into 5mm rounds

Sea salt and black pepper

Flaky sea salt, to serve

Peppery, dressed nettles make a characterful partner to creamy mozzarella or burrata. You could use chard or spinach in the same way when stingers aren't around. And any lentils that hold their shape when cooked can be substituted for the Puy. Serves 4

Bring a large pan of salted water to the boil. Add the nettles and cook, stirring once or twice, for 2–3 minutes.

Drain the nettles and rinse them immediately under cold running water to fix their green colour and stop the cooking process. Drain again, then squeeze the excess liquid from the nettles.

Tip the cooked nettles on to a large board and chop them fairly finely. Transfer to a bowl and add the garlic, olive oil and wine vinegar. Season generously with salt and pepper and stir to combine.

Place a ball (or ½ large ball) of mozzarella on each serving plate. Spoon over the nettles and scatter over the lentils and sliced spring onions. Finish with an extra trickle of olive oil and a sprinkling of flaky salt and freshly ground pepper. Serve with good bread.

Mulberries

Mark Diacono

LATIN NAME
Morus species

SEASONALITY
August–September

MORE RECIPES
Wineberries with peaches and custard (page 317); Raspberry almond streusel cake (page 526)

Mulberries have a fantastic flavour – somewhere between blackberries, raspberries, blackcurrants and the deepest flavoured grapes. Find a tree and visit it in mid- to late August for a real treat.

At their perfect state of ripeness, mulberries can barely hold themselves together, which is why you never see them in the shops and why you can expect purple stains when picking (wear old clothes). Their short shelf-life – a day, two at best – means you should decide how you intend to use them before you pick.

They make an excellent ice cream, sorbet, jam, trifle or clafoutis. And, once you've tasted the results, you'll believe vodka was invented for the sole purpose of transforming mulberries and sugar into the finest fireside drink there is. Mulberry vodka couldn't be easier to make: quarter-fill a jar with sugar, tip it out into a bowl and half-fill the jar with fruit, return the sugar and fill up with vodka. Invert the jar a few times a week and try to leave it for at least 6 months – longer if you possibly can.

Search the internet and you'll find websites listing locations of public mulberry trees across the country. They were a common sight in large nineteenth-century gardens, many of which are now open to the public, so a little light scrumping could be not too far from you.

Happily, mulberry trees are easy to grow. They rarely reach more than 3 metres in height and can always be kept at that size with a little pruning, though no ongoing pruning or training is actually required. Their heart-shaped leaves don't arrive until well into spring – the definitive sign of winter being over – and tend to grow over the fruit, which keeps most hidden from the birds.

There are red, black and white mulberry species, though the name doesn't necessarily correlate to the colour of their fruit. The trees are late developers, sometimes not fruiting for half a dozen years, so the key is to go for a variety that produces fruit relatively early in its life – 'Illinois Everbearing', 'Carmen' or 'Ivory', for example. For the same reason, get a tree that's a few years old: it will cost a little more but you'll be into delicious fruit that bit quicker.

MULBERRY AND WALNUT CRANACHAN

200g mulberries

3 tbsp clear honey

3 tbsp mulberry vodka (if you have made some) or whisky

50g medium oatmeal

40g walnuts, roughly chopped

150ml double cream

150g Greek-style yoghurt

This take on the traditional Scottish pudding, with some yoghurt stirred into the cream to make the whole thing less rich, makes stunning use of mulberries. Other soft fruit such as raspberries and loganberries are delicious alternatives. Serves 4

Start by putting the mulberries into a bowl with 1 tbsp honey and 1 tbsp mulberry vodka or whisky. Give them a good mix, crushing the fruit a little so it starts to release its juices. Set aside.

Put a non-stick frying pan over a medium-low heat. Add the oatmeal and walnuts and toast, stirring often, until they are golden and fragrant. Transfer to a plate to cool.

Whisk the cream together with the remaining honey and alcohol, until it forms soft peaks. Go gently: it's important not to over-whip the cream as it will stiffen a little further as you put the pudding together. Gently fold the yoghurt into the cream.

Add the toasted oats and macerated mulberries and gently fold them in, so that you have a rippled effect. Spoon into glasses and serve straight away.

Mullet, red

Gill Meller

LATIN NAME
Mullus surmuletus

ALSO KNOWN AS
Striped red mullet, goatfish

SEASONALITY
Avoid May–July when spawning

HABITAT
Found worldwide in warm
waters and as far north as
the British Isles

MCS RATING
3–4

REC MINIMUM SIZE
16cm

MORE RECIPES
Hot mackerel, beetroot
and horseradish sandwich
(page 373); Garfish with olives,
oregano and garlic (page 267);
Black bream with Jerusalem
artichoke purée (page 91)

SOURCING
goodfishguide.org

The red mullet is a beautiful fish: with its vivid pinks and reds, it looks almost tropical. And it is, in fact, a member of the warm-water goatfish family that long ago strayed north to swim in the Mediterranean and European Atlantic. The Ancient Romans made a cult out of the colour, keeping the fish alive until the very last minute, because the red starts to fade once it dies. Rod-and-line caught mullet still get a higher price than those that die in a net because they have a brighter hue.

Red mullet is a fish we should eat with a little caution. There is concern over fishing pressure in several areas and large numbers of juvenile red mullet are often caught – avoid any smaller than 16cm. However, a fat red mullet is a welcome, though pricey, addition to any table. Most are caught off the south and southwest coast, with a few finding their way as far north as Scotland. They are best eaten in the late summer and early autumn, avoiding the spawning season of May to July.

The well-flavoured, firm, slightly creamy-coloured flesh of red mullet puts it somewhere between a white fish and an oily one. The tradition is to cook mullet whole (a 350–500g fish is great for one portion) with the guts intact, or at least with the liver still inside, giving a slightly gamey flavour to the flesh. In fact, it is sometimes called 'the woodcock of the sea', as the game bird is cooked with its guts in too (see page 678).

I like to gut a red mullet but keep in the liver or cook it separately, perhaps with garlic, green olives, anchovies and wine, then spread it over the skin of the fried fish.

Red mullet has large scales that should be removed, taking care not to tear the skin, which has a deserved reputation for tastiness. The whole fish is lovely grilled, barbecued or roasted and works equally well with a salsa (try grapefruit, red onion and coriander) or a creamy sauce flavoured with bacon and green peppercorns. Fillets are also fantastic in a classic bouillabaisse.

RED MULLET WITH ROASTED RED PEPPER MAYO

This is fabulous with a fragrant salad of tomatoes and olives. You can happily give the same treatment to gurnard or bream. Serves 2

1 tsp cumin seeds

1 tsp coriander seeds

1 tsp fennel seeds

1 tsp dried chilli flakes

50g white breadcrumbs

4 red mullet fillets

1 tbsp olive or rapeseed oil

Sea salt and black pepper

FOR THE RED PEPPER MAYO

1 medium red pepper

4–5 tbsp good quality
mayonnaise

2 tbsp raisins

For the red pepper mayo, preheat the oven to 220°C/Fan 200°C/Gas 7 (or the grill to high). Put the pepper on a greased baking sheet and roast for about 30 minutes, turning once, or until soft, wrinkled and blackened in places. (Or blister the pepper under a hot grill, turning more often.)

Meanwhile, toast the cumin, coriander and fennel seeds in a dry frying pan for a couple of minutes, until fragrant. Using a pestle and mortar, bash the toasted seeds together with the chilli flakes until coarsely ground. Tip into a shallow dish and combine with the breadcrumbs and some salt and pepper.

Put the roasted pepper into a bowl, cover with cling film and leave for 30 minutes; this will help lift the skin. Peel, halve and deseed the pepper, discarding any white pith and juice. Chop the flesh fairly finely. When cooled completely, combine the red pepper with the mayonnaise and raisins. Taste and add salt and pepper if needed.

Press the fish fillets into the spiced breadcrumbs, patting them on to the flesh (they won't stick so readily to the skin, but don't worry about this).

Heat the oil in a large non-stick pan over a medium heat. Add the red mullet fillets, skin side down, and cook for 2–3 minutes. Carefully flip the fillets over and cook for another minute or two until the flesh is opaque right through. Serve at once, with the red pepper mayo and a salad.

Mushrooms, cultivated

Gill Meller

LATIN NAME
Agaricus bisporus

SEASONALITY
All year round

MORE RECIPES
Sautéed mushrooms with juniper (page 320); Barley and raw mushroom salad (page 47); Kohlrabi and mushroom salad with sesame (page 581); Squash, shallot and mushroom tart (page 604); Woodcock with wild mushrooms (page 678); Hedgehog mushroom and bacon omelette (page 306); Blewit, pigeon and endive salad (page 74)

While I love gathering wild mushrooms it is, of course, a seasonal activity and one that carries no guarantee of success. To enjoy the flavour of these fungi regularly, you need to buy them. Mushrooms are the 'fruit body' of a fungus. They need dead, organic material on which to grow. Spores colonise rotting matter with their mycelial threads and, if the climatic conditions are right, mushrooms are the result. Modern mushroom farmers have devised ways to mimic that environment and those conditions, and so mushrooms are now available to us every day of the year.

Mushroom cultivation is a process with a range of environmental pros and cons. There is a lot of recycling involved, but heating and cooling mushroom sheds requires a lot of energy. Some producers will use green forms of energy for this. The growing process also involves the use of peat – something for which a viable alternative has yet to be found, but at least the peat must come from a Department of the Environment (DOE) approved site.

Commercially cultivated mushrooms are grown on a special compost, made up largely of recycled agricultural waste, including chicken manure and wheat straw. Gypsum is also added. These ingredients are combined and left to break down, with regular turning, for several weeks, until a good compost forms. This is then pasteurised to destroy any pathogens.

Mushroom spawn is then mixed into the compost, which is transferred to growing beds where it is covered with a layer of 'casing soil'. Comprised of peat and spent lime (a by-product of sugar refining), this covering soil holds water and helps the fungus to develop.

Temperature and humidity manipulation, and the introduction of carbon dioxide, are then used to stress the fungus, which encourages it to throw its energies into reproduction. Around 3 weeks after the laying of the compost, a crop of mushrooms can be harvested, usually followed by a second and third flush. The spent compost is sterilised and sold to gardeners and farmers, and the process begins again.

Mushrooms can be cultivated all year round in this way, though there are still peaks and troughs. For reasons that no one has quite yet fathomed, even in carefully controlled conditions, mushrooms don't particularly like growing in the summer.

All mushrooms are rich with the 'fifth taste', umami, a delicious savouriness. To release that intense mushroom savour, it's necessary to drive off much of the mushroom's

---

CULTIVATED MUSHROOM VARIETIES

White mushrooms Taking in button mushrooms, closed cap mushrooms, open cap mushrooms and large flat mushrooms, these account for around 95 per cent of the mushrooms we buy in the UK. They are sweetly bland, but can be coaxed into flavoursomeness with the heat of the frying pan.

Chestnut mushrooms These do indeed have a lovely chestnut colour, a richer, earthier flavour than standard white mushrooms and a denser texture, so they shrink less on cooking. When still small, they are called chestnut mushrooms and when allowed to grow and mature fully, they are called portobellos.

Shiitake A dark brown mushroom with a firm-textured cap, this has a distinctive, slightly metallic, meaty flavour. Shiitake take strong seasonings very well, though their slightly chewy texture is not to everyone's taste.

Enoki With tiny white caps bobbing on long, slender stems, these look like fairy-tale mushrooms. They are very pretty used raw in a salad.

Oyster mushrooms These light brown or silvery grey mushrooms have a silky but resilient texture (rather like chicken), which makes them excellent in stir-fries. They have a slight sweetness.

considerable water content. This both concentrates the essential mushroom flavour and, if you cook them in a pan or the oven, allows the mushrooms to caramelise on the surface too. This browning of natural sugars further enhances flavours.

Use a large frying pan and don't overcrowd it: the mushrooms will release copious juices and there must be space on the pan base for that liquid to sizzle and evaporate. I often cook mushrooms in 2 or 3 batches to avoid overcrowding.

Cut the mushrooms into slices, around 5mm thick. Heat a large pan with a little oil and/or butter, over a medium to medium-high heat then add your mushrooms. Fry them quite 'hard', tossing and stirring often, until the liquid they release has bubbled away, probably 7–8 minutes. Then allow them to cook for another couple of minutes until they take on some good, golden brown colour. Their flavour will now be sweet and intense and you can enhance it with the addition of a little chopped garlic, perhaps some chopped parsley, a touch of salt and pepper and a squeeze of lemon for a fantastic breakfast, lunch or supper.

Mushrooms are also excellent in risottos, pasta dishes, soups and stocks. For a flavourful gravy suitable for vegans, sauté chopped onions, carrots, celery and bay leaves with mushrooms, bind with a little flour and then add veg stock and simmer for a few minutes. Mash the veg roughly, then pass the mix through a sieve, pressing the veg to squeeze out flavour. Season the gravy with salt, pepper, a little tamari for extra umami kick, and a shot of strong coffee, which really rounds out those savoury mushroom flavours.

Mushrooms' high water content, plus their lack of bright colour, has led to them being seen as nutritionally rather neutral, but they have hidden benefits. They've always been considered worthy of inclusion in the five-a-day matrix, being a good source of fibre, B vitamins and various minerals, including potassium. They are also a particularly rich source of an antioxidant l-ergothioneine, which may help to protect the body from cancer.

BAKED MUSHROOMS WITH ROSEMARY AND WALNUT BUTTER

4 large flat open cap mushrooms

75g butter, softened

50g walnut halves

Leaves from 3–4 small sprigs of rosemary, roughly chopped

A small handful of flat-leaf parsley leaves, roughly chopped

2 garlic cloves, grated

1 tbsp olive or rapeseed oil

Sea salt and black pepper

Big, open mushrooms are wonderful stuffed – or, topped, to be more accurate. Mushrooms' affinity with garlic is known, but both walnuts and rosemary work similarly well as partners. (Pictured on previous page.) Serves 2

Preheat the oven to 200°C/Fan 180°C/Gas 6.

Remove the stalks from the mushroom caps and place them in a food processor; set the caps aside for stuffing later.

Add the butter, walnuts, herbs, garlic, oil and a little salt and pepper to the processor and pulse until everything is well mixed but the walnuts still retain a little texture.

Place the mushrooms gills side up on a lipped baking tray. Season them lightly, then spread the stuffing evenly over the top of each mushroom. Bake for 18–20 minutes until bubbling, fragrant and golden brown. Serve with good bread and a green salad.

Mussels

LATIN NAME
Mytilus edulis

ALSO KNOWN AS
Common mussel, blue mussel

SEASONALITY
Avoid wild mussels April–September when spawning, and when water quality may be lower

HABITAT
Common all around the British Isles coast (with some gaps due to lack of habitat)

MCS RATING
1–3 (some sources not assessed)

REC MINIMUM SIZE
5cm

MORE RECIPES
Curried clams (page 184); Paella (page 163)

SOURCING
goodfishguide.org; msc.org

Mussels are farmed on many parts of our coast – though to say 'farming' is pushing it a bit, since mussel cultivation involves corralling, managing and harvesting a population of essentially wild shellfish. Some are grown on the seabed (these are hand-raked, dredged or harvested via an 'elevator' that dislodges the mussels with water jets). Others are 'rope-grown'. Both are potentially sustainable (Exmouth ground-laid mussels are MSC accredited) but rope-growing is about as ecologically friendly as aquaculture gets and produces beautifully clean, thin-shelled, grit-free mussels. The bulk of British rope-grown mussels come from Scotland, but there's a burgeoning industry in the Southwest too.

The joy of the rope-growing system is the lack of interference. There are no inputs – no chemicals are required to keep the mussels healthy. There is no captive breeding. Plastic-toggled ropes are simply fixed between heavy-duty buoys on the surface and anchors on the seabed, in sheltered tidal waters that are known to be home to a healthy population of mussels. 'Spat', or tiny baby mussels, appear, as if by magic, on the ropes.

The infant mussels are as tiny as a baby's fingernail. The real ecological gain is that you don't even have to feed them in order to get them to saleable size: 4–6cm long and filled with sweet, sea-tasting cream-to-orange coloured meat. They take the planktonic nutrients they need from the water that ebbs and flows around them. What's more, a mussel farm can provide positive ecological benefits to the waters in which it is sited. The mussel-clad ropes make a weedy underwater jungle that attracts other sea-life. It forms a natural habitat and nursery for all kinds of creatures, including anemones, starfish, marine worms, prawns and juvenile fish.

It's not perfect of course. There is a carbon footprint to the lines of giant plastic, bobbing floats – and this visible manifestation of a mussel farm may spoil the view of an otherwise flawless stretch of water. The harvesting is done by a noisy, chugging, floating diesel-powered 'mill' that drags the ropes through its clattering, mangle-type rollers and strips off the mussels. But compared to the environmental cost of other forms of fishing and aquaculture, this is a modest compromise. It is right to regard rope-grown mussels as one of the most sustainable shellfish we can choose.

Most farmed mussels – and almost all those sold in fishmongers and supermarkets – are now sold clean enough to cook with little further preparation. Still, I would always give them a shake and a rinse in a colander under cold running water. And you may need to remove their 'beards' – the tough, wiry little fibres with which they fastened themselves to their moorings. These can be gripped between your thumb and the blade of a small knife and pulled away.

You only want to cook mussels with undamaged shells that are firmly shut. This means they're alive. If they're dead, there's no way of knowing how long they've been dead – so they're best avoided. Conversely, once cooked, you should only eat those that are open.

To fully appreciate their wonderful flavour, mussels are best treated simply. Throw a knob of butter and some chopped garlic into a large, wide pan over a medium heat and follow a minute or so later with a glass of white wine or cider. Once simmering, add your *moules* and cover the pan. After 3 minutes, lift the lid, give the mussels a good stir, and pop the lid back on for a further minute. They should almost all be open, but if quite a few aren't, give them another stir and another minute. Served with all their lovely, sea-scented, savoury pan juices, and just a hunk of bread or a bowl of thin *frites*, this is seafood nirvana.

I also love mussels cooked in a simple tomato sauce – the kind made by bubbling a tin or two of tomatoes with a little garlic and olive oil – or done with a tropical twist, in half a 400ml tin of coconut milk, with some finely chopped chilli and ginger and a scattering of coriander, or with garlic, lemongrass and kaffir lime leaves.

Wild mussels

It's possible to gather wild mussels in lots of locations around the British Isles, but you do need to be careful. Firstly, be aware that in commercial mussel-growing areas, the bivalves you gather may actually belong to someone else. Secondly, mussels feed by filtering huge quantities of water, extracting microscopic sea-life as they do so. That means that anything untoward in the water will also be absorbed by the bivalve.

Most farmed British mussels are treated before sale by being stored in tanks of water treated with UV light, a process known as depuration. This doesn't happen, of course, with wild mussels, so the risk of picking up something nasty from them is greater. It pays to research the area before gathering wild shellfish. In areas where shellfish are commercially cultivated or gathered, there should be official information on water quality. In waters classed as 'category A', bacterial contamination has been measured at a very low level, but such waters are rare. The wilder, more tide-swept and cleaner-looking the location, the better. Steer clear of still water and anywhere there could be pollution from sewage or agricultural run-off. And avoid gathering mussels in the warmer months, when the chance of bacterial contamination is higher.

Pick big, mature mussels – 5cm long or more – and purge them in cold, clean salt water (35g salt per litre) for at least 8 hours, which cleans out their systems, though it won't get rid of any nasty bugs. Thorough cooking should kill any bacteria and viruses, but it won't get rid of toxins or environmental contaminants.

Wild mussels often have barnacles and beards attached. A barbecue is a great way to cook them – and means you can avoid scraping away these tenacious appendages. Just put the mussels on a grill or rack over hot charcoal or fire embers till they pop open. Pick out the meat (mind the hot shells) and eat them straight up, or dipped in a simple dressing – good olive oil, lemon juice and a pinch of dried chilli flakes is ideal.

MUSSELS IN VINEGAR WITH APPLE AND CARROT

1kg mussels

1 large carrot, peeled and cut into 2mm dice

1 large eating apple, peeled, cored and cut into 2mm dice

1 small red onion, finely diced

2 tbsp cider vinegar

2 heaped tsp caster sugar

2 bay leaves

2 sprigs of thyme

100ml apple juice

Sea salt and black pepper

Light, sharp and mildly sweet, this is an unusual and refreshing way to enjoy fresh mussels. Serves 4 as a starter

Clean the mussels thoroughly (see page 397). Combine the carrot, apple, onion, vinegar and sugar in a bowl.

Heat a heavy-based pan over a high heat. When hot, add the mussels, herbs and apple juice. Give the pan a shake and place the lid on. Cook for about 4 minutes or until the shells are open. Discard any that remain closed.

Tip the contents of the pan into a large colander set over a bowl, to catch the cooking liquor. Return this liquor to the pan and boil it until reduced by two-thirds. Leave it to cool, then combine with the pickled carrot and apple.

Pick the cooled mussels from their shells and scatter in a shallow dish. Pour over the carrot and apple and all the lovely pickling juices and place in the fridge to chill. Remove from the fridge an hour before serving and eat with brown bread and butter.

Mustard

Nikki Duffy

LATIN NAME
Yellow mustard: *Sinapis alba*.
Brown mustard: *Brassica juncea*.
Black mustard: *Brassica nigra*

ALSO KNOWN AS
Yellow mustard: white mustard

MORE RECIPES
Roasted chicory with honey,
mustard and thyme (page 166);
Walnut and blue cheese soufflés
(page 246); Leek and potato
gratin (page 344); Lobster with
béarnaise mayonnaise (page
365); Curried clams (page 184);
Lamb's kidneys with mustard
and cream (page 324); Hazelnut
and cheese biscuits (page 304);
Green tomato, cumin and green
chilli chutney (page 642)

This time-honoured condiment, with its incomparable bite, dates back to Roman times. It is made by wetting and crushing whole mustard seeds then mixing them with an acidic liquid in order to 'fix' the highly volatile, pungent compounds thus released. Centuries ago, young wine (*mustum* – hence the name of the condiment) or unripe grape juice (verjuice) would be used. These days, vinegar does the job.

In the kitchen, you can get by with nothing more than English mustard. Stained day-glo yellow with a shot of turmeric, it's the boldest of the bunch. It can deliver in almost all situations but does demand a light touch because of its famous ferocity. It is quite superb with meat, though, and excellent for seasoning a cheese sauce. If you're mixing up your own from a pot of powder, be aware that its heat will fizzle out relatively quickly. Water doesn't 'fix' the mustard flavour for long.

Dijon mustard is perhaps the best all-rounder. A duller yellow colour than English and considerably milder, the flavour can be excellent, allowing you to enjoy a little more widespread mustard taste. It's excellent in vinaigrettes and mayonnaise. There are two other French styles, Bordeaux and Meaux, which are milder still.

In farm shops and supermarkets you will also come across a wide range of 'cottage mustards' – flavoured with everything from ale to green peppercorns to lapsang souchong tea. Many of these are bobbly wholegrain types, which are almost invariably very mild, but have a lovely sweet, nutty flavour and look great in a creamy sauce.

Mustard complements rich foods most successfully – notably sausages, pork pies, juicy roast beef, bubbling Cheddar cheese on toast and thick béchamel sauces. It is at its very best when fresh, straight from the jar and unheated. Adding it to a plate of food on serving will give you the strongest hit; dressings and dips where the mustard remains uncooked will also preserve the fire. If you are adding it to a cooked sauce, do so shortly before serving because all mustards lose their character with long heating, and also with lengthy storage. Buy mustard in small quantities, store at cool room temperature and use within a couple of months.

Whole yellow mustard seeds (sometimes called white mustard) are often used in pickling mixes, and give a peppery mouth-heat when chewed. Brown mustard seeds, often fried in hot oil at the beginning of curry, have a more powerful, nose-tingling effect. Black mustard seeds are stronger still.

BRAISED SAVOY CABBAGE WITH MUSTARD

1 small or ½ large Savoy cabbage

15g butter

1 tbsp olive or rapeseed oil

1 small-medium onion, thinly sliced

2 garlic cloves, sliced

2–3 tsp black or brown mustard seeds

250ml chicken or veg stock

3–4 tbsp double cream

1 tbsp English mustard

Sea salt and black pepper

This is delicious with roast chicken or venison. Or, scattered with a handful of breadcrumbs and grated cheese and flashed under a hot grill, it makes a lovely gratin to eat on its own. Spring greens can be used in place of the cabbage. Serves 4 as a side dish, 2 as a supper

Remove the tough stalks from the cabbage and shred the leaves fairly finely; set aside.

Place a large heavy-based pan over a medium heat and add the butter and oil. When bubbling, add the onion and stir well. Cook for 4–5 minutes, then add the sliced garlic and mustard seeds. Cook, stirring regularly, for 8–10 minutes or until the onions are just beginning to take on a little colour.

Add the stock and bring to a simmer. Simmer for 3–4 minutes, letting the onions soften, then add the cream, English mustard and shredded cabbage. Bring back to a simmer. Cook, stirring regularly, until the liquid has reduced down to a sauce that coats the cabbage – about 10 minutes. By this time the cabbage will be nice and tender too. Season well with salt and pepper and serve.

Nasturtiums

Pam Corbin

LATIN NAME
Tropaeolum majus

SEASONALITY
May–August

With their intensely bright, flamboyant blooms, nasturtiums are worth growing just for their cheery good looks. But into the bargain, their flowers, leaves and seed pods are all edible and delicious. Hotter and spicier than watercress, their lively bite adds a real buzz to summer dishes.

Pre-packed bags of salad sometimes feature nasturtium flowers, but I've yet to see the leaves included. Luckily, nasturtiums are easy to grow, flowering best when grown on a poor soil in full sun. A richer soil and/or shadier site will yield more leaves than flowers. Grow them in different sites if you want lots of both. Sow seeds as soon as the frosts are over to make sure you have a good, long season for picking and eating. They do have a tendency to attract blackfly, so be vigilant and pick off affected parts of the plant as soon the bugs start to congregate.

The flowers, which are less fiery than the leaves and seeds, will radiantly grace bowls of summery soup and are brilliant tossed into green salads – stuff them with cubes of feta cheese for a treat. For a vibrant vinegar to pep up dressings, steep 20 (or more) nasturtium flowers, 2 roughly chopped garlic cloves, 1 sliced chilli, the finely grated zest of 1 lime and 1 tsp sea salt in 500ml white wine vinegar for 3–4 weeks before straining and bottling.

The tender but piquant leaves have a fiery bite. They are lovely added judiciously to any bowl of salad, blitzed into pestos, or finely chopped and sprinkled into omelettes with tomatoes and/or other herbs. Their big round leaves are also an excellent replacement for vine leaves in traditional dolma (or sarma) recipes.

Harvest nasturtium seed pods when they are fleshy, green and tender. For nasturtium butter, blitz 20 seedpods, 3 leaves and 2 flowers with 100g butter and a pinch of sea salt. This is wicked with grilled steak, fried fish or new potatoes.

Alternatively, you can pickle the pods and use them like capers: immerse in a light brine (5g salt to 100ml cold water) for 24 hours, then drain, dry and pop into a jar. Cover with white wine vinegar or cider vinegar – cold if you want them to stay crisp, hot to soften them.

NASTURTIUM AND PINK PEPPERCORN SOUP

400g lettuce leaves

50g butter

8–10 spring onions, trimmed and cut into 2cm pieces

2 garlic cloves, roughly chopped

1 tsp pink peppercorns

100g nasturtium leaves

1 rounded tbsp plain flour

1 litre hot chicken or veg stock

½–1 tsp sea salt

TO FINISH
1–2 tbsp lemon juice

Nasturtium flowers

Make this in early summer, when nasturtium leaves are young and tender. Their peppery kick is softened by the inclusion of sweet lettuce leaves: Little Gem, butterhead and iceberg are all ideal – or you could even use bolted lettuces from the garden. The soup is delicious hot or cold. Serves 4–6

Shred the lettuce into smallish pieces. Melt the butter in a large pan over a very gentle heat. Add the spring onions, garlic and peppercorns and sweat for 2–3 minutes. Now add the lettuce and nasturtium leaves, cover and cook very gently for 6–7 minutes so that the leaves wilt down without colouring.

Sprinkle in the flour and cook for a minute, stirring constantly. Then gradually pour in the hot stock, stirring well so it blends with the flour. Continue to cook gently for 8–9 minutes, stirring occasionally to prevent sticking.

Transfer the soup to a blender or food processor and blitz until lovely and smooth. Season with salt to taste.

Serve the soup hot or cold, finished with a splash of lemon juice and a nasturtium flower or two floating on top.

Nettles

LATIN NAME
Urtica dioica

SEASONALITY
Spring and autumn

HABITAT
Very common throughout
the British Isles

MORE RECIPES
Henakopita with garam
masala and eggs (page 254);
Mozzarella with nettles and
lentils (page 390)

It's worth looking out for the first peeping tips of young stingers, in verges and patches of rough ground, from mid-February. If you should luck out while looking out, you could even enjoy your first nettle soup of the year on Valentine's Day.

Presenting one's beloved with a ferocious, stinging weed may seem like an odd idea. But consider the sheer thrusting vigour of perky, nubile young nettles – the first wild crop of the year. Once cooked, of course, they relinquish their villainous bite in favour of velvety goodness. They are crammed with vitamins and minerals to nurture and fortify you as you emerge from hibernation.

A proper nettle soup is delicious, too: earthy and herbaceous, and certainly heart-warming. The best versions, in my opinion, are the simplest. Chop a large onion and a big fat carrot (or 2 medium of each) and sweat in a little oil or butter for a few minutes. Pile in 500g nettle tops (yes, that's a lot), then pour on 1 litre boiling water or light veg stock. Add ½ tsp salt and a few twists of pepper. Simmer for 3–4 minutes, stirring occasionally, then blitz the soup (in batches) in a jug blender. Return to the pan, reheat gently, stirring in another knob of butter if you like. Check the seasoning and serve with a spoonful of plain yoghurt or cream swirled on top.

In some years, you might have to wait till nearer Easter for your first nettle soup of the year. But do make a ritual, and then a habit, of it. I've been banging on about eating nettles for years. And I'm not about to stop now. They're amazing – one of the most abundant and easily gathered of all our wild foods and plentiful in early spring when so few other foods are ready for harvest.

Their long-standing use in folk medicine to treat joint and muscle pain and as an antiseptic has found vindication in modern research, which has demonstrated that extracts of nettle to have anti-inflammatory, antioxidant and antimicrobial properties. Fantastically tasty, nutritious and versatile, I'd wager there's a patch of them growing no more than 5 minutes' walk from where you now sit; they may only be metres away. If you are even mildly keen on the idea of eating local, seasonal ingredients, and not averse to a little foraging, then nettles are a free and easy entry-level option.

Following their appearance early in the year, nettles grow with unrestrained enthusiasm right through the spring and summer. But the earlier you bag them, the better. The tender growth of February, March and April is the crop to catch. When 20cm high or less, you can eat more or less the whole thing, but any bigger and you should pick only the tips – the first 4 or 6 leaves on the top of each spear – and discard any coarse stalks, to get the very best of the plant.

By late April, nettles start to become coarse and bristly, and you should not eat them once they begin to form flowers. But keep your eye out throughout late summer and autumn for secondary flushes of growth. Nettles present a perpetual headache for the horticulturalist because they grow back almost as soon as they've been mown down, while the first seedlings from an uncut patch that has flowered in early summer will start springing up as fresh new plants – often around the edges of their parent plants – in late summer and autumn. It's this abundant opportunism that makes them such a joy to the wild food gourmet.

Undeniably sting-stippled as they are, nettles are nevertheless easy to gather. Don a stout pair of gloves, roll your sleeves down and your socks up, and pick away, cramming the harvested nettle tops into a bag (a large carrier-bagful should be about 500g). Swap your gardening gloves for rubber gloves and thoroughly wash your haul in a deep sinkful of cold water, picking out the inevitable blades of grass, bugs and other unwanted

items of organic matter as they reveal themselves. Drain the clean nettles briefly in a colander, and then cook in boiling water (or other liquid such as stock) for just 2–4 minutes, depending on their tenderness, until wilted. As soon as they're immersed in the boiling liquid, their sting will be vanquished.

Unless you are actually making soup, drain your nettles and leave them until cool enough to handle, then squeeze out the excess liquid and chop, as you would spinach.

In fact, pretty much any recipe that works for spinach will also be a great vehicle for nettles. Just wilted, buttered and seasoned, they make a lovely side dish, but I've also used them in spanakopitas, saag paneer, risotto, gnocchi, pesto, savoury tart fillings, even soufflés. Their flavour falls somewhere between the brassicas, and spinach and beet leaves, with, of course, that distinctly nettly tang: an earthy, citrusy tingle on the tongue.

If you're a fan of most leafy veg, then I can pretty much guarantee you'll like nettles too – they're just great greens that have taken a walk on the wild side.

NETTLE AND POTATO CAKES

These tasty little cakes are great to try if you're new to nettles as they only require a small quantity. They're also a good way to use up leftover mash or boiled potatoes. Serves 4

A colanderful of nettle tops (about 75g)

About 500g cooked potato, roughly chopped, or leftover mash

1 medium egg, lightly beaten

4–6 spring onions, trimmed and chopped

50g well-flavoured hard cheese, such as mature Cheddar or Lancashire, grated

30g plain flour

2–3 tbsp olive or rapeseed oil

Sea salt and black pepper

Wearing rubber gloves, wash the nettle tops thoroughly, picking out any plant matter that isn't nettle and discarding the tougher nettle stalks.

Bring a large pan of well-salted water to the boil and throw in the nettles. Bring back to the boil, cook for 2–4 minutes, then drain the nettles in a colander. When they are cool enough to handle, squeeze them to extract as much water as possible, then chop.

Put the chopped potatoes or mash into a bowl. Add the egg and mix it in thoroughly, breaking down the potato as you do so. Mix in the nettles, spring onions and cheese. Sift over the flour, season with salt and pepper and mix well. You'll end up with a fairly smooth mix. Divide it into 4 portions and shape each into a patty, about 2cm thick.

Set a large non-stick frying pan over a medium heat and add the oil. When it is hot, place the nettle and potato cakes in the pan and leave to cook for 4 minutes, until nice and golden brown on the underside. Turn them over and cook for a further 4–5 minutes, until golden and hot all the way through.

Serve your potato cakes with a poached or fried egg. They are also excellent served with any leftovers from a roast chicken or pork joint, or some good sausages.

N

Nigella

Tim Maddams

LATIN NAME
Nigella sativa

ALSO KNOWN AS
Kalonji, black onion seed

MORE RECIPES
Spear-leaved orache bhajis (page 593); Crow garlic and nigella naan (page 271); Velvet crab curry (page 211)

This dark and mysterious-looking little seed is also known as kalonji or black onion seed – although, while certainly black, it has nothing to do with onions. The identity crisis of nigella does not end there. It is also called Roman coriander (though it's not a form of coriander), fennel flower (though it's not a form of fennel), black sesame (though it's not a… you get the picture) and black cumin. The latter is the most confusing because another kind of black cumin, actually related to cumin, does exist in its own right (see page 221). To avoid any confusion, the spice I am talking about is the seed harvested from the spiky pods of the flowering plant *Nigella sativa*, a native of Southwest Asia and the Middle East, and a member of the buttercup family.

Whatever you call these mini, matt black seeds, there is little doubt that they are serious flavour providers. Widely used in Indian cooking, the taste is sweet (in a treacly kind of way), mildly spicy, slightly smoky and, yes, more than a little oniony. Nigella shines when used as a solo spice: if you have ever kneaded it into bread dough, for naan, perhaps (see page 271) or sprinkled the seeds over rolls before baking, you will know what an abundance of aroma this diminutive seed can impart.

Nigella is also used in spice mixes: I love to include it in a batter mix for bhajis or pakoras, and I often add it to spiced potato dishes and marinades for meat. The striking visual effect of a shower of nigella seeds shouldn't be underestimated either – try sprinkling them on to sausage rolls or shaking them over a salad for a dramatic and delicious finish.

Nigella is also very much at home in the pickle jar, whether in a hot and fiery lime pickle or a much simpler, quicker mixture created by lightly salting fresh chopped vegetables and then dressing them in a sweetened vinegar. The nigella cuts through all the sugar and acidity and enhances almost any fruit or vegetable.

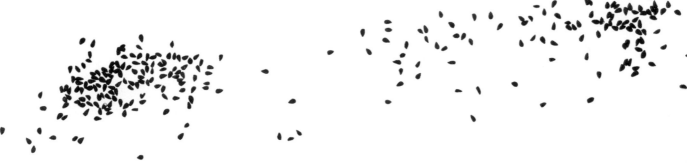

CAULIFLOWER AND NIGELLA SOUP

1 tbsp olive or rapeseed oil

15g butter

1 onion, chopped

3 garlic cloves, peeled

1 small cauliflower (about 500g)

2 tsp nigella (kalonji/black onion) seeds, plus extra to finish

500ml hot veg stock

2 tbsp double cream

Sea salt and black pepper

This creamy, delicately spiced soup can be on the table in less than 20 minutes. Serves 4

Heat the oil and butter in a large saucepan over a medium-low heat. Add the onion and garlic and sweat for about 10 minutes, until soft. Meanwhile, trim the cauliflower of its outer leaves and remove any dry or tough parts of the stalk. Roughly chop the rest.

Add the chopped cauliflower and nigella seeds to the pan of softened onion and garlic and pour on the stock, which should cover the veg. Put the lid on the pan and bring to a gentle simmer. Cook for 10 minutes or until the cauliflower is tender.

Blitz the soup using a blender until smooth and creamy. Reheat it gently in the pan if necessary, season well, stir in the cream and it's ready to eat.

Serve it scattered with a few more nigella seeds. Alternatively, embellish with some crisp shards of leftover roast meat, or a little chopped coriander and tomato.

Noodles

Tim Maddams

MORE RECIPES
Noodle salad with spicy peanut butter dressing (page 451); Pork belly with noodles, coriander and tomatoes (page 494)

These days, most noodles come in an 'instant' form. Pre-cooked and dried, or vac-packed, they take less time to cook even than pasta. In fact, a noodle meal can take just minutes to prepare – they only need the simplest sauce, dressing or broth, and perhaps some slivered raw veg or shreds of leftover meat.

Integral to the cuisines of eastern and Southeast Asia, from China to Indonesia, there are hundreds of different types of noodles in the world, made from all sorts of grains and starches (the oldest ever found, during an archaeological dig in China, were four thousand years old and made from millet). Many are wheat-based but one of the great things about noodles is that they can be made from gluten-free ingredients including rice, buckwheat, seaweed and beans. There are even noodles made from acorns; these are popular in Korea.

Noodles are not usually made from very hard varieties of wheat such as the durum wheat used for classic pasta. This is one of the things that sets them apart, and the reason why noodles are generally more tender and slippery – satisfying in a subtly different way to pasta and certainly better, in my book, in soupy dishes. Noodles also sometimes contain salt, whereas dried pasta generally does not.

The cooking time varies considerably depending on the type of noodle. Some need only brief soaking in just-boiled water, or can be fried straight from the pack. Others require a few minutes' boiling. Follow the instructions on the packet but, as with pasta, check the noodles a minute or two before the full cooking time suggested so you can catch them when they are tender but not yet soggy.

For the best results, noodles that need boiling should be cooked in excess water and stirred a few times while they simmer, as this helps to stop them sticking together. Once cooked, drain them in a colander and either toss immediately with a little oil, sauce or dressing, or rinse them first; this removes starch from their surfaces and again helps to stop them sticking. Some types of noodle – notably buckwheat – always benefit from rinsing after cooking.

TYPES OF NOODLES

Wheat noodles Often these also contain egg and are labelled 'egg noodles'. They are excellent in stir-fries and hold a thick, sticky sauce very well. Wheat-based noodles that don't usually contain egg include thick, white udon noodles, which are delicious in fragrant soups. Many of the supermarket instant or 'straight-to-wok' noodles are wheat-based. A favourite cheat of mine is to soak standard dried, quick-cook wheat noodles in cold water for half an hour or so before draining (don't rush the soaking process or they will break up into small pieces). The noodles can then be thrown straight into stir-fries or broths with no further cooking. They can also be fried in a little oil, spread out in a frying pan, to form a crispy noodle pancake.

Rice noodles These take many forms and may be made from white, wholemeal or black rice. All tend to be lighter than wheat noodles and superb in salads. Very thin rice noodles can be deep-fried, from dry, to make them crispy. Rice noodles may be gluten-free (but always check).

Soba noodles These Japanese style noodles, made with buckwheat (sometimes with wheat flour too), have an earthy, nutty flavour. They are very good cooked, drained, rinsed and served in cold salads.

Glass noodles Also known as cellophane or bean thread noodles, these are made from mung beans and cook to a translucent finish. They're often used in Thai cooking.

NOODLES WITH SEAWEED, SMOKED MACKEREL AND SOY

20g dried sea spaghetti

75g buckwheat (soba) noodles

200ml veg or fish stock, or light chicken stock

2 garlic cloves, thinly sliced

15g root ginger, finely grated

150g hot-smoked mackerel fillets (2 medium)

1 tbsp soy sauce

1 tsp sesame seeds, ideally toasted

2–3 spring onions, trimmed and thinly sliced

This simple, full-bodied broth is rich with savoury flavour from the seaweed, soy and fish. Sea spaghetti, also called thongweed, is a common seaweed with long, branching fronds, found on rocky shores around much of the British Isles. You can gather and dry it yourself (see page 579) or buy it ready-dried (see cornishseaweed.co.uk). Flaked, cooked kipper can be used in place of the mackerel. Serves 2

Soak the seaweed in cold water for 25–30 minutes (or according to the packet instructions). Drain and rinse well.

Bring a pan of water to the boil, add the seaweed and simmer for 10 minutes. Check the suggested cooking time on the packet of noodles. Add them to the cooking seaweed for this amount of time – probably 5–6 minutes. Drain the seaweed and noodles well, rinse them under the cold tap, then set aside in a colander.

Rinse out the pan and add the stock. Bring to a simmer, then add the garlic and ginger and cook for 3–4 minutes. Meanwhile, chop the seaweed and noodles a couple of times with scissors or a knife, so they are not too long. Flake the mackerel flesh off the skin.

Add the noodles to the simmering stock, followed by the soy and mackerel. Fold everything together and cook briefly, just to heat the fish through. Ladle into bowls and finish with a scattering of sesame seeds and the sliced spring onions.

Nutmeg

Nikki Duffy

LATIN NAME
Myristica fragrans

MORE RECIPES
Eccles cakes (page 340)

The name 'nutmeg' means, more or less, 'musky nut' and it's easy to see why. This hard, round, brown kernel is about the size of a grape and looks rather like a nut. Its flavour is woody, perfumed, a touch bitter and a little bit fresh – 'musky' sums it up quite well. It is subtle but has the capacity to deepen and round out the flavour of a dish. Nutmeg is not prized these days in the same way that cinnamon, vanilla or pepper are, but in the past the nutmeg trade was very lucrative.

Nutmegs are found inside a fleshy fruit, native to Indonesia. The nutmeg itself grows wrapped in a strange orange web, or 'aril', which is removed and dried to become mace. This sister spice shares nutmeg's character, but nutmeg is more pungent, more penetrating, a little more robust. Don't bother with ready-ground nutmeg; instead buy the whole 'nuts' and invest in a good, sharp, fine grater. Release the nutmeg scent, as and when you need it, by rubbing it over the grater to create a fine fall of fragrant nutmeg dust. The part-grated nutmeg can then be put back into its jar for later use.

As you grate a nutmeg, you will reveal its curious cross-section, the main, café-au-lait-coloured flesh marbled with rivulets of a darker hue. These dark veins are the rich tissue that holds the seed's essential oil, a little more of it revealed and released with each pass of the grater. That hard, tannic flesh holds the essence of the nutmeg locked so tight that the spice keeps incredibly well. They'll store almost indefinitely, in a cool, dry cupboard.

A delicately bitter, aromatic sprinkling of nutmeg is traditionally valued for the contrast it brings – visually, as well as flavourwise – to milky, eggy things. Custard tarts, béchamel sauces and savoury soufflé mixes all have more depth with a subtle dusting of nutmeg, though you may barely detect the spice itself.

Nutmeg adds complexity to baking and is often used in proprietary mixed spice blends. It lends character to meaty stews, pies and pâtés, and is found in many different kinds of curry. It is also a component of West Indian jerk seasoning. You can use it in veg dishes too: try seasoning cauliflower cheese with a sprinkle of it, or dusting it generously on to a roast pumpkin soup. It's especially welcome with dark greens such as spinach, kale and chard.

Generally, nutmeg is best added towards the end of cooking, as too much heat can emphasise its tannic bitterness.

SPICED SPINACH WITH NUTMEG

This delicately spiced veg dish is delicious alongside almost any meat or fish and is also excellent with curry. Serves 2

200g spinach

2 tbsp olive or rapeseed oil

1 medium onion, finely chopped

2 garlic cloves, finely sliced

1 tsp finely grated root ginger

1 medium-hot red chilli, deseeded and finely diced

½ tsp garam masala

A squeeze of lemon juice

Freshly grated nutmeg

Sea salt and black pepper

Wash the spinach thoroughly and drain. Remove and discard the tough stalks from any larger leaves. Set the spinach leaves aside.

Place a large frying pan or wok over a medium-low heat and add the oil. When hot, toss in the onion and fry gently for about 8 minutes, until almost translucent with little colour. Add the garlic, ginger, chilli and garam masala and fry for a further 2 minutes.

Now add the spinach leaves, along with a squeeze of lemon juice, some salt and pepper and a generous grating of nutmeg. Turn up the heat slightly and cook for 2–3 minutes, stirring often, until the spinach is nicely wilted. Taste and add more salt, pepper, lemon and/or nutmeg if needed. Serve straight away.

Oats

Gill Meller

LATIN NAME
Avena sativa

MORE RECIPES
Brazil nut, cacao and orange granola (page 85); Alexanders gratin with bacon and oats (page 14); Oat-coated puffball with sage and pancetta (page 507); Winkles in oatmeal (page 677); Mulberry and walnut cranachan (page 391); Pear and bilberry crumble tart (page 69); Olive oil and honey flapjacks (page 413)

Whether flaked, rolled or chopped, oats have taken a bashing over the years. Like many of the inexpensive foods that have traditionally sustained the poorest in society, they're easy to deride (the Romans despised the plant as a weed, while Samuel Johnson sneered at oats as mere animal fodder). But as we rediscover the benefits of wholefoods, oats are most definitely on the rise. At River Cottage, we use them pretty much daily, in various different forms. They may lack glamour, but they make up for it, in scoopfuls, with their tasty, nutritious and very versatile nature.

Unlike tough wheat, the soft grains of oats are difficult to split into parts. For this reason, they are kept intact and always eaten as a healthy wholegrain, with just the inedible hull removed. Oat 'groats', or whole hulled grains, are steamed to stop them going rancid. They can then be rolled flat to make jumbo oats (also called 'chunky', 'thick' or 'traditional' oats), or cut up first and rolled to make smaller, standard porridge oats, which cook more quickly into a finer, less-textured porridge. Quick or instant porridge oats are steamed for longer and rolled even thinner.

Some cut-up oat groats aren't rolled out at all, but kept as oatmeal and milled into different sizes from coarse pinhead, through medium and fine oatmeal, to the very finest: oat flour. Purists reckon that pinhead oatmeal makes the best porridge of all, though it takes a bit longer to cook than a flaked oat porridge and requires a little forethought. For 4 people, soak 250g pinhead oats overnight in 900ml water then, the next morning, bring it to a simmer and cook gently for around 8 minutes. Stir it lazily as you go, and add a splash more hot water if necessary.

The oat's insoluble carbohydrates mean that the grains readily retain water (the root of 'oat' is probably the Indo-European *oid*, 'to swell'). This makes them good not just for porridge but also thick drinks and moist cakes and cookies. Blend porridge oats with fruit and liquid to get creamy oat smoothies, or 'thickies'. A date, banana and oat thickie is a killer breakfast. In the same way, oats can add body to cold and hot soups. Just go cautiously and be careful not to add too much, or the texture will become gluey.

Savoury porridge is a favourite dish of mine. Soften shallots or onions with garlic in butter and olive oil, then add herbs and some pre-soaked pinhead or medium oatmeal. Stir in chicken stock so the grains absorb the liquid, just as if cooking a risotto. In the spring, I like to finish this with a bright green purée of blanched fresh nettles, and top it with more nettles wilted in butter, or some fish, scallops or crisp bacon. An all-year version can be topped with halved onions, roasted with sage until tender. This is great with roast birds, or as vegetarian comfort food with a few toasted hazelnuts.

In recent years, oats have gained great status as a health food. Eaten regularly, they can help to lower cholesterol, while the coarser, less processed forms such as oatmeal and jumbo oats are low GI. Compared to other grains, oats are high in protein (up to 17 per cent but more typically 12 per cent) and also fat. Their nourishing nature partly explains why around three-quarters of the world's supply goes into animal food, and has done for a long time. But oats grow well in northern climates and have become part of many time-honoured dishes here. In Yorkshire, oatmeal is used to make spicy parkin and in Scotland it was traditionally mixed uncooked into hot milk or water to make a drink called a brose.

Oats can give dishes a variety of textures. Medium oatmeal is a great crisp coating to a piece of fish or chicken, or Spanish *croquetas*. It doesn't absorb fat in the same way as breadcrumbs, giving a fantastic crunch while retaining the moisture of the

ingredient inside. It's especially good for pieces of delicate fish such as sole. Pinhead oatmeal is essential for our annual River Cottage haggis-making, giving the right texture and nutty taste alongside the soft offal. Oats that have been toasted in the oven – either pinhead oatmeal or rolled oats – are superb mixed with berries, honey, whisky and whipped cream in the Scottish pud, cranachan.

Oats can be a great alternative grain in a wheat-free diet, but they are not always gluten-free. They don't contain gluten themselves but are often grown or processed alongside wheat and so may be 'contaminated'. Guaranteed gluten-free oat products are increasingly available, however, not just in health food shops but mainstream retailers too. Oats do contain a protein similar to gluten called avenin. Some people with coeliac disease (an adverse reaction to gluten) are affected by avenin, but research suggests most are not.

This lack of gluten means oat flour won't make high-rise breads, but I often turn to oats when I'm baking. I like to finish off loaves by brushing them with milk and giving them a generous scattering of jumbo oats that toast in the oven to create a nice crust. Finer oats impart a light softness to cakes and there's always a place for oats in crumble toppings, combined with crushed walnuts, ground almonds, brown sugar and butter. Oat flour can be used as a flavourful alternative to wheat flour, giving the same thickening properties.

And you don't have to turn the oven on at all to make fantastic oaty flapjacks: an amazing raw version can be whipped up by whizzing dates, dried apricots, ripe banana, orange zest, coconut oil and honey in a food processor, combining the purée with oats, then pressing it into a tray and refrigerating. The fruit binds the mix, while the oats give body and nutrients: no butter, no extra sugar, no wheat – and no cooking.

CHEDDAR AND ONION OATCAKES

Plain or oat flour, to dust

100g fine oatmeal

100g porridge oats

1 medium onion, finely diced

75g Cheddar or other well-flavoured hard cheese, finely grated

½ tsp fine sea salt

About 100ml milk

Black pepper

Using both rolled oats and oatmeal, these sustaining little snacks are great to nibble on their own – but even better with a few thin slices of ham and a spoonful of crème fraîche. Makes about 20

Preheat the oven to 160°C/Fan 140°C/Gas 3 and dust 2 baking trays with flour.

Mix the oatmeal, oats, onion, cheese, salt and a grinding of black pepper in a bowl. Make a well in the centre and pour in enough milk to bring everything together into a firm, not sticky, dough. Form into a ball and leave it to rest for 5–10 minutes.

Roll out the dough on a well-floured surface to a 5mm thickness and cut out rounds with a 6cm biscuit cutter. Place on the baking trays and bake for 30 minutes, then flip all the cakes over and bake for a further 5 minutes.

Leave the oatcakes on the baking trays for a couple of minutes, then transfer to a wire rack to cool. Store in an airtight container.

Olive oil

Gill Meller

SOURCING
oilandmore.co.uk;
oilmerchant.co.uk;
oliveoil4u.co.uk

There will always be a place in most kitchens for olive oil. The best extra virgin kind is simply one of the most delicious foods in the world. With its range of fruity, peppery flavours, good olive oil has the capacity to enhance and season almost any other ingredient – even in sweet dishes.

The particular flavour of an oil depends on the type of olive used. Greek 'Kalamata' and Spanish 'Arbequina' are very good, while top-end Italian oils often contain a blend of olives such as pungent 'Frantoio', fruity 'Leccino' and grassy 'Moraiolo'. Early-harvest oils, using greener fruit, tend to be more grassy and pungent, while olives picked later produce softer, less assertive oils.

The less expensive olive oils, sometimes just called 'olive oil', but also labelled as 'light', 'blended' or 'pure' olive oil, are made by mixing lower grade, chemically extracted oil with higher grade virgin oil. This kind of olive oil is best for frying and sautéeing, because, as with most refined oils, it has a higher smoke point than the unrefined version. The flavour is generally very mild.

O

'Extra virgin' is a broad definition of quality. It signifies very low acidity in the oil, but also indicates that the olives have been carefully handled and processed, and that the oil has gone through taste tests to check for flaws such as mustiness. 'Extra virgin' oils may be mass-produced and inexpensive but the term also covers the posh, single-estate varieties that can be so exceptional in flavour (and in price).

'Cold-pressed' is another term you sometimes see on labels to indicate quality. In the past, heat was used to maximise extraction rates of some cheaper oils. However, modern methods of centrifugal production mean that no extra virgin olive oil is heated significantly during production any more. Most extra virgin olive oil is filtered, but unfiltered, cloudy examples are available too. These contain more phytonutrients and, some might argue, more flavour, but turn rancid more quickly.

Different extra virgin olive oils vary but generally their smoke point is a little too low to make them a good choice for sautéeing, searing and shallow-frying. In any case, the best way to appreciate the extraordinary flavour and aromatic quality of a good extra virgin olive oil is to use it unheated. This is particularly true with top-end extra virgin oils made from the trees of a single estate. Trickle it at the last minute on to salads, soups, simply cooked veg, pasta and rice dishes. Its gleam and flavour can turn a dish of plain white beans into something sumptuous, or a tomato salad into an utter delight. Revel in its ancient yet vibrant character – you can taste the sun and the old wood of the twisted olive trees in a great oil.

Extra virgin olive oil will deteriorate if exposed to light and heat so it is best bought in a tin or a dark glass bottle and kept in a cool place, away from direct sunlight. It is worth looking for labels that give a harvest date. Olive oil is best when freshest, though high-quality oil will keep its flavour reasonably well and mellow slightly with time.

OLIVE OIL AND HONEY FLAPJACKS

150ml extra virgin olive oil

150g clear honey

150g pitted dates, chopped

225g porridge oats (not jumbo oats)

A pinch of salt

These simple bakes are lighter and less sticky than a standard flapjack. They're dairy-free and contain no refined sugar, getting their sweetness from dates and clear honey. Use a nice, fruity extra virgin olive oil, but nothing too expensive. Makes 8–12

Preheat the oven to 170°C/Fan 150°C/Gas 3. Line a small baking tray, about 16 x 24cm, with baking parchment.

Put the olive oil, honey and dates in a food processor or blender and blitz until the dates are relatively finely chopped and form a sticky mass. Scrape into a large bowl. Add the oats with a pinch of salt and work well to combine, using a wooden spoon.

Spread the mixture out in the prepared tray and press down evenly all over. Bake for 25–30 minutes until golden brown.

Remove the tray from the oven and leave the flapjacks to cool completely before turning them out and cutting into fingers. Store in an airtight container for up to a week.

Olives

Gill Meller

LATIN NAME
Olea europaea

MORE RECIPES
Celery and walnut tapenade (page 133); Fennel and olive mash (page 257); French beans with shallots and black olives (page 265); Ewe's cheese with chickpeas, roasted chillies and olives (page 151); Pissaladière (page 419); Garfish with olives, oregano and garlic (page 267)

SOURCING
olivesetal.co.uk; therealolivecompany.co.uk

There's a huge variety of olives available to feast upon these days, from the big, juicy green Andalusian 'Gordal', to the crisp, grass-green early-harvest 'Nocellara' from Italy. The intensely fruity purple 'Kalamata' olives of Greece (pictured right), cured with red wine vinegar, are rightly famous, and then there's the prized, speckled green 'Lucques' from Languedoc or little black 'Niçoise' olives for a classic *salade niçoise*.

Served as part of a spread with charcuterie, good tomatoes, olive oil and bread, you will appreciate their unique flavours. But olives have a role in cooking too. For a classic tapenade, chop olives with garlic, anchovies, thyme and capers. Or use them to season and enrich a dairy-free pesto – try a caper and olive pesto tossed into a potato salad. Olives' briny intensity goes well with strong-flavoured fish such as mackerel and red mullet, and their salty kick is exceptionally good as a balance to juicy fruit – for example in a salad with red onions, basil and grapefruit.

Ripeness, not variety, determines the colour of olives. They can be picked when hard and green, or left on the tree to ripen to purple, then black – but in both cases remain bitter and unpalatable until cured. There are various curing methods including dry-salting and brining, and the curing can be accelerated, to a greater or lesser extent, by using an alkaline solution (lye). The best olives undergo longer fermentation.

Younger green olives have a firmer, crisper texture and sharper flavour. Mature, oil-rich, naturally ripened black olives are more complex. The cheapest tinned black olives are produced by pumping oxygen through tanks of lye-cured green olives to artificially blacken them, resulting in a dark olive with an inferior flavour. A bowlful of good quality dark olives may have slight colour variations, a sign they haven't been oxidised and colour fixed. When not pasteurised or sterilised, they will also continue to develop subtly in flavour over time. Olives sold on the stone tend to taste best and are the ones to buy if possible. A good cherry stoner makes it easy to de-stone them.

PHEASANT WITH OLIVES AND PRESERVED LEMONS

Delicate spicing, salty preserved lemon and fat green olives give this stew a North African slant. It also works well with chicken or guinea fowl. Serves 4–6

2 oven-ready pheasant (650–700g each)

2 tbsp olive oil

2 large onions, chopped

1 medium-hot red chilli

4 garlic cloves, chopped

1 tsp ground cumin

2 tsp ground coriander

150ml dry white wine

2–3 bay leaves

400g tin tomatoes, crushed

150g green olives

1 tsp sugar

250ml chicken or pheasant stock

2 tbsp roughly chopped preserved lemon rind

1–2 tbsp chopped parsley

Sea salt and black pepper

Cut off the legs of the pheasants, slicing as close to the carcass as you can. Then slice the breast meat away from the ribcages. (Use the remaining carcasses to make stock.)

Heat the oil in a large flameproof casserole over a medium heat. Season the pheasant pieces with salt and pepper, add them to the casserole, and brown them well all over. Take out the meat and set aside in a bowl.

Add the onions to the casserole, lower the heat, put the lid on and sweat gently for about 15 minutes. Meanwhile, deseed and roughly chop the chilli. Add the chilli to the casserole with the garlic, cumin and coriander and cook for a few more minutes. Turn up the heat slightly and add the wine. Let it bubble for a minute or two to reduce a little, scraping and stirring with a spatula as it cooks to release any sediment.

Return the browned pheasant to the casserole, along with any juices from the bowl. Add the bay leaves, tomatoes, olives, sugar and some salt and pepper (go easy on the salt at this stage), then the stock. Bring to the boil, then reduce the heat to a very low simmer and put the lid on. Cook for 40–50 minutes or until the pheasant leg meat is tender, rearranging the pheasant pieces halfway through, to ensure even cooking.

When cooked, stir in the preserved lemon and parsley. Season to taste and serve with a big pile of couscous and some fiery harissa paste on the side.

Onions

Mark Diacono

LATIN NAME
Allium cepa

ALSO KNOWN AS
Spring onions: scallions
or salad onions

SEASONALITY
Home-grown onions are
harvested May–October;
stored British-grown onions
are available more or less all
year round, sometimes with
a brief gap mid-summer

MORE RECIPES
English onion soup (page 613);
Roasted broccoli, red onion and
cannellini salad (page 99);
Lettuce and spring onion tarte
tatin (page 356); French beans
with shallots and black olives
(page 265); Borlottis with fennel
seeds and onion (page 81);
Sweetcorn with spring onion,
chilli and coriander (page 632);
Curried new potatoes, red onion
and lettuce (page 226); Roasted
courgettes and onions with
yoghurt dressing (page 684);
Buttermilk and sage onion rings
(page 109); Smashed chickpeas
with preserved lemon and
red onion (page 165); Squash,
shallot and mushroom tart
(page 604); Roast guinea
fowl with onions and sage
breadcrumbs (page 291);
Goat kebabs with rosemary, red
peppers and onion (page 280);
Cider onion gravy (page 182);
Bay-spiked pears with shallots
and lemon (page 53); Cheddar
and onion oatcakes (page 411)

Onions are extraordinary. Rare is the soup, stock, stew or casserole that's not improved by them, and a hot dog is simply not hot without smoky, sweet fried onions piled on top. How many dishes, the world over, start to take shape the moment a heap of glistening-white, chopped onion hits hot oil? The complexity of flavour tucked into the juicy layers of this humble-looking bulb – the sweetness, acidity, the deep savouriness – make it the hardest worker in the kitchen. It's widely available all year round, largely of fine quality, and relatively inexpensive.

Onions are nutritious too, providing vitamins B, C and E, as well as a range of minerals and antioxidants. One study found that more pungent varieties of onion are richer in antioxidants, so take that as some consolation as your eyes stream over the chopping board.

Raw onions used sparingly lend a fine bite to dips, salads and even a cheese sandwich. The secret is to slice or chop them super-thin. Soaking in cold water for 20 minutes, then draining and patting dry, will also take their ferocity down a notch or two.

However, cooking reveals the full range of the onion's characteristics. The onion plant stores its energy in the form of sugars and it also harbours harsh sulphur compounds (as a natural defence, ironically, against being eaten). Heat unlocks, mellows and blends these two elements, so that cooked onion is both richly sweet and deeply savoury, which is perhaps why it's so versatile and well loved.

The way you handle the heat makes all the difference. Onions' natural sugars mean that too high a temperature can result in black edges and bitterness. Start with a decent, heavy-based pan that will distribute heat evenly, and a reasonable amount of fat so the onions have something to fry *in*. Warm 3 tbsp olive oil in the pan over a medium heat, then add 3 finely sliced onions. A generous pinch of salt helps draw out the moisture and reduces the risk of burning. As soon as the onions start to sizzle, telling you that the heat is penetrating, reduce the heat to low and cook, stirring often.

If you put a lid on the pan, it will keep in the steam that the onions release, helping them to soften and keeping them very sweet. However, it will also reduce the extent to which they colour and caramelise – so cover them or not, depending on what you're after. Either way, after 10 minutes you'll get just-tender but still vibrant onions, ready for further cooking with other ingredients in any number of stews, risottos or curries; after 20–25 minutes, you'll have a soft, sweet/sharp tangle of onions – perfect for a pizza topping or gravy. And after 40–50 minutes, you'll have a 'melted', reduced, golden, silky mass for a luxurious onion soup or tart (see overleaf).

To make a simple onion 'marmalade' to go with cheese or cold meat, add 3 bay leaves or half a handful of thyme to the pan with the raw onions then, after about 30 minutes' cooking, throw in 75g black olives, a few glugs of wine, some balsamic vinegar and a pinch of salt. Cook for a little longer to evaporate the liquid and serve warm or cold.

Frying your onions over a slightly higher heat, uncovered, until they just catch, gives them a more savoury edge that cheers sausages so famously and works so well on top of a dhal or soup.

Roasting draws out a sweetness in onions that has a fabulous, caramelised quality to it. I often throw a few quartered onions in with roasting chicken or lamb, but I roast them on their own too. Quartered (or cut into 6 wedges for larger onions), tossed in oil and generously seasoned (perhaps with a few bay leaves or sprigs of thyme added), they are perfect after about 45 minutes in the oven at 190°C/Fan 170°C/Gas 5.

However you intend to eat your onions, peeling and some form of cutting is likely to be involved, which can raise a stinging mist to the eyes and nose. Sulphenic acids are among the compounds that make onions king in the kitchen, but also the primary culprit of this discomfort. Old wives' tales abound, but in my experience only two things help: refrigerating the onions overnight before chopping, and using a very sharp knife so that the cuts are clean without the cell-crushing that helps release those acids.

Almost all the onions in the shops have been dried for a few days, to 'set' the skins and increase their shelf life. You may find fresh onions – those that have just been harvested, without a period of drying – in markets, veg boxes or direct from the grower. They are a spring-into-summer treat. They have a certain liveliness that most onions lack. Often very strongly flavoured, fresh onions are best cooked gently and long.

White-skinned onions are usually the mildest, though rarest in the shops (and invariably imported). Red onions are stronger than white but sweeter too. Somewhere between an onion and a shallot in strength, they're a great choice for serving raw. Red onions also tend to retain their structure more than other onions: even long, slow cooking won't melt them to the same silkiness as white or yellow onions. This trait has its uses though, especially in onion tarts and when baking onions whole. Yellow (actually brown) onions are the most common, and almost always the most strongly flavoured. Whatever colour or size, look for onions that are firm and unbruised. They are best stored in cool darkness if you're not using them quickly.

Onions can be grown from seed or sets (mini onions), sown in early spring. I don't grow many though, as yellow/brown varieties are relatively inexpensive in the shops, and I can't hope to grow anything like the number I use. Any space I dedicate to this vegetable is for a few lines of red onions.

There are, however, various other long-stemmed, bobble-headed, oniony plants out there, often looking rather like giant chives, that are incredibly easy to grow. Welsh onions give you a kind of spring onion, as well as edible flowers, while many of the perennial onions (including Egyptian walking onions) will give you a few harvests, including some or all of the following: chive-like stems early in the season, with any you leave unharvested becoming like spring onions, in time forming mini shallots at the top of their stems, with the bulbs at the base swelling into small shallots too.

Shallots

Shallots are very special. Growing in clusters at the soil's surface, and wrapped in their own bronze paper, they are more subtle in flavour than onions and more approachable when raw (though you should still prepare for running eyes when chopping). Use them when just a little oniony-ness is required – raw in dressings where vinegar tempers any harshness, or lightly cooked in sauces.

Large, torpedo-shaped eschalot and echalion shallots, also known as 'banana shallots', are my favourites. Their easy sweetness is perfectly balanced by plenty of oniony edge and there's less fiddle in peeling and chopping than with smaller shallots.

Roasted and caramelised whole, shallots are fabulous with fish and meat – beef especially. Peel half a kilo (or as many as you fancy) and toss them in 2 tbsp sugar before adding to an ovenproof pan over a high heat. Allow them to caramelise for a few minutes, shaking the pan frequently so they don't burn. Add a large knob of butter and a dash of olive oil, then transfer the pan to the oven at 190°C/Fan 170°C/Gas 5 for 15–25 minutes, until the shallots are tender.

Spring onions

Thin, fleshy and with a tight pale bulb topped with hollow green leaves, spring onions carry a pretty potent kick, but one that is somehow more agreeable than raw onion. Thinly sliced, they brighten up many a dressing, soup, salad or stir-fry. If push came to shove, I'd even probably prefer an onion bhaji made with spring onions to one fashioned from normal onions. Best of all, spring onions take to the barbecue or griddle brilliantly. Peel off the outer layer, cut off the roots and coat the shaft in a little olive oil before they hit the heat. Allow 2–3 minutes each side, until softened and browned. A yoghurty garlic dressing sets them off beautifully.

PISSALADIÈRE

Few dishes celebrate onions – and the divine, silky sweetness they can achieve – better than this Provençal classic. A sort of thickly onioned pizza, it uses piquant, salty anchovies and olives to offset the onions' richness. Serves 4–6

FOR THE DOUGH

125g plain white flour, plus extra to dust

125g strong white bread flour

1 level tsp fine sea salt

½ tsp fast-acting dried yeast

1 tbsp olive oil, plus extra for oiling

FOR THE TOPPING

3 tbsp olive oil

1kg onions, halved and very thinly sliced

3 garlic cloves, finely sliced

8–10 anchovy fillets in oil

About 75g pitted black olives

2 tsp baby capers, drained and rinsed (optional)

1 tbsp thyme leaves

Sea salt and black pepper

TO FINISH

Extra virgin olive oil, or the oil from the anchovies

To make the dough, combine the flours, salt and yeast in a large bowl, add 160ml warm water and the oil, and mix to a rough dough. Turn out on to a lightly floured surface and knead for about 10 minutes, until silky and elastic.

Put the dough into a lightly oiled bowl, cover with cling film and leave in a warm place to rise for 1–2 hours, until doubled in size.

Meanwhile, make the topping. Heat the oil in a large frying pan over a medium heat. Add the onions and a good pinch of salt. When they start to sizzle, turn the heat right down, partially cover the pan and cook very gently, stirring occasionally, for about 50 minutes or until the onions are very soft, golden and translucent, but not browned. Stir in the garlic, cook for a minute or two more, then remove from the heat.

Preheat the oven to 220°C/Fan 200°C/Gas 7 and lightly oil a shallow baking tin, about 21 x 30cm.

Tip the dough out on to a well-floured surface. Pat it very roughly into a rectangle with your fingers then roll it out until it's big enough to fit the prepared tin.

Lift the dough into the tin, pressing it up the sides a little to create a rim. Spread the softened onions over the dough. Arrange the anchovies in a lattice pattern on top and place the olives, capers, if using, and thyme in between.

Grind over some pepper and bake for 20–25 minutes, until the crust is slightly browned and the onions are catching in places. Trickle over a little extra virgin olive oil or oil from the anchovy tin/jar for a more intense anchovy flavour. Serve hot, warm or cold.

Oranges

Pam Corbin

LATIN NAME
Sweet orange: *Citrus sinensis*.
Mandarin: *Citrus reticulata*.
Seville or bitter orange:
Citrus aurantium

SEASONALITY
Sweet oranges: imported all
year round. Seville oranges:
December–February. Blood
oranges: February–March

MORE RECIPES
Brazil nut, cacao and orange
granola (page 85); Roasted
chicory with honey, mustard
and thyme (page 166); Squid
with chervil and blood orange
(page 155); Sardines with
pine nuts, fennel and orange
(page 471); Slow-roasted goose
with star anise, orange and chilli
(page 283); Pistachio, orange
and honey filo tartlets (page 474);
Whisky and marmalade bread
and butter pudding (page 672);
Orange and ginger fool with
coffee syrup (page 196); Seville
orange and clove marmalade
(page 187); Candied orange and
lemon peel (page 459)

Oranges are available all year round, but they are at their best during the mid-winter months. Originating from southeast China and Burma, these citrus fruits have been used for around 4,500 years. Early fruits were a far cry from the sweet juicy ones we eat today, being both bitter and sour – characteristics still present in the Seville oranges we use for marmalade. It was not their flesh but their skin – rich with exquisite floral essence – that was valued for its perfume and fragrant flavour. The word 'orange' derives from the Sanskrit *naranga*, meaning 'perfume within' (the colour is named after the fruit, not the other way round).

Less harsh than a lemon, the modern sweet orange has a magical blend of sweetness and acidity that works well with both sweet and savoury ingredients. Add plump, succulent orange segments to a watercress and fennel salad, work the fresh juice into vinaigrettes and marinades, or heat 100g caster sugar with 100ml orange juice to make a zestful syrup to drizzle over almond or chocolate sponge cakes.

Freshly squeezed orange juice is thirst-quenching but its flavour diminishes within 20 minutes of juicing, so drink it as soon as you can. Alternatively, to make a refreshing orange barley water, put 200g pearl barley in a pan with 2 litres cold water, bring to the boil and simmer for 30 minutes, until soft. Meanwhile, put the finely grated zest of 2 lemons and 5 oranges into a large bowl. Strain over the hot water from the cooked barley (add the grain to soups). When cool, add the juice from the zested lemons and oranges, pour into clean bottles and refrigerate. Use within 2 weeks.

There are plenty of oranges to choose from, each with its own distinctive qualities (see below). Buy oranges that feel heavy, with firm skins and a soft sheen. Generally, aside from organic fruits and Sevilles, oranges are subjected to a de-greening process using ethylene gas before they are coated with wax (see page 459). A greenish tinge to an orange is usually an indication of less commercial processing and indicative of fruit picked very recently from the tree – so don't be put off!

ORANGE VARIETIES

Navel This large, seedless, easy-to-peel fruit is identified by a tiny secondary fruit growing at its apex (the 'navel'). The Navel's flavour is rarely outshone, but these oranges are far better eaters than juicers (they contain low levels of a bitter compound, limonin, which manifests when they are juiced).

Jaffa or Shamouti Oval, thick-peeled and vibrantly coloured, this is another excellent eater or dessert orange.

Valencia Relatively heavy, with sweet zesty juice, this is the best orange for juicing, although it does contain a few pips. For maximum yield, first 'loosen the juice' by rolling the fruit on a hard surface, pressing down on it to rupture some of the membranes inside, or by warming the fruit in hot water. When halving, remember to cut around the middle and not from top to bottom. A medium orange will yield approximately 100ml juice.

Blood orange The flesh within this orange-skinned fruit is deeply crimson. Red pigments (anthocyanins) develop when growing conditions combine low night temperatures and warm days. A short season, only a few weeks in February and March, makes blood oranges a treasured treat. Their blushing juice is irresistible to drink alone, to spritz into sparkling wine or to serve with vodka and ice. They also look amazing in salads. The best blood oranges come from Sicily and the western Med. (Pictured right.)

Mandarin Loose-skinned, easy to peel and deliciously sweet, the mandarin family includes tangerines, satsumas, minneolas and clementines. With their simple-to-separate segments, they are the perfect orange to stuff into pockets and lunchboxes to eat easily, out of hand. The best of them all is the clementine: its tart-sweet flavour, second to none, makes wonderfully refreshing sorbets, granitas and jellies.

Seville orange This pithy orange comes into season in January. Its unique combination of fragrance and bitterness makes it perfect for turning into marmalade. And bitter, fragrant Seville orange juice can also be employed where you would otherwise use lemon juice – in a cool and creamy *tarte*, for instance – and it's very good in duck dishes too.

To remove the white pith and the inner membranes from an orange, if required, first use a sharp knife to carefully slice off the top and bottom off the fruit, then stand the fruit on a board. Cutting downwards, work around the orange, slicing the peel and membrane away from the flesh. Now, working over a bowl to catch the segments and juice, cut the segments from between the inner membranes. Finally, for maximum yield, squeeze out the juice from the leftover membrane.

Orange flower water

The bitter orange is also the source of orange flower water – a by-product from distilling the essential oil from the orange's heady blossom. Its fragrance blissfully lifts custards, pannacottas and rice puds: use about 1 tsp orange flower water to 500ml milk or cream. A few drops splashed over fresh summer fruits will enhance their flavour, and a drop or two is delightful added to a batch of Seville marmalade – or apricot jam.

CRÊPES SUZETTE

This boozy, orangey pud is a real classic, and particularly good with the addition of fresh orange segments. Serves 4

FOR THE CRÊPES

125g plain white flour

A pinch of salt

1 medium egg, lightly beaten

About 300ml whole milk

A little vegetable oil (refined rapeseed oil), for frying

TO ASSEMBLE

4 large oranges

Juice of ½ lemon

75g butter

75g caster sugar

80ml Somerset cider brandy, Grand Marnier or Cointreau

To make the crêpes, sift the flour and salt into a bowl and make a well in the centre. Add the egg and 50ml of the milk and whisk, gradually incorporating the flour into the liquid. Continue adding more milk little by little, until you have a smooth batter, the consistency of single cream. Let rest for at least 30 minutes; if the batter thickens, add a dash of milk.

Heat a non-stick 20cm frying pan or crêpe pan over a medium heat. When hot, swirl 1 tbsp oil around the pan, then tip out the excess. Add a small ladleful (about 50ml) of batter – just enough to coat the base of the pan – and swirl it quickly to cover the base. Cook for a minute or so, until lightly coloured underneath, then flip over and cook for a minute on the other side. Repeat with all the batter – to make about 8 crêpes. As they are cooked, stack the crêpes interleaved with greaseproof paper on a large plate.

Finely grate the zest of 1 orange into a large bowl and set a large sieve over it. Slice the peel and pith off all 4 oranges (as described above) then, working over the sieve, slice out the orange segments and drop them into the sieve, so any juice drips through into the bowl. Squeeze the spent orange membranes to extract all the juice. Add the lemon juice to the bowl too. Set aside the orange segments.

Put a large frying pan over a medium heat and add the butter. When melted, add the sugar and give the pan a shake. Let bubble for a few minutes, shaking occasionally, until it turns golden brown, then add the citrus juice and zest mix. The caramel may form lumps but it should melt to a smooth syrup. Give it a good stir and let it simmer for about 4 minutes.

Now add the brandy and, standing well back, set it alight with a match. Allow the flame to die down and simmer for a further 3–4 minutes to reduce it by half: it should be nice and syrupy. Add the orange segments and simmer for another minute, then turn off the heat.

While the sauce is still hot, place one of the crêpes in the pan and turn it to coat both sides. Then fold it in half, and then in half again, to form a triangle. Move it to the side of the pan and repeat with the remaining crêpes so you end up with a pan full of syrupy, folded crêpes and slices of orange. Serve at once, with cream or ice cream.

Oregano & marjoram

Pam Corbin

LATIN NAME
Oregano: *Origanum vulgare*.
Marjoram: *Origanum majorana*

ALSO KNOWN AS
Oregano: Pot marjoram
or wild marjoram.
Marjoram: Sweet marjoram,
knotted marjoram

SEASONALITY
May–October

MORE RECIPES
Garfish with olives, oregano
and garlic (page 267); Chicken
and cider stew with rosemary
dumplings (page 617); Summer
savory scones (page 569)

Oregano and marjoram come from the same genus, but are different species. Oregano, which sports mauve flowers, is the gutsier of the two. Marjoram has subtler notes and a sweeter, more floral flavour; its flowers range in colour from white to lilac.

Oregano, with its spicy and peppery character, is great added to slow-roasted veg, rich bolognese sauces and passata. Or try rubbing it into barbecue meats or stuffing (with lemon) into mackerel before frying or griddling. To pep up roast potatoes: cut 500g spuds into 4–5cm cubes and toss with 1 tbsp olive oil, 2 tbsp finely chopped oregano and some seasoning. Roast at 200°C/Fan 180°C/Gas 6 for about 40 minutes until crisp and golden, then tip into a bowl and splash over 1 tbsp lemon juice. These spuds are lovely with roast belly of pork or pan-fried fillets of sole.

Marjoram is generally best added towards the end of cooking and works beautifully in buttery sauces for fish, with chicken or eggs, and in Provençal-style vegetable and mushroom dishes. Or try it chopped and mixed with cream cheese as a delicious filling for brown bread sandwiches. Marjoram is also particularly good in herb scones.

Both herbs bring authenticity to pizza, focaccia and ciabatta breads, and a sprig of either herb enhances vinegars and salad dressings.

Native to the Mediterranean and the South Americas, these aromatic, perennial herbs from the mint family are out-and-out sun lovers and hate getting their roots too wet. The hotter the climate, the more intense the aromatics. British-grown oregano will never match the intensity of a herb from a scorched Greek hillside, but can still be delicious. There are numerous varieties – some tender, some hardy – and a diversity of leaves: bright green, grey-green, gold and variegated. Find the flavour you enjoy the most and remember bees love all these richly scented herbs too.

Both species do well in pots – particularly marjoram, which is only half-hardy. Containing the plants also means you will be able to keep the soil relatively dry and can move them to the sunniest spots. However, you can grow them directly in beds if they are well drained and sheltered. Cut back after flowering to get fresh, leafy growth.

Both oregano and marjoram are worth drying and retain their citrusy-savoury pungency really well. Harvest just before flowering and hang bunches in a dark, dry place. Use about half as much as you would if you were using the fresh herb, crumbling the dried leaves into tomato sauces, soups and bean dishes through the winter.

SLOW-ROASTED TOMATOES WITH OREGANO

500g small-medium tomatoes

1 tbsp olive or rapeseed oil

1 tbsp soy sauce

2 tsp clear honey

1 tbsp chopped oregano, plus
extra leaves to finish

A little squeeze of lemon juice

Sea salt and black pepper

These sweet and intensely aromatic tomatoes are gorgeous heaped on to toasted sourdough. Alternatively, serve them with grilled meats or fish, or with couscous or bulgar wheat dishes. Serves 4 as a side dish

Preheat the oven to 170°C/Fan 150°C/Gas 3. Halve the tomatoes and place them cut side up in a shallow baking dish in which they fit snugly in a single layer.

In a small bowl, blend the oil, soy sauce and honey together. Add the chopped oregano and mix well to combine. Spoon the herby mix over the tomatoes, then season with a pinch of salt and a couple of grinds of pepper. Roast for about an hour until the tomatoes are utterly soft and richly red.

Remove from the oven and leave to stand for a few minutes if serving hot, or allow to cool to room temperature if serving cold. Before serving, sprinkle a little lemon juice and scatter a few fresh oregano leaves over the tomatoes.

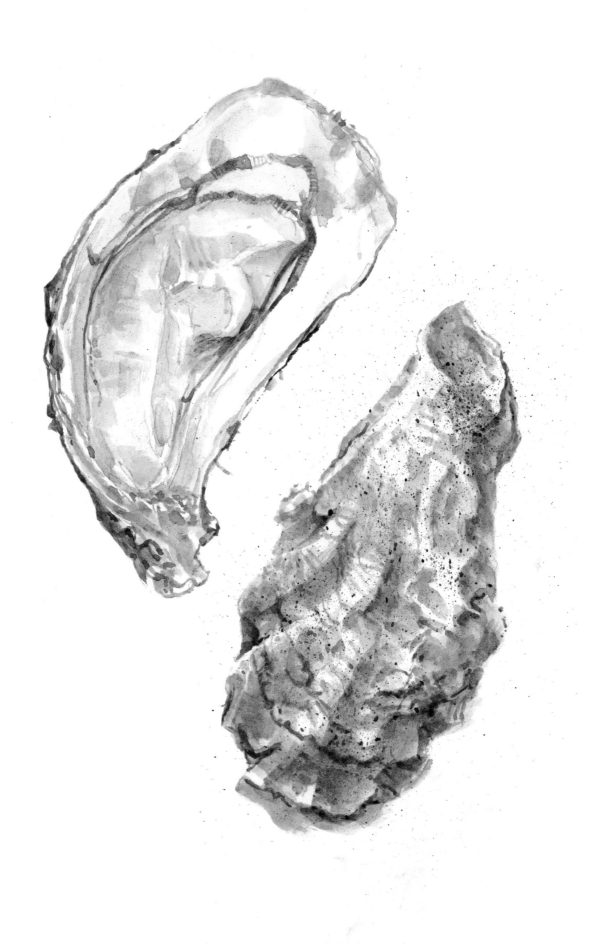

Oysters

LATIN NAME
Native oyster: *Ostrea edulis*.
Rock or Pacific oyster:
Crassostrea gigas

SEASONALITY
Native oysters September–April

MCS RATING
Wild native oysters 5, so should
not be eaten (except PDO
oysters from the Fal estuary
which are harvested sustainably).
Farmed oysters 1

SOURCING
goodfishguide.org;
faloyster.co.uk (for native
wild oysters from the Fal);
richardhawardsoysters.co.uk

Oysters are all about water quality. Suck and blow, suck and blow is all an oyster does, all day long. It can filter up to 10 litres of water an hour, from which it extracts its essential nutrients. The salinity of the water influences flavour and texture as well as determining speed of growth. An oyster from Whitstable will therefore taste different to an oyster grown in Milford Haven.

Our once abundant population of wild native oysters is now seriously depleted. Thankfully, cultivated oysters are a sustainable alternative. Oyster farming is wonderfully benign, because nothing is added to the natural environment except the oysters. The 'spat', or young oysters, often come from commercial hatcheries, or may be taken in a controlled way from designated wild areas and grown on in commercial beds.

Farmed rock oysters, also called Pacific (pictured left), are the ones you're most likely to find on sale or on a menu. They are distinct from the smaller native oysters which, though still cultivated, are more expensive and only good between September and April, outside their breeding season when their flesh may taste 'milky'. Hence the often-quoted adage to only eat oysters when there's an 'r' in the month.

Rock oysters were introduced because they could be farmed easily and eaten at any time of year – it was assumed they'd be unable to spawn in our chilly seas, so would never be out of condition. This proved to be incorrect – rocks do occasionally spawn in our waters, but it is still relatively unusual and can be managed (by keeping them in cooler areas), which is why cultivated rocks are available all year round.

Buy oysters from an oyster dealer or restaurateur who knows which farm, in which estuary, they came from. If they know neither, steer clear. A good oyster is a thing of poetic joy. A bad oyster – one that makes your stomach churn – is a disaster.

Shucking an oyster requires a special oyster knife and a certain knack. Protect your non-knife hand with a folded tea towel and secure the oyster either by gripping it in your hand, or by holding it down on a board. Start with the flatter half-shell uppermost so that the juices collect in the deeper, lower half. Insert the knife beside the 'hinge', then twist to lever the shell open. Keep your knife angled slightly upward so as not to damage the oyster. Then sever the muscle that holds the creature to its shell.

Eat oysters raw, as soon as they're open, with lemon, diced shallots and Tabasco. Revel in their salty other-worldliness. Or, if you're squeamish, barbecue them in their shells, curved side down, until they pop open, then scoop on to warm pasta with a generous squeeze of lemon and a dash of olive oil.

PAN-ROASTED OYSTERS WITH CELERIAC AND THYME

It's unusual to cook oysters for this much time, but the results are delicious: the process brings out all their umami flavours. Serves 2

FOR THE CELERIAC
150g peeled celeriac
Juice of ½ lemon
A little extra virgin olive oil
Black pepper

FOR THE OYSTERS
1 tbsp olive oil
A knob of butter
24 large rock oysters, shucked
2 sprigs of thyme

Slice the celeriac very thinly, then cut the slices into thin matchsticks (or use a mandoline to do this). Put the celeriac in a bowl and dress it lightly with a squeeze of lemon juice, a little extra virgin olive oil and a twist of pepper. Scatter the celeriac over 2 warmed plates.

Place a large non-stick frying pan over a medium heat and add the olive oil and butter. When bubbling, add the oysters and their juices (they might spit a little) with the thyme. Turn the heat down to medium. Cook the oysters for 7–8 minutes on the first side then flip them and cook for the same time on the other side, until crisp and caramelised.

Arrange the oysters over the celeriac, then scrape up all the crisp, tasty, sticky bits from the pan and sprinkle over the oysters. Serve straight away.

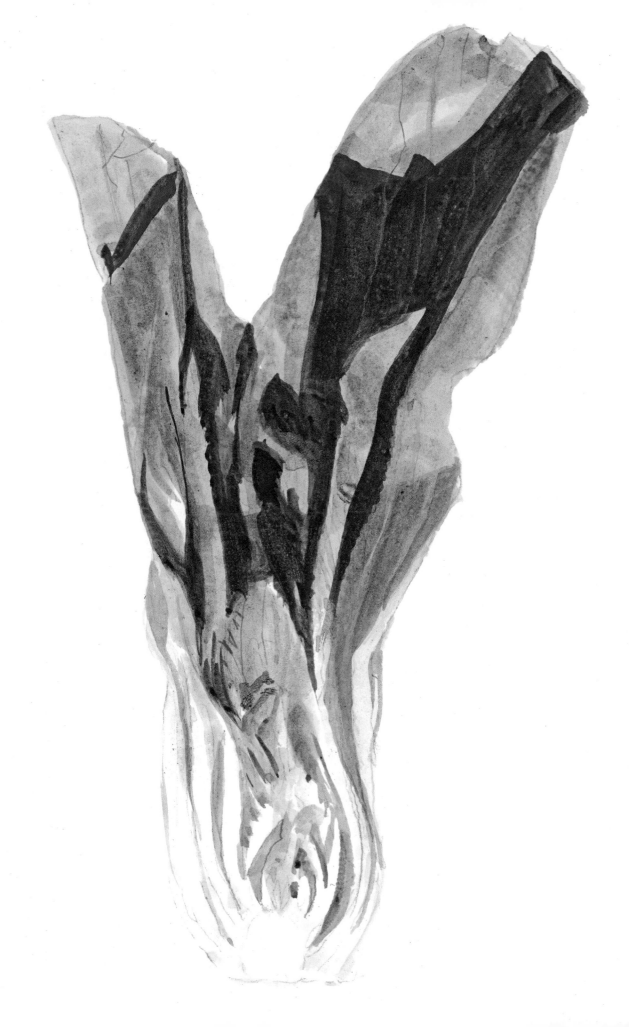

Pak choi

Nikki Duffy

LATIN NAME
Brassica rapa chinensis

ALSO KNOWN AS
Bok choy

SEASONALITY
March–December

Compact, diminutive pak choi, the *choi* meaning 'vegetable' in Cantonese, is almost two veg in one. Its white or very pale green, shovel-shaped stalks are as crunchy and succulent as a tender bit of celery, while its dark green leafy tops are wonderful wilters. The whole plant is so tender and light that you can cook it in the piece in a few minutes. Or you can slice the stalks and cook them first, then add the shredded leaves for a brief final blast. It may seem all water and crunch but, rich in vitamins, minerals and antioxidants, pak choi packs a real nutritional punch.

Although a member of the cabbage family, pak choi has no sulphurous tang or peppery kick. There's a hint of mustardy flavour but its personality is mild and ameliorating – which is what makes it complement spicy food so well. It partners hot, spicy, saucy things like nothing else. Drop it, roughly shredded, into a Thai curry or laksa a few minutes before serving; or just serve it, super-simply steamed, alongside sweet-and-sour pork or sticky, spicy, black bean beef.

My favourite way to eat pak choi is just wilted with garlic. Slice the stems thickly and throw them into a very hot wok with a little flavourless coconut oil. Toss over a high heat for 2–3 minutes until glossy and tender, then add the shredded leaves and a finely chopped garlic clove or two (and some chilli flakes if you fancy some heat). Stir-fry for another minute then add a generous splash of soy sauce and take off the heat. Finish with a few drops of toasted sesame oil and serve with rice or noodles.

Young, tender pak choi is also great served raw: sliver it into a slaw with peppers, carrots, spring onions and a fragrant dressing full of ginger, chilli, garlic and soy sauce.

Native to China, pak choi only arrived in the UK towards the end of the last century. But it's caught on to the extent that it's now widely grown here and you should be able to get British leaves for most of the year, or easily grow your own. In a sunny spot, it grows fast – you can harvest the baby leaves just a month after sowing.

Tat soi is a related and similarly lovely leaf, with longer, firmer stems that culminate in round, green leaves. Use it in all the same ways.

PAK CHOI WITH STICKY PRUNE SAUCE

2 pak choi, bases trimmed

FOR THE PRUNE SAUCE
50g pitted prunes, thinly sliced

25ml soy sauce

1 tsp clear honey

Juice of 1 large orange

1 tbsp mirin (Japanese rice wine)

1 star anise

1 tbsp toasted sesame oil

A small pinch of dried chilli flakes

TO SERVE
4 spring onions, finely sliced

A few coriander leaves

Lime wedges

This dark rich sauce makes a wonderful contrast to light and delicate pak choi (it also works well with spring greens). Serve as a vegetarian dish with rice and perhaps some stir-fried tofu, or pair it with pork chops. Serves 2

To make the sauce, put all the ingredients into a small saucepan, add 3 tbsp water and place over a medium heat. Bring to a simmer and cook for 4–5 minutes or until slightly thickened. Remove from the heat and leave to stand for 10–15 minutes, to allow the flavours to develop and the prunes to soften a little.

Halve the pak choi from top to bottom and lay them in a steamer basket over a pan of simmering water (or use an electric steamer). Cover and steam for about 5 minutes until the white part of the stem is just tender. Alternatively, cook the pak choi in a large pan of simmering water for 3 minutes or so, drain well and allow to steam off for a few minutes so there is no residual water on the leaves.

Put the pak choi on a serving plate and spoon over the sticky, spicy prune sauce. Strew with sliced spring onions and coriander leaves and serve with lime wedges.

Papaya

LATIN NAME
Carica papaya

ALSO KNOWN AS
Pawpaw (though this name
is also given to two other fruits:
Asimina triloba and *Vasconcellea pubescens*)

SEASONALITY
Imported all year round

MORE RECIPES
Mango and banana salad
(page 374)

These luscious tropical fruits are imported into the UK, from different places, all year round. Since they are usually air-freighted I see them as a once-in-a-while treat, except when I am working or holidaying in tropical climes. Then the papaya becomes my surrogate apple – an almost daily ritual, and usually the first thing to pass my lips in the morning.

A ripe one, split open, the coral flesh spritzed generously with the juice of a halved lime, then scooped straight from the skin with a teaspoon, is utterly delicious. I rarely do anything else with papaya because few things offer any improvement.

However, if I do get my hands on a few nice examples of this gorgeous fruit, I may diversify a little. It's always worth sticking with the citrus theme and mingling chunks of scooped-out papaya with segments of orange, lime and/or grapefruit in a zesty two- or three-fruit salad – or blitzing the ripe flesh into a smoothie with fresh orange and lime juice. Whizzed up with banana, papaya makes a lovely purée for babies (or grown-ups – spritzed with lime again and perhaps topped with shavings of toasted coconut). And diced or cut into julienne, papaya is a great addition to tangy-spicy salads, salsas and slaws – paired up with lots of chilli, citrus, onion and perhaps something salty such as fish sauce or tamari.

The greatest challenge is finding a perfectly ripe fruit. There are several papaya varieties – some are pear size, others as big as melons. All ripen from hard and green-skinned to soft (and fragile) and yellow or orange-skinned. So skin colour is the first indicator, a gentle squeeze the second: the fruit should feel a little tender and giving when pressed, especially at the neck end.

If you find yourself with a hard, green, unripe papaya, you won't want to scoop its flesh for breakfast (though it will ripen eventually, if left on a sunny windowsill). But it is the perfect ingredient for the classic Thai *som tum* – a sensational hot and sour salad of grated or shredded green papaya, dressed with lime juice, fish sauce and chopped peanuts.

A ripe papaya is usually cut into lengthways wedges and scooped from the inside. A green one can be peeled with a veg peeler and prepped like a courgette or cucumber. In both cases, the glossy black seeds, which resemble fish eggs, are usually scraped out and discarded (one reason that papaya plants grow almost like weeds all over the tropics). In fact these seeds are edible. You may or may not enjoy crunching them to explore their curiously tannic and peppery taste. But you won't know until you try.

SPICED PAPAYA SALSA

1 ripe papaya

1 hot green chilli, deseeded and finely chopped

1 tsp soft brown sugar

Juice of ½ lime

8 mint leaves, finely shredded

A pinch of cumin seeds

A pinch of coriander seeds

This is fresh, spicy, sweet and sour. It works beautifully with seafood, such as seared scallops or grilled fish, but is also a great thing to have on hand when the barbecue is fired up: try it with chicken, pork or burgers. Serves 4–6 as a side dish

Peel, halve and deseed the papaya, then cut into small dice and place in a bowl. Add the chilli, brown sugar, lime juice and mint, and give everything a gentle mix to get the flavours mingling.

If you have time, toast the cumin and coriander seeds lightly in a dry pan, until fragrant. (Just a pinch of each is enough, you don't want them to be overpowering.) Put the seeds into a mortar and crush with the pestle, almost to a powder.

Add the crushed seeds to the papaya and mix again. Serve straight away.

Paprika

ALSO KNOWN AS
Pimentón

MORE RECIPES
Chard and new potatoes with paprika and fennel (page 138); Spiced couscous with lemon and sultanas (page 202); Spicy kohlrabi wedges (page 327); Shrimps on sourdough with paprika and lemon (page 583); Spiced liver pâté (page 362); Squirrel and beans on toast (page 608); Sunflower seed and caraway corn crackers (page 623)

Paprika is the dried and powdered form of various varieties of mild red chilli pepper, used to infuse a dish with heat, sweetness, spice and colour. It is widely used in Spanish cuisine, where it is known as *pimentón* but is also closely associated with the cooking of Hungary where it is applied to both flavour and thicken sauces. Paprika is nowhere near as fiery as a hot chilli powder. Some paprika does carry a kick – depending on the specific peppers used, and also on how many seeds and membranes are removed during processing – but the predominant flavour is a spicy sweetness, inherent in the fruit. Paprika is also sometimes deliciously smoky – an additional flavour created by cold-smoking the peppers slowly over an oak wood fire.

On the whole, Hungarian paprika is more robust and complex. There are several different varieties, ranging from sweet to fiery. Spanish *pimentón* is a little gentler and can be sweet (*dulce*), bittersweet (*agridulce*) or hot (*picante*). The La Vera region of western Spain is famous for the particularly fine variety of smoked pimentón it produces.

It's quite usual for a recipe to call for more than one type of paprika – hot and sweet, for instance – to get a range of flavours. The one common denominator among all types is that unless paprika is cooked, it will not surrender its full flavour. This spice is often used as a dusted-on garnish, since it looks so bright and appealing. However, with even the best varieties, all you're really getting in this instance is the colour. This is not to be undervalued, though: it is quite common in Hungary for hot paprika to replace pepper in a shaker on a table.

Paprika is an essential ingredient in chorizo and when slices of chorizo are fried it colours the oil with its vibrant hue. Casseroles, soups and stews such as Hungarian goulash and paprikash are further uses for paprika, as well as a classic paella. It is also fantastic with white fish.

PORTUGUESE PAPRIKA POTATOES

3 tbsp red wine vinegar

2 tbsp sweet smoked paprika

1 medium onion, roughly chopped

2 large, ripe tomatoes (or a handful of cherry tomatoes), roughly chopped

4 large potatoes (about 700g in total), cut into 3cm chunks (unpeeled)

300g cooking chorizo, chopped into small chunks

A big handful of parsley leaves or fennel tops, chopped

Sea salt and black pepper

Plain wholemilk yoghurt or soured cream, to serve

This is an incredibly easy and delicious one-pot potato dish, rich with paprika, chorizo and tomato. Serves 6

Preheat the oven to 180°C/Fan 160°C/Gas 4. Pour 700ml water into a large, deep roasting tray and add the vinegar. Whisk in the paprika, then add the onion, tomatoes, potatoes, chorizo, half the parsley or fennel tops and some salt and pepper. Mix together.

Bake, uncovered, for 1½–2 hours, stirring after an hour and checking frequently thereafter, until the potatoes are tender and have absorbed all the other flavours.

Scatter with the remaining parsley or fennel tops and serve with a crisp, green salad and a dollop of plain yoghurt or soured cream.

Parasol mushrooms

John Wright

LATIN NAME
Macrolepiota procera.
Shaggy parasol:
Chlorophyllum rhacodes

SEASONALITY
Summer–autumn

HABITAT
Parasol mushroom: permanent
pasture and grassland.
Shaggy parasol: woodland

Few fungi are as magnificent as the parasol mushroom, or as easy to spot. While most field fungi nestle in the grass and must be searched out, at 30cm tall and 30cm wide, parasols are visible from two fields away. They also invariably grow in rings, so a find of parasols will feed the family. They are at their most succulent while the creamy white gills are soft and fresh, and the best of all are those that are just opening from their distinctive 'drumstick' stage.

The stem is tough and only useful in a clear mushroom stock; it is joined to the cap by a rather neat ball and socket joint and therefore easy to detach. The cap should not be chopped with a knife, but split radially into sections.

Parasols do not tolerate lengthy cooking as they quickly acquire the texture of a damp face flannel. However, they are delicious sautéed. The flavour is part mushroom, part chicken and the texture slightly fibrous, like chicken breast. My favourite way of cooking them is in a light tempura batter. The parasol section melts invitingly inside the crispy coating.

Appearing in summer and autumn, parasols (pictured right) are unmistakeable due to their distinctive size, habitat, scaly cap, swollen stem base and a pronounced, 'slideable' ring on the stem. 'Dapperlings', which are poisonous, look a bit like parasols, but are much smaller, seldom growing beyond 10cm in diameter.

There is also the shaggy parasol. This is smaller, greyer, with white flesh and gills that bruise orange/red, and grows in woods. Unfortunately a substantial proportion of those who eat it are unwell afterwards. It must always be cooked before eating, though even this does not guarantee a happy outcome.

BAKED PARASOL MUSHROOM WITH BRIE

A little olive or rapeseed oil,
for cooking

4 rashers of smoked streaky
bacon, derinded and cut into
lardons

1 medium onion, finely chopped

2 garlic cloves, finely chopped

80g Brie, such as Godminster
Organic or Baron Bigod

1 tbsp chopped flat-leaf parsley

60g fresh breadcrumbs

6 cooked chestnuts, chopped
(optional)

1 young, open parasol
mushroom, 25–30cm across,
stem removed, brushed clean

Sea salt and black pepper

One generous parasol, baked with a cheesy, bacony topping, feeds two amply as a starter, or makes a fine meal for one. Don't wash or peel the mushroom; instead use a brush to clean it thoroughly. Serves 1–2

Preheat the oven to 200°C/Fan 180°C/Gas 6 and grease a baking tray.

Heat a frying pan over a medium heat and add a trickle of oil, followed by the bacon lardons. Stir until the bacon starts to release its fat then add the onion and garlic. Cook for 8–10 minutes until the onion is softened.

Meanwhile, roughly dice the Brie (including the rind or not, as preferred). Add the parsley, breadcrumbs, chestnuts, if using, and Brie to the pan. Stir until the cheese melts and binds the mixture together.

Put the mushroom gill side up on a board and season with salt and pepper. Spread the hot breadcrumb mixture on top of the mushroom and place on the baking tray. Bake for 8–10 minutes or until a knife inserted into the thickest part of the mushroom passes through easily. Serve straight away, with some bitter leaves.

P

Parmesan

Steven Lamb

SOURCING

mediterraneandirect.co.uk; thehamandcheeseco.com

This unique cheese, one of only three foreign cheeses to which we've granted a stand-alone entry, originates from Northern Italy. No producer outside a defined area within Emilia Romagna and Lombardy may call their cheese Parmigiano-Reggiano. It carries a PDO, protecting its name and enshrining its distinguishing features.

Those features are very special indeed. With its dry, crystalline, granular nature and wonderful, salty flavour, Parmesan is in some ways the ultimate cook's cheese. Whether you're dissolving it into a batter or sauce, or scattering it over a dish before serving, it is both an ingredient in its own right and a superb seasoning. Its complex, nutty flavour, rich with a glutamic savouriness (umami), puts it in the same arena as soy sauce, flaky sea salt and peppery extra virgin olive oil. It finishes dishes – pasta, risottos, soups – exquisitely.

For salads and bruschette, using a vegetable peeler to produce fine 'shavings' of Parmesan can be particularly successful – spreading the flavour of the cheese in a subtle but delectable way. Generally, however, it is finely grated, forming a light dust without the gooey-stringy meltiness of most cheeses. This makes grated Parmesan particularly easy to work into mixtures such as pestos or doughs, where 'fleshier' cheeses become sticky and pasty.

Parmesan is made from unpasteurised, partially skimmed cow's milk. The cows must be fed on fodder from the correct region, but they are almost invariably housed indoors and fed dried grass, even for organic Parmesan. Free-range Parmesans don't really exist – nor vegetarian ones: it is made with animal rennet.

P

Once curdled, the milk curds are cooked until they coalesce into a mass. These solids are placed in huge, wheel-shaped moulds and tightened with a belt embedded with the name of the producer (which transfers to the rind of the cheese). The wheels are submerged in brine for up to a month and then removed to ageing rooms to mature for a year. On a cheese's first birthday it is inspected and given an official stamp. Or, should it be deemed not good enough, the markings on its rind are erased and it is sent away for grating – an ignominious fate.

Some Parmesans are eaten between 12 and 18 months, but many are aged longer. Historically, it might have been fair to say that older was better, with 3-, 4- or even 6-year-old Parmesans offering a magnificent eating experience. But these days, most Parmesan is made from the milk of Friesian cows which does not stand up to ageing quite so well.

Parmesan between 24 and 28 months old is generally at its peak and excellent as a table cheese. Try serving nuggets and crumbs of such Parmesan sprinkled with a few drops of balsamic vinegar or trickled with honey. The traditional way is to 'open' the cheese, breaking off shards with a knife, rather than attempt to slice it cleanly. Parmesan is vastly better when freshly grated or pared. Pre-grated Parmesan is almost dustily dry, with none of the complexity and sweetness of the original cheese.

So useful and versatile is Parmesan that it has become a little over-worshipped. There are other grainy, Parmesan-mimicking cheeses that can do a similar job and are ideal if you need a vegetarian substitute. But often a better choice is another hard, matured, salty cheese – good British alternatives include Berkswell and Quickes hard goat's cheese. These will never mirror Parmesan's unique, almost mineral texture and salty sweet flavour but they can be just as good in their own ways.

LITTLE GEM WITH CRUSHED BROAD BEANS AND PARMESAN

About 1kg broad beans in the pod (400–500g podded weight)

2–3 tbsp crème fraîche

100g Parmesan, finely grated, plus extra to serve

Grated zest and juice of ½ lemon

2 tbsp chopped mint, plus extra to serve

3 tbsp extra virgin olive oil, plus extra to serve

2 Little Gem lettuces

This delicious little dish makes a light and flavoursome starter and you can also serve it as part of a mezze spread or before drinks as a canapé. Of course, other hard, salty cheeses work just as well as Parmesan here. Makes 10–12; serves 3–4 as a starter

Bring a pan of water to the boil while you pod the beans. Drop the beans into the boiling water, return to a simmer and cook until they are tender – a minute or two for young beans, up to 10 minutes for mature ones.

Taste a couple of beans: if they are quite big and mealy, or the skins seem a little bitter or tough, you can skin them. With small, sweet beans, this shouldn't be necessary.

Use a fork or potato masher to break up all the beans – don't go mad, you're looking for a roughly crushed texture, not a smooth mash. Fold in the crème fraîche, Parmesan, lemon zest, mint and olive oil. Season with salt and pepper to taste.

Trim the bases from the Little Gems and discard any damaged outer leaves. Separate the leaves; you want 10–12 of the best-shaped larger leaves for this dish (save the small leaves from the centres for another dish). Wash them and spin or pat dry.

Arrange the lettuce leaves, hollow side up, on a platter. Spoon some of the crushed broad beans into each leaf, allowing a good mouthful for each one. Scatter over a little more grated Parmesan and some extra chopped mint, trickle over a little more olive oil and finally squeeze over the lemon juice before serving.

Parsley

Pam Corbin

LATIN NAME
Curly parsley: *Petroselinum crispum*. Flat-leaf parsley: *Petroselinum crispum* var. *neopolitanum*

ALSO KNOWN AS
Flat-leaf parsley: French or Italian parsley

SEASONALITY
All year round

MORE RECIPES
Chicken broth with parsley and celery seed spaetzle (page 163); Cauliflower clafoutis with ham and parsley (page 126); Quinoa with cumin-roasted roots and parsley (page 514); Crispy lentil and roasted squash salad with salsa verde (page 352); Spaghetti with whelks, garlic and parsley (page 670); Grilled langoustine with lemon and parsley butter (page 339); Grilled squid with chilli, parsley and garlic (page 607); Roast brill with air-dried ham and parsley sauce (page 92); Sautéed brains with parsley and caper sauce (page 82); Saffron speltotto with black pudding and parsley (page 548)

Parsley is an indispensable ingredient. It is the most commonly used of all culinary herbs, its versatile, grassy flavour integral to many of the great kitchen classics worldwide. We tend to take this gentle, aromatic leaf for granted, rarely giving it the kudos it deserves.

Parsley basically divides into two camps – curly-leaf and flat-leaf (pictured right). Curly parsley grows in softly rounded clumps of bright green, ruffled leaves and is a stalwart of the English kitchen garden. The crisp, springy leaves are drier and slightly more bitter than the flat-leaf variety, but their robust flavour is perfect for a traditional parsley sauce. They are also fabulous fried to serve with fish: snap off the stalks and break the leaves into sprigs. Melt 50–75g butter in a small frying pan until it sizzles, then drop in the parsley sprigs and fry for no more than a minute until crisp. Serve straight away.

With its springy texture, curly-leaf parsley makes the ideal bed for roasting a whole flatfish too: sole, brill or plaice. Place the fish, skin side uppermost, on a bed of the curly leaves, season with salt and pepper, dot with butter (or drizzle with oil) and roast at 200°C/Fan 180°C/Gas 6 for about 10 minutes per 500g. The parsley will flavour the fish while wilting down in the buttery juices – make sure you serve it all up.

Flat-leaf parsley has larger leaves, which are finer in texture and – of course – flat! In fact, it is similar in appearance to coriander, though it smells quite different. Native to the Mediterranean, flat-leaf is generally considered to have a better flavour than curly-leaf, but I think it is the lushness of the tender leaves (making it more like a vegetable) that gives it superiority. Flat-leaf parsley is a staple in Middle Eastern and Mediterranean cuisines where it is chopped and tossed in quantity into traditional tabbouleh, couscous and pasta dishes.

It certainly pays to be generous with this herb, not least because parsley's flavour is fresh and mild. But parsley also happens to be good for you, providing plenty of Vitamins C, B1, B2, carotene and iron. Raw, it makes a great addition to wholesome juices and smoothies. And flat-leaf parsley, lightly steamed, is delicious served as a vegetable – allow roughly 50g per person.

A member of the Umbelliferacae family (along with dill, lovage and carrots), parsley shares the fresh, savoury, celery-like qualities of its relatives. With its well-rounded but subtle flavour, this herb is as much about seasoning and balancing other ingredients as it is about contributing a distinctive taste of its own. It is the perfect way to finish dishes that would otherwise seem a little too rich, sweet, creamy or earthy. And the stalks are packed with fine flavour and perfect to use in meat, fish and veg stocks.

Fresh parsley is a core ingredient in many green salsas, sauces and seasonings. For example, it is one of the definitive herbs in the *fines herbes* mix – along with chervil, tarragon and chives – that elevates a simple omelette.

The French also chop parsley with raw garlic and turn it into *persillade*. This is lovely with small new potatoes – hot or cold – or mixed with oil and rubbed into chicken, fish or lamb chops prior to cooking.

The Italians use a little less garlic and add lemon zest for their fresh and zesty gremolata – which is fantastic scattered over long-cooked and earthy dishes to brighten their flavours. A capery, garlicky, sharp Italian salsa verde – so very good with plain-cooked meats, pulses and fish – would be nothing without parsley. And parsley sauce, an old-time favourite with boiled ham or poached fish, is simply made by adding *lots* of the chopped fresh herb to a smooth béchamel.

One of the simplest ways to enjoy parsley's subtle seasoning charms is in *beurre Maître d'hôtel* (parsley butter), which adds a gorgeous extra flavour to simply boiled, freshly dug new potatoes, as well as seared steak, grilled fish, vegetables, pulses – or anything you put it on. You can even spread it on crusty fresh bread. To make it, add 1 tbsp finely chopped parsley, a good squeeze of lemon juice, a little sea salt and black pepper to 100g softened unsalted butter. Blend together and shape into a roll. Wrap in greaseproof paper, keep in the fridge and use as required.

The only real skill in all these recipes is in the chopping. Make sure your parsley is clean and dry, then strip the leaves from the main stem. Roll these tightly into a cigar shape and roughly shred them, using a heavy chef's knife. Then, holding the handle of the knife in one hand and the tip with the other, chop away with a see-sawing motion, traversing across the leaves until the parsley is chopped to the required size.

Growing your own parsley is the best way to have access to a plentiful supply of the freshest and tastiest leaves. Parsley can be slow to germinate but soaking the seeds in warm water for 12–24 hours before sowing helps get them off to a good start. Nevertheless, depending on warmth, it will still take 3–6 weeks for the bright green seedlings to appear.

Parsley prefers a sunny site with a rich moist soil, and must be kept well watered in dry weather. If the plants start to turn yellow, cut them back to allow fresh growth to come through – and it will. Although usually treated as an annual, parsley is a biennial and a good outdoor clump should allow you to snip a few sprigs throughout the winter. Second best to home-grown is the pot-grown or cut parsley that's always available in supermarkets and most farm shops. So there is no excuse not to have parsley to hand – a kitchen without it is bereft indeed.

POTATO AND PARSLEY BAKE

1kg large floury potatoes, such as King Edward or Maris Piper

50–75g parsley leaves (stalks reserved)

1 onion, thinly sliced

2 garlic cloves, very roughly chopped

300ml double cream

Sea salt and black pepper

This big, vibrant bake is simple to make and incredibly parsleyish. You can use either flat-leaf or curly parsley – just be generous with it. Serves 6–8 as a side dish

Preheat the oven to 180°C/Fan 160°C/Gas 4.

Peel the potatoes, halve if very large and place them in a large pan with the parsley stalks. Cover with water, add a generous pinch of salt and bring to the boil. Lower the heat and simmer for 15 minutes to partially cook. Drain, reserving 200ml of the cooking liquid, and allow the potatoes to steam-dry in a colander. Discard the parsley stalks.

Once cool enough to handle, slice the potatoes into 1cm rounds. Lay them in a large, shallow baking dish, in as close to a single layer as possible, mingling in the sliced onion and seasoning with salt and pepper as you go.

Pour the reserved potato cooking water into a jug blender, add the parsley leaves and garlic and pulse until you have a fairly fine, vibrant green purée. Add the cream with some seasoning and pulse briefly to mix.

Pour the creamy parsley sauce over the potatoes and press everything down so it forms a fairly even layer. Bake for 25–30 minutes or until the potatoes are nice and tender and the cream is thick and bubbling.

Leave to settle for a few minutes then serve the bake on its own, with some grated hard cheese on top if you like and salad leaves on the side, or as a side dish to roast chicken or grilled fish.

Parsnip

Hugh Fearnley-Whittingstall

LATIN NAME
Pastinaca sativa

SEASONALITY
September–March

MORE RECIPES
Devilled parsnips (page 128); Curried new potatoes, red onion and lettuce (page 226); Chicken and cider stew with rosemary dumplings (page 617); Bacon and celeriac tart (page 42); Ale-braised ox cheeks with parsnips (page 64); Sticky date and parsnip cake (page 234)

The British appreciation for parsnips is something to be proud of. Few other nations have taken to this regal root in quite the same way, nor found so many wonderful ways to use it. Hop over the Channel, for instance, and the question '*Est-ce que vous aimez les panais?*' may well be met with incomprehension. The French, notwithstanding their illustrious history of gastronomic achievement, have almost no knowledge of this delicious root.

Paradoxically, it was probably a group of foreigners, namely the Romans, who introduced us to parsnips. We took a shine to them from the off, falling for their sweet flavour and delicately starchy texture, and we've been dishing them up as soups, salads and side veg for centuries. In the bleak, dark ages before sugar made an appearance in our diets, we even used parsnips to make tarts, puddings and preserves.

They remain, as far as I'm concerned, one of the finest features of the winter veg patch: something to get genuinely excited about when the first slender, ivory-skinned young roots appear in September. As well as tasting terrific, they're inexpensive, easy to work with and very, very versatile.

It's true that a parsnip does require a little bit of preparation. You can't just chuck 'em in the oven whole, like a potato, or crunch a big one raw, like a carrot. But this is only because they are packed with sweet and complex flavours: the intense, earthy pungency of the parsnip can actually make it quite an overpowering mouthful if not handled with a little care. I like to add a bit of parsnip to a stock, for instance, but never too much, or it will dominate.

If you take the right approach with parsnips, however, they can be absolutely glorious. They are, indeed, surprisingly good served raw: cut into fine matchsticks, or slivered with a mandoline, or grated. Toss them into a slaw or salad with a mustardy dressing and some winter leaves. You can even juice them – try combining with apple or pear and a spritz of lime.

Boiled parsnips make great mash when combined with potatoes, or other roots (as in the recipe overleaf), and I like parsnip mash with a little apple in it too. Or, for something a touch more refined, whiz up a smooth, silky parsnip purée with a little butter and cream, spiked with thyme and plenty of black pepper. This is a simple but very lovely way to serve parsnips with almost any meat or fish. 'Let down' the purée with some good stock and you've got yourself a parsnip soup.

Parsnips are also superb in a golden-topped gratin and can be used, grated, just like carrots in cakes. But my absolute favourite parsnip will always be one that's roasted until crispy, close to burned at the thin end, chewy and toffeeish in the middle section, and creamy, almost fluffy inside the fat end.

These roots were *made* for roasting: the dry heat concentrates and caramelises their sugars, giving them a wonderful richness. To roast your parsnips to multi-faceted perfection, peel and trim them, then cut into long, root-to-tip wedges. Or at least make sure they are suitably tapered. Toss them with rapeseed oil, or lard or goose fat, salt and pepper and roast at about 190°C/Fan 170°C/Gas 5 for 40–60 minutes, stirring once or twice.

That's your Sunday roast sorted, of course, but you've also opened the door to all sorts of hearty, warm salads because, at room temperature, that multi-textured, toasty-roasty root still packs a punch – and bounces off leaves, fruits, nuts and pulses in all kinds of pleasing ways. Try tossing roast parsnips with watercress, Puy lentils and a piquant vinaigrette, for instance.

Roasting parsnips is also a great way to prepare them for blitzing into a soup. That golden, caramelised exterior will deepen the flavours nicely – but stop short of the almost-black tip, or you might get a bitter note that is too much for your soup. (You could, of course, also get some colour on your parsnips by browning them in a pan, rather than roasting.)

Many recipes mix parsnips with honey or sugar before roasting. But, these days, I tend to avoid those additions – they burn easily and I reckon parsnips are sweet enough. What these roots really do love are herbs and spices. Try them roasted with 1–2 tsp crushed coriander or cumin seeds (or both), or plain roasted and then puréed into a soup with garlic and a dash of curry powder. Roasted parsnips' sweet and nutty flavour also marries perfectly with bacon, piquant cheeses and other salty ingredients such as capers.

It's not a myth that parsnips taste better when the weather gets colder. Low soil temperatures encourage the starches in the root to turn to sugar, and the sweetness intensifies. I eat them with increasing gusto from November through to March.

Parsnips should be peeled (unless very young and freshly dug) and topped and tailed before cooking. Really big ones can have a slightly coarse, fibrous core that cooks more slowly than the outer flesh. Some recipes suggest 'trimming out the core' of larger parsnips, but I've never bothered, and never found myself wishing I had.

As far as I'm concerned, all parts of a parsnip are too good to waste. In fact, if you give the roots a good scrub before peeling, you can even oil and roast the peelings to make delicious, curly parsnip crisps.

PARSNIP, LEEK AND POTATO MASH

50g unsalted butter

500g leeks (white and pale green parts only), washed and sliced

500g floury potatoes, such as Maris Piper or King Edward, peeled and cut into large chunks

500g parsnips, peeled and cut into large chunks

1 tbsp wholegrain mustard

Sea salt and black pepper

A hearty, flavoursome mash with a nice chunky texture, this is the perfect thing to serve with beef stew or herby pork sausages, but good enough to dish up on its own with a poached egg or a crumbling of blue cheese stirred in. Serves 4

Put a large, heavy-based frying pan over a medium-low heat and add 35g of the butter. Once it has melted, add the leeks, cover and cook gently for about 10–15 minutes, until really soft and silky.

Meanwhile, put the potatoes and parsnips into a large saucepan. Cover with cold water and salt well. Bring to the boil, lower the heat and simmer for about 20 minutes until completely tender. Drain and leave to steam-dry for a minute or two.

Return the parsnips to the pan and add the remaining butter, the leeks, mustard and a few grinds of pepper. Use a potato masher to mash the veg roughly together. Taste, add more salt and pepper as necessary, then serve immediately.

Partridge

Tim Maddams

LATIN NAME
Grey partridge: *Perdix perdix*.
Red-legged partridge:
Alectoris rufa

SEASONALITY
England, Wales and Scotland:
1 September–1 February.
Northern Ireland: 1 September–
31 January. Isle of Man
(red-legged partridge only):
13 September–31 January

HABITAT
Grey partridge: lowland
pasture and farmland.
Red-legged partridge: moorland
edges, downland and farmland

MORE RECIPES
Pigeon breasts with leeks
and mash (page 469); Indian
spiced grilled quail (page 510)

SOURCING
tasteofgame.org.uk

There are two varieties of this small game bird in the British Isles: the grey or English partridge is indigenous; the more common red-legged partridge is an interloper from the Mediterranean, introduced for the purpose of shooting.

The grey partridge is slightly smaller than its red-legged cousin and a little more tasty too. However, wild grey partridge are rare these days. The industrialisation of farming, which caused the loss of a lot of their habitat, along with high pressure from shooting, resulted in a near-collapse in the population in the second half of the last century. Thankfully, as our understanding of this bird's life cycle grows, its numbers in the wild are slowly increasing.

Greys are also reared and released specifically for shooting – but in far smaller numbers than the red-legged partridge, which is easier to keep and has the useful habit of laying two clutches of eggs a year. Around ten million partridge are reared and released every year in Britain. Most are shot in the first couple of months of the season (September and October), giving way to pheasant later on.

Partridge are probably the most user-friendly and accessible of the game birds. They don't deliver on flavour quite like pigeon or grouse, but they are certainly far more forgiving to work with. Their meat is sweet, mildly gamey and tender. As with all game birds, younger specimens are the most rewarding for a cook – but, happily, a tough partridge of any age is a rarity.

Once plucked and dressed, roasting the birds simply with garlic and herbs gives excellent results; they are perfect for pot-roasting too. I also cook partridge breasts in a pan on the hob with ceps and blackberries – a lovely seasonal feast. To do this, I often just break the skin open and peel it back, feathers and all, then remove the breast and leg meat from the birds with a stout paring knife, avoiding any plucking or gutting.

PARTRIDGES ROASTED WITH QUINCE AND BACON

2 quince or 2–3 slightly
under-ripe pears

5–6 sprigs of thyme

4 bay leaves

A handful of sage leaves

1 tbsp clear honey

2 tbsp olive or rapeseed oil

25g soft butter

2 oven-ready partridges,
at room temperature

4 rashers of streaky bacon

Sea salt and black pepper

Plump partridge and fragrant quince roast well and pair beautifully; wild duck is very good in this recipe too. If you can't get hold of quince, use pears, adding them to the roasting tray with the partridge halfway through cooking. Serves 2

Preheat the oven to 200°C/Fan 180°C/Gas 6.

Wash the quince under a running tap, rubbing the skins to remove any fine down. Use a large, sharp knife to quarter the fruit. Remove the cores with a smaller knife, then cut each quarter into 2 or 3 wedges, depending on their size. Place in a large roasting tray with the herbs and plenty of seasoning, then trickle over the honey and oil.

Smear the butter all over the partridges and season them well with salt and pepper. Wrap the rashers of bacon over the breasts of the birds. Nestle the dressed birds among the quince wedges and roast for 20 minutes.

Remove the bacon from the partridges; set it aside. Check that the quince are cooked by piercing with the tip of a knife. If they are tender, remove from the roasting tray; keep them warm with the bacon. If they need more cooking, leave them with the partridge. Roast for a further 10 minutes to brown the skin a little.

Rest the birds in the roasting tin for 10–15 minutes before serving; the meat should be just cooked and still juicy, but not rare. (If the quince are still a little firm, put them back into the oven in a separate dish during this time.) Serve one partridge per person with the roast quince and bacon. Wilted greens, such as chard, go very well with this, along with a spoonful of tender pearl barley or spelt.

P

Passionfruit

Pam Corbin

LATIN NAME
Passiflora edulis

SEASONALITY
Imported all year round

With their exquisite scent and honeyed, tangy sweetness, passionfruit throw me into a dilemma. Hardly local – not even expats – they are native to Brazil and flourish in hot climates, including Australia, New Zealand, California and South Africa. But come midwinter, when our home-grown fruits and berries are scarce, I do succumb to their charms every now and again. The only British fruit to come close to their sweet-tart succulence is a blush-red dessert gooseberry, sweet with its ripening juices.

The purple passionfruit with which we are familiar are the berries from a tropical climbing plant. Our northern passionfruit has similar-looking flowers but it's a different species and produces large golden fruits with a bland flavour.

About the size of a hen's egg, the purple passionfruit has an inedible thick skin that turns dull and wrinkled as it ripens: it's when it looks past its best that this fruit is actually most ready to fulfil its promise. Inside you'll find a heart of greenish-black seeds held in an intensely fragrant, jelly-like, golden pulp. The scented, seedy flesh is delicious on its own – simply cut the fruit in half and spoon it straight into your mouth. Or chop off the top and mix a little Greek yoghurt into the juice-filled centre. The pulp is also exquisite over meringues, or in sorbets, fruit salads and sauces.

If you don't enjoy the intense crunch of the seeds, it's easy to strain them out by pushing the pulp through a nylon sieve. Approximately 8 passionfruit will yield 150ml pulp with pips – or 100ml without. I like to spritz the juice into a glass of sparkling water – or wine – and, while its acidity is not enough to 'cook' fish in the way lime or lemon juice does, passionfruit is nevertheless a fantastic addition to a ceviche.

Choose passionfruit that feel relatively heavy in the hand, with the skin slightly wrinkled. Ripe fruits like this can be kept for a week or so in the fridge. Smooth-skinned (i.e. slightly under-ripe) fruits will ripen in a few days at room temperature. If you have a few ready to go, you can scoop out the pulp and freeze it in ice-cube trays to use when life next needs a little passion.

PASSIONFRUIT AND COCONUT CURD

150ml passionfruit pulp (with or without seeds)

100ml freshly squeezed orange or lemon juice (about 2 large lemons or 1 medium orange)

125g virgin coconut oil

350g granulated sugar

4 medium eggs, well beaten

Intensely flavoured, passionfruit pulp is perfect for a curd. This recipe is dairy-free, but you can replace the coconut oil with unsalted butter if you like. Makes 4 x 200ml jars

First sterilise your jars by washing them in hot soapy water, rinsing well, then putting them upside down on a baking tray in a very low oven (at 120°C/Fan 100°C/Gas ½) to dry and warm up.

Have ready a pan of simmering water and a heatproof bowl that fits snugly over the pan, without touching the water (a stainless steel bowl is ideal, as it conducts heat well).

Put the passionfruit pulp, orange or lemon juice, coconut oil and sugar in the bowl and set over the simmering water. Stir until the coconut oil has just melted – it should measure about 55°C on a cooking thermometer. Then slowly pour in the eggs, whisking all the time with a balloon whisk, until they are well incorporated.

Continue to cook the curd over the simmering water for a further 10 minutes or so, scraping down the sides with a spatula every now and again and giving the mix a quick whip with the balloon whisk every minute or so, until it is thick and glossy and the temperature registers at least 72°C on a cook's thermometer, but no higher than 82°C.

Remove from the heat and tip the curd into a warmed jug, immediately pour into the warm jars and seal. Label when cool and store in a cool place for up to 4 weeks. Once opened, keep in the fridge and use within a week.

Pasta

Tim Maddams

MORE RECIPES
Swede with orecchiette
(page 624); Samphire, crab and
new potato salad (page 560);
Spaghetti with whelks, garlic
and parsley (page 670);
Tagliatelle with lamb's liver,
pancetta and sage (page 551)

Since the first written record of pasta in Italy in 1154, this ingredient has assumed unbelievable status. What must have started life as a practical way of storing flour in a ready-to-cook form is now the base of some of the most wonderful food in the world. There are over 300 specific types of pasta, known by over two thousand different names, any of which can be served in myriad different ways. Every region in Italy has its own pasta dishes and opinions vary widely as to which region produces the finest pasta, which sauce pairs best with which pasta, even what different pasta shapes should be called.

Pasta is traditionally made from durum wheat flour – *semola di grano duro* – which is very 'hard' and high in gluten, but produces a dough which is uniquely malleable and inelastic (see page 262). Usually, only water is added, giving a dough that can be shaped into anything from a thin spaghetti to short twists of fusilli. Once dried, it will keep almost indefinitely. You can also buy dried pasta made with egg, though there's no great advantage in it – it's not inherently superior to non-egg pasta. Traditionally, egg-enriched doughs are used fresh, particularly for stuffed pastas such as ravioli or tortellini as well as *al forno* ('in oven') dishes such as the ubiquitous lasagne.

The many and varied shapes of pasta invite different styles of sauce or dressing. A good rule of thumb is to use simple, oily dressings such as pesto or chilli and garlic on long thin pastas such as spaghetti, and thicker sauces with more robust shapes like penne. Sauces with chunks of vegetable do well on cup-shaped pastas such as conchiglie or orecchiette, which 'catch' the pieces nicely, naturally creating a pleasing ratio of pasta to sauce with each mouthful. And tiny pasta shapes such as risoni, ditalini or pastina are perfect for soups.

Good quality pasta, once cooked, tastes great on its own – in a bland, wheaty kind of way. This leads us to the first culinary rule of cooking pasta: the sauce should never completely overpower it; you should be able to taste the pasta as well as the dressing. Another basic is to always cook your pasta in a generous quantity of boiling water to dilute the starch it releases, and to stir it from time to time so it doesn't stick to itself. The water should be liberally salted in order to season the pasta (adding salt later is never quite the same) – but never oiled, as this is utterly unnecessary and flavours the pasta in an undesirable way.

So fond are we of pasta these days that we are often guilty of tipping too much into the pan. As a guide, 75g dry pasta per person should be enough if you're serving it with a substantial sauce, 100g if it's to be only lightly dressed.

Pasta is always best when cooked *al dente*, meaning it has lost all hardness and chalkiness and will yield between the teeth – but in a spirited sort of way. It should never be soft. The cooking times suggested on packs of dried pasta are a guide, but to achieve perfection, it's always worth checking the pasta a minute or two earlier.

In the 1970s, pretty much the only pasta you could buy was spaghetti in ridiculously long packets. You can now find no end of different pastas in most supermarkets, including wholewheat versions and gluten-free varieties. Wholemeal spelt pasta is a good alternative to the classic white. If gluten is a no-no for you, you may find rice pasta a better option than maize-based varieties.

Some pasta is labelled as bronze-extruded, or bronze-die. This indicates that traditional bronze machinery has been used to shape it. As you can tell just by looking at a piece of dried bronze-die pasta, this method produces a slightly rougher surface, which makes the sauce cling more readily and has a less slippery texture in the mouth.

There are various colours of pasta out there too. Black pasta, coloured with cuttlefish ink, is well worth buying. This has a uniquely fishy edge to it, fantastic with tomato sauces. It is best used fresh rather than dried.

Making your own fresh pasta is simple. A pasta machine enables you to process the dough faster, but it isn't essential – a rolling pin will do. Traditionally, '00' pasta flour is used, which is available from delis and some supermarkets.

Don't start with anything complicated: go for simple, long strips of pappardelle or the little pinched-in-the-middle pieces known as strachetti (which means 'strangled'). If you're in a rush, you can even just roll out the dough and cut it randomly into pieces to create *malfatti* ('badly made') – amazingly good with a rich, meaty ragu. Work up to more complicated, stuffed varieties like tortellini, agnolotti, or the simple ravioli below. It's worth doing so, because home-made stuffed pasta can be absolutely divine.

GARLICKY PEA RAVIOLI WITH BROWN BUTTER

Cook this at any time of year – using parsley or a little thyme if you can't get fresh mint. A garlicky purée of broad beans is an equally tasty stuffing for the pasta in summer. Serves 4

FOR THE PASTA

265g '00' pasta flour, plus extra to dust

A pinch of salt

2 medium eggs

2 medium egg yolks

FOR THE FILLING

500g frozen peas or petits pois

20g unsalted butter

3 shallots, chopped

4 garlic cloves, chopped

2 tbsp chopped mint

50g Parmesan, finely grated

Sea salt and black pepper

TO SERVE

100g unsalted butter

To make the pasta dough, mix the flour and salt in a large bowl. Add the eggs and extra yolks and mix with your fingers, working it into a ball of dough. If it's a little dry, add 1 tbsp or so of cold water – but only enough to bind. You don't want it to be sticky. Transfer to a very lightly floured surface and knead for about 5 minutes until smooth and silky. Wrap in cling film and rest in the fridge while you make the filling.

Cook the peas in lightly salted boiling water for a few minutes (just a minute or so for petits pois), until tender. Drain and set aside. Melt the 20g butter in a saucepan over a low heat, add the shallots and fry gently for 6–8 minutes, until very soft but without much colour. Add the garlic and cook for a couple more minutes.

Put the drained peas into a food processor along with the sautéed shallot and garlic, mint, grated Parmesan, a pinch of salt and a few turns of pepper. Blitz to a smooth paste and leave to cool completely.

Cut the pasta into 4 pieces and work with one piece at a time (or the pasta sheets will be too big to handle). Using a pasta machine or a rolling pin, roll out the pasta as thinly as you can and cut the rolled pasta into 7–8cm squares.

Place 1 tbsp of pea mixture in the centre of one pasta square. Dampen the pasta edges lightly with a little water on your fingertip, then place a second pasta square on top and gently seal it all around, making sure there are no air bubbles. Trim the ravioli, leaving a neat 1cm edge around the filling. Place on a floured tray (the flour will stop it sticking) and repeat with the remaining pasta and filling. Bring a large pan of salted water to the boil.

Meanwhile, melt the 100g butter in a medium saucepan over a low heat. Increase the heat a fraction so that the butter starts to simmer. Let it cook for about 7 minutes, swirling it around often and watching it carefully, until it is at the point where it starts to foam and the butter solids on the base of the pan turn brown. Quickly, before the solids blacken, take the pan off the heat and immediately pour the brown butter into a large, warm bowl.

Add a few ravioli at a time to the boiling water and simmer for 2–3 minutes until the pasta is cooked. Scoop out carefully with a slotted spoon, letting the excess water drain away, then put the ravioli in a warmed dish, sprinkling with some of the brown butter as you go.

Serve the ravioli in warmed dishes, trickled with the remaining brown butter and a dusting of black pepper.

Pastry

Nikki Duffy

MORE RECIPES
Henakopita with garam masala and eggs (page 254); Field mushroom and celeriac pie (page 258); Jerusalem artichoke and seaweed tart (page 33); Lettuce and spring onion tarte tatin (page 356); Squash, shallot and mushroom tart (page 604); Sea beet and smoked pollack pasties (page 574); Bacon and celeriac tart (page 42); Pheasant pie (page 468); Prune, almond and caraway tart (page 505); Pear and bilberry crumble tart (page 69); Apricot and honey filo pie (page 314); Pistachio, orange and honey filo tartlets (page 474); Eccles cakes (page 340)

Flour, fat and water. That's all pastry is – literally, just a 'paste' of essentially bland ingredients. But what joy it can bring. Crisp, buttery, friable and fragile, with just enough salt included to bring out the toasty, wheaty flavour of the flour and the sweet, lactic body of the butter. It partners sweet custards, tart fruits, cream and chocolate, or rich, cheesy, meaty or earthy fillings with equal deliciousness – no mere casing or container, but a hugely pleasurable part of the whole.

On the other hand, pastry can be pretty awful. Cheap ready-made pastries are agglomerations of flour with palm oil, margarine and emulsifiers. They are bland, dull and waxy, at best. 'All butter' are the magic words to look for on a pack of pastry – as with all very simple recipes, the quality of every ingredient is blatantly evident. There are some very good pre-made pastries on the market, which are ideal if you are pushed for time or short on confidence – a good buttery puff pastry can be particularly worth buying as it's time-consuming to produce at home and takes a little practice to perfect.

Being able to make good pastry is a hallowed skill and those who are good at it are revered. My maternal grandmother was one of them. I remember watching her cut butter and pale lard into a bowlful of flour with a blunt knife, ready to encase the simplest of fillings. She had made pastry so many times, she didn't need to think about it. Now I am a mother, I've observed that a 4-year-old can make pretty good pastry too. Young children are not burdened by the idea that 'pastry is difficult' – something that makes your hands heavy before you even start. And they do not have the inclination to stand there rubbing in fat for too long. Fast, light and a bit slapdash, they don't overwork the dough and they leave a few big bits of butter in the mix which produce a delightful flakiness, even in a shortcrust.

TYPES OF PASTRY

Shortcrust pastry This is the basic flour, fat and water mix. The classic proportions are two parts flour to one part butter, with a little water or milk, and sometimes an egg yolk to bind. It can be adapted to make sweet shortcrust by adding icing sugar, chocolate pastry by adding cocoa powder and sugar, or wholemeal pastry by using brown flour. Wholemeal pastry is not as light as standard shortcrust, but it is good in certain recipes, notably those involving cheese.

Pâte sablée A rich, sweet shortcrust, this is made with a higher proportion of butter, as well as egg and sugar. It has a 'sandy' texture, hence the name. Sometimes ground almonds are included too.

Puff pastry This is made by encasing a large, rectangular piece of butter within a simple dough, then rolling out, folding, turning and re-rolling repeatedly, in order to build up a 'laminated' dough encasing many thin layers of butter. When baked, trapped air expands, while the fat melts and releases steam, puffing up the pastry into many delicious, crisp wafer-thin layers.

Flaky and rough puff pastries These are similar to puff but usually made by mixing rough chunks of fat into the dough, rather than enclosing a block, before rolling and folding.

Filo, strudel and brik pastries These are all paper-thin forms of pastry, made from a basic dough and used in several layers, each layer brushed with fat. Filo and strudel doughs are made by rolling and stretching. Preparing brik or warka pastry is an extraordinary art: a ball of soft dough is slapped against a hot plate so that a wafer-thin layer adheres to it and cooks – definitely one for the experts. These pastries all dry out very easily and become fragile and hard to handle so, when working with them, it's important to keep the unused pastry covered with a damp cloth.

Hot water crust pastry A strong pastry, this is ideal for substantial pies that need to contain a dense, heavy, juicy filling. Melting lard in lots of boiling water, then stirring in the flour (pretty much the opposite of what you do when making a light shortcrust) creates a strong gluten network, resulting in a robust, malleable pastry. Some strong bread flour may be included.

Choux pastry This is quite different from other pastries. It is made by heating water and butter in a pan then beating in flour, followed by eggs. The resulting soft dough is, again, quite strong. It's used to make choux buns and éclairs that puff up spectacularly in the oven, creating hollow centres that can be filled (usually with cream).

For the rest of us, it's helpful to understand the chemistry of pastry. For most pastries, a relatively 'soft', low-protein flour (10–11 per cent protein), such as standard plain white wheat flour, is needed. Too much gluten in the mix – as with a bread flour – and the pastry becomes tough and elastic rather than tender and nicely brittle. (This 'strength', however, can be a bonus in pastries that have to hold a high, puffed shape, which is why some choux and puff pastry recipes call for bread flour.) Salt is essential to stop the pastry being bland – just a good pinch is enough for a standard 250g flour batch of pastry.

For most pastries (shortcrust, rough puff and puff) your butter (or other fat) should be cold, and cut into small dice (5–10mm cubes) or grated coarsely, directly into the flour. The old-fashioned way is to combine butter with some lard as well. Butter lends an incomparable flavour, while lard contains almost no water and is very good for giving the pastry a particularly pleasing 'short' texture.

The idea then is to incorporate the fat into the flour – by rubbing the two together in the case of shortcrust – so the cold fat forms a coating over the flour particles. This stops the flour absorbing too much water when you add it later, and therefore inhibits the formation of gluten strands, which would make the pastry tough. (Warm or melted butter coats the flour too much, making it harder for the pastry to bind together at all.) Minimal working is the second crucial factor here, as kneading the pastry also develops gluten. This means a light touch with your hands, or the use of a mixer with a special pastry blade.

You then need to mix in just enough water, milk or egg (or a combination thereof) – again, very cold – to bring the pastry together into big clumps. Err on the side of less water rather than more. A light, brief kneading, just to get the dough to come together in one lump is all that's required.

The pastry should then be patted into a disc, wrapped in cling film and chilled for about 30 minutes. This allows the fat to solidify and the gluten strands to 'relax', giving you lighter, crumblier pastry when cooked. Flattening it into a disc rather than leaving it as a ball will make it easier to roll out once it has firmed up.

Pastry generally needs to go cold into a hot oven – the high temperature 'sets' the gluten network in the pastry before the butter can fully melt. If the oven temperature is too low, the butter melts while the flour/water dough is still soft and you get soggy, heavy pastry.

PRUNEY SAUSAGE ROLLS

FOR THE ROUGH PUFF PASTRY
200g plain flour

A pinch of salt

100g chilled, unsalted butter, cut into roughly 1cm cubes

FOR THE FILLING
400g free-range pork sausages

150g pitted prunes

TO GLAZE
1 egg, beaten with a little milk

These irresistible sausage rolls use a simple rough puff pastry, which is a mainstay in the River Cottage kitchen. Fantastic for all kinds of pies and pasties, it is buttery, flaky and delicious, and very easy to make. For best results, make the pastry a day ahead, so it has plenty of time to chill. You could substitute 400g ready-made, all-butter puff pastry if you are pushed for time. Makes 6 chunky sausage rolls

To make the rough puff pastry, in a large bowl, mix the flour with the salt, then add the cubed butter and toss until the pieces are coated in the flour. Add just enough very cold water (about 150ml) to bring the mixture together into a fairly firm, very rough dough; the chunks of butter should still be visible.

Lift the dough on to a well-floured surface and shape into a rectangle with your hands. Now roll it out in one direction, away from you, to form a long rectangle about 1cm thick. Fold the furthest third over towards you, then fold the nearest third over that (like folding a business letter), so that you now have a rectangle made up of 3 equal layers. Give the pastry a quarter-turn, then repeat the rolling, folding and turning a further 4 times. Wrap the pastry in cling film and leave to rest in the fridge for at least an hour, but up to 24.

Preheat the oven to 190°C/Fan 170°C/Gas 5. Line a baking sheet (one with a lip as the pastry may leak a little butter) with baking parchment or a silicone liner. Split the skins of the sausages, squeeze out the meat into a bowl and mash it together. Divide in half.

Cut the pastry rectangle in half crosswise. On a lightly floured surface, roll out one half into a long rectangle, about 36 x 12cm. Place half the sausagemeat in an even line down the centre of the pastry and press half the prunes into it, pushing them in and moulding the meat around them a little.

Lightly brush one long edge of the pastry with the beaten egg. Take the other side of the pastry and bring it over the top of the meat and prunes, then gently roll the sausage-filled pastry over so you have one very long sausage roll, with the pastry join underneath. With a very sharp knife, slice the roll into 4 equal pieces. Place on the prepared baking sheet. Repeat with the remaining pastry, sausagemeat and prunes.

Brush the surface of the pastry with more beaten egg. Bake for about 35 minutes, until the pastry is a rich golden brown and the sausage is cooked through. Remove to a wire rack and allow to rest for at least 30 minutes before eating, warm or cold.

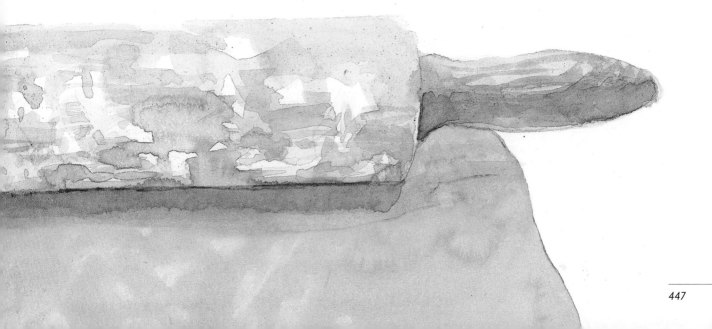

Peach & nectarine

Mark Diacono

LATIN NAME
Prunus persica

SEASONALITY
British and European fruit
July–September

MORE RECIPES
Pears with ricotta, honey and
thyme (page 536); Wineberries
with peaches and custard
(page 317); Strawberries with
lavender and honey (page 341)

My first home-grown peach was a delectable harvest. Even now, I can recall its scent, as bright and full as the summer day I ate it on. It is a tricky moment to recreate with shop-bought fruit. You will need to search out the ripest, most aromatic fruits you can find. Summer peaches from Italy are usually the best. With a relatively short distance to travel, they can be picked later and riper than fruits imported at other times of the year from far-flung America, Africa and even Australia, which are often disappointing. You'll know when you've found that peach or nectarine that has been allowed to ripen on its tree: it will smell like a peach! Buy it and all those like it, and enjoy them while swinging in a hammock.

Otherwise, it is perfectly possible to coax maximum loveliness out of peaches and nectarines by swapping the ripening sun for a little kitchen heat. Grilling, roasting or frying with a touch of sugar and (optionally) cinnamon, star anise and/or vanilla, will intensify the flavour and lend a little caramelised texture to their softened flesh. Just like apricots, peaches and nectarines work beautifully with savoury partners – a pizza topped with nectarine quarters, blue cheese and rocket is delicious.

Poaching is another way to persuade firm peaches and nectarines into soft succulence. Stud each fruit half with a clove, put into a pan and just cover with a mix of wine and water (or use all wine, water or cider). Add a split vanilla pod, a strip of lemon zest and a few sprigs of mint, and poach gently until tender. The fruit is best served just-warm with crème fraîche, or cooled then zapped in a blender with a little of the poaching liquor to be diluted 1:3 with fizz for a summer bellini.

If you're in the South and can find a sunny, sheltered spot in your garden, give peaches or nectarines a go. Dwarf varieties and fan-trained trees suit even the smallest of spaces – a modest harvest will still make you happy. To get them at their best, pick the fruit as near as possible to the point when they would fall of their own accord.

PEACH SLUMP

4 large peaches or nectarines

3–4 tbsp light muscovado sugar, to taste

Seeds scraped from ½ vanilla pod (or 1 tsp vanilla extract)

25g butter, plus extra to grease

FOR THE SLUMP TOPPING

180g plain flour

2 tsp baking powder

4 tbsp caster sugar

A pinch of salt

A pinch of ground cinnamon (optional)

80g cold butter, roughly diced

1 medium egg

100ml whole milk

75g wholemilk yoghurt, or 75ml buttermilk

This American-style pud is even easier than a crumble and a perfect way to use slightly less than ambrosial peaches or nectarines. Add a handful of raspberries or blackberries too, for a fruity contrast. Serves 4–6

Preheat the oven to 200°C/Fan 180°C/Gas 6. Lightly butter an ovenproof dish.

To peel the peaches or nectarines, score a small cross on the base of each one, then lower the fruit into a pan of boiling water. Simmer for up to a minute, until the skins are loosened. Transfer to a bowl of cold water, to cool quickly, then lift out and peel. Halve the fruit, prise out the stones and cut each half into thirds lengthways.

In a bowl, toss together the peaches, muscovado sugar and vanilla. Tip the fruit into the prepared dish and dot with the butter.

In a large bowl, mix together the flour, baking powder, caster sugar, salt and cinnamon if using, with a balloon whisk. Rub the butter into the flour mixture with your fingertips until it has the consistency of coarse breadcrumbs. Whisk together the egg, milk and yoghurt or buttermilk, and stir into the flour, being careful not to over-mix.

Drop spoonfuls of the topping on to the peaches. Try to cover them evenly, but don't worry about a few gaps – the mixture will expand as it cooks. Bake for about 25 minutes, until the top is golden and the juices are bubbling. To check that the slump topping is cooked, insert a cocktail stick into the middle – it should come out clean. Leave to stand for about 5 minutes before serving.

P

Peanuts

Gill Meller

LATIN NAME
Arachis hypogea

ALSO KNOWN AS
Groundnut

MORE RECIPES
Raw carrot salad with peanut and cumin dressing (page 123); Sweet and sour barbecued courgettes (page 201); Banana and peanut butter ice cream (page 46)

Ground, salted, dry-roasted, chocolate-covered, sugared, processed into a butter, pressed for oil – there doesn't seem to be much you can't do with this versatile, protein-packed, nutrient-rich little nut. Or, I should say, bean. Peanuts actually belong to the legume family, being the seeds of a low-growing bush. They're not a nut at all.

The peanut (or groundnut) was domesticated in South America around 2000 BC. It was initially an important animal feed crop but slowly caught on as a culinary ingredient. In the West, peanuts are largely eaten as a snack, often simply salted or dry roasted, though it's worth reminding yourself of the pleasure of buying the nuts still in their puckered shells and releasing them one by one for a messy but satisfying feast. And, of course, they are processed into peanut butter. But in other parts of the world, they have been adopted as a cooking ingredient in their own right. Typically crushed, chopped or ground into sauces and dressings, stews and soups, they form a rich, thick, slightly sweet backdrop to a host of spicy and aromatic flavours.

You will find peanuts in Indonesian, Malaysian and Thai cuisines, ground and combined with garlic, ginger and chilli, fish sauce or shrimp paste. Peanuts are important in West Africa, where they are used in stews and soups, and in their homelands of South and Central America, where they thicken moles and sauces.

Today, more peanuts are cultivated in China than anywhere else in the world. Most of the 15 million tonnes grown there annually are crushed for oil (more often labelled as 'groundnut oil'). Peanuts have a very high fat content, and their oil can be refined into an almost flavourless, general-purpose cooking medium. It has a relatively high monounsaturated fat content and a high smoke point so is useful for high-temperature frying. It contains polyunsaturated fats too. However, with a high proportion of omega-6 and almost no omega-3 fatty acids, it is one of the oils being suggested as a potential source of inflammation in the body (see page 623).

P

Peanut butter is made by roasting, skinning and grinding the nuts with salt and, more often than not, sugar. It is completely dairy-free: the butteriness comes from the peanut oil that solidifies as the puréed peanuts cool. Like any high-fat food, it should not be eaten to excess. But it's a delicious source of protein and energy and very useful in raw and vegan baking, where it binds, thickens and enriches in place of eggs, butter and gluten. Look for sugar-free versions and those that don't contain palm oil.

Peanut flour isn't yet widely available but is becoming more popular. It's very low in fat because the oil is extracted before the nut is refined. Gluten-free and low-carb, it's full of peanut flavour and rich in protein. It's used to enhance dishes rather than as a basic staple: it can be sprinkled on to porridge, added to bread doughs and flapjacks, even spooned into your favourite smoothie before blending. It's also a natural thickener and can be added to soups, stews and sauces.

Aflatoxins

Some people choose to avoid peanuts because they may be a source of aflatoxins. These are naturally occurring toxins produced by a fungus and may be found in a range of foods including nuts, maize, rice, dried foods, spices, crude vegetable oils and cocoa beans. There is a particular risk with foods stored in warm, humid conditions. Aflatoxins are carcinogenic and, at high levels, pretty lethal. Because aflatoxins are so widespread in foods, it's virtually impossible to eliminate them altogether but bodies such as the World Health Organisation recommend that levels should be reduced as far as is practicably possible. EU law sets strict limits on the levels of aflatoxins allowed in certain foods, including peanuts, and manufacturers of products such as peanut butter must test for these toxins too.

NOODLE SALAD WITH SPICY PEANUT BUTTER DRESSING

1 cucumber

1 red pepper, quartered, deseeded and thinly sliced

6 spring onions, cut into 1cm slices

A small bunch of coriander

A small bunch of mint

150g rice noodles

A little rapeseed or toasted sesame oil

FOR THE DRESSING

5 tbsp crunchy peanut butter

2 tbsp tamari (or soy sauce)

Juice of 2 limes

1 tbsp caster sugar

1 medium red chilli, deseeded and finely chopped

1 garlic clove, grated

A finger-sized piece of root ginger, grated

This dressing has all the wonderful flavours you'll find in a classic satay sauce. Aside from this lovely salad, you could use it to trickle over ricey platters or couscous dishes, as well as chicken and pork. Serves 4

To make the dressing, work the peanut butter, tamari and lime juice together, then stir in the rest of the dressing ingredients. If necessary, add a little water to thin it slightly. It wants to be loose enough to spoon over the noodles. Taste and add a little more lime or tamari if required.

Peel the cucumber, halve lengthways and scoop out the seeds, then slice and place in a large bowl with the pepper and spring onions.

Pick the coriander and mint leaves from their stalks and chop them.

Cook the noodles according to the pack instructions. Drain and refresh in cold water to stop them cooking. Drain again and toss with a little oil to prevent them sticking. Use a pair of scissors to cut the noodles into shorter lengths.

Add the noodles, two-thirds of the peanut dressing and the herbs to the vegetables and toss gently to combine. Arrange the salad over one large platter or individual plates. Spoon over the remaining dressing and serve.

Pears

LATIN NAME
Pyrus communis

SEASONALITY
August–November. Cooking
pears: January–February

MORE RECIPES
Bay-spiked pears with shallots
and lemon (page 53); Partridges
roasted with quince and bacon
(page 440); Pears with ricotta,
honey and thyme (page 536);
Upside-down chocolate plum
pudding (page 189); Pear and
bilberry crumble tart (page 69);
Cranberry and pear sauce
(page 213)

SOURCING
brogdalecollections.org (home
to the national fruit collection);
orangepippintrees.co.uk

A good, ripe pear, so ambrosial in the mouth – juicy yet curiously granular, with its complex floral flavours – is a thing of beauty. So, if you catch one at that point of perfect, fragrant ripeness, just sit down and eat it right away, letting its perfumed liquor trickle down your chin. However, I'd be the first to admit that waylaying a pear at that point of exquisite readiness isn't straightforward. Pears can be hard and crunchy one moment, mushily soft and boozily over-ripe the next.

Pears are nearly always picked when under-ripe because they actually taste better if allowed to ripen off the tree. Even if you grow your own, you should pick them when firm and ripen them indoors. The problem is, because under-ripe pears are easier to transport, some commercial crops are picked much too early, when still immature and green, and refrigerated for way too long. They'll never ripen properly and instead go from crisp to pulpy without ever having their magic moment.

Most of the pears sold in the UK are of the long, brown-freckled 'Conference' variety (pictured right, back row). They're relatively easy to grow, store and transport, and growers say they are what we, the buying public, prefer, choosing them nine times out of ten. This is a shame because, while there's nothing wrong with a Conference, it's not the most exciting pear to be had. It's also, sadly, quite likely to be imported.

Many of our pear orchards are old and not particularly productive, requiring the kind of renaissance that cherry orchards have undergone (see page 153) if we are to compete with our European neighbours. But the investment required is substantial and growers won't commit to it unless they're sure we're going to buy their pears. This is why, currently, even in the peak pear months of autumn, supermarket shelves feature so many easy-travelling, high-cropping foreign pears.

So how do you guarantee a perfect pear-eating experience? If you live in the South, start by going to an orchard or farm shop. The smaller the distance pears have had to go to get to the point of sale, the better. Not much pear-growing goes on north of Birmingham so slightly more travelled fruit will be the norm here, but you can still explore different varieties (see below).

Buy pears that are firm, but not rock hard. Don't worry about a little russeting on the skin (more likely with a British pear because it's caused by wind and rain); it won't affect flavour. When you get your pears home, leave them to ripen at cool room

FAVOURITE PEAR VARIETIES

Williams' Bon Chrétien Often just called Williams, this is a juicy, well-flavoured early variety, good in September. (Pictured right, front row.)

Beth A more unusual early variety – small, sweet, juicy and quite delicious.

Onward Related to the delectable Comice, this is plump, silky and buttery. Look for it in late September/early October.

Doyenne du Comice Often just called Comice, this is one of the most luscious of all pear varieties. Seek it out from early October and try to eat at least one raw and perfectly ripe: pear perfection.

Beurre Hardy As the name suggests, this variety is buttery and delicious – with a hint of rose fragrance. Picked in September, it's good for eating in October.

Louise Bonne of Jersey This is a lovely, tender red-flushed pear, full of fragrant flavour, good in October.

Concorde A cross between Comice and Conference, from which it inherits a longish shape, this is a reliably good late-season pear. It is available from early October.

Catillac One of the old-fashioned, late-season cooking pears, this variety can be found in orchards and farmers' markets in January and February.

temperature. There's nowhere better than the proverbial sunny windowsill, as light accelerates ripening. Mount a daily vigil, giving the fruit the merest squeeze morning and evening until you feel a gentle 'give' and detect a slight, peary fragrance. At this point the pear is perfectly ripe and ready to eat.

While a pear at the peak of ripeness is really what you want if you're eating it just as it comes, there's lots you can do with a pear that's a little under- or over-ready. Pears are magnificent cooking fruits and, actually, those that are a few days shy of spot-on tenderness will give the best results – taking the heat and softening gently while absorbing the flavours of whatever you cook them with. Almost-ripe pears are the ones to slice and fry in butter, with a squeeze of lemon and a trickle of honey, or to arrange in a fluted wheel inside a tart case or on a cake. These are the fruits to peel then poach whole in wine or apple juice with citrus zest and spices, or to bake – their cores scooped out and filled with chopped nuts and dried fruit.

Pears in this nearly-there state are also very good served raw in a salad, particularly a savoury one. They always pair well with something salty and something nutty: pears with ham and walnuts; pears with blue cheese and hazelnuts; pears with smoked mackerel and brown toast – just add a slightly lemony, mustardy dressing.

Should you come home one evening to discover your patiently waited-for pears have rushed ahead of you and become a little too soft, don't despair. Purée their melting flesh into a smoothie or use it as the base for a sorbet.

And if, despite all your pear-spicacity, pear perfection has eluded you, you can always console yourself with dried pears. These are increasingly easy to buy and lovely to eat. Chop them and add to cakes, couscous or stuffings (try them instead of fresh pears in the recipe below) – or just chew your way lazily through a handful, savouring every succulent, toffeeish morsel. You can't say pear-er than that.

PEAR AND CELERIAC STUFFING

2–3 tbsp goose fat, or olive or rapeseed oil

1 large onion, chopped

½ small celeriac, peeled

100g blanched almonds or cooked chestnuts

Finely grated zest and juice of 1 lemon

3 slightly under-ripe medium pears

500g sausagemeat

1 goose or turkey liver, or 80g chicken livers, finely chopped

A handful of fresh white breadcrumbs

1 tbsp chopped sage

1 tsp chopped thyme

A pinch of ground mace

Sea salt and black pepper

This is perfect with the Christmas goose or turkey. Ideally, for the sausagemeat, use coarsely ground free-range pork shoulder. Serves 6–8

Heat the goose fat or oil in a large frying pan over a medium-low heat, add the onion and cook gently for about 10 minutes, until soft and translucent. Meanwhile, cut the celeriac into 1cm cubes. Add the celeriac to the pan and cook for another 5 minutes, stirring occasionally. Leave to cool.

In the meantime, finely chop the almonds or crumble the cooked chestnuts; set aside.

Put the lemon juice into a large bowl. Peel, quarter and core the pears, then dice the fruit directly into the bowl, tossing it in the juice to stop it discolouring.

Add the lemon zest, sausagemeat, liver, breadcrumbs, herbs and mace, and mix together thoroughly. Add the nuts and the cooked onion and celeriac, and mix again, to combine. Season with some salt and pepper.

You can stuff this mixture under the neck skin of a chicken, turkey or goose, and also put a little inside the cavity of the bird, but don't pack it full because the stuffing will expand and may not cook through properly. Remember to include the weight of the stuffing when calculating the cooking time of your bird.

The stuffing can also be baked in a shallow, buttered dish at 190°C/Fan 170°C/Gas 5 for 35–45 minutes, depending on thickness, or until cooked through.

Peas

LATIN NAME
Pisum sativum

SEASONALITY
June–August

MORE RECIPES
Garlicky pea ravioli with brown butter (page 444); Scallops with cauliflower purée and green peppercorns (page 572)

I will always champion the superiority of fresh-picked peas over frozen ones, but only if the fresh ones are really fresh. And that basically means just-picked and eaten within a few hours, before their exquisitely leguminous natural sugars begin reverting to starch. Frozen peas, which are briefly blanched then whammed into a deep freeze almost as soon as they're off the plant, are often vastly superior to large, old, mealy 'fresh' peas that may have been sitting around in their pods on a greengrocer's shelf for far too long.

If you buy a packet of frozen peas, there's a good chance they'll be British: we grow a lot of them, our wind-scoured eastern seaboard offering their favourite dry-but-mild conditions. And an extremely handy ingredient they are – offering near-instant, vitaminaceous greenness at any time of the year. Frozen petits pois (which may be either a specific variety, or small specimens of a standard variety) barely even need cooking. You can simply let them defrost and use them. Or tip the frozen peas into a colander, pour boiling water over them and leave for a couple of minutes. This is a great start to a light and sweet pea soup or purée, or if you want to add the peas to a pasta dish, risotto or frittata.

But still, I'd never give up my tangled hazel-stick rows of curling pea vines – not for all the frozen peas in Lincolnshire. Everyone in my family loves eating raw baby peas and popping the first pods – pushing out the tiny green beads and munching them greedily is one of our favourite moments each summer. It's usually a week or two into the harvest before we eat them any other way. But freshly picked raw baby peas are also beautiful tossed into a salad with crumbled fresh ricotta and snippets of ham, or whizzed into a raw soup with spinach, mint, avocado and lemon juice.

Some pick-your-own farms now offer peas among their crops. Otherwise, you can buy peas in the pod during their season – roughly June to August – at farmers' markets, greengrocers and supermarkets. If they look fresh – vibrant, plump and bright green – or, even better, if someone can actually tell you when they were harvested, they are certainly worth buying (1kg pods yields around 400g peas). Simmer for about 5 minutes with a large sprig of mint then serve, dressed with butter, salt and black pepper. Or, for something completely different, try them in a pea and mint ice cream – a green, minty purée folded into a sweet custard and frozen.

The pods can be useful too. Add them to a simmering stock to give a layer of sweet flavour. Or make a pea pod soup – with pods, mint, potato, onion and stock – blending and passing through a sieve to take out the stringy pod fibres: a true thrifty classic.

As with broad beans (see page 94), slightly tired fresh peas or mature specimens from the garden needn't go to waste. Such veg patch veterans have a slightly floury quality, but they can work wonderfully in the right recipe. Once podded, I usually boil them for a good 10 minutes before puréeing them with mint or parsley to make soup, or a fantastic fresh pea version of mushy peas – blitzed up with sautéed onion, mint, garlic, butter and perhaps a little cheese too.

If you have room to grow your own peas – and you don't need much of it for a 6-metre row of 40 plants, or a couple of 8-stick wigwams – it's about as simple and rewarding as veg-growing gets. They will grow in most soils (just dig in some compost first) and can do well not only in conventional veg beds but also wide, fairly deep containers: roomy pots, half-barrels, even old sinks or baths will do. Train them up traditional multi-stemmed hazel sticks, or if you can only get bamboos, wrap the wigwams with pea-netting or chicken wire. Peas need plenty to cling on to.

Mid-season varieties are generally sweeter than the 'earlies'. My favourites are 'Kelvedon Wonder', which is a fast and generous cropper, and 'Saturn', while 'Douce Provence' is a good petits pois variety. Growing your own also gives you access to the young, growing shoots of the pea plant, which can be nipped off and eaten. These tasty tendrils, with their concentrated pea flavour, are fantastic in a salad with some baby peas, a lemony dressing and lots of chives. They're also great wilted in a little butter and served up in an omelette or as a simple side dish. But don't get too enthusiastic about pea shoots or you won't have any actual pea pods come harvest time.

Mangetout – literally 'eat all' – are generally tender, flat young pods, with tiny underdeveloped peas in them. They are almost always eaten whole. Personally I prefer the 'sugarsnap' type. The plumper pod is crisp and tender, like mangetout, but you get a rack of plump peas inside too: surely the best of both worlds? Very freshly picked, both types are great raw. And whether you are eating them raw or planning to cook them, it's worth stripping the fibres from the shorter edge that runs along the inside, as it were, from the frilly-skirted nose to the pointy-tipped tail.

RISI E BISI WITH PEA SHOOT PESTO

This soupy, Venetian risotto is made for home pea-growers: as well as peas it uses both the pods (to form a lovely sweet stock) and baby pea shoots (in a pesto). However, you can make the dish using about 600ml good light vegetable stock instead, and any pesto – or just a final swirl of good oil. You can also use broad beans in this recipe: small fresh ones can be added straight to the risotto, though they may need a little more cooking than peas; older ones should be cooked and skinned first. Serves 2

200g peas in the pod (or 80g podded peas, fresh or frozen)

1 carrot, thinly sliced

4 spring onions, trimmed and sliced (trimmings saved)

1 bay leaf

1 tsp black peppercorns

A few parsley stalks (optional)

10g butter

2 tsp olive or rapeseed oil

1 garlic clove, sliced

100g arborio rice

25g Parmesan, Berkswell or hard goat's cheese, finely grated

FOR THE PESTO

70g pine nuts

About 60g pea shoots

½ small garlic clove, chopped

Juice of ½ small lemon

120–150ml extra virgin olive or rapeseed oil

25g Parmesan, Berkswell or hard goat's cheese, finely grated

Sea salt and black pepper

TO FINISH

50g mild, soft goat's or ewe's cheese

Extra virgin olive or rapeseed oil

Start with the pesto: toast the pine nuts in a dry pan over a medium-low heat until lightly coloured. Transfer to a plate and leave to cool completely.

Put the pea shoots and garlic into a food processor and pulse until finely chopped (or roughly chop, then pound with a pestle and mortar). Add the pine nuts, lemon juice and some salt and pepper. Process briefly then, with the motor running (or stirring, if using a pestle and mortar), slowly pour in the extra virgin oil until the pesto is the texture you like – you may not need all of it. Stir in the cheese (and a trickle more oil if needed), then taste and add a little more salt, pepper and lemon juice as needed.

Pod the peas and set them aside. Roughly chop the pods and put them in a pan with the carrot, spring onion trimmings, bay, peppercorns and parsley stalks, if using. Pour on 750ml water, bring to a simmer and cook for 25–30 minutes. Strain, return to the pan and keep hot over a very low heat.

Heat a medium pan over a medium heat and add the butter and oil. When bubbling, add the spring onions and cook, stirring regularly, for 3–4 minutes. Add the garlic and rice and cook for a further minute.

Now add one-third of the hot pea stock and stir well. Bring back to a simmer and cook, stirring occasionally, until the stock is absorbed. Add another third and repeat, stirring regularly. Add the remaining stock along with the peas, and cook for 3–4 minutes or until the rice and peas are just tender, and the risotto has a loose consistency, almost like a soup. Take off the heat and stir in the grated cheese and some salt and pepper.

Spoon the risotto into warm bowls and top with crumbled cheese and a generous spoonful of pesto. Finish with a few more fresh pea shoots if you have them.

Pecans

Pam Corbin

LATIN NAME
Carya illinoinensis

MORE RECIPES
Brazil nut, cacao and orange granola (page 85)

Tender-sweet, rich and buttery, pecans look like elongated walnuts but taste sweeter and feel softer, with less of a distinct 'snap'. Harvested from a member of the hickory family, native to North America, they thrive best in the steamy cotton- and maize-growing regions of the deep south and the Mississippi Valley.

Pecans are harvested from October until December and, with a high oil content (70 per cent), they can quickly go rancid. To extend their life, the shelled pecans available from health food shops, farm shops and supermarkets throughout the year have been subjected to a dehydration process. Store them in an airtight container in a cool dry place and they should keep well for several months.

As proven by pecan pie – America's sticky national favourite – this nut's exceptionally creamy butteriness and delicate crunch lends itself to baking. Pile pecans into brownies, cookies, fruit cakes, bread and pastries. They make cracking good partners to – and indeed replacements for – most other nuts in these situations. Their superb flavour is heightened further if they are lightly toasted in a moderate oven for 4–5 minutes.

Often favoured as a dessert nut because of their lack of nutty bitterness, pecans are a great source of protein and fibre and work very well in savoury nut roasts and stuffings. Toasted and lightly salted, they make sustaining round-the-clock nibbles and add a wholesome bite to all kinds of salads. Place 200g shelled pecans on a baking sheet, trickle over 20ml rapeseed or olive oil and shake about a bit to coat. Roast at 180°C/Fan 160°C/Gas 4 for 5–6 minutes, remove and sprinkle with 1 tsp sea salt and a few grinds of black pepper. Return to the oven and roast for a further 5 minutes. Thankfully, the pecan is an easy nut to crack…

DOUBLE CHOCOLATE PECAN PRALINE COOKIES

125g butter, softened

175g soft light brown sugar

Seeds scraped from ½ vanilla pod (or 1 tsp vanilla extract)

150g plain flour

25g cocoa powder

1 tsp baking powder

A large pinch of salt

1 medium egg

100g dark, milk or white chocolate, coarsely chopped

FOR THE PECAN PRALINE

100g caster sugar

75g pecans, roughly chopped

TO FINISH

About 20 pecans

Use dark chocolate in these cookies for a grown-up treat; or milk or white chocolate for a sweeter result with after-school appeal. Makes about 20

For the praline, line a baking sheet with baking parchment or a silicone liner. Put the sugar in a heavy-based pan (with a light-coloured base, so you can see the sugar change colour) and place over a medium-low heat. After a couple of minutes, it will start to melt at the edges. Swirl it gently as it starts to liquefy (you can stir it a bit, but no more, or it may crystallise). By the time all the sugar has melted, some of it will be brown. Keep cooking for a minute or so, swirling gently, until all the syrup has turned a rich caramel colour.

At this point, take it off the heat, stir in the chopped pecans and tip the lot on to the prepared baking sheet; take care because the caramel will be extremely hot. Leave to cool and set, then coarsely chop the praline.

Preheat the oven to 190°C/Fan 170°C/Gas 5 and line 2 large baking sheets with baking parchment or silicone liners.

Beat together the butter, sugar and vanilla until fluffy. Combine the flour, cocoa, baking powder and salt. Add 1 tbsp to the butter and sugar mix, together with the egg, and beat until smooth. Add the remaining flour mix and work it in with a wooden spoon, then work in the praline and chocolate.

Place dessertspoonfuls of the mixture on the baking trays, shaping them roughly into rounds (leave plenty of room for spreading). Press a whole nut into the top of each and bake for 10 minutes for cookies with a slightly chewy centre, 12 minutes for a crisper finish.

Leave the cookies on the baking sheets for about 5 minutes to cool slightly, so they firm up a little, then transfer to a wire rack to cool completely.

P

Peel, citrus

All citrus fruit have a thickish, stippled rind, comprising an inner layer of bitter, creamy-white pith and an outer one of vividly tinted, fragrant skin. All of it is useful.

Citrus is available year-round but the Spanish and Mediterranean fruit in our shops from November to March tends to be particularly good. Although citrus peel is naturally waxy, most of it is sprayed with a wax, based on polyethylene or shellac, to extend its shelf-life. To avoid ingesting this, use unwaxed fruit (all organic citrus is unwaxed) or dip waxed fruits in hot water and scrub before using to remove the wax.

The vibrant outer skin, or zest, holds exquisite essential oils. To produce a very fine sprinkle of zest, use a fine, sharp grater; for longer strands, a citrus zester is good. For wider strips to add to stews or poaching liquors, pare with a veg peeler. In all cases, use a light touch – you want to skim off just the fragrant zest, not the bitter pith beneath. To make a lovely cocktail, rub a sugar lump over the whole fruit (to extract the oil alone) then drop this into a flute, pour over 20ml brandy and top up with bubbly.

The pithy layer of citrus contains an abundance of pectin – exactly what you need to get your marmalade to set. It is also full of bitter flavour that can be delicious when combined with sugar or salt. But citrus peel is tough and needs to be softened before eating. In marmalade-making, this is done by long, gentle simmering. An alternative method is to steep peels in a salty brine for a month or so, until soft. This is how Indian lime pickles and Middle Eastern preserved lemons are prepared.

Candying peel extends its uses. Home-candied peel (see below) is far superior to the shop-bought chopped stuff, but look out for large pieces of candied peel, available from delis and wholefood suppliers: it's more succulent and you can snip it to any size.

You can also dry citrus peels in a cool oven. For citrus sugar to flavour cakes, put 1kg caster sugar into a jar, add 2 or 3 dried citrus peels and seal; the peels will permeate the sugar with their flavour. Dried orange peel is good in a meat or game casserole too.

CANDIED ORANGE AND LEMON PEEL

2 lemons, scrubbed

2 medium oranges, scrubbed

1 tsp sea salt

500g granulated sugar

These translucent, succulent sweetened peels are lovely chopped into cakes, or cut into matchsticks and dipped into chocolate. Makes about 500g

With a sharp knife, lightly cut the peel of each fruit, top to bottom, into quarters, then cut it away from the fruit in neat petal-shaped pieces with the pith; you should have about 250g. Place the peel in a bowl, sprinkle with the salt and pour on cold water to cover. Place a small plate on top to keep the peel immersed and leave for 24 hours.

Drain the citrus peels and put them into a medium-large pan. Pour on 2 litres cold water, bring to the boil and simmer for 10 minutes. Drain and return the peels to the pan with 1.5 litres fresh water. Bring to the boil and simmer, covered, for about 1½ hours, until they are tender. Drain, reserving 1 litre water. Put the softened peels into a large bowl.

Return the reserved water to the pan with the sugar. Slowly bring to the boil, stirring until the sugar has dissolved. Pour this syrup over the peels. Cover and leave for 24 hours.

Strain the syrup into a saucepan and put the peels back in the bowl. Bring the syrup to the boil and boil for 1 minute, then pour over the peels. Cover, and leave for a further 24 hours. Repeat this procedure for another 2 days. On the fifth day, put the peels and syrup into the saucepan and bring to simmering point. Simmer, uncovered, turning the peels from time to time, until the syrup has nearly all disappeared. Remove from the heat.

When cool enough to handle, spread the peels out on parchment-lined trays. Leave for up to 3 days in a dry, warm spot to dry completely, then pack in an airtight container.

Pepper

Steven Lamb

LATIN NAME
Piper nigrum.
Szechuan pepper:
Zanthoxylum schinifolium,
Zanthoxylum simulans

MORE RECIPES

One of the first to be traded to Europe, pepper is the original old spice. It has become inseparable from salt as the most essential of seasonings, though it acts quite differently: where salt makes food taste more of itself, pepper gives palate-piquing heat, aroma and contrast. Pretty much any dish can be lifted by some cracked black pepper.

Black and white peppercorns are both the dried berries of a tropical vine, which is indigenous to Brazil, India and Vietnam. Black peppercorns represent the complete fruits or 'drupes' which extend in a cluster formation at the end of a branch. The peppercorn is green when it is harvested – mature but not yet fully ripened. A fully ripened peppercorn is dark red but is less pungent and aromatic than a green berry because piperine, the active ingredient which gives pepper its distinctive, hot attributes, diminishes as the berry ages.

The change in colour from green to black is the result of a short cooking process. The green berries are briefly blanched in hot water and left to dry in the sun, which activates enzymes in the outer layer of the fruit. This outer, fleshy layer darkens, hardens and shrivels to become the tough black coat of the peppercorn. It holds the pepper's essential oils and is the source of the spice's warm, woody, floral character.

Not all black pepper is the same: the generic, cheap varieties can be rather dull and characterless. For a more inspiring pepper experience, try Keralan 'Wynad', which is allowed to ripen a little longer on the vine, giving it a rich, full, complex and deliciously peppery taste. 'Tellicherry', also from Kerala, is similarly excellent. Other unique peppers to try include Cameroonian 'Penja' and Indonesian 'Lampung' – both fiery – and the fruitier Keralan 'Malabar'.

Such peppers work hard as everyday seasonings but they are also the ones to enjoy in dishes where black pepper is more than a seasoning – on steaks, in the simplest oil or butter pasta sauces or with fruit such as strawberries or peaches. As with all black peppers, they should be ground freshly before use because the aromatic flavours released fade quickly. Ready-ground black pepper is flavourless and dusty; a good quality pepper grinder is a sound investment.

A white peppercorn is a black one that has had the outer fruit layer removed; it is, in essence, the seed of the peppercorn berry. Where black peppercorns carry the full range of this spice's flavour, a white peppercorn is far less aromatic and interesting – almost musty-tasting – while still being pungent. But white pepper has its place: it's often used by chefs for seasoning white sauces and pale soups and veloutés, where visible specks of black pepper are not wanted. But I also think the relationship between hot white pepper and pork is unique and magical. White pepper can make the difference between a bland sausage and a great one.

To form green peppercorns, the same mature berries that would be turned into black peppercorns are instead preserved: either suspended in a brine or freeze-dried. Their flavour is more herbaceous than black and white pepper and still deliciously hot. Red and orange peppers are derived from the ripest drupes, which are preserved in the same way as the green ones, often with a hint of acidity or vinegar.

Pink peppercorns, which are specific to Brazil, are not really pepper at all. This is a different species, in fact more affiliated to the nut family but referred to as a peppercorn because of the fruit's visual similarity and spicy kick – which is significant though less than a true pepper's. Pink peppercorns are good with meat and fish, and can be used to add a fruity, spicy kick to fruit puddings too. They have been known to cause allergic reactions in people with nut allergies.

P

Pepper is indigenous to India and, in some parts of that country, a form of wild pepper still grows. Commercial deforestation is encroaching on its territory, making it increasingly rare, and its quality is said to be matched by the more accessible cultivated varieties. But I still imagine wild pepper to be the holy grail of pepper and hope one day to try it.

However, in the here and now, my favourite pepper by far is Szechuan. This dried berry (unrelated to black and white pepper) has a zesty, fragrant but gentle heat, which makes the tongue and lips tingle, heightening the eating experience. It's a key ingredient in the province from which it takes its name and is also used in other parts of China. It is ground with salt as a dry dip, sprinkled on chilli-hot dishes, or added to roasted meat and fried vegetables. Traditionally, it is also part of Chinese five-spice powder, though many modern supermarket blends don't include it. As with the *Piper nigrum* peppers, it should be ground just before you want to use it.

Previously grown only in its Asian homelands, Szechuan pepper is now cultivated at Otter Farm in Devon, one of the first successes of the 'climate change gardening', pioneered by our own Mark Diacono. It's exceptional too: red, vibrant and terrifically tingly; try growing your own if you possibly can.

SZECHUAN-SPICED VENISON STEAK

3 tsp Szechuan peppercorns

1 tsp flaky sea salt

2 tsp chopped thyme

2 venison haunch steaks (each 150g and about 2cm thick)

1 tbsp olive or rapeseed oil

The unique, hot, citrusy notes of Szechuan pepper are wonderful with rich venison steak. (Try adding the spice to the cooking liquor when braising venison shoulder too.) Beef steak works equally well in this recipe. Serves 2

Using a pestle and mortar, roughly crush the Szechuan pepper, flaky salt and thyme.

Season the steaks all over with the Szechuan pepper mix, patting it on to the surface. Leave to stand at cool room temperature for 30–60 minutes; this allows the pepper flavour to permeate the meat.

Set a large heavy-based non-stick frying pan over a high heat. Add the oil to the pan and when hot, add the steaks. Fry, without moving, for 1 minute then flip them over, cook for another minute or so and flip again. Repeat this process: giving the steaks a total of 2 minutes on each side if you like them rare, 3 minutes each side for medium and a fraction more if you like your venison well done.

Leave the steaks to rest in a warm place for 4–5 minutes before serving them, trickled with any pan juices or resting juices. Mashed potato, or a celeriac and potato mash, is an ideal accompaniment.

Peppers

Mark Diacono

LATIN NAME
Capsicum annuum

ALSO KNOWN AS
Bell pepper, sweet pepper, capsicum

SEASONALITY
British and European peppers available spring–autumn; peak British season June–August

MORE RECIPES
Red pepper agrodolce (page 662); Ewe's cheese with chickpeas, roasted chillies and olives (page 151); Noodle salad with spicy peanut butter dressing (page 451); Red mullet with roasted red pepper mayo (page 393); Paella (page 163); Goat kebabs with rosemary, red peppers and onion (page 280)

Peppers are ever-present on supermarket shelves, though from the height of summer into autumn there's often more variety and flavour to be had. All peppers start life that old-school semi-matt green, and colour to yellow, orange or red, depending on the variety. In other words, any green pepper that you buy is a slightly under-ripe fruit, hence the rather different flavour from their more brightly coloured brethren: more bitter, less sweet. Purple varieties are generally an under-ripe form too.

Green peppers have a place, particularly in dishes where plenty of salt and spice will balance their flavour, but I tend to go for red peppers most of the time. They are more nutritious than green ones for a start, having higher levels of vitamin C and lycopene, but they also have a more robust, complex, fruity flavour. There's not much difference, in my view, between the red and the orange or yellow varieties. I think red may have the edge on flavour, but I'm not sure I could tell the difference in a blind taste test.

A good pepper has some potential raw: sliced as thinly as you can manage, they'll add a hint of bittersweet crunch and that familiar fruity aroma to a slaw. And there's enough character in a pepper to stand up to garlic, anchovies, capers, lemon and olives in a well-dressed salad. However, to my mind, these natives of Mexico really hanker for heat: they are best cooked.

Roasting at a high temperature blackens and blisters their thin skin, which, once cooled, can be peeled away, leaving a rich, intense tongue of smoky flesh. You can even shortcut the roasting, by holding a fork-impaled pepper over a gas flame or wood fire to blister the skin, or by laying them halved and flat under a hot grill. This will impart extra smokiness and make the skin easy to slip off, but the overall texture will be firmer. Place the just-blistered peppers in a bowl with cling film over the top for 10–15 minutes and the skin will slip off easily.

That sweet, roasted flesh is now ready for tearing into strips for pasta sauces, pizza toppings or pairing with cheese – especially mild cheeses such as ricotta – but it also goes beautifully with the tang of a mild soft ewe's cheese or feta. The intense flavour works really well as a dip too (see the recipe overleaf). And peppers' bitter-sweetness pairs beautifully with beetroot in a salad, or with anchovies.

Roasted peppers also make a delicious soup. Roast 600g peppers, 400g beetroot and an onion, all sliced into 1.5cm pieces, with thyme and a good scattering of cumin, until softened, then transfer to a pan and briefly simmer in enough veg or light chicken stock to just cover. Taste and add a little lemon juice if you like, and season with salt and pepper. Serve drizzled with olive oil and topped with a little crumbled goat's or ewe's cheese and chopped parsley.

If the oven is busy with low-temperature tasks, or you want a cleaner, less smoky result than blistering gives, slice a destalked and deseeded pepper into 1cm strips and soften them in a pan over a medium-low heat with olive oil, a little garlic and a pinch of salt. After 15–20 minutes – sometimes longer, depending on the fruit – the strips will be tender and sweet, their flavour intensified. These, again, are superb in pasta sauces and pizza toppings.

Peppers love a little spiciness in their presence. The earthiness of cumin is a favourite, but nothing quite lights up a pepper like its chilli cousin, even in dried form. Paprika is especially good with peppers. For a gorgeous and simple stew, gently fry chopped chorizo until its red fat starts to seep, add a couple of finely sliced onions and sweat gently with the lid on for 10 minutes or so. Add a finely chopped medium-hot chilli (or ½ chipotle chilli if you would like smokiness with the heat), 3 finely sliced peppers, a couple of chopped garlic cloves, a good slosh of white wine and 1 tsp sweet smoked paprika to add to that in the chorizo. Cook over a low heat, lid on, for half an hour or so and serve, sprinkled with parsley and a dash of good oil as a tapas on toast or with good bread, or as a side with roast lamb or baked fish.

It's hard to judge the flavour of a pepper from its appearance but do choose firm fruit, with no cracks or wrinkles in the flesh, especially if you plan to use them raw. Feel a few in your hand: the heaviest are likely to have good, thick fleshy walls. The cold masks their flavour, so keep peppers out of the fridge, at least on the day of use.

If you fancy raising a few peppers for yourself, remember that they originate in a hot, steamy place and give them as much heat and light as you can – indoor growing is essential, I think. Sow pepper seeds in modules no later than March, to allow them the long ripening seasoning they need, then leave to germinate in a warm place such as an airing cupboard or sunny windowsill, checking them often and keeping the soil just damp. Once they are sprouting, transfer to a greenhouse, polytunnel or conservatory and wait until you can see roots at the base of the modules. At this stage transfer the plants to larger pots. Keep them in their warm spot – ideally around 20°C – and feed every couple of weeks with a tomato feed or a home-made comfrey 'tea'. Keep the soil damp but not wet, pinch out some of the growing tips to get bushier growth and support the plants with stakes if need be. God willing, you should have harvestable peppers by late summer or early autumn.

MUHAMMARA

4 red peppers

2 medium-hot red chillies

About 50g fresh breadcrumbs

120g walnuts, toasted and roughly chopped

A splash of olive oil

1 medium onion, diced

½ tsp dried chilli flakes

2 tbsp pomegranate molasses

Juice of 1 lime

½ tsp ground cumin

About 125ml extra virgin olive oil

Sea salt and black pepper

This rich, red, nutty dip, originating in Syria, makes the most of the wonderful affinity between peppers and their spicier chilli relations. Serves 6

Preheat the oven to 220°C/Fan 200°C/Gas 7. Place the peppers and chillies in a greased baking dish and roast for about 30 minutes, turning once, or until soft, wrinkled and blackened in places (as pictured on page 462). Put into a bowl, cover with cling film and leave for 10 minutes (this helps loosen the skins). When cool enough to handle, peel, core and deseed the peppers and chillies.

Meanwhile, put the breadcrumbs into a food processor with the walnuts and pulse until quite fine.

In a small pan, heat a splash of olive oil over a medium heat. Add the onion and sauté for a few minutes until lightly golden. Add the onion to the breadcrumb and walnut mixture with the pepper and chilli flesh, the chilli flakes, pomegranate molasses, lime juice, cumin and some salt and pepper. Pulse to a thick paste. Now, with the motor running, gradually incorporate the extra virgin oil until you have a thick dip consistency.

Taste and add more lime juice, pomegranate molasses, cumin and salt and pepper, if you like. Serve with crudités or toasted pitta wedges for dipping.

Perch

Nick Fisher

LATIN NAME
Perca fluviatilis

SEASONALITY
Avoid April–July when spawning.
England and Wales: closed
season on rivers generally
15 March–15 June

HABITAT
Rivers, lakes and ponds across
the British Isles

MCS RATING
Not rated

REC MINIMUM SIZE
25cm

MORE RECIPES
Potted carp (page 118);
Foil-baked trout with baby
beetroot and spring onions
(page 647)

The perch is an ancient and much-loved British freshwater delicacy, with a firm, flaky, body-builder's muscle tone and an almost mackerel-esque tinge to its flesh. A lightly butter-fried perch fillet lies somewhere in the taste and texture spectrum between brown trout and sea bass – and is a match for either of them.

Perch are predators and there aren't many fish that will better them – pike being the main exception. Roaming our rivers, lakes and reservoirs, the perch can largely take its pick from a protein-rich buffet of other freshwater fish and this results in its meaty, muscular and extremely tasty flesh. The Victorians loved it and rated perch a delicacy. In fact, it was widely enjoyed in Britain right up until the Second World War, at which point its ubiquity, thanks to it being a readily available home-grown harvest, started to work against it.

Basically, perch became passé. It lost out to cod and salmon in the popularity stakes. Which is ironic because, while stocks of those chart-topping fish are a cause for concern, perch numbers are more than healthy.

A 350g perch is the ideal size for one person. You can bake or barbecue them whole, or take their fillets and treat them as you would trout. The most difficult thing about perch is buying them. Some crop up at Billingsgate market and specialist online fish dealers. If possible, try and buy one fresh and whole: with its Teddy Boy stripes and gaudy red fins, it's an exciting fish to hold and behold.

FRIED FILLETS OF PERCH WITH SORREL AND POTATOES

The fresh, lemony flavour of sorrel is fantastic with fish – and freshwater fish in particular. This recipe also works very well with trout. Sorrel can be harvested well into the autumn, making it a great partner for later-season waxy potatoes too. Serves 2

400g waxy or salad potatoes, such as Pink Fir Apple or Belle de Fontenay

40g butter

2 tbsp olive or rapeseed oil

Fillets from 2 medium perch, scaled and pin-boned

2 bay leaves

1 garlic clove (unpeeled), bashed

1 bunch of sorrel (about 50g), de-stalked and roughly shredded

½ lemon

Sea salt and black pepper

Scrub the potatoes and cut into similar-sized large pieces. Place in a large pan, cover with water, add a large pinch of salt and bring to a simmer. Cook for 15 minutes or until tender; the tip of a knife should pass through easily. Drain and allow to steam in a colander for a few minutes to get rid of excess moisture, then place the potatoes back in the pan with half the butter and 1 tbsp oil.

Heat a large non-stick frying pan over a medium-high heat. Season the fish all over. Add the remaining oil and butter to the pan along with the bay leaves and garlic. Once the butter starts to sizzle, put the fish skin side down in the pan. Cook for 4–5 minutes, by which time the fish should have cooked at least three-quarters of the way through.

Flip the fish, squeeze over a little lemon juice and cook for a further minute. Remove the pan from the heat.

Return the potato pan to the heat for a minute or so to heat through, then take off the heat and add the shredded sorrel and some salt and pepper. Turn the sorrel briefly though the hot potatoes, until just wilted.

Spoon the sorrel and potatoes on to warmed plates and top with the perch fillets and any fishy pan juices.

Pheasant

Tim Maddams

LATIN NAME
Phasianus colchicus

SEASONALITY
England, Wales and Scotland:
1 October–1 February.
Northern Ireland and Isle of
Man: 1 October–31 January

HABITAT
Very common in rural areas

MORE RECIPES
Pheasant with olives and
preserved lemons (page 414);
Poached pheasant with star
anise (page 610); Pigeon breasts
with sloe gin gravy (page 584)

SOURCING
tasteofgame.org.uk

This non-native bird is believed to have first arrived on our shores with Greek and Turkish traders, long before the Romans landed, though no one knows exactly when. The male, or cock (pictured right), has a vividly conspicuous appearance, with vibrant burgundy and green, silver, black or purple feathers and a white pastoral collar. By contrast, the hen couldn't be more nondescript, bearing shabby, greyish-brown or deep green-black plumage that blends in remarkably well to even the sparsest cover.

Pheasants are classed as game, but they are often far from being truly wild. The vast majority of pheasants you chance upon in country lanes have been reared by gamekeepers or on game farms, then released into the woods as young 'poults' so that they can be shot later in the year.

Pheasant shooting is big business, with around 40 million birds reared and released each year to provide sport for 'guns', who pay for each day's shooting. It's the shooting itself that makes the money. The pheasant meat is more or less a by-product of this industry. Finding a market for all those dead birds can prove challenging: they are all shot at the same time of year, creating a glut, and at the height of the season birds can be got for as little as £1 a brace (pair), if not for the asking. Not very long ago, on very large shoots, birds were sometimes simply buried and left to rot due to a lack of demand for the meat. Thankfully, due to a better export market, this inexcusable waste seems to be a thing of the past.

However, reared-and-released pheasant shooting remains an area fraught with complex issues. For instance, gamekeepers treat their young birds with drugs to destroy parasites, and manage the environment around them, which includes killing predators such as foxes. On the plus side, however, shooting boosts the rural economy, and is a bonus for conservation. A lot of Britain's semi-wild habitat exists to facilitate the release and shooting of game birds: large areas of woodland, moorland and wetlands could disappear without it. And while reared and released pheasant may not experience lives as free and rich as those of truly wild game species like rabbit or pigeon, they are certainly a great deal better off than most farmed animals.

Pheasant has a reputation for being very gamey. This may have been fair 100 years ago, before reliable refrigeration, but it is no longer so. The meat at its best is sweet, juicy and similar to that of a free-range guinea fowl or chicken. But the birds must be correctly hung. Pheasant are hung with the guts in, which encourages the process of decay to start. To counteract this, they should be hung below 8°C: the meat will become more tender, but 'high', gamey flavours won't set in for about a week. Personally, I like my pheasant super-fresh, and I often eat them within 48 hours of shooting.

Roast pheasant can be fantastic early in the season when the birds are mostly very young and tender. As they age, they get tougher. As a rule, I don't roast hen birds later than Christmas, or cock birds, which toughen up more quickly, much past the end of November. With older birds, I often simply split the skin, peel it back feathers and all and remove the leg and breast meat with a knife, without plucking or gutting. This meat can be used for all sorts of dishes, from burgers and curries to game pies.

If you have a plump, young pheasant ripe for roasting, let it come to room temperature before cooking, then brush it with plenty of pork fat, butter, oil, goose or duck fat and season thoroughly. Heat a large ovenproof frying pan and place the bird in it, on its back. Cook for at least 4 minutes until the back is deep golden brown, then flip the bird on to its side and repeat the process for 3–4 minutes, and again on the other side. Now turn the bird right over and cook on the breast for just a minute or

P

two, then return it to its back. Apart from colouring and flavouring the bird, this browning phase gets the cooking process off to a good start – so don't cut corners. Add a few garlic cloves, a bay leaf or two and a sprig of thyme or rosemary to the pan, along with a little more fat if it's looking dry. Roast in the oven at 200°C/Fan 180°C/Gas 6 for about 15 minutes. More time will be required for larger cock birds and maybe a little less for smaller hens. Let the bird rest, uncovered, in a warm place for at least 10 minutes before carving (this is crucial, as it completes the cooking). The meat should be just cooked and still moist, but definitely not rare – the juices should be clear.

It's easy to get hold of oven-ready pheasant from butchers during the season, but you will probably get a better price for prepared birds from a game dealer. By far the best value pheasant will be ones bought directly from a shoot – though you will need to do the hanging, plucking and evisceration yourself. Check the birds: those that are badly shot-damaged or show excessive bruising or discoloration should be cause for concern – or at least a reason for haggling.

PHEASANT PIE

A little rapeseed or olive oil, or lard

100g bacon lardons (smoked or unsmoked)

2 onions, sliced

4 garlic cloves, sliced

2 carrots, sliced into 1cm rounds

2 oven-ready pheasants, jointed

4 tbsp plain flour

1 free-range pig's trotter, split lengthways (optional)

A small bunch of thyme

1 litre chicken or pork stock, or water

A glass of white wine

4 bay leaves

200g floury potatoes (2 medium ones), such as King Edward

750g all-butter ready-made puff pastry, or a double quantity of home-made rough puff pastry (see page 447)

Egg yolk, beaten, to glaze

Sea salt and black pepper

Bacon and a pig's trotter help to keep pheasant moist and succulent in this pie (the trotter is optional but gives magnificent body and flavour). It is also excellent made with rabbit – substitute one large, jointed rabbit for the pheasant. Serves 4

Heat a large flameproof casserole over a medium heat. Add a little oil or lard, then the bacon. Fry for a few minutes to render a little fat, then add the onions, garlic and carrots. Cook, stirring regularly, for about 10 minutes, until the onions are soft and the bacon is browning nicely, then remove everything with a slotted spoon to a plate and set aside.

Add a dash more oil to the casserole. Season the pheasant pieces and dust well with the flour, shaking off any excess. Brown the pheasant well all over in the bacon fat (do this in batches if necessary).

Return the vegetables and bacon to the casserole with the pheasant. Add the pig's trotter, if using, the thyme, stock, wine, bay and some seasoning. Bring to a low simmer and put a lid on, leaving it just ajar. Cook very gently for 1½–2 hours or until the pheasant legs are tender and giving. In the meantime, peel the potatoes and cut into roughly 4cm chunks.

Add the potatoes to the casserole and cook for another 15–20 minutes then take off the heat. When cool enough to handle, lift the pieces of pheasant out of the casserole and pick the meat from the bones, trying to keep it in fairly generous chunks. You can also pull the flesh and skin from the trotter, discarding the bones. Add the pheasant and trotter meat back to the casserole and fold together. Taste and adjust the seasoning as required. Allow to cool completely.

Preheat the oven to 190°C/Fan 170°C/Gas 5. Cut the pastry into two pieces, about two-thirds and one-third. Roll out the larger piece and use to line a lightly greased pie dish (about 1.2 litre capacity). Roll out the smaller piece of pastry to form a lid. Spoon the meat into the pastry-lined dish: it should be at least level with, and preferably a little higher than, the top of the dish. Ladle in enough juices to come 2cm short of the top of the dish (any leftover can be served with the pie).

Brush the edges of the pastry base with egg yolk, position the lid and crimp the edges together to seal. Brush the top of the pie with more egg, and cut a couple of vent holes for steam to escape at either end of the pie. Bake for 50–60 minutes, until golden brown and piping hot throughout. Leave the pie to stand and settle for around 15 minutes, then serve with mash, greens and English mustard.

Pigeon

Tim Maddams

LATIN NAME
Columba palumbus

ALSO KNOWN AS
Wood pigeon

SEASONALITY
All year round

HABITAT
Common, in woods and
farmland particularly

MORE RECIPES
Blewit, pigeon and endive
salad (page 74); Pigeon breasts
with sloe gin gravy (page 584);
Snipe with swede and bacon
(page 587)

SOURCING
tasteofgame.org.uk

Pigeon is the perfect bird in many ways – as long as you get hold of the right sort, by which I mean the common wood pigeon. This bird of woodland and farmland thrives in much of Europe – particularly where arable farming dominates over livestock. The feral pigeons that plague our towns are a different species (*Columba liva*).

Wood pigeon is one of the most ethical meats. These birds are plentiful – and the greatest agricultural pests in the land. Left unchecked, they can do immense damage to valuable crops. If the crops are to be protected, the pigeons have to be controlled. Shooters are employed by farmers and, once a pigeon has been shot, it would be madness not to eat it – not only on a point of ethical principle but because they offer some of the tastiest wild meat available (all year round too).

With the texture of rump steak and a taste like venison crossed with duck, a simple fried pigeon breast, medium-rare, is a carnivorous treat. It needs only the most basic of garnishes, such as a slice of bread and a smear of butter. But you can go further and transform it into a rare delicacy – the breast is wonderful smoked, or given the spicy treatment in a fajita or curry. My favourite way to cook pigeon breasts is to mince them with a quarter of their weight in fatty bacon and make them into burgers to be fried and served in buns with melted cheese and home-made chips.

The breast is the part most eaten – sliced off, cooked briefly and served pink (over-cooking makes them tough), but it's not the only option. Small, young birds can be roasted quickly, to keep them tender. Older, larger birds are tougher but far richer in flavour, and can be quite delicious cooked whole, long and slow, in stews or tagines.

You won't struggle to get hold of pigeon breasts from a butcher or game dealer. But if you're after whole dressed pigeons, take care that you don't get sold Continental, cage-reared birds called squabs. Ask for wild British wood pigeons and all will be well.

PIGEON BREASTS WITH LEEKS AND MASH

3–4 medium leeks, washed,
trimmed and cut into 1cm slices

1 tbsp olive or rapeseed oil

8 pigeon breasts

1 garlic clove, peeled and bashed

2 bay leaves

A knob of butter

About 2 tsp roughly chopped
thyme leaves

Sea salt and black pepper

FOR THE MASH

1kg floury potatoes, such as
Maris Piper or King Edward

75g unsalted butter

200ml whole milk

This is a lovely way to serve pigeon breasts. Partridge breasts can also be cooked like this, but you'll need to allow 3 minutes each side. Serves 4

For the mash, peel the potatoes and cut into similar-sized pieces. Place in a large pan, cover with water and add salt. Bring to the boil and simmer for about 20 minutes until completely tender. Drain the potatoes and let them steam in a colander for 5 minutes.

Put the butter and milk into the potato pan and heat gently until the butter is melted and the milk is hot but not boiling. Take off the heat. Either add the hot potatoes to the pan and mash with a potato masher until smooth and lump-free, or rice the potatoes back into the pan of hot milk and stir with a wooden spoon until smooth. Season and keep warm.

Bring a medium pan of salted water to the boil. Add the leeks and cook, covered, for 4–5 minutes until just tender. Drain, then return to the pan to keep warm.

Set a large frying pan over a medium-high heat and add the oil. Season the pigeon breasts and, when the pan is hot, add them to the pan along with the garlic and bay leaf. Sear for 1 minute each side to keep them pink inside, or 2 minutes each side for medium. (Do this in 2 batches if your pan isn't big enough.) Transfer to a warmed dish to rest for 5 minutes.

Return the pan to a low heat and add the butter and thyme. Once the butter is melted, add the leeks. Turn them in the buttery juices for a minute and then take off the heat. Spoon the mash on to warm plates and top with the leeks. Cut each pigeon breast into 4 or 5 slices and arrange on the plates. Spoon on any resting juices from the pigeon and serve.

Pike

LATIN NAME
Esox lucius

SEASONALITY
Most pike anglers target
the fish October–March.
England and Wales: closed
season on rivers generally
15 March–15 June

HABITAT
Most kinds of freshwater
habitat: rivers, lakes, ponds,
reservoirs, gravel pits

MCS RATING
Not rated

MORE RECIPES
Zander with coriander and chilli
dressing (page 685)

SOURCING
thefishsociety.co.uk

'Confident' is one word used to describe this mighty freshwater fish. 'Voracious', 'savage' and 'ruthless' get wheeled out too, but 'confident' will do for me. These green- and gold-dappled predators glide through our rivers and larger lakes, or hold themselves motionless in weed banks and root systems, their croccy, snaggle-toothed mouths ready to hinge open and obliterate whatever comes their way. Woe betide any smaller fish (including smaller pike) that swim on to their radar – not to mention unwary ducklings, frogs and small mammals. The pike's not averse to a bit of scavenging either.

This varied, meaty diet bestows the pike with well-flavoured flesh. They are among the best freshwater fish for eating – and, like carp, we used to eat them with relish. Plenty of people in Europe still do. But the fish has fallen out of favour here, partly because it has a reputation for tasting 'muddy'. My own angling experiences, however, suggest that this has as much to do with where the fish comes from, as it does with the species itself. Fish from clear, flowing water will taste 'cleaner' than those taken from gravel pits and stocked ponds. But pikes from our larger reservoirs, lakes and lochs are also often fine eating.

A modicum of care is required when tackling pike on the plate because they sport a row of fork-shaped bones. But once you know where they are – one between each flake of meat running down the creature's back – they are easily negotiated. Alternatively, you can deal with the bones by puréeing the flesh in a food processor and passing it through a sieve, which explains the popularity of classic pike mousses and quenelles. I've also had great success serving flaked and deboned pike flesh in little jellied terrines.

You're unlikely to find pike for sale on the fishmonger's slab, though it's not unheard of, and some online fishmongers sell them. Another approach, if you're not up for grabbing your waders and fishing for pike yourself, is to talk to trout farmers, river-keepers and local fishermen. For a curious piscivore it's a step well worth taking.

PIKE WITH LEEKS AND CHERVIL SAUCE

Full-flavoured pike is lovely with this creamy, herby sauce, and you can use chives instead of chervil. If you are lucky enough to have a whole pike, stuff some sliced leek into the cavity, smear the skin with butter, season and roast whole. Scoop out the leek into the roasting tray, then lift the pike on to a platter. Add about 350ml fish stock to the tray (for a 2kg pike) and make the sauce as below, increasing the quantities of cream, herbs and lemon juice. Serves 2

2 pike fillets (140–160g each)

20g butter, softened

2 small or 1 medium leek, (white and pale green parts only), trimmed and cut into 1cm slices

200ml fish stock

75ml double cream

A squeeze of lemon juice

2 tbsp chopped chervil (or chives)

Sea salt and black pepper

Preheat the oven to 200°C/Fan 180°C/Gas 6.

Season the pike fillets well with salt and pepper. Place an ovenproof frying pan over a medium heat and add half the butter then, once it starts to sizzle, add the leeks and sauté for 1 minute. Place the pike fillets, skin side up, on top of the leeks and spread the remaining butter over the fish. Transfer to the oven for 6–7 minutes, or until the fish is cooked through.

Transfer the pike to a warm plate, leaving the leeks in the frying pan; keep the fish warm. Return the pan to a medium heat, add the stock and bring to a simmer. Let bubble for 3–4 minutes until the liquor is reduced by half. Pass the stock through a sieve into a clean saucepan, saving the leeks.

Return the stock to the heat, add the cream and a small squeeze of lemon juice and simmer for 2–3 minutes until thick and creamy. Add the chervil and season with salt and pepper if needed. Pour into a warmed jug.

Serve the pike straight away with the leeks and sauce, some buttery mash and greens.

Pine nuts

Nikki Duffy

LATIN NAME
European stone pine:
Pinus pinea. Korean pine:
Pinus koraiensis

ALSO KNOWN AS
Pine kernel, piñon

MORE RECIPES
Risi e bisi with pea shoot
pesto (page 457)

SOURCING
healthysupplies.co.uk;
seedsofitaly.com

Dinky, blonde, oil- and protein-rich, pine nuts are not technically nuts at all but seeds. All pine trees produce them but only a few species yield a type that is large and tasty enough to be used. These grow in Europe, Asia and North America.

Because they take a long time to mature (1½–3 years) and are difficult to harvest, pine nuts are expensive. The pine cones are picked when still tight shut then encased in sacks and dried until they open up. The open cones are smashed, and the diminutive seeds then have to be picked out by hand from the cone debris. The seeds are still encased in a tough shell at this stage, which must also be removed.

The most famous use of pine nuts is for pesto, but they work well in vegetable patties or burgers too, and are delicious tossed into pasta dishes. You can put pine nuts in a salad but I think they are best incorporated into a clingy dressing or they tend to fall to the bottom of the bowl. They also work well in sweet dishes such as pine nut tarts, with the nuts mixed into a light, eggy filling or a rich, creamy caramel or just a moist frangipane-type sponge. You can fold pine nuts into hand-made truffles or cookies.

The finest pine nuts are the long, slender, tender fruit of the European stone pine. You can buy these delicious (usually Italian) nuts from health food suppliers or online.

However, the vast majority of those we buy in the UK are grown in China and come from the Korean pine. These nuts are short and stubby, and can be rather bland and oily. They're usually ok but unscrupulous producers have been known to mix cheap nuts from yet another species of pine – not usually considered edible – in with the crop. This has led to cases of an unpleasant 'pine nut mouth' syndrome, a form of taste disturbance that comes on hours or days after eating them. It makes everything you eat taste metallic and bitter, and can last for weeks – until the tastebuds renew.

Many people with tree nut allergy can tolerate pine nuts. However, some nut allergy sufferers do also react to pine nuts (whether to the nuts themselves or to contamination from other nuts during handling and packaging).

SARDINES WITH PINE NUTS, FENNEL AND ORANGE

50g pine nuts

2 tbsp olive oil, plus extra for oiling

1 echalion/banana shallot or small onion, chopped

2 garlic cloves, chopped

1 tsp fennel seeds

40g raisins

Finely grated zest of 1 orange, plus some of its juice

8 sardines, gutted and scaled

4 bay leaves

Sea salt and black pepper

Extra virgin olive oil, to finish

Little pine kernels make a lovely textural contrast to the rich flesh of sardines, while orange and fennel add aromatic contrast. Serves 4

Preheat the oven to 220°C/Fan 200°C/Gas 7.

Heat a dry frying pan over a medium heat, add the pine nuts and toast gently, tossing them frequently, for about 5 minutes until golden. Tip on to a plate. Return the pan to the heat and add the olive oil, followed by the shallot or onion, and fry gently for 7–10 minutes until soft.

Add the garlic and fennel seeds and cook for a minute or two longer. Stir in the toasted pine nuts, raisins, orange zest, a dash of orange juice and some salt and pepper. Stir well, then take off the heat.

Rub the sardines with a little olive oil, then season well with salt and pepper over the skin and inside the cavities. Put a bay leaf into the cavity of each fish, then stuff the pine nut mixture inside too. Lay the fish in a baking dish. Bake in the oven for about 15 minutes until cooked through and bubbling.

Transfer the fish to warm plates. Add another squeeze of orange juice and a trickle of extra virgin oil to the roasting dish and scrape up any of the filling that has escaped. Spoon this over the fish, give it a final sprinkling of pepper and serve. Small, rice-shaped pasta such as risoni are good with this, and a green salad.

Pineapple

LATIN NAME
Ananas comosus

SEASONALITY
Imported all year round

The finest fruits, to my mind, manifest a magical combination of sweetness, aroma and acidity; few have that alchemy more beguilingly arranged than this tufty-topped tropical treat. I can't say that I put a pineapple in my shopping basket every week, but when I do, I rarely regret it. And when I travel in parts of the world the pineapple calls home, I make it an almost daily treat.

This is a fruit that's had a colourful cultural journey since we first started shipping it to our shores (it was imported tinned long before fresh specimens became familiar from the 1950s onwards). We used to spike cubes of it with a cocktail stick, along with a chunk of Cheddar or Edam, and then skewer a dozen into an upturned grapefruit half. The visual recollection seems undignified, but I have to admit I liked this 1970s party piece. I'm less forgiving of the modern atrocity that is pineapple on a pizza. Or perhaps it has yet to acquire the status of historical ironic kitsch.

In truth this is a great fruit to serve with savoury ingredients. Ham and pineapple really does work – a doorstep of home-cooked, mustard-encrusted gammon with a dripping slab of fresh pineapple is a genuine thrill. I also like pineapple diced up and dosed with chilli, lime, ginger and garlic, as a salsa with fried fish.

My favourite way to serve pineapple as a treaty pud is to grill or barbecue it. Properly searing the flesh with those zebra char-stripes brings out lovely caramelised flavours; a squeeze of lime, a sprinkling of brown sugar and a dash of dark rum makes a grown-up indulgence of it.

To ascertain ripeness and readiness, look for a pineapple with golden skin from which pretty much all the greenness has faded. Give it a sniff at the base and it should reward you with a sweet, fruity (but not fermented) fragrance. Slice off the top and base with a large, sharp knife, so you can stand the pineapple up on a board, then work around it, slicing downwards to remove the skin in strips. Don't worry if you don't get out every last vestige of the pineapple's little 'eyes' at this point – just nick these out afterwards with the tip of a knife. Slice the pineapple thickly and remove the tough core, and you're good to go.

Organic and Fairtrade (see page 46) pineapples are increasingly available in both box schemes and our more enlightened supermarkets. Pineapples, like bananas, are often grown with the liberal use of pesticides and fertilisers, and those who tend them often have few rights and opportunities – compelling reasons to consider these choices.

PIÑA COLADA

1 very ripe medium pineapple

250ml coconut milk

40g caster sugar

Juice of 1 lime, plus an extra ½ lime, sliced, to serve

50ml white or dark rum

2 handfuls of ice cubes

This take on the classic cocktail is heavy on the fresh fruit and light on the rum – you can even leave out the spirit altogether for a smoothie. Serves 4

Peel, core and cut the pineapple into small chunks (as described above); you should have about 500g prepared fruit.

Put the chunked pineapple, coconut milk, sugar, lime juice and rum into a jug blender and purée until smooth.

Divide the ice between tall glasses, add the lime slices and pour over the piña colada. Serve and enjoy.

Pistachio nuts

Nikki Duffy

LATIN NAME
Pistacia vera

MORE RECIPES
Honey and apricot filo pie
(page 314)

Few foods can claim a colour so utterly distinctive as this little nut. Pistachios' greenness comes from chlorophyll, which is most evident when the nuts have been grown in cool conditions and/or harvested early. The colour can sometimes dull with cooking, but it's not easy to resist the appeal of a well-roasted and salted pistachio – a simple and lovely snack.

Native to the Middle East, most pistachios still come from Iran, but the US is also a major producer. The nuts grow on high trees in grape-like clusters, inside a thin, fleshy husk. They are unusual in that they crack themselves, forcing the miniature twin boats of their shells slightly open as they mature. In Iran, they say the nut at this stage is *khandan* (laughing). That doesn't mean they're easy to get out, however: it still takes a strong fingernail to actually prise the shell apart and release the soft little nuts. The work – and the sweet reward – is what makes eating roasted pistachios such an absorbing, vaguely addictive ritual.

Wonderful partners to spices and dried fruits in savoury dishes, pistachios are perfect in a pilaf. But this nut really comes into its own in sweet dishes – its tender texture and sweet flavour invite sugar and spices, citrus and honey.

Pistachio ice cream – pale green, sweetly nutty and delectable – is well worth making yourself because it's hard to buy a good one. A pistachio praline is lovely too: drop the nuts into searing hot, lightly salted caramel, leave to cool on a tray, then bash into coarse shards. And, of course, pistachios are at home in baklava, encased in splinteringly thin, crisp filo pastry and almost drowned in a honeyed syrup.

PISTACHIO, ORANGE AND HONEY FILO TARTLETS

Dense and sweet, these nutty tartlets are excellent with a strong coffee. Makes 12

3 sheets of ready-made filo pastry (about 30 x 27cm)

40g unsalted butter, melted

125g shelled pistachio nuts

30g caster sugar

Finely grated zest of 1 small orange

100g ricotta

1 egg yolk

A pinch of salt

1 tbsp clear honey

Preheat the oven to 180°C/Fan 160°C/Gas 4. Have ready a 12-hole muffin tin.

Place the filo sheets one on top of the other. Cut through them lengthways, down the middle, to make two long strips, then cut across the middle going in the other direction, to give 4 squares (with 3 layers each). Cut each square into four – so you end up with 48 small squares of pastry.

Brush a filo square with a little melted butter and then lay it into a hole in one of the muffin tins. Repeat the process with another 3 squares in the same hole, placing each at a slight angle to the last, brushing each piece with butter as you go. Repeat to line all of the muffin moulds. Bake the pastry cases for 5–10 minutes, until crisp and golden.

Meanwhile, put three-quarters of the pistachios (about 95g) into a food processor with the sugar and orange zest and pulse until finely chopped. Add the ricotta, egg yolk and salt and pulse again.

Spoon the mixture into the filo tart cases. Crush or roughly chop the remaining nuts and sprinkle them over the tartlets. Bake for 8 minutes or until the mixture is just firm.

Allow the tartlets to cool for 15–20 minutes, then trickle a little honey over each one before serving.

Plaice

Nick Fisher

LATIN NAME
Pleuronectes platessa

SEASONALITY
Avoid January–March when
spawning

HABITAT
From the western Mediterranean,
along the coast of Europe as far
north as Iceland. Found all
around the British Isles, most
being caught in the North Sea

MCS RATING
3–5

REC MINIMUM SIZE
30cm

MORE RECIPES
Roast brill with air-dried ham
and parsley sauce (page 92);
Grilled flounder and tomatoes
(page 260); Lemon sole
poached in butter with thyme
(page 589); Dover sole with
seaweed butter (page 588);
Herbed pouting fish fingers
(page 501); Rice and fish with
wasabi dressing (page 667)

SOURCING
goodfishguide.org; msc.org

There's something about plaice that feels very English: it's a rather 'nice' sort of fish. Its fillets are tidy and flat. Its flesh is tasty, but definitely on the bland side of fishy. And it's soft and delicate in texture, without being sensual and velvety, like sole, or abdominally ripped, like brill. It seems, all in all, a jolly decent, well-mannered fish.

Don't be fooled. Plaice are the hoover-faced gut-buckets of the wild. Mostly they are targeted by trawlers and netters over smooth sand and mud, but catch one over a mussel bed on rod and line in spring or autumn, and a big plaice's belly will rattle like a bag of marbles. A hungry plaice can suck in seed mussels the size of Brazil nuts by the dozen. I've counted over 20 whole mussels in the belly of a single plaice, making this normally svelte creature look like a python who's swallowed a poodle.

When buying plaice, try and find out where it's come from. It's a popular creature and some stocks are overfished. The best choice currently is mature (i.e. at least 30cm) plaice from the North Sea and eastern English Channel. This is one of the few fish that improves with a day or two's keeping, provided it's been well looked after. Use your eyes: the splodges on a plaice's tea-coloured back should be tangerine orange. If in doubt, flip the plaice over and have a look at its belly, which should be white as a nun's crinoline. If it's going grey or brown at the edges and has sticky mucus-y goo beginning to collect, choose something else.

Plaice fillets are very easy to cook and to eat. They don't have bones, so they can be rolled up and stuffed with anything from pine nuts to salsa verde or anchovies. Fillets will poach, steam or fry effortlessly, but, if you've bought a big whole plaice (1kg-plus) or 2 smaller ones, I'd recommend roasting it. Lay the whole plaice in a greased roasting tray, surround it with cherry tomatoes, bay, basil, rosemary (*anything green and herby*), mixed with whole or crushed garlic cloves or even slices of chorizo, and then roast it hard and serve it up like a leg of lamb. Flaking the flesh off the bone and nibbling the crispy fins is a Sunday lunch experience not to be missed.

PLAICE WITH ROSEMARY, CAPER AND ANCHOVY BUTTER

2 plaice (500–600g each), gutted

FOR THE FLAVOURED BUTTER
50g butter, softened

Leaves from 3–4 sprigs of
rosemary

1 tbsp capers, rinsed, drained
and patted dry

1 large or 2 small garlic cloves,
sliced

6 anchovy fillets in oil

1 tbsp olive or rapeseed oil

Sea salt and black pepper

This fast and fabulous dish partners plaice with a trio of big, bold flavours before it is whacked in a hot oven to sear and crisp. Brill, turbot and John Dory, even the humble flounder and dab, love this treatment too. Serves 2

Preheat the oven to 220°C/Fan 200°C/Gas 7 and grease a large baking tray.

For the flavoured butter, put the butter, rosemary, capers, garlic, anchovies and oil into a small food processor and pulse to a fine-textured butter. Alternatively, chop the rosemary, capers, garlic and anchovies finely together before beating into the butter with the oil.

Lay the plaice side by side on the baking tray, dark side upwards. Use a sharp knife to cut 1cm-deep slashes into the dark side of the fish – three or four on each side of the central line should do it.

Heap the butter on to the fish and spread it out, making sure it finds its way into all the slashes. Season the fish with a little more salt and pepper. Transfer to the hot oven and cook for 15 minutes or until just done.

Remove from the oven and leave to stand for 3–4 minutes before serving. This is great with waxy potatoes and a green salad.

Plums & gages

Hugh Fearnley-Whittingstall

LATIN NAME
Prunus domestica

SEASONALITY
July–October

MORE RECIPES
Grilled cheese salad with bullace compote (page 105); Rhubarb crème brûlée (page 532); Damson ripple parfait (page 231); Upside-down chocolate plum pudding (page 189)

SOURCING
brogdalecollections.org (home to the national fruit collection); orangepippintrees.co.uk

The word 'plum' fits in the mouth like a gorgeous fruity gobstopper. It's almost onomatopoeic – a round, full sound that reflects this plump parcel of fruity loveliness. And it's a word we can say with pride. Plums thrive in our climate and we have long been extremely good at producing them. They were grown in Roman Britain, flourished in our medieval monasteries and, in the nineteenth century, our nurserymen went plum crazy – tweaking, experimenting, cross-pollinating, and raising many new varieties, including the regal and still-ubiquitous 'Victoria'. Fat and juicy, multi-layered in flavour and delightfully, abundantly gluttish, a perfect plum can give any sun-drenched Mediterranean peach or apricot a run for its money.

As with pears, it can be a bit of a challenge to find that exquisitely ripe specimen, especially if you are buying them in a shop. Even if you grow your own, there will be a period early in the season of each variety when they come off the tree still a tad firm and sharp. But fractionally under-ripe plums are brilliant to cook with – and I cook plums far more than I eat them raw. Poached, stewed, roasted or baked, with the addition of a little sugar or honey, they effectively ripen in the pan. Like the best grapes, their skins have subtly tannic notes, while the flesh contains an excellent blend of sugars and acidity. Bubbled gently in a compote, roasted, or boiled into jam, these elements combine and develop to form some amazingly complex, winey flavours.

The Victoria still dominates the plum market. It's a fine variety that has been well marketed and is easy to grow. Just picked, they can be a bit tart, but that's precisely what you want if you're packing them into a pie. If you want to eat them raw, they benefit – like any plum – from a couple of days' ripening in a warm room before you sink your teeth in. You would be missing out, though, if you didn't partake of some of the many other available varieties.

And don't forget the gages (pictured overleaf), named after Sir Thomas Gage who introduced them to our shores from France around 200 years ago. These are small, round varieties of plum – often green, gold or yellow, though sometimes purple or flushed with pink – which are lusciously sweet. I rarely cook them because I can't resist eating them raw. They're harder to get hold of than larger plums, though you can sometimes find them in the shops during their August–September season. Mine come from my own trees. 'Cambridge Gage', 'Early Transparent', 'Reine Claude' and the extra-large 'Oullin' are my favourite varieties. The trick is to leave them on the tree as long as you dare. When the wasps take an interest, it's time to intervene.

FAVOURITE PLUM VARIETIES

Early Rivers This variety starts to come good at the end of July, and has a beautiful flavour.

Czar Following on in early August, this purple plum is traditionally used for cooking, and makes an exceptionally good jam.

Victoria Named after Queen Victoria, this ever-popular yellow-fleshed plum is usually ready for picking from around mid-August.

Avalon, Excalibur and Reeves These are all modern, mid-season varieties that you'll love if you like Victorias.

Pershore Sometimes known as 'Yellow Pershore', this is a great English cooking plum.

Ariel A sweet variety to look for in September and October.

Marjorie's Seedling This late-season plum can eat very well when ripe, but it's one that I love to cook with too.

P

Plums and gages are versatile pud-fruits, working well in dishes where you would otherwise use apricots, peaches and cherries. Try baking them in a cushion of almondy frangipane in a tart, or smother them in batter in a fluffy clafoutis.

And they can play a similar role to apples and pears in savoury dishes: they're delicious in salads with salty ham, mild cheeses and nuts. And whole plums, roasted, are wonderful with rich meats such as goose or pork. For a delicious warm salad, roast duck legs, adding halved plums for the last 30 minutes of the cooking time, then splash soy, honey and vinegar into the roasting dish to deglaze and create a beautiful dressing at the same time. Some plums will hold their shape on roasting, some will collapse, depending on the variety and ripeness.

More often than not, I cook my plums into a lightly sweetened compote, which I like to have in the fridge in late summer and autumn, to dip into for breakfast or a light pud, adding yoghurt or crème fraîche, and perhaps a sprinkling of granola. For a simple compote, put 1kg halved or quartered plums into a wide pan with a little splash of water (only enough to stop the fruit catching) and about 100g sugar or honey. I often add a split vanilla pod too, or a couple of star anise, whose warm tang is fabulous with plums. Cook very gently to start with, to get the juices flowing, then increase the heat and simmer for 10 minutes or so, until the plums are soft.

If there are large shreds of skin in your compote that bother you, pass it through a sieve to make a purée. If your compote or purée is very thin, because your plums were particularly juicy, simmer to reduce and thicken it – and intensify all those gorgeous plummy flavours. Taste while it's still warm enough to dissolve any extra sugar you may want to add. But keep it a little tart: it's all the more delicious that way.

An under-sweetened compote works well in savoury dishes. You can cook it further, with garlic, chilli, cinnamon, cloves and a splash of vinegar, to make a sweet-sour sauce – a good use for slightly under-ripe plums. Testament to the plum's versatility, this is fantastic with barbecued mackerel, cold pork, hot duck, even cheese on toast.

ROASTED PLUM FUMBLE

Combining roasted plums with an almond crumble and some cool, thick yoghurt produces a lovely, rich 'fumble' (a hybrid of a crumble and a fool). You can make the crumble well ahead if you like. In high summer, this is fantastic with a lightly spiced compote of cherries in place of the roasted plums. Serves 4

Butter, for greasing

1kg plums, halved and stoned

1 vanilla pod, split lengthways and seeds scraped out

50g caster sugar, or more if the plums are very tart

300ml plain wholemilk yoghurt

FOR THE CRUMBLE

110g plain flour

A pinch of fine sea salt

100g chilled, unsalted butter, cut into cubes

75g granulated or demerara sugar

50g ground almonds

For the 'independent crumble', preheat the oven to 180°C/Fan 160°C/Gas 4. Put all the ingredients into a large bowl and rub together with your fingertips until you have a crumbly dough. Squeeze the mix in your hands to form clumps, then crumble these on to a baking tray and spread out. Bake the lumpy crumble for 25 minutes, giving it a good stir halfway through, until golden brown and crisp. Leave to cool. You'll have more than you need for this recipe, but it keeps well in an airtight container for a couple of weeks.

Meanwhile, generously butter a roasting tin. Put the plums into the tin and distribute the vanilla seeds over them. Cut the pod into a few pieces and add these too, then sprinkle over the sugar. Roast for 20–30 minutes, ideally until the plums are really soft but still retain some shape (although some varieties will collapse, which is fine too). Allow to cool.

To serve, divide half the plums and their juices between 4 glasses. Top with a spoonful or two of yoghurt, then add the remaining plums. Top with the crumble, then give each glass a little mingle before serving.

Polenta

Tim Maddams

LATIN NAME
Zea mays

ALSO KNOWN AS
Cornmeal

MORE RECIPES
Sunflower seed and caraway
corn crackers (page 623);
Lemon, honey and courgette
cake (page 347)

Polenta is milled maize meal, aka cornmeal: dried sweetcorn ground to varying degrees of coarseness. When we think of polenta, we think of Italy but actually maize meal porridges are cooked all over the world – wherever maize is a staple crop – and notably in South America, where they are called *angu*. In fact, polenta is a relative newcomer to the European kitchen because maize was not commonly grown here until the sixteenth century, when it was first introduced from the new world. Prior to that, 'polenta' in Italy simply meant a porridge made from any grain you could lay your hands on, pulverised to a meal then boiled, with lots of stirring, until edible.

There is some confusion between the terms 'cornmeal' and 'polenta'. Technically, it's cornmeal until it's cooked, at which point it becomes polenta but the dry uncooked granules are often sold as 'polenta' too. Either way, for the finished dish we call polenta, the granules are cooked by boiling in 4–5 times their volume of liquid. The cooked polenta can be eaten as it is, 'wet', or left to set and then sliced and baked, grilled or fried to achieve a crunchy crust and soft interior. A staple of the Italian north (where corn grows easily), it's classically served with rich meaty ragus, mushrooms, cheese and wild meats, particularly pigeon.

The most common kind of polenta now is 'quick cook'. This is polenta that has actually already been cooked and is then dried and re-ground to make it effectively instant. It's so 'quick cook' that it often takes you by surprise and is ready before you planned: a brief simmer is all that's needed. Instant polenta isn't really my thing, partly because there aren't many organic brands (though some exist). I enjoy the long, gentle cooking of traditional polenta too: I think it encourages a state of focused attention on the meal at hand. But quick-cook can certainly do the job. It works well in the recipe opposite, for instance.

When I'm cooking my polenta the old-fashioned way, using 'raw' cornmeal, I start with a simmering liquid such as well-seasoned milk or stock. You can use water too, but it's important that you add plenty of salt because cornmeal is inherently bland. I add the polenta/cornmeal to this in a thin stream, stirring until it softens and thickens. I then cook it gently, stirring, for about 30 minutes. In Italy, polenta was traditionally stirred with a long wooden stick called a *cannella* until it was thick enough for the stick to stand up in it. When it reaches this point, I season the hot, soft polenta further and usually add some fat – butter, cheese, olive oil or all three. It can then be served as it is in similar ways to mashed potatoes, rice or bulgar wheat or left to set, cut into slices and fried.

Whatever kind of polenta you're cooking, it will try very hard to stick to the bottom of the pan and burn: use a good spatula and stir constantly to avoid this. And you must always watch out for white-hot volcanic outbursts as the polenta simmers and splutters away: catch some on your bare skin and you will remember the experience for some time.

Sometimes polenta is cooked and then sweetened with honey, raisins or even chocolate and eaten as a dessert. A far more common sweet use for fine cornmeal/polenta however, is in cakes – often made with olive oil rather than butter and flavoured with almonds and lemon. They can be delicious and have the added bonus of being gluten-free (maize contains no gluten). Don't, however, try to make a polenta cake with quick-cook polenta: it's the cooking of fine grains of raw polenta within the batter that makes the cake work. As the instant stuff is already cooked (and coarsely textured), it just goes horribly, heavily wrong.

P

With 'raw' polentas, or cornmeals, the main variation is the grade of the grind, ranging from very fine to very coarse, giving a subtly different end result once cooked. A good guide is to use fine polenta to serve wet or soft, and more granular polenta for the set kind – suitable for grilling and frying. But do look out for more unusual polentas with added buckwheat flour or even chestnut flour: these rustic multigrain versions can be more earthy and interesting than plain polenta.

In the cooking of the southern US, cornmeal is found in another guise. Whole grains of maize are soaked with an alkali, such as lime, which makes them more nutritious and digestible. Whole, hulled grains of this treated maize are called hominy, and can be cooked and eaten whole. However, they are often ground to produce a meal: if left coarse, the meal is used to make grits – a sort of porridge – or it can be ground finely for cornbread.

Alkali-treated maize is also used in Mexican cuisine, where it is processed into a dough, *masa harina*. This is often then dried and re-ground to make a flour, also known as *masa harina*, which is used to make cornmeal tortillas.

Cornflour

As the name suggests, this is ground from maize but it is completely different from polenta. Cornflour, known as cornstarch in the US, is the extracted starch of the maize kernel and is available in two forms, white and yellow. It is very finely powdered and is used to thicken sauces, make batters and as a coating for food to be deep-fried.

POLENTA CROQUETTES

Cornmeal is often used to give a crisp coating to fried foods, but in this recipe the roles are reversed and the polenta forms the tender, cheesy filling inside a crisp, breadcrumb crust. Serves 4–6 as a nibble

2 tbsp olive or rapeseed oil

1 medium onion, sliced

2 garlic cloves, finely chopped

Leaves from 2 sprigs of thyme

5–6 sage leaves, chopped

Leaves from 1 small sprig of rosemary, finely chopped

500ml whole milk

100g quick-cook polenta

150g mature Cheddar or other well-flavoured hard cheese, grated

25g butter

1 tbsp chopped parsley

1 small, sharp eating apple, such as a Cox or Worcester

75g plain flour

3 eggs, beaten

200g fine breadcrumbs

Vegetable oil (refined rapeseed oil), for deep-frying

Sea salt and black pepper

Line a baking tray, about 20 x 30cm and at least 2cm deep, with baking parchment.

Heat the oil in a wide saucepan over a medium-low heat. Add the onion and garlic and sweat for 10–12 minutes, until the onion softens and starts to take on a little colour. Add the thyme, sage, rosemary and milk, then stir in the polenta. Bring slowly to a simmer, stirring all the time, then cook gently for a couple of minutes until the polenta is smooth and thick.

Add the cheese, butter and parsley and mix until the cheese and butter melts in. Remove from the heat and allow the polenta to cool a little. Meanwhile, peel, quarter, core and cut the apple into roughly 3mm dice. Mix the chopped apple into the polenta mix.

Spread the mixture evenly into the lined tray. Once cool, cover with cling film and refrigerate until cold and set.

Have the flour, egg and breadcrumbs for coating ready in 3 separate bowls and add a little salt and pepper to each. Turn the slab of polenta out on to a board and cut it into finger-sized pieces. Roll each one in the flour, then the egg, then the breadcrumbs.

Heat a 5–7cm depth of oil in a deep, heavy-based pan to 180°C or until a cube of bread, dropped in, turns golden brown in about a minute. Fry the breaded polenta, a few fingers at a time, in the hot oil for 1–2 minutes, or until golden. Drain on kitchen paper.

Serve the croquettes as soon as possible, with a spicy fruity chutney (such as the green tomato chutney on page 642).

Pollack

Gill Meller

LATIN NAME
Pollachius pollachius

ALSO KNOWN AS
Lythe, pollock

SEASONALITY
Avoid January–April when spawning

HABITAT
Throughout the northeast Atlantic; common all around the British Isles

MCS RATING
3–4

REC MINIMUM SIZE
50cm

MORE RECIPES
Sea beet and smoked pollack pasties (page 574); Cod with fennel, capers and tomatoes (page 194); Coley with bacon, apples and hazelnuts (page 197); Zander with coriander and chilli dressing (page 685); Crumbed whiting goujons with curried egg tartare (page 673); Herbed pouting fish fingers (page 501); Smoked haddock jacket potatoes (page 294); Rice and fish with wasabi dressing (page 667)

SOURCING
goodfishguide.org; linecaught.org.uk; cornwallgoodseafoodguide.co.uk

Once championed as the saviour of our seas, a truly ethical fish, pollack rode high with an MCS rating of '2' – indicating we should eat more of it. But this cod cousin, also known as lythe, now carries a '3' or even a '4' rating, this last indicating it should be eaten only occasionally.

As ever with fish, it's complicated. At River Cottage, we try to get local line-caught pollack, landed by the South-West Handline Fishermen Association, which is a very sustainable choice. Caught by highly selective baited lines, there is no by-catch and no damage to the seabed. You can also buy Alaska pollack – both as the whole fish and in products such as fish fingers – which is certified by the MSC as sustainable. This is actually a different species, *Theragra chalcogramma*, but is a similarly versatile, firm white fish.

Other pollack may be more problematic. Information on numbers is patchy, but it is known that stocks in the North Sea, and Skagerrak and Kattegat (between the coasts of Norway, Sweden and Denmark) have declined to low levels. The current scientific advice is that fewer pollack should be caught there now, relative to the last few years. These pollack are also mainly taken in trawl and gill-net fisheries, both of which can have an impact on the environment and vulnerable wildlife.

This is all the more regrettable because pollack has rightly enjoyed a renaissance in recent years. Long derided as 'cat food' and cod's very poor relation, it is finally being appreciated for the delicious fish it is. It's very cod-like, though it lacks cod's pristine whiteness. Pollack flesh softens a little more quickly and easily too, if it's not swiftly and scrupulously iced – but disappointing pollack is a result of poor handling and lack of freshness, not some inherent flaw in the fish itself.

Luckily, it's the most sustainably caught pollack that is likely to be least damaged and best looked-after on its way from sea to plate. Trawled and netted pollack that are taken by fishermen looking for other species tend to be treated with less respect – and any trawled fish suffers more trauma than a line-caught specimen as it's tumbled together with a hotchpotch of other species. I continue to use South-West, line-caught pollack as an alternative to cod and haddock. And it can be used in the same ways as either of those fish, with equally handsome results.

Pollack has scales that should be removed before cooking. I usually cook it with the skin on but, if you remove the skin (which I do if steam-braising, see overleaf), it can be fried into a crisp, salty treat. Heat a little olive or rapeseed oil in a frying pan over a medium-high heat. Season the fish skin and fry it quite 'hard', turning regularly, until golden and crisp, then drain on kitchen paper and season with a bit more salt and pepper before devouring.

If you are lucky enough to come by a big, whole pollack, I highly recommend removing the head, cutting away a generous portion of 'shoulder' with it, and roasting this whole, studded with herbs and garlic, in a hot oven for about half an hour. Picking away the succulent flesh from the roasted head is hands-on eating at its most rewarding.

Pollack flesh also works very well beer-battered and deep-fried, or made into fish fingers or goujons, or as the white fish element in a fish pie, fish curry or a fishy soup or stew. But pollack is quite good enough to enjoy entirely on its own merits – as a simply cooked fillet.

You can cook the flesh just as it comes but I often give it a light salting (as with many other species of white fish) to firm and season it: this can dramatically improve the finished dish. It can then be fried in a pan, roasted or treated to what, at River

Cottage, we call 'steam-braising'. This is a simple technique that creates a lovely little pool of juices with which to sauce your fish. In a wide saucepan, heat a little oil and butter, a splash each of white wine, water and lemon juice, a little chopped garlic and some bay, and bring to a simmer. Cut some skinned pollack fillet into chunky medallions (cross-sections of the fillet), season and add them to the pan. Cover and cook very gently for 3–4 minutes, then turn the fish gently over in the juices and cook for a couple of minutes more until done.

However it's cooked, I love pollack accompanied by something a little salty such as chorizo, bacon or olives. Similarly, a spoonful of salsa verde or tapenade makes an excellent dressing. Pollack also takes on curry spices exceptionally well.

POLLACK WITH COURGETTES AND CANNELLINI BEANS

This is a lovely, light way to serve pollack – or any chunky white fish – in late summer, with lots of lemon and herbs to add fragrance and a zest. Serves 2

2 portions of pollack fillet (about 125g each)

1 tbsp fine sea salt

2 firm, small-medium courgettes

2 tbsp olive or rapeseed oil

400g tin cannellini beans, drained and rinsed

Finely grated zest and juice of 1 lemon

A knob of butter

1 tbsp chopped parsley

1 tbsp chopped dill

1 tbsp extra virgin olive or rapeseed oil

Sea salt and black pepper

Place the pieces of pollack, skin side down, on a board or plate and scatter over the salt. Leave for 20–25 minutes, then rinse well under a gently running cold tap and pat dry with kitchen paper.

Preheat your grill to high. Trim the courgettes and slice into 5mm thick rounds. Place them in a bowl, trickle over 1 tbsp oil, then season well with salt and pepper.

Lay the courgettes in a single layer on a large baking tray and place under the grill. Cook for 8–10 minutes on each side or until blistered and golden. When they're almost done, scatter over the beans, squeeze over half the lemon juice and sprinkle with the lemon zest. Place the tray back under the grill for 1–2 minutes to heat the beans through.

Heat a large non-stick frying pan over a medium-high heat. Add 1 tbsp oil and, when hot, add the lightly salted pollack, skin side down. Cook for 3–4 minutes, then turn the fish and cook for a further minute. Turn the heat off and add the butter and remaining lemon juice to the pan. Baste the fish with the butter as it melts.

Stir the parsley and dill though the courgettes and beans along with the extra virgin oil and a little salt and pepper if needed.

Divide the courgettes between warm plates and top each with a piece of fish, along with any buttery, lemony pan juices.

P

Pomegranate

Nikki Duffy

LATIN NAME
Punica granatum

SEASONALITY
Imported all year round

MORE RECIPES
Muhammara (page 464)

A pomegranate is a thing of beauty, before you have even breached the skin. Round, plump and burnished, with that curious, crown-like calyx on top, they are voluptuous and regal. Split them open and they reveal glistening, crimson seeds – more jewel-like than any other in the fruit kingdom. It's little wonder that this native of Persia has been invested with great significance for thousands of years, a symbol of plenty and of fertility, though often with darker associations too – even thought by some to be the forbidden fruit of Eden.

These fruits range in colour from rich gold to deep, burgundy red. The outer shell is tough and leathery and is not eaten, and nor is the bitter white pith beneath the skin: this rosy fruit is all about the seeds. To prepare a pomegranate, roll it on a work surface to loosen the seeds, then cut it in half. You can then scoop out the seedy pulp with a teaspoon or, much more fun, whack the shell of the fruit with a wooden spoon, showering the seeds on to your chosen dish.

These crimson gems beg to be sprinkled over foods that are pale or light in colour (sweet or savoury). Strew them on ice cream, meringue or snowy-white pannacotta, sprinkle them on to sunshine-yellow lemon tarts, pineapples and mangoes, turmeric-stained rice or chunks of pale, salty sheep's cheese – all foods that their flavour will enhance. The seeds pop between the teeth with a pleasing, juicy crunch, their flavour sweet-sour, slightly tannic, appley and refreshing. They are also very good as a finishing touch to hearty salads or big platters of roast meat – and you can even extract the juice with a lemon squeezer to use in smoothies or cocktails.

Store the whole fruits at cool room temperature and they should keep well for at least a week – much longer in the fridge. Pomegranates are a rich source of antioxidants and you can buy their juice in cartons, although it's usually processed in some way (pasteurised, concentrated, sweetened, etc.).

They also give us a fruity, sweet and tangy 'molasses' made by cooking down the juice into a thick, dark syrup. This gorgeous stuff is used throughout the Middle East, and is essential to the dip muhammara (see page 464). It's also used in dressings, sauces and glazes: try blitzing some into hummus or mixing it with a little crushed garlic to dress grilled vegetables (aubergines, particularly). It is excellent mixed into summer drinks – alcoholic or not – and can be trickled over cakes and puddings or splashed over vanilla ice cream or plain yoghurt. Sometimes called *robb-e anar, rubb* or pomegranate syrup or concentrate, the best examples contain no added sugar, and taste astonishingly fruity and fragrant.

Pomegranate molasses is not at all the same thing as grenadine, a syrup used in cocktails. Originally a pomegranate-based ingredient, these days grenadine is usually a conglomeration of sugar, colouring and various fruit juice concentrates, and rarely includes pomegranate at all.

HALLOUMI AND ROASTED CARROT SALAD WITH POMEGRANATE

500g carrots

1 tbsp clear honey

1 tbsp olive or rapeseed oil

225g halloumi cheese, cut into 5mm-thick slices

1 pomegranate

1 tbsp chopped parsley

Sea salt and black pepper

FOR THE DRESSING

1½ tbsp pomegranate molasses

1½ tbsp cider vinegar

1 tsp Dijon mustard

2 tsp clear honey

3 tbsp extra virgin olive oil

This makes a fantastic starter and is also great as part of a vegetarian main course. Serves 4

Preheat the oven to 200°C/Fan 180°C/Gas 6.

Peel the carrots and slice them into batons, about 1cm thick and 4–5cm long. Put these into a large roasting tin, spoon over the honey and oil, season with salt and pepper and then toss together well. Roast for 20 minutes.

Add the sliced halloumi cheese and toss with the carrots. Return to the oven for a further 10–15 minutes or until the edges of the cheese are looking crisp and golden.

Meanwhile make the dressing: in a bowl, whisk together the pomegranate molasses, vinegar, mustard and honey. Gradually whisk in the oil until well incorporated. Season to taste with salt and pepper.

Extract the seeds from the pomegranate (as described on page 485). Spoon the carrots and halloumi on to a warm platter. Trickle over the dressing and finish with a generous scattering of parsley and pomegranate seeds.

Serve warm, just as it comes – or make a more substantial spread of it by serving with a green salad, hummus and some warm flatbreads.

Poppy seeds

Pam Corbin

LATIN NAME
Opium poppy: *Papaver somniferum*. Common poppy: *Papaver rhoeas*

MORE RECIPES
Seedy stoneground loaf (page 263)

The teeny blue-grey seeds of the opium poppy are harvested when the seed capsule is ripe – yellowing and woody – by which time its narcotic qualities have faded.

Poppy seeds dance the line between decoration and spice – the more you use, the more their sweet, nutty flavour comes through. Most familiar as a sprinkled topping on breads and pies, or folded into zesty lemon cakes, they can also be used in quantity. In Russia and Eastern Europe, the seeds are ground and cooked with milk and sugar to fill sweet pastries. In India, the smaller, less sweet, white poppy seeds are preferred; these are ground and used to thicken sauces and curries. The best way to grind the seeds is in a coffee grinder or food mill with a little water.

Opium poppies grow in Britain (both wild and in gardens) and you can also harvest seeds from the common red (field) poppy. These are even smaller than opium poppy seeds. In both cases, collect the seedheads when they rattle, put them in a paper bag and wait for the seeds to fall out (don't eat any other parts of the poppy plant, which are toxic). But poppy seeds are easy to buy: it is more economical to buy large packs from health food shops and online suppliers than small jars from a supermarket.

Poppy seeds' affinity with citrus needn't be confined to baking. Combined with a spritz of lemon or a scattering of its zest, they also sing their souls into potato, pasta and vegetable dishes. Or try this lemony dressing: combine 75ml extra virgin olive or rapeseed oil with the juice of 1 lemon, 2 tsp clear honey and 1 tbsp toasted poppy seeds, adding salt and pepper to taste. This is lovely with soft cheeses or smoked fish, or to dress crisp, peppery salad leaves.

POPPY SEED SPELT ROLLS

1 tsp clear honey (or sugar)

15g dried yeast

1kg wholemeal spelt flour, plus a little extra to dust

20g fine salt

75g poppy seeds, plus 25g extra to coat

1 tbsp rapeseed oil, plus a little extra to grease

Full of nutty flavour from wholegrain spelt flour and a generous measure of poppy seeds (do check your teeth afterwards), these large rolls are especially good with something a little rich, such as egg mayonnaise. Makes 12

In a large bowl, dissolve the honey in 50ml warm water. Sprinkle in the dried yeast and mix well. Leave to stand for 5–10 minutes, until frothy.

Add the flour, salt and 75g poppy seeds to the yeast mixture. Pour in 600ml warm water and 1 tbsp rapeseed oil, and mix to a rough dough.

Tip the dough out on to a floured surface and knead until smooth – a good 10 minutes. Shape into a ball and rub lightly with oil.

Place the dough in a clean bowl, cover loosely with a plastic bag or cling film, and leave to rise, somewhere warm, until doubled in size – up to 1½ hours, longer if necessary.

Tip the dough out and press all over with your fingertips to deflate it. Divide into 12 pieces and shape into rolls. Pour 100ml water into a bowl and put the remaining poppy seeds in a second bowl. Dip the rolls, top first, into the water, then into the poppy seeds.

Transfer the rolls to a couple of well-floured baking trays, cover loosely with a plastic bag and leave to prove until almost doubled in size. Meanwhile, preheat the oven to 230°C/Fan 210°C/Gas 8 and put a couple of baking sheets inside to heat up.

Once the rolls have proved, slide the trays on to the hot baking sheets (if the rolls have spread out a lot during proving, push their sides in a little) and return to the oven as quickly as possible. Bake for 10 minutes, then lower the oven setting to 200°C/Fan 180°C/Gas 6 and bake for a further 10–13 minutes until the rolls are well browned and sound hollow when tapped on the base. Transfer to a wire rack and leave to cool before serving.

Pork

Gill Meller

MORE RECIPES
Spiced liver pâté (page 362);
Pork burgers with mace and
thyme (page 369); Coriander
pork chops (page 198); Pheasant
pie (page 468); Chicken and
blueberry salad with coriander
dressing (page 77); Pear and
celeriac stuffing (page 454)

SOURCING
farmsnotfactories.org
(information on pork labelling);
eversfieldorganic.co.uk;
higherhacknell.co.uk;
hughgrierson.co.uk

Pigs are wonderful animals and they produce amazing meat. They also provide a carcass that is more versatile than any other. You can eat almost every part of it, from the ears to the tail, including the skin, fat and organs and you can do so many different things with the meat: not just roasting, frying and stewing but smoking, curing, salting, drying, even fermenting, as in a traditional salami.

There's no denying that pigs have a cultural significance for us too. The pig has always been a manageable creature for even quite small households to raise themselves and so the imperative to make the most of every part of this precious animal was woven into British culinary thinking centuries ago. That's why so many fantastic traditional pork products have evolved, from Bath chaps to brawn, hams to hocks.

However, our voracious appetite for pork, rather than leading us to revere and honour the pig, has resulted in our abject abuse of the animal. Modern pork farming, where the churning out of huge quantities of lean, cheap meat is the goal, is largely a shameful business. We kill around nine million pigs a year in Britain, the majority of which have lived all their lives indoors. Our baseline animal welfare standards are higher than many other countries, but unfortunately that isn't saying much. Only 7 per cent of British 'growing' pigs (i.e animals raised for meat) spend their lives outdoors. The majority of pigs are indoors all the time; some breeding sows live outside, while some piglets are outdoor-bred before being brought inside to fatten up.

On intensive farms, pigs are kept close together and often in large numbers. In order to deal with the volumes of faeces and urine produced, they may be kept on slatted floors with no straw – the most basic environmental enrichment a pig requires. The Soil Association estimates that at least 35 per cent of pigs reared for meat in the UK are kept in barren systems without any straw bedding. Regular use of antibiotics is widespread: pig farming accounts for about 60 per cent of all British farm antibiotic use. The routine use of antibiotics in intensive farming has contributed to the rise of antibiotic-resistant strains of E. coli, salmonella, MRSA and other infections in humans.

Breeding sows on most pig farms are forced to enter a 'farrowing crate' shortly before giving birth. These crates, which are still allowed under the Red Tractor scheme, are in fact cages – bare-floored and so tiny that the sow cannot even roll over. The farrowing crate keeps the sow separate from her litter – they can reach her teats through the bars – which denies her the opportunity to express any natural mothering behaviour. The crates are the norm for indoor-reared pigs; more than half the sows in the UK give birth in them. The piglets are allowed to feed from their incapacitated mother for a month before being removed from her to begin their short, indoor lives. The sow will quickly be made pregnant again.

Only around half the pork we eat in this country even comes from British pigs. The rest is imported from countries where welfare standards are lower still. China farms around half the world's pigs, with huge numbers also raised in the EU.

Pigs are omnivores, loving to rootle and forage for roots and plants. They like to wallow in mud or water to control their temperature (they have no sweat glands so struggle to cool down in confined conditions). The natural state for female and young pigs is to live in a small family group while boars often prefer to be solitary. These are curious, intelligent, social animals that can out-perform dogs in learning tests, but they are also sometimes aggressive if confined or forced to compete for space or food. In all but the best conditions, farmers control the problems that result from crowding, competition and boredom via the short cuts of tail-docking and teeth-clipping.

P

HIGHER WELFARE PORK

Soil Association organic This is the highest welfare marker, and indicates that pigs and piglets have access to the outdoors all their lives – including pasture when conditions allow – with well-bedded shelter when required. This gives them the opportunity to express natural behaviours such as rooting and wallowing. Nose-ringing, which stops the pigs rooting, is banned, along with other practices such as tail-docking. No GM feed is permitted and antibiotics are not used prophlyactically – only to treat certain conditions. Note that this applies to pigs reared in the UK; organic standards in other countries may be different.

Free-range These pigs are born outside (without stalls or crates) and have permanent access to the outdoors throughout their lives, with adequate shelter provided.

Outdoor reared This means the breeding sows live outside, with adequate shelter provided, throughout their productive lives. The piglets, however, do not: they are born outdoors and stay there with their mothers for up to the first 10 weeks of life, then they are brought indoors to fatten up. Pigs can be slaughtered as young as 16 weeks (for small cuts of fresh pork), though many are grown on to around 30 weeks.

Outdoor bred As for 'outdoor reared', the breeding sows live outdoors with adequate shelter, for as long as they remain productive, but the piglets only stay there with their mothers for around the first 4 weeks of life. Piglets would naturally wean later than this. Piglets weaned early are more likely to suffer from diarrhoea; the treatment for this accounts for a large proportion of the industry's antibiotic use.

RSPCA assured These pigs may well have lived indoors all their lives but with more space than the most intensively reared animals. Adequate straw bedding must be provided. Farrowing crates are not allowed.

Buying pork

Farming pigs intensively is not acceptable. It doesn't even produce good pork. The most natural life a domesticated pig can lead is spent outdoors, with the sun on its back and its feet in the earth, and the taste, texture and overall quality of meat from such an animal is unquestionably superior to that of indoor-raised pigs. The various higher welfare schemes for pork in the UK are described above.

These labelling schemes allow you to make good choices in supermarkets. Small, independent retailers, who are more likely to support local producers and farmers, should be able to inform you about the products they sell. But don't assume that just because pork is local it will be high welfare. Even better, of course, is to go straight to the source. There are plenty of small producers farming high-welfare pork and selling it via mail order, direct from the farm or through farmers' markets. They may not necessarily be organic (as certification is a significant cost to the farmer) but there are many free-range pig farmers who do not compromise on welfare.

Pork breeds

You've probably heard a lot about 'rare breed' pork. Such animals are, if you like, the opposite of the commercial breeds that now dominate the pork industry. Mainstream modern breeds, including the 'Duroc', the 'Welsh', the 'British Landrace' and the 'Large White', are long and lean. They reach slaughter weight far more quickly than traditional breeds and are less hairy, which makes processing them easier. The Landrace and Large White are intensively farmed in huge numbers across the British Isles and are the source of most of the fresh and processed pork we buy.

By contrast, traditional pigs evolved in a time before factory farming, developing into distinct breeds that were uniquely suited to local conditions. The 'Berkshire', 'Gloucestershire Old Spot', 'Oxford Sandy and Black' and the wonderful 'British Saddleback' all developed distinctive individual characteristics including excellent flavours, textures and marbling. These traditional breeds don't tick the right boxes for today's intensive pork industry, however, and that's why they've become rare.

I believe that rare and traditional breed pork tastes better. It is more fatty, for instance, and that's crucial. Fat is what gives pork its unique and irresistible flavour. It makes crackling crackly, and sausages succulent. Without it, bacon is bland and roasts are disappointing. Rare breeds also grow more slowly, which means that they are more mature when slaughtered and their meat therefore carries more flavour.

Pork cuts

Ear It may not quite be possible to make a silk purse out of this part of the animal but you can certainly turn it into something very tasty. If you're removing the ears from a pig's head yourself, it's important to clean them well. Use a sharp boning knife to remove the ears close to the head, revealing the ear canals. Make a cut at the base of each ear so you can open them up and give them a really good scrub inside and out with a stiff brush or scouring pad. Ears should then be simmered gently in water for 2–3 hours until very tender. You can add aromatics such as soy sauce, chilli and garlic to produce braised ears in a sticky sauce, or just use the classic stock veg, then slice the cooked ears, coat them in breadcrumbs and bake or fry them until crisp.

Cheeks Also known as chaps, the pig's cheeks comprise a lozenge of dark muscle, as well as paler, more open-grained meat, plenty of fat and, of course, skin. The cheeks are often sold trimmed down to that 'cushion' of darker meat. There's nothing wrong with that but the whole cheek gives you a more varied eating experience – although once cooked, you should scrape away all the glandular tissue and membrane from the inner surface. Cheeks are hardworking parts of the animal and require lengthy cooking, but this renders them wonderfully soft and yielding. They were traditionally brined, cooked, pressed and breadcrumbed to produce Bath chaps – a rare treat these days. You can make your own chaps, or simply simmer pig's cheeks with stock veg, for 3–4 hours. You can then eat them as they are, slice and fry them, or press them into a terrine. Trimmed-down pig's cheeks are also great for a slow-cooked pork stew.

Shoulder Fattier than the leg, pork shoulder is a magnificent roasting joint. It's possible to roast one whole, but more often sections are boned and rolled into smaller joints. These may be called shoulder, or spare rib joints – they are exactly the same thing. After an initial hot blast to get the crackling going, shoulder responds well to long cooking at a low temperature: it's a hardworking muscle and needs time to tenderise. Cook it until falling off the bone, and you have 'pulled pork' that can be torn easily into shreds. Shoulder is also sold diced for stewing and is used in sausages.

Loin The loin is the side of the pig, from the backbone down to the belly. It is a long and relatively lean piece of meat, striated with the ribs. The loin is often divided up and those bones removed to form smaller joints for roasting. Alternatively, it can be cut into chops: loin chops from the middle of the back have a rib in them, while the larger, leaner chump chops from the top of the leg have only a small cross-section of bone. The loin also yields the delicate tenderloin, or pork fillet. It's a small, elongated muscle, the equivalent of fillet steak, and offers a combination of fine texture and leanness. It is less robustly flavoured than other parts of the pig, however, and easily overcooked. Just grilling it for 8–10 minutes each side is enough to cook it through. Sliced tenderloin is good for a super-fast stir-fry.

Chump From the back end of the loin, where it meets the leg, this small joint has a nice bit of marbling, which makes it more interesting than the leg. It makes a good roast for 2–4 people.

Belly This is inexpensive but also one of the most glorious cuts – rich with fat, and therefore flavour. A thick-end of belly makes a superb roasting cut, which is virtually impossible to overcook, while boneless strips of belly pork are delicious rubbed with herbs, salt and spices and roasted. Belly, which is what streaky bacon is made from, is also very useful cubed or minced and used to enrich leaner meats such as game, in stews or when making burgers or sausages.

Ribs Not to be confused with the spare rib joint, which is from the shoulder, ribs can come from the belly or the loin. They are inexpensive and fantastic cooked in a rich, spicy liquor until tender and sticky. Do make sure that you have ribs that have been butchered generously – i.e. with plenty of nibble-able meat on the bones.

Hand/Hock The rather misnamed 'hand', also sometimes called the 'hand and spring', is the top part of the front leg of the pig, including a section of the breast and the hock. It can be cooked bone-in (retaining its rather awkward, hard-to-carve shape) or boned-out. Either way, it responds well if slow-roasted until very tender. The hock is just the first joint of the leg, above the trotter. It contains lots of sinew and collagen, and not a huge amount of meat, and the traditional approach of cooking it slowly so that it forms a gelatinous broth, then shredding the meat and setting it within that flavoursome jelly, is hard to beat.

Leg This is also a popular roasting joint, though it is much leaner than the shoulder or loin, and so a little more prone to dryness. It's important to get a leg from a fine, well-marbled carcass to start with – if it's super-lean, no amount of care will render it tender and juicy. If you have a good butcher, you can ask them to break down the pork leg into individual muscle sets that correspond to the cuts you would get from a leg of beef (topside, silverside, rump etc.) I'm more likely to turn pork legs into ham than roast them, but I also like cubed leg of pork in a stew – again with plenty of lubrication from cream, coconut milk or some fatty belly pork.

Trotter This is a terrific cut. You can add pig's trotters to all sorts of slow-cooked meat dishes – game stews, for instance – so that they release their rich flavour and thickening gelatine into the liquor. But they make a centrepiece ingredient in their own right. I like them boned-out and slow-cooked until tender, then stuffed. By the time you've removed the bone, what's left is mostly skin but this becomes tender with long cooking. I also use trotters along with hock to make a fantastic, flavoursome and thrifty terrine, the joints cooked slowly to form a rich, jellied pork stock, then every morsel of meat and tender skin picked off the bones and folded in.

Tail Even this last scrap of the animal has potential. Tails should be split down the middle and the greater part of the bone teased out (the really slender bit at the tip can be left in – cooking will make it tender enough to eat). Simmer them in stock for an hour or so until tender. They can then be baked, fried or barbecued until golden and crisp. Tails can also be cooked with the pig's head to make into a brawn.

Faggots Not a cut as such, but a dish, the faggot is a thrifty amalgamation of minced offal, fatty pork, onions and breadcrumbs, well seasoned and formed into balls. Usually wrapped in caul fat, and fried or baked, it's a great way to put pig's liver, heart and lights (lungs) to delicious use.

Boar

Our familiar domestic pig is descended from the wild boar. These animals became extinct in Britain several hundred years ago but, with the recent advent of wild boar farming, captive animals have managed to escape and establish populations in the wild. Boar can be found roaming free in various parts of Britain – mostly in the South. Their presence is controversial: they are a native species and part of our ancient ecosystem, but they pose a threat to modern-day agriculture, to some other animals and plants, and sometimes to humans – they can cause road accidents, for example. Wild boar are shot in some areas to control their numbers. There is no closed season, and this hunting is unregulated. Numbers of wild boar are not definitively known.

Truly wild boar meat has a fantastic, deep flavour. Even the farmed version (which will still be described as 'wild boar', even though it may sometimes be cross-bred with domestic pigs), packs a punch. It tastes not unlike pork but is darker, gamier and much leaner. It responds well to slow, very gentle cooking in braises and ragus. You can also pan-cook boar escalopes or steaks more quickly – guard against overcooking but don't serve them rare (see the advice on cooking pork, below).

Cooking pork

Official advice is to always cook pork thoroughly until no pink juices remain (though even well-cooked pork can sometimes have a rosy tint in the meat itself). This is to combat various risks.

One is a parasite called *Trichinella spiralis*, which can infect pigs and be passed to humans, causing trichinosis. This is now extremely rare in commercial pork; moreover, it is easily killed by cooking. Meat only needs to reach a core temperature of around 60°C and hold it for more than 2 minutes for this to happen.

However, trichinosis is not the only area of potential concern. Pork can carry salmonella, for instance. Most strains of this are killed after 2 minutes at 70°C. But there is also a virus, Hepatitis E, which can infect pigs and be transmitted to humans. Not enough research has been done to pinpoint the time and temperature needed to kill this, though some estimates suggest as much as 20 minutes at 70°C.

Hence, the advice still tends to be relatively high temperatures and long times for cooking pork: it should reach a core temperature of 75°C for around 18 seconds, or 70°C for a minimum of 2 minutes, or 65°C for a minimum of 10 minutes etc. Or, more simply, be cooked until steaming hot to the centre, with the juices running clear.

For some, those temperatures equate to overcooking and I know of chefs so certain of the quality of their pork that they are happy to serve it rare. If I'm cooking a lean cut such as tenderloin or chump chops for myself, and I'm confident about its provenance, I err on the side of juiciness by leaving the meat just pink in the middle.

If you feel more comfortable cooking your pork until well done, stick to the fattier, more succulent cuts such as belly and shoulder, or products such as sausages. If they have come from a well-raised, properly butchered animal, they'll still come up trumps every time.

Perfect crackling

A joint from a well-fatted, thick-skinned naturally reared pig that has been hung, uncovered, in a cold store will have the firm, dry rind that engenders a good crackle. Joints that are vac-packed tend to have a waterlogged skin. When you get a joint of pork home, unwrap it and dab away any moisture from the skin with kitchen paper. Then keep it, uncovered, in the fridge for 24–48 hours before cooking.

Cut through the skin a few millimetres into the fat, but not as far as the meat, at 1–2cm intervals. A Stanley knife or similar set at about 4–5mm is the perfect tool for the job. Often, butchers will do this for you. Leaving your joint untied helps the skin curl upwards and crackle better. Oil the skin lightly, then sprinkle liberally with fine sea salt. Give the joint an initial sizzle at a very high temperature for the first half hour or so, to get the blistering going nicely on the skin, then turn the oven down. If you find that your pork is beautifully cooked but the crackling is only partway there, you can either whack up the heat again at the end (but only if it's one of the fattier roasting cuts such as shoulder) or slice the crackling off completely and grill it until blistered and beautiful – keeping a close eye, as it can burn easily.

PORK BELLY WITH NOODLES, CORIANDER AND TOMATOES

This pork belly is slow-roasted, then sliced and served in a tasty broth with noodles, tomatoes and crunchy spring onions. You can use the roasting method here for a simple pork belly roast to be served just as it comes. Serves 4–6

1kg piece free-range bone-in pork belly, cut from the thick end, skin scored

8–12 spring onions, trimmed, tops reserved

4 garlic cloves, sliced

1 finger-sized piece of root ginger, thinly sliced

1 medium-hot red chilli, roughly chopped

A large bunch of coriander, stalks removed and reserved

Finely pared zest of 1 large lime, plus some of the juice

A pinch of sugar

Tamari or soy sauce, to taste

2–3 nests of dried egg noodles (about 200g)

A drop of rapeseed or sesame oil

200g cherry tomatoes

A pinch of sugar

Sea salt and black pepper

First remove the bones from the pork: starting in the thickest corner, use a sharp meat filleting knife to make a cut immediately under the ribs. Keeping the knife tight to the underside of the bones, work carefully and slowly down from the corner, gradually releasing the ribs from the meat until you can remove them, all in one piece.

Cut between the bones to release the individual ribs. Place these in a stockpot with the spring onion tops, garlic, ginger, chilli, coriander stems and lime zest. Pour over 1 litre water and bring to a gentle simmer over a medium heat. Cook for 1½ hours.

Meanwhile, preheat the oven to 220°C/Fan 200°C/Gas 7. Place the boned pork, skin side up, in a suitably sized roasting tin. Season it well with salt and pepper and cook in the middle of the oven for about 30 minutes, or until the skin starts to blister. This is the beginning of your crackling – don't be afraid to give the joint another 5–10 minutes at this high heat to get that blistering going (though do watch that the juices aren't burning).

Now turn the heat down to 150°C/Fan 130°C/Gas 2 and add ½ glass of water to the roasting tin. Cook the pork for a further 3 hours. Add a little more water if you need to during cooking to stop the lovely juices from the pork burning.

Once the stock has simmered for long enough, pass it through a fine sieve into a clean pan. Season with salt, a good pinch of sugar, tamari or soy and lime juice to taste.

Remove the pork from the oven and allow it to rest while you cook the noodles according to the packet instructions. Drain, refresh under cold water, then drain again and toss with the tiniest drop of oil, just to stop them sticking together.

To serve, reheat the pork stock. Remove the crackling from the pork and snap it into pieces (you can give it a final blast under the grill if it's not quite crisp enough). Quarter the tomatoes and slice the spring onions on the diagonal. Tear the pork roughly into pieces.

Divide the shredded pork between large warmed bowl and add the noodles, tomatoes and spring onions. Ladle the hot stock equally into the bowls, and finish with some pieces of crackling and a generous scattering of coriander leaves.

Potatoes

Gill Meller

LATIN NAME
Solanum tuberosum

SEASONALITY
British potatoes are lifted
April–October, and available
from store the rest of the year

SOURCING
heritage-potatoes.co.uk;
thepotatoshop.com

I get just as enthused about a sack of earthy spuds as I do the more glamorous vegetables that find their way into my kitchen. With a home-grown crop available to us all year round, offering cheap-as-chips, belly-filling carbs (not to mention a good dose of vitamin C and potassium), they're an incredibly generous ingredient – and so versatile. We love them in their role as reliable side dishes: baked, mashed, boiled and roasted, but we must not overlook their potential to be major players. Potato gratins, potato-based soups, potato curries, potatoes with pasta – even potato peelings, oiled, seasoned and crisped up in the oven – can be wonderful. We should celebrate our spuds.

Potatoes are so inexpensive, so plentiful, so often used, that it's easy to suspend judgment, buy them from anywhere, store them any old how and not expect too much of them. But potatoes can taste great or disappoint, just like any other veg.

Supermarket potatoes will have been scrubbed, polished and usually sealed in a plastic bag. They are generally fine if you use them straight away, but if stored in their bag, they can sweat and moulder, and start sprouting. Take them straight out of the bag when you get home and transfer them to a fabric or paper sack. Store in a cool, dark, dry place, ideally at 7–10°C. The fridge isn't the best place to keep potatoes – very low temperatures encourage them to turn their starches into sugars. This can result in a wet texture and an unpleasant, sweet taste. When cooked at high temperatures (i.e. fried or roasted), those sugars can also convert into a potentially harmful chemical called acrylamide. So, if for some reason your spuds have been in the fridge, don't make chips with them.

I prefer to buy my spuds from a local grower who can tell me something about their crop – such as the specific variety, and when it was dug. One of the great things about spuds is that many maincrop varieties, if dug at the right time and stored correctly, can actually improve with keeping (this is due to complex changes on the cellular level). I like to buy potatoes that are a bit grubby: a light covering of soil is the best way to keep them fresh. Buy potatoes that are firm, smooth and heavy, without softening, wrinkling, bruising or greening. Spuds start to turn green when they are exposed to light. The green parts contain a substance called solanine, which is a bitter-tasting toxin. In large quantities, it can be harmful, so never use green spuds.

Growing your own spuds is uniquely rewarding – there is something so pleasing about pulling up a plant to discover the pale tubers nestling beneath like earthy jewels. Leave the mainstream spuds, such as 'King Edward' and 'Charlotte', to the commercial growers and concentrate on more specialist, hard-to-find varieties. Early potatoes are particularly worth growing yourself because they crop quickly and are best and sweetest when freshly dug.

Potato 'patio planters' – essentially sturdy bags – are a great idea if you have limited space, and can yield you a decent mini-crop. Otherwise, you'll need a sunny and not frost-prone corner of garden, manured and dug over, into which you can plant 'chitted' (sprouting) seed potatoes, around 30cm apart (a little closer if you want more, but smaller potatoes). Plant earlies in March–April and earth up the stems as they grow, protecting the developing tubers from exposure to light. Guard against slugs and keep the soil moist, and your potatoes will be ready to harvest once their flowers have died back, in June and July.

Potatoes are generally described as either 'floury', 'waxy' or somewhere in between. These terms relate to their texture when cooked, with floury potatoes being more fluffy, dry and mashable, and waxy ones smoother, firmer and better at holding their shape.

While I think the most important quality in a potato is flavour – which is why it's such a good idea to try different varieties to find those you really like – those textural characteristics are very important too.

Waxy salad potatoes don't make great mash, for instance (though they are very good if roughly 'bashed') while floury spuds won't perform well in a dish like Jansson's temptation, where the potatoes are cut into slender matchsticks. For many dishes, either type of potato works but will give different results – in a gratin dauphinoise, for instance, waxy potatoes create a more textured dish while floury ones soften more as they absorb the thickening, garlicky cream.

POPULAR POTATO VARIETIES

Anya A cross between Desiree and Pink Fir Apple, this is a lovely, knobbly, waxy, finger-shaped spud, ideal in salads or lightly roasted. It's in season early, from May.

Belle de Fontenay These early potatoes are an old French variety. Good in July and August, they are deliciously waxy, with a nutty flavour that improves with keeping if they are carefully stored.

Charlotte One of the most commonly available salad varieties, these are waxy and firm, though they lack the lovely, earthy-sweet flavour of Jersey Royals or Pink Fir Apple.

Cornish Earlies Describing the time of harvesting, rather than a specific variety, these are rivals to Jersey Royals. Small and earthy-tasting, they are sometimes sold 'dirty' to protect their fragile skins. They are available as early as late April, and through to early July.

Desiree These red-skinned potatoes have a firm, creamy flesh that mashes beautifully and also roasts and bakes well.

Estima The ubiquitous supermarket spud, these are large, smooth-skinned, mild and inoffensive all-rounders with a texture on the waxy side of centre.

Golden Wonder A really well-flavoured, super-floury spud for great mash and chips.

Jersey Royals These magnificent, buttery, waxy new potatoes are among the first to appear, finding their way to the shops as early as March and being finished by early July. The potatoes are a widely available variety known as International Kidney, but when grown on Jersey carry a PDO (the only British vegetable to do so), recognising their unique status. They are the produce of only a score or so of Jersey farmers, and much of the crop is lifted by hand because the steeply sloping fields in which they grow cannot accommodate tractors. Local seaweed is used as fertiliser.

King Edward Pale-skinned with characteristic tinges of pink, this is the ultimate floury, maincrop spud. It makes superb, fluffy-centred roasties and a magnificent mash.

Marfona A large, slightly waxy potato, this is often sold as a baking potato.

Maris Peer This is from the same breeding programme as 'Maris Piper' (see below), but quite different. Usually it is grown to produce small, round salad potatoes with an excellent flavour. Harvested May–October.

Maris Piper A fluffy, floury variety, rivalling King Edwards for its mashing, roasting and chipping abilities.

Nectar Popular with retailers because it pre-packs well, this firm potato will hold its shape in a curry.

Nicola A superb salad potato – nutty, buttery and sweet. Very easy to use as it holds its shape well, even if subjected to a little over-cooking. Crops from June to August.

Pink Fir Apple Long, knobbly, blush-skinned tuber, which looks more like some alien root than a humble spud. It has a delicious, uniquely waxy, nutty flesh, which is highly prized for salads, and rightly so. I like the fact that these are a maincrop spud – potato salads aren't just for summer.

Ratte A classic, waxy French potato, typically used for salads but also sometimes for a particularly silky *pommes purée*.

Wilja Once a supermarket favourite until it was usurped by Estima, the Wilja has a much better flavour and more robust, slightly waxier texture. It mashes well but also holds its shape nicely in a curry or pasty filling.

Yukon Gold Very popular in the US, this has a fantastic buttery flavour and fluffy flesh. It makes great mash and roasties, as well as superb fries.

P

Cooking perfect new potatoes

'Fresh' is the watchword with tender, thin-skinned little new spuds. Grow them yourself or buy them locally if you can. Earth-covered is fine – a little dirt helps keep them moist and fresh. When you get them home, wash off the bulk of the earth then give the spuds a bit of a scrape with a small knife, or a gentle scrub, to remove any stubborn dirt. In either case, don't damage the surface or you'll open it up to absorb cooking water. And, whatever you do, don't peel them: there is so much flavour in the flesh just below the skin. Cut the potatoes up if they are large, though any below the size of a small egg are best left whole. Put them in a pan of water, add salt and bring to the boil. Simmer for about 7 minutes before you start checking them with the tip of a sharp knife. Very fresh new potatoes cook surprisingly quickly. Test every minute or two until the flesh takes the knifepoint with just the merest hint of resistance, then drain immediately. Lubricate with oil or butter or soured cream, add plenty of salt and pepper and some fresh herbs if possible and off you go.

Slightly later in the season, try roasting larger new potatoes. Keep them in fairly large pieces and coat well in oil and seasoning. Roast at 190°C/Fan 170°C/Gas 5 for around 20–30 minutes until golden and tender, but not overbrowned.

Perfect mash

For mash, you need floury potatoes. Cut them into large chunks, no smaller than a large egg. Bring to the boil in well-salted water and simmer until completely tender when tested with a knife. Drain your potatoes in your largest colander and let them sit in it for several minutes, turning once or twice. This allows water on their surfaces to evaporate – you don't want that water in your mash. Meanwhile, heat some butter and milk in a large pan. The proportion of these ingredients to the potatoes is up to you, but I find 75g butter to 1kg raw potato weight, and 100–200ml whole milk to be about right. You can use other fats – cream or crème fraîche are very good and produce a less sweet mash. Unrefined oils add unique flavours. Try an olive oil mash with white fish, or a hemp oil mash with a spice-encrusted roast chicken.

Now mash your steamed-off spuds into the pan of molten butter and milk, adding plenty of salt and pepper. A potato ricer will give you the smoothest result (rubbing through a sieve does the same, but is rather labour-intensive). A good old-fashioned masher works fine as long as your potatoes are completely tender. Check the seasoning before you serve. A little freshly grated nutmeg can be an excellent addition.

Perfect roasties

The best roasties are made from floury spuds, such as King Edward, and roasted in goose or duck fat, though rapeseed oil is good too. Cut the potatoes into large-egg size pieces, put them in a pan, bring to the boil and cook for just 3–4 minutes, then steam-off as for mash (see above). Meanwhile, preheat the oven to 200°C/Fan 180°C/Gas 6. Heat the fat or oil (3–4 tbsp for 1kg potatoes) in a roasting tray big enough to allow plenty of space for the potatoes to crisp up until very hot.

Rough up the surface of your part-cooked potatoes by putting them back in the saucepan, replacing the lid, adding some seasoning and giving them a vigorous shake. (Or scratch up the surfaces with a fork.) Tip them into the searing hot fat, turn them over in it until well coated and season again. Then roast for 40–50 minutes, turning the potatoes over at least once.

PAN HAGGERTY

50g butter

2 onions, thinly sliced

500g fairly firm-fleshed maincrop potatoes, such as Maris Piper

80g well-flavoured hard cheese, such as mature Cheddar or Northumbrian Berwick Edge, grated

Sea salt and black pepper

The Northumberland take on the delicious combination of potatoes, onions and cheese. Rich and buttery, it's great with a crisp, green salad and some simply cooked pulses. Serves 6 as a side dish

Preheat the oven to 190°C/Fan 170°C/Gas 5. Melt half the butter in a 20–25cm ovenproof frying pan or shallow flameproof casserole over a medium-low heat and fry the onions for about 15 minutes, until soft and golden.

Meanwhile, peel the potatoes and slice them very thinly (use a mandoline or a food processor). Set aside a good pinch of the cheese (about 10g) for the topping.

Scoop the onions out of the pan. Layer a third of the sliced potatoes in the still-buttery pan, then add half the onions and half the cheese. Season well. Repeat the layers, then finish with a final layer of potatoes. Dot the remaining butter and the reserved cheese over the top and season.

Bake for about 40 minutes, until the potatoes are tender all the way through and the top is golden. Serve piping hot.

PAPAS ARRUGADAS

1kg smallish new potatoes

4 tbsp (50g) flaky sea salt

FOR THE GREEN HERB SAUCE

1 garlic clove, chopped

1 tsp ground cumin

A good pinch of salt

2 tbsp white wine vinegar

A small bunch of coriander (about 30g), tough stalks removed, leaves finely chopped

4 tbsp extra virgin olive oil

In the Canary Islands, this dish is served as a tempting nibble. New potatoes are boiled in very salty water, so that a dusting of salt eventually crystallises on their wrinkled ('arrugadas') skins. They are usually accompanied by a piquant sauce, or 'mojo'. The combination is also lovely alongside grilled meat or fish. Serves 4–6 as a starter or side dish

Put the whole potatoes in a large pan with the salt and pour on 1 litre water; it should just cover them. Bring to the boil, put the lid on, reduce to a simmer and cook for 15–20 minutes until the potatoes are completely tender. Drain away most of the water from the pan, leaving just 5mm covering the base.

Return the potatoes to the heat and cook gently, uncovered, for another few minutes, shaking from time to time, until the water has evaporated and the potatoes are dry and have developed a dusty coating of salt. Take off the heat and leave for 5 minutes or so. The skin of the potatoes should wrinkle slightly (some varieties do so more than others).

Meanwhile, make the sauce. Put the garlic into a large mortar along with the cumin and a good pinch of salt. Pound to a paste with the pestle. Stir in the vinegar, then add the chopped coriander and pound again to a paste. Slowly stir in the oil until you have a thick, herby dressing. (Alternatively, you can make this sauce in a blender.)

Serve the potatoes warm with the sauce either spooned over them, or served alongside for dipping.

P

Pouting

LATIN NAME
Trisopterus luscus

ALSO KNOWN AS
Pout, bib

SEASONALITY
Avoid March–April when spawning

HABITAT
Common in British inshore waters

MCS RATING
2–3

REC MINIMUM SIZE
21cm

MORE RECIPES
Black bream with Jerusalem artichoke purée (page 91); Coley with bacon, apples and hazelnuts (page 197); Cod with fennel, capers and tomatoes (page 194); Pollack with courgettes and cannellini beans (page 484); Crumbed whiting goujons with curried egg tartare (page 673)

SOURCING
goodfishguide.org

Perky little pouting, with its shimmering pinky-golden coat, is a member of the cod family. And, like all the other members of the cod family that aren't actually cod, it struggles with a lack of status. Pouting really struggles, though. It's so far down the list of white-fish-to-try, that it often falls off it altogether. This is a shame because it's a good eating fish and one that conservation bodies think we should be consuming more of, due to its relative abundance around our coast.

Everything's rather accelerated with the pouting: it lives fast, reaching reproductive age before its second birthday and likely dying before its fifth. And once you've caught one, you have to act swiftly too: its flesh is delicate and if it's been left hanging around after it's reeled in, rather than being cleaned and iced *tout de suite*, it will be soft and mushy. This perhaps accounts for its reputation as a less-than-stellar supper.

But fresh, well-kept pouting is a joy – its tender white flesh as sweet as whiting and a touch more robust in flavour. Pouting is one of the reasons why a cold box of ice (or ice packs) is a must for me when I'm boat-fishing in warmer weather. Gutted and iced on board, then fridged at home at 5°C, a fish that would have been worthless by the end of a sunny fishing trip will keep its charm for 5 days.

A fresh fillet is quite pleasing enough sizzled in butter and served with a squeeze of lemon. But it can also be partnered with more assertive ingredients. Try whole baked pouting in foil, first stuffed to the gills with bay, lemon and garlic. Fillets are fantastically versatile: fried in a pan with chorizo; thickly sliced and dropped into fish stews or curries; or given the egg-and-breadcrumb treatment (or even just egged as below), then fried until golden and served with a tangy tartare sauce.

You can sometimes buy pouting in a fishmonger's – especially close to a harbour where they are landed. Occasionally, it is also sold in supermarkets as a less expensive, more sustainable alternative to cod. Fillets should be firm and still slightly translucent.

HERBED POUTING FISH FINGERS

500g firm pouting fillet, skinned and pin-boned

3 medium eggs

About 3 tbsp finely chopped mixed herbs, such as thyme, parsley and chives

2 tbsp good quality mayonnaise

1 tbsp extra virgin olive or rapeseed oil

2 tbsp plain wholemilk yoghurt

Finely grated zest of 1 lemon

2 tbsp olive or rapeseed oil

Sea salt and black pepper

Lemon wedges, to serve

These crumb-free fish fingers, simply coated in herby beaten egg and served with a mayo dip, are a breeze to rustle up. They also work well with plaice, coley, haddock, whiting or pollack. Serves 4

Cut the fish into thick fingers. Beat the eggs lightly in a bowl, season them well and add half the chopped herbs.

For the dip, mix the mayo with the extra virgin oil, yoghurt, lemon zest and some salt and pepper. Stir in the remaining chopped herbs and transfer to a serving bowl.

Heat a large non-stick frying pan over a medium-high heat and add the 2 tbsp oil. Working in batches if necessary, dip the pieces of fish into the herby egg, then place them in the hot pan and fry for 1–2 minutes on each side until golden and just cooked through.

Pile the crispy herby fish fingers on to a board and serve with the bowl of herby mayo and lemon wedges.

Prawns

LATIN NAME
Coldwater prawn/Northern prawn: *Pandalus borealis*. Common prawn (in British inshore waters): *Palaemon serratus*. Tiger prawn: *Penaeus monodon*. King prawn: *Litopenaeus vannamei*

SEASONALITY
Coldwater prawns: not applicable (usually pre-frozen). Common prawns: spawning period is somewhat variable so difficult to avoid. Farmed prawns: not applicable

HABITAT
Coldwater prawns: widely distributed through the north Atlantic and north Pacific. Common prawns: found in the northeast Atlantic, Black Sea and the Mediterranean; common on the west coast of Scotland and Wales and southwest England; scattered elsewhere around the British Isles

MCS RATING
Coldwater prawn 1–2; common prawn not rated; king and tiger prawns (farmed) 1–5

REC MINIMUM SIZE
Common prawn 8.5cm total shell length

SOURCING
goodfishguide.org; msc.org

A pint of shell-on sweet, succulent prawns in a sun-kissed beer garden with a glug of local cider is yummy. If anything, prawns are too yummy: too easy to eat, in sandwiches, in sushi, or fork-deep in Thai green curry sauce. It's not the eating of them that's the problem. It's the catching or growing of them. The UK is the world's largest importer of prawns, opening our arms to over 400,000 tonnes a year – prawns that are either caught by trawlers or grown in farms in far-off warm places like Thailand and Vietnam.

Trawling for prawns is problematic simply because they are so small, and therefore prawn net mesh-size has to be tiny in order to catch them. Small-meshed netting will catch everything else that swims along with prawns, and so the by-catch can be massive. In some warm water tropical prawn fisheries, the ratio of by-catch to prawn can be as much as 20:1. And often by-catch is simply chucked back into the sea, dead.

There are fisheries for coldwater or Northern prawns in the North Atlantic, where fine specimens are caught and where measures to control by-catch – by fitting release panels to trawl nets – means the ratio of waste-to-prawns is much better. These Atlantic cold-water species, particularly those with MSC certification, are a good choice.

There are also some well-run, small-scale inshore prawn pot fisheries around the British Isles targeting the common prawn. These include the south coast of England, where the local prawns are known as Billy Winters, as well as Cardigan Bay in Wales and the southern and western coasts of Ireland. Using prawn pots (baited, like crab pots, with fishmonger waste), they catch nothing but prawns and, even if a small fish enters a pot, they can be easily released alive. It's a perfectly selective, sustainable method. The prawns are much more tasty and firmer of flesh than imported, trawled prawns. The downside is that they are more expensive.

The big, fat tiger and king prawns we consume so many of are mostly farmed in hot countries, and the farms can have a high impact on the surrounding land and freshwater because of the effluent they release, among other things. Like any farming of carnivorous fish, prawn farming also involves catching, killing and processing wild fish to feed the farmed species. Some would argue that prawn farming is actually the best way forward, if we do it well: the MCS rates organically farmed king and tiger prawns as a responsible choice. We're even starting to farm king prawns in Britain now, in land-based tank systems, which bypass many of the environmental issues of aquaculture. I guess it's not all bad, but I still prefer to avoid buying farmed prawns and treat myself to an occasional expensive pint of pot-caught Billy Winters instead.

DIY PRAWN COCKTAIL

About 250g live prawns

100g good mayonnaise

30g tomato ketchup

½ tbsp Worcestershire sauce

½ tbsp brandy

1 lemon

2–3 handfuls of salad leaves

1 tablespoon extra virgin olive or rapeseed oil

Sea salt and black pepper

If possible use sustainably caught live prawns and a mix of salad leaves. If live prawns are not available use MSC-certified cooked peeled prawns (skipping the boiling). Serves 4 as a starter

Bring a large pan of well-salted water (about 10g salt to a litre) to a rolling boil. Add the prawns and, once the water is boiling again, cook for 1–2 minutes. Drain and allow to cool.

To make the sauce, combine the mayonnaise with the ketchup, Worcestershire sauce and brandy. Season to taste with salt, pepper and a squeeze of lemon juice.

Dress the leaves with a little more lemon juice and the extra virgin oil. Serve the prawns with the sauce and salad, with a plate of buttered brown bread.

Either peel yourself a big pile of prawn tails, spoon on the sauce and then tuck in with gusto or peel one prawn at a time, dipping and devouring repeatedly.

Prunes

Gill Meller

MORE RECIPES
Pak choi with sticky prune sauce (page 427); Slow-cooked turkey legs with bacon and prunes (page 650); Pruney sausage rolls (page 447)

Certain varieties of plum, with an easily detached 'freestone' rather than a 'clingstone', can be dried down to 23 per cent moisture content to become prunes. Usually these days, the dark, rich, dried fruits are then slightly rehydrated before being sold. This makes them a little softer and plumper. They are labelled as 'ready to eat' and don't require soaking before use, as prunes always used to do.

However, steeping prunes in liquid is still often a step worth taking. These fruits are famously rich in fibre and this means they retain moisture, so soaking adds new layers of flavour and makes them particularly luscious. Try bathing them in fruit juice or strong tea – Earl Grey, with its spicy, aromatic nature, is a great prune-plumper. Or, for a treat, soak the fruit in brandy (better still, cider brandy). At room temperature, in unheated liquid, prunes need a good few hours to absorb liquid, but you can speed the process by heating them gently.

Throw soaked prunes into fruit salads or chop them into cake batters. Alternatively, cut out the pre-soaking and add them directly to slow-cooked dishes such as game stews, where they will swell up as everything simmers away.

Prunes' intense and complex sweetness gives them a broad range of affinities, savoury and sweet. A Christmas stuffing, rich with thyme, sage and shallots, is more luxuriant with prunes added, while a chocolate fondant is even better with chopped boozy prunes folded into the mix. At River Cottage, we use organic prunes particularly in winter, when soft fruits are not around but apples and pears are almost overwhelmingly prolific. The crisp bite of an apple has a beautiful affinity with a tender, aged dark prune.

P

The slightly minerally depth of these dried fruits also works well in dark cakes made with wholemeal flour and perhaps treacle. They are great in pulse salads, with roast pumpkin and toasted seeds, or in North African tagines with lamb or goat. Spices such as star anise, cinnamon, cloves and black peppercorns further intensify their flavour. And a prune compote made with spiced tea, sweetened and brightened with honey and orange zest, is particularly good.

Most prune plums are now produced in California, but the traditional centre of production is Southwest France. *Pruneaux d'Agen* are still a gastronomic treat: fleshy, velvety and richly flavoured. As with most dried fruit, however, non-organic prunes often contain preservatives.

Plums notoriously come in gluts and if you have a dehydrator, you can dry freestone plums at home to make your own prunes.

PRUNE, ALMOND AND CARAWAY TART

Soaked in Calvados or brandy, prunes make a luscious pudding component. In this tart, they are paired with an almondy filling, which is spiked with a little ground caraway to create a subtle aniseed tang. You can replace the caraway with a few drops of almond extract if you prefer. Serves 8–10

FOR THE PASTRY
200g plain flour
35g icing sugar
A pinch of salt
125g cold unsalted butter, cut into cubes
1 egg yolk
2–3 tbsp cold milk or water

FOR THE FILLING
250g pitted prunes
100ml Calvados or brandy
1 tsp caraway seeds
150g unsalted butter, softened
150g caster sugar
3 medium eggs, lightly beaten
150g ground almonds
50g plain flour

TO FINISH
Icing sugar, to dust (optional)

Prepare the prunes for the filling in advance. Put them in a saucepan with the Calvados or brandy and heat gently until the liquor is steaming hot, but not simmering, then take off the heat. Tip into a small bowl and leave to soak for 3–4 hours, turning the prunes every now and then. They will absorb nearly all of the liquor and be coated in a glaze.

To make the pastry, put the flour, icing sugar and salt into a food processor and blitz briefly to combine (or sift into a large bowl). Add the butter and blitz (or rub in with your fingers) until the mixture resembles breadcrumbs. Add the egg yolk, and just enough milk or water (about 2–3 tbsp) to bring the mix together into large clumps. Knead the pastry lightly into a ball, wrap in cling film and chill for 30 minutes. Preheat the oven to 180°C/Fan 160°C/Gas 4.

Roll out the pastry to about a 3mm thickness and use to line a 23cm tart tin; leave the excess pastry overhanging the rim of the tin. Prick the base of the pastry with a fork.

Line the pastry case with baking parchment and a layer of baking beans and place on a baking tray. Bake for 15 minutes, then remove the beans and parchment and return the tart case to the oven for about 10 minutes or until the pastry is dry and lightly coloured. Trim away the excess pastry. Leave the oven at 180°C/Fan 160°C/Gas 4.

For the filling, lightly toast the caraway seeds in a dry frying pan for a minute or two until they start to smell fragrant. Leave to cool, then bash to a coarse powder, using a pestle and mortar.

In a large bowl, beat the butter and sugar together until very light and fluffy. Now beat in the eggs, a little at a time. Combine the ground almonds, flour and crushed caraway and carefully fold in.

Spread this mixture in the cooled pastry case. Give the prunes a final stir, then press them into the almond mixture. Bake in the oven for about 40 minutes, until the filling is set and the pastry is golden brown.

Serve the tart warm or cold, dusted with a little icing sugar, if you like.

Puffball, giant

John Wright

LATIN NAME
Calvatia gigantea

SEASON
Late summer–autumn

HABITAT
Not common. Found in pasture, nettle beds and sometimes in woodland with rich soil

Like the hedgehog mushroom, the giant puffball is unmistakeable, and like the parasol, it is visible from a quarter of a mile away. Only small sheep or resting white ducks are likely to cause confusion. Appearing in late summer and autumn, giant puffballs should be picked while still young (about 30cm in diameter), decidedly firm and with the skin dry. After this the pure white flesh softens, goes yellow, then slimy green, then dry, brown and dusty. The fungus is not 'going off', it is maturing and the 'dust' is its spores; leave maturing specimens to their essential reproductive efforts. Even if the field has 30 puffballs in prime condition, do not take more than you can sensibly use as they do not keep well.

Unless you are feeding a crowd, cut the puffball in half, keeping one half in the fridge for another puffball dinner the next day. Peel off the thin skin. The flesh has a texture somewhere between marshmallow and feta cheese.

I am firmly opposed to any giant puffball recipe that involves baking or, worse still, stewing. This fungus is much more suited to the dry environment of the frying pan. As with most fungi, simple cooking is best. To make a giant puffball omelette, cut off thin slices, break them into biscuit-sized pieces and fry on one side in butter until golden. Remove them from the pan, add more butter and let it melt, then return the puffball pieces to the pan and fry the other side before sprinkling with salt and pouring on beaten egg and letting it set.

There are many other species of puffball, all much smaller and none as tasty as the giant puffball. The common puffball (*Lycoperdon perlatum*) is found in vast numbers in woodland and is the best of these small species as far as the cook is concerned. They reach 3cm in diameter, are white, covered in detachable granules and pestle shaped. The flavour is good, but their drawback is that they are difficult to peel. Of course you don't have to peel them; if you like eating chamois leather, you can leave the skin on.

OAT-COATED PUFFBALL WITH SAGE AND PANCETTA

1–1½ tbsp olive or rapeseed oil

4 rashers of pancetta or streaky bacon, roughly chopped

1 egg

2 tbsp milk

10–12 sage leaves

100g porridge oats (not jumbo oats)

4–6 slices of giant puffball (about 10cm in diameter and 2cm thick), skin removed

20g butter

Sea salt and black pepper

For a spicier version of this simple but rather magnificent dish, use small cubes of chorizo instead of the pancetta. You can also replace the sage with a little thyme. Serves 2

Place a large frying pan over a medium heat. Add 1 tbsp oil, then the pancetta or bacon, and cook until it starts to crisp and has rendered some of its fat. Take the pan off the heat, scoop the pancetta or bacon out, leaving some fat in the pan, and set aside.

Meanwhile, beat the egg with the milk and plenty of salt and pepper. Finely chop half the sage and combine it with the oats.

Return the frying pan to a medium heat and add a dash more oil if needed. Dip the slices of puffball first into the seasoned egg and then into the oats, to coat. Gently shake off the excess, then place the puffball slices in the pan. Cook for 3–4 minutes on each side or until golden, then transfer to warmed plates.

Return the pancetta or bacon to the pan, along with the butter and remaining sage leaves. Cook for 1 minute, or until the butter is bubbling, the pancetta is hot and the sage is fragrant. Spoon this butter over the oaty puffball slices and serve.

Pumpkin seeds

Gill Meller

With their generous size and creamy, nutty bite, pumpkin seeds are versatile and can be used in all sorts of recipes, from flapjacks to fajitas, breads to granolas – as well as being delicious, just as they come, as a snack on the go.

Leaf-shaped and greenish-blue, the seeds we buy are hulled. If taken straight from the pumpkin, they have a pale outer husk, though you can eat the husk too if you want to roast your own seeds at home. To do so, separate the seeds from any fibres or pumpkin pulp, give them a thorough wash then pat dry. Toss with oil and seasoning and roast on a baking tray at 180°C/Fan 160°C/Gas 4 for 10–15 minutes until golden and sizzling.

Pumpkins and squash belong to the gourd family, which originates in the Americas. They have been cultivated as a food for several thousand years, and the seeds have long been valued just as highly as the pumpkin's sweet flesh itself. The Mexicans eat them raw, salted, toasted, fried and spiced; they are also used in Mexican salsas, soups, moles, and drinks.

Pumpkins and squashes are grown in huge quantities today, and many just for the seeds. China produces more pumpkin seeds than any other country: varieties such as 'Kakai', which produce close to hull-less seeds, are a popular choice.

Pumpkin seeds are rich in fibre and protein and contain antioxidants, as well as beneficial minerals including zinc, iron and magnesium. Lightly toasting the seeds in a dry frying pan invigorates the flavour and awakens their sweetness. They are lovely tossed with tamari and dried chilli flakes and pan-roasted for a few minutes, or tumbled through a mix of crushed fennel seed, sugar and salt and baked until fragrant. Or, try tossing plain toasted pumpkin seeds in olive oil, salt and lemon juice and scattering them over freshly dressed crab or swapping them for pine nuts in classic pesto recipes.

Velvety green pumpkin seed oil is made by pressing the roasted, hulled seeds. The rich, earthy, intense oil is delicious in salad dressings, adds character when trickled over winter soups (pumpkin soup especially, of course!) and can even be used in, or over, ice cream. It has a low smoke point so it's best left unheated. Styrian pumpkin seed oil, made from a variety of Austrian pumpkin that produces shell-less seeds, has PDO status and is particularly prized for its flavour.

MEXICAN PUMPKIN SEED DIP

Serve this spicy Mexican-style seed-based dip with crudités, such as carrots and cucumber, or scoop and devour on good tortilla chips. Use a milder chilli if you prefer less heat. Serves 6–8

200g pumpkin seeds

1 tsp coriander seeds

2 tsp cumin seeds

350g large, ripe tomatoes, skinned (see page 21)

1 tbsp olive or rapeseed oil

3 garlic cloves, sliced

½–1 habanero chilli, deseeded and sliced

1 medium onion, roughly chopped

Juice of 1 lime

2 tbsp chopped coriander

Sea salt and black pepper

Heat a dry frying pan over a medium heat. Add the pumpkin, coriander and cumin seeds and toast for 2–3 minutes until fragrant and beginning to pop. Transfer to a plate and allow to cool.

In the meantime, roughly chop the tomatoes. Heat a medium frying pan over a medium-high heat. Add the oil, then the tomatoes, garlic, chilli, onion and a little salt and pepper. Cook, stirring regularly, for 10–12 minutes or until soft and beginning to caramelise. Set aside to cool.

Tip the cooled seeds into a food processor and add the cooked tomato mixture. Process until you have a coarse paste.

Transfer to a serving bowl and stir in the lime juice and chopped coriander. Adjust the seasoning with salt and pepper to taste.

Purslane

Portulaca oleracea

SEASONALITY
June–September

This humble little plant – common purslane to give it its full name – has a natural range that spreads all the way from North Africa to Australia, via India. Although it's often viewed as a weed, due to its propensity to grow fast and low, it's been eaten for millennia. The ancient Egyptians, Greeks and Romans were very fond of it and we used to eat it in this country too, but it has been rather lost in the clutter of modern cultivation. It is now absent from the table in all but the most horticultural of households, which is a real shame, though we have pinched its name for other, unrelated plants such as sea purslane (*Halimione portulacoides*) and winter purslane (*Claytonia perfoliata*) because they share its defining characteristics: succulent leaves and an acidic flavour.

Growing your own purslane is easy: it will thrive in even the most neglectful of environments, with the added bonus that as it swiftly covers the ground, it stops other, less tasty weeds getting a foothold. If you don't grow it yourself, you will probably need to get hold of a local salad grower as it's not widely available in the shops. But I promise you it's worth the effort. Its small, shovel-shaped, greyish-green leaves are both succulent and crunchy. The taste mingles acidity and earthiness – somewhere between a salty sorrel and a crisp spinach. In a salad, the leaves offer little pops of natural seasoning, the perfect counterpoint to sweet tomatoes or pungent herbs.

Purslane can be cooked too, though it's mucilaginous, meaning it holds a glue-like substance in its leaves, which becomes evident when heated. This characteristic is sometimes employed to thicken soups or stews but for me, purslane is best lightly wilted, or kept fresh and raw.

Purslane has surprisingly high levels of omega-3 fatty acids. It also contains malic acid (found in apples), which is partly responsible for its lovely, fruity-sour flavour. Purslane picked in the morning tastes best, when its acid levels are highest. The acid turns to glucose through the day, and the leaf is noticeably less zingy in the afternoon.

NEW POTATO, MACKEREL AND PURSLANE SALAD

Purslane's slightly sour, fruity flavour is fantastic in salads. It's a wonderful partner for rich, oily mackerel – although you could use fried herring, or cold, shredded chicken or ham here instead. Serves 4

4 mackerel fillets

A little rapeseed or olive oil

Lemon juice, to taste

500g new potatoes, cooked and cooled

40g purslane leaves

Sea salt and black pepper

FOR THE DRESSING

1 small garlic clove, finely chopped

1 tsp clear honey

1 tsp English mustard

1½ tbsp cider vinegar

4 tbsp extra virgin olive or rapeseed oil

6 spring onions, finely sliced

Season the mackerel fillets with salt and pepper. Heat a thin film of oil in a frying pan over a medium heat. When it is fairly hot, lay the mackerel fillets in the pan, skin side down. Cook for 2–3 minutes until the fillets are almost completely opaque, then turn them over and cook for a minute only, to finish cooking. Spritz with a little lemon juice, then set aside to cool down.

Meanwhile, to make the dressing, whisk the garlic, honey, mustard, cider vinegar and extra virgin oil together in a bowl to emulsify. Season with salt and pepper, then stir through the sliced spring onions.

Cut the cooked new potatoes into bite-sized pieces and put them into a large bowl. Flake in the flesh from the cooled mackerel, checking for any bones as you go. Add the dressing, and mix everything together gently, adding a trickle more extra virgin oil if you think it needs it.

Taste and adjust the seasoning, adding a little more salt or pepper if required. Gently fold the purslane leaves through the salad and it's ready to serve.

Quail

Tim Maddams

LATIN NAME
Common quail: *Coturnix
coturnix.* Japanese quail:
Coturnix japonica

SOURCING
littlewindsor.com;
norfolkquail.co.uk

Quail are a delight to eat – more nutty and full-flavoured than chicken, with little or no gameyness. But the quail story is a fairly sad one. This is the smallest of the game birds to live on our shores, but you won't come across wild British quail for sale as they are currently very rare and the hunting of them is banned. Breeding pairs are on the increase and a few migrate here from parts of Europe where they are more abundant, but this is a struggling species in the wild.

Many quail are farmed, however, particularly on the Continent. Generally speaking, these are Japanese quail, a sub species of the wild quail with a greater tolerance to captivity. Most of the birds are farmed for their little eggs but the birds themselves are easy enough to come by. The problem is that imported quail are often from big, low-welfare units.

The ideal alternative – British quail from a small, free-range farm – doesn't really exist at the moment. Quail do not like the cold or damp and require protection from predators so farming them in a genuinely free-range system is challenging. 'Free-range' quail eggs are available, though even these are likely to come from birds raised in aviaries – albeit, large outdoor ones with grass underfoot. Farming quail successfully for meat or eggs on a larger scale usually means keeping them in sheds. Look for the term 'free to fly', which indicates that the birds, while kept indoors, do at least have space on the ground and above it to forage and fly.

If you do get hold of a responsibly produced local quail or two, one of the best ways to cook them is to roast them simply. Start them on their backs in a hot pan with a little fat, seasoning and a bay leaf or two. Once well coloured on the back, flip them on to each side for a minute or two and then finally give them a minute or two on the breasts before returning them to their backs and popping into a hot oven for 4–5 minutes. Leave to rest for at least 12 minutes before serving.

INDIAN SPICED GRILLED QUAIL

4 quail

2 tsp fenugreek seeds

4 cloves

¼ cinnamon stick

1 tsp dried chilli flakes

1 tsp black peppercorns

Seeds from 6 cardamom pods

6 garlic cloves, grated

1 tsp ground turmeric

Finely grated zest of 1 lemon

2 tbsp rapeseed or virgin
coconut oil

Sea salt and black pepper

These spatchcocked quail are rubbed with an intense paste of freshly ground spices then left overnight to let the flavours penetrate. Grilled until blistered and crisp, they are a sticky, finger-licking treat; you could also barbecue them. Partridges and poussins can be cooked in the same way, increasing the cooking time accordingly. Serves 4

Turn one quail breast side down and, using a pair of kitchen scissors, cut down each side of the backbone and lift the bone away. Turn the quail breast side up and push down on the breast with your hand to open out and flatten the bird. This is 'spatchcocking'. Repeat with the other quail. The backbones can be frozen and added to your next chicken stock.

Toast the fenugreek, cloves, cinnamon, chilli, peppercorns and cardamom in a small dry frying pan over a medium heat for 1–2 minutes until fragrant. Blitz the spices in a spice mill or crush them with a pestle and mortar until quite finely ground. Combine the ground spices with the garlic, turmeric, lemon zest, oil and a good pinch of salt.

Place the spatchcocked birds in a large dish and rub the spice paste all over them. Cover and leave to marinate in the fridge for 12 hours, or overnight.

When ready to cook, preheat the grill to high. Place the quail on a grill tray, breast side up, and grill for 8–10 minutes. Turn on to the other side and grill for a further 5–6 minutes; the juices should run clear. Remove the quail to a warmed platter, turning them breast side up again; brush over any pan juices. Cover and leave to rest in a warm place for 10 minutes. The quail are delicious served with flatbreads, roughly mashed avocado and plain yoghurt.

Q

Quince

Mark Diacono

LATIN NAME
Cydonia oblonga

SEASONALITY
October–December

MORE RECIPES
Partridges roasted with quince and bacon (page 440)

SOURCING
claybarnquinces.co.uk

I'd like to doff my cap to Edward I, for it was he who helped the quince across the Channel on its long journey from Asia to our islands. We owe him much. Quince are one of the great consolations for mid-autumn's shortening days and dipping temperatures. These firm, pear-like fruit are harvested in October, and can be stored for about a couple of months thereafter. Get them while you can. They're not easy to find, but are well worth seeking out. Specialist greengrocers and markets or online food suppliers are your best bet, or small local growers and farm shops.

The fruit can look like anything from a small pear to an almost-spherical baseball and, although hard and unpromising when picked, quinces reveal their finer qualities when shown a little warmth and patience. Once indoors, they turn increasingly yellow. Their soft, downy covering falls away and they release the most fabulous sweet perfume – a single, ripening fruit can fill the room. It's worth finding a few for this alone. The scent also tells you they're ready to use.

For most quince recipes, peeling and coring is necessary. It requires caution: a sharp knife and even keener attention is needed as the flesh is very hard. Take your time; a full complement of fingers is the preferred outcome. Once peeled, cored and quartered, submerge the fruit in water acidulated with lemon juice to prevent discolouring. From here, your options are many.

Poached quince is a wonderful thing, and provides a springboard for any number of delicious preparations. For the simplest option, put 4 peeled, quartered and cored quinces in a pan with 150g sugar or 100g honey and enough water to cover. Alternatively, try using cider or white wine to make up some or all of the poaching liquid. Simmer until tender, checking frequently – quince can take anything from 15 minutes to 1½ hours until they'll take the point of a knife. Add spices or aromatics as you see fit (see recipe overleaf). A little lemon or orange juice doesn't go amiss either.

Once poached, the fruit and liquid will have turned a gorgeous rosy pink. Take the fruit out of the liquor: you can then either reduce it over a medium-high heat to make a syrup to serve with the poached fruit (along with a little cream and/or chocolate sauce), or roast the quinces in a fairly high oven, basting with a little of the liquid, to lightly caramelise them. The result is subtly but delightfully different to poaching.

Don't waste any of that fragrant liquid: frozen, then scratched into crystals with a fork, it makes for an incredible granita, especially if wine or cider has played a part in its making (reduce the liquor a little first to intensify it, if you like). The quince peelings can also be gently simmered in a solution of equal weights sugar to water, creating the most wonderfully aromatic, fruity syrup that insists on being diluted with three parts sparkling wine and drunk in haste.

Quince is as much a spice as a fruit. A little can lift other ingredients beautifully: just a few thin slices added to an apple pie, crumble or compote bring that characteristic warmth, colour and flavour without overpowering the apple, and poached quince in place of the traditional apricots in a lamb tagine may even top the original.

Membrillo, quince paste, quince cheese – they're all the same thing – is a must-make recipe. Poach cored and chopped (but unpeeled) quinces in water. Once soft, pass the fruit through a sieve or mouli to exclude the skin (which will have imparted its pectin) and create a smooth purée. To this, add an equal weight of caster or granulated sugar and cook over a moderate heat. Don't let the heat get too high or it will spit molten sugar at you. Cook, stirring constantly, until you can draw a spoon across the base of the pan and the paste pauses before closing over the spoon's path.

Grease a shallow tin and pour in the purée to a 1–3cm depth. Allow to set overnight. Turn the quince paste out of the tin and cut it into pieces, coating each with caster sugar. It's delightful with game, salty meats and blue cheese as well as the classic salty sheep's cheese Manchego, but also pretty good just as a sweet nibble with coffee.

Quince were commonly grown here until a century or so ago, when our love for softer, sweeter, more immediately edible fruit – especially pears and apples – took over. Thankfully, quince are easy to grow for yourself. I've never eaten a variety that tasted distinct from others, but 'Krymsk' and 'Leskovac' (occasionally spelt with the odd stray 'z') are perhaps a little hardier than the rest, for those in more northerly or exposed locations. Never making huge trees, quinces are available on a range of rootstocks, including true dwarf rootstocks, keeping their size to 1.4m tall – perfect for a large pot on a balcony. They are self-fertile, so a single tree will produce fruit. If you're picking your own, don't wait for any hint of softness in the fruit: they should be harvested firm, just as the skin yellows from pale apple green.

QUINCE IN STAR ANISE AND HONEY SYRUP

Finely pared zest and juice
of 1 small orange

4 star anise

12 black peppercorns

4 bay leaves

100g granulated sugar

3 tbsp clear honey

4 quince (about 800g in total)

These sweetened quince are very versatile. Submerged in their syrup, they will keep for several weeks in the fridge and can be served cold with pheasant or pork, or warmed gently and eaten with custard or yoghurt. You can even drop a chunk into your favourite fruit smoothie. Bay, peppercorns and star anise work beautifully here, but you could use other spices such as cloves, cinnamon, cardamom and fennel. Makes 2 x 500ml jars

Put the orange zest and juice, star anise, peppercorns, bay leaves, sugar, honey and 300ml water in a large, wide pan. Set over a medium heat and bring to a gentle simmer, stirring to dissolve the sugar and honey. Meanwhile peel, quarter and core the quince.

Carefully place the quince in the simmering, fragrant liquor. They should be in a single layer – add a splash more water if necessary to just cover the fruit. Cook very gently until tender: anything from 15 minutes to 1½ hours, depending on the variety of quince and the ripeness of the fruit. If your quince cook very quickly and are in danger of collapsing, remove them from the pan as soon as they are soft. If, on the other hand, you have slow-cooking quince, you may need to top up the cooking liquor with a little hot water to keep them submerged during the lengthy cooking time.

Meanwhile, sterilise a couple of sealable 500ml jars, such as Kilner jars, by washing them in hot soapy water, rinsing well, then putting them upside down on a baking tray in a very low oven (at 120°C/Fan 100°C/Gas ½) to dry and warm up.

Pack the hot, tender quince quarters neatly into the warm jars. Pour over the hot fruity liquor – which must completely cover the fruit – then seal the jars immediately. Once cooled, store in the fridge and use within 4–6 weeks. Once opened, store in the fridge and eat within a week or so.

Q

Quinoa

Gill Meller

LATIN NAME
Chenopodium quinoa

MORE RECIPES
Minted spelt and tomato salad
(page 386)

SOURCING
britishquinoa.co.uk;
hodmedods.co.uk

Quinoa is a small, South American seed with a big profile. Originally pronounced *keen-wah*, the name is now often anglicised to *quin-oah*. It is eaten like a grain but is naturally gluten-free, so it makes a great alternative to wheaty options such as couscous and bulgar. The staple diet of the Incas for thousands of years, quinoa offers protein of an unusually high quality for a plant food, containing good amounts of all the essential amino acids. It's also a better source of minerals than most grains – particularly iron, magnesium and zinc – and richer in B vitamins and folate.

However, the increasing popularity of this 'superfood' around the world has led to rising prices in its original territory, the Andes. This might be good for quinoa farmers but the price of the crop has rocketed so much that many local people can no longer afford this nourishing seed themselves. Fortunately, there is an alternative – some enterprising farmers are now growing quinoa in Britain.

Quinoa has an unusual, nutty texture, a slightly sweet, seedy flavour and an interesting appearance: the cooked seeds unfurl a little 'tail'. White quinoa is the most common variety but you also get red and black types. It can be sold as flakes, which can be made into porridge or stirred into cakes and biscuits; it also makes an especially nourishing flour. If you're avoiding gluten altogether, check your quinoa is guaranteed gluten-free as, like some grains, it can be 'contaminated' by proximity to other foods during processing.

The seeds have a coating of saponins – naturally occurring substances which are bitter and soapy-tasting. Sometimes this outer layer is removed during processing but it's always a good idea to rinse the seeds thoroughly before cooking anyway.

Quinoa doesn't need pre-soaking. Cook it in about three times its volume of water or stock for 10–12 minutes, until tender. Drain and leave it to sit for 5 minutes or so after cooking so excess moisture can evaporate.

Quinoa is a great vehicle for other flavours. It works brilliantly in salads, carrying the taste of the dressing – try it with roasted pumpkin, apples and tarragon. And it's a great alternative to couscous in tabbouleh or as a more nutritious alternative to rice. You can also incorporate it, once cooked, into breads, flapjacks and other treats.

QUINOA WITH CUMIN-ROASTED ROOTS AND PARSLEY

500g small carrots, scrubbed and halved lengthways

500g small beetroot, scrubbed and quartered

1 large onion, peeled and cut into thin wedges

2 tsp ground cumin

Finely grated zest and juice of 1 lemon

4 tbsp olive or rapeseed oil

1 tbsp clear honey

200g quinoa

Leaves from a small bunch of flat-leaf parsley, chopped

Sea salt and black pepper

Earthy roots, sweet onion and nutty quinoa make this a highly comforting and colourful dish. You could use couscous in place of quinoa – cook it as per the recipe on page 202 but without the spices and seasonings. Serves 6–8 as a side dish, 4–6 as a main

Preheat the oven to 190°C/Fan 170°C/Gas 5. Put the carrots, beetroot and onion into a roasting tray. Add the cumin, lemon zest and half the oil. Season with salt and pepper and toss together. Roast for 40–50 minutes, turning occasionally, or until the veg are tender when pierced with the tip of a knife, and starting to caramelise at the edges. Trickle over the honey and set aside to cool.

Meanwhile, cook the quinoa. Rinse it thoroughly, drain and then put into a pan and cover with plenty of cold water – about 3 times the volume of the quinoa. Bring to the boil, then simmer for about 10 minutes until the grains are tender.

Drain the quinoa well, leave in the sieve for 5 minutes and then tip into a large bowl. Add a little salt and pepper and a trickle of oil and toss well. Leave to cool completely.

Tip the quinoa into the tray of cooled roots along with the lemon juice, remaining oil and chopped parsley. Tumble everything together, taste for seasoning and serve.

Rabbit

LATIN NAME
Oryctolagus cuniculus

SEASONALITY
All year round; best late
summer to winter

HABITAT
Common and widespread

MORE RECIPES
Roasted chilli mole (page 173);
Pheasant pie (page 468); Rabbit
ragu with tarragon (page 633);
Braised rabbit with turnips
(page 652); Chicken and cider
stew with rosemary dumplings
(page 617); Squirrel and beans
on toast (page 608)

SOURCING
tasteofgame.org.uk

Before I tell you what a delicious, wholesome and versatile meat rabbit is, I want to make it clear that I am talking exclusively about the wild creature. I don't consider farmed rabbit to be the same – and I don't view it as an acceptable choice, either. Most of the farmed rabbit sold in the UK comes from the Continent, from animals kept in cages and fattened on pelleted feeds. It's a cruel system that produces flabby, flavourless flesh. The meat is also paler, and the animals larger, than wild rabbit – so it's fairly easy to spot. Even if conditions were better, farming rabbit seems like folly to me when we have healthy, wild rabbit – not just plentiful but often troublesomely over-abundant.

Wild rabbit has the depth of flavour that all grass-fed wild meat shares – and is also readily and cheaply available. Even if you're ordinarily a little shy of game, rabbit is a great entry-level ingredient, more delicate than much other wild flesh, with a comfortingly chickeny texture.

Yet rabbit still only bobs about on the fringes of even the most committed carnivorous diet. This is, no doubt, partly down to mawkishness ('but they're so cute') though it can't be the whole story. Lambs and chicks and even piglets are just as endearing and we don't seem to have much trouble eating them. A more profound issue, I think, is that non-farmed meat is increasingly an anomaly in our diets. Many of us are distrustful of food that has not been manipulated and processed in some industrial system. But that's the wrong way round, surely?

It's certainly true that wild rabbit offers a different experience to farmed flesh. There's not a lot of lard on a bunny and you shouldn't expect it to be super-succulent. But if you add a little supplementary fat, you can render it tender and moist as well as flavourful. Streaky bacon or pancetta goes into most of my rabbit stews, but liquid lubrication works well too: consider yoghurt, cream or coconut milk.

If I find myself with a rabbit that I'm sure is still in the first flush of youth, I often roast it. Wrapped in streaky bacon and given a fast, hot blast in the oven, it can be wonderful. But my default way of cooking this animal is slow and low, in some kind of a stew. Keeping it at a tremulous simmer is the safest way to save the meat from dryness and toughness. Check on it several times: some rabbit is tender in an hour, but an older animal can take two, sometimes more.

As with any shot animal, you must look out for the little balls of lead shot and bits of sharp bone in the meat. Alternatively, try one of the many recipes – such as a rabbit pie – that calls for jointed pieces of rabbit to be cooked, then the meat stripped off the bones. I often do this when I've stewed a rabbit and want to make a family-friendly meal of it. The picked-over meat goes back in the lovely sauce and my stew becomes a ragu – very often served with pasta, or mash, or, most agreeably, wet polenta. And once in a while I like to whittle the rabbit meat off the bones before cooking, mince it, mix with some decent sausagemeat and use it to make bunny burgers – just delicious.

Technically, rabbit is vermin, rather than game (it's a great nuisance to farmers, especially market gardeners trying to grow vegetables) and there is no closed season for it. However, I avoid rabbit between March and July when the does are likely to be carrying or feeding young. I particularly like rabbits shot in the early autumn, which are usually pleasingly plump from their summer grazing.

There are various ways to acquire rabbit, including shooting it yourself. That is something you should only undertake with an appropriate gun, certification, permission and knowledge of the area you're shooting in – not to mention a reasonable level of skill with the weapon you are using. A quicker way is to order rabbit from a butcher or game dealer, and there are lots of good online sources of wild rabbit these days too. You can buy the whole animal 'in the fur', or you can ask for a skinned, de-headed carcass, or choose a rabbit that has already been cut up into joints.

The advantage to skinning the rabbit yourself is that it's much easier to judge the age when the creature is still entire. And age has a significant effect on tenderness. With a young rabbit, you should be able to tear the ears fairly easily, and the claws should be smooth and sharp. Young 'uns are also much easier to skin than a big old buck or doe, for whom you will have to apply some strength to prise the skin away.

Preparing a rabbit

Rabbits should be gutted as soon as they are killed. If you've shot the rabbit yourself, the first thing you should do is empty its bladder so urine cannot taint the meat. Turn the rabbit on its back and apply pressure between its hind legs, over the bladder, to release what may be quite a considerable quantity of liquid. Then, make a long cut with a very sharp knife – just through the skin – from the urinary tract up to the base of the breast bone. Pull out the stomach and intestines. Discard the lungs but keep the heart, kidneys and liver. Rinse the cavity as soon as you get to a stream or a tap.

To skin the animal, first cut off all four feet, above the 'knees'. Lay the rabbit on its back and make a slit across the belly and the tops of the thighs. Pull the skin down and off the legs like a pair of tights. Then turn the rabbit over, get a good grip on the skin and pull it down towards the head as far as it will go. Ease out the front legs. Cut off the head (skinned, this can be used in stock).

To joint the rabbit, cut between the ball and socket joints that connect the rear legs to the hips and remove the legs. Cut off the front legs behind the shoulder muscles. Cut away the thin flaps of meat that join the ribs to the belly (keep these for cooking, or for stock). Chop off the thin, bony section of ribcage from the body (again, good for stock), then cut the remaining meaty 'saddle' into two pieces.

RABBIT WITH ANCHOVIES, ROSEMARY AND CREAM

1 rabbit, jointed

8–10 anchovy fillets in oil

2 medium onions, thinly sliced

3 garlic cloves, finely chopped or grated

1 medium-hot red chilli, deseeded and sliced

1–2 bay leaves, torn

3–4 sprigs of rosemary

200ml double cream

Sea salt and black pepper

Salty, sweet anchovies work well in this rich dish, rounding out the flavour without being overpowering or fishy. You can also make it with a couple of plump squirrels. Serves 2–4

Put the rabbit pieces on a plate, trickle over 2 tbsp of the oil from the anchovies and season well with salt and pepper. Turn the rabbit pieces over in the oil and seasoning. Heat a flameproof casserole dish over a medium heat, add the rabbit pieces and brown them well all over. Remove the rabbit and set aside.

Add the onions to the casserole, with a splash more oil if needed. Cook gently for about 8 minutes until they begin to soften, then add the garlic and chilli and cook for a further few minutes. Return the rabbit pieces to the pan, along with any juices that have seeped from them. Add 800ml water, the bay leaves and rosemary and bring to a simmer. Put a lid on the pan but leave it slightly ajar to allow some steam to escape. Turn the heat down low and cook for about an hour, until the rabbit is beginning to feel tender.

Add the cream and cook, uncovered, for a further 30–45 minutes or until the rabbit is completely tender. The sauce should have reduced to a nice coating consistency. If it's not quite there, remove the rabbit to a warm dish and simmer the sauce until it has thickened, then return the rabbit to the casserole. Add the anchovy fillets and check the seasoning.

Serve with sauté potatoes and a green salad.

Radicchio

Nikki Duffy

LATIN NAME
Cichorium intybus

ALSO KNOWN AS
Chicory

SEASONALITY
November–March

MORE RECIPES
Roasted chicory with honey, mustard and thyme (page 166); Grilled cheese salad with bullace compote (page 105); John Dory with creamed radicchio (page 318); Endive with chicken livers and bacon (page 250); Venison salad with apple, celeriac and hazelnuts (page 660)

A form of chicory, this startling red and white leaf is as fantastic to eat as it is stunning to look at. Its pure white stems, thick at the bases, extend their snowy, branch-like veins into glossy, deep maroon leaves. These good looks – the result of the radicchio heads being blanched in dark sheds – are reason alone to use this leaf in a salad. But the flavour is also exceptional. Radicchio offers a wonderful thing: refined bitterness. If it is seasoned and dressed well, that sharp edge becomes quite delectable.

Although, of course, you can grow it yourself, radicchio is classically an Italian ingredient and different varieties bear the names of various towns in the Veneto, where it is produced. The finest, 'Radicchio Rosso di Treviso', has slender leaves and an amazing, full, bitter, nutty flavour. The earlier variety, 'Precoce', forms a tight, bullet-shaped head while the later, highly prized 'Tardivo' (illustrated right) has distinctive, narrow leaves that are much more separate on the plant. 'Radicchio rosso di Verona' is rounder, and mild 'Chioggia' is rounder still, looking rather like a cabbage. There is also an almost all-white variety, 'Castelfranco', that looks like a big, blowsy rose.

In season from November to early spring, radicchio is the perfect counterpoint to rich, cold-weather foods: fatty meats, bubbling gratins and roasted roots. It is exquisite paired with salty ingredients, such as olives, bacon or cheese, and it enlivens starchy foods such as bread, potato and pasta. Roughly torn and dressed sparingly with a little olive oil and salt, you can serve it up as a side dish just as it comes. In Italy, they often just trickle it with hot lard and a splash of vinegar. But a radicchio salad can be quite special: try tossing the shredded leaves with mozzarella and smashed black olives, sprinkle with chopped parsley and trickle with a dressing made with olive oil, orange juice and a little balsamic vinegar. Radicchio and blue cheese is another stunning combination, especially if dressed with oil, salt and honey and served with sourdough.

But radicchio takes well to cooking too. Heat dulls its colour to a reddish-brown, but the flavour stays strong. As you might expect, it's the Italians who have all the best ideas: quartered whole radicchios, fried until caramelised and tender, then topped with Taleggio cheese and whacked under a hot grill; wilted and stirred into pasta with bacon and garlic; or worked through a red-wine-stained risotto with lots of Parmesan.

ROAST POTATOES WITH RADICCHIO AND CHEESE

This is an amazingly easy and delicious all-in-one lunch or supper. It also works brilliantly with 2–3 heads of chicory or a big head of endive. Serves 6 as a side dish or 4 as a main

1.5kg largish, not-too-floury potatoes, such as Desiree or Marfona

1 large or 2 small heads of radicchio

2 garlic cloves, thickly sliced

Leaves from 2 sprigs of rosemary

Leaves from 3 sprigs of thyme

4 tbsp olive oil

5–6 tbsp crème fraîche

100g mature hard cheese, such as Cheddar, Shipcord or a good Lancashire, grated

Sea salt and black pepper

Preheat the oven to 200°C/Fan 180°C/Gas 6.

Peel the potatoes and cut them into similar-sized pieces – halves or quarters, depending on size. Put into a pan, cover with water and add a pinch of salt. Bring to the boil and par-cook for 10 minutes. Drain the potatoes and leave them to steam in a colander for a few minutes. In the meantime, halve, core and roughly shred the radicchio.

Transfer the potatoes to a roasting tray and scatter the radicchio, garlic, rosemary and thyme over them. Trickle all over with the olive oil and season well with salt and pepper. Tumble everything together and bake for 25–30 minutes or until the radicchio is wilted and the potatoes are beginning to crisp a little.

Take the tray from the oven, dot the crème fraîche over the potatoes and radicchio and scatter with the cheese. Return to the oven for 10 minutes or until the cheese is melted and bubbling. Serve straight away.

Radishes

Gill Meller

LATIN NAME
Raphanus sativus

SEASONALITY
April–September

MORE RECIPES
Raw asparagus and radish salad
(page 36)

The radish is one of those garden vegetables that signify a shift in the culinary year. Asparagus arrives, the elderflower comes out and then, after all the browns and greys of winter, there's the bright red of the radish. But I think lots of people don't appreciate quite how good these little roots can be, perhaps because those on sale in supermarkets are usually rather dull.

The first rule of radishes is that they should be very fresh: a just-picked, home-grown bunch will be juicy, crunchy and peppery. Keep the fresh roots in a half-full jug of water in the fridge and they will remain crisp, and the edible leaves vibrant, for 4 or 5 days.

The best way to enjoy such tip-top radishes is to take them cold from the fridge and serve them on a plateful of ice. The chill emphasises their bite and offers a satisfying contrast to the peppy, hot flavour (which lies mainly in the skin). Smear the radishes with softened unsalted butter and then dip into good flaky sea salt, or serve with an anchovy and caper sauce, perhaps alongside some other early summer crudités such as slim, raw asparagus and the first baby carrots. Raw and grated, radishes also work well stirred into a raita of yoghurt, with chopped mint and coriander.

Less-than-sparkling radishes are not a disaster, however: cook them in soups and sautés or throw them into Asian-style stir-fries with chilli, garlic, a little lime and coriander and other quick-cook crunchy veg such as sugarsnap peas.

If you plant radish seeds throughout the spring and summer, you'll have a steady supply of this characterful little root – and they'll be ready, seed to plate, in just 4 weeks. I even like to use thinned-out radish seedlings as fresh little garnishes. The slightly elongated 'French Breakfast' variety is very good, as is 'Pink Beauty'. Just water your radishes well so they swell up, rather than dry out and bolt.

The radish comes in many colours – white, pink, purple and black – and many sizes, including larger autumn-harvest varieties and long Asian daikon or mooli radishes. But there is always something special about those first little globes of the year: the perky, pinky-scarlet harbingers of summer food.

RADISHES WITH CHICKEN LIVERS AND LOVAGE

250g free-range or organic
chicken livers

1 garlic clove, thinly sliced

Finely grated zest of ½ lemon

1 tbsp olive oil, plus extra for
frying

12 small firm radishes, with tops
if available

3 tbsp double cream

1 tsp chopped lovage

Sea salt and black pepper

Tender chicken livers and crunchy radishes work superbly together. The lovage adds a warming, spicy edge – but you could use a blend of finely chopped celery leaves and parsley if you don't have any. Serves 2

Trim the chicken livers and cut any larger ones in half. Put the livers in a bowl with the garlic, lemon zest, olive oil and some salt and pepper. Stir together, then leave to stand for 5–10 minutes.

Meanwhile, halve the radishes and give them a quick wash (set aside the leafy tops, if you have them). Heat a large frying pan over a high heat, add a dash of oil followed by the radishes, and cook for 1 minute, tossing regularly.

Now add the chicken livers in an even layer. Cook for 4 minutes, turning 2 or 3 times. Add the cream and lovage, along with any saved radish leaves, and bring up to a simmer. Cook for 1–2 minutes until the cream has thickened. The livers should be still a little pink inside, but not bloody or raw-looking.

Spoon the mixture on to warmed plates and serve at once, with bread and salad leaves.

R

Raisins, sultanas & currants

Pam Corbin

Sweet, succulent and wholesome, raisins, sultanas and currants are simply grapes preserved by drying. And this is still done, largely, via the age-old method of leaving the fruit in the sun.

The term 'raisin' is sometimes used to refer to any type of dried grape, but in the UK we generally distinguish between the types. Currants, the smallest of the vine fruit bunch, have nothing to do with fresh currants, but are dried black seedless 'Zante' grapes and come mainly from Greece. Their charm is in their dense, chewy texture and intense, black-grape flavour, which is best appreciated in baking.

With some exceptions, such as sticky 'Lexia' raisins which are made from 'Muscatel' grapes, raisins and sultanas come from the same type of grape. These days, that's usually the white 'Thompson Seedless'. The difference is in how they are dried. Raisins are left in the sun for longer, which gives them their dark colour and rich, almost toffeeish flavour. Sultanas are pre-treated by being dipped in a solution of alkaline potassium carbonate. This 'breaks', or splits, the skins, allowing the fruit to dry more quickly, hence their juicy succulence, lighter colour and slightly fruitier flavour. Raisins and sultanas are, however, more or less interchangeable in recipes.

The moisture content of grapes needs to be reduced by around 75 per cent to ensure that the natural sugars are sufficiently high to preserve the fruit, so raisins, sultanas and currants are packed with concentrated fructose and glucose. Light to carry and with a lengthy shelf-life, it's no wonder they have helped fuel some of the world's most significant journeys: they traversed the Alps with Hannibal; journeyed with Christopher Columbus across the Atlantic; were rations on Peary's North Pole expedition; and have fired up astronauts in outer space. Today, they're still regarded as a great energy-boosting snack.

Vine fruits are available as a single variety or they can be bought ready mixed for cake-making. Look out for Fairtrade and/or organic options in health food stores and supermarkets. Very light, bright-looking fruits, such as 'golden' or 'crimson' sultanas, may have been processed with the preservative sulphur dioxide. Some vine fruits also contain potassium sorbate. To make them aesthetically pleasing and prevent them clumping together, most dried vine fruits (including organic varieties) are sprayed with vegetable oil – usually sunflower.

Vine fruits, even the more succulent kinds, often benefit from being plumped up a little before use. This is particularly true in salads and slaws, and in baking. You'll find some cakes, such as bara brith (Welsh teabread) or boiled fruit cakes, incorporate plumping-up as part of the recipe. Otherwise, it's never a bad idea to soak the fruit in something delicious beforehand, such as fruit juice or booze. However, you can add lusciousness by simply dunking the fruits in hot water for 5–10 minutes, then lightly tossing them in a sieve to drain them before using.

For rich fruit cakes, my favourite way of reviving dried vine fruits is to put them in an ovenproof dish with orange juice or whisky (or both), cover, then warm in a low oven at 130°C/Fan 110°C/Gas ½ for about 30 minutes. Alternatively (and this needs a bit of forethought) soak them overnight in a warm room.

Sometimes fruit sinks to the bottom in a cake batter. It shouldn't happen if the batter is thoroughly mixed and thick enough to hold the fruit, but you can help prevent it by tossing the fruit in a little of the recipe's flour before adding them (this also helps to distribute the fruit evenly throughout the batter). If you're going do to this, however, it's best not to soak the fruit first or they'll end up coated in a gluey mess.

Ideal storecupboard standbys, vine fruits are called into service for classic Welsh cakes and rock cakes, and to perk up plain scones, flapjacks or yeasty bread dough. At Christmas, they feature in figgy pudding, stollen, Christmas cake and mincemeat.

Give baked eating apples – 'Cox' or 'Russets' – a festive twist by peeling and coring, then stuffing with sultanas and chopped marzipan. Lightly toss the whole apples in cinnamon and sugar before baking at 180°C/Fan 160°C/Gas 4 for 35–40 minutes or until soft. Serve with brandy butter or rum and raisin ice cream.

A few raisins added to cereal or muesli makes breakfast more wholesome. Or try this warming porridge that can be mixed up the night before and quickly cooked for early risers: put 50g porridge oats, 250ml water or milk, 1 tbsp raisins or sultanas, 1 small, finely chopped apple and a big pinch of cinnamon in a saucepan. Cook over a gentle heat for 4–5 minutes until thick and creamy and the raisins are plump. This is enough for one gargantuan portion or two smaller ones.

Vine fruits play a wonderful part in savoury dishes too. Their sweetness and fragrance pair marvellously with nuts, spices and herbs to elevate simple starches – rice, couscous, semolina – into more nutritious meals. They add a lovely sweetness to a crunchy coleslaw: in a large bowl, whisk together 150ml soured cream, 2 tbsp lemon juice and 1 tsp toasted caraway or cumin seeds. Add 500g finely sliced green cabbage, 6 finely chopped spring onions, a couple of grated carrots and 100g raisins. Toss together, season and serve.

And, of course, grapes, grains and spices grown in the same locality have long been combined in fantastic dishes, such as spicy pilafs and fragrant tagines.

SPOTTED DICK WITH APPLE-BRANDY RAISINS

125g raisins

4 tbsp Somerset cider brandy (or other good brandy)

A little softened butter, to grease

75g plain flour

75g wholegrain spelt flour

2 tsp baking powder

½ tsp ground mace

75g shredded suet

100g caster sugar

100ml whole milk

1 tsp vanilla extract

Grated zest of 1 large orange

This traditional pudding is given a West Country twist with a little spelt flour and raisins soaked in cider brandy. Serves 4–6

Put the raisins into a bowl, pour on the brandy and leave in a warm place to plump up for at least 4 hours, overnight if possible (or cover and put in a very low oven for 30 minutes).

Generously grease a 1.5 litre pudding basin with butter.

In a large bowl, thoroughly combine the flours, baking powder, mace, suet and sugar; set aside.

Combine the milk, vanilla extract and orange zest. Make a well in the centre of the dry ingredients and gradually stir in the milk mixture, followed by the raisins, stirring until everything is evenly combined. Spoon the mixture into the prepared basin.

Take a double layer of foil or baking parchment and butter one side of it, then fold a large pleat into the centre. Place the foil or parchment, buttered side down, over the pudding and use kitchen string to tie it in place under the rim of the basin. Loop a length of string over the top of the basin, securing it at each side, to form a 'handle'.

Put a trivet or upturned heatproof plate in a large saucepan and stand the basin on it. Pour in boiling water to come about halfway up the side of the basin. Put the lid on and bring to a gentle simmer. Simmer for 1¼ hours, topping up the simmering water if needed.

Take the basin from the saucepan and leave it to stand for 10 minutes before turning out the pud. Serve with thick cream or custard.

R

Rapeseed oil

Hugh Fearnley-Whittingstall

MORE RECIPES
Brazil nut, cacao and orange granola (page 85); Roasted almond aïoli (page 19); Dill salsa verde (page 235); Risi e bisi with pea shoot pesto (page 457)

SOURCING
riverford.co.uk

Drive any distance through the British countryside in May and you'll likely be witness to great vistas of yellow rapeseed in flower. The dazzling blooms have dominated our early summer landscape for decades. Oilseed rape is traditionally grown as a commodity crop, the oil extracted with heat and chemical solvents, then deodorised into a bland, multi-purpose cooking oil, or used in processed foods. The fibre also finds its way into livestock feeds. But that's been changing and, recently, enterprising farmers have learned how to treat their seeds differently and produce from them a high quality, cold-pressed culinary oil.

There is a challenge here. The conventional rapeseed crop has rightly concerned environmentalists because the plant is hungry for fertiliser and demanding of pesticides and herbicides. It's undeniably quite a tall order to produce rapeseed organically in Britain. However, it can be done, as growers such as Stringers in Yorkshire, have proved. I'm one of many who would like to see more organic British rapeseed oil on our shelves – and I'm hopeful this will come to pass, particularly as EU rules suspending the use of groups of pesticides such as neonicotinoids encourage farmers to find alternative approaches to growing this crop.

When I first tried rapeseed oil, a good decade ago, I wasn't prepared for quite how much of a fan I would become. Like many cooks, I'd long been a devotee of olive oil. But I can honestly say that rapeseed is a far more important ingredient for me now.

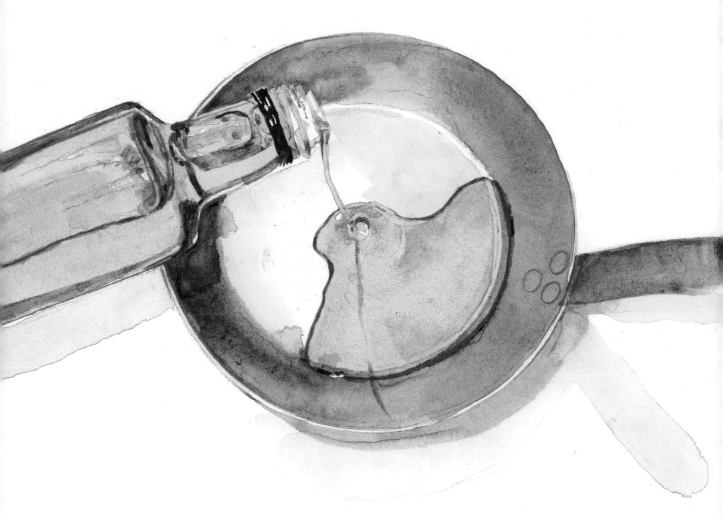

Organic rapeseed is my default oil for trickling on to salads and for mixing into dressings – it is a very good partner to the earthy flavours of root veg such as carrots, parsnips and beetroot. I sometimes use it for cooking if I am looking to bring a bit of flavour to the pan or roasting tray – for example when roasting root veg – while its vibrant yellow colour makes it a striking finishing touch when splashed over hummus, yoghurt dips or soups. Rapeseed oil finds its way into my breads, cakes, scones and pancakes, gets stirred into home-made granola before baking, and I even trickle it on my breakfast toast.

The flavour of rapeseed oil is far more delicate than olive oil, but still distinctive and unique. There can be a slight pungency that lets you know this plant is part of the brassica family, but the predominant notes are sweet, nutty and floral. Experiment: use it anywhere you would normally use olive oil, and I think you will find it grows on you. It has won a place in the hearts, and by the stoves, of many British chefs – you may find it does the same for you.

When tested, cold-pressed British rapeseed oils typically reveal a high smoke point, which makes them a good choice for frying and roasting. They are also high in monounsaturated fat and a source of vitamin E, with a healthy ratio of omega-6 to omega-3 fatty acids.

Look for cold-pressed rapeseed oil, which may also be called 'extra virgin' (though this is a rather vague term in relation to this oil). Cheaper, refined rapeseed oil is also on sale and a great deal of what is sold as generic 'vegetable oil' is rapeseed, also of a highly refined kind. This has some uses – deep-frying, for instance – but it boasts none of the flavour or golden viscosity of the cold-pressed variety.

ROOTS AND FRUITS SALAD WITH RAPESEED DRESSING

Rapeseed's nutty flavour works exceptionally well with root veg, whether cooked or, as here, raw. Serves 4

2 medium oranges

50g raisins or sultanas

120g peeled celeriac

120g carrot (1 large one)

1 medium eating apple

3–4 good handfuls of watercress, tough stalks removed

50g lightly toasted cashews, roughly chopped (optional)

FOR THE DRESSING

3 tbsp extra virgin rapeseed oil

2 tsp English mustard

½ garlic clove, crushed or grated

Sea salt and black pepper

Cut a slice off the top and base of each orange and stand them on a board. Use a sharp knife to slice down, removing the peel and pith in sections. Slice the segments of fruit out from between the membranes, dropping them directly into a bowl. Add the raisins or sultanas, stir and set aside.

For the dressing, whisk the rapeseed oil, mustard and garlic together with some salt and pepper (don't worry if the mustard doesn't blend completely). Pour into a large bowl.

Cut the celeriac into fine matchsticks and drop them straight into the dressing, so they don't discolour. Peel the carrot, cut into matchsticks and add to the celeriac. Quarter and core the apple, then slice it thinly into the bowl. Stir well, making sure the mustard is distributed.

Add the orange segments and raisins and any residual juice in the bowl. Stir well again, then taste and add more salt and pepper if needed.

Roughly tear up the watercress and spread it over a serving platter. Spoon the rooty, fruity salad on top, add the cashews if using, and serve.

Raspberries

Pam Corbin

LATIN NAME
Rubus idaeus

SEASONALITY
July–November

MORE RECIPES
Barbecued fennel and courgettes with loganberries (page 367); Mulberry and walnut cranachan (page 391); Wineberries with peaches and custard (page 317); Basil pannacotta with minted raspberries (page 50); Peach slump (page 448); Strawberry salad with raspberry basil sauce (page 616)

Soft, juicy, beautiful raspberries rank high in the fruit world. Their tender flesh belies their intense, rich aroma and outstanding, sweet-sharp flavour. They are members of the rose family – and you can taste it in their clear, fragrant, floral tones. They are superior to many of the strawberries on sale, which are often picked under-ripe and can disappoint in taste and texture. Raspberries, on the other hand, can only be harvested when the berries are ripe and will readily slide off their creamy white cores. Perfection when fresh, raspberries also freeze well and are incredibly versatile.

These intense little fruits grow best in a moist, rich, free-draining loam. They prefer a coolish summer with long daylight hours but not too much hot sun – all of which means they are quite the perfect berry to grow in the British Isles. Cultivated in the right conditions, they can crop abundantly anywhere on our islands, but Scotland's misty softness and slightly acidic soil produce the best berries of all.

Raspberries fall into summer- or autumn-fruiting varieties. 'Glen Moy', 'Glen Ample' and 'Leo' are summer favourites, with 'Autumn Bliss' and pale yellow 'All Gold' stalwarts in the autumn. If you grow both types, you'll have plenty of fruit from early July until late into October. They are reasonably easy to grow, with little work, and their yield is priceless. Summer berries grow on canes (stems) produced the summer before, and the canes should be cut down after fruiting to allow new growth. Autumn berries grow on canes produced in that same year and should be cut back early in the following spring. Raspberries grow wild too, mostly in shaded woodlands or hedgerow.

Robust in flavour, raspberries are nevertheless very delicate in texture. Each berry (or drupe) is made up of a mass of tiny, thin-skinned individual fruits with a pip in every fleshy globule. Washing is disastrous – it crushes and waterlogs the fruit. Instead, just check for any tiny grubs (unlikely to be found in commercial berries). The berries don't keep well, spoiling within a day or two of picking. But there are plenty of ways to capture their utter loveliness.

Freshly picked raspberries are gorgeous simply sprinkled with caster sugar and eaten with cream or yoghurt. Alternatively, toss them into cakes and muffins; dot them through pie and cobbler fillings (they're amazing with early-season apples); or drop them into breakfast muesli or granola. A handful of berries stuffed inside the cavity of roasting duck, guinea fowl, pheasant or chicken moistens the flesh while adding mellow fruitiness to any accompanying *jus* from the pan; a welcome change from cherries, oranges or apples with your roast.

If you dislike raspberries' pippiness, crush and sieve them to make purées and fruity jellies. Fresh raspberry coulis is a gem of a sauce to ripple over poached pears, fresh peaches, melon slices or ice creams, and blissful swirled into breakfast porridge with a couple of spoonfuls of yoghurt. Simply crush or blitz 500g raspberries with 50–100g icing sugar and push through a nylon sieve. Store in the fridge for up to a week or portion up in small containers and freeze.

If time is short, pop raspberries in the freezer to use later: place them in a single layer on a parchment-lined tray and freeze until solid before transferring to freezer bags or sealable containers. They'll keep for a year, though I'm sure you'll use them up long before that in fruit tarts, crumbles and gorgeous gooey meringue cases.

British-grown berries are available in supermarkets and farm shops from summer well into late autumn. Generally their quality is excellent although they can be a bit pricey. For larger quantities – to make jams, jellies and liqueurs – pick-your-own fruit farms are a more economical bet.

Raspberries make one of the best jams – a must for any good Bakewell tart or sherry trifle and essential in a classic Victoria sponge. For a glorious soft-set jam, mix 1kg crushed, ripe berries with 650g jam sugar (with added pectin), heat to dissolve, then boil rapidly for a mere 5 minutes. Pot into small, warm sterilised jars (about 200g), filling them to the brim, and seal immediately with twist-on lids. The sugar content is lower than for many traditional jams so it won't keep as long (use within 6 months). Once opened, keep in the fridge and eat within 3 weeks.

Raspberry vinegar, a traditional accompaniment to Yorkshire pud in the Northeast, is another fine way to preserve the flavour. It's simply made by infusing the berries in sweetened vinegar. The resulting tangy, fruity syrup makes a soothing drink when diluted with water – hot or cold. Used neat, it adds piquancy to fresh and toasted cheeses, and it can be drizzled over smoked oily fish, rich meats and pâtés. It's also great for deglazing the lovely caramelised residues from meaty roast or grill pans.

And raspberries' vivacious tones lend themselves wonderfully to a ruby red sorbet too. Dissolve 115g sugar in 200ml water and simmer for 5 minutes, then cool. Purée and sieve 500g raspberries then combine with the cooled sugar syrup before churning in an ice-cream maker. You can add the seeds from a vanilla pod or some grated orange zest to the purée to tweak the flavour deliciously – either way, this frozen delight is delectable melting over a chunk of warm chocolate brownie.

RASPBERRY ALMOND STREUSEL CAKE

100g unsalted butter, softened

100g caster sugar

2 medium eggs

100g self-raising flour

200g raspberries, plus extra to serve

FOR THE STREUSEL TOPPING

50g butter

100g plain flour

A good pinch of salt

25g caster sugar

50g toasted flaked almonds

TO FINISH

Icing sugar, to dust

This gorgeous, light cake can be enjoyed with a cup of tea or served as a pudding, with crème fraîche or clotted cream and more luscious raspberries. It is delicious made with other berries too: try loganberries, blackberries, mulberries or Japanese wineberries. Serves 6

Preheat the oven to 180°C/Fan 160°C/Gas 4. Grease a 20cm springform cake tin and line the base with greased baking parchment.

For the streusel topping, melt the butter in a small pan, stir in the flour, salt and sugar to make a crumbly mixture, then stir in the almonds and set aside.

For the cake, in a large bowl, cream together the butter and sugar until light and fluffy. Beat in the eggs one at a time, adding a spoonful of self-raising flour with each egg. Gently fold in the remaining self-raising flour, using a large metal spoon or spatula.

Spread the cake batter in the tin and distribute the raspberries on top, then scatter with the streusel mix, making sure it stays nicely coarse and lumpy. Bake in the oven for about 45 minutes, until a skewer inserted into the middle of the cake comes out clean. Leave to cool completely in the tin.

To serve, dust with icing sugar and top with a few more raspberries. Serve with a little cream, if you like.

R

Razor clams

LATIN NAME
Ensis species

ALSO KNOWN AS
Razorfish, spoots

SEASONALITY
Easiest to hand-gather in spring and summer

HABITAT
Sheltered beaches, bays and estuaries with sand or gravel; found all around the British Isles, though rare on the east coast and north Devon and Cornwall coastline

MCS RATING
3 if hand-gathered;
5 if electric-fished

REC MINIMUM SIZE
10cm

SOURCING
goodfishguide.org

The razor clam spends its life beneath soft sand inside a sharp-edged, elongated shell, from which its fleshy 'foot' extends as both anchor and digging device. When captured, the foot dangles in a manner that calls to mind… well, less pedestrian parts of the body. However, that protruberance is the tastiest part of this very tasty bivalve.

Razors in the shell occasionally appear in fishmongers. These can be worth buying, particularly if alive and spankingly fresh. But there is an environmental caveat. Diving for the clams has long been considered the more sustainable way to gather them (as opposed to dredging). However, in recent years, some divers have been illegally electrocuting whole swathes of seabed, which stuns the clams, bringing them out of the sand. We do not know how much damage it does to marine life, but it's certainly not harmless. Unfortunately, it is very hard to know when electrocution has been employed. Razors labelled 'hand-dived' could have been caught this way.

Probably the only sure-fire way to acquire a sustainable feed's-worth of razors is to gather them yourself by the time-honoured 'salt-squirting method'. You can find them all around the British coastline. They dislike rough conditions so estuaries, inlets and beaches that don't bear the brunt of the worst storms are the best hunting grounds.

Razors live buried in the sand, vertically. Most congregate just below the low tide line but a few always find themselves, at the lowest tides, in exposed ground. Spring tides are a good time to search, i.e. when there is the greatest difference between high and low water. Collect only a few at a time, and ensure they are mature (over 10cm).

Take a tub of cheap salt, or a squeezy bottle filled with a saturated saline solution. Look for a small, oval hole in the sand that signifies a razor's presence beneath, and tip or squirt a little salt into the opening. The irritated clam should send up its siphon, with its be-shelled body following behind, and all you need do is grasp the shell by the edges (so as not to crush the body) and firmly but gently persuade the clam upwards.

Hand-gathered razors must be purged in a bucket of clean seawater for a few hours then rinsed in fresh water. Steam them open like other clams, in a small amount of wine, cider or water, with butter, garlic and a few herbs. They also barbecue well. All of the meat, barring the black stomach, is edible; the muscular foot is the sweetest part. Fried bacon or chorizo makes a wonderful partner, as does herby gremolata.

RAZOR CLAMS WITH CHERRY TOMATOES AND BASIL

200g cherry tomatoes, quartered (or smaller pieces if you prefer)

½ small red onion, finely diced

8 basil leaves, shredded

1kg razor clams, purged (see above)

3 garlic cloves, chopped

Juice of ½ lemon

300ml dry white wine

40g butter

Black pepper

Lemon wedges, to serve

This makes a fantastic summer starter. Cherry tomatoes are usually particularly sweet, but you can use any tasty tomato, chopped small. Serves 4

Combine the tomatoes, red onion and basil, season with black pepper and set aside.

Place a heavy-based saucepan (that is wide enough to fit the clams, lying flat, no more than two deep and has a lid) over a high heat. Once hot, add the clams, then the garlic, lemon juice and wine. Cover and cook for 2–3 minutes, giving it a shake now and again, until all the shells have opened and the clams have come out. Discard any that won't open. Take out the clams and shells, leaving the liquor in the pan.

Simmer the liquor until reduced by half, then whisk in the butter. Pour into a warmed bowl. Pull the black stomach sacs away from the clams and discard. Slice the clam meat and add to the sauce. Stir in the tomato mixture and taste; you probably won't need to add salt.

Choose one good opened-up clam shell per person, spoon the mixture into the shells, and serve, with lemon wedges for squeezing.

R

Rhubarb

Pam Corbin

LATIN NAME
Rheum x hybridum

SEASONALITY
Forced rhubarb: December–
April. Maincrop: April–September

MORE RECIPES
Rhubarb compote with angelica
and honey (page 22); Strawberry,
rhubarb and sweet cicely salad
(page 627); Vanilla and rhubarb
ice cream (page 655)

SOURCING
yorkshirerhubarb.co.uk

Alluring rhubarb is one of the great shoots of the edible garden, just as pert and exciting, in its own way, as asparagus or purple sprouting broccoli. This sharp, bright multi-tasker works with both sweet and savoury ingredients. Although technically a vegetable, rhubarb is generally given honorary fruit status.

The first edible crop in the yearly growing cycle, rhubarb bridges the spring 'hungry gap'. Its succulent, slender stalks appear long before the first of the summer berries. The earliest rhubarb of all is the forced variety, which brings the natural season forward by at least 8 weeks, appearing from early January – or even late December.

Home-grown forced rhubarb is a traditional crop produced in a small area between Leeds, Bradford and Wakefield, known as the Rhubarb Triangle. For over a century, this early northern harvest has been renowned for its fabulous colour and flavour – due mainly to the skill of the growers, but also to the heavy soil and cold, frosty climate of the eastern Pennines which is thought to mimic rhubarb's original home in Siberia. So special is this rhubarb that it now boasts PDO (Protected Designation of Origin) status. The crowns (plants) are cultivated in darkened and heated sheds. The lack of light forces them to send out slender stems – intensely pink, succulent and tender – which have a particularly lovely, effervescent flavour. To ensure that no beam of sunlight ever reaches them, they are hand harvested, by candlelight.

Forced rhubarb is pricey, but unparalleled as a winter treat. If you grow rhubarb, you can force it yourself by tucking in straw or manure around garden crowns and placing forcing pots over the top of them.

Field or maincrop rhubarb (pictured left) is normally available from early April in the South, a little later in the North. Its stalks are thicker and crisper than the early forced sticks, with a deep red-green hue. Despite their differing characteristics, you can use early and maincrop rhubarb in the same recipes – just be aware that the later crop is sharper and tarter and needs more sugar.

In the past, lack of sugar or culinary care, coupled with the use of aged stalks, have given rhubarb something of a bad name. But these days the tart sticks are valued for their sharp tone, texture and colour. Rhubarb now appears raw in crisp winter salads or light, quick pickles with celery, carrot and onion. The stems' sourness excites in savoury dishes: add it to lamb for rich, slow-cooked North African tagines, or chop and mix it raw into forcemeat to stuff into pork or lamb joints or Christmas roast goose, where its bright acidity cuts through the fatty richness. Rhubarb even works with fish: serve pan-fried oily fish with roasted rhubarb lightly seasoned with a dash or two of balsamic vinegar and the juices from the pan.

Flavour-wise, rhubarb stands alone. There's nothing else like it. But you'll find its acidity softens pleasingly when ginger, orange zest, sweet cicely or rosewater is added.

You will need to chop off rhubarb's leaves before cooking – they are poisonous to eat, though they can be composted. A quick wipe to remove any dust or dirt from the stalks is the only other preparation required.

For sweet affairs, the simplest way to cook rhubarb is to lightly poach or roast it. To poach, cut the stalks diagonally into 5cm pieces, place in a shallow pan and sprinkle with sugar: 10–15g sugar per 100g rhubarb is a good starting point, although you may need more, especially with maincrop rhubarb. Then add just a splash of water or orange juice (rhubarb has plenty of juice of its own). Cover and poach gently over a low heat for around 10 minutes. To roast, cook the same ingredients in a covered shallow baking dish at 150°C/Fan 130°C/Gas 2 for about 30 minutes until tender. In both cases, you should be able to keep the rhubarb holding its shape rather than collapsing into a purée – but it will taste just as good either way.

Rhubarb's sharp, fresh taste lends itself willingly to the preserving pan. Both early and maincrop shoots can be turned into piquant ketchups to serve with sausages, lamb chops or fried fish, or spiced up a little to make storecupboard chutney. Rhubarb is lovely in sweet preserves too, though it does lack the pectin essential for jam-making so needs to be partnered with other fruits, or added pectin. A few stalks added to a batch of strawberry jam sharpens and defines it deliciously in place of lemon juice.

To make good old-fashioned rhubarb and ginger jam, slice 1kg rhubarb into 2.5cm pieces, place in a preserving pan with 100g grated fresh ginger and 100ml orange juice and sprinkle over 900g jam sugar (with pectin). Leave for an hour or so for the juices to draw. Gently bring the mixture to the boil, stirring carefully to prevent catching. Boil hard for about 6 minutes to reach setting point. Pot into sterilised jars and seal immediately. This jam is lovely on crisp buttered toast or crumpets.

Blushing forced rhubarb can be transformed into a gorgeous pink cordial. Poach 1.5kg sliced rhubarb with 150ml water until soft. Strain through a jelly bag or fine sieve, then return to the pan, adding 50g sugar per 100ml juice. Heat gently until dissolved and the liquid is steaming hot, but not boiling. Remove from the heat and pour immediately into warm sterilised bottles, leaving a 1cm gap at the top, and seal. Store in a cool, dry place. Drink alone or mix with sparkling wine, or add to gin or vodka.

RHUBARB CRÈME BRÛLÉE

FOR THE RHUBARB LAYER
500g rhubarb, trimmed and cut into 1–2cm chunks

100g caster sugar

FOR THE CUSTARD
500ml double cream

100ml whole milk

1 vanilla pod, split lengthways

6 medium egg yolks

100g caster sugar, plus extra to finish

Tangy rhubarb is a superb counterpoint to the rich, creamy sweetness of a crème brûlée. Other compotes of tart fruit (cooking apple, plum, gooseberry etc.) can be used in the same way. Serves 6–8

Put the rhubarb into a wide pan, in a single layer (or as close as possible). Add the sugar and 2 tbsp water. Cover and cook over a low heat for 10–15 minutes until the rhubarb is tender but not collapsed.

Carefully spoon the rhubarb into a sieve to drain off excess liquor (use this in another dish). Allow to cool, then divide between 6–8 ramekins or other small heatproof dishes. Chill thoroughly in the fridge. Preheat the oven to 150°C/Fan 130°C/Gas 2.

To make the custard, pour the cream and milk into a heavy-based pan. Scrape the vanilla seeds into the cream mix and add the pod too. Bring to a simmer over a low heat, then set aside for a few minutes to infuse. Meanwhile, mix together the egg yolks and sugar in a large bowl. Pour on the hot cream mixture, whisking well. Pass through a sieve into a jug.

Pour the hot custard gently over the chilled rhubarb – pour it over the back of a spoon held just above the ramekin to avoid disturbing the fruit too much. Stand the ramekins in a roasting tin and pour in hot water to come halfway up the side of the dishes. Cook for 25–30 minutes or until the custard is just set but with a slight wobble in the centre.

Remove the custards from the tin and leave to cool, then chill until shortly before serving. (Make them up to 48 hours in advance, covering with cling film if preparing well ahead).

To serve, scatter 1 tsp caster sugar evenly over the top of each crème. Put them briefly under a very hot grill or use a cook's blowtorch to caramelise the sugar until golden and bubbling. Leave for 5–10 minutes so the sugary top cools and sets to a crisp caramel shell.

Serve straight away or refrigerate for an hour or two (no longer or the caramel will soften).

Rice

Tim Maddams

LATIN NAME
Oryza sativa

MORE RECIPES
Fairy ring champignon risotto (page 252); Lemon verbena pilaf (page 348); Risi e bisi with pea shoot pesto (page 457); Rice and fish with wasabi dressing (page 667); Paella (page 163)

SOURCING
traidcraftshop.co.uk and shop.jts.co.uk for fairly traded rice

Rice is the seed of a grass, farmed extensively across Asia, India, Italy, Australia and the US. It is the most widely eaten food in the world, accounting for around one fifth of the calories consumed on this planet.

Traditional rice-growing is highly labour-intensive. Seed is planted, then seedlings pulled up and replanted in a small field or paddy, surrounded by a low bank. The field is then flooded with nutrient-rich water in which the plants thrive. Once the crop is ripe, the harvest is carried out by hand. Even the threshing of the grain is often still done manually.

In some Asian countries, rice-farming occupies more than half of the entire national workforce – and life is often tough for these producers. Their crop must compete with rice grown in a very different way, in places such as Australia and the US, where seed is planted via air-drop from a satellite-guided plane and harvested by giant combines. Buying fairly traded rice helps to ensure small farmers in developing countries get a fair price.

There are thousands of different varieties of cultivated rice worldwide. Common to most of them is a large 'water footprint'. Modern rice farmers have developed strains that use less water than older varieties – but in order to flourish, rice still needs lots of water, as well as plenty of nutrients, heat and sunshine. If we all bought organic rice, we could make a real difference to the global consumption of fossil fuels: a tonne of nitrogen fertiliser requires over 7 barrels of crude oil in its manufacture.

Rice can be brown (basically wholemeal) or white (with the bran and germ milled away). It is also described by the length of its grain, the shorter grain types being usually more sticky. The starch in rice is made up of amylopectin and amylose. The more amylopectin it contains, relative to amylose, the more sticky it will be.

TYPES OF RICE

Basmati This aromatic long-grained rice from northern India and Pakistan is one of the finest rices in the world and accounts for nearly half the rice we eat in the UK.

Fragrant jasmine rice Often from Thailand, this is similar to basmati but a little more fragrant and sticky.

Long grain white rice This is a good all-rounder, less fragrant and flavourful than basmati, but high in amylose and therefore un-sticky and very easy to cook.

Wild rices Now cultivated so not technically 'wild' at all, these are ancient forms of rice (or similar grasses). Usually sold in their wholegrain form, they are often dramatically coloured, with a good nutty flavour.

Camargue red rice This takes its name from the drained salt marshes of southern France, where it was first grown in the 1980s. A cross between a wild and cultivated rice, it is sweet with a reddy-brown bran, and exceptionally good.

Easy-cook rice This is par-boiled in the husk prior to milling. It actually takes longer to cook than standard long grain rice but crucially is less likely to stick together.

Sushi rice This short grain rice is heavily milled, which means it is virtually all starch and therefore slightly sticky. As well as sushi, it also makes a good (if inauthentic) risotto.

Paella rice A short grain rice, used particularly for Spanish paella, but also excellent for risotto and rice pudding. Bomba is a favoured variety.

Glutinous or sticky rice This short grain rice is high in amylopectin, so very sticky – ideal for serving with thin sauces. ('Glutinous' is a misnomer as rice is gluten-free.)

Risotto rices There are three main types: arborio, carnaroli and vialone nano. All are medium to short grain and high in amylopectin. The starch they release is ideal for stabilising the rich emulsion of butter and stock that is the hallmark of a great risotto. **Arborio** is the most common and least expensive risotto rice. **Carnaroli** is considered superior and produces a creamy risotto while retaining the crucial *al dente* texture of the grains. **Vialone nano**, a rice of the Veneto, is perfect for the soupy risottos of that region.

Pudding rice A very short grain rice that can absorb a lot of liquid, making it ideal in a baked rice pudding.

R

Rice flour

This is gluten-free but still capable of producing light cakes and crunchy biscuits. To adapt a baking recipe to be gluten-free, I swap rice flour for wheat, increase the flour content by 10 per cent, lower the baking temperature and increase the baking time. As long as there are eggs and raising agents in the mix too, this is usually successful.

Cooking rice

The easiest way to cook rice, in my opinion, is in a rice cooker. Controlled electronically and non-stick, it virtually eliminates the possibility of undercooking or overcooking.

However, if you don't have a rice cooker, here is a fail-safe absorption method for white basmati. Wash your rice in a sieve under the cold tap until the water runs clear. Weigh the rice, then weigh out twice as much water. Put the water and rice into a heavy-based pan (preferably non-stick) with a tight-fitting lid. Bring to the boil, add salt, turn down to a low simmer and put the lid on. Cook for 12 minutes, then check the rice is cooked. If not, give it another minute or two, turn off the heat then cover the pan again and rest for at least 5 minutes. Fluff up the rice with a fork before serving.

Rice can also be boiled in excess liquid, then drained. This method works well for wholegrain rices, which are much less likely to absorb too much water and turn mushy.

And then there is the pilaf method – similar to the method for risotto – where the grains are fried first, coating them in oil which makes them less sticky, before being simmered in a small amount of liquid.

Storing cooked rice

Cooked rice can be inhabited by a nasty bacteria, *Bacillus cereus*, which causes food poisoning. The bacteria multiplies when rice is left standing at room temperature, producing an emetic toxin. Reheating the rice will not get rid of the toxin – no matter how hot it gets. So, if preparing rice in advance, be sure to cool it quickly (on a chilled plate or tray) and get it in the fridge as rapidly as possible – ideally within 30 minutes.

SPICY BROWN RICE AND BROCCOLI

200g brown basmati rice, rinsed

1 head of broccoli (about 350g)

2 tbsp rapeseed or olive oil

1 large onion, thinly sliced

1 heaped tsp cumin seeds

2 garlic cloves, thinly sliced

2 tsp grated root ginger

2 tsp ground coriander

1 tbsp harissa paste

2 tbsp chopped preserved lemon (rind and flesh)

Sea salt and black pepper

TO FINISH

50g flaked almonds, toasted

Coriander leaves

This is lovely with a dollop of hummus. It's also a great accompaniment to barbecued lamb or fish. You can use other brown rice, or Camargue red rice. It's also very good (and quicker) made with couscous. Serves 3–4 as a main, 4–6 as a side dish

Bring a large pan of water to the boil, add salt, then tip in the rice. Lower the heat and simmer for about 25 minutes until the rice is tender, topping up with more boiling water if necessary. (Or cook your rice of choice according to the pack instructions.)

Meanwhile, cut the broccoli into small florets. Heat a large frying pan over a medium heat. Add the broccoli, season with salt and cook for 4–5 minutes, without stirring, until it starts to char, then give it a stir and cook for another 6–8 minutes, shaking and stirring from time to time, until tender but still *al dente*. Remove the broccoli to a plate; set aside.

Return the frying pan to a medium-low heat. Add the oil, then the onion. Cook for about 10 minutes until soft and golden. Add the cumin seeds and garlic and cook for a minute. Add the ginger, ground coriander and harissa. Cook gently for a couple of minutes.

Drain the rice, let it steam in the colander for a couple of minutes, then combine with the broccoli and spicy onion mix. Stir in the preserved lemon and season with salt and pepper to taste. Heap into a serving dish and scatter with the almonds and coriander to serve.

Ricotta

Nikki Duffy

MORE RECIPES
Barley and raw mushroom salad (page 47); Dandelion and ricotta salad with bacon (page 232); Griddled fennel and apple with ricotta (page 255); Apricot and honey filo pie (page 314)

SOURCING
highwealddairy.co.uk; locharthur.org.uk; westcombedairy.com

Ricotta is a light and delicate 'whey cheese', made by reheating the whey drained off during the making of other cheeses. (The word ricotta means 'recooked'). Heat and acid cause lactoglobulin, a protein abundant in whey, to bind into tiny, delicate clots, giving ricotta its characteristic, slightly grainy, texture. This unique, light dairy product can be made from ewe's whey (as with the celebrated ricotta Romana), though cow's, buffalo's or goat's may also be used.

All ricotta is effectively pasteurised, even if made with the whey from unpasteurised cheese-making, because of the heat needed to form the curds. However, mass-produced ricotta is quite different from the artisan cheese. The bland stuff, filled into plastic tubs, that you find in supermarkets and delis is perfectly ok for a cheesecake or ravioli filling, but it is pretty forgettable.

Although traditionally Italian, excellent ricotta is now made in Britain. Try a good, fresh one from a small dairy and you will really appreciate the difference. The good stuff has a delicate lactic, slightly 'cooked', flavour and the most wonderful texture – some is fluffy, soft and melt-in-the-mouth, while other varieties are a little firmer and beautifully crumbly, breaking obligingly into semi-soft nuggets that mingle beautifully into salads.

Try any good ricotta dotted over buttered peas or broad beans, snippets of bacon, slices of new potato or cherry tomatoes. Crumble or spoon it into summer veg soups at the last minute, and anoint with green-gold olive oil. Or, for a wonderful pud, serve ricotta with berries, a squeeze of lemon and a trickle of honey. In Italy, ricotta is eaten with honey alone, or sometimes sieved and beaten then served sprinkled with a mixture of sugar, finely ground coffee and a few drops of liqueur.

Ricotta salata is rather a different ingredient. Drained, seasoned and aged, it is salty and firm, and traditionally used as a grating cheese for pasta dishes.

PEARS WITH RICOTTA, HONEY AND THYME

2 medium-sized pears, such as Conference or Comice

4 sprigs of thyme

150–200g ricotta

2 tbsp clear honey

FOR POACHING THE PEARS (OPTIONAL)

500ml pear or apple juice

50g caster sugar

2 star anise

½ cinnamon stick

4 black peppercorns

Use a traditional, artisan ricotta, if you can, to fully appreciate this simple dish. It makes a lovely pudding, but you could also serve it as a starter, perhaps trickled with a little good oil. If you have beautifully ripe pears, there's no need to cook them – just use them raw. Ripe peaches or nectarines are also gorgeous in this recipe. Serves 4

If you are poaching the pears, peel, then quarter and remove the cores. Place the pears in a pan in which they fit fairly snugly. Pour over the pear or apple juice and add the sugar and spices. Strip the thyme leaves from the stems and set the leaves aside; add the stems to the pan. Bring the liquid gently to a simmer, stirring occasionally to dissolve the sugar. Simmer until the pears are tender but not soft. This will take 5–20 minutes, depending on their ripeness.

Remove the pears from the poaching liquor and leave to cool. (Save the liquor to use as a cordial and drink it diluted with sparkling water, or boil it to reduce it to a fruity syrup.)

If you are using perfectly ripe, raw pears, peel, quarter and core them just before serving.

To serve, arrange a couple of pieces of pear on each plate and spoon or crumble over the ricotta. Trickle all over with honey and sprinkle with thyme leaves.

Rocket

Mark Diacono

LATIN NAME
Salad rocket: *Eruca vesicaria sativa*. Wild rocket: *Diplotaxis tenuifolia, Diplotaxis muralis*

ALSO KNOWN AS
Roquette, arugula

SEASONALITY
All year round

MORE RECIPES
Walnut, barley, rocket and blue cheese salad (page 666)

It wasn't until the late twentieth century that rocket made it to British shop shelves. As novel as it seemed, however, rocket was only new to us, not the rest of the world. It has a long history of cultivation that stretches from northern India, through the Med and the Sahel countries that together form the widest part of Africa. The ancient Greeks viewed its leaves and the oil from its seeds as powerful aphrodisiacs, and it purportedly has medicinal properties.

In any event, it now seems impossible to imagine life without this splendid, peppery leaf, thanks as much to its versatility as its incredible flavour. It is welcome in the kitchen, whether as a single-ingredient salad, simply dressed with good olive oil and salt, or whizzed up in place of basil for a punchy pesto, or strewn on to pizza. Cooking seems not to dull its individuality, as can happen with some leaves, which makes it wonderful as a wilted vegetable. Rocket can also be used as a herb, as a little of its oomph goes a long way. Try it wilted into risotto, as a peppery bed for a poached egg, or in a mozzarella and tomato salad.

There are two kinds of rocket: 'wild' and salad. Both are superb in their own way. Wild rocket (actually the one usually found in bags of salad) has narrower leaves with much more incised edges, and is stronger in flavour. Given the choice, I would plump for salad rocket for a single leaf salad, and wild for just about everything else, but there's very little in it.

Rocket (of both kinds) is simple to grow yourself, even in a pot. It will do well outside most of the time, though it fares better undercover in the winter. If you sow it regularly, you can keep yourself supplied almost year round. Salad rocket has a tendency to go to seed in hot, dry weather. Wild rocket is a little more forgiving – which partly explains why it is more widely cultivated. Both types of rocket can be harvested by cutting the leaves 2–3cm above the soil, then leaving to regrow for repeated picking, making them great money-saving, home-grown harvests. Young leaves, and those grown in cooler weather, are less peppery.

Should you allow your rocket to grow uncut, you'll find the flowers it forms are much-loved by pollinators. They're also tasty, carrying a peppery punch similar to the leaves. Try them scattered in leafy salads, on soups, or with freshly picked strawberries.

BEETROOT, STRAWBERRY AND ROCKET SALAD

250–300g small beetroot (golf ball size or smaller), scrubbed

200g ripe strawberries

About 50g rocket leaves

A scattering of cashew nuts, toasted, or sunflower or pumpkin seeds (optional)

FOR THE DRESSING
Juice of 1 lemon

1 tsp sugar

2 tbsp extra virgin olive or rapeseed oil

Sea salt and black pepper

Strawberries and beetroot are a great combination – and a good foil to rocket's heat. This salad is also delicious scattered with a little diced Brie or Camembert, or some crumbled ricotta, if you want to up the protein and make it more substantial. Finish this off with a few rocket flowers, if you have any. Serves 4 as a starter, 2 as a light lunch with extras

Put the whole beetroot in a pan with a good pinch of salt. Cover with water and bring to the boil. Simmer, covered, for 45–50 minutes or until tender. Drain and allow to cool, then peel the skin away.

Cut the beetroot into quarters and place in a large bowl. Hull and halve the strawberries and add these to the beetroot, along with the rocket.

For the dressing, put all the ingredients into a jam jar, screw on the lid and shake to emulsify. Taste it and tweak the flavour with more salt, pepper or sugar if needed.

Spoon the dressing over the fruit and veg. Toss lightly together, then arrange on plates and add a scattering of toasted cashews or seeds if you like. Serve straight away.

Rose hips & petals

Pam Corbin

LATIN NAME
Rosa species

SEASONALITY
Petals: June–July.
Hips: September–October

SOURCING
greensofdevon.com;
maddocksfarmorganics.co.uk

A symbol of love, the rose has been cherished for centuries. Its fragrance is prized in the perfume industry, but the rose is also highly valued as an ingredient in Middle Eastern, North African and Indian cooking. Rose petals are infused in tisanes and jams and ground into beguiling spice mixes such as ras-el-hanout. Captured in rose water, their mystical redolence is also used to enhance Turkish delight and milk puddings. From the British hedgerow, meanwhile, we can help ourselves to an abundance of the rose's plump progeny, the rose hip, which can be cooked to reveal a unique and wonderfully fruity flavour.

All rose petals are edible, but not all are imbued with the exquisite hallmark rose fragrance. It is those heady with a fruity-musky, myrrh-and-old-rose perfume that the cook should seek out. Pink- and yellow-bloomed varieties generally have the richest scents. The damask rose (*Rosa damascena*), the apothecary's rose (*Rosa gallica*) and *Rosa rugosa*, also called the Japanese rose, all have fabulous culinary pedigrees, but there are many other gorgeous varieties out there for you to sniff out. The soft-pink blooms of our native dog rose (*Rosa canina*) only have five, lightly scented petals, so I prefer to leave the blooms to grow into the prettiest of hips to use later in the year.

Rose water is made by steeping petals in water, oil or alcohol to extract their fragrance. It is available from most supermarkets but note that the intensity can vary considerably. Some brands are very strong, so use it judiciously. To make your own, delicate version, you will need plenty of flowerheads. Pink petals give a particularly lovely colour, but don't be prejudiced – it's their fragrance you're after.

Make sure the petals are fresh and dry. Put them in a saucepan and barely cover with water. Place a lid on the pan and simmer the petals gently for 15 minutes until the water has drawn both colour and fragrance. Strain the mixture, squeezing every drop of loveliness from the wilted petals. Measure the warm liquid and stir in 20g caster sugar for every 100ml, then decant into a sterilised, sealable bottle and keep in the fridge for up to 4 weeks. Add a splash of this nectar to summer fruits such as raspberries, strawberries, blackcurrants, plums and apricots; infuse into milk or cream to delicately flavour desserts; or use to imbue cakes and pastries.

Rose petals make outstanding jams and jellies. Begin with a simple hot water infusion; or add them to simmering cooking apples before straining; or add a handful of petals to strawberry jam when it has reached setting point, for an extra dimension.

Strewn upon plain or iced sponge cakes, fresh petals make pretty decorations. Brushed with beaten egg white, lightly dusted with caster sugar and dried, the petals will keep in an airtight container for use on celebration cakes. The white 'heel' at the base of the petal is a little bitter; remove it if you're aiming for total perfection.

Most commercially grown blooms will have been sprayed with herbicide or pesticide at some stage, though it is possible to buy organic roses. If you are planting a new, non-organic rose in bloom, allow the flowers to die back and wait for the new blooms before picking for culinary use – and of course, don't spray them yourself!

Rose petals can also be dried, though you'll need a mountain of blooms to get a half decent quantity: place them in a single layer on a small-meshed wire cake rack and leave in a warm, airy place for 24–48 hours to dry. Otherwise, dried rose petals are available from health food stores or spice specialists (make sure you get those suitable for eating, rather than for perfume). To make rose-scented sugar for baking, toss 5g dried petals with 250g caster sugar and leave to infuse for 4 weeks. Sieve out the petals before using the sugar – in cakes, shortbread and custards.

Even after their petals have faded, many roses still flaunt their beauty in scarlet rose hips, which have quite a different, but equally delicious, flavour. Hips form after the flowers have been fertilised by another rose via wind or insect pollination. Many rose cultivars are sterile and do not produce hips. The wild dog rose, however, is abundant with hips in the autumn hedgerow. Not only are they beautiful and bright, they also have an exceptionally high vitamin C content.

Cooking and straining the hips for a syrup is the perfect way to make the most of the hip's unique fruity flavour; it also avoids the mass of hairy white seeds within the core of the hip, which are a skin irritant and should not be eaten. Rose hip syrup has many delectable uses: mix into ice creams and cakes, squiggle over pancakes, porridge and creamy rice puds; drizzle over fruity cakes; or spritz into sparkling wine. Or, for a warming cordial, mix 1 part to 6 parts hot water.

A few radiant rose hips included with poaching crab apples or cookers (again, the fruit pulp itself must be strained out) will make fruit jellies and fruit cheeses blush with a rosy hue. Harvest hips in early autumn when the fruits are well coloured and the waxy skins are starting to soften.

Dried rose hips, available ground, from health food shops, make a richly flavoured tisane. Allow ½ tsp dried hips to 500ml boiling water. The infusion is lovely for soaking dried fruits for moist fruit teabreads and cakes: allow 150ml rose hip tea to 250g fruit.

ROSE PETAL HONEY

340g jar clear honey

About 50g deeply fragrant rose petals (probably 5–6 roses), free from pesticides

Genuine rose honey, from bees that feast on roses, is rare but you can make your own in just a few days. Choose a mild honey, such as acacia or clover, or a mild mixed wildflower honey – get a raw, local one if you can (see page 312). Makes 1 jar

First gently warm the honey by sitting the jar, unopened, in a bowl of hot water.

Making sure they are bug-free, pack the rose petals into a clean 400ml jam jar (one that has a well-fitting metal lid). Pour the jarful of warmed honey over the petals. Seal the jar and give it a good shake to mix the honey and petals together. Leave to infuse on a sunny windowsill for 6–7 days. The petals will rise to the surface so give the jar a quick shake each day to keep everything combined.

Lightly warm the honey again by standing the jar in a bowl of hot water for a few minutes. Strain the scented honey through a fine sieve into a clean jar. Store in a cool dark place, where it should keep indefinitely.

Rosemary

Nikki Duffy

LATIN NAME
Rosmarinus officinalis

SEASONALITY
All year round

MORE RECIPES
Roasted broccoli, red onion
and cannellini salad (page 99);
Baked mushrooms with
rosemary and walnut butter
(page 396); Roasted beetroot
orzotto with lavender (page 68);
Grilled sardines with potatoes
and rosemary (page 565); Plaice
with rosemary, caper and
anchovy butter (page 476);
Chicken and cider stew with
rosemary dumplings (page 617);
Barbecued duck breasts with
rosemary and figs (page 240);
Rabbit with anchovies, rosemary
and cream (page 516); Goat
kebabs with rosemary, red
peppers and onion (page 280);
Damson and rosemary vodka
(page 663)

SOURCING
downderry-nursery.co.uk;
rosemaries.co.uk

Resinous, piney, orangey and warm, rosemary's powerful scent is one of the most wonderful in the herb garden. Its aroma is comforting, reassuring and inspiring. Closely associated since ancient times with memory and intellect, this herb is still appreciated today for the mind-clearing, stimulating effect of its essential oils.

Although a native of the Mediterranean, evergreen rosemary's hardy nature means it grows beautifully in cooler climes too, and it's been a favoured British herb for hundreds of years: Sir Thomas More was a fan and Shakespeare, famously, wrote of it. Like some other strong and pungent herbs, rosemary was initially appreciated more for its perfume and its medicinal value than its flavour. When plague ravaged the land, it was burned in a bid to drive off the contagion, and even in more wholesome times rosemary was strewn on the floors of churches – a symbol of remembrance and a prophylactic against the stink of life.

When it comes to cooking, I think rosemary's qualities are unique and enticing, though not everyone would agree. Elizabeth David counselled that rosemary is a 'treacherous' herb. The Italians, with their liberal love of it, tend to 'over-do' it, she said, pointing out that rosemary's penetrating pungency can overwhelm other flavours and that the needles themselves are not nice to eat. It's important to bear in mind that she was talking about rosemary actually eaten in Italy, scythed from some hillside bush or stone-walled *giardino* where it had soaked up the solar heat for months on end. Rosemary grown in the British Isles will always be a little milder, less muscular. But in any event, there are simple ways to manage rosemary's robustness.

One wonderful way to use rosemary is as an infuser. Simmered whole in a soup or stew, soaked in a hot syrup or torn into tufts and roasted alongside hearty meats or chunky veg, you don't need to eat the herb itself in order to enjoy its character. But finely chopped, it can be stirred directly into everything from a meaty stuffing to a cake batter. The leaves are tough, waxy and bitter if eaten whole, but a bit of knife-work is all that's required to render them more approachable.

Rosemary is a fantastic partner to roast chicken and lamb, and is brilliant with fish – especially oily fish, which can take on all that lovely piney flavour. It's possibly even better with veg though – especially any kind of roasted root or squash. The flavour is too strident for tender peas, beans or courgettes, but roasted aubergines and tomatoes are both wonderful with a hint of rosemary.

This pungent herb can be great with fruit too. In autumn and winter it's a delicious partner to orchard fruit and to citrus: add a sprig to the liquid for poaching pears or roasting plums, or tuck some under baking apples. Chop it finely and combine with grated lemon zest and butter to keep a roasting chicken succulent, or orange zest to season fish. Orange segments poached in a caramel syrup taste amazing if you replace the more usual spices with a large sprig of rosemary. Or make a simple sugar syrup flavoured with rosemary and use in citrusy cocktails, or a virgin lemon- or limeade.

Rosemary is one herb I would not want to be without in my garden. Generous and undemanding, it stands sentinel all year, its glossy, dark green needles never fading or wavering in flavour, throwing up spear after spear of new growth in the warmer months, and spraying out a little froth of blue flowers for the bees in the early summer. (Rosemary honey is surprisingly delicate and beautifully floral.)

Hard to establish from seed, it's best to buy a well-rooted young rosemary plant and site it in the sunniest spot you have in the garden, in well-drained soil. Heat-loving Mediterranean herb that it is, it should nevertheless tolerate pretty much all that the

British climate can throw at it, as long as it's not sitting in cold, waterlogged ground. The name, *Rosmarinus*, actually means 'dew of the sea', a reference to its liking for the sandy-soiled Mediterranean coast. If you have heavy clay soil, digging in grit before you plant rosemary – or keeping it in a large pot – will serve you well.

Rosemary has a tendency to woodiness and can grow into a small tree – beautiful but not ideal if you want lots of tender, aromatic leaves for the kitchen. Regular, judicious pruning/harvesting throughout the spring and summer is the best tack: drastic cutting, especially in cold weather, can leave rosemary very disgruntled indeed.

Any fragrant spears you don't find use for in the kitchen can be burned on a barbecue or in a fireplace. Their scent is intoxicating, heady and divine and will subtly perfume food cooked over them.

Rosmarinus officinalis is the most familiar form of this plant, and an excellent one, but there are many good cultivars. The flavours vary: some are quite gingery, some very citric. 'Prostratus Group' is a low-growing, spreading rosemary that will cling to rockeries and spill beautifully out of pots. 'Miss Jessop's Upright', with a slightly more astringent, spicy flavour than the standard *officinalis*, produces many sky-reaching spears that make wonderful barbecue skewers, while 'Lady in White' has beautiful white flowers and an excellent flavour. Go to one of the many specialist growers in the UK for quality and good advice.

ROASTED APPLES WITH ROSEMARY

6 medium eating apples

50g light muscovado or soft light brown sugar

1 tsp ground cinnamon

Finely grated zest of 1 lemon

Leaves stripped from 2 good sprigs of rosemary

25g butter

Rosemary brings out all the aromatic qualities in these caramelised apples, and enhances both their sweetness and their sharpness. You can serve them either as a pudding, with cream or yoghurt, or as an accompaniment to roast meat such as pork. Choose an eating apple variety that will hold its shape, such as Cox or Russet. Serves 4

Preheat the oven to 200°C/Fan 180°C/Gas 6.

Peel the apples, then cut them into quarters and cut out the cores. Place the apple pieces in a non-stick baking dish. Add the sugar, cinnamon, lemon zest and rosemary and toss together well.

Cut the butter into small pieces and scatter over the top of the fruit. Roast in the oven until tender and caramelised, giving the apples a gentle stir 2 or 3 times during cooking. It will take between 30 and 45 minutes, depending on the apple variety. Cover the apples with foil if the sticky juices look like they are burning before the apples are done.

Serve the sweet, herby roasted apples straight away.

Rowan

John Wright

LATIN NAME
Sorbus aucuparia

ALSO KNOWN AS
Mountain ash

SEASONALITY
Berries August–November

HABITAT
Common in mountainous or hilly areas, though often as lone trees, and widely planted in urban areas

The lovely rowan is one of the most widespread of all trees in the British Isles, appearing from Shetland to the Channel Islands. It is also a most prolific fruiter, producing sprays of bright orange fruit from every twig in late summer and autumn. What a pity, then, that its flavour is bitter and it smells distinctively of sick. Unlike the nearly-as-common hawthorn, it doesn't even have the decency to be tasteless.

While rowanberries redeem themselves slightly by containing vitamin C and antioxidants, as an ingredient (and a poisonous one when raw), they may be the least promising entry in this book. But challenges are there to be met and a few, sensible culinary possibilities exist.

The classic, indeed the only, common recipe is for rowan jelly, traditionally served with game, where robust opposing flavours are welcome. On its own in a jelly, rowan would be too bitter, so cooking apples or crab apples are added. Put equal quantities of roughly chopped apples and berries in a pan, just cover with water, and boil until the apples are soft, then mash lightly. Allow the purée to drip through a muslin bag overnight into a heavy-based saucepan. For every 500ml liquid, add 375g sugar. Bring to a fast boil for a few minutes until it reaches setting point, leave to settle for a few minutes, skimming off any froth, and pour into hot sterilised jars.

Working on the principle that adding sugar, butter and cream to just about anything is bound to improve it, I tried the following recipe for rowan toffee, given to me by my friend Monica Wilde. It is actually pretty good, resulting in a fruity, slightly astringent toffee.

ROWAN TOFFEE

300g rowanberries

300g granulated sugar

30g butter

100ml double cream

The sweetness in this fruity hedgerow treat is tempered by a hint of bitterness from the berries – just the thing to keep you going during foraging expeditions. Makes about 400g

Line a 20cm square baking tin with baking parchment.

Put the rowanberries into a saucepan and pour on enough water to cover by 2cm. Bring to the boil, lower the heat and simmer for 15 minutes. Mash with a potato masher, then push the pulp through a fine sieve to extract the juice. You need 300ml rowanberry juice (if you have less, scale down the other ingredients accordingly).

Put the juice and sugar into a large, deep saucepan over a low heat and stir until the sugar has dissolved.

Stop stirring, turn up the heat a little and bring to the boil. As the solution heats up, it will start to darken. Cook until the temperature registers 120°C on a sugar thermometer (i.e. the 'hard ball' stage, when a little piece of the toffee dropped into ice-cold water holds a firm ball).

When this stage is reached, remove the pan from the heat and add the butter, stirring as it melts. Then add the cream.

Return the toffee to the heat and cook until it registers 140°C on a sugar thermometer (i.e. the 'soft crack' stage, when a little piece of the toffee dropped into ice-cold water will separate into hard threads that will flex a little before snapping). The mixture will have become much darker and the bubbles will be smaller and closer together.

Immediately pour the toffee into the prepared baking tin and leave to set completely before cutting. Store in an airtight container in a cool place, but not the fridge.

R

Runner beans

Mark Diacono

LATIN NAME
Phaseolus coccineus

SEASONALITY
June–October

MORE RECIPES
French beans with shallots and
black olives (page 265)

We are creatures of habit. Almost any veg patch in the land will feature runner beans climbing their way up tepees or avenues of canes, their carers waiting impatiently for the flowers to pass and the beans to form. Once picked, the crop is invariably boiled until just tender and served as a side dish. And perfectly reasonable they are like that too. But I think we can aim a little higher when it comes to this vegetable.

The reputation of runners as fibrous, stringy things is due to too many middle-aged examples being dished up at Sunday lunch. Modern varieties, thankfully, have been bred to be far less stringy than beans of old. Even so, the ones you buy in the shops have often been left on the plant far too long.

Buy the smallest ones you can find and give any that are longer than 15cm (probably most of them) a swipe down each side of the bean with a potato peeler to remove the tougher fibres, before slicing. And that slicing should be done with a little finesse: slender, diagonally-slanted cross sections of bean, or those long ribbons of runner you can produce with a special little slicer, will further shorten any troublesome fibres.

Very fresh home-grown runners less than 15cm long can usually be cooked whole and certainly without de-stringing. And a young, raw one, no longer than 10cm, pinched straight from the plant is a fresh-from-the-garden treat – up there with the first peas.

Sliced runners, cooked in just a little water, olive oil and garlic, were made to go with lamb or roasted veg; they soften beautifully into a stew with garlic and tomatoes; and they're great tempura-ed with a sweet chilli dip. With their robust texture, runners are great pickled, too, either as the solo veg in a chutney or in a mixed fruit and veg preserve or piccalilli. Runner beans seem to form a happy alliance with most herbs – especially dill and basil. Cream is often the best medium to hold that alliance together: creamy, herby runner beans (see the recipe below) make a fantastic pasta sauce.

We tend to eat runner beans as whole pods, but if they are allowed to grow and swell at the end of season, the pink beans inside can be eaten: they are delicious fresh or dried (as for borlotti beans, see page 81). Use them as you might borlotti or cannellini beans: pork, chorizo and chicken stews are a good place to start.

The fine floral flourish of a runner bean vine in the summer, resplendent with red or white flowers, is a delight. Grow your own and your veg patch will look a treat as well as offering you the best varieties that you can pick at the perfect, short-and-sweet moment. 'Polestar' and 'Scarlet Emperor' are hard to beat for a sweet, stringless harvest.

R

RUNNER BEANS WITH CREAM AND TARRAGON

500g runner beans

20g butter

2 garlic cloves, thinly sliced

4 tbsp double cream or
crème fraîche

1 tbsp chopped tarragon

Sea salt and black pepper

This is a lovely way to serve runner beans – or French beans – great with chicken or fish, or a heap of Puy lentils. Or you can up the cream a bit and serve it as a pasta sauce. Serves 4

Top and tail the runner beans. Very small, tender ones can be left whole. Otherwise, use a potato peeler to remove the long fibres running along each side then, working at a sharp angle, cut them into 5mm slices, so you get nice, elongated cross-sections of bean.

Bring a large pan of water to a rolling boil, add salt, then drop in the beans. Cook for 3–4 minutes until tender but not soft. Drain the beans and leave to steam in a colander.

Meanwhile, melt the butter in a large pan. When it's bubbling, add the sliced garlic and cook for 30 seconds then add the cream and tarragon and stir well.

When the cream is bubbling, add the beans and some salt and pepper. Stir the beans through the cream until everything is piping hot. Serve straight away.

Rye

Gill Meller

LATIN NAME
Secale cereale

MORE RECIPES
Field mushroom and celeriac pie (page 258); Rye and caraway scones (page 114); Tortillas with cumin and garlic oil (page 221)

SOURCING
bakerybits.co.uk

A graceful-looking crop, rye is hardy and resilient, thriving in cold climates where other grains struggle. Popular in Scandinavia and Eastern Europe, it's often planted in the autumn as the ground cools, and thrives even in snow and harsh winter winds. The grain itself is fairly difficult to refine, so rye flour is usually wholemeal and, as it includes the nutritious bran and germ, it is a good source of soluble fibre.

Rye's traditional use is in bread-making. Related to wheat, it contains some gluten but does not form the same kind of elastic, springy dough that wheat does. Rye is sometimes combined with wheat flour to produce a lighter bread, but pure rye breads are classic too. The dough itself is sticky and dense and bakes into bread with a characteristically moist texture, close crumb and intense nutty flavour. Rye breads are often made with a fermenting leaven or sourdough starter, which results in a better texture than if yeast is used, and, of course, contributes to flavour.

Pumpernickel is a typical German rye bread, made with cracked and whole rye grains. Its dark colour and complex, sweet flavour come from fantastically long baking times – in some cases as long as 24 hours at a very low temperature. *Rugbrød* is a Danish fermented rye loaf, full of seeds and wholegrains (and occasionally wheat flour too). It's delicious eaten for breakfast with cheese and ham or used for *smørrebrød* – open sandwiches, buttered and topped with pickled fish, eggs and cured meats.

But rye flour should not be reserved for bread alone. Its nutty aroma and earthy texture will lend character to cakes, scones, biscuits, crispbreads and pancake batters. If you use rye flour in a recipe where you would normally use wheat, be prepared to add more liquid, as it is more absorbent. The results will be a little more dense and crumbly but also more richly flavoured.

Dark, wholemeal rye flour is widely available. A lighter version, which has some of the bran sifted out, can also be found. Rye flakes are roasted, rolled whole grains – ideal for an easy porridge, or fried in butter until crisp and sprinkled on veg dishes.

RYE CHOCOLATE CAKE

250g dark chocolate (about 70% cocoa solids), broken into chunks

250g unsalted butter, cut into cubes

4 medium eggs, separated

200g caster sugar (or half caster/ half soft light brown sugar)

100g light rye flour

A pinch of salt

1 tsp baking powder

Rye adds a lovely nutty taste to this rich, fudgey chocolate cake. If you can't find light rye, dark rye works well too. Serves 8

Preheat the oven to 170°C/Fan 150°C/Gas 3. Grease and line a 23cm springform cake tin.

Put the chocolate and butter in a heatproof bowl and set over a pan of barely simmering water, making sure the water doesn't touch the base of the bowl. Stir occasionally until melted. Leave to cool slightly.

Meanwhile, whisk the egg yolks and sugar together in a large bowl until well combined, then stir in the melted chocolate and butter. Combine the rye flour, salt and baking powder and fold into the mixture.

In a separate bowl, whisk the egg whites until they hold firm peaks. Stir a large spoonful into the chocolate mixture to loosen it, then carefully fold in the rest of the egg whites, using a large metal spoon or spatula, trying to keep in as much air as possible.

Pour the mixture into the prepared tin and bake for about 30 minutes, until only just set. It should still wobble slightly in the centre – this means the cake will have a divinely sticky, fudgey texture. Leave to cool for 10–15 minutes before releasing from the tin.

Serve the cake warm or cold, on its own or with a dollop of thick cream, crème fraîche or Greek yoghurt.

Saffron

Gill Meller

LATIN NAME
Crocus sativus

MORE RECIPES
Paella (page 163)

SOURCING
englishsaffron.co.uk;
norfolksaffron.co.uk

This spice is famously more expensive than gold, gram for gram, so it's fortunate that you need just a small pinch to get the best of its woody, musky and curiously perfumed flavour. Saffron is the dried stigma of the purple crocus. Its high cost is a reflection of the laborious work of production. Each flower must be gathered, by hand, at just the right time of day. The long stigma are then picked out of the bloom and carefully dried to capture their power. It takes around 16,000 flowers to make 100g of usable saffron.

Saffron is largely imported now, the best coming from the arid plains of Spain, Iran and Kashmir. However, back in the seventeenth century, East Anglian 'crokers' exported cargo-loads of home-grown saffron and there was a vibrant saffron-growing tradition in the West Country too, manifested in the Cornish saffron buns and breads still made today. A few intrepid British growers are now reviving the tradition of growing saffron.

The magical filaments come to us rusty red, often wrapped in yellow cellophane, ready to stain all they touch a rich, golden hue. The name comes from *za'faran*, the Arabic for 'yellow'. Look for whole strands of saffron with a deep orangey colour. Beware cheap offerings, which can be adulterated – or at least bulked with safflower petals – and avoid powdered saffron, which may include turmeric and synthetic dyes. Stored in a cool, dark space, good saffron keeps its potency for a couple of years.

To best release the colour and flavour, saffron stigmas need to be infused in liquid to dissolve their waxy coating. Soak for 20 minutes in warm milk, booze, stock or water, then add both the saffron and the liquid to your dish.

With its fragrant quality, saffron is fantastic in ricey things, such as pilafs and risottos, and in rustic, French-style fish soups too. Saffron has a delicate bitterness and is a good counterpoint to sugary sweetness, not just in saffron buns, but in simple, buttery sponge cakes. And saffron custard is delectable, either churned into ice cream or just chilled and served with a tart compote of young gooseberries.

SAFFRON SPELTOTTO WITH BLACK PUDDING AND PARSLEY

Saffron is a classic ingredient in many risottos but it works just as well with pearled spelt. For a sustaining meal, this is wonderful with a poached egg. Serves 2

About 650ml veg or light chicken stock

A large pinch of saffron strands

1½ tbsp olive oil

25g butter

1 onion, finely chopped

2 garlic cloves, thinly sliced

125g pearled spelt (or pearl barley), rinsed

½ small glass of dry white wine

100g black pudding, cut into 1cm slices

30g Parmesan or other hard matured cheese, finely grated

1 tbsp chopped parsley

1 tbsp chopped fennel herb (optional)

Sea salt and black pepper

Bring the stock to a gentle simmer in a saucepan. Add the saffron and keep the stock hot over a very low heat.

Heat 1 tbsp oil and half the butter in a large saucepan over a medium heat. Add the onion and garlic and cook gently for 8–10 minutes or until soft but not coloured. Add the spelt or barley and cook, stirring, for a further 2 minutes. Add the wine and cook for a couple of minutes, stirring, until it has all been absorbed.

Add a couple of ladlefuls of the hot stock (with the saffron) and simmer gently, stirring from time to time, until it is absorbed by the grain. Continue in this way until the grain is tender: spelt should take about 25 minutes, barley a little longer. You may not need all the stock, or you may need a little more.

Meanwhile, when the spelt is almost cooked, heat a splash of oil in a frying pan over a medium heat and fry the black pudding for 3–4 minutes on each side.

When the grain is tender, take the speltotto off the heat. Stir in the cheese and remaining butter and season with salt and pepper to taste. Add the parsley and fennel, if using, and give it a final stir. Divide between warm plates, crumble over the black pudding and serve.

S

Sage

LATIN NAME
Salvia officinalis

SEASONALITY
All year round

MORE RECIPES
Buttermilk and sage onion rings (page 109); Roasted squash with chestnuts, sausage and sage (page 158); Oat-coated puffball with sage and pancetta (page 507); Roast guinea fowl with onions and sage breadcrumbs (page 291); Snipe with swede and bacon (page 587); Hare ragu (page 301); Saltimbocca (page 657); Pear and celeriac stuffing (page 454); Cider onion gravy (page 182); Crab apple jelly with thyme, juniper and mint (page 204)

Sage was once seen as a herb for the physic garden rather than the potager, said to help everything from colds to rheumatism, snakebites to infertility. Modern science confirms that sage does possess antibacterial, antioxidant and anti-inflammatory properties. In fact it's a potent plant that should be used with restraint, and avoided in any quantity when pregnant.

But we've learned to embrace this pungent, edgy ingredient for all it can do in the kitchen. Like several other herbs, sage contains camphor and it's the bitterness from this that sets some people against it. But it's also this quality that makes sage so fantastic with fatty meats such as pork, and with strong vegetable flavours such as the alliums and earthy-sweet squashes and pumpkins. It's famously good with onion, and makes a tart apple sauce quite special.

For a reasonably subtle sage flavour, make a sage butter. Infuse finely slivered sage leaves in gently bubbling butter for a few minutes, then trickle over fresh pasta, pork chops – even a poached egg. Fried whole sage leaves, crisped very briefly in hot oil (see below) are likewise delicious, cutting through richness with their delectable, aromatic bitterness. Another way to wield sage well is to cook it for a long time, so it mellows. Use it chopped in stews, soups and stuffings, or, best of all, slow-cooked pulse dishes. Sage is a fantastic seasoning for beans' creamy, starchy mildness.

Sage is not hard to grow, as long as you choose a well-drained, reasonably sunny location. It's an evergreen perennial and in the summer casts out plumes of purple flowers – much beloved by bees – but you'll need to cut them off if you want the leaves to continue growing tender and tasty. The flowers are edible, however, with a lovely, delicate sagey flavour. Sage can be harvested all year round but can become more harsh and bitter in the colder months – still good, but worth using more carefully. Good old *Salvia officinalis* is the only plant you really need in the kitchen but there are cultivars – everything from pineapple sage to blackcurrant sage, and varieties with purple, white or variegated leaves – which can put on a display in the garden.

TAGLIATELLE WITH LAMB'S LIVER, PANCETTA AND SAGE

This wonderfully quick dish is also good with calf's, chicken or duck livers. Serves 4

250g dried tagliatelle

300g very fresh lamb's liver, trimmed

1 tbsp olive oil, lard or bacon fat

75g pancetta, diced

1 small garlic clove, sliced

150ml double cream

8 large sage leaves, chopped

Sea salt and black pepper

FOR THE SAGE GARNISH

3 tbsp olive oil

About 24 whole sage leaves

TO SERVE

Finely grated Parmesan or other hard, well-flavoured cheese, such as Berkswell

Put a large pan of salted water on to boil for the pasta.

Meanwhile, prepare the sage garnish. Heat the olive oil in a small pan over a medium-high heat. To test the heat, throw in a sage leaf: it should sizzle instantly. Add the whole sage leaves and fry for about 30 seconds, until crisp, turning them with a fork so they cook evenly. Drain on kitchen paper, season with salt and set aside.

Add the tagliatelle to the pan of boiling water and cook until *al dente*. Cut the liver into 1cm thick slices.

About 5 minutes before the pasta will be ready, start making the sauce. Heat the oil or fat in a large, heavy-based frying pan over a medium-high heat and fry the pancetta for 2 minutes or until it just begins to colour. Add the garlic and fry for 20–30 seconds.

Now add the liver and sauté for about a minute. Tip in the cream and chopped sage, season, turn down the heat and let the mixture bubble for a minute. If the sauce seems too thick, add a splash of water to 'let it down' to a nice coating consistency.

Drain the pasta well and divide between warmed dishes. Spoon over the creamy liver mix and grate on some cheese. Finish with the fried sage leaves and a grinding of pepper.

Salmon

Nick Fisher

LATIN NAME
Atlantic salmon: *Salmo salar*.
Pacific salmon: *Oncorhynchus*
species

SEASONALITY
Wild Pacific salmon: avoid
late summer–autumn when
spawning but note that most
on sale is previously frozen.
Farmed: not applicable

MCS RATING
Wild Atlantic salmon 5;
conventionally farmed Atlantic
salmon 3; organically farmed
Atlantic salmon 2; Pacific
salmon 1–2

REC MINIMUM SIZE
Varies with species

MORE RECIPES
Cucumber, smoked mackerel
and dill salad (page 220); Dab
in a bag (page 230); Steamed
sea bass with kale and ginger
(page 573); Rice and fish with
wasabi dressing (page 667)

SOURCING
goodfishguide.org; msc.org

A once-noble creature, salmon has sadly lost its way. Historically known as 'the king of fish', it has been transformed into a flabby, farmed pink thing that slouches across every finger of sushi nigiri from here to Hirosaki.

The Atlantic salmon, which swims our rivers and seas, is an awesome example of aquatic evolution, of survival-against-all-odds. It's an illustration of how nature can devise a strategy to allow a species under constant threat to not just continue to exist, but to transform itself from a tiny minnow into a hulking 20kg beast of a thing, jam-packed with millions of ripe eggs, ready to spawn a new generation.

Salmon is a version of trout, born in tiny, often inhospitable streams in places like the Highlands of Scotland, where to even last the winter is unlikely. Baby salmon know survival in a sterile river is not easy and take the gamble of leaving the rivers and heading out to sea. Apart from the risks of predation from birds, seals and every other fish, the young salmon also has to undergo a physiological transformation, enabling it to leave a freshwater environment and enter corrosive salt water – a change that would be fatal to almost all other freshwater fish (rather like you and me deciding to swap breathing oxygen for carbon monoxide). Then this tiny mite has to make its way to the rich feeding grounds near Greenland where it spends a couple of years gorging on the all-you-can-eat buffet of the sea.

Once large (anything over 3kg) and beginning to mature sexually, the salmon will run the gauntlet of nets, trawlers, seals, dolphins, pollution and poachers, to re-enter the very same river from which it first came. At this point it has to go through the salt-to-freshwater change, an equally demanding physical transformation in reverse, only to find itself faced with the job of running up a river, which may have been accessible to a wee fingerling fish moving downstream, but is not so easy for a huge silver thing going against the current, across weirs, through towns, over dams, while everything with teeth and a belly wants to eat it.

For a wild Atlantic salmon to survive the journey and actually manage to lay eggs and have them fertilised is miraculous. This is perhaps partly why our wild stocks are seriously depleted (though overfishing, pollution, migration barriers and environmental conditions are also in play) and why buying a wild Atlantic salmon to eat is just about impossible. Some Irish companies are allowed to smoke a portion of their healthier river-run fish. Otherwise, the sale of wild salmon is thankfully rigidly controlled.

And so, every piece of Atlantic salmon you buy, smoked or fresh, cooked or raw, is farmed – grown in net cages, fed on fishmeal pellets. There are a lot more farmed Atlantic salmon in the world than there are wild ones.

The farming of salmon has been mired in controversy because of a number of factors. These include pollution: there's an awful lot of salmon shit falls out of a cage full of fish, and it can affect the biodiversity of the seabed below. Then there's sea lice: these parasites occur naturally in the sea, finding fish to attach themselves to, and farmed salmon provide a dense collection of ready hosts. If lice numbers build up, it can cause malnutrition and death for both farmed and wild salmon and sea trout. One new solution to such threats is to put 'cleaner fish', who eat the lice, in the pens with the salmon. But many farmers also still rely on a range of chemicals to treat their stock, which can impact the sea-life underneath and around the net pens.

In addition, hundreds of thousands of farmed salmon have escaped over the years. Those that survive can interbreed with wild salmon causing genetic dilution as well as competing with them for food. And then, there's the complicated issue of feed.

Farmed fish are mostly fed on pellets containing fishmeal and fish oil from industrially caught wild fish. These may be species, like capelin and sand eels, which we don't want to eat – but they are important in the diet of other wild species, including wild salmon.

Some of our cold-smoked salmon is world class, but the fish itself still comes from a farm. Some of the loins and cutlets of salmon in fishmongers' displays are inviting – the marbling of fat through the flesh looks gorgeous and the price per kilo value is excellent. But it's still a farmed fish. The truth is, salmon farming is a necessity if we want to continue eating salmon on the scale we do.

In fairness to the industry, organic salmon farmers make their feed from trimmings from fish processed for human consumption and/or from sustainable stocks and are intelligent and careful about what, if any, chemicals they introduce into the environment. However, personally, I still don't want to eat a version of such an amazing fish that has been forced to live its life in a netted cage, fed on pellets.

But there is an alternative: wild Pacific salmon, which is widely available. There are five types: 'Chinook' (also known as king), 'Sockeye' (red), 'Chum' (dog or keta), 'Coho' (silver), and pink (humpback or spring). On first sight, their meat might look weird because it's a much deeper red than the (often dye-enhanced) pink of Atlantic. But it's fabulous oily, rich, muscly fish that you can eat with a clear conscience. In 2015 the run of Pacific salmon on the east coast of Canada was the largest ever recorded.

You could argue that to eat farmed is better than eating wild, because each fish you eat has been produced by man and therefore has not been removed from the natural wild world. And you might be right. After all, the meat we eat is from farmed animals. If it's not a problem for you, then you can't beat steamed Atlantic salmon loins with spring greens and mustard dressing, grilled salmon cutlets with capers and lime, or cold-smoked salmon pieces in lightly scrambled eggs on zingy rye bread toast.

However, if you do eat our farmed fish, I think you have to accept that the farming might not be doing our seas much good. The alternative is to eat wild, and admittedly imported, from a fishery that is very well controlled. I would buy wild Pacific salmon from an MSC-certified fishery every time.

FRIED SALMON WITH CUCUMBER AND GOOSEBERRY SALAD

2 salmon fillet portions (about 150g each)

1 tbsp olive or rapeseed oil

A small knob of butter

FOR THE SALAD

½ small cucumber

100g ripe, raw, not-too-sharp gooseberries

Juice of ½ lemon

1 tsp caster sugar

1 tbsp chopped mint

1 tbsp extra virgin olive or rapeseed oil

Sea salt and black pepper

This clean-tasting salad, with its sharp, fruity notes and delicate crunch, goes beautifully with rich, oily salmon. Outside the gooseberry season, you can make it just with cucumber – use a bit more of it and be generous with the lemon juice. You could also use tarragon instead of mint. This recipe works well with sea trout and with fresh mackerel too. Serves 2

To prepare the salad, peel the cucumber, halve it lengthways and scoop out the seeds, then slice into 1cm thick half-moons and place in a bowl. Halve the gooseberries and add these to the cucumber. Add the lemon juice, sugar, mint, extra virgin oil and some salt and pepper. Stir everything together very gently then set aside while you cook the fish.

Heat a large non-stick frying pan over a medium-high heat. Season the salmon all over with salt and pepper. Add the oil to the pan along with the butter. When it's bubbling away, lay the fish, skin side down, in the pan. Cook for 5–6 minutes, by which time the fish should have cooked at least three-quarters of the way through. Flip the fish over and give it a further minute, until just cooked through.

Transfer the fish to warmed plates. Give the salad a final turn and spoon it over and/or next to the fish. Serve straight away, with new potatoes.

S

Salsify & scorzonera

Gill Meller

LATIN NAME
Salsify: *Tragopogon porrifolius*.
Scorzonera: *Scorzonera hispanica*

ALSO KNOWN AS
Scorzonera: black salsify

SEASONALITY
October–November

These slender roots are unknown to many, but they are among the most delicious and delicately flavoured of all the winter veg. Salsify looks rather like a long, scrawny parsnip. Scorzonera (pictured left) is beautifully black-skinned and has a less tapering shape (though it may be labelled salsify too, or 'black salsify'). Both vegetables boast a subtle, sweet, nutty flavour, which is also sometimes described as either oysterish or artichoke-like.

Rarely to be found in mainstream retailers, these roots are treats that turn up in veg boxes and at farm shops in the autumn. Usually, they will be caked in earth, which is fine, as it protects their delicate skins. Take them home and wash off the soil, then peel them (with a light hand – otherwise you'll have hardly any root left!).

The flesh of both salsify and scorzonera browns very quickly so they should be dropped into a bowl of water with the juice of a lemon added as soon as they are peeled. Fish them out again, root by root, to slice them into discs or long fingers, or leave them whole if you prefer. They can then be simply simmered for 15–20 minutes, until tender, and served with butter, salt and pepper.

Alternatively, well-cooked salsify or scorzonera make fantastic pale purées, if blitzed up with butter and a splash of cream. They also roast well and the roots are fantastic part-cooked then layered in a dish with butter, a little crème fraîche and some cheese, and baked as a gratin.

Some people prefer to scrub these roots then cook them unpeeled, rubbing off the skins later. This allows you to avoid the sticky white latex that the roots can exude when peeled, but I still find it a bit of a faff.

Both salsify and scorzonera are hardy members of the daisy family – and not much more difficult to grow. Sow them in the spring, thin out the seedlings, keep them well watered and pull them up in the autumn – unless they're very small, in which case, grow them on for another year. That's about it. You can even eat the leaves and the flowers, if you like.

SLOW-BAKED SALSIFY WITH BUTTER AND THYME

Juice of 1 lemon

400g salsify

80g unsalted butter

100ml chicken or veg stock, or water

Leaves from 3–4 sprigs of thyme

2 garlic cloves, sliced

Sea salt and black pepper

Slow-roasted with a generous quantity of butter, salsify becomes meltingly tender and forms a lovely, rich liquor that will sauce whatever you serve it with. It makes a great side dish to fish but is also fantastic alongside wilted nettles or sea beet. You can do exactly the same thing with scorzonera. Serves 2

Preheat the oven to 140°C/Fan 120°C/Gas 1. Have ready a bowl of cold water acidulated with the juice of the lemon.

Rinse any earth from the salsify, then trim and peel the roots, dropping them straight into the lemon water once peeled. When all are done, drain the salsify and place the whole roots in a small roasting tin or baking dish in which they fit quite snugly. Dot over the butter and pour in the stock or water. Scatter over the thyme leaves, the garlic and plenty of salt and pepper.

Cover with a sheet of foil, crimping it tightly over the edges of the tin so as to trap all the steam as the salsify is cooking. Cook in the oven for 2½–3 hours or until the salsify is beautifully tender, giving the tin or dish a little shake partway through cooking to baste the veg. Serve straight away, with the roasting juices.

S

Salt

Steven Lamb

LATIN NAME
Sodium chloride

MORE RECIPES
Papas arrugadas (page 500);
Coley with bacon, apples and
hazelnuts (page 197); Pollack
with courgettes and cannellini
beans (page 484); Lemon-cured
herring (page 310); Tea-brined
chicken (page 634); Slow-cooked
turkey legs with bacon and
prunes (page 650); Salt beef with
carrots and potatoes (page 559);
Seared ox heart (page 305)

SOURCING
cornishseasalt.co.uk;
halenmon.com

Salt is a central ingredient in just about every kitchen across the planet. An exceptional mineral, older than civilisation, it is essential to our survival. Our bodies would cease to function without it and we instinctively hunger for it. Human beings have been finding ways to harvest salt since before the beginning of recorded history – and when we learned that it could not just flavour but preserve food too, it opened up new worlds to us. Have salt, will travel.

Salt has amazing properties. It enhances flavours but also tones down bitterness. It can preserve an ingredient almost indefinitely, or season it in the lightest way, so it can be served at its peak. Salt has its place in every culinary genre, from baking to cocktail-shaking. And, when it is absent, you know that it is needed.

Aside from its straight role in savoury dishes, salt forms an amazing partnership with sugar, either in quantity – in a cure, for instance – or even in tiny amounts. A pinch of salt enhances cakes, pastries and biscuits, and noticeably salty sweet treats, such as salted chocolate caramels, have a uniquely addictive quality.

In addition to its seasoning role, salt has a magical part to play in the alchemy of curing and preserving food. Salt is made up of tiny atoms that penetrate food and remove fluid from cells via osmosis. Since it is the residual fluid in meat, fish and poultry that attracts the bacteria which cause it to spoil, the removal of liquid by salt is an efficient way to preserve food. Salt also increases acidity, lowering the pH in meat, which makes it less hospitable to the microbes that cause spoilage.

By drastically slowing down deterioration in these ways, salt also creates a window of opportunity for flavour to develop. Salt applied to the surface of meat causes enzymes

TYPES OF SALT

This elemental ingredient is either rock salt, mined from below the earth's surface, or sea salt, which is evaporated from seawater. (Though rock salt was once sea salt too – it comes from huge deposits of sodium chloride, the ghosts of ancient oceans, buried beneath the land.)

Table salt This is the most common form of culinary rock salt. It is pumped from below the earth as a brine, refined by having trace elements such as magnesium and calcium removed, evaporated by boiling in a series of pressurised containers, and finally dried. It is then combined with additives that stop it caking and sticking together. Table salt is very inexpensive but generally has a more dull, chemical flavour than additive-free salt. The additives don't dissolve readily, either, which is why a brine made with fine, free-flowing salt may look cloudy. Iodine is occasionally added to table salt – the idea being to help prevent iodine deficiency which can lead to thyroid-related illnesses. Iodised salts carry a distinct taste of seaweed, particularly when dissolved in tap water that has a high level of chlorine.

Coarse rock salt Also generally recrystallised from a purified brine, this rock salt has large, hard, crunchy crystals that work very well dispensed from salt grinders (although, unlike pepper, there is no great advantage to using your salt freshly ground).

Fine sea salt This may be produced from purified sea water, evaporated under controlled conditions to create small, regularly shaped crystals. As with fine-grained rock salts, it may well have anti-caking agents added. Other fine sea salts are formed by simply grinding down flaky sea salt.

Flaky sea salt If seawater is filtered and then heated to evaporation point, either under the sun or in broad vats, it forms large, delicate, flat, flaky crystals. The best flaky salts retain traces of natural minerals but are additive-free. Flaky sea salts are much more expensive than standard table salts but they have a sweet, full flavour that makes them ideal for seasoning and finishing dishes. They look beautiful and also add an appealing, crunchy texture when sprinkled on at the last minute. In the UK, we produce some fantastic flaky sea salts that are the rival of any in the world. Welsh Halen Môn (which has a PDO and is Soil Association approved), Maldon Sea Salt and Cornish Sea Salt are all superb. Fleur de sel from Southwest France is similarly excellent.

Pure dried vacuum salt (PDV) This is evaporated in such a way as to produce tiny, equally sized grains; it can be rock or sea salt. I find it the best salt for curing and preserving because, when applied to meat, the grains have an even, aggressive action, making for a predictable and effective curing process.

to digest natural sugars within it and then release lactic or acetic acid. These acids in turn break down proteins and fats into smaller molecules, such as peptides. Over the course of several weeks or months, peptides convert into a complex array of flavoursome compounds with citrus and nutty notes.

If you add salt to water it dissolves into liquid brine, which can both flavour ingredients and suspend the process of decay. A brine also relaxes the protein strands in meat, which are usually grouped together tightly. This allows the brine to be deposited in the spaces, making the meat moister on cooking.

Of course, there are health issues related to consuming an excess of salt. The recommended maximum daily amount for adults is 6g: about 1 tsp. If salt is applied knowingly to good ingredients within that parameter, as opposed to being consumed in a hidden form via processed foods, it can be kept in balance and its flavour-enhancing magic can be enjoyed.

SALTED CARAMEL SAUCE

150g caster or granulated sugar

50g unsalted butter, at room temperature, cut into small pieces

150ml double cream, ideally not fridge-cold

A good pinch of salt

It's essential to have your ingredients measured out and ready before you start here. Use on ice cream, pancakes and other fruity puddings. For an unusual twist, try stirring in a pinch of ground cumin. Makes about 300ml

Put the sugar in a heavy-based saucepan with a reasonably wide base, or a small frying pan. A stainless steel pan is better than a dark-based one, so you can see the colour of the caramel. Shake the pan to spread the sugar evenly, and place over a medium-low heat.

After a couple of minutes, the sugar will start to melt at the edges. Shake and swirl it gently as it starts to liquefy and brown. You can stir it a little but be restrained – stirring can cause the sugar to re-crystallise. By the time all the sugar has melted, some of it will be quite brown. Keep cooking for a minute or so, swirling the pan gently, until all the syrup has turned a rich, dark golden brown with a reddish tint.

As soon as the caramel has reached the right colour, take the pan off the heat. Add the butter and let it melt – be careful, the mix will bubble and steam. Gently stir the melted butter into the caramel – don't worry if it doesn't seem to amalgamate fully at this stage.

Now, working fairly quickly but in a controlled fashion, gradually add the cream, stirring in each addition before adding the next, and adding the salt about halfway through, to make a velvety smooth sauce. There may be a few little sticky bits lurking at the edges of the pan but, if your caramel was smooth to start with and you work quickly, you shouldn't get any crystallised lumps. If this does happen, put the sauce back over a gentle heat and stir to dissolve them as far as possible, then pass through a sieve before serving.

Serve the sauce warm or at room temperature. It will keep for a week in the fridge, and can be gently reheated.

S

Salt beef

Steven Lamb

SOURCING
graigfarm.co.uk;
turnerandgeorge.co.uk

While we enjoy it today for its deliciousness, salt beef has its roots in the tradition of curing meat out of necessity. In Britain, this ingredient can be traced back to the sixteenth century at least, when barrels of brined beef were a staple of the English Navy.

There is a tradition of salt beef in the Jewish communities of New York and London too, and it is their style of salt beef that is perhaps most familiar to us today: a gently brined, slow-cooked, open-grained joint of brisket. The best examples are only delicately salty, but unbelievably moist and deeply flavoured. There are delis and restaurants that specialise in salt beef, particularly in London, but it is a bit of a rare find. Making it yourself, using brisket or foreflank, is a good option.

The beef is brined before cooking (this is what makes it 'salt beef'). Recipes may suggest brines with anything from 10–30 per cent salinity, and brining time anything from one day to several days. I like to use a moderate amount of salt and the minimum time (as in the recipe below) because I find this seasons the beef beautifully.

Beef contains less residual liquid than other meats and deteriorates more slowly. And, of course, a modern recipe like this is not designed to preserve the meat for long keeping, so the brining can be relatively light. But you must suit your own palate: a heavier brine and/or longer soaking time will just give you more salty salt beef.

After brining, the beef is gently poached with stock veg and aromatics such as garlic and bay until it is so tender that a skewer passes through it easily. This will take around 3 hours. Salt beef can be served hot with boiled potatoes, lentils or beans or cold, in sandwiches with mustard and gherkins. Leftover beef can be fried into a delicious salt beef hash.

SALT BEEF WITH CARROTS AND POTATOES

If you don't have time to brine your own beef, you can use a piece of shop-bought boned and rolled raw salt beef. Serves 6 with leftovers

1.5–2kg piece of beef brisket (or foreflank), boned and rolled

3 medium onions, halved but root left on, and peeled

6 medium carrots, peeled and left whole

3–4 celery stalks, halved

1 head of garlic, halved through the middle

A small bunch of thyme

4 bay leaves

A small bunch of parsley

750g large potatoes

Sea salt and black pepper

FOR THE BRINE

360g soft light brown sugar

600g fine salt

½ tsp black peppercorns

½ tsp juniper berries

2–3 bay leaves

A large sprig of thyme

If you are brining your own beef, put all the brine ingredients into a large pan with 3 litres water. Stir over a low heat until the sugar and salt have dissolved, then bring to the boil. Simmer for 1–2 minutes, then take off the heat. Allow to cool, then refrigerate.

Put the beef into a non-metallic container and pour over the cold brine. If necessary, place a plate on top to keep the meat submerged. Leave to cure in the fridge, allowing 24 hours per kg.

Remove the meat from the brine, rinse and pat dry. Wrapped in muslin, it will keep for a few days in the fridge.

When ready to cook, put the salted beef into a large pan that has a tight-fitting lid and pour in enough fresh water to cover. Add the onions, carrots, celery, garlic, thyme and bay. Pick the leaves from the parsley stalks and reserve them, then add the stalks to the pan. Bring to a simmer and cook very gently, covered, for around 3 hours, until very tender (start checking it after a couple of hours).

Peel the potatoes and cut into large pieces. Transfer the beef to a warm plate to rest. Add the potatoes to the pan of salt beef stock and return to a simmer. Cook for 15–25 minutes or until the potatoes are just tender. Chop the parsley leaves and add them to the pan along with some pepper (and salt if needed).

Slice the beef and serve in dishes, with the chunky vegetables and a few spoonfuls of the well-flavoured broth. This is very good with some mustard.

Samphire, marsh

John Wright

LATIN NAME
Salicornia species

ALSO KNOWN AS
Glasswort

SEASONALITY
June–September

HABITAT
Salt marshes and mud flats

SOURCING
riverford.co.uk;
fishforthought.co.uk

Marsh samphire is a common, native plant of muddy estuaries and shores, occasionally making an appearance in brackish water behind pebble beaches. The bright green, sometimes purple, branching leaves have the appearance of tiny cacti, and for good reason – their succulence and shape is to protect them from what is, in effect, a very dry, or at least very drying, habitat. It is sometimes thought that samphire is a seaweed, but, despite spending half its time under water, it is a true flowering plant and related to spinach. (Rock samphire is a completely unrelated plant, found on sea walls, pebble beaches and cliffs; never marshes. It was once highly prized, though I have no idea why, as it tastes horribly of paraffin.)

Although common, marsh samphire is a plant to pick only occasionally and then with care. By law, it must be cut, not uprooted – even though this is of no help to what is, after all, an annual plant. Tread carefully when picking so that you damage as few plants as possible, and just take what you need. In some parts of the country, notably East Anglia, samphire is jealously guarded by the locals who collect it as a cash crop. The decent and safe path is to ask them and, if you get a frosty look, search elsewhere.

The plant first appears in spring but is generally not large enough to pick until, traditionally, 21 June, midsummer's day. It loses its fresh appearance by mid–September and disappears by late October.

When fresh, the leaves are extremely salty and succulent. The older specimens have a central thread, which is usually stripped out through the teeth in as lady-like a manner as is possible. Once lightly sautéed in butter (the simplest and most common method of cooking) much of the saltiness seems to disappear. Generally, samphire is used as a simple and appropriate accompaniment to fish. When used in dishes such as a fish quiche or omelette, bear in mind that there is still a lot of salt left in the samphire and no more need be added.

If you are not gathering your own, getting hold of samphire is easy enough; many fishmongers and even supermarkets sell it. However, little of that on sale is British, even during its season. You can often ferret it out in the summer, though, in independent shops near samphire-growing areas like the Norfolk coast.

SAMPHIRE, CRAB AND NEW POTATO SALAD

500–600g new potatoes,
scrubbed

200g marsh samphire, trimmed
and washed

200g fresh crabmeat

3 tbsp extra virgin olive or
rapeseed oil

Finely grated zest of ½ lemon
and the juice of the whole lemon

Sea salt and black pepper

Lemon wedges, to serve

This delicate warm salad makes a lovely starter or light lunch. You can use brown or spider crab, adding just the white meat or a mixture of white and brown as you prefer, or even lobster. You can also substitute penne pasta for the new potatoes. Serves 4

Cut the potatoes into bite-sized pieces. Add to a pan of cold water with a generous pinch of salt and bring to a simmer. Cook gently for 8–10 minutes or until just barely tender.

Drop the samphire into the pan and simmer for another 2 minutes. Drain the potatoes and samphire and place in a large salad bowl.

Add the crabmeat to the bowl, trickle over the oil and add the lemon zest. Squeeze over the juice of the lemon and season the salad with pepper and a little salt (go easy on the salt because of the samphire's natural saltiness).

Tumble everything together gently and serve straight away, with some lemon wedges and brown bread and butter.

Sardines

LATIN NAME
Sardina pilchardus

ALSO KNOWN AS
Pilchards (big sardines)

SEASONALITY
Best eaten August–February, outside peak spawning times

HABITAT
Found throughout European waters, with the British Isles usually the northernmost limit

MCS RATING
2–3

REC MINIMUM SIZE
15cm

MORE RECIPES
Garfish with olives, oregano and garlic (page 267); Roast gurnard with pepper, lemon, thyme and chilli (page 292); Lemon-cured herring (page 310); Grilled sprats with harissa dressing (page 600); Sardines with pine nuts, fennel and orange (page 471)

SOURCING
goodfishguide.org; msc.org; fish4ever.co.uk; pilchardworks.co.uk (for tinned Cornish sardines)

Seafood sustainability will always be a thorny issue, if not an outright minefield. In a world where appetite for fish rages on, while stock levels fluctuate, fishing methods constantly change and international politics muddy the waters, choosing the 'right' fish is rarely simple. However, we can fairly unequivocally say that it's a good idea to eat British sardines. Not all sardine stocks are as robust as they could be, but those fished around our coast – mainly in the Southwest – are both healthy and well managed.

This means it's also good to eat British pilchards. That's not a hard conclusion to draw, because sardines and pilchards are in fact the same thing, the only difference being size. A pilchard is a big sardine. A sardine is a small pilchard. But the nomenclature is also, these days, linked to branding. 'Pilchard' is not an elegant word, and most of us think of these fish coming from a tin, coated in gloopy sauce. 'Sardine', on the other hand, conjures images of the Mediterranean island, Sardinia, after which these fish may or may not have been named – either way, the association with a hot, sunny and sexy place is good for sales. There's nothing wrong with that. Anything that encourages us to eat this oily-fleshed, wholesome and sustainable little fish is good in my book.

There are several related species known internationally as 'sardine', but only one, Sardina pilchardus, which swims as far north as the British Isles. It's been an important commercial fish on the south coast as far back as the sixteenth century, at least.

In days gone by, the Cornish pilchard industry relied in part on lookouts, or 'huers', who would be stationed on cliff tops in the season, scouting for masses of the silvery fish. A shout of 'hevva!' (which comes from the Cornish word for 'shoal'), channelled through a tin trumpet, signalled that they had been spotted and, by means of special signals, the scout would then help guide the boats with their nets to the right spot.

Most of the fish caught would be packed in salt and these were exported in great quantity to European countries, particularly Italy, where they were much valued on days of Catholic abstinence. Oil pressed from the fish would also be burnt for lighting (and a pilchard lamp does not smell as bad as you might think). They remained an important commodity up until the beginning of the last century. At this point, alternative forms of preservation took precedence over salting, and the popularity of other tinned fish such as tuna and salmon grew. These factors conspired to diminish trade to the point where, in 1995, only a minuscule 7 tonnes of pilchard were landed off Cornwall.

However, within the last couple of decades, the pilchard fishers of Cornwall have taken steps to revive their industry – and have chalked up a remarkable success story. They re-branded their catch (out with 'pilchards' in with 'Cornish sardines') and formed a trade body that both promotes the product and works to keep stock levels healthy. The catch for 2014 was 4,000 tonnes – and there are still, for now, plenty more of those silvery little fish in the Cornish sea. These days, skippers use sonar, rather than a cliff-top lookout, to locate the fish, but Cornish sardines are still caught by small boats using traditional methods such as ring and drift nets, within 6 miles of the coast.

Old-fashioned, salted pilchards are sadly no longer available but fresh Cornish sardines and tinned Cornish pilchards most certainly are. The fishery has MSC certification, and also has European PGI (Protected Geographical Indication) status, meaning that they are recognised as uniquely linked to their area. They are particularly delicious in late summer and early autumn, when they are plump with maximum oil content. For good eating and good conscience, they're one of the very best piscine choices you can make.

S

Sardines reach sexual maturity at a precocious 2 years old – one of the factors that enables stocks to 'bounce back' relatively quickly after catches are taken. The most sustainable sardine to buy is one over 15cm in length because this signifies the creature has reached that stage of maturity and so may well have already reproduced. Confusingly, that technically makes it an old-school pilchard, but 15cm-plus specimens are more likely to be called sardines these days.

As a shoaling species, most sardines are caught using netting methods that operate within the water column (rather than by methods that drag heavy gear along the bottom). These techniques are usually very selective because sardines tend to swim together, but away from other species. Such methods are not ecologically flawless. Some by-catch can occur, and as with any fishing, we can always take too much – in fact, sardines are currently being overfished in some European waters – but they are caught without damaging the seabed and its benthic flora and fauna.

The rich flesh of sardines is delicate. As with any oil-rich fish, they can soften and start to go off very soon after catching, so should be nabbed as fresh as possible. However, once gutted, there's little preparation needed beyond rubbing off the fish's soft scales with your thumb and giving them a good rinse.

Related to herring, sardines are similarly blessed with lots of very fine bones. De-boning them is a tricky and time-consuming task, likely to leave you with a very mauled-looking, bruised fillet. You just have to enjoy those fine, calcium-rich little bits as part of the sardine experience (or eat tinned fillets, where the cooking process renders the small bones all but undetectable).

It is, however, very easy to remove the main 'backbone' part of the skeleton of a sardine. This is done by simply laying a whole, gutted fish on a board, belly down and belly flaps flaring outward, then pressing along the backbone until you feel the flesh release from it. Flip the sardine back over, grasp the tail and pull it gently up, bringing the spine and ribcage with it. You'll be left with a filleted sardine ready to throw on the barbecue or toss into a roasting dish.

And few fish respond so well to the fierce crackle of an open flame or the hard heat of a high oven. The oil sizzles in the rich flesh, basting it from within, while the skin (well salted, please) crisps to a glorious, fragrant, fishy toothsomeness. Sardines are just made for the barbie. I like these char-skinned beauties partnered with something a little sharp and punchy: a salsa verde, for example, or a simple spritz of lemon juice is good. Like mackerel, sardines are also very good with gooseberries or tomatoes.

Eating a sardine escabeche – where the fish are first fried, then bathed in a hot, spicy, onion- and chilli-fragranced vinegar and left to cool – is one of the nicest ways I know to end a summer day. And, perfect as they are for the fast blast or the quick fry, sardines are also ripe for the slow-cook treatment. Barely simmered in a tomato sauce over a very low heat for up to 4 hours, they emerge tender and delicious, with all the bones and even the head soft enough to eat.

Tinned sardines (or pilchards) are such a different animal from the fresh ones, that to me they hardly suffer by comparison, but can be enjoyed for a separate set of virtues. They are all about that yielding oily flesh that flakes so lightly yet tastes so rich. And somehow you know they are doing you good, oiling your joints and feeding your brain. In fact, fast food (I can open a tin in *seconds*) is rarely so virtuous. Not only do they provide oodles of healthy omega-3 fats, but the bones, softened within the fish flesh by the canning process, deliver a healthy shot of calcium too. I like tinned sardines crushed on to hot toast just as they come, but I also sometimes 'bloody mary' them first by mixing them with tomato ketchup, Tabasco, Worcestershire sauce, lemon juice and a pinch of celery salt. I've even been known to add a shot of vodka to take this superb snack to its logical conclusion. Tinned sardines are also fantastic flaked into a potato salad, strewn on to an omelette, folded into hot pasta, crushed into a coarse pâté (with crème fraîche and lots of lemon) or mashed into a steaming jacket potato with a generous amount of butter and perhaps some capers and a little chopped parsley. I like tinned Cornish sardines, as well as the MSC-certified ones from Fish4Ever.

GRILLED SARDINES WITH POTATOES AND ROSEMARY

750g cooked new or waxy salad potatoes, cut into 3–4mm slices

2 garlic cloves, cut into 1–2mm slices

Leaves from a large sprig of rosemary, finely chopped

4 tbsp olive oil

12 fresh sardines, scaled and gutted

Lemon juice

Sea salt and black pepper

As the sardines cook under the high heat of the grill, their lovely juices soak into the layer of potatoes underneath, lending them a fabulous flavour. This works with herring too. Serves 4

Preheat the grill to its hottest setting.

Put the sliced potatoes into a large bowl and add the sliced garlic and chopped rosemary. Add the olive oil and a little seasoning and turn the whole lot together gently with your hands, trying to keep the potato slices from breaking up too much.

Choose a large, lipped baking tray that will contain any juices. Spread the garlicky, herby potatoes in a single layer on the tray. Place under the grill and cook for a few minutes until the tops of most of the potatoes have taken on a little colour. Remove the tray and turn the potatoes over with a spatula. Don't worry if you miss the odd one or two.

Season the sardines inside and out with salt and pepper and lay them randomly over the potatoes. Return the tray to the grill. Cook for 3–4 minutes or until the fish are a little blistered and golden, then carefully flip each one over and grill for a further 2–3 minutes until just cooked through.

Squeeze a little lemon juice over the sardines and potatoes then serve them with any juices from the baking tray, with a green salad and some good bread on the side.

Sausages

MORE RECIPES
Roasted squash with chestnuts, sausage and sage (page 158); Pruney sausage rolls (page 447); Pear and celeriac stuffing (page 454)

SOURCING
gazegillorganics.co.uk, graigfarm.co.uk, rhug.co.uk and wellhungmeat.com (for fresh sausages); capreolusfinefoods.co.uk and good-game.co.uk (for British charcuterie)

Sausages are one of the oldest known forms of processed food. Dating back thousands of years, they were made by countless civilisations, including the Ancient Egyptians.

Sadly, in more recent years, this product has veered far away from its classic form, and many sausages on sale are a blend of cheap ingredients and additives, overly processed in large factories. Commerciality needn't mean the end of quality but, as a general rule, the further away you go from sausages made by a skilled butcher or producer and towards products made on an industrial scale, the more likely that quality will plummet.

A sausage is, or should be, a simple combination of minced raw meat and fat, seasoned with herbs, spices and salt, mixed with a small amount of rusk or breadcrumb to hold the fat in the sausage, then encased in a skin. The percentage of meat should not drop too far below 70 per cent. In my view, not only must the ingredients be of the highest quality, there should not be too many of them. Always check the label.

Sausages come in different skins. Natural casings are made from the intestines of sheep, pigs and cows, while synthetic casings are spun from collagen. Synthetic skins are the industry norm as they are cheaper but they often feel like a barrier – as though the sausage is still in the wrapper – whereas natural casings feel like a more integral part of the product.

There's a fashion now for 'gourmet' sausages: pork and leek or beef and Stilton, and such like. At best, these flavoured sausages can be outstanding. At worst, the meat and the flavouring are paired up in a bid to mask the inferiority of both.

It's the meat that really dictates overall quality. A sausage should not be a vessel for flesh of such dubious provenance that it would not otherwise make it on to your plate. Some cheap British bangers still include 'mechanically separated meat', for instance – a fine mince formed by removing vestigial scraps of meat, sinew and membrane from bones in a machine. It's not allowed to be counted as part of the meat content – though in some cases, by means of creative labelling, it still is.

Since good quality, high-welfare meat naturally costs more, any sausages labelled 'value' or 'basic' should give you pause for thought. And a sausage that is only, say 40 per cent pork (as with some of the 'catering' or 'economy' sausages out there) obviously begs some questions about what else is filling the skins.

The welfare of the animals that produce the meat has a huge impact on the quality of a sausage. The meat should be at least free-range, if not organic. See page 490 for other higher welfare indicators you might find on pork sausages. If you buy unlabelled sausages at the butchers, ask about their provenance.

Other kinds of sausage

As well as fresh sausages of the breakfast banger type, there are cured sausages, which don't require cooking. This group includes salami, which undergoes a process of fermentation and air-drying, as well as classic Continental sausages such as Bologna, frankfurter and mortadella, which contain enough salt to cure them but are then either smoked to help preserve them further or poached to cook them through before being eaten hot or cold.

It is often even harder to be sure of the provenance of sausages like these, since the majority of them are imported. But this is an exciting area because British charcuterie is very much on the rise. You can buy great, ethically produced British salamis now, for instance.

Home-made sausages

The best way to make sure that the ingredients of a sausage satisfy your standards is to make it yourself: something that can easily be done with a small amount of kit (i.e. a mincer and a sausage-stuffer). Home-made bangers are both pleasurable to make and delicious to eat. There's lots of advice and detailed instructions on home sausage-making in River Cottage's *Curing & Smoking* and *Pigs & Pork* handbooks, not to mention *The River Cottage Cookbook*, but here are a few salient points:

Sausages can be made with any meat but there must always be some form of fat in the mix so that the sausage is moist and tender when cooked. You can either use a cut of meat with a nice marbling of fat already inherent in it, such as pork shoulder, or combine a lean meat, such as venison, with something fatty, like pork belly. In salami, small cubes of pure back fat are mosaic-ed through meat to give a soft texture.

Sausages can take lots of seasoning, and there is no end to the variety of additions you can make. In pork sausages, I like to combine mace and white pepper with a hit of garam masala, while my beef sausages tend to be laced with hot spices such as cayenne and chilli.

If you are using breadcrumbs in your sausage mix, make sure that all the residual active yeast has been 'baked out' of them, by putting them in a low oven for about 10 minutes, then cooling them completely. Residual yeast in breadcrumbs sometimes has a souring effect on sausage meat, particularly pork.

Home-made or shop-bought, fresh sausages can be poached, smoked, roasted, grilled or fried. I cook mine by placing them in a cold pan with a splash of oil and cooking over a medium heat, shaking the pan every now and then, until the sausages are cooked all the way through with a nice colour and even caramelisation. This can take a good 20 minutes. If you want to avoid the classic barbecue offering – blackened on the outside and still semi-raw within – then the cooking of sausages cannot be rushed. Slow-cooking also stops the sausage from splitting and exploding in the pan – they're not called bangers for nothing.

SAUSAGES WITH SQUASH AND KALE

1 tbsp rapeseed oil

8 sausages

1 large onion, thinly sliced

2 garlic cloves, thinly sliced

4 bay leaves

2–3 sprigs of rosemary

1 small or ½ larger squash, such as a butternut or Crown Prince (about 500g)

350ml chicken, veg or pork stock

150g kale

Sea salt and black pepper

A fantastic, one-pot supper, this is hearty but not heavy. You can use any type of good, fresh sausage, and any variety of squash. (Pictured on page 566.) Serves 4

Place a large flameproof casserole over a medium heat. Add the oil, followed by the sausages. Brown them well all over – 6–8 minutes should do it – then remove them to a plate. Add the onion, garlic, bay and rosemary to the casserole and cook gently for 8–10 minutes until the onion is soft and just beginning to colour.

Meanwhile, peel and deseed the squash, then cut into large bite-sized chunks. Add to the casserole, along with the sausages and stock. Bring to a simmer, put the lid and cook gently over a low heat for 20–30 minutes or until the squash is almost tender.

In the meantime, remove the stalks from the kale and roughly shred the leaves. Add the kale to the casserole, stir and replace the lid. Cook for a further 10 minutes or so. Season with salt and pepper to taste.

Serve with some good bread for mopping up the juices.

Savory, summer & winter

Nikki Duffy

LATIN NAME
Summer savory: *Satureja hortensis*. Winter savory: *Satureja montana*

SEASONALITY
Summer savory: May–September. Winter savory: all year round

MORE RECIPES
Roasted beetroot orzotto with lavender (page 68); Goat kebabs with rosemary, red peppers and onion (page 280)

These are two underused herbs: lovely, aromatic things with robust, penetrating personalities – more akin to thyme and rosemary than, say, parsley or tarragon.

They are related but fairly different. Summer savory is a hardy annual, good between May and September, and the more delicate of the two. It's not *very* delicate, however. The flavour is aromatic – a little peppery, with a slightly resinous edge. It's a versatile herb that works well with green veg, root veg, fish and meat, and rich, creamy things. Add it, finely chopped, to meaty dishes such as stews – putting in some at the beginning and some at the end to get layers of flavour. It's great in a burger too, or the crumb coating for chicken goujons or baked fish. I love it strewn into vegetable bakes, or beaten into butter and used to dress green veg such as chard or French beans. Keep it away from your most delicate dishes and you can't go wrong.

Summer savory grows readily from seed, and thrives in pots as well as sunny, well-drained beds, blooming into a very pretty plant that looks rather like a long-leaved thyme. It froths with tiny white flowers in the early summer – but you should pinch these out if you want the leaves to stay tender and sweet.

Winter savory is more robust in flavour and darker in colour – a hardy perennial that looks a little like a miniature rosemary. It's got a wonderful, assertive flavour, with hints of mint, menthol and pine. It's exactly what a dish of simply cooked beans or lentils calls for. It is also very good in rich, meaty, fruit-studded stuffings for lamb or pork, and it's great roasted with slightly sweet, earthy veg such as parsnips and squashes. Use it as an infuser, without eating the actual herb, or chop it finely and add it judiciously for a more distinct flavour.

Winter savory can be raised from seed, taken as a cutting or bought as a young plant. Like its summer sibling, it prefers Mediterranean-style conditions, so a sunny, sheltered position and light, well-drained soil are ideal. It does well in pots. However, it's a tough little thing and, as long as it doesn't get too wet, you should be able to harvest from it all year round.

SUMMER SAVORY SCONES

180g plain flour

A good pinch of salt

20g caster sugar

2 tsp baking powder

85g cold butter, cubed

2 tbsp finely chopped summer savory

140ml single cream

Savory adds a wonderful fragrant note to these simple scones. Serve them still warm with butter and cheese or ham. They are also delicious made with thyme or marjoram. Makes 9

Preheat the oven to 200°C/Fan 180°C/Gas 6. Line a baking sheet with baking parchment.

Put the flour, salt, sugar and baking powder into a large bowl and whisk to combine and aerate. Add the cold butter and, using your fingertips, lightly rub it in until most of the pieces of butter are the size of petits pois or a little smaller; don't overwork the mix. Stir in the chopped savory. Set aside 1 tbsp cream, then stir in the rest until the mixture just comes together into a slightly sticky dough.

Turn out on to a lightly floured surface and roll or press the dough lightly with your hands until it's about 1.5cm thick. Stamp out 6.5cm rounds using a cutter, then gently re-roll or re-pat the dough scraps to cut the final scones.

Place the rounds on the baking sheet and brush the tops with the remaining cream. Bake for 15–17 minutes, until golden and well risen. Transfer to a wire rack to cool, then serve them warm or cold, split and buttered. These are best eaten within a day of making.

Scallops

LATIN NAME
King scallop: *Pecten maximus*.
Queen scallop: *Aequipecten opercularis*

SEASONALITY
King scallop: avoid April–
September when spawning.
Queen scallop: avoid in spring
and autumn when spawning

HABITAT
Main scallop-fishing areas
around the British Isles are
the English Channel, Isle of
Man, West of Scotland and
Moray Firth

MCS RATING
2–4

REC MINIMUM SIZE
King scallop: 10cm shell
width (minimum landing size
in some areas is 11cm).
Queen scallop: 4cm shell width
(minimum landing size in some
areas is 5cm)

MORE RECIPES
John Dory with creamed
radicchio (page 318)

SOURCING
goodfishguide.org; msc.org

Scallop divers hand-pick mature specimens from the seabed without damaging their ecologically rich territory. They do need a licence to sell their catch, but beyond that this form of fishing is largely unregulated and relies on good self-management – as well as the natural limitations imposed by time, water and weather – to be ecologically sound. However, when practised responsibly, it is a highly sustainable form of fishing.

It's a very different story for most scallops, which are dredged – raked up by heavy, sharp-toothed gear – which has huge repercussions in terms of damage to and destruction of marine flora and fauna. In some fisheries, measures are in place to limit the impact of dredging: the closure of certain sections of seabed, for instance, or restrictions on the size of the dredging equipment. Some would argue that carefully managed dredging is sustainable: there's even a scallop dredge fishery off Shetland that has been certified by the MSC. But hand-dived scallops remain the best option.

Scallops are so compactly meaty because they are all muscle. Unlike many other shellfish, they are very mobile, moving often underwater to find the best places for hoovering up plankton. The function of that big white puck of meat is to open and close the shell and propel the scallop forward. A 'flock' of scallops speeding along in this way is one of the most magnificent sights of the seabed.

The filtering frill or mantle around the edge of the scallop muscle holds a fringe of photoreceptors. These primitive eyes can sense if a shadow passes and the scallop then uses its jet propulsion to escape danger. The vibrantly coloured coral, meanwhile, is the scallop's formidable, all-in-one sexual organ. The orange-pink tip contains up to 100 million eggs whilst the creamy part contains the sperm. Both are released into the sea at different times and places so this hermaphrodite doesn't mate with itself.

As a scallop grows and fattens, it adds rings of growth to its shell. However, if disturbed, it will divert energy to forming extra shell. The best scallops are heavy in their shell, indicating that they have lived a relaxed life, and more of their energy has gone into building up meat.

If you are lucky enough to get scallops live and super-fresh in the shell, they are amazingly sweet. In this condition, they are delicious served raw: just slice the muscle into thin rounds and season with lime juice, a little sugar, freshly chopped coriander and a pinch of salt. However, due to complex processing regulations that make it easier and cheaper for fishmongers to sell them 'cut', you are more likely to buy them already released from the shell and therefore dead. Cut scallops can still be sublime, as long as they are very fresh – but I wouldn't serve them raw.

Scallops are best cooked very simply. Oil them lightly and flash-fry on a griddle or hot frying pan for about 1 minute on each side, or cook them quickly in butter with a whisper of garlic. You can keep the orange roe attached if you like to eat it (it has a rich flavour and velvety texture), though if the scallops are super-big you may want to cut off the coral so it is easier to get it into contact with the hot pan to cook properly.

Cooking should be done with a high heat, long enough to form a speckled golden crust on the outside of the scallop while leaving it barely cooked within – the centre should be just hot and have lost its pearly translucence. Serve simply with lemon juice and herbs or with cured pork; or barbecue scallops on skewers with chunks of chorizo; or fry chorizo in a pan and cook the scallops in the spicy oil it releases.

If you are buying live scallops in the shell, store them rounded side down in the fridge for no more than a couple of days. The shell will be shut tight at first but may well open up a few centimetres over 48 hours. To open or shuck the scallop, you need

S

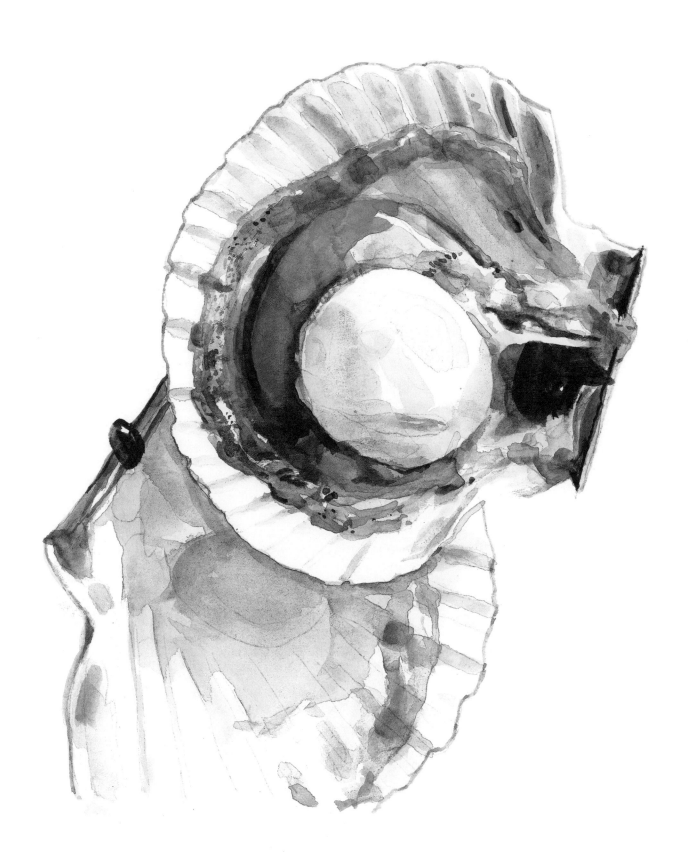

a thin-bladed knife with a little flex to it, such as a filleting knife. Hold the shell vertically, round edge down, hinge at the top, on a board, with the flat side of the shell facing towards you. Find an opening partway down the side of shell and wangle the knife-tip in. The idea is to keep the knife tight to the flat of the shell and cut down through the muscle at the point it meets the shell. With luck and practice, the shell will open and the scallop remain whole.

You need to get rid of the black sac of guts at the back of the scallop, plus a small strand of black intestine, as these can harbour toxins. Make a little incision just behind where the orange roe joins the white meat and peel away the unwanted parts, leaving the roe with the main muscle. Trim off and discard the two frilly pieces of mantle. Chefs also tend to cut off the small piece of tough, extra-white muscle on the edge of the more tender flesh. Rinse the scallops and pat dry.

If you are buying your scallops ready-shucked, look for ones that haven't been frozen at sea and are still attached to their orange-and-tan coral.

Most scallops are taken from the wild although scallop 'ranchers' do exist: licensed individuals who have been granted rights to the shellfish in a certain area. Ranchers will place their scallops in a good situation, both for feeding and harvesting.

In Britain, we favour king scallops, which are found all around our coast. These can live for 20 years but generally reach their legal size for landing at around 4 years. Kings are generally best in the colder months before they spawn and their bisexual tackle shrivels. Smaller and shorter-living queenies are especially abundant near the Isle of Man, where they are caught by otter-trawl when they swim off the seabed between June and October. Often exported, otter-trawled Manx queenies have been MSC-certified in the past but certification is currently suspended because stocks are too low.

SCALLOPS WITH CAULIFLOWER PURÉE AND GREEN PEPPERCORNS

This combination of sweet, seared scallops, silky cauliflower and zesty green peppercorns is amazing. A purée of peas or broad beans works beautifully here too. Serves 2 as a starter

25g butter

1 tbsp olive or rapeseed oil

½ small onion, sliced

1 garlic clove, sliced

½ small cauliflower (about 200g), trimmed and roughly chopped

Leaves from 2 sprigs of thyme

150ml whole milk

A few drops of cider vinegar

6 scallops

2 tsp green peppercorns in brine, drained

Sea salt and black pepper

Put a medium saucepan over a medium-low heat and add half the butter and half the oil. When bubbling, add the onion and garlic and cook gently for about 10 minutes until soft and beginning to caramelise a little. Now add the cauliflower and the thyme and season with a little salt and pepper. Stir well and cook for a further 3–4 minutes.

Pour in the milk, bring to a simmer, place a lid on the pan and cook for 6–8 minutes until the cauliflower is tender (don't worry if the milk looks a little grainy). Take off the heat and use a stick blender in the pan (or transfer to a jug blender) to purée the cauliflower until smooth. Add the cider vinegar and more salt or pepper as required. Keep warm.

Heat a medium non-stick frying pan over a high heat. Add the remaining oil and, when the pan is hot, add the scallops. Season them with salt and pepper and cook for about 1 minute on each side or until they have a nice golden crust. Remove the pan from the heat and add the remaining butter and the green peppercorns. Swirl them around in the pan as the butter melts.

Put a couple of spoonfuls of cauliflower purée on each warmed plate. Top with the scallops and spoon over the green peppercorn butter. Serve at once.

Sea bass

Nick Fisher

LATIN NAME
Dicentrarchus labrax

ALSO KNOWN AS
Bass

SEASONALITY
Avoid February–May when
spawning

HABITAT
Found around the British
Isles but more common
off the south coast

MCS RATING
3–5

REC MINIMUM SIZE
42cm

MORE RECIPES
Black bream with Jerusalem
artichoke purée (page 91)

SOURCING
goodfishguide.org;
linecaught.org.uk

Bass are homicidal thugs, ruthless killers who come armed to the teeth with hardened plates on their gills, thick, tough scales and sharp fin spines. Bass love to hunt. On wrecks and reefs, when the tide starts to bubble fizzy oxygen into the water, the blood rushes to bass' brains and they switch to kill-mode. Anyone who's ever caught a bass will have felt the sheer psychopathic violence of this predator vibrating through the line. It is no wonder that the French call them *loups de mer* – wolves of the sea.

Sadly, however, wild bass are in big trouble. As slow-growing fish, they are vulnerable to over-exploitation. Their numbers are in free-fall and scientific advice is that the current catch is far too high. Fishing for bass by hand-line – as the South-West Handline Fishermen's Association do in Cornwall – is the most selective, low-impact method. But right now, even catches from these fisheries are not thought to be sustainable.

Not even recreational bass fishermen can relax – angling for this fish is such a popular sport that it's contributing to the decline of this magnificent fish and the angling fraternity are now, quite correctly, prohibited from keeping more than one fish per day for half the year – and any fish at all for the other half.

The alternative to wild bass is the farmed fish, which accounts for most of the bass you'll find on sale. Much of it is grown in net-confined farms in Turkey, Cyprus, Greece or Malta, while some now comes from land-based tank systems, which avoid many of the problems of traditional aquaculture and are considered a good environmental choice. But I'm afraid farmed bass is not for me. This fish lives for rough, oxygenated water, rugged rocky ground and fast prey to chase and kill; wild bass flesh is slightly oily, protein-packed killer-meat. Farmed is distinctly dull by comparison.

So, while I wait in sure and certain hope of the stock recovering, I'm not eating much bass these days. If you do want to shop for bass, be aware that the small portion-sized fish you see for sale (under 1kg) will *always* be farmed fish. It's illegal for commercial fishermen to land these plate-sized specimens. Big bass over 42cm long, or fillets that are two-fingers deep, are likely to be wild.

STEAMED SEA BASS WITH KALE AND GINGER

2 garlic cloves, grated

A thumb-sized piece of root ginger, grated

2 tbsp soy sauce

1 tsp toasted sesame oil

1 small hot red chilli, deseeded and thinly sliced (optional)

2 sea bass fillets (about 150g each)

150g kale or cavolo nero, leaves stripped from the stalk

This is a very simple, quick dish, which also works with bream, John Dory, gurnard, hake and trout or sustainable salmon. Everything is steamed together so the flavours mingle beautifully. You'll need a steamer with a basket large enough to hold the fish fillets in one layer – though you can cut them into pieces if need be. Serves 2

Combine the garlic, ginger, soy and sesame oil, and the chilli if using. Rub this mixture into the fish and leave to marinate for 15–20 minutes.

Meanwhile, wash and drain the kale or cavolo nero and lay in the base of the steamer basket. Pour 200–300ml water into the steaming pan and bring to a brisk simmer.

Place the fish on top of the kale or cavolo nero leaves, pouring over any marinating juices. Set the basket of kale and fish on top of the steaming pan and cover with a lid. Steam for 4–5 minutes or until the fish is just cooked.

Serve the fish and kale or cavolo nero on warmed plates, with rice or noodles.

Sea beet

Hugh Fearnley-Whittingstall

LATIN NAME
Beta vulgaris subsp. *maritima*

ALSO KNOWN AS
Sea spinach

SEASONALITY
From late March

HABITAT
Upper beach, pebble beaches, coastal paths, cliff tops. Common around most of the British Isles, though less so in the far north of Scotland

MORE RECIPES
Chard and new potatoes with paprika and fennel (page 138); Henakopita with garam masala and eggs (page 254); Spinach, egg and potato curry (page 599)

If you love spinach and Swiss chard, then sea beet will certainly float your boat. You can use this delicious leaf in place of either, or indeed of pretty much any leafy green vegetable, in countless recipes, from tarts and soups to curries and bhajis. But you won't find sea beet in the shops.

Sea beet is a wild plant, with fleshy, sometimes red-tinged leaves, which look like a more leathery version of spinach, and nodding flower spikes in summer. As you would expect, it's usually found by the sea – generally on cliff-tops or paths, well above the tideline (but within the reach of the sea spray).

As with many wild greens, the early season growth is the most sweet and tender. Start keeping your eye out for sea beet's thick, glossy clumps from late March. The leaves can be picked right through to the winter, but as with many leafy greens, this plant is less tasty when it has thrown its energy into flowering. The beet-like root, while edible, should not be dug up without the permission of the landowner.

Once home, wash sea beet leaves thoroughly (changing the water at least once) and remove the tough stalks. Steam it, wilt it in boiling water (then squeeze out excess liquid and chop) or sweat it down in a pan with butter, then serve just as it is, well seasoned with black pepper. Or try a creamed sea beet gratin – the cooked, chopped leaves folded into a good béchamel, topped with cheese and breadcrumbs and grilled – one of my all-time favourite foraged-veg meals.

SEA BEET AND SMOKED POLLACK PASTIES

Glorious picnic fare, these golden-crusted pastry parcels are bursting with smoky, sea-scented deliciousness. They're also excellent made with spinach or chard. Makes 4

Shortcrust pastry (see page 33) OR home-made rough puff pastry (see page 447), made with 400g flour and 200g butter

1 egg, beaten with a little milk, to glaze

FOR THE FILLING

200g sea beet

350–400g smoked pollack or smoked haddock

15g butter

1 tbsp olive or rapeseed oil

1 onion, thinly sliced

2 garlic cloves, sliced

1 tbsp plain flour

150ml double cream

1 tsp Dijon mustard

1 tbsp chopped dill

Sea salt and black pepper

Remove the coarse stems from the sea beet. Wash the leaves, shake off excess water and place them in a large pan. Season with a little salt and pepper, cover and cook over a medium-high heat for 4–5 minutes or until wilted and tender. Meanwhile, cut the fish into finger-sized strips, checking for pin-bones as you do so.

Drain the sea beet and leave until cool enough to handle, them squeeze out the excess water and roughly chop.

Put the butter and oil in a large saucepan over a medium heat. When bubbling, add the onion and garlic. Cook, stirring often for 8–10 minutes or until starting to colour. Sprinkle over the flour, stir well and cook for a further minute. Stir in the cream, then the fish, chopped sea beet, mustard, dill and some salt and pepper. Cook for a couple of minutes more – the cream will thicken quickly. You don't need to cook the fish through at this point. Remove from the heat and leave to cool completely.

Preheat the oven to 190°C/Fan 170°C/Gas 5 and line a baking tray with baking parchment or a silicone liner (with rough puff pastry, use a baking tray with a lip as the pastry may leak a little butter). Divide the pastry into 4 equal pieces. Roll out each one to a thickness of 4–5mm then cut a circle from each, about 20cm in diameter.

Place one quarter of the sea beet filling on one half of each pastry circle, leaving a 2–3cm margin at the edge. Brush beaten egg over the pastry edge, next to the filling. Fold over the pastry to encase the filling and crimp the edges together securely. Repeat for each pasty, brush the tops with more egg wash, and place on the prepared baking tray.

Bake for 30–35 minutes until the pastry is a rich golden brown. Allow the pasties to cool a little, or completely, before eating.

Sea buckthorn

John Wright

LATIN NAME
Hippophae rhamnoides

SEASONALITY
Berries: August–October

HABITAT
Seashore, sand dunes and
roadsides. Fairly common
around the entire British coast

Sea buckthorn, famed through history for its health-bestowing properties, is a native shrub of eastern coasts. It has now been planted on roadsides just about everywhere, and as a stabiliser of sand dunes, where it has made an impenetrable nuisance of itself.

With its narrow, grey-green leaves and clustered, vivid orange berries, sea buckthorn is easy to spot. The berries ripen in late August and are available until late October. The best time to pick them is when they are bright orange and very juicy – easily crushed between the fingers. September is generally peak season, but this does vary from year to year and with location.

The bright berries cluster among the vicious thorns along the branches and are extremely difficult to pick. Since it is only the juice that is required, rather than the whole berry, I often hold a bucket under a branch and, protected by a thick rubber glove, squidge out the juice. A neat alternative is to freeze entire berry laden branches, then beat and shake the berries on to a sheet, transfer them to a bowl and let them defrost – at which point they will collapse and give up their juice.

Occasionally, with under-ripe berries that don't burst easily, it's necessary to coax the juice out of them by simmering them in a little water. But ripe berries don't even need heating. The key thing is to strain out all debris, twigs, leaves and unwanted matter by squeezing the juice/pulp through fine muslin or a jelly bag.

The flavour is a bit of a shock the first time you try it – orangey but highly acidic – though sweetening does wonders, transforming it into an intense, head-clearing fruitiness. If brought to the boil and sugar is added, the extracted juice gives you a cordial that will keep for a couple of weeks. This is useful, not just as the base of a fruity drink, but in a champagne cocktail or a sauce for fish. If the juice is boiled with sugar for a little longer, you will get a jelly; longer still and you get a fruit cheese, superb with, well, cheese.

SEA BUCKTHORN JUICE

400ml strained sea buckthorn
juice

About 200g caster sugar,
to taste

The idea here is to produce a sweet-tart, juicy liquor, 'pasteurised' by heating but not containing enough sugar to be fully preserved and syrupy, as with a traditional cordial. You will have to judge the amount of sugar to add because the acidity and flavour of the berries can vary a good deal over the season – but 50 per cent sugar to juice should be about right. Extract your buckthorn juice as described above. Makes about 500ml

Put the strained juice into a pan and heat gently until steaming hot but not boiling. Whisk in the sugar until it is dissolved. Taste and add more sugar as needed to get a still-tart but palatable result. Pour the sweetened juice into a sterilised jug or bottle, leave to cool then refrigerate.

Keep the sweetened juice in the fridge and use up within a week. It makes a fantastically refreshing drink, diluted with a little sparkling water and poured over a glass full of ice.

You can also add a couple of teaspoonfuls of the juice to a sweet-and-sour sauce, or set the juice with a little gelatine for an intensely flavoured, almost orangey jelly. Try a sea buckthorn syllabub too, whisking the juice into softly whipped, sweetened cream.

S

Seaweed

John Wright

LATIN NAME
Dulse: *Palmaria palmate*.
Kelp: *Laminaria digitata*.
Sugar kelp: *Saccharina latissima*.
Laver: *Porphyra* spp.
Gutweed: *Ulva intestinalis*.
Carragheen: *Chondrus crispus*,
Mastocarpus stellatus.
Sea spaghetti: *Himanthalia
elongata*

SEASONALITY
Most varieties can be foraged
all year round but many are
best in spring and summer

HABITAT
Many varieties are common
and widely distributed

MORE RECIPES
Jerusalem artichoke and
seaweed tart (page 33);
Noodles with seaweed, smoked
mackerel and soy (page 407);
Dover sole with seaweed butter
(page 588); Hake with root and
seaweed broth (page 297)

SOURCING
clearspring.co.uk;
cornishseaweed.co.uk;
justseaweed.com;
maraseaweed.com

It is extraordinary that so abundant a food resource as seaweed is all but ignored by the British. Apart from dulse in Northern Ireland and Scotland, and laver in Wales, there is little traditional use for this food and most people's experience of seaweed is as an unsuspected food additive or in sushi. Nori – the thin, dark green sheet you find rolled elegantly around sushi rice – is made from an oriental species of laver which has been put through a paper-making process and then toasted.

Half the reason why the British eschew seaweed is its former lack of mainstream availability. The other half is that they have absolutely no idea what to do with the stuff. And the third half (yes, I know) is that it really, really doesn't look very tasty. The first problem is well on the way to being solved. These days, seaweeds are available dried from delicatessens, health food shops and supermarkets and can be fantastically convenient ingredients: with all the hard work done for you, they usually just need soaking – though some can even be used straight from the pack.

And of course you can also gather your own fresh seaweed. There is certainly no shortage of it and it can be truly delicious. It is all down to how you prepare it. The flavour of raw seaweeds is mild and slightly fishy and the texture a bit of a challenge. So, apart from using it raw as a decorative addition to a dish or dried (as described below), seaweeds should be cooked. This breaks down the cell structure and a transformation takes place. The umami flavours – those intense meaty, yeasty, fishy, mushroomy tastes within – are released.

If the taste is not enough to tempt you, then perhaps the health benefits are. Seaweeds' balance of minerals, antioxidants, amino acids and proteins makes them instant food supplements. In particular they are high in iron and iodine, the latter element lacking in much of our diet. Seaweeds also perform the welcome trick of making you feel full, swelling up inside you and satisfying you for longer. Finally, some seaweeds make an excellent replacement for salt. The effect comes partly from a small amount of sodium chloride plus other salts, but mostly from the glutamates with which seaweeds are packed.

Rocky shores and spring (big) low tides are where and when to look. Spring to early autumn is the best time, though some are available during the winter. There is no legal right to forage seaweeds, but no one is likely to complain about you carefully removing the odd kilo here and there. Any detached seaweeds in good condition are fair game however, so you may never need to transgress.

Wherever possible, cut the seaweed a third of its length from its holdfast. With kelp, just remove a single frond from each specimen. Do bring a separate net bag for each species as sorting them out later can take hours. Mercifully, there are no poisonous seaweeds, but only a dozen or so are worth eating (see opposite).

But how on earth do you cook the stuff? Boiling it up for 15 minutes in a saucepan will usually result in a slimy mess. For each of the seaweeds described opposite I give an indication of which methods work best, only two of which will end up as a slimy mess, but in a good way.

To dry your own seaweed, first wash it very thoroughly in fresh water then spread it out evenly on a cotton sheet in the garden and leave until fairly dry. To finish the process, transfer the seaweed to a baking tray and dry it in the lowest possible oven to complete crispness.

EDIBLE SEAWEEDS

Dulse The red fronds of this seaweed grow attached to almost anything, but most often to the fronds of another seaweed, serrated wrack. Wash and trim dulse as soon as you get home and cook as soon as possible. Steam (like cabbage) for 15 minutes and serve with butter and black pepper or chop and use in a smoked fish tart or a maritime bubble and squeak. It is very good deep-fried too: dust with flour and cook (very carefully, a little at a time) in vegetable oil at 180°C until the fizzing stops. Dulse also dries very well and is often eaten this way, but most of the time I put the dried fronds into a blender to form dulse powder. This can be used as a salt substitute to season everything from omelettes to curries to soups.

Kelp and Sugar kelp While these large, brown seaweeds can be dried and powdered, their main use is as a flavour enhancer akin to kombu in broths and stocks. Like bay leaves, they are removed before serving. Dashi, the stock used in miso soup, can be made with our native kelps.

Laver Thin, brown, translucent fronds of laver can be found draped over rocks in huge quantities. Use scissors to pick it, to avoid little bits of the rock coming with it. To make traditional Welsh laver bread, simmer the laver in water in a lidded pan for 8 hours, then remove the lid and stir every few minutes for another 2 hours until a thick and, yes, slimy,

paste is left. The flavour? Fishy Marmite. I love it. Mix with oatmeal and crumbled crispy bacon, shape into little cakes and fry until golden brown on both sides.

Gutweed This bright green seaweed of the upper shore can be eaten raw in a salad, though requires considerable chewing, but it makes the best ever crispy seaweed. Deep-fry thoroughly washed and partially dried fronds in vegetable oil at 180°C for a few seconds, then drain on kitchen paper.

Carragheen The wiry brown fronds of this seaweed can be found attached to rocks. Throw about 80g fresh carragheen in a pan, cover with 2–3cm water and simmer for 30 minutes. The resulting slimy mess is the start of a fantastic seaweed pannacotta. Heat 200ml milk with elderflower or lemon verbena to flavour it, strain, and stir in 50g sugar. Squeeze the hot, sticky seaweed mix through muslin into the hot milk. Whisk in 200ml cream and pour into darioles to set.

Sea spaghetti This is a magnificent-looking seaweed related to the familiar (and less edible) wracks, including the bladder wrack. The long, branching, flattened fronds lay like a mass of thick hair between rocks at low tide, though they float and wave around when the tide is in. It has a mild flavour with an *al dente* bite when lightly cooked. I like it stir-fried with noodles. It is not fibrous, unlike its thin, round, unbranched look-alike, which actually looks more like spaghetti.

DHAL WITH CRISPY SEAWEED

1 tbsp rapeseed oil

1 medium onion, sliced

4 garlic cloves, thinly sliced

1 medium-hot red chilli, deseeded and finely chopped, or a pinch of dried chilli flakes

½ tbsp cumin seeds

A few fresh or dried curry leaves

2 tsp curry powder

175g red lentils

1 litre vegetable stock

½ tbsp tomato purée

1 tsp garam masala

Sea salt and black pepper

FOR THE CRISPY SEAWEED

About 250g fresh gutweed, thoroughly washed

Vegetable oil (refined rapeseed oil), for deep-frying

Gutweed works brilliantly in this dish, frying to a delightfully brittle crispness with a sweet, minerally flavour. Serves 4–6

First prepare the seaweed. Squeeze all the excess water from the gutweed, then lay it out on a clean, dry tea towel placed over a tray. Thoroughly pat it dry, then leave in the fridge for several hours to dry – the drier it is, the less it will spit when fried.

To make the dhal, heat a large saucepan over a medium-low heat, then add the oil. When hot, add the onion, garlic, chilli, cumin seeds, curry leaves and curry powder. Cook, stirring regularly, for 12–15 minutes, without colouring.

Rinse the lentils briefly in a sieve under a cold running water, drain and add to the onion and spice mix, along with the stock and the tomato purée. Bring to a gentle simmer and cook, stirring regularly, for 45 minutes, adding a splash more stock or water if necessary. Add the garam masala, then taste the dhal and add a little salt and pepper if required. Remove from the heat and allow it to stand for 5–10 minutes while you cook the seaweed.

Heat an 8–10cm depth of oil in a deep, heavy-based pan, to 160°C (a few fronds of the gutweed dropped into the hot oil should fizz and pop instantly). Deep-fry the gutweed in small batches, for 30–60 seconds at a time, until it is crisp but still nice and green. Be very careful because the seaweed can spit a great deal. Scoop it out, drain on kitchen paper and scatter with a little fine sea salt.

Spoon the dhal into a warmed serving bowl and top with the seaweed. Serve with plain yoghurt and fresh naan bread.

Sesame seeds & oil

Gill Meller

LATIN NAME
Sesamum indicum

MORE RECIPES
Raw sprout salad with sesame, ginger and lime (page 102); Raw kale with yoghurt and tahini (page 322); Pak choi with sticky prune sauce (page 427); Sweet and sour barbecued courgettes (page 201); Mackerel with tamari and sesame glaze (page 592); Noodles with seaweed, smoked mackerel and soy (page 407); Steamed sea bass with kale and ginger (page 573); Lamb, labneh and spinach salad (page 335); Seedy stoneground loaf (page 263); Quick za'atar crispbreads (page 637)

This tiny seed punches above its weight: it's 50 per cent oil, one of the richest of all seeds, and, when toasted, reveals a wonderful nutty, smoky character. It also has a rich portfolio of nutrients, including lignans, which may help reduce cholesterol, antioxidants, which help to boost the immune system and fight inflammation, and minerals such as calcium and magnesium.

The little oval seeds first grew wild in Africa and India but are now farmed in many parts of the world, with Myanmar currently the world's largest producer. They form in four neat ranks inside small pods, which are the fruits of a slender, flowering plant. The seeds of some varieties burst open when ripe – which is believed to be the origin of the phrase 'Open sesame!'.

There are many different strains of sesame, all are white inside, but the hulls range in colour from the familiar off-white through yellow and brown to a jet-black variety popular in China and Southeast Asia. These are a little harder to come by in the UK, but are worth seeking out for their rich flavour and the unusual lick of colour they add to dishes: they are stunning on sushi, and a jar of black sesame tahini looks almost like a jar of ink.

As with any seeds, I tend to buy sesame seeds in relatively small quantities – about 250g at a time – store them in a Le Parfait jar and try to use them up fairly quickly, so they are at their freshest and best.

First and foremost, I use sesame seeds for baking. They are always incorporated into my seeded doughs and often sprinkled on top of breads too, from baps to large loaves. Not only are they aesthetically pleasing, but they offer a nice texture contrast with the soft crumb. I also use sesame seeds in flatbreads, crackers, seedy breakfast bars and all sorts of biscuits, whether praline-style brittles or shortbready petits fours.

Sesame seeds also go into dukkah, a Middle Eastern dry dip made from nuts, seeds and spices – a fantastic nibble. To make it, briefly roast 50g hazelnuts, rub off their skins if necessary, then put them into a mortar. Toast 75g sesame seeds in a small dry pan until fragrant, then add to the mortar. Repeat with 30g coriander seeds and 15g cumin seeds. Crush the nuts and seeds with the pestle to a rough, crunchy powder (or grind in a food processor, taking care not to over-process). Add salt to taste. Serve in a little dish with bread and good olive oil: dip the bread first into the oil and then the dukkah.

I also use sesame seeds in Asian-influenced salads. I toss them with grated raw carrot, along with ginger and coriander, to make a delicious little side dish, or mix them with sliced cucumber and radish, soy sauce and a touch of sugar and rice vinegar, to serve with bream.

If I'm using the seeds as an ingredient in this way, I always treat them to a light toasting first. (Of course, this is not necessary if using them in baking.) Toasting brings out the flavour and aroma of all seeds but it seems to have a particularly magical effect with sesame. Simply scatter the seeds in a small frying pan set over a low heat and toast for 1–2 minutes, shaking the pan often. When the seeds start to pop, tip them on to a plate to cool. Because they are tiny, sesame seeds burn easily, so do take care.

You can actually save yourself this small task and buy sesame seeds ready-toasted. These are a favourite Japanese ingredient, so look for them in Japanese shops or online specialists. Japan is the world's biggest importer of sesame, and the seeds and oil are especially appreciated there. The seeds, toasted and roughly crushed with salt, form *gomashio*, a delicious seasoning.

S

Tahini

This thick, pale paste of roasted, ground-up sesame seeds makes a fantastic base for all sorts of dressing, dips and sauces and even soups. It also goes into sweet dishes, such as halva, the dense, crumbly Middle Eastern sweetmeat.

Tahini has a delicately bitter, nutty flavour, which is generally best balanced by sweet, creamy or earthy ingredients; it also boasts a useful binding quality. Be aware that when liquid is added to tahini, it will initially thicken up or 'seize', but gradually adding more liquid will loosen it again.

Tahini is part of the classic aubergine dip, baba ganoush, but is perhaps best known as the base of hummus. I use it in the traditional chickpea version but I also love its warm, nutty edge and thickening nature in any hummus made with root veg, such as beetroot or carrot. And a little tahini beaten into yoghurt and seasoned well with lemon juice, garlic, salt and pepper makes a wonderful simple dressing for roasted vegetables, or pulse or grain salads: try trickling a yoghurt, tahini and green peppercorn dressing over ripe sliced tomatoes.

Tahini comes in two forms: light, made from hulled seeds; and dark, made with whole seeds, which is more bitter. You can even make it yourself, like a nut butter, if you have a high-power blender. Home-made or shop-bought, tahini keeps well in a cool, dark place or the fridge, though chilling makes it stiffer. If the oil separates out – as is often the case even with shop-bought tahini – just stir it back in before using.

Sesame oil

Sesame seeds have long been prized for their oil. If this is pressed from the untoasted seeds, it forms a mildly nutty, general-purpose cooking oil (though high in omega-6 fatty acids, see page 623). The seeds are usually toasted before being pressed and then yield an oil with an intense, roasted, fragrant, seedy flavour with hints of nuts, smoke and coffee. This powerful flavour dissipates if the oil is heated so it is best reserved for briefly cooked sauces, or trickled on to dishes just before serving. Splash it on to stir-fries, soups and noodles, or trickle it over roast pork rubbed with ginger, star anise and chilli. You only need a teaspoonful or two of sesame oil to get that extraordinary flavour all the way through a dish.

KOHLRABI AND MUSHROOM SALAD WITH SESAME

This makes a lovely side dish to some simply cooked fish or pork. Use small, fresh kohlrabi and peel them well to reveal the most tender flesh. Serves 4

2 tbsp sesame seeds

1 small red onion, halved and very thinly sliced

Juice of 2 limes

1 tsp caster sugar

A small pinch of dried chilli flakes

1 tbsp toasted sesame oil

2 kohlrabi (about 500g in total)

50–75g chestnut mushrooms

Sea salt and black pepper

Set a small frying pan over a low heat. Add the sesame seeds and toast for 1–2 minutes, shaking the pan often. When they start to pop, take off the heat and set aside.

Put the sliced red onion into a bowl. Add the lime juice, sugar, chilli, sesame oil and some salt and pepper. Mix well, then set aside to marinate.

Peel the kohlrabi and trim back the tops and bases. Cut the kohlrabi into matchsticks using a sharp knife or, better still, a mandoline. Remove and discard the stalks from the mushrooms; slice the caps thinly.

Tumble the kohlrabi and mushroom slices through the dressed onion, along with the toasted sesame seeds. Taste and add more salt, pepper, sugar or lime juice as required. Serve straight away.

Shrimps

Nick Fisher

LATIN NAME
Crangon crangon

ALSO KNOWN AS
Brown shrimp

SEASONALITY
Spawning peaks April–September so commercially harvested shrimps are best eaten October–March

HABITAT
Sandy estuaries all around the British coast

MCS RATING
3–4

REC MINIMUM SIZE
4cm total shell length

SOURCING
goodfishguide.org;
cleysmokehouse.com;
eastlincsseafood.co.uk;
fishfanatics.co.uk;
morecambebayshrimps.com

Wetsuits and boogie-boards are all well and good, but personally, if I'm off with the family to a sandy beach for the day, it's shrimp nets I want to see cluttering up my rear view mirror. The best shrimps to eat are brown shrimps. You can buy them – there are shrimp fisheries around our coast – but the finest brown shrimps are ones you've caught yourself and boiled in a bucket of seawater, sitting on the beach.

Shrimp nets are a basic tool: a broom-handle-like shaft attached to an angled, hardwood board with a fine-meshed net, which billows in the water behind the board as you push it through knee-deep, sea-covered flat sand. Clever people make their own shrimp nets, the rest of us buy them. Apart from having a delicious pay off, shrimping provides hours of obsessively exciting, joyously competitive fun for all the family. It's a low tide, summer activity, which takes planning and a very flat sandy beach like those of Morecambe or Hunstanton. Look for knee-deep, warm lagoons left by the outgoing tide.

Shrimps take minutes to cook: drop them into boiling, salty water (about 10g salt per litre, if you're not doing it there and then on the beach), return to the boil and cook for another couple of minutes, then drain and cool.

If you don't want to eat your shrimps just as they come, another option is to make classic potted shrimps: peeling cooked shrimps and preserving them in spicy butter to be spread on sourdough toast. Flash-frying them in hot, spiced fat and eating them whole, heads and tails too, is another great way to go (see below). But in the same way that shrimp gathering is a leisurely activity, I feel that shrimp eating should also require an investment of time. For me, the best way to eat shrimps is from the shell, one at a time, sucking each nugget-like tail from its shell while crunch-sucking each head – not a wham-bam snack but an exercise in meditative, mindful eating.

Shell-on, peeled or potted brown shrimp are available in shops and online all year. Most of these are the harvest of beam trawlers, with all the attendant issues of by-catch and habitat damage. The small Solway Firth fishery is relatively good, however, while off Norfolk they're making improvements with a view to going for MSC accreditation. In Lancashire's Morecambe Bay, meanwhile, the shrimp are still caught in nets towed by small boats or tractors.

SHRIMPS ON SOURDOUGH WITH PAPRIKA AND LEMON

25g butter

1 garlic clove, grated or crushed

Finely grated zest and juice of ½ lemon

1 tsp sweet smoked paprika

1 tbsp chopped parsley

150g cooked shrimp, shell-on or peeled

2–4 slices of sourdough bread (depending on size)

Extra virgin olive oil, to trickle

Sea salt and black pepper

Plump brown shrimps have so much flavour that they can take an intense hit of smoky paprika and sharp lemon and come up smiling. If you have shell-on shrimps, you can fry them whole in the spiced butter and eat them, shell and all, or peel them as you go. Otherwise, peeled shrimps work just as well. Serves 2

Place a large frying pan over a medium-high heat and add the butter. When it is melted and bubbling, add the garlic and lemon zest. Cook for 1–2 minutes, until the garlic is fragrant but not coloured.

Add the smoked paprika, parsley and most of the lemon juice. Finally add the shrimps and toss well to combine. Cook for a further minute, but no more.

Meanwhile, toast the sourdough and trickle with extra virgin olive oil.

Season the shrimps with salt and pepper to taste and pile on to the toasted sourdough. Trickle with a little more extra virgin olive oil and lemon juice to serve.

Sloes

LATIN NAME
Prunus spinosa

ALSO KNOWN AS
Blackthorn (the shrub on which the berries grow)

SEASONALITY
September–November

HABITAT
Common in wood edges, scrub and hedgerow throughout the British Isles, with the exception of northern Scotland

MORE RECIPES
Damson and rosemary vodka (page 663)

Wait until after the first frost before you pick your sloes. This is sage advice – that freezing and thawing process begins to break down the cell walls within the fruit, and helps to develop flavour. But I find it rather hard to heed those words. Sloes appear sooner and sooner in our warming climate and it's not uncommon to see them weighing down the blackthorn bushes in early September, when a spell of Indian summer is a more likely prospect than freezing temperatures. And once they're there, all dark and ripe and duskily bloomed, it's tough to muster the discipline not to pick them.

Blackthorn bushes are barbed with vicious spines so the wise sloe-picker dons thick gloves. The compulsion to plunder is made that much stronger by the knowledge that the birds, and indeed many foraging humans, will have few compunctions about the weather. It's lucky, then, that there is a way to cheat. Putting sloes into a domestic freezer then allowing them to thaw again mimics the action of a real frost.

Once your sloes are thus prepared, naturally or otherwise (and to be honest, unfrosted sloes still work well in recipes), the time-honoured use for them is as the rich, fruity, almost spicy flavouring for a home-made liqueur. And it is very hard to beat. Fresh off the bush, sloes have a powerfully bitter, tannic kick that makes them no fun to eat raw. But when sweetened, booze-soaked and matured, they mellow and soften and reveal layers of winey, chocolatey, tarry loveliness.

Gin is the classic base, of course, but I actually prefer vodka, its neutrality allowing the complex flavours of the sloes to come through. My advice for a great sloe vodka is to keep the sugar content lower than most recipes stipulate (around 250g sugar to 1kg sloes and 1 litre spirit) and to mature it as long as you can before drinking. A couple of years minimum, I'd say. Three or four will only improve it. Forgetting a bottle in some dark corner of your larder or garage, then rediscovering it a decade or so later, is when you discover just how special this hedgerow liqueur can be.

The boozy sloe pulp left over from a batch of gin or vodka can be de-stoned and combined with melted dark chocolate to make some rather gorgeous after-dinner treats. Or, to get more immediate joy from your sloes, use the just-picked fruit to make a syrup or, combined with cooking or crab apples, a jelly.

PIGEON BREASTS WITH SLOE GIN GRAVY

4 pigeon breasts

A little olive or rapeseed oil

2 small knobs of butter

A sprig of thyme

3 tbsp sloe gin (or sloe vodka)

3 tbsp red wine

150ml game or chicken stock

Sea salt and black pepper

This lovely, delicately sweet gravy is fantastic against the gaminess of pigeon and also goes well with pheasant, duck or venison. If you have whole pigeons, take off the breasts ahead of time and use the carcasses to make the stock. Serves 2

Season the pigeon breasts well with salt and pepper. Place a frying pan over a medium-high heat and, when hot, add a dash of oil and a knob of butter. As soon as the butter starts to bubble, add the pigeon breasts, skin side down, along with the thyme. Cook for 1 minute each side, if you like them quite rare, or 2 minutes each side for medium, basting with the pan juices during cooking. Transfer to a warmed dish and let rest for 5 minutes.

Meanwhile make the gravy. Discard the thyme, then add the sloe gin and wine to the pan and boil for about 30 seconds to reduce the liquid. Add the stock and boil to reduce this by two-thirds. Add a knob of butter, whisk it in and then pass the sauce through a tea strainer into a small, warmed jug. Add any resting juices from the pigeon. Taste and add more salt or pepper if needed.

Slice the pigeon breasts thickly and serve with the gravy, along with some celeriac and/or potato mash (with some chives stirred through) and simply cooked greens or cabbage.

Snails

LATIN NAME
Helix aspersa,
Cornu aspersum

ALSO KNOWN AS
Garden snail, common garden
snail, petit-gris

SEASONALITY
All year round, but they
hibernate in the winter

HABITAT
Common in gardens, hedgerow,
fields and woodland

MORE RECIPES
Spaghetti with whelks, garlic
and parsley (page 670)

SOURCING
dorsetsnails.co.uk (for cooked
snails); hrh-escargots.co.uk
(for live snails)

There is always something pleasing about eating a wild food that you've gathered yourself. But in the case of the small but surprisingly voracious garden snail, which munches its way through my spring lettuce, the satisfaction is somewhat increased. And gathering them is so easy – I can think of no other quarry so ill-equipped to make a break for freedom. A dish of snails in garlic butter is not only delicious, it also represents the settling of a score. Fortunately, the common garden snail, which thrives in the wild too, is the best type to eat. (The larger and much rarer Roman snail, *Helix pomatia*, is also prized for food but is now a protected species in England.)

In the warmer months, search for garden snails after rain – you can even encourage them out with a little artificial downpour from a garden hose. Largely nocturnal, they are easier to gather in the dark, by torchlight. Snails hibernate in winter so during the colder months you will have to look a little harder, peering under plant pots or in woody nooks and crannies to find them sleeping in their shells. Obviously, you should only gather snails from places free of toxins such as garden chemicals or animal waste.

Preparation is more time-consuming as snails need to be purged before you eat them (unless you've gathered them deep in hibernation, in which case their guts will already be empty). Put the snails in a large, clean bucket with some mesh or netting over the top to allow airflow and feed them on a one-ingredient diet, such as lettuce, for 5 days. Rinse them regularly before returning to the bucket. Starve the snails completely for a further 48 hours, rinse again, and they are then ready to cook.

Put your purged snails in a bowl and shake it to make them retract into their shells. Now drop them into a large pan of boiling salted water with a few bay leaves and peppercorns added (plus some roughly sliced stock vegetables and other herbs if you have them). Once it comes back to the boil, simmer for 10 minutes, then drain and leave to cool. The meat can be extracted from the shells with a pin, the black cloaca trimmed away and the meat is ready for further cooking. If the cooked snails seem at all slimy at this point, toss them in a little salt, leave them for a few minutes, then rinse.

A well-cooked snail is a meaty, succulent nugget – nicely chewy, mildly earthy – and it's hard to beat the simple, time-honoured preparations, such as the recipe below. I also like them in a risotto or a gratin. Of course, you don't have to gather snails yourself to enjoy them – you can buy British farmed snails either live or pre-cooked.

GARLICKY SNAILS WITH BREADCRUMBS

A classic French dish, this is a great way to try snails for the first time. Serves 4 as a starter

3 tbsp olive oil

30g fairly fine, slightly stale
breadcrumbs

50g unsalted butter

2–3 garlic cloves, finely chopped

48 snails, purged, cooked and
removed from their shells
(see above)

A good squeeze of lemon juice

1–2 tbsp dry white wine
(optional)

2 tbsp coarsely chopped parsley

Sea salt and black pepper

Heat the olive oil in a wide frying pan over a medium heat. Add the breadcrumbs with some salt and pepper. Stir the breadcrumbs until they have absorbed the oil evenly, then toast in the pan for a couple of minutes until golden and crisp, tossing them often so they do not burn. Tip on to a plate lined with kitchen paper and set aside.

Wipe out the pan, then return it to a medium-low heat and add the butter. When it is foaming, add the garlic and cook gently for a minute; don't let it colour too much. Add the prepared snails, with some salt and pepper, and cook gently, tossing them frequently in the butter, for about 2 minutes. Add the lemon juice, and the wine if using, and cook for 30 seconds more, then throw in most of the chopped parsley.

Return the crisp breadcrumbs to the pan and shake briefly to mix everything together. Taste and add more salt, pepper or lemon juice if needed, then transfer to small warmed bowls. Finish with a sprinkling of parsley and a touch of flaky salt, then serve.

Snipe

Tim Maddams

LATIN NAME
Common snipe:
Gallinago gallinago.
Jacksnipe: *Lymnocryptes minimus*

SEASONALITY
England, Wales and Scotland:
12 August–31 January.
Northern Ireland and Isle of
Man: 1 September–31 January.

HABITAT
Water meadows, wetlands,
heathland and moorland

SOURCING
tasteofgame.org.uk

MORE RECIPES
Woodcock with wild
mushrooms (page 678)

This diminutive bird is a bit of a deceiver. It's so small that it seems hardly worth the bother of shooting it, let alone plucking and cooking it, yet the flavour it delivers is immense – utterly delightful in its richness and rare character. There are two kinds of snipe in the British Isles: the common snipe and the slightly smaller jacksnipe, which is protected here – except in Northern Ireland, where it is more abundant.

Common snipe are small brown birds with white undersides that flit up out of nowhere in damp meadow and scrubland locations. They are incredibly difficult to shoot as they rise swiftly and suddenly from the ground and climb higher and higher, following an erratic path. It's this unwillingness to comply with hunters' wishes that has given rise to the term 'sniper' to describe a marksman of exceptional talent.

Traditionally, most wildfowl are sold in a 'brace', meaning two birds, but little snipe are sold in threes. This is known as a 'finger' due to the fact that you can carry three between the fingers of one hand.

Unless you know someone who shoots a few snipe each year, getting hold of a 'finger' will probably prove rather tricky: only the most dedicated of game dealers are likely to be able to get them and even a solitary snipe is a rare treat for the wild meat fan. If you are lucky enough to have one come your way, it's well worth the hassle of plucking it. Snipe should then be cooked guts in, in the same fashion as woodcock (see page 678) but for about half the time.

The birds can be locally abundant but we must remain cautious – no one wants to see a decline in the species. However, the difficulty of shooting them and the small number of people dedicated enough to try are, I believe, limiting factors that will ensure the survival of this wonderful creature.

SNIPE WITH SWEDE AND BACON

These delicate little game birds need only brief cooking: this meal can be ready in under half an hour. You could use woodcock or small pigeon instead of snipe, increasing the cooking time accordingly, and celeriac instead of swede. Serves 2

1 swede, about 500g, peeled and cut into smallish chunks

2 tbsp double cream or crème fraîche

40g butter

A dash of rapeseed oil or lard

4 thick rashers of smoked bacon, roughly chopped

2 sprigs of thyme

4–6 oven-ready snipe, at room temperature

1 medium onion, thinly sliced

2 garlic cloves, sliced

6–8 sage leaves

25ml brandy

75ml red wine

300ml game or chicken stock

Sea salt and black pepper

Put the swede into a pan of salted water and bring to the boil. Simmer for 12–15 minutes, until completely tender. Drain well, then mash together with the cream, about two-thirds of the butter, some salt and lots of black pepper. Keep warm.

Meanwhile, preheat the oven to 200°C/Fan 180°C/Gas 6 and place a large, heavy-based frying pan over a medium-high heat. Add a dash of oil or lard, followed by the bacon. Cook for a couple of minutes until the bacon starts to render some fat, then add the thyme.

Season the snipe and add them to the frying pan, pushing the bacon to one side. Brown well on all sides for 4–5 minutes. Lift the birds out into a small roasting tray, leaving the bacon in the pan. Add the onion, garlic and sage to the frying pan and cook over a medium-low heat for 8–10 minutes, until soft.

Meanwhile, roast the snipe in the oven for about 5 minutes or until the guts just pop out.

Add the brandy to the frying pan and stir for a minute as it bubbles, to deglaze the pan. Pour in the wine and let it simmer until reduced by half. Add the stock, bring to a simmer and reduce it by half too.

Remove the birds from the oven and leave to rest in a warm place for a few minutes. Meanwhile, finish the sauce. Whisk in the remaining butter, along with any resting juices from the snipe, then taste and adjust the seasoning. Serve the snipe alongside the swede, with the smoky bacon sauce.

Sole, Dover

Nick Fisher

LATIN NAME
Solea solea

ALSO KNOWN AS
Common sole, black sole, slip sole (when undersized)

SEASONALITY
Avoid April–June when spawning

HABITAT
Most are caught in the North Sea; also from the Irish Sea, English Channel and off the French Atlantic coast

MCS RATING
2–5

REC MINIMUM SIZE
30cm

MORE RECIPES
Grilled flounder and tomatoes (page 260); Megrim with crab and chives (page 380); Lemon sole poached in butter with thyme (page 589); Rice and fish with wasabi dressing (page 667)

SOURCING
goodfishguide.org; msc.org

Like turbot, Dover sole is an intimidating fish to buy and cook, mostly because it comes with such culinary baggage. The French may have been historically rude about English cuisine, but one thing they've always waxed lyrical about is our Dover sole. Legendary chef Auguste Escoffier gave no fewer than 180 recipes for Dover sole in just one book, *Le Répertoire de La Cuisine*. Most of them are over-complicated, involving champagne-flavoured custards and the like. However, such avid focus goes to illustrate just how crazy gourmands were for this great British *poisson*.

Dover sole do not come from Dover; this was simply the port that historically supplied the best sole to London and Paris. But 'Dover' has become so synonymous with great-tasting sole, that a species of Pacific sole has now been re-branded as 'Dover sole' too, just to up its cachet.

Because Dover sole is a classy fish with a classy reputation it's in great demand, which in turn means it's overfished in some areas, including the Irish Sea. The best choice is mature sole (over 30cm) from the North Sea, Celtic Sea or English Channel. If you can buy from an MSC-certified fishery such as the Hastings Fleet Dover sole fishery, so much the better.

However, Dover sole is a fish much loved by the restaurant trade, so there's fierce competition at fish markets to buy plate-sized soles, which means much of the catch is diverted before it reaches the retail market. Dovers can be bought online and from some fishmongers and supermarkets. They can also sometimes be bought directly from one of the small trammel netting boats that work out of the harbours along the south coast. If you do manage to get your hands on one, by all means punch the air in fish-tastic victory. But then, forget about it, for 2 days at least. A fresh sole needs fridge time to 'mature'. Not to get more fishy, but to let the muscle firm up (like hanging beef) and develop its natural ripened flavour.

The cooking part is simple. Rip off the top brown skin, leaving on the bottom white one. Massage with herby, salty butter and stick under a hot grill, or in the hottest part of an oven. Shower with lemon juice and devour with warm granary bread.

DOVER SOLE WITH SEAWEED BUTTER

2 Dover sole, dark skin removed

Sea salt and black pepper

FOR THE SEAWEED BUTTER

75g unsalted butter, softened

½ garlic clove, grated

Finely grated zest of ½ lemon

1 tbsp chopped fine-textured dried seaweed (such as pre-dried 'sea salad', or dried dulse)

Butter infused with the intense, salty-savoury flavour of seaweed brings heaps of character to Dover – or any flatfish. It's worth making a large batch. Freeze until firm, then slice into rounds, bag up and keep in the freezer for other dishes: try dropping the pats, still frozen, into risotto; or allow to melt over just-boiled potatoes. Serves 2

To make the seaweed butter, put all the ingredients into a large bowl and beat to combine. Spoon the soft butter into the centre of a double layer of cling film. Even it out into a little sausage, then fold the cling film over and roll it up tightly by twisting the ends of the cling film. Place in the fridge until required.

Preheat the oven to 220°C/Fan 200°C/Gas 7. Line a roasting tray with baking parchment.

Season the soles all over with salt and pepper. Place them in the roasting tray, skinned side up. Slice the seaweed butter into 6 pats and put three on each sole. Bake in the oven for about 7 minutes, until the fish is just cooked through and the butter is bubbling and smelling delicious.

Serve with waxy potatoes and fresh peas, or salad leaves dressed with a little lemon juice and olive oil.

S

Sole, lemon

Nick Fisher

LATIN NAME
Microstomus kitt

SEASONALITY
Avoid April–August, when
spawning

HABITAT
Found in the northeast Atlantic
from Iceland to the Bay of Biscay.
Common around the southwest
coast of the British Isles, the
North Sea and the Irish Sea

MCS RATING
3–4

REC MINIMUM SIZE
25cm

MORE RECIPES
Grilled flounder and tomatoes
(page 260); Megrim with crab
and chives (page 380); Dover
sole with seaweed butter
(page 588); Rice and fish with
wasabi dressing (page 667)

SOURCING
goodfishguide.org

If cooking the likes of turbot or Dover sole makes you nervous, then by all means practise on a lemon. It might not offer quite the same edible-velvet experience as Dover sole, but there's a pleasing musculature to the lemon sole's flesh, reminiscent of slightly pumped plaice – and it will fit into any of the recipes that the more fancy flatfish are famous for, at a fraction of the price. Because it's cheaper, you can do things with a lowly lemon you'd never dream of doing to a delicate Dover.

Off the bone is the proper, or at least traditional, way to eat the flesh – and there are some who like to roll their lemon sole fillets around things like capers and anchovies, roasted tomatoes and stoned olives. But if you fancy just hacking off a couple of fillets, coating them in breadcrumbs, deep-frying and serving them with double-cooked jumbo chips and shop-bought mayonnaise – no one's going to report you to the Taste Police. Sometimes you just need a fat, cheap lemon to help you relax and get in your sole groove.

Lemon sole neither tastes nor looks like a lemon, nor is it a true-blue sole. It is actually from the plaice and dab family. This doesn't make a whole lot of difference in the kitchen – though in the sea, it does. Lemon sole like deeper, colder water than the Soleidae family and are found from the Bay of Biscay northwards as far as Iceland.

This is rarely a target species. Until modern deep-water trawl methods were perfected, lemon sole were rarely seen on a deck, let alone on a plate, and many fisheries remain largely unmanaged. Lemons are most likely to come in as a by-catch on trawlers hunting for demersal, bottom-feeding white fish, like cod or haddock. Or they are caught up in the prodigious northern langoustine fishery (see page 339). There is a lack of information regarding lemon sole numbers. Surveys suggest the stock in the Southwest is likely to be overfished but that numbers are high and stable in the North Sea. If you can find sole that's been caught in a seine net, it's a better choice than trawled.

LEMON SOLE POACHED IN BUTTER WITH THYME

75g unsalted butter

Finely pared zest of ½ lemon

A small bunch of thyme,
torn into sprigs

2 lemon sole, filleted

Sea salt and black pepper

Any flatfish will be enhanced and enriched by this gentle cooking process, but it's particularly good with sweet-fleshed lemon sole. Use good quality unsalted butter, as it will really make a difference to the flavour of the finished dish. Soles can be filleted into 4 small fillets per fish, or 2 larger 'double' fillets. The smaller, single fillets are easier to fit into a pan for this dish. Serves 2

Heat a large, heavy-based, non-stick pan over a low heat. Add the butter, lemon zest and thyme sprigs. Allow the herbs and lemon to cook very gently in the butter for 2–3 minutes.

Season the sole fillets all over with salt and pepper then nestle them, flesh side down, in the pan, in as close to a single layer as possible. Poach very gently for 6–8 minutes, basting the fish with the fragrant butter every so often.

When the fish is just cooked through, transfer it to warmed plates, giving each person a couple of top and bottom fillets. Spoon over the butter from the pan, along with the thyme and lemon zest, and serve with waxy potatoes and a green salad.

Sorrel

LATIN NAME
Common sorrel: *Rumex acetosa*.
Wood sorrel: *Oxalis acetosella*

SEASONALITY
Often found all year round
but spring and autumn are
the best times

HABITAT
Common sorrel: often found
in rough pasture and hedgerow.
Wood sorrel: common in all
types of woodland

MORE RECIPES
Fried fillets of perch with sorrel
and potatoes (page 465)

One of my favourite leafy greens, sorrel bridges the divide rather splendidly between herb and vegetable. It doesn't look much – like a frail spinach, perhaps – so the lemony punch it packs can be a delightful surprise the first time you try it. Sorrel's leaves are among the earliest to reveal themselves as the ground warms in February or March, and they provide a wonderful tonic for palates tired of starchy winter fare.

My favourite sorrel is the kind I pick in the wild. Common sorrel can be found fairly easily in hedgerows and permanent pastures where chemical fertilisers and weedkillers aren't used (avoid the similar-looking, but toxic, 'Lords and Ladies'). Also the unrelated wood sorrel with its pretty trefoiled leaves is widespread in mixed woodland. A handful of leaves of either variety makes a fantastic accompaniment to grilled fish, a great partner to sautéed mushrooms and a lovely addition to a lettuce salad. Raw sorrel wants only a few drops of olive or rapeseed oil and some salt and pepper – no lemon or vinegar is needed as the leaf provides its own sharpness.

Cultivated sorrel (pictured right) is perhaps easier to come by – certainly if you grow your own (which I always do). It's a perennial that flourishes enthusiastically in pretty much any situation. Some farmers' markets and greengrocers, organic suppliers and even supermarkets now sell it too. When young, the leaves are good in salads but I tend to cook the more mature, robustly flavoured leaves. Like spinach, sorrel wilts down alarmingly when heated, shrinking to a fraction of its former volume, its lovely bright green turning to a dull khaki as it does so. Keep stirring and wilting and the leaves actually dissolve into a purée. It looks messy, but the flavour remains a delight.

You can harness this dissolving tendency to make a superb, intensely flavoured sauce for fish – especially oily fish; it also partners a poached egg, or warm new potatoes happily. Just wilt a good handful of shredded sorrel leaves in a generous knob of butter to the purée stage, then remove from the heat and stir in an egg yolk and a little cream. Sorrel also works beautifully in soups and risottos – dishes where its acidity can be balanced by starchy, buttery, creamy elements.

When you're cooking the larger leaves, strip out and discard the stalks first. Unless they are very small, the leaves are generally best shredded: roll them up first into fat 'cigars', then slice them across thinly. Avoid aluminium or cast-iron pans, because the oxalic acid in the leaves reacts with the metal and affects the flavour.

MERINGUE WITH STRAWBERRIES AND SORREL

Sorrel's lemony acidity is fantastic with sweet meringue – and the vibrant green of the raw leaves contrasts beautifully with strawberries. Serves 4

FOR THE MERINGUE
2 medium egg whites

100g caster sugar

TO ASSEMBLE
150ml double cream

40g caster sugar

Finely grated zest of ½ lemon

200g strawberries, hulled and
thickly sliced

A handful of small sorrel leaves
(or larger ones, shredded)

Preheat the oven to 120°C/Fan 120°C/Gas ½. Line a baking tray with baking parchment.

To make the meringue, whisk the egg whites in a scrupulously clean bowl until they hold soft peaks, then slowly whisk in the sugar, 1 tbsp at a time. When it is all incorporated, whisk for another couple of minutes until the meringue is very thick and glossy.

Spoon on to the baking sheet to form a round, about 15cm in diameter and 4–5cm high. Bake for 3 hours (for a meringue with a nicely marshmallowy middle). Remove from the oven and allow to cool.

Shortly before serving, whisk the cream with the sugar and lemon zest until it holds soft peaks. Spoon the lemony cream over the meringue. Top with the strawberries and sorrel just before serving.

S

Soy sauce

Nikki Duffy

ALSO KNOWN AS
Shoyu, tamari

MORE RECIPES
Raw carrot salad with peanut and cumin dressing (page 123); Noodle salad with spicy peanut butter dressing (page 451); Wilted mizuna with chilli, garlic and sunflower seeds (page 387); Pak choi with sticky prune sauce (page 427); Marinated tofu with spring greens (page 638); Noodles with seaweed, smoked mackerel and soy (page 407); Steamed sea bass with kale and ginger (page 573); Rice and fish with wasabi dressing (page 667); Roast jerk chicken (page 16); Ginger-braised lamb (page 278); Pork belly with noodles, coriander and tomatoes (page 494); Barbecued tripe (page 644)

SOURCING
clearspring.co.uk; sanchi.co.uk

Fermentation is a wonderful thing, creating flavour in a magical, alchemical way – in the case of this ingredient, taking the bland, pale sweetness of a soya bean and turning it into a rich, red-black, immensely flavourful liquor. Full of glutamate – which gives us that super-savoury fifth taste, umami – soy can work as a subtle thread of salty-rich flavour in a dressing or sauce or stand alone as a dip, perhaps augmented with garlic and chilli. Soy sauce is salty but it is not the same as salt. Used well, salt makes ingredients taste more of themselves. Soy contributes a deep, complex character of its own.

Traditionally made Japanese soy sauces – *shoyu* – are the best. Made by slowly fermenting roughly equal quantities of soaked, steamed soya beans and crushed roasted wheat with salt and water, for 6–18 months, they have a rich, complex flavour. There are only a handful of producers still making shoyu in this way.

More mainstream Japanese soy sauces are based not on whole soya beans but on defatted soy meal – the matter left over after oil has been extracted from soya beans. They are brewed for 6 months and alcohol may be added as a preservative.

Tamari is a Japanese soy sauce made with little or no wheat. It has a similar flavour to *shoyu* but is stronger and more intense (wheat gives a layer of sweetness and aroma to soy) so you generally need a little less of it.

Chinese soy sauces also contain less wheat than Japanese ones. Although made in a similar way, they are generally brewed for less time so are less rich and complex. Many of the Chinese soys in our shops these days are diluted and may contain additives such as colourings and preservatives. Light Chinese soys are thinner and saltier. Dark soys have traditionally been allowed to ferment for longer, and are thick and intense but more mellow. They are used for flavour but also colour. The qualities of light and dark are distinct enough that Chinese recipes may call for both.

Some cheap soy sauces are not fermented at all, but processed in days from soya flour mixed with hydrochloric acid to produce a hydrolysed protein. To this, flavours, colours and preservatives are added. There aren't many 'chemical soy sauces' like this on the market in the UK but it pays to check the label of any soy you buy.

MACKEREL WITH TAMARI AND SESAME GLAZE

Robust, rich mackerel holds its own with strong, bold flavours like tamari in this very quick and simple dish. Serves 2

3 tbsp tamari (or soy sauce)

2 tsp clear honey

1 tbsp sesame seeds

1 tbsp cider vinegar

1 tsp fish sauce

1 tbsp toasted sesame oil

A dash of rapeseed oil

2 small-medium mackerel, filleted

1 garlic clove, thinly sliced

2–3cm knob of root ginger, thinly sliced

½–1 red chilli (to taste), deseeded and thinly sliced

Leaves from a small bunch of coriander, roughly chopped

In a small bowl, whisk together the tamari, honey, sesame seeds, vinegar, fish sauce, sesame oil and 3 tbsp water and set aside.

Heat a large non-stick pan over a medium-high heat. Add the rapeseed oil, followed by the mackerel fillets, skin side down. Cook for 2 minutes, then add the garlic, ginger and chilli to the pan, scattering them around the fillets so they start to cook quickly. Let them sizzle for a minute or so, then flip the mackerel fillets over.

Add the tamari mixture to the pan. Let the liquid come up to a simmer, by which point the mackerel should be cooked through (check that the flesh is opaque and comes away from the skin easily). Carefully remove the fillets to a warm plate.

Continue to simmer the sauce for a further 1–2 minutes or until it is well reduced and sticky. Return the mackerel to the pan and turn it over in the sauce, coating it well. Sprinkle the coriander over the fish then remove it from the heat.

Serve the mackerel and its sticky glaze straight away, with rice or noodles.

Spear-leaved orache

LATIN NAME
Atriplex prostrate

SEASONALITY
Late spring–summer

HABITAT
Found throughout the British Isles, on waste ground, in gardens and on the coast

MORE RECIPES
Henakopita with garam masala and eggs (page 254); Spinach, egg and potato curry (page 599)

This leaf is certainly not something you can pick up from the greengrocers, though you can very often find it in your veg garden, even if you haven't planted it. 'Aw-rak' (as I pronounce it) is a weed. Not that it is confined to domestic situations – it can be found on waste ground, along roadsides and on the upper seashore too. It is extremely common as far north as Sheffield, beyond which it becomes increasingly confined to the coast.

It is a fairly easy plant to recognise with its distinctly triangular leaves that sport a coarsely saw-toothed edge. The young leaves are covered in fine, white granules just like those of fat hen (page 254). It is a plant often mistaken for the relatively rare and equally edible Good King Henry, but this has longer triangular leaves.

Over all, members of the goosefoot family, to which spear-leaved orache belongs, are notoriously difficult to identify. Since no goosefoot to my knowledge is actually poisonous there will be no problem as long as you are sure that it is, indeed, of the goosefoot clan. The nearest dangerous look-alike is datura, a member of the treacherous nightshade family. Unfortunately, it too has a fondness for vegetable plots – but is easily distinguished by its sharply lobed leaves.

Although available from May to October, late spring and early summer is the best time to pick the leaves of spear-leaved orache; beyond this the plant runs to seed and only the sparse side leaves are available. If you find a very young plant you can eat everything but the roots. The leaves are fairly fleshy and the texture and flavour very like that of spinach.

SPEAR-LEAVED ORACHE BHAJIS

These spicy treats can also be made with fat hen, chard or good old spinach, of course. Serves 4 as a side dish

1 small onion, halved and finely sliced

1 small leek, trimmed and finely sliced

1 small carrot, peeled, halved lengthways and finely sliced

100g spear-leaved orache, stems removed, shredded

1 garlic clove, crushed or finely grated

1 tsp fennel seeds

2 tsp nigella (kalonji/black onion) seeds

1 tsp ground ginger

1 tsp ground turmeric

2 tsp sweet paprika

1 tbsp ground cumin

140g chickpea (gram) flour

Vegetable oil (refined rapeseed oil), for frying

Sea salt

Put the onion, leek, carrot, orache and garlic into a bowl and mix well, breaking up the half-rings of onion and leek with your hands.

Toast the fennel and nigella seeds in a dry frying pan for a few minutes, until fragrant, then add to the veg, along with the other spices. Add a generous pinch of salt and mix well.

Scatter the flour over the spicy veg and toss to coat well, then add 125ml cold water and work it in so all the veg are coated in batter.

Heat a 2–3cm depth of oil in a deep, heavy-based pan until it reaches about 160°C. If you don't have a cook's thermometer, cook one bhaji to test the temperature of the oil: drop a dessertspoonful of the mixture into the hot oil. It should take around 3 minutes, turning once or twice, for the bhaji to turn a deep golden brown. Remove and check that the batter is cooked through to the middle. Drain on kitchen paper. This test-bhaji will also tell you if you have enough salt in the mix.

Cook the remaining mixture, in small batches, as above; you should be able to make about 16 bhajis from the mix. Once cooked, drain on kitchen paper and keep warm while you cook the rest.

Serve the bhajis hot, with raita or other yoghurty dip.

Spelt

Nikki Duffy

LATIN NAME
Triticum spelta

MORE RECIPES
Roasted beetroot orzotto with lavender (page 68); Minted spelt and tomato salad (page 386); Saffron speltotto with black pudding and parsley (page 548); Walnut, barley, rocket and blue cheese salad (page 666); Roast grouse with barley, apples and squash (page 290); Upside-down chocolate plum pudding (page 189); Spotted dick with apple-brandy raisins (page 522); Spelt and honey pikelets (page 680); Poppy seed spelt rolls (page 487)

SOURCING
bacheldremill.co.uk;
dovesfarm.co.uk;
sharphampark.com

Spelt, a form of wheat, is an old, old food and this is precisely why it has become a brand new trend. Modern wheat has been hybridised and cross-bred to be high yielding, easy to harvest and amenable to fast, modern bread-making processes. However, it seems this process may also have made wheat less digestible than older forms. Enter spelt, a grain used by our Bronze Age ancestors, which has changed very little over the millennia, and retains a different type of gluten.

Although grown for centuries in many parts of the world, spelt fell out of favour around the time of the Industrial Revolution, because its tough husk and its stature (it grows to 1.5 metres) meant harvesting and milling it was labour-intensive. However, it is now enjoying a renaissance, with excellent organic spelt being grown in Britain.

A lot of claims are made for spelt: that it is inherently more nutritious than modern wheat, for instance, and that it's a fail-safe alternative for people who avoid that grain. But studies on spelt are not quite so conclusive. Generally, spelt does have a higher protein and lipid content than modern wheat. And some studies have shown wholemeal spelt to be higher in nutrients, including iron and zinc, and to contain less phytic acid, which can reduce the absorption of minerals from food.

But perhaps the most interesting thing about spelt is that, while it does contain gluten – and people with coeliac disease or wheat allergy should not eat it – it's definitely not the same as the gluten in modern wheat. The ratio of the proteins that form the gluten are different, resulting in a gluten matrix that is variously described as softer, more soluble, more fragile and less elastic. This, it is suggested, may be why many people find spelt easier to digest than wheat.

The different nature of spelt gluten is something you can observe yourself if you make bread with it. The dough is softer, more pliable, less elastic. Spelt doughs rise quickly so they can save you time. In fact, they can be used for quick breads, such as soda bread, just as readily as for a yeasted loaf – something you can't say about standard wheat bread flours. In all cases, spelt can make delicious breads. The gluten in spelt produces a 'shorter' texture so the loaves are often a little closer textured than standard wheat bread – not the same kind of light, airy, big-bubbled loaf you'll get with strong Canadian wheat flour – but flavoursome, full-bodied and satisfying.

Spelt flour can be used to make good fruit cakes, scones, crackers and biscuits, and it works well as a sauce thickener. In fact, it will add depth of colour, an earthy taste and bags of character to pretty much anything you use it in. You can even produce decent pastry with it – not ethereal perhaps, but certainly tasty. Spelt has a really good, nutty, very slightly sweet flavour, without the strident character you can detect with, say, rye or buckwheat.

Much of the spelt on the market now is organic. And this points to one of the other great attractions of the grain – it's a more environmentally friendly crop than wheat. Hardy and resilient, spelt is able to grow in difficult conditions. It does not respond well to the use of nitrogen fertilisers – they tend to make the tall stems bend under their own weight – so growers use less of them. Spelt's tough husk protects the growing kernel naturally, so it doesn't need chemical spraying. And the husk also keeps the inner grain fresher for longer and means it retains its nutrients more easily than modern wheat.

Spelt flour is usually wholemeal, and often stoneground – leading to a tastier, less heat-affected, lower GI result. But you can also buy white spelt flour (though, like all white flours, it has less flavour).

Besides flour, you can buy spelt pasta (the wholemeal version is a particular favourite of mine for quick, very filling meals), spelt cookies, crackers and breakfast cereals. Pearled spelt (pictured on page 594), meanwhile – the whole grain of the plant, polished to remove the bran layer – is a favourite River Cottage ingredient. It can be used just like pearl barley but is quicker to cook, a little sweeter and, I think, a little tastier. Substitute it in any pearl barley recipe, or cook it, toss with a rich dressing and use as the base of a hearty salad. Use cooked, oiled and seasoned pearled spelt in place of plain pasta or rice too. It makes a great 'speltotto' (see page 548).

CREAMY SPELT AND ALMOND PUDDING

200g pearled spelt

800ml unsweetened almond milk

200ml double cream

1 vanilla pod

Finely grated zest of 1 lemon

70g caster sugar

This simple variation on a classic rice pud makes great use of whole grains of pearled spelt. A combination of almond milk and dairy cream gives a beautifully nutty, creamy flavour but, for a dairy-free pud, you can replace the cream with extra almond milk. Serves 4–6

Place the spelt in a bowl, pour on cold water to cover and leave to stand for 3–4 hours to soften the grain. Drain and set aside.

Combine the almond milk and cream in a large, heavy-based saucepan. Split the vanilla pod lengthways and scrape out the seeds with the tip of a small, sharp knife. Add the seeds and the pod to the milk, along with the lemon zest, sugar and drained spelt.

Bring to a simmer and cook for 30–40 minutes, stirring regularly, especially towards the end of cooking as the pudding starts to thicken. Test the grains to make sure they are cooked as you like them. If they are a little too *al dente*, add a splash more almond milk and continue to cook until you're happy with the texture of the spelt and the consistency of the pudding. Remove the pan from the heat and allow the pudding to sit for a few minutes before serving.

Serve with a trickle of honey or maple syrup, or a spoonful of jam and some toasted almonds. Buttery fried apples (perhaps with a splash of cider brandy), roasted apples or caramelised bananas also make delicious accompaniments.

S

Spinach

LATIN NAME
Spinach: *Spinacia oleracea*.
Perpetual spinach: *Beta vulgaris* var. *cicla*

SEASONALITY
All year round

MORE RECIPES
Spiced spinach with nutmeg (page 408); Coconut, spinach and apple sambal (page 192); Spear-leaved orache bhajis (page 593); Chanterelle and chard bruschetta (page 137); Mozzarella with nettles and lentils (page 390); Henakopita with garam masala and eggs (page 254); Cockle and chard rarebit (page 188); Cucumber, smoked mackerel and dill salad (page 220); Velvet crab curry (page 211); Sea beet and smoked pollack pasties (page 574); Lamb, labneh and spinach salad (page 335); Kiwi, spinach and avocado smoothie (page 325)

Spinach crops up in seemingly every cuisine, from classic Mediterranean to Chinese, Indian and Middle Eastern. It is both characterful and individual, with its 'green-tasting', almost metallic bite, yet combines easily with strong, salty ingredients such as bacon and anchovies, chorizo or other highly flavoured meats. It wakes up (and is beautifully moderated by) the big carbs, such as rice, potatoes and pasta. Perhaps best of all, spinach loves spices and seasonings and takes to them without being drowned out. *Aloo gobi* (spinach and cauliflower), *saag aloo* (spinach and potato) and spinach and chickpea curry are three favourites.

This delicate leaf, like so many of our now-familiar foods, is well travelled. It originated in the East. The Persians were cultivating it by the fourth century, and the Chinese by the seventh. The Moors brought it with them when they invaded Spain in the eighth century and it was probably from here that the leaf found its way to Britain. In a simple dish, 'spynoches yfryed', it made an appearance in the fourteenth century *The Forme of Cury*, the earliest known English cookbook. Gradually, spinach came to dominate over the wild, wiltable greens in use in earlier times. It was cooked into soups, served raw in salads and even made into sweet tarts. The term 'Florentine' to describe dishes containing spinach probably reflects the fact that Florence-born Catherine de Medici, Queen of France from 1547 until 1559, was a big fan.

We still love spinach for its versatility and the speed with which it can be cooked but, of course, it also has a cast-iron reputation, if you'll excuse the pun, as a source of nutrients. It provides vitamins K, A, C, B12 and folic acid, as well as antioxidants and fibre. But the idea of it being rammed with iron needs qualifying: it does contain plenty of the mineral, but this is of the 'non-haem' sort, which is less easily absorbed than iron from animal products. Spinach is also rich in oxalic acid (which gives it that metallic edge) and this slows iron absorption.

You might say that spinach's only other downside is its incredible wiltability: a heap will vanish into a thimbleful when cooked. But I like to think of this as nature's way of getting us to eat more of it. That super-shrinking nature is explained by spinach's high water content. So what you don't want to add, when cooking it, is more water. With stir-fries, pasta sauces or simple side dishes, the leaves can be added straight to a hot pan, with other ingredients, and allowed to collapse (which they'll quickly do).

If your spinach needs to be cooked before you add it to a dish (for a quiche filling, say), here's the technique: drop it, with just the residual water that clings to it after washing, into a capacious pan (it's often easiest to cook it in batches). Cover and place over a moderate heat, where it will quickly wilt, then tip into a colander and allow to cool. Now grab the leafy heap with your hands and squeeze out as much water as you can. It will seem to reduce down to almost nothing, but don't panic: its flavour, character and colour are now concentrated, and it won't make your soufflé soggy.

As well as spices and seasoning, spinach loves creaminess and dairy products. For the comforting River Cottage classic creamed spinach, wilt 500g spinach as above, then chop and combine with a rich béchamel sauce (350ml bay- and onion-infused milk cooked into a roux made with 50g butter and 25g flour). The addition of a generous grating of nutmeg, as so often with spinach, lifts and defines the dish.

Spinach has an affinity with cheese too, especially salty cheeses. Whether in a tart, salad or held within folds of filo in the classic Greek spanakopita, spinach and feta is a marriage made in heaven, yet milder cheeses are also happily partnered. In ravioli, cannelloni or even lasagne, spinach and ricotta is a delicious, classic pasta filling.

S

598

And for something out of the every day, try Oysters Rockefeller. This extravagance – oysters topped with buttery, garlicky, wilted spinach, Pernod and breadcrumbs then grilled – should be enjoyed in the sunshine with slightly too much dry white wine.

In most shops these days, spinach is sold in its young form, as 'baby leaf'. The appeal of this is that it can be used raw or, if you want to cook it, with no preparation. More mature spinach leaves – for which you will probably need a farm shop, good greengrocer or veg box scheme – do have the edge on flavour and body, however. All you need to do is tear out the tougher stalks – the work of moments. Always wash spinach very thoroughly before use because it has a tendency to harbour grit.

Raw spinach is one of my most-used salad leaves. Picked small, young and delicate, it adds a delicious, minerally edge to a leafy salad. If you grow your own, it takes very well to a cut-and-come-again approach, which will keep you in small leaves pretty much all year round. It's easy to grow. Sow directly into the ground from March until autumn – a 6-weekly sowing will mean you never run out. Space the seeds at 20cm intervals in rows 30cm apart, water little and often to prevent bolting. Harvest regularly, cutting or picking a few centimetres above ground to encourage replacement leaves to grow, and reduce the chances of bolting. 'Dominant' and 'Bordeaux' are the best varieties for growing through the cold months, and 'Matador' seems to be slowest to bolt through the summer than most. New Zealand spinach is a hardy, beautiful spinach worth trying – it stands winter cold well and has delicate leaves even when large.

There is also perpetual spinach, which is actually a form of green-stemmed chard. Also incredibly easy to grow, all year round, this is a real veg-patch winner and a must if you love your leaves.

SPINACH, EGG AND POTATO CURRY

3 tbsp rapeseed oil

2 large onions, halved and finely sliced

4 garlic cloves, finely sliced

2–3 medium-hot green chillies, sliced

40g root ginger, finely chopped

2 tbsp korma or other curry powder

400ml coconut milk

400ml vegetable stock

6 eggs

500g cooked small waxy or salad potatoes, halved

400g spinach, any tough stems removed, large leaves shredded

Juice of 1 small lemon

A large handful of coriander, stalks removed, leaves chopped

30g flaked almonds, toasted

Sea salt and black pepper

Coconut milk adds an appealing edge of sweetness to this curry, mellowing the spiciness. In place of the spinach, you can use tender leaves from wild greens such as sea beet, spear-leaved orache or fat hen. If you prefer less heat, remove the seeds and membrane from the chillies. Serves 6

Heat the oil in a large saucepan over a medium heat. Add the onions with a pinch of salt and sweat for about 10–12 minutes until soft. Add the garlic, chillies and ginger and fry for another couple of minutes. Stir in the curry powder and cook for a minute, then add the coconut milk and stock. Season with some salt and pepper and simmer for 15 minutes.

Meanwhile, put the eggs in a pan of boiling water, bring back to a simmer and cook for 5 minutes. Drain, put them in a bowl of cold water for a couple of minutes, then peel.

Add the eggs, cooked potatoes and spinach to the curry. Put the lid on the pan and cook for 2 minutes, to encourage the spinach to wilt, then uncover and simmer gently for a further 5 minutes. Stir in the lemon juice and half of the chopped coriander. Taste and add more salt and pepper if necessary.

Scatter the rest of the coriander and the flaked almonds over the curry and serve with basmati rice.

Sprats

LATIN NAME
Sprattus sprattus

ALSO KNOWN AS
Brisling

SEASONALITY
Avoid spring and summer,
particularly May and June
when spawning

HABITAT
Found all around the British
Isles, also as far north as the
Baltic, as far south as North
Africa, and in the Mediterranean

MCS RATING
2–4

REC MINIMUM SIZE
8cm

SOURCING
goodfishguide.org

Delicious, easy to cook and dripping with omega-3 oils, sprats are a gift from the sea. They are also a crucial link at the base of the marine food chain, preyed upon by many other creatures – piscine, mammal and avian – so it's vital we don't deplete their stocks.

Sprats are a migratory species that moves to our inshore waters in autumn in search of food. On beaches along the south coast, vast shoals of these glimmering creatures sometimes find themselves caught in the thrashing tide, chased by other fish, by gulls, by the sea itself and driven towards the shore. Occasionally they may even be thrown ashore by the waves, left fluttering on the beach, easy prey for any opportunist. On several occasions, I have managed to bag a supper of these tasty, fishy morsels with no more effort than it takes to bend down and pick them up off the Dorset shingle.

That's not the only way to catch a sprat of course. These tiny shoaling creatures are easy to scoop up in nets – of varying types and sizes. In the North Sea, large quantities are taken by industrial vessels and turned into fishmeal and oil (both used in salmon farming). The sprats you find on the fishmonger's counter are more likely to come from small boats taking advantage of the seasonal influx. But both kinds of fishing should continue with caution. As very fast-growing little creatures, sprats are good at replacing themselves – but any species can be overfished if we are greedy. North Sea sprats are doing well at the moment and are still the best choice but look for those caught by seine nets, mid-water trawlers or, ideally, small inshore boats. And avoid whitebait, which is generally comprised largely or entirely of baby sprats.

Sprats are generally sold whole, guts and all, but they take little time to prepare (see recipe below). Like all oily fish, they respond beautifully to searing heat. I usually grill or barbecue sprats, or fling them into a very hot frying pan. They need no more flavouring than salt and pepper, though a few hot spices thrown into the mix can be good too. Cook seasoned sprats under a hot grill for about 2 minutes each side until the skin is browned and the juices bubbling; or cram them on to barbecue skewers in silvery ranks, oil and salt them, then grill over charcoal to blistered perfection. You can also bake sprats in the top of a hot oven for 8–10 minutes. Give them a good squeeze of lemon and a sprinkle more salt and eat straight away, with your fingers.

GRILLED SPRATS WITH HARISSA DRESSING

Bathed with a slightly sweet, spicy dressing then grilled until blistered and brown, these sprats are irresistible. Sardines are also fantastic grilled with this dressing. Serves 6

1kg sprats (at least 10 per person)

Sea salt and black pepper

FOR THE HARISSA DRESSING
2 tbsp harissa paste

Finely grated zest and juice of 1 lemon

1 garlic clove, grated

2 tsp caster sugar

1 tbsp finely chopped parsley

4 tbsp olive or rapeseed oil

TO FINISH
A little lemon or lime juice

Chopped coriander (optional)

To make the dressing, put all the ingredients into a small bowl and whisk to combine.

Holding a sprat in one hand, use scissors to cut away a strip, about 5mm wide along the belly, from the tail to the gills. Pull this away then hold the fish, head down, under a running cold tap. Use your thumb to push out the guts, rinsing as you go. Transfer to a plate lined with kitchen paper and pat dry. Repeat with the remaining sprats.

Preheat the grill to high. Lay a piece of foil over a large grill pan, oil it lightly and lay out the sprats in a single layer. Brush them with about one-third of the harissa dressing, then season with salt and pepper. Slide under the hot grill. Cook for a couple of minutes until brown and blistered then turn over, brush with more dressing and cook the second side for another 2 minutes or so.

Serve straight away, with the remaining dressing, spritzed with a little lemon or lime juice and sprinkled with chopped coriander, if you have some. Crisp salad leaves and waxy potatoes are good on the side.

Spring greens

Mark Diacono

LATIN NAME
Brassica oleracea

SEASONALITY
March–May

MORE RECIPES
Braised white beans with greens (page 55); Marinated tofu with spring greens (page 638); Braised Savoy cabbage with mustard (page 400); Pak choi with sticky prune sauce (page 427)

This is a loose term for a loose and lovely vegetable – essentially a less than fully mature cabbage. Some varieties form little or no heart, 'Wintergreen' for example. Others are cabbages that, in the right conditions, would form a tight, compact ball of leaves in the centre but which can be harvested while still loose and open. 'Duncan' is an excellent choice. The cold tolerance of these varieties means they can be grown through the winter and are ready to harvest from early spring, when other veg pickings are relatively slim. Pointed summer cabbages, planted close together so they don't grow too big, often produce very good 'spring' greens too, and can be cropped well into the summer.

While heartless, these greens are far from soulless, having a rich but sweet flavour and a relatively tender texture. This makes them a welcome change from the firm crunch of many mature winter cabbages. All but the thickest or most damaged outer leaves can be eaten. The coarser stalks should be removed too, because they can be tough and fibrous, but there's no need to worry about the more slender stems. The leaves themselves cook to a silky texture.

Most of the time, I treat their sweet, gentle nuttiness very simply, just rolling the leaves into a 'cigar' and finely shredding them before steaming or boiling for just a few minutes until tender. A little salt, pepper and butter are all that's needed to ready them for whatever main course needs a little green side.

Spring greens work deliciously with pasta too. For a quick midweek supper or lunch, finely slice a rasher or two of bacon and fry until lightly browned, before adding a handful of shredded spring greens and a finely chopped garlic clove and cooking for 5–6 minutes. Add a splash of cream and/or wild garlic if it is still in season, along with salt and pepper, and serve with spaghetti. That affinity between greens and gentle wild garlic is something to exploit in a delicious side dish – just stir wild garlic leaves into steamed or boiled shredded greens and their heat will wilt them deliciously.

'Crispy seaweed' is often, in fact, deep-fried spring greens and is easy to make. Remove the central rib from each leaf and thinly shred the fleshy part of the leaves, blanch in boiling water, drain and thoroughly pat dry. The shredded leaves can then be deep-fried, but I prefer to drizzle them with a little olive oil and bake them in a hot oven (220°C/Fan 200°C/Gas 7) for 5–7 minutes, turning halfway through if need be. Salt and pepper, sesame seeds, Chinese five-spice or a blend of mild chilli powder and smoked paprika sprinkled over them works wonders.

SPRING GREENS WITH LEMON AND GARLIC

2 good heads of spring greens

20g butter

1 tbsp olive or rapeseed oil

1 small garlic clove, grated

Finely grated zest of 1 lemon and a squeeze of lemon juice

Sea salt and black pepper

Sharp lemon and sweet garlic bring out all the vegetal deliciousness of spring greens. This makes a fantastic side dish for almost any meat or fish, or serve it up next to a potato gratin and a dish of pulses. Serves 2–4

Cut the base away from the bunches of spring greens and discard any rough or damaged outer leaves. Strip out the coarser stems. Roll several leaves at a time into fat 'cigars' then slice them across their length into thick ribbons.

Bring a large pan of salted water to the boil. Add the greens, stirring them into the water, then cook for 3–4 minutes, until just done but retaining a little bite. Drain thoroughly.

Return the pan to a low heat and add the butter, oil, garlic and lemon zest. Let sizzle gently for a minute or so, then return the greens to the pan and stir to combine. Season well with salt and pepper and a little squeeze of lemon juice. Serve straight away.

Squashes

Hugh Fearnley–Whittingstall

LATIN NAME
Cucurbita maxima, Cucurbita pepo, Cucurbita moschata

SEASONALITY
Harvested October–November, can be stored through to spring

MORE RECIPES
Squash and cinnamon soup with roasted seeds (page 183); Crispy lentil and roasted squash salad with salsa verde (page 352); Roast grouse with barley, apples and squash (page 290); Roasted squash with chestnuts, sausage and sage (page 158); Sausages with squash and kale (page 568); Tongue, kale and apple hash with horseradish (page 643); North African shepherd's pie (page 335)

I get more excited about squashes than is strictly seemly. The generosity of their form is more than tempting – all those voluptuous curves – and their gorgeous colours are hard to resist. But it's the taste and texture of their flesh that woos me every time. I should say tastes and textures as there is much delightful variance between the different types. And if I can get a dozen or so squashes, embracing at least 3 or 4 varieties, across the kitchen threshold between October and March, then I know I will have a winter's worth of fabulous, earthy-sweet dishes under my belt.

Every year, I set myself the little challenge of coming up with a couple of new ways to eat squash. And, so inspiring are these cheery vegetable-fruits, I've not failed yet. I halve them and fill them with herbs and cream, or purée the flesh with butter and thyme. I transform them into spicy, sweet tarts, savoury risottos and thick, velvety soups. I indulge repeatedly in roasted, burnt-edged chunks of squash, served with leaves, with mushrooms, with nubbly grains of spelt, with seeds or nuts. I grate squash flesh for fruity tea breads and mash it to fill ravioli. And I simmer it with coconut milk, lentils and spices to make the most soothing of curries.

These splendid members of the Cucurbit family (related to melons, courgettes and cucumbers) love our mild climate, and we produce some fabulous examples. They are harvested in early autumn and have amazing staying power – keeping happily for weeks, if not months, once cut from the vine. In a good year, I'll be enjoying squash right up until March. To keep them in prime condition, they should be stored in a dry, cool room (not the fridge); 15°C or so is about right.

Pumpkins are a kind of squash, of course, but they are often bred for size rather than flavour – fodder for the burgeoning Halloween market – and I'm suspicious of any specimen larger than my head. The more swollen it is, the more likely it will be fibrous and watery – I mean the pumpkin, not my head.

Squashes, however, reliably offer a range of lovely flavours and textures, from honeyed, silky sweetness through to chestnutty fluffiness. Trying new varieties is all part of the fun but you can almost always substitute one type for another.

FAVOURITE SQUASH VARIETIES

Acorn Dark green, this has a lovely fluted form that just begs to be deconstructed into neat wedges for roasting.

Butternut This bell-shaped, parchment-coloured squash is ubiquitous. For most of the year, butternuts are imported but when in season, British ones can be excellent. They are among the wetter-fleshed of the squashes so I like them best for soups and purées.

Crown Prince This large squash (illustrated right), with its ethereal, blue-grey skin and tender, velvety flesh, is one of my favourites and a great all-rounder. Brilliant for skin-on wedges, roasted with garlic and chilli if you are so minded.

Gem Small and round, this is perfect for baking whole, hollowed out and filled with a rich savoury stuffing.

Harlequin This is shaped like the Acorn, but has glorious motley-coloured skin.

Iron Bark This Australian variety, now catching on here, is known for its excellent keeping qualities, no doubt helped by its hard, green-black rind. The rich orange flesh has a dryish texture rather like cooked potato and a lovely sweet taste.

Kabocha This has a rough, mottled green skin, golden flesh and a beautifully sweet flavour. 'Sweet Mama' is a particularly tasty example.

Onion squash Also know as 'Uchiki Kuri', this is a small squash with glossy orange skin (the name refers to its shape, not its flavour). It has a relatively dry, fluffy flesh, which is wonderful mashed.

Spaghetti squash This yellow torpedo should be boiled whole or halved and baked, cut side down. Once tender, the flesh can be broken up with a fork into spaghetti-like strands. Toss them with butter, salt and pepper.

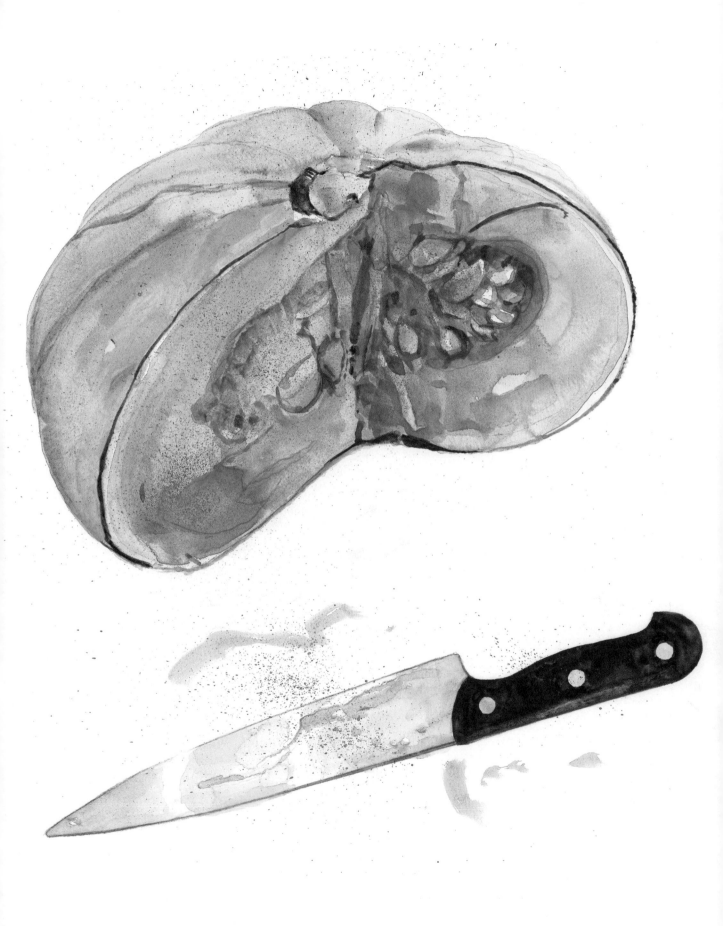

A ripe, raw specimen is so heavy, hard and unyielding that it could qualify as an offensive weapon, and prepping one requires firm discipline, a heavy, sharp knife and a sturdy wooden board. Don't try to cut through the hard, woody stalk – make your knife cut right next to it. As soon as the initial breach is made and you have halved the squash, you can steady it on its cut surface, and things start to get easier. For roasted wedges, leave the skin on. If you need to remove it, use a good potato peeler on thin-skinned varieties such as butternut, or your knife for tough-skinned squashes. Quarter or otherwise segment the squash and scoop out the seeds with a spoon or small knife. You needn't discard them: wash to remove the sticky, stringy bits of flesh, scatter on a baking tray, then oil, salt and roast at 180°C/Fan 160°C/Gas 4 for 10–15 minutes until golden and tempting.

The dense, hard flesh of squash is actually mostly water and it tastes best when the cooking process has driven off some of that moisture, concentrating the sweet, nutty flavour. That's why roasting is so successful. Sloshed with oil, scattered with bashed garlic cloves, salt, pepper, chilli flakes and herbs, and whacked into a hot oven (190°C/Fan 170°C/Gas 5) for 30–60 minutes, depending on the size of the chunks, squash reveals all its rich colour and flavour.

Growing your own squashes is hugely rewarding. If you're buying seeds, you'll have a huge range to choose from. Or if you've prepared a meal with squash you find particularly delicious, set the seeds aside. Let them dry out in a warm place and save them for sowing the following May.

Squash plants take up a reasonable amount of space but are undemanding. Treat them to several wheelbarrows full of good manure early on, pray for a decent mix of wet and warm weather over the summer, and they will repay you by blossoming spectacularly and flinging tendrils all over the garden before, in a final autumnal flourish, offering up a cornucopia of curvaceous, colourful, sweet-fleshed fruit.

SQUASH, SHALLOT AND MUSHROOM TART

350g peeled, deseeded squash (about 500g unprepared weight)

175g shallots, halved or quartered

2 tbsp olive or rapeseed oil

A few rosemary and/or thyme sprigs

150g large, firm mushrooms, such as portobello or field mushrooms, thickly sliced

1 sheet of ready-rolled all-butter puff pastry

100g Stinking Bishop, Baronet, Taleggio or other washed rind cheese

Sea salt and black pepper

This glorious supper is easy to put together. If you don't want to take the pastry route, give the squash, shallot and mushroom mix a little longer in the oven and serve on a bed of leaves as a salad, dressed with a tad more oil and a trickle of good balsamic vinegar. Serves 4

Preheat the oven to 190°C/Fan 170°C/Gas 5. Cut the squash into 1cm slices. Lay the squash slices and shallots on a large baking tray. Pour over the oil, season with salt and pepper and scatter on half of the herbs. Roast for 30 minutes.

Stir in the mushrooms and return to the oven for 20 minutes, until everything is cooked and starting to caramelise (don't let it colour too much, because it will be cooked further later on). Remove from the oven and tip the roasted veg into a dish. Turn up the oven to 200°C/Fan 180°C/Gas 6.

Lay the pastry sheet on a large baking tray and score a border 2cm in from the edge all round; don't cut right through. Spread the veg over the pastry, leaving the border clear.

Slice the cheese thickly and arrange on top of the veg. Strip the leaves off the remaining rosemary and/or thyme and scatter these over, then add some more seasoning. Bake for 15–20 minutes, until golden brown and bubbling.

Serve with a salad of bitter or peppery leaves to balance the sweet squash and shallots.

Squid

Gill Meller

LATIN NAME
Loligo vulgaris, Loligo forbesi

SEASONALITY
Avoid December–May when
spawning

HABITAT
Widespread throughout the
northeast Atlantic and the
Mediterranean

MCS RATING
3–4; squid from Scotland and
Cornwall are currently the best
choices, with jigged squid being
a particularly selective method

REC MINIMUM SIZE
16cm body length (not including
the tentacles)

MORE RECIPES
Squid with chervil and blood
orange (page 155); Cuttlefish
with fennel and white beans
(page 228); Paella (page 163)

SOURCING
goodfishguide.org

This is a seafood that requires a little understanding. But once you've got squid sussed, it will reward you with tender, sea-sweet flesh that can be cooked in minutes, and works deliciously well with all sorts of rich and spicy partners.

First off, it's important to know that squid's slightly bouncy texture is natural, and one of its unique charms. You bite into the smooth cooked flesh and there should be a slight resistance there. However, no one wants to eat squid that feels like chewing rubber – something that can happen if squid is overdone or, conversely, underdone. Squid needs to be cooked either very quickly or long and slow. Like certain cuts of meat, it becomes tender, then tough, then tender again.

A really fresh, young squid (300–600g), will yield flesh that needs as little as 30 seconds on a searing hot barbecue or griddle – 1 minute max – just enough to char the exterior and drive the heat in. The slight bitterness of the char accentuates the sweetness of the flesh. If you have a larger, older squid (700g or more), you can tenderise it in several ways. Open out the body and cut it into large squares (about 8cm), then score the inner surface in a diamond pattern, with the lines 2–3cm apart. This helps the heat to get into the thicker flesh and also stops the meat from curling up too much in the heat – the technique is good with younger squid, too.

Another neat trick is to mash up kiwi fruit, spread it on to raw squid and leave it for anything from 1–6 hours. The flesh will be transformed by an enzyme in the fruit, actinidin, which breaks down proteins. You can also soften squid by long, slow cooking – anything from 1½–3 hours, depending on the age of the squid. With time, the flesh develops a deep, rich, lingering savouriness while retaining that unique cephalopod sweetness, also found in octopus and cuttlefish. I like to slow-cook whole squid bodies that have been stuffed with a mixture of uncooked rice, chorizo and fennel seed, in a rich tomato sauce, and I also love squid braised with chunks of bacon and white beans for a hearty seafood stew.

For quick cooking, the classic is calamari – deep-fried squid rings – dipped in garlicky mayonnaise. It's hard to beat. Dip your squid rings in seasoned flour or batter and fry in oil heated to around 180°C for just 45–60 seconds. Don't overwhelm the pan with too much calamari, especially if you are using batter, or you'll cool the oil and the calamari won't crisp up.

When buying squid, look for freshness, signified by bright eyes and a reddish-purple, speckled skin. If the skin is reasonably intact, this is a sign that the squid has been carefully handled during its journey to the fishmonger's slab. A lot of the squid in our supermarkets is imported and may have been previously frozen. Most of the squid caught in British waters is landed in Scotland, often brought in as by-catch by trawl or seine nets aimed at white fish species such as cod and haddock. It's rarely a specifically targeted species but here in the Southwest, we are lucky enough to have access to jig-caught squid from the area around Sennen Cove. Jigging is a very selective form of fishing, similar to hand-lining. However, it's still the case that many of the squid caught are immature ones that haven't reproduced (the females die immediately after spawning). So as with any species, it's important to be judicious and to avoid the spawning period.

To prepare squid, hold on to the body with one hand and gently pull the head away with your other hand. It'll bring out the squid's internal workings in one fell swoop. Squid don't carry much ink but if you find an intact pouch, the contents will add a hint of colour and a punch of flavour to a fish soup or stew. Cut away the tentacles

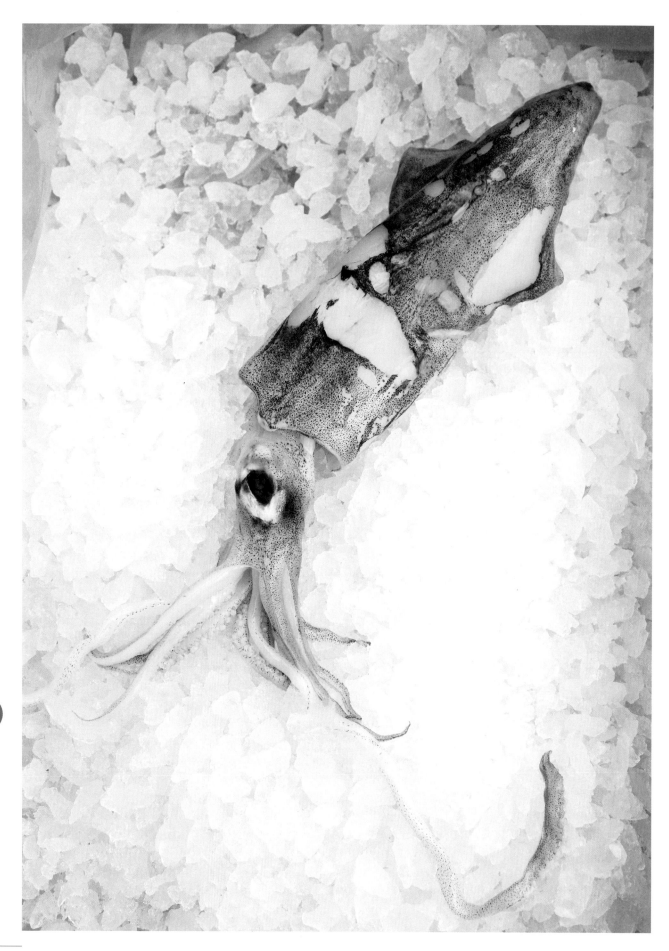

from just in front of the eyes. There's a small, oft-forgotten moustache-shaped piece of edible flesh that sits just below the head and alongside the guts – easily missed but fine and tender. The rest of the head and guts should be discarded. Pull out the piece of clear cartilage that is the squid's only skeletal structure and looks like a transparent feather. To separate the wings, which propel the squid through the water, reach under them with thumb and forefinger and pull them off – try and do this so the majority of the skin comes away too. Otherwise, peel off any remaining skin with your fingers.

To prepare squid rings, cut off the tip of the body at the 'tail' end so you can run fresh water through the body and get rid of any remaining guts, grit or sand (trawled squid tend to have more of this than jigged ones as they've been rolled along the seabed). Cut the body tube into rings. If it's a young squid, you can make the rings up to 2cm wide to give the flesh some bite. Make them about 5mm wide if the squid is older and has thicker flesh. With bigger squid, the ring of tentacles can be divided in half or quarters – they should be shared among the plates so everyone gets both body and legs, which have slightly different tastes as well as textures.

Squid is often seen as something to cook in the summer but I also like it in the autumn: chargrilled and mixed with broccoli as a warm salad; or flash-fried and mixed with roasted aubergines, chickpeas and tahini; or with warm chickpea hummus, toasted almonds and smoked paprika. Heading east, it can be paired with zesty flavours such as coriander, ginger and basil, or you can drop rings into a green curry at the last minute, perhaps with some pieces of fish. Squid is great marinated with combinations of ginger, soy, honey, spring onions and sesame oil, then cooked in a stir-fry. The Italians also eat squid preserved in oil and even enjoy super-fresh squid raw in very thin slices, appreciating yet another of its remarkable textures.

GRILLED SQUID WITH CHILLI, PARSLEY AND GARLIC

1 large garlic clove, grated

2 tsp dried chilli flakes

1 tbsp finely chopped parsley, plus extra to finish

2 tbsp olive or rapeseed oil

4 small squid, cleaned, bodies left whole

Sea salt and black pepper

Extra virgin olive oil, to finish

This is fantastic treatment for small, tender squid. Keeping the body whole means the squid doesn't curl up too much on the hot grill. Serves 2

Combine the grated garlic, chilli and parsley in a large bowl. Stir in the olive or rapeseed oil and some salt and pepper.

Place the squid on a board and insert a cook's knife carefully into the body pouch from the open end so it fills the cavity. Use another sharp knife to cut through the squid body at 1.5–2cm intervals – you won't be able to cut through to the board because of the other knife inside. Turn the squid over and slice this side too, without the cuts meeting up at the sides, so that you end up with a whole but 'ribboned' squid. Repeat with all the squid.

Put the slashed squid bodies and tentacles into the bowl of flavoured oil. Rub it into the squid and season with salt and pepper.

Heat a griddle pan over a fiercely high heat (or heat up the barbecue). Lay the squid bodies and tentacles on it and cook for 1 minute on each side.

Remove the squid to a warmed plate and trickle with a little extra virgin olive oil and a final scattering of chopped parsley. Rest for 1–2 minutes, turning the squid once or twice in the oil, before serving with new potatoes and a crisp salad.

Squirrel, grey

Hugh Fearnley-Whittingstall

LATIN NAME
Sciurus carolinensis

SEASONALITY
Available all year round, but
best eaten in the autumn

HABITAT
Common in woodland, parks
and gardens

MORE RECIPES
Rabbit with anchovies, rosemary
and cream (page 516); Rabbit
ragu with tarragon (page 633)

SOURCING
tasteofgame.org.uk

Squirrels may be bright-eyed and charming, but that's no reason not to eat them – particularly when you consider that they are delicious, very much free-range and that there are far too many of the bushy-tailed little blighters about.

Grey squirrels are a pest. These non-native interlopers dwarf our resident red squirrels – both in terms of individual size (they're more than twice as big) and overall population. Estimates vary but most suggest there are 2.5–3 million of them in Britain and they out-compete the reds for food and habitat. They can also carry a virus that's fatal to red squirrels. Plus they eat a lot of birds' eggs and damage young trees.

There's not a lot of meat on a squirrel, but its muscular hind legs, combined with the saddle, provide a good portion for one – or two in a stew. To joint a squirrel, divide the front quarters from the rear, cutting just below the front legs. The rear portion can be cooked whole or halved for a stew. The front legs, shoulders and head are good for the stock pot.

Squirrel meat is partridge-like: lean, fine-textured and very tasty without being particularly gamey. The older the squirrel, the tougher it will be, and the more it will benefit from long, slow cooking. Once skinned and prepared, the only clue to age is size. But if you acquire your squirrel whole and in the fur, look out for ragged claws and worn teeth – a sign of age. Young animals are tender enough to simply pan-cook or barbecue – you can use them in most recipes designed for rabbit or chicken pieces. Older squirrels are best for stews and pie fillings; again, use rabbit recipes as your guide. My default procedure for a senior squirrel (jointed) is to stew it gently then take the meat off the bones and return it to the sauce – as in the recipe below.

If you're buying squirrels, make sure you know where the animals have come from: one common method of squirrel-culling is poisoning. Buying from a good game dealer is the best bet, and there are online sources too. Squirrel is best in the autumn, when it will be plump from a summer of fruit and nut eating, and very delicious indeed.

SQUIRREL AND BEANS ON TOAST

This rustic dish makes a generous lunch if you use a couple of squirrels, though it can even be used to make the most of just one. It works well with a small rabbit too. Serves 4

2 tbsp olive or rapeseed oil

1–2 squirrels, jointed

1 medium onion, chopped

2 garlic cloves, thinly sliced

½ tsp hot smoked paprika

1–2 large sprigs of rosemary

2 bay leaves

A small glass of red wine

400g tin chopped tomatoes

400g tin cannellini or other
white beans, rinsed and drained

Sea salt and black pepper

TO SERVE

4 slices of sourdough or ciabatta,
toasted

Extra virgin olive oil, to finish

Grated hard cheese (optional)

Heat a heavy-based saucepan over a medium-high heat and add the oil. When hot, add the squirrel pieces and a little salt and pepper. Fry for 3–4 minutes, turning often, until the meat is just starting to brown. Reduce the heat, add the onion, garlic, paprika, rosemary and bay and fry gently for a further 5 minutes.

Add the wine and chopped tomatoes; if necessary, add a little water to barely cover the meat. Bring up to a gentle simmer. Place a lid on the pan, turn down the heat and cook for 1½–2 hours or until the squirrel meat is tender.

Lift the squirrel pieces out of the sauce on to a tray. When cool enough to handle, flake the meat off the bones on to a large plate. Go over the meat thoroughly to make sure you haven't missed any small sharp bones, then return it to the pan.

Add the beans, bring back to a simmer and cook, uncovered, for a further 15–20 minutes. This will help the sauce thicken.

Season to taste and pile on to toast, drizzle with some good extra virgin olive oil and sprinkle with a little cheese if you like, before bringing to the table.

St George's mushrooms

LATIN NAME
Calocybe gambosa

SEASONALITY
Late April and May

HABITAT
Locally abundant in short grass, old pasture, lawns, sometimes woodland

MORE RECIPES
Blewit, pigeon and endive salad (page 74); Field mushroom and celeriac pie (page 258); Sautéed mushrooms with juniper (page 320)

These mushrooms are on my list of a dozen or so species which are tasty, common and unmistakeable. They start to appear in rings in permanent pasture or other grassland, on path sides and sometimes woodland around St George's Day, 23 April, hence the name. Fairly stocky in stature, St George's are about the size of a portobello mushroom – typically up to 10cm in diameter. Off-white in colour (cap, gills and stem), they smell strongly of raw pastry. I know of no other large, white-all-over mushroom that grows in spring – but do check in an illustrated guide before you decide that you have the right species.

As with many mushrooms, it is well worth learning your spot, as the St George's is likely to appear in the same place year after year, sometimes for many decades. I have one location that has reliably produced between 100 and 200 St George's mushrooms every spring for the last 15 years.

The strong, mealy smell that makes this mushroom so distinctive can be a little off-putting, but do not worry – it is moderated to pleasantness by cooking. Being very fleshy, St George's can take a good while to soften – 10 minutes at least. Like other wild mushrooms, they are best cooked simply: sautéed with cream and garlic, then served on toast, takes an awful lot of beating.

ST GEORGE'S MUSHROOM AND ASPARAGUS PIZZA

As these mushrooms coincide seasonally with glorious early asparagus, it is particularly satisfying to combine them in a recipe. Makes 3 pizzas, each serving 2–3

FOR THE PIZZA DOUGH
250g plain white flour

250g strong white bread flour

1½ tsp fine sea salt

1 tsp fast-acting dried yeast

1 tbsp olive or rapeseed oil, plus a little extra to oil

Flour or polenta, to sprinkle

FOR THE TOPPING
25g butter

1–2 tbsp olive or rapeseed oil

3 large onions, finely sliced

400–500g St George's mushrooms, trimmed and cut into 3–4mm slices

300g slender asparagus spears, woody ends snapped off

Sea salt and black pepper

Extra virgin olive oil, to finish

To make the dough, put the flours into a large bowl with the salt and yeast. Mix well. Add the oil and 325ml warm water and mix to a rough dough.

Turn out on to a clean surface and knead for 5–10 minutes until smooth, using as little flour as possible. Trickle a little oil into a bowl, add the dough and turn it in the oil. Cover with a tea towel and leave in a warm place until doubled in size, 1–2 hours.

Preheat the oven to 250°C/Fan 230°C/Gas 9, if it goes that high, or to at least 220°C/Fan 200°C/Gas 7. Put a baking sheet in to warm up.

For the topping, place a medium-large frying pan over a medium heat and add the butter and 1 tbsp oil. Once the butter is melted, add the onion and season with salt and pepper. When sizzling, turn the heat down, put a lid on the pan and cook the onions gently for about 20 minutes until soft and golden.

Tip the dough on to a lightly floured surface and deflate it gently with your fingers. Let it rest for a few minutes, then cut into 3 equal pieces. Roll out one piece as thinly as you can. Scatter a peel (pizza shovel) or another baking sheet with a little flour (or polenta) and place the dough base on it.

Spread one-third of the onions over the base, then lay one-third of the sliced mushrooms on top. Add a few spears of asparagus then trickle with a little more oil and season well.

Slide the pizza on to the hot baking sheet in the oven (for a really crisp crust). Or, simply place the baking sheet on top of the hot one in the oven. Bake for 10–12 minutes until crisp and well browned at the edges. Repeat with the remaining dough and toppings. Trickle a little extra virgin olive oil over the surface to serve.

Star anise

Mark Diacono

LATIN NAME
Illicium verum

MORE RECIPES
Slow-roasted goose with star anise, orange and chilli (page 283); Quince in star anise and honey syrup (page 512); Pears with ricotta, honey and thyme (page 536); Chocolate, brandy and star anise ice cream (page 178); Seville orange and clove marmalade (page 187)

This exquisite-looking spice is the sun-dried fruit of an evergreen tree. Its flavour is pungent, heavy and warm, yet bright. It is not related to aniseed but shares a distinctive flavour compound, anethole, which is both sweet and penetratingly aromatic. Star anise is a strong spice: too much can ruin the pleasure, so use it judiciously. But it is fabulous with so many things – meat and fruit dishes are where I use it most.

Star anise can be infused whole in a stew, broth or syrup, lending its qualities but being removed before eating. Just a single 'star' imparts plenty of sweet warmth and depth: try cooking it with apples as they collapse into a compote, with poaching peaches or pears, or in a pan of mulling cider. It even works in tomato sauces. And if you have a cold that requires hot honey, lemon and a tot of whisky, ½ star anise will bring them together with soothing style.

For a more intense zap of star anise, use it ground. It's not so widely available in this form, but you can grind your own in a mortar or coffee grinder. Efficiently crushing the whole stars can be a challenge: as an alternative, release the tiny glossy seeds from inside each 'spoke' of the star and crush these, saving the star pod for an infusion.

Star anise is native to China and Vietnam and you'll find it used extensively in dishes from these lands. It's essential to the broth for a steaming bowl of Vietnamese pho, for instance. And to my Western tastebuds, its unique, aromatic pungency is one of the defining notes in Chinese food. It's one of the crucial ingredients in Chinese five-spice seasoning. For an unbeatable, lively freshness, make it yourself: lightly toast 2 star anise, 2 tsp each of fennel seeds and Szechuan pepper, a 5cm piece of cinnamon stick and 7 cloves in a dry pan, shaking often to avoid burning. Blitz in a coffee grinder or pound in a mortar until reduced to a fine powder.

Goose, duck, pork and squid all benefit from a dusting of or marinating in five-spice before roasting, and sprinkling the mix over plums before baking with honey results in a deeply satisfying autumn pud.

POACHED PHEASANT WITH STAR ANISE

Legs and breasts from
1 pheasant

40g butter

1 onion, finely sliced

1 tsp black peppercorns

2 garlic cloves, crushed

3–4 sprigs of thyme

3 star anise

1 litre pheasant or chicken stock

1 tsp clear honey

Sea salt and black pepper

Pheasant responds well to poaching in this way. The legs, which need more time to tenderise, are cooked first; adding the breasts later ensures they remain moist. This recipe is equally delicious with guinea fowl. In either case, if you start with the whole bird, you can use the carcass, skin and wings to make the stock ahead of time. Serves 2

Remove the skin from the legs and breasts of the pheasant. Lightly season the meat.

Place a medium saucepan over a low heat and add half the butter. When it's melted, add the onion, peppercorns, garlic, thyme and star anise. Cook, stirring regularly, for 8–10 minutes, until the onion is starting to soften and the spices are fragrant.

Pour in the stock and bring to a gentle simmer, then drop in the pheasant legs, adding a little more stock to cover them if needed. Cover and cook over a low heat, allowing the stock to barely simmer, for about 1 hour or until the leg meat is tender and coming away from the bone. Add the pheasant breasts and simmer for a further 15–20 minutes, until just cooked through. Top up with a little more stock or water during cooking if needed.

Remove the meat to a plate. Strain the broth into a clean pan and bring to the boil. Let bubble until reduced by three-quarters, to a richly flavoured sauce. Stir in the honey and remaining butter and take off the heat. Season with salt and pepper to taste then return the pheasant to the sauce to warm through briefly before serving. Serve with rice and chopped coriander, or some wet polenta and steamed greens.

Stock

Steven Lamb

SOURCING

barfieldsbutchers.co.uk and pegotyhedge.co.uk (for liquid stocks)

A good stock makes all the difference to soups, stews, sauces, gravy and risottos, which is extraordinary when you consider that most stocks are comprised essentially of leftovers, trimmings and remains. Making your own is a deeply satisfying process.

All stocks begin with a collection of aromatic vegetables, herbs and spices. Meat and fish stocks also need bones, scraps and trimmings, skin, sinew and even selected items of offal, to give them their full-bodied flavours.

Carrots, onions and celery stems are the holy trinity of stock vegetables. You need at least two of each and they should be chopped, but you can leave them chunky and even unpeeled as long as they are clean. You can either start your stock with raw veg or sauté them first to get some browning flavours going.

To the vegetable base, it's usual to add herbs such as bay and parsley, and sometimes spices or aromatics such as peppercorns. To this, you can add whatever bones, giblets, skins and frames are appropriate. A slosh of white wine often goes in and the last thing to add is cold water to cover the ingredients. Add only enough to cover them – there is no point diluting the flavours any more than you have to.

Slowly bring the stock to the boil, then turn the heat down to a gentle simmer. Leave the pan uncovered. With meat stocks, it is best to ladle off any 'scum' that rises to the surface (this is just protein from the meat). To get the most flavour out of the ingredients, meat stocks should simmer for 3–4 hours, being topped up with a little water only as much as necessary to keep the ingredients submerged. You can let the liquid level drop towards the end to concentrate the stock's flavour. Vegetable and fish stocks need only about 30 minutes' simmering, and fish stocks actually start to take on some undesirable flavours after this time. At the end of the cooking process, your stock needs to be strained (see page 613).

STOCK-BUILDING INGREDIENTS

Essentials For any stock, you need onion, celery, carrot and bay leaves.

Desirable extras For any stock, the following are a bonus: parsley stalks, thyme, black peppercorns, white wine, leek tops, celeriac trimmings (well-scrubbed).

Possible extras For a veg stock: fried mushrooms, parsnip (just a little), tomato skins and seeds, a little garlic; for a fish stock: fennel trimmings, garlic; for chicken and other poultry stocks: giblets such as gizzards and necks, but not liver; for red meat and game stocks: red wine, strip of orange zest, star anise (just one), garlic, a few leaves of lovage.

What not to put in a stock Avoid adding salt or salty seasonings such as soy or Worcestershire sauce (these will become concentrated and make the stock too salty), cabbages or other brassicas (these will make your stock sulphurous), potato (adds nothing and makes stocks cloudy), liver (this makes meat stocks bitter).

TYPES OF STOCK

Vegetable stock Use lots of celery and alliums, such as onions and leeks, lots of herbs (particularly bay) and not too much carrot (which can make the stock oddly sweet). Make sure the veg is not over-diluted. And if you can add some tasty, umami-rich fried mushrooms or tomatoes you'll be creating another welcome layer of flavour. Vegetable is a good basic stock for almost any soup, risotto or stew but not ideal in rich gravies where you need more heft.

Fish stock This utilises the skeletons ('frames') and skins of filleted fish – it can be supplemented with the shells from crabs, lobster, crayfish or prawns, or these can be used alone to make a shellfish stock. If using a fish head, remove the eyes as these make the stock cloudy, and the gills, which can give an 'off' taste. Stick to white-fleshed fish, avoiding oily fish such as mackerel. A fish or shellfish stock needs only 30 minutes' gentle simmering. It is the obvious choice for a fish soup, chowder, risotto or fish pie.

Chicken stock This is often made with the stripped carcass of a roast chicken. If you have a bird with giblets, add these too (minus the liver). If you have jointed a chicken for a dish and have the raw bones left, it will make excellent stock, though not a large quantity. A light chicken stock is good in soups and risottos but if it's too strong, it can also detract from delicate ingredients. Chicken stock comes into its own for broths (see below), casseroles, stews, gravies, curries – any slow-cooked meaty dish.

Game bird and other poultry stocks These are made in the same way as a chicken stock and can similarly be turned into wonderful, warming broths with the addition of noodles, small pasta or rice, and some chopped vegetables and/or leftover meat. Game bird stocks work well, of course, in game dishes such as pies, stews and curries but you can also use them in non-game recipes.

Meat bone stocks
These stocks traditionally fall into the categories of dark (or brown) and white meat stocks. Dark meat stocks begin with the deliberate overcooking of meat bones in a hot oven for long enough to make them richly caramelised and coloured. The 'Maillard reaction' that goes on when meat is browned releases intense flavours. A white meat stock is made using meat bones (classically veal) but without the initial caramelisation.

Lamb stock This is one of the strongest tasting and most distinctive red meat stocks, so it is generally best reserved for lamb dishes. A good lamb stock, with the addition of pot barley, carrots, onions and some greens such as spinach or kale, gives you a fine Scotch Broth.

Beef stock The best, most full-bodied beef stock is made from a combination of roasted beef bones (including, ideally a marrow bone) and also some raw bones, plus a good spectrum of stock veg (ideally the onions and carrots well-browned) and aromatics (crucially bay and parsley), simmered very gently for upwards of 5 hours. Too rich for most soups or risottos, it's a fine addition to beefy stews, ragus, and chillies. It's also a great addition to your roast beef gravy (see pages 62–3). Strained and boiled down hard with a dash of red wine, it makes the ultimate beef reduction.

Pork stock There's no reason not to make a stock from pork bones as you would any others. It's a good all-purpose base for gravy, spicy broths and sauces or, if jellified with trotters, can be used to fill a pork pie. Pork bones can be added to beef or chicken stock too.

Ham stock The salty, savoury stock made from cooking a ham bone is a classic base for pea and ham soup but can also go into other vegetable soups.

S

You can strain your stock through a colander but, for a very clear stock, you need to pass it through a muslin-lined sieve. This fine straining is necessary if you want to boil meat stocks further, to a rich reduction or *jus* (see page 62). Stocks should not be seasoned at this point unless they are not being cooked further in another dish.

A meat stock that is left to cool will almost certainly form a layer of fat on the surface. This is easily removed once the fat has cooled and set. Stocks freeze well, either in plastic containers or, if very concentrated, in ice-cube trays.

Making stock from fresh bones

If you can get a supply of fresh, raw bones from your butcher (cheaply or even for free) then your stock-making need not depend on leftover bones generated in your own kitchen (or you can combine both sources). This is particularly important if you want to make beef or lamb stock in any quantity, as the joints we buy rarely have enough bones to make a decent amount of stock from the leftover roast. Using a combination of raw and roasted bones produces the best flavoured meat stocks, as each contributes different flavours. Online suppliers are a good source of organic and free-range bones.

Ready-made stocks

There are many off-the-shelf options if you don't have time to make your own stocks. Instant stocks can often be overly salty, however, in which case dilute them more than the packet suggests. And do check the label for unwelcome additives if you are buying stock cubes. Look for instant stocks that use organic and/or free-range meat, at least. Pre-made liquid stocks can be useful too – though the quality varies considerably.

ENGLISH ONION SOUP

60g butter

1.5kg onions, quartered and thinly sliced

4–5 garlic cloves, sliced

1 bay leaf

A few sprigs of thyme

150ml dry cider

750ml chicken stock

750ml beef stock

2 tbsp rapeseed oil

12–18 sage leaves

Sea salt and black pepper

TO SERVE

4 slices of sourdough bread

120g Cheddar or other well-flavoured hard cheese, grated

This Anglicised version of the classic French soupe à l'oignon uses two kinds of stock, plus West Country cider, to provide a wonderful richness. Serves 6

Melt the butter in a large heavy-based pan over a medium-low heat. Add the onions and sauté slowly for around 45 minutes, until soft, tender and browned.

Now add the garlic, bay and thyme. Cook gently for 5 minutes, then pour in the cider and simmer for about 3 minutes until reduced to a glaze. Remove the herbs. Pour in the stocks, bring to a simmer and simmer gently for 20 minutes. Season with salt and pepper to taste.

Heat the oil in a small pan over a medium-high heat. When it seems hot, throw in a sage leaf to test the heat: it should sizzle instantly. Add all the whole sage leaves and fry for about 30 seconds, until they are crisp.

Preheat the grill to high. Toast the slices of sourdough on both sides. Ladle the onion soup into heatproof bowls, top each serving with a slice of toasted sourdough, sprinkle on the cheese and grill until melted and bubbling.

Serve the soup topped with the crisp sage leaves.

Strawberries

Mark Diacono

LATIN NAME
Fragaria ananassa

SEASONALITY
May–October

MORE RECIPES
Beetroot, strawberry and rocket salad (page 537); Strawberry, rhubarb and sweet cicely salad (page 627); Strawberries with lavender and honey (page 341); Meringue with strawberries and sorrel (page 590)

A strawberry that has been loved by the sun, picked at its peak by the person who's going to eat it, and enjoyed during Wimbledon, is a pleasure apart. The first few of the summer set the soul dancing like no other fruit, though late-season strawberries may taste great too (depending on the variety, they can be worth eating as late as October).

Strawberries are tricky devils to buy, though. Most in the shops are sealed up in plastic, ensuring their scent, flavour and texture remains a mystery until you get them home. Buying British strawberries is the best option in such situations: not only does it support our growers but the shorter journey to the shelves means there's more chance of the fruit being picked near to optimum ripeness. This is a critical factor: strawberries don't ripen further after picking – what you buy is as good as it gets.

I recommend buying summer strawberries from a pick-your-own fruit farm. You get to sniff them (they should smell strongly of strawberry), taste some and choose them at the perfect point of ripeness, giving you the best deal. And buying direct supports the growers. However, in fairness, supermarket strawberries are much improved on the offering of even a few years ago. Better, more flavoursome varieties are undoubtedly the main reason: 'Jubilee', 'Sweet Eve' and (if you're lucky enough to find them) 'Honeoye' are streets ahead of the blandest. 'Elsanta', the butt of many jibes when it comes to supermarket strawberries, is actually a perfectly fine variety grown at home, where it can be given time to ripen under the sun properly, but rarely a stellar strawberry when bought in the shops.

Whatever variety, it's the weather that is the key to superb flavour: in almost all cases, the more sun a strawberry gets, the sweeter it's likely to taste. Not that we should consider sweetness above all else. As with tomatoes, I find a strawberry with a balance between sweet and acid the most satisfying: that touch of sharpness often makes the sweetness even more pleasurable.

Once you pick up on this delicious duality, you might find yourself moved to try strawberries in savoury recipes. Risk a handful on a pizza, ideally partnered with salty ingredients such as prosciutto, olives and cheese, and you'll be hooked – those little fruitful explosions set everything else off perfectly. If that sounds a step too far, try a dusting of freshly ground black pepper with the faintest sprinkle of sugar over a few strawberries. Fennel, rocket, cucumber, parsley (as a salad leaf), tomato, almonds, celery and onion are other pairings to experiment with in salads.

Growing your own strawberries is easy; they take well to container growing too. Plants will produce well for 4 or 5 years, which makes them a good investment. Start with young plants, planting them in full sun, with 50cm between plants, a little less if in containers. Water well, especially in dry spells, and feed with tomato or seaweed feed to promote good fruiting. I grow a handful of varieties that overlap in productivity, to give a long season of fruit. 'Honeoye' is the best of the earlies, for June; the old corker 'Cambridge Favourite' is at its peak through July; 'Mara des Bois' has a deliciously complex flavour, producing over a long season that is at its height from August into early October; 'Royal Sovereign' may be too small for the supermarkets, but its depth of flavour is remarkable; 'Florence' is dark, highly aromatic and full of flavour, thanks to its late season of ripeness.

Now I grow strawberries, I often find I have a few going over the top during the peak of summer production. These soft fruits usually find themselves in a smoothie (often as not, sweetening a veg-heavy concoction). Or in a superb, yet quick and easy, granita: zap a kilo of ripe strawberries in the blender, then push through a nylon sieve into a bowl to extract the seeds. Whisk in 200g icing sugar and the juice of 1–2 lemons; as with most ices, it should be sweeter and sharper than you'd like it when frozen, as the flavours will soften. Pour into a large plastic tub –wide enough that the purée is no more than 4cm deep, so that it freezes quickly and is easily attacked with a fork. Freeze. Take the tub from the freezer about 20 minutes before serving, then use a fork to scrape the mix into frozen shards. Serve immediately, before the shards have time to melt. A punnet or two that are out of date and cheap will work just as well in this dish as perfectly ripe strawberries.

If you are ever in any doubt as to what to do with strawberries, allow cream and something crunchy to come to the rescue. Eton mess is as marvellous as it is simple: swirl 500g roughly crushed strawberries through 350g whipped double cream with as much broken meringue as you fancy. Strawberries take surprisingly well to a crumble too, though I like them paired with apricots, peaches or nectarines rather than solo.

I love a strawberry fool, and though fine in itself, it also makes a starting point for other tempting variations. Hull and chop 400g strawberries, sprinkle with caster sugar and allow them to macerate for an hour or so. Before serving, scrape the seeds from a vanilla pod into 200ml double cream, stir in 100g plain yoghurt and whisk until very soft peaks form. Gently stir in the strawberries – you are after a ripple rather than complete incorporation. This will serve 4 as it is. For something a little more substantial, top with an 'independent crumble' (see page 479) to make a fumble (a fool with a crumble). Cranachan is a fabulous idea too, essentially a fool with a little booze (traditionally whisky) stirred in with the fruit and topped with toasted oats and honey.

Whether you buy or pick your strawberries, by all means extend their life by keeping them in the fridge, but let them get to room temperature before eating or you will sacrifice most of their flavour and aroma. (They don't freeze well.)

If you are lucky enough to come across a patch of wild strawberries, don't tell anyone. They are not uncommon in woodland clearings or patches of open, grassy ground, but rarely abundant. These tiny, intensely fragrant fruits (a slightly different species to our cultivated strawberries) are best eaten straight off the plant or enjoyed with just a little sugar or honey.

STRAWBERRY SALAD WITH RASPBERRY BASIL SAUCE

75g raspberries

Juice of 1 lemon

2 tsp clear honey

150g strawberries

6–8 large basil leaves

The anise scent and natural sweetness of basil enhances both strawberries and raspberries in this simple fruit salad. Try it with blueberries as well as, or instead of, the strawberries too.
Serves 2

Place the raspberries in large bowl with the lemon juice and honey and use a fork to crush them together.

Hull the strawberries and slice them thickly into the raspberry mixture. Shred the basil and add this too. Tumble the fruit and basil together and allow to stand for 15–20 minutes at room temperature.

Serve the strawberry salad just as it is, or with a little fresh ricotta dotted over the top.

Suet

Pam Corbin

SOURCING
graigfarm.co.uk and
greenpasturefarms.co.uk
(for fresh beef suet)

MORE RECIPES
Spotted dick with apple-brandy
raisins (page 522)

There are few ingredients that exemplify the post-war changes in our diet as much as suet – or the lack of it. Dumplings, spotted dick, jam roly-poly, steak and kidney pudding: such wonderful, energy-packed dishes for a time when we needed muscle power to toil the land. These no longer merit a place as daily fare, but we still need a bit of comfort once in a while.

Suet is a creamy-white fat from the kidney and loin region in cows and sheep. It is the hardest and most saturated of all animal fats and has a very high melting point: 45–50°C, in contrast to butter's 32–35°C. This means that a dough can rise and 'set' before the suet in it melts, leaving a mass of tiny air holes. Hence suet makes astonishingly light pastry and the fluffiest of dumplings.

Most of the suet used these days is from cattle, often from Northern Ireland or Holland. It's hard to know much about its provenance. The fat is dehydrated, pre-grated, stabilised with a little flour and stores well at ambient temperatures. Vegetarian 'suet' is made from palm and sunflower oils.

Fresh suet can be bought from a butcher (you may need to order it), or found online. It needs to be rendered down: cut it into small pieces and place in a heatproof bowl set over a pan of barely simmering water until it has melted. Strain the fat into a clean basin, to remove any bits of tissue, cool it down then chill it well before grating coarsely. Store in the fridge.

CHICKEN AND CIDER STEW WITH ROSEMARY DUMPLINGS

2 tbsp olive or rapeseed oil

1 medium-large chicken, jointed into 8 pieces

2 medium onions, chopped

4 garlic cloves, chopped

Leaves from 2 sprigs of thyme

500ml dry or medium cider

1–2 bay leaves

Leaves from a handful of marjoram, chopped (optional)

About 250g swede

About 250g turnips (2 medium)

About 250g carrots (3 large)

About 250g parsnips (2 large)

2 tbsp tomato purée

850ml chicken stock

Sea salt and black pepper

FOR THE DUMPLINGS

250g self-raising flour

125g suet

1 tbsp chopped rosemary

Leaves from a small bunch of parsley, chopped

The key to good dumplings is a light touch: don't work the dough for any longer than it takes to just bring it together. This warming stew also works well with rabbit. Serves 6–8

Preheat the oven to 160°C/Fan 140°C/Gas 3. Heat the oil in a large flameproof casserole over a medium-high heat. Season the chicken pieces and brown, in batches, in the pan, transferring them to a bowl as they are done.

Add the onions to the casserole and sauté over a medium heat until just turning golden, about 8 minutes. Add the garlic and thyme, cook for another minute, then turn up the heat and add the cider, bay leaves and marjoram, if using. Let the cider bubble until it is reduced by half.

Meanwhile, peel the swede and turnips and cut into 1.5cm cubes. Peel and halve the carrots and parsnips lengthways, then cut into 1cm half-moon slices.

Stir the tomato purée into the onion mix and return the chicken to the casserole, along with any resting juices. Add the prepared vegetables, pour over the stock and season with salt and pepper. Bring to a simmer, cover, then place in the oven for 1¼ hours.

When the chicken has been in the oven for an hour or so, make the dumplings. Mix the flour, suet and chopped herbs together with some salt and pepper, then stir in sufficient water to form a soft dough – about 175ml. Divide the mixture into 12 equal pieces and shape into dumplings.

Take the stew from the oven, drop the dumplings into it, cover the dish again and return to the oven for a further 20 minutes or until the dumplings are nicely puffed up. Remove the lid and return to the oven for a further 20 minutes until the dumplings are golden brown. Poke a cocktail stick into the centre of one, to check it's cooked through.

Serve the stew and dumplings with a heap of winter greens.

Sugar

Nikki Duffy

Sugar is made one of two ways: from sugar beet or from sugar cane. All types of sugar are processed – even soft, brown, crumbly sugars are the result of a chain of interventions, but not all sugar is refined.

Refining refers to the process of removing everything that is not pure sucrose. But either way, sugar is a highly extracted food – the sweetness stripped out of a plant, with little or none of its actual vegetable goodness remaining. That's why sugar is such a controversial ingredient these days – our bodies are not really designed to process carbohydrate in such a concentrated form. However, eaten in moderate amounts – and, crucially, combined with other wholesome ingredients – sugar can be useful in terms of providing energy. And, of course, it can make things taste delicious.

Sugar beets are lumpen, pale roots that look like fat parsnips. One of the plus points with beet sugar is that it is home-grown. We produce about 1.2 million tonnes of beet sugar in Britain each year (the beet tops are used as animal fodder) and, on average, the beets travel only around 30 miles from farm to factory – the factories being sited in beet-producing areas such as East Anglia and Nottinghamshire.

Beet sugar is always refined because the natural molasses in beets does not taste good – an unrefined brown beet sugar would be unpleasant. After washing, sugar beets are chopped, then soaked in hot water until their sugars have diffused into the liquid. This brown liquor is treated with lime and carbon dioxide to remove impurities, then filtered and boiled in a vacuum to produce a syrup. This sugar syrup is 'seeded' with existing sugar crystals, which encourages the rest of the syrup to crystallise. The sugar crystals are separated from the liquor in a centrifuge and then washed and dried to form white sugar. The remaining brown syrup is molasses – a mix of sugar, water, salts and minerals.

Cane sugar is produced all over the world in tropical regions, the main suppliers being Brazil, India, China and Thailand. The production process is similar to that for beet sugar: cane is crushed to release its sugary juice and this is again 'cleaned' with lime before being boiled to a syrup, which is seeded with sugar dust. The resultant crystals are then separated out centrifugally but left as a raw brown sugar which still contains molasses.

Unrefined sugars, such as muscovado, retain this molasses content. It gives them colour, moistness and – crucially – flavour. Refined white sugar just tastes sweet. Molasses-containing sugars have a range of toasty, nutty, caramel flavours that inform your cooking. Raw cane sugar, however, is often then refined to remove any remaining molasses. The crystals are re-dissolved in water, purified using milk of lime and the juice is then processed to get straight, white sucrose.

Some manufacturers in some parts of the world use charcoal derived from animal bones as part of the filtering process for cane sugar, which means those sugars are not suitable for vegans. Check with the manufacturer, but many of the widely available British brands of sugar are suitable for vegans.

Table sugar (sucrose) has a medium-high GI (glycaemic index rating), ranking higher than naturally occurring sugars such as fructose, but lower than pure glucose. GI measures the speed at which a food elevates blood glucose. High GI foods cause a sharp spike in blood sugar followed by a sudden drop that can leave you feeling sluggish and craving more sugar. Low GI foods make for more stable energy levels. GI is significantly affected by factors including the way a food is cooked, and what it is served with.

TYPES OF SUGAR

Caster sugar This is very fine and therefore ideal for baking, where you need the sugar to dissolve easily into non-liquid ingredients i.e. in egg white for meringues or for creaming with butter for a cake. It is available as white or golden (unrefined) caster. The golden type is never quite as fine as the white, so you have to work harder to get it to dissolve.

Granulated sugar Slightly coarser and cheaper than caster, this everyday sugar is used for sweetening tea or coffee, or dissolving to make syrups etc. It is not ideal for delicate cakes as it may stay undissolved in the batter.

Demerara sugar With its characteristic large, crunchy brown granules, this sugar is fabulous on top of cakes or crumbles. It can be made by mixing molasses back into refined, granulated white sugar. However, you can also get unrefined demerara, produced from cane juice syrup that is heated for longer to get a larger crystal size.

Muscovado sugars These are the most flavourful of all unrefined sugars, containing a good proportion of molasses. They are very moist and can stick together in lumps. If these lumps get hard, put the sugar in a bowl and cover with a damp tea towel so that the sugar reabsorbs moisture. Light muscovado has a wonderful caramel flavour and is fantastic in flapjacks and granolas, carrot cakes or tea breads. Dark muscovado is really rich, with an edge of bitter-sweetness from the extra molasses. It's masterful in dark fruit cakes and intense chocolate cakes. Molasses sugar is darker and stronger still and ideal in sticky barbecue glazes or in rich, spicy chutneys.

Soft brown sugars These have similar colours but less flavour and moisture than muscovado. Like demerara, they can be refined – formed by mixing molasses back into pure white sugar – or they can be unrefined cane sugar that retains some of its natural molasses.

Palm sugar Also called jaggery, this is made by boiling the sap from various types of palm, including coconut palms. It is unrefined, so it retains a golden colour and rich flavour. Palm sugar is sold in lumps or large crystals and gives an authentic flavour to Southeast Asian curries, salad dressings and puddings.

Jam and Preserving sugars Jam sugar has pectin added so it can be used with fruits which are low in pectin (such as strawberries) to make jam with a good set. Preserving sugar does not contain pectin: it is simply refined white sugar with extra-large grains. These are less prone to sticking to the base of the preserving pan and burning than finer caster or granulated sugars.

Golden syrup This super-sweet viscous syrup is an invert syrup and technically a light form of treacle. It is created by treating a sugar syrup (a by-product of the refining process) with an acid or an enzyme to break down its sucrose into fructose and glucose. As with honey, the 'free' fructose gives the syrup a sweeter taste than sugar. Unlike honey, golden syrup does not crystallise, so it is useful as a stabiliser in certain recipes, such as home-made fudge or caramel.

Treacle Another invert syrup, this is very rich in molasses, which gives it a tarry black colour and a distinct bitter note. (In the US, it would be called molasses.) Treacle is typically used in dark fruit cakes, gingery biscuits and parkins, and glazes for baked hams. Like golden syrup, it helps retain moisture in baked things.

Fructose Pure fructose is now available in the sugar aisle of most supermarkets, often labelled as 'fruit sugar', though it is usually refined from corn, beet or cane. You can use it just like caster sugar. It is sweeter than standard sugar (sucrose), so you can use less, and it has a lower GI.

S

Sugar can have a significant effect on a dish, even in small quantities. In fact, in savoury food, it can be used as a seasoning akin to salt: a pinch of sugar in a tomato sauce balances acidity beautifully, for example. But of course we often use sugar in much larger amounts. In treats such as caramel and fudge, it is not just sugar's intense sweetness that we value, but the brown colours and toasty flavours created when it is strongly heated. And sugar is integral to the deliciousness of brownies, biscuits and buns. Having said that, I do think some modern baking recipes use more than is strictly necessary. You can often lose 25 per cent of the sugar from a cake recipe and barely notice the difference.

If you balk at the volume of sugar added to traditional jams, you can reduce that too – by up to half. But the sugar's bacteria-inhibiting power will be affected. Low-sugar preserves taste fresher but don't keep so well: once opened, they should be stored in the fridge and eaten within weeks rather than months.

NUTTY BROWN SUGAR MERINGUES

4 medium egg whites

300g soft light brown sugar

100g skinned hazelnuts, toasted and crushed or very finely chopped

These have subtle caramel notes from the brown sugar. Hazelnuts work brilliantly in the mix, giving a praline-like flavour, but pistachios are good too. Makes 8–10

Preheat the oven to 120°C/Fan 120°C/Gas ½. Line a baking sheet with baking parchment.

Use either a freestanding mixer or a bowl and electric hand mixer with a whisk attachment. Make sure all is scrupulously clean and free of any grease. Put the egg whites into the bowl and whisk for several minutes until they are thick and holding firm peaks.

Still beating, gradually add the sugar a spoonful at a time. Make sure each spoonful is fully incorporated before you add the next. Stop beating only when all the sugar is assimilated and you have a very thick, glossy meringue that holds firm peaks. Use a spatula or large metal spoon to fold in the hazelnuts as lightly as you can.

Spoon the meringue on to the baking tray in 8–10 blobs. Try to keep them the same size, but don't worry too much about making them neat or uniform.

Bake for 3 hours, then remove from the oven and leave to cool completely. When cool, use the meringues at once or store in an airtight container for a few days. (Airtight is important, or they will start to soften.)

Serve the meringues with whipped cream and fresh fruit such as crushed raspberries.

Sumac

Tim Maddams

LATIN NAME
Rhus coriaria

MORE RECIPES
Quick za'atar crispbreads
(page 637)

Sumac is a shrub that grows on rocky upland in the more arid regions of the world. Its berries, dried and crushed, are used as a spice in Middle Eastern cookery – especially Lebanese food, but it's happy in many dishes. Dark plum red in colour, sumac has a unique, vibrant flavour: lemony and acidic, but also smoky and rich. The citrusy tang means it performs a little like lemon zest in a dish – adding a lovely, bright top note of flavour and enhancing other ingredients.

It's a spice that is very easy to work with – it doesn't need grinding or toasting. Simply sprinkle it on to just-grilled meats and fish, or mix it into a zingy, rich coriander dressing. I also love sumac on pancakes with some exceptional honey and maybe a few fresh or dried apricots.

Sumac is perhaps best known as an ingredient in fattoush – the Lebanese crispy bread salad – and it's a great way to try it. Split open some pitta breads and dry them out in the oven until crisp, while you make a dressing of sumac, finely chopped garlic, olive oil and a little chopped chilli. Dress the bread with this mixture, then add chopped tomato, cucumber and loads of torn mint and basil.

Many versions of za'atar (see page 635) include sumac. This Middle Eastern spice mix makes a great dry dip, used in the same way as dukkah – dunk bread in oil before dipping it into the za'atar and you are in paradise. It is also excellent as a marinade for anything you're planning on barbecuing. Simply add a little oil to the dry spices and rub into meat, fish or vegetables.

Sumac also works rather well with tequila in a sort of Middle Eastern version of a Margarita. Add a little pomegranate juice too and you're really into new territory.

You can buy sumac from good health food shops and spice suppliers. The spice keeps well for several months (especially in the fridge).

SUMAC EGGS

A great weekend breakfast or a delicious meat-free lunch. Serves 2–4

3 tbsp olive or rapeseed oil

2 onions, halved and finely sliced

2 tsp thyme leaves

2 garlic cloves, finely chopped

¼ tsp dried chilli flakes

400g tin peeled tomatoes, crushed or chopped

4 eggs

1 tsp sumac

150g feta or any mild, salty ewe's cheese, or Lancashire, crumbled

A small handful of coriander leaves

A small knob of butter

Sea salt and black pepper

Heat the oil in a medium frying pan over a medium-low heat. Add the onion and thyme and sauté gently for about 8–10 minutes, until the onions are softened and starting to turn golden. Add the garlic and chilli, stir for a minute, then add the tomatoes, season and simmer for about 10 minutes until thickened slightly.

Break an egg into a saucer and slide it into the sauce. Repeat with the other eggs so they are evenly distributed around the pan. Sprinkle half the sumac and some pepper over the whole thing, then continue to cook gently (effectively poaching the eggs) until the egg whites are set but the yolks are still runny. Remove the pan from the heat, crumble over the cheese and sprinkle on the coriander.

Heat the butter in a small saucepan, add the rest of the sumac, stir, then trickle this spiced butter over the eggs. Serve with warm flatbreads.

Sunflower seeds & oil

Nikki Duffy

LATIN NAME

Helianthus annuus

MORE RECIPES

Roasted almond aïoli (page 19); Squash and cinnamon soup with roasted seeds (page 183); Wilted mizuna with chilli, garlic and sunflower seeds (page 387); Mujadara (page 104); Lobster with béarnaise mayonnaise (page 365); Dandelion and ricotta salad with bacon (page 232); Seedy stoneground loaf (page 263)

SOURCING

clearspring.co.uk (for unrefined and high-oleic sunflower oils)

Sunflower oil is produced from vast fields of heavy-headed blooms, particularly in Russia and the Ukraine. Although it has long been seen as a flavourless, go-to frying medium, it doesn't start life bland. When left unrefined, it has a distinctive, nutty flavour. You can buy it in this form but it should only be used for dressings and other 'cold' applications because it has a low smoke point – around 100°C (the smoke point is the temperature at which oil starts to smoke and break down).

Refined sunflower oil (the most readily available kind) has a much higher smoke point (around 230°C) though the refining process involves heating the oil, treating it with a chemical solvent, bleaching and deodorising it. However, research is showing that polyunsaturated fats like sunflower oil are particularly susceptible to oxidative damage during cooking, even when refined and even before they reach their smoke point. Studies have found that standard refined sunflower oil produces very nasty toxic compounds (aldehydes) when used for ordinary frying.

For everyday frying or sautéeing, I prefer oils rich in monounsaturated fat, such as olive oil or rapeseed oil, or for gentle frying, saturated fats such as virgin coconut oil or butter. You can also find 'high-oleic' sunflower oils, pressed from a type of sunflower seed that has a higher monounsaturated fat content than normal, making the oil more stable when heated, up to about 190°C. I only use standard sunflower oil occasionally, unheated, when I want a neutral-tasting oil in a mayonnaise.

The latest health advice is also steering us away from standard sunflower oil because of its omega-6 content. Like many other seed oils, sunflower is a rich source of omega-6 fatty acids. We need these, but modern diets contain far too much omega-6 compared to omega-3. Ideally, you want somewhere between 3:1 and 1:1 omega-6 to omega-3, but the ratio in our diets ranges from 10:1 to 30:1. Some types of omega-6 can cause inflammation in the body (whereas omega-3 reduces it) and excessive amounts are associated with some diseases. At the very least, we should be consuming sources of omega-6 moderately while upping our omega-3 intake (from oily fish, for instance).

Whole sunflower seeds contain omega-6, of course, but you get the goodness of the rest of the seed too – protein, fibre, vitamin E and minerals such as magnesium and selenium. Lightly toasted, they are a great finishing sprinkle for salads and soups.

SUNFLOWER SEED AND CARAWAY CORN CRACKERS

Delightfully moreish, these are good with cheese or dips, or on their own. Makes about 60

A little olive or rapeseed oil

100g fine polenta/cornmeal (not quick-cook)

200g plain flour

1 tsp smoked paprika (hot or sweet)

1 tsp caraway seeds, finely ground to a powder (using a pestle and mortar)

1 tsp fine sea salt

60g sunflower seeds, plus extra for topping

Flaky sea salt, to finish

Lightly oil a couple of baking trays. Put the polenta, flour, paprika, caraway and fine salt into a large bowl. Lightly toast the sunflower seeds in a dry frying pan for a few minutes until golden, then crush them, using a pestle and mortar or food processor, almost to a powder (in batches if necessary). Add to the other dry ingredients and mix in enough warm water (about 100–110ml) to form a stiff, smooth dough (like pasta).

Knead the dough on a clean surface for 3–4 minutes, then cut into 3 pieces. Wrap each in cling film and leave to rest for 20 minutes. Preheat the oven to 160°C/Fan 140°C/Gas 3.

Roll out one piece of dough to a very thin sheet, about 2mm thick. Scatter more sunflower seeds over the dough, then go over lightly with the rolling pin to press them in. Cut into 7–8cm squares and place on a baking tray. Repeat with the rest of the dough. Trickle a little oil over the crackers, then bake (in 2 batches) for 12–15 minutes, until golden brown.

Sprinkle the crackers with a little flaky sea salt then leave to cool. Store in an airtight tin for up to a couple of weeks.

Swede

Tim Maddams

LATIN NAME
Brassica napus subsp. *rapifera*,
Brassica napus subsp.
napobrassica

ALSO KNOWN AS
Neeps, rutabaga

SEASONALITY
October–February

MORE RECIPES
Chicken and cider stew with
rosemary dumplings (page 617);
Snipe with swede and bacon
(page 587); Roasted haggis,
swede and kale salad (page
295); Bacon and celeriac tart
(page 42)

It's hard to think of a vegetable with a less glamorous image than this one. It's a root we tend to use as an also-ran in soups, stews and other dishes that need a little bulking out: it rarely gets the starring role. Yet it's such a useful veg, with a flavour all its own.

Swede is a member of the Brassica family, a cross between a cabbage and a turnip, and similarly contains beneficial phytochemicals. It has a sweet, slightly mustardy pungency, which for some is off-putting. However, like so many things, it can be absolutely delicious if you add butter (a lot) and the right seasoning (indecent quantities of black pepper).

It is a very good, flavoursome alternative to potatoes and can be cooked in many of the same ways: boiled, mashed, roasted or even chipped. The classic mashed neeps (as swede is known in Scotland) is hard to beat: the root is peeled, cubed, boiled, then mashed with the aforementioned butter and black pepper. And swede soup is a winner – especially if laced with roasted garlic. Less conventionally, small chunks of roasted swede make a great topping for pizza along with sweated onion, a scattering of thyme and a trickle of cream.

Swede takes only around 12 minutes' simmering and, like all brassicas, gets a little bitter when overcooked – so keep an eye on it. It's tasty when raw too: a winter slaw of finely shredded or grated swede, apple, beetroot and cabbage, dressed in a little yoghurt with chilli powder and a pinch of turmeric, makes an excellent side dish or sandwich filling.

Growing your own swede is easy. You might argue that it's barely worth it as it's so cheap to buy, but the leaves that grow atop the root are rarely included when you buy it in the shops and they make an excellent and welcome addition to the range of winter greens. A root will keep in the fridge for at least a fortnight, as long as it's not wrapped in plastic – it needs to be allowed to breathe.

SWEDE WITH ORECCHIETTE

1 swede (about 850g), peeled
and cut into 1cm cubes

2 tbsp olive or rapeseed oil

20g butter

1 medium onion, chopped

1 medium-hot red chilli,
deseeded and chopped

2 garlic cloves, chopped

Swede tops, if available, or
about 100g curly kale, cavolo
nero or chard, tough stalks
removed, leaves finely sliced

300g orecchiette (or other
smallish pasta shapes)

Sea salt and black pepper

Extra virgin olive or rapeseed
oil, to finish

Mature Cheddar or other
well-flavoured hard cheese,
grated, to serve

This recipe makes use of the swede tops, as well as the root – so it's a great one if you grow your own swede. However, if you don't, substitute kale or chard. Serves 4

Preheat the oven to 200°C/Fan 180°C/Gas 6. Put the swede cubes into a roasting dish, trickle over the oil and season with salt and pepper. Roast for about 30 minutes, until soft and golden brown.

When the swede is almost done, put a pan of water on to boil for the pasta. Meanwhile, heat the butter in a large, wide saucepan over a low heat. Add the onion, chilli and garlic and sweat for 8–10 minutes, until the onion is soft but not coloured. Then turn up the heat to medium and add the swede tops or other greens. Season and stir for 1–2 minutes until wilted.

While the veg are sweating, salt the boiling water and cook the orecchiette for about 12 minutes until *al dente* – use the time suggested on the pack as a guide.

When the swede is ready, add it to the pan of onions and wilted greens. Drain the pasta and stir it in, along with a slosh of extra virgin oil, and more salt and pepper if needed. Toss together.

Serve straight away, in warmed bowls, topped with a generous sprinkling of cheese.

S

Sweet cicely

Mark Diacono

LATIN NAME
Myrrhis odorata

SEASONALITY
February–November

I fell in love with sweet cicely the first year I grew it. It has a gentle but generous presence in all but winter, emerging as early as any edible plant and peppering the next nine months with leaves, flowers and seeds that carry the sweetest, smoothest aniseed there is. Even the long tap root carries those qualities, though I don't harvest it because, left in the ground, it will re-grow in subsequent years.

Sweet cicely's warm aniseed character is most known for its ability to draw the sourness from rhubarb, gooseberries and other sharp fruit (meaning you can reduce the sugar you might otherwise add). But it also lends itself beautifully to seafood – try seared scallops sprinkled with finely chopped sweet cicely leaves, and a little lemon juice and zest, for a gorgeous midsummer starter. Eggs and, perhaps peculiarly, earthy root vegetables such as parsnips, also take a delicious and interesting turn under this herb's gentle influence.

Sweet cicely pods, which appear after the flowers fade, are well worth gathering when they first form and are bright green. At this stage they'll be juicy, succulent and full of sweet aniseed flavour – lovely to use in a fruit salad (see below). After a week or so, the pods become a bit dull and fibrous.

If you're sceptical of anise flavours, do give sweet cicely a chance. The flavour makes me think of a happy alliance of fennel, star anise and liquorice, with which it shares a common essential oil, anethole. Even if you remain unconvinced after tasting it, grow sweet cicely for its ability to give, as seventeenth-century botanist John Parkinson wrote, 'a better taste to any other herb put with it'.

While its gifts are widely appreciated in much of Europe, sweet cicely remains largely unknown and unavailable in British shops: you have to grow it yourself. Happily, few plants are as idiot-proof as this one. Start with a young plant and it will flourish in a position of part shade. If starting with seed, bear in mind that it is viable for one year only and that it needs a period of cold to germinate, so sow it before winter. Sweet cicely's long tap root means it grows poorly in any containers other than large, deep pots that are kept well watered.

STRAWBERRY, RHUBARB AND SWEET CICELY SALAD

300g strawberries

200g rhubarb stalks

1 tbsp chopped sweet cicely pods or leaves

Juice of ½ orange

2–3 tbsp caster sugar

This light and refreshing fruit salad is a perfect use for sweet cicely pods, which appear after the flowers fade. Gather them when they first form and are bright green – otherwise use finely chopped leaves instead. Serves 4

Hull the strawberries, cut them into 4–5mm slices and place in a bowl.

Trim the rhubarb and slice it very thinly across the stalk – a mandoline is ideal for this. Add it to the bowl, along with the sweet cicely, orange juice and 2 tbsp sugar. Stir well and leave to macerate and soften at cool room temperature for 2 hours (or leave it for longer in the fridge).

Taste and add a little more sugar if needed. Serve in small bowls or glasses, with a spoonful of natural yoghurt if you like.

Sweet potato

Nikki Duffy

LATIN NAME
Ipomoea batatas

ALSO KNOWN AS
Kumara

SEASONALITY
Imported all year round

MORE RECIPES
Carrot soup with ginger and coriander (page 123); Crispy lentil and roasted squash salad with salsa verde (page 352); Spicy kohlrabi wedges (page 327)

Sweet potatoes are not potatoes – at least, they are not related to our familiar spuds. They belong to a different family and although both tubers are native to South America, the sweet potato has not made the transition to the West as successfully. The ones we eat are usually grown in China, Africa or the US.

The bright orange flesh of the sweet potato is coloured by lavish quantities of beta-carotene; it's also rich in vitamin A and other antioxidants. Although sometimes touted as a low GI food (meaning it releases energy slowly) this is only true if you cook sweet potatoes fairly quickly. They undergo quite profound chemical changes during cooking, owing to an enzyme that breaks down their starches into maltose (a sugar). Generally, longer cooking, such as baking and roasting, allows more time for the enzyme activity and therefore a sweeter result. It also raises the GI, making slow-baked sweet potatoes actually a high GI food. If boiled fast or steamed, their GI is low to medium.

Sweet potatoes have an exceptionally sweet flavour – more like parsnips or carrots than potatoes. These tubers have a high water content so, while they can be mashed, they tend to turn into more of a purée than a fluff. They're best combined with standard spuds for mashing. They can also be baked whole and served in their jackets (you can eat the skin and it carries a concentration of nutrients).

Sweet potatoes are delicious roasted, which helps to drive off their moisture. But be aware that they cook more quickly and burn more easily than potatoes, and will brown rather than crisp up. Keep the temperature lower than you would for classic roast spuds, cook for less time and check them often. Alternatively, capitalise on their smooth, moist nature by using them in soups or adding them, puréed, to cakes.

Most of the sweet potatoes on sale in Britain have russet skins and orange flesh, though there are also white-fleshed varieties, which are a little more chestnutty and less sweet. They are best stored in a cool place, but not the fridge. Sweet potatoes are sometimes inaccurately called yams, but these are quite different tubers.

ROASTED SWEET POTATOES AND AUBERGINE

2 large sweet potatoes (about 500g in total)

1 large aubergine (about 350g)

1 tsp cumin seeds

1 tsp coriander seeds

3 garlic cloves, chopped

Leaves from 2 rosemary sprigs, chopped

3 tbsp olive oil

Sea salt and black pepper

FOR THE DRESSING

A small bunch of parsley (about 30g), large stalks removed

60g walnuts, lightly toasted

1 garlic clove, chopped

Juice of ½ lemon

4 tbsp extra virgin olive oil

Flavoured with spices and rosemary and served with a piquant parsley and walnut dressing, this hearty veg dish is great on its own, or served with roast chicken or pork chops. Serves 4

Preheat the oven to 200°C/Fan 180°C/Gas 6. Scrub the sweet potatoes but leave the skins on. Slice them into 1cm thick rounds. Slice the aubergine in the same way. Put all the veg on a large roasting tray.

Crush the cumin and coriander seeds using a pestle and mortar, then tip into a small bowl and add the chopped garlic, rosemary and olive oil. Mix well, then trickle over the sweet potatoes and aubergines. Season with salt and pepper and toss together well, making sure the veg are evenly coated.

Spread out the veg evenly on the roasting tray and place in the oven. Roast, giving the veg a turn once or twice during cooking, for 35–40 minutes until the sweet potatoes are cooked through and browned.

Meanwhile, make the dressing. Roughly chop the parsley and put into a food processor with the walnuts, garlic and lemon juice. Blitz briefly to chop up the walnuts, then add the olive oil and a pinch of salt and blitz again to form a paste. Add about 2 tbsp water to thin it slightly.

Serve the roasted veg hot from the oven, with the dressing dotted over the top.

S

Sweetbreads

Steven Lamb

MORE RECIPES
Sautéed brains with parsley and caper sauce (page 82)

SOURCING
turnerandgeorge.co.uk

Sweetbreads is the rather euphemistic culinary name given to two different glands from an animal: throat sweetbreads are the thymus gland; heart sweetbreads are the pancreas. Both deserve to be celebrated for their innate deliciousness and mild, creamy richness. Both appear pale pink and multi-lobed and are not always easy to tell apart – though the heart sweetbread is often rounder and plumper and may be a little fattier. Some say that the throat sweetbread has the edge on flavour but there's not much in it. (Testicles are sometimes thought to be sweetbreads, but this is not the case.)

It is only calf's and lamb's sweetbreads that make it to our tables. To prepare them for cooking, wash under cold running water then put into a bowl, cover with fresh water and leave in the fridge for at least an hour to help draw out any blood. Rinse the sweetbreads again and put into a saucepan. Cover with plenty of fresh cold water, add a bay leaf and some black peppercorns if you like, then slowly bring to a simmer. Simmer for 3–4 minutes, then scoop the sweetbreads into a colander and run under cold water to cool quickly. Peel off any membranes and cut out any remaining little pockets of blood, fat or gristle, then gently pat dry. The sweetbreads can now be briefly roasted, braised or coated in breadcrumbs and fried until golden brown.

Sweetbreads can be bought from butchers but might need to be ordered in advance. They are also available from some supermarkets and online. Although they should be available all year round, heart sweetbreads are harder to find in the winter; spring is the best time for these. Most of the calf's sweetbreads you come across will be from Continental calves, likely not kept in high-welfare conditions. But British rose veal sweetbreads can now be found and British lamb's sweetbreads are an equally delicious option. In all cases, look for very fresh sweetbreads, which should be glossy and pale pink, and use them within a day or two, or freeze them.

SWEETBREAD KIEVS

500g lamb's sweetbreads

80g salted butter, softened

2 large garlic cloves, finely chopped

4 tbsp finely chopped parsley

A squeeze of lemon juice

Sea salt and black pepper

FOR THE CRUMB COATING

40g plain flour

3 medium eggs

About 150g fine breadcrumbs

Vegetable oil (refined rapeseed oil), for frying

This is a take on the more traditional chicken Kiev. The sweetbreads stay beautifully soft and succulent inside their crisp crumb coating. Serves 4

Prepare the sweetbreads as described above but, once simmering, cook for just 30 seconds (no longer or they will become too soft to stuff). Leave to cool completely.

In a bowl, mix the butter with the garlic, parsley, lemon juice and some pepper. Spread, about 1cm thick, on a sheet of cling film, wrap up and put in the fridge to firm up.

With a sharp knife, carefully cut a slit into the side of each sweetbread. Cut the butter into pieces and stuff as much as you can into each sweetbread, leaving just enough space to close them. (Don't worry if they split a little.) Refrigerate while you prepare the coating.

Put the flour in a bowl and season it well. Lightly whisk the eggs in a second bowl. Put the breadcrumbs in a third. Coat one sweetbread in the flour and dust off any excess, then dip into the egg, and finally dip into the breadcrumbs, patting them on with your fingers. Repeat the egg and crumb layers to get a good coating. Do this with all the sweetbreads.

Heat a 3cm depth of oil in a large, heavy-based saucepan to about 160°C. To test the tepmerature, drop in a cube of bread: it should turn golden brown in about 90 seconds. Cook the Kievs, in 2 or 3 batches so as not to overcrowd the pan, for about 6 minutes, giving any very large ones an extra minute. Lift out with a slotted spoon and drain on kitchen paper. Don't worry if a little butter seeps out of the Kievs when cooking.

Serve at once, with crisp salad leaves or wilted spinach and creamy mashed potatoes.

Sweetcorn

Tim Maddams

LATIN NAME
Zea mays

ALSO KNOWN AS
Corn on the cob, maize,
popping corn

SEASONALITY
Fresh corn cobs:
August–September

Maize is one of the world's most versatile staple foods. It was domesticated thousands of years ago and since then, on every continent, it has been used for everything from flour (see page 480) to biofuel.

Sweetcorn – maize in its fresh form – is at its best cooked simply, still on the cob, so you can enjoy the sensation of biting off those little popping cushions of sweetness, as well as the lovely earthy flavour. Pull away the outer husk and remove all the white pithy strands (known as silk) that lie beneath. Boil the corn cobs in plenty of salted water for around 8 minutes, until tender, then drain. Try serving the cobs with a nice smoked paprika butter – add 2 tsp smoked paprika and a little salt to 100g butter and beat until soft.

Sweetcorn is particularly good barbecued: the outer husk protects the tender grains from the fierce heat, while infusing them with a charcoal flavour that suits them well. To prepare the cobs for barbecuing, carefully pull the outer husk down, being sure not to tear it off the cob, and remove all the silk, then reposition the outer husk to protect the cob. Soak the whole cobs in cold salted water for at least 10 minutes, then shake off the excess water. Cook on the barbecue for around 12 minutes or until the kernels inside are tender. Leave to stand for at least 5 minutes, to avoid burning your fingers when peeling and eating. This also allows the corn kernels time to soften a little more.

Maize is actually a giant kind of grass and the golden kernels that we eat are technically grains, rather than a vegetable. Even when super fresh, the kernels have a starchy quality, which is why they work so well puréed or creamed, turned into fritters, or added to soups and stews, especially a rich and hearty chowder that includes fish and/or roasted red peppers.

Fresh corn on the cob is only around for a relatively short time during late summer, and the glut seems to be over almost as soon as it has started. The lovely sweetness of fresh corn evaporates rapidly once it is cut from the plant, so locally grown corn is always best. If you can't get hold of really fresh corn cobs, frozen corn kernels are a good alternative. They may not have the same hands-on appeal as a whole, hot, buttery cob but, as a rule, they are cut from the cobs soon after picking and frozen quickly, so they taste far better than imported corn cobs.

However, those packets of baby sweetcorn that you come across in supermarkets are really not worth buying. The little cobs may look pretty in a stir-fry but they are tasteless. And tinned, cooked sweetcorn kernels – invariably salty and soggy – are a far cry from the sweet little kernels you slice straight off a cob and cook yourself.

Growing your own sweetcorn can be something of a hit-and-miss affair. In the British climate, starting the plants off indoors or under glass will get you the best results. The American system of growing beans up the long stems of the sweetcorn plant is a great way of saving on space and benefits both plants: they use different nutrients from the soil and the bean plant shades the ground, lessening moisture loss.

There are many different varieties of sweetcorn available for home growing, some bi- or even tri-coloured. 'Merit' and 'Swift' are common varieties and easy to grow. I like to try to grow two different varieties a year, on the basis that at least one is likely to survive.

Whole kernels of dried corn form the basis of the cinema favourite, popcorn, which is very easy and a lot of fun to make at home. Good quality kernels are available from health food stores and supermarkets. Then all you need is a large pan with a good lid,

S

a little oil and a sprinkling of salt. Heat the pan to a good temperature but not so hot as to burn the oil when you pour it in. Add 1 tbsp or so of oil (olive or rapeseed) and then add a cup of popping corn kernels. Place the lid on the pan and, holding it in place with a decent oven cloth, give the pan a good shake to coat the kernels in the hot oil. Try not to move the pan around too much after that.

The popping should start inside the pan within a minute, build to a crescendo in another minute and then, a minute later, almost stop. You can then take the lid off the pan to reveal the fluffy, exploded kernels within. There are always a few unpopped kernels at the bottom of the pan that never pop no matter how long you leave them on the heat; it's better to take the pan off the heat after the popping slows down so as to protect the rest of the popcorn from burning.

Season with salt or sugar, or try curry powder and salt, or chilli powder and dried herbs. Or you can make an unbelievably moreish version by popping the corn in bacon fat, then seasoning it with a mix of pulverised crisp-cooked bacon, sugar and sea salt.

SWEETCORN WITH SPRING ONION, CHILLI AND CORIANDER

2 large corn on the cobs, husk and silk removed

2 tbsp olive or rapeseed oil

1 bunch of spring onions, trimmed and sliced into 1cm pieces

2 garlic cloves, grated

1 tsp dried chilli flakes

A good pinch of sweet smoked paprika

Finely grated zest and juice of ½ orange

1 tbsp chopped coriander

Sea salt and black pepper

This punchy little dish is a fantastic accompaniment to grilled chicken or fish. Alternatively, try scattering it over lettuce leaves for a smoky-sweet salad, or spoon into freshly cooked flatbreads and serve with soured cream. Serves 2

Stand each cob on its end on a board and slice downwards with a sharp knife, as close to the core as you can, cutting off the kernels.

Heat a large frying pan over a high heat. Add the oil followed by the sweetcorn kernels and spring onions. Fry 'hard' for 3–4 minutes, or until the corn is taking on a little colour. Add the garlic, chilli, smoked paprika and orange zest and continue to cook for 2 minutes.

Remove from the heat and add the coriander and orange juice. Season with salt and pepper, toss to mix and serve.

S

T

Tarragon

LATIN NAME
Artemisia dracunculus

ALSO KNOWN AS
French tarragon

SEASONALITY
May–September

MORE RECIPES
Runner beans with cream and tarragon (page 546); Lobster with béarnaise mayonnaise (page 365); Fried salmon with cucumber and gooseberry salad (page 553)

A glorious, underused herb, tarragon is packed with a fabulous and unique flavour: vegetal, anise-tinged and sweet. The taste is quite refined but also penetrating – it's certainly not a background herb. There really is no completely satisfactory substitute for it (chervil is probably the closest you'll get, though it's more subtle). Tarragon is a herb to grow or buy freshly picked rather than pre-packed from a supermarket. Forced, cut and plastic-wrapped, this herb is wan, wilted and lacking by the time it gets to the shops.

Tarragon is best used fresh and raw, or nearly raw. It loses its potency if cooked for too long (though the stems can go into a stew). It is quite characterful enough to stand up to other strong flavours and also has a welcome ability to cut through and enliven creamy, buttery, eggy dishes. Chop it – fairly roughly, if you like, since the leaves are tender – and throw over chicken, fish or eggs. It works well with red meat too, particularly in a classic béarnaise sauce, which owes its subtle but unmistakable flavour to tarragon.

Pair the herb with almost any green vegetable, perhaps with a spoonful of crème fraîche too, or combine it with new potatoes and mayonnaise. Cast it into summer vegetable soups, strew over an omelette or add to a tomato salad in place of the more usual basil, with which it shares a certain aniseedy tone.

In the garden, tarragon likes space to stretch its roots. It propagates itself by putting out underground runners, so if you grow it in a pot make it a big one. It likes full sun and well-drained soil. You can take cuttings from the underground runners – just dig up a mature plant and break off sections of root with growing shoots attached.

Tarragon's alternative name, French tarragon, distinguishes it from Russian tarragon (*Artemesia dracunculoides*), which is a similar herb but with an inferior flavour.

RABBIT RAGU WITH TARRAGON

2 tbsp olive oil

25g butter

1 rabbit, jointed

1 large red or yellow onion, halved and thinly sliced

2 garlic cloves, thinly sliced

2 celery stalks, trimmed and thinly sliced

600ml veg or chicken stock

A bunch of tarragon (15–20g), leaves picked, stalks reserved

A squeeze of lemon juice

Sea salt and black pepper

This rustic dish, which also works well with a couple of squirrels, is rich and delicious, yet very simple to prepare. Serves 2–4

Preheat the oven to 160°C/Fan 140°C/Gas 3.

Place a large flameproof casserole over a medium-high heat and add the olive oil and half the butter. When bubbling, add the rabbit pieces and season with salt and pepper. Cook for 8–10 minutes on each side, or until nicely coloured. Transfer the rabbit to a plate.

Add the onion, garlic and celery to the hot casserole, lower the heat and cook, stirring, for 8–10 minutes, without colouring. Return the rabbit pieces to the casserole then add the stock and tarragon stalks. Bring up to a gentle simmer.

Put a lid on the casserole, leaving it slightly ajar, then place in the middle of the oven. Cook for 1–1½ hours or until the rabbit meat is lovely and tender, and falling off the bone.

Using tongs, lift the rabbit out on to a clean plate. When it's cool enough to handle, gently flake the meat from the bones. Place the casserole of stock back over a medium heat and bring up to a simmer. Cook, uncovered, until the liquid has reduced by at least two-thirds and is quite thick. In the meantime, chop the tarragon leaves.

Remove the tarragon stalks. Return the rabbit meat to the casserole. Taste the liquor and season with salt and pepper as needed. Add the tarragon leaves, along with the remaining butter and a squeeze of lemon juice. Serve with rice or pasta, with a dressed green salad on the side.

Tea

LATIN NAME
Camellia sinensis

MORE RECIPES
Sticky date and parsnip cake
(page 234)

SOURCING
tregothnan.co.uk
(for Cornish-grown tea)

Aside from water, tea is the most widely consumed beverage on the planet. The many different kinds all originate from the same leafy evergreen plant. The colour, taste and aroma of the final brew depend on how – and when – the leaves and buds are treated.

Plucked when fully open, the leaves for green tea are dried immediately, locking in their liveliness and retaining health-benefiting antioxidants. Green tea has a distinct bitterness and a light, fragrant flavour. White tea is made from the youngest leaves and buds of the bush, which are briefly withered before drying. The result is sweetly floral and, like green tea, nicest without milk. Black tea gains its briskness and rich colour from a lengthier process. The leaves are fully wilted, rolled and left to ferment before they are dried, yielding the dark brew that so many of us drink so often. Also gracing the teashop shelves these days is matcha – a vivid green powder of finely ground tea leaves, taken from bushes that have been shaded from the sun. The leaf is consumed, as well as the infusion, giving maximum antioxidant benefits.

With its complex, fragrant quality – both herbal and spice-like – tea plays a role in cooking too. Black tea is perfect for steeping dried fruits for compotes, tea breads and moist fruit cakes. Fragrant teas such as jasmine or lapsang souchong can be used to flavour cream or milk for puddings or ice creams. You can even perfume rice by cooking it in tea. And matcha can be used in smoothies, baking and puddings.

For a beautifully light jelly, infuse 2 tbsp green or white tea leaves in 650ml boiling water while you soak gelatine leaves (sufficient for 700ml liquid) in cold water for 5 minutes. Combine the juice of 1 lemon and 50g sugar in a measuring jug and top up with the strained hot tea to make 700ml. Stir in the squeezed-out gelatine, divide between 4–6 small glasses and set in the fridge.

Use a good English Breakfast blend for cooking, or lapsang souchong if you like smoky flavours, or a strong brew of bergamot orange-scented Earl Grey.

There are many Fairtrade and/or organic teas to choose from. To keep them in the very best condition, store all teas in airtight containers, away from the light.

TEA-BRINED CHICKEN

1 chicken, jointed into 4 pieces (2 breasts with wing attached and 2 legs), or 1kg chicken pieces on the bone

A little rapeseed oil

Sea salt and black pepper

FOR THE BRINE

4 heaped tbsp lapsang souchong tea leaves

30g fine sea salt

100g caster sugar

Finely grated zest and juice of 1 lemon

A few sprigs of thyme, rosemary or oregano

Brining makes chicken particularly succulent and gives a delicate sweetness to the roasted skin. Smoky lapsang souchong tea imbues the meat with a subtle, aromatic flavour. This recipe is also good with guinea fowl. Serves 4–6

For the brine, put the tea into a large jug and pour on 1 litre just-boiled water. Add the salt and sugar, stir well and leave until completely cold. Strain the liquid and combine with the lemon zest and juice.

Put the chicken pieces into a container in which they will fit fairly snugly. Pour on the cold tea brine to cover and add the herbs. Leave, covered, in the fridge for 24 hours.

When ready to cook, preheat the oven to 220°C/Fan 200°C/Gas 7. Take the chicken joints from the brine, pat them dry with kitchen paper and place in a large roasting tin, skin side up. Brush with oil and sprinkle the skin with black pepper and just a pinch of salt.

Add 3–4 tbsp water to the roasting tin. Roast for 15 minutes, then reduce the heat to 180°C/Fan 160°C/Gas 4 and cook for a further 15 minutes or until the chicken is done. To check, pierce a couple of pieces in the thickest part and make sure the juices run clear.

Leave to rest in the roasting tin for at least 10 minutes before serving. This is delicious with spicy brown rice and broccoli (page 535) or French beans with shallots and black olives (page 265).

Thyme

Nikki Duffy

LATIN NAME
Thymus vulgaris.
Lemon thyme:
Thymus x citriodorus

SEASONALITY
All year round

MORE RECIPES
Cardoon bruschetta with honey and thyme (page 116); Roasted chicory with honey, mustard and thyme (page 166); Slow-baked salsify with butter and thyme (page 555); Pan-roasted oysters with celeriac and thyme (page 425); Lemon sole poached in butter with thyme (page 589); Turbot with white wine, lemon zest and thyme (page 648); Roast gurnard with pepper, lemon, thyme and chilli (page 292); Pork burgers with mace and thyme (page 369); Pears with ricotta, honey and thyme (page 536); Blackcurrant and thyme sorbet (page 224); Cherry, thyme and marzipan muffins (page 154); Crab apple jelly with thyme, juniper and mint (page 204)

Thyme has a flavour so unique and wonderful that a phenolic compound 'thymol' has been named after it. In addition to being an integral part of thyme itself, thymol is also found in the herbs bergamot, oregano and winter savory, as well as more unexpected places, including lamb.

Thyme was burned by the ancient Greeks in their sacrificial rites – the name is derived from the Greek *thuein*, for 'burnt offering'. And you can see why the gods might have been pleased, for thyme has one of the most wonderful characters of any herb. With its aromatic, smoky, floral pungency, it's on a par with rosemary and bay, but it has a sweetness, an amenability, that those slightly more robust herbs lack. You can eat raw thyme leaves and flowers far more pleasurably than you can those of other woody herbs.

Thyme is a hardy evergreen perennial and its combination of flavour, fragrance and approachability makes it the most versatile of all the 'hard', year-round herbs. Use it during cooking to impart a mellow tone to a dish, or add it raw at the end for a stronger, brighter thyme taste. Or, even better, do both. It's very hard to go wrong with thyme.

It adds a lot of value to home-made stock, and is one of the classic bouquet garni herbs. Chopped, it is almost essential in stuffings for meat and vegetables, great in a burger or home-made sausage, and wonderful in a tomato sauce. But don't stop there. Thyme works wonders with roasted roots, alliums and squashes. It is superb combined with chestnuts, especially if they're crumbled and fried with butter and salt first, and amazing in scones, soda breads and dumplings. Thyme – especially lemon thyme – is also very good with fish. Put some torn sprigs inside a red mullet or bream before roasting, or chop it and use in a pan-made sauce for fillets of white fish.

Thyme is a good base for za'atar, a classic herb blend of the Arab world that also includes sesame, sumac and salt. Za'atar is traditionally served as a dry dip with bread and oil, or sprinkled on to labneh or dips, or it may be dusted over meat or vegetables – before or after cooking.

Versatile thyme also has sweet applications: it can be delicious with fruit – everything from summer blueberries to autumn's plums, apples and pears. It even works with chocolate in a mousse or a biscuit. Little thyme flowers, which should be nipped off as soon as they appear in the early summer to keep the leaves growing sweet and tender, are delicious sprinkled on to pizzas, pasta dishes, tomato salads, even ice cream.

Thyme is easy to buy, though I would avoid the 'growing pots' on offer in many supermarkets. These invariably feature thyme that's been forced so hard and so fast that it can't support its own weight and tastes like little more than mildly scented grass. Cut bunches, if the leaves have some depth of colour and the stems some robustness, are far more likely to do the job you want thyme to do.

But grow your own thyme at home if you can – once you've got it, you'll certainly use it, and you don't need a lot of space. It likes sun and dryness and it's not a big fan of the rain, so pot-growing is a good idea as it protects the plant, keeps the roots well-drained and means you can site it in the sunniest position you can find. Thyme is a slow-grower, so start off with a young plant rather than seeds, unless you are very patient. Cosset it as much as you can, keeping it warm, sheltered from wind and dry (though of course it does need some water), but not fed, as it prefers poor soil.

One advantage of very young thyme is that its stems are tender, so you can chop them up along with the leaves for adding to a dish. Older thyme will have a richer

flavour but the stems are too woody to eat and you need to pick the leaves off them. This is, undeniably, a bit of a fiddly task, but worth it. Either way, never cut thyme too brutally. Just take a sprig here and a sprig there or you'll cut it all away before you know it. This is one reason why a few thyme plants are a good idea – they will keep you well stocked (and your stocks well). And if you're up for that, make sure at least one of them is lemon thyme.

Lemon thyme is so lemonily fragrant as to be a different herb in its own right to standard thyme. It's fantastic with fish, lamb and chicken, wonderful in biscuits and fluffy sponge cakes, and makes an interesting addition to custard. The leaves are also lovely floating on a cocktail or home-made lemonade.

Warm, spicy orange thyme is another good one, and broad-leaved thyme is a reliable kitchen all-rounder – or choose one of the many prostrate or creeping thymes which can be grown alongside paths, in lawns, or even between paving slabs, to release their heady, floral fragrance where you tread.

QUICK ZA'ATAR CRISPBREADS

3 pitta breads

FOR THE ZA'ATAR
3 tbsp sesame seeds
2 tbsp very finely chopped thyme leaves
2 tsp ground sumac
½ tsp flaky sea salt
Olive oil, to mix

The aromatic herb blend za'atar is often sprinkled on raw bread dough before baking. This quick, cheaty version gives you toasty, fragrant crispbreads to nibble with a cold beer, or dip into a steaming tagine or a bowl of creamy hummus. Serves 2–3

Preheat the oven to 180°C/Fan 160°C/Gas 4.

To make the za'atar, first heat a dry frying pan over a medium heat. Add the sesame seeds and toast them gently for just a couple of minutes, until golden. Tip them out and leave to cool, then combine with the thyme, sumac and salt and mix thoroughly. Trickle in enough olive oil to create a thick paste.

Toast the pitta breads lightly in a toaster, just enough to make them puff up a little. Then use a sharp bread knife to slit each pitta in half through its steamy centre. Cut each half into 2 or 3 pieces.

Spread the za'atar paste over the cut, fluffy sides of the pitta bread and place them on a baking sheet. Bake for 12 minutes, or until crisp and sizzling, then eat as soon as they are cool enough to handle.

Tofu

ALSO KNOWN AS
Bean curd

Tofu is made from the 'milk' pressed from soaked, dried soya beans. The creamy liquid is curdled by the addition of magnesium chloride and the curds are pressed to become tofu. Bland, pale and a little wet – looking rather like a block of soft cheese – it's not the most promising of ingredients, but the texture can be very pleasing. It is particularly valuable in a vegetarian diet – as a non-animal source of 'complete' protein, having all eight essential amino acids, and a good source of minerals and vitamins.

Pressing tofu with kitchen paper to dry it as much as possible before cooking is a good idea. It pairs well with rice and crunchy vegetables, and dusting it in cornflour and frying it hard produces a lovely delicate crust. Tofu also has an amazing ability to soak up the flavours of other ingredients, such as chillies, ginger, garlic and lime. Just marinate tofu in a simple mix of soy sauce and aromatics (see the recipe below) before frying it.

Standard tofu is spongy and breaks down into crumbly curds if pressed. But you can also buy 'silken' tofu, which is very smooth, almost jelly-like, and can be puréed into dips and even smoothies.

Soya

In recent years, the amount of soya in Western diets has increased significantly. Of greater concern than traditional sources – such as tofu and soy sauce – is the 'hidden' kind: soya flour and oil are found in everything from bread to breakfast cereals and large amounts of soya (often GM) are fed to farm animals. This has led to environmental issues – the mass production of soya in countries such as Brazil has caused major deforestation, for instance. As soya is rich in hormone-mimicking phyto-oestrogens, there has also been much discussion about its potential effects on our health – good and bad – with research as yet being far from conclusive.

MARINATED TOFU WITH SPRING GREENS

250g firm tofu

250–300g spring greens

2–3 tbsp rapeseed oil

1 medium-hot red chilli, deseeded and finely sliced

FOR THE MARINADE

4 tbsp soy sauce or tamari

3 tbsp mirin (Japanese rice wine) or Chinese cooking wine

1 tbsp rice wine vinegar

1 tbsp clear honey

1 garlic clove, grated

1 tsp freshly grated root ginger

A pinch of dried chilli flakes

½ tsp Chinese five-spice powder

TO FINISH

1 tbsp sesame seeds, toasted

A trickle of toasted sesame oil

If you marinate the tofu overnight, it will really take up the flavours, but just a few hours' soaking is still worthwhile. Serves 4 as side dish, 2 as a main

For the marinade, combine all the ingredients in a bowl and mix until well combined. Cut the tofu into roughly 2cm cubes. Add these to the marinade and turn gently. Cover and leave to marinate in the fridge overnight, or for at least a couple of hours.

When ready to cook, remove any tough stalks from the spring greens. Roll up the leaves and slice across into roughly 1cm thick ribbons.

Scoop the tofu from the bowl, reserving the marinade. Heat a large non-stick frying pan or wok over a high heat. Add 2 tbsp oil and, when hot, add the tofu. Cook for 3–4 minutes, stirring or tossing often, until golden and beginning to crisp. Remove and set aside.

Add the ribboned spring greens to the pan with a splash more oil if needed and stir-fry over a high heat for 3–4 minutes until wilted. Add the chilli and season lightly with salt and pepper.

Return the tofu to the pan, toss together with the greens for a minute or so, then transfer to a warmed serving dish.

Pour the reserved marinade into the pan, bring to a simmer and cook for 2–3 minutes until reduced by a third. Pour the reduced liquor over the tofu and greens. Sprinkle with sesame seeds and a trickle of sesame oil. Serve with rice or noodles.

Tomatoes

Hugh Fearnley-Whittingstall

LATIN NAME
Solanum lycopersicum

SEASONALITY
July–October

MORE RECIPES
Chilled avocado soup with tomatoes (page 40); Slow-roasted tomatoes with oregano (page 423); Minted spelt and tomato salad (page 386); Tomato and anchovy sauce (page 21); Razor clams with cherry tomatoes and basil (page 528); Cod with fennel, capers and tomatoes (page 194); Grilled flounder and tomatoes (page 260); Cuttlefish with fennel and white beans (page 228); White beans with chorizo and tomato (page 180); Squirrel and beans on toast (page 608); Pork belly with noodles, coriander and tomatoes (page 494); Grapefruit, tomato and coriander salsa (page 287); Scented tomato jelly (page 275)

Seasonal they may be – the fragrant, juicy, sweet-sharp gifts of the summer and early autumn – but in their tinned, sauced, puréed or preserved form, I use tomatoes all year round. They are rich in glutamic acid – a substance found more often in meat than in fruit – and are characterised by a richly savoury, 'umami' taste. Assuming they are ripe, tomatoes carry enormous depth, adding rich flavour and satisfying sensory texture to whatever you put them in.

These ruddy fruits are relative newcomers to our tables. Native to South America, they turned up in Europe a mere 500 years ago and, initially, were rebuffed. Correctly identifying them as a member of the nightshade family (along with peppers, potatoes and aubergines), we treated them with deep suspicion, describing them as 'stinking' and 'poisonous'. In fact, they could be poisonous: if you put a sliced tomato on a pewter platter, the acidic fruit absorbs lead from the metal and becomes toxic. Luckily, this *faux pas* is easily avoided.

Once we got past our initial, not unfounded, fears, however, we learned to love the tomato. In fact, now we really love them – to the point where we never want to be without them. British tomato-growers manage to produce fruit from March to November. And when our own crop is exhausted, we haul them in from southern Europe, Israel and Africa. More than 75 per cent of the tomatoes we eat are imported.

The consequence of this over-reliance on fresh tomatoes is that we so often eat them in less than optimum condition. We have forgotten that they are seasonal fruits, best eaten very fresh, and expect them to turn up on our plates – rosy, red and bursting with flavour – all year round.

But, believe me, no tomato eaten in December or March is ever going to fill you with joy. Those are the fruits – insipid, pale and wet – that remind me why, as a child, I hated tomatoes. It wasn't until my dad starting growing tomatoes in my teens that I saw the light. Fresh, in-season tomatoes of really good varieties, I learned, pack almost as much flavour, sweetness and intensity as the ketchup that I certainly didn't have any trouble eating. And if they're home-grown, they also radiate that edgy, pungent scent that becomes really quite addictive.

I still rate home-grown tomatoes the best of all and I raise plenty every year. I favour meaty 'Brandywine', Provençal 'Marmande' (pictured overleaf) and the lovely 'Cuor di Bue' for my salads. If I'm cooking a fresh tomato sauce, I plump for plum toms: less seedy and more fleshy than other types, they cook down swiftly and retain a fruity flavour – 'San Marzano' is a great variety. When it comes to cherry tomatoes, the ultimate flavour-bomb is sweet, orange 'Sungold'. But also good are 'Gardener's Delight' and 'Tumbling Tom', which can be grown in baskets, window boxes or pots.

If you are buying your tomatoes in the shops, the best way to avoid disappointment is to stick to the natural season: July to October – maybe a week or two either side if you're lucky. Really, you want to be guided by your nose – if it doesn't smell like a tomato, it won't taste like a tomato. Don't be diverted by tomatoes sold on the vine – the vine itself gives off a strong scent, but it doesn't guarantee that the fruit on it will be flavour-packed. It's actually easier to judge tomatoes if they're *off* the vine.

One of the problems with supermarket tomatoes is that they are usually encased in plastic so you have no idea what they smell like at all. As a guide, cherry tomatoes are almost without exception the most flavourful type in the big retailers. And when you get your tomatoes home, don't refrigerate them: it dulls their flavour. Store them in a cool larder.

In late summer, when my tomatoes are at their musky, fragrant best, I eat them most often simply sliced and served with extra virgin olive oil and flaky sea salt. They also get chopped into a great many salsas and salady side dishes with herbs and something from the allium family, whether that's spring onions, shallots or a tiny dab of raw, grated garlic.

When I have a real glut, including the inevitable tithe of tomatoes that I've allowed to grow over-ripe, it's time to get out the roasting tray. I make litres of home-made roast tomato passata every year because it so utterly, deliciously useful. Curries, stews, chillies, soups, lasagnes – all are enriched by it. I scatter thyme, olive oil, chopped garlic, salt and pepper on to huge trays of halved tomatoes, sling them into the oven until bubbling, soft and slightly charred, then rub them through a sieve to get their sweet, rich, roasty pulp. It freezes like a dream.

My final home harvest is not of over-ripe tomatoes, but of the green ones born too late in the year to ever fully ripen. Even these have their uses. Lightly salted then coated in egg and breadcrumbs, fried green tomatoes are fantastic for breakfast. They also make even better chutney than red tomatoes, particularly alongside apples (see recipe overleaf).

And the good news for tomato-lovers like me is that, when the crop is finally over, the tomato fun is certainly not. These fruits take to preserving exceptionally well. In their variously processed forms they offer, if not the same juicy sweetness and lively tang as the fresh fruit, then certainly that crucial, savoury depth and body. Concentrated tomato purée is a very handy standby: the best ones are pure, concentrated, cooked-down tomato – no salt, no preservatives – and give richness to everything from bolognese to barbecue sauces. Tomato ketchup has its place as a sweet-sour condiment but a squirt or two can also be used to round out a shepherd's pie filling or quick chilli. And even a tin of concentrated tomato soup can be pressed into service – its dense sweetness means it can be baked into a surprisingly good cake.

But my favourite form of preserved tomato comes in a tin. These might not actually be an improvement on their fresh, juicy brethren straight out of the greenhouse, but they can be just as good in their own way. I buy tins of whole plum tomatoes – ready-chopped ones always seem to me to lack sauciness and intensity. Brands vary considerably, though, and it's worth paying a few pence extra to get more tomatoes, in a thicker juice (I like the organic ones from Biona). Italian tinned tomatoes are generally the best – they need to be: their home market is exceptionally demanding.

Before cooking, I tip tinned tomatoes into a bowl and use my hands to crush them, picking out any scraps of skin or tough, stalky end bits as I go. Most often, they are then used to make a sauce, tipped into a wide pan where some sliced garlic has already started to cook in a generous puddle of olive oil. Beyond the crucial salt and pepper, I'll also add a couple of bay leaves or sprigs of thyme, if they're to hand. I simmer all this – for as little as 10 minutes, but up to 40 – to concentrate sweetness and flavour. And I often finish with a pinch of sugar, to round out the tomatoes' acidity.

The resulting reduced, garlicky, tomato sauce can make friends with almost any bulky carbohydrate. Pasta is an obvious vehicle (particularly if you add some scraps of fried bacon too), or you can cook the sauce down to a really thick pulp and use it on pizzas. I also like to chilli-up the sauce and combine it with roast potatoes to create patatas bravas – and a chilli-spiked tomato sauce is fantastic on gnocchi or with slabs of cheesy polenta.

Preparing fresh tomatoes

There are times when silky, skinless and/or seedless raw tomato flesh is just the thing, in a salsa or dressing, for instance, or in a raw tomato sauce for hot pasta.

To skin tomatoes, fill a large bowl with just-boiled water. Submerge the tomatoes in it for 2 minutes, then fish one out. Knick the skin with the tip of a sharp knife and it should shrink back readily, then peel away in your fingers. Hoik all the others out of the hot water and get peeling. If the skin isn't coming off easily, return the tomatoes to the hot water for a minute and try again (though don't leave them too long or they'll become mushy). If the skin still won't budge, you've got under-ripe fruit – abandon the skinning agenda and do something else with them.

Once sliced open, cut out the tough white stalk end of the tomato. The seeds and their surrounding juicy jelly are then easily scooped out with a small knife, teaspoon or your thumb. Don't discard this seedy pulp. Put it in a sieve and press the juice through – it's incredibly flavoursome and should be added to a sauce or dressing.

GREEN TOMATO, CUMIN AND GREEN CHILLI CHUTNEY

This is a really fresh, vibrant chutney that will go with almost anything. It is a great way to use year-end tomatoes that will never fully ripen. Makes 1.6kg, 5 x 320g jars

4 medium-hot green chillies, deseeded and roughly chopped

1 head of garlic, cloves separated and peeled

30g root ginger, roughly chopped

2 tbsp olive or rapeseed oil

2 tbsp mustard seeds

3 tsp ground cumin

2 tsp ground coriander

500g onions, chopped

350ml cider vinegar

1kg green tomatoes, chopped

500g cooking apples, peeled, cored and chopped

250g soft brown sugar

Grated zest and juice of 2 limes

1 tsp sea salt

1 tsp ground white pepper

Put the chillies, garlic and ginger into a food processor and blitz to a paste. Set aside.

Heat the oil in a preserving pan or very large saucepan over a medium heat. Add the mustard seeds and fry for a minute or so until they start to pop. Add the garlicky paste and fry it for a couple of minutes, stirring continually so it doesn't burn. Then add the cumin and coriander, followed by the chopped onions, and fry for a further 4–5 minutes to wake up the spices and start to soften the onions.

Add the vinegar and give everything a good stir: this will help loosen any spices stuck to the bottom of the pan before you add the remaining ingredients.

Now add the tomatoes, apples, sugar, lime zest and juice, salt and pepper. Give it a good stir and bring to the boil. Now turn the heat right down and simmer very gently, uncovered, for 2½–3 hours until rich and thick. Stir frequently, particularly towards the end of cooking, to ensure it doesn't stick.

While your chutney is cooking, sterilise your jars by washing them in hot soapy water, rinsing well, then putting them upside down on a baking tray in a very low oven (at 120°C/Fan 100°C/Gas ½) to dry and warm up. Wash the lids with soapy water, rinse, then place in a heatproof container and pour boiling water over them to sterilise.

When your chutney is ready, spoon it while still scalding hot into the warm jars and seal tightly with the lids. Leave to cool before labelling. Store in a cool dry place. This chutney is good to eat straight away but will get better over time. Use within a couple of years.

Tongue

SOURCING
eversfieldorganic.co.uk;
turnerandgeorge.co.uk

Tongue is a cut that deserves more respect. There's no denying that cooking one from scratch is never a quick option. But once poached or braised, tongue can be pressed, sliced, fried or frittered, served hot or cold, and is wonderfully meaty and dense without being offaly or pungent. Lamb and ox tongues are by far the most commonly sold in the UK, but you can also use the tongues from pork and venison.

Tongue is a powerful muscle and needs long cooking. You can cook it from fresh, but soaking it in a brine for a day or two beforehand softens the texture and gives more definition to the flavour. Poach it in water with a few stock veg for around 3 hours then drain and peel off the coarse outer skin before eating.

Once cooked, tongue is traditionally combined with some of its own gelatinous juices and pressed in a mould of some sort – largely so as to disguise it. It's hard to deny that a whole tongue is an ungainly and rather ugly-looking thing. But pressing is not essential – you can always just let the tongue speak for itself.

I particularly like a pork tongue that has been cooked in stock with the rest of the pig's head. When the meat falls away from the head bones, it can be reassembled around the whole tongue and pressed in a terrine mould. After setting overnight, this brawn and tongue 'gala' can be sliced so that the different meats mosaic around the tongue to give a glorious cross section of flavours. But tongue can be cooked much more simply than that – just boiled and sliced is wonderful. Serve it hot with salsa verde or cold in sandwiches with mustard.

A single ox tongue can weigh as much as 2kg and feed a crowd. Tongues from young cattle are much smaller (as little as 750g) and will serve 4–6 people. Pig's tongues are smaller – allow one per person – and lamb's tongues smaller again. Tongue in general represents great value for money. It is available from good butchers and increasingly from online sources too. Do ask about provenance – some calf's tongues are from Continental veal calves, but higher welfare or rose British veal tongue is available. Tongue freezes well and, once you get past its appearance, offers a splendid culinary experience.

TONGUE, KALE AND APPLE HASH WITH HORSERADISH

2 tbsp beef dripping or lard,
or rapeseed oil

2 red onions, sliced

3–4 sprigs of thyme

About 500g cooked potato or
squash/pumpkin (or a mixture)

2 crisp eating apples, peeled,
cored and roughly diced

250g cooked ox tongue, cut into
1–2cm dice

2 tsp grated horseradish (from
a jar or a fresh root)

About 200g shredded cooked
kale (or cabbage or sliced
Brussels sprouts)

Sea salt and black pepper

This delicious, thrown-together dish works wonderfully with a slab of good tongue bought from a deli. Alternatively, brine and cook a tongue yourself, following the recipe for salt beef on page 559. Serves 4

Heat the dripping, lard or rapeseed oil in a large, non-stick frying pan over a medium heat. Add the onions and thyme and fry gently for about 10 minutes until soft.

Meanwhile, cut the potato and/or squash into 2cm chunks and place in a bowl. Add the apple, chopped tongue and horseradish and tumble everything together, breaking up the potato/squash a bit as you stir.

Add the potato and tongue mixture to the onions, with some salt and pepper, and toss everything together well. Cook for around 10 minutes, stirring often, until the potato/squash starts to colour. Add a little more fat if you need to, and use a spatula to keep scraping up the golden, crisp veg as it browns on the base of the pan. Add the greens and cook for a further 2–3 minutes.

Taste and adjust the seasoning if necessary, then serve straight away, with poached or fried eggs if you like.

Tripe

Hugh Fearnley-Whittingstall

SOURCING
greenpasturefarms.co.uk

Ask for tripe in your average supermarket and the chances are you'll be directed to the pet food aisle. This is a shame. It's a classic part of our food heritage, a cheap and nourishing source of protein when more glamorous meats were scarce, and a one-time beloved staple of the North, sold in countless eating houses across Lancashire, to sustain the working people.

I'm not going to pretend that the stomach lining of an ox is to everyone's taste, but meat-eaters owe it to themselves, and to the cows, to at least give tripe a try. As with eating any offal, it is a way to ensure we make the most of the animals we kill for food. And tripe certainly offers flavours and textures you won't get from any other cut.

The problem is that it's hard to find. And, though I know of one online supplier of grass-fed, free-range tripe, I've never seen organic tripe at all. Presumably, this is due to lack of demand. Conventionally produced tripe is also processed extensively: by the time it gets to a butcher's counter, it's been not only boiled but bleached, a treatment that considerably mutes its character. Should you get your hands on tripe fresh from the animal – something I'm fortunate to be able to do from time to time from my local abattoir – it has a fuller and more potent flavour and a darker colour, and needs to be scrubbed very thoroughly before cooking.

Processed tripe tastes only mildly 'gutty'. And even though it has been 'pre-cooked' it still needs long, gentle cooking, to tenderise it. But it's important not to overcook it – it's much nicer when it retains a little bite and texture. The old English way is to simmer it in milk, with thinly sliced onions, until the tripe is tender and the milk and onions are reduced to a sweet, almost toffeeish sauce. I prefer a more Continental approach, simmering it slowly with chickpeas or beans, chorizo or bacon, tomatoes and a dash of wine. Simply simmered, tripe is also very good sliced into strips, breadcrumbed and fried, and served with a mild mustard or tartare sauce.

BARBECUED TRIPE

2 sheets of processed tripe, about 10 x 15cm

A thumb-sized piece of root ginger, thinly sliced

6 garlic cloves, roughly chopped

1 green chilli, sliced

2 onions, roughly chopped

2 celery stalks, roughly chopped

2 lemongrass stems, bashed

1 star anise

½ tsp black peppercorns

TO FINISH

A little rapeseed oil

Sea salt

A large bunch of coriander, coarse stems removed, chopped

Juice of 2 limes

2 tbsp soy sauce or tamari

Earthy tripe is excellent cooked in an aromatic Asian-inspired stock then grilled. The charring from the barbecue is particularly appealing. Serves 4

Rinse the tripe under a cold running tap, then place it in a pan and cover with water. Bring to the boil over a high heat, then drain the tripe and return it to the pan.

Add the ginger, garlic, chilli, onions, celery, lemongrass, star anise and black peppercorns and pour in enough fresh water just to cover. Bring to a simmer over a medium-high heat, then reduce the heat. Cook gently for 1½–2 hours, or until tender, topping up the water as required. When cooked, drain and allow the tripe to cool.

Heat up your barbecue. When it's nice and hot, cut the tripe into roughly 5 x 10cm pieces. Rub each with little oil, season with salt, then place them on the grid over the hot coals. Cook the tripe for 3–4 minutes on each side, or until it is beginning to char and caramelise a little at the edges. Remove to a warm serving platter. Repeat with the remaining tripe.

To serve, dress the tripe with chopped coriander, lime juice and soy or tamari. Toss together before bringing to the table. This is great with plain boiled rice and sliced spring onions, and some extra chopped chilli for more heat if you like.

Trout, sea trout & grayling

Nick Fisher

LATIN NAME
Brown trout and sea trout: *Salmo trutta*. Rainbow trout: *Oncorhynchus mykiss*. Grayling: *Thymallus thymallus*

SEASONALITY
Farmed trout: not applicable. Wild trout, sea trout and grayling: closed seasons are determined by local byelaws

HABITAT
Largely farmed; some healthy stocks of wild brown trout in Scotland and Ireland; sea trout can be found in freshwater rivers and coastal waters across the British Isles

MCS RATING
Farmed trout 1–3

REC MINIMUM SIZE
Wild brown trout 25cm; wild sea trout 40cm; grayling 30cm (but in all cases, check local byelaws)

MORE RECIPES
Potted carp (page 118); Dab in a bag (page 230); Fried salmon with cucumber and gooseberry salad (page 553); Fried fillets of perch with sorrel and new potatoes (page 465); Steamed sea bass with kale and ginger (page 573); Rice and fish with wasabi dressing (page 667); Cucumber, smoked mackerel and dill salad (page 220)

SOURCING
graigfarm.co.uk; streamfarm.co.uk; thefishsociety.co.uk

In taxonomic terms, trout, sea trout and grayling are members of the Salmonid family. They share with the salmon tribe an adipose fin (a nubby little thing between dorsal fin and tail), and a propensity to *sometimes* migrate to salt water. I say sometimes, because it's complicated. Grayling don't migrate and trout do, but only some trout and only when it suits them.

There are many different kinds of trout: brown, rainbow, blue, ferox, tiger and dollaghan, all of which can be fascinating if you're an angler, but cooks need only concern themselves with brown and rainbow.

Brown trout is a native fish. Rainbow trout originates from America. Native brown trout range from tiny tarns in the high hills of Scotland and the Lake District to the chalk-stream rivers of Hampshire and Dorset. Rainbows don't breed in Britain (apart from one or two small freak populations) because conditions don't suit.

Both these fish are farmed in the British Isles. The trout you buy, in any form, will mostly be farmed rainbows because they do best in an aquaculture set-up. They're aggressive, hungry feeders and in the right conditions will quickly pile on the pounds. But farmed brown trout occasionally turn up on fish slabs too. There's not much to choose between them flavourwise. Both species are fed on the same fishmeal pellets, which means their flesh tends to be highly coloured and their flavour very salmony.

There are some excellent trout farms with lovely, clean water, which produce very fine fish – and organic farms that use carefully sourced fishmeal. But the flavour of a farmed trout will never be as good as that of a wild fish that has foraged its way through nature's aquatic-insect buffet.

Many fish farms also grow trout for restocking rivers and lakes. When released, these are caught by anglers, who pay to take them home. These fish, once they have naturalised and started eating flies and the like, have paler flesh than their farmed relatives, with more of a natural, freshwater fish flavour.

Truly wild brown trout are delicious, especially the little ones taken from highland tarns and small rivers. But stocks are precarious and vary from region to region, so catch-and-release is mandatory in most well-managed rivers these days; i.e. the fish must be returned to the water alive. However, in some unpolluted, lightly fished Irish and Scottish lochs, large heads of wild brown trout still thrive. So my dream breakfast of wee wild brownies fried in butter with foraged mushrooms is, while a very rare treat, still just about possible.

Grayling are just as delicious as trout. They used to be considered vermin in chalk-stream rivers because of their assumed propensity to eat valuable trout eggs. However, those beliefs have evaporated in the last 20 years and now even the fanciest river fishery is proud to boast a healthy head of grayling. Hugh and I once fried a few on a riverbank with wild garlic leaves and salty butter – an exceptional wild meal.

The chances of finding grayling at the fishmonger are very slim because there is no fishery that targets them. Should you ever see one on the slab – or on a menu, or in a friendly angler's creel – don't even draw breath. Buy it and bake, steam, fry or grill it. The flesh is firm, creamy white, lovely with herbs, hot or cold, perhaps augmented with a lovingly hand-made mayonnaise.

On the rare occasion when I cook farmed trout, I'll cook it whole, on the barbecue, with a bellyful of bay leaves and butter, or some chives and dill to pep up the flavour, wrapped in foil for the first 5–10 minutes then opened up to let the steam out for another 5 minutes or so.

Sea trout

Excellent as trout and grayling can be, sea trout (illustrated below) is altogether superior. Delicately salty but firmly muscular, it tastes like a cross between a bass and a truly wild salmon. But a sea trout is actually just a brown trout – a spotty, cheeky, mini-banana-sized, river-born wild native brown trout that has decided to follow its salmon cousins' macho migratory habits and take to the ocean. This is nature's way of preserving the species. A brown trout that overwinters in an inhospitable winter river will probably die. Even if it lives, it won't produce a heap of eggs because it is half-starved. However, if some of the brown trout are programmed to go out to sea (we still have no idea how this programming works), they will, if they survive the process, get big.

A sea trout doesn't go across the Atlantic, like the Atlantic salmon. Mostly it just mooches around the coast, in and out of estuaries, feeding on crabs and worms and shrimps for a year or two, getting big and turning from brown to saltwater silver. Then, once it weighs anything up to 5kg, it'll head back up a river to lay some beefy, fit, fertile eggs – of which it now carries millions.

Just to ensure the brown trout bloodline continues, there is perfect interbreeding capability. A huge, sleek, prawn-fed female sea trout can still mate with the tiny finger-long brown trout male who never left the home river in the first place. Sea trout are an enigmatic miracle of nature.

Some sea trout find their way into the retail fishmonger chains during the summer. Not surprisingly, shoppers are often confused by them and will plump for farmed salmon instead, which means that this life-changing fish is very reasonably priced. For my money, poached or steamed sea trout with fresh samphire and a lemony vinaigrette is pretty much heaven on a plate.

FOIL-BAKED TROUT WITH BABY BEETROOT AND SPRING ONIONS

2 tbsp olive or rapeseed oil, plus extra to oil

10 cooked golf-ball-sized baby beetroot (see page 68), or 2–3 cooked larger beetroot

A small bunch of spring onions (about 8), trimmed and sliced

2 trout (325–375g each), gutted and descaled

2 garlic cloves, crushed

6 sprigs of thyme

6 sprigs of dill (optional)

2 bay leaves

1 lemon, sliced

40g butter

60ml dry white wine

Sea salt and black pepper

Baking fish whole in foil is a great way to keep it moist and full of flavour. Trout are an ideal size for this treatment and their juices taste wonderful when mingled with beetroot, butter, wine and herbs. Perch are also excellent cooked this way. Serves 2

Preheat the oven to 200°C/Fan 180°C/Gas 6.

Put two double-layered pieces of foil, big enough to comfortably envelop each trout, shiny side down, on your work surface. Lightly oil the foil.

Quarter the baby beetroot (or slice, if using large ones), then arrange in the middle of each foil sheet to make a 'bed' for the fish. Scatter over the spring onions. If you have any nice, tender beetroot leaves left over, tear out the stalks, and add a few leaves to each parcel. Trickle 1 tbsp oil over the veg and add a pinch of salt.

Slash the fish flesh 3 times on each side, then season the fish inside and out. Stuff the cavity of each fish with the garlic, herbs and lemon. Lay the fish on top of the beetroot. Dot with the butter and add a few more drops of oil.

Bring up the foil around each fish to create a 'bowl' then trickle half the wine into each. Bring the foil right over the fish (but not tightly) and crimp the edges together so the fish are completely sealed in baggy foil parcels. Place on a baking tray.

Bake for 15–20 minutes, or until the trout is cooked through – the flesh nearest the head (the fattest part) should pull away from the bone easily. Place the foil parcels on warmed plates and take to the table, where they can be opened up. Serve with a green salad.

Turbot

Nick Fisher

LATIN NAME
Psetta maxima,
Scophthalmus maximus

SEASONALITY
Avoid wild turbot April–August
when spawning

HABITAT
Northeast Atlantic; the majority
are caught in the North Sea

MCS RATING
Farmed 2; wild 3–4

REC MINIMUM SIZE
30cm

MORE RECIPES
Roast brill with air-dried ham
and parsley sauce (page 92);
Plaice with rosemary, caper and
anchovy butter (page 476)

SOURCING
goodfishguide.org

One illustration of just how highly the turbot is revered is the fact that it has merited the design and manufacture of its very own cooking vessel. Most fish are cooked in a generic pan. The turbot demanded the creation of the *turbotière*, a turbot-shaped steamer, ornately crafted out of copper and brass, to be used exclusively for the preparation of this king of the flatties.

But no one needs a *turbotière*. Roasting, poaching, poach-frying or even simple pan-frying are all perfect ways to render your turbot tasty. In all honesty, unless you catch your own, or have unlimited cash, you're unlikely to be dining on turbot often enough to need a special pan anyway. Nor should you. Wild stocks are not well managed so turbot should remain a treat. The best turbot are caught using lines. Others are caught using static nets and bottom trawls but, as both these methods can damage fragile marine habitats and other wildlife, I would not recommend them.

Increasingly, turbot are also being farmed. They need to eat fishmeal, which remains one of the thornier problems of aquaculture but, because they are grown in huge indoor tanks, rather than the open sea, the overall environmental impact of farming them is lower than for, say, salmon.

Turbot are often cut into tranches: cross-section slices of the body – or more often, one half of the body – including the bone. I love a tranche because the muscular flakes of flesh are exposed and, when cooked, begin to separate and leak out those heavenly high-end fish flavours.

The thick skin, which peels off easily when cooked, is rubbery and tough, with tubercles (little, gnarly bumps) rather than scales. The flesh, though, is legendary: meaty, muscly and flaky, with hints of lobster and scallop, and notes of goat's cheese and coconut. It will make your eyes lose focus as your heart skips a beat. Famous and fabulous though it is, there is nothing too difficult about cooking turbot – except maybe not cooking it for too long, and affording it.

TURBOT WITH WHITE WINE, LEMON ZEST AND THYME

4 thick tranches of turbot,
on the bone (180–200g each)

Finely grated zest of 1 lemon

2 tsp roughly chopped thyme
or lemon thyme leaves

A pinch of dried chilli flakes
(optional)

2 tbsp olive or rapeseed oil

25g butter

A small glass of dry white wine

Sea salt and black pepper

Chunky tranches on the bone are cooked with just a few complementary flavours to enhance the magnificent flavour of this fish. If you're lucky enough to have a whole turbot, you can cook it the same way, giving it around 30 minutes' roasting. It's a winning dish for brill, too. (Pictured right.) Serves 4

Preheat the oven to 220°C/Fan 200°C/Gas 7.

Season the fish all over with salt and pepper. Combine the lemon zest, thyme leaves and chilli, if using, with a few drops of the oil, then rub this mix all over the fish.

Put the tranches in a roasting dish. Dot with the butter and trickle over the remaining oil. Pour the wine into the base of the dish (not over the fish) and roast in the oven for 10–12 minutes.

Take the tranches out of the oven, baste with the herby, winey juices, then cover loosely with foil and leave somewhere warm to rest for 4–5 minutes, by which time they should be just cooked and coming away from the bone easily. Serve the tranches with their delicious juices, chips and a salad.

T

Turkey

Steven Lamb

LATIN NAME
Meleagris gallopavo

SOURCING
johnwrightturkeys.co.uk;
organicbutcher.net

Turkey is often seen as *the* celebratory culinary symbol of Christmas – an indulgent centrepiece – yet it can be disappointing, and unhappy on the welfare front too. The typical turkey is bred indoors in an overcrowded warehouse without environmental enrichment. We eat around ten million turkeys each December and only a small percentage of these come from higher welfare farms. In recent years, the birds have been selectively bred to achieve enormous weights, particularly in the breast, in a short space of time – all just to tick the Christmas box.

Even if you secure yourself a free-range or organic bird, one of the problems with turkey is that the differential between the leg and the breast meat, in terms of the cooking needed, is significant. This is actually a greater problem with a bird that has ranged freely – its legs have had to do a fair amount of work so they are strong, but tough. The problem is magnified with larger birds too. But, of course, there are ways around it and a well-reared organic or free-range turkey, properly cooked, can be delicious.

In the US, Thanksgiving turkeys are often brined before they are roasted. This tenderises, moistens and flavours the meat. It was a revelation when I first tried it, so now putting an organic turkey to soak in a herby brine bath has become a Christmas Eve ritual for me. Cooked the next day for the usual time at the usual temperature it comes out plump, full of flavour and juice – even the legs are tender and giving.

The second approach is to simply remove the legs and cook them separately. You then have the freedom to cure, brine, braise, slow-roast or even confit them, stopping the cooking only when they are deliciously tender, with no worries about the breast meat. The legless crown roasts quickly and is easy to carve.

Turkeys range hugely in size. A smallish bird of around 3.5kg serves 6, while a monster of 7kg or more will easily feed a dozen, with copious leftovers. Always get your turkey with giblets if you can – minus the liver, and augmented with a few aromatic veg, they make a superb stock.

SLOW-COOKED TURKEY LEGS WITH BACON AND PRUNES

Turkey leg meat is rich and dark and responds well to a light overnight curing, followed by slow cooking. Serves 4–6

2 turkey legs, thigh and drumstick (1.5–2kg in total)

2–3 tbsp lard or rapeseed oil

200g streaky bacon or pancetta, roughly chopped

100g prunes, roughly chopped

250ml hot chicken, turkey or veg stock

Sea salt and black pepper

FOR THE LIGHT CURE

30g coarse sea salt

1 tsp freshly ground black pepper

6–8 sprigs of thyme

2–3 bay leaves, torn

Combine the ingredients for the cure and rub the mixture all over the turkey legs. Place them in a tray or dish, and refrigerate for 24 hours.

Scrape off the cure and rinse the legs then pat them dry with kitchen paper. Preheat the oven to 150°C/Fan 130°C/Gas 2.

Heat the lard or oil in a frying pan over a medium heat. Add the bacon or pancetta and fry it for 5–6 minutes or until beginning to colour. Using a slotted spoon, transfer the bacon to a medium baking dish, leaving as much fat as possible in the pan.

Add the turkey legs to the frying pan and brown them all over, then nestle them into the dish with the bacon. Scatter over the prunes and pour over the hot stock. Cover tightly with foil and cook in the oven for about 2½ hours or until the meat is tender and giving, removing the foil for the last 30 minutes or so, to allow the juices to reduce and intensify.

To serve, pull the meat from the legs with a spoon and fork and place on warm plates with the rich juices, prunes and bacon. This is excellent with mash or polenta and some simply cooked kale or purple sprouting broccoli.

T

Turmeric

Nikki Duffy

LATIN NAME
Curcuma longa

MORE RECIPES
Lemon verbena pilaf (page 348); Curried clams (page 184); Velvet crab curry (page 211); Crumbed whiting goujons with curried egg tartare (page 673); Indian spiced grilled quail (page 510); Fragrant beef curry (page 350)

This glowing yellow spice comes from the rhizome (underground stem) of a plant of the ginger family. You can buy the whole fresh root, which looks like a smaller version of root ginger, from spice specialists or stores that cater to Thai and Indian cooks. Its bright orange flesh can be grated, just like fresh ginger, and added to pickles and preserves, used to colour rice, or employed in recipes that call for dried turmeric, where it will impart a slightly more vibrant flavour. Usually, however, we buy the dried and finely ground root, where the colour has relaxed into a lovely, acid yellow and the flavour is a little more subtle but nonetheless distinctive. If you are substituting one for the other, 1 tbsp finely grated fresh root is equivalent to 1 tsp dried ground turmeric.

Either way, turmeric's flavour is wonderful: bitter, earthy and warm. It does not have spicy heat but it adds depth, a welcome sourness and of course its glorious colour, to curries especially (turmeric stains like anything – a turmeric-rich curry will dye your wooden spoons and grating the root will yellow your fingers).

Ground turmeric is nearly always found in pre-blended curry powders but this spice works well wherever you want a touch of musky, grounding earthiness – particularly in combination with toasted and ground whole spices. It's great in a simple fish curry, and pretty much essential in a dhal. It's fantastic in spiced vegetable mixes, whether served alone or tucked inside samosas. And, like saffron, turmeric is wonderful with rice. You can even use a little in sweet dishes such as ice creams and cakes.

Turmeric has long been celebrated for its medicinal properties, prized in folk medicine as an antiseptic and said to be a good remedy in a case of cobra bite. It contains curcumin, which is thought to have a host of benefits, including anti-cancer and anti-inflammatory properties. Research is in its early stages but, nevertheless, curcumin and turmeric extracts are available in health food shops, many also containing black pepper extract, which is supposed to help the body absorb curcumin.

STIR-FRIED CABBAGE WITH TURMERIC AND GARLIC

1 tbsp rapeseed or virgin coconut oil

1 tbsp finely grated fresh turmeric (about 3 little knobs) or 1 tsp ground turmeric

2 garlic cloves, finely grated

½ white cabbage (about 500g), finely shredded

Sea salt and black pepper

TO SERVE
Lemon or lime juice (optional)

Coriander leaves (optional)

This very simple, quick recipe is a delicious way to serve cabbage – very good alongside spicy curries, dhals or grilled fish. You can even eat it with just a dollop of plain yoghurt as a light meal or healthy snack. It tastes particularly good if you use fresh turmeric but dried works well too. Serves 4 as a side dish

Put a large, non-stick frying pan over a medium heat and add the oil. When it's hot, add the turmeric and garlic and stir for 30 seconds or so until sizzling. Before they start to burn, add the shredded cabbage and ½ tsp salt. Stir well so that all the cabbage is coated in the yellow, turmeric-stained oil.

Cook over a medium heat, stirring often, for 7–10 minutes, until the cabbage is slightly wilted but still quite crunchy. It's rather nice if some of the cabbage picks up a little colour from the base of the pan but don't let it burn.

Take the pan off the heat. Taste and add some pepper and more salt if necessary. A light spritz of lemon or lime juice and/or a scattering of fresh coriander leaves is good too. Serve straight away.

Turnip

LATIN NAME
Brassica rapa subsp. *rapa*

SEASONALITY
June–December

MORE RECIPES
Chicken and cider stew with rosemary dumplings (page 617)

I first grew turnips after noticing how much my pigs seemed to love them, strimming off the leafy green tops then nosing up the roots until not a scrap remained. I subsequently added both turnips and the leafy, rootless variation, *cime di rapa*, to my veg patch and they've kept their place ever since.

Turnips are far too good to consider as winter ballast: they are a superb summer-into-autumn treat that starts to come good in June. Pick or buy them small – snooker rather than cricket ball – and you'll find they are full of sweetness and pepperiness in perfect balance. Baby ones can be simply boiled whole and buttered. They can still be very good when larger, later in the year, though they often veer slightly more towards swede in flavour and may get a little woody with size. They should certainly be sliced or chopped relatively small.

At any size, roasted in oil with a little honey and a pinch of cumin and/or coriander, sliced and sautéed in butter or braised in stock, turnips' sweetness and spice come to the fore beautifully, and work especially well with beef or salty meats such as ham. That combination of sweet and heat also sits brilliantly with cream, especially in a dauphinoise (I tend to split it 50/50 with potato) or finely diced in a risotto. And don't cast the leafy tops into the compost bin; they have a fabulous, nutty, spicy flavour and are wonderful shredded and sautéed with olive oil and garlic for a pasta sauce, or combined with the braised roots.

Cime di rapa (turnip tops) belongs to the same Brassica subspecies as turnips, and is essentially the same plant with an exaggerated leafy top but no bulbous root – perfect as a hardy, leafy green if the roots aren't to your fancy. It is easy to grow, as are turnips themselves, though be aware that the roots are a little unpredictable, tasting better or worse depending on where they're grown. However, 'Snowball' and 'Purple Top Milan' are great varieties to try.

BRAISED RABBIT WITH TURNIPS

4 bay leaves (fresh or dried)

2 tsp fennel seeds

200g smoked streaky bacon, cut into lardons

1 rabbit, jointed into 6 pieces (2 shoulders, 2 legs and saddle split into 2)

6 sprigs of thyme

8 small-medium turnips, peeled and cut into wedges

2 crisp eating apples, such as Cox's, peeled, cored and diced

4 garlic cloves, peeled and bashed

250ml dry cider

250ml chicken stock

Sea salt and black pepper

This hearty, pared-back stew is scented with fennel seeds and bay, which are toasted at the beginning to help release their earthy flavours. Serves 4

Preheat the oven to 160°C/Fan 140°C/Gas 3.

Scatter the bay leaves and fennel seeds over the base of a sturdy roasting dish or deep flameproof casserole. Place over a medium-high heat on the hob for 3–4 minutes until the bay and fennel are fragrant.

Add the lardons, rabbit pieces, thyme, turnips, apple and garlic, and season with plenty of salt and pepper. Pour in the cider and allow it to bubble rapidly until reduced by half.

Now add the stock – the liquid should just cover the ingredients. Bring to a simmer, then place a lid on the pan or seal it tightly with foil. Transfer to the oven and braise for 1–1½ hours, or until the rabbit is tender and yielding, and the turnips are nicely done.

Served the braised rabbit and turnips, along with the cidery pan juices, with a heap of buttered cabbage.

Vanilla

LATIN NAME
Vanilla planifolia

MORE RECIPES
Cashew pannacotta (page 124);
Chocolate, brandy and star
anise ice cream (page 178);
Wineberries with peaches and
custard (page 317); Lime and
coconut mousse (page 358);
Peach slump (page 448);
Rhubarb crème brûlée
(page 532); Creamy spelt and
almond pudding (page 596);
Whisky and marmalade bread
and butter pudding (page 672);
Double chocolate pecan praline
cookies (page 458)

SOURCING
ndali.net; steenbergs.co.uk

Vanilla – real vanilla – is heady and sensuous, even sexy, laying down its spicy aroma of smoky-dates-with-a-hint-of-musk and adding lingering depth, breadth and warmth wherever it is strewn. And the tell-tale presence of those tiny black seeds gives a visual tease of anticipation. It's a curious irony that the word 'vanilla' is sometimes associated with the plain, safe, unexciting options in life.

The time was when vanilla character was delivered to our cakes and trifles via little bottles of brown vanilla 'essence' – essentially caramel-coloured water with synthetic flavouring added. This wan imitation has now been all but pushed off the shelves by products that burst with the perfumed richness of the pod itself. Alongside liquid vanilla extracts (made by steeping vanilla pods in alcohol), are oozingly thick, seed-flecked vanilla bean pastes, fragrant vanilla sugars and vanilla powders, and the long, sticky, ribbed black pods themselves.

It is fitting that this most sensual of spices begins life as one of the most suggestive of flowers: the orchid – specifically, an orchid vine that flourishes in steamy tropical regions. Vanilla originated in Central America, and a small quantity, of a particularly rich and spicy character, is still produced in Mexico. The vast majority is now from Madagascar and other sources include India, Indonesia, Tahiti and Uganda – which is where my favourite vanilla, Ndali, comes from.

Vanilla farming is an extraordinarily demanding and frankly intimate affair. In order to guarantee pollination, the male and female parts of each flower have to be gently brought together by hand (only a special little Mexican bee can do the job naturally). It's an operation that has to be performed within a few hours of the flower opening. Fertilised flowers form fat vanilla 'beans', which are harvested when still smooth, green and bland. It takes a 5- or 6-month process of fermentation – including exposure to the scorching sun and periods wrapped in blankets so the beans 'sweat' – to turn them into the dark, sweet black pods, heady with scent, that are so beloved of pastry chefs the world over. The intense curing process causes inert phenolic compounds within the pods, including the crucial vanillin, to develop and intensify.

Around 600 years ago, the Aztecs were blending vanilla with chocolate in their bracing drink *xocoatl* (chilli was another ingredient) and it's fair to say the idea has caught on. Vanilla's sweetness and slightly smoky, new-leathery character are perfect partners to chocolate's dark, fruity bitterness in cakes, brownies and mousses. Vanilla's most classic uses are with creamy, sweet things such as pannacotta and ice cream – custard would be nothing without it – but it's lovely with fruit too. I love vanilla added to the liquor for poaching pears, or blended into butter for roasting plums or apricots. I rarely make a rhubarb compote without vanilla in it, and a little vanilla and sugar stirred into crème fraîche makes a superb partner to raspberries or strawberries.

Vanilla will always be most at home in creamy puddings and fruity combinations but it is now fashionable to use it in savoury dishes too. You need to be restrained here, but it can be very successful with fish. Try adding a knife-tip of scraped-out seeds to the citrus juice for a ceviche, or gently infusing ½ pod in the oil before frying scallops. Added to tomato sauces, vanilla helps to round out and mellow them in the way a pinch of sugar does. You can also add it to mixtures of dry spices to be rubbed on to meat before cooking.

Vanilla extracts and pastes are very convenient – I often splash them into batters when I'm baking. But even the best do not come close to the extraordinary intensity of flavour you get from the seed-packed pod itself. I use one whenever I can –

particularly in a custard or pannacotta where the vanilla flavour really needs to shine through. Vanilla pods should be black, moist and flexible – you should be able to tie one in a knot without it splitting. If left whole and stored in an airtight jar, they'll keep well for months. Once sliced open with the tip of a knife, their tiny seeds will appear as a thick paste – and the aroma at this point should knock your socks off.

Occasionally, you can buy pods that have developed a frosty coating of white filaments – these are vanillin crystals. Some claim they signify the very best vanilla flavour, while others say flavour is the result of skilful curing and crystal-free pods can be just as good. Either way, they're certainly not a bad sign.

Many recipes call for the seeds to be scraped out and added to liquid (cream, milk, wine etc.) to infuse, with the pod thrown in after them. But if you are using only the seeds, keep the pod for another day: it will dry and harden but can be snipped up and added to a rice pudding or custard, or buried in a jar of sugar where it will scent it deliciously. You can even fish pods out of a pan of hot liquid, once they have done their job, rinse them, dry them and set them aside for later use. The flavour will be a little diminished, but still significant, and it's a thrifty idea given that quality vanilla pods are expensive.

VANILLA AND RHUBARB ICE CREAM

250ml whole milk

250ml double cream

1 vanilla pod

4 medium egg yolks

175g caster sugar

250g rhubarb, trimmed and sliced into 3cm chunks

This gorgeous ice has a wonderful, almost sherbety flavour. You can, if you prefer, keep the rhubarb purée separate and swirl it into the soft-set ice cream to make a rhubarb ripple. Serves 4–6

Put the milk and cream into a heavy-based pan. Use a sharp knife to split the vanilla pod from top to bottom, then use the tip of the blade to scrape out all the tiny, sticky vanilla seeds within. Add the seeds and pod to the creamy milk, place over a low heat and bring to a tremulous simmer.

Whisk the egg yolks and 100g of the sugar together thoroughly in a large bowl, then pour on the hot vanilla cream, whisking as you go. Pour this mixture into a clean pan and cook over a medium heat, stirring continuously, until thickened. Don't let the mixture boil or the custard will curdle.

Take the pan off the heat. Lay a piece of baking parchment or cling film directly on the surface of the custard to prevent a skin forming and leave to stand for 1–2 hours, so the vanilla flavour is deeply infused. Then pass through a sieve into a bowl, cover and chill.

Meanwhile, put the rhubarb in a pan with the remaining 75g sugar and 2 tbsp water. Bring to a gentle simmer over a medium heat and cook, stirring often, for about 10 minutes until the rhubarb is tender. Tip into a sieve set over a bowl and use a ladle or spatula to push as much of the juice and pulp through as possible (you can eat the pulp left in the sieve – it's delicious with yoghurt). Leave the purée to cool, then chill it.

Once chilled, combine the vanilla custard and rhubarb purée. Churn in an ice-cream machine until soft-set (or freeze, beating at intervals, see page 178), then transfer to a fairly shallow freezerproof container and freeze until solid. Place in the fridge about 30 minutes before serving to soften and make scooping easier.

Note You can use this, or any other great vanilla ice cream, to make a gorgeous vanilla milkshake: in a blender, blitz 2–3 scoops with 250ml whole milk, ½ banana, ½ tsp vanilla extract and a dusting of freshly grated nutmeg. Pour into a couple of glasses and serve.

MORE RECIPES

Skirt steak and chips (page 64);
Fragrant beef curry (page 350);
Coriander pork chops (page 198);
Goat kebabs with rosemary, red
peppers and onion (page 280)

SOURCING

bocaddonfarmveal.com;
brookfieldfarmdorset.co.uk;
gazegillorganics.co.uk;
helenbrowningorganics.co.uk

Until fairly recently, veal was a dirty word. Anyone with a modicum of food knowledge understood that this, the meat of calves, was the product of a cruel and inhumane system, and it was widely shunned – or, if eaten, done so in the same atmosphere of controversy that surrounds foie gras.

If you keep a young calf in a restricted space so that it can move very little, and feed it on a milk diet that lacks iron, its meat remains pale and very delicate in flavour. A desirable thing, for some. However, the shocking cruelties of the traditional crate-rearing system are undeniable: calves were exported (alive, obviously) to the Continent, where they were kept in 'crates' so tiny that the creature within them couldn't turn around. No exercise, no contact with other animals. Thankfully, this regime is now illegal in the EU, banned in 2007.

But calves are still raised for veal in Europe in poor conditions. Every year, thousands of them are transported long distances to reach veal farms where they may be confined to sheds with uncomfortable, bare, slatted floors that allow excrement to fall through – a benchmark of low welfare. (Straw bedding is a more humane option.)

Although EU law now stipulates that the animals be fed at least some roughage (without it, their stomachs cannot develop normally), the diet of European veal calves is still usually milk-based and low in iron – the whiteness of the meat a greater priority than the welfare of the animals.

However, when it comes to British veal, the story these days is far more positive. Veal is a brand that's hard to sell, because of its ingrained association with animal cruelty. But it's important to understand that the option of simply not eating veal at all is equally wrong-headed.

Veal is a by-product of the dairy industry and I think anyone who eats dairy products has a responsibility to consider it. Most veal calves are not pure-bred meat animals. They are almost exclusively the unwanted offspring of dairy cows – mostly male. If there is no market for them as meat, those calves are shot shortly after birth. This is an indefensible waste.

If, like me, you want to enjoy dairy products at least sometimes, you can cast a vote in support of a more sane and holistic solution to the 'problem' of male dairy calves. And that is exactly what's happening. There's been a renaissance in the British veal industry, with the realisation that eating male calves raised in a higher-welfare system is a better choice than having them slaughtered and incinerated at birth.

Various bodies have done a lot of work of late to rehabilitate British veal. In 2006, Compassion in World Farming and the RSPCA established a 'Calf Forum', bringing together a group of 'stakeholder bodies' – including beef and dairy farmers, processors and retailers – to try to find a better alternative to destroying or exporting unwanted dairy calves.

Since then, the number of calves being exported to Europe has massively reduced (partly due to an export ban by the Netherlands, linked to bovine TB). The Forum has done a lot to change the way male dairy calves are viewed in the UK and the number of calves being killed shortly after birth has dropped by 36 per cent, with far more dairy calves being raised for meat. Just as importantly, consumer understanding about exactly what veal represents, and how ethical choices can be made, has vastly increased.

Hence higher welfare British veal is now on the high street. As with all meats, there is a spectrum. In order to produce a relatively pale meat, some British veal calves are raised on a milk-based diet in a completely indoor system. But they are in straw-bedded barns (UK law requires that all calves are provided with bedding), loose-housed in social groups and, along with formula milk, their diet includes enough fibre and iron to keep them healthy. They are slaughtered at 6–8 months. Welfare can be good, and the RSPCA includes some of this veal in its Assured scheme.

'Rose' veal comes from calves that are raised more like traditional beef cattle, with a more mixed diet, and slaughtered between 8 and 12 months. They're still likely to be indoors most or all of the time. Rose veal is pink and tender: not as robust and characterful as beef, but not so pale as milk-fed veal.

Rather harder to find, but the best option, in my book, is organic rose veal (a lot of organic veal comes from beef calves, which are not linked to the dairy industry). These animals are still raised indoors at least some of the time, and eat some cereal-based feed, but have access to organic pasture in the warmer months. And, in some cases, calves are reared by surrogate mothers, so they can suckle when they want to.

Why, you could argue, do we need to eat veal at all? Why don't we raise those animals to be mature beef carcasses? Well, sometimes we do – a lot of excess dairy cattle is raised as beef (see page 56) – and one of the points realised by the Calf Forum mentioned earlier is that rearing calves for beef, rather than veal, can be more profitable for farmers. But it's not easy: pure dairy calves don't tend to put on bulky, meaty muscle quickly and intensive finishing is necessary.

In addition, veal does offer something unique: a delicate, tender version of beef. It is lamb to beef's mutton, if you like. A classic *saltimbocca* (see below), or a veal chop, grilled with garlic and rosemary, is delicious. Osso buco – veal shank – has a wonderful flavour and texture, with a nugget of sweet marrow as an additional treat. As long as we are producing male dairy calves, we should continue to explore the possibilities of this delicate meat – raised in the highest welfare conditions possible.

SALTIMBOCCA

4 rose veal escalopes
(about 150g each)

8 large sage leaves

8 slices of air-dried ham
or 12 thin rashers of
streaky bacon

A little rapeseed oil

75g butter

350ml dry cider

Sea salt and black pepper

This West Country take on the classic veal saltimbocca (which means 'jumps in the mouth') replaces the traditional Marsala with good English scrumpy to create a rich and delicious little sauce. Serves 4

Trim the escalopes of any sinew. Put them between two sheets of greaseproof paper and bash them with a rolling pin until they are around 5mm thick. Season the escalopes with black pepper (you don't need salt).

Lay 2 sage leaves on top of each escalope then wrap 2 slices of ham (or 3 bacon rashers) around each, tucking the ends under the escalope to make a neat parcel. You can secure the ham/bacon with a cocktail stick if you like.

Cook the escalopes in two batches. Put a large frying pan over a medium-high heat and add a splash of oil and 25g of the butter. When the butter is foaming, add 2 escalopes and cook for 1½–2 minutes each side. Remove and keep them warm while you repeat with the other 2 escalopes.

Put the pan back on the heat and add the remaining butter and the cider. Simmer the liquid briskly to reduce it down to a thick, glossy sauce. Season with a pinch of salt.

Serve the saltimbocca on warmed plates with the cider sauce. Roast parsnips and apples and some wilted spinach are great accompaniments, or you could just go for mash or soft polenta.

Venison

LATIN NAME
Red deer: *Cervus elaphus*.
Roe deer: *Capreolus capreolus*.
Sika deer: *Cervus nippon*.
Fallow deer: *Dama dama*.
Muntjac: *Muntiacus reevesi*.
Chinese water deer: *Hydropotes inermis*

SEASONALITY
Different types available at different times of year but November–March is the most abundant time

MORE RECIPES
Szechuan-spiced venison steak (page 461)

SOURCING
tasteofgame.org.uk

Venison is the meat of a deer. As there are six species of deer in Britain and the males and females have slightly varying flavours, this actually means 12 subtly different meats. There are only two indigenous species: the red and the roe. The former is the biggest of all the species, and an icon of the Scottish Highlands, though it is actually even more at home in lowland forests, where it grows larger owing to an easier life. The meat has a rich intensity, which I find pleasing as long as it's been hung, cooked and served well, but it can be too strong for many – particularly if it is from a stag in rut.

The roe deer is also a creature of the woods, with a ghost-like ability to appear and vanish in silence. Its reclusive habits belie the fact that it is prevalent over almost all of the British Isles. The meat is among the best and most rewarding there is – rich and subtly gamey, with a mild ferrous note – and the carcass is an easy-to-manage size. Meat from a female roe is my very favourite venison.

The sika deer is the largest of the non-indigenous species and has the ability to cross-breed with the native red. Its meat has a rich complexity and is less lean than other types of venison due to the sika's ability to put on fat. Many would say sika meat is even finer than roe. Fallow deer, though interlopers, have been resident in Britain for a very long time and are common over most of the country. Fallow venison does not have quite the same depth of flavour as sika or roe but it does carry a little bit of tasty fat, particularly in animals from park herds.

The remaining two species are both small deer, about the size of a large dog. The Chinese water deer is slightly the bigger of the two and gives excellent meat; the meat of the smaller muntjac is not quite as flavoursome but it is easier to get hold of. Both species are very recent incomers, being the progeny of escapees from parks and zoos, but the muntjac has colonised suburbia at an astonishing rate while the Chinese water deer is far more localised.

Some deer are truly wild and shot by trained hunters known as stalkers – or, more commonly these days, deer 'managers'. Since deer lack any natural predators in the British Isles, stalking keeps their numbers in check, thereby protecting crops and indeed the health of the deer herd itself. There is a strong argument for wild venison being one of the most ethical meats available.

Other deer may be farmed in much the same way as sheep or cows, or 'parked' – contained within a specific place and then left to their own devices, with animals being periodically culled to provide meat. Only the larger deer species are suitable for farming or parking and so sika, red and fallow venison is often far easier to obtain than that from the smaller deer, and should be available from any decent butcher. If you're after roe, Chinese water deer or muntjac – or any wild venison – you will need to go to a specialist game dealer. Wild meat, for me, just has the edge in the flavour stakes and, if I have the choice, I choose doe or hind (female) meat over stag or buck (male). It's common for meat from male deer to have a stronger, more metallic taste. Also, males are often larger, making them a little tougher as their muscles have had to work harder.

All deer species in Britain, wild or otherwise, have hunting seasons to protect their breeding cycle. No single type of venison is available all year but there is always some in season. November to March is the best period, however, with a wide range available.

Many supermarkets now stock venison too, which is good news. It is a very low-fat meat, largely grass-fed, and even farmed venison is effectively free-range. Unfortunately, however, as demand rises, retailers are looking outside the UK to fill gaps in supply and increasing quantities are imported from as far afield as the Antipodes.

Cooking venison

Venison is butchered into two legs – or 'haunches' – two shoulders, a saddle from the back of the animal and breasts from the rib cage. The trim, shoulders and breasts provide meat that's good for longer cooking, while the saddle and haunches yield roasting joints and steaks. Venison offal can be good too, if extremely fresh – and the liver is the star of the show.

Venison carcasses are generally hung to develop flavour and tenderise the meat: 6–7 days in a chilled cold store is about right. Once butchered into basic cuts, venison can be hung further – perhaps a week – to really tenderise it. More time than that, or a higher temperature, and the meat can become too 'high' and gamey.

Cooking any venison requires care. It is very lean, particularly the saddle and haunch, and will be unforgiving if overcooked. The golden rule is to add some fat: that might be a good knob of butter when browning the meat, a handful of chopped fatty bacon when stewing, or some minced pork back fat if you're making venison burgers. Make sure that venison is not fridge-cold when you start and, for best results from the leaner cuts, cook them hot and fast and allow the meat to rest well before serving. Success is more easily achieved with less complicated cuts, such as seamed-out haunch steaks or small roasting cuts, rather than whole roast haunches. The tougher cuts from the shoulder, breast and neck make excellent stewing meat for casseroles, curries or pies, and also mince well for burgers, sausages and ragu.

My favourite venison dish of all is the liver sliced and fried in butter then served with a little salad of wilted parsley, shallots and capers. I make a reduction of balsamic vinegar and stock, add the butter from the venison pan and trickle this over the lot.

VENISON SALAD WITH APPLE, CELERIAC AND HAZELNUTS

This beautifully coloured and textured autumnal salad is very simple to put together: everything is cooked in the same pan. (Pictured on previous page.) Serves 2

1 tbsp olive or rapeseed oil

150g peeled celeriac, cut into roughly 2cm chunks

A sprig of rosemary

2 small eating apples, such as Russets

150g venison loin, trimmed

A handful of hazelnuts (about 25g), lightly bashed

50g bitter leaves, such as radicchio or chicory

1 tsp thyme leaves

Sea salt and black pepper

FOR THE DRESSING

1 tsp English mustard

1 tsp caster sugar

2 tsp cider vinegar

2 tbsp extra virgin olive or rapeseed oil

Place a large non-stick frying pan over a medium-high heat. Add the oil and, when hot, add the celeriac and rosemary. Season with salt and pepper and cook for 3–5 minutes, turning the celeriac regularly.

Meanwhile, quarter the apples, core them, then cut each quarter in half again. Season the venison loin all over.

Push the celeriac to one side of the pan. Add the venison and put the apple pieces next to it. Cook for 5 minutes, then flip both the venison and apple pieces over and cook for another 5 minutes. (Give the celeriac a little stir every now and then so it doesn't catch.) This will give you medium-rare meat. Remove the venison to a board to rest.

Add the bashed hazelnuts to the pan and give it a good shake to mix everything. Cook for a few more minutes (the celeriac should still be a little *al dente*) then remove and allow to cool a little.

For the dressing, whisk all the ingredients together in a bowl and season with salt and pepper to taste.

To serve, shred the bitter leaves and arrange them over a large platter. Scatter over the warm celeriac, nuts and apples. Slice the venison thinly and arrange this on top. Sprinkle over the thyme then trickle over the mustardy dressing and serve.

Vinegar

Vin aigre is simply sour wine or, more accurately, the natural end state of wine, or any alcoholic liquor, if fermentation is not halted. Certain specialised, booze-loving bacteria work on the alcohol, turning it into acetic acid, which is the source of vinegar's sharpness.

During the process, a vinegar 'mother' is formed – this is a gel-like layer of cellulose produced by the bacteria and containing many of them. You may find it forming in organic, unpasteurised shop-bought vinegars – and some brands actually advertise the mother as a positive health benefit, since it means the product is essentially 'live'. Whatever your view, vinegar mother is not going to do you any harm – you can just strain it out.

Traditional vinegars, where wine or cider is simply inoculated with vinegar mother and allowed to ferment, take months to produce – and the process is rather unpredictable. There are not many of these around any more – health food shops and the internet are your best hunting grounds. Vinegar bacteria need oxygen to work and modern vinegar-making methods focus on ways to increase the amount of oxygen they get, thus speeding the process. Most vinegar is now produced by 'submerged fermentation', where the alcoholic liquid is housed in large, temperature-controlled vats called acetators. Acetobacter (essentially, vinegar mother) is added to the liquid and air is pumped through it. This system can turn out vinegar in 24 hours.

It's easy to be reticent about using vinegar. It's so very sharp, harsh and bold and too much really is too much. Like salt, it's a flavour you can't take back. But acidity is such a crucial element in well-balanced cooking, it pays to get to grips with the sharp stuff. Just add it drop by cautious drop.

Don't be afraid to add vinegar to ingredients that are already acidic, like fruit or tomatoes. Just like lemon juice, vinegar's acidity has a seasoning effect – although you should choose one of the sweeter vinegars, like balsamic or sherry, here. One of my favourite ways to serve strawberries is coated in a sauce made by blitzing raspberries, sugar and balsamic vinegar into a purée, then sieving out the pips.

Conversely, vinegar is a welcome counterpoint to the sweet and rich. It's crucial in mayonnaise and, combined with honey or sugar, mustard and garlic, it forms the basis of a classic vinaigrette dressing, the embroidery on the olive oil backdrop. But a tiny dash of vinegar in rich stews and soups, often added right at the end, can be the thing that defines their flavours.

Vinegar can be infused with herbs to make flavoured vinegars. Its make-up means it dissolves aromatic compounds more readily than water so it can really bring out the flavours of other things. Choose a good quality, light vinegar such as rice, white wine or cider with an acidity of at least 5 per cent (check the label). Pack your chosen flavouring – anything from raspberries to rose petals, grated horseradish to lemon peel – into a sterilised jar and pour over the cold vinegar. Make sure the flavourings are completely submerged and leave to infuse for at least 2 weeks in the fridge before straining the vinegar and decanting into a clean bottle. White wine vinegar infused with tarragon is one of the best (use it in salad dressings with olive oil, or in béarnaise sauce), while a syrupy, sweetened raspberry vinegar can be used like a cordial in drinks.

Vinegar is an ingredient we use for its chemical properties as much as its flavour. Once one of the only reliable methods of preserving food, since it is so inhospitable to harmful bacteria, it remains essential in pickles and chutneys. Vinegar is also crucial in some meat marinades, where the acetic acid 'denatures' protein, altering it on a molecular level so that it becomes softer.

TYPES OF VINEGAR

Malt vinegar Made from a basic malted barley beer, this is strident in character and dark in colour. It's great for fish and chips, and hearty chutneys, but too harsh for subtle dressings. Barley contains gluten but the fermentation process renders the amount in malt vinegar negligible.

White wine vinegar This is one of the great all-rounder vinegars, perfect for a classic vinaigrette and ideal for herb-flavoured vinegars.

Red wine vinegar With its lovely, full, winey quality, this is great for seasoning meaty stews and gravies.

Cider vinegar Having a distinct fruitiness and a softer, mellower flavour than wine vinegars, cider vinegar is hugely versatile. Use it for everything from subtle vinaigrettes to pickles. Unfiltered versions are cloudy and may be sold with the 'mother' still in the bottle.

Distilled vinegar Made from malted barley or corn, distilled vinegars have little flavour beyond their acetic tang, but they are useful for pickles where you want other flavours to dominate. They are also very handy for descaling your kettle.

Rice vinegar With a light, sweet character, this is good with Asian flavours: soy sauce, garlic, ginger, chilli. Use in dipping sauces, dressings for noodles and sweet-sour stir-fries.

Sherry vinegar Dark, glossy and richly flavoured, this has a lovely caramel sweetness. Like traditional balsamic, fine sherry vinegars are aged in a range of wooden barrels. The method is known as the solera system.

Balsamic vinegar True, traditional balsamic is technically not a vinegar at all because it is made not from wine, but from concentrated, cooked-down fresh grape juice – known as grape must or *mosto*. Fermentation begins only after it has been reduced. The slowly fermenting, acidifying *mosto* is aged – for at least 12 years – in a succession of barrels made from different woods that impart a spectrum of subtle flavours. Really good *balsamico* is aged for much longer and is so rich and sweet that it can be enjoyed as a digestif. Look for the label Aceto Balsamico Tradizionale di Modena, DOP (*Denominazione di Origine Protetta*). The price tag is another good indication – *tradizionale* starts at £50–60 for 100ml. Use neat, in tiny, precious droplets on the finest ingredients, such as aged Parmesan, milky *mozzarella di bufala* or a dish of perfect strawberries.

Nearly all the balsamic vinegar on our shop shelves is the cheaper *aceto balsamico di Modena*. Confusingly, this may have an IGP (*Indicazione Geografica Protteta*), but not a DOP. This is still made from grape must, but it has actual vinegar added, and sometimes sugar and colouring too. These vinegars may still be aged and can be excellent (and expensive, though not *tradizionale* expensive), but some are thin and disappointing – inferior to a good cider or wine vinegar. British apple balsamic vinegar is a nice ingredient, however: an appley approximation of grape-based balsamic, using concentrated apple juice (essentially the *mosto*) and cider vinegar (and colour). There is also a white balsamic – a lighter, clearer alternative, but still with the sweetness that comes from the cooked-down *mosto*.

RED PEPPER AGRODOLCE

A little rapeseed oil

2 large red (or orange or yellow) peppers

25g raisins

A small sprig of rosemary

1 bay leaf

1 garlic clove, peeled and bashed

2 tbsp cider vinegar

2 tsp caster sugar

2 tsp capers in vinegar, rinsed

2 tbsp extra virgin olive oil

Sea salt and black pepper

The Italian way of preparing vegetables agrodolce (literally 'sour-sweet') involves seasoning with a blend of vinegar and sugar. Here, the sweetness is enhanced with raisins and the sharpness with capers. Serves 4 as an antipasti dish

Preheat the oven to 220°C/Fan 200°C/Gas 7.

Place the peppers on a greased baking sheet and roast for about 30 minutes, turning once, or until soft, wrinkled and blackened in places. While they are still hot, transfer to a bowl and cover with cling film. Leave for 15–20 minutes.

Meanwhile, put the raisins, rosemary, bay, bashed garlic, vinegar and sugar in a small pan. Bring to a simmer over a low heat, stirring to dissolve the sugar, then turn off the heat and leave to infuse.

Remove the stalks and seeds from the peppers then peel off the skin, which should come away easily. Slice the peppers into thick strips and place in a bowl.

Pour the warm, infused vinegar-sugar mixture over the peppers, add the capers and olive oil and season with salt and pepper. Turn the peppers in the sweet and sour dressing, then leave to stand for an hour or two before serving.

This is delicious with bread and a creamy mild cheese such as buffalo mozzarella or soft sheep's cheese, or with a selection of antipasti-style dishes.

V

Vodka

MORE RECIPES
Mulberry and walnut cranachan
(page 391)

SOURCING
blackcow.co.uk;
ghostvodka.co.uk;
twobirdsspirits.co.uk;
williamschase.co.uk

Vodka, being a very strong distilled spirit, is famously flavourless, or at least it tastes mostly of alcohol, possessing just a few hints of its base ingredient. That base can be almost anything fermentable: potato, barley, wheat and corn are the most traditional, but vodka can be based on sugar beet, rice, milk – even Fairtrade quinoa – these days. The versatility of the basic technique means you can make vodka almost anywhere and there's now a thriving British distilling industry capitalising on that.

Vodka is a bracing tipple on its own, of course, but its neutrality also make it a great choice for an alcoholic infusion. My favourites are sloe vodka, raspberry vodka, rose petal vodka (*Rosa rugosa* is best) and the rather unlikely sweet vernal grass vodka (a British version of bison grass vodka). On their own they are terrific but most are even better in a cocktail. Rose petal vodka with rosehip syrup, raspberry juice, soda water, lemonade and ice, for example, makes a quite superb summer drink which I call a 'pink pint'. A vodka infusion will always make the flavour of the infused ingredient immediately accessible. So, if you want your sponge cake to taste of rose petals, look no further, just add rose vodka to the mix.

Vodka infusions can also form the basis of vodka shots, where vodka is turned into a more than usually invigorating jelly. Sloe vodka shot, watermint shot, jelly bean shot – endless fun can be had by choosing different infusions, layering different jellies, sprinkling coloured sugar or using unusual moulds. The basic process is to make a plain jelly with sweetened water, using leaf gelatine, and stir in an equal volume of vodka infusion while the water is still slightly warm (calculate the gelatine needed according to the total quantity of liquid, i.e. water plus vodka). Of course, infusions are not always essential: you can use fruit juices mixed with neat vodka instead.

Straight vodka can also be mixed into preserves and fruit sauces to give them an extra bite. Try vodka in fruit jam for a Victoria sponge, vodka in marmalade to top a cheesecake, or vodka and plum sauce to pour over a pudding.

DAMSON AND ROSEMARY VODKA

500g ripe damsons

350g caster sugar

2 large sprigs of rosemary,
lightly bashed

700ml vodka

This is fragrant and floral, with a fruity tang from the damsons and heady notes from the rosemary. If you can't find wild fruit, cultivated damsons work too – as do sloes. It makes for a wonderful Christmas snifter. Makes about 1 litre

With a small, sharp knife, make a couple of cuts in each damson, through to the stone. Place the fruit in a large, sealable jar, such as a Kilner jar, along with the sugar, rosemary and vodka. Give the jar a good shake and set it aside.

Shake the jar several times over the next few days to encourage all the sugar to dissolve. Then place the jar somewhere cool and dark and away from temptation for 2–3 months.

Now strain out the fruit and rosemary by pouring the mixture through a sieve lined with muslin or a clean tea towel. Funnel the strained, fruity liquor into a clean bottle and seal with a cork or screw cap.

Store the vodka in a cool, dark cupboard. You can drink it straight away but it will improve with keeping. The longer you can store it, the better. The strained-out damsons can be used in all manner of delicious ways – add to sauces, game stews, jams and puddings, or just warm them through and serve with ice cream. (Just watch out for the stones!)

Note For a more complex, mellow flavour, reduce the sugar to 175g and let the fruit sit in the vodka for 6 months before bottling, then mature the strained liquor for 2–3 years before drinking.

Walnuts

LATIN NAME
Juglans regia

SEASONALITY
Wet walnuts:
October–November

MORE RECIPES
Muhammara (page 464); Celery
and walnut tapenade (page 133);
Walnut and blue cheese soufflés
(page 246); Baked mushrooms
with rosemary and walnut butter
(page 396); Cheddar, apple and
celeriac salad (page 140);
Henakopita with garam masala
and eggs (page 254); Roasted
sweet potatoes and aubergine
(page 628); Roasted grapes
(page 288); Mulberry and walnut
cranachan (page 391); Pear and
bilberry crumble tart (page 69)

SOURCING
kentishcobnuts.com;
orangepippintrees.co.uk

Originating in central Asia, the walnut does not grow with unbounded enthusiasm in the British Isles. However, you may be lucky and have a productive tree in your garden or access to an accommodating roadside tree nearby. The nuts are likely to be smaller than their more southerly cousins, but still a treat.

If you really like walnuts, though, you will likely have to buy them. Fortunately they are no longer the Christmas-only treat they once were. Increasingly available these days are British 'wet' walnuts, usually sold locally – look out for them in farm shops and at roadside stalls from mid-October to early November. These are walnuts that are fully formed but fresh off the tree: the shell is firm but the flesh inside is pale, not yet bitter, soft and not wet, exactly, but juicy. They offer a different eating experience to the standard shop-bought walnut, which has been kiln-dried and so is darker, crisper and more strident. Wet walnuts are best enjoyed one by one as you release them from the shell, with a crisp apple or some assertive Cheddar alongside. They do not keep well once exposed to air but can be stored in their shells for a couple of weeks if kept cool, preferably in the fridge or even freezer. Shelled nuts also need to be kept cool and closely packed in airtight bags or containers.

Very immature nuts – picked in the summer before the shell has formed – can be pickled. To check their suitability, gently push a pin into the end of the nut – if it meets strong resistance after a few millimetres then you are too late. The whole nuts must be soaked in brine for 2 weeks, changing the brine once. After that, they should be dried then boiled in malt vinegar with pickling spices. They are an acquired taste, but some people seem to like them.

The high calorific value of nuts can dissuade people from eating them, but the calories come from oils that are essential to health. Walnuts are a good source of beneficial omega-3 fatty acids – more so than other nuts. They also contain essential minerals and vitamins and are rich in antioxidants.

If that is not enough, walnuts are incredibly useful in the kitchen. Their relatively soft texture gives a pleasant bite, and their flavour is unique – rich and toasty but with a distinct, tannic bitterness from their paper-thin skins that makes them as much at home in savoury dishes as in sweet.

Perhaps the most everyday use for walnuts is in salads. They make great partners to everything from the classic celery and apple of Waldorf salad, through rocket and strawberry, spinach and caramelised onions, to green beans and sun-dried tomatoes, providing robust crunch and texture. They are particularly good in salads if lightly roasted first.

Walnuts are also excellent chopped for use in a stuffing. Peppers stuffed with breadcrumbs, sautéed onions, chopped dried tomatoes, feta cheese and walnuts and then slow-baked, take some beating, but this mixture, or something similar, works equally well in cannelloni or mushrooms.

Walnuts are by far the best nuts for that staple vegetarian fare, the nut roast. This can be made with any likely combination of ingredients you fancy provided that none of them are meat, at least one of them is a nut and the whole thing remains intact once baked. My ingredients of choice are walnuts (obviously), breadcrumbs, freshly cooked mushrooms, powdered dried mushrooms, onion, celery, carrot, a little chopped dried tomato, herbs and a beaten egg or two to hold everything together, though water will do this too if you prefer. This mixture, provided you lightly cook the onion, celery and carrot first, will also make excellent walnut burgers.

W

For dessert, I like walnut and honey ice cream, or apple with a walnut crumble topping, or walnut torte or walnut meringue. I always make my pancakes with half plain flour, half sweet chestnut flour, but this is even richer and nuttier with 1 tbsp of ground walnuts thrown in the batter too.

Walnuts make an elevating addition to what one might call the more industrial variety of home-made bread. You can even over-egg a pudding by serving it with walnut butter – mix ground walnuts with a little walnut oil, salt and sugar and pound to a butter in a pestle and mortar. Walnuts, ground in a food processor with flour, also give a nutty depth to shortcrust pastry for anything from a fruit tart to a game pie. And a good chocolate brownie is always so very much better with chopped walnuts.

You can even make a refreshing drink by blitzing 30g walnuts with 200ml semi-skimmed milk and straining out the solids through muslin. And of course I must mention the ubiquitous smoothie – a breakfast of date and walnut smoothie will keep you going until 3pm. Do take into account in all walnut dishes that bitter skin and use this wonderful nut with some restraint.

Hidden among the exotic and flavoured oils on the delicatessen's shelf you may be lucky enough to find walnut oil. Not all walnut oils are the same – some are rather bland. But a good one is a rich delight. French walnut oil is often exceptional, and quite unsurpassable for dressings – better than olive oil, in my opinion. Walnut oil is expensive and does not keep for very long once opened – two good reasons to buy it in small quantities. Keep it in a dark glass bottle or a tin, in the fridge. Don't cook with it; use it cold for dressings.

WALNUT, BARLEY, ROCKET AND BLUE CHEESE SALAD

125g walnut halves

200ml apple juice

150g pearl barley (or pearled spelt)

½ small red onion, very finely sliced

2 good handfuls of rocket

75g blue cheese, such as Dorset Blue Vinney or Cornish Blue

Sea salt and black pepper

FOR THE DRESSING

About 1 tsp thyme leaves

2 tsp clear honey

2 tbsp extra virgin olive or rapeseed oil

1 tbsp cider vinegar

Soaking nuts, rather like soaking dried fruit, makes them deliciously moist and plump. In this salad, walnuts are soaked in apple juice, which gives them a lovely fruity tang. Serves 3–4 as a starter, 2 as a main dish

Soak the walnut halves in the apple juice for about an hour. This will soften them slightly, and they'll plump up and become fruity and sweet.

Meanwhile, soak the pearl barley or spelt in cold water for 20 minutes. Drain and tip into a saucepan, cover with fresh water and bring to a simmer. Cook for 25–30 minutes (a little less for spelt) or until tender but with a nutty bite. Drain and allow to cool.

To make the dressing, put the ingredients in a jam jar with a little salt and pepper and shake vigorously to combine.

Drain the walnuts (you can drink the apple juice, or use it for another recipe such as poached pears). Combine the nuts with the red onion, the cooled pearl barley and 2 tbsp of the dressing. Season with salt and pepper and mix well.

Spoon the dressed walnuts and barley on to individual plates or a serving platter. Scatter over the rocket leaves and crumble over the blue cheese. Trickle with the remaining dressing and serve.

Wasabi

LATIN NAME
Wasabia japonica

SOURCING
thewasabicompany.co.uk

Why is an eye-watering, sinus-blasting hit of wasabi so enjoyable on a piece of pure, raw seafood? The delicate, sweet blandness of sashimi just seems to beg for a hot spot of this zesty green freshness. It's thought wasabi was originally served with sushi so that the plant's anti-bacterial properties would guard against food poisoning. But there's more to it than that. The fiery green paste brings out the flavour of the seafood and does something else in the mouth that's hard to explain: it just works.

The wasabi plant is part of the brassica family, and the condiment comes from the grated stem. Wasabi is related to horseradish, which it resembles all too well. In fact, many commercial wasabi pastes largely comprise horseradish and/or mustard powder, with vivid colouring added, and very little actual wasabi. Look on the label and you'll see what's in the tube or pot of powder. Genuine wasabi has a subtler shade of green and a broader spectrum of flavours, with sweet, pungent and herbal aspects to its nose-prickling heat.

Like its sister horseradish, wasabi is best eaten freshly grated. Grating unleashes an enzymatic chain reaction that gives wasabi its kick. Whole wasabi stems can be kept for a few weeks in the fridge and you can grate them as you need them. The best tool for this is a Japanese *oroshigane* grater (which you can use for ginger too). Some graters still feature the traditional sharkskin but often they are made from more sustainable metal or china, with small, sharp bumps that mash up the root as you rub it over the surface, forming a fine purée. Ideally, wait 3–4 minutes after grating, which allows the wasabi to become slightly sweeter, then eat or use within 20 minutes.

Aside from sushi, wasabi can be served with steak or sausages, added to dipping sauces, or used to spice up butter before dotting on meat or fish. It's also good in a peppy dip for crudités: soak a couple of handfuls of whole blanched almonds overnight in cold water. Drain, then put in a blender with 1 tsp grated fresh ginger, 1 small grated garlic clove, a good dash of soy sauce and 1–2 tsp freshly grated wasabi root. Blitz to a thick, coarse purée, adding a little water, check the seasoning and serve.

RICE AND FISH WITH WASABI DRESSING

150g long-grain white or
brown rice

200–300g cold, cooked fish flesh,
all skin and bone removed

2 tbsp tamari or soy sauce

1 tbsp rice wine vinegar

4 spring onions, finely sliced

FOR THE DRESSING

2 tsp wasabi paste or freshly
grated wasabi

1 tsp freshly grated root ginger

1 small garlic clove, grated

Juice of 1 large lime

2 tsp clear honey

2 tbsp rapeseed oil

Sea salt

This salad takes the elements of sushi and re-imagines them in salad form. The fish is cooked rather than raw. You can use any cold, cooked fish – roast, steamed or grilled, white or oily – so this recipe is a great vehicle for leftovers. Serves 4

Cook the rice as described on the packet. Drain and spread out on a large plate, then leave in a cool spot to cool quickly and completely. It's important not to leave cooked rice standing for long at room temperature – ideally you want to get the rice cool within about 20 minutes of cooking. Give it a stir every now and then to speed the process.

Flake the cooked fish and stir it gently through the rice. Then sprinkle over the tamari or soy sauce and the vinegar, and stir once more. Spoon the fish and rice over a large platter. Scatter over the spring onions.

For the dressing, whisk all the ingredients together thoroughly in a bowl. Trickle the dressing over the rice and fish and serve straight away.

Watercress

John Wright

LATIN NAME
Nasturtium officinale

SEASONALITY
British watercress
April–November;
imported all year round

HABITAT
Wild watercress is common
in streams of lowland England
and Wales

MORE RECIPES
Roots and fruits salad with
rapeseed dressing (page 524);
Curried new potatoes, red
onion and lettuce (page 226);
Pot-roasted mallard with celeriac
and watercress (page 241); Kiwi,
spinach and avocado smoothie
(page 325)

SOURCING
organicwatercress.co.uk

Watercress is in the cabbage family and shares the peppery flavours of its cousins, wild rocket, horseradish, mustard and more. It also has the property of becoming more peppery with chewing – the hot-tasting chemicals taking a few seconds to form. Sadly, cooking dramatically reduces that piquant quality.

You can buy watercress all year round from shops and markets. It is also possible to pick your own during the British season, summer and early autumn being the best time. However, while wild picking is always a tempting proposition – not least because watercress in the shops is twice the price of spinach –wild watercress is, unfortunately, perilous stuff. For the inexperienced forager it can be confused with one or two other water plants (most commonly the harmless and rather carroty fool's watercress) and, worse, it can bear one of the life-stages of the very dangerous liver fluke. The metacercaria, as it is known, is only a fifth of a millimetre in diameter at this stage, so you will never be able to spot it. Once inside you, it wanders aimlessly about your body until settling contentedly in your bile ducts and transforming itself into a slug-like creature of considerable size. Fast-running streams lacking muddy banks and away from grazing animals should be safe – the fluke is carried by sheep and cattle – but you may feel *should* is just not enough.

Soaking your wild watercress in a very mild solution of food-grade chlorine bleach for 10 minutes and then rinsing twice will kill the parasite. This is not as terrible as it sounds; it is a process used with many pre-packed salad vegetables and you would ingest more chlorine in a single intake of breath in the average swimming pool. Cooking is the safest option for wild watercress, but the peppery flavour is very quickly lost.

Commercially produced watercress is grown in large watery beds fed by spring water and does not suffer from liver fluke infestations. If you buy watercress it will be

safe to eat it raw – and that is truly the best way to enjoy it. Few plants are more welcome in a salad. Its flavour, pepperiness and succulence form a unique combination that will go with most other salad ingredients.

Cooking notoriously reduces the health benefits of many foods and with watercress this is a great shame. It is considered to be a 'superfood' as it is packed with antioxidants, including a substantial amount of vitamin C and beta-carotene. Indeed the second part of its name, *officinale,* indicates that it has long been considered an important component of the apothecary's storecupboard.

To get the fullest flavour from raw watercress, it is necessary to sacrifice its texture in a blender, as puréeing allows the peppery chemicals to form. For a simple salsa verde, blend 85g raw watercress with a little fresh basil, lemon juice and 1–2 tsp olive or walnut oil. Watercress works nicely in green smoothies too, in combination with, well, anything you like – orange juice, melon, carrot and so on. A flavoured butter or cream cheese can also be made with the raw leaf.

If not serving raw, the rule is to cook watercress as little as possible or the flavour will be turned to bitterness. Watercress and sweet chestnut dumplings are particularly good – made with suet and a half-and-half mix of self-raising flour and sweet chestnut flour mixed with water and lightly chopped watercress.

Blending ever-so-slightly-cooked watercress is an excellent way of retaining its pepperiness in anything served hot – you can purée briefly blanched watercress and simply add it to soups before serving, for instance. Most of the peppery quality we love will be preserved, and the soup will be a beautiful green. Similarly you can add puréed watercress to a white sauce to go with, say, trout.

Lightly sautéed watercress also keeps much of its flavour and makes a great accompaniment to steak. And wilted watercress can be used as an alternative to spinach in just about anything: cannelloni stuffing, pasta verde, quiche, stuffed chicken and so on. It retains at least some flavour, most of its goodness and is still very green.

CHILLED SPICED WATERCRESS AND YOGHURT SOUP

2 tbsp olive or rapeseed oil

2 medium onions, finely sliced

2 small garlic cloves, thinly sliced

700ml veg or light chicken stock

400g watercress

1½ tsp garam masala

3 tbsp plain wholemilk yoghurt, plus extra to serve

Sea salt and black pepper

Extra virgin olive or rapeseed oil, to finish

This is a great soup for summer and early autumn – lightly peppery with a nice bit of spice coming through from the garam masala. Serves 4

Heat the oil in a saucepan over a medium-low heat and add the onions, with a pinch each of salt and pepper. Cook, stirring regularly, for about 10 minutes, until the onions are soft and translucent but not coloured. Add the garlic and cook gently for a further 2 minutes.

Now add the stock, bring to the boil, lower the heat and simmer for 4 minutes. Pour the whole lot into a bowl, leave to cool, then refrigerate to chill.

Bring a pan of water to the boil and add a pinch of salt. Add the watercress and blanch for 2 minutes or until the tougher stalks are just tender (i.e. can be squashed between your fingers). Drain and then plunge the watercress into iced water to 'refresh' it before draining again. This will help keep it green and vibrant.

Put the watercress into a blender with the chilled stock mixture, the garam masala and yoghurt. Blitz to a fine purée, then chill for a further 20–25 minutes or until ready to serve.

Serve the soup cold, topped with a small extra spoonful of yoghurt, a twist of black pepper and a trickle of extra virgin oil.

Whelks

Nick Fisher

LATIN NAME
Buccinum undatum

SEASONALITY
Avoid during autumn and winter when breeding

HABITAT
Found from Iceland to the Bay of Biscay and can be locally abundant around the British Isles. Occasionally found at low water mark, but more commonly underwater

MCS RATING
4

REC MINIMUM SIZE
Shell length 7.7cm

SOURCING
goodfishguide.org; msc.org association-ifca.org.uk (for whelk-potting regulations)

If ever there was a maligned mollusc, it is the whelk. As a teenager, I used to 'enjoy' saucers of malt vinegar-soaked whelks in Norwich market, every Saturday. Somehow, the whelk, whose texture is somewhere between escargot and Haribo, won a place in my heart. Not so the rest of the nation. Although we have a busy, and at times lucrative, whelk fishery all around the British Isles, most of our catch is exported to South Korea.

Nevertheless, such is the fishing pressure on this slow-maturing mollusc, that alarm bells are being rung concerning its future. It would be good to see more fisheries following the example of the Granville Bay whelk fishery in Normandy, where thousands of tonnes of whelks are landed every year. This fishery is putting in place regulations on boat size and the number of whelk pots fished per boat, and is currently undergoing assessment by the MSC.

My theory as to why whelks are big in East Asia and a fading seaside attraction in Britain is simple: sauces and slicing. Whelks in the UK are traditionally boiled, cooled and drenched in industrial strength vinegar. Whelks in Korea are typically simmered with herbs and aromatics, cooled, then sliced and served in a range of spicy sauces. The rubbery texture of a huge mouthful of chewy whelk is not to everyone's liking, but thin-sliced cross-sections, served warm in a carefully crafted dressing, are much more inviting. My favourite way to eat whelks now is in my own version of a spicy Thai salad in which the down-at-rubbery-heel whelk takes on exotic and enigmatic qualities.

If you have a boat, you can pot for whelks yourself – the kind of pot you need is very basic and easy to make, or can be cheaply bought. I use very stinky pot bait or fish frames and heads and I always let them rot a bit first. Whelks like bait best when it's honking. You should check local byelaws regarding permits and regulations for whelk-potting.

If you are buying whelks, buy them live if possible and prepare as described in the recipe below. Frozen whole whelks are good too, but forget pickled ones.

SPAGHETTI WITH WHELKS, GARLIC AND PARSLEY

This simple dish is a great way to appreciate the unique texture and subtle marine flavour of whelks. It's also a good treatment for land snails, purged, cooked and shelled as described on page 586. Serves 2 as a main dish, or 4 as a starter

15–20 live whelks, depending on size

A bay leaf and/or a sprig of thyme (optional)

1 small carrot, roughly chopped (optional)

1 celery stalk, roughly chopped (optional)

200g spaghetti

50g butter

A dash of olive or rapeseed oil

2 garlic cloves, grated

1 medium-hot red chilli, deseeded and chopped, or ½ –1 tsp dried chilli flakes

2 tbsp chopped flat-leaf parsley

Sea salt and black pepper

½ lemon, to serve

Scrub the whelks under a cold tap. As you handle them, you may find that some of them release a certain amount of slime – don't worry about this, just rinse it away.

Bring a large pan of water to the boil and add the herbs, carrot and celery if you have them. Drop in the whelks and cook at a gentle simmer for 8–10 minutes. Drain and leave to cool, then prise the whelks from their shells with a fork. Remove the cap from the front end of the body, and the dark digestive sac from the tail end. If any are still a bit slimy, wipe with a cloth. Cut the whelks in half (or 3–4 pieces if very large). Season well with salt and pepper.

Bring a large pan of water to the boil, salt it well and add the spaghetti. Cook for about 12 minutes until *al dente* – use the time suggested on the packet as a guide.

Meanwhile, place a large non-stick frying pan over a medium-high heat. Add the butter and a dash of oil, then add the sliced whelks and sauté for 4–5 minutes. Toss in the garlic, chilli and parsley and cook for a further minute. Season well.

Drain the cooked spaghetti, retaining a little of the cooking water. Add the spaghetti to the whelks in the pan, with about 3 tbsp of the reserved cooking water, and toss well to combine. Give everything a good squeeze of lemon juice, and serve.

W

Whisky

MORE RECIPES
Mulberry and walnut cranachan
(page 391)

SOURCING
thewhiskyexchange.com;
whiskymerchants.co.uk

Whisky (whiskey in Ireland and the Americas) is a spirit distilled from fermented grains, deriving its name from the Celtic *uisge beatha* meaning 'water of life'. Single malt Scotch whiskies, the product of one distillery, made from malted, toasted barley and matured in oak for years, are complex, rich, spicy, citrusy, woody and strong. If the malted grain has been dried over a peat fire, the whisky will also have a distinctive, smoky, slightly medicinal tang.

The much more widely drunk type of Scotch is blended – a mix of spirits from different distilleries, comprising some from unmalted grain as well as malted barley. Blended Scotch whiskies offer a gentler, more rounded drinking experience. They're not inferior to single malts, just different, and can work well in cooked dishes where their smooth character is less disruptive to other flavours. Malt whisky has its place in the kitchen too, but go for slightly lighter, sweeter types such as those from Speyside. Big, smoky, peaty beasts, such as the Islay malts, can do rather wild things in a dish and are best, I think, enjoyed in a glass.

Whisky is a traditional ingredient in many Scottish recipes, not infrequently combined with oats, honey and cream – bland, sweet, cushioning ingredients that form the ideal backdrop to whisky's bright, hot complexity. You can even put a nip in your porridge in the morning (though only if you're about to stride off up a snowy Cairngorm, not drive the kids to school). For a gorgeous pud of crushed fruit, toasted oatmeal and cream spiked with Scotch, try cranachan. In such recipes, the whisky is used unheated, and its blithe alcoholic tang is much in evidence.

There are also lots of cooked uses for whisky, where that edge is mellowed. It works well in marinades and bastes, and with fruit – try adding a dram to a rich fruit cake or a batch of marmalade. In all cases, add whisky judiciously… it's powerful stuff.

American bourbon whiskey is made primarily from corn and has a sweeter character than Scotch, hence its frequent use in glazes for barbecued meat.

WHISKY AND MARMALADE BREAD AND BUTTER PUDDING

Rich, hot, comforting and indulgent, this is best served with lots of cold double cream.
Serves 8–10

About 100g butter, softened, plus extra to grease

450g slightly stale, crustless white bread

3 medium eggs

1 medium egg yolk

125g caster sugar

300ml whole milk

200ml double cream

100ml whisky

1 tsp vanilla extract

100g orange marmalade

100g dried cranberries or raisins

A little demerara or granulated sugar, to finish

Lightly butter an ovenproof dish, about 2 litre capacity. Cut the bread into slices, about 1cm thick. Butter the bread lightly on both sides and cut it into squares or triangles.

In a bowl, whisk the eggs, egg yolk and sugar together thoroughly, then stir in the milk, cream, whisky and vanilla.

Line the bottom of the buttered dish with a third of the bread slices and spread half of the marmalade over them. Cover with half of the cranberries or raisins, then spoon on a third of the whisky custard. Repeat these layers. Finish with the rest of the bread and pour on the remaining custard. Leave the pudding to stand for 15 minutes, so the bread can really soak up the custard before baking. Preheat the oven to 180°C/Fan 160°C/Gas 4.

Just before baking, push the bread down slightly with a spatula to make sure the custard is all soaked in, and sprinkle a little sugar over the surface. Stand the dish in a roasting tin and pour boiling water from the kettle into the roasting tin, to come halfway up the sides of the dish. Bake for 25 minutes, then turn up the heat to 200°C/Fan 180°C/Gas 6 and bake for a further 15 minutes until the pudding is set and golden on top.

Lift the dish out of the roasting tin and leave the pudding to stand for at least 10 minutes before serving.

Whiting

LATIN NAME
Merlangius merlangus

SEASONALITY
Avoid February–May when spawning

HABITAT
Northeast Atlantic, including all around the British coast

MCS RATING
2–5

REC MINIMUM SIZE
30cm

MORE RECIPES
Pollack with courgettes and cannellini beans (page 484); Zander with coriander and chilli dressing (page 685); Herbed pouting fish fingers (page 501); Rice and fish with wasabi dressing (page 667)

SOURCING
goodfishguide.org

Whiting doesn't get enough respect. The insults begin out at sea: once hauled up in a net, the chances are this fish will be chucked right back. The discard rate is as high as 80 per cent in some fisheries – a shocking figure. This is partly due to restrictive quotas but also because fishermen won't land what people won't buy. Whiting is not generally a targeted fish but taken as by-catch by trawlers looking for other species. And we value this slender, bug-eyed brother of the cod so little, that it is seen as dispensable.

One thing that would help the whiting's cause is more selective fishing gear. This would prevent such high discard rates of juvenile fish, allowing consistently larger fish to reach the market. And when we do see such specimens, or their pleasingly tapering fillets, on sale, we should vote with our frying pans. Whiting from the Celtic Sea, Cornwall and English Channel are the ones to buy: stocks are in rude health here and MCS have this British whiting on their 'Fish to Eat' list of good, sustainable choices.

Give whiting the plain frying or grilling treatment and it won't compete with the flavour and texture of gurnard or wild bream. But whiting's soft white flesh is perfect for battering or breadcrumbing. It's a great choice for goujons, or a hot fish sandwich piled with salad and mayo. And it works a treat in stews, soups, curries and fish pies.

Like many white fish, whiting is also a prime candidate for a light salting, which firms and seasons its delicate fillets. Apply a generous sprinkling of fine sea salt to the flesh, leave for just 10–15 minutes then rinse and pat dry. Try lightly salted whiting cubed and combined with grated potato and a trickle of beaten egg, then fried into rösti-style fish cakes. Served with a blob of home-made tartare sauce, they are out of this world.

Seek out whiting in the autumn and early winter, when it's at its best, and cook it as soon as possible to make the most of the flesh in its firmest, sweetest state.

CRUMBED WHITING GOUJONS WITH CURRIED EGG TARTARE

Crisp, crunchy goujons, dipped into a spiced-up tartare sauce, make irresistible finger food. Any white fish can be used here, but it's a great way to make the most of whiting. Serves 4

4 whiting fillets (500g in total)

5 tbsp plain flour

2 medium eggs, lightly beaten

125g fresh fine breadcrumbs

1 tsp crushed fenugreek seed

A pinch of cayenne pepper

1 tsp ground turmeric

Vegetable oil (refined rapeseed oil), for frying

Sea salt and black pepper

FOR THE CURRIED TARTARE

2 tbsp good mayonnaise

1 tbsp plain wholemilk yoghurt

1 hard-boiled egg, chopped

1–2 gherkins, finely chopped

1 tbsp chopped coriander

2 tbsp raisins

1 tsp curry powder

1 tsp English mustard

To make the curried egg tartare, simply mix all the ingredients together in a bowl and season with salt and pepper if required. Set aside while you cook the fish.

Slice each whiting fillet into 5–6 long fingers, cutting at an angle across the fillet.

Put the flour on a plate and season it well. Pour the beaten egg into a shallow dish. Put the breadcrumbs on another plate and mix with a little salt, the ground fenugreek, cayenne and turmeric.

Dip each fillet first in the seasoned flour, shaking off the excess, then into the egg and finally in the seasoned breadcrumbs, patting them on so they form an even layer all over.

Heat about a 5mm depth of oil in a large frying pan over a medium-high heat. To test whether it is hot enough, throw in a few breadcrumbs; they should immediately 'fizz' and bubble vigorously in the oil.

Put the crumbed goujons into the pan (you might need to cook them in a couple of batches). Fry for 2–3 minutes, without moving the fish, until the breadcrumbs are crisp and crunchy underneath. Carefully turn the goujons over and cook for 2–3 minutes on the other side. Transfer to a plate lined with kitchen paper to drain.

Serve the goujons hot, with the curried egg tartare.

Wine

Gill Meller

MORE RECIPES
Morels and potatoes braised with red wine and garlic (page 388); Cuttlefish with fennel and white beans (page 228); Razor clams with cherry tomatoes and basil (page 528); Turbot with white wine, lemon zest and thyme (page 648); Figs poached in red wine (page 259); Blackcurrant and red wine jelly (page 274); Bay syllabub (page 217)

Good wine can be a delicious element in good cooking. As an ingredient, it is very versatile – less harsh and strong than other alcohols such as brandy or whisky, and full of flavours – ranging from blackcurrant to black tar, from buttered toast to bananas. It can be mellow, or rich and bright, depending on how you use it.

Choosing wine for cooking is easy if you follow one simple rule: don't put anything in a pan that you wouldn't put in a glass. There is no such thing as 'cooking wine'; it's either good wine or it's not. Acidic, thin, overly sweet or even corked wines will not be disguised by the cooking process – far from it. Cooking tends to concentrate wine's character. That's not to say you should use your very best wines for cooking – their finer, subtler qualities are best appreciated in the glass. But good-to-excellent quality should be the benchmark. And of course, you might want to drink more of the same wine with the dish you're cooking: don't sell yourself short.

Organic wines have lower levels of sulphur dioxide added than conventional wines. This chemical is widely used in wine-making to destroy unwanted yeasts and moulds, and as a preservative, but some people are sensitive to it.

Generally, when you cook with wine, you are looking to alter it slightly. All wine has an alcoholic edge to its flavour, and a dish containing wine is generally more enjoyable if this has been blunted. This usually means reducing the wine with heat, which softens it, while concentrating its complex fruity flavours. Sometimes wines are greatly reduced – to make a syrupy *jus*, for instance – and sometimes only a little, when simmered in a bolognese sauce, for example. Occasionally, wines are not reduced at all, as in some jellies and fruit puddings. In this case, they are often sweetened.

Wine is excellent for deglazing. A pan that has been used to brown meat bears a residue of caramelised, almost-burnt, well-seasoned meaty loveliness that must not be wasted. The best way to release all that delicious savoury flavour is with a hot liquid – and none better than wine. After browning meat, remove it from the pan. Pour a glassful of wine into the pan, bring to a simmer and let bubble for a few minutes, using a spatula to stir and scrape, releasing those cooked-on scraps of meaty flavour. As it dissolves the meat-browning residues, the wine will also reduce and concentrate. If you are making a stew-type dish, you can then tip the contents of the pan into your stew pot. For a quick sauce, add a little butter, stock and/or cream to the simmering wine, cook for a few minutes more, and it's ready to serve.

It's a bit of a myth, by the way, that alcohol is instantly 'burned off' when wine is heated. Certainly some evaporates, but not all of it. The longer a dish is cooked, the more alcohol is lost, but even a slow-cooked stew may still retain a tiny amount.

Red wines are most often used for cooking meat – either in quite large quantities, added at the beginning of a long, slow braise, or in smaller shots for deglazing. But red wines have other uses: combined with a fruit purée, they make amazingly rich jellies, sorbets and granitas. Pears are delicious poached in red wine, and peaches are lovely marinated in it. In general, fruity red wines without too much tannin are best for cooking – Pinot Noir or Beaujolais, perhaps, or a lighter Cabernet Sauvignon. I tend not to use really oaky reds, as I think they have a curious sweetness to them.

Dry white wine is essential in the early stages of a risotto – the first liquid to be absorbed by the rice, it forms a base of rich flavour. Dry whites are also excellent in a sauce for fish or chicken. Again, I avoid the oakier whites like New World Chardonnays. Sweeter white wines are exquisite with fruit. And sparkling wines are a luxurious ingredient: a jelly made with Champagne, its bubbles caught in the gel, is particularly

W

special. Sometimes I just pour a slosh of chilled Champagne over a scoop of home-made fruit sorbet so that the two mingle together in a glorious cocktail-cum-pudding.

Fortified wines have a special place in the kitchen. Port, sherry and Marsala are all produced by adding distilled spirits to a base wine. Rich, ruby port is based on red wine but has a lovely, subtle sweetness. Use it when you want an intense punch of tarry, fruity flavour without a lot of extra liquid – in pâtés, sauces and gravies for game or red meat, for example. Ruby ports are the least costly and a good quality one is fine for cooking.

Sherry begins life as a white wine, which is then fortified and matured via the complex *solera* system. This involves keeping the sherry in part-empty casks, so that it oxidises and evaporates, developing its unique flavour. Wine from newer vintages is regularly added to the older sherries, creating a complex blend. Medium sherry, rather than sweet or dry, is best for cooking.

Marsala is a Sicilian fortified wine, prized for its nutty, datey, toffee-ish flavours. It's lovely served lightly chilled with crisp cantuccini biscuits for dunking, and essential to zabaglione, a feather-light mousse of whisked eggs, sugar and Marsala. It's great in game and offal recipes too – its treacly character providing a counterpoint to ferrous meat flavours. I prefer dry (*secco*) Marsala for cooking.

REDCURRANT AND RED WINE JELLY

1kg redcurrants, stripped off their stalks

200ml red wine

About 450g granulated sugar

Redcurrants make a beautiful, tart-sweet jelly, which is wonderful when enriched with a good shot of red wine. Serve it with roast meats or use it to enhance a gravy. It's also excellent with cheese. Makes 3–4 x 200ml jars

Tip the redcurrants into a large saucepan or preserving pan. Pour in the red wine and 200ml water and bring to a simmer. Cook for 30 minutes or until the currants are very soft and pulpy, crushing them with a wooden spoon to split the skins.

Strain the redcurrant pulp through a jelly bag, leaving it to drip for several hours, or overnight, until no more juices come through. Give the jelly bag a squeeze if you like, but remember the jelly may end up a bit cloudy if you do this.

Sterilise your jars by washing them in hot soapy water, rinsing well, then putting them upside down on a baking tray in a very low oven (at 120°C/Fan 100°C/Gas ½) to dry and warm up. Put a saucer in the fridge to chill.

Measure the strained juice into a clean saucepan or preserving pan – you should have about 600ml. For every 600ml juice, weigh out 450g sugar. Bring the juice slowly to the boil, then add the sugar, stirring to dissolve it fully. When it is completely dissolved, bring to a rolling boil and boil for 6–8 minutes, then turn off the heat and test for setting point.

Drop a small spoonful of the jelly on to the chilled saucer. Leave for a few seconds to cool, and then push your finger through the jelly. If it wrinkles, it is ready. If the jelly floods back into the space where your finger was, place the pan back on the heat and cook for a further 2–3 minutes. Place the saucer back in the freezer and test again in the same way.

Once setting point is reached, pour the hot jelly into the hot jars and seal immediately.

W

Winkles

John Wright

LATIN NAME
Littorina littorea

SEASONALITY
Some areas have a closed season, generally 15 May–15 September

HABITAT
Found all around the British Isles on rocky shores and in seaweed-rich estuaries

MCS RATING
Not rated

REC MINIMUM SIZE
2cm shell length

SOURCING
goodfishguide.org

I have a great affection for the winkle as it was part of my seaside childhood. Then, as now, winkles are easier to collect than to purchase. Visit any rocky shore at low tide and you will find enough winkles to fill half a bucket. They are much easier to find in the warmer months, though in some areas there is a closed season to be observed.

They are easy to recognise, though it won't matter at all if you get it wrong, as all similar shellfish are edible. Winkles form a distinctly rounded shell with a sharp conical point. They also possess an inedible little trapdoor (operculum) in the rounded hole at the base. Pulled gently from the rocks, they will make a little sucking sound.

Occasionally, you'll find these molluscs at a fishmonger's stall; if buying, hand-gathered winkles are preferable to those that have been mechanically harvested.

Being grazers, rather than filter feeders such as mussels and oysters, winkles seldom carry the same toxic perils and are perfectly safe to eat. They do not need to be purified. However, 3 or 4 hours in salted water (3.5 per cent salt) will clean them a little. Do not leave them longer as they will drown.

The humble winkle is simple food and demands simple cooking. I like to steam them in a lidded saucepan with butter, garlic and a little white wine for 10 minutes. There are two methods of extracting the cooked meat – picking and cracking. A pin is traditionally used for picking but I find pointed tweezers to be more reliable. The flesh is in a spiral and a certain rotatory flourish is required to extract it intact. The other method involves cracking them gently with a hammer (or rock, if you are on the beach). Once the bits of shell have been removed, you will be left with a perfect spiral of winkle.

The flavour is remarkably sweet and the texture nicely chewy without being at all rubbery. However, like oysters, winkles should always be eaten with eyes closed – they really aren't very pretty. Not even a bit.

WINKLES IN OATMEAL

500g live winkles in the shell, well scrubbed

1 egg

20g butter, melted and cooled slightly

50g fine oatmeal

2 tbsp very finely chopped chives

2 tbsp rapeseed oil

1 garlic clove, finely sliced

Sea salt and black pepper

Cider vinegar, to finish

A fine oatmeal coating makes these winkles crisp and crunchy. Seasoned with garlic, salt and vinegar, they're irresistible finger food. Serves 2

Bring a large saucepan of salted water to a rolling boil. Add the winkles and cook them for 4–5 minutes. Drain and allow to cool. Use a pin or tweezers to remove the 'trapdoor' from the open end of each shell, then skewer out the winkle meat into a bowl.

In a large bowl, whisk the egg together with half the melted butter and some salt and pepper. Combine the oatmeal with half the chives in another bowl.

Drop the winkles into the egg mixture, then lift them out and drop them into the oatmeal to coat all over.

Heat the remaining butter with the oil in a non-stick frying pan over a medium-high heat. When bubbling, add the winkles and cook for 3–4 minutes until golden, tossing them gently every 30 seconds or so. Add the sliced garlic a minute before the end of cooking and toss well.

Drain the winkles on kitchen paper. Shake over a few drops of cider vinegar, the remaining chives and a sprinkling of salt, then serve straight away.

Woodcock

Tim Maddams

LATIN NAME
Scolopax rusticola

SEASONALITY
England, Wales and Northern
Ireland: 1 October–31 January.
Scotland: 1 September–
31 January

HABITAT
Woodland, sometimes also
heath and marsh

MORE RECIPES
Snipe with swede and bacon
(page 587)

SOURCING
tasteofgame.org.uk

The woodcock is without doubt one of the finest eating birds nature has seen fit to provide us with – though getting hold of one is not easy. These wild, migratory birds make their way to us from Scandinavia and Russia, arriving in autumn to overwinter in the comparative warmth of the British Isles. It is not unusual for woodcock to fly over 4,000 miles to make it here. Before the migratory habits of this bird were understood, they were believed to hatch from mermaid's purses on the beach, where they were often found sitting on the sand, utterly exhausted.

They soon move inland, however. Woodcock are worm eaters and use long, proboscis-like bills to probe soft earth and mud for tiny invertebrates. In colder winters, our woods can be surprisingly busy with these enigmatic creatures. But it's unlikely that you will be able to find woodcock at the butcher's. Even a good game dealer will struggle to get them on demand. Most woodcock are jealously guarded by those who shoot them. Not only are they tricky birds to hit, but they are unfeasibly good to eat. If you are keen to get hold of a few, a local game keeper or shooter is your best bet, but a note of caution is needed. We are only just starting to understand these nocturnal birds and it is thought there may be a small decline in male woodcock numbers in Britain. While a few taken for the pot each year is unlikely to cause lasting damage to the overall population, woodcock should remain the rarest of culinary treats.

The tradition is to roast the bird whole, plucked but not gutted, and then spread the cooked guts on a piece of toast to serve alongside. This isn't as grim as it may sound: the birds defecate upon taking flight and therefore the intestines are free of faecal matter. I do cook woodcock like this myself, though I often give the guts a minute or two in the pan with some chopped garlic before mashing them with a fork and spreading on the toast. This makes them more enjoyable and reveals their nutty flavour.

Woodcock should be roasted as for other small game birds, i.e. started off in a pan, being browned first on the back and then working round to the breasts, then finished in a hot oven for just a few minutes (see page 587). They are cooked and ready to begin resting when the guts just pop out of the body cavity.

WOODCOCK WITH WILD MUSHROOMS

You could use almost any wild mushrooms for this dish (or cultivated chestnut mushrooms), but ceps, chanterelles, blewits and hedgehog mushrooms are all very good. This dish also works with snipe in place of the woodcock; allow a few minutes less in the oven. Serves 2

75g butter, lard or bacon fat

A dash of rapeseed oil (optional)

2 prepared woodcock, guts in or out as you prefer, at room temperature

1 large onion, finely sliced

3 or 4 handfuls of wild mushrooms (about 200g), cleaned and cut into pieces as necessary

2 sprigs of thyme

2 garlic cloves, sliced

50ml Madeira or sherry

Sea salt and black pepper

Preheat the oven to 200°C/Fan 180°C/Gas 6.

Set an ovenproof frying pan over a medium-high heat and add half the butter or lard (if using butter, add a dash of oil too, to stop it burning). Season the birds all over, add them to the pan and cook for 4–5 minutes, turning to brown all over. Transfer to a plate.

Add the remaining fat to the pan and lower the heat a little. Add the onion, mushrooms, thyme and a little salt and pepper. Cook, stirring regularly, for 8–10 minutes or until the mushroom liquor has evaporated and the mushrooms are starting to brown, then add the garlic. Nestle the birds back into the pan, pour in the Madeira or sherry and roast in the oven for 8–10 minutes. Take out, cover loosely with foil and let rest for 10 minutes.

If you've cooked your woodcook with the guts in, spoon them out and stir through the mushrooms. Serve the woodcock and mushrooms with celeriac mash or roast potatoes. Alternatively, stir some hot, buttery pasta such as pappardelle through the mushroom mix.

Yeast

Gill Meller

MORE RECIPES
Seedy stoneground loaf
(page 263); Poppy seed spelt
rolls (page 487); Crow garlic
and nigella naan (page 271);
Chive buckwheat blinis with
hard-boiled eggs (page 175);
St George's mushroom and
asparagus pizza (page 609);
Lancashire, apple and leek pizza
(page 151); Pulla (page 115)

Yeast is a magical thing, a fungus that we have, if not exactly tamed, then certainly bent to our will. Yeasts are single-celled organisms that hunger always for carbohydrate (sugar). Once they have some, they consume it voraciously and this activity begins a chain of effects that can result in a nicely brewed pint of beer – and a beautifully risen loaf of bread.

Long ago, people realised that they could harness the wild yeasts that exist naturally in the environment. These yeasts are hungry and resilient and, given the chance, they will grow. They will grow on fruit or vegetables and on meats – and when they grow in a paste of flour and water, something amazing happens. The yeast consumes the carbohydrates in the flour. As it does so, it releases alcohol and carbon dioxide. The alcohol gives flavour to the developing dough and the carbon dioxide forms bubbles that are trapped in it, causing it to rise. The complex chemical reactions that take place while yeast works also have the effect of making the gluten in the dough stronger and stretchier.

For thousands of years, all bread was sourdough bread, leavened only with natural yeasts 'captured' from the air. We make sourdough bread in the same way today, simply leaving a flour and water paste sitting for a day or two until wild yeasts populate it and start to work. A little fruit can be included in the mix, to stimulate yeasty activity, but even that's not essential. Yeast doesn't need much encouragement to get to work.

Bakers also learned to capitalise on the brewing industry, scooping the yeasty froth ('barm') that formed on top of fermenting beer and using that to leaven their bread. This is one reason why breweries and bakeries were often sited close by each other. But yeast became such an essential ingredient, used so extensively, that it was inevitable that we would find a way to produce it, in vast quantities and in a very consistent form, on an industrial level.

The yeast we use most often now is produced in a lab with strict hygiene controls so that no wild, natural yeast can get involved. Instead, carefully selected yeasts are allowed to grow in temperature-controlled vats, fed with molasses and a variety of minerals and pumped with air, all calculated to maximise yeast growth. The resultant product, the finely tuned athlete of the yeast world, is honed to work efficiently and predictably when added to recipes. After washing and cooling, it is pressed into a cake (fresh yeast) or dried and granulated.

There are three basic types of yeast available today. Dried yeast comes in plump, buff-coloured granules and needs to be 'activated' before use. This is done by adding yeast to warm water or milk (or whatever liquid you are putting into your bread), and 'feeding' it with a little sugar or honey. Whisked together, this yeasty brew will start to froth and foam within 15 minutes and it is then ready to add to dry flour. If it doesn't have a decent head on it after that time, it's yeast that's past its best. Discard it, because it will let your loaf down. Most dried yeast is good for around 6 months after purchase.

Many recipes now use 'fast-acting', 'quick' or 'easy-blend' dried yeast (all the same thing). This comes in very fine, rod-shaped granules that absorb water easily and so do not need to be activated but can be added straight to flour, saving you a little time.

The third option is fresh yeast (pictured overleaf), which comes in a creamy block and needs to be dissolved in warm water, with a little sugar to get it frothing. Apart from the tactile and sensory pleasure of it, there's no real advantage to using fresh yeast over dried. They are essentially the same thing: a processed ingredient, bred in controlled conditions. Fresh yeast is no more 'natural' than dried yeast granules. It does, however, have a much shorter shelf life – just a couple of weeks, so buy it in small quantities as and when needed.

You can use whatever yeast you have to hand in any recipe, but you'll have to adjust the quantity and the method. There's an amazing range of diverging advice on how much fresh yeast replaces how much quick yeast. Some sources suggest twice as much, some say four times as much. The important thing is not to panic – adding a bit less yeast won't stop your recipe working, it might just slow the rate of rising, which can be a good thing. I work on the principle that you need about twice as much fresh yeast (by weight) as you would quick yeast. Crumble it with your fingers into warm water, whisking until completely dissolved, and add a little sugar. To use ordinary dried yeast in a recipe that calls for quick yeast, I use the same amount plus a pinch more as it can be slightly slower working, and activate it in warm liquid with a spoonful of sugar.

Yeast has an ambivalent relationship with salt. A little of it slows down yeast's activity to a desirable degree (see below) but too much will kill it – or at least stop it working effectively. So always follow bread recipes carefully for quantities of salt – and don't let yeast come into contact with all the salt at once – i.e. mix the salt into your flour first. Other ingredients can also affect the way yeast works. Although it likes a bit of sugar, larger quantities will slow it down, as will fats such as butter and milk, and egg. This is why rich doughs for, say, brioche, take much longer to rise than plain loaves.

Yeast likes to grow in a warm environment: it is most active at around 35°C. It is killed by temperatures above about 55°C, so only ever mix it with warm rather than hot liquids. Keeping a rising bread dough at very warm room temperature will maximise yeast activity. However, yeast is enthusiastic stuff and will work even at fridge temperatures – just much more slowly. This can be a very good thing: as yeast works, various other enzymatic and bacterial activities take place in the dough – activities which result in a deeper, richer, more bready flavour. The longer the dough takes to rise, the more time there is for these flavour-producing processes to go on. This is why sourdough bread, which might take 20 times as long to rise as a commercial yeast loaf, also has about 20 times as much flavour.

SPELT AND HONEY PIKELETS

300g wholemeal spelt flour

5g fast-acting dried yeast

200ml warm whole milk

2 tbsp clear honey

1 tsp fine sea salt

1 tsp baking powder

A little rapeseed oil, for frying

A pikelet is a sort of freeform crumpet, made with a thick, yeasted batter. Once cooked, it is full of bubbly holes – perfect for soaking up melted butter, honey or jam. Makes about 24

In a medium bowl, whisk together the flour and yeast, then whisk in the warm milk and 200ml warm water, and finally the honey, to create a smooth and fairly thick batter. Cover with cling film and leave in a warm place for at least an hour, until it is really bubbly. You can leave it for up to 3 hours if need be.

When you are ready to cook, heat a large heavy-based frying pan over a medium heat. Whisk the salt and baking powder into the batter. Add a little oil to the frying pan, then wipe out any excess with some kitchen paper.

Cook the pikelets in batches (wiping the pan with more oil if needed). Drop tablespoonfuls of the batter into the pan, leaving some space between them, as they will spread a little. Cook for 2½–3 minutes on the first side until they are almost cooked all the way through and full of holes, then flip them over and cook for a further 1 minute until golden brown and cooked through. Serve straight away, allowing about 4 pikelets each.

Y

Yoghurt

Gill Meller

SOURCING

browncoworganics.co.uk; daylesford.com

Yoghurt is fermented milk. Bacterial cultures convert lactose (sugar) in the milk to lactic acid, resulting in a slightly sharp, lactic flavour. The acid also causes the milk proteins to coagulate, giving yoghurt a thickened texture. This form of semi-preserved milk originated in some of the hotter parts of the world – Asia and the Middle East – and is interwoven in their cuisines. But it has become a culinary mainstay across the globe. Easier to digest and with a longer shelf life than milk itself, yoghurt is nutritious, incredibly useful and deliciously versatile.

Much of the yoghurt on sale these days is labelled as 'live' or 'bio-live'. Actually, unless heat-treated, all yoghurt is 'live', containing the bacteria that made it yoghurt in the first place. But in most 'live' or 'bio' yoghurts, there are additional cultures, chosen because they are 'friendly' bacteria that already exist in the human gut. Bifidobacteria and lactobacilli – both groups of probiotics – are the most common. There is substantial evidence that probiotic bacteria can have a range of health benefits, and that yoghurt can deliver them effectively to the gut.

You can also capitalise on yoghurt's 'live'ness by making your own yoghurt at home using a shop-bought product as a starter. First heat 1 litre whole milk to 85°C (this denatures the proteins so they set in a gel rather than clumping into curds). When the milk has cooled to 45°C, stir in 4–6 tbsp plain live yoghurt. Keep the mixture as close to this temperature as you can, either by sealing it in a warmed vacuum flask, or by putting it in a warmed jar, wrapped in a towel, and placing in an airing cupboard. After 4–7 hours, or overnight, it should be thickened. Cool and then refrigerate.

Many of the yoghurts on the market these days are reduced fat but I prefer plain, wholemilk yoghurt for its naturally creamy mouth-feel and full flavour. It is also more stable when heated. With a fat content ranging from about 3–6 per cent, it's still not a high-fat food. Greek-style yoghurt is thicker and richer because some of the whey is strained off; sometimes it also contains cream. Fruity flavoured yoghurts often contain sugar as well as thickeners and stabilisers.

Goat's and sheep's milks also make great yoghurt and are both more stable than cow's milk yoghurt when heated. Both can be amazingly mild and creamy, though some goat's yoghurt can have a distinguishable 'goaty' flavour.

Yoghurt is great just as it comes – creamy but not cloying, with that welcome hint of sharpness. It's also lovely for breakfast with a home-made compote of Bramley apples or ripe plums, or a purée of strawberries or peaches, finished with a trickle of honey and a scattering of pistachios.

For a simple salad dressing, whisk yoghurt with olive oil, lemon juice, finely grated lemon zest and chopped herbs; this is great spooned over hearty salads that include roasted root veg, particularly beetroot and carrots, as well as seeds and robust leaves (or see the recipe overleaf). Yoghurt combined with a little tahini also makes a lovely dressing, spiked with garlic, nigella seeds and finely diced red onion; try it spooned over tomatoes, or chargrilled aubergines, or as a condiment for barbecued lamb.

When added to a marinade, yoghurt's gentle acidity helps to tenderise meat. Use it with chicken – and with wild rabbit in particular, which can be tough. After a few hours in the marinade, shake off the excess, but keep some of the yoghurty mix clinging to the meat. It cooks to a delicious, sweet-sour crust that locks in flavour and moistness.

Yoghurt is often employed as a lighter, fresher alternative to cream, as with frozen yoghurt. For an instant version, blitz plain yoghurt with frozen fruits such as berries or sliced bananas in a food processor, sweetening with honey as needed. But cream

Y

and yoghurt also work well mixed together, with the yoghurt imparting a welcome, subtle acidity. I almost always add yoghurt to the mix for a pannacotta, for instance.

Yoghurt's affinity with chilli-hot foods is another reason to love it. Not only does it feel physically cool in the mouth, it actually softens the 'burn' of spicy foods by helping to absorb the substance capsaicin, responsible for chilli heat. A dollop of thick, plain yoghurt is delicious with curries, chillies and tagines; it's also great combined with other cooling ingredients such as tomatoes and cucumbers, mint and coriander, in side dishes to serve with curries, such as raitas.

The acidity of yoghurt is often employed in baking; it reacts with alkaline bicarbonate of soda to give a lift to muffins and cakes, for example. And yoghurt's body and thickness mean it can even be used in cakes with little or no flour (see page 73), combining with eggs to give a soufflé-like texture. Yoghurt cakes are wonderful flavoured with honey, citrus zest and spices.

Yoghurt is also used in other forms of cooking – you just need to be slightly cautious when adding it to hot dishes such as soups or curries, as it has a tendency to 'split' or curdle when heated. Add it at the last minute, when you've taken the dish off the heat, to avoid this.

Finally, you can use yoghurt to make a delicious, simple fresh 'cheese', known in the Middle East as labneh. Put 500g plain wholemilk yoghurt in a bowl and stir in ½ tsp fine sea salt. Line a sieve with muslin or a fine cotton cloth. Put the salted yoghurt into the centre, flip the cloth over to cover and place the sieve over a bowl. Leave in the fridge for 2–4 hours, until enough whey has drained off to give the labneh the texture of crème fraîche. Leave it longer if you want it thicker. You can eat it plain or stir in chopped herbs, lemon zest, black pepper and chilli.

Labneh is great with hot flatbreads, flaky salt and extra virgin olive oil. Alternatively, dollop it over chargrilled veg, or serve with seared squid and chickpeas, or a dish of artichoke hearts and preserved lemons.

ROASTED COURGETTES AND ONIONS WITH YOGHURT DRESSING

4 medium-large red onions

3 medium courgettes (about 700g in total)

2 tbsp olive or rapeseed oil

Sea salt and black pepper

FOR THE YOGHURT DRESSING

4 tbsp plain wholemilk yoghurt

1 small garlic clove, grated

Juice of ½ lemon

2 tbsp chopped mint

1 tbsp extra virgin olive or rapeseed oil

Minty yoghurt makes a lovely accompaniment to sweet roasted red onions and courgettes. However, you could use this thick, tangy, fragrant dressing with any barbecued or roasted veg, or alongside charred lamb or chicken. Serves 4

Preheat the oven to 180°C/Fan 160°C/Gas 4.

Peel the red onions and cut each into 6–8 wedges. Place in a large roasting tin. Slice the courgettes into 2cm rounds, add to the onions and trickle with the oil. Season well with salt and pepper and toss together gently.

Place the tray in the oven and roast the vegetables for 40–45 minutes, stirring once or twice, until soft and beginning to caramelise. Remove from the oven and allow to cool.

For the yoghurt dressing, combine all the ingredients in a bowl and season with salt and pepper to taste.

Put the cooled vegetables into a large serving bowl and spoon over the yoghurt dressing. Turn together briefly, then serve straight away, with good bread or roast chicken.

Zander

Nick Fisher

LATIN NAME
Sander lucioperca

ALSO KNOWN AS
Pike-perch

SEASONALITY
England and Wales: closed
season on rivers generally
15 March–15 June

MCS RATING
Not rated

REC MINIMUM SIZE
30cm

MORE RECIPES
Cod with fennel, capers and
tomatoes (page 194)

Zander is often lumped together with perch – so much so that it is even called the 'pike-perch' by anglers and fishmongers. This catchy moniker derives from some curious notion that the two-fanged, mirror-eyed, spooky-looking, night-hunting zander was created in a Frankensteinian hybridisation of two of our deadliest fresh water killers, the pike and the perch. Much as I love this idea, it is total bunkum. These fish are quite different. While perch boasts an almost oily quality to its firm meat, zander is just like a freshwater cod. Flaky and tender of flesh, white as the driven snow, with none of the 'muddy' taste often associated with freshwater fish.

In addition, while perch is a long-time inhabitant of the British waterways, zander is an illegal alien introduced to England a mere century and a half ago, to Woburn Abbey by the 9th Duke of Bedford, who knew of its culinary fame on the Continent.

Sadly, because of a badly planned 'naturalisation scheme' attempted by the National Rivers Authority in the 1960s, in which they were introduced into the fen drains of East Anglia, zander have been blamed for decimating our indigenous stocks of coarse fish. They are voracious predators who, as a result of their incredible ocular physiology, are able to hunt in muddy, opaque water, and at night. Since zander live on a diet of finger-sized roach and bream, British coarse anglers have grown to hate them.

However, European cooks love them. Zander is now successfully farmed throughout northern Europe where it appears regularly on fishmonger's slabs and menus and, in some regions of Eastern Europe, is more popular than trout. The firm, white, cod-like nature of its flesh is uncanny. Zander can grow very large too; fish just shy of 20lb (9kg) have been caught from the River Severn. So, should you ever come across a zander (some online suppliers and fishmongers sell them), don't be deterred by its grey skin, glassy eyes and vampire fangs – snap it up. Try it in any recipe where you would otherwise use cod, pollack or haddock.

ZANDER WITH CORIANDER AND CHILLI DRESSING

This slightly spicy dressing is excellent with zander, but works equally well with pike, pollack, whiting – most white fish, in fact. You can use it with chicken or pork too. Serves 4

1 tbsp olive or rapeseed oil

4 zander fillets, skin on
(about 150g each)

A small knob of butter

A squeeze of lemon juice

Sea salt and black pepper

FOR THE DRESSING

A small bunch of coriander,
(about 30g), finely chopped,
including stalks

2 garlic cloves, finely chopped

1 medium-hot red chilli
(deseeded for less heat, if
preferred), finely chopped

Juice of ½ lemon

1 tsp ground cumin

1 tsp hot smoked paprika

5 tbsp extra virgin olive oil

For the dressing, either mix all the ingredients together in a bowl, or blitz in a blender to create a smoother dressing (using the blender to chop the coriander, garlic and chilli first). Season with salt and pepper to taste and set aside.

Put a large frying pan over a medium-high heat and add the oil. Season the zander fillets all over with salt and pepper and place them, skin side down, in the hot pan. Press down on the flesh for a few seconds to help stop the fish curling up and enable it to cook more evenly. Cook the fillets, without moving, for 3 minutes, then turn them over; the skin should be nice and brown by now.

Add the butter and lemon juice to the pan, and cook the fillets on the second side for 1–2 minutes, basting with the pan juices once or twice, until just cooked through – the flesh should flake apart easily.

Transfer the zander fillets to warmed plates and spoon over some of the dressing. Bring the remaining dressing to the table. Serve the fish with freshly cooked Puy lentils, tossed with spring onions and herbs, or some roasted sweet potatoes.

Further resources

ORGANISATIONS
Campaign groups and useful sources of further information:

association-ifca.org.uk Association of Inshore Fisheries and Conservation Authorities, for local fishing byelaws and regulations

basc.org.uk The British Association for Shooting and Conservation, provides information on shooting and game seasons

bigbarn.co.uk For local food suppliers

ciwf.org.uk Compassion in World Farming, who campaign to stop factory farming worldwide and provide information on the alternatives

cornwallgoodseafoodguide.org.uk Information on seafood from Cornish waters, with details on seasonality and sustainability

ethicalconsumer.org Magazine and website focused on ethical shopping, including regular buyers' guides on a range of ingredients

fairtrade.org.uk The Fairtrade Foundation, lists Fairtrade products

farma.org.uk National Farmers' Retail and Markets Association, lists farm shops, farmers' markets and pick-your-own-farms

farmsnotfactories.org Working to end factory farming. Good information on higher welfare pork in particular

feedbackglobal.org Campaigns to end food waste

fishmongers.info The National Federation of Fishmongers, lists independent fishmongers in Britain

gwct.org.uk Game and Wildlife Conservation Trust, promotes game and wildlife management

hsa.org.uk The Humane Slaughter Association, promotes the humane treatment of all food animals worldwide

mcsuk.org The Marine Conservation Society is a British charity caring for our seas, shores and wildlife. At goodfishguide.org, MCS provides ratings for fish and shellfish species, assessing the relative 'health' of different fisheries and farming systems against a number of sustainability criteria

msc.org The Marine Stewardship Council, certifies sustainable seafood, identified via its blue eco-labels

pickyourownfarms.org.uk Lists pick-your-own farms and farm shops selling fresh produce across Britain

soilassociation.org The Soil Association is a charity campaigning for planet-friendly food and farming. It is also the UK's leading organic certifier

sustainweb.org Works for better food and farming. Campaigns include The Real Bread Campaign and The Alliance to Save Our Antibiotics

tasteofgame.org.uk Offers information on game dealers around Britain

thegoodshoppingguide.com Promotes ethical shopping, with information on thousands of brands

GENERAL SUPPLIERS
Sources of specific ingredients are included in the relevant A–Z entries. The following suppliers offer a range of ingredients:

Herbs and spices

jekkasherbfarm.com The largest collection of culinary herbs in the UK (not mail order)

laurelfarmherbs.co.uk A broad selection of herb plants

seasonedpioneers.com For spices and spice blends

steenbergs.co.uk A huge range of organic and Fairtrade spices

thespiceshop.co.uk Supplies dried and fresh herbs and spices

Veg patch

brogdaleonline.co.uk Linked to the National Fruit Collection at Brogdale, sells fruit trees and soft fruit bushes

organicplants.co.uk Organic vegetable seedlings and plants

otterfarm.co.uk Sells fruit, veg, herb and spice seeds and plants

seaspringseeds.co.uk For herb, vegetable and chilli seeds

walcotnursery.co.uk Organic fruit trees and soft fruit bushes

Storecupboard

goodnessdirect.co.uk Online supplier of health foods and a range of eco-friendly products

healthysupplies.co.uk Broad range of health foods and storecupboard ingredients, including organic and Fairtrade products

riverford.co.uk Organic veg box delivery plus organic storecupboard ingredients

abelandcole.co.uk Organic vegetables and storecupboard ingredients

Fish and shellfish online

andyrace.co.uk Wide range of fresh and smoked Scottish fish and shellfish

crabmeat.co.uk Cornish brown crab, spider crab and lobster

dorsetoysters.com Oysters, clams, cockles and other shellfish

fishforthought.co.uk A wide range of fish and shellfish

thecornishfishmonger.co.uk Fish and shellfish largely from Cornish waters

Index

holey cheeses 144
hominy 481
honey 312–14
  apricot and honey filo pie 314
  gooseberry, cream and honey pudding 286
  honeycomb 44
  lemon, honey and courgette cake 347
  mead 314
  olive oil and honey flapjacks 413
  pistachio, orange and honey filo tartlets 474
  quince in star anise and honey syrup 512
  rose petal honey 540
  spelt and honey pikelets 680
  strawberries with lavender and honey 341
horse mackerel 373
horse mushrooms 315
  drying 315
  spiced horse mushroom and beetroot 'burger' 315
horseradish 316, 667
  creamed apple and horseradish sauce 316
  hot mackerel, beetroot and horseradish sandwich 373
  tongue, kale and apple hash with horseradish 643
hot dogfish dog 236
hot water crust pastry 445
hummus 165
  broad bean 96
  hempy 308
Hungarian hot wax chillies 168

I

ice cream: banana and peanut butter 46
  beer 65
  chocolate, brandy and star anise 178
  damson ripple parfait 231
  vanilla and rhubarb 655
Iceberg lettuce 355
Indian spiced grilled quail 510
Iron Bark squash 602

J

jacksnipe 587
Jaffa oranges 420
Jamaica pepper see allspice
Jamaican pimento see allspice
James Grieve apples 25
jamón serrano 300
jams: raspberry 526
  rhubarb and ginger 532
  sugars for 620
  see also jelly (preserve); marmalade

January King cabbage 110
Japanese quail 510
Japanese wineberries 317
  wineberries with peaches and custard 317
jeera see cumin
jelly: blackcurrant and red wine 274
  elderflower 249
  redcurrant and red wine 675
jelly (preserve): blackberry 73
  crab apple 204
  hot haw 302
  rowan 544
  scented tomato 275
jerk chicken 16
Jersey Royal potatoes 498
Jerusalem artichokes see artichokes, Jerusalem
John Dory 318
  John Dory with creamed radicchio 318
jostaberries 284
juniper 320
  crab apple jelly with thyme, juniper and mint 204
  sautéed mushrooms with juniper 320

K

kabocha squash 602
kaffir lime 357, 358
kaffir lime leaves 358
kai-lan 387
kale 322
  'kale crisps' 322
  raw kale with yoghurt and tahini 322
  roasted haggis, swede and kale salad 295
  sausages with squash and kale 568
  steamed sea bass with kale and ginger 573
  tongue, kale and apple hash 643
kalonji see nigella
kasha see buckwheat
kebabs, goat 280
kelp 578, 579
key lime 357–8
kid 280
kidney beans 54, 55
kidneys 324
  lamb's kidneys with mustard and cream 324
King Edward potatoes 498
king prawns 502
king scallops 570, 572
kippers 309
kiwi fruit 325
  kiwi, spinach and avocado smoothie 325
knotted marjoram see marjoram

kohlrabi 327
  kohlrabi and mushroom salad 581
  spicy kohlrabi wedges 327
Korean pine 471

L

labneh 684
  lamb, labneh and spinach salad 335
lactic bacteria 88, 106, 143
lager 65
lamb 328–35
  cuts 330–4
  ginger-braised lamb 278
  lamb, labneh and spinach salad 335
  North African shepherd's pie 335
  roast lamb with lovage 368
  stock 612
lamb's brains 82
  sautéed brains with parsley and caper sauce 82
lamb's hearts 305
lamb's kidneys 324
  lamb's kidneys with mustard and cream 324
lamb's lettuce 336
  chicken and blueberry salad 77
  lamb's lettuce salad with poached egg 336
lamb's liver 360
  tagliatelle with lamb's liver, pancetta and sage 551
lamb's sweetbreads 629
lamb's tongues 643
Lancashire cheese 144, 147
  Lancashire, apple and leek pizza 151
langoustine 339
  grilled langoustine with lemon and parsley butter 339
lard 340
  Eccles cakes 340
lavender 341
  roasted beetroot orzotto with lavender 68
  strawberries with lavender and honey 341
laver 578, 579
leathers, fruit: crab apple and haw 302
leeks 342–4
  carrot soup with ginger and coriander 123
  Lancashire, apple and leek pizza 151
  leek and potato gratin 344
  parsnip, leek and potato mash 438
  pigeon breasts with leeks and mash 469
  pike with leeks and chervil sauce 470
leftovers, bread 89

pearl barley 47
  roasted beetroot orzotto 68
pears 452–4
  bay-spiked pears 53
  cranberry and pear sauce 213
  pear and bilberry crumble tart 69
  pear and celeriac stuffing 454
  pears with ricotta, honey and thyme 536
peas 455–7
  garlicky pea ravioli 444
  growing 455–7
  risi e bisi with pea shoot pesto 457
peas, split see split peas
pecans 458
  double chocolate pecan praline cookies
    458
Pecorino 433
pectin 459
peel, citrus 459
  candied orange and lemon peel 459
pelargonium, scented see geranium,
    scented
penny bun see ceps
pepper 460–1
peppermint 385
peppers 463–4
  goat kebabs with rosemary, red peppers
    and onion 280
  growing 464
  muhammara 464
  pepper stew 463–4
  red pepper agrodolce 662
  red pepper mayo 393
  roasted pepper soup 463
perch 465, 685
  fried fillets of perch with sorrel and
    potatoes 465
Perl Las cheese 150
perpetual spinach 597, 599
Pershore plums 477
Persian lime see lime
persillade 434
pesto 48–50
  pea shoot pesto 457
petit-gris see snails
petits pois 457
pheasant 466–8
  pheasant pie 468
  pheasant with olives and preserved
    lemons 414
  poached pheasant with star anise 610
  roasting 466–8
pheasant eggs 243
pickles: bread and butter 218–20
  cherry 153
  fairy ring champignons 252

ginger 278
  lemon-cured herring 310
  nasturtium pods 401
  preserved lemons 347
  walnuts 664
pies: apricot and honey filo pie 314
  field mushroom and celeriac pie 258
  henakopita with garam masala and eggs
    254
  North African shepherd's pie 335
  pheasant pie 468
  sea beet and smoked pollack pasties 574
  see also pastries; tarts
pigeon 469
  blewit, pigeon and endive salad 74
  pigeon breasts with leeks and mash 469
  pigeon breasts with sloe gin gravy 584
pigeon peas 54
pigs 488–91
  see also pork
pig's brains 82
  sautéed brains with parsley and caper
    sauce 82
pig's heart 305
pig's kidneys 324
pig's liver 360
  spiced liver pâté 362
pig's tongues 643
pike 470, 685
  pike with leeks and chervil sauce 470
pike-perch see zander
pikelets, spelt and honey 680
pilaf, lemon verbena 348
pilchards 562–5
piltlock see coley
pimentón see paprika
pine nuts 471
  pea shoot pesto 457
  pesto 50
  sardines with pine nuts, fennel and
    orange 471
pineapple 472
  piña colada 472
pineapple mint 385
Pink Fir Apple potatoes 498
pink peppercorns 460
  nasturtium and pink peppercorn soup
    401
piñon see pine nuts
pinto beans 54, 81
Piri-piri chillies 170
pissaladière 419
pistachio nuts 474
  pistachio, orange and honey filo tartlets
    474
pistou 50

pizza: Lancashire, apple and leek 151
  St George's mushroom and asparagus
    609
plaice 476
  plaice with rosemary, caper and
    anchovy butter 476
plain brown flour 262
plain white flour 262
plantains 45
plum brandy 83
plums 477–9
  plum compote 479
  roasted plum fumble 479
  upside-down chocolate plum pudding
    189
  wild plums 105
  see also cherry plums; prunes
poblano chillies 168
polenta 480–1
  polenta croquettes 481
  sunflower seed and caraway corn
    crackers 623
pollack 483–4
  pollack with courgettes and cannellini
    beans 484
  sea beet and smoked pollack pasties 574
  'steam-braising' 484
pomace brandy 83
pomegranate 485–6
  halloumi and roasted carrot salad 486
pomegranate molasses 486
pomelo 287
popcorn 632
poppy seeds 487
  poppy seed dressing 487
  poppy seed spelt rolls 487
porcini see ceps
porgy see bream, black
pork 488–94
  breeds of pig 490–1
  buying 490
  cooking safely 493
  coriander pork chops 198
  crackling 493–4
  cuts 491–2
  lard 340
  pork belly with noodles, coriander and
    tomatoes 494
  pork burgers 369
  spiced liver pâté 362
  stock 612
  see also bacon; ham; sausages
porridge 522
  savoury porridge 409
porridge oats see oats
port 675

Acknowledgements

The River Cottage family is a large one and we are grateful to everyone who has been part of it over the years. We would particularly like to thank the following people, whose hard work and support have helped to make this book possible:

Gelf Alderson, Maddy Allen, Will Anderson, Adrian Andrews, Kirsten Baptist, Zam Baring, George Barson, Kirsty Bate, Jessica Booth, Claire Botten, Rachael Boughton, Roly Boughton, Lydia Brammer, Lucy Brazier, Lucy Broad, Sophie Broad, Jim Budden, Cat Bugler, Ben Bulger, Emma Burlingham, Trish Bye, Marcus Campbell, Stephanie Carley-Smith, Daryl Clapp, Dawn Coghlan, Bruce Cole, Mihaela Constantinescu, Annie Coplestone, Philippa Corbin, Tara Crabb, Freyja Davis, Simon Deverell, Emma Dixon, Lucy Dixon, Simon Dodd, Matt Downing, Joe Draper, Charles Dunn, George Dunn, Nonie Dwyer, Joe Fox, Mahler Fox, Charles Gabriel, Sally Gale, Oliver Gladwin, Matthew Gojevic, Bob Hains, Fran Hall, Ryan Hanson, Craig Hearn, Alex Heaton, Joe Hunt, Tom Hunt, David Gedye, Daniel Gollop, Joel Gostling, Simon Greenwood, Harriet Grose, Christopher Griffin, Kate Humphreys, Charlie James, Crona Kelly, Sophie Keywood, Victoria Keywood, Paul Kidson, Rachael Kinsella, Elli Lamb, Jake Lea-Wilson, Rebecca Leech, Sarah Little, William Livingstone, Jason Locke, Lucy Lomas, Sam Lomas, Trevor Lopez de Vergara, Kerenza Love, Rob Love, Mandy Loveridge, Debbie Manners, Hoi Ling Mak, Jade Miller-Robinson, Sushila Moles, Emma Moore, Jemma Moran, Sam North, Matt Norton, Chris Onions, Andrew Palmer, Andrew Park, Kate Parr, Deborah Parsons, Abigail Perry, Joshua Pethybridge, Pirjetta Plucinska, Marie Potter, Daniel Powell, Mark Price, Lucy Pugsley, Connor Reed, Dan Richards, Lucy Richards, Gary Richmond, Lawrence Roberts, Debora Robertson, Sam Rom, Abigail Rowden, Ian Rowswell, Graeme Roy, Craig Rudman, Katherine Sakowska, Mark Stavrakakis, Daniel Stevens, Michael Stone, Theresa Tipping, Murry Toms, Michelle Tucker, Sarah Turner, Fiona Tyne, Andrew Tyrell, Malwina Tyrell, Jessamy Upton, Michael Wakley, Joanna Walker, Shelley Wallis, Callum Webster, Harriet Welch, Christine Whyman and Harriet Wild.

Our thanks go to the creative team who have brought the book together: Janet Illsley, Lawrence Morton, Simon Wheeler, Michael Frith and Sally Somers. Also to Antony Topping of Greene & Heaton literary agents, Hattie Ellis for additional research, and the in-house team at Bloomsbury: Richard Atkinson, Natalie Bellos, Alison Cowan, Marina Asenjo, Lena Hall, Alison Glossop, Xa Shaw Stewart, Tess Viljoen, Ellen Williams and Sarah Williams.

The recipes that feature in the book were developed and tested by: Gelf Alderson, Ben Bulger, Pam Corbin, Joe Draper, Nikki Duffy, Hugh Fearnley-Whittingstall, Anna Horsburgh, Gill Meller, Sarah Turner and Andrew Tyrell.

For expert advice and information, we would like to thank: William Bolton of Saxa; Katie Brian at AHDB Beef and Lamb; Luisa Candido at Dairy UK; David Cotton at AHDB Dairy; Sally Dimartino at Whitworths; Peter Fairs of Fairking Ltd.; Duncan Farrington at Farrington Oils; Professor Glenn Gibson of Reading University; Guy Grieve of The Ethical Shellfish Company; Professor Martin Grootveld of De Montfort University; Juliet Harbutt of thecheeseweb.com; Patrick Hearne at Capel Mushrooms; Jimmie Hepburn of Aquavision; David Jarrad of the Shellfish Association of Great Britain; Richard Lawley at foodsafetywatch.org; Harold McGee; David and Ben Oakes of Sconser Scallops; Nele Okojie of The Silver Spoon Company; Jonathan Olins of Poupart; Robert Parker at Wilkin & Sons; Martin Savage at The National Association of British and Irish Millers; James Simpson of the Marine Stewardship Council; Axel Steenberg of steenbergs.co.uk; Samuel Stone from the Marine Conservation Society; Andrew Trump of Organic Arable and Guy Watson of riverford.co.uk.

Contributors

Pam Corbin A specialist in preserving, Pam began her food career with Thursday Cottage, a small artisanal company producing quality jams and marmalades. In 2001 it won The Guild of Fine Food's *Best Speciality Food Business*, and Pam continues to act as a consultant for the company. She is also an expert baker and has worked closely with River Cottage for many years, appearing in the Channel 4 River Cottage TV series and writing the River Cottage *Preserves* and *Cakes* handbooks. Pam lives on the Devon/Dorset border, where she and her husband raised their daughters, and shares her passion for preserves by teaching at venues around the country.

Mark Diacono A former environmental consultant, Mark is a cook, writer and green gardening expert. In 2006, he established his Otter Farm smallholding in Devon, where he lives with his wife and daughter and grows everything from wine grapes to Szechuan pepper. Mark is currently expanding the operation to create a kitchen garden school. Previously head gardener at River Cottage, Mark is author of the River Cottage *Veg Patch*, *Fruit*, and *Chicken & Eggs* handbooks, as well as the award-winning *A Year at Otter Farm* and *A Taste of the Unexpected*.

Nikki Duffy A food writer and editor for the past 15 years, with a broad range of expertise, Nikki wrote a regular column in the *Guardian*, was Deputy Editor of *Waitrose Food Illustrated*, and is the author of the *River Cottage Baby & Toddler Cookbook* and the River Cottage *Herbs* handbook. She has worked closely with Hugh and the team since 2006, collaborating on many River Cottage projects and developing and testing numerous recipes. She lives in Suffolk with her two daughters.

Hugh Fearnley-Whittingstall An award-winning writer, journalist and broadcaster, Hugh is widely known for his uncompromising commitment to seasonal, ethically produced food. His early smallholding experiences, shown in the Channel 4 River Cottage TV series, led to the publication of *The River Cottage Cookbook* (2001). Eleven more books have followed, including the acclaimed *River Cottage Meat Book* and *River Cottage Veg Every Day*. Hugh's broadcasting work includes influential campaigns such as the BAFTA-winning *Hugh's Fish Fight*, and *Hugh's War on Waste*. Hugh established the current River Cottage HQ, a cookery school and organic smallholding, near Axminster, in 2006. He lives in the Southwest with his wife, their four children, and assorted livestock.

Nick Fisher Nick is a BAFTA-winning TV scriptwriter and series creator, who also just happens to be one of the UK's foremost experts on fishing and fish cookery. As well as creating, writing and presenting four series of *Screaming Reels* (Channel 4) and the Sony-Award-winning *Dirty Tackle* (BBC Radio 5 live), Nick co-authored *The River Cottage Fish Book* with Hugh, and wrote the River Cottage *Sea Fishing* handbook. Nick lives in rural Dorset with his family, where he recently completed his debut novel, *Pot Luck*, a crime thriller set in the Weymouth crab fishing industry.

Steven Lamb A teacher, presenter and writer, Steven is also the resident River Cottage curing and smoking expert. He leads courses at HQ, appears in the TV series, and is author of the award-winning River Cottage *Curing & Smoking* handbook. Part of the River Cottage operation since 2005, Steven works closely with the rest of the team, representing River Cottage both in the UK and abroad. He writes on an array of culinary subjects for print and online and is now completing another handbook. Steven lives on the Devon/Dorset border with his wife and three daughters.

Tim Maddams A chef, writer and cookery teacher, Tim lives in Devon with his family. He grew up in rural Wiltshire, where he developed a love of the British countryside and an in-depth knowledge of the game and wild foods it offers. After working with some of the UK's leading chefs, Tim returned to his roots and became head chef at the River Cottage Canteen in Axminster. He appeared often on the Channel 4 River Cottage series and wrote the River Cottage *Game* handbook. In 2012, Tim set up his own company, which now takes him around Britain and Europe, teaching, writing, cooking and consulting on ethical food.

Gill Meller A Dorset native, Gill joined Hugh in the very early days. River Cottage Head Chef for over 10 years, Gill is now a writer, food stylist and teacher. Author of the River Cottage *Pigs & Pork* handbook and *Gather*, his first solo cookbook, he is a contributor to the *Guardian*, *Waitrose Food*, *Delicious* and *BBC Countryfile Magazine* and is currently food columnist for *Country Living*. Gill appears regularly on the River Cottage TV series and Food Tube channel, and teaches both at River Cottage HQ and internationally. He lives with his wife and daughters on the West Dorset coast.

John Wright John is the author of four River Cottage handbooks: *Mushrooms*, *Edible Seashore*, *Hedgerow* and *Booze*, as well as *The Natural History of the Hedgerow* and *The Naming of the Shrew: A Curious History of Latin Names*. In addition to writing and appearing on the *River Cottage* TV series, he gives lectures on natural history and leads 'forays', showing people how to collect wild food from hedgerow, seashore, pasture and woodland. Fungi are John's greatest passion and he is a member of the British Mycological Society as well as a Fellow of the Linnaean Society. He lives in rural West Dorset with his wife and two daughters.

Bloomsbury Publishing
An imprint of Bloomsbury Publishing Plc

50 Bedford Square   1385 Broadway
London   New York
WC1B 3DP   NY 10018
UK   USA

www.bloomsbury.com

First published in Great Britain 2016

The recipes on pages 89, 178, 192, 259, 419, 429, 438, 448, 454, 458, 464, 500, 526, 558, 599, 604,
613 and 622 first appeared in the *Guardian*.

British Library Cataloguing-in-Publication Data
A catalogue record for this book is available from the British Library.

ISBN: HB: 978-1-4088-2860-1
         ePub: 978-1-4088-6365-7

2 4 6 8 10 9 7 5 3

Project editor: Janet Illsley
Designer: Lawrence Morton
Photographer and stylist: Simon Wheeler (simonwheeler.eu)
Illustrator: Michael Frith (michaelfrith.com)
Indexer: Hilary Bird

Printed and bound in Italy by Graphicom

To find out more about our authors and books visit www.bloomsbury.com. Here you will find extracts,
author interviews, details of forthcoming events and the option to sign up for our newsletters.